Volume II

DOCUMENTS
of
AMERICAN HISTORY
Since 1898

ninth edition

DOCUMENTS

of

AMERICAN HISTORY

volume II   since 1898

edited by

Henry Steele Commager

PRENTICE-HALL, INC., Englewood Cliffs, New Jersey

Library of Congress Cataloging in Publication Data

Commager, Henry Steele, ed.
  Documents of American history.

  CONTENTS: v. 1. To 1898.—v. 2. Since 1898.
  1. United States—History—Sources. I. Title.
E173.C66 1973b   973'.08
ISBN 0-13-217000-0 (v. 2)
Library of Congress Catalog Card Number: 73-11490

© 1973
by PRENTICE-HALL, Inc.,
Englewood Cliffs, New Jersey

Printed in the United States of America

10 9 8 7 6 5 4 3

PRENTICE-HALL INTERNATIONAL, INC., *London*
PRENTICE-HALL OF AUSTRALIA, PTY. LTD., *Sydney*
PRENTICE-HALL OF CANADA, LTD., *Toronto*
PRENTICE-HALL OF INDIA PRIVATE LIMITED, *New Delhi*
PRENTICE-HALL OF JAPAN, INC., *Tokyo*

To

EVAN

WHO LIKED THEM

PREFACE

These documents are designed to illustrate the course of American history from the Age of Discovery to the present. Exigencies of space and of circumstance have required that the term document be interpreted in a very narrow sense. Properly speaking, almost everything of an original character is a document: letters, memoirs, ballads, folk-lore, poetry, fiction, newspaper reports and editorials, sermons and speeches, to say nothing of inscriptions, stamps, coins, buildings, painting and sculpture, and all the innumerable memorials which man has left in his effort to understand and organize his world. I have tried to limit my selection to documents of an official and quasi-official character, though I have been no more consistent in this than in other things. I have not included selections often, and mistakenly, referred to as "readings"; even partially to illuminate American history from letters, memoirs, travelers' descriptions, etc. would require many volumes; this material, too, should be read in its entirety rather than in excerpt, and is readily available to students.

What is presented here, then, is part of the official record, and students know that the official record is neither the whole record nor in every case the real record. I cannot say that I have been guided in my choice of material by any rigid principles of selection. The choice has been determined by the experience of the class-room, by personal interest, and by availability. I have attempted to include those documents with which students should be familiar, such as the Northwest Ordinance or *Marbury* v. *Madison;* those which are illustrative or typical, such as colonial charters or land laws; those which focussed upon themselves the attention of the country, such as the Missouri Compromise or the Lincoln-Douglas Debates; those which serve as a convenient point of departure for the study of some economic or political development, such as labor cases or party platforms; those which illuminate some phase of our social life, such as the constitution of the Brook Farm Association or the Mooney-Billings Report; those which have certain qualities of interest, eloquence or beauty, such as Lee's Farewell to his Army or Holmes' dissent in the Abrams Case.

No one can be more acutely conscious of the inadequacies of such a collection than is the editor. Students familiar with the sources of American history will find many omissions and will discover many episodes unilluminated. To most of these charges I can plead only the exigencies of space; to some I must confess personal idiosyncrasy and fallibility. Students will look in vain for Webster's Reply to Hayne or Stephen's Cornerstone speech, for Hamilton's Report on Manufactures or the Federal Reserve Act, for the diplomatic correspondence on the X.Y.Z. affair or the Trent episode. These, and scores of similar selections, were omitted because I was not able to achieve a satisfactory condensation and did not feel that they could be included *in extenso*. While I have made efforts to find documents which would illustrate phases of our social and economic history, there are fewer of these than is desirable. Such documents are hard to come by: spiritual forces do not readily translate themselves into documents. I would have liked to have included Emerson's *Divinity School Address,* Fitzhugh's *Pro-Slavery Argument,* the platform of the American Economic Association; to have yielded to this temptation would have opened the flood-gates of miscellaneous source material. It cannot be pretended that presidential messages, supreme court decisions, or statutes, reveal much of the undercurrents of our social life. To discover these it would be necessary to go to church records, school reports, the minutes of fraternal orders, the records of labor organizations and agricultural societies, the records of probate courts, etc. American historians have been distressingly backward in the appreciation and publication of such material. These records therefore are not readily available, nor would a lifetime be sufficient to canvass them and take from them that which is typical.

Neither the notes nor the bibliographies which accompany these documents pretend to be extensive. In the notes I have attempted to state only what is essential for an understanding of the background of the document; the bibliographies are designed to indicate additional reading for the orientation of the document and additional bibliographical references. I have only occasionally included references to the rich deposits of material in

periodicals and the publications of learned societies: for these the student will have to go
to specialized bibliographical guides and to the invaluable *Writings on American History*
which Miss Griffin has compiled. The documents themselves have been taken from and
collated with the sources indicated. No effort has been made to standardize spelling, capital
ization or punctuation, or even to correct obvious errors in the originals: to have undertaken this, even granting its propriety, would have produced confusion. I have taken very
few liberties with these documents. Omissions have been indicated by the customary ellipsis
sign, but I have omitted such phrases as "be it also enacted" and "done at the city of
Washington, etc." without any indication. I have in most instances abbreviated Article to
Art. and Section to Sec., and I have frequently substituted numbered dates for the lengthier
form. I have no doubt that in the many processes of copying, collating, and printing, numerous errors have crept in; for these I beg the indulgence of the reader.

I am under obligation to many people for coöperation in the compilation of this volume.
The officials of the libraries of New York University bore patiently with my demands. To
my colleagues in the Department of History, Mr. Cochran, Mr. Craven, Mr. Hoffman,
Mr. Musser, and Mr. Wettereau, to Mr. Stein of the Department of Economics, Mr. Thach
of the Department of Government, and Dean Sommer of the Law School of New York
University, I am grateful for suggestions. Without the faithful and intelligent assistance of
Miss Margaret Carroll this volume could never have been prepared.

                                                    HENRY STEELE COMMAGER

PREFACE TO THE NINTH EDITION

In order to avoid an enlargement that would make *Documents of American History* un-
wieldy, I have had to drop some of the documents of the seventh and eighth editions. In
every case these documents illustrated events which, from the perspective of 1973, seem
somewhat less important than they did when originally inserted, or, as in the case of some
judicial opinions, have been superseded by more recent decisions. We have included here
new documents from the period since 1966—an era that has seen far-reaching developments
in constitutional, political, diplomatic, and social realms. In the selection and editing of the
documents I have been greatly aided by Professor Milton Cantor of the University of
Massachusetts.

                                                    HENRY STEELE COMMAGER

TABLE OF CONTENTS

DOCUMENTS OF
AMERICAN HISTORY

Since 1898

346. McKINLEY'S WAR MESSAGE
April 11, 1898

(Richardson, ed. *Messages and Papers*, Vol. X, p. 139 ff.)

In this message to Congress President McKinley recounted the events which in his opinion justified intervention in Cuba. Filled with suggestion and innuendo, the account is thoroughly misleading, but it struck a responsive note in Congress and in the public mind. In as much as Spain, in the note received by McKinley April 10, promised to order an immediate cessation of hostilities in Cuba, the principal basis for intervention had disappeared. For recognition of Cuban independence, see Doc. No. 347. See W. Millis, *The Martial Spirit;* F. E. Chadwick, *Relations of the United States and Spain*, Vol. I; C. S. Olcott, *Life of William McKinley*, 2 Vols.; J. H. Latané, *America as a World Power*, ch. i. For diplomatic correspondence, see *Foreign Relations of the United States*, 1898; and *Spanish Diplomatic Correspondence and Documents, 1896–1900.* An analysis of this is in H. E. Flack, *Spanish-American Diplomatic Relations Preceding the War of 1898.*

EXECUTIVE MANSION, *April 11, 1898.*
To the Congress of the United States:

Obedient to that precept of the Constitution which commands the President to give from time to time to the Congress information of the state of the Union and to recommend to their consideration such measures as he shall judge necessary and expedient, it becomes my duty to now address your body with regard to the grave crisis that has arisen in the relations of the United States to Spain by reason of the warfare that for more than three years has raged in the neighboring island of Cuba. . . .

The present revolution is but the successor of other similar insurrections which have occurred in Cuba against the dominion of Spain, extending over a period of nearly half a century, each of which during its progress has subjected the United States to great effort and expense in enforcing its neutrality laws, caused enormous losses to American trade and commerce, caused irritation, annoyance, and disturbance among our citizens, and, by the exercise of cruel, barbarous, and uncivilized practices of warfare, shocked the sensibilities and offended the human sympathies of our people. . . .

Our trade has suffered, the capital invested by our citizens in Cuba has been largely lost, and the temper and forbearance of our people have been so sorely tried as to beget a perilous unrest among our own citizens, which has inevitably found its expression from time to time in the National Legislature, so that issues wholly external to our own body politic engross attention and stand in the way of that close devotion to domestic advancement that becomes a self-contained commonwealth whose primal maxim has been the avoidance of all foreign entanglements. All this must needs awaken, and has, indeed, aroused, the utmost concern on the part of this Government, as well during my predecessor's term as in my own.

In April, 1896, the evils from which our country suffered through the Cuban war became so onerous that my predecessor made an effort to bring about a peace through the mediation of this Government in any way that might tend to an honorable adjustment of the contest between Spain and her revolted colony, on the basis of some effective scheme of self-government for Cuba under the flag and sovereignty of Spain. It failed through the refusal of the Spanish government then in power to consider any form of mediation or, indeed, any plan of settlement which did not begin with the actual submission of the insurgents to the mother country, and then only on such terms as Spain herself might see fit to grant. The war continued unabated. The resistance of the insurgents was in no wise diminished. . . .

The overtures of this Government made through its new envoy, General Woodford, and looking to an immediate and effective amelioration of the condition of the island, although not accepted to the extent of admitted mediation in any shape, were met by assurances that home rule in an advanced phase would be forthwith offered to Cuba, without waiting for the war to end, and that more humane methods should thenceforth prevail in the conduct of hostilities. Coincidentally with these declarations the new government of Spain continued and completed the policy, already begun by its predecessor, of testifying friendly regard for this nation by releasing American citizens held under one charge or another connected with the insurrection, so that by the end of November not a single person entitled in any way to our national protection remained in a Spanish prison. . . .

The necessity for a change in the condition of the reconcentrados is recognized by the Spanish Government. Within a few days past the orders of General Weyler have been revoked. The reconcentrados, it is said, are to be permitted to return to their homes and aided to resume the self-supporting pursuits of peace. Public works have been ordered to give them employment and a sum of $600,000 has been appropriated for their relief.

The war in Cuba is of such a nature that, short of subjugation or extermination, a final military victory for either side seems impracticable. The alternative lies in the physical exhaustion of the one or the other party, or perhaps of both—a condition which in effect ended the ten years' war by the truce of Zanjon. The prospect of such a protraction and conclusion of the present strife is a contingency hardly to be contemplated with equanimity by the civilized world, and least of all by the United States, affected and injured as we are, deeply and intimately, by its very existence.

Realizing this, it appeared to be my duty, in a spirit of true friendliness, no less to Spain than to the Cubans, who have so much to lose by the prolongation of the struggle, to seek to bring about an immediate termination of the war. To this end I submitted on the 27th ultimo, as a result of much representation and correspondence, through the United States minister at Madrid, propositions to the Spanish Government looking to an armistice until October 1 for the negotiation of peace with the good offices of the President.

In addition I asked the immediate revocation of the order of reconcentration, so as to permit the people to return to their farms and the needy to be relieved with provisions and supplies from the United States, co-operating with the Spanish authorities, so as to afford full relief.

The reply of the Spanish cabinet was received on the night of the 31st ultimo. It offered, as the means to bring about peace in Cuba, to confide the preparation thereof to the insular parliament, inasmuch as the concurrence of that body would be necessary to reach a final result, it being, however, understood that the powers reserved by the constitution to the central Government are not lessened or diminished. As the Cuban parliament does not meet until the 4th of May next, the Spanish Government would not object for its part to accept at once a suspension of hostilities if asked for by the insurgents from the general in chief, to whom it would pertain in such case to determine the duration and conditions of the armistice. . . .

With this last overture in the direction of immediate peace, and its disappointing reception by Spain, the Executive is brought to the end of his effort.

In my annual message of December last I said.

Of the untried measures there remain only: recognition of the insurgents as belligerents; recognition of the independence of Cuba; neutral intervention to end the war by imposing a rational compromise between the contestants, and intervention in favor of one or the other party. I speak not of forcible annexation, for that can not be thought of. That, by our code of morality, would be criminal aggression.

Thereupon I reviewed these alternatives in the light of President Grant's measured words, uttered in 1875, when, after seven years of sanguinary, destructive, and cruel hostilities in Cuba, he reached the conclusion that the recognition of the independence of Cuba was impracticable and indefensible and that the recognition of belligerence was not warranted by the facts according to the tests of public law. I commented especially upon the latter aspect of the question, pointing out the inconveniences and positive dangers of a recognition of belligerence, which, while adding to the already onerous burdens of neutrality within our own jurisdiction, could not in any way extend our influence or effective offices in the territory of hostilities.

Nothing has since occurred to change my view in this regard, and I recognize as fully now as then that the issuance of a proclamation of neutrality, by which process the so-called recognition of belligerents is published, could of itself and unattended by other action accomplish nothing toward the one end for which we labor—the instant pacification of Cuba and the cessation of the misery that afflicts the island. . . .

There remain the alternative forms of intervention to end the war, either as an impartial neutral, by imposing a rational compromise between the contestants, or as the active ally of the one party or the other.

As to the first, it is not to be forgotten that during the last few months the relation of the United States has virtually been one of friendly intervention in many ways, each not of itself conclusive, but all tending to the exertion of a potential influence toward an ultimate pacific result, just and honorable to all interests concerned. The spirit of all our acts hitherto has been an earnest, unselfish desire for peace and prosperity in Cuba, untarnished by differences between us and Spain and unstained by the blood of American citizens.

The forcible intervention of the United States as a neutral to stop the war, according to the large dictates of humanity and following many historical precedents where neighboring states have interfered to check the hopeless sacrifices of life by internecine conflicts beyond their borders, is justifiable on rational grounds. It involves, however, hostile constraint upon both the parties to the contest, as well to enforce a truce as to guide the eventual settlement.

The grounds for such intervention may be briefly summarized as follows:

First. In the cause of humanity and to put an end to the barbarities, bloodshed, starvation, and horrible miseries now existing there, and which the parties to the conflict are either unable or unwilling to stop or mitigate. It is no answer to say this is all in another country, belonging to another nation, and is therefore none of our business. It is specially our duty, for it is right at our door.

Second. We owe it to our citizens in Cuba to afford them that protection and indemnity for life and property which no government there can or will afford, and to that end to terminate the conditions that deprive them of legal protection.

Third. The right to intervene may be justified by the very serious injury to the commerce, trade, and business of our people and by the wanton destruction of property and devastation of the island.

Fourth, and which is of the utmost importance. The present condition of affairs in Cuba is a constant menace to our peace and entails upon this Government an enormous expense. With such a conflict waged for years in an island so near us and with which our people have such trade and business relations; when the lives and liberty of our citizens are in constant danger and their property destroyed and themselves ruined; where our trading vessels are liable to seizure and are seized at our very door by war ships of a foreign nation; the expeditions of fili-bustering that we are powerless to prevent al-together, and the irritating questions and entanglements thus arising—all these and others that I need not mention, with the resulting strained relations, are a constant menace to our peace and compel us to keep on a semi-war footing with a nation with which we are at peace.

These elements of danger and disorder al-ready pointed out have been strikingly il-lustrated by a tragic event which has deeply and justly moved the American people. I have already transmitted to Congress the re-port of the naval court of inquiry on the destruction of the battle ship *Maine* in the harbor of Havana during the night of the 15th of February. The destruction of that noble vessel has filled the national heart with inexpressible horror. Two hundred and fifty-eight brave sailors and marines and two of-ficers of our Navy, reposing in the fancied security of a friendly harbor, have been hurled to death, grief and want brought to their homes and sorrow to the nation.

The naval court of inquiry, which, it is needless to say, commands the unqualified confidence of the Government, was unani-mous in its conclusion that the destruction of the *Maine* was caused by an exterior ex-plosion—that of a submarine mine. It did not assume to place the responsibility. That remains to be fixed.

In any event, the destruction of the *Maine*, by whatever exterior cause, is a patent and impressive proof of a state of things in Cuba that is intolerable. That condition is thus shown to be such that the Spanish Govern-ment can not assure safety and security to a vessel of the American Navy in the harbor of Havana on a mission of peace, and right-fully there. . . .

The long trial has proved that the object for which Spain has waged the war can not be attained. The fire of insurrection may flame or may smolder with varying seasons, but it has not been and it is plain that it can not be extinguished by present methods. The only hope of relief and repose from a condition which can no longer be endured is the enforced pacification of Cuba. In the name of humanity, in the name of civiliza-tion, in behalf of endangered American in-terests which give us the right and the duty to speak and to act, the war in Cuba must stop.

In view of these facts and of these con-siderations I ask the Congress to authorize and empower the President to take measures to secure a full and final termination of hostilities between the Government of Spain and the people of Cuba, and to secure in the island the establishment of a stable govern-ment, capable of maintaining order and ob-serving its international obligations, insuring peace and tranquillity and the security of its citizens as well as our own, and to use the military and naval forces of the United States as may be necessary for these purposes.

And in the interest of humanity and to aid in preserving the lives of the starving people of the island I recommend that the distribution of food and supplies be continued and that an appropriation be made out of the public Treasury to supplement the charity of our citizens.

The issue is now with the Congress. It is a solemn responsibility. I have exhausted every effort to relieve the intolerable condition of affairs which is at our doors. Prepared to execute every obligation imposed upon me by the Constitution and the law, I await your action.

Yesterday, and since the preparation of the foregoing message, official information was received by me that the latest decree of the Queen Regent of Spain directs General Blanco, in order to prepare and facilitate peace, to proclaim a suspension of hostilities, the duration and details of which have not yet been communicated to me.

This fact, with every other pertinent con-sideration, will, I am sure, have your just and careful attention in the solemn delibera-tions upon which you are about to enter. If this measure attains a successful result, then our aspirations as a Christian, peace-loving people will be realized. If it fails, it will be only another justification for our contem-plated action.

WILLIAM McKINLEY.

347. THE INDEPENDENCE OF CUBA
April 20, 1898

(U. S. Statutes at Large, Vol. XXX, p. 738)

April 11, McKinley sent his message to Congress recommending intervention in Cuba. See Doc. No. 346. The Joint Resolution of April 20 authorized the use of the army and the navy to effect Cuban independence; the formal declaration of war followed April 25. The most important of the resolutions of April 20 was the fourth, known as the Teller Amendment. See references, Doc. No. 346.

Joint resolution for the recognition of the independence of the people of Cuba, demanding that the Government of Spain relinquish its authority and government in the Island of Cuba, and to withdraw its land and naval forces from Cuba and Cuban waters, and directing the President of the United States to use the land and naval forces of the United States to carry these resolutions into effect.

Whereas the abhorrent conditions which have existed for more than three years in the Island of Cuba, so near our own borders, have shocked the moral sense of the people of the United States, have been a disgrace to Christian civilization, culminating, as they have, in the destruction of a United States battle ship, with two hundred and sixty-six of its officers and crew, while on a friendly visit in the harbor of Havana, and can not longer be endured, as has been set forth by the President of the United States in his message to Congress of April eleventh, eighteen hundred and ninety-eight, upon which the action of Congress was invited: Therefore,

Resolved, First. That the people of the Island of Cuba are, and of right ought to be, free and independent.

Second. That it is the duty of the United States to demand, and the Government of the United States does hereby demand, that the Government of Spain at once relinquish its authority and government in the Island of Cuba and withdraw its land and naval forces from Cuba and Cuban waters.

Third. That the President of the United States be, and he hereby is, directed and empowered to use the entire land and naval forces of the United States, and to call into the actual service of the United States the militia of the several States, to such extent as may be necessary to carry these resolutions into effect.

Fourth. That the United States hereby disclaims any disposition or intention to exercise sovereignty, jurisdiction, or control over said Island except for the pacification thereof, and asserts its determination, when that is accomplished, to leave the government and control of the Island to its people.

348. THE ANNEXATION OF HAWAII
July 7, 1898

(U. S. Statutes at Large, Vol. XXX, p. 750-51)

Though President Cleveland withdrew from the Senate the Treaty of 1893 providing for the annexation of the Hawaiian Islands and denounced the methods by which the Hawaiian revolution had been brought about, Queen Liliuokalani was not restored to the throne. In July 1894 the Republic of Hawaii was established, and was recognized by the United States. Agitation for annexation continued, and a second treaty of annexation was concluded in 1897. While this treaty was still pending in the Senate the war with Spain broke out and the United States used the islands as a naval base. The islands were then annexed by joint resolution in order to avoid the danger of rejection by one-third of the Senate.

Joint Resolution To provide for annexing, the Hawaiian Islands to the United States.

WHEREAS the Government of the Republic of Hawaii having, in due form, signified its consent, in the manner provided by its constitution, to cede absolutely and without reserve to the United States of America all rights of sovereignty of whatsoever kind in and over the Hawaiian Islands and their dependencies, and also to cede and transfer to the United States the absolute fee and ownership of all public, Government, or Crown lands, public buildings or edifices, ports, harbors, military equipment, and all other public property of every kind and description belonging to the Government of the Hawaiian Islands, together with every right and appurtenance thereunto appertaining: Therefore,

Resolved, That said cession is accepted, ratified, and confirmed, and that the said Hawaiian Islands and their dependencies be, and they are hereby, annexed as a part of the territory of the United States and are subject to the sovereign dominion thereof, and that all and singular the property and rights hereinbefore mentioned are vested in the United States of America.

The existing laws of the United States relative to public lands shall not apply to such lands in the Hawaiian Islands; but the Congress of the United States shall enact special laws for their management and disposition: *Provided,* That all revenue from or proceeds of the same, except as regards such part thereof as may be used or occupied for the civil, military, or naval purposes of the United States, or may be assigned for the use of the local government, shall be used solely for the benefit of the inhabitants of the Hawaiian Islands for educational and other public purposes.

Until Congress shall provide for the government of such islands all the civil, judicial, and military powers exercised by the officers of the existing government in said islands shall be vested in such person or persons and shall be exercised in such manner as the President of the United States shall direct; and the President shall have power to remove said officers and fill the vacancies so occasioned.

The existing treaties of the Hawaiian Islands with foreign nations shall forthwith cease and determine, being replaced by such treaties as may exist, or as may be hereafter concluded, between the United States and such foreign nations. The municipal legislation of the Hawaiian Islands, not enacted for the fulfillment of the treaties so extinguished, and not inconsistent with this joint resolution nor contrary to the Constitution of the United States nor to any existing treaty of the United States, shall remain in force until the Congress of the United States shall otherwise determine.

Until legislation shall be enacted extending the United States customs laws and regulations to the Hawaiian Islands the existing customs relations of the Hawaiian Islands with the United States and other countries shall remain unchanged.

The public debt of the Republic of Hawaii, lawfully existing at the date of the passage of this joint resolution, including the amounts due to depositors in the Hawaiian Postal Savings Bank, is hereby assumed by the Government of the United States; but the liability of the United States in this regard shall in no case exceed four million dollars. So long, however, as the existing Government and the present commercial relations of the Hawaiian Islands are continued as hereinbefore provided said Government shall continue to pay the interest on said debt.

There shall be no further immigration of Chinese into the Hawaiian Islands, except upon such conditions as are now or may hereafter be allowed by the laws of the United States; and no Chinese, by reason of anything herein contained, shall be allowed to enter the United States from the Hawaiian Islands.

The President shall appoint five commissioners, at least two of whom shall be residents of the Hawaiian Islands, who shall, as soon as reasonably practicable, recommend to Congress such legislation concerning the Hawaiian Islands as they shall deem necessary or proper. . . .

349. TREATY OF PEACE WITH SPAIN
Concluded at Paris
December 10, 1898

(U. S. Statutes at Large, Vol. XXX, p. 1754 ff.)

The American commissioners were William R. Day, Cushman K. Davis, William P. Frye, George Gray, and Whitelaw Reid. For the history of the negotiations see, *Papers relating to the Treaty with Spain,* 56 Cong. 1 Sess. Senate Doc. No. 148; R. Cortissoz, *Whitelaw Reid,* Vol. II, chs. xii, xiii; J. H. Latané, *America as a World Power,* ch. iv; W. S. Holt, *Treaties Defeated by the Senate,* ch. viii. The cession of the Philippines to the United States precipitated a contest over ratification that seriously threatened the fate of the treaty.

ART. I. Spain relinquishes all claim of sovereignty over and title to Cuba.

And as the island is, upon its evacuation by Spain, to be occupied by the United States, the United States will, so long as such occupation shall last, assume and discharge the obligations that may under international law result from the fact of its occupation, for the protection of life and property.

ART. II. Spain cedes to the United States the island of Porto Rico and other islands now under Spanish sovereignty in the West Indies, and the island of Guam in the Marianas or Ladrones.

ART. III. Spain cedes to the United States the archipelago known as the Philippine Islands, and comprehending the islands lying within the following line:

A line running from west to east along or near the twentieth parallel of north latitude, and through the middle of the navigable channel of Bachi, from the one hundred and eighteenth (118th) to the one hundred and twenty seventh (127th) degree meridian of longitude east of Greenwich, thence along the one hundred and twenty seventh (127th) degree meridian of longitude east of Greenwich to the parallel of four degrees and forty five minutes (4° 45') north latitude, thence along the parellel of four degrees and forty five minutes (4° 45') north latitude to its intersection with the meridian of longitude one hundred and nineteen degrees and thirty five minutes (119° 35') east of Greenwich, thence along the meridian of longitude one hundred and nineteen degrees and thirty five minutes (119° 35') east of Greenwich to the parallel of latitude seven degrees and forty minutes (7° 40') north, thence along the parallel of latitude seven degrees and forty minutes (7° 40') north to its intersection with the one hundred and sixteenth (116th) degree meridian of longitude east of Greenwich, thence by a direct line to the intersection of the tenth (10th) degree parallel of north latitude with the one hundred and eighteenth (118th) degree meridian of longitude east of Greenwich, and thence along the one hundred and eighteenth (118th) degree meridian of longitude east of Greenwich to the point of beginning.

The United States will pay to Spain the sum of twenty million dollars ($20,000,000) within three months after the exchange of the ratifications of the present treaty.

ART. IV. The United States will, for the term of ten years from the date of the exchange of the ratifications of the present treaty, admit Spanish ships and merchandise to the ports of the Philippine Islands on the same terms as ships and merchandise of the United States. . . .

ART. VII. The United States and Spain mutually relinquish all claims for indemnity, national and individual, of every kind, of either Government, or of its citizens or subjects, against the other Government, that may have arisen since the beginning of the late insurrection in Cuba and prior to the exchange of ratifications of the present treaty, including all claims for indemnity for the cost of the war.

The United States will adjudicate and settle the claims of its citizens against Spain relinquished in this article.

ART. VIII. In conformity with the provisions of Articles I, II, and III of this treaty, Spain relinquishes in Cuba, and cedes in Porto Rico and other islands in the West Indies, in the island of Guam, and in the Philippine Archipelago, all the buildings, wharves, barracks, forts, structures, public highways and other immovable property which, in conformity with law, belong to the public domain, and as such belong to the Crown of Spain.

And it is hereby declared that the relinquishment or cession, as the case may be, to which the preceding paragraph refers, cannot in any respect impair the property or rights which by law belong to the peaceful possession of property of all kinds, of provinces, municipalities, public or private establishments, ecclesiastical or civic bodies, or any other associations having legal capacity to acquire and possess property in the aforesaid territories renounced or ceded, or of private individuals, of whatsoever nationality such individuals may be.

The aforesaid relinquishment or cession, as the case may be, includes all documents exclusively referring to the sovereignty relinquished or ceded that may exist in the archives of the Peninsula. Where any document in such archives only in part relates to said sovereignty, a copy of such part will be furnished whenever it shall be requested. Like rules shall be reciprocally observed in favor of Spain in respect of documents in the archives of the islands above referred to.

In the aforesaid relinquishment or cession, as the case may be, are also included such rights as the Crown of Spain and its authorities possess in respect of the official archives and records, executive as well as judicial, in the islands above referred to, which relate to said islands or the rights and property of their inhabitants. Such archives and records shall be carefully preserved, and private persons shall without distinction have the right to require, in accordance with law, authenticated copies of the contracts, wills and other instruments forming part of notarial protocols or files, or which may be contained in the executive or judicial archives, be the latter in Spain or in the islands aforesaid. . . .

ART. X. The inhabitants of the territories over which Spain relinquishes or cedes her sovereignty shall be secured in the free exercise of their religion.

ART. XI. The Spaniards residing in the territories over which Spain by this treaty cedes or relinquishes her sovereignty shall be subject in matters civil as well as criminal to the jurisdiction of the courts of the country wherein they reside, pursuant to the ordinary laws governing the same; and they shall have the right to appear before such courts, and to pursue the same course as citizens of the country to which the courts belong. . . .

ART. XIII. The rights of property secured by copyrights and patents acquired by Spaniards in the Island of Cuba, and in Porto Rico, the Philippines and other ceded territories, at the time of the exchange of the ratifications of this treaty, shall continue to be respected. Spanish scientific, literary and artistic works, not subversive of public order in the territories in question, shall continue to be admitted free of duty into such territories, for the period of ten years, to be reckoned from the date of the exchange of the ratifications of this treaty. . . .

ART. XV. The Government of each country will, for the term of ten years, accord to the merchant vessels of the other country the same treatment in respect of all port charges, including entrance and clearance dues, light dues, and tonnage duties, as it accords to its own merchant vessels, not engaged in the coastwise trade.

This article may at any time be terminated on six months' notice given by either Government to the other.

ART. XVI. It is understood that any obligations assumed in this treaty by the United States with respect to Cuba are limited to the time of its occupancy thereof; but it will upon the termination of such occupancy, advise any Government established in the island to assume the same obligations.

350. THE OPEN DOOR IN CHINA
1899–1900

In both England and the United States there was at the close of the century a growing apprehension that the encroachments of the European powers and of Japan on China would destroy the territorial integrity and sovereignty of China and would lead to discriminations at the expense of English and American rights. In March 1898 the English Ambassador approached the United States with a suggestion for joint action to protect the integrity of China; eventually the agitation of Lord Charles Beresford, the influence of W. W. Rockhill of the American State Department, and of Alfred Hippisley, an Englishman, led to the concrete formulation of the famous Open Door policy. This policy was first announced in the circular note of September 6, 1899. For the various replies of the Powers, many of them far from "final and definitive," see *Foreign Relations of the United States,* 1899, p. 128 ff. Evasive as these replies were, Hay interpreted them to indicate acceptance of the Open Door policy and promptly announced such acquiescence in the circular note of March 20, 1900. Shortly thereafter the outbreak of the Boxer uprising seriously endangered the Open Door policy, and Hay moved once again to formulate and apply that policy. To the note of July 3 there were, however, no satisfactory replies. Of these Open Door notes, Dr. Tyler Dennett says, "It would have taken more than a lawyer to define what new rights had been recognized, or required, or even what had actually been said, but such comment is beside the point. These notes had not been put forward by a lawyer as a contribution to the law of nations, but by a publicist to crystallize public opinion." (*Hay,* p. 293). See, T. Dennett, *John Hay,* chs. xxiv–xxvi; W. W. Willoughby, *Foreign Rights and Interests in China,* 2 Vols.; T. F. Millard, *Democracy and the Eastern Question;* H. Chung, *The Oriental Policy of the United States;* M. J. Bau, *The Open Door Doctrine.* For a critical evaluation of the Open Door policy see J. Barnes, ed. *Empire in the East.* An appreciation of Hay's gesture is "The Quarry" by William Vaughn Moody.

1. HAY'S CIRCULAR LETTER,
September 6, 1899

(Malloy, ed. *Treaties, Conventions, etc.,* Vol. I, p. 246)

MR. HAY TO MR. WHITE

DEPARTMENT OF STATE

WASHINGTON, September 6, 1899.

SIR: At the time when the Government of the United States was informed by that of Germany that it had leased from His Majesty the Emperor of China the port of Kiao-chao and the adjacent territory in the province of Shantung, assurances were given to the ambassador of the United States at Berlin by the Imperial German minister for foreign affairs that the rights and privileges insured by treaties with China to citizens of the United States would not thereby suffer or be in anywise impaired within the area over which Germany had thus obtained control.

More recently, however, the British Government recognized by a formal agreement with Germany the exclusive right of the latter country to enjoy in said leased area and the contiguous "sphere of influence or interest" certain privileges, more especially those relating to railroads and mining enterprises; but, as the exact nature and extent of the rights thus recognized have not been clearly defined, it is possible that serious conflicts of interest may at any time arise, not only between British and German subjects within said area, but that the interests of our citizens may also be jeopardized thereby.

Earnestly desirous to remove any cause of irritation and to insure at the same time to the commerce of all nations in China the undoubted benefits which should accrue from a formal recognition by the various powers claiming "spheres of interest" that they shall enjoy perfect equality of treatment for their commerce and navigation within such "spheres," the Government of the United States would be pleased to see His German Majesty's Government give formal assurances and lend its coöperation in securing like assurances from the other interested powers that each within its respective sphere of whatever influence—

First. Will in no way interfere with any treaty port or any vested interest within any so-called "sphere of interest" or leased territory it may have in China.

Second. That the Chinese treaty tariff of the time being shall apply to all merchandise landed or shipped to all such ports as are within said "sphere of interest" (unless they be "free ports"), no matter to what nationality it may belong, and that duties so leviable shall be collected by the Chinese Government.

Third. That it will levy no higher harbor dues on vessels of another nationality frequenting any port in such "sphere" than shall be levied on vessels of its own nationality, and no higher railroad charges over lines built, controlled, or operated within its "sphere" on merchandise belonging to citizens or subjects of other nationalities transported through such "sphere" than shall be levied on similar merchandise belonging to its own nationals transported over equal distances.

The liberal policy pursued by His Imperial German Majesty in declaring Kiao-chao a free port and in aiding the Chinese Government in the establishment there of a custom-house are so clearly in line with the proposition which this Government is anxious. to see recognized that it entertains the strongest hope that Germany will give its acceptance and hearty support.

The recent ukase of His Majesty the Emperor of Russia declaring the port of Ta-lien-wan open during the whole of the lease under which it is held from China, to the merchant ships of all nations, coupled with the categorical assurances made to this Government by His Imperial Majesty's representative at this capital at the time, and since repeated to me by the present Russian ambassador, seem to insure the support of the Emperor to the proposed measure. Our ambassador at the Court of St. Petersburg has, in consequence, been instructed to submit it to the Russian Government and to request their early consideration of it. A copy of my instruction on the subject to Mr. Tower is herewith inclosed for your confidential information.

The commercial interests of Great Britain and Japan will be so clearly served by the desired declaration of intentions, and the views of the Governments of these countries as to the desirability of the adoption of measures insuring the benefits of equality of treatment of all foreign trade throughout China are so similar to those entertained by the United States, that their acceptance of the propositions herein outlined and their co-operation in advocating their adoption by the other powers can be confidently expected. I inclose herewith copy of the instruction which I have sent to Mr. Choate on the subject.

In view of the present favorable conditions, you are instructed to submit the above considerations to His Imperial German Majesty's minister for foreign affairs, and to request his early consideration of the subject.

Copy of this instruction is sent to our ambassadors at London and at St. Petersburg for their information.

I have, etc.,   JOHN HAY.

2. HAY'S LETTER OF INSTRUCTION
March 20, 1900

(Malloy, ed. *Treaties, Conventions, etc.*, Vol. I, p. 260)

Instructions sent mutatus mutandis to the United States ambassadors at London, Paris, Berlin, St. Petersburg, and Rome, and to the United States Minister at Tokyo.

Department of State,
Washington, March 20, 1900.

SIR: The —— Government having accepted the declaration suggested by the United States concerning foreign trade in China, the terms of which I transmitted to you in my instruction No. — of ——, and like action having been taken by all the various powers having leased territory or so-called "spheres of interest" in the Chinese Empire, as shown by the notes which I herewith transmit to you, you will please inform the government to which you are accredited, that the condition originally attached to its acceptance— that all other powers concerned should likewise accept the proposals of the United States —having been complied with, this Government will therefore consider the assent given to it by —— as final and definitive.

You will also transmit to the minister of foreign affairs copies of the present inclosures, and by the same occasion convey to him the expression of the sincere gratification which the President feels at the successful termination of these negotiations, in which he sees proof of the friendly spirit which animates the various powers interested in the untrammeled development of commerce and industry in the Chinese Empire and a source of vast benefit to the whole commercial world.

I am, etc.,   JOHN HAY.

3. HAY'S CIRCULAR LETTER OF
July 3, 1900

(Foreign Relations of the United States, 1900, p. 345)

Circular telegram sent to the United States embassies in Berlin, Paris, London, Rome, and St. Petersburg, and to the United States missions in Vienna, Brussels, Madrid, Tokyo, The Hague, and Lisbon.

Department of State,
Washington, July 3, 1900.

In this critical posture of affairs in China it is deemed appropriate to define the attitude of the United States as far as present circumstances permit this to be done. We adhere to the policy initiated by us in 1857, of peace with the Chinese nation, of furtherance of lawful commerce, and of protection of lives and property of our citizens by all means guaranteed under extraterritorial treaty rights and by the law of nations. If wrong be done to our citizens we propose to hold the responsible authors to the uttermost accountability. We regard the condition at Pekin as one of virtual anarchy, whereby power and responsibility are practically devolved upon the local provincial authorities. So long as they are not in overt collusion with rebellion and use their power to protect foreign life and property we regard them as representing the Chinese people, with whom we seek to remain in peace and friendship. The purpose of the President is, as it has been heretofore, to act concurrently with the other powers, first, in opening up communication with Pekin and rescuing the American officials, missionaries, and other Americans who are in danger; secondly, in affording all possible protection everywhere in China to American life and property; thirdly, in guarding and protecting all legitimate American interests; and fourthly, in aiding to prevent a spread of the disorders to the other provinces of the Empire and a recurrence of such disasters. It is, of course, too early to forecast the means of attaining this last result; but the policy of the government of the United States is to seek a solution which may bring about permanent safety and peace to China, preserve Chinese territorial and administrative entity, protect all rights guaranteed to friendly powers by treaty and international law, and safeguard for the world the principle of equal and impartial trade with all parts of the Chinese Empire.

You will communicate the purport of this instruction to the minister for foreign affairs.

Hay.

351. PLATFORM OF THE AMERICAN ANTI-IMPERIALIST LEAGUE
October 18, 1899

(C. Schurz, Speeches, Correspondence and Political Speeches, Vol. V, p. 77 ff.)

This platform was adopted at the Anti-imperialist Congress which met in Chicago, October 17, 1899. The league was composed of various local and sectional anti-imperialist leagues; George S. Boutwell of Massachusetts was elected president of the new organization. For anti-imperialism, see M. Lanzar-Carpia, "The Anti-Imperialist League," *Philippine Social Science Review*, Vol. IV; M. A. DeWolfe Howe, *Portrait of an Independent: Moorfield Storey;* M. Storey and M. P. Lichauco, *Conquest of the Philippines by the United States;* R. F. Pettigrew, *The Course of Empire.*

We hold that the policy known as imperialism is hostile to liberty and tends toward militarism, an evil from which it has been our glory to be free. We regret that it has become necessary in the land of Washington and Lincoln to reaffirm that all men, of whatever race or color, are entitled to life, liberty, and the pursuit of happiness. We maintain that governments derive their just powers from the consent of the governed. We insist that the subjugation of any people is "criminal aggression" and open disloyalty to the distinctive principles of our Government.

We earnestly condemn the policy of the present National Administration in the Philippines. It seeks to extinguish the spirit of

1776 in those islands. We deplore the sacrifice of our soldiers and sailors, whose bravery deserves admiration even in an unjust war. We denounce the slaughter of the Filipinos as a needless horror. We protest against the extension of American sovereignty by Spanish methods.

We demand the immediate cessation of the war against liberty, begun by Spain and continued by us. We urge that Congress be promptly convened to announce to the Filipinos our purpose to concede to them the independence for which they have so long fought and which of right is theirs.

The United States have always protested against the doctrine of international law which permits the subjugation of the weak by the strong. A self-governing state cannot accept sovereignty over an unwilling people. The United States cannot act upon the ancient heresy that might makes right.

Imperialists assume that with the destruction of self-government in the Philippines by American hands, all opposition here will cease. This is a grievous error. Much as we abhor the war of "criminal aggression" in the Philippines, greatly as we regret that the blood of the Filipinos is on American hands, we more deeply resent the betrayal of American institutions at home. The real firing line is not in the suburbs of Manila. The foe is of our own household. The attempt of 1861 was to divide the country. That of 1899 is to destroy its fundamental principles and noblest ideals.

Whether the ruthless slaughter of the Filipinos shall end next month or next year is but an incident in a contest that must go on until the Declaration of Independence and the Constitution of the United States are rescued from the hands of their betrayers. Those who dispute about standards of value while the Republic is undermined will be listened to as little as those who would wrangle about the small economies of the household while the house is on fire. The training of a great people for a century, the

aspiration for liberty of a vast immigration are forces that will hurl aside those who in the delirium of conquest seek to destroy the character of our institutions.

We deny that the obligation of all citizens to support their Government in times of grave National peril applies to the present situation. If an Administration may with impunity ignore the issues upon which it was chosen, deliberately create a condition of war anywhere on the face of the globe, debauch the civil service for spoils to promote the adventure, organize a truth-suppressing censorship and demand of all citizens a suspension of judgement and their unanimous support while it chooses to continue the fighting, representative government itself is imperiled.

We propose to contribute to the defeat of any person or party that stands for the forcible subjugation of any people. We shall oppose for reëlection all who in the White House or in Congress betray American liberty in pursuit of un-American gains. We still hope that both of our great political parties will support and defend the Declaration of Independence in the closing campaign of the century.

We hold, with Abraham Lincoln, that "no man is good enough to govern another man without that man's consent. When the white man governs himself, that is self-government, but when he governs himself and also governs another man, that is more than self-government—that is despotism". "Our reliance is in the love of liberty which God has planted in us. Our defense is in the spirit which prizes liberty as the heritage of all men in all lands. Those who deny freedom to others deserve it not for themselves, and under a just God cannot long retain it."

We cordially invite the coöperation of all men and women who remain loyal to the Declaration of Independence and the Constitution of the United States.

352. DOWNES v. BIDWELL
182 U. S. 244
1901

Error to the United States circuit court for the   Southern district of New York. This was an action brought by Downes against Bidwell, collector of the port of New York, to recover back duties paid under protest upon a consignment shipped to the plaintiff from Porto Rico in November, 1900. The duties were collected under the Foraker Act of April 2, 1900, providing a temporary government for the island. This is one of the earliest of the so-called Insular Cases, dealing with the vexed question of the constitutional relations of the United States with the territories acquired through the War with Spain. Mr. John W. Davis said of these Insular Cases that "there may be found in these opinions the most hotly contested and long continued duel in the life of the Supreme Court." The literature, technical and controversial, on the insular cases and the general question of imperialism is enormous. The briefs and arguments in the insular cases were published in *House Documents, 56 Cong. 2 Sess. No. 509*. For general treatments of the constitutional questions involved, see, W. F. Willoughby, *Territories and Dependencies of the United States;* C. F. Randolph, *Law and Policy of Annexation;* and C. E. Magoon, *Legal Status of the Territory and Inhabitants of the Islands Acquired by the United States during the War with Spain.*

BROWN, J. This case involves the question whether merchandise brought into the port of New York from Porto Rico, since the passage of the Foraker act, is exempt from duty, notwithstanding the third section of that act, which requires the payment of "fifteen per centum of the duties which are required to be levied, collected and paid upon like articles of merchandise imported from foreign countries.". . .

In the case of *De Lima* v. *Bidwell* just decided, we held that upon the ratification of the treaty of peace with Spain, Porto Rico ceased to be a foreign country, and became a territory of the United States, and that duties were no longer collectible upon merchandise brought from that island. We are now asked to hold that it became a part of the *United States* within that provision of the Constitution which declares that "all duties, imposts and excises shall be uniform throughout the United States." Art. I, Sec. 8. If Porto Rico be a part of the United States, the Foraker act imposing duties upon its products is unconstitutional, not only by reason of a violation of the uniformity clause, but because by section 9 "vessels bound to or from one State" cannot "be obliged to enter, clear or pay duties in another."

The case also involves the broader question whether the revenue clauses of the Constitution extend of their own force to our newly acquired territories. The Constitution itself does not answer the question. Its solution must be found in the nature of the government created by that instrument, in the opinion of its contemporaries, in the practical construction put upon it by Congress and in the decisions of this court. . . .

[Here follows some consideration of the Articles of Confederation, the Ordinance of 1787, and the Constitution.]

It is sufficient to observe in relation to these three fundamental instruments that it can nowhere be inferred that the territories were considered a part of the United States. The Constitution was created by the people of the *United States,* as a union of *States,* to be governed solely by representatives of the *States;* and even the provision relied upon here, that all duties, imposts and excises shall be uniform "throughout the United States," is explained by subsequent provisions of the Constitution, that "no tax or duty shall be laid on articles exported from any *State,"* and "no preference shall be given by any regulation of commerce or revenue to the ports of one *State* over those of another; nor shall vessels bound to or from one State be obliged to enter, clear or pay duties in another." In short, the Constitution deals with *States,* their people and their representatives. . . .

The question of the legal relations between the States and the newly acquired territories first became the subject of public discussion in connection with the purchase of Louisiana in 1803. . . .

Notwithstanding these provisions for the incorporation of territories into the Union, Congress, not only in organizing the territory of Louisiana by Act of March 26, 1804, but all other territories carved out of this vast inheritance, has assumed that the Constitution did not extend to them of its own force, and has in each case made special provision, either that their legislatures shall pass no law inconsistent with the Constitution of the United States, or that the Constitution or laws of the United States shall be the supreme law of such territories. Finally, in Rev. Stat., Sec. 1891, a general provision was enacted that "the Constitution and all laws of the United States which are not locally inapplicable shall have the same force and effect within all the organized territories, and in every territory hereafter organized, as elsewhere within the United States". . . .

Indeed, whatever may have been the fluctuations of opinion in other bodies, (and even this court has not been exempt from them), Congress has been consistent in recognizing the difference between the States and territories under the Constitution.

The decisions of this court upon this subject have not been altogether harmonious. Some of them are based upon the theory that the Constitution does not apply to the territories without legislation. Other cases, arising from territories where such legislation has been had, contain language which would justify the inference that such legislation was unnecessary, and that the Constitution took effect immediately upon the cession of the territory to the United States. It may be remarked, upon the threshold of an analysis of these cases, that too much weight must not be given to general expressions found in several opinions that the power of Congress over territories is complete and supreme, because these words may be interpreted as meaning only supreme under the Constitution; nor upon the other hand, to general statements that the Constitution covers the territories as well as the States, since in such cases it will be found that acts of Congress had already extended the Constitution to such territories, and that thereby it subordinated not only its own acts, but those of the territorial legislatures, to what had become the supreme law of the land. . . . [Here follows a review of the decisions.]

Eliminating, then, from the opinions of this court all expressions unnecessary to the disposition of the particular case, and gleaning therefrom the exact point decided in each, the following propositions may be considered as established:

1. That the District of Columbia and the territories are not States, within the judicial clause of the Constitution giving jurisdiction in cases between citizens of different States;

2. That territories are not States, within the meaning of Revised Statutes, sec. 709, permitting writs of error from this court in cases where the validity of a *state* statute is drawn in question;

3. That the District of Columbia and the territories are States, as that word is used in treaties with foreign powers, with respect to the ownership, disposition and inheritance of property;

4. That the territories are not within the clause of the Constitution providing for the creation of a Supreme Court and such inferior courts as Congress may see fit to establish;

5. That the Constitution does not apply to foreign countries or to trials therein conducted, and that Congress may lawfully provide for such trials before consular tribunals, without the intervention of a grand or petit jury;

6. That where the Constitution has been once formally extended by Congress to territories, neither Congress nor the territorial legislature can enact laws inconsistent therewith. . . .

To sustain the judgment in the case under consideration it by no means becomes necessary to show that none of the articles of the Constitution apply to the Island of Porto Rico. There is a clear distinction between such prohibitions as go to the very root of the power of Congress to act at all, irrespective of time or place, and such as are operative only "throughout the United States" or among the several States.

Thus, when the Constitution declares that "no bill of attainder or ex post facto law shall be passed," and that "no title of nobility shall be granted by the United States," it goes to the competency of Congress to pass a bill *of that description.* Perhaps the same remark may apply to the First Amendment, that "Congress shall make no law respecting an establishment of religion, or prohibiting the free exercise thereof, or abridging the freedom of speech, or of the press, or the right of the people to peacefully assemble and to petition the government for a redress of grievances." We do not wish, however, to be understood as expressing an opinion how far the bill of rights contained in the first eight amendments is of general and how far of local application.

Upon the other hand, when the Constitution declares that all duties shall be uniform "throughout the United States," it becomes necessary to inquire whether there be any territory over which Congress has jurisdiction which is not a part of the "United States," by which term we understand the *States* whose people *united* to form the Constitution, and such as have since been admitted to the Union upon an equality with them. Not only did the people in adopting the Thirteenth Amendment thus recognize a distinction between the United States and "any place subject to their jurisdiction," but Congress itself, in the Act of March 27, 1804, c. 56, 2 Stat. 298, providing for the proof of public records, applied the provisions of the act, not only to "every court and office within the United States," but to the "courts and offices of the respective territories of the United States and countries subject to the jurisdiction of the United States.". . . Unless these words are to be rejected as meaningless, we must treat them as a recognition by Congress of the fact that there may be territories subject to the jurisdiction of the United States, which are not *of* the United States. . . .

Indeed, the practical interpretation put by Congress upon the Constitution has been long continued and uniform to the effect that the Constitution is applicable to territories acquired by purchase or conquest only when and so far as Congress shall so direct. . . .

We are also of opinion that the power to acquire territory by treaty implies, not only the power to govern such territory, but to prescribe upon what terms the United States will receive its inhabitants, and what their status shall be in what Chief Justice Marshall termed the "American empire." There seems to be no middle ground between this position and the doctrine that if their inhabitants do not become, immediately upon annexation, citizens of the United States, their children thereafter born, whether savages or civilized, are such, and entitled to all the rights, privileges and immunities of citizens. If such be their status, the consequences will be extremely serious. Indeed, it is doubtful if Congress would ever assent to the annexation of territory upon the condition that its inhabitants, however foreign they may be to our habits, traditions, and modes of life, shall become at once citizens of the United States. In all its treaties hitherto the treaty-making power has made special provisions for this subject. . . . In all these cases there is an implied denial of the right

of the inhabitants to American citizenship until Congress by further action shall signify its assent thereto. . . .

It is obvious that in the annexation of outlying and distant possessions grave questions will arise from differences of race, habits, laws and customs of the people, and from differences of soil, climate and production, which may require action on the part of Congress that would be quite unnecessary in the annexation of contiguous territory inhabited only by people of the same race, or by scattered bodies of native Indians.

We suggest, without intending to decide, that there may be a distinction between certain natural rights enforced in the Constitution by prohibitions against interference with them, and what may be termed artificial or remedial rights which are peculiar to our own system of jurisprudence. Of the former class are the rights to one's own religious opinions and to a public expression of them, or, as sometimes said, to worship God according to the dictates of one's own conscience; the right to personal liberty and individual property; to freedom of speech and of the press; to free access to courts of justice, to due process of law, and to an equal protection of the laws; to immunities from unreasonable searches and seizures, as well as cruel and unusual punishments; and to such other immunities as are indispensable to a free government. Of the latter case are the rights to citizenship, to suffrage (*Minor v. Happersett,* 21 Wall. 162), and to the particular methods of procedure pointed out in the Constitution, which are peculiar to Anglo-Saxon jurisprudence, and some of which have already been held by the States to be unnecessary to the proper protection of individuals. . . .

We do not desire, however, to anticipate the difficulties which would naturally arise in this connection, but merely to disclaim any intention to hold that the inhabitants of these territories are subject to an unrestrained power on the part of Congress to deal with them upon the theory that they have no rights which it is bound to respect. . . .

In passing upon the questions involved in this and kindred cases, we ought not to overlook the fact that, while the Constitution was intended to establish a permanent form of government for the States which should elect to take advantage of its conditions, and continue for an indefinite future, the vast possibilities of that future could never have entered the minds of its framers. . . . The difficulties of bringing about a union of the States were so great, the objections to it seemed so formidable, that the whole thought of the convention centered upon surmounting these obstacles. The question of territories was dismissed with a single clause, apparently applicable only to the territories then existing, giving Congress the power to govern and dispose of them. . . .

. . . If it be once conceded that we are at liberty to acquire foreign territory, a presumption arises that our power with respect to such territories is the same power which other nations have been accustomed to exercise with respect to territories acquired by them. If, in limiting the power which Congress was to exercise within the United States, it was also intended to limit it with regard to such territories as the people of the United States should thereafter acquire, such limitations should have been expressed. Instead of that, we find the Constitution speaking only to States, except in the territorial clause, which is absolute in its terms, and suggestive of no limitations upon the power of Congress in dealing with them. . . .

. . . The liberality of Congress in legislating the Constitution into all our contiguous territories has undoubtedly fostered the impression that it went there by its own force, but there is nothing in the Constitution itself, and little in the interpretation put upon it, to confirm that impression. There is not even an analogy to the provisions of an ordinary mortgage for its attachment to after-acquired property, without which it covers only property existing at the date of the mortgage. In short, there is absolute silence upon the subject. The executive and legislative departments of the government have for more than a century interpreted this silence as precluding the idea that the Constitution attached to these territories as soon as acquired, and unless such interpretation be manifestly contrary to the letter or spirit of the Constitution, it should be followed by the judicial department. . . .

Patriotic and intelligent men may differ widely as to the desirableness of this or that acquisition, but this is solely a political question. We can only consider this aspect of the case so far as to say that no construction of the Constitution should be adopted which would prevent Congress from considering each case upon its merits, unless the language of the instrument imperatively demand it. A false step at this time might be fatal to the development of what Chief Justice Marshall called the American empire. Choice in some cases, the natural gravitation of small bodies towards large ones in others, the result of a successful war in still others, may bring about conditions which would render the annexation of distant possessions desirable. If those possessions are inhabited by alien races, differing from us in religion, customs, laws, methods of taxation and modes of thought, the administration of government and justice, according to Anglo-Saxon principles, may for a time be impossible; and the question at once arises whether large concessions ought not to be made for a time, that, ultimately, our own theories may be carried out, and the blessings of a free government under the Constitution extended to them. We decline to hold that there is anything in the Constitution to forbid such action.

We are therefore of opinion that the Island of Porto Rico is a territory appurtenant and belonging to the United States, but not a part of the United States within the revenue clauses of the Constitution; that the Foraker act is constitutional, so far as it imposes duties upon imports from such island, and that the plaintiff cannot recover back the duties exacted in this case.

The judgment of the Circuit Court is therefore affirmed.

[WHITE, J. delivered a separate opinion concurring in the judgment, but for different reasons. Justices SHIRAS and McKENNA concurred in this opinion. Chief Justice FULLER delivered a dissenting opinion, in which Justices HARLAN, BREWER, and PECKHAM concurred. HARLAN, J., also delivered a separate dissenting opinion.]

FULLER, C. J. dissenting. . . . The inquiry is stated to be: "Had Porto Rico, at the time of the passage of the act in question, been incorporated into and become an integral part of the United States?" And the answer being given that it had not, it is held that the rule of uniformity was not applicable.

I submit that that is not the question in

this case. The question is whether, when Congress has created a civil government for Porto Rico, has constituted its inhabitants a body politic, has given it a governor and other officers, a legislative assembly, and courts, with right of appeal to this court, Congress can, in the same act and in the exercise of the power conferred by the first clause of section eight, impose duties on the commerce between Porto Rico and the States and other territories in contravention of the rule of uniformity qualifying the power. If this can be done, it is because the power of Congress over commerce between the States and any of the territories is not restricted by the Constitution. This was the position taken by the Attorney General, with a candor and ability that did him great credit.

But that position is rejected, and the contention seems to be that, if an organized and settled province of another sovereignty is acquired by the United States, Congress has the power to keep it, like a disembodied shade, in an intermediate state of ambiguous existence for an indefinite period; and, more than that, that after it has been called from that limbo, commerce with it is absolutely subject to the will of Congress, irrespective of constitutional provisions. . . .

Great stress is thrown upon the word "incorporation" as if possessed of some occult meaning, but I take it that the act under consideration made Porto Rico, whatever its situation before, an organized territory of the United States. Being such, and the act undertaking to impose duties by virtue of clause 1 sec. 8, how is it that the rule which qualifies the power does not apply to its

exercise in respect of commerce with that territory? The power can only be exercised as prescribed, and even if the rule of uniformity could be treated as a mere regulation of the granted power—a suggestion as to which I do not assent—the validity of these duties comes up directly, and it is idle to discuss the distinction between a total want of power and a defective exercise of it.

The concurring opinion recognizes the fact that Congress, in dealing with the people of new territories or possessions, is bound to respect the fundamental guarantees of life, liberty, and property, but assumes that Congress is not bound, in those territories or possessions, to follow the rule of taxation prescribed by the Constitution. And yet the power to tax involves the power to destroy, and the levy of duties touches all our people in all places under the jurisdiction of the government.

The logical result is that Congress may prohibit commerce altogether between the States and territories, and may prescribe one rule of taxation in one territory, and a different rule in another.

That theory assumes that the Constitution created a government empowered to acquire countries throughout the world, to be governed by different rules than those obtaining in the original States and territories, and substitutes for the present system of republican government a system of domination over distant provinces in the exercise of unrestricted power.

In our judgment, so much of the Porto Rican act as authorized the imposition of duties is invalid, and plaintiffs were entitled to recover. . . .

353. THE GOLD STANDARD ACT OF 1900
March 14, 1900

(U. S. Statutes at Large, Vol. XXXI, p. 45 ff.)

The election of McKinley in 1896 had temporarily ended the agitation for free silver. The return of prosperity during the McKinley administration, the great increase in world production of gold, and the failure of the half-hearted efforts of the administration to arrive at some international agreement for bimetallism, all

made the enactment of the gold standard inevitable. See, A. B. Hepburn, *History of Currency*, p. 371 ff.; D. R. Dewey, *Financial History*, p. 468 ff.

An act to define and fix the standard of value, to maintain the parity of all forms of money issued or coined by the United States. . . .

Be it enacted, That the dollar consisting of twenty-five and eight-tenths grains of gold nine-tenths fine, as established by section thirty-five hundred and eleven of the Revised Statutes of the United States, shall be the standard unit of value, and all forms of money issued or coined by the United States shall be maintained at a parity of value with this standard, and it shall be the duty of the Secretary of the Treasury to maintain such parity.

Sec. 2. That United States notes, and Treasury notes issued under the Act of July 14, 1890, when presented to the Treasury for redemption, shall be redeemed in gold coin of the standard fixed in the first section of this Act, and in order to secure the prompt and certain redemption of such notes as herein provided it shall be the duty of the Secretary of the Treasury to set apart in the Treasury a reserve fund of one hundred and fifty million dollars in gold coin and bullion, which fund shall be used for such redemption purposes only, and whenever and as often as any of said notes shall be redeemed from said fund it shall be the duty of the Secretary of the Treasury to use said notes so redeemed to restore and maintain such reserve fund. . . .

Sec. 3. That nothing contained in this Act shall be construed to affect the legal-tender quality as now provided by law of the silver dollar, or of any other money coined or issued by the United States. . . .

Sec. 14. That the provisions of this Act are not intended to preclude the accomplishment of international bimetallism whenever conditions shall make it expedient and practicable to secure the same by concurrent action of the leading commercial nations of the world and at a ratio which shall insure permanence of relative value between gold and silver.

354. McKINLEY'S RECIPROCITY SPEECH
Buffalo, New York, September 5, 1901

(Richardson, ed. *Messages and Papers,* Vol. X, p. 393 ff.)

In this, McKinley's last public address, the high-priest of protective tariffs announced that "the period of exclusiveness is past" and suggested a modification of the traditional tariff policy of the Republican party. The following day he was shot by the anarchist Czolgosz, and he died September 14. Roosevelt, who succeeded him, cautiously avoided the tariff issue. See, C. S. Olcott, *Life of William McKinley,* 2 Vols.

. . . My fellow citizens: Trade statistics indicate that this country is in a state of unexampled prosperity. The figures are almost appalling. They show that we are utilizing our fields and forests and mines, and that we are furnishing profitable employment to the millions of working-men throughout the United States, bringing comfort and happiness to their homes, and making it possible to lay by savings for old age and disability. That all the people are participating in this great prosperity is seen in every American community, and shown by the enormous and unprecedented deposits in our savings banks. Our duty is the care and security of these deposits, and their safe investment demands the highest integrity and the best business capacity of those in charge of these depositories of the people's earnings.

We have a vast and intricate business, built up through years of toil and struggle, in which every part of the country has its stake, which will not permit either of neglect or of undue selfishness. No narrow, sordid, policy will subserve it. The greatest skill and wisdom on the part of manufacturers and producers will be required to hold and increase it. Our industrial enterprises, which have grown to such proportions, affect the homes and occupations of the people and the welfare of the country. Our capacity to produce has developed so enormously, and our products have so multiplied, that the problem of more markets requires our urgent and immediate attention. Only a broad and enlightened policy will keep what we have. No other policy will get more. In these times of marvellous business energy and gain we ought to be looking to the future, strengthening the weak places in our industrial and commercial systems, that we may be ready for any storm or strain.

By sensible trade arrangements which will not interrupt our home production, we shall extend the outlets for our increasing surplus. A system which provides a mutual exchange of commodities is manifestly essential to the continued and healthful growth of our export trade. We must not repose in fancied security that we can forever sell everything and buy little or nothing. If such a thing were possible, it would not be best for us or for those with whom we deal. We should take from our customers such of their products as we can use without harm to our industries and labor. Reciprocity is the natural outgrowth of our wonderful industrial develop-

ment under the domestic policy now firmly established. What we produce beyond our domestic consumption must have a vent abroad. The excess must be relieved through a foreign outlet, and we should sell everywhere we can and buy wherever the buying will enlarge our sales and production, and thereby make a greater demand for home labor.

The period of exclusiveness is past. The expansion of our trade and commerce is the pressing problem. Commercial wars are unprofitable. A policy of good will and friendly trade relations will prevent reprisals. Reciprocity treaties are in harmony with the spirit of the times; measures of retaliation are not.

If perchance some of our tariffs are no longer needed for revenue or to encourage and protect our industries at home, why should they not be employed to extend and promote our markets abroad? . . .

355. HAY-PAUNCEFOTE TREATY
November 18, 1901

(Malloy, ed. *Treaties, Conventions, etc.* Vol. I, p. 782 ff.)

The first Hay-Pauncefote Treaty was ratified by the Senate, December 20, 1900, but with amendments unacceptable to Great Britain. See, T. Dennett, *John Hay*, ch. xxi; L. M. Keasby, *Nicaragua Canal*, chs. xxi, xxii; H. G. Miller, *The Isthmian Highway*, ch. xi; W. S. Holt, *Treaties Defeated by the Senate*, ch. ix.

TREATY TO FACILITATE THE CONSTRUCTION OF A SHIP CANAL

The United States of America and His Majesty Edward the Seventh, of the United Kingdom of Great Britain and Ireland, . . . being desirous to facilitate the construction of a ship canal to connect the Atlantic and Pacific Oceans, by whatever route may be considered expedient, and to that end to remove any objection which may arise out of the convention of the nineteenth of April, 1850, commonly called the Clayton-Bulwer treaty, to the construction of such canal under the auspices of the Government of the United States, without impairing the "general principle" of neutralization established

in Article VIII of that convention, have . . . agreed upon the following articles:

ART. I. The High Contracting Parties agree that the present treaty shall supersede the afore-mentioned Convention of the 19th April, 1850.

ART. II. It is agreed that the canal may be constructed under the auspices of the Government of the United States either directly at its own cost, or by gift or loan of money to individuals or Corporations, or through subscription to or purchase of stock or shares, and that, subject to the provisions of the present Treaty, the said Government shall have and enjoy all the rights incident to such construction, as well as the exclusive right of providing for the regulation and management of the canal.

ART. III. The United States adopts, as the basis of the neutralization of such ship canal, the following Rules, substantially as embodied in the Convention of Constantinople signed the twenty-eighth of October,

1888, for the free navigation of the Suez Canal, that is to say:

1. The canal shall be free and open to the vessels of commerce and of war of all nations observing these Rules, on terms of entire equality, so that there shall be no discrimination against any such nation, or its citizens or subjects, in respect of the conditions or charges of traffic or otherwise. Such conditions and charges of traffic shall be just and equitable.

2. The canal shall never be blockaded, nor shall any right of war be exercised nor any act of hostility be committed within it. The United States, however, shall be at liberty to maintain such military police along the canal as may be necessary to protect it against lawlessness and disorder.

3. Vessels of war of a belligerent shall not revictual nor take any stores in the canal except so far as may be strictly necessary; and the transit of such vessels through the canal shall be effected with the least possible delay in accordance with the Regulations in force, and with only such intermission as may result from the necessities of the service.

Prizes shall be in all respects subject to the same rules as vessels of war of the belligerents.

4. No belligerent shall embark or disembark troops, munitions of war, or warlike materials in the canal, except in case of accidental hindrance of the transit, and in such case the transit shall be resumed with all possible dispatch.

5. The provisions of this Article shall apply to waters adjacent to the canal, within 3 marine miles of either end. Vessels of war of a belligerent shall not remain in such waters longer than twenty-four hours at any one time, except in case of distress, and in such case shall depart as soon as possible; but a vessel of war of one belligerent shall not depart within twenty-four hours from the departure of a vessel of war of the other belligerent.

6. The plant, establishments, buildings and all works necessary to the construction, maintenance and operation of the canal shall be deemed to be part thereof, for the purposes of this treaty, and in time of war, as in time of peace, shall enjoy complete immunity from attack or injury by belligerents, and from acts calculated to impair their usefulness as part of the canal.

ART. IV. It is agreed that no change of territorial sovereignty or of international relations of the country or countries traversed by the beforementioned canal shall affect the general principle of neutralization or the obligation of the High Contracting Parties under the present Treaty. . . .

356. PRESIDENT ROOSEVELT AND THE TRUSTS

Extract from First Annual Message to Congress
December 3, 1901

(Richardson, ed. *Messages and Papers,* Vol. X, p. 417 ff.)

With this message President Roosevelt, who succeeded to the Presidency on the death of McKinley, gave warning that he would wield the "big stick" on lawless business. The message was succinctly summarized by Mr. Dooley, "Th' trusts, says he, are heejoous monsthers built up be th' enlightened intherprise iv th' men that have done so much to advance progress in our beloved country, he says. On wan hand I wud stamp thim undher fut; on th' other hand not so fast."

To the Senate and House of Representatives:
    . . . The tremendous and highly complex industrial development which went on with ever-accelerated rapidity during the latter half of the nineteenth century brings us face to face, at the beginning of the twentieth, with very serious social problems. The old laws, and the old customs which had almost the binding force of law, were once quite sufficient to regulate the accumulation and

distribution of wealth. Since the industrial changes which have so enormously increased the productive power of mankind, they are no longer sufficient.

The growth of cities has gone on beyond comparison faster than the growth of the country, and the upbuilding of the great industrial centres has meant a startling increase, not merely in the aggregate of wealth, but in the number of very large individual, and especially of very large corporate, fortunes. The creation of these great corporate fortunes has not been due to the tariff nor to any other governmental action, but to natural causes in the business world, operating in other countries as they operate in our own.

The process has aroused much antagonism, a great part of which is wholly without warrant. . . . The captains of industry who have driven the railway systems across this continent, who have built up our commerce, who have developed our manufactures, have on the whole done great good to our people. Without them the material development of which we are so justly proud could never have taken place. Moreover, we should recognize the immense importance of this material development by leaving as unhampered as is compatible with the public good the strong and forceful men upon whom the success of business operations inevitably rests. The slightest study of business conditions will satisfy any one capable of forming a judgment that the personal equation is the most important factor in a business operation; that the business ability of the man at the head of any business concern, big or little, is usually the factor which fixes the gulf between striking success and hopeless failure.

An additional reason for caution in dealing with corporations is to be found in the international commercial conditions of today. The same business conditions which have produced the great aggregations of corporate and individual wealth have made them very potent factors in international commercial competition. Business concerns which have the largest means at their disposal and are managed by the ablest men are naturally those which take the lead in the strife for commercial supremacy among the nations of the world. America has only just begun to assume that commanding position in the international business world which we believe will more and more be hers. It is of the utmost importance that this position be not jeopardized, especially at a time when the overflowing abundance of our own natural resources and the skill, business energy, and mechanical aptitude of our people make foreign markets essential. Under such conditions it would be most unwise to cramp or to fetter the youthful strength of our nation.

Moreover, it cannot too often be pointed out that to strike with ignorant violence at the interests of one set of men almost inevitably endangers the interests of all. The fundamental rule in our national life—the rule which underlies all others—is that, on the whole, and in the long run, we shall go up or down together. . . .

The mechanism of modern business is so delicate that extreme care must be taken not to interfere with it in a spirit of rashness or ignorance. Many of those who have made it their vocation to denounce the great industrial combinations which are popularly, although with technical inaccuracy, known as "trusts", appeal especially to hatred and fear. These are precisely the two emotions, particularly when combined with ignorance, which unfit men for the exercise of cool and steady judgment. In facing new industrial conditions, the whole history of the world shows that legislation will generally be both unwise and ineffective unless undertaken after calm inquiry and with sober self-restraint. . . .

All this is true; and yet it is also true that there are real and grave evils, one of the chief being overcapitalization because of its many baleful consequences; and a resolute and practical effort must be made to correct these evils.

There is a widespread conviction in the minds of the American people that the great corporations known as trusts are in certain of their features and tendencies hurtful to the general welfare. This . . . is based upon sincere conviction that combination and concentration should be, not prohibited, but supervised and within reasonable limits controlled; and in my judgment this conviction is right.

It is no limitation upon property rights or freedom of contract to require that when men receive from government the privilege of doing business under corporate form, which frees them from individual responsibility, and enables them to call into their enterprises the capital of the public, they shall do so upon absolutely truthful representations as to the value of the property in which the capital is to be invested. Corporations engaged in interstate commerce should be regulated if they are found to exercise a license working to the public injury. It should be as much the aim of those who seek for social betterment to rid the business world of crimes of cunning as to rid the entire body politic of crimes of violence. Great corporations exist only because they are created and safeguarded by our institutions; and it is therefore our right and our duty to see that they work in harmony with these institutions.

The first essential in determining how to deal with the great industrial combinations is knowledge of the facts—publicity. In the interest of the public, the government should have the right to inspect and examine the workings of the great corporations engaged in interstate business. Publicity is the only sure remedy which we can now invoke. What further remedies are needed in the way of governmental regulation, or taxation, can only be determined after publicity has been obtained, by process of law, and in the course of administration. The first requisite is knowledge, full and complete—knowledge which may be made public to the world. . . .

The large corporations, commonly called trusts, though organized in one State, always do business in many States, often doing very little business in the State where they are incorporated. There is utter lack of uniformity in the State laws about them; and as no State has any exclusive interest in or power over their acts, it has in practice proved impossible to get adequate regulation through State action. Therefore, in the interest of the whole people, the nation should, without interfering with the power of the States in the matter itself, also assume power of supervision and regulation over all corporations doing an interstate business. This is especially true where the corporation derives a portion of its wealth from the existence of some monopolistic element or tendency in its business. There would be no hardship in such supervision; banks are subject to it, and in their case it is now accepted as a simple matter of course. Indeed, it is now probable that supervision of corporations by the National Government need not go so far as is now the case with the supervision exercised over them by so conservative a State as Massachusetts, in order to produce excellent results.

When the Constitution was adopted, at the end of the eighteenth century, no human wisdom could foretell the sweeping changes, alike in industrial and political conditions, which were to take place by the beginning of the twentieth century. At that time it was accepted as a matter of course that the several States were the proper authorities to regulate, so far as was then necessary, the comparatively insignificant and strictly localized corporate bodies of the day. The conditions are now wholly different and wholly different action is called for. I believe that a law can be framed which will enable the National Government to exercise control along the lines above indicated; profiting by the experience gained through the passage and administration of the Interstate Commerce Act. If, however, the judgment of the Congress is that it lacks the constitutional power to pass such an act, then a constitutional amendment should be submitted to confer the power.

357. W.C.T.U. DECLARATION OF PRINCIPLES
1902

(National Woman's Christian Temperance Union, *Annual Leaflet,* 1902)

The W. C. T. U. was, with the Anti-Saloon League and the Methodist Church, the most ef- fective of the numerous agencies working for prohibition. For background of the prohibition movement see J. A. Krout, *The Origins of Prohibition*. See also, P. Odegard, *Pressure Politics: The Story of the Anti-Saloon League;* E. H. Cherrington, *Evolution of Prohibition in the United States;* D. L. Colvin, *Prohibition in the United States.*

We believe in the coming of His Kingdom whose service is perfect freedom, because His laws, written in our members as well as in nature and in grace, are perfect, converting the soul.

We believe in the gospel of the Golden Rule, and that each man's habits of life should be an example safe and beneficent for every other man to follow.

We believe that God created both man and woman in His own image, and therefore, we believe in one standard of purity for both men and women, and in the equal right of all to hold opinions and to express the same with equal freedom.

We believe in a living wage; in an eight hour day; in courts of conciliation and arbitration; in justice as opposed to greed of gain; in "peace on earth and good-will to men."

We therefore formulate, and for ourselves adopt the following pledge, asking our sisters and brothers of a common danger and a common hope, to make common cause with us, in working its reasonable and helpful precepts into the practice of everyday life:

I hereby solemnly promise GOD HELPING ME, to abstain from all distilled, fermented and malt liquors, including wine, Beer and Cider, and to employ all proper means to discourage the use of and traffic in the same.

To conform and enforce the rationale of this pledge, we declare our purpose to educate the young; to form a better public sentiment; to reform so far as possible, by religious, ethical and scientific means, the drinking classes; to seek the transforming power of divine grace for ourselves and all for whom we work, that they and we may willfully transcend no law of pure and wholesome living; and finally we pledge ourselves to labor and to pray that all of these principles, founded upon the Gospel of Christ, may be worked out into the customs of Society and the Laws of the Land.

358. THE DRAGO DOCTRINE
December 29, 1902

(Foreign Relations of the United States, 1903, p. 1 ff.)

This announcement of the doctrine that the use of coercion for the collection of claims would constitute a violation of the principles of the Monroe Doctrine arose out of the Venezuelan situation of 1902. On the failure of Venezuela to make any arrangements for the payment of claims of German, English and other foreign claimants, Great Britain and Germany established a blockade of the Venezuela coast; Italy shortly joined the blockading powers. The claims were eventually arbitrated, and the powers induced to withdraw their blockade. The Drago doctrine was embodied in Convention II of the Second Hague Convention, 1907. See, Malloy, ed. *Treaties, Conventions, etc.,* Vol. II, p. 2254. The Venezuela situation can be followed in Moore's *Digest,* Vol. VI; *Foreign Relations of the United States,* 1903 and 1904; H. C. Hill, *Roosevelt and the Caribbean.*

THE DRAGO DOCTRINE: LETTER OF DR. LUIS

M. DRAGO, MINISTER OF FOREIGN RELATIONS OF THE ARGENTINE REPUBLIC, TO MR. MÉROU, ARGENTINE MINISTER TO THE UNITED STATES, DECEMBER 29, 1902

BUENOS AIRES, *December 29, 1902.*

MR. MINISTER: I have received your excellency's telegram of the 20th instant concerning the events that have lately taken place between the Government of the Republic of Venezuela and the Governments of Great Britain and Germany. According to your excellency's information the origin of the disagreement is, in part, the damages suffered by subjects of the claimant nations during the revolutions and wars that have recently occurred within the borders of the Republic mentioned, and in part also the fact that certain payments on the external debt of the nation have not been met at the proper time.

Leaving out of consideration the first class of claims the adequate adjustments of which it would be necessary to consult the laws of the several countries, this Government has deemed it expedient to transmit to your excellency some considerations with reference to the forcible collection of the public debt suggested by the events that have taken place.

At the outset it is to be noted in this connection that the capitalist who lends his money to a foreign state always takes into account the resources of the country and the probability, greater or less, that the obligations contracted will be fulfilled without delay.

All governments thus enjoy different credit according to their degree of civilization and culture and their conduct in business transactions; and these conditions are measured and weighed before making any loan, the terms being made more or less onerous in accordance with the precise data concerning them which bankers always have on record.

In the first place the lender knows that he is entering into a contract with a sovereign entity, and it is an inherent qualification of all sovereignty that no proceedings for the execution of a judgment may be instituted or carried out against it, since this manner of collection would compromise its very existence and cause the independence and freedom of action of the respective government to disappear.

Among the fundamental principles of public international law which humanity has consecrated, one of the most precious is that which decrees that all states, whatever be the force at their disposal, are entities in law, perfectly equal one to another, and mutually entitled by virtue thereof to the same consideration and respect.

The acknowledgment of the debt, the payment of it in its entirety, can and must be made by the nation without diminution of its inherent rights as a sovereign entity, but the summary and immediate collection at a given moment, by means of force, would occasion nothing less than the ruin of the weakest nations, and the absorption of their governments, together with all the functions inherent in them, by the mighty of the earth. The principles proclaimed on this continent of America are otherwise. "Contracts between a nation and private individuals are obligatory according to the conscience of the sovereign, and may not be the object of compelling force," said the illustrious Hamilton. "They confer no right of action contrary to the sovereign will."

The United States has gone very far in this direction. The eleventh amendment to its Constitution provided in effect, with the unanimous assent of the people, that the judicial power of the nation should not be extended to any suit in law or equity prosecuted against one of the United States by citizens of another State, or by citizens or subjects of any foreign State. The Argentine Government has made its provinces indictable, and has even adopted the principle that the nation itself may be brought to trial before the supreme court on contracts which it enters into with individuals.

What has not been established, what could in no wise be admitted, is that, once the amount for which it may be indebted has been determined by legal judgment, it should be deprived of the right to choose the manner and the time of payment, in which it has as much interest as the creditor himself, or more, since its credit and its national honor are involved therein.

This is in no wise a defense for bad faith, disorder, and deliberate and voluntary insolvency. It is intended merely to preserve the dignity of the public international entity which may not thus be dragged into war with detriment to those high ends which determine the existence and liberty of nations.

The fact that collection can not be accomplished by means of violence does not, on the other hand, render valueless the acknowledgment of the public debt, the definite obligation of paying it.

The State continues to exist in its capacity as such, and sooner or later the gloomy situations are cleared up, resources increase, common aspirations of equity and justice prevail, and the most neglected promises are kept.

The decision, then, which declares the obligation to pay a debt, whether it be given by the tribunals of the country or by those of international arbitration, which manifest the abiding zeal for justice as the basis of the political relations of nations, constitutes an indisputable title which can not be compared to the uncertain right of one whose claims are not recognized and who sees himself driven to appeal to force in order that they may be satisfied.

As these are the sentiments of justice, loyalty, and honor which animate the Argentine people and have always inspired its policy, your excellency will understand that it has felt alarmed at the knowledge that the failure of Venezuela to meet the payments of its public debt is given as one of the determining causes of the capture of its fleet, the bombardment of one of its ports, and the establishment of a rigorous blockade along its shores. If such proceedings were to be definitely adopted they would establish a precedent dangerous to the security and the peace of the nations of this part of America.

The collection of loans by military means implies territorial occupation to make them effective, and territorial occupation signifies the suppression or subordination of the governments of the countries on which it is imposed.

Such a situation seems obviously at variance with the principles many times proclaimed by the nations of America, and particularly with the Monroe doctrine, sustained and defended with so much zeal on all occasions by the United States, a doctrine to which the Argentine Republic has heretofore solemnly adhered. . . .

But in very recent times there has been observed a marked tendency among the publicists and in the various expressions of European opinion to call attention to these countries as a suitable field for future territorial expansion. . . .

And it will not be denied that the simplest way to the setting aside and easy ejectment of the rightful authorities by European governments is just this way of financial interventions—as might be shown by many examples. We in no wise pretend that the South American nations are, from any point of view, exempt from the responsibilities of all sorts which violations of international law impose on civilized peoples. We do not nor can we pretend that these countries occupy an exceptional position in their relations with European powers, which have the indubitable right to protect their subjects as completely as in any other part of the world against the

persecutions and injustices of which they may be the victims. The only principle which the Argentine Republic maintains and which it would, with great satisfaction, see adopted, in view of the events in Venezuela, by a nation that enjoys such great authority and prestige as does the United States, is the principle, already accepted, that there can be no territorial expansion in America on the part of Europe, nor any oppression of the peoples of this continent, because an unfortunate financial situation may compel some one of them to postpone the fulfillment of its promises. In a word, the principle which she would like to see recognized is: that the public debt can not occasion armed intervention nor even the actual occupation of the territory of American nations by a European power.

The loss of prestige and credit experienced by States which fail to satisfy the rightful claims of their lawful creditors brings with it difficulties of such magnitude as to render it unnecessary for foreign intervention to aggravate with its oppression the temporary misfortunes of insolvency.

The Argentine Government could cite its own example to demonstrate the needlessness of armed intervention in these cases. . . .

At this time, then, no selfish feeling animates us, nor do we seek our own advantage in manifesting our desire that the public debt of States should not serve as a reason for an armed attack on such States. Quite as little do we harbor any sentiment of hostility with regard to the nations of Europe. On the contrary, we have maintained with all of them since our emancipation the most friendly relations, especially with England, to whom we have recently given the best proof of the confidence which her justice and equanimity inspire in us by intrusting to her decision the most important of our international questions, which she has just decided, fixing our limits with Chile after a controversy of more than seventy years.

We know that where England goes civilization accompanies her, and the benefits of political and civil liberty are extended. Therefore we esteem her, but this does not mean that we should adhere with equal sympathy to her policy in the improbable case of her attempting to oppress the nationalities of this continent which are struggling for their own progress, which have already overcome the greatest difficulties and will surely triumph—to the honor of democratic institutions. Long, perhaps, is the road that the South American nations still have to travel. But they have faith enough and energy and worth sufficient to bring them to their final development with mutual support.

And it is because of this sentiment of continental brotherhood and because of the force which is always derived from the moral support of a whole people that I address you, in pursuance of instructions from His Excellency the President of the Republic, that you may communicate to the Government of the United States our point of view regarding the events in the further development of which that Government is to take so important a part, in order that it may have it in mind as the sincere expression of the sentiments of a nation that has faith in its destiny and in that of this whole continent, at whose head march the United States, realizing our ideals and affording us examples.

Luis M. Drago.

359. THE LOTTERY CASE (CHAMPION v. AMES)
188 U. S. 321
1903

Appeal from the U. S. circuit court for the Northern district of Illinois. Congress, by act of March 2, 1895, had made it a criminal offense to send lottery tickets through the mails. This case involved the question whether such a prohibition was a valid exercise of the power of Congress over commerce. How far Congress can go in regulating morals, health, etc. under the authority of the commerce clause, is subject to dispute. Compare this case to *Hammer* v. *Dagenhart,* Doc. No. 413.

HARLAN, J. . . . We come then to inquire whether there is any solid foundation upon which to rest the contention that Congress may not regulate the carrying of lottery tickets from one State to another, at least by corporations or companies whose business it is, for hire, to carry tangible property from one State to another.

It was said in argument that lottery tickets are not of any real or substantial value in themselves, and therefore are not subjects of commerce. If that were conceded to be the only legal test as to what are to be deemed subjects of commerce that may be regulated by Congress, we cannot accept as accurate the broad statement that such tickets are of no value. . . .

We are of opinion that lottery tickets are subjects of traffic and therefore are subjects of commerce, and the regulation of the carriage of such tickets from State to State, at least by independent carriers, is a regulation of commerce among the several States.

But it is said that the statute in question does not regulate the carrying of lottery tickets from State to State, but by punishing those who cause them to be so carried Congress in effect prohibits such carrying; that in respect of the carrying from one State to another of articles or things that are, in fact, or according to usage in business, the subjects of commerce, the authority given Congress was not to *prohibit*, but only to *regulate*. This view was earnestly pressed at the bar by learned counsel, and must be examined.

It is to be remarked that the Constitution does not define what is to be deemed a legitimate regulation of interstate commerce. In Gibbons v. Ogden it was said that the power to regulate such commerce is the power to prescribe the rule by which it is to be governed. But this general observation leaves it to be determined, when the question comes before the court, whether Congress in prescribing a particular rule, has exceeded its power under the Constitution. . . .

We have said that the carrying from State to State of lottery tickets constitutes interstate commerce, and that the regulation of such commerce is within the power of Congress under the Constitution. Are we prepared to say that a provision which is, in effect a *prohibition* of the carriage of such articles from State to State is not a fit or appropriate mode for the *regulation* of that particular kind of commerce? If lottery traffic, *carried on through interstate commerce,* is a matter of which Congress may take cognizance and over which its power may be exerted, can it be possible that it must tolerate the traffic, and simply regulate the manner in which it may be carried on? Or may not Congress, for the protection of the people of all the States, and under the power to regulate interstate commerce, devise such means, within the scope of the Constitution, and not prohibited by it, as will drive that traffic out of commerce among the States?

In determining whether regulation may not under some circumstances properly take the form or have the effect of prohibition, the nature of the interstate traffic which it was sought by the act of May 2d, 1895, to suppress cannot be overlooked. . . .

If a State, when considering legislation for the suppression of lotteries within its own limits, may properly take into view the evils that inhere in the raising of money in that mode, why may not Congress, invested with the power to regulate commerce among the several States, provide that such commerce shall not be polluted by the carrying of lottery tickets from one State to another? In this connection it must not be forgotten that the power of Congress to regulate commerce among the States is plenary, is complete in itself, and is subject to no limitations except such as may be found in the Constitution. What provision in that instrument can be regarded as limiting the exercise of the power granted? What clause can be cited which, in any degree, countenances the suggestion that one may, of right, carry or cause to be carried from one State to another that which will harm the public morals? We cannot think of any clause of that instrument that could possibly be invoked by those who assert their right to send lottery tickets from State to State except the one providing that no person shall be deprived of his liberty without due process of law. . . . But surely it will not be said to be a part of anyone's liberty, as recognized by the supreme law of the land, that he shall be allowed to introduce into commerce among the States an element that will be confessedly injurious to the public morals.

If it be said that the act of 1895 is incon-sistent with the Tenth Amendment, reserving to the States respectively, or to the people, the powers not delegated to the United States, the answer is that the power to regulate commerce among the States has been expressly delegated to Congress.

Besides, Congress, by that act, does not assume to interfere with traffic or commerce in lottery tickets carried on exclusively within the limits of any State, but has in view only commerce of that kind among the several States. It has not assumed to interfere with the completely internal affairs of any State, and has only legislated in respect of a matter which concerns the people of the United States. As a State may, for the purpose of guarding the morals of its own people, forbid all sales of lottery tickets within its limits, so Congress, for the purpose of guarding the people of the United States against the "wide-spread pestilence of lotteries" and to protect the commerce which concerns all the States, may prohibit the carrying of lottery tickets from one State to another. In legislating upon the subject of the traffic in lottery tickets, as carried on through interstate commerce, Congress only supplemented the action of those States—perhaps all of them—which, for the protection of the public morals, prohibit the drawing of lotteries, as well as the sale or circulation of lottery tickets, within their respective limits. It said, in effect, that it would not permit the declared policy of the States, which sought to protect their people against the mischiefs of the lottery business, to be overthrown or disregarded by the agency of interstate commerce. We should hesitate long before adjudging that an evil of such appalling character, carried on through interstate commerce, cannot be met and crushed by the only power competent to that end. We say competent to that end, because Congress alone has the power to occupy, by legislation, the whole field of interstate commerce. . . . If the carrying of lottery tickets from one State to another be interstate commerce, and if Congress is of opinion that an effective regulation for the suppression of lotteries, carried on through such commerce, is to make it a criminal offense to cause lottery tickets to be carried from one State to another, we know of no authority in the Courts to hold that the means thus devised are not appropriate and necessary to protect the country at large against a species of inter-state commerce which, although in general use and somewhat favored in both national and state legislation in the early history of the country, has grown into disrepute, and has become offensive to the entire people of the nation. It is a kind of traffic which no one can be entitled to pursue as of right. . . .

That regulation may sometimes appropriately assume the form of prohibition is also illustrated by the case of diseased cattle, transported from one State to another. . . .

The Act of July 2, 1890, known as the Sherman Anti-Trust Act . . . is an illustration of the proposition that regulation may take the form of prohibition . . . [Cites other examples].

It is said, however, that if, in order to suppress lotteries carried on through interstate commerce, Congress may exclude lottery tickets from such commerce, that principle leads necessarily to the conclusion that Congress may arbitrarily exclude from commerce among the States any article, commodity, or thing, of whatever kind or nature, or however useful or valuable, which it may choose, no matter with what motive, to declare shall not be carried from one State to another. It will be time enough to consider the constitutionality of such legislation when we must do so. The present case does not require the court to declare the full extent of the power that Congress may exercise in the regulation of commerce among the States. We may, however, repeat, in this connection, what the court has heretofore said, that the power of Congress to regulate commerce among the States, although plenary, cannot be deemed arbitrary, since it is subject to such limitations or restrictions as are prescribed by the

Constitution. This power, therefore, may not be exercised so as to infringe rights secured or protected by that instrument. It would not be difficult to imagine legislation that would be justly liable to such an objection as that stated, and be hostile to the objects for the accomplishment of which Congress was invested with the general power to regulate commerce among the several States. But, as often said, the possible abuse of a power is not an argument against its existence. There is probably no governmental power that may not be exerted to the injury of the public. . . .

The whole subject is too important, and the questions suggested by its consideration are too difficult of solution, to justify any attempt to lay down a rule for determining in advance the validity of every statute that may be enacted under the commerce clause.

We decide nothing more in the present case than that lottery tickets are subjects of traffic among those who choose to sell or buy them; that the carriage of such tickets by independent carriers from one State to another is therefore interstate commerce; that under its power to regulate commerce among the several States Congress—subject to the limitations imposed by the Constitution upon the exercise of the powers granted—has plenary authority over such commerce, and may prohibit the carriage of such tickets from State to State; and that legislation to that end, and of that character, is not inconsistent with any limitation or restriction imposed upon the exercise of the powers granted to Congress.

The judgment is affirmed.

FULLER, C. J., delivered a dissenting opinion in which Justices BREWER, SHIRAS, and PECKHAM concurred.

360. THE PLATT AMENDMENT

Treaty with Cuba Embodying the Platt Amendment
May 22, 1903

(Malloy, ed. *Treaties, Conventions, etc.* Vol. I, p. 362 ff.)

By the so-called Teller Amendment of the Resolutions of April 19, 1898, the United States disclaimed any intention of exercising sovereignty over the Island of Cuba and promised to leave the government in the hands of the Cuban people. On the conclusion of the war, General Leonard Wood, military governor of the island, provided for the meeting of a constitutional convention to draw up a form of government. The convention met in November 1900, and drew up a constitution modeled upon that of the United States, but without any provision for future relations with the United States. The American government was unwilling to acquiesce in this situation, and a series of provisions known as the Platt Amendments were added to the Army Appropriation Bill of March 2, 1901. These Amendments were drafted by Elihu Root, with the exception of the fifth, drafted by General Wood. The Cuban convention duly added them as an appendix to the Cuban Constitution, and in 1903 they were incorporated into a Treaty with the United States. See, *Documentary History of the Inauguration of the Cuban Government*, Annual Report of the Secretary of War, 1902, Appendix A.; Foreign Policy Association *Information Service Reports*, "Cuba and the Platt Amendment," April, 1929; H. Hagedorn, *Leonard Wood*, 2 Vols.; G. H. Stuart, *Cuba and its International Relations;* L. H. Jenks, *Our Cuban Colony;* H. C. Hill, *Roosevelt and the Caribbean;* E. Root, *Military and Colonial Policy of the United States;* A. G. Robinson, *Cuba and the Intervention;* C. J. Chapman, *History of the Cuban Republic.* The Platt Amendment was abrogated by Treaty of May 31, 1934, Doc. No. 485.

ART. I. The Government of Cuba shall never enter into any treaty or other compact with any foreign power or powers which will impair or tend to impair the independence of Cuba, nor in any manner authorize or permit any foreign power or powers to obtain by colonization or for military or naval purposes, or otherwise, lodgement in or control over any portion of said island.

ART. II. The Government of Cuba shall not assume or contract any public debt to pay the interest upon which, and to make reasonable sinking-fund provision for the ultimate discharge of which, the ordinary revenues of the Island of Cuba, after defraying the current expenses of the Government, shall be inadequate.

ART. III. The Government of Cuba consents that the United States may exercise the right to intervene for the preservation of Cuban independence, the maintenance of a government adequate for the protection of life, property, and individual liberty, and for discharging the obligations with respect to Cuba imposed by the treaty of Paris on the United States, now to be assumed and undertaken by the government of Cuba.

ART. IV. All Acts of the United States in Cuba during its military occupancy thereof are ratified and validated, and all lawful rights acquired thereunder shall be maintained and protected.

ART. V. The Government of Cuba will execute, and as far as necessary extend, the plans already devised or other plans to be mutually agreed upon, for the sanitation of the cities of the island, to the end that a recurrence of epidemics and infectious diseases may be prevented thereby assuring protection to the people and commerce of Cuba, as well as to the commerce of the southern ports of the United States and the people residing therein.

ART. VI. The Isle of Pines shall be omitted from the boundaries of Cuba, specified in the Constitution, the title thereto being left to future adjustment by treaty.

ART. VII. To enable the United States to maintain the independence of Cuba, and to protect the people thereof, as well as for its own defense, the government of Cuba will sell or lease to the United States lands necessary for coaling or naval stations at certain specified points to be agreed upon with the President of the United States. . . .

361. CONVENTION WITH PANAMA FOR THE CONSTRUCTION OF A CANAL

Concluded November 18, 1903

(Malloy, ed. *Treaties, Conventions, etc.,* Vol. II, p. 1349 ff.)

Upon the failure of the United States to come to any satisfactory agreement with Colombia on

the question of an Isthmian Canal, Panama revolted from Colombia and, with the benevolent
protection of the United States, declared her independence. The revolt took place November 3,
1903; our government recognized the Republic of
Panama on the 6th, and concluded a canal
treaty on the 18th of November. The terms are
practically the same as those offered to
Colombia. In order "to remove all misunderstandings growing out of the political events in
Panama in November 1903", the United States
paid to Colombia, in 1922, the sum of $25,-
000,000. The literature on the diplomacy of
the Canal is extensive, but see H. Pringle,
Theodore Roosevelt, Book II, chs. v–vi; W. F.
McCaleb, *Theodore Roosevelt,* p. 145 ff.; H. C.
Hill, *Roosevelt and the Caribbean;* P. Bunau-
Varilla, *Panama.* There is a wealth of material
in Congressional Investigations. See "The Story
of Panama," *Hearings on the Rainey Resolution,*
House Committee on Foreign Affairs, 1912;
Diplomatic History of the Panama Canal, 63d
Congress, 2nd Session, Sen. Doc. No. 474;
Senate Committee on Inter-Oceanic Canals, 59th
Congress, 2nd Session, Sen. Doc. No. 401.

ART. I. The United States guarantees and
will maintain the independence of the Republic of Panama.

ART. II. The Republic of Panama grants
to the United States in perpetuity the use,
occupation and control of a zone of land and
land under water for the construction, maintenance, operation, sanitation and protection
of said Canal of the width of ten miles extending to the distance of five miles on each
side of the center line of the route of the
canal to be constructed; the said zone beginning in the Caribbean Sea, three marine
miles from mean low water mark, and extending to and across the Isthmus of Panama
into the Pacific Ocean to a distance of three
marine miles from mean low water mark,
with the proviso that the cities of Panama
and Colon and the harbors adjacent to said
cities, which are included within the boundaries of the zone above described, shall not
be included within this grant. The Republic
of Panama further grants to the United
States in perpetuity the use, occupation and
control of any other lands and waters outside of the zone above described which may
be necessary and convenient for the construction, maintenance, operation, sanitation
and protection of the said Canal or of any
auxiliary canals or other works necessary and
convenient for the construction, maintenance,

operation, sanitation and protection of the
said enterprise.

The Republic of Panama further grants
in like manner to the United States in perpetuity all islands within the limits of the
zone above described and in addition thereto
the group of small islands in the Bay of
Panama, named Perico, Naos, Culebra and
Flamenco.

ART. III. The Republic of Panama grants
to the United States all the rights, power
and authority within the zone mentioned and
described in Article II of this agreement and
within the limits of all auxiliary lands and
waters mentioned and described in said Article II which the United States would
possess and exercise if it were the sovereign
of the territory within which said lands and
waters are located to the entire exclusion of
the exercise by the Republic of Panama of
any such sovereign rights, power or authority. . . .

ART. V. The Republic of Panama grants
to the United States in perpetuity a monopoly for the construction, maintenance
and operation of any system of communication by means of canal or railroad across its
territory between the Caribbean Sea and the
Pacific Ocean. . . .

ART. VII. The Republic of Panama grants
to the United States within the limits of the
cities of Panama and Colon and their adjacent harbors and within the territory adjacent thereto the right to acquire by purchase or by the exercise of the right of
eminent domain, any lands, buildings, water
rights or other properties necessary and convenient for the construction, maintenance,
operation and protection of the Canal and of
any works of sanitation, such as the collection and disposition of sewage and the distribution of water in the said cities of Panama and Colon, which, in the discretion of
the United States may be necessary and
convenient for the construction, maintenance,
operation, sanitation and protection of the
said Canal and railroad.

The Republic of Panama agrees that the
cities of Panama and Colon shall comply
in perpetuity with the sanitary ordinances
whether of a preventive or curative character
prescribed by the United States and in case
the Government of Panama is unable or
fails in its duty to enforce this compliance

by the cities of Panama and Colon with the sanitary ordinances of the United States the Republic of Panama grants to the United States the right and authority to enforce the same.

The same right and authority are granted to the United States for the maintenance of public order in the cities of Panama and Colon and the territories and harbors adjacent thereto in case the Republic of Panama should not be, in the judgment of the United States, able to maintain such order.

ART. VIII. The Republic of Panama grants to the United States all rights which it now has or hereafter may acquire to the property of the New Panama Canal Company and the Panama Railroad Company as a result of the transfer of sovereignty from the Republic of Colombia to the Republic of Panama over the Isthmus of Panama and authorizes the New Panama Canal Company to sell and transfer to the United States its rights, privileges, properties and concessions as well as the Panama Railroad and all the shares or part of the shares of that company.

ART. IX. The United States agrees that the ports at either entrance of the Canal and the waters thereof and the Republic of Panama agrees that the towns of Panama and Colon shall be free for all time so that there shall not be imposed or collected custom house tolls, tonnage, anchorage, lighthouse, wharf, pilot or quarantine dues or any other charges or taxes of any kind upon any vessel using or passing through the Canal or belonging to or employed by the United States, directly or indirectly, in connection with the construction, maintenance, operation, sanitation and protection of the main Canal, or auxiliary works, or upon the cargo, officers, crew or passengers of any such vessels, except such tolls and charges as may be imposed by the United States for the use of the Canal and other works, and except tolls and charges imposed by the Republic of Panama upon merchandise destined to be introduced for the consumption of the rest of the Republic of Panama, and upon vessels touching at the ports of Colon and Panama and which do not cross the Canal.

The Government of the Republic of Panama shall have the right to establish in such ports and in the towns of Panama and Colon such houses and guards as it may deem necessary to collect duties on importations destined to other portions of Panama and to prevent contraband trade. The United States shall have the right to make use of the towns and harbors of Panama and Colon as places of anchorage, and for making repairs, for loading, unloading, depositing or trans-shipping cargoes either in transit or destined for the service of the canal and for other works pertaining to the canal.

ART. X. The Republic of Panama agrees that there shall not be imposed any taxes, national, municipal, departmental or of any other class upon the Canal, the railways and auxiliary works, tugs and other vessels employed in the service of the canal, storehouse, workshops, offices, quarters for laborers, factories of all kinds, warehouses, wharves, machinery and other works, property, and effects appertaining to the Canal or railroad and auxiliary works, or their officers or employees, situated within the cities of Panama and Colon, and that there shall not be imposed contributions or charges of a personal character of any kind upon officers, employees, laborers and other individuals in the service of the Canal and railroad and auxiliary works. . . .

ART. XIV. As the price or compensation for the rights, powers and privileges granted in this convention by the Republic of Panama to the United States, the Government of the United States agrees to pay to the Republic of Panama the sum of ten million dollars ($10,000,000) in gold coin of the United States on the exchange of the ratification of this convention and also an annual payment during the life of this convention of two hundred and fifty thousand dollars ($250,000) in like gold coin, beginning nine years after the date aforesaid.

The provisions of this article shall be in addition to all other benefits assured to the Republic of Panama under this convention.

But no delay or difference of opinion under this article or any other provisions of this treaty shall affect or interrupt the full operation and effect of this convention in all other respects. . . .

ART. XVIII. The Canal, when constructed, and the entrances thereto shall be neutral in perpetuity, and shall be opened upon the terms provided for by Section 1 of Article III of, and in conformity with all the stipulations of, the treaty entered into by the Governments of the United States and Great Britain on November 18, 1901.

ART. XIX. The Government of the Republic of Panama shall have the right to transport over the Canal its vessels and its troops and munitions of war in such vessels at all times without paying charges of any kind. The exemption is to be extended to the auxiliary railway for the transportation of persons in the service of the Republic of Panama, or of the police force charged with the preservation of public order outside of said zone, as well as to their baggage, munitions of war and supplies.

ART. XX. If by virtue of any existing treaty in relation to the territory of the Isthmus of Panama, whereof the obligations shall descend or be assumed by the Republic of Panama, there may be any privilege or concession in favor of the Government or the citizens and subjects of a third power relative to an interoceanic means of communication which in any of its terms may be incompatible with the terms of the present convention, the Republic of Panama agrees to cancel or modify such treaty in due form, for which purpose it shall give to the said third power the requisite notification within the term of four months from the date of the present convention, and in case the existing treaty contains no clause permitting its modifications or annulment, the Republic of Panama agrees to procure its modifications or annulment in such form that there shall not exist any conflict with the stipulations of the present convention. . . .

ART. XXII. The Republic of Panama renounces and grants to the United States the participation to which it might be entitled in the future earnings of the Canal under Article XV of the concessionary contract with Lucien N. B. Wyse, now owned by the New Panama Canal Company, and any and all other rights or claims of a pecuniary nature arising under or relating to said concession, or arising under or relating to the concessions to the Panama Railroad Company or any extension or modification thereof; and it likewise renounces, confirms and grants to the United States, now and

hereafter, all the rights and property reserved in the said concessions which otherwise would belong to Panama at or before the expiration of the terms of ninety-nine years of the concessions granted to or held by the above-mentioned party and companies, and all right, title and interest which it now has or may hereafter have, in and to the lands, canal, works, property and rights held by the said companies under said concessions or otherwise, and acquired or to be acquired by the United States from or through the New Panama Canal Company, including any property and rights which might or may in the future either by lapse of time, forfeiture or otherwise, revert to the Republic of Panama under any contracts or concessions, with said Wyse, the Universal Panama Canal Company, the Panama Railroad Company and the New Panama Canal Company.

The aforesaid rights and property shall be and are free and released from any present or reversionary interest in or claims of Panama and the title of the United States thereto upon consummation of the contemplated purchase by the United States from the New Panama Canal Company, shall be absolute, so far as concerns the Republic of Panama, excepting always the rights of the Republic specifically secured under this treaty.

ART. XXIII. If it should become necessary at any time to employ armed forces for the safety or protection of the Canal, or of the ships that make use of the same, or the railways and auxiliary works, the United States shall have the right, at all times and in its discretion, to use its police and its land and naval forces or to establish fortifications for these purposes.

ART. XXIV. No change either in the Government or in the laws and treaties of the Republic of Panama shall, without the consent of the United States, affect any right of the United States under the present convention, or under any treaty stipulation between the two countries that now exists or may hereafter exist touching the subject matter of this convention.

If the Republic of Panama shall hereafter enter as a constituent into any other Government or into any union or confederation of States, so as to merge her sovereignty or independence in such Government, union or confederation, the rights of the United States under this convention shall not be in any respect lessened or impaired.

Art. XXV. For the better performance of the engagements of this convention and to the end of the efficient protection of the Canal and the preservation of its neutrality, the Government of the Republic of Panama will sell or lease to the United States lands adequate and necessary for naval or coaling stations on the Pacific coast and on the western Caribbean coast of the Republic at certain points to be agreed upon with the President of the United States. . . .

John Hay—Bunau-Varilla

362. THE ROOSEVELT COROLLARY TO THE MONROE DOCTRINE
1904, 1905

Roosevelt's experience in the Venezuela episode and the outbreak of disorder in Santo Domingo led him to develop the so-called Roosevelt corollary to the Monroe Doctrine—the principle that inasmuch as we permit no European nation to intervene in the affairs of Latin-American countries we must ourselves assume the responsibility of preserving order and protecting life and property in those countries. This principle led to protracted intervention in Santo Domingo and, subsequently, to intervention in Haiti, Nicaragua and Cuba. There is no necessary connection between this principle of moral and police responsibility and the original Monroe Doctrine. Roosevelt formulated his "corollary" in his annual messages of 1904 and 1905. See references, Docs. No. 398, 460, 469.

1. Roosevelt's Annual Message
December 6, 1904

(Messages and Papers of the Presidents,
Vol. XIV, p. 6923 ff.)

. . . It is not true that the United States feels any land hunger or entertains any projects as regards the other nations of the Western Hemisphere save such as are for their welfare. All that this country desires is to see the neighboring countries stable, orderly, and prosperous. Any country whose people conduct themselves well can count upon our hearty friendship. If a nation shows that it knows how to act with reasonable efficiency and decency in social and political matters, if it keeps order and pays its obligations, it need fear no interference from the United States. Chronic wrongdoing, or an impotence which results in a general loosening of the ties of civilized society, may in America, as elsewhere, ultimately require intervention by some civilized nation, and in the Western Hemisphere the adherence of the United States to the Monroe Doctrine may force the United States, however reluctantly, in flagrant cases of such wrongdoing or impotence, to the exercise of an international police power. If every country washed by the Caribbean Sea would show the progress in stable and just civilization which with the aid of the Platt amendment Cuba has shown since our troops left the island, and which so many of the republics in both Americas are constantly and brilliantly showing, all question of interference by this Nation with their affairs would be at an end. Our interests and those of our southern neighbors are in reality identical. They have great natural riches, and if within their borders the reign of law and justice obtains, prosperity is sure to come to them. While they thus obey the primary laws of civilized society they may rest assured that they will be treated by us in a spirit of cordial and helpful sympathy. We would interfere with them only in the last resort, and then only if it became evident that their inability or unwillingness to do justice at home and abroad had violated the rights of the United States or had invited foreign aggression to the detriment of the entire body of American nations. It is a mere truism to say that every nation, whether in America or anywhere else, which desires to maintain its freedom, its independence, must ultimately realize that the right of such independence can not be separated from the responsibility of making good use of it.

In asserting the Monroe Doctrine, in taking such steps as we have taken in regard to Cuba, Venezuela, and Panama, and in endeavoring to circumscribe the theater of war in the Far East, and to secure the open door in China, we have acted in our own interest as well as in the interest of humanity at large. There are, however, cases in which, while our own interests are not greatly involved, strong appeal is made to our sympathies. . . . But in extreme cases action may be justifiable and proper. What form the action shall take must depend upon the circumstances of the case; that is, upon the degree of the atrocity and upon our power to remedy it. The cases in which we could interfere by force of arms as we interfered to put a stop to intolerable conditions in Cuba are necessarily very few.

2. ROOSEVELT'S ANNUAL MESSAGE
December 5, 1905

(Messages and Papers of the Presidents, Vol. XIV, p. 6994 ff.)

. . . It must be understood that under no circumstances will the United States use the Monroe Doctrine as a cloak for territorial aggression. We desire peace with all the world, but perhaps most of all with the other peoples of the American Continent. There are, of course, limits to the wrongs which any self-respecting nation can endure. It is always possible that wrong actions toward this Nation, or toward citizens of this Nation, in some State unable to keep order among its own people, unable to secure justice from outsiders, and unwilling to do justice to those outsiders who treat it well, may result in our having to take action to protect our rights; but such action will not be taken with a view to territorial aggression, and it will be taken at all only with extreme reluctance and when it has become evident that every other resource has been exhausted.

Moreover, we must make it evident that we do not intend to permit the Monroe Doctrine to be used by any nation on this Continent as a shield to protect it from the consequences of its own misdeeds against foreign nations. If a republic to the south of us commits a tort against a foreign nation. such as an outrage against a citizen of that nation, then the Monroe Doctrine does not force us to interfere to prevent punishment of the tort, save to see that the punishment does not assume the form of territorial occupation in any shape. The case is more difficult when it refers to a contractual obligation. Our own Government has always refused to enforce such contractual obligations on behalf of its citizens by an appeal to arms. It is much to be wished that all foreign governments would take the same view. But they do not; and in consequence we are liable at any time to be brought face to face with disagreeable alternatives. On the one hand, this country would certainly decline to go to war to prevent a foreign government from collecting a just debt; on the other hand, it is very inadvisable to permit any foreign power to take possession, even temporarily, of the custom houses of an American Republic in order to enforce the payment of its obligations; for such temporary occupation might turn into a permanent occupation. The only escape from these alternatives may at any time be that we must ourselves undertake to bring about some arrangement by which so much as possible of a just obligation shall be paid. It is far better that this country should put through such an arrangement, rather than allow any foreign country to undertake it. To do so insures the defaulting republic from having to pay debt of an improper character under duress, while it also insures honest creditors of the republic from being passed by in the interest of dishonest or grasping creditors. Moreover, for the United States to take such a position offers the only possible way of insuring us against a clash with some foreign power. The position is, therefore, in the interest of peace as well as in the interest of justice. It is of benefit to our people; it is of benefit to foreign peoples; and most of all it is really of benefit to the people of the country concerned. . . .

363. NORTHERN SECURITIES COMPANY v. UNITED STATES
193 U. S. 197
1904

Appeal from the circuit court of United States for the district of Minnesota. It was with this celebrated suit that President Roosevelt made his first bid for popularity as a "trust-buster". A struggle between the Harriman and the Hill interests for the control of the stock of the Northern Pacific Railway had ended, in 1901, with the formation of the Northern Securities Company as a holding company to hold the stock of the competing interests. This was the first great holding company, and the question whether such a device constituted a violation of the Sherman Anti-Trust Act was one of great importance. The opinion of Mr. Justice Holmes, who had just been appointed to the Supreme Court, was awaited with particular interest. See, B. H. Meyer, *A History of the Northern Securities Case;* F. B. Clark, *Constitutional Doctrines of Justice Harlan;* D. Richardson, *Constitutional Doctrines of Justice O. W. Holmes.*

HARLAN, J. . . . The Government charges that if the combination was held not to be in violation of the act of Congress, then all efforts of the National Government to preserve to the people the benefits of free competition among carriers engaged in interstate commerce will be wholly unavailing, and all transcontinental lines, indeed the entire railway systems of the country, may be absorbed, merged and consolidated, thus placing the public at the absolute mercy of the holding corporation.

. . . In our judgment, the evidence fully sustains the material allegations of the bill, and shows a violation of the act of Congress, in so far as it declares illegal every combination or conspiracy in restraint of commerce among the several States and with foreign nations, and forbids attempts to monopolize such commerce or any part of it.

. . . Is the act to be construed as forbidding every combination or conspiracy in restraint of trade or commerce among the States or with foreign nations? Or, does it embrace only such restraints as are unreasonable in their nature? Is the motive with which a forbidden combination or conspiracy was formed at all material when it appears that the necessary tendency of the particular combination or conspiracy in ques-

tion is to restrict or suppress free competition between competing railroads engaged in commerce among the States? Does the act of Congress prescribe, as a *rule* for *interstate* or *international* commerce, that the operation of the natural laws of competition between those engaged in *such* commerce shall not be restricted or interfered with by any contract, combination or conspiracy? . . .

. . . The first case in this court arising under the Anti-Trust Act was *United States* v. *E. C. Knight Co.*, 156 U. S. 1. The next case was that of *United States* v. *Trans-Missouri Freight Association*, 166 U. S. 290. That was followed by *United States* v. *Joint Traffic Association*, 171 U. S. 505, *Hopkins* v. *United States*, 171 U. S. 578, *Anderson* v. *United States*, 171 U. S. 604, *Addyston Pipe & Steel Co.* v. *United States* 175 U. S. 211, and *Montague & Co.* v. *Lowry*, 193 U. S. 38. To these may be added *Pearsall* v. *Great Northern Railway*, 161 U. S. 646, which, although not arising under the Anti-Trust Act, involved an agreement under which the Great Northern and Northern Pacific Railway companies should be consolidated and by which competition between those companies was to cease.

. . . We will not incumber this opinion by extended extracts from the former opinions of this court. It is sufficient to say that from the decisions in the above cases certain propositions are plainly deducible and embrace the present case. Those propositions are:

That although the act of Congress known as the Anti-Trust Act has no reference to the mere manufacture or production of articles or commodities within the limits of the several States, it does embrace and declare illegal every contract, combination or conspiracy, in whatever form, of whatever nature, and whoever may be parties to it, which directly or necessarily operates *in restraint* of trade or commerce *among the several States or with foreign nations;*

That the act is not limited to restraints of interstate and international trade or commerce that are unreasonable in their nature, but embraces *all* direct *restraints* imposed by any combination, conspiracy or monopoly upon such trade or commerce;

That railroad carriers engaged in interstate or international commerce are embraced by the act;

That combinations even among *private* manufacturers or dealers whereby interstate or international commerce is restrained are equally embraced by the act;

That Congress has the power to establish *rules* by which *interstate and international* commerce shall be governed, and, by the Anti-Trust Act, has prescribed the rule of free competition among those engaged in such commerce;

That *every* combination or conspiracy which would extinguish competition between otherwise competing railroads engaged in *interstate trade or commerce,* and which would *in that way* restrain such trade or commerce, is made illegal by the act;

That the natural effect of competition is to increase commerce, and an agreement whose direct effect is to prevent this play of competition restrains instead of promotes trade and commerce;

That to vitiate a combination, such as the act of Congress condemns, it need not be shown that the combination, in fact, results or will result in a total suppression of trade or in a complete monopoly, but it is only essential to show that by its necessary operation it tends to restrain interstate or international trade or commerce and to deprive the public of the advantages that flow from free competition;

That the constitutional guarantee of liberty of contract does not prevent Congress from prescribing the rule of free competition for those engaged in *interstate and international* commerce; and,

That under its power to regulate commerce among the several States and with foreign nations, Congress had authority to enact the statute in question. . . .

It is said that whatever may be the power of a State over such subjects Congress cannot forbid single individuals from disposing of their stock in a state corporation, even if such corporation be engaged in interstate and international commerce; that the holding or purchase by a state corporation or the purchase by individuals, of the stock of another corporation, for whatever purposes, are matters in respect of which Congress has no authority under the Constitution. . . . It is unnecessary in this case to consider such abstract, general questions. The court need not now concern itself with them. . . .

In this connection, it is suggested that the contention of the Government is that the acquisition is itself interstate commerce, if that corporation be engaged in interstate commerce. . . . For instance, it is said that the question here is whether the power of Congress over interstate commerce extends to the regulation of the ownership of the stock in state railroad companies, by reason of their being engaged in such commerce. Again it is said that the only issue in this case is whether the Northern Securities Company can acquire and hold stock in other state corporations. . . . Such statements as to the issues in this case are, we think, wholly unwarranted and are very wide of the mark; it is the setting up of mere men of straw to be easily stricken down. . . . What the Government particularly complains of, indeed, all that it complains of here, is the existence of a combination among the stockholders of competing railroad companies which in violation of the act of Congress restrains interstate and international commerce through the agency of a common corporate trustee designated to act for both companies in repressing free competition between them. . . .

Whether the free operation of the normal laws of competition is a wise and wholesome rule for trade and commerce is an economic question which this court need not consider or determine. Undoubtedly, there are those who think that the general business interests and prosperity of the country will be best promoted if the rule of competition is not applied. But there are others who believe that such a rule is more necessary in these days of enormous wealth than it ever was in any former period of our history. Be all this as it may, Congress has, in effect, recognized the rule of free competition by declaring illegal every combination or conspiracy in restraint of . . . commerce.

Indeed, if the contentions of the defendants are sound, why may not *all* the railway companies in the United States, that are engaged, under state charters, in interstate and international commerce, enter into a combination such as the one here in question, and by the device of a holding corporation obtain the absolute control throughout the entire country of rates for passengers and freight, beyond the power of Congress to protect the public against their exactions? The argument in behalf of the defendants necessarily leads to such results and places Congress, although invested by the people of the United States with full authority to regulate . . . commerce, in a condition of utter helplessness, so far as the protection of the public against such combinations is concerned. . . .

It was said in argument that the circumstances under which the Northern Securities Company obtained the stock of the constituent companies imported simply an investment in the stock of other corporations, a purchase of that stock; which investment or purchase, it was contended was not forbidden by the charter of the company and could not be made illegal by any act of Congress. This view is wholly fallacious. . . . There was no actual investment, in any substantial sense, by the Northern Securities Company in the stock of the two constituent companies. . . . However that company may have acquired for itself the stock in the Great Northern and Northern Pacific Railway companies . . . all the stock it held or acquired in the constituent companies was acquired and held to be used in suppressing competition between those companies. It came into existence only for that purpose. . . .

Guided by these long established rules of construction, it is manifest that if the Anti-Trust Act is held not to embrace a case such as is now before us, the plain intention of the legislative branch of the Government will be defeated. If Congress has not, by the words used in the act, described this and like cases, it would, we apprehend, be impossible to find words that would describe them. . . .

The judgement of the court is that the decree below be and hereby is affirmed. . . .

HOLMES, J., with whom concurred Chief Justice FULLER, Justice WHITE and Justice PECKHAM, dissenting.

. . . Great cases like hard cases make bad law. For great cases are called great, not by reason of their real importance in shaping the law of the future, but because of some accident of immediate overwhelming interest which appeals to the feelings and distorts the judgement. These immediate interests exercise a kind of hydraulic pressure which makes what previously was clear seem doubtful, and before which even well settled principles of law will bend. What we have to do in this case is to find the meaning of some not very difficult words. . . .

. . . We must try, I have tried, to do it with the same freedom of natural and spontaneous interpretation that one would be sure of if the same question arose upon an indictment for a similar act which excited no public attention, and was of importance only to a prisoner before the court. Furthermore, while at times judges need for their work the training of economists or statesmen, and must act in view of their foresight and of consequences, yet when their task is to interpret and apply the words of a statute, their function is merely academic to begin with—to read English intelligently—and a consideration of consequences comes into play, if at all, only when the meaning of the words used is open to reasonable doubt.

The question to be decided is whether, under the act of July 2, 1890, it is unlawful, at any stage of the process, if several men unite to form a corporation for the purpose of buying more than half the stock of each of two competing interstate railroad companies, if they form the corporation, and the corporation buys the stock. I will suppose further that every step is taken, from the beginning, with the single intent of ending competition between the companies. . . .

This act is construed by the Government to affect the purchasers of shares in two railroad companies because of the effect it may have, or, if you like, is certain to have, upon the competition of these roads. If such a remote result of the exercise of an ordinary incident of property and personal freedom is enough to make that exercise unlawful, there is hardly any transaction concerning commerce between the States that may not be made a crime by the finding of a jury or a court. The personal ascendency of one man may be such that it would give to his advice the effect of a command, if he owned but a single share in each road. The tendency of his presence in the stockholders' meetings might be certain to prevent competition, and thus his advice, if not his mere existence, become a crime.

. . . Contracts in restraint of trade are dealt with and defined by the common law. They are contracts with a stranger to the contractor's business, (although in some cases carrying on a similar one,) which wholly or partially restrict the freedom of the contractor in carrying on that business as otherwise he would. The objection of the common law to them was primarily on the contractor's own account. The notion of monopoly did not come in unless the contract covered the whole of England. . . .

. . . The provision of the statute against contracts in restraint of trade has been held to apply to contracts between railroads, otherwise remaining independent, by which they restricted their respective freedom as to rates. This restriction by contract with a stranger to the contractor's business is the ground of the decision in *United States* v. *Joint Traffic Association,* following and affirming *United States* v. *Trans-Missouri Freight Association.* I accept those decisions absolutely, not only as binding upon me, but as decisions which I have no desire to criticize or abridge. But the provision has not been decided, and, it seems to me, could not be decided without perversion of plain language, to apply to an arrangement by which competition is ended through community of interest—an arrangement which leaves the parties without external restriction. That provision, taken alone, does not require that all existing competitions shall be maintained. It does not look primarily, if at all, to competition. It simply requires that a party's freedom in trade between the States shall not be cut down by contract with a stranger. . . .

. . . According to popular speech, every concern monopolizes whatever business it does, and if that business is trade between two States it monopolizes a part of the trade among the States. Of course the statute does not forbid that. It does not mean that all business must cease. A single railroad down a narrow valley or through a mountain gorge monopolizes all the railroad transportation through that valley or gorge. Indeed every railroad monopolizes, in a popular sense, the trade of some area. Yet I suppose that no one would say that the statute forbids a combination of men into a corporation to build and run such a railroad between the States.

. . . I will suppose that three parties apply to a State for charters; one for each of two new and possibly competing lines respectively, and one for both of these lines, and that the charter is granted to the last. I think that charter would be good, and I think the whole argument to the contrary rests on a popular instead of an accurate and legal conception of what the word "monopolize" in the statute means. I repeat, that in my opinion there is no attempt to monopolize, and what, as I have said, in my judgment amounts to the same thing, that there is no combination in restraint of trade, until something is done with the intent to exclude strangers to the combination from competing with it in some part of the business which it carries on.

Unless I am entirely wrong in my understanding of what a "combination in restraint of trade" means, then the same monopoly may be attempted and effected by an individual, and is made equally illegal in that case by Sec. 2. But I do not expect to hear it maintained that Mr. Morgan could be sent to prison for buying as many shares as he liked of the Great Northern and the Northern Pacific, even if he bought them both at the same time and got more than half the stock of each road. . . .

A partnership is not a contract or combination in restraint of trade between the partners unless the well known words are to be given a new meaning invented for the purpose of this act. . . . The law, I repeat, says nothing about competition, and only prevents its suppression by contracts or combinations in restraint of trade, and such contracts or combinations derive their character as restraining trade from other features than the suppression of competition alone. To see whether I am wrong, the illustrations put in the argument are of use. If I am, then a partnership between two stage drivers who had been competitors in driving across a state line, or two merchants once engaged in rival commerce among the States whether made after or before the act, if now continued, is a crime. For, again I repeat, if the restraint on the freedom of the members of a combination caused by their entering into partnership is a restraint of trade, every such combination, as well the small as the great, is within the act. . . .

I am happy to know that only a minority of my brethren adopt an interpretation of the law which in my opinion would make eternal the *bellum omnium contra omnes* and disintegrate society so far as it could

into individual atoms. If that were its intent I should regard calling such a law a regulation of commerce as a mere pretense. It would be an attempt to reconstruct society. I am not concerned with the wisdom of such an attempt, but I believe that Congress was not entrusted by the Constitution with the power to make it and I am deeply persuaded that it has not tried.

364. LOCHNER v. NEW YORK
198 U. S. 45
1905

Error to the County Court of Oneida County, New York. A New York law limited the hours of labor in bakeries to not more than sixty hours a week or ten hours a day. The validity of this law was challenged on the ground that it was not a proper exercise of the police power, but a violation of the rights of contract and of property guaranteed in the Fourteenth Amendment. Compare the decision of the Court here with the decision in *Holden* v. *Hardy,* Doc. No. 344, and *Bunting* v. *Oregon,* Doc. No. 421.

PECKHAM, J. . . . The statute necessarily interferes with the right of contract between the employer and employees, concerning the number of hours in which the latter may labor in the bakery of the employer. The general right to make a contract in relation to his business is part of the liberty of the individual protected by the Fourteenth Amendment of the Federal Constitution. . . . There are, however, certain powers, existing in the sovereignty of each State in the Union, somewhat vaguely termed police powers, the exact description and limitation of which have not been attempted by the courts. These powers, broadly stated and without, at present, any attempt at a more specific definition, relate to the safety, health, morals and general welfare of the public. . . .

The State, therefore, has power to prevent the individual from making certain kinds of contracts, and in regard to them the Federal Constitution offers no protection. If the contract be one which the State, in the

legitimate exercise of its police power, has the right to prohibit, it is not prevented from prohibiting it by the Fourteenth Amendment. . . .

. . . This court has recognized the existence and upheld the exercise of the police powers of the States in many cases which might fairly be considered as border ones, and it has, in the course of its determination of questions regarding the asserted invalidity of such statutes, on the ground of their violation of the rights secured by the federal Constitution, been guided by rules of a very liberal nature, the application of which has resulted, in numerous instances, in upholding the validity of state statutes thus assailed. Among the later cases where the state law has been upheld by this court is that of *Holden* v. *Hardy,* 169 U. S. 366. . . .

It will be observed that, even with regard to that class of labor, the Utah statute provided for cases of emergency wherein the provisions of the statute would not apply. The statute now before this court has no emergency clause in it, and, if the statute is valid, there are no circumstances and no emergencies under which the slightest violation of the provisions of the act would be innocent. There is nothing in *Holden* v. *Hardy* which covers the case now before us. . . .

It must, of course, be conceded that there is a limit to the valid exercise of the police power by the State. There is no dispute concerning this general proposition. Otherwise the Fourteenth Amendment would have no efficacy and the legislatures of the States would have unbounded power, and it would be enough to say that any piece of legislation was enacted to conserve the morals, the health, or the safety of the people; such legislation would be valid, no matter how absolutely without foundation the claim might be. The claim of the police power would be a mere pretext—become another and delusive name for the supreme sovereignty of the State to be exercised free from constitutional restraint. This is not contended for. In every case that comes before this court, therefore, where legislation of this character is concerned, and where the protection of the federal Constitution is sought, the question necessarily arises: Is this a fair, reasonable, and appropriate exercise of the police power of the State, or is it an unreasonable, unnecessary, and arbitrary interference with the right of the individual to his personal liberty or to enter into those contracts in relation to labor which may seem to him appropriate or necessary for the support of himself and his family? Of course the liberty of contract relating to labor includes both parties to it. The one has as much right to purchase as the other to sell labor.

This is not a question of substituting the judgment of the court for that of the legislature. If the act be within the power of the State it is valid, although the judgment of the court might be totally opposed to the enactment of such a law. But the question would still remain: Is it within the police power of the State? and that question must be answered by the court.

The question whether this act is valid as a labor law, pure and simple, may be dismissed in a few words. There is no reasonable ground for interfering with the liberty of person or the right of free contract, by determining the hours of labor, in the occupation of a baker. There is no contention that bakers as a class are not equal in intelligence and capacity to men in other trades or manual occupations, or that they are not able to assert their rights and care for themselves without the protecting arm of the State, interfering with their independence of judgment and of action. They are in no sense wards of the State. Viewed in the light of a purely labor law, with no reference whatever to the question of health, we think that a law like the one before us involves neither the safety, the morals, nor the welfare, of the public, and that the interest of the public is not in the slightest degree affected by such an act. The law must be upheld, if at all, as a law pertaining to the health of the individual engaged in the occupation of a baker. It does not affect any other portion of the public than those who are engaged in that occupation. Clean and wholesome bread does not depend upon whether the baker works but ten hours per day or only sixty hours a week. The limitation of the hours of labor does not come within the police power on that ground.

It is a question of which of two powers or rights shall prevail—the power of the State to legislate or the right of the individual to liberty of person and freedom of contract. The mere assertion that the subject relates, though but in a remote degree, to the public health, does not necessarily render the enactment valid. The act must have a more direct relation, as a means to an end, and the end itself must be appropriate and legitimate, before an act can be held to be valid which interferes with the general right of an individual to be free in his person and in his power to contract in relation to his own labor. . . .

We think the limit of the police power has been reached and passed in this case. There is, in our judgment, no reasonable foundation for holding this to be necessary or appropriate as a health law to safeguard the public health, or the health of the individuals who are following the trade of a baker. If this statute be valid, and if, therefore, a proper case is made out in which to deny the right of an individual, *sui juris,* as employer or employee, to make contracts for the labor of the latter under the protection of the provisions of the federal Constitution, there would seem to be no length to which legislation of this nature might not go. . . .

It is impossible for us to shut our eyes to the fact that many of the laws of this character, while passed under what is claimed to be the police power for the purpose of protecting the public health or welfare, are, in reality, passed from other motives. We are justified in saying so when, from the character of the law and the subject upon which it legislates, it is apparent that the public health or welfare bears but the most remote relation to the law. The purpose of a statute must be determined from the natural and legal effect of the language employed; and whether it is or is not repugnant to the Constitution of the United States must be determined from the natural effect of such statutes when put into operation, and not from their proclaimed purpose. . . . The court looks beyond the mere letter of the law in such cases.

. . . The act is not, within any fair meaning of the term, a health law, but is an illegal interference with the rights of individuals, both employers and employees, to make contracts regarding labor upon such terms as they may think best, or which they may agree upon with the other parties to such contracts. Statutes of the nature of that under review, limiting the hours in which grown and intelligent men may labor to earn their living, are mere meddlesome interferences with the rights of the individual, and they are not saved from condemnation by the claim that they are passed in the exercise of the police power and upon the subject of the health of the individual whose rights are interfered with, unless there be some fair ground, reasonable in and of itself, to say that there is material danger to the public health, or to the health of the employees, if the hours of labor are not curtailed. . . .

It is manifest to us that the limitation of the hours of labor as provided for in this section of the statute . . . has no such direct relation to and no such substantial effect upon the health of the employee, as to justify us in regarding the section as really a health law. It seems to us that the real object and purpose were simply to regulate the hours of labor between the master and his employees . . . in a private business, not dangerous in any degree to morals or in any real and substantial degree, to the health of the employees. Under such circumstances the freedom of master and employee to contract with each other in relation to their employment, and in defining the same, cannot be prohibited or interfered with, without violating the Federal Constitution.

Judgement reversed.

HOLMES, J., dissenting. . . . The case is decided upon an economic theory which a large part of the country does not entertain. If it were a question whether I agreed with that theory, I should desire to study it further and long before making up my mind. But I do not conceive that to be my duty, because I strongly believe that my agreement or disagreement has nothing to do with the right of a majority to embody their opinions in law. It is settled by various decisions of this court that state constitutions and state laws may regulate life in many ways which we as legislators might think as injudicious, or if you like as tyrannical, as this, and which, equally with this, interfere with the liberty to contract. Sunday laws and usury laws are ancient examples. A more modern one is the prohibition of lotteries. The liberty of the citizen to do as he likes so long as he does not interfere with the liberty of others to do the same, which has been a shibboleth for some well-known writers, is interfered with by school laws, by the post-office, by every state or municipal institution which takes his money for purposes thought desirable, whether he likes it or not. The Fourteenth Amendment does not enact Mr. Herbert Spencer's Social Statics. . . . United States and state statutes and decisions cutting down the liberty to contract by way of combination are familiar to this court. . . . Some of these laws embody convictions or prejudices which judges are likely to share. Some may not. But a constitution is not intended to embody a particular economic theory, whether of paternalism and the organic relation of the citizen to the state or of *laissez faire*. It is made for people of fundamentally differing views, and the accident of our finding certain opinions natural and familiar, or novel, and even shocking, ought not to conclude our judgement upon the question whether statutes embodying them conflict with the Constitution of the United States.

General propositions do not decide concrete cases. The decision will depend on a judgement or intuition more subtle than any articulate major premise. But I think that the proposition just stated, if it is accepted, will carry us far toward the end. Every opinion tends to become a law. I think that the word "liberty," in the Fourteenth Amendment, is perverted when it is held to prevent the natural outcome of a dominant opinion, unless it can be said that a rational and fair man necessarily would admit that the statute proposed would infringe fundamental principles as they have been understood by the traditions of our people and our law. It does not need research to show that no such sweeping condemnation can be passed upon the statute before us. A reasonable man might think it a proper measure on the score of health. Men whom I certainly could not pronounce unreasonable would uphold it as a first instalment of a general regulation of the hours of work. Whether in the latter aspect it would be open to the charge of inequality I think it unnecessary to discuss.

365. PEOPLE v. WILLIAMS
189 New York, 131
1907

Appeal from order of the Appellate Division of the Supreme Court. Compare the decision in this case to the decision in *Commonwealth* v. *Hamilton Manufacturing Company*, Doc. No. 295.

GRAY, J. The defendant was arrested and convicted upon the charge of having violated the provisions of section 3841 of the Penal Code. . . . The provision of the Labor Law now in question is contained in section 77; which is entitled: "Hours of labor of minors and women" and reads that "No minor under the age of eighteen years, and no female shall be employed, permitted or suffered to work in any factory in this state before six o'clock in the morning, or after nine o'clock in the evening of any day; or for more than ten hours in any one day except to make a shorter work day on the last day of the week; or for more than sixty hours in any one week, or more hours in any one week than will make an average of ten hours per day for the whole number of days so worked." (L. 1903, ch. 184, sec. 2.) The information and the proof were that a female, named Katie Mead, over twenty one years of age, was found by the factory inspector at work in a book binding establishment, in the city of New York, at twenty minutes after ten o'clock in the evening. . . . If the inhibition against employing a female in any factory after that hour was a valid act of legislation, then the defendant came within its operation and he was amenable to punishment. After the defendant had been found guilty, the trial court granted his motion in arrest of judgment and discharged him; holding that the legislative enactment was unconstitutional. The justices of the Appellate Division, in the first department, by a divided vote, have affirmed the order of the trial court.

In my judgment, the determination below was correct. I think that the legislature, in preventing the employment of an adult woman in a factory, and in prohibiting her to work therein, before six o'clock in the morning, or after nine o'clock in the evening has overstepped the limits set by the Constitution of the state to the exercise of the power to interfere with the rights of citizens. The fundamental law of the state, as embodied in its Constitution, provides that "no person shall . . . be deprived of life, liberty or property without due process of law." (Art. 1, sec. 6.) The provisions of the State and the Federal Constitutions protect every citizen in the right to pursue any lawful employment in a lawful manner. He enjoys the utmost freedom to follow his chosen pursuit and any arbitrary distinction against, or deprivation of, that freedom by the legislature is an invasion of the constitutional guaranty. Under our laws men and women now stand alike in their constitutional rights and there is no warrant for making any discrimination between them with respect to the liberty of person, or of contract. It is claimed, however, in this case, that the enactment in question can be justified as an exercise of the police power of the state; having for its purpose the general welfare of the state in a measure for the preservation of the health of the female citizens. It is to be observed that it is not a regulation of the number of hours of labor for working women; the enactment goes far beyond this. It attempts to take away the right of a woman to labor before six in the morning, or after nine o'clock in the evening without any reference to other considerations. . . . Except as to women under twenty one years of age, this was the first attempt on the part of the state to restrict their liberty of person, or their freedom of contract, in the pursuit of a vocation. I find nothing in the language of the section which suggests the purpose of promoting health, except as it might be inferred that for a woman to work during the forbidden hours of night would be unhealthful. If the inhibition of the section in question had been framed to prevent the ten hours of work from being performed at night, or to prolong them beyond nine o'clock in the evening, it might, more readily, be appreciated that the health of women was the matter of legislative concern. That is not the effect, nor the sense, of the provision of the section with which, alone, we are dealing. It was not the case upon which this defendant was convicted. If this enactment is to be sustained, then an adult woman, although a citizen and entitled as such to all the rights of citizenship under our laws, may not be employed, nor contract to work, in any factory for any period of time, no matter how short, if it is within the prohibited hours; and this, too, without any regard to the healthfulness of the employment. It is clear, as it seems to me, that this legislation cannot, and should not, be upheld as a proper exercise of the police power. It is, certainly, discriminative against female citizens, in denying to them equal rights with men in the same pursuit. The courts have gone very far in upholding legislative enactments, framed clearly for the welfare, comfort and health of the community, and that a wide range in the exercise of the police power of the state should be conceded, I do not deny; but, when it is sought under the guise of a labor law, arbitrarily, as here, to prevent an adult female citizen from working at any

time of the day that suits her, I think it is time to call a halt. It arbitrarily deprives citizens of their right to contract with each other. The tendency of legislatures, in the form of regulatory measures, to interfere with the lawful pursuits of citizens is becoming a marked one in this country, and it behooves the courts, firmly and fearlessly, to interpose the barriers of their judgments, when invoked to protect against legislative acts, plainly transcending the powers conferred by the Constitution upon the legislative body. . . .

Without extended reference to the cases bearing upon the much discussed subject of the exercise of the police power, I need only refer to the recent case of *Lochner* v. *State of New York*, (198 U. S. 45); where the Supreme Court of the United States had before it a case arising in this state under a provision of the Labor Law, which restricted the hours of labor for the employés of bakers. . . . It was held that bakers "are in no sense wards of the State.". . .

So I think, in this case, that we should say, as an adult female is in no sense a ward of the state, that she is not to be made the special object of the exercise of the paternal power of the state and that the restriction, here imposed upon her privilege to labor, violates the constitutional guarantees. In the gradual course of legislation upon the rights of a woman in this state, she has come to possess all of the responsibilities of the man and she is entitled to be placed upon an equality of rights with the man.

It might be observed that working in a factory in the night hours is not the only situation of menace to the working woman; but such occupation is, arbitrarily, debarred her.

For these reasons, I advise that the order appealed from should be affirmed.

366. MULLER v. OREGON
208 U. S. 412
1908

Error to the supreme court of Oregon. An Oregon law of 1903 prohibited the employment of any female in any factory or laundry for more than ten hours a day. Mr. Louis Brandeis, subsequently Justice of the Supreme Court, was one of the counsel for the state of Oregon, and pro-

duced a mass of evidence of a statistical, sociological, and historical character bearing on the reasonableness of the law in question, which was admitted by the court. Mr. Brandeis's brief was printed by the National Consumers' League as *Women in Industry*.

BREWER, J. . . . The single question is the constitutionality of the statute under which the defendant was convicted, so far as affects the work of a female in a laundry. . . .

It is the law of Oregon that women, whether married or single, have equal contractual and personal rights with men. . . .

It thus appears that, putting to one side the elective franchise, in the matter of personal and contractual rights they stand on the same plane as the other sex. Their rights in these respects can no more be infringed than the equal rights of their brothers. We held in Lochner v. New York, 198 U. S. 45, that a law providing that no laborer shall be required or permitted to work in a bakery more than sixty hours in a week or ten hours in a day was not as to men a legitimate exercise of the police power of the State, but an unreasonable, unnecessary, and arbitrary interference with the right and liberty of the individual to contract in relation to his labor, and as such was in conflict with, and void under, the federal Constitution. That decision is invoked by plaintiff in error as decisive of the question before us. But this assumes that the difference between the sexes does not justify a different rule respecting a restriction of the hours of labor.

. . . It may not be amiss, in the present case, before examining the constitutional question, to notice the course of legislation, as well as expressions of opinion from other than judicial sources. In the brief filed by Mr. Louis D. Brandeis for the defendant in error is a very copious collection of all these matters. . . .

The legislation and opinions referred to . . . may not be, technically speaking, authorities, and in them is little or no discussion of the constitutional question presented to us for determination, yet they are significant of a widespread belief that woman's physical structure, and the functions she performs in consequence thereof, justify special legislation restricting or qualifying the conditions under which she should be permitted to toil. Constitutional questions, it is true, are not settled by even a consensus of present public opinion, for it is the peculiar value of a written constitution that it places in unchanging form limitations upon legislative action, and thus gives a permanence and stability to popular government which other-wise would be lacking. At the same time, when a question of fact is debated and debatable, and the extent to which a special constitutional limitation goes is affected by the truth in respect to that fact, a widespread and long-continued belief concerning it is worthy of consideration. We take judicial cognizance of all matters of general knowledge. . . .

That woman's physical structure and the performance of maternal functions place her at a disadvantage in the struggle for subsistence is obvious. This is especially true when the burdens of motherhood are upon her. Even when they are not, by abundant testimony of the medical fraternity continuance for a long time on her feet at work, repeating this from day to day, tends to injurious effects upon the body, and, as healthy mothers are essential to vigorous offspring, the physical well-being of woman becomes an object of public interest and care in order to preserve the strength and vigor of the race. . . .

Differentiated by these matters from the other sex, she is properly placed in a class by herself, and legislation designed for her protection may be sustained, even when like legislation is not necessary for men, and could not be sustained. It is impossible to close one's eyes to the fact that she still looks to her brother and depends upon him. Even though all restrictions on political, personal, and contractual rights were taken away, and she stood, so far as statutes are concerned, upon an absolutely equal plane with him, it would still be true that she is so constituted that she will rest upon and look to him for protection; that her physical structure and a proper discharge of her maternal functions—having in view not merely her own health, but the well-being of the race—justify legislation to protect her from the greed as well as the passion of man. The limitations which this statute places upon her contractual powers, upon her right to agree with her employer as to the time she shall labor, are not imposed solely for her benefit, but also largely for the benefit of all. Many words cannot make this plainer. The two sexes differ in structure of body, in the functions to be performed by each, in the amount of physical strength, in the capacity for long continued labor, particularly when done standing, the influence of vigorous health upon the future well-being of the race, the self-reliance which enables one to assert full rights, and in the capacity to maintain the struggle for subsistence. This difference justifies a difference in legislation, and upholds that which is designed to compensate for some of the burdens which rest upon her. . . .

For these reasons, and without questioning in any respect the decision in *Lochner* v. *New York,* we are of the opinion that it cannot be adjudged that the act in question is in conflict with the federal Constitution, so far as it respects the work of a female in a laundry, and the judgment of the supreme court of Oregon is
Affirmed.

367. JAPANESE IMMIGRATION—THE GENTLEMEN'S AGREEMENT
1908

(Report of the Commissioner General of Immigration, 1908, p. 125)

The growing number of Japanese in California, and the hostility of labor to Oriental competition, led to an agitation against Japanese immigration that culminated in the San Francisco school laws of 1906. These laws required, in insulting terms, that Chinese, Japanese, and Korean children attend a separate Oriental Public School. The danger of further hostile legislation led President Roosevelt to conclude with Japan the famous Gentlemen's Agreement,—an executive agreement, the exact terms of which have never been revealed. The agreement salved the pride of Japan, and temporarily placated the Californians. By permitting the immigration of wives, it increased the Japanese population in California materially, and was eventually superseded by the Immigration Act of 1924. See, E. G. Mears, *Resident Orientals on the American Pacific Coast;* S. L. Gulick, *The American Japanese Problem;* E. Root, "The Real Questions under the Japanese Treaty and the San Francisco School Board Resolution," *Proc. Am. Soc. of International Law,* 1907; K. K. Amakami, *The Real Japanese Question;* T. Iyenaga and K. Sato, *Japan and the California Problem;* R. D. McKenzie, *Oriental Exclusion;* J. E. Johnsen, ed. *Japanese Exclusion.*

In order that the best results might follow from an enforcement of the regulations, an understanding was reached with Japan that the existing policy of discouraging emigra-

tion of its subjects of the laboring classes to continental United States should be continued, and should, by co-operation with the governments, be made as effective as possible. This understanding contemplates that the Japanese government shall issue passports to continental United States only to such of its subjects as are non-laborers or are laborers who, in coming to the continent, seek to resume a formerly acquired domicile, to join a parent, wife, or children residing there, or to assume active control of an already possessed interest in a farming enterprise in this country, so that the three classes of laborers entitled to receive passports have come to be designated "former residents," "parents, wives, or children of residents," and "settled agriculturists."

With respect to Hawaii, the Japanese government of its own volition stated that, experimentally at least, the issuance of passports to members of the laboring classes proceeding thence would be limited to "former residents" and "parents, wives, or children of residents." The said government has also been exercising a careful supervision over the subject of emigration of its laboring class to foreign contiguous territory.

368. ADAIR v. UNITED STATES
208 U. S. 161
1908

Error to the District Court of United States for Eastern District of Kentucky to review conviction of an agent of an interstate carrier for discharging an employee from service because of his membership in a labor organization.

HARLAN, J. This case involves the con-

stitutionality of certain provisions of the act of Congress of June 1, 1898, . . . concerning carriers engaged in interstate commerce and their employees. . . .

The 10th section upon which the present prosecution is based is in these words:

"That any employer subject to the provisions of this act, . . . who shall require any employee, or any person seeking employment, as a condition of such employment, to enter into an agreement, either written or verbal, not to become or remain a member of any labor corporation, association, or organization; . . . is hereby declared to be guilty of a disdemeanor. . . ."

The specific charge . . . was "that said William Adair, agent and employee of said common carrier and employer, . . . did unlawfully and unjustly discriminate against O. B. Coppage, employee, . . . by then and there discharging said O. B. Coppage from such employment . . . *because of his membership in said labor organization and thereby did unjustly discriminate against an employee of a common carrier and employer engaged in interstate commerce because of his membership in a labor organization,* contrary to the forms of the Statute.". . .

May Congress make it a criminal offense against the United States—as, by the 10th section of the Act of 1898 it does,—for an agent or officer of an interstate carrier, . . . to discharge an employee from service simply because of his membership in a labor organization? . . .

The first inquiry is whether the part of the 10th section of the Act of 1898 upon which the first count of the indictment is based is repugnant to the 5th Amendment of the Constitution, declaring that no person shall be deprived of liberty or property without due process of law. In our opinion that section in the particular mentioned is an invasion of the personal liberty, as well as of the right of property, guaranteed by that Amendment. Such liberty and right embrace the right to make contracts for the purchase of the labor of others, and equally the right to make contracts for the sale of one's own labor; each right, however, being subject to the fundamental condition that no contract, whatever its subject-matter, can be sustained which the law, upon reasonable grounds, forbids as inconsistent with the public interest, or as hurtful to the public order, or as detrimental to the common good. . . . It is sufficient in this case to say that, as agent of the railroad company, and, as such, responsible for the conduct of the business of one of

its departments, it was the defendant Adair's right—and that right inhered in his personal liberty, and was also a right of property—to serve his employer as best he could, so long as he did nothing that was reasonably forbidden by law as injurious to the public interest. It was the right of the defendant to prescribe the terms upon which the services of Coppage would be accepted, and it was the right of Coppage to become or not, as he chose, an employee of the railroad company upon the terms offered to him. . . .

In every case that comes before this court, therefore, where legislation of this character is concerned, . . . the question necessarily arises: Is this a fair, reasonable, and appropriate exercise of the police power of the state, or is it an unreasonable, unnecessary, and arbitrary interference with the right of the individual to his personal liberty or to enter into those contracts in relation to labor which may seem to him appropriate or necessary for the support of himself and his family? . . .

While, . . . the right of liberty and property guaranteed by the Constitution against deprivation without due process of law is subject to such reasonable restraints as the common good or the general welfare may require, it is not within the functions of government . . . to compel any person in the course of his business and against his will, to accept or retain the personal services of another, or to compel any person, against his will, to perform personal services for another. . . .

As the relations and the conduct of the parties towards each other was not controlled by any contract other than a general employment on one side to accept the services of the employee and a general agreement on the other side to render services to the employer,—no term being fixed for the continuance of the employment,—Congress could not, consistently with the 5th Amendment, make it a crime against the United States to discharge the employee because of his being a member of a labor organization.

But it is suggested that the authority to make it a crime . . . can be referred to the power of Congress to regulate interstate commerce, without regard to any question of personal liberty or right of property arising under the 5th Amendment. This suggestion can have no bearing, in the present discussion unless the statute, in the particular just stated, is, within the meaning of the Constitution, a regulation of commerce among the States. If it be not, then clearly the government cannot invoke the commerce clause of the Constitution as sustaining the indictment against Adair. . . .

Looking alone at the words of the statute for the purpose of ascertaining its scope and effect, and of determining its validity, we hold that there is no such connection between interstate commerce and membership in a labor organization as to authorize Congress to make it a crime against the United States for an agent of an interstate carrier to discharge an employee because of such membership on his part. . . .

It results, on the whole case, that the provision of the statute under which the defendant was convicted must be held to be repugnant to the 5th Amendment and as not embraced by nor within the power of Congress to regulate interstate commerce, but, under the guise of regulating commerce, and as applied to this case, it arbitrarily sanctions an illegal invasion of the personal liberty as well as the right of property of the defendant Adair.

Judgement reversed.

HOLMES, J., dissenting: I . . . think that the statute is Constitutional, and, but for the decision of my brethren, I should have felt pretty clear about it.

As we all know, there are special labor unions of men engaged in the service of carriers. These unions exercise a direct influence upon the employment of labor in that business, upon the terms of such employment, and upon the business itself. Their very existence is directed specifically to the business, and their connection with it is, at least, as intimate and important, as that of safety couplers, and, I should think, as the liability of master to servant,—matters which, it is admitted, Congress might regulate so far as they concerned commerce among the states. I suppose that it hardly would be denied that some of the relations of railroads with unions of railroad employees are closely enough connected with commerce to justify legislation by Congress. If so, legislation to prevent the exclusion of such unions from employment is sufficiently near.

The ground on which this particular law is held bad, is not so much that it deals with matters remote from commerce among the states, as that it interferes with the paramount individual rights secured by the 5th Amendment. The section is, in substance, a very limited interference with freedom of contract, no more. It does not require the carriers to employ anyone. It does not forbid them to refuse to employ anyone, for any reason they deem good, even where the notion of a choice of persons is a fiction and wholesale employment is necessary upon general principles that it might be proper to control. The section simply prohibits the more powerful party to exact certain undertakings, or to threaten dismissal or unjustly discriminate on certain grounds against those already employed. I hardly can suppose that the grounds on which a contract lawfully may be made to end are less open to regulation than other terms. So I turn to the general question whether the employment can be regulated at all. I confess that I think that the right to make contracts at will that has been derived from the word "liberty" in the Amendments, has been stretched to its extreme by the decisions; but they agree that sometimes the right may be restrained. Where there is, or generally is believed to be, an important ground of public policy for restraint, the Constitution does not forbid it, whether this court agrees or disagrees with the policy pursued. It cannot be doubted that to prevent strikes and, so far as possible, to foster its scheme of arbitration, might be deemed by Congress an important point of policy, and I think it impossible to say that Congress might not reasonably think that the provision in question would help a good deal to carry its policy along. But suppose the only effect really were to tend to bring about the complete unionizing of such railroad laborers as Congress can deal with, I think that object alone would justify the act. I quite agree that the question what and how much good labor unions do, is one on which intelligent people may differ; I think that laboring men sometimes attribute to them advantages, as many attribute to combinations of capital, disadvantages, that really are due to economic conditions of a far wider and deeper kind; but I could not pronounce it unwarranted if Congress should decide that to foster a strong union was for the best interests, not only of the men, but of the railroads and the country at large.

369. THE CONSERVATION OF NATURAL RESOURCES
Roosevelt's Seventh Annual Message to Congress
Dec. 3, 1907

(The Works of Theodore Roosevelt, Vol. XV, p. 443 ff.)

Of all Roosevelt's policies, that of conservation of the natural resources of the nation was of the most permanent significance. In his first message to Congress he had announced that the forest and water problems were the most vital domestic problems facing the American people, and during his administration he succeeded in setting aside almost 150,000,000 acres of timber land and some 85,000,000 acres of mineral lands in Alaska. More than this, he dramatized the problem of conservation before the country by his speeches, his actions, and by the convening of the Conservation Conference, Doc. No. 370. On Roosevelt and conservation, see, *Theodore Roosevelt, an Autobiography,* ch. xi; the various *Reports* of the Public Lands Commission, the Inland Waterways Commission, and the National Conservation Commission; C. R. Van Hise, *Conservation of Natural Resources in the United States;* F. H. Newell, *Irrigation in the United States;* W. E. Smyth, *The Conquest of Arid America;* G. Pinchot, *The Fight for Conservation;* B. H. Hibbard, *History of Public Land Policies,* ch. xxii; on the enduring nature of the problem, see S. Chase, *The Tragedy of Waste.*

To the Senate and House of Representatives:
   . . . The conservation of our natural resources and their proper use constitute the fundamental problem which underlies almost every other problem of our national life. . . . As a nation we not only enjoy a wonderful measure of present prosperity but if this prosperity is used aright it is an earnest of future success such as no other nation will have. The reward of foresight for this nation is great and easily foretold. But there must be the look ahead, there must be a realization of the fact that to waste, to destroy, our natural resources, to skin and exhaust the land instead of using it so as to increase its usefulness, will result in undermining in the days of our children the very prosperity which we ought by right to hand down to them amplified and developed. For the last few years, through several agencies, the government has been endeavoring to get our people to look ahead and to substitute a planned and orderly development of our resources in place of a haphazard striving for immediate profit. Our great river systems should be developed as national water highways, the Mississippi, with its tributaries, standing first in importance, and the Columbia second, although there are many others of importance on the Pacific, the Atlantic, and the Gulf slopes. The National Government should undertake this work, and I hope a beginning will be made in the present Congress; and the greatest of all our rivers, the Mississippi, should receive special attention. From the Great Lakes to the mouth of the Mississippi there should be a deep waterway, with deep waterways leading from it to the East and the West. Such a waterway would practically mean the extension of our coastline into the very heart of our country. It would be of incalculable benefit to our people. If begun at once it can be carried through in time appreciably to relieve the congestion of our great freight-carrying lines of railroads. The work should be systematically and continuously carried forward in accordance with some well-conceived plan. The main streams should be improved to the highest point of efficiency before the improvement of the branches is attempted; and the work should be kept free from every taint of recklessness or jobbery. The inland waterways which lie just back of the whole Eastern and Southern coasts should likewise be developed. Moreover, the development of our waterways involves many other important water problems, all of which should be considered as part of the same general scheme. The government dams should be used to produce hundreds of thousands of horse-power as an incident to improving nav-

igation; for the annual value of the unused water-power of the United States perhaps exceeds the annual value of the products of all our mines. As an incident to creating the deep waterways down the Mississippi, the government should build along its whole lower length levees which, taken together with the control of the headwaters, will at once and forever put a complete stop to all threat of floods in the immensely fertile delta region. The territory lying adjacent to the Mississippi along its lower course will thereby become one of the most prosperous and populous, as it already is one of the most fertile, farming regions in all the world. I have appointed an inland waterways commission to study and outline a comprehensive scheme of development along all the lines indicated. Later I shall lay its report before the Congress.

Irrigation should be far more extensively developed than at present, not only in the States of the great plains and the Rocky Mountains, but in many others, as, for instance, in large portions of the South Atlantic and Gulf States, where it should go hand in hand with the reclamation of swamp-land. The Federal Government should seriously devote itself to this task, realizing that utilization of waterways and water-power, forestry, irrigation, and the reclamation of lands threatened with overflow, are all interdependent parts of the same problem. The work of the Reclamation Service in developing the larger opportunities of the Western half of our country for irrigation is more important than almost any other movement. The constant purpose of the government in connection with the Reclamation Service has been to use the water resources of the public lands for the ultimate greatest good of the greatest number; in other words, to put upon the land permanent home-makers, to use and develop it for themselves and for their children and children's children. . . .

The effort of the government to deal with the public land has been based upon the same principle as that of the Reclamation Service. The land law system which was designed to meet the needs of the fertile and well-watered regions of the Middle West has largely broken down when applied to the drier regions of the great plains, the mountains, and much of the Pacific slope, where

a farm of 160 acres is inadequate for self-support. . . . Three years ago a public-lands commission was appointed to scrutinize the law, and defects, and recommend a remedy. Their examination specifically showed the existence of great fraud upon the public domain, and their recommendations for changes in the law were made with the design of conserving the natural resources of every part of the public lands by putting it to its best use. Especial attention was called to the prevention of settlement by the passage of great areas of public land into the hands of a few men, and to the enormous waste caused by unrestricted grazing upon the open range. The recommendations of the Public-Lands Commission are sound, for they are especially in the interest of the actual home-maker; and where the small home-maker cannot at present utilize the land they provide that the government shall keep control of it so that it may not be monopolized by a few men. The Congress has not yet acted upon these recommendations; but they are so just and proper, so essential to our national welfare, that I feel confident, if the Congress will take time to consider them, that they will ultimately be adopted.

Some such legislation as that proposed is essential in order to preserve the great stretches of public grazing-land which are unfit for cultivation under present methods and are valuable only for the forage which they supply. These stretches amount in all to some 300,000,000 acres, and are open to the free grazing of cattle, sheep, horses, and goats, without restriction. Such a system, or lack of system, means that the range is not so much used as wasted by abuse. As the West settles, the range becomes more and more overgrazed. Much of it cannot be used to advantage unless it is fenced, for fencing is the only way by which to keep in check the owners of nomad flocks which roam hither and thither, utterly destroying the pastures and leaving a waste behind so that their presence is incompatible with the presence of home-makers. The existing fences are all illegal. . . . All these fences, those that are hurtful and those that are beneficial, are alike illegal and must come down. But it is an outrage that the law should necessitate such action on the part of the Administration. The unlawful fencing of public lands for private grazing must be stopped, but the necessity which occasioned it must be provided for. The Federal Government should have control of the range, whether by permit or lease, as local necessities may determine. Such control could secure the great benefit of legitimate fencing, while at the same time securing and promoting the settlement of the country. . . . The government should part with its title only to the actual home-maker, not to the profit-maker who does not care to make a home. Our prime object is to secure the rights and guard the interests of the small ranchman, the man who ploughs and pitches hay for himself. It is this small ranchman, this actual settler and home-maker, who in the long run is most hurt by permitting thefts of the public land in whatever form.

Optimism is a good characteristic, but if carried to an excess it becomes foolishness. We are prone to speak of the resources of this country as inexhaustible; this is not so. The mineral wealth of the country, the coal, iron, oil, gas, and the like, does not reproduce itself, and therefore is certain to be exhausted ultimately; and wastefulness in dealing with it today means that our descendants will feel the exhaustion a generation or two before they otherwise would. But there are certain other forms of waste which could be entirely stopped—the waste of soil by washing, for instance, which is among the most dangerous of all wastes now in progress in the United States, is easily preventable, so

that this present enormous loss of fertility is entirely unnecessary. The preservation or replacement of the forests is one of the most important means of preventing this loss. We have made a beginning in forest preservation, but . . . so rapid has been the rate of exhaustion of timber in the United States in the past, and so rapidly is the remainder being exhausted, that the country is unquestionably on the verge of a timber famine which will be felt in every household in the land. . . . The present annual consumption of lumber is certainly three times as great as the annual growth; and if the consumption and growth continue unchanged, practically all our lumber will be exhausted in another generation, while long before the limit to complete exhaustion is reached the growing scarcity will make itself felt in many blighting ways upon our national welfare. About twenty per cent of our forested territory is now reserved in national forests; but these do not include the most valuable timber-lands, and in any event the proportion is too small to expect that the reserves can accomplish more than a mitigation of the trouble which is ahead for the nation. . . . We should acquire in the Appalachian and White Mountain regions all the forest-lands that it is possible to acquire for the use of the nation. These lands, because they form a national asset, are as emphatically national as the rivers which they feed, and which flow through so many States before they reach the ocean. . . .

370. DECLARATION OF THE CONSERVATION CONFERENCE
May 15, 1908

(Proceedings of a Conference of Governors, May 13–15, 1908, p. 192 ff.)

To cap his work for the conservation of natural resources, President Roosevelt called a conference of governors, congressmen, supreme court justices, members of the cabinet, and other distinguished public men, to consider the broad problem of conservation. The conference adopted the resolution given below, and provided for the appointment of thirty-six state conservation commissions and a national conservation commission. The national commission, of which Gifford Pinchot was chairman, prepared an inventory of the natural resources of the country. On conservation see references in Doc. No. 369.

DECLARATION

We the Governors of the States and Territories of the United States of America, in Conference assembled, do hereby declare the conviction that the great prosperity of our country rests upon the abundant resources of the land chosen by our forefathers for their homes and where they laid the foundation of this great Nation.

We look upon these resources as a heritage to be made use of in establishing and promoting the comfort, prosperity, and happiness of the American People, but not to be wasted, deteriorated, or needlessly destroyed.

We agree that our country's future is involved in this; that the great natural resources supply the material basis on which our civilization must continue to depend, and on which the perpetuity of the Nation itself rests.

We agree, in the light of facts brought to our knowledge and from information received from sources which we can not doubt, that this material basis is threatened with exhaustion. Even as each succeeding generation from the birth of the Nation has performed its part in promoting the progress and development of the Republic, so do we in this generation recognize it as a high duty to perform our part; and this duty in large degree lies in the adoption of measures for the conservation of the natural wealth of the country.

We declare our firm conviction that this conservation of our natural resources is a subject of transcendent importance, which should engage unremittingly the attention of the Nation, the States, and the People in earnest cooperation. These natural resources include the land on which we live and which yields our food; the living waters which fertilize the soil, supply power, and form great avenues of commerce; the forests which yield the materials for our homes, prevent erosion of the soil, and conserve the navigation and other uses of our streams; and the minerals which form the basis of our industrial life, and supply us with heat, light, and power.

We agree that the land should be so used that erosion and soil-wash shall cease; that there should be reclamation of arid and semi-arid regions by means of irrigation, and of swamp and overflowed regions by means of drainage; that the waters should be so conserved and used as to promote navigation, to enable the arid regions to be reclaimed by irrigation, and to develop power in the interests of the People; that the forests which regulate our rivers, support our industries, and promote the fertility and productiveness of the soil should be preserved and perpetuated; that the minerals found so abundantly beneath the surface should be so used as to prolong their utility; that the beauty, healthfulness, and habitability of our country should be preserved and increased; that the

sources of national wealth exist for the benefit of the People, and that monopoly thereof should not be tolerated.

We commend the wise forethought of the President in sounding the note of warning as to the waste and exhaustion of the natural resources of the country, and signify our high appreciation of his action in calling this Conference to consider the same and to seek remedies therefor through cooperation of the Nation and the States.

We agree that this cooperation should find expression in suitable action by the Congress within the limits of and coextensive with the national jurisdiction of the subject, and, complementary thereto, by the legislatures of the several States within the limits of and coextensive with their jurisdiction.

We declare the conviction that in the use of the natural resources our independent States are interdependent and bound together by ties of mutual benefits, responsibilities and duties.

We agree in the wisdom of future conferences between the President, Members of Congress, and the Governors of States on the conservation of our natural resources with a view of continued cooperation and action on the lines suggested; and to this end we advise that from time to time, as in his judgment may seem wise, the President call the Governors of the States and Members of Congress and others into conference.

We agree that further action is advisable to ascertain the present condition of our natural resources and to promote the conservation of the same; and to that end we recommend the appointment by each State of a Commission on the Conservation of Natural Resources, to cooperate with each other and with any similar commission of the Federal Government.

We urge the continuation and extension of forest policies adapted to secure the husbanding and renewal of our diminishing timber supply, the prevention of soil erosion, the protection of headwaters, and the maintenance of the purity and navigability of our streams. We recognize that the private ownership of forest lands entails responsibilities in the interests of all the People, and we favor the enactment of laws looking to the protection and replacement of privately owned forests.

We recognize in our waters a most valuable asset of the People of the United States, and we recommend the enactment of laws looking to the conservation of water resources for irrigation, water supply, power, and navigation, to the end that navigable and source streams may be brought under complete control and fully utilized for every purpose. We especially urge on the Federal Congress the immediate adoption of a wise, active, and thorough waterway policy, providing for the prompt improvement of our streams and the conservation of their watersheds required for the uses of commerce and the protection of the interests of our People.

We recommend the enactment of laws looking to the prevention of waste in the mining and extraction of coal, oil, gas, and other minerals with a view to their wise conservation for the use of the People, and to the protection of human life in the mines.

Let us conserve the foundations of our prosperity.

Respectfully submitted,

[SIGNATURES]

371. THE SOCIAL CREED OF THE CHURCHES

Statement Adopted by the General Conference of the Methodist Episcopal Church
May 1908

(A Year Book of the Church and Social Service in the United States, ed. by H. F. Ward, 1916, p. 197–8)

One of the most significant developments in the history of the church in America is the movement for the socialization of Christianity. While the roots of this movement go back to the period of the rise of Unitarianism, it reached its climax in the first two decades of the twentieth century. See, A. M. Schlesinger, *The Rise of the City,* ch. x; W. E. Garrison, *The March of Faith;* W. Gladden, *Recollections;* S. Matthews, "The Development of Social Christianity in America," in G. B. Smith, ed. *Religious Thought in the Last Quarter Century;* J. R. Commons, *Social Reform and the Church;* W. Rauschenbusch, *Christianity and the Social Crisis;* H. F. Ward, *The Social Creed of the Churches;* R. T. Ely, *Social Aspects of Christianity;* F. G. Peabody, *Jesus Christ and the Social Question;* G. Taylor, *Social Idealism and the Changing Theology.*

The Methodist Episcopal Church stands:

For equal rights and complete justice for all men in all stations of life.

For the principle of conciliation and arbitration in industrial dissensions.

For the protection of the worker from dangerous machinery, occupational disease, injuries and mortality.

For the abolition of child labor.

For such regulation of the conditions of labor for women as shall safeguard the physical and moral health of the community.

For the suppression of the "sweating system."

For the gradual and reasonable reduction of the hours of labor to the lowest practical point, with work for all; and for that degree of leisure for all which is the condition of the highest human life.

For a release from employment one day in seven.

For a living wage in every industry.

For the highest wage that each industry can afford, and for the most equitable division of the products in industry that can ultimately be devised.

For the recognition of the Golden Rule, and the mind of Christ as the supreme law of society and the sure remedy for all social ills.

372. THE ROOT-TAKAHIRA AGREEMENT
November 30, 1908

(Foreign Relations of the United States, 1908, p. 510–511)

This agreement was brought about by an exchange of notes between the Japanese Ambassador and Secretary of State Root. By it Japan apparently confirmed the Open Door policy in China, and both nations bound themselves to maintain the existing *status quo* in China. In as much as Japan had, in the preceding years, concluded a number of secret agreements with

China and with Russia, giving to her exceptional privileges in China and Manchuria, the significance of the agreement is somewhat ambiguous. See, W. W. Willoughby, *Foreign Rights and Interests in China*, 2 Vols.; G. H. Blakeslee, ed., *Japan and Japanese-American Relations;* H. K. Norton, *China and the Powers;* P. J. Treat, *Japan and the United States, 1853–1921.*

The Japanese Ambassador to the Secretary of State

Imperial Japanese Embassy
Washington, November 30, 1908

Sir: The exchange of views between us, which has taken place at the several interviews which I have recently had the honor of holding with you, has shown that Japan and the United States holding important outlying insular possessions in the region of the Pacific Ocean, the Governments of the two countries are animated by a common aim, policy, and intention in that region.

Believing that a frank avowal of that aim, policy, and intention would not only tend to strengthen the relations of friendship and good neighborhood, which have immemorially existed between Japan and the United States, but would materially contribute to the preservation of the general peace, the Imperial Government have authorized me to present to you an outline of their understanding of that common aim, policy and intention.

1. It is the wish of the two Governments to encourage the free and peaceful development of their commerce on the Pacific Ocean.

2. The policy of both Governments, uninfluenced by any aggressive tendencies, is directed to the maintenance of the existing status quo in the region above mentioned and to the defense of the principle of equal opportunity for commerce and industry in China.

3. They are accordingly firmly resolved reciprocally to respect the territorial possessions belonging to each other in said region.

4. They are also determined to preserve the common interest of all powers in China by supporting by all pacific means at their disposal the independence and integrity of China and the principle of equal opportunity for commerce and industry of all nations in that Empire.

5. Should any event occur threatening the status quo as above described or the principle of equal opportunity as above defined, it remains for the two Governments to communicate with each other in order to arrive at an understanding as to what measures they may consider it useful to take.

If the foregoing outline accords with the view of the Government of the United States, I shall be gratified to receive your confirmation.

I take this opportunity to renew to your excellency the assurance of my highest consideration.

K. Takahira.

373. THE INJUNCTION IN LABOR DISPUTES

Extract from Inaugural Address of President Taft
March 4, 1909

(Supplement to the Messages and Papers of the Presidents Covering the Administration of W. H. Taft, p. 7758)

Before his entry into politics, Taft had been a Judge of the Circuit Court, and his decisions had aroused the hostility of labor. His position on questions involving the power, prestige, and independence of the judiciary was consistently conservative; see Doc. No. 378. See in connection with the opinion here expressed, the Norris-LaGuardia Anti-Injunction Law, Doc. No. 474. On Taft, see H. S. Duffy, *William Howard Taft,* and the forthcoming biography by Henry Pringle.

. . . Another labor question has arisen which has awakened the most excited discussion. That is in respect to the power of the federal courts to issue injunctions in industrial disputes. As to that, my convictions are fixed. Take away from the courts, if it could be taken away, the power to issue injunctions in labor disputes, and it would create a privileged class among the laborers and save the lawless among their number from a most needful remedy available to all men for the protection of their business against lawless invasion. The proposition that business is not a property or pecuniary right which can be protected by equitable injunction is utterly without foundation in precedent or reason. The proposition is usually linked with one to make the secondary boycott lawful. Such a proposition is at variance with the American instinct, and will find no support, in my judgment, when submitted to the American people. The secondary boycott is an instrument of tyranny, and ought not to be made legitimate.

The issue of a temporary restraining order without notice has in several instances been abused by its inconsiderate exercise, and to remedy this the platform upon which I was elected recommends the formulation in a statute of the conditions under which such a temporary restraining order ought to issue. A statute can and ought to be framed to embody the best modern practice, and can bring the subject so closely to the attention of the court as to make abuses of the process unlikely in the future. The American people, if I understand them, insist that the authority of the courts shall be sustained, and are opposed to any change in the procedure by which the powers of a court may be weakened and the fearless and effective administration of justice be interfered with.

374. TAFT'S DEFENCE OF THE PAYNE-ALDRICH TARIFF

Speech at Winona, Minnesota
September 1909

(Supplement to the Messages and Papers of the Presidents Covering the Administration of W. H. Taft, p. 7773 ff.)

The Republican platform of 1908 called for a revision of the tariff, and shortly after his accession to the Presidency, Taft called a special session of Congress to carry out this pledge. The result was the Payne-Aldrich Tariff which Taft signed August 5, 1909. The high-protectionist character of the tariff aroused widespread dissatisfaction, and partly to allay this dissatisfaction Taft undertook a speaking tour through the mid-western states. In his Winona speech he declared that this bill was the best tariff bill that the Republican Party had ever passed, a statement which brought down upon him a storm of derisive criticism. See, N. W. Stephenson, *Nelson W. Aldrich*, p. 346 ff.; C. G. Bowers, *Beveridge and the Progressive Era*, Book IV; R. M. La Follette, *La Follette's Autobiography*, chs. x–xi; F. A. Ogg, *National Progress*, ch. xxii; F. W. Taussig, *Tariff History of the United States* (5th ed.), ch. viii; I. M. Tarbell, *Tariff in Our Times*, ch. xiii.

. . . The Ways and Means Committee of the House, with Mr. Payne at its head, spent a full year in an investigation, assembling evidence in reference to the rates under the tariff, and devoted an immense amount of work in the study of the question where the tariff rates could be reduced and where they ought to be raised with a view to maintaining a reasonably protective rate, under the principles of the platform, for every industry that deserved protection. They found that the determination of the question, what was the actual cost of production and whether an industry in this country could live under a certain rate and withstand threatened competition from abroad, was most difficult. The manufacturers were prone to exaggerate the injury which a reduction in the duty would give and to magnify the amount of duty that was needed; while the importers, on the other hand, who were interested in developing the importation from foreign shores, were quite likely to be equally biased on the other side.

Mr. Payne reported a bill—the Payne Tariff bill—which went to the Senate and was amended in the Senate by increasing the duty on some things and decreasing it on others. The difference between the House bill and the Senate bill was very much less than the newspapers represented. . . .

One way of stating what was done is to say what the facts show—that under the Dingley law there were 2,024 items. This included dutiable items only. The Payne law leaves 1,150 of these items unchanged. . . .

Now, the promise of the Republican platform was not to revise everything downward, and in the speeches which have been taken as interpreting that platform, which I made in the campaign, I did not promise that everything should go downward. What I promised was, that there should be many decreases, and that in some few things increases would be found to be necessary; but that on the whole I conceived that the change of conditions would make the revision necessarily downward—and that, I contend, under the showing which I have made, has been the result of the Payne bill. I did not agree, nor did the Republican party agree, that we would reduce rates to such a point as to reduce prices by the introduction of foreign competition. That is what the free traders desire. That is what the revenue tariff reformers desire; but that is not what the Republican platform promised, and it is not what the Republican party wished to bring about. To repeat the statement with which I opened this speech, the proposition of the Republican party was to reduce rates so as to maintain a difference between the cost of production abroad and the cost of production here, insuring a reasonable profit to the manufacturer on all articles produced in this country; and the proposition to reduce rates and prevent their being excessive was to avoid the opportunity for monopoly and the suppression of competition, so that the excessive rates could be taken advantage of to force prices up.

With respect to the wool schedule, I agree that it probably represents considerably more than the difference between the cost of production abroad and the cost of production here. The difficulty about the woolen sched-

ule is that there were two contending factions early in the history of Republican tariffs, to wit, woolgrowers and the woolen manufacturers, and that finally, many years ago, they settled on a basis by which wool in the grease should have 11 cents a pound, and by which allowance should be made for the shrinkage of the washed wool in the differential upon woolen manufactures. The percentage of duty was very heavy—quite beyond the difference in the cost of production, which was not then regarded as a necessary or proper limitation upon protective duties. . . .

On the whole, however, I am bound to say that I think the Payne tariff bill is the best tariff bill that the Republican party ever passed. . . .

If the country desires free trade, and the country desires a revenue tariff and wishes the manufacturers all over the country to go out of business, and to have cheaper prices at the expense of the sacrifice of many of our manufacturing interests, then it ought to say so and ought to put the Democratic party in power if it thinks that party can be trusted to carry out any affirmative policy in favor of a revenue tariff. Certainly in the discussions in the Senate there was no great manifestation on the part of our Democratic friends in favor of reducing rates on necessities. They voted to maintain the tariff rates on everything that came from their particular sections. If we are to have free trade, certainly it can not be had through the maintenance of Republican majorities in the Senate and House and a Republican administration. . . .

375. THE RULE OF REASON
1897–1911

Did the Sherman Anti-Trust Act prohibit *all* contracts in restraint of trade between the States, or only unreasonable restraints? Unreasonable or undue restraint of trade had long been illegal at common law. Inasmuch as the Federal Courts had no common law jurisdiction, was the Sherman Act intended merely to grant the Federal Courts such jurisdiction, or was the act intended to go further than the common law in outlawing contracts in restraint of trade? The evolution of the so-called "rule of reason" is indicated in the following extracts. The literature on the Sherman Act is voluminous. See, on the question of the rule of reason, P. L. Anderson, *The Rule of Reason;* A. H. Walker, *History of the Sherman*

Law, passim; W. H. Taft, *The Anti-Trust Act and the Supreme Court;* and the illuminating bibliography in Warren, *The Supreme Court* (1928 ed.) Vol. II, p. 733, 734, n.

1 *United States* v. *Trans-Missouri Freight Association,* 166 U. S. 290. (1897)

PECKHAM, J. . . . The next question to be discussed is as to what is the true construction of the statute. . . . What is the meaning of the language as used in the statute "that every contract, combination in the form of trust or otherwise, or conspiracy in restraint of trade or commerce among the several States . . . is hereby declared to be illegal"? Is it confined to a contract or combination which is only in unreasonable restraint of trade or commerce, or does it include what the language of the act plainly and in terms covers, all contracts of that nature? It is now . . . urged that the statute, in declaring illegal every combination in the form of trust or otherwise, or conspiracy in restraint of trade or commerce, does not mean what the language therein plainly imports, but that it only means to declare illegal any such contract which is in *unreasonable* restraint of trade, while leaving all others unaffected by the provisions of that act; that the common law meaning of the term "contract in restraint of trade" includes only such contracts as are in *unreasonable* restraint of trade, and when that term is used in the Federal statute it is not intended to include all contracts in restraint of trade, but only those which are in unreasonable restraint thereof. . . . By the simple use of the term "contract in restraint of trade", all contracts of that nature, whether valid or otherwise, would be included and not alone that kind of contract which was invalid and unenforceable as being in unreasonable restraint of trade. When, therefore, the body of an act pronounces illegal every contract or combination in restraint of trade . . . among the several States etc. the plain and ordinary meaning of such language is not limited to that kind of contract alone which is in unreasonable restraint of trade, but all contracts are included in such language, and no exception or limitation can be added without placing in the act that which has been omitted by Congress. . . . The arguments which have been addressed to us against the inclusion of all contracts in restraint of trade, as provided for by the language of the act, have been based on the alleged presumption that Congress, notwithstanding the language of the act, could not have intended to embrace all contracts, but only such contracts as were in unreasonable restraint of trade. . . . In other words, we are asked to read into the act by way of judicial legislation an exception that is not placed there by the lawmaking branch of the Government, and this is to be done upon the theory that the impolicy of such legislation is so clear

that it cannot be supposed Congress intended the natural import of the language to be used. This we cannot and ought not to do. . . . If the act ought to read as contended for by the defendants, Congress is the body to amend it and not this court, by a process of judicial legislation wholly unjustifiable. . . .

2 Report of Senator Nelson, on behalf of Senate Judiciary Committee, in reference to bill to amend the Anti-Trust Act in certain particulars. *Federal Anti-Trust Decisions.* Vol. IV, p. 160 ff. (1909).
    . . . The Anti-Trust Act makes it a criminal offense to violate the law, and provides a punishment both by fine and imprisonment. To inject into the act the question of whether an agreement or combination is *reasonable or unreasonable* would render the act as a criminal or penal statute indefinite and uncertain, and hence, to that extent, utterly nugatory and void, and would practically amount to a repeal of that part of the act. . . . And while the same technical objection does not apply to civil prosecutions, the injection of the rule of reasonableness or unreasonableness would lead to the greatest variableness and uncertainty in the enforcement of the law. The defense of reasonable restraint would be made in every case and there would be as many different rules of reasonableness as cases, courts and juries. What one court or jury might deem unreasonable another court or jury might deem reasonable. A court or jury in Ohio might find a given agreement or combination reasonable, while a court and jury in Wisconsin might find the same agreement and combination unreasonable. In the case of *People* v. *Sheldon* 139 N. Y. 264, Chief Justice Andrews remarks, "If agreements and combinations to prevent competition in prices are or may be hurtful to trade, the only sure remedy is to prohibit all agreements of that character. . . ." To amend the Anti-Trust Act, as suggested by this bill, would be to entirely emasculate it, and for all practical purposes render it nugatory as a remedial statute. Criminal prosecutions would not lie and civil remedies would labor under the greatest doubt and uncertainty. The act as it exists is clear, comprehensive, certain, and highly remedial. It practically

covers the field of Federal jurisdiction and is in every respect a model law. To destroy or undermine it at the present juncture, when combinations are on the increase . . . would be a calamity.

3 *Standard Oil Company of New Jersey et al v. The United States.* 221 U. S. 1. (1911) WHITE, C. J. . . . It is certain that only one point of concord between the parties is discernible, which is, that the controversy in every aspect is controlled by a correct conception of the meaning of the first and second sections of the Anti-Trust Act. . . . We shall make our investigation under four separate headings: First, the text of the first and second sections of the act originally considered and its meaning in the light of the common law and the law of this country at the time of its adoption; second, the contentions of the parties concerning the act, and the scope and effect of the decisions of this court upon which they rely. . . .

In view of the common law and the law in this country as to restraint of trade, which we have reviewed, and the illuminating effect which that history must have under the rule to which we have referred, we think it results:

(a) That the context manifests that the statute was drawn in the light of the existing practical conception of the law of restraint of trade, because it groups as within that class, not only contracts which were in restraint of trade in the subjective sense, but all contracts or acts which theoretically were attempts to monopolize, yet which in practice had come to be considered as in restraint of trade in a broad sense.

(b) That in view of the many new forms of contracts and combinations which were being evolved from existing economic conditions, it was deemed essential by an all-embracing enumeration to make sure that no form of contract or combination by which an undue restraint of interstate or foreign commerce was brought about could save such restraint from condemnation. The statute under this view evidenced the intent not to restrain the right to make and enforce contracts, whether resulting from combination or otherwise, which did not unduly restrain interstate or foreign commerce, but to pro-

tect that commerce from being restrained by methods, whether old or new, which would constitute an interference that is an undue restraint.

(c) And as the contracts or acts embraced in the provision were not expressly defined, since the enumeration addressed itself simply to classes of acts, those classes being broad enough to embrace every conceivable contract or combination which could be made concerning trade or commerce or the subjects of such commerce, and thus caused any act done by any of the enumerated methods anywhere in the whole field of human activity to be illegal if in restraint, it inevitably follows that the provision necessarily called for the exercise of judgement which required that some standard should be resorted to for the purpose of determining whether the prohibitions contained in the statute had or had not in any given case been violated. Thus not specifying, but indubitably contemplating and requiring a standard, it follows that it was intended that the standard of reason which had been applied at the common law and in this country in dealing with subjects of the character embraced by the statute, was intended to be the measure used for the purpose of determining whether in a given case a particular act had or had not brought about the wrong against which the statute provided. . . .

4 Dissenting opinion of Justice Harlan in Standard Oil case.

. . . After what has been adjudged, upon full consideration, as to the meaning and the scope of the Anti-Trust Act, and in view of the usages of this court when attorneys for litigants have attempted to reopen questions that have been deliberately decided, I confess to no little surprise as to what has occurred in the present case. The court says that the previous cases, above cited, "cannot by any possible conception be treated as authoritative without the certitude that *reason* was resorted to for the purpose of deciding them." . . . It is more than once intimated, if not suggested, that if the Anti-Trust Act is to be construed as prohibiting *every* contract or combination, of whatever nature, which is in fact in restraint of commerce, regardless of the reasonableness or unreasonableness of such restraint, that fact would show that the court had not proceeded, in its decision, according to "the light of reason", but had disregarded the "rule of reason" . . . Now this court is asked to do that which it has distinctly declared it could not and would not do, and has now done what it then said it could .not constitutionally do. It has, by mere interpretation, modified the act of Congress, and deprived it of practical value as a defensive measure against the evils to be remedied. . . . In effect, the court says, that it will now, for the first time, bring the discussion under the "light of reason" and apply the "rule of reason" to the questions to be decided. I have the authority of this court for saying that such a course of proceeding on its part would be "judicial legislation".

Still more, what is now done involves a serious departure from the settled usages of this court. Counsel have not ordinarily been allowed to discuss questions already settled by previous decisions. . . .

But my brethren, in their wisdom, have deemed it best to pursue a different course. They have now said to those who condemn our former decisions and who object to all legislative prohibitions of contracts, combinations, and trusts in restraint of interstate commerce, "You may *now* restrain such commerce, provided you are reasonable about it; only take care that the restraint is not undue." . . .

It remains for me to refer, more fully than I have heretofore done, to another, and, in my judgment—if we look to the future—the most important aspect of this case. That aspect concerns the usurpation by the judicial branch of the Government of the functions of the legislative department. . . . I said at the outset that the action of the court in this case might well alarm thoughtful men who revered the Constitution. I meant by this that many things are intimated and said in the court's opinion which will not be regarded otherwise than as sanctioning an invasion by the judiciary of the constitutional domain of Congress—an attempt by interpretation to soften or modify what some regard as a harsh public policy. This court, let me repeat, solemnly adjudged many years ago that it could not, except by *"judicial legislation"* read words into the Anti-Trust Act not put there by Congress, and which,

being inserted, give it a meaning which the words of the act, as passed, if properly interpreted, would not justify. The Court has decided that it could not thus change a public policy formulated and declared by Congress; that Congress has paramount authority to regulate interstate commerce, and that it alone can change a policy once inaugurated by legislation. The courts have nothing to do with the wisdom or policy of an act of Congress. Their duty is to ascertain the will of Congress, and if the statute embodying the expression of that will is constitutional, the courts must respect it. They have no function to declare a public policy, nor to *amend* legislative enactments. . . . Nevertheless, if I do not misapprehend its opinion, the court has now read into the act of Congress words which are not to be found there, and has thereby done that which it adjudged in 1896 and in 1898 could not be done without violating the Constitution, namely, by interpretation of a statute, changed a public policy declared by the legislative department. . . .

5 Extract from Special Message of President Taft, December 5, 1911, *Supplement to the Messages and Papers of the Presidents Covering the Administration of William Howard Taft*, p. 8025–6.

. . . In two early cases, where the statute was invoked to enjoin a transportation rate agreement between interstate railroad companies, it was held that it was no defense to show that the agreement as to rates complained of was reasonable at common law, because it was said that the statute was directed against all contracts and combinations in restraint of trade whether reasonable at common law or not. It was plain from the record, however, that the contracts complained of in those cases would not have been deemed reasonable at common law. In subsequent cases the court said that the statute should be given a reasonable construction and refused to include within its inhibition, certain contractual restraints of trade which it denominated as incidental or as indirect.

These cases of restraint of trade that the court excepted from the operation of the statute were instances which, at common law, would have been called reasonable. In the Standard Oil and Tobacco cases, therefore, the court merely adopted the tests of the common law, and in defining exceptions to the literal application of the statute, only substituted for the test of being incidental or indirect, that of being reasonable, and this, without varying in the slightest the actual scope and effect of the statute. In other words, all the cases under the statute which have now been decided would have been decided the same way if the court had originally accepted in its construction the rule at common law.

It has been said that the court, by introducing into the construction of the statute common-law distinctions, has emasculated it. This is obviously untrue. By its judgment every contract and combination in restraint of interstate trade made with the purpose or necessary effect of controlling prices by stifling competition, or of establishing in whole or in part a monopoly of such trade, is condemned by the statute. The most extreme critics can not instance a case that ought to be condemned under the statute which is not brought within its terms as thus construed.

The suggestion is also made that the Supreme Court by its decision in the last two cases has committed to the court the undefined and unlimited discretion to determine whether a case of restraint of trade is within the terms of the statute. This is wholly untrue. A reasonable restraint of trade at common law is well understood and is clearly defined. It does not rest in the discretion of the court. It must be limited to accomplish the purpose of a lawful main contract to which, in order that it shall be enforceable at all, it must be incidental. If it exceed the needs of that contract, it is void.

The test of reasonableness was never applied by the court at common law to contracts or combinations or conspiracies in restraint of trade whose purpose was or whose necessary effect would be to stifle competition, to control prices, or establish monopolies. The courts never assumed power to say that such contracts or combinations or conspiracies might be lawful if the parties to them were only moderate in the use of the power thus secured and did not exact from the public too great and exorbitant prices. It is true that many theorists, and others engaged in business violating the statute, have hoped that some such line could be drawn by courts; but no court of authority has ever attempted it. Certainly there is nothing in the decisions of the latest two cases from which such a dangerous theory of judicial discretion in enforcing this statute can derive the slightest sanction.

376. DECLARATION OF PRINCIPLES OF THE NATIONAL PROGRESSIVE REPUBLICAN LEAGUE
January 21, 1911

(The Autobiography of Robert La Follette, p. 495–6)

Insurgency, which had been stirring in the Republican Party ever since the fight on the Hepburn Act of 1906, was crystallized by the administration support to the Payne-Aldrich Tariff. See Doc. No. 374. Robert La Follette of Wisconsin was by common consent the natural leader of the progressive element in the Republican party. "During the holiday recess in the last days of December, 1910," he says in his *Autobiography*, "I drafted a Declaration of Principles and form of constitution for the organization of a league, and submitted the same to Senators Bourne and Bristow. . . . The organization was effected at a meeting held at my residence on the 21st day of January, 1911. Jonathan Bourne was elected President; Frederic C. Howe, Secretary; Charles R. Crane, Treasurer". For the campaign of 1912 see references, Doc. No. 379. A provocative appreciation of La Follette is in J. Chamberlain, *Farewell to Reform*, ch. viii.

We, the undersigned, associate ourselves together as The National Progressive Republican League.

The object of the League is the promotion of popular government and progressive legislation.

Popular government in America has been thwarted and progressive legislation strangled by the special interests, which control caucuses, delegates, conventions, and party organizations; and, through this control of the machinery of government, dictate nominations and platforms, elect administrations, legislatures, representatives in Congress, United States Senators, and control cabinet officers.

Under existing conditions legislation in the public interest has been baffled and defeated. This is evidenced by the long struggle to secure laws but partially effective for the control of railway rates and services, the revision of the tariff in the interest of the producer and consumer, statutes dealing with trusts and combinations, based on sound economic principles, as applied to modern industrial and commercial conditions; wise, comprehensive and impartial reconstruction of banking and monetary laws, the conservation of coal, oil, gas, timber, waterpowers, and other natural resources belonging to the people, and for the enactment of all legislation solely for the common good.

Just in proportion as popular government has in certain states superseded the delegate convention system, and the people have assumed control of the machinery of government, has government become responsive to the popular will, and progressive legislation been secured.

The Progressive Republican League believes that popular government is fundamental to all other questions. To this end it advocates:

(1) The election of United States Senators by direct vote of the people.

(2) Direct primaries for the nomination of elective officials.

(3) The direct election of delegates to national conventions with opportunity for the voter to express his choice for President and Vice-President.

(4) Amendment to state constitutions providing for the Initiative, Referendum and Recall.

(5) A thoroughgoing corrupt practices act.

377. CANADIAN RECIPROCITY
Special Message of President Taft
January 26, 1911

(Supplement to the Messages and Papers of the Presidents Covering the Administration of W. H. Taft, p. 7961 ff.)

A reciprocity treaty with Canada had been concluded in 1854, only to be denounced by the United States in 1866. The Payne-Aldrich Tariff of 1909 precipitated what appeared to be a dangerous tariff war between the United States and Canada, and Taft attempted to avoid this by concluding another reciprocity agreement. An agreement negotiated by Secretary Knox received the assent of Congress, and was signed by the President July 26, 1911. In the course of the debates on the measure, however, the argument had been advanced that reciprocity was a step toward ultimate annexation; this argument aroused nationalistic sentiment in Canada, and led to the rejection of the agreement by the Dominion Parliament. See, United States Tariff Commission, *Reciprocity with Canada;* S. F. Bemis, ed. *American Secretaries of States,* Vol. IX, p. 344 ff.; H. Keenleyside, *Canada and the United States.*

THE WHITE HOUSE, January 26, 1911.
To the Senate and House of Representatives:

. . . One by one the controversies resulting from the uncertainties which attended the partition of British territory on the American Continent at the close of the Revolution, and which were inevitable under the then conditions, have been eliminated—some by arbitration and some by direct negotiation. The merits of these disputes, many of them extending through a century, need not now be reviewed. They related to the settlement of boundaries, the definition of rights of navigation, the interpretation of treaties, and many other subjects.

The path having been thus opened for the improvement of commercial relations, a reciprocal trade agreement is the logical sequence of all that has been accomplished in disposing of matters of a diplomatic and controversial character. The identity of interest of two peoples linked together by race, language, political institutions, and geographical proximity offers the foundation. . . .

The guiding motive in seeking adjustment of trade relations between two countries so situated geographically should be to give play to productive forces as far as practicable, regardless of political boundaries. While equivalency should be sought in an arrangement of this character, an exact balance of financial gain is neither imperative nor attainable. No yardstick can measure the benefits to the two peoples of this freer commercial intercourse and no trade agreement should be judged wholly by custom house statistics.

We have reached a stage in our own development that calls for a statesmanlike and broad view of our future economic status and its requirements. We have drawn upon our natural resources in such a way as to invite attention to their necessary limit. This has properly aroused effort to conserve them, to avoid their waste, and to restrict their use to our necessities. We have so increased in population and in our consumption of food products and the other necessities of life, hitherto supplied largely from our own country, that unless we materially increase our production we can see before us a change in our economic position, from that of a country selling to the world food and natural products of the farm and forest, to one consuming and importing them. Excluding cotton, which is exceptional, a radical change is already shown in our exports in the falling off in the amount of our agricultural products sold abroad and a correspondingly marked increase in our manufactures exported. A farsighted policy requires that if we can enlarge our supply of natural resources, and especially of food products and the necessities of life, without substantial injury to any of our producing and manufacturing classes, we should take steps to do so now. We have on the north of us a country contiguous to ours for three thousand miles, with natural resources of the same character as ours which have not been drawn upon as ours have been, and in the development of which the conditions as to wages and character of the wage earner and transportation to market differ but little from those prevailing with us. The difference is not greater than it is between different States of our own country or between different Provinces of the Dominion of Canada. Ought we not, then, to arrange a commercial agreement with Canada, if we can, by which we shall have direct access to her great supply of natural products without an obstructing or prohibitory tariff? This is not a violation of the protective principle, as that has been authoritatively announced by those who uphold it, because that princi-

ple does not call for a tariff between this country and one whose conditions as to production, population, and wages are so like ours, and when our common boundary line of three thousand miles in itself must make a radical distinction between our commercial treatment of Canada and of any other country. . . .

In the reciprocal trade agreement numerous additions are made to the free list. These include not only food commodities, such as cattle, fish, wheat and other grains, fresh vegetables, fruits, and dairy products, but also rough lumber and raw materials useful to our own industries. Free lumber we ought to have. By giving our people access to Canadian forests we shall reduce the consumption of our own, which, in the hands of comparatively few owners, now have a value that requires the enlargement of our available timber resources.

Natural, and especially food, products being placed on the free list, the logical development of a policy of reciprocity in rates on secondary food products, or foodstuffs partly manufactured, is, where they cannot also be entirely exempted from duty, to lower the duties in accord with the exemption of the raw material from duty. This has been followed in the trade agreement which has been negotiated. As an example, wheat is made free and the rate on flour is equalized on a lower basis. In the same way, live animals being made free, the duties on fresh meats and on secondary meat products and on canned meats are substantially lowered. Fresh fruits and vegetables being placed on the free list, the duties on canned goods of these classes are reduced. . . .

This trade agreement, if entered into, will cement the friendly relations with the Dominion which have resulted from the satisfactory settlement of the controversies that have lasted for a century, and further promote good feeling between kindred peoples. It will extend the market for numerous products of the United States among the inhabitants of a prosperous neighboring country with an increasing population and an increasing purchasing power. It will deepen and widen the sources of food supply in contiguous territory, and will facilitate the movement and distribution of these foodstuffs.

The geographical proximity, the closer relation of blood, common sympathies, and identical moral and social ideas furnish very real and striking reasons why this agreement ought to be viewed from a high plane.

Since becoming a nation, Canada has been our good neighbor, immediately contiguous across a wide continent without artificial or natural barrier except navigable waters used in common.

She has cost us nothing in the way of preparations for defense against her possible assault, and she never will. She has sought to agree with us quickly when differences have disturbed our relations. She shares with us common traditions and aspirations. I feel I have correctly interpreted the wish of the American people by expressing, in the arrangement now submitted to Congress for its approval, their desire for a more intimate and cordial relationship with Canada. I therefore earnestly hope that the measure will be promptly enacted into law.

WILLIAM H. TAFT.

378. TAFT'S VETO OF ARIZONA ENABLING ACT
August 22, 1911

(Supplement to the Messages and Papers of the Presidents Covering the Administration of W. H. Taft, p. 8016 ff.)

Taft based his veto of the joint resolution admitting New Mexico and Arizona to the Union on the clause in the Arizona constitution providing for the recall of judges. Arizona changed the Constitution to conform to Taft's objections, and, after admission, restored the objectionable provision. Roosevelt, in 1911 and 1912, had given his support to the principle of the recall of judges, and Colorado had an arrangement for the recall of judicial decisions. See, C. A. Beard and B. E. Schultz, *Documents on the Initiative, Referendum, and Recall;* W. B. Munro, *The Initiative, Referendum and Recall.* On the struggle of Arizona and New Mexico for statehood, the most elaborate account is in C. A. Bowers, *Beveridge and the Progressive Era, passim.*

THE WHITE HOUSE, *August 22, 1911.*

To the House of Representatives:

I return herewith, without my approval, House joint resolution No. 14, "To admit the Territories of New Mexico and Arizona as States into the Union on an equal footing with the original States." . . .

I have not approved the Arizona constitution, nor have the two Houses of Congress, except as they have done so by the joint resolution under consideration. The resolution admits [Arizona] to statehood . . . on condition . . . that Arizona shall submit to its electors, at the time of the election of its State officers, a proposed amendment to its constitution by which judicial officers shall be excepted from the section permitting a recall of all elective officers.

If I sign this joint resolution, I do not see how I can escape responsibility for the judicial recall of the Arizona constitution. The joint resolution admits Arizona with the judicial recall, but requires the submission of the question of its wisdom to the voters. In other words, the resolution approves the admission of Arizona with the judicial recall, unless the voters themselves repudiate it. Under the Arizona constitution all elective officers, and this includes county and State judges, six months after their election are subject to the recall. . . .

This provision of the Arizona constitution, in its application to county and State judges, seems to me so pernicious in its effect, so destructive of independence in the judiciary, so likely to subject the rights of the individual to the possible tyranny of a popular majority, and, therefore, to be so injurious to the cause of free government, that I must disapprove a constitution containing it. . . . I am discharging my constitutional function in respect to the enactment of laws, and my discretion is equal to that of the Houses of Congress. I must therefore withhold my approval from this resolution if in fact I do not approve it as a matter of governmental policy. Of course, a mere difference of opinion as to the wisdom of details in a State constitution ought not to lead me to set up my opinion against that of the people of the Territory. It is to be their government, and while the power of Congress to withhold or grant statehood is absolute, the people about to constitute a State should generally know better the kind of government and constitution suited to their needs than Congress or the Executive. But when such a constitution contains something so destructive of free government as the judicial recall, it should be disapproved.

A government is for the benefit of all the people. . . . Now, as the government is for all the people, and is not solely for a majority of them, the majority in exercising control either directly or through its agents is bound to exercise the power for the benefit of the minority as well as the majority. But all have recognized that the majority of a people, unrestrained by law, when aroused and without the sobering effect of deliberation and discussion, may do injustice to the minority or to the individual when the selfish interest of the majority prompts. Hence arises the necessity for a constitution by which the will of the majority shall be permitted to guide the course of the government only under controlling checks that experience has shown to be necessary to secure for the minority its share of the benefit to the whole people that a popular government is established to bestow. A popular government is not a government of a majority, by a majority, for a majority of the people. It is a government of the whole people, by a majority of the whole people under such rules and checks as will secure a wise, just, and beneficent government for all the people. It is said you can always trust the people to do justice. If that means all the people and they all agree, you can. But ordinarily they do not all agree, and the maxim is interpreted to mean that you can always trust a majority of the people. This is not invariably true; and every limitation imposed by the people upon the power of the majority in their constitutions is an admission that it is not always true. No honest, clear-headed man, however great a lover of popular government, can deny that the unbridled expression of the majority of a community converted hastily into law or action would sometimes make a government tyrannical and cruel. Constitutions are checks upon the hasty action of the majority. They are the self-imposed restraints of a whole people upon a majority of them to secure sober action and a respect for the rights of the minority, and

of the individual in his relation to other individuals, and in his relation to the whole people in their character as a state or government. . . .

By the recall in the Arizona constitution it is proposed to give to the majority power to remove arbitrarily, and without delay, any judge who may have the courage to render an unpopular decision. By the recall it is proposed to enable a minority of 25 per cent of the voters of the district or State, for no prescribed cause, after the judge has been in office six months, to submit the question of his retention in office to the electorate. The petitioning minority must say on the ballot what they can against him in 200 words, and he must defend as best he can in the same space. Other candidates are permitted to present themselves and have their names printed on the ballot, so that the recall is not based solely on the record or the acts of the judge, but also on the question whether some other and more popular candidate has been found to unseat him. Could there be a system more ingeniously devised to subject judges to momentary gusts of popular passion than this? We can not be blind to the fact that often an intelligent and respectable electorate may be so roused upon an issue that it will visit with condemnation the decision of a just judge, though exactly in accord with the law governing the case, merely because it affects unfavorably their contest. Controversies over elections, labor troubles, racial or religious issues as to the construction or constitutionality of liquor laws, criminal trials of popular or unpopular defendants, the removal of county seats, suits by individuals to maintain their constitutional rights in obstruction of some popular improvement—these and many other cases could be cited in which a majority of a district electorate would be tempted by hasty anger to recall a conscientious judge if the opportunity were open all the time. No period of delay is interposed for the abatement of popular feeling. The recall is devised to encourage quick action, and to lead the people to strike while the iron is hot. The judge is treated as the instrument and servant of a majority of the people and subject to their momentary will, not after a long term in which his qualities as a judge and his character as a man have been subjected to a test of all the varieties of judicial work and duty so as to furnish a proper means of measuring his fitness for continuance in another term. On the instant of an unpopular ruling, while the spirit of protest has not had time to cool and even while an appeal may be pending from his ruling in which he may be sustained, he is to be haled before the electorate as a tribunal, with no judicial hearing, evidence, or defense, and thrown out of office, and disgraced for life because he has failed, in a single decision, it may be, to satisfy the popular demand. Think of the opportunity such a system would give to unscrupulous political bosses in control, as they have been in control not only of conventions but elections! Think of the enormous power for evil given to the sensational, muckraking portion of the press in rousing prejudice against a just judge by false charges and insinuations, the effect of which in the short period of an election by recall it would be impossible for him to meet and offset! Supporters of such a system seem to think that it will work only in the interest of the poor, the humble, the weak and the oppressed; that it will strike down only the judge who is supposed to favor corporations and be affected by the corrupting influence of the rich. Nothing could be further from the ultimate result. The motive it would offer to unscrupulous combinations to seek to control politics in order to control judges is clear. Those would profit by the recall who have the best opportunity of rousing the majority of the people to action on a sudden impulse. Are they likely to be the wisest or the best people in a community? Do they not include those who have money enough to employ the firebrands and slanderers in a community and the stirrers-up of social hate? Would not self-respecting men well hesitate to accept judicial office with such a sword of Damocles hanging over them? What kind of judgments might those on the unpopular side expect from courts whose judges must make their decisions under such legalized terrorism? The character of the judges would deteriorate to that of trimmers and time-servers, and independent judicial action would be a thing of the past. As the possibilities of such a system pass in review, is it too much to characterize it as one which will destroy the judiciary, its standing, and its usefulness? . . .

Attempt is made to defend the principle of judicial recall by reference to States in which judges are said to have shown themselves to be under corrupt corporate influence and in which it is claimed that nothing but a desperate remedy will suffice. If the political control in such States is sufficiently wrested from corrupting corporations to permit the enactment of a radical constitutional amendment like that of judicial recall, it would seem possible to make provision in its stead for an effective remedy by impeachment in which the cumbrous features of the present remedy might be avoided, but the opportunity for judicial hearing and defense before an impartial tribunal might be retained. Real reforms are not to be effected by patent short cuts or by abolishing those requirements which the experience of ages has shown to be essential in dealing justly with everyone. Such innovations are certain in the long run to plague the inventor or first user and will come readily to the hand of the enemies and corrupters of society after the passing of the just popular indignation that prompted their adoption.

Again judicial recall is advocated on the ground that it will bring the judges more into sympathy with the popular will and the progress of ideas among the people. It is said that now judges are out of touch with the movement toward a wider democracy and a greater control of governmental agencies in the interest and for the benefit of the people. The righteous and just course for a judge to pursue is ordinarily fixed by statute or clear principles of law, and the cases in which his judgment may be affected by his political, economic, or social views are infrequent. But even in such cases, judges are not removed from the people's influence. Surround the judiciary with all the safeguards possible, create judges by appointment, make their tenure for life, forbid diminution of salary during their term, and still it is impossible to prevent the influence of popular opinion from coloring judgments in the long run. Judges are men, intelligent, sympathetic men, patriotic men, and in those fields of the law in which the personal equation unavoidably plays a part, there will be found a response to sober popular opinion as it changes to meet the exigency of social, political, and economic changes. Indeed this should be so. Individual instances of a hidebound and retrograde conservatism on the part of courts in decisions which turn on the individual economic or sociological views of the judges may be pointed out; but they are not many, and do not call for radical action. In treating of courts we are dealing with a human machine, liable like all the inventions of man to err, but we are dealing with a human institution that likens itself to a divine institution because it seeks and preserves justice. It has been the corner stone of our gloriously free government in which the rights of the individual and of the minority have been preserved, while governmental action of the majority has lost nothing of beneficent progress, efficacy, and directness. This balance was planned in the Constitution by its framers and has been maintained by our independent judiciary. . . .

But it is said that the people of Arizona are to become an independent State when created, and even if we strike out judicial recall now, they can reincorporate it in their constitution after statehood.

To this I would answer that in dealing with the courts, which are the corner stone of good government, and in which not only the voters, but the nonvoters and nonresidents, have a deep interest as a security for their rights of life, liberty, and property, no matter what the future action of the State may be, it is necessary for the authority which is primarily responsible for its creation to assert in no doubtful tones the necessity for an independent and untrammeled judiciary. . . .

WILLIAM H. TAFT.

379. ROOSEVELT'S CANDIDACY IN 1912

(*The Works of Theodore Roosevelt*, National ed. Vol. XVII, p. 149–150)

When Roosevelt returned from his European trip in June, 1910, he was drawn, though with apparent reluctance, into State and national politics. As early as August 31, 1910, in his speech at Ossawatomie, Kansas he sounded a note of protest against the conservatism of the Taft administration. With the apparent waning of the La Follette movement, progressives turned to Roosevelt to assume the leadership of the insurgents in the Republican Party. Roosevelt himself had definitely decided to enter the race for the nomination early in 1912, and he was instrumental in having the Progressive Governors draw up the letter of February 10. Roosevelt replied from New York February 24. See H. Pringle, *Theodore Roosevelt*, Book III; J. B. Bishop, *Theodore Roosevelt and His Time*, Vol. II, ch. xx–xxiv; L. Einstein, *Roosevelt: His Mind in Action;* R. La Follette, *Autobiography,* chs. x–xiii; H. S. Duffy, *W. H. Taft*, chs. xxviii–xxix. The speeches of the campaign can be found in Roosevelt's *Works,* Vol. XVII, and in W. Wilson, *The New Freedom.*

Chicago, Illinois, February 10, 1912

We, the undersigned Republican Governors, assembled for the purpose of considering what will best insure the continuation of the Republican Party as a useful agency of good government, declare it our belief, after a careful investigation of the facts, that a large majority of the Republican voters of the country favor your nomination, and a large majority of the people favor your election as the next President of the United States.

We believe that your candidacy will insure success in the next campaign. We believe that you represent as no other man represents those principles and policies upon which we must appeal for a majority of the votes of the American people, and which, in our opinion, are necessary for the happiness and prosperity of the country.

We believe that, in view of this public demand, you should soon declare whether, if the nomination for the presidency comes to you unsolicited and unsought, you will accept it.

In submitting this request we are not considering your personal interests. We do not regard it as proper to consider either the interests or the preference of any man as regards the nomination for the presidency. We are expressing our sincere belief and best judgment as to what is demanded of you in the interests of the people as a whole, and we feel that you would be unresponsive to a plain public duty if you should decline to accept the nomination coming as the voluntary expression of the wishes of a majority of the Republican voters of the United States through the action of their delegates in the next National Convention.

Yours truly,

William E. Glasscock,	West Virginia.
Chester H. Aldrich,	Nebraska.
Robert P. Bass,	New Hampshire.
Joseph M. Cary,	Wyoming.
Chase S. Osborn,	Michigan.
W. R. Stubbs,	Kansas.
Herbert S. Hadley,	Missouri.

New York, February 24, 1912

GENTLEMEN:

I deeply appreciate your letter, and I realize to the full the heavy responsibility it puts upon me, expressing as it does the carefully considered convictions of the men elected by popular vote to stand as the heads of government in their several States.

I absolutely agree with you that this matter is not one to be decided with any reference to the personal preferences or interests of any man, but purely from the standpoint of the interests of the people as a whole.

I will accept the nomination for President if it is tendered to me, and I will adhere to this decision until the convention has expressed its preference.

One of the chief principles for which I have stood, and for which I now stand, and which I have always endeavored and always shall endeavor to reduce to action, is the genuine rule of the people, and therefore I hope that so far as possible the people may be given the chance, through direct primaries, to express their preference as to who shall be the nominee of the Republican Presidential Convention.

Very truly yours,

THEODORE ROOSEVELT.

380. ROOSEVELT AND THE NEW NATIONALISM

Speech of Theodore Roosevelt before the Ohio Constitutional Convention, Columbus Ohio

February 21, 1912

(*The Works of Theodore Roosevelt*, National ed. Vol. XVII, p. 119 ff.)

Roosevelt had already decided, when he delivered this speech, to enter the race in 1912. The speech can therefore be regarded as the opening note in the pre-convention campaign. Three days later, February 24, Roosevelt formally accepted the invitation of the Seven Governors to be a candidate on the Republican ticket. The principal interest of this address lies in Roosevelt's energetic advocacy of the recall of judicial decisions. Roosevelt's attitude toward the Courts alienated many of his more conservative followers such as Root, Stimson, Knox, Lodge, etc., and was partly responsible for his subsequent defeat. For the origins of this attitude, see Doc. No. 310.

. . . The only safe course to follow in this great American democracy, is to provide for making the popular judgement really effective.

When this is done, then it is our duty to see that the people, having the full power, realize their heavy responsiblity for exercising that power aright.

But it is a false constitutionalism, a false statesmanship, to endeavor by the exercise of a perverted ingenuity to seem to give the people full power and at the same time to trick them out of it. Yet this is precisely what is done in every case where the State permits its representatives, whether on the bench or in the legislature or in executive office, to declare that it has not the power to right grave social wrongs, or that any of the officers created by the people, and rightfully the servants of the people, can set themselves up to be the masters of the people. Constitution-makers should make it clear beyond shadow of doubt that the people in their legislative capacity have the power to enact into law any measure they deem necessary for the betterment of social and industrial conditions. The wisdom of framing any particular law of this kind is a proper subject of debate; but the power of the people to enact the law should not be subject to debate. To hold the contrary view is to be false to the cause of the people, to the cause of American democracy. . . .

We stand for the rights of property, but we stand even more for the rights of man.

We will protect the rights of the wealthy

man, but we maintain that he holds his wealth subject to the general right of the community to regulate its business use as the public welfare requires. . . .

Moreover, shape your constitutional action so that the people will be able through their legislative bodies, or, failing that, by direct popular vote, to provide workmen's compensation acts to regulate the hours of labor for children and for women, to provide for their safety while at work, and to prevent overwork or work under unhygienic or unsafe conditions. See to it that no restrictions are placed upon legislative powers that will prevent the enactment of laws under which your people can promote the general welfare, the common good. Thus only will the "general welfare" clause of our Constitution become a vital force for progress, instead of remaining a mere phrase. This also applies to the police powers of the government. Make it perfectly clear that on every point of this kind it is your intention that the people shall decide for themselves how far the laws to achieve their purposes shall go, and that their decision shall be binding upon every citizen in the State, official or non-official, unless, of course, the Supreme Court of the nation in any given case decides otherwise. . . .

There remains the question of the recall of judges. . . .

I do not believe in adopting the recall save as a last resort, when it has become clearly evident that no other course will achieve the desired result.

But either the recall will have to be adopted or else it will have to be made much easier than it now is to get rid, not merely of a bad judge, but of a judge who, however virtuous, has grown so out of touch with social needs and facts that he is unfit longer to render good service on the bench.

It is nonsense to say that impeachment meets the difficulty. In actual practice we have found that impeachment does not work, that unfit judges stay on the bench in spite of it, and indeed because of the fact that impeachment is the only remedy that can be used against them. Where such is the actual fact it is idle to discuss the theory of the case. Impeachment as a remedy for the ills of which the people justly complain is a complete failure. A quicker, a more sum-

mary, remedy is needed; some remedy at least as summary and as drastic as that embodied in the Massachusetts constitution. And whenever it be found in actual practice that such remedy does not give the needed results, I would unhesitatingly adopt the recall.

But there is one kind of recall in which I very earnestly believe, and the immediate adoption of which I urge.

There are sound reasons for being cautious about the recall of a good judge who has rendered an unwise and improper decision. Every public servant, no matter how valuable—and not omitting Washington or Lincoln or Marshall—at times makes mistakes. Therefore we should be cautious about recalling the judge, and we shall be cautious about interfering in any way with the judge in decisions which he makes in the ordinary course as between individuals. But when a judge decides a constitutional question, when he decides what the people as a whole can or cannot do, the people should have the right to recall that decision if they think it wrong. We should hold the judiciary in all respect; but it is both absurd and degrading to make a fetich of a judge or of any one else. . . .

Again and again in the past justice has been scandalously obstructed by State courts declaring State laws in conflict with the Federal Constitution, although the Supreme Court of the nation had never so decided or had even decided in a contrary sense.

When the supreme court of the State declares a given statute unconstitutional, because in conflict with the State of the National Constitution, its opinion should be subject to revision by the people themselves. Such an opinion ought always to be treated with great respect by the people, and unquestionably in the majority of cases would be accepted and followed by them. But actual experience has shown the vital need of the people reserving to themselves the right to pass upon such opinion. If any considerable number of the people feel that the decision is in defiance of justice, they should be given the right by petition to bring before the voters at some subsequent election, special or otherwise, as might be decided, and after the fullest opportunity for deliberation and debate, the question whether or not the judges' interpretation of the Constitution is to be sustained. If it is sustained, well and good. If not, then the popular verdict is to be accepted as final, the decision is to be treated as reversed, and the construction of the Constitution definitely decided—subject only to action by the Supreme Court of the United States. . . .

381. RECOMMENDATIONS OF THE ALDRICH COMMISSION
1912

(Publications of the National Monetary Commission, Vol. XXVI, p. 6 ff.)

The Monetary Commission was authorized by Act of Congress in 1908, under the chairmanship of Nelson W. Aldrich. It submitted numerous volumes dealing with the financial history of the United States and European nations, and some recommendations for the reconstruction of the American banking system. Some of these were adopted by Congress in 1913–14 in the Federal Reserve Act. On Aldrich and the Monetary Commission, see N. W. Stephenson, *Nelson W. Aldrich,* ch. xxi.

We have made a thorough study of the defects of our banking system, which were largely responsible for these disasters and have sought to provide effective remedies for these and other defects, in the legislation we propose.

The principal defects in our banking system we believe may be summarized as follows:

1. We have no provision for the concentration of the cash reserves of the banks and for their mobilization and use wherever needed in times of trouble. Experience has shown that the scattered cash reserves of our banks are inadequate for purposes of assistance or defense at such times.

2. Antiquated Federal and State laws restrict the use of bank reserves and prohibit the lending power of banks at times when, in the presence of unusual demands, reserves should be freely used and credit liberally extended to all deserving customers.

3. Our banks also lack adequate means available for use at any time to replenish their reserves or increase their loaning powers when necessary to meet normal or unusual demands.

4. Of our various forms of currency the bank-note issue is the only one which we might expect to respond to the changing needs of business by automatic expansion and contraction, but this issue is deprived of all such qualities by the fact that its volume is largely dependent upon the amount and price of United States bonds.

5. We lack means to insure such effective coöperation on the part of banks as is necessary to protect their own and the public interests in times of stress or crisis. There is no coöperation of any kind among banks outside the clearing-house cities. While clearing-house organizations of banks have been able to render valuable services within a limited sphere for local communities, the lack of means to secure their coöperation or affiliation in broader fields makes it impossible to use these or similar local agencies to prevent panics or avert calamitous disturbances affecting the country at large. These organizations have, in fact, never been able to prevent the suspension of cash payments by financial institutions in their own localities in cases of emergency.

6. We have no effective agency covering the entire country which affords necessary facilities for making domestic exchanges between different localities and sections, or which can prevent disastrous disruption of all such exchanges in times of serious trouble.

7. We have no instrumentality that can deal effectively with the broad questions which, from an international standpoint, affect the credit and status of the United States as one of the great financial powers of the world. In times of threatened trouble or of actual panic these questions, which involve the course of foreign exchange and the international movements of gold, are even more important to us from a national than from an international standpoint.

8. The lack of commercial paper of an established standard, issued for agricultural, industrial, and commercial purposes, available for investments by banks, leads to an unhealthy congestion of loanable funds in

great centers and hinders the development of the productive forces of the country.

9. The narrow character of our discount market, with its limited range of safe and profitable investments for banks, results in sending the surplus money of all sections, in excess of reserves and local demands, to New York, where it is usually loaned out on call on Stock Exchange securities, tending to promote dangerous speculation and inevitably leading to injurious disturbances in reserves. This concentration of surplus money and available funds in New York imposes upon the managers of the banks of that city the vast responsibilities which are inherent in the control of a large proportion of the banking resources of the country.

10. The absence of a broad discount market in our system, taken together with the restrictive treatment of reserves, creates at times when serious financial disturbances are anticipated a condition of dependence on the part of individual banks throughout the country, and at the same time places the farmers and others engaged in productive industries at a great disadvantage in securing the credit they require for the growth, retention, and distribution of their products.

11. There is a marked lack of equality in credit facilities between different sections of the country, reflected in less favored communities, in retarded development, and great disparity in rates of discount.

12. Our system lacks an agency whose influence can be made effective in securing greater uniformity, steadiness, and reasonableness of rates of discount in all parts of the country.

13. We have no effective agency that can surely provide adequate banking facilities for different regions promptly and on reasonable terms to meet the ordinary or unusual demands for credit or currency necessary for moving crops or for other legitimate purposes.

14. We have no power to enforce the adoption of uniform standards with regard to capital, reserves, examinations, and the character and publicity of reports of all banks in the different sections of the country.

15. We have no American banking institutions in foreign countries. The organization of such banks is necessary for the development of our foreign trade.

16. The provision that national banks shall not make loans upon real estate restricts their power to serve farmers and other borrowers in rural communities.

17. The provision of law under which the Government acts as custodian of its own funds results in irregular withdrawals of money from circulation and bank reserves in periods of excessive Government revenues, and in the return of these funds into circulation only in periods of deficient revenues. Recent efforts to modify the Independent Treasury system by a partial distribution of the public moneys among national banks have resulted, it is charged, in discrimination and favoritism in the treatment of different banks.

382. SOCIALIST PARTY PLATFORM OF 1912
Indianapolis, Indiana, May 12, 1912

(K. Porter, ed. *National Party Platforms*, p. 361 ff.)

The Socialist Party offered its first candidate in a national election in 1892. The history of the party is closely identified with the career of Eugene V. Debs, who became converted to socialism during his imprisonment at the time of the Pullman Strike. In 1912 the party nominated Debs for the presidency for the fourth time: Emil Seidel of Milwaukee was the nominee for the vice-presidency. Debs polled a popular vote of almost nine hundred thousand. On the Socialist Party, see N. Fine, *Labor and Farmer Parties in the United States, 1828–1928;* J. Macy, *Socialism in the United States;* M. Hillquit, *History of Socialism in the United States;* F. E. Haynes, *Social Politics in the United States,* chs. ix, xii. On Debs see D. Karsner, *Debs, His Authorized Life and Letters;* M. Coleman, *Eugene V. Debs.*

The Socialist party declares that the capitalist system has outgrown its historical function, and has become utterly incapable of meeting the problems now confronting society. We denounce this outgrown system as incompetent and corrupt and the source of unspeakable misery and suffering to the whole working class.

Under this system the industrial equipment of the nation has passed into the absolute control of a plutocracy which exacts an annual tribute of hundreds of millions of dollars from the producers. Unafraid of any organized resistance, it stretches out its greedy hands over the still undeveloped resources of the nation—the land, the mines, the forests and the water powers of every State of the Union.

In spite of the multiplication of labor-saving machines and improved methods in industry which cheapen the cost of production, the share of the producers grows ever less, and the prices of all the necessities of life steadily increase. The boasted prosperity of this nation is for the owning class alone. To the rest it means only greater hardship and misery. The high cost of living is felt in every home. Millions of wage-workers have seen the purchasing power of their wages decrease until life has become a desperate battle for mere existance.

Multitudes of unemployed walk the streets of our cities or trudge from State to State awaiting the will of the masters to move the wheels of industry.

The farmers in every state are plundered by the increasing prices exacted for tools and machinery and by extortionate rents, freight rates and storage charges.

Capitalist concentration is mercilessly crushing the class of small business men and driving its members into the ranks of propertyless wage-workers. The overwhelming majority of the people of America are being forced under a yoke of bondage by this soulless industrial despotism.

It is this capitalist system that is responsible for the increasing burden of armaments, the poverty, slums, child labor, most of the insanity, crime and prostitution, and much of the disease that afflicts mankind.

Under this system the working class is exposed to poisonous conditions, to frightful and needless perils to life and limb, is walled around with court decisions, injunctions and unjust laws, and is preyed upon incessantly for the benefit of the controlling oligarchy of wealth. Under it also, the children of the working class are doomed to ignorance, drudging toil and darkened lives.

In the face of these evils, so manifest that all thoughtful observers are appalled at them, the legislative representatives of the Republican and Democratic parties remain the faithful servants of the oppressors. Measures designed to secure to the wage-earners of this Nation as humane and just treatment as is already enjoyed by the wage-earners of all other civilized nations have been smothered in committee without debate, the laws ostensibly designed to bring relief to the farmers and general consumers are juggled and transformed into instruments for the exaction of further tribute. The growing unrest under oppression has driven these two old parties to the enactment of a variety of regulative measures, none of which has limited in any appreciable degree the power of the plutocracy, and some of which have been perverted into means of increasing that power. Anti-trust laws, railroad restrictions and regulations, with the prosecutions, indictments and investigations based upon such legislation, have proved to be utterly futile and ridiculous.

Nor has this plutocracy been seriously restrained or even threatened by any Republican or Democratic executive. It has continued to grow in power and insolence alike under the administration of Cleveland, McKinley, Roosevelt and Taft.

We declare, therefore, that the longer sufferance of these conditions is impossible, and we purpose to end them all. We declare them to be the product of the present system in which industry is carried on for private greed, instead of for the welfare of society. We declare, furthermore, that for these evils there will be and can be no remedy and no substantial relief except through Socialism under which industry will be carried on for the common good and every worker receive the full social value of the wealth he creates.

Society is divided into warring groups and classes, based upon material interests. Fundamentally, this struggle is a conflict between the two main classes, one of which, the capitalist class, owns the means of production, and the other, the working class, must use these means of production, on terms dictated by the owners.

The capitalist class, though few in numbers, absolutely controls the government, legislative, executive and judicial. This class owns the machinery of gathering and disseminating news through its organized press. It subsidizes seats of learning—the colleges and schools—and even religious and moral agencies. It has also the added prestige which established customs give to any order of society, right or wrong.

The working class, which includes all those who are forced to work for a living whether by hand or brain, in shop, mine or on the soil, vastly outnumbers the capitalist class. Lacking effective organization and class solidarity, this class is unable to enforce its will. Given such a class solidarity and effective organization, the workers will have the power to make all laws and control all industry in their own interest. All political parties are the expression of economic class interests. All other parties than the Socialist party represent one or another group of the ruling capitalist class. Their political conflicts reflect merely superficial rivalries between competing capitalist groups. However they result, these conflicts have no issue of real value to the workers. Whether the Democrats or Republicans win politically, it is the capitalist class that is victorious economically.

The Socialist party is the political expression of the economic interests of the workers. Its defeats have been their defeats and its victories their victories. It is a party founded on the science and laws of social development. It proposes that, since all social necessities to-day are socially produced, the means of their production and distribution shall be socially owned and democratically controlled.

In the face of the economic and political aggressions of the capitalist class the only reliance left the workers is that of their economic organizations and their political power. By the intelligent and class conscious use of these, they may resist successfully the capitalist class, break the fetters of wage slavery, and fit themselves for the future society, which is to displace the capitalist system. The Socialist party appreciates the full significance of class organization and urges the wage-earners, the working farmers and all other useful workers to organize for economic and political action, and we pledge ourselves to support the toilers of the fields as well as those in the shops, factories and mines of the nation in their struggles for economic justice.

In the defeat or victory of the working class party in this new struggle for freedom lies the defeat or triumph of the common people of all economic groups, as well as the failure or triumph of popular government. Thus the Socialist party is the party of the present day revolution which makes the transition from economic individualism to socialism, from wage slavery to free co-operation, from capitalist oligarchy to industrial democracy.

Working Program

As measures calculated to strengthen the working class in its fight for the realization of its ultimate aim, the co-operative commonwealth, and to increase its power against capitalist oppression, we advocate and pledge ourselves and our elected officers to the following program:

Collective Ownership

1. The collective ownership and democratic management of railroads, wire and wireless telegraphs and telephones, express service, steamboat lines, and all other social means of transportation and communication and of all large scale industries.

2. The immediate acquirement by the municipalities, the states or the federal government of all grain elevators, stock yards, storage warehouses, and other distributing agencies, in order to reduce the present extortionate cost of living.

3. The extension of the public domain to include mines, quarries, oil wells, forests and water power.

4. The further conservation and development of natural resources for the use and benefit of all the people: . . .

5. The collective ownership of land wherever practicable, and in cases where such ownership is impracticable, the appropriation by taxation of the annual rental value of all the land held for speculation and exploitation.

6. The collective ownership and democratic management of the banking and currency system.

Unemployment

The immediate government relief of the unemployed by the extension of all useful public works. All persons employed on such works to be engaged directly by the government under a work day of not more than eight hours and at not less than the prevailing union wages. The government also to establish employment bureaus; to lend money to states and municipalities without interest for the purpose of carrying on public works, and to take such other measures within its power as will lessen the widespread misery of the workers caused by the misrule of the capitalist class.

Industrial Demands

The conservation of human resources, particularly of the lives and well-being of the workers and their families:

1. By shortening the work day in keeping with the increased productiveness of machinery.
2. By securing for every worker a rest period of not less than a day and a half in each week.
3. By securing a more effective inspection of workshops, factories and mines.
4. By the forbidding the employment of children under sixteen years of age.
5. By the co-operative organization of the industries in the federal penitentiaries for the benefit of the convicts and their dependents.
6. By forbidding the interstate transportation of the products of child labor, of convict labor and of all uninspected factories and mines.
7. By abolishing the profit system in government work and substituting either the direct hire of labor or the awarding of contracts to co-operative groups of workers.
8. By establishing minimum wage scales.
9. By abolishing official charity and substituting a non-contributary system of old age pensions, a general system of insurance by the State of all its members against unemployment and invalidism and a system of compulsory insurance by employers of their workers, without cost to the latter, against industrial diseases, accidents and death.

Political Demands

1. The absolute freedom of press, speech and assemblage.
2. The adoption of a graduated income tax and the extension of inheritance taxes, graduated in proportion to the value of the estate and to nearness of kin—the proceeds of these taxes to be employed in the socialization of industry.

3. The abolition of the monopoly ownership of patents and the substitution of collective ownership, with direct rewards to inventors by premiums or royalties.
4. Unrestricted and equal suffrage for men and women.
5. The adoption of the initiative, referendum and recall and of proportional representation, nationally as well as locally.
6. The abolition of the Senate and of the veto power of the President.
7. The election of the President and Vice-President by direct vote of the people.
8. The abolition of the power usurped by the Supreme Court of the United States to pass upon the constitutionality of the legislation enacted by Congress. National laws to be repealed only by act of Congress or by a referendum vote of the whole people.
9. Abolition of the present restrictions upon the amendment of the constitution, so that instrument may be made amendable by a majority of the voters in a majority of the States.
10. The granting of the right of suffrage in the District of Columbia with representation in Congress and a democratic form of municipal government for purely local affairs.
11. The extension of democratic government to all United States territory.
12. The enactment of further measures for the conservation of health. The creation of an independent bureau of health, with such restrictions as will secure full liberty to all schools of practice.
13. The enactment of further measures for general education and particularly for vocational education in useful pursuits. The Bureau of Education to be made a department.
14. The separation of the present Bureau of Labor from the Department of Commerce and Labor and its elevation to the rank of a department.
15. Abolition of all federal districts courts and the United States circuit court of appeals. State courts to have jurisdiction in all cases arising between citizens of several states and foreign corporations. The election of all judges for short terms.
16. The immediate curbing of the power of the courts to issue injunctions.
17. The free administration of the law.
18. The calling of a convention for the revision of the constitution of the U. S.

Such measures of relief as we may be able to force from capitalism are but a preparation of the workers to seize the whole powers of government, in order that they may thereby lay hold of the whole system of socialized industry and thus come to their rightful inheritance.

383. BRYAN'S RESOLUTIONS, DEMOCRATIC NATIONAL CONVENTION
June 27, 1912

(Official Proceedings of the Democratic National Convention, 1912, p. 149)

With the rupture of the Republican Party, and the probability that the Democratic nominee would be elected to the Presidency, Bryan began an intensive campaign to nominate a liberal candidate. The first step was the contest over the temporary chairmanship of the Convention. The second, designed as a dramatic gesture to influence public opinion, was the Resolution below. "If (the convention) passed the resolution," wrote Bryan, "it excluded anyone who was the representative of Morgan, Belmont, or Ryan or under their influence; if they voted it down, the rebuke from the country would make it impossible for New York to select a candidate." The resolution passed, 883 to 201, even New York voting for it. The second paragraph in these resolutions was withdrawn by Bryan, but this was not generally understood by the delegates. See, Bryan, *A Tale of Two Conventions;* R. S. Baker, *Woodrow Wilson, Life and Letters,* Vol. III, p. 340 ff.

Resolved, That in this crisis in our party's career and in our country's history this convention sends greetings to the people of the United States, and assures them that the party of Jefferson and Jackson is still the champion of popular government and equality before the law. As proof of our fidelity to the people, we hereby declare ourselves opposed to the nomination of any candidate for President who is the representative of or under obligation to J. Pierpont Morgan, Thomas F. Ryan, August Belmont, or any other member of the privilege-hunting and favor-seeking class.

Be It Further Resolved, That we demand the withdrawal from this convention of any delegate or delegates constituting or representing the above-named interests.

384. THE PROGRESSIVE PARTY PLATFORM
August 5, 1912

(K. Porter, ed. National Party Platforms, p. 334 ff.)

The steam-roller tactics of the Republican National Convention of 1912 in ruling against the Roosevelt delegates to that convention led to the formation of the Progressive Party. June 22, Roosevelt's followers met at Orchestra Hall, Chicago, and pledged support to him and to his principles. July 7, the call for a nominating convention was issued, and the convention duly met at Chicago August 5 and nominated Roosevelt by acclamation. Hiram Johnson of California was nominated to the Vice-Presidency. The third party succeeded in winning 88 electoral votes and a popular vote of over four millions. See, G. H. Payne, *The Birth of a New Party;* V. Rosewater, *Backstage in 1912;* O. K. Davis, *Released for Publication;* M. Sullivan, *Our Times,* Vol. III; R. M. La Follette, *Autobiography,* chs. xi–xii; H. Pringle, *Theodore Roosevelt.*

The conscience of the people, in a time of grave national problems, has called into being a new party, born of the nation's sense of justice. We of the Progressive party here dedicate ourselves to the fulfillment of the duty laid upon us by our fathers to maintain the government of the people, by the people and for the people whose foundations they laid. . . .

THE OLD PARTIES

Political parties exist to secure responsible government and to execute the will of the people.

From these great tasks both of the old parties have turned aside. Instead of instruments to promote the general welfare, they have become the tools of corrupt interests which use them impartially to serve their selfish purposes. Behind the ostensible government sits enthroned an invisible government owing no allegiance and acknowledging no responsibility to the people.

To destroy this invisible government, to

dissolve the unholy alliance between corrupt business and corrupt politics is the first task of the statesmanship of the day.

The deliberate betrayal of its trust by the Republican party, the fatal incapacity of the Democratic party to deal with the new issues of the new time, have compelled the people to forge a new instrument of government through which to give effect to their will in laws and institutions.

Unhampered by tradition, uncorrupted by power, undismayed by the magnitude of the task, the new party offers itself as the instrument of the people to sweep away old abuses, to build a new and nobler commonwealth. . . .

THE RULE OF THE PEOPLE

. . . In particular, the party declares for direct primaries for the nomination of State and National officers, for nation-wide preferential primaries for candidates for the presidency; for the direct election of United States Senators by the people; and we urge on the States the policy of the short ballot, with responsibility to the people secured by the initiative, referendum and recall. . . .

EQUAL SUFFRAGE

The Progressive party, believing that no people can justly claim to be a true democracy which denies political rights on account of sex, pledges itself to the task of securing equal suffrage to men and women alike.

CORRUPT PRACTICES

We pledge our party to legislation that will compel strict limitation of all campaign contributions and expenditures, and detailed publicity of both before as well as after primaries and elections.

PUBLICITY AND PUBLIC SERVICE

We pledge our party to legislation compelling the registration of lobbyists; publicity of committee hearings except on foreign affairs, and recording of all votes in committee; and forbidding federal appointees from holding office in State or National political organizations, or taking part as officers or delegates in political conventions for the nomination of elective State or National officials.

THE COURTS

The Progressive party demands such restriction of the power of the courts as shall leave to the people the ultimate authority to determine fundamental questions of social welfare and public policy. To secure this end, it pledges itself to provide:

1. That when an Act, passed under the police power of the State, is held unconstitutional under the State Constitution, by the courts, the people, after an ample interval for deliberation, shall have an opportunity to vote on the question whether they desire the Act to become law, notwithstanding such decision.

2. That every decision of the highest appellate court of a State declaring an Act of the Legislature unconstitutional on the ground of its violation of the Federal Constitution shall be subject to the same review by the Supreme Court of the United States as is now accorded to decisions sustaining such legislation.

ADMINISTRATION OF JUSTICE

. . . We believe that the issuance of injunctions in cases arising out of labor disputes should be prohibited when such injunctions would not apply when no labor disputes existed.

We believe also that a person cited for contempt in labor disputes, except when such contempt was committed in the actual presence of the court or so near thereto as to interfere with the proper administration of justice, should have a right to trial by jury.

SOCIAL AND INDUSTRIAL JUSTICE

The supreme duty of the Nation is the conservation of human resources through an enlightened measure of social and industrial justice. We pledge ourselves to work unceasingly in State and Nation for:

Effective legislation looking to the prevention of industrial accidents, occupational diseases, overwork, involuntary unemployment, and other injurious effects incident to modern industry;

The fixing of minimum safety and health standards for the various occupations, and the exercise of the public authority of State and Nation, including the Federal Control over interstate commerce, and the taxing power, to maintain such standards;

The prohibition of child labor;

Minimum wage standards for working women, to provide a "living wage" in all industrial occupations;

The general prohibition of night work for women and the establishment of an eight hour day for women and young persons;

One day's rest in seven for all wage workers;

The eight hour day in continuous twenty-four-hour industries;

The abolition of the convict contract labor system; substituting a system of prison production for governmental consumption only; and the application of prisoners' earnings to the support of their dependent families;

Publicity as to wages, hours and conditions of labor; full reports upon industrial accidents and diseases, and the opening to public inspection of all tallies, weights, measures and check systems on labor products;

Standards of compensation for death by industrial accident and injury and trade disease which will transfer the burden of lost earnings from the families of working people to the industry, and thus to the community;

The protection of home life against the hazards of sickness, irregular employment and old age through the adoption of a system of social insurance adapted to American use;

The development of the creative labor power of America by lifting the last load of illiteracy from American youth and establishing continuation schools for industrial education under public control and encouraging agricultural education and demonstration in rural schools;

The establishment of industrial research laboratories to put the methods and discoveries of science at the service of American producers;

We favor the organization of the workers, men and women, as a means of protecting their interests and of promoting their progress. . . .

CURRENCY

. . . The issue of currency is fundamentally a Government function and the system should have as basic principles soundness and elasticity. The control should be lodged with the Government and should be protected from domination or manipulation by Wall Street or any special interests.

We are opposed to the so-called Aldrich currency bill, because its provisions would place our currency and credit system in private hands, not subject to effective public control. . . .

CONSERVATION

. . . We believe that the remaining forests, coal and oil lands, water powers and other natural resources still in State or National control (except agricultural lands) are more likely to be wisely conserved and utilized for the general welfare if held in the public hands.

In order that consumers and producers, managers and workmen, now and hereafter, need not pay toll to private monopolies of power and raw material, we demand that such resources shall be retained by the State or Nation, and opened to immediate use under laws which will encourage development and make to the people a moderate return for benefits conferred. . . .

385. THE LODGE COROLLARY TO THE MONROE DOCTRINE
August 2, 1912

(*Congressional Record,* 62d Congress, 2d Session, Vol. XXXXVIII, pt. 10, p. 10045)

In 1911 an American syndicate proposed to sell a four hundred thousand acre tract of land in Lower California, including Magdalena Bay, to a Japanese syndicate. On hearing of the proposal, Senator Lodge introduced a resolution which, with slight alterations, was passed by the Senate by a vote of 51 to 4. This resolution was the first extension of the Monroe Doctrine to an Asiatic power, and the first extension of the Doctrine to cover control of American soil which had a potential military value by a foreign corporation. See, T. A. Bailey, "The Lodge Corollary," *Pol. Sci. Qt.,* Vol. XLVIII, p. 220 ff.; S. F. Bemis, ed., *American Secretaries of State,* Vol.

IX, p. 340 ff.; J. M. Callahan, *American Foreign Policy in Mexican Relations.*

Resolved, That when any harbor or other place in the American continents is so situated that the occupation thereof for naval or military purposes might threaten the communications or the safety of the United States, the Government of the United States could not see without grave concern the actual or potential possession of such harbor or other place by any Government, not American, as to give that Government practical power of control for naval or military purposes.

386. DOLLAR DIPLOMACY

Extract from Fourth Annual Message of President Taft
December 3, 1912

(Supplement to the Messages and Papers of the Presidents Covering the Administration of Taft, p. 8152–3)

American surplus capital had flowed largely into South American investments, but prior to the accession of Taft to the Presidency there had been little investment in China. The financing of Chinese development was almost entirely in the hands of English, Japanese and European bankers. In 1909, however, Taft made official representations to the Chinese Government on behalf of some American banking houses for participation in the Hukuang railroad in the Yangtse Valley. As a result American bankers were admitted to a four power consortium. In 1912 American bankers were about to co-operate in floating a Chinese loan for £25,000,000, but the advent of Wilson to the Presidency brought a sharp repudiation of "dollar diplomacy" in the Far East, and the Americans withdrew. For the Hukuang Railroad loan, see *Foreign Relations of the United States,* 1910, 1912, and for the consortium, *Foreign Relations,* 1912. On dollar diplomacy, see, S. Nearing and J. Freeman, *Dollar Diplomacy;* J. W. Overlach, *Foreign Financial Control in China;* B. H. Williams, *Economic Foreign Policy of the United States;* M. C. Hsu, *Railway Problems in China;* H. Croly, *Willard Straight;* F. V. Field, *American Participation in the Chinese Consortiums.*

CHINA

In China the policy of encouraging financial investment to enable that country to help itself has had the result of giving new life and practical application to the open-door policy. The consistent purpose of the present administration has been to encourage the use of American capital in the development of China by the promotion of those essential reforms to which China is pledged by treaties with the United States and other powers. The hypothecation to foreign bankers in connection with certain industrial enterprises, such as the Hukuang railways, of the national revenues upon which these reforms depended, led the Department of State early in the administration to demand for American citizens participation in such enterprises, in order that the United States might have equal rights and an equal voice in all questions pertaining to the disposition of the public revenues concerned. The same policy of promoting international accord among the powers having similar treaty rights as ourselves in the matters of reform, which could not be put into practical effect without the common consent of all, was likewise adopted in the case of the loan desired by China for the reform of its currency. The principle of international cooperation in matters of common interest upon which our policy had already been based in all of the above instances has admittedly been a great factor in that concert of the powers which has been so happily conspicuous during the perilous period of transition through which the great Chinese nation has been passing.

CENTRAL AMERICA NEEDS OUR HELP IN DEBT ADJUSTMENT

In Central America the aim has been to help such countries as Nicaragua and Honduras to help themselves. They are the immediate beneficiaries. The national benefit to the United States is twofold. First, it is obvious that the Monroe doctrine is more vital in the neighborhood of the Panama Canal and the zone of the Caribbean than anywhere else. There, too, the maintenance of that doctrine falls most heavily upon the United States. It is therefore essential that the countries within that sphere shall be removed from the jeopardy involved by heavy foreign debt and chaotic national finances and from the ever-present danger of international complications due to disorder at home. Hence the United States has been glad to encourage and support American bankers who were willing to lend a helping hand to the financial rehabilitation of such countries because this financial rehabilitation and the protection of their customhouses from being the prey of would-be dictators would remove at one stroke the menace of foreign creditors and the menace of revolutionary disorder.

The second advantage of the United States is one affecting chiefly all the southern and

Gulf ports and the business and industry of the South. The Republics of Central America and the Caribbean possess great natural wealth. They need only a measure of stability and the means of financial regeneration to enter upon an era of peace and prosperity, bringing profit and happiness to themselves and at the same time creating conditions sure to lead to a flourishing interchange of trade with this country.

I wish to call your especial attention to the recent occurrences in Nicaragua, for I believe the terrible events recorded there during the revolution of the past summer—the useless loss of life, the devastation of property, the bombardment of defenseless cities, the killing and wounding of women and children, the torturing of noncombatants to exact contributions, and the suffering of thousands of human beings—might have been averted had the Department of State, through approval of the loan convention by the Senate, been permitted to carry out its now well-developed policy of encouraging the extending of financial aid to weak Central American States with the primary objects of avoiding just such revolutions by assisting those Republics to rehabilitate their finances, to establish their currency on a stable basis, to remove the customhouses from the danger of revolutions by arranging for their secure administration, and to establish reliable banks.

387. TAFT'S VETO OF LITERACY TEST FOR IMMIGRANTS
February 14, 1913

(Supplement to the Messages and Papers of the Presidents Covering the Administration of William Howard Taft, p. 8228 ff.)

The veto message is accompanied by the opinion of Secretary of Commerce, Charles Nagel. For Wilson's veto of the literacy test, see Doc. No. 404.

To the Senate:

I return herewith, without my approval, Senate Bill No. 3175.

I do this with great reluctance. The bill contains many valuable amendments to the present immigration law which will insure greater certainty in excluding undesirable immigrants.

The bill received strong support in both Houses and was recommended by an able commission after an extended investigation and carefully drawn conclusions.

But I can not make up my mind to sign a bill which in its chief provision violates a principle that ought, in my opinion, to be upheld in dealing with our immigration. I refer to the literacy test. For the reasons stated in Secretary Nagel's letter to me, I can not approve that test. The Secretary's letter accompanies this.

WM. H. TAFT.

My Dear Mr. President:

. . . I am of the opinion that this provision can not be defended upon its merits. It was originally urged as a selective test. For some time recommendations in its support upon that ground have been brought to our attention. The matter has been considered from that point of view, and I became completely satisfied that upon that ground the test could not be sustained. The older argument is now abandoned, and in the later conferences, at least, the ground is taken that the provision is to be defended as a practical measure to exclude a large proportion of undesirable immigrants from certain countries. The measure proposes to reach its result by indirection, and is defended purely upon the ground of practical policy, the final purpose being to reduce the quantity of cheap labor in this country. I can not accept this argument. No doubt the law would exclude a considerable percentage of immigration from southern Italy, among the Poles, the Mexicans, and the Greeks. This exclusion would embrace probably in large part undesirable but also a great many desirable people, and the embarrassment, expense, and distress to those who seek to enter would be out of all proportion to any good that can possibly be promised for this measure.

My observation leads me to the conclusion that, so far as the merits of the individual immigrant are concerned, the test is altogether overestimated. The people who come from the countries named are frequently illiterate because opportunities have been denied them. The oppression with which these people have to contend in modern times is not religious, but it consists of a denial of the opportunity to acquire reading and writing. Frequently the attempt to learn to read and write the language of the particular people is discouraged by the Government, and these immigrants in coming to our shores are really striving to free themselves from the conditions under which they have been compelled to live.

So far as the industrial conditions are concerned, I think the question has been superficially considered. We need labor in this country, and the natives are unwilling to do the work which the aliens come over to do. It is perfectly true that in a few cities and localities there are congested conditions. It is equally true that in very much larger areas we are practically without help. In my judgment, no sufficiently earnest and intelligent effort has been made to bring our wants and our supply together, and so far the same forces that give the chief support to this provision of the new bill have stubbornly resisted any effort looking to an intelligent distribution of new immigration to meet the needs of our vast country. In my judgment, no such drastic measure based upon a ground which is untrue and urged for a reason which

we are unwilling to assert should be adopted until we have at least exhausted the possibilities of a rational distribution of these new forces. . . .

The census returns show conclusively that the importance of illiteracy among aliens is overestimated, and that these people are prompt after their arrival to avail [themselves] of the opportunities which this country affords. While, according to the reports of the Bureau of Immigration, about 25 per cent of the incoming aliens are illiterate, the census shows that among the foreign-born people of such States as New York and Massachusetts where most of the congestion complained of has taken place, the proportion of illiteracy represents only about 13 per cent.

I am persuaded that this provision of the bill is in principle of very great consequence, and that it is based upon a fallacy in undertaking to apply a test which is not calculated to reach the truth and to find relief from a danger which really does not exist. This provision of the bill is new, and it is radical. It goes to the heart of the measure. It does not permit of compromise, and, much as I regret it, because the other provisions of the measure are in most respects excellent and in no respect really objectionable, I am forced to advise that you do not approve this bill. Very sincerely, yours,

CHARLES NAGEL, *Secretary*.

388. THE CONCENTRATION OF CONTROL OF MONEY AND CREDIT
Report of the Pujo Committee
1913

(U. S. 62d Congress, 3rd. Session, *House Report,* No. 1593, ch. iii)

Ever since the publication of Henry D. Lloyd's *Wealth Against Commonwealth* in 1894 the charge that a small group of money masters controlled American industry, transportation and credit, had gained acceptance. With the muckraking campaign of the first decade of the new century this charge was substantiated in many details and given wide popularity. In February 1912 the House of Representatives directed the Committee on Banking and Currency to investigate banking and currency with a view to necessary legislation. A subcommittee, headed by Arsene P. Pujo, investigated banking abuses. The chief examiner of the Pujo committee was Samuel Untermeyer of New York. The material unearthed by the

Pujo committee was valuable for the campaign of 1912 and served to strengthen the hands of the reformers in the first Wilson administration. See for relevant material, *The Autobiography of Robert La Follette,* p. 762 ff.; L. Brandeis, *Other Peoples' Money;* J. Moody, *The Truth About the Trusts;* H. W. Laidler, *Concentration of Control in American Industry;* J. Moody, *Masters of Capital;* W. I. King, *Wealth and Income of the People of the United States;* G. Myers, *History of Great American Fortunes,* 3 Vols.; L. Corey, *The House of Morgan;* C. C. Regier, *The Era of the Muckrakers;* A. A. Berle and G. C. Means, *Modern Corporation and Private Property.*

Section 2—Fact of Increasing Concentration Admitted

The resources of the banks and trust companies of the city of New York on 1911 were $5,121,245,175, which is 21.73 per cent of the total banking resources of the country as reported by the Comptroller of the Currency. This takes no account of the unknown resources of the great private banking houses whose affiliations to the New York financial institutions we are about to discuss.

That in recent years concentration of control of the banking resources and consequently of credit by the groups to which we will refer has grown apace in the city of New York is defended by some witnesses and regretted by others, but acknowledged by all to be a fact.

As appears from statistics compiled by accountants for the committee, in 1911, of the total resources of the banks and trust companies in New York City, the 20 largest held 42.97 per cent; in 1906, the 20 largest held 38.24 per cent of the total; in 1901, 34.97 per cent.

Section 3—Processes of Concentration

This increased concentration of control of money and credit has been effected principally as follows:

First, through consolidations of competitive or potentially competitive banks and trust companies, which consolidations in turn have recently been brought under sympathetic management.

Second, through the same powerful interests becoming large stockholders in potentially competitive banks and trust companies. This is the simplest way of acquiring control, but since it requires the largest investment of capital, it is the least used, although the recent investments in that direction for that apparent purpose amount to tens of millions of dollars in present market values.

Third, through the confederation of potentially competitive banks and trust companies by means of the system of interlocking directorates.

Fourth, through the influence which the more powerful banking houses, banks, and trust companies have secured in the management of insurance companies, railroads, producing and trading corporations, and public utility corporations, by means of stockholdings, voting trusts, fiscal agency contracts, or representation upon their boards of directors, or through supplying the money requirements of railway, industrial, and public utilities corporations and thereby being enabled to participate in the determination of their financial and business policies.

Fifth, through partnership or joint account arrangements between a few of the leading banking houses, banks, and trust companies in the purchase of security issues of the great interstate corporations, accompanied by understandings of recent growth—sometimes called "banking ethics"—which have had the effect of effectually destroying competition between such banking houses, banks, and trust companies in the struggle for business or in the purchase and sale of large issues of such securities.

Section 4—Agents of Concentration

It is a fair deduction from the testimony that the most active agents in forwarding and bringing about the concentration of control of money and credit through one or another of the processes above described have been and are—

J. P. Morgan & Co.
First National Bank of New York
National City Bank of New York
Lee, Higginson & Co., of Boston and New York
Kidder, Peabody & Co., of Boston and New York
Kuhn, Loeb & Co.

. . . . . .

Combined Power of Morgan & Co., the First National, and National City Banks.—In earlier pages of the report the power of these three great banks was separately set forth. It is now appropriate to consider their combined power as one group.

First, as regards banking resources:

The resources of Morgan & Co. are unknown; its deposits are $163,000,000. The resources of the First National Bank are $150,000,000 and those of its appendage, the First Security Co., at a very low estimate, $35,000,000. The resources of the National City Bank are $274,000,000; those of its appendage, the National City Co., are unknown, though the capital of the latter is alone

$10,000,000. Thus, leaving out of account the very considerable part which is unknown, the institutions composing this group have resources of upward of $632,000,000, aside from the vast individual resources of Messrs. Morgan, Baker, and Stillman.

Further, as heretofore shown, the members of this group, through stockholdings, voting trusts, interlocking directorates, and other relations, have become in some cases the absolutely dominant factor, in others the most important single factor, in the control of the following banks and trust companies in the city of New York:

(a) Bankers Trust Co., resources	$250,000,000
(b) Guaranty Trust Co., resources	232,000,000
(c) Astor Trust Co., resources	27,000,000
(d) National Bank of Commerce, resources	190,000,000
(e) Liberty National Bank, resources	29,000,000
(f) Chase National Bank, resources	150,000,000
(g) Farmers Loan & Trust Co., resources	135,000,000

in all, 7, with total resources of 968,000,000 which, added to the known resources of members of the group themselves, makes $1,600,000,000 as the aggregate of known banking resources in the city of New York under their control or influence.

If there be added also the resources of the Equitable Life Assurance Society controlled through stock ownership of J. P. Morgan 504,000,000

the amount becomes $2,104,000,000

Second, as regards the greater transportation systems.

(a) Adams Express Co.: Members of the group have two representatives in the directorate of this company.

(b) Anthracite coal carriers: With the exception of the Pennsylvania, the Reading, the Central of New Jersey (a majority of whose stock is owned by the Reading), the Lehigh Valley, the Delaware, Lackawanna & Western, the Erie (controlling the New York, Susquehanna & Western), and the New York, Ontario & Western, afford the only transportation outlets from the anthracite coal fields. As before stated, they transport 80 per cent of the output moving from the mines and own and control 88 per cent of the entire deposits. The Reading, as now organized, is the creation of a member of this banking group—Morgan & Co. One or more members of the group are stockholders in that system and have two representatives in its directorate; are stockholders of the Central of New Jersey and have four representatives in its directorate; are stockholders of the Lehigh Valley and have four representatives in its directorate; are stockholders of the Delaware, Lackawanna & Western and have nine representatives in its directorate; are stockholders of the Erie, and have four representatives in its directorate; have two representatives in the directorate of the New York, Ontario & Western; and have purchased or marketed practically all security issues made by these railroads in recent years.

(c) Atchison, Topeka & Sante Fe Railway: One or more members of the group are stockholders and have two representatives in the directorate of the company; and since 1907 have purchased or procured the marketing of its security issues to the amount of $107,244,000.

(d) Chesapeake & Ohio Railway: Members of the group have two directors in common with this company; and since 1907, in association with others, have purchased or procured the marketing of its security issues to the amount of $85,000,000.

(e) Chicago Great Western Railway: Members of the group absolutely control this system through a voting trust.

(f) Chicago, Milwaukee & St. Paul Railway: Members of the group have three directors or officers in common with this company, and since 1909, in association with others, have purchased or procured the marketing of its security issues to the amount of $112,000,000.

(g) Chicago & Northwestern Railway: Members of the group have three directors in common with this company, and since 1909, in association with others, have purchased or procured the marketing of its security issues to the amount of $31,250,000.

(h) Chicago, Rock Island & Pacific Railway: Members of the group have four directors in common with this company.

(i) Great Northern Railway: One or more members of the group are stockholders of and have marketed the only issue of bonds made by this company.

(j) International Mercantile Marine Co.; A member of the group organized this company, is a stockholder, dominates it through a voting trust, and markets its securities.

(k) New York Central Lines: One or more members of the group are stockholders and have four representatives in the directorate of the company, and since 1907 have purchased from or marketed for it and its principal subsidiaries security issues to the extent of $343,000,000, one member of the group being the company's sole fiscal agent.

(l) New York, New Haven & Hartford Railroad: One or more members of the group are stockholders and have three representatives in the directorate of the company, and since 1907 have purchased from or marketed for it and its principal subsidiaries security issues in excess of $150,000,000, one member of the group being the company's sole fiscal agent.

(m) Northern Pacific Railway: One member of the group organized this company and is its fiscal agent, and one or more members are stockholders and have six representatives in its directorate and three in its executive committee.

(n) Southern Railway: Through a voting trust, members of the group have absolutely controlled this company since its reorganization in 1894.

(o) Southern Pacific Co.: Until its separation from the Union Pacific, lately ordered by the Supreme Court of the United States, members of the group had three directors in common with this company.

(p) Union Pacific Railroad: Members of the group have three directors in common with this company.

Third, as regards the greater producing and trading corporations.

(a) Amalgamated Copper Co.: One member of the group took part in the organization of the company, still has one leading director in common with it, and markets its securities.

(b) American Can Co.: Members of the group have two directors in common with this company.

(c) J. L. Case Threshing Machine Co.: The president of one member of the group is a voting trustee of this company and the group also has one representative in its directorate and markets its securities.

(d) William Cramp Ship & Engine Building Co.: Members of the group absolutely control this company through a voting trust.

(e) General Electric Co.: A member of the group was one of the organizers of the company, is a stockholder, and has always had two representatives in its directorate and markets its securities.

(f) International Harvester Co.: A member of the group organized the company, named its directorate and the chairman of its finance committee, directed its management, through a voting trust, and markets its securities.

(g) Lackawanna Steel Co.: Members of the group have four directors in common with the company and, with associates, marketed its last issue of securities.

(h) Pullman Co.: The group has two representatives, Mr. Morgan and Mr. Baker, in the directorate of this company.

(i) United States Steel Corporation: A member of the group organized this company, named its directorate, and the chairman of its finance committee (which also has the powers of an executive committee) is its sole fiscal agent and a stockholder, and has always controlled its management.

Fourth, as regards the great public utility corporations.

(a) American Telephone and Telegraph Co.: One or more members of the group are stockholders, have three representatives in its directorate, and since 1906, with other associates, have marketed for it and its subsidiaries security issues in excess of $300,-000,000.

(b) Chicago Elevated Railways: A member of the group has two officers or directors in common with the company, and in conjunction with others marketed for it in 1911 security issues amounting to $66,000,000.

(c) Consolidated Gas Co. of New York: Members of the group control this company through majority representation on its directorate.

(d) Hudson & Manhattan Railroad: One or more members of the group marketed and have large interests in the securities of this company, though its debt is now being adjusted by Kuhn, Loeb & Co.

(e) Interborough Rapid Transit Co. of New York: A member of the group is the banker of this company, and the group has agreed to market its impending bond issue of $170,000,000.

(f) Philadelphia Rapid Transit Co.: Members of the group have two representatives in the directorate of this company.

(g) Western Union Telegraph Co.: Members of the group have seven representatives in the directorate of this company.

Summary of Directorships Held by These Members of the Group.—Exhibit 134-B . . . shows the combined directorships in the more important enterprises held by Morgan & Co., the First National Bank, the National City Bank, and the Bankers and Guaranty Trust Cos., which latter two, as previously shown, are absolutely controlled by Morgan & Co. through voting trusts. It appears there that firm members or directors of these institutions together hold:

One hundred and eighteen directorships in 34 banks and trust companies having total resources of $2,679,000,000 and total deposits of $1,983,000,000.

Thirty directorships in 10 insurance companies having total assets of $2,293,000,000.

One hundred and five directorships in 32 transportation systems having a total capitalization of $11,784,000,000 and a total mileage (excluding express companies and steamship lines) of 150,200.

Sixty-three directorships in 24 producing and trading corporations having a total capitalization of $3,339,000,000.

Twenty-five directorships in 12 public utility corporations having a total capitalization of $22,245,000,000.

In all, 341 directorships in 112 corporations having aggregate resources or capitalization of $42,340,000,000.

The members of the firm of J. P. Morgan & Co. held 72 directorships in 47 of the greater corporations: George F. Baker, chairman of the board, F. L. Hine, president, and George F. Baker, Jr., and C. D. Norton, vice-presidents, of the First National Bank of New York, hold 46 directorships in 37 of the greater corporations; and James Stillman, chairman of the board, Frank A. Vanderlip, president, and Samuel McRoberts, J. T. Talbert, W. A. Simonson, vice-presidents, of the National City Bank of New York, hold 32 directorships in 26 of the greater corporations; making in all for these members of the group 150 directorships in 110 of the greater corporations. . . .

389. WILSON'S FIRST INAUGURAL ADDRESS
March 4, 1913

(U. S. 63d Congress, Special Session, *Senate Doc.* 3)

In his first Inaugural Address Woodrow Wilson reaffirmed the philosophy of the New Freedom which he had enunciated during his campaign for election. The address is one of the most notable statements of democratic faith in our political literature, and for eloquence compares favorably with Jefferson's First Inaugural and Lincoln's Second Inaugural. On Wilson, see R. S. Baker, *Woodrow Wilson, Life and Letters*, Vol. IV; W. E. Dodd, *Woodrow Wilson;* J. Kerney, *The Political Education of Woodrow Wilson*.

MY FELLOW CITIZENS:

There has been a change of government. It began two years ago, when the House of Representatives became Democratic by a decisive majority. It has now been completed.

The Senate about to assemble will also be Democratic. The offices of President and Vice-President have been put into the hands of Democrats. What does the change mean? That is the question that is uppermost in our minds to-day. That is the question I am going to try to answer, in order, if I may, to interpret the occasion.

It means much more than the mere success of a party. The success of a party means little except when the Nation is using that party for a large and definite purpose. No one can mistake the purpose for which the Nation now seeks to use the Democratic Party. It seeks to use it to interpret a change in its own plans and point of view. Some old things with which we had grown familiar, and which had begun to creep into the very habit of our thought and of our lives, have altered their aspect as we have latterly looked critically upon them, with fresh, awakened eyes; have dropped their disguises and shown themselves alien and sinister. Some new things, as we look frankly upon them, willing to comprehend their real character, have come to assume the aspect of things long believed in and familiar, stuff of our own convictions. We have been refreshed by a new insight into our own life.

We see that in many things that life is very great. It is incomparably great in its material aspects, in its body of wealth, in the diversity and sweep of its energy, in the industries which have been conceived and built up by the genius of individual men and the limitless enterprise of groups of men. It is great, also, very great, in its moral force.

Nowhere else in the world have noble men and women exhibited in more striking forms the beauty and the energy of sympathy and helpfulness and counsel in their efforts to rectify wrong, alleviate suffering, and set the weak in the way of strength and hope. We have built up, moreover, a great system of government, which has stood through a long age as in many respects a model for those who seek to set liberty upon foundations that will endure against fortuitous change, against storm and accident. Our life contains every great thing, and contains it in rich abundance.

But the evil has come with the good, and much fine gold has been corroded. With riches has come inexcusable waste. We have squandered a great part of what we might have used, and have not stopped to conserve the exceeding bounty of nature, without which our genius for enterprise would have been worthless and impotent, scorning to be careful, shamefully prodigal as well as admirably efficient. We have been proud of our industrial achievements, but we have not hitherto stopped thoughtfully enough to count the human cost, the cost of lives snuffed out, of energies overtaxed and broken, the fearful physical and spiritual cost to the men and women and children upon whom the dead weight and burden of it all has fallen pitilessly the years through. The groans and agony of it all had not yet reached our ears, the solemn, moving undertone of our life, coming

up out of the mines and factories and out of every home where the struggle had its intimate and familiar seat. With the great Government went many deep secret things which we too long delayed to look into and scrutinize with candid, fearless eyes. The great Government we loved has too often been made use of for private and selfish purposes, and those who used it had forgotten the people.

At last a vision has been vouchsafed us of our life as a whole. We see the bad with the good, the debased and decadent with the sound and vital. With this vision we approach new affairs. Our duty is to cleanse, to reconsider, to restore, to correct the evil without impairing the good, to purify and humanize every process of our common life without weakening or sentimentalizing it. There has been something crude and heartless and unfeeling in our haste to succeed and be great. Our thought has been "Let every man look out for himself, let every generation look out for itself," while we reared giant machinery which made it impossible that any but those who stood at the levers of control should have a chance to look out for themselves. We had not forgotten our morals. We remembered well enough that we had set up a policy which was meant to serve the humblest as well as the most powerful, with an eye single to the standards of justice and fair play, and remembered it with pride. But we were very heedless and in a hurry to be great.

We have come now to the sober second thought. The scales of heedlessness have fallen from our eyes. We have made up our minds to square every process of our national life again with the standards we so proudly set up at the beginning and have always carried at our hearts. Our work is a work of restoration.

We have itemized with some degree of particularity the things that ought to be altered and here are some of the chief items: A tariff which cuts us off from our proper part in the commerce of the world, violates the just principles of taxation, and makes the Government a facile instrument in the hands of private interests; a banking and currency system based upon the necessity of the Government to sell its bonds fifty years ago and perfectly adapted to concentrating cash and restricting credits; an industrial system which, take it on all its sides, financial as well as administrative, holds capital in leading strings, restricts the liberties and limits the opportunities of labor, and exploits without renewing or conserving the natural resources of the country; a body of agricultural activities never yet given the efficiency of great business undertakings or served as it should be through the instrumentality of science taken directly to the farm, or afforded the facilities of credit best suited to its practical needs; water-courses undeveloped, waste places unreclaimed, forests untended, fast disappearing without plan or prospect of renewal, unregarded waste heaps at every mine. We have studied as perhaps no other nation has the most effective means of production, but we have not studied cost or economy as we should either as organizers of industry, as statesmen, or as individuals.

Nor have we studied and perfected the means by which government may be put at the service of humanity, in safeguarding the health of the Nation, the health of its men and its women and its children, as well as their rights in the struggle for existence. This is no sentimental duty. The firm basis of government is justice, not pity. These are matters of justice. There can be no equality or opportunity, the first essential of justice in the body politic, if men and women and children be not shielded in their lives, their very vitality, from the consequences of great industrial and social processes which they can not alter, control, or singly cope with. Society must see to it that it does not itself crush or weaken or damage its own constituent parts. The first duty of law is to keep sound the society it serves. Sanitary laws, pure food laws, and laws determining conditions of labor which individuals are powerless to determine for themselves are intimate parts of the very business of justice and legal efficiency.

These are some of the things we ought to do, and not leave the others undone, the old-fashioned, never-to-be-neglected, fundamental safeguarding of property and of individual right. This is the high enterprise of the new day: To lift everything that concerns our life as a Nation to the light that shines from the hearthfire of every man's conscience and vision of the right. It is inconceivable that we should do this as partisans; it is inconceivable we should do it in ignorance of the facts as they are or in blind haste. We shall restore, not destroy. We shall deal with our economic system as it is and as it may be modified, not as it might be if we had a clean sheet of paper to write upon; and step by step we shall make it what it should be, in the spirit of those who question their own wisdom and seek counsel and knowledge, not shallow self-satisfaction or the excitement of excursions whither they can not tell. Justice, and only justice, shall alway be our motto.

And yet it will be no cool process of mere science. The Nation has been deeply stirred, stirred by a solemn passion, stirred by the knowledge of wrong, of ideals lost, of government too often debauched and made an instrument of evil. The feelings with which we face this new age of right and opportunity sweep across our heartstrings like some air out of God's own presence, where justice and mercy are reconciled and the judge and the brother are one. We know our task to be no mere task of politics but a task which shall search us through and through, whether we be able to understand our time and the need of our people, whether we be indeed their spokesmen and interpreters, whether we have the pure heart to comprehend and the rectified will to choose our high course of action.

This is not a day of triumph; it is a day of dedication. Here muster, not the forces of party, but the forces of humanity. Men's hearts wait upon us; men's lives hang in the balance; men's hopes call upon us to say what we will do. Who shall live up to the great trust? Who dares fail to try? I summon all honest men, all patriotic, all forward-looking men, to my side. God helping me, I will not fail them, if they will but counsel and sustain me!

390. THE REPUDIATION OF "DOLLAR DIPLOMACY"

Statement from President Wilson
March 19, 1913

(American Journal of International Law, Vol. VII, p. 338-9)

For the history of the Chinese loan see Doc. No. 386. The American bankers acquiesced in the position of the Government and withdrew from the consortium.

We are informed that at the request of the last administration a certain group of American bankers undertook to participate in the loan now desired by the Government of China (approximately $125,000,000.) Our government wished American bankers to participate along with the bankers of other nations, because it desired that the good will of the United States towards China should be exhibited in this practical way, that American capital should have access to that great country, and that the United States should be in a position to share with the other Powers any political responsibilities that might be associated with the development of the foreign relations of China in connection with her industrial and commercial enterprises. The present administration has been asked by this group of bankers whether it would also request them to participate in the loan. The representatives of the bankers through whom the administration was approached declared that they would continue to seek their share of the loan under the proposed agreements only if expressly requested to do so by the government. The administration has declined to make such request because it did not approve the conditions of the loan or the implications of responsibility on its own part which it was plainly told would be involved in the request.

The conditions of the loan seem to us to touch very nearly the administrative independence of China itself; and this administration does not feel that it ought, even by implication, to be a party to those conditions. The responsibility on its part which would be implied in requesting the bankers to undertake the loan might conceivably go to the length in some unhappy contingency of forcible interference in the financial, and even the political, affairs of that great oriental state, just now awakening to a consciousness of its power and its obligations to its people. The conditions include not only the pledging of particular taxes, some of them antiquated and burdensome, to secure the loan, but also the administration of those taxes by foreign agents. The responsibility on the part of our government implied in the encouragement of a loan thus secured and administered is plain enough and is obnoxious to the principles upon which the government of our people rests.

The Government of the United States is not only willing, but earnestly desirous, of aiding the great Chinese people in every way that is consistent with their untrammeled development and its own immemorial principles. The awakening of the people of China to a consciousness of their possibilities under free government is the most significant, if not the most momentous event of our generation. With this movement and aspiration the American people are in profound sympathy. They certainly wish to participate, and participate very generously, in opening to the Chinese and to the use of the world the almost untouched and perhaps unrivalled resources of China.

The Government of the United States is earnestly desirous of promoting the most extended and intimate trade relationships between this country and the Chinese Republic. . . . This is the main material interest of its citizens in the development of China. Our interests are those of the open door—a door of friendship and mutual advantage. This is the only door we care to enter.

391. TARIFF REVISION UNDER WILSON

Address of President Wilson to Congress asking revision of the Payne-Aldrich Tariff
April 8, 1913

(Congressional Record, 63d Congress, 1st Session, Vol. L, p. 130 ff.)

Wilson had pledged tariff reform in his campaign for the presidency; immediately upon his accession to office he called Congress into a special session, and on April 8, reviving a custom that had not been observed since Jefferson, addressed Congress in person. In response to Wilson's demand for downward revision Congress promptly passed the Underwood tariff which became law October 3, 1913. See, R. S. Baker, *Woodrow Wilson, Life and Letters,* Vol. IV, ch. iii.; F. W. Taussig, *Tariff History of the United States,* 1931 ed.; H. P. Willis, "The Tariff of 1913," *Journal Pol. Econ.* Vol. XXII.

GENTLEMEN OF THE CONGRESS:

. . . I have called the Congress together in extraordinary session because a duty was laid upon the party now in power at the recent elections which it ought to perform promptly, in order that the burden carried by the people under existing law may be lightened as soon as possible, and in order, also, that the business interests of the country may not be kept too long in suspense as to what the fiscal changes are to be to which they will be required to adjust themselves. It is clear to the whole country that the tariff duties must be altered. They must be changed to meet the radical alteration in the conditions of our economic life which the country has witnessed within the last generation. While the whole face and method of our industrial and commercial life were being changed beyond recognition the tariff schedules have remained what they were before the change began, or have moved in the direction they were given when no large circumstance of our industrial development was what it is to-day. Our task is to square them with the actual facts. The sooner that is done the sooner we shall escape from suffering from the facts and the sooner our men of business will be free to thrive by the law of nature—the nature of free business—instead of by the law of legislation and artificial arrangement.

We have seen tariff legislation wander very far afield in our day—very far indeed from the field in which our prosperity might have had a normal growth and stimulation. No one who looks the facts squarely in the face or knows anything that lies beneath the surface of action can fail to perceive the principles upon which recent tariff legislation has been based. We long ago passed beyond the modest notion of "protecting" the industries of the country and moved boldly forward to the idea that they were entitled to the direct patronage of the Government. For a long time—a time so long that the men now active in public policy hardly remember the conditions that preceded it—we have sought in our tariff schedules to give each group of manufacturers or producers what they themselves thought that they needed in order to maintain a practically exclusive market as against the rest of the world. Consciously or unconsciously, we have built up a set of privileges and exemptions from competition behind which it was easy by any, even the crudest, forms of combination to organize monopoly; until at last nothing is normal, nothing is obliged to stand the tests of efficiency and economy, in our world of big business, but everything thrives by concerted arrangement. Only new principles of action will save us from a final hard crystallization of monopoly and a complete loss of the influences that quicken enterprise and keep independent energy alive.

It is plain what those principles must be. We must abolish everything that bears even the semblance of privilege or of any kind of artificial advantage, and put our business men and producers under the stimulation of a constant necessity to be efficient, economical, and enterprising, masters of competitive supremacy, better workers and merchants than any in the world. Aside from the duties laid upon articles which we do not, and probably can not, produce, therefore, and the duties laid upon luxuries and merely for the sake of the revenues they yield, the object of the tariff duties henceforth laid must be effective competition, the whetting of American wits by contest with the wits of the rest of the world.

It would be unwise to move toward this end headlong, with reckless haste, or with strokes that cut at the very roots of what has grown up amongst us by long process and at our own invitation. It does not alter a thing to upset it and break it and deprive it of a chance to change. It destroys it. We must make changes in our fiscal laws, in our fiscal system, whose object is development, a more free and wholesome development, not revolution or upset or confusion. We must build up trade, especially foreign trade. We need the outlet and the enlarged field of energy more than we ever did before. We must build up industry as well, and must adopt freedom in the place of artificial stimulation only so far as it will build, not pull down. In dealing with the tariff the method by which this may be done will be a matter of judgment exercised item by item. To some not accustomed to the excitements and responsibilities of greater freedom our methods may in some respects and at some points seem heroic but remedies may be heroic and yet be remedies. It is our business to make sure that they are genuine remedies. Our object is clear. If our motive is above just challenge and only an occasional error of judgment is chargeable against us, we shall be fortunate.

We are called upon to render the country a great service in more matters than one. Our responsibility should be met and our methods should be thorough, as thorough as moderate and well considered, based upon the facts as they are, and not worked out as if we were beginners. We are to deal with the facts of our own day, with the facts of no other and to make laws which square with those facts. It is best, indeed it is necessary, to begin with the tariff. . . .

392. WILSON'S DENUNCIATION OF THE TARIFF LOBBY

Statement to the Press
May 26, 1913

(Associated Press Dispatch, Washington, May 26, 1913)

I think that the public ought to know the extraordinary exertions being made by the lobby in Washington to gain recognition for certain alterations of the Tariff bill. Washington has seldom seen so numerous, so industrious or so insidious a lobby. The newspapers are being filled with paid advertisements calculated to mislead the judgement of public men not only, but also the public opinion of the country itself. There is every evidence that money without limit is being spent to sustain this lobby and to create an appearance of a pressure of opinion antagonistic to some of the chief items of the Tariff bill.

It is of serious interest to the country that the people at large should have no lobby and be voiceless in these matters, while great bodies of astute men seek to create an artificial opinion and to overcome the interests of the public for their private profit. It is thoroughly worth the while of the people of this country to take knowledge of this matter. Only public opinion can check and destroy it.

The Government in all its branches ought to be relieved from this intolerable burden and this constant interruption to the calm progress of debate. I know that in this I am speaking for the members of the two Houses who would rejoice as much as I would to be released from this unbearable situation.

393. WILSON'S SPECIAL MESSAGE ON MEXICAN RELATIONS
August 27, 1913

(Congressional Record, 63d Congress, 1st. Sess., Vol. 50, p. 3803–04)

The Mexican situation reached a crisis in the summer of 1913. For the diplomatic and political background of our relations with Mexico at this time, see J. F. Rippy, *The United States and Mexico*, ch. xx; E. E. Robinson and V. J. West, *The Foreign Policy of Woodrow Wilson, passim;* R. S. Baker, *Woodrow Wilson, Life and Letters,* Vol. IV, ch. vi; J. M. Callahan, *American Foreign Policy in Mexican Relations,* ch. xiv.

Gentlemen of the Congress: It is clearly my duty to lay before you, very fully and without reservation, the facts concerning our present relations with the Republic of Mexico. The deplorable posture of affairs in Mexico I need not describe, but I deem it my duty to speak very frankly of what this Government has done and should seek to do in fulfillment of its obligation to Mexico herself, as a friend and neighbor, and to American citizens whose lives and vital interests are daily affected by the distressing conditions which now obtain beyond our southern border. . . .

The peace, prosperity and contentment of Mexico mean more, much more, to us than merely an enlarged field for our commerce and enterprise. They mean an enlargement of the field of self-government and the realization of the hopes and rights of a nation with whose best aspirations, so long suppressed and disappointed, we deeply sympathize. We shall yet prove to the Mexican people that we know how to serve them without first thinking how we shall serve ourselves. . . .

Mexico has a great and enviable future before her, if only she choose and attain the paths of honest constitutional government.

The present circumstances of the Republic, I deeply regret to say, do not seem to promise even the foundations of such a peace. We have waited many months, months full of peril and anxiety for the conditions there to improve, and they have not improved. They have grown worse, rather. . . . War and disorder, devastation and confusion, seem to threaten to become the settled fortune of the distracted country. As friends we could wait no longer for a solution which every week seemed further away. It was our duty at least to volunteer our good offices—to offer to assist, if we might, in effecting some arrangement which would bring relief and peace and set up a universally acknowledged political authority there.

Accordingly, I took the liberty of sending the Hon. John Lind, formerly governor of Minnesota, as my personal spokesman and representative, to the City of Mexico, with the following instructions:
[Instructions follow]. . . .

Mr. Lind executed his delicate and difficult mission with singular tact, firmness, and good judgement, and made clear to the authorities at the City of Mexico not only the purpose of his visit but also the spirit in which it had been undertaken. But the proposals he submitted were rejected. . . .

I am led to believe that they were rejected partly because the authorities at Mexico City had, been grossly misinformed and misled upon two points. They did not realize the spirit of the American people in this matter, their earnest friendliness and yet sober determination that some just solution be found for the Mexican difficulties; and they did not believe that the present administration spoke through Mr. Lind for the people of the United States. The effect of this unfortunate misunderstanding on their part is to leave them singularly isolated and without friends who can effectually aid them. So long as the misunderstanding continues we can only await the time of their awakening to a realization of the actual facts. We can not thrust our good offices upon them. The situation must be given a little more time to work itself out in the new circumstances; and I believe that only a little more will be necessary. For the circumstances are new. The rejection of our friendship makes them new and will inevitably bring its own alterations in the whole aspect of affairs. The actual situation of the authorities at Mexico City will presently be revealed.

Meanwhile what is it our duty to do? Clearly everything that we do must be rooted in patience and done with calm and disinterested deliberation. Impatience on our part would be childish, and would be fraught with every risk of wrong and folly. We can afford to exercise the self-restraint of a really great nation which realizes its own strength and scorns to misuse it. It was our duty to offer our active assistance. It is now our duty to show what true neutrality will do to enable the people of Mexico to set their affairs in order again, and wait for a further opportunity to offer our friendly counsels. The door is not closed against the resumption, either upon the initiative of Mexico or upon our own, of the effort to bring order out of the confusion by friendly cooperative action, should fortunate occasion offer.

While we wait, the contest of the rival forces will undoubtedly for a little while be sharper than ever, just because it will be plain that an end must be made of the existing situation, and that very promptly; and with the increased activity of the contending factions will come, it is to be feared, increased danger to the non-combatants in Mexico, as well as to those actually in the field of battle. The position of outsiders is always particularly trying and full of hazard where there is civil strife and a whole country is upset. We should earnestly urge all Americans to leave Mexico at once, and should assist them to get away in every way possible—not because we would mean to slacken in the least our efforts to safeguard their lives and their interests, but because it is imperative that they should take no unnecessary risks when it is physically possible for them to leave the country. We should let every one who assumes to exercise authority in any part of Mexico know in the most unequivocal way that we shall vigilantly watch the fortunes of those Americans who can not get away, and shall hold those responsible for their sufferings and losses to a definite reckoning. That can be and will be made plain beyond the possibility of a misunderstanding.

For the rest, I deem it my duty to exercise the authority conferred upon me by the law of March 14, 1912, to see to it that neither side of the struggle now going on in Mexico receive any assistance from this side the border. I shall follow the best practice of nations in the matter of neutrality by forbidding the exportation of arms or munitions of war of any kind from the United States to any part of the Republic of Mexico—a policy suggested by several interesting precedents and certainly dictated by many manifest considerations of practical expediency. We can not in the circumstances be partisans of either party to the contest that now distracts Mexico, or constitute ourselves the virtual umpire between them.

I am happy to say that several of the great Governments of the world have given this Government their generous moral support in urging upon the provisional authorities at the City of Mexico the acceptance of our proffered offices in the spirit in which they were made. . . .

394. WILSON'S MOBILE ADDRESS
October 27, 1913

(U. S. 63d Congress, 1st Session, *Senate Doc. 226*)

This address delivered before the Southern Commercial Congress at Mobile, Alabama, announced the Wilson policy toward Latin-America. Though the promises of this address were not consistently observed, relations with the Latin-American states were materially improved during the Wilson administrations. See, E. E. Robinson and V. J. West, *The Foreign Policy of Woodrow Wilson;* J. F. Rippy, *The United States and Mexico*, ch. xx; R. S. Baker, *Woodrow Wilson, Life and Letters,* Vol. IV, chs. ii, vi.

. . . The future, ladies and gentlemen, is going to be very different for this hemisphere from the past. These States lying to the south of us, which have always been our neighbors, will now be drawn closer to us by innumerable ties, and, I hope, chief of all, by the tie of a common understanding of each other. Interest does not tie nations together; it sometimes separates them. But sympathy and understanding does unite them, and I believe that by the new route that is just

about to be opened, while we physically cut two continents asunder, we spiritually unite them. It is a spiritual union which we seek. . . .

There is one peculiarity about the history of the Latin American States which I am sure they are keenly aware of. You hear of "concessions" to foreign capitalists in Latin America. You do not hear of concessions to foreign capitalists in the United States. They are not granted concessions. They are invited to make investments. The work is ours, though they are welcome to invest in it. We do not ask them to supply the capital and do the work. It is an invitation, not a privilege; and States that are obliged, because their territory does not lie within the main field of modern enterprise and action, to grant concessions are in this condition, that foreign interests are apt to dominate their domestic affairs, a condition of affairs always dangerous and apt to become intolerable.

What these States are going to see, therefore, is an emancipation from the subordination, which has been inevitable, to foreign enterprise and an assertion of the splendid character which, in spite of these difficulties, they have again and again been able to demonstrate. The dignity, the courage, the self-possession, the self-respect of the Latin American States, their achievements in the face of all these adverse circumstances, deserve nothing but the admiration and applause of the world. They have had harder bargains driven with them in the matter of loans than any other peoples in the world. Interest has been exacted of them that was not exacted of anybody else, because the risk was said to be greater; and then securities were taken that destroyed the risk—an admirable arrangement for those who were forcing the terms! I rejoice in nothing so much as in the prospect that they will now be emancipated from these conditions, and we ought to be the first to take part in assisting in that emancipation. I think some of these gentlemen have already had occasion to bear witness that the Department of State in recent months has tried to serve them in that wise. In the future they will draw closer and closer to us because of circumstances of which I wish to speak with moderation and, I hope, without indiscretion.

We must prove ourselves their friends, and champions upon terms of equality and honor. You cannot be friends upon any other terms than upon the terms of equality. You cannot be friends at all except upon the terms of honor. We must show ourselves friends by comprehending their interest whether it squares with our own interest or not. It is a very perilous thing to determine the foreign policy of a nation in the terms of material interest. It not only is unfair to those with whom you are dealing, but it is degrading as regards your own actions.

Comprehension must be the soil in which shall grow all the fruits of friendship, and there is a reason and a compulsion lying behind all this which is dearer than anything else to the thoughtful men of America. I mean the development of constitutional liberty in the world. Human rights, national integrity, and opportunity as against material interests—that, ladies and gentlemen, is the issue which we now have to face. I want to take this occasion to say that the United States will never again seek one additional foot of territory by conquest. She will devote herself to showing that she knows how to make honorable and fruitful use of the territory she has, and she must regard it as one of the duties of friendship to see that from no quarter are material interests made superior to human liberty and national opportunity. I say this, not with a single thought that anyone will gainsay it, but merely to fix in our consciousness what our real relationship with the rest of America is. It is the relationship of a family of mankind devoted to the development of true constitutional liberty. We know that that is the soil out of which the best enterprise springs. We know that this is a cause which we are making in common with our neighbors, because we have had to make it for ourselves.

Reference has been made here to-day to some of the national problems which confront us as a Nation. What is at the heart of all our national problems? It is that we have seen the hand of material interest sometimes about to close upon our dearest rights and possessions. We have seen material interests threaten constitutional freedom in the United States. Therefore we will now know how to sympathize with those in the rest of America who have to contend with such powers, not only within their borders but from outside their borders also. . . .

In emphasizing the points which must unite us in sympathy and in spiritual interest with the Latin American peoples, we are only emphasizing the points of our own life, and we should prove ourselves untrue to our own traditions if we proved ourselves untrue friends to them. . . .

395. THE TAMPICO INCIDENT

Address of President Wilson to Congress on the Mexican Crisis
April 20, 1914

(Foreign Relations of the United States, 1914, p. 474 ff.)

On April 9 several sailors from the U. S. S. *Dolphin* were arrested at Tampico by officers of President Huerta. Admiral Mayo at once demanded an apology and a salute of twenty-one guns. This demand was sustained by the American government, though in as much as the United States did not recognize Huerta, it presented obvious legal difficulties. Huerta refused to comply with the American demands, and April 20 Wilson appeared before Congress and asked for authority to take such action as the situation required. The House, by a vote of 323–29, and the Senate by a vote of 72–13, gave Wilson the necessary authority. On the 22d, Admiral Fletcher landed marines at Vera Cruz, seized the customs house and prevented the landing of munitions from a German ship. This action brought the United States and Mexico to the verge of war, and threatened, moreover, to unite all of Mexico behind Huerta. From this unhappy situation both nations were rescued by the timely intervention of the A.B.C. powers with the offer of mediation. See Doc. No. 396. For the Tampico incident, see R. S. Baker, *Woodrow Wilson*, Vol. IV, p. 313 ff.; M. E. Curti, *Bryan and World Peace*, p. 181 ff.; C. P. Lamar, *Life of Joseph Rucker Lamar;* J. M. Callahan, *American Foreign Relations in Mexican Policy*. The official correspondence can be found in *Foreign Relations of the United States*, 1914.

Gentlemen of the Congress:

It is my duty to call your attention to a situation which has arisen in our dealings with General Victoriano Huerta at Mexico City which calls for action, and to ask your advice and cooperation in acting upon it. On the 9th of April a paymaster of the U.S.S. *Dolphin* landed at the Iturbide Bridge landing at Tampico with a whaleboat and boat's crew to take off certain supplies needed by his ship, and while engaged in loading the boat was arrested by an officer and squad of men of the army of General Huerta. . . . Admiral Mayo regarded the arrest as so serious an affront that he was not satisfied with the apologies offered, but demanded that the flag of the United States be saluted with special ceremony by the military commander of the port.

The incident can not be regarded as a trivial one, especially as two of the men arrested were taken from the boat itself—that is to say, from the territory of the United States—but had it stood by itself it might have been attributed to the ignorance or arrogance of a single officer. Unfortunately, it was not an isolated case. A series of incidents have recently occurred which can not but create the impression that the representatives of General Huerta were willing to go out of their way to show disregard for the dignity and rights of this Government and felt perfectly safe in doing what they pleased, making free to show in many ways their irritation and contempt. . . .

The manifest danger of such a situation was that such offenses might grow from bad to worse until something happened of so gross and intolerable a sort as to lead directly and inevitably to armed conflict. It was necessary that the apologies of General Huerta and his representatives should go much further, that they should be such as to attract the attention of the whole population to their significance, and such as to impress upon General Huerta himself the necessity of seeing to it that no further occasion for explanations and professed regrets should arise. I, therefore, felt it my duty to sustain Admiral Mayo in the whole of his demand and to insist that the flag of the United States should be saluted in such a way as to indicate a new spirit and attitude on the part of the Huertistas.

Such a salute, General Huerta has refused, and I have come to ask your approval and support in the course I now propose to pursue.

This Government can, I earnestly hope, in no circumstances be forced into war with the people of Mexico. Mexico is torn by civil strife. If we are to accept the tests of its own constitution, it has no government. General Huerta has set his power up in the City of Mexico, such as it is, without right and by methods for which there can be no justification. Only part of the country is under his control. If armed conflict should unhappily come as a result of his attitude of personal resentment toward this Government, we should be fighting only General Huerta and those who adhere to him and give him their support, and our object would be only to restore to the people of the distracted Republic the opportunity to set up again their own laws and their own government.

But I earnestly hope that war is not now in question. I believe I speak for the American people when I say that we do not desire to control in any degree the affairs of our sister Republic. Our feeling for the people of Mexico is one of deep and genuine friendship, and every thing that we have so far done or refrained from doing has proceeded from our desire to help them, not to hinder or embarrass them. We would not wish even to exercise the good offices of friendship without their welcome and consent. The people of Mexico are entitled to settle their own domestic affairs in their own way, and we sincerely desire to respect their right. The present situation need have none of the grave

implications of interference if we deal with it promptly, firmly, and wisely.

No doubt I could do what is necessary in the circumstances to enforce respect for our Government without recourse to the Congress, and yet not exceed my constitutional powers as President; but I do not wish to act in a manner possibly of so grave consequence except in close conference and cooperation with both the Senate and House. I, therefore, come to ask your approval that I should use the armed forces of the United States in such ways and to such an extent as may be necessary to obtain from General Huerta and his adherents the fullest recognition of the rights and dignity of the United States, even amidst the distressing conditions now unhappily obtaining in Mexico.

There can in what we do be no thought of aggression or of selfish aggrandizement. We seek to maintain the dignity and authority of the United States only because we wish always to keep our great influence unimpaired for the uses of liberty, both in the United States and wherever else it may be employed for the benefit of mankind.

396. MEDIATION PROTOCOL OF THE A.B.C. CONFERENCE
Niagara Falls, New York, June 12, 1914

(Foreign Relations of the United States, 1914, p. 548–9)

President Wilson's opposition to Huerta led to retaliations by Huerta against American citizens; when the Mexican President refused to apologize for arresting American marines at Tampico, Wilson ordered the occupation of Vera Cruz. The situation was rapidly shaping up for war when Wilson was saved by an offer of mediation by Argentina, Brazil and Chile. Huerta was soon driven out of Mexico, and another conference of the A.B.C. powers, several lesser Latin American states and the United States, decided to recognize Carranza. The A.B.C. Conference is important not so much for its accomplishments as for the indication of the willingness of the United States to admit Latin American nations to joint responsibility for the maintenance of American policies. Other documents on the Conference can be found in *Foreign Relations of the United States,* 1914, p. 487 ff. A convenient summary is in *Publications of the World Peace Foundation,* Vol. VI, No. 3. See also, J. F. Rippy, *The United States and Mexico,* ch. xx; E. E. Robinson and V. J. West, *Foreign Policy of Woodrow Wilson;* J. M. Callahan, *American Foreign Policy in Mexican Relations.*

Protocol No. 3, June 12, 1914.

A Provisional Government for the United Mexican States, constituted as hereinafter provided, shall be recognized at Mexico City at noon on the ——— day of ——— 1914, from which time it shall exercise governmental power until the inauguration of a Constitutional President.

Protocol No. 4, June 24, 1914.

I.

The Provisional Government referred to in protocol No. 3 shall be constituted by agreement of the delegates representing the parties between which the internal struggle in Mexico is taking place.

II.

A. Upon the constitution of the Provisional Government in the City of Mexico, the Government of the United States of

America will recognize it immediately and thereupon diplomatic relations between the two countries will be restored.

B. The Government of the United States of America will not in any form whatsoever claim a war indemnity or other international satisfaction.

C. The Provisional Government will proclaim an absolute amnesty to all foreigners for any and all political offenses committed during the period of civil war in Mexico.

D. The Provisional Government will negotiate for the constitution of international commission for the settlement of the claims of foreigners on account of damages sustained during the period of civil war as a consequence of military acts or the acts of national authorities.

III.

The three mediating Governments agree on their part to recognize the Provisional Government organized as provided by Section I of this protocol.

397. WILSON'S PANAMA CANAL TOLLS MESSAGE
Address to Congress March 5, 1914

(Congressional Record, 63d Congress, 2d Session, Vol. LI, p. 4313)

The Panama Canal Act of August 24, 1912 exempted vessels engaged in the coastwise trade of the United States from payment of the customary canal tolls. Great Britain protested that this exemption constituted a breach of the Canal Treaty of 1901, Article III, sec. 1; see Doc. No. 355. Congress yielded to the President's demand and required equality of charges on all vessels. Wilson's position on this question aroused general approval in the United States and Great Britain, and was instrumental in persuading Great Britain to follow Wilson's leadership in Mexican relations. See, R. S. Baker, *Woodrow Wilson,* Vol. IV, ch. viii.

Gentlemen of the Congress:

I have come to you upon an errand which can be very briefly performed, but I beg that you will not measure its importance by the number of sentences in which I state it. No communication I have addressed to the Congress carried with it graver or more far-reaching implications as to the interest of the country, and I come now to speak upon a matter with regard to which I am charged in a peculiar degree, by the Constitution itself, with personal responsibility.

I have come to ask you for the repeal of that provision of the Panama Canal Act of August 24, 1912, which exempts vessels engaged in the coastwise trade of the United States from payment of tolls, and to urge upon you the justice, the wisdom, and the large policy of such a repeal with the utmost earnestness of which I am capable.

In my own judgment, very fully considered and maturely formed, that exemption constitutes a mistaken economic policy from every point of view, and is, moreover, in plain contravention of the treaty with Great Britain concerning the canal concluded on November 18, 1901. But I have not come to urge upon you my personal views. I have come to state to you a fact and a situation. Whatever may be our own differences of opinion concerning this much debated measure, its meaning is not debated outside the United States. Everywhere else the language of the treaty is given but one interpretation, and that interpretation precludes the exemption I am asking you to repeal. We consented to the treaty; its language we accepted, if we did not originate it; and we are too big, too powerful, too self-respecting a nation to interpret with a too strained or refined reading the words of our own promises just because we have power enough to give us leave to read them as we please. The large thing to do is the only thing we can afford to do, a voluntary withdrawal from a position everywhere questioned and misunderstood. We ought to reverse our action without raising the question whether we were right or wrong, and so once more deserve our reputation for generosity and for the redemption of every obligation without quibble or hesitation.

I ask this of you in support of the foreign policy of the administration. I shall not know how to deal with other matters of even greater delicacy and nearer consequence if you do not grant it to me in ungrudging measure.

398. THE BRYAN-CHAMORRO CONVENTION
August 5, 1914

(*U. S. Statutes at Large,* Vol. XXXIX, p. 1661 ff.)

The United States had been interested in an Isthmian canal across Nicaragua for three-quarters of a century. For the first convention granting the United States right of transit, that of 1867, see Malloy, ed., *Treaties, Conventions,* etc., Vol. II, p. 1279 ff. The Bryan-Chamorro Convention by which the United States secured lease to the Great Corn and Little Corn islands and the Gulf of Fonseca was regarded by other Central American States as an infringement on Nicaraguan sovereignty. Costa Rica and Salvador denounced the convention before the Central American Court of Justice. The Court upheld this protest and ruled against the United States. Both Nicaragua and the United States disregarded the ruling of the Court, and it came to an inglorious end. See S. Nearing and J. Freeman, *Dollar Diplomacy;* D. G. Munro, *The Five Republics of Central America;* I. J. Cox, *Nicaragua and the United States;* M. W. Williams, *Anglo-American Isthmian Diplomacy;* H. G. Miller, *The Isthmian Highway,* ch. xvi.

ART. I. The Government of Nicaragua grants in perpetuity to the Government of the United States, forever free from all taxation or other public charge, the exclusive proprietary rights necessary and convenient for the construction, operation and maintenance of an inter-oceanic canal by way of the San Juan River and the great Lake of Nicaragua or by way of any route over Nicaraguan territory, the details of the terms upon which such canal shall be constructed, operated and maintained to be agreed to by the two governments whenever the Government of the United States shall notify the Government of Nicaragua of its desire or intention to construct such canal.

ART. II. To enable the Government of the United States to protect the Panama Canal and the proprietary rights granted to the Government of the United States by the foregoing article, and also to enable the Government of the United States to take any measure necessary to the ends contemplated herein, the Government of Nicaragua hereby leases for a term of ninety-nine years to the Government of the United States the islands in the Caribbean Sea known as Great Corn Island and Little Corn Island; and the Gov-

ernment of Nicaragua further grants to the Government of the United States for a like period of ninety-nine years the right to establish, operate and maintain a naval base at such place on the territory of Nicaragua bordering upon the Gulf of Fonseca as the Government of the United States may select. The Government of the United States shall have the option of renewing for a further term of ninety-nine years the above leases and grants upon the expiration of their respective terms, it being expressly agreed that the territory hereby leased and the naval base which may be maintained under the grant aforesaid shall be subject exclusively to the laws and sovereign authority of the United States during the terms of such lease and grant and of any renewal or renewals thereof.

ART. III. In consideration of the foregoing stipulations and for the purposes contemplated by this Convention and for the purpose of reducing the present indebtedness of Nicaragua, the Government of the United States shall, upon the date of the exchange of ratification of this Convention, pay for the benefit of the Republic of Nicaragua the sum of three million dollars United States gold coin, of the present weight and fineness, to be deposited to the order of the Government of Nicaragua in such bank or banks or with such banking corporation as the Government of the United States may determine, to be applied by Nicaragua upon its indebtedness or other public purposes for the advancement of the welfare of Nicaragua in a manner to be determined by the two High Contracting Parties, all such disbursements to be made by orders drawn by the Minister of Finance of the Republic of Nicaragua and approved by the Secretary of State of the United States or by such person as he may designate.

This Convention shall be ratified by the High Contracting Parties in accordance with their respective laws, and the ratifications thereof shall be exchanged at Washington as soon as possible. . . .

WILLIAM JENNINGS BRYAN.
EMILIANO CHAMORRO.

399. HOUSTON, EAST & WEST TEXAS RAILWAY COMPANY v. UNITED STATES
234 U. S. 342
1914

Appeal from the United States Commerce Court. Suit to set aside order of the Interstate Commerce Commission regulating railway rates. This case is generally known as the Shreveport Case.

HUGHES, C. J. These suits were brought in the commerce court . . . to set aside an order of the Interstate Commerce Commission, dated March 11, 1912, upon the ground that it exceeded the Commission's authority. . . .

The gravamen of the complaint, said the Interstate Commerce Commission, was that the carriers made rates out of Dallas and other Texas points into eastern Texas which were much lower than those which they extended into Texas from Shreveport. The situation may be briefly described: Shreveport, Louisiana, is about 40 miles from the Texas state line, and 231 miles from Houston, Texas, on the line of the Houston, East & West Texas and Houston and Shreveport Companies; it is 189 miles from Dallas, Texas, on the line of the Texas & Pacific. Shreveport competes with both cities for the trade of the intervening territory. The rates on these lines from Dallas and Houston, respectively, eastward to intermediate points, in Texas, were much less, according to distance, than from Shreveport westward to the same points. It is undisputed that the difference was substantial, and injuriously affected the commerce of Shreveport. . . .

The Interstate Commerce Commission found that the interstate class rates out of Shreveport to named Texas points were unreasonable, and it established maximum class rates for this traffic. . . .

The point of the objection to the order is that, as the discrimination found by the Commission to be unjust arises out of the relation of intrastate rates, maintained under state authority, to interstate rates that have been upheld as reasonable, its correction was beyond the Commission's power. . . . The invalidity of the order is challenged upon two grounds:

1. That Congress is impotent to control the intrastate charges of an interstate carrier even to the extent necessary to prevent injurious discrimination against interstate traffic. . . .

Congress is empowered to regulate,—that is, to provide the law for the government of interstate commerce; to enact "all appropriate legislation" for its protection and advancement . . . As it is competent for Congress to legislate to these ends, unquestionably it may seek their attainment by requiring that the agencies of interstate commerce shall not be used in such manner as to cripple, retard, or destroy it. The fact that carriers are instruments of intrastate commerce, as well as of interstate commerce, does not derogate from the complete and paramount authority of Congress over the latter, or preclude the Federal power from being exerted to prevent the intrastate operations of such carriers from being made a means of injury to that which has been confided to Federal care. Wherever the interstate and intrastate transactions of carries are so related that the government of the one involves the control of the other, it is Congress, and not the state, that is entitled to prescribe the final and dominant rule, for otherwise Congress would be denied the exercise of its constitutional authority, and the state, and not the nation, would be supreme within the national field. . . .

It is for Congress to supply the needed correction where the relation between intrastate and interstate rates presents the evil to be corrected, and this it may do completely, by reason of its control over the interstate carrier in all matters having such a close and substantial relation to interstate commerce that it is necessary or appropriate to exercise the control for the effective government of that commerce.

It is also clear that, in removing the injurious discriminations against interstate traffic arising from the relation of intrastate to interstate rates, Congress is not bound to reduce the latter below what it may deem to be a proper standard fair to the carrier and to the public. Otherwise, it could prevent the injury to interstate commerce only by the sacrifice of its judgement as to interstate rates. Congress is entitled to maintain its own standard as to these rates, and to forbid any discriminatory action by interstate carriers which will obstruct the freedom of movement of interstate traffic over their lines in accordance with the terms it establishes.

Having this power, Congress could provide for its execution through the aid of a subordinate body; and we conclude that the order of the Commission now in question cannot be held invalid upon the ground that it exceeded the authority which Congress could lawfully confer. . . .

Decree of the Commerce Court affirmed. Justices LURTON and PITNEY dissenting.

400. WILSON'S APPEAL FOR NEUTRALITY
Message to Senate, August 19, 1914

(U. S. 63 Congress, 2nd Sess. *Senate Doc.* 566)

The outbreak of the World War in August, 1914 brought an immediate Proclamation of Neutrality, August 4, together with a proposal to "act in the interest of peace". Two weeks later President Wilson reinforced this official proclamation with an appeal for neutrality "in thought as well as in action."

My fellow countrymen: I suppose that every thoughtful man in America has asked himself, during these last troubled weeks, what influence the European war may exert upon the United States, and I take the liberty of addressing a few words to you in order to point out that it is entirely within our own choice what its effects upon us will be and to urge very earnestly upon you the sort of speech and conduct which will best safeguard the Nation against distress and disaster.

The effect of the war upon the United States will depend upon what American citizens say and do. Every man who really loves America will act and speak in the true spirit of neutrality, which is the spirit of impartiality and fairness and friendliness to all concerned. The spirit of the Nation in this critical matter will be determined largely by what individuals and society and those gathered in public meetings do and say, upon what newspapers and magazines contain, upon what ministers utter in their pulpits, and men proclaim as their opinions on the street.

The people of the United States are drawn from many nations, and chiefly from the nations now at war. It is natural and inevitable that there should be the utmost variety of sympathy and desire among them with regard to the issues and circumstances of the conflict. Some will wish one nation, others another, to succeed in the momentous struggle. It will be easy to excite passion and difficult to allay it. Those responsible for exciting it will assume a heavy responsibility, responsibility for no less a thing than that the people of the United States, whose love of their country and whose loyalty to its Government should unite them as Americans all, bound in honor and affection to think first of her and her interests, may be divided in camps of hostile opinion, hot against each other, involved in the war itself in impulse and opinion if not in action.

Such divisions amongst us would be fatal to our peace of mind and might seriously stand in the way of the proper performance of our duty as the one great nation at peace, the one people holding itself ready to play a part of impartial mediation and speak the counsels of peace and accommodation, not as a partisan, but as a friend.

I venture, therefore, my fellow countrymen, to speak a solemn word of warning to you against that deepest, most subtle, most essential breach of neutrality which may spring out of partisanship, out of passionately taking sides. The United States must be neutral in fact as well as in name during these days that are to try men's souls. We must be impartial in thought as well as in action, must put a curb upon our sentiments as well as upon every transaction that might be construed as a preference of one party to the struggle before another.

My thought is of America. I am speaking, I feel sure, the earnest wish and purpose of every thoughtful American that this great country of ours, which is, of course, the first in our thoughts and in our hearts, should show herself in this time of peculiar trial a Nation fit beyond others to exhibit the fine poise of undisturbed judgment, the dignity of self-control, the efficiency of dispassionate action; a Nation that neither sits in judgment upon others nor is disturbed in her own counsels and which keeps herself fit and free to do what is honest and disinterested and truly serviceable for the peace of the world.

Shall we not resolve to put upon ourselves the restraints which will bring to our people the happiness and the great and lasting influence for peace we covet for them?

401. TREATY OF ARBITRATION WITH CHINA
September 15, 1914

(American Journal of International Law, Supplement, Vol. X, p. 268)

When Bryan became Secretary of State he proceeded to put into effect a policy of the arbitration of international disputes that he had advocated since the beginning of his public career. These treaties called for the erection of arbitration commissions to adjudicate issues in dispute between the United States and other nations, and the suspension of all preparation for war for the period of one year. Bryan succeeded in concluding thirty of these treaties, and he regarded them as his most permanent claim to fame. See, M. E. Curti, *Bryan and World Peace;* C. L. Lange, *The American Peace Treaties;* P. Hibben, *The Peerless Leader,* ch. xxvii; the treaties are collected in *Treaties for the Advancement of Peace Negotiated by William Jennings Bryan.*

TREATY BETWEEN CHINA AND THE UNITED STATES FOR THE ADVANCEMENT OF PEACE

Signed at Washington, September 15, 1914; ratifications exchanged, October 22, 1915.

Art. I. Any disputes arising between the Government of the United States of America and the Government of the Republic of China, of whatever nature they may be, shall, when ordinary diplomatic proceedings have failed and the high contracting parties do not have recourse to arbitration, be submitted for investigation and report to a permanent international commission constituted in the manner prescribed in the following article.

The high contracting parties agree not to resort, with respect to each other, to any act of force during the investigation to be made by the commission and before its report is handed in.

Art. II. The international commission shall be composed of five members appointed as follows: each government shall designate two members, only one of whom shall be of its own nationality; the fifth member shall be designated by common consent and shall not belong to any of the nationalities already represented on the commission; he shall perform the duties of president.

In case the two governments should not be able to agree on the choice of the fifth commissioner, the other four shall be called upon to designate him, and failing an understanding between them, the provisions of Article 45 of the Hague Convention of 1907 shall be applied.

The commission shall be organized within six months from the exchange of ratification of the present convention.

The members shall be appointed for one year and their appointment may not be renewed. They shall remain in office until superseded or reappointed, or until the work on which they are engaged at the time their office expires is completed. . . .

Art. III. In case a dispute should arise between the high contracting parties which is not settled by the ordinary methods, each party shall have a right to ask that the investigation thereof be intrusted to the international commission charged with making a report. Notice shall be given to the President of the international commission, who shall at once communicate with his colleagues.

In the same case the president may, after consulting his colleagues and upon receiving the consent of a majority of the commission, offer the services of the latter to each of the contracting parties. Acceptance of that offer declared by one of the two governments shall be sufficient to give jurisdiction of the case to the commission in accordance with the foregoing paragraph.

The place of meeting shall be determined by the commission itself.

Art. IV. The two high contracting parties shall have a right, each on its own part, to state to the president of the commission what is the subject matter of the controversy. No difference in these statements, which shall be furnished by way of suggestion, shall arrest the action of the commission.

In case the cause of the dispute should consist of certain acts already committed or about to be committed, the commission shall as soon as possible indicate what measures to preserve the rights of each party ought in its opinion to be taken provisionally and pending the delivery of its report.

Art. V. . . . The work of the commission shall be completed within one year from the date on which it has taken jurisdiction of the case, unless the high contracting parties should agree to set a different period.

The conclusion of the commission and the terms of its report shall be adopted by a majority. The report, signed by virtue of his office, shall be transmitted by him to each of the contracting parties.

The high contracting parties reserve full liberty as to the action to be taken on the report of the commission.

Art. VI. The present treaty shall be ratified by the President of the United States of America, with the advice and consent of the Senate of the United States, and by the President of the Republic of China.

It shall go into force immediately after the exchange of ratifications and shall last five years.

Unless denounced six months at least before the expiration of the said period of five years, it shall remain in force until the expiration of a period of twelve months after either party shall have notified the other of its intention to terminate it. . . .

> William Jennings Bryan.
> Kai Fu Shah.

402. THE FEDERAL TRADE COMMISSION ACT
September 26, 1914

(*U. S. Statutes at Large,* Vol. XXXVIII, p. 717 ff.)

January 20, President Wilson delivered to Congress a message on trusts in which he recommended, among other things, a law creating a federal trade commission to advise, inform and guide business. A bill in harmony with these suggestions was promptly introduced into Congress and with the energetic support of Senator Newlands and Representatives Adamson, Clayton and others, passed and approved September 26. The purpose of this and the Clayton Bill, according to Wilson, was "to make men in a small way of business as free to succeed as men in a big way, and to kill monopoly in the seed." See, G. C. Henderson, *The Federal Trade Commission;* R. S. Baker, *Woodrow Wilson,* Vol. IV, ch. vii; H. R. Seager and C. A. Gulick, *Trust and Corporation Problems.*

An act to create a Federal Trade Commission, to define its powers and duties, and for other purposes.

Be it enacted, That a commission is hereby created and established, to be known as the Federal Trade Commission (hereinafter referred to as the commission), which shall be composed of five commissioners, who shall be appointed by the President, by and with the advice and consent of the Senate. Not more than three of the commissioners shall be members of the same political party. The first commissioners appointed shall continue in office for terms of three, four, five, six, and seven years, respectively, from the date of the taking effect of this Act, the term of each to be designated by the President, but their successors shall be appointed for terms of seven years, except that any person chosen to fill a vacancy shall be appointed only for the unexpired term of the commissioner whom he shall succeed. . . .

SEC. 3. That upon the organization of the commission and election of its chairman, the Bureau of Corporations and the offices of Commissioner and Deputy Commissioner of Corporations shall cease to exist; and all pending investigations and proceedings of the Bureau of Corporations shall be continued by the commission. . . .

SEC. 5. That unfair methods of competition in commerce are hereby declared unlawful.

The commission is hereby empowered and directed to prevent persons, partnerships, or corporations, except banks, and common carriers subject to the Acts to regulate commerce, from using unfair methods of competition in commerce.

Whenever the commission shall have reason to believe that any such person, partnership, or corporation has been or is using any unfair method of competition in commerce, . . . it shall issue and serve upon such person, partnership, or corporation a complaint stating its charges in that respect, and containing a notice of a hearing upon a day and at a place therein fixed at least thirty days after the service of said complaint. The person, partnership, or corporation so complained of shall have the right to appear at the place and time so fixed and show cause why an order should not be entered by the commission requiring such person, partnership, or corporation to cease and desist from the violation of the law so charged in said complaint. . . . If upon such hearing the commission shall be of the opinion that the method of competition in question is prohibited by this Act, it shall make a report in writing in which it shall state its findings as to the facts, and shall issue and cause to be served on such person, partnership, or corporation an order requiring such person, partnership, or corporation to cease and desist from using such method of competition. . . .

SEC. 6. That the commission shall also have power—

(a) To gather and compile information concerning and to investigate from time to time the organization, business, conduct, practices, and management of any corporation engaged in commerce, excepting banks and common carriers subject to the Act to regulate commerce, and its relation to other corporations and to individuals, associations, and partnerships.

(b) To require, . . . corporations engaged in commerce, excepting banks, and common carriers subject to the Act to regulate commerce, . . . to file with the commission in such form as the commission may prescribe annual or special, or both annual and special, reports or answers in writing to specific questions, furnishing to the commission such information as it may require as to the organization, business, conduct, practices, management, and relation to other corporations, partnerships, and individuals of the respective corporations filing such reports. . . .

(c) Whenever a final decree has been entered against any defendant corporation in any suit brought by the United States to prevent and restrain any violation of the antitrust Acts, to make investigation, . . . of the manner in which the decree has been or is being carried out, . . . it shall be its duty to make such investigation. It shall transmit to the Attorney General a report embodying its findings and recommendations as a result of any such investigation, and the report shall be made public in the discretion of the commission.

403. THE CLAYTON ANTI-TRUST ACT
October 15, 1914

(*U. S. Statutes at Large* XXXVIII, p. 730 ff.)

This act and the Federal Trade Commission Act embodied a large part of Wilson's ideas of the regulation of business. For a general expression of the Wilsonian policy, see *The New Freedom*. The most important sections of the Clayton law were those dealing with labor. For the judicial construction of these labor provisions, see Doc. No. 445. The legislative history of the Clayton Act is told in R. S. Baker, *Woodrow Wilson, Life and Letters*, Vol. IV.

. . . SEC. 2. That it shall be unlawful for any person engaged in commerce, in the course of such commerce, either directly or indirectly to discriminate in price between different purchasers of commodities which commodities are sold for use, consumption, or resale within the United States or any . . . other place under the jurisdiction of the United States, where the effect of such discrimination may be to substantially lessen competition or tend to create a monopoly in any line of commerce: . . .

SEC. 3. That it shall be unlawful for any person engaged in commerce, to lease or make a sale of goods, . . . or other commodities, . . . for use, consumption or resale within the United States or . . . other place under the jurisdiction of the United States, or fix a price charged therefor, or discount from, or rebate upon, such price, on the condition, . . . that the lessee or purchaser thereof shall not use or deal in the goods, . . . or other commodities of a competitor or competitors of the lessor or seller, where the effect of such lease, sale, or contract for sale or such condition, agreement, or understanding may be to substantially lessen competition or tend to create a monopoly in any line of commerce. . . .

SEC. 6. That the labor of a human being is not a commodity or article of commerce. Nothing contained in the anti-trust laws shall be construed to forbid the existence and operation of labor, agricultural, or horticultural organizations, instituted for the purposes of mutual help, and not having capital stock or conduced for profit, or to forbid or restrain individual members of such organizations from lawfully carrying out the legitimate objects thereof; nor shall such organizations, or the members thereof, be held or construed to be illegal combinations or conspiracies in restraint of trade, under the anti-trust laws.

SEC. 7. That no corporation engaged in commerce shall acquire, directly or indirectly, the whole or any part of the stock or other share capital of another corporation engaged also in commerce, where the effect of such acquisition may be to substantially lessen competition between the corporation whose stock is so acquired and the corporation making the acquisition, or to restrain such commerce in any section or community, or tend to create a monopoly of any line of commerce. . . .

This section shall not apply to corporations purchasing such stock solely for investment and not using the same by voting or otherwise to bring about, or in attempting to bring about, the substantial lessening of competition. . . .

SEC. 8. That from and after two years

from the date of the approval of this act no person shall at the same time be a director or other officer or employee of more than one bank, banking association or trust company, organized or operating under the laws of the United States, either of which has deposits, capital, surplus, and undivided profits aggregating more than $5,000,000; and no private banker or person who is a director in any bank or trust company, organized and operating under the laws of a State, having deposits, capital, surplus, and undivided profits aggregating more than $5,000,000, shall be eligible to be a director in any bank or banking association organized or operating under the laws of the United States. . . .

That from and after two years from the date of the approval of this Act no person at the same time shall be a director in any two or more corporations, any one of which has capital, surplus, and undivided profits aggregating more than $1,000,000, engaged in whole or in part in commerce, other than banks, banking associations, trust companies and common carriers subject to the Act to regulate commerce, approved February 4th, 1887, if such corporations are or shall have been theretofore, by virtue of their business and location of operation, competitors, so that the elimination of competition by agreement between them would constitute a violation of any of the provisions of any of the anti-trust laws. . . .

SEC. 10. That after two years from the approval of this Act no common carrier engaged in commerce shall have any dealings in securities, supplies, or other articles of commerce, . . . to the amount of more than $50,000, in the aggregate, in any one year, with another corporation, firm, partnership or association when the said common carrier shall have upon its board of directors or as its president, manager, or as its purchasing or selling officer, or agent in the particular transaction, any person who is at the same time a director, manager, or purchasing or selling officer of, or who has any substantial interest in, such other corporation, firm, partnership, or association, unless and except such purchases shall be made from, or such dealings shall be with, the bidder whose bid is the most favorable to such common carrier, to be ascertained by competitive bidding under regulations to be prescribed by rule or otherwise by the Interstate Commerce Commission. . . .

SEC. 20. That no restraining order or injunction shall be granted by any court of the United States, or a judge or the judges thereof, in any case between an employer and employees or between employers and employees, or between employees, or between persons employed and persons seeking employment, involving, or growing out of, a dispute concerning terms or conditions of employment, unless necessary to prevent irreparable injury to property, or to a property right, of the party making the application, for which injury there is no adequate remedy at law, and such property or property right must be described with a particularity in the application, which must be in writing and sworn to by the applicant or by his agent or attorney.

And no such restraining order or injunction shall prohibit any person or persons, whether singly or in concert, from terminat-ing any relation of employment, or from ceasing to perform any work or labor, or from recommending, advising, or persuading others by peaceful means so to do; or from attending at any place where any such person or persons may lawfully be, for the purpose of peacefully obtaining or communicating information, or from peacefully persuading any person to work or to abstain from working; or from ceasing to patronize or to employ any party to such dispute, or from recommending, advising, or persuading others by peaceful and lawful means so to do; or from paying or giving to, or withholding from, any person engaged in such dispute, any strike benefits or other moneys or things of value; or from peaceably assembling in a lawful manner, and for lawful purposes; or from doing any act or thing which might lawfully be done in the absence of such dispute by any party thereto; nor shall any of the acts specified in this paragraph be considered or held to be violations of any law of the United States.

404. WILSON'S VETO OF LITERACY TEST FOR IMMIGRANTS
January 28, 1915

(*Congressional Record,* 63d Congress, 3d. session, Vol. LII, p. 2481–2)

A similar act had been vetoed by Presidents Cleveland and Taft; a bill incorporating the main features of the Act of 1915 was passed over President Wilson's veto, in 1917.

To the House of Representatives: It is with unaffected regret that I find myself constrained by clear conviction to return this bill without my signature. Not only do I feel it to be a very serious matter to exercise the power of veto in any case, because it involves opposing the single judgement of the President to the judgement of a majority of both Houses of the Congress . . . but also because this particular bill is in so many important respects admirable, well conceived, and desirable. Its enactment into law would undoubtedly enhance the efficiency and improve the methods of handling the important branch of the public service to which it relates. But candor and a sense of duty with regard to the responsibility so clearly imposed upon me by the Constitution in matters of legislation leave me no choice but to dissent.

In two particulars of vital consequence this bill embodies a radical departure from the traditional and long established policy of this country, a policy in which our people have conceived the very character of their Government to be expressed, the very mission and spirit of the Nation in respect of its relations to the peoples of the world outside their borders. It seeks to all but close entirely the gates of asylum which have always been open to those who could find nowhere else the right and opportunity of constitutional agitation for what they conceived to be the natural and inalienable rights of men; and it excludes those to whom the opportunities of elementary education have been denied, without regard to their character, their purposes, or their natural capacity.

Restrictions like these, adopted earlier in our history as a Nation, would very materially have altered the course and cooled the humane ardors of our politics. The right of political asylum has brought to this country many a man of noble character and elevated purpose who was marked as an outlaw in his own less fortunate land, and who has yet become an ornament to our citizenship and to our public councils. The children and compatriots of these illustrious Americans must stand amazed to see the representatives of their Nation now resolved, in the fullness of our national strength and at the maturity of our great institutions, to risk turning such men back from our shores without test of quality or purpose. It is difficult for me to believe that the full effect of this feature of the bill was realized when it was framed and adopted, and it is im-· possible for me to assent to it in the form in which it is here cast.

The literacy test and the tests and restrictions which accompany it constitute an even more radical change in the policy of the Nation. Hitherto we have generously kept our doors open to all who were not unfitted by reason of disease or incapacity for self-support or such personal records and antecedents as were likely to make them a menace to our peace and order or to the wholesome and essential relationships of life. In this bill it is proposed to turn away from tests of character and of quality and impose tests which exclude and restrict; for the laws here embodied are not tests of quality or of character or of personal fitness, but tests of opportunity. Those who come seeking opportunity are not to be admitted unless

they have already had one of the chief of the opportunities they seek, the opportunity of education. The object of such provisions is restriction, not selection.

If the people of this country have made up their minds to limit the number of immigrants by arbitrary tests and so reverse the policy of all the generations of Americans that have gone before them, it is their right to do so. I am their servant and have no license to stand in their way. But I do not believe that they have. I respectfully submit that no one can quote their mandate to that effect. Has any political party ever avowed a policy of restriction in this fundamental matter, gone to the country on it, and been commissioned to control its legislation? Does this bill rest upon the conscious and universal assent and desire of the American people? I doubt it. It is because I doubt it that I make bold to dissent from it. I am willing to bide by the verdict, but not until it has been rendered. Let the platforms of parties speak out upon this policy and the people pronounce their wish. The matter is too fundamental to be settled otherwise.

I have no pride of opinion in this question. I am not foolish enough to profess to know the wishes and ideals of America better than the body of her chosen representatives know them. I only want instruction direct from those whose fortunes with ours, and all men's are involved.

405. THE FIRST *LUSITANIA* NOTE
May 13, 1915

(Foreign Relations of the United States, 1915, Supplement, p. 393 ff.)

On May 7, 1915, the British passenger ship *Lusitania* was torpedoed and sunk by a German submarine with a loss of life of over eleven hundred passengers and crew, including one hundred and twenty-four Americans. This act brought the United States and Germany to the verge of war. The first *Lusitania* note was written by President Wilson, and without the qualifying clauses which Secretary Bryan was anxious to insert. Because of a misunderstanding of a conversation which the Austrian Ambassador Dumba held with Bryan, Germany was at first inclined to take the note less seriously than was required by the circumstances. The German government attempted to justify the act of the submarine commander on the ground that the *Lusitania*

was, in fact, armed and carried contraband of war. In his second *Lusitania* note of June 9, Wilson brushed aside these allegations as irrelevant, and again insisted upon a disavowal from the German government and assurances that the German government would recognize "the obligation to take sufficient precaution to ascertain whether a suspected merchantman is in fact of belligerent nationality or is in fact carrying contraband of war under a neutral flag. The Government of the United States therefore deems it reasonable to expect that the Imperial German Government will adopt the measures necessary to put these principles into practice in respect to the safeguarding of American lives and American ships." (*For. Rel. of the U. S., 1915,* Suppl.,

p. 436 ff.) Bryan felt unable to sign this note, and resigned from the Cabinet: the note went out over the signature of Secretary Lansing. The negotiations dragged out for some time, but after a further exchange of notes, and the sinking of the *Arabic,* August 19, 1915, Germany promised to accept the President's terms. See, C. Seymour, *American Diplomacy during the World War,* p. 89 ff.; C. Seymour, *Intimate Papers of Colonel House,* Vol. I, ch. xiv, Vol. II, chs. i–ii; W. J. Bryan, *Memoirs,* Part II, chs. xiv–xv; S. F. Bemis, ed., *American Secretaries of States,* Vol. X, p. 23 ff.; J. B. Scott, *Survey of International Relations Between the United States and Germany, 1914–1917;* C. H. Grattan, *Why We Fought.*

The Secretary of State to Ambassador Gerard.
DEPARTMENT OF STATE,
Washington, May 13, 1915.
Please call on the Minister of Foreign Affairs and after reading to him this communication leave with him a copy.

In view of recent acts of the German authorities in violation of American rights on the high seas which culminated in the torpedoing and sinking of the British steamship *Lusitania* on May 7, 1915, by which over 100 American citizens lost their lives, it is clearly wise and desirable that the Government of the United States and the Imperial German Government should come to a clear and full understanding as to the grave situation which has resulted.

The sinking of the British passenger steamer *Falaba* by a German submarine on March 28, through which Leon C. Thrasher, an American citizen, was drowned; the attack on April 28 on the American vessel *Cushing* by a German aeroplane; the torpedoing on May 1 of the American vessel *Gulflight* by a German submarine, as a result of which two or more American citizens met their death; and, finally, the torpedoing and sinking of the steamship *Lusitania,* constitute a series of events which the Government of the United States has observed with growing concern, distress, and amazement.

Recalling the humane and enlightened attitude hitherto assumed by the Imperial German Government in matters of international right, and particularly with regard to the freedom of the seas; having learned to recognize the German views and the German influence in the field of international obligation as always engaged upon the side of justice and humanity; and having understood the instructions of the Imperial German Government to its naval commanders to be upon the same plane of humane action prescribed by the naval codes of other nations, the Government of the United States was loath to believe—it can not now bring itself to believe—that these acts, so absolutely contrary to the rules, the practices, and the spirit of modern warfare, could have the countenance or sanction of that great Government. It feels it to be its duty, therefore, to address the Imperial German Government concerning them with the utmost frankness and in the earnest hope that it is not mistaken in expecting action on the part of the Imperial German Government which will correct the unfortunate impressions which have been created and vindicate once more the position of that Government with regard to the sacred freedom of the seas.

The Government of the United States has been apprised that the Imperial German Government considered themselves obliged by the extraordinary circumstances of the present war and the measures adopted by their adversaries in seeking to cut Germany off from all commerce, to adopt methods of retaliation which go much beyond the ordinary methods of warfare at sea, in the proclamation of a war zone from which they have warned neutral ships to keep away. This Government has already taken occasion to inform the Imperial German Government that it can not admit the adoption of such measures or such a warning of danger to operate as in any degree an abbreviation of the rights of American shipmasters or of American citizens bound on lawful errands as passengers on merchant ships of belligerent nationality; and that it must hold the Imperial German Government to a strict accountability for any infringement of those rights, intentional or incidental. It does not understand the Imperial German Government to question those rights. It assumes, on the contrary, that the Imperial Government accept, as of course, the rule that the lives of noncombatants, whether they be of neutral citizenship or citizens of one of the nations at war, can not lawfully or rightfully be put in jeopardy by the capture or destruction of an unarmed merchantman, and recognize also, as all other nations do, the obligation to take the usual precaution of visit and search to ascertain whether a suspected merchantman is in fact of belligerent nationality or is in fact carrying contraband of war under a neutral flag.

The Government of the United States, therefore, desires to call the attention of the Imperial German Government with the utmost earnestness to the fact that the objection to their present method of attack against the trade of their enemies lies in the practical impossibility of employing submarines in the destruction of commerce without disregarding those rules of fairness, reason, justice, and humanity which all modern opinion regards as imperative. It is practically impossible for the officers of a submarine to visit a merchantman at sea and examine her papers and cargo. It is practically impossible for them to make a prize of her; and, if they can not put a prize crew on board of her, they can not sink her without leaving her crew and all on board of her to the mercy of the sea in her small boats. These facts it is understood the Imperial German Government frankly admit. We are informed that in the instances of which we have spoken time enough for even that poor measure of safety was not given, and in at least two of the cases cited not so much as a warning was received. Manifestly submarines can not be used against merchantmen, as the last few weeks have shown, without an inevitable violation of many sacred principles of justice and humanity.

American citizens act within their indisputable rights in taking their ships and in traveling wherever their legitimate business calls them upon the high seas, and exercise those rights in what should be the well-justified confidence that their lives will not be endangered by acts done in clear violation of universally acknowledged international obligations, and certainly in the confidence that their own Government will sustain them in the exercise of their rights.

There was recently published in the newspapers of the United States, I regret to inform the Imperial German Government, a formal warning, purporting to come from the Imperial German Embassy at Washington, addressed to the people of the United States, and stating, in effect, that any citizen of the United States who exercised his right of free travel upon the seas would do so at his peril if his journey should take him within the zone of waters within which the Imperial German Navy was using submarines against the commerce of Great Britain and France, notwithstanding the respectful but very earnest protest of his Government, the Government of the United States. I do not refer to this for the purpose of calling the attention of the Imperial German Government at this time to the surprising irregularity of a communication from the Imperial German Embassy at Washington addressed to the people of the United States through the newspapers, but only for the purpose of pointing out that no warning that an unlawful and inhumane act will be committed can possibly be accepted as an excuse or palliation for that act or as an abatement of the responsibility for its commission.

Long acquainted as this Government has been with the character of the Imperial German Government and with the high principles of equity by which they have in the past been actuated and guided, the Government of the United States can not believe that the commanders of the vessels which committed these acts of lawlessness did so except under a misapprehension of the orders issued by the Imperial German naval authorities. It takes it for granted that, at least within the practical possibilities of every such case, the commanders even of submarines were expected to do nothing that would involve the lives of noncombatants or the safety of neutral ships, even at the cost of failing of their object of capture or destruction. It confidently expects, therefore, that the Imperial German Government will disavow the acts of which the Government of the United States complains, that they will make reparation so far as reparation is possible for injuries which are without measure, and that they will take immediate steps to prevent the recurrence of anything so obviously subversive of the principles of warfare for which the Imperial German Government have in the past so wisely and so firmly contended.

The Government and people of the United

States look to the Imperial German Government for just, prompt, and enlightened action in this vital matter with the greater confidence because the United States and Germany are bound together not only by special ties of friendship but also by the explicit stipulations of the treaty of 1828 between the United States and the Kingdom of Prussia.

Expressions of regret and offers of reparation in the case of the destruction of neutral ships sunk by mistake, while they may satisfy international obligations, if no loss of life results, can not justify or excuse a practice, the natural and necessary effect of which is to subject neutral nations and neutral persons to new and immeasurable risks.

The Imperial German Government will not expect the Government of the United States to omit any word or any act necessary to the performance of its sacred duty of maintaining the rights of the United States and its citizens and of safeguarding their free exercise and enjoyment.

BRYAN.

406. ELIHU ROOT ON INVISIBLE GOVERNMENT

Speech to the New York Constitutional Convention
August 30, 1915

(Record of the Constitutional Convention of the State of New York, 1915, Vol. III, p. 3381 ff.)

These remarks by Mr. Root apropos of the reorganization of the executive power in the State, constitute an excellent analysis of "invisible government" and boss rule. On Boss Platt, see *The Autobiography of Thomas Collier Platt;* H. S. Gosnell, *Boss Platt and his New York Machine;* D. S. Alexander, *Four Famous New Yorkers.*

Mr. Chairman, I have had great doubt whether or not I should impose any remarks on this bill upon the Convention, especially after my friend Mr. Quigg has so ingeniously made it difficult for me to speak; but I have been so long deeply interested in the subject of the bill, and I shall have so few opportunities hereafter, perhaps never another, that I cannot refrain from testifying to my faith in the principles of government which underlie the measure, and putting upon this record for whatever it may be worth the conclusions which I have reached upon the teachings of long experience in many positions, through many years of participation in the public affairs of this State and in observation of them. . . .

The governments of our cities: Why, twenty years ago, when James Bryce wrote his "American Commonwealth," the government of American cities was a byword and a shame for Americans all over the world. Heaven be thanked, the government of our cities has now gone far toward redeeming itself and us from that disgrace, and the government of American cities today is in the main far superior to the government of American States. I challenge contradiction to that statement. How has it been reached? How have our cities been lifted up from the low grade of incompetency and corruption on which they stood when the "American Commonwealth" was written? It has been done by applying the principles of this bill to city government, by giving power to the men elected by the people to do the things for which they were elected. But I say it is quite plain that that is not all. It is not all.

I am going to discuss a subject now that goes back to the beginning of the political life of the oldest man in this Convention, and one to which we cannot close our eyes, if we keep the obligations of our oath. We talk about the government of the Constitution. We have spent many days in discussing the powers of this and that and the other officer. What is the government of this State? What has it been during the forty years of my acquaintance with it? The government of the Constitution? Oh, no; not half the time, or half way. When I ask what do the people find wrong in our State government, my mind goes back to those periodic fits of public rage in which the people rouse up and tear down the political leader, first of one party and then of the other party. It goes on to the public feeling of resentment against the control of party organizations, of both parties and of all parties.

Now, I treat this subject in my own mind not as a personal question to any man. I am talking about the system. From the days of Fenton, and Conkling, and Arthur and Cornell, and Platt, from the days of David B. Hill, down to the present time the government of the State has presented two different lines of activity, one of the constitutional and statutory officers of the State, and the other of the party leaders,—they call them party bosses. They call the system —I don't coin the phrase, I adopt it because it carries its own meaning—the system they call "invisible government." For I don't remember how many years, Mr. Conkling was the supreme ruler in this State; the Governor did not count, the legislatures did not count; comptrollers and secretaries of state and what not, did not count. It was what Mr. Conkling said, and in a great outburst of public rage he was pulled down.

Then Mr. Platt ruled the State; for nigh upon twenty years he ruled it. It was not the Governor; it was not the Legislature; it was not any elected officers; it was Mr. Platt. And the capitol was not here; it was at 49 Broadway; Mr. Platt and his lieutenants. It makes no difference what name you give, whether you call it Fenton or Conkling or Cornell or Arthur or Platt, or by the names of men now living. The ruler of the State during the greater part of the forty years of my acquaintance with the State government has not been any man authorized by the Constitution or by the law; and, sir, there is throughout the length and breadth of this State a deep and sullen and long-continued resentment at being governed thus by men not of the people's choosing. The party leader is elected by no one, accountable to no one, bound by no oath of office, removable by no one. Ah! My friends here have talked about this bill's creating an autocracy. The word points with admirable facility the very opposite reason for the bill. It is to destroy autocracy and restore power so far as may be to the men elected by the people, accountable to the people, removable by the people. I don't criticise the men of the invisible government. How can I? I have known them all, and among them have been some of my dearest friends.

I can never forget the deep sense of indignation that I felt in the abuse that was heaped upon Chester A. Arthur, whom I honored and loved, when he was attacked because he held the position of political leader. But it is all wrong. It is all wrong that a government not authorized by the people should be continued superior to the government that is authorized by the people.

How is it accomplished? How is it done? Mr. Chairman, it is done by the use of patronage, and the patronage that my friends on the other side of this question have been arguing and pleading for in this Convention is the power to continue that invisible government against that authorized by the people. Everywhere, sir, that these two systems of government co-exist, there is a conflict day by day, and year by year, between two principles of appointment to office, two radically opposed principles. The elected officer or the appointed officer, the lawful officer who is to be held responsible for the administration of his office, desires to get men into the different positions of his office who will do their work in a way that is creditable to him and his administration. Whether it be a president appointing a judge, or a governor appointing a superintendent of public works, whatever it may be, the officer wants to make a success, and he wants to get the man selected upon the ground of his ability to do the work.

How is it about the boss? What does the boss have to do? He has to urge the appointment of a man whose appointment will consolidate his power and preserve the organization. The invisible government proceeds to build up and maintain its power by a reversal of the fundamental principle of good government, which is that men should be selected to perform the duties of the office; and to substitute the idea that men should be appointed to office for the preservation and enhancement of power of the political leader. The one, the true one, looks upon appointment to office with a view to the service that can be given to the public. The other, the false one, looks upon appointment to office with a view to what can be gotten out of it. Gentlemen of the Convention, I appeal to your knowledge of facts. Every one of you knows that what I say about the use of patronage under the system of invisible government is true. Louis Marshall told us the other day about the appointment of wardens in the Adirondacks, hotel keepers and people living there, to render no service whatever. They were appointed not for the service that they were to render to the State; they were appointed for the service they were to render to promote the power of a political organization. Mr. Chairman, we all know that the halls of this capitol swarm with men during the session of the Legislature on pay day. A great number, seldom here, rendering no service, are put on the payrolls as a matter of patronage, not of service, but of party patronage. Both parties are alike; all parties are alike. The system extends through all. Ah, Mr. Chairman, that system finds its opportunity in the division of powers, in a six headed executive, in which, by the natural workings of human nature there shall be opposition and discord and the playing of one force against the other, and so, when we refuse to make one Governor elected by the people the real chief executive, we make inevitable the setting up of a chief executive not selected by the people, not acting for the people's interest, but for the selfish interest of the few who control the party, whichever party it may be. Think for a moment of what this patronage system means. How many of you are there who would be willing to do to your private client, or customer, or any private trust, or to a friend or neighbor, what you see being done to the State of New York every year of your lives in the taking of money out of her treasury without service? We can, when we are in a private station, pass on without much attention to inveterate abuses. We can say to ourselves, I know it is wrong, I wish it could be set right; it cannot be set right, I will do nothing. But here, here, we face the duty, we cannot escape it, we are bound to do our work, face to face, in clear recognition of the truth, unpalatable, deplorable as it may be and the truth is that what the unerring instinct of the democracy of our State has seen in this government is that a different standard of morality is applied to the conduct of affairs of States than that which is applied in private affairs. I have been told forty times since this Convention met that you cannot change it. We can try, can't we? I deny that we cannot change it. I repel that cynical assumption which is born of the lethargy that comes from poisoned air during all these years. I assert that this perversion of democracy, this robbing democracy of its virility, can be changed as truly as the system under which Walpole governed the commons of England, by bribery, as truly as the atmosphere which made the *credit mobilier* scandal possible in the Congress of the United States has been blown away by the force of public opinion. We cannot change it in a moment, but we can do our share. We can take this one step toward, not robbing the people of their part in government, but toward robbing an irresponsible autocracy of its indefensible and unjust and undemocratic control of government, and restoring it to the people to be exercised by the men of their choice and their control. . . .

407. THE CONCENTRATION OF WEALTH

Final Report of the Commission on Industrial Relations
1915

(U. S. Commission on Industrial Relations: Final Report and Testimony, Vol. I, p. 80 ff. U. S. 64th Congress, 1st Session, *Sen. Doc.* No. 415)

By Act of August 23, 1912, Congress provided for a Commission on Industrial Relations to survey the condition of industry in the United States with special reference to labor. The Commission's Report is in eleven volumes; the first contains the final report and conclusions. For references, see Doc. No. 388, and E. Clark, *American Foundations and Their Fields.*

The Concentration of Wealth and Influence

The evidence developed by the hearings and investigations of the commission is the basis for the following statements:

1. The control of manufacturing, mining, and transportation industries is to an in-

creasing degree passing into the hands of great corporations through stock ownership, and control of credit is centralized in a comparatively small number of enormously powerful financial institutions. These financial institutions are in turn dominated by a very small number of powerful financiers.

2. The final control of American industry rests, therefore, in the hands of a small number of wealthy and powerful financiers.

3. The concentration of ownership and control is greatest in the basic industries upon which the welfare of the country must finally rest.

4. With few exceptions each of the great basic industries is dominated by a single large corporation, and where this is not true the control of the industry through stock ownership in supposedly independent corporations and through credit is almost, if not quite, as potent.

5. In such corporations, in spite of the large number of stockholders, the control through actual stock ownership rests with a very small number of persons. For example, in the United States Steel Corporation, which had in 1911 approximately one hundred thousand share holders, 1.5 percent of the stockholders held 57 percent of the stock, while the final control rested with a single private banking house.

Similarly, in the American Tobacco Company before the dissolution, 10 stockholders owned sixty percent of the stock.

6. Almost without exception the employees of the large corporations are unorganized as a result of the active and aggressive "nonunion" policy of the corporation management.

Furthermore, the labor policy of the large corporations almost inevitably determines the labor policy of the entire industry.

7. A careful and conservative study shows that the corporations controlled by six financial groups and affiliated interests employ 2,651,684 wage earners and have a grand total capitalization of $19,875,200,000. These six financial groups control 28 percent of the total number of wage earners engaged in the industries covered by the report of our investigation. The Morgan-First National Bank group alone controls corporations employing 785,499 wage earners. . . .

8. The lives of millions of wage earners are therefore subject to the dictation of a relatively small number of men.

9. These industrial dictators for the most part are totally ignorant of every aspect of the industries which they control except the finances, and are totally unconcerned with regard to the working and living conditions of the employees in those industries. Even if they were deeply concerned, the position of the employees would be merely that of the subjects of benevolent industrial despots.

10. Except, perhaps, for improvements in safety and sanitation, the labor conditions of these corporation-control industries are subject to great criticism and are a menace to the welfare of the Nation.

11. In order to prevent the organization of employees for the improvement of working conditions, elaborate systems of espionage are maintained by the large corporations which refuse to deal with labor unions, and the employees suspected of union affiliations are discharged.

12. The domination by the men in whose hands the final control of a large part of American industry rests is not limited to their employees, but is being rapidly extended to control the education and "social service" of the Nation.

13. This control is being extended largely through the creation of enormous privately managed funds for indefinite purposes, hereinafter designated "foundations," by the endowment of colleges and universities, by the creation of funds for the pensioning of teachers, by contributions to private charities, as well as through controlling or influencing the public press. . . .

22. The entrance of the foundations into the field of industrial relations, through the creation of a special division by the Rockefeller Foundation, constitutes a menace to the national welfare to which the attention not only of Congress but of the entire country should be directed. Backed by the $100-000,000 of the Rockefeller Foundation, this movement has the power to influence the entire country in the determination of its most vital policy. . . .

26. Apart from these foundations there is developing a degree of control over the teachings of professors in our colleges and

universities which constitutes a most serious menace. In June of this year two professors, known throughout their professions as men of great talent and high character, were dropped from the positions they had occupied and no valid reason for such action was made public. Both were witnesses before the commission, and made statements based upon their own expert knowledge and experience which were given wide publicity. One was a professor of law in a State university, who had acted as counsel for the strikers in Colorado; the other a professor of economics, who had not only been active in fights in behalf of child-labor legislation and other progressive measures, but had recently published a work comparing the incomes paid for all classes of service.

In the face of such an enormous problem one can only frankly confess inability to suggest measures which will protect the Nation from the grave dangers described. It is believed, however, that if Congress will enact the measures already recommended, providing for a heavy tax on large inheritances with a rigid limitation on the total amount of the bequest, for the reclamation by the Federal Government of all parts of the public domain (including mineral rights) which have been secured by fraud, and for a tax on nonproductive land and natural resources, a great step in the right direction will have been taken.

As regards the "foundations" created for unlimited general purposes and endowed with enormous resources, their ultimate possibilities are so grave a menace, not only as regards their own activities and influence but also the benumbing effect which they have on private citizens and public bodies, that if they could be clearly differentiated from other forms of voluntary altruistic effort it would be desirable to recommend their abolition. It is not possible, however, at this time to devise any clear-cut definition upon which they can be differentiated.

As the basis for effective action, it is suggested that the commission recommend:

1. The enactment by Congress of a statute providing that all incorporated nonprofit-making bodies whose present charters empower them to perform more than a single specific function and whose funds exceed $1,000,000 shall be required to secure a Federal charter.

The Federal charter should contain the following provisions:

(a) Definite limitation of the funds to be held by any organization, at least not to exceed the largest amount held by any at the time of the passage of the act.

(b) Definite and exact specifications of the powers and functions which the organization is empowered to exercise, with provision for heavy penalties if its corporate powers are exceeded.

(c) Specific provision against the accumulation of funds by the compounding of unexpended income and against the expenditure in any one year of more than 10 per cent of the principal.

(d) Rigid inspection of the finances as regards both investment and expenditure of funds.

(e) Complete publicity through open reports to the proper Government officials.

(f) Provision that no line of work which is not specifically and directly mentioned in the articles of incorporation shall be entered upon without the unanimous consent and approval of the board of trustees, nor unless Congress is directly informed of such intention through communication to the Clerk of the House and the Clerk of the Senate, which shall be duly published in the Congressional Record, nor until six months after such intention has been declared.

2. Provision by Congress for the thorough investigation, by a special committee or commission, of all endowed institutions, both secular and religious, whose property holdings or income exceeds a moderate amount. The committee or commission should be given full power to compel the production of books and papers and the attendance and testimony of witnesses. It should be authorized and directed to investigate not only the finances of such institutions but all their activities and affiliations.

3. As the only effective means of counteracting the influence of the foundations, as long as they are permitted to exist, consists in the activities of governmental agencies along similar lines, the appropriations of the Federal Government for education and social service should be correspondingly increased.

408. THE GORE-McLEMORE RESOLUTION AND WILSON'S REPLY
February, March, 1916
(*Current History,* April, 1916, p. 15 ff.)

As Secretary of State Mr. Bryan had urged that many of the most dangerous problems of our relations with belligerents might be avoided if Americans were forbidden to travel on the armed ships of belligerent powers. Mr. Wilson refused to accept this point of view as either reasonable or necessary. The German threat of a renewal of unrestricted submarine warfare March 1, 1916, aroused widespread hostility in Congress to the Wilson program. The Democratic Congressional leaders served notice on the President that unless he placed an embargo upon American travel on armed merchantmen, Congress would recommend such action. The Gore-McLemore Resolution embodied the Bryan attitude toward this perplexing question. President Wilson's letter to Senator Stone indicated his refusal to accept any limitation on American rights or any modification of international law. As a result of Presidential pressure the resolution was defeated in the Senate, 68–14 and in the House 276–142. A considerable part of the administration support came from Republicans. See C. Seymour, *American Diplomacy During the World War* p. 116 ff.; "Armed Liner Issue," *Current History,* April, 1916.

1. THE GORE-McLEMORE RESOLUTION

Resolved . . . That it is the sense of the Congress, vested as it is with the sole power to declare war, that all persons owing allegiance to the United States should in behalf of their own safety and the vital interest of the United States, forbear to exercise the right to travel as passengers on any armed vessel of any belligerent power, whether such vessel be armed for offensive or defensive purposes, and it is the further sense of Congress that no passport should be issued or renewed by the Secretary of State, or anyone acting under him, to be used by any person owing allegiance to the United States for the purpose of travel upon any such armed vessel of a belligerent power.

2. PRESIDENT WILSON'S LETTER TO SENATOR STONE

The White House,
Washington, February 24, 1916.

My Dear Senator: I very warmly appreciate your kind and frank letter of to-day, and feel that it calls for an equally frank reply.

You are right in assuming that I shall do everything in my power to keep the United States out of war. I think the country will feel no uneasiness about my course in that respect. Through many anxious months I have striven for that object, amidst difficulties more manifold than can have been apparent upon the surface, and so far I have succeeded. I do not doubt that I shall continue to succeed. The course which the Central European powers have announced their intention of following in the future with regard to undersea warfare seems for the moment to threaten insuperable obstacles, but its apparent meaning is so manifestly inconsistent with explicit assurances recently given us by those powers with regard to their treatment of merchant vessels on the high seas, that I must believe that explanations will presently ensue which will put a different aspect upon it. We have had no reason to question their good faith or their fidelity to their promises in the past, and I for one feel confident that we shall have none in the future.

But in any event our duty is clear. No nation, no group of nations, has the right while war is in progress to alter or disregard the principles which all nations have agreed upon in mitigation of the horrors and sufferings of war; and if the clear rights of American citizens should ever unhappily be abridged or denied by any such action, we should, it seems to me, have in honor no choice as to what our own course should be.

For my own part, I cannot consent to any abridgment of the rights of American citizens in any respect. The honor and self-respect of the nation is involved. We covet peace, and shall preserve it at any cost but the loss of honor. To forbid our people to exercise their rights for fear we might be called upon to vindicate them would be a deep humiliation indeed. It would be an implicit, all but an explicit, acquiescence in the violation of the rights of mankind everywhere, and of whatever nation or allegiance. It would be a deliberate abdication of our hitherto proud position as spokesmen, even amidst the turmoils of war, for the law and the right. It would make everything this Government has attempted, and everything that it has achieved during this terrible struggle of nations meaningless and futile.

It is important to reflect that if in this instance we allowed expediency to take the place of principle, the door would inevitably be opened to still further concessions. Once accept a single abatement of right, and many other humiliations would certainly follow, and the whole fine fabric of international law might crumble under our hands piece by piece. What we are contending for in this matter is of the very essence of the things that have made America a sovereign nation. She cannot yield them without conceding her own impotency as a nation, and making virtual surrender of her independent position among the nations of the world.

I am speaking, my dear Senator, in deep solemnity, without heat, with a clear consciousness of the high responsibilities of my office, and as your sincere and devoted friend. If we should unhappily differ, we shall differ as friends; but where issues so momentous as these are involved we must, just because we are friends, speak our minds without reservation.

Faithfully yours,
Woodrow Wilson

409. THE *SUSSEX* AFFAIR

Wilson's Address to Congress
April 19, 1916

(U. S. 64th Congress, 1st Session, *House Doc.* 1034)

After the sinking of the *Arabic*, August 18, 1915, Germany gave a pledge that in the future liners would not be sunk by submarines without warning and without safety for the lives of noncombatants. This period of quiet in submarine warfare came to an end with the sinking of the French cross-channel steamer *Sussex,* March 24, 1916. Wilson warned Germany that unless she ceased her unrestricted submarine warfare, the United States would be forced to break off diplomatic relations. On May 4, Germany promised that merchant vessels would not be sunk without warning, unless they should attempt to escape or to offer resistance. The crisis was temporarily passed, but in January, 1917, Germany renewed her policy of unrestricted submarine warfare. See, J. S. Bassett, *Our War with Germany,* chs. i–v; J. B. McMaster, *The United States and the World War,* Vol. I; J. B. Scott, *Survey of International Relations Between the United States and Germany, 1914–1917,* ch. ix.

A situation has arisen in the foreign relations of the country of which it is my plain duty to inform you very frankly. . . .

In February of the present year the Imperial German Government informed this Government . . . that the Imperial German Government felt justified in the circumstances in treating all armed merchantmen of belligerent ownership as auxiliary vessels of war, which it would have the right to destroy without warning. . . .

One of the latest and most shocking instances of this method of warfare was that of the destruction of the French cross-channel steamer *Sussex*. It must stand forth, as the sinking of the *Lusitania* did, as so singularly tragical and unjustifiable as to constitute a truly terrible example of the inhumanity of submarine warfare as the commanders of German vessels have for the past twelvemonth been conducting it. If this instance stood alone, some explanation, some disavowal by the German Government, some evidence of criminal mistake or wilful disobedience on the part of the commander of the vessel that fired the torpedo might be sought or entertained; but unhappily it does not stand alone. . . .

The Government of the United States has been very patient. At every stage of this distressing experience of tragedy after tragedy in which its own citizens were involved, it has sought to be restrained from any extreme course of action or of protest by a thoughtful consideration of the extraordinary circumstances of this unprecedented war, and actuated in all that it said or did by the sentiments of genuine friendship which the people of the United States have always entertained and continue to entertain towards the German nation. It has of course accepted the successive explanations and assurances of the Imperial German Government as given in entire sincerity and good faith, and has hoped, even against hope, that it would prove to be possible for the German Government so to order and control the acts of its naval commanders as to square its policy with the principles of humanity as embodied in the law of nations. It has been willing to wait until the significance of the facts became absolutely unmistakable and susceptible of but one interpretation.

That point has now unhappily been reached. The facts are susceptible of but one interpretation. The Imperial German Government has been unable to put any limits or restraints upon its warfare against either freight or passenger ships. It has therefore become painfully evident that the position which this Government took at the very outset is inevitable, namely, that the use of submarines for the destruction of an enemy's commerce is, of necessity, because of the very character of the vessels employed and the very methods of attack which their employment of course involves, incompatible with the principles of humanity, the long established and incontrovertible rights of neutrals, and the sacred immunities of non-combatants.

I have deemed it my duty, therefore, to say to the Imperial German Government, that if it is still its purpose to prosecute relentless and indiscriminate warfare against vessels of commerce by the use of submarines, notwithstanding the now demonstrated impossibility of conducting that warfare in accordance with what the Government of the United States must consider the sacred and indisputable rules of international law and the universally recognized dictates of humanity, the Government of the United States is at last forced to the conclusion that there is but one course it can pursue; and that unless the Imperial German Government should now immediately declare and effect an abandonment of its present methods of warfare against passenger and freight carrying vessels this Government can have no choice but to sever diplomatic relations with the Government of the German Empire altogether.

This decision I have arrived at with the keenest regret; the possibility of the action contemplated I am sure all thoughtful Americans will look forward to with unaffected reluctance. But we cannot forget that we are in some sort and by the force of circumstances the responsible spokesmen of the rights of humanity, and that we cannot remain silent while those rights seem in process of being swept utterly away in the maelstrom of this terrible war. We owe it to a due regard for our own rights as a nation, to our sense of duty as a representative of the rights of neutrals the world over, and to a just conception of the rights of mankind to take this stand now with the utmost solemnity and firmness. . . .

410. AMERICAN CONTROL OF HAITI
Treaty Between the United States and Haiti
May 3, 1916
(*U. S. Statutes at Large*, Vol. XXXIX, p. 1654)

Long continued anarchy in Haiti led to American intervention in January and February, 1914; in December of that year American naval officers, acting under instructions from the Navy Department, removed half a million dollars of reserve funds from the Banque Nationale and secured them in the National City Bank of New York until monetary reforms had been carried into effect. Continued revolutions led to a demand for American control of the finances, customs and police force of the island, but not until the terrible massacre of July 27, 1915, did the United States invest the capital with marines. Such investment was held imperative in order to establish order and to forestall the intervention of European powers. A Convention satisfactory to the United States was signed September 16, ratified by the Haitian government November 11, and by the United States Senate in February, 1916. American forces continued to occupy Haiti until 1930. The occupations of Haiti and of Santo Domingo are illuminating examples of the effects of the Monroe Doctrine and of economic imperialism. An excellent treatise on American occupation is H. P. Davis, *Black Democracy*, Part II; R. L. Buell, "American Occupation of Haiti," Foreign Policy Association, *Information Service*, Vol. V, C. Kelsey, "American Intervention in Haiti", Am. Academy of Pol. and Social Science, *Annals*, 1922, E. G. Balch, et al., *Occupied Haiti*,

F. Bausman, et al., *The Seizure of Haiti by the United States*, are for the most part critical. See also *Inquiry into the Occupation and Administration of Haiti and Santo Domingo*, United States, 67th Congress, 2nd Sess. Sen. *Report* 794, and A. C. Millspaugh, *Haiti Under American Control, 1915–1930*.

Art. I. The Government of the United States will, by its good offices, aid the Haitian Government in the proper and efficient development of its agricultural, mineral and commercial resources and in the establishment of the finances of Haiti on a firm and solid basis.

Art. II. The President of Haiti shall appoint, upon nomination by the President of the United States, a General Receiver and such aids and employees as may be necessary, who shall collect, receive and apply all customs duties on imports and exports accruing at the several custom houses and ports of entry of the Republic of Haiti.

The President of Haiti shall appoint, upon nomination by the President of the United States, a Financial Adviser, who shall be an officer attached to the Ministry of Finance, to give effect to whose proposals and labours the Minister will lend efficient aid. The Financial Adviser shall devise an adequate system of public accounting, aid in increasing the revenues and adjusting them to the expenses, inquire into the validity of the debts of the Republic, enlighten both Governments with reference to all eventual debts, recommend improved methods of collecting and applying the revenues, and make such other recommendations to the Minister of Finance as may be deemed necessary for the welfare and prosperity of Haiti.

Art. III. The Government of the Republic of Haiti will provide by law or appropriate decrees for the payment of all customs duties to the General Receiver, and will extend to the Receivership, and to the Financial Adviser, all needful aid and full protection in the execution of the powers conferred and duties imposed herein; and the United States on its part will extend like aid and protection.

Art. IV. Upon the appointment of the Financial Adviser, the Government of the Republic of Haiti, in co-operation with the Financial Adviser, shall collate, classify, arrange and make full statement of all the debts of the Republic, the amounts, character, maturity and condition thereof, and the interest accruing and the sinking fund requisite to their final discharge.

Art. V. All sums collected and received by the General Receiver shall be applied, first, to the payment of the salaries and allowances of the General Receiver, his assistants and employees and expenses of the Receivership, including the salary and expenses of the Financial Adviser, which salaries will be determined by previous agreement; second, to the interest and sinking fund of the public debt of the Republic of Haiti; and, third, to the maintenance of the constabulary referred to in Article X, and then the remainder to the Haitian Government for purposes of current expenses. . . .

Art. VI. The expenses of the Receivership, including salaries and allowances of the General Receiver, his assistants and employees, and the salary and expenses of the Financial Adviser, shall not exceed five per centum of the collections and receipts from customs duties, unless by agreement by the two Governments.

Art. VII. The General Receiver shall make monthly reports of all collections, receipts and disbursements to the appropriate officer of the Republic of Haiti and to the Department of State of the United States, which reports shall be open to inspection and verification at all times by the appropriate authorities of each of the said Governments.

The Republic of Haiti shall not increase its public debt except by previous agreement with the President of the United States, and shall not contract any debt or assume any financial obligation unless the ordinary revenues of the Republic available for that purpose, after defraying the expenses of the Government, shall be adequate to pay the interest and provide a sinking fund for the final discharge of such debt.

Art. IX. The Republic of Haiti will not without a previous agreement with the President of the United States, modify the customs duties in a manner to reduce the revenues therefrom; and in order that the revenues of the Republic may be adequate to meet the public debt and the expenses of the Government, to preserve tranquillity and to promote material prosperity, the Republic of Haiti will co-operate with the Financial

Adviser in his recommendations for improvement in the methods of collecting and disbursing the revenues and for new sources of needed income.

Art. X. The Haitian Government obligates itself, for the preservation of domestic peace, the security of individual rights and full observance of the provisions of this treaty, to create without delay an efficient constabulary, urban and rural, composed of native Haitians. This constabulary shall be organized and officered by Americans, appointed by the President of Haiti, upon nomination by the President of the United States. . . . These officers will be replaced by Haitians as they, by examination, conducted under direction of a board to be selected by the senior American officer of this constabulary and in the presence of a representative of the Haitian Government, are found to be qualified to assume such duties. The constabulary herein provided for, shall, under the direction of the Haitian Government, have supervision and control of arms and ammunition, military supplies, and traffic therein, throughout the country. The high contracting parties agree that the stipulations in this Article are necessary to prevent factional strife and disturbances.

Art. XI. The Government of Haiti agrees not to surrender any of the territory of the Republic of Haiti by sale, lease or otherwise, or jurisdiction over such territory, to any foreign government or power, not to enter into any treaty or contract with any foreign power or powers that will impair or tend to impair the independence of Haiti.

Art. XII. The Haitian Government agrees to execute with the United States a protocol for the settlement, by arbitration or otherwise, of all pending pecuniary claims of foreign corporations, companies, citizens or subjects against Haiti.

Art. XIII. The Republic of Haiti, being desirous to further the development of its natural resources, agrees to undertake and execute such measures as in the opinion of the high contracting parties may be necessary for the sanitation and public improvement of the Republic, under the supervision and direction of an engineer or engineers, to be appointed by the President of Haiti upon nomination by the President of the United States, and authorized for that purpose by the Government of Haiti.

Art. XIV. The high contracting parties shall have authority to take such steps as may be necessary to insure the complete attainment of any of the objects comprehended in this treaty; and, should the necessity occur, the United States will lend an efficient aid for the preservation of Haitian Independence and the maintenance of a Government adequate for the protection of life, property and individual liberty. . . .

Art. XVI. The present treaty shall remain in full force and virtue for the term of ten years, to be counted from the day of exchange of ratifications, and further for another term of ten years if, for specific reasons presented by either of the high contracting parties, the purpose of this treaty has not been fully accomplished. . . .

411. AGRICULTURAL LEGISLATION IN THE FIRST WILSON ADMINISTRATION
Letter of President Wilson to A. F. Lever
August 11, 1916

(*Congressional Record*, 64th Congress, 1st Session, App., p. 1762–3)

This letter from Wilson to the chairman of the Committee on Agriculture furnishes a succinct summary of the agricultural legislation of the first Wilson administration. See, E. R. A. Seligman, *Economics of Farm Relief;* W. S. Holt, *Federal Farm Loan Bureau;* J. B. Morman, *Farm Credits in the United States and Canada;* E. S. Spahr, *History and Theory of Agricultural Credit in the United States.*

My Dear Mr. Lever: It has given me much satisfaction to approve to-day the bill making appropriations for the Department of Agriculture for the fiscal year ending June 30, 1917, and for other purposes, because the bill not only makes very generous provision for the improvement of farm production in the Nation and for investigations and demonstrations in the field of marketing of farm crops and of the organization of rural life, but also contains three well-conceived measures designed to improve market practices and the storage and financing of staple crops. As the passage of this bill marks the practical completion of an important part of the program for the betterment of rural life which was mapped out at the beginning of the administration, I feel that I cannot let the occasion pass without conveying to you and your associates in both Houses my appreciation of the great service rendered to the nation in strengthening its great agricultural foundations.

The record, legislative as well as administrative, is a remarkable one. It speaks for itself and needs only to be set forth.

1. Appreciation of the importance of agriculture has been shown through greatly and intelligently increased appropriations for its support.

2. Particular pains have been taken to foster production by every promising means, and careful thought has been given especially to the matter of increasing the meat supply of the Nation.

3. Greatly increased provision has been made, through the enactment of the co-operative agricultural extension act, for conveying agricultural information to farmers, and for inducing them to apply it. This piece of legislation is one of the most significant and far-reaching measures for the education of adults ever adopted by any Government. It provides for co-operation between the States and the Federal Government. This is a highly important and significant principle. When the act is in full operation there will be expended annually under its terms, from Federal and State sources alone, a total of over $8,600,000 in the direct education of the farmer; this amount is being and will be increasingly supplemented by contributions from local sources. It will permit the placing in each of the 2,850 rural counties of the Nation two farm demonstrators and specialists, who will assist the demonstrators in the more difficult problems confronting them.

4. Systematic provision for the first time has been made for the solution of problems in that important half of agriculture which concerns distribution marketing, rural finance, and rural organization.

5. Provision was made promptly for the creation of an Office of Markets and Rural Organization, and the appropriations for this office, including those for enforcing new laws designed to promote better marketing, have been increased to $1,200,000. The more difficult problems of marketing are being investigated and plans are in operation for furnishing assistance to producers of perishables through a market news service. A similar service for the live-stock interest will be inaugurated during the year.

6. The problem of securing the uniform grading of staple crops, of regulating dealings and traffic in them, of developing a better system of warehouses, and of providing more available collateral for farm loans has been successfully dealt with.

7. Under the cotton-futures act standards for cotton have been established, the operations of the future exchanges have been put under supervision, and the sale of cotton has been placed on a firmer basis.

8. The United States grain-standards act will secure uniformity in the grading of grain, enable the farmer to obtain fairer prices for his product, and afford him an incentive to raise better grades of grain.

9. The United States warehouse act will enable the Department of Agriculture to license bonded warehouses in the various States. It will lead to the development of better storage facilities for staple crops and will make possible the issuance of reliable warehouse receipts which will be widely and easily negotiable.

10. Of no less importance for agriculture and for national development is the Federal Aid road act. This measure will conduce to the establishment of more effective highway machinery in each State, strongly influence the development of good road building along right lines, stimulate larger production and better marketing, promote a fuller and more attractive rural life, add greatly to the convenience and economic welfare of all the people, and strengthen the national foundations. The act embodies sound principles of road legislation and will safeguard the expenditure of funds arising under the act not only, but will also result in the more efficient

use of the large additional sums made available by States and localities.

11. The Federal Reserve Act benefits the farmer, as it does all the other people of the Nation, by guaranteeing better banking, safeguarding the credit structure of the country, and preventing panics. It takes particular note of the special needs of the farmer by making larger provision for loans through national banks on farm mortgages and by giving farm paper a maturity period of six months.

12. It was essential, however, that banking machinery be devised which would reach intimately into the rural districts, that it should operate on terms suited to the farmer's needs, and should be under sympathetic management. The need was for machinery which would introduce business methods into farm finance, bring order out of chaos, reduce the cost of handling farm loans, place upon the market mortgages which would be a safe investment for private funds, attract into agricultural operations a fair share of the capital of the Nation, and lead to a reduction of interest. These needs and these ideals have been met by the enactment of the Federal farm-loan act. . . .

Faithfully yours,

Woodrow Wilson

412. ORGANIC ACT OF THE PHILIPPINE ISLANDS
August 29, 1916

(*U. S. Statutes at Large,* Vol. XXXIX, p. 545 ff.)

The act of July 1, 1902 had provided a territorial government for the Philippines. Inhabitants of the islands were made citizens of the Philippines, not of the United States; partial self-government was extended to the islands, and these rights were enlarged in 1907. Many Filipinos continued to hope for independence, and their demands met with some support among various idealistic and economic groups in the United States. The Democratic Party in 1912 pledged its support to ultimate independence; in accordance with this traditional Democratic position, President Wilson appointed native Filipinos to a majority of the seats in the Philippine upper house. The Jones Act of August 29, 1916, not only greatly enlarged Philippine self-government, but promised independence as soon as a stable government was established. This promise was finally fulfilled by the Philippine Independence Act of 1934, Doc. No. 484. The literature on the Philippines is extensive and controversial; see D. C. Worcester, *Philippines: Past and Present;* W. C. Forbes, *The Philippine Islands,* 2 Vols.; J. S. Reyes, *Legislative History of America's Economic Policy Toward the Philippines;* C. B. Elliott, *The Philippines to the End of the Commission Government;* F. B. Harrison, *The Cornerstone of Philippine Independence.* On military conquest and occupation, see M. Storey and M. P. Lichauco, *Conquest of the Philippines by the United States, 1898–1925.*

An Act to declare the purpose of the people of the United States as to the future political status of the people of the Philippine Islands, and to provide a more autonomous government for those islands.

Whereas it was never the intention of the people of the United States in the incipiency of the War with Spain to make it a war of conquest or for territorial aggrandizement; and

Whereas it is, as it has always been, the purpose of the people of the United States to withdraw their sovereignty over the Philippine Islands and to recognize their independence as soon as a stable government can be established therein; and

Whereas for the speedy accomplishment of such purpose it is desirable to place in the hands of the people of the Philippines as large a control of their domestic affairs as can be given them without, in the meantime, impairing the exercise of the rights of sovereignty by the people of the United States, in order that, by the use and exercise of popular franchise and governmental powers, they may be the better prepared to fully assume the responsibilities and enjoy all the privileges of complete independence: Therefore

Be it enacted, . . .

SEC. 2. That all inhabitants of the Philippine Islands who were Spanish subjects on [April 11, 1899] and then resided in said islands, and their children born subsequent thereto, shall be deemed and held to be citizens of the Philippine Islands, except such as shall have elected to preserve their allegiance to the Crown of Spain in accordance with the provisions of the treaty of peace between the United States and Spain, . . . and except such others as have since become citizens of some other country: . . .

SEC. 3. [Bill of rights for the Philippines.] . . .

SEC. 5. That the statutory laws of the United States hereafter enacted shall not apply to the Philippines Islands, except when they specifically so provide, or it is so provided in this Act.

SEC. 6. That the laws now in force in the Philippines shall continue in force and effect, except as altered, amended, or modified herein, until altered, amended or repealed by the legislative authority herein provided or by Act of Congress of the United States.

SEC. 7. That the legislative authority herein provided shall have power, when not inconsistent with this Act, by due enactment to amend, alter, modify, or repeal any law, civil or criminal, continued in force by this Act as it may from time to time see fit.

This power shall specifically extend with the limitation herein provided as to the tariff to all laws relating to revenue and taxation in effect in the Philippines.

SEC. 8. That general legislative power, except as otherwise herein provided, is hereby granted to the Philippine Legislature, authorized by this Act. . . .

SEC. 10. That while this Act provides that the Philippine government shall have the authority to enact a tariff law the trade relations between the islands and the United States shall continue to be governed exclusively by laws of the Congress of the United States: *Provided,* That tariff acts or acts amendatory to the tariff of the Philippine Islands shall not become law until they shall receive the approval of the President of the United States, nor shall any act of the Philippine Legislature affecting immigration or the currency or coinage laws of the Philippines become a law until it has been approved by the President of the United States: *Provided further,* That the President shall approve or disapprove any act mentioned in the foregoing proviso within six months from and after its enactment and submission for his approval, and if not disapproved within such

time it shall become a law the same as if it had been specifically approved.

SEC. 11. . . . That the entire indebtedness of the Philippine government . . . shall not exceed at any one time the sum of $15,000,000. . . .

SEC. 12. That general legislative powers in the Philippines, except as herein otherwise provided, shall be vested in a legislature which shall consist of two houses, one the senate and the other the house of representatives, and the two houses shall be designated "The Philippine Legislature": . . .

SEC. 13. [The Senate]

SEC. 14. [The House of Representatives]

SEC. 15. . . . Until otherwise provided by the Philippine Legislature herein provided for the qualifications of voters for senators and representatives in the Philippines and all officers elected by the people shall be as follows:

Every male person who is not a citizen or subject of a foreign power twenty-one years of age or over . . . who shall have been a resident of the Philippines for one year and of the municipality in which he shall offer to vote for six months next preceding the day of voting, and who is comprised within one of the following classes:

(a) Those who under existing law are legal voters and have exercised the right of suffrage.

(b) Those who own real property to the value of 500 pesos, or who annually pay 30 pesos or more of the established taxes.

(c) Those who are able to read and write either Spanish, English or a native tongue.

. . . The first election under the provisions of this Act shall be held on the first Tuesday of October, nineteen hundred and sixteen, . . . *Provided,* That the Governor General of the Philippine Islands shall appoint, without the consent of the senate and without restriction as to residence, senators and representatives who will, in his opinion, best represent the senate district and those representative districts which may be included in the territory not now represented in the Philippine Assembly: . . .

SEC. 19. . . . Every bill and joint resolution which shall have passed both houses shall, before it becomes a law, be presented to the Governor General. If he approve the same, he shall sign it; but if not, he shall return it with his objections to that house in which it shall have originated, which shall enter the objections at large on its journal and proceed to reconsider it. If, after such reconsideration, two-thirds of the members elected to that house shall agree to pass the same, it shall be sent, together with the objections, to the other house, by which it shall likewise be reconsidered, and if approved by two-thirds of all the members elected to that house it shall be sent to the Governor General, who, in case he shall then not approve, shall transmit the same to the President of the United States. . . . If the President of the United States approve the same, he shall sign it and it shall become a law. If he shall not approve same, he shall return it to the Governor General, so stating, and it shall not become a law: . . .

All laws enacted by the Philippine Legislature shall be reported to the Congress of the United States, which hereby reserves the power and authority to annul the same. If at the termination of any fiscal year the appropriations necessary for the support of government for the ensuing fiscal year shall not have been made, the several sums appropriated in the last appropriation bills for the objects and purposes therein specified, so far as the same may be done, shall be deemed to be reappropriated for the several objects and purposes specified in said last appropriation bill; . . .

SEC. 20. That at the first meeting of the Philippine Legislature created by this Act and triennially thereafter there shall be chosen by the legislature two Resident Commissioners to the United States, who shall hold their office for a term of three years beginning with the fourth day of March following their election, and which shall be entitled to an official recognition as such by all departments upon presentation to the President of a certificate of election by the Governor General of said islands. . . .

SEC. 21. That the supreme executive power shall be vested in an executive officer, whose official title shall be "The Governor General of the Philippine Islands." He shall be appointed by the President, by and with the advice and consent of the Senate of the United States, and hold his office at the pleasure of the President and until his successor is chosen and qualified. The Governor General shall reside in the Philippine Islands during his official incumbency, and maintain his office at the seat of government. He shall, unless otherwise herein provided, appoint, by and with the consent of the Philippine Senate, such officers as may now be appointed by the Governor General, or such as he is authorized by this Act to appoint, or whom he may hereafter be authorized by law to appoint; . . . He . . . shall be commander in chief of all locally created armed forces and militia. . . . He shall be responsible for the faithful execution of the laws of the Philippine Islands and of the United States operative within the Philippine Islands, and whenever it becomes necessary he may call upon the commanders of the military and naval forces of the United States in the islands, or summon the *posse comitatus*, or call out the militia or other locally created armed forces, to prevent or suppress lawless violence, invasion, insurrection, or rebellion; and he may, in case of rebellion or invasion, or imminent danger thereof, when the public safety requires it, suspend the privileges of the writ of habeas corpus, or place the islands, or any part thereof, under martial law. . . .

SEC. 26. . . . The chief justice and associate justices of the Supreme Court shall hereafter be appointed by the President, by and with the advice and consent of the Senate of the United States. The judges of the court of first instance shall be appointed by the Governor General by and with the advice and consent of the Philippine Senate. . . .

SEC. 27. That the Supreme Court of the United States shall have jurisdiction to review, revise, reverse, modify, or affirm the final judgements and decrees of the Supreme Court of the Philippine Islands in all actions, cases, causes, and proceedings now pending therein or hereafter determined thereby in which the Constitution or any statute, treaty, title, right, or privilege of the United States is involved, or in causes in which the value in controversy exceeds $25,000. . . .

SEC. 28. . . . It shall be unlawful for any corporation organized under this Act, or for any person, company, or corporation receiving any grant, franchise, or concession from the government of said islands, to use, employ, or contract for the labor of persons held in involuntary servitude; . . .

SEC. 29. That, except as in this Act otherwise provided, the salaries of all the officials of the Philippines not appointed by the President, including deputies, assistants, and other employees, shall be such and be so paid out of the revenues of the Philippines as shall from time to time be determined by the Philippine Legislature; and

if the legislature shall fail to make an appropriation for such salaries, the salaries so fixed shall be paid without the necessity of further appropriations therefor. The salaries of all officers and all expenses of the offices of the various officials of the Philippines appointed as herein provided by the President shall also be paid out of the revenues of the Philippines. . . .

413. HAMMER v. DAGENHART ET AL.
247 U. S. 251
1918

Appeal from the U. S. district court for the Western District of North Carolina. This case involved the interpretation of the Keating-Owen Act of 1916. *Stat. at Large,* Vol. XXXIX, p. 675.

DAY, J. . . . The attack upon the act rests upon three propositions:

First. It is not a regulation of interstate and foreign commerce.

Second. It contravenes the Tenth Amendment to the Constitution.

Third. It conflicts with the Fifth Amendment to the Constitution.

The controlling question for decision is: Is it within the authority of Congress in regulating commerce among the States to prohibit the transportation in interstate commerce of manufactured goods, the product of a factory in which, within thirty days prior to their removal therefrom, children under the age of fourteen have been employed or permitted to work, or children between the ages of fourteen and sixteen years have been employed or permitted to work more than eight hours in any day, or more than six days in any week, or after the hour of 7 o'clock P. M. or before the hour of 6 o'clock A. M.?

The power essential to the passage of this act, the government contends, is found in the commerce clause of the Constitution which authorizes Congress to regulate commerce with foreign nations and among the States. . . .

But it is insisted that adjudged cases in this court establish the doctrine that the power to regulate given to Congress incidentally includes the authority to prohibit the movement of ordinary commodities, and

therefore that the subject is not open for discussion. The cases demonstrate the contrary. They rest upon the character of the particular subjects dealt with and the fact that the scope of governmental authority, state or national, possessed over them, is such that the authority to prohibit is, as to them, but the exertion of the power to regulate.

The first of these cases is *Champion* v. *Ames,* 188 U. S. 321, the so-called *Lottery Case,* in which it was held that Congress might pass a law having the effect to keep the channels of commerce free from use in the transportation of tickets used in the promotion of lottery schemes. In *Hipolite Egg Co.* v. *United States,* 220 U. S. 45, this court sustained the power of Congress to pass the Pure Food and Drugs Act which prohibited the introduction into the States by means of interstate commerce of impure foods and drugs. In *Hoke* v. *United States,* 227 U. S. 308, this court sustained the constitutionality of the so-called "White Slave Traffic Act" whereby the transportation of a woman in interstate commerce for the purpose of prostitution was forbidden. . . . [Cites other cases.]

In each of these instances the use of interstate transportation was necessary to the accomplishment of harmful results. In other words, although the power over interstate transportation was to regulate, that could only be accomplished by prohibiting the use of the facilities of interstate commerce to effect the evil intended.

This element is wanting in the present case. The thing intended to be accomplished by this statute is the denial of the facilities of interstate commerce to those manufacturers in the States who employ children within the prohibited ages. The act in its effect does not regulate transportation among the States, but aims to standardize the ages at which children may be employed in mining and manufacturing within the States. The goods shipped are of themselves harmless. The act permits them to be freely shipped after thirty days from the time of their removal from the factory. When offered for shipment, and before transportation begins, the labor of their production is over, and the mere fact that they were intended for interstate commerce transportation does not make their production subject to federal control under the commerce power.

Commerce "consists of intercourse and traffic . . . and includes the transportation of persons and property, as well as the purchase, sale and exchange of commodities." The making of goods and the mining of coal are not commerce, nor does the fact that these things are to be afterwards shipped, or used in interstate commerce, make their production a part thereof.

Over interstate transportation, or its incidents, the regulatory power of Congress is ample, but the production of articles intended for interstate commerce is a matter of local regulation. . . . If it were otherwise, all manufacture intended for interstate shipment would be brought under federal control to the practical exclusion of the authority of the states, a result certainly not contemplated by the framers of the Constitution when they vested in Congress the authority to regulate commerce among the states.

It is further contended that the authority of Congress may be exerted to control interstate commerce in the shipment of child-made goods because of the effect of the circulation of such goods in other States where the evil of this class of labor has been recognized by local legislation, and the right to thus employ child labor has been more rigorously restrained than in the state of production. In other words, that the unfair competition thus engendered may be controlled by closing the channels of interstate commerce to manufacturers in those States where the local laws do not meet what

Congress deems to be the more just standard of other States.

There is no power vested in Congress to require the States to exercise their police power so as to prevent possible unfair competition. Many causes may coöperate to give one State, by reason of local laws or conditions, an economic advantage over others. The commerce clause was not intended to give to Congress a general authority to equalize such conditions. In some of the States laws have been passed fixing minimum wages for women, in others the local law regulates the hours of labor of women in various employments. Business done in such States may be at an economic disadvantage when compared with States which have no such regulation; surely, this fact does not give Congress the power to deny transportation in interstate commerce to those who carry on business where the hours of labor and the rate of compensation for women have not been fixed by a standard in use in other States and approved by Congress.

The grant of power to Congress over the subject of interstate commerce was to enable it to regulate such commerce, and not to give it authority to control the States in their exercise of the police power over local trade and manufacture.

The grant of authority over a purely federal matter was not intended to destroy the local power always existing and carefully reserved to the States in the Tenth Amendment to the Constitution. . . .

That there should be limitations upon the right to employ children in mines and factories in the interest of their own and the public welfare, all will admit. That such employment is generally deemed to require regulation is shown by the fact that the brief of counsel states that every state in the Union has a law upon the subject, limiting the right to thus employ children. In North Carolina, the State wherein is located the factory in which the employment was had in the present case, no child under twelve years of age is permitted to work.

It may be desirable that such laws be uniform, but our federal government is one of enumerated powers. . . .

To sustain this statute would not be, in our judgment, a recognition of the lawful exertion of congressional authority over interstate commerce, but would sanction an invasion by the federal power of the control of a matter purely local in its character, and over which no authority has been delegated to Congress in conferring the power to regulate commerce among the states. . . .

In our view the necessary effect of this act is, by means of a prohibition against the movement in interstate commerce of ordinary commercial commodities, to regulate the hours of labor of children in factories and mines within the States, a purely state authority. Thus the act in a twofold sense is repugnant to the Constitution. It not only transcends the authority delegated to Congress over commerce, but also exerts a power as to a purely local matter to which the federal authority does not extend. The far-reaching result of upholding the act cannot be more plainly indicated than by pointing out that if Congress can thus regulate matters intrusted to local authority by prohibition of the movement of commodities in interstate commerce, all freedom of commerce will be at an end, and the power of the states over local matters may be eliminated, and thus our system of government be practically destroyed.

For these reasons we hold that this law exceeds the constitutional authority of Congress. It follows that the decree of the district court must be affirmed.

HOLMES, J., dissenting:

The single question in this case is whether Congress has power to prohibit the shipment in interstate or foreign commerce of any product of cotton mill [etc.]. . . . The objection urged against the power is that the States have exclusive control over their methods of production and that Congress cannot meddle with them, and taking the proposition in the sense of direct intermeddling I agree to it and suppose that no one denies it. But if an act is within the powers specifically conferred upon Congress, it seems to me that it is not made any less constitutional because of the indirect effects that it may have, however obvious it may be that it will have those effects, and that we are not at liberty upon such grounds to hold it void.

The first step in any argument is to make plain what no one is likely to dispute—that

the statute in question is within the power expressly given to Congress if considered only as to its immediate effects, and that if invalid it is so only upon some collateral ground. The statute confines itself to prohibiting the carriage of certain goods in interstate or foreign commerce. Congress is given power to regulate such commerce in unqualified terms. It would not be argued to-day that the power to regulate does not include the power to prohibit. Regulation means the prohibition of something, and when interstate commerce is the matter to be regulated I cannot doubt that the regulations may prohibit any part of such commerce that Congress sees fit to forbid. At all events it is established by the Lottery Case and others that have followed it that a law is not beyond the regulative power of Congress merely because it prohibits certain transportation out and out. So I repeat that this statute in its immediate operation is clearly within the Congress's constitutional power.

The question, then, is narrowed to whether the exercise of its otherwise constitutional power by Congress can be pronounced unconstitutional because of its possible reaction upon the conduct of the States in a matter upon which I have admitted that they are free from direct control. I should have thought that that matter had been disposed of so fully as to leave no room for doubt. I should have thought that the most conspicuous decisions of this court had made it clear that the power to regulate commerce and other constitutional powers could not be cut down or qualified by the fact that it might interfere with the carrying out of the domestic policy of any state.

The manufacture of oleomargarine is as much a matter of state regulation as the manufacture of cotton cloth. Congress levied a tax upon the compound when colored so as to resemble butter that was so great as obviously to prohibit the manufacture and sale. In a very elaborate discussion the present chief justice excluded any inquiry into the purpose of an act which, apart from that purpose, was within the power of Congress. *McCray* v. *United States*, 195 U. S. 27. . . . Fifty years ago a tax on state banks, the obvious purpose and actual effect of which was to drive them, or at least their circulation, out of existence, was sustained, although the result was one that Congress had no constitutional power to require. The court made short work of the argument as to the purpose of the act. "The judicial cannot prescribe to the legislative departments of the government limitations upon the exercise of its acknowledged powers." *Veazie Bank* v. *Fenno*, 8 Wallace 533. . . . And to come to cases upon interstate commerce, . . . the Sherman Act has been made an instrument for the breaking up of combinations in restraint of trade and monopolies, using the power to regulate commerce as a foothold, but not proceeding because that commerce was the end actually in mind. The objection that the control of the states over production was interfered with was urged again and again, but always in vain. . . .

The Pure Food and Drug Act which was sustained in *Hipolite Egg Co.* v. *United States*, 220 U. S. 45, with the intimation that "no trade can be carried on between the states to which it [the power of Congress to regulate commerce] does .not extend," applies not merely to articles that the changing opinions of the time condemn as intrinsically harmful, but to others innocent in themselves, simply on the ground that the order for them was induced by a preliminary fraud. It does not matter whether the supposed evil precedes or follows the transportation. It is enough that, in the opinion of Congress, the transportation encourages the evil. . . .

The notion that prohibition is any less prohibition when applied to things now thought evil I do not understand. But if there is any matter upon which civilized countries have agreed,—far more unanimously than they have with regard to intoxicants and some other matters over which this country is now emotionally aroused,—it is the evil of premature and excessive child labor. I should have thought that if we were to introduce our own moral conceptions where, in my opinion, they do not belong, this was preëminently a case for upholding the exercise of all its powers by the United States.

But I had thought that the propriety of the exercise of a power admitted to exist in some cases was for the consideration of Congress alone, and that this court always had disavowed the right to intrude its judgment upon questions of policy or morals. It is not for this court to pronounce when prohibition is necessary to regulation if it ever may be necessary—to say that it is permissible as against strong drink, but not as against the product of ruined lives.

The act does not meddle with anything belonging to the States. They may regulate their internal affairs and their domestic commerce as they like. But when they seek to send their products across the state line they are no longer within their rights. If there were no Constitution and no Congress their power to cross the line would depend upon their neighbors. Under the Constitution such commerce belongs not to the States, but to Congress to regulate. It may carry out its views of public policy whatever indirect effect they may have upon the activities of the States. Instead of being encountered by a prohibitive tariff at her boundaries, the State encounters the public policy of the United States which it is for Congress to express. The public policy of the United States is shaped with a view to the benefit of the nation as a whole. If, as has been the case within the memory of men still living, a State should take a different view of the propriety of sustaining a lottery from that which generally prevails, I cannot believe that the fact would require a different decision from that reached in *Champion* v. *Ames*. Yet in that case it would be said with quite as much force as in this that Congress was attempting to intermeddle with the State's domestic affairs. The national welfare as understood by Congress may require a different attitude within its sphere from that of some self-seeking State. It seems to me entirely constitutional for Congress to enforce its understanding by all the means at its command.

MR. JUSTICE MCKENNA, MR. JUSTICE BRANDEIS, and MR. JUSTICE CLARKE concur in this opinion.

414. THE ADAMSON ACT
September 3, 5, 1916

(*U. S. Statutes at Large,* Vol. XXXIX, p. 721 ff.)

In March, 1916, the Four Brotherhoods of Railway workers demanded an eight-hour day without reduction of wages, and threatened a nation-wide strike unless their demands were complied with. As a tie-up in our transportation system at that time would have been disastrous, Wilson appeared before Congress and asked for the enactment of a law providing for an eight-hour day without reduction in wages: Congress responded with the Adamson Act. On the constitutionality of the measure, see *Wilson* v. *New,* Doc. No. 415.

An act to establish an eight-hour day for employees of carriers engaged in interstate and foreign commerce, and for other purposes

BE it enacted, That beginning January first, nineteen hundred and seventeen, eight hours shall, in contracts for labor and service, be deemed a day's work and the measure or standard of a day's work for the purpose of reckoning the compensation for services of all employees who are now or may hereafter be employed by any common carrier by railroad, except railroads independently owned and operated not exceeding one hundred miles in length, electric street railroads, and electric interurban railroads, which is subject to the provisions of the Act of February 4, 1887, entitled "An Act to regulate commerce," as amended, and who are now or may hereafter be actually engaged in any capacity in the operation of trains used for the transportation of persons or property on railroads, . . . from any State or Territory of the United States or the District of Columbia to any other State or Territory of the United States or the District of Columbia or from one place in a Territory to another place in the same Territory, or from any place in the United States to an adjacent foreign country, or from any place in the United States through a foreign country to any other place in the United States: *Provided,* That the above exceptions shall not apply to railroads though less than one hundred miles in length whose principal business is leasing or furnishing terminal or transfer facilities to other railroads, or are themselves engaged in transfers of freight between railroads or between railroads and industrial plants. . . .

Sec. 2. That the President shall appoint a commission of three, which shall observe the operation and effects of the institution of the eight-hour standard workday. . . .

Sec. 3. That pending the report of the commission . . . and for a period of thirty days thereafter, the compensation of railway employees subject to this Act for a standard eight-hour workday shall not be reduced below the present standard day's wage. . . .

415. WILSON v. NEW
243 U. S. 332
1917

Appeal from the District Court for Western District of Missouri. Suit to enjoin enforcement of the Adamson Act fixing an eight-hour work day for and regulating wages of railway employees on interstate carriers. On the constitutionality of emergency legislation see the Minnesota Mortgage Moratorium Case, Doc. No. 483.

WHITE, C. J. Was there power in Congress, under the circumstances existing, to deal with the hours of work and wages of railroad employees engaged in interstate commerce, is the principal question here to be considered. . . .

[Review of history of passage of Adamson Act by Congress]

All the propositions relied upon and arguments advanced ultimately come to two questions: first, the entire want of constitutional power to deal with the subjects embraced by the statute, and second, such abuse of the power, if possessed as rendered its exercise unconstitutional. We will consider these subjects under distinct propositions separately.

I. The entire want of constitutional power to deal with the subjects embraced by the statute. . . .

. . . Concretely stated, therefore, the question is this: Did Congress have power, . . . to provide a permanent eight-hour standard and to create by legislative action a standard of wages to be operative upon the employers and employees for such reasonable time as it deemed necessary to afford an opportunity for the meeting of the minds of employers and employees on the subject of wages? Or, in other words, did it have the power, in order to prevent the interruption of interstate commerce, to exert its will to supply the absence of a wage scale resulting from the disagreement as to wages between the employers and employees, and to make its will on that subject controlling for the limited period provided for?

Coming to the general considerations by which both subjects must be controlled, to simplify the analysis for the purpose of considering the question of inherent power, we put the question as to the eight-hour standard entirely out of view, on the ground that the authority to permanently establish it is so clearly sustained as to render the subject not disputable. . . .

That the business of common carriers by rail is in a sense a public business because of the interest of society in the continued operation and rightful conduct of such business, and that the public interest begets a public right of regulation to the full extent necessary to secure and protect it, is settled by so many decisions, state and Federal, and is illustrated by such a continuous exertion of state and Federal legislative power, as to leave no room for question on the subject. It is also equally true that as the right to fix by agreement between the carrier and its employees a standard of wages to control their relations is primarily private, the establishment and giving effect to such agreed-on standard is not subject to be controlled or prevented by public authority. But, taking all these propositions as undoubted, if the situation which we have described and with which the act of Congress dealt be taken into view,—that is, the dispute between the employers and employees

as to a standard of wages, their failure to agree, the resulting absence of such standard, the entire interruption of interstate commerce which was threatened, and the infinite injury to the public interest which was imminent,—it would seem inevitably to result that the power to regulate necessarily obtained and was subject to be applied to the extent necessary to provide a remedy for the situation, which included the power to deal with the dispute, to provide by appropriate action for a standard of wages to fill the want of one caused by the failure to exert the private right on the subject, and to give effect by appropriate legislation to the regulations thus adopted. This must be unless it can be said that the right to so regulate as to save and protect the public interest did not apply to a case where the destruction of the public right was imminent as the result of a dispute between the parties and their consequent failure to establish by private agreement the standard of wages which was essential; in other words, that the existence of the public right and the public power to preserve it was wholly under the control of the private right to establish a standard by agreement. Nor is it an answer to this view to suggest that the situation was one of emergency, and that emergency cannot be made the source of power. The proposition begs the question, since although an emergency may not call into life a power which has never lived, nevertheless emergency may afford a reason for the exertion of a living power already enjoyed. . . .

Let us . . . briefly recapitulate some of the more important of the regulations which have been enacted in the past in order to show how necessarily the exertion of the power to enact them manifests the existence of the legislative authority to ordain the regulation now before us, and how completely the whole system of regulations adopted in the past would be frustrated or rendered unavailing if the power to regulate under the conditions stated, which was exerted by the act before us, was not possessed. . . .

In the presence of this vast body of acknowledged powers there would seem to be no ground for disputing the power which was exercised in the act which is before us . . . to exert the legislative will for the purpose of settling the dispute, and bind both parties to the duty of acceptance and compliance, to the end that no individual dispute or difference might bring ruin to the vast interests concerned in the movement of interstate commerce, for the express purpose of protecting and preserving which the plenary legislative authority granted to Congress was reposed. . . .

We are of the opinion that the reasons stated conclusively establish that, from the point of view of inherent power, the act which is before us was clearly within the legislative power of Congress to adopt, and that, in substance and effect, it amounted to an exertion of its authority under the circumstances disclosed to compulsorily arbitrate the dispute between the parties by establishing as to the subject-matter of that dispute a legislative standard of wages operative and binding as a matter of law upon the parties,—a power none the less efficaciously exerted because exercised by direct legislative act instead of by the enactment of other and appropriate means providing for the bringing about of such result. If it be conceded that the power to enact the statute was in effect the exercise of the right to fix wages where, by reason of the dispute, there had been a failure to fix by agreement, it would simply serve to show the nature and character of the regulation essential to protect the public right and safeguard the movement of interstate commerce, not involving any denial of the authority to adopt it. . . .

We conclude that the court below erred in holding the statute was not within the power of Congress to enact and its decree must therefore be . . . reversed.

Justices Day, Pitney, Van Devanter and McReynolds dissenting.

416. PEACE WITHOUT VICTORY

Address of President Wilson to the United States Senate
January 22, 1917

(U. S. 64th Congress, 2nd Sess., *Sen. Document* 685)

This memorable speech, calling for a peace without victory, anticipated in many respects the Fourteen Points speech, and indicated Wilson's determination to provide machinery for the maintenance of international peace. The term "peace without victory" inspired a great deal of contemporary derision. See C. Seymour, *American Diplomacy During the World War.*

Gentlemen of the Senate: . . .

. . . I have sought this opportunity to address you because I thought that I owed it to you, as the counsel associated with me in the final determination of our international obligations, to disclose to you without reserve the thought and purpose that have been taking form in my mind in regard to the duty of our Government in the days to come when it will be necessary to lay afresh and upon a new plan the foundations of peace among the nations.

It is inconceivable that the people of the United States should play no part in that great enterprise. . . . They cannot in honor withhold the service to which they are now about to be challenged. They do not wish to withhold it. But they owe it to themselves and to the other nations of the world to state the conditions under which they will feel free to render it.

That service is nothing less than this, to add their authority and their power to the authority and force of other nations to guarantee peace and justice throughout the world. Such a settlement cannot now be long postponed. It is right that before it comes this Government should frankly formulate the conditions upon which it would feel justified in asking our people to approve its formal and solemn adherence to a League for Peace. I am here to attempt to state those conditions.

The present war must first be ended; but we owe it to candor and to a just regard for the opinion of mankind to say that, so far as our participation in guarantees of future peace is concerned, it makes a great deal of difference in what way and upon what terms it is ended. The treaties and agreements which bring it to an end must embody terms which will create a peace that is worth guaranteeing and preserving, a peace that will win the approval of mankind, not merely a peace that will serve the several interests and immediate aims of the nations engaged. . . .

No covenant of co-operative peace that does not include the peoples of the New World can suffice to keep the future safe against war; and yet there is only one sort of peace that the peoples of America could join in guaranteeing. The elements of that peace must be elements that engage the confidence and satisfy the principles of the American governments, elements consistent with their political faith and with the practical convictions which the peoples of America have once for all embraced and undertaken to defend. . . .

It will be absolutely necessary that a force be created as a guarantor of the permanency of the settlement so much greater than the force of any nation now engaged or any alliance hitherto formed or projected that no nation, no probable combination of nations could face or withstand it. If the peace presently to be made is to endure, it must be a peace made secure by the organized major force of mankind.

The terms of the immediate peace agreed upon will determine whether it is a peace for which such a guarantee can be secured. The question upon which the whole future peace and policy of the world depends is this: Is the present war a struggle for a just and secure peace, or only for a new balance of power? If it be only a struggle for a new balance of power, who will guarantee, who can guarantee the stable equilibrium of the new arrangement? Only a tranquil Europe can be a stable Europe. There must be, not a balance of power, but a community of power; not organized rivalries, but an organized common peace.

Fortunately we have received very explicit assurances on this point. . . . I think it will be serviceable if I attempt to set forth what we understand them to be.

They imply, first of all, that it must be a peace without victory. It is not pleasant to say this. I beg that I may be permitted to put my own interpretation upon it and that it may be understood that no other interpretation was in my thought. I am seeking only to face realities and to face them without soft concealments. Victory would mean peace forced upon the loser, a victor's terms imposed upon the vanquished. It would be accepted in humiliation, under duress, at an intolerable sacrifice, and would leave a sting, a resentment, a bitter memory upon which terms of peace would rest, not permanently, but only as upon quicksand. Only a peace between equals can last. Only a peace the very principle of which is equality and a common participation in a common benefit. The right state of mind, the right feeling between nations, is as necessary for a lasting peace as is the just settlement of vexed questions of territory or of racial and national allegiance.

The equality of nations upon which peace must be founded if it is to last must be an equality of rights; the guarantees exchanged must neither recognize nor imply a difference between big nations and small, between those that are powerful and those that are weak. Right must be based upon the common strength, not upon the individual strength, of the nations upon whose concert peace will depend. Equality of territory or of resources there of course cannot be; nor any sort of equality not gained in the ordinary peaceful and legitimate development of the peoples themselves. But no one asks or expects anything more than an equality of rights. Mankind is looking now for freedom of life, not for equipoises of power.

And there is a deeper thing involved than even equality of right among organized nations. No peace can last, or ought to last, which does not recognize and accept the principle that governments derive all their just powers from the consent of the governed, and that no right anywhere exists to hand peoples about from sovereignty to sovereignty as if they were property. I take it for granted, for instance, if I may venture upon a single example, that statesmen everywhere are agreed that there should be a united, independent, and autonomous Poland, and that henceforth inviolable security of life, of worship, and of industrial and social development should be guaranteed to all peoples who have lived hitherto under the power of governments devoted to a faith and purpose hostile to their own. . . .

So far as practicable, moreover, every great people now struggling towards a full development of its resources and of its powers should be assured a direct outlet to the great highways of the sea. Where this cannot be done by the cession of territory, it can no doubt be done by the neutralization of direct rights of way under the general guarantee which will assure the peace itself. With a right comity of arrangement no nation need be shut away from free access to the open paths of the world's commerce.

And the paths of the sea must alike in law and in fact be free. The freedom of the seas is the *sine qua non* of peace, equality, and co-operation. No doubt a somewhat radical reconsideration of many of the rules of international practice hitherto thought to be established may be necessary in order to make the seas indeed free and common in practically all circumstances for the use of mankind, but the motive for such changes is convincing and compelling. There can be no trust or intimacy between the peoples of the world without them. The free, constant, unthreatened intercourse of nations is an essential part of the process of peace and of development. It need not be difficult either to define or to secure the freedom of the seas if the governments of the world sincerely desire to come to an agreement concerning it.

It is a problem closely connected with the limitation of naval armaments and the co-operation of the navies of the world in keeping the seas at once free and safe. And the question of limiting naval armaments opens the wider and perhaps more difficult question of the limitation of armies and of all programs of military preparation. Difficult and delicate as these questions are, they must be faced with the utmost candor and decided in a spirit of real accommodation if peace is to come with healing in its wings, and come to stay. Peace cannot be had without concession and sacrifice. There can be no sense of safety and equality among the nations if great preponderating armaments are henceforth to continue here and there to be built up and maintained. The statesmen of the world must plan for peace and nations must adjust and accommodate their policy to it as they have planned for war and made ready for pitiless contest and rivalry. The question of armaments, whether on land or sea, is the most immediately and intensely practical question connected with the future fortunes of nations and of mankind.

I have spoken upon these great matters without reserve and with the utmost explicitness because it has seemed to me to be necessary if the world's yearning desire for peace was anywhere to find free voice and utterance. Perhaps I am the only person in high authority amongst all the peoples of the world who is at liberty to speak and hold nothing back. I am speaking as an individual, and yet I am speaking also, of course, as the responsible head of a great government, and I feel confident that I have said what the people of the United States would wish me to say. . . .

I am proposing, as it were, that the nations should with one accord adopt the doctrine of President Monroe as the doctrine of the world: that no nation should seek to extend its polity over any other nation or people, but that every people should be left free to determine its own polity, its own way of development, unhindered, unthreatened, unafraid, the little along with the great and powerful.

I am proposing that all nations henceforth avoid entangling alliances which would draw them into competitions of power; catch them in a net of intrigue and selfish rivalry, and disturb their own affairs with influences intruded from without. There is no entangling alliance in a concert of power. When all unite to act in the same sense and with the same purpose all act in the common interest and are free to live their own lives under a common protection.

I am proposing government by the consent of the governed; that freedom of the seas which in international conference after conference representatives of the United States have urged with the eloquence of those who are the convinced disciples of liberty; and that moderation of armaments which makes of armies and navies a power for order merely, not an instrument of aggression or of selfish violence.

These are American principles, American policies. We could stand for no others. And they are also the principles and policies of forward looking men and women everywhere, of every modern nation, of every enlightened community. They are the principles of mankind and must prevail.

417. THE ZIMMERMANN NOTE
Released March 1, 1917

(J. B. Scott, ed. *Diplomatic Correspondence between the United States and Germany,*
p. 338)

This note from the German Foreign Secretary to the German Minister in Mexico, was received by the United States Department of State from the British Naval Intelligence Service, February 26. It was promptly given to the press, and was very effective in consolidating public opinion in favor of war against Germany. See, C. H. Grattan, *Why We Fought;* J. B. Scott, *Survey of International Relations Between the United States and Germany, 1914–1917.*

Berlin, January 19, 1917

On the first of February we intend to begin submarine warfare unrestricted. In spite of this it is our intention to keep neutral the United States of America.

If this attempt is not successful we propose an alliance on the following basis with Mexico: That we shall make war together and together make peace. We shall give general financial support, and it is understood that Mexico is to reconquer the lost territory in New Mexico, Texas, and Arizona. The details are left for your settlement.

You are instructed to inform the President of Mexico of the above in the greatest confidence as soon as it is certain there will be an outbreak of war with the United States, and we suggest that the President of Mexico on his own initiative should communicate with Japan suggesting adherence at once to this plan; at the same time offer to mediate between Germany and Japan.

Please call to the attention of the President of Mexico that the employment of ruthless submarine warfare now promises to compel England to make peace in a few months.

Zimmermann.

418. WILSON'S SPEECH FOR DECLARATION OF WAR AGAINST GERMANY

Address delivered at Joint Session of the Two Houses of Congress, April 2, 1917

(U. S. 65th Congress, 1st Session, *Senate Doc.* 5)

Wilson had been successful during his first administration in avoiding entry into the World War, and the slogan "he kept us out of war" had considerable influence in his re-election in November, 1916. In January, 1917, however, Germany informed the United States that she intended to resume unrestricted submarine warfare; on February 3, Ambassador Bernstorff received his passports, and diplomatic relations with Germany were severed. During March three American merchant ships were sunk by submarines, and Wilson called Congress into extraordinary session, for April 2. Four days later Congress declared war with Germany; war was not declared upon Austria until December 7, 1917. Wilson's speech to Congress was one of the most notable of all his addresses: only the First Inaugural can be compared to it for eloquence. On the causes of the War, see, C. H. Grattan, *Why* *We Fought;* C. Seymour, ed., *The Intimate Papers of Colonel House,* Vol. II; C. Seymour, *American Diplomacy During the World War.*

I have called the Congress into extraordinary session because there are serious, very serious, choices of policy to be made, and made immediately, which it was neither right nor constitutionally permissible that I should assume the responsibility of making.

On the third of February last I officially laid before you the extraordinary announcement of the Imperial German Government that on and after the first day of February it was its purpose to put aside all restraints of law or of humanity and use its submarines to sink every vessel that sought to approach either the ports of Great Britain and Ireland or the western coasts of Europe or any of the ports controlled by the enemies of Germany within the Mediterranean. That had seemed to be the object of the German submarine warfare earlier in the war, but since April of last year the Imperial Government had somewhat restrained the commanders of its undersea craft in conformity with its promise then given to us that passenger boats should not be sunk and that due warning would be given to all other vessels which its submarines might seek to destroy, when no resistance was offered or escape attempted, and care taken that their crews were given at least a fair chance to save their lives in their open boats. The precautions taken were meager and haphazard enough, as was proved in distressing instance after instance in the progress of the cruel and unmanly business, but a certain degree of restraint was observed. The new policy has swept every restriction aside. Vessels of every kind, whatever their flag, their character, their cargo, their destination, their errand, have been ruthlessly sent to the bottom without warning and without thought of help or mercy for those on board, the vessels of friendly neutrals along with those of belligerents. Even hospital ships and ships carrying relief to the sorely bereaved and stricken people of Belgium, though the latter were provided with safe conduct through the proscribed areas by the German Government itself and were distinguished by unmistakable marks of identity, have been sunk with the same reckless lack of compassion or of principle.

I was for a little while unable to believe that such things would in fact be done by any government that had hitherto subscribed to the humane practices of civilized nations. International law had its origin in the attempt to set up some law which would be respected and observed upon the seas, where no nation had right of dominion and where lay the free highways of the world. . . . This minimum of right the German Government has swept aside under the plea of retaliation and necessity and because it had no weapons which it could use at sea except these which it is impossible to employ as it is employing them without throwing to the winds all scruples of humanity or of respect for the

understandings that were supposed to underlie the intercourse of the world. I am not now thinking of the loss of property involved, immense and serious as that is, but only of the wanton and wholesale destruction of the lives of non-combatants, men, women, and children, engaged in pursuits which have always, even in the darkest periods of modern history, been deemed innocent and legitimate. Property can be paid for; the lives of peaceful and innocent people cannot be. The present German submarine warfare against commerce is a warfare against mankind.

It is a war against all nations. American ships have been sunk, American lives taken, in ways which it has stirred us very deeply to learn of, but the ships and people of other neutral and friendly nations have been sunk and overwhelmed in the waters in the same way. There has been no discrimination. The challenge is to all mankind. Each nation must decide for itself how it will meet it. The choice we make for ourselves must be made with a moderation of counsel and a temperateness of judgment befitting our character and our motives as a nation. We must put excited feeling away. Our motive will not be revenge or the victorious assertion of the physical might of the nation, but only the vindication of right, of human right, of which we are only a single champion.

When I addressed the Congress on the twenty-sixth of February last I thought that it would suffice to assert our neutral rights with arms, our right to use the seas against unlawful interference, our right to keep our people safe against unlawful violence. But armed neutrality, it now appears, is impracticable. Because submarines are in effect outlaws when used as the German submarines have been used against merchant shipping, it is impossible to defend ships against their attacks as the law of nations has assumed that merchantmen would defend themselves against privateers or cruisers, visible craft giving chase upon the open sea. It is common prudence in such circumstances, grim necessity indeed, to endeavor to destroy them before they have shown their own intention. They must be dealt with upon sight, if dealt with at all. The German Government denies the right of neutrals to use arms at all within the areas of the sea which it has proscribed, even in the defense of rights which no modern publicist has ever before questioned their right to defend. The intimation is conveyed that the armed guards which we have placed on our merchant ships will be treated as beyond the pale of law and subject to be dealt with as pirates would be. Armed neutrality is ineffectual enough at best; in such circumstances and in the face of such pretensions it is worse than ineffectual: it is likely only to produce what it was meant to prevent; it is practically certain to draw us into the war without either the rights or the effectiveness of belligerents. There is one choice we cannot make, we are incapable of making: we will not choose the path of submission and suffer the most sacred rights of our Nation and our people to be ignored or violated. The wrongs against which we now array ourselves are no common wrongs; they cut to the very roots of human life.

With a profound sense of the solemn and even tragical character of the step I am taking and of the grave responsibilities which it involves, but in unhesitating obedience to what I deem my constitutional duty, I advise that the Congress declare the recent course of the Imperial German Government to be in fact nothing less than war against the government and people of the United States; that it formally accept the status of belligerent which has thus been thrust upon it; and that it take immediate steps not only to put the country in a more thorough state of defense but also to exert all its power and employ all its resources to bring the Government of the German Empire to terms and end the war.

What this will involve is clear. It will involve the utmost practicable coöperation in counsel and action with the governments now at war with Germany, and, as incident to that, the extension to those governments of the most liberal financial credits, in order that our resources may so far as possible be added to theirs. It will involve the organization and mobilization of all the material resources of the country to supply the materials of war and serve the incidental needs of the Nation in the most abundant and yet the most economical and efficient way possible. It will involve the immediate full equipment of the navy in all respects but particularly in supplying it with the best means of dealing with the enemy's submarines. It will involve

the immediate addition to the armed forces of the United States already provided for by law in case of war at least five hundred thousand men, who should, in my opinion, be chosen upon the principle of universal liability to service, and also the authorization of subsequent additional increments of equal force so soon as they may be needed and can be handled in training. It will involve also, of course, the granting of adequate credits to the Government, sustained, I hope, so far as they can equitably be sustained by the present generation, by well conceived taxation. . . .

While we do these things, these deeply momentous things, let us be very clear, and make very clear to all the world what our motives and our objects are. My own thought has not been driven from its habitual and normal course by the unhappy events of the last two months, and I do not believe that the thought of the Nation has been altered or clouded by them. I have exactly the same things in mind now that I had in mind when I addressed the Senate on the twenty-second of January last; the same that I had in mind when I addressed the Congress on the third of February and on the twenty-sixth of February. Our object now, as then, is to vindicate the principles of peace and justice in the life of the world as against selfish and autocratic power and to set up amongst the really free and self-governed peoples of the world such a concert of purpose and of action as will henceforth insure the observance of those principles. Neutrality is no longer feasible or desirable where the peace of the world is involved and the freedom of its peoples, and the menace to that peace and freedom lies in the existence of autocratic governments backed by organized force which is controlled wholly by their will, not by the will of their people. We have seen the last of neutrality in such circumstances. We are at the beginning of an age in which it will be insisted that the same standards of conduct and of responsibility for wrong done shall be observed among nations and their governments that are observed among the individual citizens of civilized states.

We have no quarrel with the German people. We have no feeling towards them but one of sympathy and friendship. It was not upon their impulse that their government acted in entering this war. It was not with their previous knowledge or approval. It was a war determined upon as wars used to be determined upon in the old, unhappy days when peoples were nowhere consulted by their rulers and wars were provoked and waged in the interest of dynasties or of little groups of ambitious men who were accustomed to use their fellow men as pawns and tools. . . .

We are accepting this challenge of hostile purpose because we know that in such a Government, following such methods, we can never have a friend; and that in the presence of its organized power, always lying in wait to accomplish we know not what purpose, there can be no assured security for the democratic Governments of the world. We are now about to accept gauge of battle with this natural foe to liberty and shall, if necessary, spend the whole force of the nation to check and nullify its pretensions and its power. We are glad, now that we see the facts with no veil of false pretense about them, to fight thus for the ultimate peace of the world and for the liberation of its peoples, the German peoples included: for the rights of nations great and small and the privilege of men everywhere to choose their way of life and of obedience. The world must be made safe for democracy. Its peace must be planted upon the tested foundations of political liberty. We have no selfish ends to serve. We desire no conquest, no dominion. We seek no indemnities for ourselves, no material compensation for the sacrifices we shall freely make. We are but one of the champions of the rights of mankind. We shall be satisfied when those rights have been made as secure as the faith and the freedom of nations can make them.

Just because we fight without rancor and without selfish object, seeking nothing for ourselves but what we shall wish to share with all free peoples, we shall, I feel confident, conduct our operations as belligerents without passion and ourselves observe with proud punctilio the principles of right and of fair play we profess to be fighting for.

I have said nothing of the Governments allied with the Imperial Government of Germany because they have not made war upon us or challenged us to defend our right and our honor. The Austro-Hungarian Government has, indeed, avowed its unqualified indorsement and acceptance of the reckless and lawless submarine warfare adopted now without disguise by the Imperial German Government, and it has therefore not been possible for this Government to receive Count Tarnowski, the Ambassador recently accredited to this Government by the Imperial and Royal Government of Austria-Hungary; but that Government has not actually engaged in warfare against citizens of the United States on the seas, and I take the liberty, for the present at least, of postponing a discussion of our relations with the authorities at Vienna. We enter this war only where we are clearly forced into it because there are no other means of defending our rights.

It will be all the easier for us to conduct ourselves as belligerents in a high spirit of right and fairness because we act without animus, not in enmity towards a people or with the desire to bring any injury or disadvantage upon them, but only in armed opposition to an irresponsible government which has thrown aside all considerations of humanity and of right and is running amuck. We are, let me say again, the sincere friends of the German people, and shall desire nothing so much as the early reëstablishment of intimate relations of mutual advantage between us,—however hard it may be for them, for the time being, to believe that this is spoken from our hearts. We have borne with their present Government through all these bitter months because of that friendship,—exercising a patience and forbearance which would otherwise have been impossible. We shall, happily, still have an opportunity to prove that friendship in our daily attitude and actions towards the millions of men and women of German birth and native sympathy who live amongst us and share our life, and we shall be proud to prove it towards all who are in fact loyal to their neighbors and to the Government in the hour of test. They are, most of them, as true and loyal Americans as if they had never known any other fealty or allegiance. They will be prompt to stand with us in rebuking and restraining the few who may be of a different mind and purpose. If there should be disloyalty, it will be dealt with with a firm hand of stern repression; but, if it lifts its head at all, it will lift it only here and there and without countenance except from a lawless and malignant few.

It is a distressing and oppressive duty, Gentlemen of the Congress, which I have performed in thus addressing you. There are, it may be, many months of fiery trial and sacrifice ahead of us. It is a fearful thing to lead this great peaceful people into war, into the most terrible and disastrous of all wars, civilization itself seeming to be in the balance. But the right is more precious than peace, and we shall fight for the things which we have always carried nearest our hearts,— for democracy, for the right of those who submit to authority to have a voice in their own Governments, for the rights and liberties of small nations, for a universal dominion of right by such a concert of free peoples as shall bring peace and safety to all nations and make the world itself at last free. To such a task we can dedicate our lives and our fortunes, everything that we are and everything that we have, with the pride of those who know that the day has come when America is privileged to spend her blood and her might for the principles that gave her birth and happiness and the peace which she has treasured. God helping her, she can do no other.

419. THE LEVER ACT
August 10, 1917
(U. S. Statutes at Large, Vol. XL, p. 276 ff.)

This act authorized the President to conserve food and fuel during the prosecution of the War. The guarantee of two dollars a bushel for wheat was to last until May 1, 1919; actually the price was fixed at $2.20 a bushel. Herbert Hoover was made Food Commissioner, and H. A. Garfield Fuel Commissioner. See, C. R. Van Hise, *Conservation and Regulation in the United States during the World War;* F. M. Surface, *The Stabilization of the Price of Wheat during the War;* W. F. Willoughby, *Government Organization in War Time and After.*

An Article to provide for the national security and defense by encouraging the production, conserving the supply, and controlling the distribution of food products and fuel.

Be it enacted, That by reason of the existence of a state of war, it is essential to the national security and defense, for the successful prosecution of the war, and for the support and maintenance of the Army and Navy, to assure an adequate supply and equitable distribution, and to facilitate the movement, of foods, feeds, fuel . . . and equipment required for the actual production of foods, feeds, and fuel, hereafter in this Act called necessaries; to prevent, . . . scarcity, monopolization, hoarding, injurious speculation, manipulations . . . and private controls, affecting such supply, . . . and to establish and maintain governmental control of such necessaries during the war. For such purposes the instrumentalities . . . and prohibitions hereinafter set forth are created. The President is authorized to make such regulations and to issue such orders as are essential effectively to carry out the provisions of this Act. . . .

SEC. 14. That whenever the President shall find that an emergency exists requiring stimulation of the production of wheat and that it is essential that the producers of wheat, produced within the United States, shall have the benefits of the guaranty provided for in this section, he is authorized, . . . to determine and fix and to give public notice of what, under specified conditions, is a reasonable guaranteed price for wheat, in order to assure such producers a reasonable profit. The President shall thereupon fix such guaranteed price. . . . Thereupon, the Government of the United States hereby guarantees every producer of wheat produced within the United States, that, upon compliance by him with the regulations prescribed, he shall receive for any wheat produced in reliance upon this guarantee within the period, not exceeding eighteen months, prescribed in the notice, a price not less than the guaranteed price therefor as fixed pursuant to this section. . . . The guaranteed prices for the several standard grades of wheat for the crop of nineteen hundred and eighteen, shall be based upon number one northern spring or its equivalent at not less than $2 per bushel at the principal interior primary markets. This guaranty shall not be dependent upon the action of the President under the first part of this section, but is hereby made absolute and shall be binding until May first, nineteen hundred and nineteen. . . .

For the purpose of making any guaranteed price effective under this section, or whenever he deems it essential . . . the President is authorized also, in his discretion, to purchase any wheat for which a guaranteed price shall be fixed . . . and to hold, transport, or store it, or to sell, dispose of, and deliver the same. . . .

SEC. 15. That from and after thirty days from the date of the approval of this Act no foods, fruits, food materials, or feeds shall be used in the production of distilled spirits for beverage purposes: . . . Nor shall there be imported into the United States any distilled spirits. Whenever the President shall find that limitation, regulation, or prohibition of the use of foods, fruits, food materials, or feeds in the production of malt or vinous liquors for beverage purposes, or that reduction of the alcoholic content of any such malt or vinous liquor, is essential, in order to assure an adequate and continuous supply of food, or that the national security and defense will be subserved thereby, he is authorized, from time to time, to prescribe and give public notice of the extent of the limitation, regulation, prohibition, or reduction so necessitated. . . .

SEC. 16. That the President is authorized and directed to commandeer any or all distilled spirits in bond or in stock at the date of the approval of this Act for redistillation, in so far as such redistillation may be necessary to meet the requirements of the Government in the manufacture of munitions and other military and hospital supplies. . . .

SEC. 24. That the provisions of this Act shall cease to be in effect when the existing state of war between the United States and Germany shall have terminated. . . .

SEC. 25. That the President of the United States shall be, . . . empowered, whenever and wherever in his judgment necessary for the efficient prosecution of the war, to fix the price of coal and coke, wherever and whenever sold . . . to regulate the method of production, sale, shipment, distribution, apportionment, or storage thereof among dealers and consumers. . . .

420. THE LANSING–ISHII AGREEMENT
November 2, 1917
(*Foreign Relations of the United States,* 1917, p. 264)

In 1915 Japan had given notice to the world that she would not, in fact, be bound by the Open Door policy. At this time she had presented to China the notorious Twenty-One Demands, fifteen of which China was compelled to accept. By a series of secret agreements with the Allied Powers, during 1916 and 1917, she had secured special concessions and promises of territorial acquisitions in the Far East. In the summer of 1917 Viscount Ishii came to the United States on a special mission for the purpose of quieting American apprehensions of Japanese policies and securing from the United States a modification of the Open Door policy. Ishii insisted that the United States recognize Japan's "paramount" interest in China. The Lansing-Ishii agreement, while apparently confirming the Open Door policy, did actually recognize that Japan had "special interests" in China; to that extent it represented a diplomatic victory for Japan. See, S. F. Bemis, ed. *American Secretaries of State,* Vol. X, p. 126 ff.; J. V. A. MacMurray, *Treaties* *and Agreements with and Concerning China,* Vol. II; W. W. Willoughby, *Foreign Rights and Interests in China,* 2 Vols.; T. F. Millard, *Democracy and the Eastern Question;* H. Chung, *The Oriental Policy of the United States.*

Department of State
Washington, November 2, 1917

Excellency: I have the honor to communicate herein my understanding of the agreement reached by us in our recent conversations touching the questions of mutual interest to our Governments relating to the Republic of China.

In order to silence mischievous reports that have from time to time been circulated, it is believed by us that a public announcement once more of the desires and intentions shared by our two Governments with regard to China is advisable.

The Governments of the United States and Japan recognize that territorial propinquity creates special relations between countries, and consequently the Government of the United States recognizes that Japan has special interests in China, particularly in that part to which her possessions are contiguous.

The territorial sovereignty of China, nevertheless, remains unimpaired, and the Government of the United States has every confidence in the repeated assurances of the Imperial Japanese Government that while geographical position gives Japan such special interests, they have no desire to discriminate against the trade of other nations or to disregard the commercial rights heretofore granted by China in treaties with other powers.

The Governments of the United States and Japan deny that they have any purpose to infringe in any way the independence or territorial integrity of China, and they declare, furthermore, that they always adhere to the principle of the so-called "open-door" or equal opportunity for commerce and industry in China.

Moreover, they mutually declare that they are opposed to the acquisition by any government of any special rights or privileges that would affect the independence or territorial integrity of China, or that would deny to the subjects or citizens of any country the full enjoyment of equal opportunity in the commerce and industry of China.

I shall be glad to have Your Excellency confirm this understanding of the agreement reached by us.

Robert Lansing.

His Excellency Viscount Kikujiro Ishii

421. BUNTING v. OREGON
243 U. S. 426
1917

Error to the supreme court of Oregon. This case involved the interpretation of an Oregon statute of 1913 establishing a ten hour day for all employees in manufacturing establishments and providing that overtime work not to exceed three hours in one day must be paid at the rate of time and one-half of the regular wage.

McKENNA, J. . . . The consonance of the Oregon law with the Fourteenth Amendment is the question in the case, and this depends upon whether it is a proper exercise of the police power of the State, as the supreme court of this State decided that it is.

That the police power extends to health regulations is not denied, but it is denied that the law has such purpose or justification. It is contended that it is a wage law, not a health regulation, and takes the property of plaintiff in error without due process. . . .

There is a certain verbal plausibility in the contention that it was intended to permit thirteen hours' work if there be fifteen and one-half-hours' pay, but the plausibility disappears upon reflection. The provision for overtime is permissive, in the same sense that any penalty may be said to be permissive. Its purpose is to deter by its burden, and its adequacy for this was a matter of legislative judgment under the particular circumstances. . . . We cannot know all of the conditions that impelled the law or its particular form. The supreme court, nearer to them, describes the law as follows: "It is clear that the intent of the law is to make ten hours a regular day's labor in the occupations to which reference is made. Apparently the provisions permitting labor for the overtime on express conditions were made in order to facilitate the enforcement of the law, and in the nature of a mild penalty for employing one not more than three hours overtime. It might be regarded as more difficult to detect violations of the law by an employment for a shorter time than for a longer time. This penalty also goes to the employee in case the employer avails himself of the overtime clause." . . .

But passing general considerations and coming back to our immediate concern, which is the validity of the particular exertion of power in the Oregon law, our judgment of it is that it does not transcend constitutional limits. . . .

There is a contention made that the law, even regarded as regulating hours of service, is not either necessary or useful "for preservation of the health of employees in mills, factories and manufacturing establishments."

The record contains no facts to support the contention, and against it is the judgment of the legislature and the supreme court, which said: "In view of the well-known fact that the custom in our industries does not sanction a longer service than 10 hours per day, it cannot be held, as a matter of law, that the legislative requirement is unreasonable or arbitrary as to hours of labor. Statistics show that the average daily working time among workingmen in different countries is, in Australia, 8 hours; in Great Britain, 9; in the United States, 9¾; in Denmark, 9¾; in Norway, 10; Sweden, France, and Switzerland, 10½; Germany, 10¼; Belgium, Italy, and Austria, 11; and in Russia, 12 hours." . . .

Judgment affirmed.

WHITE, C. J., and VAN DEVANTER, J., and MCREYNOLDS, J., dissented. BRANDEIS, J., took no part in the decision.

422. IMMIGRATION RESTRICTION
The Laws of 1917 and 1921

(U. S. Bureau of Immigration, *Annual Report of the Commissioner-General of Immigration,* 1923, p. 2 ff.)

The law of 1917, passed over the veto of President Wilson, marked a definite end to our traditional immigration policy: the act of 1921 with its quota system inaugurated the present policy of severe restriction. This summary of the two important laws is given in lieu of the acts themselves. For a collection of Documents on Immigration, see E. Abbott, *Selected Documents on Immigration; Historical Aspects of the Immigration Problem.* A brief history of the legislation of the nineteen-twenties can be found in C. P. Howland, ed. *Survey of American Foreign Relations: 1929.*

Perhaps it is not very generally realized that the per centum limit law marked the beginning of actual restriction or limitation of immigration to the United States from Europe, Africa, Australia, and a considerable part of Asia. The Chinese exclusion act of 1882, the passport agreement with Japan which became effective in 1908, and the "barred zone" provision in the general immigration law of 1917 had already stopped or greatly reduced the influx of oriental peoples, but so far as others, and particularly Europeans, were concerned, all applicants who met the various tests prescribed in the general law were admitted. This general law, first enacted in 1882 and several times revised and strengthened, was and still is based on the principle of selection rather than of numerical restriction. It is probably true that the provision barring illiterate aliens from admission, which was added to the general law in 1917, was intended as a restrictive measure rather than a quality test, but in its practical effect it was only another addition to the already numerous class of alleged undesirables who were denied admission, and obviously could not be relied upon actually to limit the volume of immigration.

The immigration act of 1882, which, as already indicated, was the first general law upon the subject, provided for the exclusion from the United States of the following classes only: Convicts, lunatics, idiots, and persons likely to become a public charge. This law underwent more or less important revisions in 1891, 1893, 1903, 1907, and 1917, until the last-mentioned act, which is the present general immigration law, denies admission to many classes of aliens, including the following: Idiots, imbeciles, feeble-minded persons, epileptics, insane persons; persons who have had one or more attacks of insanity at any time previously; persons of constitutional psychopathic inferiority; persons with chronic alcoholism; paupers; professional beggars; vagrants; persons afflicted with tuberculosis in any form or with a loathsome or dangerous contagious disease; persons certified by the examining physician as being mentally or physically defective, such physical defect being of a nature which may affect the ability of the alien to earn a living; persons who have been convicted of or admit having committed a felony or other crime or misdemeanor involving moral turpitude; polygamists, or persons who practice polygamy or believe in or advocate the practice of polygamy; anarchists and similar classes; immoral persons and persons coming for an immoral purpose; contract laborers;

persons likely to become a public charge; persons seeking admission within one year of date of previous debarment or deportation; persons whose ticket or passage is paid for with the money of another or who are assisted by others to come, unless it is affirmatively shown that such persons do not belong to one of the foregoing excluded classes; persons whose ticket or passage is paid for by any corporation, association, society, municipality, or foreign government, either directly or indirectly; stowaways; children under 16 years of age unless accompanied by one or both of their parents; persons who are natives of certain geographically defined territory; aliens over 16 years of age who are unable to read some language or dialect; certain accompanying aliens, as described in the last proviso of section 18 of the act; and persons who have arrived in Canada or Mexico by certain steamship lines. Persons who fail to meet certain passport requirements were added to the excluded classes in subsequent legislation.

Obviously it would be difficult to find, or even to invent, many other terms denoting individual undesirability which might be added to the foregoing list, but, as already pointed out, the general law is essentially selective in theory, for even its most rigid application with respect to the excludable classes above enumerated could not be depended upon to prevent the coming of unlimited numbers of aliens who were able to meet the tests imposed.

Even a casual survey of congressional discussions of the immigration problem during the past quarter of a century demonstrates very clearly that while the law makers were deeply concerned with the mental, moral, and physical quality of immigrants, there developed as time went on an even greater concern as to the fundamental racial character of the constantly increasing numbers who came. The record of alien arrivals year by year had shown a gradual falling off in the immigration of northwest European peoples, representing racial stocks which were common to America even in colonial days, and a rapid and remarkably large increase in the movement from southern and eastern European countries and Asiatic Turkey. Immigration from the last-named sources reached an annual average of about 750,000 and in some

years nearly a million came, and there seems to have been a general belief in Congress that it would increase rather than diminish. At the same time no one seems to have anticipated a revival of the formerly large influx from the "old sources," as the countries of northwest Europe came to be known.

This remarkable change in the sources and racial character of our immigrants led to an almost continuous agitation of the immigration problem both in and out of Congress, and there was a steadily growing demand for restriction, particularly of the newer movement from the south and east of Europe. During the greater part of this period of agitation the so-called literacy test for aliens was the favorite weapon of the restrictionists, and its widespread popularity appears to have been based quite largely on a belief, or at least a hope, that it would reduce to some extent the stream of "new" immigration, about one-third of which was illiterate, without seriously interfering with the coming of the older type, among whom illiteracy was at a minimum.

Presidents Cleveland and Taft vetoed immigration bills because they contained a literacy test provision, and President Wilson vetoed two bills largely for the same reason. In 1917, however, Congress passed a general immigration bill which included the literacy provision over the President's veto, and, with certain exceptions, aliens who are unable to read are no longer admitted to the United States. At that time, however, the World War had already had the effect of reducing immigration from Europe to a low level, and our own entry into the conflict a few days before the law in question went into effect practically stopped it altogether. Consequently, the value of the literacy provision as a means of restricting European immigration was never fairly tested under normal conditions.

The Congress, however, seemingly realized that even the comprehensive immigration law of 1917, including the literacy test, would afford only a frail barrier against the promised rush from the war-stricken countries of Europe, and in December, 1920, the House of Representatives, with little opposition, passed a bill to suspend practically all immigration for the time being. The per centum limit plan was substituted by the Senate, however, and the substitute prevailed in Congress, but it failed to become a law at the time because President Wilson withheld executive approval. Nevertheless, favorable action was not long delayed, for at the special session called at the beginning of the present administration the measure was quickly enacted, and, with President Harding's approval, became a law on May 19, 1921. This law expired by limitation June 30, 1922, but by the act of May 11, 1922, its life was extended to June 30, 1924, and some strengthening amendments were added.

The principal provisions of the per centum limit act, or the "quota law," as it is popularly known, are as follows:

The number of aliens of any nationality who may be admitted to the United States in any fiscal year shall not exceed 3 per cent of the number of persons of such nationality who were resident in the United States according to the census of 1910.

Monthly quotas are limited to 20 per cent of the annual quota.

For the purposes of the act, "nationality" is determined by country of birth.

The law does not apply to the following classes of aliens: Government officials; aliens in transit; aliens visiting the United States as tourists or temporarily for business or pleasure; aliens from countries immigration from which is regulated in accordance with treaties or agreement relating solely to immigration, otherwise China and Japan; aliens from the so-called Asiatic barred zone; aliens who have resided continuously for at least five years in Canada, Newfoundland, Cuba, Mexico, Central or South America, or adjacent islands; aliens under the age of 18 who are children of citizens of the United States.

Certain other classes of aliens who are counted against quotas are admissible after a quota is exhausted. The following are included in this category: Aliens returning from a temporary visit abroad; aliens who are professional actors, artists, lecturers, singers, ministers of any religious denomination, professors for colleges or seminaries, members of any recognized learned profession, or aliens employed as domestic servants.

So far as possible preference is given to the wives and certain near relatives of citizens of the United States, applicants for citizenship and honorably discharged soldiers, eligible to citizenship, who served in the United States military or naval forces at any time between April 6, 1917, and November 11, 1918.

Transportation companies are liable to a fine of $200 for each alien brought to a United States port in excess of the quota and where such fine is imposed the amount paid for passage must be returned to the rejected alien.

The quota limit law is in addition to and not in substitution for the provisions of the immigration laws.

423. THE FOURTEEN POINTS
1. Wilson's Address to Congress January 8, 1918

(Supplement to the Messages and Papers of the Presidents Covering the Second Administration of Woodrow Wilson, p. 8421 ff.)

In this famous speech on War Aims and Peace Terms, President Wilson laid down fourteen points as the "only possible" program for world peace. These points were subsequently taken as the basis for peace negotiations. The immediate background of this speech was the failure of the Interallied Conference to agree upon a formulation of war aims, and the overtures of Russia toward Germany. The fourteen points were based on a report prepared for Mr. Wilson by The Inquiry—a commission organized by Mr. House for the purpose of studying Allied and American policy. See, C. Seymour, *American Diplomacy During the World War*, p. 277 ff.; R. S. Baker,

Woodrow Wilson and the World Settlement, Vol. I, ch. vi. See also, J. B. Scott, ed. *Official Statements of War Aims and Peace Proposals, December 1916 to November 1919.*

Gentlemen of the Congress:

. . . It will be our wish and purpose that the processes of peace, when they are begun, shall be absolutely open and that they shall involve and permit henceforth no secret understandings of any kind. The day of conquest and aggrandizement is gone by; so is also the day of secret covenants entered into in the interest of particular governments and likely at some unlooked-for moment to upset the peace of the world. It is this happy fact, now clear to the view of every public man whose thoughts do not still linger in an age that is dead and gone, which makes it possible for every nation whose purposes are consistent with justice and the peace of the world to avow now or at any other time the objects it has in view.

We entered this war because violations of right had occurred which touched us to the quick and made the life of our own people impossible unless they were corrected and the world secured once for all against their recurrence. What we demand in this war, therefore, is nothing peculiar to ourselves. It is that the world be made fit and safe to live in; and particularly that it be made safe for every peace-loving nation which, like our own, wishes to live its own life, determine its own institutions, be assured of justice and fair dealing by the other peoples of the world as against force and selfish aggression. All the peoples of the world are in effect partners in this interest, and for our own part we see very clearly that unless justice be done to others it will not be done to us. The program of the world's peace, therefore, is our program; and that program, the only possible program, as we see it, is this:

I. Open covenants of peace, openly arrived at, after which there shall be no private international understandings of any kind but diplomacy shall proceed always frankly and in the public view.

II. Absolute freedom of navigation upon the seas, outside territorial waters, alike in peace and in war, except as the seas may be closed in whole or in part by international action for the enforcement of international covenants.

III. The removal, so far as possible, of all economic barriers and the establishment of an equality of trade conditions among all the nations consenting to the peace and associating themselves for its maintenance.

IV. Adequate guarantees given and taken that national armaments will be reduced to the lowest point consistent with domestic safety.

V. A free, open-minded, and absolutely impartial adjustment of all colonial claims, based upon a strict observance of the principle that in determining all such questions of sovereignty the interests of the populations concerned must have equal weight with the equitable claims of the government whose title is to be determined.

VI. The evacuation of all Russian territory and such a settlement of all questions affecting Russia as will secure the best and freest coöperation of the other nations of the world in obtaining for her an unhampered and unembarrassed opportunity for the independent determination of her own political development and national policy and assure her of a sincere welcome into the society of free nations under institutions of her own choosing; and, more than a welcome, assistance also of every kind that she may need and may herself desire. The treatment accorded Russia by her sister nations in the months to come will be the acid test of their good will, of their comprehension of her needs as distinguished from their own interests, and of their intelligent and unselfish sympathy.

VII. Belgium, the whole world will agree, must be evacuated and restored, without any attempt to limit the sovereignty which she enjoys in common with all other free nations. No other single act will serve as this will serve to restore confidence among the nations in the laws which they have themselves set and determined for the government of their relations with one another. Without this healing act the whole structure and validity of international law is forever impaired.

VIII. All French territory should be freed and the invaded portions restored, and the wrong done to France by Prussia in 1871 in the matter of Alsace-Lorraine, which has unsettled the peace of the world for nearly fifty years, should be righted, in order that peace may once more be made secure in the interest of all.

IX. A readjustment of the frontiers of Italy should be effected along clearly recognizable lines of nationality.

X. The peoples of Austria-Hungary, whose place among the nations we wish to see safeguarded and assured, should be accorded the freest opportunity of autonomous development.

XI. Rumania, Serbia, and Montenegro should be evacuated; occupied territories restored; Serbia accorded free and secure access to the sea; and the relations of the several Balkan states to one another determined by friendly counsel along historically established lines of allegiance and nationality; and international guarantees of the political and economic independence and territorial integrity of the several Balkan states should be entered into.

XII. The Turkish portions of the present Ottoman Empire should be assured a secure sovereignty, but the other nationalities which are now under Turkish rule should be assured an undoubted security of life and an absolutely unmolested opportunity of autonomous development, and the Dardanelles should be permanently opened as a free passage to the ships and commerce of all nations under international guarantees.

XIII. An independent Polish state should be erected which should include the territories inhabited by indisputably Polish populations, which should be assured a free and secure access to the sea, and whose political and economic independence and territorial integrity should be guaranteed by international covenant.

XIV. A general association of nations must be formed under specific covenants for the purpose of affording mutual guarantees of political independence and territorial integrity to great and small states alike.

In regard to these essential rectifications of wrong and assertions of right we feel ourselves to be intimate partners of all the governments and peoples associated together against the Imperialists. We cannot be separated in interest or divided in purpose. We stand together until the end.

For such arrangements and covenants we are willing to fight and to continue to fight until they are achieved; but only because we wish the right to prevail and desire a just and stable peace such as can be secured only by removing the chief provocations to war, which this program does not remove. We have no jealousy of German greatness, and there is nothing in this program that impairs it. We grudge her no achievement or distinction of learning or of pacific enterprise such as have made her record very bright and very enviable. We do not wish to injure her or to block in any way her legitimate influence or power. We do not wish to fight her either with arms or with hostile arrangements of trade if she is willing to associate herself with us and the other peace-loving nations of the world in covenants of justice and law and fair dealing. We wish her only to accept a place of equality among the peoples of the world,—the new world in which we now live, —instead of a place of mastery.

Neither do we presume to suggest to her any alteration or modification of her institutions. But it is necessary, we must frankly say, and necessary as a preliminary to any intelligent dealings with her on our part, that we should know whom her spokesmen speak for when they speak to us, whether for the Reichstag majority or for the military party and the men whose creed is imperial domination.

We have spoken now, surely, in terms too concrete to admit of any further doubt or question. An evident principle runs through the whole program I have outlined. It is the principle of justice to all peoples and nationalities, and their right to live on equal terms of liberty and safety with one another, whether they be strong or weak. Unless this principle be made its foundation no part of the structure of international justice can stand. The people of the United States could act upon no other principle; and to the vindication of this principle they are ready to devote their lives, their honor, and everything that they possess. The moral climax of this the culminating and final war for human liberty has come, and they are ready to put their own strength, their own highest purpose, their own integrity and devotion to the test.

2. The American Interpretation of the Fourteen Points

(Foreign Relations of the United States, 1918, Supplement, Vol. I, p. 405 ff.)

This semi-official interpretation of the Fourteen Points was prepared under the supervision of Colonel House by Frank Cobb and Walter Lippman. "These interpretations," wrote Colonel House, "were on the table day after day when we sat in conference. . . . Many times they asked the meaning of this or that point and I would read from the accepted interpretation." (*Intimate Papers of Colonel House*, Vol. IV, p. 154.) See C. Seymour, *American Diplomacy During the World War*, p. 372 ff.

1. The purpose is clearly to prohibit treaties, sections of treaties of understandings that are secret, such as the [Triple Alliance], etc.

The phrase "openly arrived at" need not cause difficulty. In fact, the President explained to the Senate last winter that the phrase was not meant to exclude confidential diplomatic negotiations involving delicate matters. The intention is that nothing which occurs in the course of such confidential negotiations shall be binding unless it appears in the final covenant made public to the world.

The matter may perhaps be put this way: it is proposed that in future every treaty be part of the public law of the world, and that every nation assume a certain obligation in regard to its enforcement. Obviously, nations cannot assume obligations in matters of which they are ignorant; and therefore any secret treaty tends to undermine the solidity of the whole structure of international covenants which it is proposed to erect.

2. This proposition must be read in connection with number 14 which proposes a league of nations. It refers to navigation under the three following conditions: (1) general peace; (2) a general war, entered into by the League of Nations for the purpose of enforcing international covenants; (3) limited war, involving no breach of international covenants.

Under "(1) General peace" no serious dispute exists. There is implied freedom to come and go [on the high seas].

No serious dispute exists as to the intention under "(2) A general war entered into by the League of Nations to enforce international covenants." Obviously such a war is conducted against an outlaw nation and complete non-intercourse with that nation is intended.

"(3) A limited war, involving no breach of international covenants" is the crux of the whole difficulty. The question is, what are to be the rights of neutral shipping and private property on the high seas during a war between a limited number of nations when that war involves no issue upon which the League of Nations cares to take sides. In other words, a war in which the League of Nations remains

neutral. Clearly, it is the intention of the proposal that in such a war the rights of neutrals shall be maintained against the belligerents, the rights of both to be clearly and precisely defined in the law of nations.

3. The proposal applies only to those nations which accept the responsibilities of membership in the League of Nations. It means the destruction of all special commercial agreements, each putting the trade of every other nation in the League on the same basis, the most-favored-nation clause applying automatically to all members of the League of Nations. Thus a nation could legally maintain a tariff or a special railroad rate or a port restriction against the whole world, or against all the signatory powers. It could maintain any kind of restriction which it chose against a nation not in the League. But it could not discriminate as between its partners in the League.

This clause naturally contemplates fair and equitable understanding as to the distribution of raw materials.

4. "Domestic safety" clearly implies not only internal policing, but the protection of territory against invasion. The accumulation of armaments above this level would be a violation of the intention of the proposal.

What guarantees should be given and taken, or what are to be the standards of judgment have never been determined. It will be necessary to adopt the general principle and then institute some kind [of international commission of investigation] to prepare detailed projects for its execution.

5. Some fear is expressed in France [and England] that this involves reopening of all colonial questions. Obviously it is not so intended. It applies clearly [to those] colonial claims which have been created by the war. That means the German colonies and any other colonies which may come under international consideration as a result of the war. . . .

What are the "interests of the populations"? That they should not be militarized, that exploitation should be conducted on the principle of the "open door", and under the strictest regulation as to labor conditions, profits and taxes, that a sanitary regime be maintained, that permanent improvements in the way of roads, etc., be made, that native organization and custom be respected, that the protecting authority be stable and experienced enough to thwart intrigue and corruption, that the [protecting] power have adequate resources in money and competent administrators to act successfully.

It would seem as if the principle involved in this proposition is that a colonial power acts not as owner of its colonies, but as trustee for the natives and for the interests of the society of nations, that the terms on which the colonial administration is conducted are a matter of international concern and may legitimately be the subject of international inquiry, and that the peace conference may, therefore, write a code of colonial conduct binding upon [all] colonial powers.

6. The first question is whether Russian territory is synonymous with territory belonging to the former Russian Empire. This is clearly not so, because proposition 13 stipulates an independent Poland, a proposal which excludes the territorial reëstablishment of the Empire. What is recognized as valid for the Poles will certainly have to be recognized for the Finns, the Lithuanians, the Letts, and perhaps also for the Ukrainians. Since the formulating of this condition these subject nationalities have emerged, and there can be no doubt that they will have to be granted an opportunity of free development.

The problem of these nationalities is complicated by two facts: (1) that they have conflicting claims; (2) that the evacuation called for in the proposal may be followed by Bolshevist revolutions in all of them. . . .

This can mean nothing less than the [recognition] by the peace conference of a series of [de facto] governments representing Finns, Esths, Lithuanians, Ukrainians. This primary [act] of recognition should be conditional upon the calling of national assemblies for the creation of de facto governments, as soon as the peace conference has drawn frontiers for these new states. The frontiers should be drawn so far as possible on ethnic lines, but in [every] case the right of unhampered economic [transit] should be reserved. No dynastic ties with German [or] Austrian or Romanoff princes should be permitted, and every inducement should be [given] to encourage federal [relations] between these new states. Under proposition 3 the economic sections of the treaty of Brest-Litovsk are obliterated, but this proposition should not be construed as forbidding a customs union, a monetary union, a railroad union, etc., of these states. Provision should also be made by which Great Russia can federate with these states on the same terms. . . .

The essence of the Russian problem then in the immediate future would seem to be: (1) the recognition of provisional governments; (2) assistance extended to and through these governments. . . .

In any case the treaties of Brest-Litovsk and Bucharest must be cancelled as palpably fraudulent. Provision must be made for the withdrawal of all German troops in Russia and the peace conference [will] have a clean slate on which to write a policy for all the Russian peoples.

7. The only problem raised here is in the word "restored". Whether restoration is to be in kind or how the amount of the indemnity is to be determined is a matter of detail, not of principle. The principle that should be established is that in the case of Belgium there exists no distinction between "legitimate" and "illegitimate" destruction. The initial act of invasion was illegitimate and therefore all the consequences of that act are of the same character. Among the consequences may be put the war debt of Belgium. The recognition of this principle would constitute "the healing act" of which the President speaks.

8. In regard to the restoration of French territory it might well be argued that the invasion of northern France, being the result of the illegal act as regards Belgium, was in itself illegal. But the case is not perfect. As the world stood in 1914, war between France and Germany was not in itself a violation of international law, and great insistence should be put upon keeping the Belgian case distinct and symbolic. Thus Belgium might well, as indicated above, claim reimbursement not only for destruction but for the cost of carrying on the war. France could not claim payment, it would seem, for more than the damage done to her northeastern departments.

The status of Alsace-Lorraine was settled by the official statement issued a few days ago. It is to be restored completely to French sovereignty.

Attention is called to the strong current of French opinion which claims "the boundaries of 1914 [1814]" rather than of 1871. The territory claimed is the valley of the Saar with its coalfields. No claim on grounds of nationality can be established, but the argument leans on the possibility of taking this territory in lieu of indemnity; it would seem to be a clear violation of the President's proposal.

Attention is called also to the fact that no reference is made to status of Luxemburg. The best solution would seem to be a free choice by the [people of] Luxemburg themselves.

9. This proposal is less than the Italian claim; less, of course, than the territory allotted by the treaty of London; less than the arrangement made between the Italian Government and the Jugo-Slav state.

In the region of Trent the Italians claim a strategic rather than ethnic frontier. It should be noted in this connection that [Italy] and Germany will become neighbors if German Austria joins the German Empire. And if Italy obtains the best geographical frontier she will assume sovereignty over a large number of Germans. This is a violation of principle. But it may be argued that by drawing a sharp line along the crest of the Alps, Italy's security will be enormously enhanced and the necessity of heavy armaments reduced. It might, therefore, be provided that Italy should have her claim in the Trentino, but that the northern part, inhabited by Germans, should be completely autonomous and that the population should not be liable to military service in the Italian Army. Italy could thus occupy the uninhabited Alpine peaks for military purposes, but would not govern the cultural life of the alien population to the south of her frontier.

The other problems of the frontier are questions between Italy and Jugo-Slavia, Italy and the Balkans, Italy and Greece.

The agreement reached with Jugo-Slavs may well be allowed to stand, although it should be insisted for [the protection of] the hinterland that both Trieste and Fiume be free ports. This is [essential] to Bohemia, German Austria, Hungary, as well as to prosperity of the cities themselves. . . .

Italy's claims in Turkey belong to the problem of the Turkish Empire.

10. This proposition no longer holds. Instead we have [today] the following elements:

(1) Czecho-Slovakia. Its territories include at least a million Germans for whom some provision must be made.

The independence of Slovakia means the dismemberment of the northwestern countries of Hungary.

(2) Galicia. Western Galicia is clearly Polish. Eastern Galicia is in large measure Ukrainian (or Ruthenian) and does not of right belong to Poland.

There also are several hundred thousand Ukrainians among the north and northeastern borders of Hungary and in parts of Bukowina (which belonged to Austria).

(3) German Austria. This territory should of right be permitted to join Germany, but there is strong objection in [France] because of the increase of [population] involved.

(4) Jugo-Slavia. It faces the following problems: (a) Frontier questions with Italy in Istria and the Dalmatian coast; with Roumania in the Banat. (b) An international problem arises out of the refusal of the Croats to accept the domination of the Serbs of Servian Kingdom. (c) A problem of the Mohammedan Serbs of Bosnia who are said to be loyal to the Hapsburgs. They constitute a little less than one-third of the population.

(5) Transylvania. Will undoubtedly join Roumania, but provision must be made for the protection of the Magyars, Szeklers and Germans who constitute a large minority.

(6) Hungary. Now independent and very democratic in form, but governed by Magyars whose aim is to prevent the detachment of territory of nationalities on the fringe.

The United States is clearly committed to the program of national unity and independence. It must stipulate, however, for the protection of national minorities, for freedom of access to the Adriatic and the Black Sea, and it supports a program aiming at a confederation of southeastern Europe.

11. This proposal is also altered by events. Servia will appear as Jugo-Slavia with access to the Adriatic. Roumania will have acquired the Dobrudja, Bessarabia and probably Transylvania. These two states will have eleven or twelve million inhabitants and will be far greater and stronger than Bulgaria.

Bulgaria should clearly have her frontier in the southern Dobrudja as it stood before the second Balkan War. She should also have Thrace up to the Enos-Midia line and perhaps even to the Midia-Rodosto line.

Macedonia should be allotted after an impartial investigation. The line which might be taken as a basis of investigation is the southern line of the "contested zone" agreed upon by Serbia and Bulgaria before the first Balkan War.

Albania could be under a protectorate, no doubt of Italy, and its frontiers in the north might be essentially those of the London conference.

12. The same difficulty arises here as in the case of Austria-Hungary concerning the word "autonomous".

It is clear that the Straits and Constantinople, while they may remain nominally Turkish, should be under international control. This control may be collective or be in the hands of one power as mandatory of the League.

Anatolia should be reserved for the Turks. The coast lands, where Greeks predominate, should be under special international control, perhaps with Greece as mandatory.

Armenia must be [given] a port on the Mediterranean, and a protecting power established. France may claim it, but the Armenians would prefer Great Britain.

Syria has already been allotted to France by agreement with Great Britain.

Great Britain is clearly the best mandatory for Palestine, Mesopotamia and Arabia.

A general code of guarantees binding upon all mandatories in Asia Minor should be written into the treaty of peace.

This should contain provisions for minorities and the "open door". The trunk railroad lines should be internationalized.

13. The chief problem is whether Poland is to obtain territory west of the Vistula, which would cut off the Germans of East Prussia from the Empire, or whether Danzig can be made a free port and the Vistula internationalized.

On the east, Poland should receive no territory in which Lithuanians or Ukrainians predominate.

If Posen and Silesia go to Poland, rigid protection must be afforded the minorities of Germans and Jews living there, as well as in other parts of the Polish state.

The principle on which frontiers will be [delimited] is contained in the President's word "indisputably". This may imply the taking of an impartial census before frontiers are marked.

14. The principle of a league of nations as the primary essential of a permanent peace has been so clearly presented by President Wilson in his speech of September 27, 1918, that no further elucidation is required. It is the foundation of the whole diplomatic structure of a permanent peace.

3. The Allies Accept the Fourteen Points
November 5, 1918

(Foreign Relations of the United States, 1918, Supplement, Vol. I, p. 468–9)

In October, 1918, the German Government opened negotiations with President Wilson looking to an armistice on the basis of the Fourteen Points. While Wilson was willing to conclude an armistice on this basis as far as the United States was concerned, he could not bind the Allies to any such agreement. The diplomacy of Colonel House and the threat from Wilson of independent action by the United States finally forced the Allies to agree to accept the Fourteen Points as a basis for the Armistice, but with an important reservation on the interpretation of the second point—the freedom of the seas. See C. Seymour, *American Diplomacy During the World War,* chs. viii–x; R. S. Baker, *Woodrow Wilson and the World Settlement,* Vol. I, ch. x.

The Allied Governments have given careful consideration to the correspondence which has passed between the President of the United States and the German Government. Subject to the qualifications which follow they declare their willingness to make peace with the Government of Germany on the terms of peace laid down in the President's address to Congress of January, 1918, and the principles of settlement enunciated in his subsequent addresses. They must point out, however, that clause 2, relating to what is usually described as the freedom of the seas, is open to various interpretations, some of which they could not accept. They must, therefore, reserve to themselves complete freedom on this subject when they enter the peace conference.

Further, in the conditions of peace laid down in his address to Congress of January 8, 1918, the President declared that invaded territories must be restored as well as evacuated and freed, the Allies feel that no doubt

ought to be allowed to exist as to what this provision implies. By it they understand that compensation will be made by Germany for all damage done to the civilian population of the Allies and their property by the aggression of Germany by land, by sea and from the air.

424. RAILWAY ADMINISTRATION ACT
March 21, 1918
(*U. S. Statutes at Large*, Vol. XL, p. 451 ff.)

Shortly after the outbreak of the war the Railroads created a Railroads' War Board to secure more unified administration of the roads; the results were disappointing and in December 1917 the Government took over control of the railroads. The Act of March 21, 1917 provided for the operation of the roads and for compensation to the owners. Governmental operation aroused considerable criticism on grounds of extravagance, but on the whole the roads were operated efficiently and soundly. For the return of the roads to private ownership and control, see the Transportation Act of 1920, Doc. No. 438. On government operation, see F. H. Dixon, *Railroads and Government, 1910–1921;* W. D. Hines, *War History of American Railroads;* R. MacVeagh, *Transportation Act of 1920.*

An Act To provide for the operation of transportation systems while under Federal control, for the just compensation of their owners, and for other purposes.
BE *it enacted* . . . That the President, having in time of war taken over the possession, use, control, and operation (called herein Federal control) of certain railroads and systems of transportation (called herein carriers), is hereby authorized to agree with and to guarantee to any such carrier making operating returns to the Interstate Commerce Commission, that during the period of such Federal control it shall receive as just compensation an annual sum, payable from time to time in reasonable installments, for each year and pro rata for any fractional year of such Federal control, not exceeding a sum equivalent as nearly as may be to its average annual railway operating income for the three years ended June thirtieth, nineteen hundred and seventeen.

That any railway operating income accruing during the period of Federal control in excess of such just compensation shall remain the property of the United States. . . .

Every such agreement shall also contain adequate and appropriate provisions for the maintenance, repair, renewals, and depreciation of the property, for the creation of any reserves or reserve funds found necessary in connection therewith, and for such accounting and adjustments of charges and payments, both during and at the end of Federal control as may be requisite in order that the property of each carrier may be returned to it in substantially as good repair and in substantially as complete equipment as it was in at the beginning of Federal control, and also that the United States may, by deductions from the just compensations or by other proper means and charges, be reimbursed for the cost of any additions, repairs, renewals, and betterments to such property not justly chargeable to the United States; in making such accounting and adjustments, due consideration shall be given to the amounts expended or reserved by each carrier for maintenance, repairs, renewals, and depreciation during the three years ended June thirtieth, nineteen hundred and seventeen, to the condition of the property at the beginning and at the end of Federal control and to any other pertinent facts and circumstances. . . .

SEC. 5. That no carrier while under Federal control shall, without the prior approval of the President, declare or pay any dividend in excess of its regular rate of dividends during the three years ended June thirtieth, nineteen hundred and seventeen: *Provided, however,* That such carriers as have paid no regular dividends or no dividends during said period may, with the prior approval of the President, pay dividends at such rate as the President may determine.

SEC. 6. That the sum of $500,000,000 is hereby appropriated, out of any moneys in the Treasury not otherwise appropriated, which, together with any funds available from any operating income of said carriers, may be used by the President as a revolving fund for the purpose of paying the expenses of the Federal control, and so far as necessary the amount of just compensation, and to provide terminals, motive power, cars, and other necessary equipment, such terminals, motive power, cars, and equipment to be used and accounted for as the President may direct and to be disposed of as Congress may hereafter by law provide.

The President may also make or order any carrier to make any additions, betterments, or road extensions, and to provide terminals, motive power, cars and other equipment necessary or desirable for war purposes or in the public interest on or in connection with the property of any carrier. He may from said revolving fund advance to such carrier all or any part of the expense of such additions, betterments, or road extensions, and to provide terminals, motive power, cars, and other necessary equipment so ordered and constructed by such carrier or by the President, such advances to be charged against such carrier and to bear interest at such rate and be payable on such terms as may be determined by the President, to the end that the United States may be fully reimbursed for any sums so advanced. . . .

From said revolving fund the President may expend such an amount as he may deem necessary or desirable for the utilization and operation of canals, or for the purchase . . . and operation of boats . . . and other transportation facilities on the inland, canal, or coastwise waterways. . . .

SEC. 10. . . . That during the period of Federal control, whenever in his opinion the public interest requires, the President may initiate rates, fares, charges, classifications, regulations, and practices by filing the same with the Interstate Commerce Commission, which said rates, fares, charges, classifications, regulations, and practices shall not be suspended by the commission pending final determination. . . .

SEC. 14. That the Federal control of railroads and transportation systems herein and heretofore provided for shall continue for and during the period of the war and for a reasonable time thereafter, which shall not exceed one year and nine months next following the date of the proclamation by the President of the exchange of ratifications of the treaty of peace: *Provided, however,* That the President may, prior tu July first, nineteen hundred and eighteen, relinquish control of all or any part of any railroad or system of transportation, further Federal control of which the President shall deem not needful or desirable; and the President may at any time during the period of Federal control agree with the owners thereof to relinquish all or any part of any railroad or system of transportation. The President may relinquish all railroads and systems of transportation under the Federal control at any time he shall deem such action needful or desirable. No right to compensation shall accrue to such owners from and after the date of relinquishment for the property so relinquished. . . .

SEC. 16. That this Act is expressly declared to be emergency legislation enacted to meet conditions growing out of war; and nothing herein is to be construed as expressing or prejudicing the future policy of the Federal Government concerning the ownership, control, or regulation of carriers or the method or basis of the capitalization thereof.

425. THE ESPIONAGE ACT
May 16, 1918
(*U. S. Statutes at Large,* Vol. XL, p. 553 ff.)

This Act was far more drastic than the act of June 15, 1917, and made the Sedition Act of 1798 look very mild indeed. Under Attorney-General Palmer the Espionage Act was drastically enforced, and freedom of speech and of the press temporarily disappeared. See, Z. Chafee, *Freedom of Speech.* For the judicial interpretation of the act, see *Schenck,* v. *U. S.,* Doc. No. 426 and *Abrams* v. *U. S.,* Doc. No. 427.

Be it enacted, That section three of the Act . . . approved June 15, 1917, be . . . amended so as to read as follows:

"Sec. 3. Whoever, when the United States is

at war, shall wilfully make or convey false reports or false statements with intent to interfere with the operation or success of the military or naval forces of the United States, or to promote the success of its enemies, or shall wilfully make or convey false reports, or false statements, or say or do anything except by way of bona fide and not disloyal advice to an investor . . . with intent to obstruct the sale by the United States of bonds . . . or the making of loans by or to the United States, or whoever, when the United States is at war, shall wilfully cause . . . or incite . . . insubordination, disloyalty, mutiny, or refusal of duty, in the military or naval forces of the United States, or shall wilfully obstruct . . . the recruiting or enlistment service of the United States, and whoever, when the United States is at war, shall wilfully utter, print, write, or publish any disloyal, profane, scurrilous, or abusive language about the form of government of the United States, or the Constitution of the United States, or the military or naval forces of the United States, or the flag . . . or the uniform of the Army or Navy of the United States, or any language intended to bring the form of government . . . or the Constitution . . . or the military or naval forces . . . or the flag . . . of the United States into contempt, scorn, contumely, or disrepute . . . or shall wilfully display the flag of any foreign enemy, or shall wilfully . . . urge, incite, or advocate any curtailment of production in this country of any thing or things . . . necessary or essential to the prosecution of the war . . . and whoever shall wilfully advocate, teach, defend, or suggest the doing of any of the acts or things in this section enumerated and whoever shall by word or act support or favor the cause of any country with which the United States is at war or by word or act oppose the cause of the United States therein, shall be punished by a fine of not more than $10,000 or imprisonment for not more than twenty years, or both. . . .

426. SCHENCK v. UNITED STATES
249 U. S. 47
1919

Error to the United States district court for the Eastern district of Pennsylvania. This case involved the constitutionality of the Espionage Act of June 15, 1917, Doc. No. 425. The defendants alleged that the act violated the First Amendment to the Constitution. Compare this opinion to the dissenting opinion of Mr. Justice Holmes in the *Abrams* v. *United States,* Doc. No. 427.

HOLMES, J. This is an indictment in three counts. The first charges a conspiracy to violate the Espionage Act of June 15, 1917 . . . by causing and attempting to cause insubordination, &c., in the military and naval forces of the United States, and to obstruct the recruiting and enlistment service of the United States, when the United States was at war with the German Empire, to wit, that the defendants wilfully conspired to have printed and circulated to men who had been called and accepted for military service under the Act of May 18, 1917, a document set forth and alleged to be calculated to cause such insubordination and obstruction. The count alleges overt acts in pursuance of the conspiracy, ending in

the distribution of the document set forth. . . . They set up the First Amendment to the Constitution forbidding Congress to make any law abridging the freedom of speech, or of the press, and bringing the case here on that ground have argued some other points also of which we must dispose.

It is argued that the evidence, if admissible, was not sufficient to prove that the defendant Schenck was concerned in sending the documents. According to the testimony Schenck said he was general secretary of the Socialist party and had charge of the Socialist headquarters from which the documents were sent. He identified a book found there as the minutes of the Executive Committee of the party. The book showed a resolution of August 13, 1917, that 15,000 leaflets should be printed on the other side of one of them in use, to be mailed to men who had passed exemption boards, and for distribution. Schenck personally attended to the printing. On August 20 the general secretary's report said, "Obtained new leaflets from printer and started work addressing envelopes" &c.; and there was a resolve that Comrade Schenck be allowed $125 for sending leaflets through the mail. He said that he had about fifteen or sixteen thousand printed. There were files of the circular in question in the inner office which he said were printed on the other side of the one sided circular and were there for distribution. Other copies were proved to have been sent through the mails to drafted men. Without going into confirmatory details that were proved, no reasonable man could doubt that the defendant Schenck was largely instrumental in sending the circulars about. . . .

The document in question upon its first printed side recited the first section of the Thirteenth Amendment, said that the idea embodied in it was violated by the Conscription Act and that a conscript is little better than a convict. In impassioned language it intimated that conscription was despotism in its worse form and a monstrous wrong against humanity in the interest of Wall Street's chosen few. It said, "Do not submit to intimidation," but in form at least confined itself to peaceful measures such as a petition for the repeal of the act. The other and later printed side of the sheet was headed "Assert Your Rights." It stated reasons for alleging that any one violated the Constitution when he refused to recognize "your right to assert your opposition to the draft," and went on "If you do not assert and support your rights, you are helping to deny or disparage rights which it is the solemn duty of all citizens and residents of the United States to retain." It described the arguments on the other side as coming from cunning politicians and a mercenary capitalist press, and even silent consent to the conscription law as helping to support an infamous conspiracy. It denied the power to send our citizens away to foreign shores to shoot up the people of other lands, and added that words could not express the condemnation such cold-blooded ruthlessness deserves, &c., &c., winding up "You must do your share to maintain, support and uphold the rights of the people of this country." Of course the document would not have been sent unless it had been intended to have some effect, and we do not see what effect it could be expected to have upon persons subject to the draft except to influence them to obstruct the carrying of it out. The defendants do not deny that the jury might find against them on this point.

But it is said, suppose that that was the tendency of this circular, it is protected by the First Amendment to the Constitution. . . . We admit that in many places and in ordinary times the defendants in saying all that was said in the circular would have been within their constitutional rights. But the character of every act depends upon the circumstances in which it is done. The most stringent protection of free speech would not protect a man in falsely shouting fire in a theatre and causing a panic. It does not even protect a man from an injunction against uttering words that may have all the effect of force. The question in every case is whether the words used are used in such circumstances and are of such a nature as to create a clear and present danger that they will bring about the substantive evils that Congress has a right to prevent. It is a question of proximity and degree. When a nation is at war many things that might be said in time of peace are such a hindrance to its effort that their utterance will not be endured so long as men fight and that no Court could regard them as protected by any constitutional right. It seems to be admitted that if an actual obstruction of the recruiting service were proved, liability for words that produced that effect might be enforced. The statute of 1917 in sec. 4 punishes conspiracies to obstruct as well as actual obstruction. If the act, (speaking, or circulating a paper,) its tendency and the intent with which it is done are the same, we perceive no ground for saying that success alone warrants making the act a crime. . . .

Judgements affirmed.

427. ABRAMS v. UNITED STATES
250 U. S. 616
1919

We have included only the dissenting opinion in this case. The position of the Court on the interpretation of laws limiting freedom of speech can be read in *Schenck* v. *United States,* Doc. No. 426, and *Gitlow* v. *New York,* Doc. No. 456. Mr. Justice Holmes's dissent is significant because it expresses much of his legal philosophy and because of its literary quality. For Mr. Justice Holmes, see, S. Bent, *Mr. Justice Holmes;* F. Frankfurter, ed. *Mr. Justice Holmes;* A. Lief, ed. *The Dissenting Opinions of Mr. Justice Holmes;* D. Richardson, *The Constitutional Doctrines of Justice Holmes.*

HOLMES, J., dissenting. This indictment is found wholly upon the publication of two leaflets which I shall describe in a moment. The first count charges a conspiracy pending the war with Germany to publish abusive language about the form of government of the United States, laying the preparation and publishing of the first leaflet as overt acts. The second count charges a conspiracy pending the war to publish language intended to bring the form of government into contempt, laying the preparation and publishing of the two leaflets as overt acts. The third count alleges a conspiracy to encourage resistance to the United States in the same war and to attempt to effectuate the purpose by publishing the same leaflets. The fourth count lays a conspiracy to incite curtailment of production of things necessary to the prosecution of the war and to attempt to accomplish it by publishing the second leaflet to which I have referred. . . .

No argument seems to me necessary to show that these pronunciamentos in no way attack the form of government of the United States, or that they do not support either of the first two counts. What little I have to say about the third count may be postponed until I have considered the fourth. With regard to that it seems too plain to be denied that the suggestion to workers in the ammunition factories that they are producing bullets to murder their dearest, and the further advocacy of a general strike, both in the second leaflet, do urge curtailment of production of things necessary to the prosecution of the war within the meaning of

the Act of May 16, 1918, c. 75, 40 Stat. 553, amending part 3 of the earlier Act of 1917. But to make the conduct criminal that statute requires that it should be "with intent by such curtailment to cripple or hinder the United States in the prosecution of the war." It seems to me that no such intent is proved.

I am aware of course that the word intent as vaguely used in ordinary legal discussion means no more than knowledge at the time of the act that the consequences said to be intended will ensue. Even less than that will satisfy the general principle of civil and criminal liability. A man may have to pay damages, may be sent to prison, at common law might be hanged, if at the time of his act he knew facts from which common experience showed that the consequences would follow, whether he individually could foresee them or not. But, when words are used exactly, a deed is not done with intent to produce a consequence unless that consequence is the aim of the deed. It may be obvious, and obvious to the actor, that the consequence will follow, and he may be liable for it even if he regrets it, but he does not do the act with intent to produce it unless the aim to produce it is the proximate motive of the specific act, although there may be some deeper motive behind. . . .

I do not see how anyone can find the intent required by the statute in any of the defendants' words. The second leaflet is the only one that affords even a foundation for the charge, and there, without invoking the hatred of German militarism expressed in the former one, it is evident from the beginning to the end that the only object of the paper is to help Russia and stop American intervention there against the popular government—not to impede the United States in the war that it was carrying on. To say that two phrases taken literally might import a suggestion of conduct that would have interference with the war as an indirect and probably undesired effect seems to me by no means enough to show an attempt to produce that effect. . . .

In this case sentences of twenty years imprisonment have been imposed for the publishing of two leaflets that I believe the defendants had as much right to publish as the Government has to publish the Constitution of the United States now vainly invoked by them. Even if I am technically wrong and enough can be squeezed from these poor and puny anonymities to turn the color of legal litmus paper; I will add, even if what I think the necessary intent were shown; the most nominal punishment seems to me all that possibly could be inflicted, unless the defendants are to be made to suffer not for what the indictment alleges but for the creed that they avow—a creed that I believe to be the creed of ignorance and immaturity when honestly held, as I see no reason to doubt that it was held here, but which, although made the subject of examination at the trial, no one has a right even to consider in dealing with the charges before the Court.

Persecution for the expression of opinions seems to me perfectly logical. If you have no doubt of your premises or your power and want a certain result with all your heart you naturally express your wishes in law and sweep away all opposition. To allow opposition by speech seems to indicate that you think the speech impotent, as when a man says that he has squared the circle, or that you do not care whole-heartedly for the result, or that you doubt either your power or your premises. But when men have realized that time has upset many fighting faiths, they may come to believe even more than they believe the very foundations of their own conduct that the ultimate good desired is better reached by free trade in ideas—that the best test of truth is the power of the thought to get itself accepted in the competition of the market, and that truth is the only ground upon which their wishes safely can be carried out. That at any rate is the theory of our Constitution. It is an experiment, as all life is an experiment. Every year if not every day we have to wager our salvation upon some prophecy based upon imperfect knowledge. While that experiment is part of our system I think that we should be eternally vigilant against attempts to check the expression of opinions that we loathe and believe to be fraught with death, unless they so imminently threaten immediate interference with the lawful and pressing purposes of the law that an immediate check is required to save the country. I wholly disagree with the argument of the Government that the First Amendment left the common law as to seditious libel in force. History seems to me against the notion. I had conceived that the United States through many years had shown its repentence for the Sedition Act of 1798, by repaying fines that it imposed. Only the emergency that makes it immediately dangerous to leave the correction of evil counsels to time warrants making any exception to the sweeping command, "Congress shall make no law . . . abridging the freedom of speech." Of course I am speaking only of expressions of opinion and exhortations, which were all that were uttered here, but I regret that I cannot put into more impressive words my belief that in their conviction upon this indictment the defendants were deprived of their rights under the Constitution of the United States.

Mr. Justice Brandeis concurs with the foregoing opinion.

428. THE ARCHANGEL EXPEDITION
The Aide-Mémoire of July 17, 1918

(Foreign Relations of the United States, 1918, Russia, Vol. II, p. 287 ff.)

This aide-mémoire states the terms upon which the United States would participate with the Allied Powers in intervention in Russia. Though the mémoire states that "military intervention . . . would be of no advantage" and that the United States "cannot take part in such intervention", it pledges the Government to do just that. In accordance with this agreement, three battalions of infantry and three companies of engineers were sent to Archangel to protect supplies, and a small American force co-operated with the Japanese at Vladivostock. These forces were withdrawn in 1919 and 1920. See, J. R. Moore, ed. *American Expedition in North Russia; F. L. Schuman, American Policy Toward Russia since 1917,* chs. v, vii; R. Albertson,

Fighting Without a War; W. S. Graves, *America's Siberian Adventure, 1918–1920;* C. K. Cummins and W. W. Pettit, *Russian-American Relations, 1913–1920: Documents and Papers.*

The Secretary of State to the Allied Ambassadors Aide-Mémoire

. . . It is the clear and fixed judgment of the Government of the United States, arrived at after repeated and very searching reconsiderations of the whole situation in Russia, that military intervention there would add to the present sad confusion in Russia rather than cure it, injure her rather than help her, and that it would be of no advantage in the prosecution of our main design, to win the war against Germany. It can not, therefore, take part in such intervention or sanction it in principle. Military intervention would, in its judgment, even supposing it to be efficacious in its immediate avowed object of delivering an attack upon Germany from the east, be merely a method of making use of Russia, not a method of serving her. Her people could not profit by it, if they profited by it at all, in time to save them from their present distresses, and their substance would be used to maintain foreign armies, not to reconstitute their own. Military action is admissible in Russia, as the Government of the United States sees the circumstances, only to help the Czecho-Slovaks consolidate their forces and get into successful cooperation with their Slavic kinsmen and to steady any efforts at self-government or self-defense in which the Russians themselves may be willing to accept assistance. Whether from Vladivostok or from Murmansk and Archangel, the only legitimate object for which American or Allied troops can be employed, it submits, is to guard military stores which may subsequently be needed by Russian forces and to render such aid as may be acceptable to the Russians in the organization of their own self-defense. For helping the Czecho-Slovaks there is immediate necessity and sufficient justification. Recent developments have made it evident that that is in the interest of what the Russian people themselves desire, and the Government of the United States is glad to contribute the small force at its disposal for that purpose. It yields, also, to the judgment of the Supreme Command in the matter of establishing a small force at Murmansk, to guard the military stores at Kola, and to make it safe for Russian forces to come together in organized bodies in the north. But it owes it to frank counsel to say that it can go no further than these modest and experimental plans. It is not in a position, and has no expectation of being in a position, to take part in organized intervention in adequate force from either Vladivostok or Murmansk and Archangel. It feels that it ought to add, also, that it will feel at liberty to use the few troops it can spare only for the purposes here stated and shall feel obliged to withdraw those forces, in order to add them to the forces at the western front, if the plans in whose execution it is now intended that they should cooperate should develop into others, inconsistent with the policy to which the Government of the United States feels constrained to restrict itself.

At the same time the Government of the United States wishes to say with the utmost cordiality and good will that none of the conclusions here stated is meant to wear the least color of criticism of what the other governments associated against Germany may think it wise to undertake. It wishes in no way to embarrass their choices of policy. All that is intended here is a perfectly frank and definite statement of the policy which the United States feels obliged to adopt for herself and in the use of her own military forces. The Government of the United States does not wish it to be understood that in so restricting its own activities it is seeking, even by implication, to set limits to the action or to define the policies of its associates.

It hopes to carry out the plans for safeguarding the rear of the Czecho-Slovaks operating from Vladivostok in a way that will place it and keep it in close cooperation with a small military force like its own from Japan, and if necessary from the other Allies, and that will assure it of the cordial accord of all the Allied powers; and it proposes to ask all associated in this course of action to unite in assuring the people of Russia in the most public and solemn manner that none of the governments uniting in action either in Siberia or in northern Russia contemplates any interference of any kind with the political sovereignty of Russia, any intervention in her internal affairs, or any impairment of her territorial integrity either now or hereafter, but that each of the associated powers has the single object of affording such aid as shall be acceptable, and only such aid as shall be acceptable, to the Russian people in their endeavor to regain control of their own affairs, their own territory, and their own destiny.

It is the hope and purpose of the Government of the United States to take advantage of the earliest opportunity to send to Siberia a commission of merchants, agricultural experts, labor advisers, Red Cross representatives, and agents of the Young Men's Christian Association accustomed to organizing the best methods of spreading useful information and rendering educational help of a modest sort, in order in some systematic manner to relieve the immediate economic necessities of the people there in every way for which opportunity may open. The execution of this plan will follow and will not be permitted to embarrass the military assistance rendered in the rear of the westward-moving forces of the Czecho-Slovaks.

429. PRESIDENT WILSON'S APPEAL TO THE VOTERS TO RETURN A DEMOCRATIC CONGRESS
October 24, 1918

(Associated Press Dispatch)

With the end of the World War rapidly approaching, President Wilson was preparing to go to Europe to secure a just peace. His appeal for political support met with popular disapproval. The elections of November 5 resulted in Republican majorities in both Houses of Congress. Wilson's partial failure at Paris may be attributed to the fact that European diplomats knew that he had been repudiated by his own people. Just before Wilson sailed for Europe, ex-President Roosevelt issued a statement that "Our allies and our enemies and Mr. Wilson himself should all understand that Mr. Wilson has no authority whatever to speak for the American people at this time. His leadership has just been emphatically repudiated by them. Mr. Wilson and his Fourteen Points and his four supplementary points and his five complementary points and all his utterances every which way have ceased to have any shadow of right to be accepted as expressive of the will of the American people."

My Fellow Countrymen:

The Congressional elections are at hand. They occur in the most critical period our country has ever faced or is likely to face in our time. If you have approved of my leadership and wish me to continue to be your unembarrassed spokesman in affairs at home and abroad, I earnestly beg that you will express yourselves unmistakably to that effect by returning a Democratic majority to both the Senate and the House of Representatives.

I am your servant and will accept your judgment without cavil. But my power to administer the great trust assigned to me by the Constitution would be seriously impaired should your judgment be adverse, and I must frankly tell you so because so many critical issues depend upon your verdict. No scruple or taste must in grim times like these be allowed to stand in the way of speaking the plain truth.

I have no thought of suggesting that any political party is paramount in matters of patriotism. I feel too deeply the sacrifices which have been made in this war by all our citizens, irrespective of party affiliations, to harbor such an idea. I mean only that the difficulties and delicacies of our present task are of a sort that makes it imperatively necessary that the nation should give its undivided support to the Government under a unified leadership, and that a Republican Congress would divide the leadership.

The leaders of the minority in the present Congress have unquestionably been pro-war, but they have been anti-administration. At almost every turn since we entered the war they have sought to take the choice of policy and the conduct of the war out of my hands and put it under the control of instrumentalities of their own choosing.

This is no time either for divided counsels or for divided leadership. Unity of command is as necessary now in civil action as it is upon the field of battle. If the control of the House and the Senate should be taken away from the party now in power an opposing majority could assume control of legislation and oblige all action to be taken amid contest and obstruction.

The return of a Republican majority to either house of the Congress would, moreover, be interpreted on the other side of the water as a repudiation of my leadership. Spokesmen of the Republican party are urging you to elect a Republican Congress in order to back up and support the President, but, even if they should in this impose upon some credulous voters on this side of the water, they would impose on no one on the other side. It is well understood there as well as here that Republican leaders desire not so much to support the President as to control him.

The peoples of the allied countries with whom we are associated against Germany are quite familiar with the significance of elections. They would find it very difficult to believe that the voters of the United States had chosen to support their President by electing to the Congress a majority controlled by those who are not in fact in sympathy with the attitude and action of the Administration.

I need not tell you, my fellow countrymen, that I am asking your support not for my own sake or for the sake of a political party, but for the sake of the nation itself in order that its inward duty of purpose may be evident to all the world. In ordinary times I would not feel at liberty to make such an appeal to you. In ordinary times divided counsels can be endured without permanent hurt to the country. But these are not ordinary times.

If in these critical days it is your wish to sustain me with undivided minds, I beg that you will say so in a way which it will not be possible to misunderstand, either here at home or among our associates on the other side of the sea. I submit my difficulties and my hopes to you.

WOODROW WILSON.

430. THE CHILD LABOR ACT
February 24, 1919

(U. S. Statutes at Large, Vol. XL, p. 1138)

The decision of the Supreme Court in *Hammer v. Dagenhart* defeated the effort of Congress to prohibit child labor through the exercise of its control over interstate commerce. In 1919 a section of the general taxation bill assessed a tax upon the products of child labor. For the fate of this section, see Doc. No. 431. In 1924 Congress passed an amendment to the Constitution giving Congress the right to regulate child labor: fifteen years later 28 states had ratified this amendment, but the prospects for obtaining a sufficient number of ratifications were dim. See, R. Fuller, *Child Labor and the Constitution.*

. . . Sec. 1200. Every person (other than a bona fide boys' or girls' canning club recognized by the Agricultural Department of a State and of the United States) operating (a) any mine or quarry situated in the United States in which children under the age of sixteen years have been employed or permitted to work during any portion of the taxable year; or (b) any mill, cannery, workshop, factory, or manufacturing establishment situated in the United States in which children under the age of fourteen years have been employed or permitted to work, or children between the ages of fourteen and sixteen have been employed or permitted to work more than eight hours in any day or more than six days in any week, or after the hour of seven o'clock post meridian, or before the hour of six o'clock ante meridian, during any portion of the taxable year, shall pay for each taxable year, in addition to all other taxes imposed by law, an excise tax equivalent to 10 per centum of the entire net profits received or accrued for such year from the sale or disposition of the product of such mine, quarry, mill, cannery, workshop, factory, or manufacturing establishment. . . .

431. BAILEY v. DREXEL FURNITURE COMPANY
259 U. S. 20
1922

Error to the U. S. district court for the western district of North Carolina. This case involved the constitutionality of the Child Labor tax law of February 24, 1919, Doc. No. 430.

TAFT, C. J. . . . The law is attacked on the ground that it is a regulation of the employment of child labor in the States—an exclusively state function under the Federal Constitution and within the reservations of the Tenth Amendment. It is defended on the ground that it is a mere excise tax levied by the Congress of the United States under its broad power of taxation conferred by § 8, Article I, of the federal Constitution. We must construe the law and interpret the intent and meaning of Congress from the language of the act. The words are to be given their ordinary meaning unless the context shows that they are differently used. Does this law impose a tax with only that incidental restraint and regulation which a tax must inevitably involve? Or does it regulate by the use of the so-called tax as a penalty? If a tax, it is clearly an excise. If it were an excise on a commodity or other thing of value we might not be permitted under previous decisions of this court to infer solely from its heavy burden that the act intends a prohibition instead of a tax. But this act is more. It provides a heavy exaction for a departure from a detailed and specified course of conduct in business. That course of business is that employers shall employ in mines and quarries, children of an age greater than sixteen years; in mills and factories, children of an age greater than fourteen years, and shall prevent children of less than sixteen years in mills and factories from working more than eight hours a day or six days in the week. If an employer departs from this prescribed course of business, he is to pay to the Government one-tenth of his entire net income in the business for a full year. The amount is not to be proportioned in any degree to the frequency of the departures, but is to be paid by the employer in full measure whether he employs five hundred

children for a year, or employs only one for a day. Moreover, if he does not know the child is within the named age limit, he is not to pay; that is to say, it is only where he knowingly departs from the prescribed course that payment is to be exacted. . . .

In the light of these features of the act, a court must be blind not to see that the so-called tax is imposed to stop the employment of children within the age limits prescribed. Its prohibitory and regulatory effect and purpose are palpable. All others can see and understand this. How can we properly shut our minds to it?

It is the high duty and function of this court in cases regularly brought to its bar to decline to recognize or enforce seeming laws of Congress, dealing with subjects not entrusted to Congress but left or committed by the supreme law of the land to the control of the States. We can not avoid the duty even though it requires us to refuse to give effect to legislation designed to promote the highest good. The good sought in unconstitutional legislation is an insidious feature because it leads citizens and legislators of good purpose to promote it without thought of the serious breach it will make in the ark of our covenant or the harm which will come from breaking down recognized standards. In the maintenance of local self government, on the one hand, and the national power on the other, our country has been able to endure and prosper for near a century and a half.

Out of a proper respect for the acts of a co-ordinate branch of the Government, this court has gone far to sustain taxing acts as such, even though there has been ground for suspecting from the weight of the tax it was intended to destroy its subject. But in the act before us the presumption of validity cannot prevail, because the proof of the contrary is found on the very face of its provisions. Grant the validity of this law, and all that Congress would need to do, hereafter, in seeking to take over to its control any one of the great number of subjects of public interests, jurisdiction of which the

States have never parted with, and which are reserved to them by the Tenth Amendment, would be to enact a detailed measure of complete regulation of the subject and enforce it by a so-called tax upon departures from it. To give such magic to the word "tax" would be to break down all constitutional limitation of the powers of Congress and completely wipe out the sovereignty of the State. . . .

For the reasons given, we must hold the Child Labor Tax Law invalid and the judgment of the district court is

Affirmed.

CLARKE, J., dissents.

432. THE VOLSTEAD ACT
October 28, 1919

(*U. S. Statutes at Large,* Vol. XXXXI, p. 305 ff.)

Ratification of the Eighteenth Amendment was proclaimed January 29, 1919: the amendment went into effect January 16, 1920. The National Prohibition Act, known popularly as the Volstead Act after its sponsor, Volstead of Minnesota, was passed over the veto of President Wilson. On the constitutionality of the Act, see Doc. No. 433. The literature on Prohibition is enormous, but most of it is of a controversial character. See E. H. Cherrington, *Evolution of Prohibition in the United States;* P. Odegard, *Pressure Politics;* C. Merz, *The Dry Decade;* H. Feldman, *Prohibition, Its Economic and Industrial Aspects;* I. Fisher, *Prohibition at Its Worst;* F. Franklin, *The A.B.C. of Prohibition;* The Federal Council of Churches of Christ in America, *The Prohibition Situation; Annals* of the American Academy of Pol. and Social Science, Vol. CIX. The famous Wickersham Report is in the U. S. 71st Congress, 3d Sess., *House Doc. No. 722.*

Be it Enacted. . . . That the short title of this Act shall be the "National Prohibition Act."

TITLE I.
TO PROVIDE FOR THE ENFORCE-MENT OF WAR PROHIBITION.

The term "War Prohibition Act" used in this Act shall mean the provisions of any Act or Acts prohibiting the sale and manufacture of intoxicating liquors until the conclusion of the present war and thereafter until the termination of demobilization, the date of which shall be determined and proclaimed by the President of the United States. The words "beer, wine, or other intoxicating malt or vinous liquors" in the War Prohibition Act shall be hereafter construed to mean any such beverages which contain one-half of 1 per centum or more of alcohol by volume: . . .

SEC. 2. The Commissioner of Internal Revenue, his assistants, agents, and inspectors, shall investigate and report violations of the War Prohibition Act to the United States attorney for the district in which committed, who shall be charged with the duty of prosecuting, subject to the direction of the Attorney General, the offenders as in the case of other offenses against laws of the United States; and such Commissioner of Internal Revenue, his assistants, agents, and inspectors may swear out warrants before United States commissioners or other officers or courts authorized to issue the same for the apprehension of such offenders, and may, subject to the control of the said United States attorney, conduct the prosecution at the committing trial for the purpose of having the offenders held for the action of a grand jury. . . .

TITLE II.
PROHIBITION OF INTOXICATING BEVERAGES.

SEC. 3. No person shall on or after the date when the eighteenth amendment to the Constitution of the United States goes into effect, manufacture, sell, barter, transport, import, export, deliver, furnish or possess any intoxicating liquor except as authorized in this Act, and all the provisions of this Act shall be liberally construed to the end that the use of intoxicating liquor as a beverage may be prevented.

Liquor for nonbeverage purposes and wine for sacramental purposes may be manufactured, purchased, sold, bartered, transported, imported, exported, delivered, furnished and possessed, but only as herein provided, and the commissioner may, upon application, issue permits therefor: *Provided,* That nothing in this Act shall prohibit the purchase and sale of warehouse receipts covering distilled spirits on deposit in Government bonded warehouses, and no special tax liability shall attach to the business of purchasing and selling such warehouse receipts. . . .

SEC. 6. No one shall manufacture, sell, purchase, transport, or prescribe any liquor without first obtaining a permit from the commissioner so to do, except that a person may, without a permit, purchase and use liquor for medicinal purposes when prescribed by a physician as herein provided, and except that any person who in the opinion of the commissioner is conducting a bona fide hospital or sanatorium engaged in the treatment of persons suffering from alcoholism, may, under such rules, regulations, and conditions as the commissioner shall prescribe, purchase and use, in accordance with the methods in use in such institution, liquor, to be administered to the patients of such institution under the direction of a duly qualified physician employed by such institution.

All permits to manufacture, prescribe, sell, or transport liquor, may be issued for one year, and shall expire on the 31st day of December next succeeding the issuance thereof: . . . Permits to purchase liquor shall specify the quantity and kind to be purchased and the purpose for which it is to be used. No permit shall be issued to any person who within one year prior to the application therefor or issuance thereof shall have violated the terms of any permit issued under this Title or any law of the United States or of any State regulating traffic in liquor. No permit shall be issued to anyone to sell liquor at retail, unless the sale is to be made through a pharmacist designated in the permit and duly licensed under the laws of his State to compound and dispense medicine prescribed by a duly licensed physician. No one shall be given a permit to prescribe liquor unless he is a physician duly licensed to practice medicine and actively engaged in the practice of such profession. . . .

Nothing in this title shall be held to apply to the manufacture, sale, transportation, importation, possession, or distribution of wine for sacramental purposes, or like religious rites, except section 6 (save as the same requires a permit to purchase) and section 10 hereof, and the provisions of this Act prescribing penalties for the violation of either of said sections. No person to whom a permit may be issued to manufacture, transport, import, or sell wines for sacramental purposes or like religious rites shall sell, barter, exchange, or furnish any such to any person not a rabbi, minister of the gospel, priest, or an officer duly authorized for the purpose by any church or congregation, nor to any such except upon an application duly subscribed by him, which application, authenticated as regulations may prescribe, shall be filed and preserved by the seller. The head of any conference or diocese or other ecclesiastical jurisdiction may designate any rabbi, minister, or priest to supervise the manufacture of wine to be used for the purposes and rites in this section mentioned, and the person so designated may, in the discretion of the commissioner, be granted a permit to supervise such manufacture.

SEC. 7. No one but a physician holding a permit to prescribe liquor shall issue any prescription for liquor. And no physician shall prescribe liquor unless after careful physical examination of the person for whose use such prescription is sought, or if such examination is found impracticable, then upon the best information obtainable, he in good faith believes that the use of such liquor as a medicine by such person is necessary and will afford relief to him from some known ailment. Not more than a pint of spiritous liquor to be taken internally shall be prescribed for use by the same person within any period of ten days and no prescription shall be filled more than once. Any pharmacist filling a prescription shall at the time indorse upon it over his own signature the word "canceled," together with the date when the liquor was delivered, and then make the same a part of the record that he is required to keep as herein provided. . . .

SEC. 18. It shall be unlawful to advertise, manufacture, sell, or possess for sale any utensil, contrivance, machine, preparation, compound, tablet, substance, formula direction, recipe advertised, designed, or intended for use in the unlawful manufacture of intoxicating liquor. . . .

SEC. 21. Any room, house, building, boat,

vehicle, structure, or place where intoxicating liquor is manufactured, sold, kept, or bartered in violation of this title, and all intoxicating liquor and property kept and used in maintaining the same, is hereby declared to be a common nuisance, and any person who maintains such a common nuisance shall be guilty of a misdemeanor and upon conviction thereof shall be fined not more than $1,000 or be imprisoned for not more than one year, or both. . . .

SEC. 25. It shall be unlawful to have or possess any liquor or property designed for the manufacture of liquor intended for use in violating this title or which has been so used, and no property rights shall exist in any such liquor or property. . . . No search warrant shall issue to search any private dwelling occupied as such unless it is being used for the unlawful sale of intoxicating liquor, or unless it is in part used for some business purposes such as a store, shop, saloon, restaurant, hotel, or boarding house. . . .

SEC. 29. Any person who manufactures or sells liquor in violation of this title shall for a first offense be fined not more than $1,000, or imprisoned not exceeding six months, and for a second or subsequent offense shall be fined not less than $200 nor more than $2,000 and be imprisoned not less than one month nor more than five years.

Any person violating the provisions of any permit, or who makes any false record, report, or affidavit required by this title, or violates any of the provisions of this title, for which offense a special penalty is not prescribed, shall be fined for a first offense not more than $500; for a second offense not less than $100 nor more than $1,000, or be imprisoned not more than ninety days; for any subsequent offense he shall be fined not less than $500 and be imprisoned not less than three months nor more than two years. . . .

SEC. 33. After February 1, 1920, the possession of liquors by any person not legally permitted under this title to possess liquor shall be prima facie evidence that such liquor is kept for the purpose of being sold, bartered, exchanged, given away, furnished, or otherwise disposed of in violation of the Provisions of this title. . . . But it shall not be unlawful to possess liquors in one's private dwelling while the same is occupied and used by him as his dwelling only and such liquor need not be reported, provided such liquors are for use only for the personal consumption of the owner thereof and his family residing in such dwelling and of his bona fide guests when entertained by him therein; and the burden of proof shall be upon the possessor in any action concerning the same to prove that such liquor was lawfully acquired, possessed, and used. . . .

433. NATIONAL PROHIBITION CASES
253 U. S. 350
1920

These were seven cases involving the constitutionality of the Volstead Act of 1919 and the validity of the Eighteenth Amendment. This is the only case in the history of the court where the court stated its opinion of a question of constitutional law without giving its reasoning.

VAN DEVANTER, J., announced the conclusions of the court.

Power to amend the Constitution is reserved by Article V, which reads: . . . The text of the Eighteenth Amendment, proposed by Congress in 1917 and proclaimed as ratified in 1919, 40 Stat. at L. 1050, 1941, is as follows: . . .

The cases have been elaborately argued at the bar and in printed briefs; and the

arguments have been attentively considered, with the result that we reach and announce the following conclusions on the questions involved.

1. The adoption by both houses of Congress, each by a two-thirds vote, of a joint resolution proposing an amendment to the Constitution sufficiently shows that the proposal was deemed necessary by all who voted for it. An express declaration that they regarded it as necessary is not essential. None of the resolutions whereby prior amendments were proposed contained such a declaration.

2. The two-thirds vote in each house which is required in proposing an amendment is a vote of two-thirds of the members

present—assuming the presence of a quorum —and not a vote of two thirds of the entire membership, present and absent. *Missouri Pacific Ry. Co.* v. *Kansas,* 248 U. S. 276.

3. The referendum provisions of state constitutions and statutes cannot be applied, consistently with the Constitution of the United States, in the ratification or rejection of amendments to it. *Hawke* v. *Smith,* 253 U. S. 221.

4. The prohibition of the manufacture, sale, transportation, importation and exportation of intoxicating liquors for beverage purposes, as embodied in the Eighteenth Amendment, is within the power to amend reserved by Article V of the Constitution.

5. That amendment, by lawful proposal and ratification, has become a part of the Constitution, and must be respected and given effect the same as other provisions of that instrument.

6. The first section of the amendment— the one embodying the prohibition—is operative throughout the entire territorial limits of the United States, binds all legislative bodies, courts, public officers and individuals within those limits, and of its own force invalidates every legislative act— whether by Congress, by a state legislature, or by a territorial assembly—which authorizes or sanctions what the section prohibits.

7. The second section of the amendment— the one declaring "The Congress and the several States shall have concurrent power to enforce this article by appropriate legislation"—does not enable Congress or the several States to defeat or to thwart the prohibition, but only to enforce it by appropriate means.

8. The words "concurrent power" in that section do not mean joint power, or require that legislation thereunder by Congress, to be effective, shall be approved or sanctioned by the several States or any of them; nor

do they mean that the power to enforce is divided between Congress and the several States along the lines which separate or distinguish foreign and interstate commerce from intrastate affairs.

9. The power confided to Congress by that section, while not exclusive, is territorially co-extensive with the prohibition of the first section, embraces manufacture and other intrastate transactions as well as importation, exportation and interstate traffic, and is in no wise dependent on or affected by action or inaction on the part of the several States or any of them.

10. That power may be exerted against the disposal for beverage purposes of liquors manufactured before the amendment became effective just as it may be against subsequent manufacture for those purposes. In either case it is a constitutional mandate or prohibition that is being enforced.

11. While recognizing that there are limits beyond which Congress cannot go in treating beverages as within its power of enforcement, we think these limits are not transcended by the provision of the Volstead Act (Title II, § 1), wherein liquors containing as much as one-half of one per cent. of alcohol by volume and fit for use for beverage purposes are treated as within that power. *Jacob Ruppert* v. *Caffey,* 251 U. S. 264.

WHITE, C. J., concurring. I profoundly regret that in a case of this magnitude, affecting as it does an amendment to the Constitution dealing with the powers and duties of the national and state governments, and intimately concerning the welfare of the whole people, the court has deemed it proper to state only ultimate conclusions without an exposition of the reasoning by which they have been reached. . . .

McKENNA, J., and CLARKE, J., delivered dissenting opinions.

434. PREAMBLE OF THE INDUSTRIAL WORKERS OF THE WORLD
Chicago, 1919

(P. F. Brissenden, *The I. W. W., A Study of American Syndicalism,* p. 351)

The Industrial Workers of the World was organized in 1905 and lasted about twenty years. It represented the extreme left wing of the American labor movement, advocated the general strike, and practised sabotage and violence.

Its membership, extremely fluctuating and recruited chiefly among the casual laborers of the western lumber camps, mines and harvest fields, never exceeded sixty thousand. See, P. F. Brissenden, *The I. W. W.;* J. S. Gambs, *The Decline of the I. W. W.;* W. D. Haywood, *Bill Haywood's Book;* D. L. Saposs, *Left Wing Unionism;* J. Oneal, *American Communism.*

The working class and the employing class have nothing in common. There can be no peace so long as hunger and want are found among millions of working people and the few, who make up the employing class, have all the good things of life.

Between these two classes a struggle must go on until the workers of the world organize as a class, take possession of the earth and the machinery of production and abolish the wage system.

We find that the centering of the management of industries into fewer and fewer hands makes the trade unions unable to cope with the ever growing power of the employing class. The trade unions foster a state of affairs which allows one set of workers to be pitted against another set of workers in the same industry, thereby helping defeat one another in wage wars. Moreover the trade unions aid the em-ploying class to mislead the workers into the belief that the working class have interests in common with their employers.

These conditions can be changed and the interest of the working class upheld only by an organization formed in such a way that all its members in any one industry, or in all industries if necessary, cease work whenever a strike or lockout is on in any department thereof, thus making an injury to one an injury to all.

Instead of the conservative motto, "A fair day's wage for a fair day's work," we must inscribe on our banner the revolutionary watchword, "Abolition of the wage system." It is the historic mission of the working class to do away with capitalism. The army of production must be organized not only for the everyday struggle with capitalists, but also to carry on production when capitalism shall have been overthrown. By organizing industrially we are forming the structure of the new society within the shell of the old.

435. PRESIDENT WILSON'S EXPOSITION OF THE LEAGUE OF NATIONS TO THE SENATE COMMITTEE ON FOREIGN RELATIONS
August 19, 1919

(U. S. 66th Congress, 1st. Session, *Sen. Doc.* No. 76)

In July, 1919, the Treaty of Versailles and the Covenant of the League of Nations were formally transmitted to the Senate. In order to allay strong Senatorial opposition to ratification, Wilson invited the members of the Senate Committee on Foreign Relations to discuss with him their objections to the Covenant of the League. The most irreconcilable of Wilson's opponents, Senator Lodge of Massachusetts, was chairman of the Foreign Affairs Committee, and Wilson's appeal was without apparent effect. See, H. C. Lodge, *The Senate and the League of Nations;* W. E. Dodd, *Woodrow Wilson;* J. C. Malin, *The United States After the World War,* chs. ii–iv.

MR. CHAIRMAN:

I have taken the liberty of writing out a little statement in the hope that it might faciliate discussion by speaking directly on some points that I know have been points of controversy and upon which I thought an expression of opinion would not be unwelcome. . . .

Nothing, I am led to believe, stands in the way of ratification of the treaty except certain doubts with regard to the meaning and implication of certain articles of the Covenant of the League of Nations; and I must frankly say that I am unable to understand why such doubts should be entertained. You will recall that when I had the pleasure of a conference with your committee and with the committee of the House of Representatives on Foreign Affairs at the White House in March last the questions now most frequently asked about the League of Nations were all canvassed with a view to their immediate clarification. The Covenant of the League was then in its first draft and subject to revision. It was pointed out that no express recognition was given to the Monroe Doctrine; that it was not expressly provided that the League should have no authority to act or to express a judgment on matters of domestic policy; that the right to withdraw from the League was not expressly recognized; and that the constitutional right of the Congress to determine all questions of peace and war was not sufficiently safeguarded. On my return to Paris all these matters were taken up again by the Commission on the League of Nations and every suggestion of the United States was accepted.

The views of the United States with regard to the questions I have mentioned had, in fact, already been accepted by the commission and there was supposed to be nothing inconsistent with them in the draft of the Covenant first adopted—the draft which was the subject of our discussion in March —but no objection was made to saying explicitly in the text what all had supposed to be implicit in it. There was absolutely no doubt as to the meaning of any one of the resulting provisions of the Covenant in the minds of those who participated in drafting them, and I respectfully submit that there is nothing vague or doubtful in their wording.

The Monroe Doctrine is expressly mentioned as an understanding which is in no way to be impaired or interfered with by anything contained in the covenant and the expression "regional understandings like the Monroe Doctrine" was used, not because any one of the conferees thought there was any comparable agreement anywhere else in existence or in contemplation, but only because it was thought best to avoid the appearance of dealing in such a document with the policy of a single nation. Absolutely nothing is concealed in the phrase.

With regard to domestic questions Article 16 of the Covenant expressly provides that, if in case of any dispute arising between members of the League the matter involved is claimed by one of the parties "and is found by the council to arise out of a matter which by international law is solely within the domestic jurisdiction of that party, the council shall so report, and shall make no recommendation as to its settlement." The United States was by no means the only Government interested in the explicit adoption of this provision, and there is no doubt in the mind of any authoritative student of international law that such matters as immigration, tariffs, and naturalization are incontestably domestic questions with which no international body could deal without ex-

press authority to do so. No enumeration of domestic questions was undertaken because to undertake it, even by sample, would have involved the danger of seeming to exclude those not mentioned.

The right of any sovereign State to withdraw had been taken for granted, but no objection was made to making it explicit. Indeed, so soon as the views expressed at the White House conference were laid before the commission it was at once conceded that it was best not to leave the answer to so important a question to inference. No proposal was made to set up any tribunal to pass judgment upon the question whether a withdrawing nation had in fact fulfilled "all its international obligations and all its obligations under the covenant." It was recognized that that question must be left to be resolved by the conscience of the Nation proposing to withdraw; and I must say that it did not seem to me worth while to propose that the article be made more explicit, because I knew that the United States would never itself propose to withdraw from the League if its conscience was not entirely clear as to the fulfillment of all its international obligations. It has never failed to fulfill them and never will.

Article 10 is in no respect of doubtful meaning when read in the light of the covenant as a whole. The council of the League can only "advise upon" the means by which the obligations of that great article are to be given effect to. Unless the United States is a party to the policy or action in question, her own affirmative vote in the council is necessary before any advice can be given, for a unanimous vote of the council is required. If she is a party, the trouble is hers anyhow. And the unanimous vote of the council is only advice in any case. Each Government is free to reject it if it pleases. Nothing could have been made more clear to the conference than the right of our Congress under our Constitution to exercise its independent judgment in all matters of peace and war. No attempt was made to question or limit that right.

The United States will, indeed, undertake under Article 10 to "respect and preserve as against external aggression the territorial integrity and existing political independence of all members of the League," and that engagement constitutes a very grave and solemn moral obligation. But it is a moral, not a legal, obligation, and leaves our Congress absolutely free to put its own interpretation upon it in all cases that call for action. It is binding in conscience only, not in law.

Article 10 seems to me to constitute the very backbone of the whole covenant. Without it the League would be hardly more than an influential debating society.

It has several times been suggested, in public debate and in private conference, that interpretations of the sense in which the United States accepts the engagements of the covenant should be embodied in the instrument of ratification. There can be no reasonable objection to such interpretations accompanying the act of ratification provided they do not form a part of the formal ratification itself. Most of the interpretations which have been suggested to me embody what seems to me the plain meaning of the instrument itself. But if such interpretations should constitute a part of the formal resolution of ratification, long delays would be the inevitable consequence, inasmuch as all the many Governments concerned would have to accept, in effect, the language of the Senate as the language of the treaty before ratification would be complete. The assent of the German Assembly at Weimar would have to be obtained, among the rest, and I must frankly say that I could only with the greatest reluctance approach that Assembly for permission to read the treaty as we understand it and as those who framed it quite certainly understood it. If the United States were to qualify the document in any way, moreover, I am confident from what I know of the many conferences and debates which accompanied the formulation of the treaty that our example would immediately be followed in many quarters, in some instances with very serious reservations, and that the meaning and operative force of the treaty would presently be clouded from one end of its clauses to the other.

Pardon me, Mr. Chairman, if I have been entirely unreserved and plain-spoken in speaking of the great matters we all have so much at heart. If excuse is needed, I trust that the critical situation of affairs may serve as my justification. The issues that manifestly hang upon the conclusions of the Senate with regard to peace and upon the time of its action are so grave and so clearly insusceptible of being thrust on one side or postponed that I have felt it necessary in the public interest to make this urgent plea, and to make it as simply and as unreservedly as possible.

I thought that the simplest way, Mr. Chairman, to cover the points that I knew to be points of interest.

436. THE DEFEAT OF THE LEAGUE OF NATIONS

Resolution of Ratification of Treaty of Peace with Germany and the League of Nations
March 19, 1920

(*Congressional Record*, Vol. LIX, p. 4599)

Wilson called Congress into special session for consideration of the Treaty with Germany, May 19, 1919. An unofficial copy of the treaty was read to the Senate June 9, but the treaty was not officially before the Senate until July 10; then debate on the Treaty and the League was under way. After a vigorous and at times embittered debate, the treaty, both with and without reservations, was rejected November 19, 1919. Efforts to arrive at a compromise between the moderate reservationist Republicans and the moderate Democrats were unavailing. The Treaty was brought up for reconsideration again on February 11, but again with reservations dictated largely by Senator Lodge and unacceptable to the President. The final vote on the Treaty, with reservations, came March 19. It resulted in 49 for ratification and 35 against ratification, and the treaty thus lacking the necessary two-thirds vote was defeated. Subsequent efforts to make peace by resolution were defeated in 1920 and successful the following year. See Doc. No. 442. Separate treaties concluding peace with Germany, Austria and Hungary were ratified October 18, 1921. See, H. C. Lodge, *The Senate and the League of Nations;* D. F. Fleming, *The United States and the League of Nations, 1918–1920;* C. P. Howland, ed. *Survey of American Foreign Relations, 1928,* Sec. III; W. S. Holt, *Treaties Defeated by the Senate,* ch. x; J. C. Malin, *The United States After the World War,* chs. i–iv; A. Nevins, *Henry White,* ch. xxiii;

S. F. Bemis, ed. *American Secretaries of State,* Vol. X, p. 47 ff.

The PRESIDENT pro tempore. Upon agreeing to the resolution of ratification the yeas are 49 and the nays are 35. Not having received the affirmative votes of two-thirds of the Senators present and voting, the resolution is not agreed to, and the Senate does not advise and consent to the ratification of the treaty of peace with Germany.

The resolution of ratification voted upon and rejected is as follows:

Resolution of ratification.

Resolved (two-thirds of the Senators present concurring therein), That the Senate advise and consent to the ratification of the treaty of peace with Germany concluded at Versailles on the 28th day of June, 1919, subject to the following reservations and understandings, which are hereby made a part and condition of this resolution of ratification, which ratification is not to take effect or bind the United States until the said reservations and understandings adopted by the Senate have been accepted as a part and a condition of this resolution of ratification by the allied and associated powers and a failure on the part of the allied and associated powers to make objection to said reservations and understandings prior to the deposit of ratification by the United States shall be taken as a full and final acceptance of such reservations and understandings by said powers:

1. The United States so understands and construes article 1 that in case of notice of withdrawal from the League of Nations, as provided in said article, the United States shall be the sole judge as to whether all its international obligations and all its obligations under the said covenant have been fulfilled, and notice of withdrawal by the United States may be given by a concurrent resolution of the Congress of the United States.

2. The United States assumes no obligation to preserve the territorial integrity or political independence of any other country by the employment of its military or naval forces, its resources, or any form of economic discrimination, or to interfere in any way in controversies between nations, including all controversies relating to territorial integrity or political independence, whether members of the league or not, under the provisions of article 10, or to employ the military or naval forces of the United States, under any article of the treaty for any purpose, unless in any particular case the Congress, which, under the Constitution, has the sole power to declare war or authorize the employment of the military or naval forces of the United States, shall, in the exercise of full liberty of action, by act or joint resolution so provide.

3. No mandate shall be accepted by the United States under article 22, part 1, or any other provision of the treaty of peace with Germany, except by action of the Congress of the United States.

4. The United States reserves to itself exclusively the right to decide what questions are within its domestic jurisdiction and declares that all domestic and political questions relating wholly or in part to its internal affairs, including immigration, labor, coastwise traffic, the tariff, commerce, the suppression of traffic in women and children and in opium and other dangerous drugs, and all other domestic questions, are solely within the jurisdiction of the United States and are not under this treaty to be submitted in any way either to arbitration or to the consideration of the council or of the assembly of the League of Nations, or any agency thereof, or to the decision or recommendation of any other power.

5. The United States will not submit to arbitration or to inquiry by the assembly or by the council of the League of Nations, provided for in said treaty of peace, any questions which in the judgment of the United States depend upon or relate to its long-established policy, commonly known as the Monroe doctrine; said doctrine is to be interpreted by the United States alone and is hereby declared to be wholly outside the jurisdiction of said League of Nations and entirely unaffected by any provision contained in the said treaty of peace with Germany.

6. The United States withholds its assent to articles 156, 157, and 158, and reserves full liberty of action with respect to any controversy which may arise under said articles.

7. No person is or shall be authorized to represent the United States, nor shall any citizen of the United States be eligible, as a member of any body or agency established

or authorized by said treaty of peace with Germany, except pursuant to an act of the Congress of the United States providing for his appointment and defining his powers and duties.

8. The United States understands that the reparation commission will regulate or interfere with exports from the United States to Germany, or from Germany to the United States, only when the United States by act or joint resolution of Congress approves such regulation or interference.

9. The United States shall not be obligated to contribute to any expenses of the League of Nations, or of the secretariat, or of any commission, or committee, or conference, or other agency, organized under the League of Nations or under the treaty or for the purpose of carrying out the treaty provisions, unless and until an appropriation of funds available for such expenses shall have been made by the Congress of the United States: *Provided,* That the foregoing limitation shall not apply to the United States' proportionate share of the expense of the office force and salary of the secretary general.

10. No plan for the limitation of armaments proposed by the council of the League of Nations under the provisions of article 8 shall be held as binding the United States until the same shall have been accepted by Congress, and the United States reserves the right to increase its armament without the consent of the council whenever the United States is threatened with invasion or engaged in war.

11. The United States reserves the right to permit, in its discretion, the nationals of a covenant-breaking State, as defined in article 16 of the covenant of the League of Nations, residing within the United States or in countries other than such covenant-breaking State, to continue their commercial, financial, and personal relations with the nationals of the United States.

12. Nothing in articles 296, 297, or in any of the annexes thereto or in any other article, section, or annex of the treaty of peace with Germany shall, as against citizens of the United States, be taken to mean any confirmation, ratification, or approval of any act otherwise illegal or in contravention of the rights of citizens of the United States.

13. The United States withholds its assent to Part XIII (articles 387 to 427, inclusive) unless Congress by act or joint resolution shall hereafter make provision for representation in the organization established by said Part XIII, and in such event the participation of the United States will be governed and conditioned by the provisions of such act or joint resolution.

14. Until Part I, being the covenant of the League of Nations, shall be so amended as to provide that the United States shall be entitled to cast a number of votes equal to that which any member of the league and its self-governing dominions, colonies, or parts of empire, in the aggregate shall be entitled to cast, the United States assumes no obligation to be bound, except in cases where Congress has previously given its consent, by any election, decision, report, or finding of the council or assembly in which any member of the league and its self-governing dominions, colonies, or parts of empire, in the aggregate have cast more than one vote.

The United States assumes no obligation to be bound by any decision, report, or finding of the council or assembly arising out of any dispute between the United States and any member of the league if such member, or any self-governing dominion, colony, empire, or part of empire united with it politically has voted.

15. In consenting to the ratification of the treaty with Germany the United States adheres to the principle of self-determination and to the resolution of sympathy with the aspirations of the Irish people for a government of their own choice adopted by the Senate June 6, 1919, and declares that when such government is attained by Ireland, a consummation it is hoped is at hand, it should promptly be admitted as a member of the League of Nations.

437. MISSOURI v. HOLLAND
252 U. S. 416
1920

Appeal from the United States district court for the Western District of Missouri. This case involved the constitutionality of the Migratory Bird Treaty Act of July 3, 1918, which sought to enforce certain provisions of a convention between the United States and Canada. The important question raised was whether Congress could, in pursuance of the provisions of a treaty, enact legislation otherwise beyond its powers. The opinion of the Court in this case is one of the most far-reaching assertions of national power in our constitutional history.

HOLMES, J. This is a bill in equity brought by the State of Missouri to prevent a game warden of the United States from attempting to enforce the Migratory Bird Treaty Act of July 3, 1918, and the regulations made by the Secretary of Agriculture in pursuance of the same. The ground of the bill is that the statute is an unconstitutional interference with the rights reserved to the States by the Tenth Amendment, and that the acts of the defendant done and threatened under that authority invade the sovereign right of the State and contravene its will manifested in statutes. The State also alleges a pecuniary interest, as owner of the wild birds within its borders and otherwise, admitted by the government to be sufficient, but it is enough that the bill is a reasonable and proper means to assert the alleged quasi sovereign rights of a State. A motion to dismiss was sustained by the district court on the ground that the act of Congress is constitutional. 258 Fed. Rep. 479. The State appeals.

On December 8, 1916, a treaty between the United States and Great Britain was proclaimed by the President. It recited that many species of birds in their annual migrations traversed certain parts of the United States and of Canada, that they were of great value as a source of food and in destroying insects injurious to vegetation, but were in danger of extermination through lack of adequate protection. It therefore provided for specified closed seasons and protection in other forms, and agreed that the two powers would take or propose to their law-making bodies the necessary measures for carrying the treaty out. 39 Stat. 1702. The above mentioned Act of July 3, 1918, entitled an act to give effect to the convention, prohibited the killing, capturing or selling any of the migratory birds included in the terms of the treaty except as permitted by regulations compatible with those terms, to be made by the Secretary of Agriculture. Regulations were proclaimed on July 31, and October 25, 1918. It is unnecessary to go into any details, because, as we have said, the question raised is the general one whether the treaty and statute are void as an interference with the rights reserved to the States.

To answer this question it is not enough to refer to the Tenth Amendment, reserving the powers not delegated to the United States, because by Article II, §2, the power to make treaties is delegated expressly, and by Article VI treaties made under the authority of the United States, along with the Constitution and laws of the United States made in pursuance thereof, are declared the supreme law of the land. If the treaty is valid there can be no dispute about the validity of the statute under Article I, §8, as a necessary and proper means to execute the powers of the Government. The language of the Constitution as to the supremacy of treaties being general, the question before us is narrowed to an inquiry into the ground upon which the present supposed exception is placed.

It is said that a treaty cannot be valid if it infringes the Constitution, that there are limits, therefore, to the treaty-making power, and that one such limit is that what an act of Congress could not do unaided, in derogation of the powers reserved to the States, a treaty cannot do. An earlier act of Congress that attempted by itself and not in pursuance of a treaty to regulate the killing of migratory birds within the States had been held bad in the District Court. *United States* v. *Shauver,* 214 Fed. Rep. 154; *United States* v. *McCullagh,* 221 Fed. Rep. 288. Those decisions were supported by arguments that migratory birds were owned by the States in their sovereign capacity for the benefit of their people, and that under cases like *Geer*

v. *Connecticut,* 161 U. S. 519, this control was one that Congress had no power to displace. The same argument is supposed to apply now with equal force.

Whether the two cases cited were decided rightly or not they cannot be accepted as a test of the treaty power. Acts of Congress are the supreme law of the land only when made in pursuance of the Constitution, while treaties are declared to be so when made under the authority of the United States. It is open to question whether the authority of the United States means more than the formal acts prescribed to make the convention. We do not mean to imply that there are no qualifications to the treaty-making power; but they must be ascertained in a different way. It is obvious that there may be matters of the sharpest exigency for the national well being that an act of Congress could not deal with but that a treaty followed by such an act could, and it is not lightly to be assumed that, in matters requiring national action, "a power which must belong to and somewhere reside in every civilized government" is not to be found. *Andrews* v. *Andrews,* 188 U. S. 14. What was said in that case with regard to the powers of the States applies with equal force to the powers of the nation in cases where the States individually are incompetent to act. We are not yet discussing the particular case before us but only are considering the validity of the test proposed. . . . The treaty in question does not contravene any prohibitory words to be found in the Constitution. The only question is whether it is forbidden by some invisible radiation from the general terms of the Tenth Amendment. We must consider what this country has become in deciding what that amendment has reserved.

The State as we have intimated founds its claim of exclusive authority upon an assertion of title to migratory birds, an assertion that is embodied in statute. No doubt it is true that as between a State and its inhabitants the State may regulate the killing and sale of such birds, but it does not follow that its authority is exclusive of paramount powers. To put the claim of the State upon title is to lean upon a slender reed. Wild birds are not in the possession of anyone; and possession is the beginning of ownership. The whole foundation of the State's rights is the presence within their jurisdiction of birds that yesterday had not arrived, tomorrow may be in another State and in a week a thousand miles away. If we are to be accurate we cannot put the case of the State upon higher ground than that the treaty deals with creatures that for the moment are within the state borders, that it must be carried out by officers of the United States within the same territory, and that but for the treaty the State would be free to regulate this subject itself.

As most of the laws of the United States are carried out within the States and as many of them deal with matters which in the silence of such laws the State might regulate, such general grounds are not enough to support Missouri's claim. Valid treaties of course "are as binding within the territorial limits of the States as they are elsewhere throughout the dominion of the United States." *Baldwin* v. *Franks,* 120 U. S. 678. No doubt the great body of private relations usually fall within the control of the State, but a treaty may override its power. We do not have to invoke the later developments of constitutional law for this proposition; it was recognized as early as *Hopkirk* v. *Bell,* 3 Cranch, 454, with regard to statutes of limitation, and even earlier, as to confiscation, in *Ware* v. *Hylton,* 3 Dall. 199. . . . Further illustration seems unnecessary, and it only remains to consider the application of established rules to the present case.

Here a national interest of very nearly the first magnitude is involved. It can be protected only by national action in concert with that of another power. The subject-matter is only transitorily within the State and has no permanent habitat therein. But for the treaty and the statute there soon might be no birds for any powers to deal with. We see nothing in the Constitution that compels the government to sit by while a food supply is cut off and the protectors of our forests and our crops are destroyed. It is not sufficient to rely upon the States. The reliance is vain, and were it otherwise, the question is whether the United States is forbidden to act. We are of opinion that the treaty and statute must be upheld.

Decree affirmed.

Justices VAN DEVANTER and PITNEY dissented.

438. THE TRANSPORTATION ACT OF 1920
February 28, 1920

(*U. S. Statutes at Large,* Vol. XLI, p. 456 ff.)

This act, sometimes known as the Esch-Cummins Act, terminated the war-time period of government operation of the railroads and provided for the return of the roads to private ownership and operation under careful regulations. The most interesting feature of the Transportation Act of 1920 was the so-called "recapture" clause which provided for the setting aside of a reserve fund from railroad earnings over a "fair return." See A. R. Ellingwood and W. Coombs, *The Government and Railroad Transportation;* W. M. Splawn, *Government Ownership and Operation of Railroads;* R. MacVeagh, *The Transportation Act of 1920;* F. H. Dixon, *Railroads and Government;* W. D. Hines, *War History of American Railroads.*

TITLE II.
TERMINATION OF FEDERAL CONTROL

SEC. 200. (a) Federal control shall terminate at 12.01 A.M., March 1, 1920; and the President shall then relinquish possession and control of all railroads and systems of transportation then under Federal control and cease the use and operation thereof. . . .

SEC. 202. The President shall, as soon as practicable after the termination of Federal control, adjust, settle, liquidate, and wind up all matters, including compensation, and all questions and disputes of whatsoever nature, arising out of or incident to Federal control. . . .

SEC. 208. (a) All rates, fares, and charges, . . . which on February 29, 1920, are in effect on the lines of carriers subject to the Interstate Commerce Act, shall continue in force and effect until thereafter changed by State or Federal authority, respectively, or pursuant to authority of law; but prior to September 1, 1920, no such rate, fare, or charge shall be reduced, . . . unless such reduction or change is approved by the Commission. . . .

SEC. 209. . . .

(c) The United States hereby guarantees—

(1) With respect to any carrier with which a contract . . . has been made . . . that the railway operating income of such carrier for the guaranty period as a whole shall not be less than one-half the amount named in such contract as annual compensation, . . .

TITLE III.
DISPUTES BETWEEN CARRIERS AND THEIR EMPLOYEES AND SUBORDINATE OFFICIALS

SEC. 301. It shall be the duty of all carriers and their officers, employees, and agents, to exert every reasonable effort . . . to avoid any interruption to the operation of any carrier growing out of any dispute between the carrier and the employees or subordinate officials thereof. All such disputes shall be considered and, if possible, decided in conference between representatives designated and authorized so to confer by the carriers, or the employees or subordinate officials thereof, directly interested in the dispute. If any dispute is not decided in such conference, it shall be referred by the parties thereto to the board which under the provisions of this title is authorized to hear and decide such dispute.

SEC. 302. Railroad Boards of Labor Adjustment may be established by agreement between any carrier, . . . or the carriers as a whole, and any employees or subordinate officials of carriers, or organization or group of organizations thereof.

SEC. 303. Each such Adjustment Board shall, (1) upon the application of the chief executive of any carrier or organization of employees or subordinate officials whose members are directly interested in the dispute, (2) upon the written petition signed by not less than 100 unorganized employees or subordinate officials directly interested in the dispute, (3) upon the Adjustment Board's own motion, or (4) upon the request of the Labor Board whenever such board is of the opinion that the dispute is likely substantially to interrupt commerce, receive for hearing, and as soon as practicable and with due diligence decide, any dispute involving only grievances, rules, or working conditions, not decided as provided in section 301, between the carrier and its employees or subordinate officials. . . .

SEC. 304. There is hereby established a board to be known as the "Railroad Labor Board" and to be composed of nine members as follows:

(1) Three members constituting the labor group, representing the employees and subordinate officials of the carriers, to be appointed by the President, by and with the advice and consent of the Senate, from not less than six nominees whose nominations shall be made and offered by such employees in such manner as the Commission shall by regulation prescribe;

(2) Three members, constituting the management group, representing the carriers, to be appointed by the President, by and with the advice and consent of the Senate, from not less than six nominees whose nominations shall be made and offered by the carriers in such manner as the Commission shall by regulation prescribe; and

(3) Three members, constituting the public group, representing the public, to be appointed directly by the President, by and with the advice and consent of the Senate. . . .

SEC. 306. (a) Any member of the Labor Board who during his term of office is an active member or in the employ of or holds any office in any organization of employees or subordinate officials, or any carrier, or owns any stock or bond thereof, or is pecuniarily interested therein, shall at once become ineligible for further membership upon the Labor Board; but no such member is required to relinquish honorary membership in, or his rights in any insurance or pension or other benefit fund maintained by, any organization of employees or subordinate officials or by a carrier.

SEC. 307. (a) The Labor Board shall hear, and . . . decide, any dispute involving grievances, rules, or working conditions, in respect to which any Adjustment Board certifies to the Labor Board that in its opinion the Adjustment Board has failed or will fail to reach a decision within a reasonable time, or in respect to which the Labor Board determines that any Adjustment Board has so failed or is not using due diligence in its consideration thereof. . . .

(b) The Labor Board shall receive for hearing, and as soon as practicable and with due diligence decide, all disputes with respect to the wages or salaries of employees or subordinate officials of carriers, not decided as provided in section 301. . . .

(c) A decision by the Labor Board under the provisions of paragraphs (a) or (b) of this section shall require the concurrence therein of at least 5 of the 9 members of the Labor Board: *Provided,* That in case of any decision under paragraph (b), at least one of the representatives of the public shall concur in such decision. . . .

(d) . . . In determining the justness and reasonableness of . . . wages and salaries or working conditions the board shall, so far as applicable, take into consideration among other relevant circumstances:

(1) The scale of wages paid for similar kinds of work in other industries;

(2) The relation between wages and the cost of living;

(3) The hazards of the employment;

(4) The training and skill required;

(5) The degree of responsibility;

(6) The character and regularity of employment; and

(7) Inequalities of increases in wages or of treatment, the result of previous wage orders or adjustments.

SEC. 407 . . .

(4) The Commission shall as soon as practicable prepare and adopt a plan for the consolidation of the railway properties of the continental United States into a limited number of systems. In the division of such railways into such systems under such plan, competition shall be preserved as fully as possible and wherever practicable the existing routes and channels of trade and commerce shall be maintained. . . .

(6) It shall be lawful for two or more carriers by railroad, subject to this Act, to consolidate their properties or any part thereof, into one corporation for the ownership, management, and operation of the properties theretofore in separate ownership, management, and operation, under the following conditions:

(a) The proposed consolidation must be in harmony with and in furtherance of the complete plan of consolidation mentioned in paragraph (5) and must be approved by the Commission; . . .

(8) The carriers affected by any order made under the foregoing provisions of this section and any corporation organized to effect a consolidation approved and authorized in such order shall be, and they are hereby, relieved from the operation of the "antitrust laws," as designated in section 1 of the Act entitled "An Act to supplement existing laws against unlawful restraints and monopolies, and for other purposes," approved October 15, 1914, and of all other restraints or prohibitions by law, State or Federal, in so far as may be necessary to enable them to do anything authorized or required by any order made under and pursuant to the foregoing provisions of this section. . . .

SEC. 422. . . .

(2) In the exercise of its power to prescribe just and reasonable rates the Commission shall initiate, modify, establish or adjust such rates so that carriers as a whole . . . will, under honest, efficient and economical management and reasonable expenditures for maintenance of way, structures and equipment, earn an aggregate annual net railway operating income equal, as nearly as may be, to a fair return upon the aggregate value of the railway property of such carriers held for and used in the service of transportation. . . .

(3) The Commission shall from time to time determine and make public what percentage of such aggregate property value constitutes a fair return thereon, and such percentage shall be uniform for all rate groups or territories which may be designated by the Commission. In making such determination it shall give due consideration, among other things, to the transportation needs of the country and the necessity . . . of enlarging such facilities in order to provide the people of the United States with adequate transportation: *Provided,* That during the two years beginning March 1, 1920, the Commission shall take as such fair return a sum equal to 5½ per centum of such aggregate value to make provision in whole or in part for improvements, betterments, or equipment, which, according to the accounting system prescribed by the Commission, are chargeable to capital account. . . .

(5) Inasmuch as it is impossible . . . to establish uniform rates upon competitive traffic which will adequately sustain all the carriers which are engaged in such traffic and which are indispensable to the communities to which they render the service of transportation, without enabling some of such carriers to receive a net railway operating income substantially and unreasonably in excess of a fair return upon the value of their railway property held for and used in the service of transportation, it is hereby declared that any carrier which receives such an income so in excess of a fair return, shall hold such part of the excess, as hereinafter prescribed, as trustee for, and shall pay it to, the United States.

(6) If, under the provisions of this section, any carrier receives for any year a net railway operating income in excess of 6 per centum of the value of the railway property held for and used by it in the service of transportation, one-half of such excess shall be placed in a reserve fund established and maintained by such carrier, and the remaining one-half thereof shall, within the first four months following the close of the period for which such computation is made, be recoverable by and paid to the Commission for the purpose of establishing and maintaining a general railroad contingent fund as hereinafter described. . . .

439. RAILROAD COMMISSION OF WISCONSIN v. CHICAGO, BURLINGTON, & QUINCY RAILROAD COMPANY
257 U. S. 563
1922

Appeal from the District Court for Eastern District of Wisconsin. Decree to enjoin state railroad commission from interfering with maintenance of rates fixed by the Interstate Commerce Commission. The Interstate Commerce Commission, acting under authority of the Transportation Act of 1920, ordered an increase of twenty per cent in passenger rates on railroads in the group which embraced the Wisconsin carriers. This order conflicted with a state statute of February 28, 1920, fixing a maximum rate of 2 cents a mile for intrastate passenger transportation. The Interstate Commerce Commission consequently ordered an increase in intrastate rates to bring them into conformity with those charged over interstate transportation.

TAFT, C. J. The Commission's order, interference with which was enjoined by the district court, effects the removal of the unjust discrimination found to exist against persons in interstate commerce, and against interstate commerce, by fixing a minimum for intrastate passenger fares in Wisconsin at 3.6 cents per mile. . . .

We have two questions to decide.

First, Do the intrastate passenger fares work undue prejudice against persons in interstate commerce, such as to justify a horizontal increase of them all?

Second, Are these intrastate fares an undue discrimination against interstate commerce as a whole which it is the duty of the Commission to remove? . . .

The order in this case . . . is much wider than the orders made in the proceedings following the Shreveport and Illinois C. R. Co. Cases. There, as here, the report of the Commission showed discrimination against persons and localities at border points and the orders were extended to include all rates or fares from all points in the state to border points. But this order is not so restricted. It includes fares between all interior points, although neither may be near the border, and the fares between them may not work a discrimination against interstate travelers at all. Nothing in the precedents cited justifies an order affecting all rates of a general description when it is clear that this would include many rates not within the proper class or reason of the order. . . .

Intrastate rates and the income from them must play a most important part in maintaining an adequate national railway system. Twenty per cent of the gross freight receipts of the railroads of the country are from intrastate traffic, and 50 per cent of the passenger receipts. The ratio of the gross intrastate revenue to the interstate revenue is a little less than one to three. If the rates, on which such receipts are based, are to be fixed at a substantially lower level than in interstate traffic, the share which the intrastate traffic will contribute will be proportionately less. . . .

It is objected here, as it was in the Shreveport Case, that orders of the Commission which raise the intrastate rates to a level of the interstate structure violate the specific proviso of the original Interstate Commerce Act . . . that the Commission is not to regulate traffic wholly within a state. To this the same answer must be made as was made in the Shreveport Case, that such orders as to intrastate traffic are merely incidental to the regulation of interstate commerce, and necessary to its efficiency. Effective control of the one must embrace some control over the other, in view of the blending of both in actual operation. The same rails and the same cars carry both. The same men conduct them. Commerce is a unit and does not regard state lines, and while, under the Constitution, interstate and intrastate commerce are ordinarily subject to regulation by different sovereignties, yet when they are so mingled together that the supreme authority, the nation, cannot exercise complete effective control over interstate commerce without incidental regulation of intrastate commerce, such incidental regulation is not an invasion of state authority or a violation of the proviso. . . .

Congress in its control of its interstate commerce system, is seeking in the Transportation Act to make the system adequate to the needs of the country by securing for it a reasonably compensatory return for all the work it does. The states are seeking to use that same system for intrastate traffic. That entails large duties and expenditures on the interstate commerce which may burden it unless compensation is received for the intrastate business reasonably proportionate to that for the interstate business. Congress, as the dominant controller of interstate commerce, may, therefore, restrain undue limitations of the earning power of the interstate commerce system in doing state work. The affirmative power of Congress in developing interstate commerce agencies is clear. In such development, it can impose any reasonable condition on a state's use of interstate carriers for intrastate commerce it deems necessary or desirable. This is because of the supremacy of the national power in this field. Order of the District Court affirmed.

440. DAYTON–GOOSE CREEK RAILWAY COMPANY v. UNITED STATES
263 U. S. 456
1924

Appeal from decree of District Court for Eastern District of Texas dismissing a bill to restrain enforcement of order from Interstate Commerce Commission. The Transportation Act of 1920 (see Doc. No. 438) provided that any railroad receiving an income in excess of such fair return as shall be established by the Interstate Commerce Commission shall hold the excess earnings as a trustee for the United States. One half of the excess is to constitute a reserve fund to be maintained by the carrier, and the other half a general railroad revolving fund to be maintained and administered by the Interstate Commerce Commission.

TAFT, C. J. The main question in this case is whether the so-called "recapture" paragraphs of the Transportation Act of February 28, 1920 are constitutional. . . .

This court has recently had occasion to construe the Transportation Act. . . . It was pointed out that the Transportation Act adds a new and important object to previous interstate commerce legislation, which was designed primarily to prevent unreasonable or discriminatory rates against persons and localities. The new act seeks affirmatively to build up a system of railways prepared to handle promptly all the interstate traffic of the country. It aims to give the owners of the railways an opportunity to earn enough to maintain their properties and equipment in such a state of efficiency that they can carry well this burden. To achieve this great purpose, it puts the railroad systems of the country more completely than ever under the fostering guardianship and control of the Commission, which is to supervise their issue of securities, their car supply and distribution, their joint use of terminals, their construction of new lines, their abandonment of old lines, and by a proper division of joint rates, and by fixing adequate rates, for interstate commerce, and, in case of discrimination, for intrastate commerce, to secure a fair return upon the properties of the carriers engaged. . . .

We have been greatly pressed with the argument that the cutting down of income actually received by the carrier for its service to a so-called fair return is a plain appropriation of its property without any compensation; that the income it receives for the use of its property is as much protected by the 5th Amendment as the property itself. The statute declares the carrier to be only a trustee for the excess over a fair return received by it. Though in its possession, the excess never becomes its property, and it accepts custody of the product of all the rates with this understanding. It is clear, therefore, that the carrier never has such a title to the excess as to render the recapture of it by the government a taking without due process.

It is then objected that the government has no right to retain one half of the excess, since, if it does not belong to the carrier, it belongs to the shippers, and should be returned to them. If it were valid, it is an objection which the carrier cannot be heard to make. It would be soon enough to consider such a claim when made by the shipper. But it is not valid. The rates are reasonable from the standpoint of the shipper, as we have shown, though their net product furnishes more than a fair return for the carrier. The excess caused by the discrepancy between the standard of reasonableness for the shipper and that for the carrier, due to the necessity of maintaining uniform rates to be charged the shippers, may properly be appropriated by the government for public uses because the appropriation takes away nothing which equitably belongs either to the shipper or to the carrier. . . .

The third question for our consideration is whether the recapture clause, by reducing the net income from intrastate rates, invades the reserved power of the States and is in conflict with the 10th Amendment. In solving the problem of maintaining the efficiency of an interstate commerce railway system which serves both the states and the nation, Congress is dealing with a unit, in which state and interstate operations are often inextricably commingled. When the adequate maintenance of interstate commerce involves and makes necessary on this account the incidental and partial control of intrastate commerce, the power of Congress to exercise such control has been clearly established. (Minnesota Rate Cases, 230 U. S. 352; Shreveport Case, 234 U. S. 342; Railway Commission v. Chicago B & Q R. R. 257 U. S. 563.) The combination of uniform rates with the recapture clauses is necessary to the better development of the country's in-terstate transportation system as Congress has planned it. The control of the excess profit due to the level of the whole body of rates is the heart of the plan. To divide that excess and attempt to distribute one part to interstate traffic and the other to intrastate traffic would be impracticable and defeat the plan. . . .

Decree of District Court affirmed.

441. GREEN v. FRAZIER
253 U. S. 233
1920

Error to the Supreme Court of the State of North Dakota. This case involved the legality of taxation for the maintenance of State-managed manufacturing and banking institutions. The decision in *Loan Association* v. *Topeka,* Doc. No. 286, had established the rule that public moneys could not be used for the support of private business, but it remained to determine what businesses were private and what public in character. For the background, see P. R. Fossum, *The Agrarian Movement in North Dakota.*

DAY, J. . . . The only ground of attack involving the validity of the legislation which requires our consideration concerns the alleged deprivation of rights secured to the plaintiffs by the Fourteenth Amendment to the federal Constitution. It is contended that taxation under the laws in question has the effect of depriving plaintiffs of property without due process of law.

The legislation involved consists of a series of acts passed under the authority of the state constitution, which are (1) An Act creating an Industrial Commission of North Dakota which is authorized to conduct and manage on behalf of that State certain utilities, enterprises, and business projects, to be established by law . . . (2) The Bank of North Dakota Act, which establishes a Bank operated by the State . . . (4) An Act providing for the issuing of bonds in the sum of not exceeding $10,000,000 . . . These bonds are to be issued for the purpose of raising money to produce funds for the Bank of North Dakota . . . (5) An Act declaring the purpose of the State of North Dakota to engage in the business of manufacturing and marketing farm products and to establish a warehouse, elevator, and flour mill system . . . (6) An Act providing for the issuing of bonds of the State of North Dakota in a sum not exceeding $5,000,000 . . . These bonds are to be issued and sold for the purpose of carrying on the business of the Mill & Elevator Association. The faith and credit of the state are pledged for the payment of the bonds, both principle and interest . . . (7) The Home Building Act. . . .

There are certain principles which must be borne in mind in this connection, and which must control the decision of this court upon the federal question herein involved. This legislation was adopted under the broad power of the state to enact laws raising by taxation such sums as are deemed necessary to promote purposes essential to the general welfare of its people. Before the adoption of the Fourteenth Amendment this power of the state was unrestrained by any federal authority. That amendment introduced a new limitation upon state power into the federal Constitution. The states were forbidden to deprive persons of life, liberty and property without due process of law. What is meant by due process of law this court has had frequent occasion to consider, and has always declined to give a precise meaning, preferring to leave its scope to judicial decisions when cases from time to time arise.

The due process of law clause contains no specific limitation upon the right of taxation in the states, but it has come to be settled that the authority of the states to tax does not include the right to impose taxes for merely private purposes. . . .

Accepting this as settled by the former adjudications of this court, the enforcement of the principle is attended with the application of certain rules equally well settled.

The taxing power of the states is primarily

vested in their legislatures, deriving their authority from the people. When a state legislature acts within the scope of its authority it is responsible to the people, and their right to change the agents to whom they have intrusted the power is ordinarily deemed a sufficient check upon its abuse. When the constituted authority of the state undertakes to exert the taxing power, and the question of the validity of its action is brought before this court, every presumption in its favor is indulged, and only clear and demonstrative usurpation of power will authorize judicial interference with legislative action.

In the present instance under the authority of the constitution and laws prevailing in North Dakota the people, the legislature, and the highest court of the state have declared the purpose for which these several acts were passed to be of a public nature, and within the taxing authority of the state. With this united action of people, legislature and court, we are not at liberty to interfere unless it is clear beyond reasonable controversy that rights secured by the federal Constitution have been violated. What is a public purpose has given rise to no little judicial consideration. Courts, as a rule, have attempted no judicial definition of a "public" as distinguished from a "private" purpose, but have left each case to be determined by its own peculiar circumstances. . . . Questions of policy are not submitted to judicial determination, and the courts have no general authority of supervision over the exercise of discretion which under our system is reposed in the people or other departments of government.

With the wisdom of such legislation, and the soundness of the economic policy involved we are not concerned. Whether it will result in ultimate good or harm it is not within our province to inquire.

We come now to examine the grounds upon which the supreme court of North Dakota held this legislation not to amount to a taking of property without due process of law. The questions involved were given elaborate consideration in that court, and it held, concerning what may in general terms be denominated the "banking legislation," that it was justified for the purpose of providing banking facilities, and to enable the state to carry out the purposes of the other acts, of

which the Mill and Elevator Association Act is the principal one. It justified the Mill and Elevator Association Act by the peculiar situation in the State of North Dakota, and particularly by the great agricultural industry of the state. It estimated from facts of which it was authorized to take judicial notice, that 90 per cent. of the wealth produced by the state was from agriculture; and stated that upon the prosperity and welfare of that industry other business and pursuits carried on in the state were largely dependent; that the state produced 125,000,000 bushels of wheat each year. The manner in which the present system of transporting and marketing this great crop prevents the realization of what are deemed just prices was elaborately stated. It was affirmed that the annual loss from these sources (including the loss of fertility to the soil and the failure to feed the by-products of grain to stock within the state), amounted to fifty-five millions of dollars to the wheat raisers of North Dakota. It answered the contention that the industries involved were private in their nature, by stating that all of them belonged to the State of North Dakota, and therefore the activities authorized by the legislation were to be distinguished from business of a private nature having private gain for its objective.

As to the Home Building Act, that was sustained because of the promotion of the general welfare in providing homes for the people, a large proportion of whom were tenants moving from place to place. It was believed and affirmed by the supreme court of North Dakota that the opportunity to secure and maintain homes would promote the general welfare, and that the provisions of the statutes to enable this feature of the system to become effective would redound to the general benefit.

As we have said, the question for us to consider and determine is whether this system of legislation is violative of the federal Constitution because it amounts to a taking of property without due process of law. The precise question herein involved so far as we have been able to discover has never been presented to this court. The nearest approach to it is found in Jones v. City of Portland, 245 U. S. 217, in which we held that an act of the State of Maine authorizing cities or towns to establish and maintain wood, coal and fuel yards for the purpose of selling these necessaries to the inhabitants of cities and towns, did not deprive taxpayers of due process of law within the meaning of the Fourteenth Amendment. In that case we reiterated the attitude of this court towards state legislation, and repeated what had been said before, that what was or was not a public use was a question concerning which local authority, legislative and judicial, had especial means of securing information to enable them to form a judgment; and particularly that the judgment of the highest court of the state declaring a given use to be public in its nature, would be accepted by this court unless clearly unfounded. In that case the previous decisions of this court, sustaining this proposition, were cited with approval, and a quotation was made from the opinion of the supreme court of Maine justifying the legislation under the conditions prevailing in that state. We think the principle of that decision is applicable here.

This is not a case of undertaking to aid private institutions by public taxation as was the fact in Citizens' Savings and Loan Association v. Topeka, 20 Wallace 655. In many instances states and municipalities have in late years seen fit to enter upon projects to promote the public welfare which in the past have been considered entirely within the domain of private enterprise.

Under the peculiar conditions existing in North Dakota, which are emphasized in the opinion of its highest court, if the state sees fit to enter upon such enterprises as are here involved, with the sanction of its constitution, its legislature and its people, we are not prepared to say that it is within the authority of this court, in enforcing the observance of the Fourteenth Amendment, to set aside such action by judicial decision.

Affirmed.

442. TREATY OF PEACE WITH GERMANY
August 25, 1921

(*U. S. Statutes at Large,* Vol. XXXXII, p. 1939)

The United States of America and Germany:

Considering that the United States, acting in conjunction with its co-belligerents, entered into an Armistice with Germany on November 11, 1918, in order that a Treaty of Peace might be concluded;

Considering that the Treaty of Versailles was signed on June 28, 1919, and came into force according to the terms of its Article 440, but has not been ratified by the United States;

Considering that the Congress of the United States passed a Joint Resolution, approved by the President July 2, 1921, which reads in part as follows:

"Resolved by the Senate and House of Representatives of the United States of America in Congress Assembled:

"That the state of war declared to exist between the Imperial German Government and the United States of America by the joint resolution of Congress approved April 6, 1917, is hereby declared at an end.

"Section 2. That in making this declaration, and as a part of it, there are expressly reserved to the United States of America and its nationals any and all rights, privileges, indemnities, reparations or advantages, together with the right to enforce the same, to which it or they have become entitled under the terms of the Armistice signed November 11, 1918, or any extensions or modifications thereof; or which were acquired by or are in the possession of the United States of America by reason of its participation in the war or to which its nationals have thereby become rightfully entitled; or which, under the Treaty of Versailles, have been stipulated for its or their benefit; or to which it is entitled as one of the Principal Allied and Associated powers; or to which it is entitled by virtue of any Act or Acts of Congress; or otherwise."

. . . Being desirous of restoring the friendly relations existing between the two Nations prior to the outbreak of war:

Have for that purpose appointed their plenipotentiaries:

The President of the United States of America

Ellis Loring Dresel, Commissioner of the United States of America to Germany, and

The President of the German Empire

Dr. Friedrich Rosen, Minister for Foreign Affairs,

Who, having communicated their full powers, found to be in good and due form have agreed as follows:

Art. 1. Germany undertakes to accord to the United States, and the United States shall have and enjoy, all the rights, privileges, indemnities, reparations or advantages specified in the aforesaid Joint Resolution of the Congress of the United States of July 2, 1921, including all the rights and advantages stipulated for the benefit of the United States in the Treaty of Versailles which the United States shall fully enjoy notwithstanding the fact that such Treaty has not been ratified by the United States.

Art. 2. With a view to defining more particularly the obligations of Germany under the foregoing Article with respect to certain provisions in the Treaty of Versailles, it is understood and agreed between the High Contracting Parties:

(1) That the rights and advantages stipulated in that Treaty for the benefit of the United States, which it is intended the United States shall have and enjoy, are those defined in Section 1 of Part IV, and Parts V, VI, VIII, IX, X, XI, XII, XIV, and XV.

The United States, in availing itself of the rights and advantages stipulated in the provisions of that Treaty mentioned in this paragraph, will do so in a manner consistent with the rights accorded to Germany under such provisions.

(2) That the United States shall not be bound by the provisions of Part 1 of that Treaty, nor by any provisions of that Treaty, including those mentioned in Paragraph (1) of this Article, which relate to the Covenant of the League of Nations, or by the Council or by the Assembly thereof, unless the United States shall expressly give the assent to such action.

(3) That the United States assumes no obligations under or with respect to the provisions of Part II, Part III, Sections 2 to 8 inclusive of Part IV, and Part XIII of that Treaty.

(4) That, while the United States is privileged to participate in the Reparation Commission, according to the terms of Part VIII of that Treaty, and in any other Commission established under the Treaty or under any agreement supplemental thereto, the United States is not bound to participate in any such commission unless it shall elect to do so.

(5) That the periods of time to which reference is made in Article 440 of the Treaty of Versailles shall run, with respect to any act or election on the part of the United States, from the date of the coming into force of the present Treaty.

Art. 3. The present Treaty shall be ratified in accordance with the constitutional forms of the High Contracting Parties and shall take effect immediately on the exchange of ratifications, which shall take place as soon as possible at Berlin.

In witness whereof, the respective plenipotentiaries have signed this Treaty and have hereunto affixed their seals.

Done in duplicate in Berlin this twenty-fifth day of August, 1921.

Ellis Loring Dresel.

Rosen.

443. THE SHEPPARD–TOWNER ACT
November 23, 1921

(*U. S. Statutes at Large,* Vol. XXXXII, p. 224 ff.)

This act, extending federal aid to states for welfare work, was regarded by many critics as an unwarranted intrusion on the jurisdiction of the states, and many states refused to avail themselves of the provisions of the act. See A. F. Macdonald, *Federal Aid: a Study of the American Subsidy System;* W. Thompson, *Federal Centralization.*

An Act For the promotion of the welfare and hygiene of maternity and infancy, and for other purposes.

Be it enacted That there is hereby authorized to be appropriated annually, out of any money in the Treasury not otherwise appropriated, the sums specified in section 2 of this Act, to be paid to the several States for the purpose of cooperating with them in promoting the welfare and hygiene of maternity and infancy as hereinafter provided.

Sec. 2. For the purpose of carrying out the provisions of this Act, there is authorized to be appropriated, out of any money in the Treasury not otherwise appropriated, for the current fiscal year $480,000, to be equally apportioned among the several States, and for each subsequent year, for the period of five years, $240,000, to be equally apportioned among the several States in the manner hereinafter provided: Provided, That there is hereby authorized to be appropriated for the use of the States, subject to the provisions of this Act, for the fiscal year ending to June 30, 1922, an additional sum of $1,000,000 and annually thereafter, for the period of five years, an additional sum not to exceed $1,000,000: Provided further, That the additional appropriations herein authorized shall be apportioned $5,000 to each State and the balance among the States in the proportion which their population bears to the total population of the States of the United States, according to the last preceding United States census: And provided further, That no payment out of the additional appropriation herein authorized shall be made in any year to any State until an equal sum has been appropriated for that year by the legislature of such State for the maintenance of the services and facilities provided for in this Act. . . .

Sec. 4. In order to secure the benefits of the appropriations authorized in section 2 of this Act, any State shall, through the legislative authority thereof, accept the provisions of this Act and designate or authorize the creation of a State agency with which the Children's Bureau shall have all necessary powers to co-operate as herein provided in the administration of the provisions of this Act: Provided, That in any State having a child-welfare or child-hygiene division in its State agency of health, the said State agency of health shall administer the provisions of this Act through such divisions. If the legislature of any State has not made provision for accepting the provisions of this Act the governor of such State may in so far as he is authorized to do so by the laws of such State accept the provisions of this Act and designate or create a State agency to co-operate with the Children's Bureau until six months after the adjournment of the first regular session of the legislature in such State following the passage of this Act. . . .

Sec. 8. Any State desiring to receive the benefits of this Act shall, by its agency described in section 4, submit to the Children's Bureau detailed plans for carrying out the provisions of this Act within such State, which plans shall be subject to the approval of the board: . . .

Sec. 14. This Act shall be construed as intending to secure to the various States control of the administration of this Act within their respective States, subject only to the provisions and purposes of this Act.

444. TRUAX v. CORRIGAN
257 U. S. 312
1921

Error to the supreme court of Arizona. This is one of the leading cases on the right of labor to picket or to employ a boycott in labor disputes. The facts of the controversy are stated in the case below. For a general discussion, see F. Frankfurter and N. Greene, *The Labor Injunction;* P. F. Brissenden, "The Labor Injunction," *Pol. Sci. Qt.,* Vol. XLVIII.

TAFT, C. J. . . . The complaint further averred that the defendants were relying for immunity on Paragraph 1464 of the Revised Statutes of Arizona, 1913, which is in part as follows:

"No restraining order or injunction shall be granted by any court of this state, or a judge or the judges thereof, in any case between an employer and employees, or between employers and employees, or between employees, or between persons employed and persons seeking employment, involving or growing out of a dispute concerning terms or conditions of employment, unless necessary to prevent irreparable injury to property or to a property right of the party making the application, for which injury there is no adequate remedy at law, and such property or property right must be described with particularity in the application, which must be in writing and sworn to by the applicant or by his agent or attorney.

"And no such restraining order or injunction shall prohibit any person or persons from terminating any relation of employment, or from ceasing to perform any work or labor, or from recommending, advising, or persuading others by peaceful means so to do; or from attending at or near a house or place where any person resides or works, or carries on business, or happens to be for the purpose of peacefully obtaining or communicating information, or of peacefully persuading any person to work or to abstain from working; or from ceasing to patronize or to employ any party to such dispute; or from recommending, advising, or persuading others by peaceful means so to do; . . ."

The plaintiffs alleged that this paragraph if it made lawful defendants' acts contravened the Fourteenth Amendment to the Constitution of the United States by depriving plaintiffs of their property without due process of law, and by denying to plaintiffs the equal protection of the laws, and was, therefore, void and of no effect. Upon the case thus stated the plaintiffs asked a temporary, and a permanent, injunction.

. . . The Superior Court for Chocise County . . . dismissed the complaint, and this judgment was affirmed by the supreme court of Arizona. . . .

The effect of this ruling is that, under the statute, loss may be inflicted upon the plaintiffs' property and business by "picketing" in any form if violence be not used, and that, because no violence was shown or claimed, the campaign carried on, as described in the complaint and exhibits, did not unlawfully invade plaintiffs' rights. . . .

The complaint and its exhibits make this case:

The defendants conspired to injure and destroy plaintiffs' business by inducing their theretofore willing patrons and would be patrons not to patronize them. . . .

The result of this campaign was to reduce the business of the plaintiffs from more than $55,000 a year to one of $12,000.

Plaintiffs' business is a property right (Duplex Printing Press Co. v. Deering, 254 U. S. 443) and free access for employees,

owner, and customers to his place of business is incident to such right. Intentional injury caused to either right or both by a conspiracy is a tort. . . .

A law which operates to make lawful such a wrong as is described in plaintiffs' complaint deprives the owner of the business and the premises of his property without due process, and cannot be held valid under the Fourteenth Amendment. . . .

If, however, contrary to the construction which we put on the opinion of the Supreme Court of Arizona, it does not withhold from the plaintiffs all remedy for the wrongs they suffered, but only the equitable relief of injunction, there still remains the question whether they are thus denied the equal protection of the laws. . . .

The necessary effect of . . . paragraph 1464 is that the plaintiffs in error would have had the right to an injunction against such a campaign as that conducted by the defendants in error, if it had been directed against the plaintiffs' business and property in any kind of a controversy which was not a dispute between employer and former employees. . . .

This brings us to consider the effect in this case of that provision of the Fourteenth Amendment which forbids any State to deny to any person the equal protection of the laws. The clause is associated in the amendment with the due process clause and it is customary to consider them together. . . .

The guaranty was aimed at undue favor and individual or class privilege, on the one hand, and at hostile discrimination or the oppression of inequality, on the other. It sought an equality of treatment of all persons, even though all enjoyed the protection of due process. Mr. Justice Field, delivering the opinion of this court in Barbier v. Connolly, 113 U. S. 27, of the equality clause, said— "Class legislation, discriminating against some and favoring others, is prohibited, but legislation which, in carrying out a public purpose, is limited in its application, if within the sphere of its operation it affects alike all persons similarly situated, is not within the amendment." . . .

Mr. Justice Matthews, in Yick Wo v. Hopkins, 118 U. S. 356, speaking for the court of both the due process and the equality clause of the Fourteenth Amendment, said:

"These provisions are universal in their application, to all persons within the territorial jurisdiction, without regard to any differences of race, of color, or nationality; *and the equal protection of the laws is a pledge of the protection of equal laws.*" . . .

With these views of the meaning of the equality clause, it does not seem possible to escape the conclusion that by the clauses of Paragraph 1464 of the Revised Statutes of Arizona, here relied on by the defendants, as construed by its supreme court, the plaintiffs have been deprived of the equal protection of the law. . . . Here is a direct invasion of the ordinary business and property rights of a person, unlawful when committed by any one, and remediable because of its otherwise irreparable character by equitable process, except when committed by ex-employees of the injured person. If this is not a denial of the equal protection of the laws, then it is hard to conceive what would be. . . .

Classification is the most inveterate of our reasoning processes. We can scarcely think or speak without consciously or unconsciously exercising it. It must therefore obtain in and determine legislation; but it must regard real resemblances and real differences between things and persons, and class them in accordance with their pertinence to the purpose in hand. Classification like the one with which we are here dealing is said to be the development of the philosophic thought of the world and is opening the door to legalized experiment. When fundamental rights are thus attempted to be taken away, however, we may well subject such experiment to attentive judgment. The Constitution was intended, its very purpose was, to prevent experimentation with the fundamental rights of the individual. We said through Mr. Justice Brewer, in Muller v. Oregon, 208 U. S. 412, 52 L. ed. 551, 28 S. Ct. R. 324, that "it is the peculiar value of a written constitution that it places in unchanging form limitations upon legislative action, and thus gives a permanence and stability to popular government which otherwise would be lacking." . . .

We conclude that the demurrer in this case should have been overruled, the defendants required to answer, and that if the evidence sustained the averments of the complaint, an injunction should issue as prayed. . . .

Judgment reversed.

HOLMES, J., dissenting. The dangers of a delusive exactness in the application of the Fourteenth Amendment have been adverted to before now. Delusive exactness is a source of fallacy throughout law. By calling a business "property" you make it seem like land, and lead up to the conclusion that a statute cannot substantially cut down the advantages of ownership existing before the statute was passed. An established business no doubt may have pecuniary value and commonly is protected by law against various unjustified injuries. But you cannot give it definiteness of contour by calling it a thing. It is a course of conduct and like other conduct is subject to substantial modification according to time and circumstances both in itself and in regard to what shall justify doing it harm. I cannot understand the notion that it would be unconstitutional to authorize boycotts and the like in aid of the employees' or the employers' interest by statute when the same result has been reached constitutionally without statute by Courts with whom I agree. In this case it does not even appear that the business was not created under the laws as they now are.

I think further that the selection of the class of employers and employees for special treatment, dealing with both sides alike, is beyond criticism on principles often asserted by this Court. And especially I think that without legalizing the conduct complained of the extraordinary relief by injunction may be denied to the class. Legislation may begin where an evil begins. If, as many intelligent people believe, there is more danger that the injunction will be abused in labor cases than elsewhere I can feel no doubt of the power of the legislature to deny it in such cases. . . .

I must add one general consideration. There is nothing that I more deprecate than the use of the Fourteenth Amendment beyond the absolute compulsion of its words to prevent the making of social experiments that an important part of the community desires, in the insulated chambers afforded by the several States, even though the experiments may seem futile or even noxious to me and to those whose judgment I most respect. I agree with the more elaborate expositions of my brothers PITNEY and BRANDEIS and in their conclusion that the judgment should be affirmed.

(PITNEY, J., delivered a dissenting opinion.

in which CLARKE, J., concurred. BRANDEIS, J., also delivered a dissenting opinion.)

445. DUPLEX PRINTING PRESS COMPANY v. DEERING
254 U. S. 443
1921

Appeal from the U.S. circuit court of appeals for the second district. Suit to enjoin an alleged unlawful conspiracy in restraint of trade. The facts are stated in the opinion. This is the leading case on the interpretation of the labor clauses of the Clayton Anti-Trust Act of 1914. See Doc. No. 403.

PITNEY, J. This was a suit in equity brought by appellant in the District Court for the Southern District of New York for an injunction to restrain a course of conduct carried on by defendants in that district . . . in maintaining a boycott against the products of complainant's factory, in furtherance of a conspiracy to injure and destroy its good will, trade, and business,—especially to obstruct and destroy its interstate trade. . . .

The suit was begun before but brought to hearing after, the passage of the Clayton Act of October 15, 1914. Both parties invoked the provisions of the later act, and both Courts created them as applicable. Complainant relied also upon the common law; but we shall deal first with the effect of the acts of Congress.

The facts . . . may be summarized as follows: Complainant conducts its business on the "open-shop" policy, without discrimination against either union or nonunion men. The individual defendants and the local organization of which they are the representatives are affiliated with the International Association of Machinists . . . and are united in a combination, . . . having the object of compelling complainant to unionize its factory. . . .

In August, 1913 . . . the International Association called a strike at complainant's factory in Battle Creek, as a result of which union machinists to the number of about eleven in the factory, and three who supervised the erection of presses in the field, left complainant's employ. . . . The acts complained of made up the details of an elaborate program adopted and carried out by defendants in their organizations in and

about the city of New York as part of a country-wide program adopted by the International Association, for the purpose of enforcing a boycott of complainant's product. . . .

All the judges of the Circuit Court of Appeals concurred in the view that defendants' conduct consisted essentially of efforts to render it impossible for complainant to carry on any commerce in printing presses between Michigan and New York; and that defendants had agreed to do and were endeavoring to accomplish the very thing pronounced unlawful by this court in *Lowe* v. *Lawler*. The judges also agreed that the interference with interstate commerce was such as ought to be enjoined, unless the Clayton Act of October 15, 1914, forbade such injunction. . . .

That . . . complainant has sustained substantial damage to its interstate trade,—and is threatened with further and irreparable loss and damage in the future,—is proved by clear and undisputed evidence. Hence, the right to an injunction is clear if the threatened loss is due to a violation of the Sherman Act, as amended by the Clayton Act. . . .

The substance of the matters here complained of is an interference with complainant's interstate trade intended to have coercive effect upon complainant, and produced by what is commonly known as a "secondary boycott"; that is, a combination not merely to refrain from dealing with complainant, or to advise or by peaceful means persuade complainant's customers to refrain ("primary boycott") but to exercise coercive pressure. . . .

As we shall see, the recognized distinction between a primary and a secondary boycott is material to be considered upon the question of a proper construction of the Clayton Act. . . .

The principal reliance is upon sec. 20 (of Clayton Act). . . . The second paragraph declares that "no such restraining order or injunction" shall prohibit certain conduct specified,—manifestly still referring to a "case between an employer and an employee, . . . involving, or growing out of, a dispute concerning terms or conditions of employment", as designated in the first paragraph. It is very clear that the restriction upon the use of the injunction is in favor only of those concerned as parties to such a dispute as is described. . . .

The majority of the Circuit Court of Appeals appear to have entertained the view that the words "employers and employees" as used in sec. 20 should be treated as referring to "the business class or clan to which the parties ligitant respectively belong;" and that, . . . sec. 20 operated to permit members of the Machinists' Union elsewhere—some 60,000 in number,—although standing in no relation of employment under complainant, past, present, or prospective, to make that dispute their own, and proceed to instigate sympathetic strikes, picketing, and boycotting against employers wholly unconnected with complainant's factory, and having relations with complainant only in the way of purchasing its product in the ordinary course of interstate commerce, —and this where there was no dispute between such employers and their employees respecting terms or conditions of employment.

We deem this construction altogether inadmissible. . . .

The emphasis placed on the words "lawful" and "lawfully," "peaceful" and "peacefully", and the references to the dispute and the parties to it, strongly rebut a legislative intent to confer a general immunity for conduct violative of the Anti-Trust laws, or otherwise unlawful. The subject of the boycott is dealt with specifically in the "ceasing to patronize" provision, and by the clear force of the language employed the exemption is limited to pressure exerted upon a "party to such dispute" by means of "peaceful and *lawful*" influence upon neutrals. There is nothing here to justify defendants or the organizations they represent in using either threats or persuasion to bring about strikes or a cessation of work on the part of employees of complainant's customers or prospective customers, or of the trucking company employed by the customers, with the object of compelling such customers to withdraw or refrain from commercial relations with complainant, and of thereby constraining complainant to yield the matter in dispute. To instigate a sympathetic strike in aid of a secondary boycott cannot be deemed "peaceful and lawful" persuasion. . . .

The question whether the bill legalized a secondary boycott having been raised (in the House), it was emphatically and unequivocally answered . . . in the negative. The subject . . . was under consideration when the bill was framed, and the section as reported was carefully prepared with the settled purpose of excluding the secondary boycott, and confining boycotting to the parties to the dispute, allowing parties to cease to patronize and to ask others to cease to patronize a party to the dispute; it was the opinion of the committee that it did not legalize the secondary boycott; it was not their purpose to authorize such a boycott; not a member of the committee would vote to do so; clarifying amendment was unnecessary; the section as reported expressed the real purpose so well that it could not be tortured into a meaning authorizing the secondary boycott. . . .

There should be an injunction against defendants and the associations represented by them.

Justices BRANDEIS, HOLMES and CLARKE dissenting.

446. BALZAC v. PORTO RICO
258 U. S. 298
1922

Error to the supreme court of Porto Rico. Balzac, an editor, was convicted for criminal libel without a jury trial. He appealed on the ground that the Sixth Amendment to the Federal Constitution guaranteed him the right of trial by jury. This case involved the question of the application of such procedural rights to the inhabitants of our insular possessions. For the constitutional problems involved, see references under *Downes* v. *Bidwell*, Doc. No. 352.

TAFT, C. J. . . . We have now to inquire whether that part of the Sixth Amendment to the Constitution, which requires that, in all criminal prosecutions, the accused shall enjoy the right to a speedy and public trial, by an impartial jury of the State and district wherein the crime shall have been committed, which district shall have been previously ascertained by law, applies to Porto Rico. Another provision on the subject is in Article III of the Constitution providing that the trial of all crimes, except in cases of impeachment, shall be by jury; and such trial shall be held in the State where the said crimes shall have been committed; but, when not committed within any State, the trial shall be at such place or places as the Congress may by law have directed. The Seventh Amendment of the Constitution provides that in suits at common law, where the value in controversy shall exceed twenty dollars, the right of trial by jury shall be preserved. It is well settled that these provisions for jury trial in criminal and civil cases apply to the territories of the United States. . . . But it is just as clearly settled that they do not apply to territory belonging to the United States, which has not been incorporated into the Union. *Hawaii* v. *Mankichi,* 190 U. S. 197, *Dorr* v. *United States,* 195 U. S. 138. It was further settled in *Downes* v. *Bidwell,* 182 U. S. 244, and confirmed by *Dorr* v. *United States,* 195 U. S. 138, R. 808, that neither the Philippines nor Porto Rico was territory which had been incorporated in the Union or become a part of the United States, as distinguished from merely belonging to it; and that the acts giving temporary governments to the Philippines, 32 Stat. 691, and to Porto Rico, 31 Stat. 77, had no such effect. The *Insular Cases* revealed much diversity of opinion in this court as to the constitutional status of the territory acquired by the Treaty of Paris ending the Spanish War, but the *Dorr Case* shows that the opinion of Mr. Justice White of the majority, in *Downes* v. *Bidwell,* has become the settled law of the court. The conclusion of this court in the *Dorr Case,* 195 U. S. 149, was as follows:

"We conclude that the power to govern territory, implied in the right to acquire it, and given to Congress in the Constitution in Article IV, § 3, to whatever other limitations it may be subject, the extent of which must be decided as questions arise, does not require that body to enact for ceded territory, not made a part of the United States by Con-gressional action, a system of laws which shall include the right of trial by jury, and that the Constitution does not, without legislation and of its own force, carry such right to territory so situated."

The question before us, therefore, is: Has Congress, since the Foraker Act of April 12, 1900, enacted legislation incorporating Porto Rico into the Union? Counsel for the plaintiff in error give, in their brief, an extended list of acts, to which we shall refer later, which they urge as indicating a purpose to make the island a part of the United States, but they chiefly rely on the Organic Act of Porto Rico of March 2, 1917, known as the Jones Act.

The act is entitled "An Act to provide a civil government for Porto Rico, and for other purposes." It does not indicate by its title that it has a purpose to incorporate the island into the Union. It does not contain any clause which declares such purpose or effect. While this is not conclusive, it strongly tends to show that Congress did not have such an intention. Few questions have been the subject of such discussion and dispute in our country as the status of our territory acquired from Spain in 1899. The division between the political parties in respect to it, the diversity of the views of the members of this court in regard to its constitutional aspects, and the constant recurrence of the subject in the Houses of Congress, fixed the attention of all on the future relation of this acquired territory to the United States. Had Congress intended to take the important step of changing the treaty status of Porto Rico by incorporating it into the Union, it is reasonable to suppose that it would have done so by the plain declaration, and would not have left it to mere inference. Before the question became acute at the close of the Spanish War, the distinction between acquisition and incorporation was not regarded as important, or at least it was not fully understood and had not aroused great controversy. Before that, the purpose of Congress might well be a matter of mere inference from various legislative acts; but in these latter days, incorporation is not to be assumed without express declaration, or an implication so strong as to exclude any other view. . . .

The section of the Jones Act which counsel press on us is § 5. This in effect declares that all persons who under the Foraker Act were made citizens of Porto Rico and certain other residents shall become citizens of the United States, unless they prefer not to become such, in which case they are to declare such preference within six months, and thereafter they lose certain rights under the new government. . . . When Porto Ricans passed from under the government of Spain, they lost the protection of that government as subjects of the King of Spain, a title by which they had been known for centuries. They had a right to expect, in passing under the dominion of the United States, a status entitling them to the protection of their new sovereign. . . . It became a yearning of the Porto Ricans to be American citizens, therefore, and this act gave them the boon. What additional rights did it give them? It enabled them to move into the continental United States and becoming residents of any State there to enjoy every right of any other citizen of the United States, civil, social and political. A citizen of the Philippines must be naturalized before he can settle and vote in this country. Not so the Porto Rican under the Organic Act of 1917.

In Porto Rico, however, the Porto Rican can not insist upon the right of trial by jury, except as his own representatives in his legislature shall confer it on him. The citizen of the United States living in Porto Rico can not there enjoy a right of trial by jury under the Federal Constitution, any more than the Porto Rican. It is locality that is determinative of the application of the Constitution, in such matters as judicial procedure, and not the status of the people who live in it.

It is true that, in the absence of other and countervailing evidence, a law of Congress or a provision in a treaty acquiring territory, declaring an intention to confer political and civil rights on the inhabitants of the new lands as American citizens, may be properly interpreted to mean an incorporation of it into the Union, as in the case of Louisiana and Alaska. This was one of the chief grounds upon which this court placed its conclusion that Alaska had been incorporated in the Union, in *Rassmussen* v. *United States*, 197 U. S. 516. But Alaska was a very different case from that of Porto Rico. It was an enormous territory, very sparsely settled and offering opportunity for immigration and settlement by American citizens. It was on the American

Continent and within easy reach of the then United States. It involved none of the difficulties which incorporation of the Philippines and Porto Rico presents, and one of them is in the very matter of trial by jury. This court refers to the difficulties in *Dorr* v. *United States*, 195 U. S. 138, 148:

"If the right to trial by jury were a fundamental right which goes wherever the jurisdiction of the United States extends, or if Congress, in framing laws for outlying territory belonging to the United States was obliged to establish that system by affirmative legislation, it would follow that, no matter what the needs or capacities of the people, trial by jury, and in no other way, must be forthwith established, although the result may be to work injustice and provoke disturbance rather than to aid the orderly administration of justice. . . . Again, if the United States shall acquire by treaty the cession of territory having an established system of jurisprudence, where jury trials are unknown, but a method of fair and orderly trial prevails under an acceptable and long-established code, the preference of the people must be disregarded, their established customs ignored and they themselves coerced to accept, in advance of incorporation into the United States, a system of trial unknown to them and unsuited to their needs. We do not think it was intended, in giving power to Congress to make regulations for the territories, to hamper its exercise with this condition."

The jury system needs citizens trained to the exercise of the responsibilities of jurors. In common-law countries centuries of tradition have prepared a conception of the impartial attitude jurors must assume. The jury system postulates a conscious duty of participation in the machinery of justice which it is hard for people not brought up in fundamentally popular government at once to acquire. One of its greatest benefits is in the security it gives the people that they, as jurors actual or possible, being a part of the judicial system of the country can prevent its arbitrary use or abuse. Congress has thought that a people like the Filipinos or the Porto Ricans, trained to a complete judicial system which knows no juries, living in compact and ancient communities, with definitely formed customs and political conceptions, should be permitted themselves to determine how far they wish to adopt this institution of Anglo-Saxon origin, and when. . . . We cannot find any intention to depart from this policy in making Porto Ricans American citizens. . . .

We need not dwell on another consideration which requires us not lightly to infer, from acts thus easily explained on other grounds, an intention to incorporate in the Union these distant ocean communities of a different origin and language from those of our continental people. Incorporation has always been a step, and an important one, leading to statehood. Without, in the slightest degree, intimating an opinion as to the wisdom of such a policy, for that is not our province, it is reasonable to assume that when such a step is taken it will be begun and taken by Congress deliberately and with a clear declaration of purpose, and not left a matter of mere inference or construction. . . .

On the whole, therefore, we find no features in the Organic Act of Porto Rico of 1917 from which we can infer the purpose of Congress to incorporate Porto Rico into the United States with the consequences which would follow. . . .

The judgments of the Supreme Court of Porto Rico are affirmed.

Mr. Justice HOLMES concurs in the result.

447. NAVAL LIMITATION TREATY
Signed February 6, 1922
Proclaimed August 21, 1923

(U. S. Statutes at Large, Vol. XXXXIII, p. 1655 ff.)

December 14, 1920, Senator Borah introduced a resolution requesting the President to call an international conference for the reduction of naval armaments. The resolution was appended to the Naval Appropriations Bill for 1921. In accordance with this resolution President Harding invited the principal powers to a conference to consider not only naval disarmaments, but questions relating to the Pacific as well. The conference convened in Washington November 12, 1921, and Secretary Hughes presented the American program for disarmament. That program was embodied in the Naval Limitation Treaty, given below. On the Washington Conference see R. L. Buell, *The Washington Conference;* Y. Ichihashi, *The Washington Conference and After;* G. H. Blakeslee, *The Pacific Area,* World Peace Foundation Pamphlets, Vol. XII, no. 3; S. F. Bemis, ed. *American Secretaries of State,* Vol. X, p. 242 ff. The *Report of the Conference* is in *Senate Document 126,* 67th Congress, 2nd Session. See also, Docs. No. 448, 449.

The United States of America, the British Empire, France, Italy and Japan;

Desiring to contribute to the maintenance of the general peace, and to reduce the burdens of competition in armament;

Have resolved, with a view to accomplishing these purposes, to conclude a treaty to limit their respective naval armament, and to that end have appointed as their Plenipotentiaries; . . .

Who, having communicated to each other their respective full powers, found to be in good and due form, have agreed as follows:

CHAPTER I

ART. I. The Contracting Powers agree to limit their respective naval armament as provided in the present Treaty.

ART. II. The Contracting Powers may retain respectively the capital ships which are specified in Chapter II, Part 1. On the coming into force of the present Treaty, but subject to the following provisions of this Article, all other capital ships, built or building, of the United States, the British Empire and Japan shall be disposed of as prescribed in Chapter II, Part 2.

In addition to the capital ships specified in Chapter II, Part 1, the United States may complete and retain two ships of the *West Virginia* class now under construction. On the completion of these two ships the *North Dakota* and *Delaware* shall be disposed of as prescribed in Chapter II, Part 2.

The British Empire may, in accordance with the replacement table in Chapter II, Part 3, construct two new capital ships not exceeding 35,000 tons (35,560 metric tons) standard displacement each. On the completion of the said two ships the *Thunderer, King George V, Ajax* and *Centurion* shall be disposed of as prescribed in Chapter II, Part 2.

ART. III. Subject to the provisions of

Article II, the Contracting Powers shall abandon their respective capital ship building programs, and no new capital ships shall be constructed or acquired by any of the Contracting Powers except replacement tonnage which may be constructed or acquired as specified in Chapter II, Part 3.

Ships which are replaced in accordance with Chapter II, Part 3, shall be disposed of as prescribed in Part 2 of that Chapter.

ART. IV. The total capital ship replacement tonnage of the Contracting Powers shall not exceed in standard displacement, for the United States 525,000 tons (533,400 metric tons); for the British Empire 525,000 tons (533,400 metric tons); for France 175,000 tons (177,800 metric tons); for Italy 175,000 tons (177,800 metric tons); for Japan 315,000 tons (320,040 metric tons).

ART. V. No capital ship exceeding 35,000 tons (35,560 metric tons) standard displacement shall be acquired by, or constructed by, for, or within the jurisdiction of, any of the Contracting Powers.

ART. VI. No capital ship of any of the Contracting Powers shall carry a gun with a calibre in excess of 16 inches (405 millimetres).

ART. VII. The total tonnage for aircraft carriers of each of the Contracting Powers shall not exceed in standard displacement, for the United States 135,000 tons (137,160 metric tons); for the British Empire 135,000 tons (137,160 metric tons); for France 60,000 tons (60,960 metric tons); for Italy 60,000 tons (60,960 metric tons); for Japan 81,000 tons (82,296 metric tons). . . .

ART. IX. No aircraft carrier exceeding 27,-000 tons (27,432 metric tons) standard displacement shall be acquired by, or constructed by, for or within the jurisdiction of, any of the Contracting Powers. . . .

ART. XI. No vessel of war exceeding 10,000 tons (10,160 metric tons) standard displacement, other than a capital ship or aircraft carrier, shall be acquired by, or constructed by, for, or within the jurisdiction of, any of the Contracting Powers. Vessels not specifically built as fighting ships nor taken in time of peace under government control for fighting purposes, which are employed on fleet duties or as troop transports or in some other way for the purpose of assisting in the prosecution of hostilities otherwise than as fighting ships, shall not be within the limitations of this Article.

ART. XII. No vessel of war of any of the Contracting Powers, hereafter laid down, other than a capital ship, shall carry a gun with a calibre in excess of 8 inches (203 millimetres).

ART. XIII. Except as provided in Article IX, no ship designated in the present Treaty to be scrapped may be reconverted into a vessel of war.

ART. XIV. No preparations shall be made in merchant ships in time of peace for the installation of warlike armaments for the purpose of converting such ships into vessels of war, . . .

ART. XIX. The United States, the British Empire and Japan agree that the status quo at the time of the signing of the present Treaty, with regard to fortifications and naval bases, shall be maintained in their respective territories and possessions specified hereunder:

(1) The insular possessions which the United States now holds or may hereafter acquire in the Pacific Ocean, except (a) those adjacent to the coast of the United States, Alaska and Panama Canal Zone, not including the Aleutian Islands, and (b) the Hawaiian Islands;

(2) Hongkong and the insular possessions which the British Empire now holds or may hereafter acquire in the Pacific Ocean, east of the meridian of 110° east longitude, except (a) those adjacent to the coast of Canada, (b) the Commonwealth of Australia and its Territories, and (c) New Zealand;

(3) The following insular territories and possessions of Japan in the Pacific Ocean, to wit: the Kurile Islands, the Bonin Islands, Amami-Oshima, the Loochoo Islands, Formosa and the Pescadores, and any insular territories or possessions in the Pacific Ocean which Japan may hereafter acquire.

The maintenance of the status quo under the foregoing provisions implies that no new fortifications or naval bases shall be established in the territories and possessions specified; that no measures shall be taken to increase the existing naval facilities for the repair and maintenance of naval forces, and that no increase shall be made in the coast defences of the territories and possessions above specified. This restriction, however, does not preclude such repair and replacement of worn-out weapons and equipment as is customary in naval and military establishments in time of peace. . . .

CHAPTER II
PART 1.

CAPITAL SHIPS WHICH MAY BE RETAINED BY THE CONTRACTING POWERS

[Lists]

PART 2.

RULES FOR SCRAPPING VESSELS OF WAR.

The following rules shall be observed for the scrapping of vessels of war which are to be disposed of in accordance with Articles II and III.

I. A vessel to be scrapped must be placed in such condition that it cannot be put to combatant use.

II. This result must be finally effected in any one of the following ways:

(a) Permanent sinking of the vessel;

(b) Breaking the vessel up.

This shall always involve the destruction or removal of all machinery, boilers and armour, and all deck, side and bottom plating;

(c) Converting the vessel to target use exclusively. . . . Not more than one capital ship may be retained for this purpose at one time by any of the Contracting Powers. . . .

PART 3.
SEC. I.

RULES FOR REPLACEMENT.

(a) Capital ships and aircraft carriers twenty years after the date of their completion may, except as otherwise provided in Article VIII and in the tables in Section II of this Part, be replaced by new construction, but within the limits prescribed in Article IV and Article VII. The keels of such new construction may, except as otherwise provided in Article VIII and in the tables in Section II of this Part, be laid down not earlier than seventeen years from the date of completion of the tonnage to be replaced, provided, however, that no capital ship tonnage, with the exception of the ships referred to in the third paragraph of Article II, and replacement tonnage specifically mentioned in Section II of this Part, shall be laid down until ten years from November 12, 1921. . . .

CHAPTER III

ART. XXIII. The present Treaty shall remain in force until December 31st, 1936, and in case none of the Contracting Powers shall have given notice two years before that date of its intention to terminate the Treaty, it shall continue in force until the expiration of two years from the date on which notice of termination shall be given by one of the Contracting Powers. . . .

448. THE FOUR-POWER TREATY
December 13, 1921. In Force, August 17, 1923

(U. S. Statutes at Large, Vol. XXXXIII, p. 1646 ff.)

This was one of the treaties that emerged from the Washington Arms Conference. For references, see under Doc. No. 447.

Treaty between the United States, the British Empire, France and Japan relating to their Insular Possessions and Insular Dominions in the Region of the Pacific Ocean

The United States of America, the British Empire, France and Japan,

With a view to the preservation of the general peace and the maintenance of their rights in relation to their insular possessions and insular dominions in the region of the Pacific Ocean,

Have determined to conclude a treaty to this effect and have appointed as their plenipotentiaries: . . .

Who, having communicated their full powers, found in good and due form, have agreed as follows:

I. The high contracting parties agree as between themselves to respect their rights in relation to their insular possessions and insular dominions in the region of the Pacific Ocean.

If there should develop between any of the

high contracting parties a controversy arising out of any Pacific question and involving their said rights which is not satisfactorily settled by diplomacy and is likely to affect the harmonious accord now happily subsisting between them, they shall invite the other high contracting parties to a joint conference to which the whole subject will be referred for consideration and adjustment.

II. If the said rights are threatened by the aggressive action of any other power, the high contracting parties shall communicate with one another fully and frankly in order to arrive at an understanding as to the most efficient measures to be taken, jointly or separately, to meet the exigencies of the particular situation.

III. This treaty shall remain in force for 10 years from the time it shall take effect, and after the expiration of said period it shall continue to be in force subject to the right of any of the high contracting parties to terminate it upon 12 months' notice.

IV. This treaty shall be ratified as soon as possible in accordance with the constitutional methods of the high contracting parties and shall take effect on the deposit of ratifications, which shall take place at Washington, and thereupon the agreement between Great Britain and Japan, which was concluded at London on July 13, 1911, shall terminate. . . .

449. THE NINE-POWER TREATY
February 6, 1922. Proclaimed August 5, 1925

(U.S. Statutes at Large, Vol. XXXXIV, p. 2113 ff.)

This treaty, one of several to emerge from the Washington Conference, apparently gave international sanction to the traditional Open Door policy toward China. The principles which this treaty attempted to establish were, however, shortly violated by Japan. A number of other treaties and resolutions concerning China were adopted by the Conference. Of these the most important were: a treaty relating to the Chinese tariff; an adjustment of the Shantung controversy; and a resolution providing for a commission to study the problem of extraterritoriality in China. For references, see Doc. No. 447.

A Treaty . . . relating to principles and policies to be followed in matters concerning China.

The United States of America, Belgium, the British Empire, China, France, Italy, Japan, the Netherlands and Portugal:

Desiring to adopt a policy designed to stabilize conditions in the Far East, to safeguard the rights and interests of China, and to promote intercourse between China and the other Powers upon the basis of equality of opportunity;

Have resolved to conclude a treaty for that purpose and to that end have appointed as their respective Plenipotentiaries: . . .

Who, having communicated to each other their full powers, found to be in good and due form, have agreed as follows:

I. The Contracting Powers, other than China, agree:

(1) To respect the sovereignty, the independence, and the territorial and administrative integrity of China;

(2) To provide the fullest and most unembarrassed opportunity to China to develop and maintain for herself an effective and stable government;

(3) To use their influence for the purpose of effectually establishing and maintaining the principle of equal opportunity for the commerce and industry of all nations throughout the territory of China;

(4) To refrain from taking advantage of conditions in China in order to seek special rights or privileges which would abridge the rights of subjects or citizens of friendly States, and from countenancing action inimical to the security of such States.

II. The Contracting Powers agree not to enter into any treaty, agreement, arrangement, or understanding, either with one another, or, individually or collectively, with any Power or Powers, which would infringe or impair the principles stated in Article I.

III. With a view to applying more effectually the principles of the Open Door or equality of opportunity in China for the trade and industry of all nations, the Contracting Powers, other than China, agree that they will not seek nor support their respective nationals, in seeking

(a) any arrangement which might purport to establish in favor of their interests any general superiority of rights with respect to commercial or economic development in any designated region of China.

(b) any such monopoly or preference as would deprive the nationals of any other Power of the right of undertaking any legitimate trade or industry in China, or of participating with the Chinese Government, or with any local authority, in any category of public enterprise, or which by reason of its scope, duration or geographical extent is calculated to frustrate the practical application of the principle of equal opportunity.

It is understood that the foregoing stipulations of this Article are not to be so construed as to prohibit the acquisition of such properties or rights as may be necessary to the conduct of a particular commercial, industrial, or financial undertaking or to the encouragement of invention and research.

China undertakes to be guided by the principles stated in the foregoing stipulations of this Article in dealing with applications for economic rights and privileges from Governments and nationals of all foreign countries, whether parties to the present Treaty or not.

IV. The Contracting Powers agree not to support any agreements by their respective nationals with each other designed to create Spheres of Influence or to provide for the enjoyment of mutually exclusive opportunities in designated parts of Chinese territory.

V. China agrees that, throughout the whole of the railways in China, she will not exercise or permit unfair discrimination of any kind. In particular there shall be no discrimination whatever, direct or indirect, in respect of charges or of facilities on the ground of the nationality of passengers or the countries from which or to which they are proceeding, or the origin or ownership of goods or the country from which or to which they are consigned, or the nationality or ownership of the ship or other means of conveying such passengers or goods before or after their transport on the Chinese railways.

The Contracting Powers, other than China, assume a corresponding obligation in respect of any of the aforesaid railways over which they or their nationals are in a position to exercise any control in virtue of any concession, special agreement or otherwise.

VI. The Contracting Powers, other than China, agree fully to respect China's rights as a neutral in time of war to which China is not a party; and China declares that when she is a neutral she will observe the obligations of neutrality.

VII. The Contracting Powers agree that, whenever a situation arises which in the opinion of any one of them involves the application of the stipulations of the present Treaty, and renders desirable discussion of such application, there shall be full and frank communication between the Contracting Powers concerned.

VIII. Powers not signatory to the present Treaty, which have Governments recognized by the Signatory Powers and which have treaty relations with China, shall be invited to adhere to the present Treaty. To this end the Government of the United States will make the necessary communications to non-signatory Powers and will inform the Contracting Powers of the replies received. Adherence by any Power shall become effective on receipt of notice thereof by the Government of the United States.

IX. The present Treaty shall be ratified by the Contracting Powers in accordance with their respective constitutional methods and shall take effect on the date of the deposit of all the ratifications, which shall take place at Washington as soon as possible. The Government of the United States will transmit to the other Contracting Powers a certified copy of the procès-verbal of the deposit of ratifications.

The present Treaty, of which the French and English texts are both authentic, shall remain deposited in the archives of the Government of the United States, and duly certified copies thereof shall be transmitted by that Government to the other Contracting Powers.

In faith whereof the above-named Plenipotentiaries have signed the Present Treaty.

Done at the City of Washington the sixth day of February One Thousand Nine Hundred and Twenty-Two.

450. WOLFF PACKING CO. v. COURT OF INDUSTRIAL RELATIONS
OF KANSAS
262 U. S. 522
1923

Writ of Error to Supreme Court of Kansas.

TAFT, C. J. This case involves the validity of the Court of Industrial Relations Act of Kansas (1920). The act declares the following to be affected with a public interest: First, manufacture and preparation of food for human consumption; . . . fifth, public utilities and common carriers. The act vests an industrial court of three judges with power, upon its own initiative or on complaint, to summon the parties and hear any dispute over wages or other terms of employment in any such industry, and if it shall find the peace and health of the public imperiled by such controversy, it is required to make findings and fix the wages and other terms for the future conduct of the industry. . . .

The Charles Wolff Packing Co., the plaintiff in error, is a corporation of Kansas engaged in slaughtering hogs and cattle and preparing the meat for sale and shipment. . . .

In January, 1921, the president and secretary of the Meat Cutters Union filed a complaint with the Industrial Court against the Packing Company, respecting the wages its employees were receiving. The Company appeared and answered and a hearing was had. The Court made findings, including one of an emergency, and an order as to wages, increasing them over the figures to which the company had recently reduced them. The Company refused to comply with the order, and the Industrial Court then instituted mandamus proceedings in the Supreme Court to compel compliance. . . . The Industrial Court conceded that the Wolff Company could not operate on the schedule fixed without a loss, but relied on the statement by its president that he hoped for more prosperous times.

The Packing Company brings this case here on the ground that the validity of the Industrial Court Act was upheld, although as in conflict with the provision of the 14th Amendment that no State shall deprive any person of liberty or property without due process of law. . . .

The necessary postulate of the Industrial Court Act is that the state, representing the people, is so much interested in their peace, health, and comfort, that it may compel those engaged in the manufacture of food and clothing, and the production of fuel, whether owners or workers, to continue in their business and employment on terms fixed by an agency of the state, if they cannot agree. Under the construction adopted by the state supreme court, the act gives the Industrial Court authority to permit the owner or employer to go out of the business if he shows that he can only continue on the terms fixed at such heavy loss that collapse will follow; but this privilege, under the circumstances, is generally illusory. A laborer dissatisfied with his wages is permitted to quit, but he may not agree with his fellows to quit, or combine with others to induce them to quit.

These qualifications do not change the essence of the act. It curtails the right of the employer, on the one hand, and that of the employee, on the other, to contract about his affairs. This is part of the liberty of the individual protected by the guaranty of the due process clause of the 14th Amendment. . . .

It is manifest from an examination of the cases cited . . . that the mere declaration by a legislature that a business is affected with a public interest is not conclusive of the question whether its attempted regulation on that ground is justified. The circumstances of its alleged change from the status of a private business and its freedom from regulation into one in which the public have come to have an interest, are always a subject of judicial inquiry. . . .

It has never been supposed, since the adoption of the Constitution, that the business of the butcher, or the baker, the tailor, the woodchopper, the mining operator, or the miner, was clothed with such a public interest that the price of his product or his wages could be fixed by state regulation. . . .

To say that a business is clothed with a public interest is not to determine what regulation is permissible in view of the private rights of the owner. The extent to which an inn or cab system may be regulated may differ widely from that allowable as to a railroad or other common carrier. It is not a matter of legislative discretion solely. It depends upon the nature of the business, on the feature which touches the public, and on the abuses reasonably to be feared. To say that business is clothed with a public interest is not to import that the public may take over its entire management and run it at the expense of the owner. The extent to which regulation may reasonably go varies with different kinds of business. The regulation of rates to avoid monopoly, is one thing. The regulation of wages is another. A business may be of such character that only the first is permissible, while another may involve such a possible danger of monopoly on the one hand, and such disaster from stoppage on the other, that both come within the public concern and power of regulation.

If, as, in effect, contended by counsel for the state, the common callings are clothed with a public interest by a mere legislative declaration, which necessarily authorizes full and comprehensive regulation within legislative discretion, there must be a revolution in the relation of government to general business. This will be running the public-interest argument into the ground. . . . It will be impossible to reconcile such result with the freedom of contract and of labor secured by the 14th Amendment.

This brings to the nature and purpose of the regulation under the Industrial Court Act. The avowed object is continuity of food, clothing, and fuel supply. By sec. 6 reasonable continuity and efficiency of the industries specified are declared to be necessary for the public peace, health, and general welfare, and all are forbidden to hinder, limit, or suspend them. Sec. 7 gives the Industrial Court power, in case of controversy between employers and workers which may endanger the continuity or efficiency of service, to bring the employer and employee before it, and after hearing and investigation, to fix the terms and conditions between them. The employer is bound by this act to pay the wages fixed; and while the worker is not required to work at the wages fixed, he is forbidden on penalty of fine or imprisonment, to strike against them, and thus is compelled to give up that means of putting himself on an equality with his employer which action in concert with his fellows gives him. . . .

The minutely detailed government supervision, including that of their relations to their employees, to which the railroads of the country have been gradually subjected by Congress through its power over interstate commerce, furnishes no precedent for regulation of the business of the plaintiff, whose classification as public is, at the best, doubtful. It is not too much to say that the ruling in *Wilson* v. *New* went to the borderline, although it concerned an interstate common carrier in the presence of a nation-wide emergency and the possibility of great disaster. Certainly there is nothing to justify extending the drastic regulation sustained in that exceptional case to the one before us.

We think that Industrial Court Act . . . in conflict with the 14th Amendment. Judgement reversed.

451. ADKINS v. CHILDREN'S HOSPITAL
261 U. S. 525
1923

Appeal from the Court of Appeals for the District of Columbia. Suit to enjoin the Wage Board for the District of Columbia from enforcing its orders fixing minimum wages for women under authority of an act of Congress of September 19, 1918. The statute authorized the Board to ascertain and declare standards of minimum wages for women and minors adequate to the cost of living and to maintain them in health and protect their morals. The Court of Appeals affirmed decrees granting the injunction. See *The Su-* *preme Court and Minimum Wage Legislation,* pub. by the National Consumers' League.

SUTHERLAND, J. The question presented for determination by these appeals is the constitutionality of the Act of September 19, 1918, providing for the fixing of minimum wages for women and children in the District of Columbia. . . .

It is declared that the purposes of the act

are "to protect the women and minors of the District from conditions detrimental to their health and morals, resulting from wages which are inadequate to maintain decent standards of living; and the act in each of its provisions and in its entirety, shall be interpreted to effectuate these purposes." . . .

The statute now under consideration is attacked upon the ground that it authorizes an unconstitutional interference with the freedom of contract included within the guaranties of the due process clause of the 5th Amendment. That the right to contract about one's affairs is a part of the liberty of the individual protected by this clause is settled by the decisions of this Court and is no longer open to question. Within this liberty are contracts of employment of labor. In making such contracts, generally speaking, the parties have an equal right to obtain from each other the best terms they can as the result of private bargaining. . . .

There is, of course, no such thing as absolute freedom of contract. It is subject to a great variety of restraints. But freedom of contract is, nevertheless, the general rule and restraint the exception; and the exercise of legislative authority to abridge it can be justified only by the existence of exceptional circumstances. Whether these circumstances exist in the present case constitutes the question to be answered. It will be helpful to this end to review some of the decisions where the interference has been upheld and consider the grounds upon which they rest. [Here an elaborate review of the decisions.] . . .

If now, in the light furnished by the foregoing exceptions to the general rule forbidding legislative interference with freedom of contract, we examine and analyze the statute in question, we shall see that it differs from them in every material respect. It is not a law dealing with any business charged with a public interest, or with public work, or to meet and tide over a temporary emergency. It has nothing to do with the character, methods or periods of wage payments. It does not prescribe hours of labor or conditions under which labor is to be done. It is not for the protection of persons under legal disability or for the prevention of fraud. It is simply and exclusively a price-fixing law, confined to adult women (for we are not now considering the provisions relating to minors), who are legally as capable of contracting for themselves as men. It forbids two parties having lawful capacity—under penalties as to the employer—to freely contract with one another in respect of the price for which one shall render service to the other in a purely private employment where both are willing, perhaps anxious, to agree, even though the consequence may be to oblige one to surrender a desirable engagement and the other to dispense with the services of a desirable employee. The price fixed by the board need have no relation to the capacity or earning power of the employee, the number of hours which may happen to constitute the day's work, the character of the place where the work is to be done, or the circumstances or surroundings of the employment; and, while it has no other basis to support its validity than the assumed necessities of the employee, it takes no account of any independent resources she may have. It is based wholly on the opinions of the members of the board and their advisers —perhaps an average of their opinions, if they do not precisely agree—as to what will be necessary to provide a living for a woman, keep her in health and preserve her morals. It applies to any and every occupation in the District, without regard to its nature or the character of the work.

The standard furnished by the statute for the guidance of the board is so vague as to be impossible of practical application with any reasonable degree of accuracy. What is sufficient to supply the necessary cost of living for a woman worker and maintain her in good health and protect her morals is obviously not a precise or unvarying sum—not even approximately so. The amount will depend upon a variety of circumstances: the individual temperament, habits of thrift, care, ability to buy necessaries intelligently, and whether the woman live alone or with her family. To those who practice economy, a given sum will afford comfort, while to those of a contrary habit the same sum will be wholly inadequate. The coöperative economies of the family group are not taken into account though they constitute an important consideration in estimating the cost of living, for it is obvious that the individual expense will be less in the case of a member of a family than in the case of one living alone. The relation between earnings and morals is not capable of standardization. It cannot be shown that well paid women safeguard their morals more carefully than those who are poorly paid. Morality rests upon other considerations than wages; and there is, certainly, no such prevalent connection between the two as to justify a broad attempt to adjust the latter with reference to the former. As a means of safeguarding morals the attempted classification in our opinion, is without reasonable basis. No distinction can be made between women who work for others and those who do not; nor is there ground for distinction between women and men, for, certainly, if women require a minimum wage to preserve their morals men require it to preserve their honesty. For these reasons, and others which might be stated, the inquiry in respect of the necessary cost of living and of the income necessary to preserve health and morals, presents an individual and not a composite question, and must be answered for each individual considered by herself and not by a general formula prescribed by a statutory bureau. . . .

The law takes account of the necessities of only one party to the contract. It ignores the necessities of the employer by compelling him to pay not less than a certain sum, not only whether the employee is capable of earning it, but irrespective of the ability of his business to sustain the burden, generously leaving him, of course, the privilege of abandoning his business as an alternative for going on at a loss. Within the limits of the minimum sum, he is precluded, under penalty of fine and imprisonment, from adjusting compensation to the differing merits of his employees. It compels him to pay at least the sum fixed in any event, because the employee needs it, but requires no service of equivalent value from the employee. It therefore undertakes to solve but one-half of the problem. The other half is the establishment of a corresponding standard of efficiency, and this forms no part of the policy of the legislation, although in practice the former half without the latter must lead to ultimate failure, in accordance with the inexorable law that no one can continue indefinitely to take out more than he puts in without ultimately exhausting the supply. The law . . . takes no account of periods of stress and business depression, of crippling losses, which may leave the employer himself without adequate means of livelihood. To the extent that the sum fixed exceeds the fair value of the services rendered, it amounts to a compulsory exaction from the employer for the support of a partially indigent person, for whose condition there rests upon him no peculiar responsibility, and therefore, in effect, arbitrarily shifts to his shoulders a burden which, if it belongs to anybody, belongs to society as a whole.

The feature of this statute which perhaps more than any other, puts upon it the stamp of invalidity is that it exacts from the employer an arbitrary payment for a purpose and upon a basis having no causal connection with his business, or the contract or the work the employee engages to do. The declared basis as already pointed out, is not the value of the service rendered but the extraneous circumstances that the employee needs to get a prescribed sum of money to insure her subsistence, health and morals. The ethical right of every worker, man or woman, to a living wage, may be conceded. One of the declared and important purposes of trade organizations is to secure it. And with that principle and with every legitimate effort to realize it in fact, no one can quarrel; but the fallacy of the proposed method of attaining it is that it assumes that every employer is bound at all events to furnish it. . . .

It is said that great benefits have resulted from the operation of such statutes, not alone in the District of Columbia but in the several States, where they have been in force. A mass of reports, opinions of special observers and students of the subject, and the like, has been brought before us in support of this statement, all of which we have found interesting, but only mildly persuasive. . . .

Finally, it may be said that if, in the interest of the public welfare, the police power may be invoked to justify the fixing of a minimum wage, it may, when the public welfare is thought to require it, be invoked to justify a maximum wage. The power to fix high wages connotes, by like reasoning, the power to fix low wages. If, in the face of the guaranties of the 5th Amendment, this form of legislation shall be legally justified, the field for the operation of the police power will have been widened to a great and dangerous degree. If, for example, in the opinion of future lawmakers, wages in the building trades shall become so high as to preclude people of ordinary means from building and owning homes, an authority which sustains the minimum wage will be invoked to support a maximum wage for building laborers and artisans, and the same argument which has been here urged to strip the employer of his constitutional liberty of contract in one direction will be utilized to strip the employee of his constitutional liberty of contract in the opposite direction. A wrong decision does not end with itself; it is a precedent, and, with the swing of sentiment, its bad influence may run from one extremity of the arc to the other.

It has been said that legislation of the kind now under review is required in the interest of social justice, for whose ends freedom of contract may lawfully be subjected to restraint. The liberty of the individual to do as he pleases, even in innocent matters, is not absolute. It must frequently yield to the common good, and the line beyond which the power of interference may not be pressed is neither definite nor unalterable but may be made to move, within limits not well defined, with changing need and circumstance. Any attempt to fix a rigid boundary would be unwise and futile. But, nevertheless, there are limits to the power, and when these have been passed, it becomes the plain duty of the courts in the proper exercise of their authority to so declare. To sustain the individual freedom of action contemplated by the Constitution, is not to strike down the common good but to exalt it; for surely the good of society as a whole cannot be better served than by the preservation against arbitrary restraint of the liberties of its constituent members.

It follows from what has been said that the act in question passes the limit prescribed by the Constitution, and, accordingly, the decrees of the court below are

Affirmed.

TAFT, C. J. dissenting. . . . Legislatures, in limiting freedom of contract between employee and employer by a minimum wage, proceed on the assumption that employees in the class receiving least pay are not upon a full level of equality of choice with their employer, and in their necessitous circumstances are prone to accept pretty much anything that is offered. They are peculiarly subject to the overreaching of the harsh and greedy employer. The evils of the sweating system and of the long hours and low wages which are characteristic of it are well known. Now, I agree that it is a disputable question in the field of political economy, how far a statutory requirement of maximum hours or minimum wages may be a useful remedy for these evils, and whether it may not make the case of the oppressed employee worse than it was before. But it is not the function of this court to hold Congressional acts invalid simply because they are passed to carry out economic views which the court believes to be unwise or unsound. . . .

The right of the legislature under the 5th and 14th Amendments to limit the hours of employment on the score of the health of the employee, it seems to me, has been firmly established. As to that, one would think, the line had been pricked out so that it has become a well-formulated rule. . . .

However, the opinion herein does not overrule the Bunting case in express terms, and therefore I assume that the conclusion in this case rests on the distinction between a minimum of wages and a maximum of hours in the limiting of liberty to contract. I regret to be at variance with the court as to the substance of this distinction. . . .

If it be said that long hours of labor have a more direct effect upon the health of the employee than the low wage, there is every respectable authority from close observers, disclosed in the record and in the literature on the subject, quoted at length in the briefs, that they are equally harmful in this regard; Congress took this view, and we cannot say it was not warranted in so doing. . . .

HOLMES, J., dissenting: The question in this case is the broad one, whether Congress can establish minimum rates of wages for women in the District of Columbia, with due provision for special circumstances, or whether we must say that Congress has no power to meddle with the matter at all. To me, notwithstanding the deference due to the prevailing judgement of the court, the power of Congress seems absolutely free from doubt. The end—to remove conditions leading to ill health, immorality, and the deterioration of the race—no one would deny to be within the scope of constitutional legislation. The means are means that have the approval of Congress, of many states, and of those governments from which we have learned our greatest lessons. When so many intelligent persons who have studied the matter more than any of us can, have thought that the means are effective and are worth the price, it seems to me impossible to deny that the belief reasonably may be held by reasonable men. . . . But, in the present instance, the only objection that can be urged is founded in the vague contours of the 5th Amendment, prohibiting the depriving any person of liberty or of property without due process of law. To that I turn.

The earlier decisions upon the same words in the 14th Amendment began within our memory, and went no farther than an unpretentious assertion of the liberty to follow the ordinary callings. Later that innocuous generality was expanded into the dogma Liberty of Contract. Contract is not specially mentioned in the text that we have to construe. It is merely an example of doing what you want to do, embodied in the word "liberty". But pretty much all law, consists in forbidding men to do some things that they want to do, and contract is no more exempt from law than other acts. . . .

[Cites numerous examples.]

The criterion of constitutionality is not whether we believe the law to be for the public good. We certainly cannot be prepared to deny that a reasonable man reasonably might have that belief, in view of the legislation of Great Britain, Victoria, and a number of the states of this Union. The belief is fortified by a very remarkable collection of documents submitted on behalf of the appellants, material here, I conceive, only as showing that the belief reasonably may be held. . . .

452. TEAPOT DOME

Joint Resolution of Congress Respecting Prosecution for Cancellation of Oil Leases
February 8, 1924

(U. S. Statutes at Large, Vol. XXXXIII, p. 5)

The scandals of the Harding were no less shocking than those of the Grant administration. Of all the revelations, none more profoundly stirred the indignation of the nation than those concerning the leasing of rich oil reserves to private interests by the Secretaries of the Navy and of the Interior. These reserves, originally under the control of the Department of the Navy, were transferred to the Department of the Interior. In 1922, Secretary Albert B. Fall of this Department secretly leased the Teapot Dome reserve to Harry F. Sinclair, and the Elk Hill reserve to E. L. Doheny. The civil suits instituted for the cancellation of these leases were finally successful; on the criminal charges arising from corruption, Secretary Fall was convicted and imprisoned. See, U.S. 68 Cong. 1st. Sess. *Sen. Rep.* 794; M. E. Ravage, *Teapot Dome.*

A joint resolution directing the President to institute and prosecute suits to cancel certain leases of oil lands and incidental contracts, and for other purposes.

Whereas it appears from evidence taken by the Committee on Public Lands and Surveys of the United States Senate that certain lease of naval reserve No. 3, in the State of Wyoming, bearing date April 7, 1922, made in form by the Government of the United States, through Albert B. Fall, Secretary of the Interior, and Edwin Denby, Secretary of the Navy, as lessor, to the Mammoth Oil Co., as lessee, and that certain contract between the Government of the United States and the Pan American Petroleum & Transport Co., dated April 25, 1922, signed by Edward C. Finney, Acting Secretary of the Interior, and Edwin Denby, Secretary of the Navy, relating among other things to the construction of oil tanks at Pearl Harbor, Territory of Hawaii, and that certain lease of naval reserve No. 1, in the State of California, bearing date December 11, 1922, made in form by the Government of the United States through Albert B. Fall, Secretary of the Interior, and Edwin Denby, Secretary of the Navy, as lessor, to the Pan American Petroleum Co., as lessee, were executed under circumstances indicating fraud and corruption; and

Whereas the said leases and contract were entered into without authority on the part of the officers purporting to act in the execution of the same for the United States and in violation of the laws of Congress; and

Whereas such leases and contract were made in defiance of the settled policy of the Government adhered to through three successive administrations, to maintain in the ground a great reserve supply of oil adequate to the needs of the Navy in any emergency threatening the national security: Therefore be it

Resolved, etc., That the said leases and contract are against the public interest and that the lands embraced therein should be recovered and held for the purpose to which they were dedicated; and

Resolved further, That the President of the United States be, and he hereby is, authorized and directed immediately to cause suit to be instituted and prosecuted for the annulment and cancellation of the said leases and contract and all contracts incidental or supplemental thereto, to enjoin further extraction of oil from the said reserves under said leases or from the territory covered by the same, to secure any further appropriate incidental relief, and to prosecute such other actions or proceedings, civil and criminal, as may be warranted by the facts in relation to the making of the said leases and contract.

And the President is further authorized and directed to appoint, by and with the advice and consent of the Senate, special counsel who shall have charge and control of the prosecution of such litigation, anything in the statutes touching the powers of the attorney General of the Department of Justice to the contrary notwithstanding.

453. THE IMMIGRATION ACT OF 1924
May 26, 1924

(U. S. Bureau of Immigration, *Annual Report of the Commissioner-General of Immigration,* 1924, p. 24 ff.)

The quotas established by the immigration act of 1921, Doc. No. 422, were unsatisfactory for two reasons: they admitted too large a number of immigrants; they did not discriminate sufficiently in favor of immigration from Northern and Western Europe. The act of 1924 sought to remedy the first defect by reducing the percentage of immigrants admitted in relation to nationals already in the country from three to two, and remedied the second by establishing 1890 rather than 1910 as the basic date. The report and summary of the law of 1924 is given in lieu of the law itself for purposes of conciseness.

. . . The "Immigration act of 1924" . . . which supplants the so-called quota limit act of May 19, 1921, the latter having expired by limitation at the close of the fiscal year just ended, makes several very important changes not only in our immigration policy but also in the administrative machinery of the Immigration Service. Some of the more important changes in these respects will be briefly referred to.

It will be remembered that the quota limit act of May, 1921, provided that the number of aliens of any nationality admissible to the United States in any fiscal year should be limited to 3 per cent of the number of persons of such nationality who were resident in the United States according to the census of 1910, it being also provided that not more than 20 per cent of any annual quota could be admitted in any one month. Under the act of 1924 the number of each nationality who may be admitted annually is limited to 2 per cent of the population of such nationality resident in the United States according to the census of 1890, and not more than 10 per cent of any annual quota may be admitted in any month except in cases where such quota is less than 300 for the entire year.

Under the act of May, 1921, the quota area was limited to Europe, the Near East, Africa, and Australasia. The countries of North and South America, with adjacent islands, and countries immigration from which was otherwise regulated, such as China, Japan, and countries within the Asiatic barred zone, were not within the scope of the quota law. Under the new act, however, immigration from the entire world, with the exception of the Dominion of Canada, Newfoundland, the Republic of Mexico, the Republic of Cuba, the Republic of Haiti, the Dominican Republic, the Canal Zone, and independent countries of Central and South America, is subject to quota limitations. The various quotas established under the new law are shown in the following proclamation of the President, issued on the last day of the present fiscal year:

BY THE PRESIDENT OF THE UNITED STATES OF AMERICA

A PROCLAMATION

Whereas it is provided in the act of Congress approved May 26, 1924, entitled "An act to limit the immigration of aliens into the United States, and for other purposes" that—

"The annual quota of any nationality shall be two per centum of the number of foreign-born individuals of such nationality resident in continental United States as determined by the United States census of 1890, but the minimum quota of any nationality shall be 100 (Sec. 11(a)). . . .

"The Secretary of State, the Secretary of Commerce, and the Secretary of Labor, jointly, shall, as soon as feasible after the enactment of this act, prepare a statement showing the number of individuals of the various nationalities resident in continental United States as determined by the United States census of 1890, which statement shall be the population basis for the purposes of subdivision (a) of section 11 (sec. 12(b)).

"Such officials shall, jointly, report annually to the President the quota of each nationality under subdivision (a) of section 11, together with the statements, estimates, and revisions provided for in this section. The President shall proclaim and make known the quotas so reported." (Sec. 12 (e)).

Now, therefore, I, Calvin Coolidge, President of the United States of America acting under and by virtue of the power in me vested by the aforesaid act of Congress, do hereby proclaim and make known that on and after July 1, 1924, and throughout the fiscal year 1924–1925, the quota of each nationality provided in said Act shall be as follows:

Country or area of birth

	Quota 1924–1925
Afghanistan	100
Albania	100
Andorra	100
Arabian peninsula (1, 2)	100
Armenia	124
Australia, including Papua, Tasmania, and all islands appertaining to Australia	
(3, 4)	121
Austria	785
Belgium (5)	512
Bhutan	100
Bulgaria	100
Cameroon (proposed British mandate)	100
Cameroon (French mandate)	100
China	100
Czechoslovakia	3,073
Danzig, Free City of	228
Denmark (5, 6)	2,789
Egypt	100
Esthonia	124
Ethiopia (Abyssinia)	100
Finland	170
France (1, 5, 6)	3,954
Germany	51,227
Great Britain and Northern Ireland (1, 3, 5, 6)	34,007
Greece	100
Hungary	473
Iceland	100
India (3)	100
Iraq (Mesopotamia)	100
Irish Free State (3)	28,567
Italy, including Rhodes, Dodekanesia, and Castellorizzo (5)	3,845
Japan	100
Latvia	142
Liberia	100
Liechtenstein	100
Lithuania	344
Luxemburg	100
Monaco	100
Morocco (French and Spanish Zones and Tangier)	100
Muscat (Oman)	100
Nauru (proposed British mandate) (4)	100
Nepal	100
Netherlands (1, 5, 6)	1,648
New Zealand (including appertaining islands (3, 4)	100
Norway (5)	6,453
New Guinea, and other Pacific Islands under proposed Australian mandate (4)	100
Palestine (with Trans-Jordan, proposed British mandate)	100

Quota
1924–1925

Persia (1) 100
Poland 5,982
Portugal (1, 5) 503
Ruanda and Urundi (Belgium
mandate) 100
Rumania 603
Russia, European and Asiatic
(1) 2,248
Samoa, Western (4) (pro-
posed mandate of New
Zealand) 100
San Marino 100
Siam 100
South Africa, Union of (3) . 100
South West Africa (proposed
mandate of Union of
South Africa) 100
Spain (5) 131
Sweden 9,561
Switzerland 2,081
Syria and The Lebanon
(French mandate) 100
Tanganyika (proposed Brit-
ish mandate) 100
Togoland (proposed British
mandate) 100
Togoland (French mandate) 100
Turkey 100
Yap and other Pacific islands
(under Japanese mandate)
(4) 100
Yugoslavia 671

1. (a) Persons born in the portions of Persia, Russia, or the Arabian peninsula situated
within the barred zone, and who are admissible under the immigration laws of the United
States as quota immigrants, will be charged
to the quotas of these countries; and (b) persons born in the colonies, dependencies, or
protectorates, or portions thereof, within the
barred zone, of France, Great Britain, the
Netherlands, or Portugal, who are admissible

under the immigration laws of the United
States as quota immigrants, will be charged to
the quota of the country to which such colony
or dependency belongs or by which it is administered as a protectorate.

2. The quota-area denominated "Arabian
peninsula" consists of all territory except
Muscat and Aden, situated in the portion of
that peninsula and adjacent islands, to the
southeast of Iraq, of Palestine with Trans-
Jordan, and of Egypt.

3. Quota immigrants born in the British
self-governing dominions or in the Empire of
India, will be charged to the appropriate
quota rather than to that of Great Britain
and Northern Ireland. There are no quota
restrictions for Canada and Newfoundland. . . .

4. Quota immigrants eligible to citizenship
in the United States, born in a colony, dependency, or protectorate of any country to
which a quota applies will be charged to the
quota of that country.

5. In contrast with the law of 1921, the
immigration act of 1924 provides that persons born in the colonies or dependencies of
European countries situated in Central America, South America, or the islands adjacent to
the American continents (except Newfoundland and islands pertaining to Newfoundland,
Labrador and Canada), will be charged to the
quota of the country to which such colony
or dependency belongs.

GENERAL NOTE.—The immigration quotas
assigned to the various countries and quota-
areas should not be regarded as having any
political significance whatever, or as involving
recognition of new governments, or of new
boundaries, or of transfers of territory except
as the United States Government has already
made such recognition in a formal and official
manner. . . .

CALVIN COOLIDGE.

454. THE LA FOLLETTE PLATFORM OF 1924

(K. Porter, ed. *National Party Platforms,* p. 516 ff.)

The apparent failure of the Farmer-Labor
movement in 1920 led to the disintegration of
that organization. Its place was taken by the
Conference for Progressive Political Action,
which had the support of the Four Railroad
Brotherhoods. The Conference, dissatisfied with

the nominations and platforms of the two major
parties in 1924, offered the nomination on a
third party ticket to Robert La Follette of Wisconsin, long leader of the progressive element
in the Republican party. The American Federation of Labor, the Socialist Party, and other

minor organizations rallied to the La Follette standard, and in the subsequent election he polled 4,822,900 votes—the largest number ever polled by a third party candidate. La Follette's *Autobiography* was written prior to this election: there is no adequate biography of La Follette but several are promised. See N. Fine, *Labor and Farmer Parties in the United States, 1828–1928.*

The great issue before the American people today is the control of government and industry by private monopoly.

For a generation the people have struggled patiently, in the face of repeated betrayals by successive administrations, to free themselves from this intolerable power which has been undermining representative government.

Through control of government, monopoly has steadily extended its absolute dominion to every basic industry.

In violation of law, monopoly has crushed competition, stifled private initiative and independent enterprise, and without fear of punishment now exacts extortionate profits upon every necessity of life consumed by the public.

The equality of opportunity proclaimed by the Declaration of Independence and asserted and defended by Jefferson and Lincoln as the heritage of every American citizen has been displaced by special privilege for the few, wrested from the government of the many.

FUNDAMENTAL RIGHTS IN DANGER

That tyrannical power which the American people denied to a king, they will no longer endure from the monopoly system. The people know they cannot yield to any group the control of the economic life of the nation and preserve their political liberties. They know monopoly has its representatives in the halls of Congress, on the Federal bench, and in the executive departments; that these servile agents barter away the nation's natural resources, nullify acts of Congress by judicial veto and administrative favor, invade the people's rights by unlawful arrests and unconstitutional searches and seizures, direct our foreign policy in the interests of predatory wealth, and make wars and conscript the sons of the common people to fight them.

The usurpation in recent years by the federal courts of the power to nullify laws duly enacted by the legislative branch of the government is a plain violation of the Constitution. . . .

DISTRESS OF AMERICAN FARMERS

The present condition of American agriculture constitutes an emergency of the gravest character. The Department of Commerce report shows that during 1923 there was a steady and marked increase in dividends paid by the great industrial corporations. The same is true of the steam and electric railways and practically all other large corporations. On the other hand, the Secretary of Agriculture reports that in the fifteen principal wheat growing states more than 108,000 farmers since 1920 have lost their farms through foreclosure or bankruptcy; that more than 122,-000 have surrendered their property without legal proceedings, and that nearly 375,000 have retained possession of their property only through the leniency of their creditors, making a total of more than 600,000 or 26 percent of all farmers who have virtually been bankrupted since 1920 in these fifteen states alone.

Almost unlimited prosperity for the great corporations and ruin and bankruptcy for agriculture is the direct and logical result of the policies and legislation which deflated the farmer while extending almost unlimited credit to the great corporations; which protected with exorbitant tariffs the industrial magnates, but depressed the prices of the farmers' products by financial juggling while greatly increasing the cost of what he must buy; which guaranteed excessive freight rates to the railroads and put a premium on wasteful management while saddling an unwarranted burden on to the backs of the American farmer; which permitted gambling in the products of the farm by grain speculators to the great detriment of the farmer and to the great profit of the grain gambler.

A COVENANT WITH THE PEOPLE

Awakened by the dangers which menace their freedom and prosperity the American people still retain the right and courage to exercise their sovereign control over their government. In order to destroy the economic and political power of monopoly, which has come between the people and their government, we pledge ourselves to the following principles and policies:

THE HOUSE CLEANING

1. We pledge a complete housecleaning in the Department of Justice, the Department of the Interior, and the other executive departments. We demand that the power of the Federal Government be used to crush private monopoly, not to foster it.

NATURAL RESOURCES

2. We pledge recovery of the navy's oil reserves and all other parts of the public domain which have been fraudulently or illegally leased, or otherwise wrongfully transferred, to the control of private interests; vigorous prosecution of all public officials, private citizens and corporations that participated in these transactions; complete revision of the water-power act, the general leasing act, and all other legislation relating to the public domain. We favor public ownership of the nation's water power and the creation and development of a national super-water-power system, including Muscle Shoals, to supply at actual cost light and power for the people and nitrate for the farmers, and strict public control and permanent conservation of all the nation's resources, including coal, iron and other ores, oil and timber lands, in the interest of the people.

RAILROADS

3. We favor repeal of the Esch-Cummins railroad law and the fixing of railroad rates upon the basis of actual, prudent investment and cost of service. . . .

TAX REDUCTION

4. We favor reduction of Federal taxes upon individual incomes and legitimate business, limiting tax exactions strictly to the requirements of the government administered with rigid economy, particularly by the curtailment of the eight hundred million dollars now annually expended for the army and navy in preparation for future wars; by the recovery of the hundreds of millions of dollars stolen from the Treasury through fraudulent war contracts and the corrupt leasing of the public resources; and by diligent action to collect the accumulated interest upon the eleven billion dollars owing us by foreign governments.

We denounce the Mellon tax plan as a device to relieve multi-millionaires at the expense of other tax payers, and favor a taxation policy providing for immediate reductions upon moderate incomes, large increases in the inheritance tax rates upon large estates to prevent the indefinite accumulation by inheritance of great fortunes in a few hands; taxes upon excess profits to penalize profiteering, and complete publicity, under proper safeguards, of all Federal tax returns.

THE COURTS

5. We favor submitting to the people, for their considerate judgment, a constitutional amendment providing that Congress may by enacting a statute make it effective over a judicial veto.

We favor such amendment to the constitution as may be necessary to provide for the election of all Federal Judges, without party designation, for fixed terms not exceeding ten years, by direct vote of the people.

THE FARMERS

6. We favor drastic reduction of the exorbitant duties on manufactures provided in the Fordney-McCumber tariff legislation, the prohibiting of gambling by speculators and profiteers in agricultural products; the reconstruction of the Federal Reserve and Federal Farm Loan Systems, so as to eliminate control by usurers, speculators and international financiers, and to make the credit of the nation available upon fair terms to all and without discrimination to business men, farmers, and home-builders. We advocate the calling of a special session of Congress to pass legislation for the relief of American agriculture. We favor such further legislation as may be needful or helpful in promoting and protecting co-operative enterprises. We demand that the Interstate Commerce Commission proceed forthwith to reduce by an approximation to pre-war levels the present freight rates on agricultural products, including live stock, and upon the materials required upon American farms for agricultural purposes.

LABOR

7. We favor abolition of the use of injunctions in labor disputes and declare for complete protection of the right of farmers and industrial workers to organize, bargain collectively through representatives of their own

choosing, and conduct without hindrance co-operative enterprises.

We favor prompt ratification of the Child Labor amendment, and subsequent enactment of a Federal law to protect children in industry. . . .

PEACE ON EARTH

12. We denounce the mercenary system of foreign policy under recent administrations in the interests of financial imperialists, oil monopolies and international bankers, which has at times degraded our State Department from its high service as a strong and kindly intermediary of defenseless governments to a trading outpost for those interests and concession-seekers engaged in the exploitations of weaker nations, as contrary to the will of the American people, destructive of domestic development and provocative of war. We favor an active foreign policy to bring about a revision of the Versailles treaty in accordance with the terms of the armistice, and to promote firm treaty agreements with all nations to outlaw wars, abolish conscription, drastically reduce land, air and naval armaments, and guarantee public referendum on peace and war.

455. PIERCE v. SOCIETY OF THE SISTERS
268 U. S. 510
1925

Appeal from the District Court of United States for Oregon. Suit to enjoin enforcement of Oregon Compulsory Education Act of 1922 requiring children to attend public schools.

MCREYNOLDS, J. These appeals are from decrees . . . which granted preliminary orders restraining appellants from threatening or attempting to enforce the Compulsory Education Act adopted November 7, 1922, under the initiative provision of her Constitution by the voters of Oregon. . . .

The challenged act, effective September 1, 1926, requires every parent . . . of a child between eight and sixteen years to send him "to a public school for the period of time a public school shall be held during the current year" in the district where the child resides; and failure to do so is declared a misdemeanor. . . . The manifest purpose is to compel general attendance at public schools by normal children between eight and sixteen, who have not completed the eighth grade. And without doubt enforcement of the statute would seriously impair, perhaps destroy, the profitable features of appellees' business, and greatly diminish the value of their property.

Appellee the Society of Sisters is an Oregon corporation, organized in 1880, with power to care for orphans, educate and instruct the youth, establish and maintain academies or schools, and acquire necessary real and personal property. . . . It conducts interdependent primary and high schools and junior colleges, and maintains orphanages for the custody and control of children between eight and sixteen. In its primary schools many children between those ages are taught the subjects usually pursued in Oregon public schools during the first eight years. Systematic religious instruction and moral training according to the tenets of the Roman Catholic Church are also regularly provided. . . . The business is remunerative . . . and the successful conduct of this business requires long-time contracts with teachers and parents. The Compulsory Education Act of 1922 has already caused the withdrawal from its schools of children who would otherwise continue, and their income has steadily declined. . . .

The bill alleges that the enactment conflicts with the right of parents to choose schools where their children will receive appropriate mental and religious training . . . and the right of schools and teachers therein to engage in a useful business or profession, and is accordingly repugnant to the Constitution and void. . . .

No question is raised concerning the power of the State reasonably to regulate all schools, to inspect, supervise and examine them, their teachers and pupils; to require that all children of proper age attend some school, that teachers shall be of good moral character and patriotic disposition, that certain studies plainly essential to good citizenship must be taught, and that nothing be taught which is manifestly inimical to the public welfare.

The inevitable practical result of enforcing the act under consideration would be destruction of appellees' primary schools, and perhaps all other private primary schools for normal children within the State of Oregon. Appellees are engaged in a kind of undertaking not inherently harmful, but long regarded as useful and meritorious. Certainly there is nothing in the present records to indicate that they have failed to discharge their obligations to patrons, students, or the State. And there are no peculiar circumstances or present emergencies which demand extraordinary measures relative to primary education.

Under the doctrine of *Meyer* v. *Nebraska,* 262 U. S. 390, we think it entirely plain that the Act of 1922 unreasonably interferes with the liberty of parents and guardians to direct the upbringing and education of children under their control. As often heretofore pointed out rights guaranteed by the Constitution may not be abridged by legislation which has no reasonable relation to some purpose within the competency of the State. The fundamental theory of liberty upon which all governments in this Union repose excludes any general power of the State to standardize its children by forcing them to accept instruction from public teachers only. The child is not the mere creature of the State; those who nurture him and direct his destiny have the right, coupled with the high duty, to recognize and prepare him for additional obligations. . . .

Decree affirmed.

456. GITLOW v. PEOPLE OF NEW YORK
268 U. S. 652
1925

Error to the Supreme Court of the State of New York. Both the Federal and the State Constitutions guarantee the right of freedom of speech, but the question of how far that right may be used is one of the most perplexing that the Courts have to face. As Mr. Justice Holmes said in the case of *U.S.* v. *Schenck,* Doc. No. 426, "The most stringent protection of free speech would not protect a man in falsely shouting fire in a theatre and causing a panic." The present case involved the validity of the New York Criminal Anarchy Act of 1902. Compare the opinion of the Court in this case with the opinions in *U.S.* v. *Schenck* and *Abrams* v. *United States,* 250 U.S. 616, and *Patterson* v. *Colorado,* 205 U. S. 454. For a general discussion, see Z. Chafee, *Freedom of Speech.*

SANFORD, J. Benjamin Gitlow was indicted in the supreme court of New York, with three others, for the statutory crime of criminal anarchy. . . .

The contention here is that the statute, by its terms and as applied in this case, is repugnant to the due process clause of the Fourteenth Amendment. Its material provisions are:

"Section 160. *Criminal anarchy defined.*— Criminal anarchy is the doctrine that organized government should be overthrown by force or violence, or by assassination of the executive head or of any of the executive officials of government, or by any unlawful means. The advocacy of such doctrine either by word of mouth or writing is a felony.

"Section 161. *Advocacy of criminal anarchy.*—Any person who:

"1. By word of mouth or writing advocates, advises or teaches the duty, necessity or propriety of overthrowing or overturning organized government by force or violence, or by assassination of the executive head or of any of the executive officials of government, or by any unlawful means; or,

"2. Prints, publishes, edits, issues or knowingly circulates, sells, distributes or publicly displays any book, paper, document, or written or printed matter in any form, containing or advocating, advising or teaching the doctrine that organized government should be overthrown by force, violence or any unlawful means . . . ,

"Is guilty of a felony and punishable" by imprisonment or fine, or both.

The indictment was in two counts. The first charged that the defendants had advocated, advised, and taught the duty, necessity, and propriety of overthrowing and overturning organized government by force, violence, and unlawful means, by certain writings therein set forth, entitled, "The Left Wing Manifesto"; the second, that the defendants had printed, published, and knowingly circulated and distributed a certain paper called "The Revolutionary Age," containing the writings set forth in the first count, advocating, advising, and teaching the doctrine that organized government should be overthrown by force, violence, and unlawful means. . . .

There was no evidence of any effect resulting from the publication and circulation of the Manifesto.

No witnesses were offered in behalf of the defendant.

Extracts from the Manifesto are set forth in the margin. Coupled with a review of the rise of Socialism, it condemned the dominant "moderate Socialism" for its recognition of the necessity of the democratic parliamentary state; repudiated its policy of introducing Socialism by legislative measures; and advocated, in plain and unequivocal language, the necessity of accomplishing the "Communist Revolution" by a militant and "revolutionary Socialism," based on "the class struggle" and mobilizing the "power of the proletariat in action," through mass industrial revolts developing into mass political strikes and "revolutionary mass action," for the purpose of conquering and destroying the parliamentary state and establishing in its place, through a "revolutionary dictatorship of the proletariat," the system of Communist Socialism. The then recent strikes in Seattle and Winnipeg were cited as instances of a development already verging on revolutionary action and suggestive of proletarian dictatorship, in which the strike workers were "trying to usurp the functions of municipal government"; and Revolutionary Socialism, it was urged, must use these mass industrial revolts to broaden the strike, make it general and militant, and develop it into mass political strikes and revolutionary mass action for the annihilation of the parliamentary state. . . .

. . . The sole contention here is, essentially, that, as there was no evidence of any concrete result flowing from the publication of the Manifesto, or of circumstances showing the likelihood of such result, the statute as construed and applied by the trial court penalizes the mere utterance, as such, of

"doctrine" having no quality of incitement, without regard either to the circumstances of its utterance or to the likelihood of unlawful sequences; and that, as the exercise of the right of free expression with relation to government is only punishable "in circumstances involving likelihood of substantive evil," the statute contravenes the due process clause of the Fourteenth Amendment. The argument in support of this contention rests primarily upon the following propositions: first, that the "liberty" protected by the Fourteenth Amendment includes the liberty of speech and of the press; and second, that while liberty of expression "is not absolute," it may be restrained "only in circumstances where its exercise bears a causal relation with some substantive evil, consummated, attempted, or likely"; and as the statute "takes no account of circumstances," it unduly restrains this liberty, and is therefore unconstitutional.

The precise question presented, and the only question which we can consider under this writ of error, then, is whether the statute, as construed and applied in this case by the state courts, deprived the defendant of his liberty of expression, in violation of the due process clause of the Fourteenth Amendment.

The statute does not penalize the utterance or publication of abstract "doctrine" or academic discussion having no quality of incitement to any concrete action. It is not aimed against mere historical or philosophical essays. It does not restrain the advocacy of changes in the form of government by constitutional and lawful means. What it prohibits is language advocating, advising, or teaching the overthrow of organized government by unlawful means. . . .

The Manifesto, plainly, is neither the statement of abstract doctrine nor, as suggested by counsel, mere prediction that industrial disturbances and revolutionary mass strikes will result spontaneously in an inevitable process of evolution in the economic system. It advocates and urges in fervent language mass action which shall progressively foment industrial disturbances, and, through political mass strikes and revolutionary mass action, overthrow and destroy organized parliamentary government. . . .

The means advocated for bringing about the destruction of organized parliamentary government, namely, mass industrial revolts usurping the functions of municipal government, political mass strikes directed against the parliamentary state, and revolutionary mass action for its final destruction, necessarily imply the use of force and violence, and in their essential nature are inherently unlawful in a constitutional government of law and order. That the jury was warranted in finding that the Manifesto advocated not merely the abstract doctrine of overwhelming organized government by force, violence, and unlawful means, but action to that end, is clear.

For the present purposes we may and do assume that freedom of speech and of the press—which are protected by the First Amendment from abridgment by Congress—are among the fundamental personal rights and "liberties" protected by the due process clause of the Fourteenth Amendment from impairment by the states. . . .

It is a fundamental principle, long established, that the freedom of speech and of the press which is secured by the Constitution does not confer an absolute right to speak or publish, without responsibility, whatever one may choose, or an unrestricted and unbridled license that gives immunity for every possible use of language, and prevents the punishment of those who abuse this freedom. . . .

That a state, in the exercise of its police power, may punish those who abuse this freedom by utterances inimical to the public welfare, tending to corrupt public morals, incite to crime, or disturb the public peace, is not open to question. . . .

And, for yet more imperative reasons, a State may punish utterances endangering the foundations of organized government and threatening its overthrow by unlawful means. These imperil its own existence as a constitutional state. Freedom of speech and press, said Story (supra), does not protect disturbances of the public peace or the attempt to subvert the government. It does not protect publications or teachings which tend to subvert or imperil the government, or to impede or hinder it in the performance of its governmental duties. It does not protect publications prompting the overthrow of government by force; the punishment of those who publish articles which tend to destroy organized society being essential to the security of

freedom and the stability of the state. And a State may penalize utterances which openly advocate the overthrow of the representative and constitutional form of government of the United States and the several states, by violence or other unlawful means. In short, this freedom does not deprive a State of the primary and essential right of self-preservation, which, so long as human governments endure, they cannot be denied. . . .

By enacting the present statute the State has determined, through its legislative body, that utterances advocating the overthrow of organized government by force, violence, and unlawful means, are so inimical to the general welfare, and involve such danger of substantive evil, that they may be penalized in the exercise of its police power. That determination must be given great weight. Every presumption is to be indulged in favor of the validity of the statute. . . . That utterances inciting to the overthrow of organized government by unlawful means present a sufficient danger of substantive evil to bring their punishment within the range of legislative discretion is clear. Such utterances, by their very nature, involve danger to the public peace and to the security of the state. They threaten breaches of the peace and ultimate revolution. And the immediate danger is none the less real and substantial because the effect of a given utterance cannot be accurately foreseen. The state cannot reasonably be required to measure the danger from every such utterance in the nice balance of a jeweler's scale. A single revolutionary spark may kindle a fire that, smoldering for a time, may burst into a sweeping and destructive conflagration. It cannot be said that the state is acting arbitrarily or unreasonably when, in the exercise of its judgment as to the measures necessary to protect the public peace and safety, it seeks to extinguish the spark without waiting until it has enkindled the flame or blazed into the conflagration. It cannot reasonably be required to defer the adoption of measures for its own peace and safety until the revolutionary utterances lead to actual disturbances of the public peace or imminent and immediate danger of its own destruction; but it may, in the exercise of its judgment, suppress the threatened danger in its incipiency. . . .

We cannot hold that the present statute

is an arbitrary or unreasonable exercise of the police power of the state, unwarrantably infringing the freedom of speech or press; and we must and do sustain its constitutionality.

This being so it may be applied to every utterance—not too trivial to be beneath the notice of the law—which is of such a character and used with such intent and purpose as to bring it within the prohibition of the statute. . . . In other words, when the legislative body has determined generally, in the constitutional exercise of its discretion, that utterances of a certain kind involve such danger of substantive evil that they may be punished, the question whether any specific utterance coming within the prohibited class is likely, in and of itself, to bring about the substantive evil, is not open to consideration. It is sufficient that the statute itself be constitutional, and that the use of the language comes within its prohibition. . . .

And finding, for the reasons stated, that the statute is not in itself unconstitutional, and that it has not been applied in the present case in derogation of any constitutional right, the judgment of the court of appeals is affirmed.

HOLMES, J., dissenting:

Mr Justice Brandeis and I are of opinion that this judgment should be reversed. The general principle of free speech, it seems to me, must be taken to be included in the Fourteenth Amendment, in view of the scope that has been given to the word "liberty" as there used, although perhaps it may be accepted with a somewhat larger latitude of interpretation than is allowed to Congress by the sweeping language that governs, or ought to govern, the laws of the United States. If I am right, then I think that the criterion sanctioned by the full court in *Schenck* v. *United States*, 249 U. S. 47,

52, applies: "The question in every case is whether the words used are used in such circumstances and are of such a nature as to create a clear and present danger that they will bring about the substantive evils that [the state] has a right to prevent." . . . If what I think the correct test is applied, it is manifest that there was no present danger of an attempt to overthrow the government by force on the part of the admittedly small minority who shared the defendant's views. It is said that this Manifesto was more than a theory, that it was an incitement. Every idea is an incitement. It offers itself for belief, and, if believed, it is acted on unless some other belief outweighs it, or some failure of energy stifles the movement at its birth. The only difference between the expression of an opinion and an incitement in the narrower sense is the speaker's enthusiasm for the result. Eloquence may set fire to reason. But whatever may be thought of the redundant discourse before us, it had no chance of starting a present conflagration. If, in the long run, the beliefs expressed in proletarian dictatorship are destined to be accepted by the dominant forces of the community, the only meaning of free speech is that they should be given their chance and have their way.

If the publication of this document had been laid as an attempt to induce an uprising against government at once, and not at some indefinite time in the future, it would have presented a different question. The object would have been one with which the law might deal, subject to the doubt whether there was any danger that the publication could produce any result; or, in other words, whether it was not futile and too remote from possible consequences. But the indictment alleges the publication and nothing more.

457. THE UNITED STATES AND THE WORLD COURT

Senate Reservations to Accession of the United States, and World Court Modifications
January 27, 1926

The World Court of International Justice was provided for by the Covenant of the League of Nations. A committee of ten distinguished jurists, including Mr. Elihu Root, drew up the Rules for the Court; these were adopted by the As-

sembly of the League of Nations, December 13, 1920, and the Court was organized the following year. Every administration has apparently favored our accession to the Court, but not until 1926 was President Coolidge able to secure the consent of the Senate, and then with the reservations below. These reservations were incorporated with slight modifications into the Protocol of March 19, 1929, and the signature of the United States affixed November 25, 1929. The Senate has not yet (1934) acted upon the ratification of the protocol. The Senate reservations are in *Congressional Record,* Vol. LXVII, p. 2306; the World Court Protocol in Foreign Policy Association, *Information Service,* Vol. V, No. 21. See, P. C. Jessup, *The United States and the World Court,* World Peace Foundation Pamphlets, Vol XII, No. 4.

1. CONDITIONS UPON WHICH THE UNITED STATES WILL ENTER THE WORLD COURT

THE SWANSON RESOLUTION

Whereas the President, under date of February 24, 1923, transmitted a message to the Senate accompanied by a letter from the Secretary of State, dated February 17, 1923, asking the favorable advice and consent of the Senate to the adherence on the part of the United States to the protocol of December 16, 1920, of signature of the statute for the Permanent Court of International Justice, set out in said message of the President (without accepting or agreeing to the optional clause for compulsory jurisdiction contained therein), upon the conditions and understandings hereafter stated, to be made a part of the instrument of adherence: Therefore be it

Resolved (two-thirds of the Senators present concurring), That the Senate advise and consent to the adherence on the part of the United States to the said protocol of December 16, 1920, and the adjoined statute for the Permanent Court of International Justice (without accepting or agreeing to the optional clause for compulsory jurisdiction contained in said statute), and that the signature of the United States be affixed to the said protocol, subject to the following reservations and understandings, which are hereby made a part and condition of this resolution, namely:

1. That such adherence shall not be taken to involve any legal relation on the part of the United States to the League of Nations or the assumption of any obligations by the United States under the treaty of Versailles.

2. That the United States shall be permitted to participate, through representatives designated for the purpose and upon an equality with the other states, members, respectively, of the Council and Assembly of the League of Nations, in any and all proceedings of either the council or the assembly for the election of judges or deputy judges of the Permanent Court of International Justice or for the filling of vacancies.

3. That the United States will pay a fair share of the expenses of the court, as determined and appropriated from time to time by the Congress of the United States.

4. That the United States may at any time withdraw its adherence to the said protocol and that the statute for the Permanent Court of International Justice adjoined to the protocol shall not be amended without the consent of the United States.

5. That the court shall not render any advisory opinion except publicly after due notice to all states adhering to the court and to all interested states and after public hearing or opportunity for hearing given to any state concerned; nor shall it, without the consent of the United States, entertain any request for an advisory opinion touching any dispute or question in which the United States has or claims an interest.

The signature of the United States to the said protocol shall not be affixed until the powers signatory to such protocol shall have indicated, through an exchange of notes, their acceptance of the foregoing reservations and understandings as a part and a condition of adherence by the United States to the said protocol.

Resolved further, As a part of this act of ratification that the United States approve the protocol and statute hereinabove mentioned, with the understanding that recourse to the Permanent Court of International Justice for the settlement of differences between the United States and any other state or states can be had only by agreement thereto through general or special treaties concluded between the parties in dispute; and

Resolved further, That adherence to the said protocol and statute hereby approved shall not be so construed as to require the United States to depart from its traditional policy of not intruding upon, interfering with, or entangling itself in the political questions of policy or internal administration of any foreign state; nor shall adherence to the said protocol and statute be construed to imply a relinquishment by the United States of its traditional attitude toward purely American questions.

2. DRAFT PROTOCOL FOR THE ACCESSION OF THE UNITED STATES

The States signatories of the Protocol of Signature of the Permanent Court of International Justice, dated December 16th, 1920, and the United States of America, through the undersigned duly authorized representatives, have mutually agreed upon the following provisions regarding the adherence of the United States of America to the said Protocol, subject to the five reservations formulated by the United States in the resolution adopted by the Senate on January 27th, 1926.

ART. 1. The States signatories of the said Protocol accept the special conditions attached by the United States in the five reservations mentioned above to its adherence to the said Protocol upon the terms and conditions set out in the following Articles.

ART. 2. The United States shall be admitted to participate, through representatives designated for the purpose and upon an equality with the signatory States Members of the League of Nations represented in the Council or in the Assembly, in any and all proceedings of either the Council or the Assembly for the election of judges or deputy-judges of the Permanent Court of International Justice, provided for in the Statute of the Court. The vote of the United States shall be counted in determining the absolute majority of votes required by the Statute.

ART. 3. No amendment of the Statute of the Court may be made without the consent of all the Contracting States.

ART. 4. The Court shall render advisory opinions in public session after notice and opportunity for hearing substantially as provided in the now existing Articles 73 and 74 of the Rules of Court.

ART. 5. With a view to ensuring that the Court shall not, without the consent of the United States, entertain any request for an advisory opinion touching any dispute or question in which the United States has or claims an interest, the Secretary-General of the League of Nations shall, through any channel designated for that purpose by the United States, inform the United States of any proposal before the Council or the Assembly of the League for obtaining an advisory opinion from the Court, and thereupon, if desired, an exchange of views as to whether an interest of the United States is affected shall proceed with all convenient speed between the Council or Assembly of the League and the United States.

Whenever a request for an advisory opinion comes to the Court, the Registrar shall notify the United States thereof, among other States mentioned in the now existing Article 73 of the Rules of Court, stating a reasonable time-limit fixed by the President within which a written statement by the United States concerning the request will be received. If for any reason no sufficient opportunity for an exchange of views upon such request should have been afforded and the United States advises the Court that the question upon which the opinion of the Court is asked is one that affects the interests of the United States, proceedings shall be stayed for a period sufficient to enable such an exchange of views between the Council or the Assembly and the United States to take place.

With regard to requesting an advisory opinion of the Court in any case covered by the preceding paragraphs, there shall be attributed to an objection of the United States the same force and effect as attaches to a vote against asking for the opinion given by a Member of the League of Nations in the Council or in the Assembly.

If, after the exchange of views provided for in paragraphs 1 and 2 of this Article, it shall appear that no agreement can be reached and the United States is not prepared to forego its objection, the exercise of the powers of withdrawal provided for in Article 8 hereof will follow naturally without any imputation of unfriendliness or unwillingness to co-operate generally for peace and goodwill.

ART. 6. Subject to the provisions of Article 8 below, the provisions of the present Protocol shall have the same force and effect as the provisions of the Statute of the Court and any future signature of the Protocol of December 16th, 1920, shall be deemed to be an acceptance of the provisions of the present Protocol.

ART. 7. The present Protocol shall be ratified. Each State shall forward the instrument of ratification to the Secretary-General of the League of Nations, who shall inform all the other signatory States. The instruments of ratification shall be deposited in the archives of the Secretariat of the League of Nations.

The present Protocol shall come into force as soon as all States which have ratified the Protocol of December 16th, 1920, and also the United States, have deposited their ratifications.

ART. 8. The United States may at any time notify the Secretary-General of the League of Nations that it withdraws its adherence to the Protocol of December 16th, 1920. The Secretary-General shall immediately communicate this notification to all the other States signatories of the Protocol.

In such case, the present Protocol shall cease to be in force as from the receipt by the Secretary-General of the notification by the United States.

On their part, each of the other Contracting States may at any time notify the Secretary-General of the League of Nations that it desires to withdraw its acceptance of the special conditions attached by the United States to its adherence to the Protocol of December 16th, 1920. The Secretary-General shall immediately give communication of this notification to each of the States signatories of the present Protocol. The present Protocol shall be considered as ceasing to be in force if and when, within one year from the date of receipt of the said notification, not less than two-thirds of the Contracting States other than the United States shall have notified the Secretary-General of the League of Nations that they desire to withdraw the above-mentioned acceptance.

458. TYSON v. BANTON
273 U. S. 418
1926

Appeal from United States district court for Southern district of New York. The facts of the case are stated in the opinion below. The dissenting opinion of Mr. Justice Holmes is particularly important as foreshadowing the attitude of the Court at the present time.

SUTHERLAND, J. Appellant is engaged in the business of reselling tickets of admission to theatres and other places of entertainment in the city of New York. . . . Section 167 of ch. 590 (New York laws) declares that the price of or charge for admission to theatres, etc., is a matter affected with a public interest and subject to state supervision in order to safeguard the public against fraud, extortion, exorbitant rates, and similar abuses. Section 172 forbids the resale of any ticket . . . to any theatre, etc., "at a price in excess of fifty cents in advance of the price printed on the face of such ticket." . . .

Strictly, the question for determination relates only to the maximum price for which an entrance ticket to a theatre, etc., may be resold. But the answer necessarily must be to a question of greater breadth. The statutory declaration is that the price of or charge for admission to a theatre . . . is a matter affected with a public interest. To affirm the validity of section 172 is to affirm this declaration completely since appellant's business embraces the resale of entrance tickets to all forms of entertainment therein enumerated. And since the ticket broker is a mere appendage of the theatre, etc., and the price of or charge for admission is the essential element in the statutory declaration, it results that the real inquiry is whether every public exhibition, game, contest or performance, to which an admission charge is made, is clothed with a public interest, so as to authorize a law-making body to fix the maximum amount of the charge, which its patrons may be required to pay. . . .

A business is not affected with a public interest merely because it is large or because the public are warranted in having a feeling of concern in respect of its maintenance. Nor is the interest meant such as arises from the mere fact that the public derives benefit, accommodation, ease or enjoyment from the existence or operation of the business; and while the word has not always been limited narrowly as strictly denoting "a right", that synonym, more nearly than any other, expresses the sense in which it is to be understood. . . .

. . . The mere declaration by the legislature that a particular kind of property or business is affected with a public interest is not conclusive upon the question of the validity of the regulation. The matter is one which is always open to judicial inquiry.

From the foregoing review it will be seen that each of the decisions of this court upholding governmental price regulation aside from cases involving legislation to tide over temporary emergencies, has turned upon the existence of conditions, peculiar to the business under consideration, which bore such a substantial and definite relation to the public interest as to justify an indulgence of the legal fiction of a grant by the owner to the public of an interest in the use.

Lord Hale's statement that when private property is "affected with a public interest, it ceases to be *juris privati* only" is accepted by this court as the guiding principle in cases of this character. . . .

A theatre or other place of entertainment does not meet this conception of Lord Hale's aphorism or fall within the reasons of the decisions of this court based upon it. A theatre is a private enterprise, which, in its relation to the public, differs obviously and widely, both in character and degree, from a grain elevator, standing at the gateway of commerce and exacting toll . . .; or stock yards, standing in like relation to the commerce in live stock; or insurance company engaged as a sort of common agency, in collecting and holding a guarantee fund in which definite and substantial rights are enjoyed by a considerable portion of the public. . . . Sales of theatre tickets bear no relation to the commerce of the country; and they are not interdependent transactions, but stand, both in form and effect, separate and apart from each other, "terminating in their effect with the instances." And, certainly a place of entertainment is in no legal sense a public utility; and, quite as certainly, its activities are not such that their enjoyment can be regarded under any conditions from the point of view of an emergency. . . .

The statute assailed contravenes the 14th Amendment, and the decree must be reversed.

Holmes, J., dissenting. We fear to grant power and are unwilling to recognize it when it exists. The States very generally have stripped jury trials of one of their most important characteristics by forbidding the judges to advise the jury upon the facts, and when legislatures are held to be authorized to do anything considerably affecting public welfare, it is covered by apologetic phrases like the police power, or the statement that the business concerned has been dedicated to a public use. The former expression is convenient, to be sure, to conciliate the mind to something that needs explanation; the fact that the constitutional requirement of compensation when property is taken cannot be pressed to its grammatical extreme; that property rights may be taken for public purposes without pay if you do not take too much; that some play must be allowed to the joints if the machine is to work. But police power often is used in a wide sense to cover and, as I said, to apologize for the general power of the legislature to make a part of the community uncomfortable by a change.

I do not believe in such apologies. I think the proper course is to recognize that a state legislature can do whatever it sees fit to do unless it is restrained by some express prohibition in the Constitution of the United States or of the state, and that courts should be careful not to extend such prohibitions beyond their obvious meaning by reading into them conceptions of public policy that the particular court may happen to entertain.

Coming down to the case before us, I think, as I intimated in *Adkins* v. *Children's Hospital,* that the notion that a business is clothed with a public interest and has been devoted to the public use is little more than a fiction intended to beautify what is disagreeable to the sufferers. The truth seems to me to be that, subject to compensation when compensation is due, the legislature may forbid or restrict any business when it has a sufficient force of public opinion behind it. Lotteries were thought useful adjuncts of the state a century or so ago; now they are believed to be immoral and they have been stopped. Wine has been thought good for man from the time of the Apostles until recent years. But when public opinion changed it did not need the 18th Amendment, notwithstanding the 14th, to enable a state to say that the business should end. What has happened to lotteries and wine might happen to theatres in some moral storm of the future, not because theatres were devoted to a public use, but because people had come to think that way.

But if we are to yield to fashionable conventions, it seems to me that theatres are as much devoted to public use as anything well can be. We have not that respect for art that is one of the glories of France. But to many people the superfluous is the necessary,

and it seems to me that government does not go beyond its sphere in attempting to make life livable for them. I am far from saying that I think this particular law a wise and rational provision. That is not my affair. But if the people of the state of New York speaking by their authorized voice say that they want it, I see nothing in the Constitution of the United States to prevent their having their will.

459. MYERS v. UNITED STATES
272 U. S. 52
1926

Appeal from the Court of Claims. It will be remembered that President Johnson challenged the validity of the Tenure of Office Act of March 2, 1867 (see Doc. No. 263) and that his impeachment rested largely on his defiance of this Act. He was unable, at the time, to bring the question of the constitutionality of the Act before the Courts, and not until 1926 did the Court hand down an opinion on the vexed question of the power of removal. The opinion of the Court in this case may be taken as a complete vindication of the position of President Johnson.

TAFT, C. J. This case presents the question whether under the Constitution the President has the exclusive power of removing executive officers of the United States whom he has appointed by and with the advice and consent of the Senate.

Meyers was on July 21, 1917 appointed by the President, by and with the advice and consent of the Senate, to be a postmaster of the first class at Portland, Oregon, for a term of four years. On January 20, 1920, Myers's resignation was demanded. He refused the demand. On February 2, 1920, he was removed from office by order of the Postmaster General, acting by direction of the President. . . .

By the 6th section of the Act of Congress of July 12, 1876, under which Myers was appointed with the advice and consent of the Senate as a first class postmaster, it is provided that "Postmasters of the first, second and third classes shall be appointed and may be removed by the President by and with the advice and consent of the Senate and shall hold their offices for four years unless

sooner removed or suspended according to law".

The Senate did not consent to the President's removal of Myers during his term. If this statute in its requirement that his term should be four years unless sooner removed by the President by and with the consent of the Senate is valid, the appellant . . . is entitled to recover his unpaid salary for his full term and the judgement of the court of claims must be reversed. The government maintains that the requirement is invalid, for the reason that under article 2 of the Constitution, the President's power of removal of executive officers appointed by him with the advice and consent of the Senate is full and complete without consent of the Senate. If this view is sound, the removal of Myers by the President without the Senate's consent was legal. . . .

[There follows a learned discussion of the history of the President's power of removal.]

Our conclusion on the merits sustained by the arguments before stated is that article 2 grants to the President the executive power of the Government, i. e. the general administrative control of those executing the laws, including the power of appointment and removal of executive officers, a conclusion confirmed by his obligation to take care that the laws be faithfully executed; that article 2 excludes the legislative of executive power by Congress to provide for appointments and removals except only as granted therein to Congress in the matter of inferior offices; that Congress is only given power to provide for appointments and removals of inferior officers after it has vested, and on condition that it does vest, their appointment in other authority than the President with the Senate's consent; that the provisions of the second section of article 2, which blend action by the legislative branch, or by part of it, in the work of the executive, are limitations to be strictly construed and not to be extended by implication; that the President's power of removal is further established as an incident to his specifically enumerated function of appointment by and with the advice of the Senate, but that such incident does not by implication extend to removals of the Senate's power of checking appointment; and finally that to hold otherwise would make it impossible for the President in case of political or other difference with the Senate or Congress to take care that the laws be faithfully executed.

We come now to a period in the history of the Government when both houses of Congress attempted to reverse this constitutional construction and to subject the power of removing executive officers appointed by the President and conformed by the Senate to the control of the Senate, indeed finally to the assumed power in Congress to place the removal of such officers anywhere in the Government.

This reversal grew out of the serious political difference between the two Houses of Congress and President Johnson. . . . The chief legislation in support of the reconstruction policy of Congress was the Tenure of Office Act of March 2, 1867, providing that all officers appointed by and with the consent of the Senate should hold their offices until their successors should have in like manner been appointed and qualified, that certain heads of departments, including the Secretary of War, should hold their offices during the terms of the President by whom appointed and one month thereafter subject to removal by consent of the Senate. The Tenure of Office Act was vetoed, but it was passed over the veto. . . .

In spite of the foregoing Presidential declarations, it is contended that since the passage of the Tenure of Office Act, there has been a general acquiescence by the Executive in the power of Congress to forbid the President alone to remove executive officers, an acquiescence which has changed any formerly accepted constitutional construction to the contrary. Instances are cited of the signed approval by President Grant and other Presidents of legislation in derogation of such construction. We think these are all to be explained not by acquiescence therein, but by reason of the otherwise valuable effect of the legislation approved. Such is doubtless the explanation of the executive approval of the Act of 1867, which we are considering, for it was an appropriation act on which the section here in question was imposed as rider. . . .

When, then, are the elements that enter into our decision of this case? We have first a construction of the Constitution made by a Congress which was to provide by legislation for the organization of the Government in accord with the Constitution which had just then been adopted, and in which there were, as representatives and senators, a considerable number of those who had been members of the Convention that framed the Constitution and presented it for ratification. It was the Congress that launched the Government. It was the Congress that rounded out the Constitution itself by the proposing of the first ten amendments which had in effect been promised to the people as a consideration for the ratification. . . . It was a Congress whose constitutional decisions have always been regarded as they should be regarded as of the greatest weight in the interpretation of that fundamental instrument. . . . We are now asked to set aside this construction thus buttressed and adopt an adverse view because the Congress of the United States did so during a heated political difference of opinion between the then President and the majority leaders of Congress over the reconstruction measures adopted as a means of restoring to their proper status the States which attempted to withdraw from the Union at the time of the Civil War. . . . When on the merits we find our conclusions strongly favoring the view which prevailed in the First Congress, we have no hesitation in holding that conclusion to be correct; and it therefore follows that the Tenure of Office Act of 1867, in so far as it attempted to prevent the President from removing executive officers who had been appointed by him by and with the advice and consent of the Senate, was invalid and that subsequent legislation to the same effect was equally so.

For the reasons given we must therefore hold that the provision of the law of 1876 by which the unrestricted power of removal of first class postmasters is denied to the President is in violation of the Constitution and invalid. This leads to an affirmation of the judgement of the Court of Claims. . . .

HOLMES, J., dissenting. . . . The arguments (for the President's power of removal) drawn from the executive power of the President, and from his duty to appoint officers of the United States (when Congress does not vest the appointment elsewhere), to take care that the laws be faithfully executed, and to commission all officers of the United States, seem to me spider's webs inadequate to control the dominant facts.

We have to deal with an office that owes its existence to Congress and that Congress may abolish tomorrow. Its duration and the pay attached to it while it lasts depend on Congress alone. Congress alone confers on the President the power to appoint to it and at any time may transfer the power to other hands. With such power over its own creation, I have no more trouble in believing that Congress has power to prescribe a term of life for it free from any interference than I have in accepting the undoubted power of Congress to decree its end. I have equally little trouble in accepting its power to prolong the tenure of an incumbent until Congress or the Senate shall have assented to his removal. The duty of the President to see that the laws be executed is a duty that does not go beyond the laws or require him to achieve more than Congress sees fit to leave within his power.

McREYNOLDS, J., and BRANDEIS, J., joined in this dissent.

460. AMERICAN INTERVENTION IN NICARAGUA

Message of President Coolidge to Congress
January 10, 1927

(U. S. 69th Congress, 2d Session, *House Doc*. No. 633)

Dissatisfaction of the liberals in Nicaragua with the Diaz government resulted in disturbances which led in 1927 to a renewal of American intervention. In his special message to Congress of January 10, President Coolidge sketched the background of American intervention and pointed out the circumstances which, in his opinion, made intervention imperative. Within a few months over 5000 American marines were sent to Nicaragua to preserve order. In April Mr. Henry Stimson went to Nicaragua as special commissioner to work out some agreement among the warring factions. He succeeded in providing for a new election to take place in 1928 under American supervision. At this election General Moncada, the liberal candidate, was elected over General Diaz who had been maintained by American arms and diplomacy. Moncada promptly appointed Dr. Sacasa, who had been deposed by Diaz and whose appeal to the United States had been spurned, minister to the United States! Sandino, a Sacasa supporter, refused to be bound by the election of 1928, and for the next four years he carried on a desultory warfare against the government. In 1932 Dr. Sacasa was elected to the Presidency, and Sandino voluntarily laid down his arms. American marines were withdrawn from Nicaragua in 1933. See, I. J. Cox, *Nicaragua and the United States, 1909–1927;* H. A. Stimson, *American Policy in Nicaragua;* C. P. Howland, ed. *Survey of American Foreign Relations, 1929;* M. Winkler, *Investments of United States Capital in Latin America.*

The White House

To the Congress of the United States:

. . . It is well known that in 1912 the United States intervened in Nicaragua with a large force and put down a revolution, and that from that time to 1925 a legation guard of American marines was, with the consent of the Nicaraguan Government, kept in Managua to protect American lives and property. In 1923 representatives of the five Central American countries, namely, Costa Rica, Guatemala, Honduras, Nicaragua, and Salvador, at the invitation of the United States, met in Washington and entered into a series of treaties. These treaties dealt with limitation of armament, a Central American tribunal for arbitration, and the general subject of peace and amity. The treaty last referred to specifically provides in Article II that the Governments of the contracting parties will not recognize any other government which may come into power in any of the five Republics through a coup d'état, or revolution, and disqualifies the leaders of such coup d'état, or revolution, from assuming the presidency or vice presidency. . . .

The United States was not a party to this treaty, but it was made in Washington under the auspices of the Secretary of State, and this Government has felt a moral obligation to apply its principles in order to encourage the Central American States in their efforts to prevent revolution and disorder. . . .

The Nicaraguan constitution provides in article 106 that in the absence of the President and Vice President the Congress shall designate one of its members to complete the unexpired term of President . . . the action of Congress in designating Senor Diaz was perfectly legal and in accordance with the constitution. Therefore the United States Government on November 17 extended recognition to Senor Diaz. . . .

Immediately following the inauguration of President Diaz and frequently since that date he has appealed to the United States for support, has informed this Government of the aid which Mexico is giving to the revolutionists, and has stated that he is unable solely because of the aid given by Mexico to the revolutionists to protect the lives and property of American citizens and other foreigners. When negotiations leading up to the Corinto conferences began, I immediately placed an embargo on the shipment of arms and ammunition to Nicaragua. . . .

. . . At the end of November, after spending some time in Mexico City, Doctor Sacasa went back to Nicaragua, landing at Puerto Cabezas, near Bragmans Bluff. He immediately placed himself at the head of the insurrection and declared himself President of Nicaragua. He has never been recognized by any of the Central American Republics nor by any other government, with the exception of Mexico, which recognized him immediately. As arms and munitions in large quantities were reaching the revolutionists, I deemed it unfair to prevent the recognized government from purchasing arms abroad, and, accordingly, the Secretary of State has notified the Diaz Government that licenses would be issued for the export of arms and munitions purchased in this country. It would be thoroughly inconsistent for this country not to

support the government recognized by it while the revolutionists were receiving arms and munitions from abroad. . . .

For many years numerous Americans have been living in Nicaragua, developing its industries and carrying on business. At the present time there are large investments in lumbering, mining, coffee growing, banana culture, shipping, and also in general mercantile and other collateral business.

In addition to these industries now in existence, the Government of Nicaragua, by a treaty entered into on the 5th day of August, 1914, granted in perpetuity to the United States the exclusive proprietary rights necessary and convenient for the construction, operation, and maintenance of an oceanic canal. . . .

There is no question that if the revolution continues American investments and business interests in Nicaragua will be very seriously affected, if not destroyed.

Manifestly the relation of this Government to the Nicaraguan situation and its policy in the existing emergency, are determined by the facts which I have described. The proprietary rights of the United States in the Nicaraguan canal route, with the necessary implications growing out of it affecting the Panama Canal, together with the obligations flowing from the investments of all classes of our citizens in Nicaragua, place us in a position of peculiar responsibility. I am sure it is not the desire of the United States to intervene in the internal affairs of Nicaragua or of any other Central American Republic. Nevertheless it must be said that we have a very definite and special interest in the maintenance of order and good government in Nicaragua at the present time, and that the stability, prosperity, and independence of all Central American countries can never be a matter of indifference to us. The United States can not, therefore, fail to view with deep concern any serious threat to stability and constitutional government in Nicaragua tending toward anarchy and jeopardizing American interests, especially if such state of affairs is contributed to or brought about by outside influences or by any foreign power. It has always been and remains the policy of the United States in such circumstances to take the steps that may be necessary for the preservation and protection of the lives, the property, and the interests of its citizens and of this Government itself. In this respect I propose to follow the path of my predecessors.

Consequently, I have deemed it my duty to use the powers committed to me to insure the adequate protection of all American interests in Nicaragua, whether they be endangered by internal strife or by outside interference in the affairs of that Republic.

Calvin Coolidge.

461. THE McNARY–HAUGEN BILL
February 25, 1927

(*The Congressional Record,* 69th Congress, 2d Session, Vol. LXVIII, part 4, p. 3869 ff.)

The prolonged agricultural depression that set in about 1921 resulted in a persistent demand that the Government extend relief of a more positive character than any heretofore attempted. In the face of an agricultural surplus which tended to level down all prices to the world price, the Farm Bloc in Congress attempted to solve the problem by extending the protective system to the farmers. The McNary-Haugen Act sought to maintain a high domestic price by permitting the government to buy up the surplus agricultural commodities, dispose of them at a loss in the foreign market, and make good the loss through an "equalization fee" to be paid by the farmers. The bill was roundly denounced by President Coolidge as dangerously socialistic in character. It was repassed in May, 1928, and again vetoed by President Coolidge. The second veto can be found in *Supplement to the Messages and Papers of the Presidents Covering the Administration of President Coolidge,* p. 9777 ff. George N. Peek, who drafted the bill, explained it in *Current History,* November 1928. See also E. R. A. Seligman, *The Economics of Farm Relief;* J. D. Black, *Agricultural Reform in the United States.*

SEC. 1. It is hereby declared to be the policy of Congress to promote the orderly marketing of basic agricultural commodities in interstate and foreign commerce and to that end to provide for the control and disposition of surpluses of such commodities, to enable producers of such commodities to stabilize their markets against undue and excessive fluctuations, to preserve advantageous domestic markets for such commodities, to minimize speculation and waste in marketing such commodities, and to encourage the organization of producers of such commodities into cooperative marketing associations.

SEC. 2. (a) A Federal Farm Board is hereby created which shall consist of the Secretary of Agriculture, who shall be a member ex officio, and 12 members, one from each of the 12 Federal land-bank districts, appointed by the President of the United States, by and with the advice and consent of the Senate, from lists of eligibles submitted by the nominating committee for the district, as hereinafter in this section provided.

(b) There is hereby established a nominating committee in each of the 12 Federal land-bank districts, to consist of seven members. Four of the members of the nominating committee in each district shall be elected by the bona fide farm organizations and cooperative associations in such district at a convention of such organizations and associations, to be held at the office of the Federal land bank in such district, or at such other place, in the city where such Federal land bank is located, to which the convention may adjourn. Two of the members of the nominating committee in each district shall be elected by a majority vote of the heads of the agricultural departments of the several States of each Federal land-bank district, at a meeting to be held in the same city and at the same time of the meeting of the convention of the bona fide farm organizations and cooperative associations in each district. One of the members of the nominating committee in each district shall be appointed by the Secretary of Agriculture. . . .

SEC. 6. (a) For the purposes of this act, cotton, wheat, corn, rice, tobacco, and swine shall be known and are referred to as "basic agricultural commodities," except that the board may, in its discretion, treat as a separate basic agricultural commodity one or more of such classes or types of tobacco as are designated in the classification of the Department of Agriculture.

(b) Whenever the board finds that the conditions of production and marketing of any other agricultural commodity are such that the provisions of this act applicable to a basic agricultural commodity should be made applicable to such other agricultural commodity, the board shall submit its report thereon to Congress.

(c) Whenever the board finds, first, that there is or may be during the ensuing year either (1) a surplus above the domestic requirements for wheat, corn, rice, tobacco, or swine, or (2) a surplus above the requirements for the orderly marketing of cotton, or of wheat, corn, rice, tobacco, or swine; and, second, that both the advisory council hereinafter created for the commodity and a substantial number of cooperative associations or other organizations representing the producers of the commodity favor the full cooperation of the board in the stabilization of the commodity, then the board shall publicly declare its findings and commence, upon a date to be fixed by the board and published in such declaration, the operations in such commodity authorized by this act: . . .

(d) During the continuance of such operations in any basic agricultural commodity, the board is authorized to enter into agreements, for the purpose of carrying out the policy declared in section 1, with any cooperative association engaged in handling the basic agricultural commodity, or with a corporation created by one or more of such cooperative associations, or with processors of the basic agricultural commodity.

(e) Such agreements may provide for (1) removing or disposing of any surplus of the basic agricultural commodity, (2) withholding such surplus, (3) insuring such commodity against undue and excessive fluctuations in market conditions, and (4) financing the purchase, storage, or sale or other disposition of the commodity. The moneys in the stabilization fund of the basic agricultural commodity shall be available for carrying out such agreements. In the case of any agreement in respect of the removal or disposal of the surplus of a basic agricultural commodity, the agreement shall provide both for the payment from the stabilization fund for the commodity of the amount of losses, costs, and charges, arising out of the purchase, storage, or sale or other disposition of the commodity or out of contracts therefor, and for the payment into the stabilization fund for the commodity of profits (after deducting all costs and charges provided for in the agreement) arising out of such purchase, storage, or sale or other disposition, or contracts therefor. In the case of agreements insuring such commodity against undue and excessive fluctuations in market conditions, the board may insure any cooperative marketing association against decline in the market price for the commodity at the time of sale by the association, from the market price for such commodity at the time of delivery to the association.

SEC. 7. (a) The board is hereby authorized and directed to create for each basic agricultural commodity an advisory council of seven members fairly representative of the producers of such commodity. . . .

SEC. 8. In order that each marketed unit of a basic agricultural commodity may contribute ratably its equitable share to the stabilization fund hereinafter established for such commodity; in order to prevent any unjust discrimination against, any direct burden or undue restraint upon, and any suppression of commerce with foreign nations in basic agricultural commodities in favor of interstate or intrastate commerce in such commodities; and in order to stabilize and regulate the current of foreign and interstate commerce in such commodities—there shall be apportioned and paid as a regulation of such commerce an equalization fee as hereinafter provided.

SEC. 9. Prior to the commencement of operations in respect of any basic agricultural commodity, and thereafter from time to time, the board shall estimate the probable advances, losses, costs, and charges to be paid in respect of the operations in such commodity. Having due regard to such estimates, the board shall from time to time determine and publish the amount for each unit of weight, measure, or value designated by it, to be collected upon such unit of such basic agricultural commodity during the operations in such commodity. Such amount is hereinafter referred to as the "equalization fee." At the time of determining and publishing an equalization fee the board shall specify the period during which it shall remain in effect, and the place and manner of its payment and collection.

SEC. 10. (a) Under such regulations as the board may prescribe there shall be paid, during operations in a basic agricultural commodity and in respect of each unit of such commodity, an equalization fee upon one of the following: the transportation, processing, or sale of such unit. . . .

(b) The board may by regulation require any person engaged in the transportation, processing, or acquisition by sale of a basic agricultural commodity—

(1) To file returns under oath and to report, in respect of his transportation, processing, or acquisition of such commodity, the amount of equalization fees payable thereon and such other facts as may be necessary for their payment or collection.

(2) To collect the equalization fee as directed by the board, and to account therefor.

(3) In the case of cotton, to issue to the producer a serial receipt for the commodity which shall be evidence of the participating interest of the producer in the equalization fund for the commodity. The board may in such case prepare and issue such receipts and prescribe the terms and conditions thereof. The Secretary of the Treasury, upon the request of the board, shall have such receipts prepared at the Bureau of Engraving and Printing.

(c) Every person who, in violation of the regulations prescribed by the board, fails to collect or account for any equalization fee shall be liable for its amount and to a penalty equal to one-half its amount. Such amount and penalty may be recovered together in a civil suit brought by the board in the name of the United States.

SEC. 11. (a) In accordance with regulations prescribed by the board, there shall be established a stabilization fund for each basic agricultural commodity. Such funds shall be administered by and exclusively under the control of the board, and the board shall have the exclusive power of expending the moneys in any such fund. There shall be deposited to the credit of the stabilization fund for a basic agricultural commodity, advances from the revolving fund hereinafter established, premiums paid for insurance under section 12, and the equalization fees and profits in connection with operations by the board in

the basic agricultural commodity or its food products. . . .

SEC. 12. (a) The board is authorized, upon such terms and conditions and in accordance with such regulations as it may prescribe, to make loans out of the revolving fund to any cooperative association engaged in the purchase, storage, or sale or other disposition of any agricultural commodity (whether or not a basic agricultural commodity) for the purpose of assisting such cooperative association in controlling the surplus of such commodity in excess of the requirements for orderly marketing.

(b) For the purpose of developing continuity of cooperative services, including unified terminal marketing facilities and equipment, the board is authorized, upon such terms and conditions and in accordance with such regulations as it may prescribe, to make loans out of the revolving fund to any cooperative association engaged in the purchase, storage, sale, or other disposition, or processing of any agricultural commodity, (1) for the purpose of assisting any such association in the acquisition, by purchase, construction, or otherwise, of facilities to be used in the storage, processing, or sale of such agricultural commodity, or (2) for the purpose of furnishing funds to such associations for necessary expenditures in federating, consolidating, or merging cooperative associations, or (3) for the purpose of furnishing to any such association funds to be used by it as capital for any agricultural credit corporation eligible for receiving rediscounts from an intermediate-credit bank. In making any such loan the board may provide for the payment of such charge, to be determined by the board from time to time, upon each unit of the commodity handled by the association, as will within a period of not more than 20 years repay the amount of such loan, together with interest thereon. The aggregate amounts loaned under this subdivision and remaining unpaid shall not exceed at any one time the sum of $25,000,000.

(c) Any loan under subdivision (a) or (b) shall bear interest at the rate of 4 per cent per annum.

(d) The board may at any time enter into a contract with any cooperative marketing association engaged in marketing any basic agricultural commodity, insuring such association for periods of 12 months against decline in the market price for such commodity at the time of sale by the association from the market price for such commodity at the time of delivery to the association. For such insurance the association shall pay such premium, to be determined by the board, upon each unit of the basic agricultural commodity reported by the association for coverage under the insurance contract, as will cover the risks of the insurance. . . .

SEC. 16. (a) There is hereby authorized to be appropriated, out of any money in the Treasury not otherwise appropriated, the sum of $250,000,000, which shall be administered by the board and used as a revolving fund, in accordance with the provisions of this act. . . .

462. COOLIDGE'S VETO OF THE McNARY–HAUGEN BILL
February 25, 1927

(*Congressional Record,* 69th Congress, 2d Session, Vol. LXVIII, p. 4771 ff.)

To the Senate:

THE conditions which Senate bill 4808 is designed to remedy have been, and still are, unsatisfactory in many cases. No one can deny that the prices of many farm products have been out of line with the general price level for several years. No one could fail to want every proper step taken to assure to agriculture a just and secure place in our economic scheme. Reasonable and constructive legislation to that end would be thoroughly justified and would have the hearty support of all who have the interests of the Nation at heart. The difficulty with this particular measure is that it is not framed to aid farmers as a whole, and it is, furthermore, calculated to injure rather than promote the general public welfare.

It is axiomatic that progress is made through building on the good foundations that already exist. For many years—indeed, from before the day of modern agricultural science—balanced and diversified farming has been regarded by thoughtful farmers and scientists as the safeguard of our agriculture. The bill under consideration throws this aside as of no consequence. It says in effect that·all the agricultural scientists and all the thinking farmers of the last 50 years are wrong, that what we ought to do is not to encourage diversified agriculture but instead put a premium on one-crop farming.

The measure discriminates definitely against products which make up what has been universally considered a program of safe farming. The bill upholds as ideals of American farming the men who grow cotton, corn, rice, swine, tobacco, or wheat, and nothing else. These are to be given special favors at the expense of the farmer who has toiled for years to build up a constructive farming enterprise to include a variety of crops and livestock that shall, so far as possible, be safe, and keep the soil, the farmer's chief asset, fertile and productive.

The bill singles out a few products, chiefly sectional, and proposes to raise the prices of those regardless of the fact that thousands of other farmers would be directly penalized. If this is a true farm-relief measure, why does it leave out the producers of beef cattle, sheep, dairy products, poultry products, potatoes, hay, fruit, vegetables, oats, barley, rye, flax, and the other important agricultural lines? So far as the farmers as a whole are concerned this measure is not for them. It is for certain groups of farmers in certain sections of the country. Can it be thought that such legislation could have the sanction of the rank and file of the Nation's farmers?

This measure provides specifically for the payment by the Federal board of all losses, costs, and charges of packers, millers, cotton spinners, or other processors who are operating under contract with the board. It contemplates that the packers may be commissioned by the Government to buy hogs enough to create a near scarcity in this country, slaughter the hogs, sell the pork products abroad at a loss, and have their losses, costs, and charges made good out of the pockets of farm taxpayers. The millers would be similarly commissioned to operate in wheat or corn and have their losses, costs, and charges paid by farm taxpayers. . . .

It seems almost incredible that the producers of hogs, corn, wheat, rice, tobacco, and cotton should be offered a scheme of legislative relief in which the only persons who are guaranteed a profit are the exporters, packers, millers, cotton spinners, and other processors.

Clearly this legislation involves government fixing of prices. It gives the proposed Federal board almost unlimited authority to fix prices on the designated commodities. This is price fixing, furthermore, on some of the Nation's basic foods and materials. Nothing is more certain than that such price fixing would upset the normal exchange relationships existing in the open market and that it would finally have to be extended to cover a multitude of other goods and services. Government price fixing, once started, has alike no justice and no end. It is an economic folly from which this country has every right to be spared.

This legislation proposes, in effect, that Congress shall delegate to a Federal Farm Board, nominated by farmers, the power to fix and collect a tax, called an equalization fee, on certain products produced by those farmers. That certainly contemplates a remarkable delegation of the taxing power. The purpose of that tax, it may be repeated, is to pay the losses incurred in the disposition of the surplus products in order to raise the price on that portion of the products consumed by our own people.

This so-called equalization fee is not a tax for purposes of revenue in the accepted sense. It is a tax for the special benefit of particular groups. As a direct tax on certain of the vital necessaries of life it represents the most vicious form of taxation. Its real effect is an employment of the coercive powers of Government to the end that certain special groups of farmers and processors may profit temporarily at the expense of other farmers and of the community at large.

The chief objection to the bill is that it would not benefit the farmer. Whatever may be the temporary influence of arbitrary interference, no one can deny that in the long run prices will be governed by the law of supply and demand. To expect to increase prices and then to maintain them on a higher level by means of a plan which must of necessity increase production while decreasing consumption, is to fly in the face of an economic law as well established as any law of nature. Experience shows that high prices in any given year mean greater acreage the next year. This does not necessarily mean a larger crop the following year, because adverse weather conditions may produce a smaller crop on a larger acreage, but in the long run a constantly increasing acreage must of necessity mean a larger average crop. . . .

A board of 12 men are granted almost unlimited control of the agricultural industry and can not only fix the price which the producers of five commodities shall receive for their goods, but can also fix the price which the consumers of the country shall pay for these commodities. The board is expected to obtain higher prices for the American farmer by removing the surplus from the home market and dumping it abroad at a below-cost price. To do this, the board is given the authority by implication to fix the domestic price level, either by means of contracts which it may make with processors or cooperatives, or by providing for the purchase of the commodities in such quantities as will bring the prices up to the point which the board may fix.

Except as it may be restrained by fear of foreign importations, the farm board, composed of representatives of producers, is given the power to fix the prices of these necessities of life at any point it sees fit. The law fixes no standards, imposes no restrictions, and requires no regulation of any kind. There could be no appeal from the arbitrary decision of these men, who would be under constant pressure from their constituents to push prices as high as possible. To expect moderation under these circumstances is to disregard experience and credit human nature with qualities it does not possess. It is not so long since the Government was spending vast sums and through the Department of Justice exerting every effort to break up combinations that were raising the cost of living to a point conceived to be excessive. This bill, if it accomplishes its purpose, will raise the price of the specified agricultural commodities to the highest possible point and in doing so the board will operate without any restraints imposed by the antitrust laws. The granting of any such arbitrary power to a Government board is to run counter to our traditions, the philosophy of our Government, the spirit of our institutions, and all principles of equity.

The administrative difficulties involved are sufficient to wreck the plan. No matter how simple an economic conception may be, its application on a large scale in the modern world is attended by infinite complexities and difficulties. The principle underlying this bill, whether fallacious or not, is simple and easy to state; but no one has outlined in definite and detailed terms how the principle is to be carried out in practice. How can the board be expected to carry out after the enactment of the law what can not even be described prior to its passage? In the meanwhile, existing channels and methods of distribution and marketing must be seriously dislocated.

This is even more apparent when we take into consideration the problem of administering the collection of the equalization fee. The bureau states that the fee will have to be collected either from the processors or the transportation companies, and dismisses as impracticable collections at the point of sale. In the case of transportation companies it points out the enormous difficulties of collecting the fee in view of the possibility of shipping commodities by unregistered vehicles. In so far as processors are concerned, it estimates the number at 6,632, without considering the number of factories engaged in the business of canning corn or manufacturing food products other than millers. Some conception of the magnitude of the task may be had when we consider that if the wheat, the corn, and the cotton crops had been under operation in the year 1925, collection would have been required from an aggregate of 16,034,466,679 units. The bureau states that it will be impossible to collect the equalization fee in full.

The bill will not succeed in providing a practical method of controlling the agricultural surplus, which lies at the heart of the whole problem. In the matter of controlling output, the farmer is at a disadvantage as compared with the manufacturer. The latter is better able to gauge his market, and in the face of falling prices can reduce production. The farmer, on the other hand, must operate over a longer period of time in producing his crops and is subject to weather conditions and disturbances in world markets which can never be known in advance. In trying to find a solution for this fundamental problem of the surplus, the present bill offers no constructive suggestion. It seeks merely to increase the prices paid by the consumer, with the inevitable result of stimulating production on the part of the farmer and decreasing consumption on the part of the public. It ignores the fact that production is curbed only by decreased, not increased, prices. In the end the equalization fee and the entire machinery provided by the bill under construction will merely aggravate conditions which are the cause of the farmer's present distress.

We must be careful in trying to help the farmer not to jeopardize the whole agricultural industry by subjecting it to the tyranny of bureaucratic regulation and control. That is what the present bill will do. But aside from all this, no man can foresee what the effect on our economic life will be of disrupting the long-established and delicately adjusted channels of commerce. That it will be far-reaching is undeniable, nor is it beyond the range of possibility that the present bill, if enacted into law, will threaten the very bases of our national prosperity, through dislocation, the slowing up of industry, and the disruption of the farmer's home market, which absorbs 90 per cent of his products. . . .

The effect of this plan will be continuously to stimulate American production and to pile up increasing surpluses beyond the world demand. We are already overproducing. It has been claimed that the plan would only be used in the emergency of occasional surplus which unduly depresses the price. No such limitations are placed in the bill. But on the other hand the definition of surplus is the "surplus over domestic requirements" and as we have had such a surplus in most of the commodities covered in the bill for 50 years and will have for years to come it means continuous action. It is said that by the automatic increase of the equalization fee to meet the increasing losses on enlarged dumping of increasing surplus that there would be restraint on production. This can prove effective only after so great an increase in production as will greatly enlarge our exports on all the commodities except cotton. With such increased surpluses dumped from the United States on to foreign markets the world prices will be broken down and with them American prices upon which the premium is based will likewise be lowered to the point of complete disaster to American farmers. It is impossible to see how this bill can work.

Several of our foreign markets have agriculture of their own to protect and they have laws in force which may be applied to dumping and we may expect reprisals from them against dumping agricultural products which will even more diminish our foreign markets.

The bill is essentially a price-fixing bill, because in practical working the board must arrive in some way at the premium price which will be demanded from the American consumer, and it must fix these prices in the contracts at which it will authorize purchases by flour millers, packers, other manufacturers, and such cooperatives as may be used, for the board must formulate a basis upon which the board will pay losses on the export of their surplus. . . .

The main policy of this bill is an entire reversal of what has been heretofore thought to be sound. Instead of undertaking to secure a method of orderly marketing which will dispose of products at a profit, it proposes to dispose of them at a loss. It runs counter to the principle of conservation, which would require us to produce only what can be done at a profit, not to waste our soil and resources producing what is to be sold at a loss to us for the benefit of the foreign consumer. It runs counter to the well-considered principle that a healthy economic condition is best maintained through a free play of competition by undertaking to permit

a legalized restraint of trade in these commodities and establish a species of monopoly under Government protection. . . . For many generations such practices have been denounced by law as repugnant to the public welfare. It can not be that they would now be found to be beneficial to agriculture.

This measure is so long and involved that it is impossible to discuss it without going into many tiresome details. Many other reasons exist why it ought not to be approved, but it is impossible to state them all without writing a book. The most decisive one is that it is not constitutional. This feature is discussed in an opinion of the Attorney General, herewith attached and made a part hereof, so that I shall not consider the details of that phase of my objections. Of course it includes some good features. Some of its provisions, intended to aid and strengthen cooperative marketing, have been borrowed from proposals that do represent the general trend of constructive thought on the agricultural problem. In this measure, however, these provisions are all completely subordinated to the main objective, which is to have the Government dispose of exportable surpluses at a loss and make some farmer taxpayers foot the bill. This is not a measure to help cooperative marketing. Its effect, on the contrary, is to eliminate the very conditions of advantage that now induce farmers to join together to regulate and improve their own business. . . .

CALVIN COOLIDGE.

463. BUCK v. BELL
274 U. S. 200
1927

Error to the Supreme Court of Appeals of State of Virginia. A statute of Virginia, March 20, 1924, provided for the sterilization of inmates of State-supported institutions who should be found to be affected with hereditary insanity.

HOLMES, J. . . . An Act of Virginia . . . recites that the health of the patient and the welfare of society may be promoted in certain cases by the sterilization of mental defectives, under careful safeguard, etc. . . . ; that the Commonwealth is supporting in various institutions many defective persons who if now discharged would become a

menace but if incapable of procreating might be discharged with safety and become self-supporting with benefit to themselves and to society. . . .

We have seen more than once that the public welfare may call upon the best citizens for their lives. It would be strange if it could not call upon those who already sap the strength of the State for these lesser sacrifices, often not felt to be such by those concerned, in order to prevent our being swamped with incompetence. It is better for all the world, if instead of waiting to execute degenerate offspring for crime, or to let them starve for their imbecility, society can prevent those who are manifestly unfit from continuing their kind. The principle that sustains compulsory vaccination is broad enough to cover cutting the Fallopian. . . . Three generations of imbeciles are enough.

But, it is said, however it might be if this reasoning were applied generally, it fails when it is confined to the small number who are in the institutions named and is not ap-plied to the multitudes outside. It is the usual last resort of constitutional arguments to point out shortcomings of this sort. But the answer is that the law does all that is needed when it does all that it can, indicates a policy, applies it to all within the lines, and seeks to bring within the lines all similarly situated so far and so fast as its means allow. . . .

Judgment affirmed. BUTLER, J., dissenting.

464. NIXON v. HERNDON (TEXAS WHITE PRIMARY CASE)
273 U. S. 536
1927

Writ of error to the district court of the United States for Western District of Texas. After Reconstruction, the Southern States resorted to a great variety of contrivances to evade the requirements of the Fifteenth Amendment. The most popular of these devices of recent years has been the expedient of excluding negroes from participation in party primaries. This exclusion is generally attained by indirection: the effort of Texas to exclude negroes from participation in the primaries of the Democratic party took the form of an express prohibition. For an excellent discussion of negro participation in politics in the South, see P. Lewinsohn, *Race, Class and Party.*

HOLMES, J. This is an action against the judges of elections for refusing to permit the plaintiff to vote at a primary election in Texas. It lays the damages at $5,000. The petition alleges that the plaintiff is a negro, a citizen of the United States and of Texas and a resident of El Paso, and in every way qualified to vote, as set forth in detail, except that the statute to be mentioned interferes with his right; that on July 26, 1924, a primary election was held at El Paso for the nomination of candidates for a senator and representatives in Congress and state and other offices, upon the Democratic ticket; that the plaintiff, being a member of the Democratic party, sought to vote, but was denied the right by defendants; that the denial was based upon a statute of Texas enacted in May, 1923, and designated article 3093a, by the words of which "in no event shall a negro be eligible to participate in a Democratic party primary election held in the state of Texas," etc., and that this statute is contrary to the 14th and 15th Amend-ments to the Constitution of the United States. The defendants moved to dismiss upon the ground that the subject matter of the suit was political and not within the jurisdiction of the court and that no violation of the Amendments was shown. The suit was dismissed and a writ of error was taken directly to this court. Here no argument was made on behalf of the defendants but a brief was allowed to be filed by the attorney general of the state. . . .

The important question is whether the statute can be sustained. But although we state it as a question the answer does not seem to us open to a doubt. We find it unnecessary to consider the 15th Amendment, because it seems to us hard to imagine a more direct and obvious infringement of the 14th. That Amendment, while it applies to all, was passed, as we know, with a special intent to protect the blacks from discrimination against them. . . . That Amendment "not only gave citizenship and the privileges of citizenship to persons of color, but it denied to any state the power to withhold from them the equal protection of the laws. . . . What is this but declaring that the law in the states shall be the same for the black as for the white; that all persons, whether colored or white, shall stand equal before the laws of the states, and, in regard to the colored race, for whose protection the Amendment was primarily designed, that no discrimination shall be made against them by law because of their color?" [*Buchanan* v. *Wailey*, 245 U.S. 60] . . . The statute of Texas, in the teeth of the prohibitions referred to, assumes to forbid negroes to take part in a primary election the importance of which we have indicated, discriminating against them by the distinction of color alone. States may do a good deal of classifying that it is difficult to believe rational, but there are limits, and it is too clear for extended argument that color cannot be made the basis of a statutory classification affecting the right set up in this case.

Judgment reversed.

465. BARTOLOMEO VANZETTI'S LAST STATEMENT IN COURT
April 9, 1927

(O. K. Fraenkel, *The Sacco-Vanzetti Case,* p. 138 ff.)

Probably no criminal case in American history attracted as much attention as did the trial of Nicola Sacco and Bartolomeo Vanzetti for the murder of Alexander Beradelli at South Braintree, Massachusetts, April 15, 1920. In the course of the trial much was made of the radical beliefs and activities of the defendants, and it was alleged that Judge Thayer had been guilty of prejudice against the defendants and of conduct unbecoming in a judge. The widespread belief that the defendants had not received a fair trial and that the conviction had been found on grounds having to do with their political doctrines and their foreign character, led to extraordinary efforts on their behalf by liberals throughout the world. After the sentence of death was imposed on the defendants, Governor Fuller was persuaded to appoint a distinguished committee, consisting of President Lowell of Harvard University, President Stratton of the M.I.T. and Judge Robert Grant, to review the case. The committee's report sustained the findings of the Court, but concluded that Judge Thayer had been guilty of a "grave breach of official decorum". The execution of Sacco and Vanzetti on August 23, 1927 was regarded by many as on a par with the execution of witches in seventeenth century Salem. The *Records* of the Trial were published in six volumes by Holt and Co.

Yes. What I say is that I am innocent, not only of the Braintree crime but also of the Bridgewater crime. That I am not only innocent of these two crimes, but in all my life I have never stole and I have never killed and I have never spilled blood. That is what I want to say. And it is not all. Not only am I innocent of these two crimes, not only in all my life I have never stole, never killed, never spilled blood, but I have struggled all my life, since I began to reason, to eliminate crime from the earth.

Everybody that knows these two arms knows very well that I did not need to go in between the street and kill a man to take the money. I can live with my two arms and live well. But besides that, I can live even without work with my arm for other people. I have had plenty of chance to live independently and to live what the world conceives to be a higher life than not to gain our bread with the sweat of our brow. . . .

Well, I want to reach a little point farther, and it is this—that not only have I not been trying to steal in Bridgewater, not only have I not been in Braintree to steal and kill and have never steal or kill or spilt blood in all my life, not only have I struggled hard against crimes, but I have refused myself the commodity or glory of life, the pride of life of a good position because in my consideration it is not right to exploit man. . . .

Now, I should say that I am not only innocent of all these things, not only have I never committed a real crime in my life—though some sins, but not crimes—not only have I struggled all my life to eliminate crimes that the official law and the official moral condemns, but also the crime that the official moral and the official law sanctions and sanctifies,—the exploitation and the oppression of the man by the man, and if there is a reason why I am here as a guilty man, if there is a reason why you in a few minutes can doom me, it is this reason and none else.

I beg your pardon. There is the more good man I ever cast my eyes upon since I lived, a man that will last and will grow always more near and more dear to the people, as far as into the heart of the people, so long as admiration for goodness and for sacrifice will last. I mean Eugene Debs. . . . He know, and not only he but every man of understanding in the world, not only in this country but also in the other countries, men that we have provided a certain amount of a record of the times, they all stick with us, the flower of mankind of Europe, the better writers, the greatest thinkers, of Europe, have pleaded in our favor. The scientists, the greatest scientists, the greatest statesmen of Europe, have pleaded in our favor. The people of foreign nations have pleaded in our favor.

Is it possible that only a few on the jury, only two or three men, who would condemn their mother for worldly honor and for earthly fortune; is it possible that they are right against what the world, the whole world has say it is wrong and that I know that it is wrong? If there is one that I should know it, if it is right or if it is wrong, it is I and this man. You see it is seven years that we are in jail. What we have suffered during those years no human tongue can say, and yet you see me before you, not trembling, you see me looking you in your eyes straight, not blushing, not changing color, not ashamed or in fear. . . .

We have proved that there could not have been another Judge on the face of the earth more prejudiced and more cruel than you have been against us. We have proved that. Still they refuse the new trial. We know, and you know in your heart, that you have been against us from the very beginning, before you see us. Before you see us you already know that we were radicals, that we were underdogs, that we were the enemy of the institution that you can believe in good faith in their goodness—I don't want to condemn that—and that it was easy on the time of the first trial to get a verdict of guiltiness.

We know that you have spoke yourself and have spoke your hostility against us, and your despisement against us with friends of yours on the train, at the University Club, of Boston, on the Golf Club of Worcester, Massachusetts. I am sure that if the people who know all what you say against us would have the civil courage to take the stand, maybe your Honor—I am sorry to say this because you are an old man, and I have an old father—but maybe you would be beside us in good justice at this time.

When you sentenced me at the Plymouth trial you say, to the best part of my memory, of my good faith, that crimes were in accordance with my principle,—something of that sort—and you take off one charge, if I remember it exactly, from the jury. The jury was so violent against me that they found me guilty of both charges, because there were only two. . . .

We were tried during a time that has now passed into history. I mean by that, a time when there was hysteria of resentment and hate against the people of our principles, against the foreigner, against slackers, and it seems to me—rather, I am positive, that both you and Mr. Katzmann has done all what it were in your power in order to work out, in order to agitate still more the passion of the juror, the prejudice of the juror, against us. . . .

Well, I have already say that I not only am not guilty of these crimes, but I never commit a crime in my life,—I have never steal and I have never kill and I have never spilt blood, and I have fought against the crime, and I have fought and I have sacrificed myself even to eliminate the crimes that the law and the church legitimate and sanctify.

This is what I say: I would not wish to a dog or to a snake, to the most low and misfortunate creature on the earth—I would not wish to any of them what I have had to suffer for things that I am not guilty of. But my conviction is that I have suffered for things that I am guilty of. I am suffering because I am a radical and indeed I am a radical; I have suffered because I was an Italian, and indeed I am an Italian; I have suffered more for my family and for my beloved than for myself; but I am so convinced to be right that if you could execute me two times, and if I could be reborn two other times, I would live again to do what I have done already. I have finished. Thank you.

466. TREATIES OF ARBITRATION AND CONCILIATION WITH GERMANY
May 5, 1928

(*United States Treaty Series*, No. 774, 775)

Article II of the Kellogg Pact provided that "the settlement of all disputes or conflicts . . . shall never be sought except by pacific means." It remained to provide the machinery by which this sentiment might be converted into reality. In December 1927 the United States submitted to France the text of a treaty for arbitration; this was ratified the following February, and the Department of State at once entered into negotiations with other powers for the conclusion of treaties of arbitration and conciliation. Unlike the traditional treaties of arbitration, these treaties made no exception for disputes involving "national honor and vital interest", though the treaty of arbitration did except disputes involving the maintenance of the Monroe Doctrine. The Treaties with Germany are given as examples of those entered into with most of the powers of the world. See references, Doc. No. 467.

1. TREATY OF ARBITRATION

The President of the United States of America and the President of the German Reich

Determined to prevent so far as in their power lies any interruption in the peaceful relations now happily existing between the two nations;

Desirous of reaffirming their adherence to the policy of submitting to impartial decision all justiciable controversies that may arise between them; and

Eager by their example not only to demonstrate their condemnation of war as an instrument of national policy in their mutual relations, but also to hasten the time when the perfection of international arrangements for the pacific settlement of international disputes shall have eliminated forever the possibility of war among any of the powers of the world;

Have decided to conclude a treaty of arbitration and for that purpose they have appointed as their respective plenipotentiaries

The President of the United States of America, Frank B. Kellogg, Secretary of State of the United States, and

The President of the German Reich, Herr Friedrich von Prittwitz und Gaffron, German Ambassador to the United States of America:

Who, having communicated to one another their full powers found in good and due form, have agreed upon the following articles:

ART. I. All differences relating to international matters in which the high contracting parties are concerned by virtue of a claim of right made by one against the other under treaty or otherwise, which it has not been possible to adjust by diplomacy, which have not been adjusted as a result of reference to an appropriate commission of conciliation, and which are justiciable in their nature by reason of being susceptible of decision by the application of the principles of law or equity, shall be submitted to the Permanent Court of Arbitration established at The Hague by the convention of October 18, 1907, or to some other competent tribunal, as shall be decided in each case by special agreement, which special agreement shall provide for the organization of such tribunal if necessary, define its powers, state the question or questions at issue, and settle the terms of reference.

The special agreement in each case shall be made on the part of the United States of America by the President of the United States of America by and with the advice and consent of the Senate thereof, and on the part of Germany in accordance with its constitutional laws.

ART. II. The provisions of this treaty shall not be invoked in respect of any dispute the subject matter of which

(a) is within the domestic jurisdiction of either of the high contracting parties,

(b) involves the interests of third parties.

(c) depends upon or involves the maintenance of the traditional attitude of the United States concerning American questions, commonly described as the Monroe doctrine,

(d) depends upon or involves the observance of the obligations of Germany in accordance with the Covenant of the League of Nations.

ART. III. The present treaty shall be ratified by the President of the United States of America by and with the advice and consent of the Senate thereof and by the President of the German Reich in accordance with German constitutional laws.

The ratifications shall be exchanged at Washington as soon as possible, and the treaty shall take effect on the date of the exchange of the ratifications. It shall thereafter remain in force continuously unless and until terminated by one year's written notice given by either high contracting party to the other.

In faith whereof the respective plenipotentiaries have signed this treaty in duplicate in the English and German languages, both texts having equal force, and hereunto affix their seals.

Done at Washington the fifth day of May in the year of our Lord one thousand nine hundred and twenty-eight.

FRANK B. KELLOGG,
F. VON PRITTWITZ.

2. TREATY OF CONCILIATION

The President of the United States of America and the President of the German Reich, being desirous to strengthen the bonds of amity that bind them together and also to advance the cause of general peace, have resolved to enter into a treaty for that purpose, and have agreed upon and concluded the following articles:

ART. I. Any disputes arising between the Government of the United States of America and the Government of Germany, of whatever nature they may be, shall, when ordinary diplomatic proceedings have failed and the high contracting parties do not have recourse to adjudication by a competent tribunal, be submitted for investigation and report to a permanent International Commission constituted in the manner prescribed in the next succeeding article; the high contracting parties agree not to declare war or begin hostilities during such investigation and before the report is submitted.

ART. II. The International Commission shall be composed of five members, to be appointed as follows: One member shall be chosen from each country, by the Government thereof; one member shall be chosen by each Government from some third country; the fifth member shall be chosen by common agreement between the two Governments, it being understood that he shall not be a citizen of either country. The expenses of the Commission shall be paid by the two Governments in equal proportions.

The International Commission shall be appointed within six months after the exchange of ratifications of this treaty; and vacancies shall be filled according to the manner of the original appointment.

ART. III. In case the high contracting parties shall have failed to adjust a dispute by diplomatic methods, and they do not have recourse to adjudication by a competent tribunal, they shall at once refer it to the International Commission for investigation and report. The International Commission may, however, spontaneously by unanimous agreement offer its services to that effect, and in such case it shall notify both Governments and request their cooperation in the investigation.

The high contracting parties agree to furnish the Permanent International Commission with all the means and facilities required for its investigation and report.

The report of the commission shall be completed within one year after the date on which it shall declare its investigation to have begun, unless the high contracting parties shall shorten or extend the time by mutual agreement. The report shall be prepared in triplicate; one copy shall be presented to each Government, and the third retained by the commission for its files.

The high contracting parties reserve the right to act independently on the subject matter of the dispute after the report of the commission shall have been submitted. . . .

Washington the fifth of May one thousand nine hundred and twenty-eight.

FRANK B. KELLOGG.
F. VON PRITTWITZ.

467. THE KELLOGG PEACE PACT
August 27, 1928

(U. S. Statutes at Large, Vol. XXXXVI, p. 2343)

In June, 1927, Aristide Briand proposed to the United States government a treaty outlawing war between France and the United States. Secretary of State Kellogg proposed to broaden the pact to embrace all nations. In April, 1928, notes were forwarded to the major European powers requesting their adherence to the pact, and August 27 the pact was signed by fifteen powers: subsequently sixty-two nations adhered to the agreement. The Treaty was introduced to the Senate December 4, 1928, and passed with only one dissenting vote—that of Senator Blaine of Wisconsin. See, D. P. Myers, *Origin and Conclusion of the Paris Pact;* D. H. Miller, *The*

Peace Pact of Paris; A. J. Toynbee, *Survey of International Relations, 1928,* Part I.

The President of the German Reich, the President of the United States of America, His Majesty the King of the Belgians, the President of the French Republic, His Majesty the King of Great Britain, Ireland and the British Dominions beyond the Seas, Emperor of India, His Majesty the King of Italy, His Majesty the Emperor of Japan, the President of the Republic of Poland, the President of the Czechoslovak Republic,

Deeply sensible of their solemn duty to promote the welfare of mankind;

Persuaded that the time has come when a frank renunciation of war as an instrument of national policy should be made to the end that the peaceful and friendly relations now existing between their peoples may be perpetuated;

Convinced that all changes in their relations with one another should be sought only by pacific means and be the result of a peaceful and orderly process, and that any signatory power which shall hereafter seek to promote its national interests by resort to war should be denied the benefits furnished by this treaty;

Hopeful that, encouraged by their example, all the other nations of the world will join in this humane endeavor and by adhering to the present treaty as soon as it comes into force bring their peoples within the scope of its beneficent provisions, thus uniting the civilized nations of the world in a common renunciation of war as an instrument of their national policy;

Have decided to conclude a treaty and for that purpose have appointed as their respective plenipotentiaries: . . .

Who, having communicated to one another their full powers found in good and due form have agreed upon the following articles:

ART. 1. The high contracting parties solemnly declare in the names of their respective peoples that they condemn recourse to war for the solution of international controversies, and renounce it as an instrument of national policy in their relations with one another.

ART. 2. The high contracting parties agree that the settlement or solution of all disputes or conflicts of whatever nature or of whatever origin they may be, which may arise among them, shall never be sought except by pacific means.

ART. 3. The present treaty shall be ratified by the high contracting parties named in the preamble in accordance with their respective constitutional requirements, and shall take effect as between them as soon as all their several instruments of ratification shall have been deposited at Washington.

This treaty shall, when it has come into effect as prescribed in the preceding paragraph, remain open as long as may be necessary for adherence by all the other powers of the world. Every instrument evidencing the adherence of a power shall be deposited at Washington and the treaty shall immediately upon such deposit become effective as between the power thus adhering and the other powers parties hereto. . . .

468. THE PHILOSOPHY OF RUGGED INDIVIDUALISM

Speech by Herbert Hoover, New York City
October 22, 1928

(The New Day. Campaign Speeches of Herbert Hoover, p. 149 ff.)

With this speech Hoover closed his campaign for the Presidency in 1928. It expresses the philosophy not only of Hoover, but of the Republican party in the years after the World War. For the campaign, see, R. V. Peel and T. C. Donnelly, *The 1928 Campaign: An Analysis.* For an earlier exposition of the doctrines herein announced, see H. Hoover, *American Individualism; The Challenge to Liberty.*

This campaign now draws near a close. The platforms of the two parties defining principles and offering solutions of various national problems have been presented and are being earnestly considered by our people. . . .

In my acceptance speech I endeavored to outline the spirit and ideals by which I would be guided in carrying that platform into administration. Tonight I will not deal with the multitude of issues which have been already well canvassed. I intend rather to discuss some of those more fundamental principles and ideals upon which I believe the government of the United States should be conducted. . . .

After the war, when the Republican party assumed administration of the country, we were faced with the problem of determination of the very nature of our national life. During one hundred and fifty years we have builded up a form of self-government and a social system which is peculiarly our own. It differs essentially from all others in the world. It is the American system. It is just as definite and positive a political and social system as has ever been developed on earth. It is founded upon a particular conception of self-government in which decentralized local responsibility is the very base. Further than this, it is founded upon the conception that only through ordered liberty, freedom, and equal opportunity to the individual will his initiative and enterprise spur on the march of progress. And in our insistence upon equality of opportunity has our system advanced beyond all the world.

During the war we necessarily turned to the government to solve every difficult economic problem. The government having absorbed every energy of our people for war, there was no other solution. For the preservation of the state the Federal Government became a centralized despotism which undertook unprecedented responsibilities, assumed autocratic powers, and took over the business of citizens. To a large degree we regimented our whole people temporarily into a socialistic state. However justified in time of war if continued in peace-time it would destroy not only our American system but with it our progress and freedom as well.

When the war closed, the most vital of all issues both in our own country and throughout the world was whether governments should continue their wartime ownership and operation of many instrumentalities of production and distribution. We were challenged with a peace-time choice between the American system of rugged individualism and a European philosophy of diametrically opposed doctrines—doctrines of paternalism and state socialism. The acceptance of these ideas would have meant the destruction of self-government through centralization of government. It would have meant the undermining of the individual initiative and enterprise through which our people have grown to unparalleled greatness.

The Republican Party from the beginning resolutely turned its face away from these ideas and these war practices. . . . When the Republican Party came into full power it went at once resolutely back to our fundamental conception of the state and the rights and responsibilities of the individual. Thereby it restored confidence and hope in the American people, it freed and stimulated enterprise, it restored the government to its position as an umpire instead of a player in the economic game. For these reasons the American people have gone forward in progress while the rest of the world has halted, and some countries have even gone backwards. If anyone will study the causes of retarded recuperation in Europe, he will find much of it due to stifling of private initiative on one hand, and overloading of the government with business on the other.

There has been revived in this campaign, however, a series of proposals which, if adopted, would be a long step toward the abandonment of our American system and a surrender to the destructive operation of governmental conduct of commercial business. Because the country is faced with difficulty and doubt over certain national problems—that is prohibition, farm relief, and electrical power—our opponents propose that we must thrust government a long way into the businesses which give rise to these problems. In effect, they abandon the tenets of their own party and turn to state socialism as a solution for the difficulties presented by all three. It is proposed that we shall change from prohibition to the state purchase and sale of liquor. If their agricultural relief program means anything, it means that the government shall directly or indirectly buy and sell and fix prices of agricultural products. And we are to go into the hydroelectric power business. In other words, we are confronted with a huge program of government in business.

There is, therefore, submitted to the American people a question of fundamental principle. That is: shall we depart from the principles of our American political and economic system, upon which we have advanced beyond all the rest of the world, in order to adopt methods based on principles destructive of its very foundations? And I wish to emphasize the seriousness of these proposals. I wish to make my position clear; for this goes to the very roots of American life and progress.

I should like to state to you the effect that this projection of government in business would have upon our system of self-government and our economic system. That effect would reach to the daily life of every man and woman. It would impair the very basis of liberty and freedom not only for those left outside the fold of expanded bureaucracy but for those embraced within it.

Let us first see the effect upon self-government. When the Federal Government undertakes to go into commercial business it must at once set up the organization and administration of that business, and it immediately finds itself in a labyrinth, every alley of which leads to the destruction of self-government.

Commercial business requires a concentration of responsibility. Self-government requires decentralization and many checks and balances to safeguard liberty. Our Government to succeed in business would need to become in effect a despotism. There at once begins the destruction of self-government. . . .

It is a false liberalism that interprets itself into the government operation of commercial business. Every step of bureaucratizing of the business of our country poisons the very roots of liberalism—that is, political equality, free speech, free assembly, free press, and equality of opportunity. It is the road not to more liberty, but to less liberty. Liberalism should be found not striving to spread bureaucracy but striving to set bounds to it. True liberalism seeks all legitimate freedom first in the confident belief that without such freedom the pursuit of all other blessings and benefits is vain. That belief is the foundation of all American progress, political as well as economic.

Liberalism is a force truly of the spirit, a force proceeding from the deep realization that economic freedom cannot be sacrificed if political freedom is to be preserved. Even if Governmental conduct of business could give us more efficiency instead of less efficiency, the fundamental objection to it would remain unaltered and unabated. It would destroy political equality. It would increase rather than decrease abuse and corruption. It would stifle initiative and invention. It would undermine the development of leadership. It would cramp and cripple the mental and spiritual energies of our people. It would extinguish equality and opportunity. It would dry up the spirit of liberty and progress. For these reasons primarily it must be resisted. For a hundred and fifty years liberalism has found its true spirit in the American system, not in the European systems.

I do not wish to be misunderstood in this statement. I am defining a general policy. It does not mean that our government is to part with one iota of its national resources without complete protection to the public interest. I have already stated that where the government is engaged in public works for purposes of flood control, of navigation, of irrigation, of scientific research or national defense, or in pioneering a new art, it will at times necessarily produce power or commodities as a by-product. But they must be a by-product of the major purpose, not the major purpose itself.

Nor do I wish to be misinterpreted as believing that the United States is free-for-all and devil-take-the-hindmost. The very essence of equality of opportunity and of American individualism is that there shall be no domination by any group or combination in this republic, whether it be business or political. On the contrary, it demands economic justice as well as political and social justice. It is no system of laissez faire.

I feel deeply on this subject because during the war I had some practical experience with governmental operation and control. I have witnessed not only at home but abroad the many failures of government in business. I have seen its tyrannies, its injustices, its destructions of self-government, its undermining of the very instincts which carry our people forward to progress. I have witnessed the lack of advance, the lowered standards of living, the depressed spirits of people working under such a system. My objection is based not upon theory or upon a failure to recognize wrong or abuse, but I know the adoption of such methods would strike at the very roots of American life and would destroy the very basis of American progress.

Our people have the right to know whether we can continue to solve our great problems without abandonment of our American system. I know we can. . . .

And what have been the results of the American system? Our country has become the land of opportunity to those born without inheritance, not merely because of the wealth of its resources and industry but because of this freedom of initiative and enterprise. Russia has natural resources equal to ours. Her people are equally industrious, but she has not had the blessings of one hundred and fifty years of our form of government and our social system.

By adherence to the principles of decentralized self-government, ordered liberty, equal opportunity, and freedom to the individual, our American experiment in human welfare has yielded a degree of well-being unparalleled in all the world. It has come nearer to the abolition of poverty, to the abolition of fear of want, than humanity has ever reached before. Progress of the past seven years is the proof of it. This alone furnishes the answer to our opponents, who ask us to introduce destructive elements into the system by which this has been accomplished. . . .

I have endeavored to present to you that the greatness of America has grown out of a political and social system and a method of control of economic forces distinctly its own —our American system—which has carried this great experiment in human welfare farther than ever before in all history. We are nearer today to the ideal of the abolition of poverty and fear from the lives of men and women than ever before in any land. And I again repeat that the departure from our American system by injecting principles destructive to it which our opponents propose, will jeopardize the very liberty and freedom of our people, and will destroy equality of opportunity not alone to ourselves but to our children. . . .

469. THE STIMSON DOCTRINE

Address by Secretary of State Stimson before the Council on Foreign Relations
February 6, 1931

(W. Lippmann and W. O. Scroggs, eds. *The United States in World Affairs,* 1931, p. 332 ff.)

President Wilson had attempted to establish moral standards as a test for recognition of new governments in foreign states. This policy had involved the United States in no little embarrassment and difficulty in dealing with Latin American countries. It was abandoned by the Hoover administration, and the abandonment formalized in this statement by Secretary Stimson. President Roosevelt has followed the Stimson rather than the Wilson policy in his dealings with foreign nations.

. . . The practice of this country as to the recognition of new governments has been substantially uniform from the days of the administration of Secretary of State Jefferson in 1792 to the days of Secretary of State Bryan in 1913. There were certain slight departures from this policy during the Civil War, but they were manifestly due to the exigencies of warfare and were abandoned immediately afterwards. This general policy, as thus observed, was to base the act of recognition not upon the question of the constitutional legitimacy of the new government but upon its *de facto* capacity to fulfill its obligations as a member of the family of nations. This country recognized the right of other nations to regulate their own internal affairs of government and disclaimed any attempt to base its recognition upon the correctness of their constitutional action.

Said Mr. Jefferson in 1792:

We certainly cannot deny to other nations that principle whereon our own Government is founded, that every nation has a right to govern itself internally under what forms it pleases, and to change these forms at its own will; and externally to transact business with other nations through whatever organ it chooses, whether that be a king, convention, assembly, committee, president, or whatever it be.

In these essentials our practice corresponded with the practice of the other nations of the world.

The particular considerations upon which our action was regularly based were well stated by Mr. Adee, long the trusted Assistant Secretary of State of this Government, as follows:

Ever since the American Revolution entrance upon diplomatic intercourse with foreign states has been *de facto,* dependent upon the existence of three conditions of fact: the control of the administrative machinery of the state; the general acquiescence of its people; and the ability and willingness of their government to discharge international and conventional obligations. The form of government has not been a conditional factor in such recognition; in other words, the *de jure* element of legitimacy of title has been left aside.

With the advent of President Wilson's administration this policy of over a century was radically departed from in respect to the Republic of Mexico, and, by a public declaration on March 11, 1913, it was announced that

Cooperation (with our sister republics of Central and South America) is possible only when supported at every turn by the orderly processes of just government based upon law, not upon arbitrary or irregular force. We hold, as I am sure that all thoughtful leaders of republican government everywhere hold, that just government rests always upon the consent of the governed, and that there can be no freedom without order based upon law and upon the public conscience and approval. We shall look to make these principles the basis of mutual intercourse, respect, and helpfulness between our sister republics and ourselves.

Mr. Wilson's government sought to put this new policy into effect in respect to the recognition of the then Government of Mexico held by President Victoriano Huerta. Although Huerta's government was in *de facto* possession, Mr. Wilson refused to recognize it, and he sought through the influence and pressure of his great office to force it from power. Armed conflict followed with the forces of Mexico, and disturbed relations between us and that republic lasted until a comparatively few years ago.

In his sympathy for the development of free constitutional institutions among the people of our Latin American neighbors, Mr. Wilson did not differ from the feelings of the great mass of his countrymen in the United States . . . but he differed from the practice of his predecessors in seeking actively to propagate these institutions in a foreign country by the direct influence of this Government and to do this against the desires of the authorities and people of Mexico.

The present administration has declined to follow the policy of Mr. Wilson and has followed consistently the former practice of this Government since the days of Jefferson. As soon as it was reported to us, through our diplomatic representatives, that the new governments in Bolivia, Peru, Argentina, Brazil, and Panama were in control of the administrative machinery of the state, with the apparent general acquiescence of their people, and that they were willing and apparently able to discharge their international and conventional obligations, they were recognized by our Government. And, in view of the economic depression, with the consequent need for prompt measures of financial stabilization, we did this with as little delay as possible in order to give those sorely pressed countries the quickest possible opportunities for recovering their economic poise.

470. HOOVER'S VETO OF THE MUSCLE SHOALS BILL
Message to the Senate, March 3, 1931

(Message from the President of the United States, Government Printing Office)

In 1918 President Wilson had authorized, as a wartime measure, the construction of government plants at Muscle Shoals on the Tennessee River for the manufacture of nitrates, and of dams to generate electric power. After the war the disposition of these plants and dams became a matter of prolonged and bitter controversy. Conservatives insisted that they be turned over to private companies; progressives under the leadership of Senator Norris of Nebraska advocated government ownership and operation. Henry Ford at one time offered to take over the plants, but no satisfactory arrangement could be made. In 1928 a bill providing for government operation passed Congress only to be vetoed by President Coolidge. A similar bill of 1931 was vetoed by President Hoover: the veto message reiterated the Republican doctrine of individualism in business and the belief that government ownership and operation was an approach to socialism. For the ultimate settlement of the question, see Doc. No. 478.

To the Senate:

I return herewith, without my approval, Senate Joint Resolution 49, "To provide for the national defense by the creation of a corporation for the operation of the Government properties at and near Muscle Shoals in the State of Alabama; to authorize the letting of the Muscle Shoals properties under certain conditions; and for other purposes."

This bill proposes the transformation of the war plant at Muscle Shoals, together with important expansions, into a permanently operated Government institution for the production and distribution of power and the manufacture of fertilizers. . . .

The plants at Muscle Shoals were originally built for a production of nitrates for use in war explosives. I am advised by the War Department that the very large development in the United States by private enterprise in the manufacture of synthetic nitrogen now affords an ample supply covering any possible requirements of war. It is therefore unnecessary to maintain this plant for any such purposes.

This bill provides that the President for a period of 12 months may negotiate a lease of the nitrate plants for fertilizer manufacture under detailed limitations, but in failure to make such a lease the bill makes it mandatory upon the Government to manufacture nitrogen fertilizers at Muscle Shoals by the employment of existing facilities or by modernizing existing plants or by any other process. . . .

I am firmly opposed to the Government entering into any business the major purpose of which is competition with our citizens. There are national emergencies which require that the Government should temporarily enter the field of business, but they must be emergency actions and in matters where the cost of the project is secondary to much higher considerations. There are many localities where the Federal Government is justified in the construction of great dams and reservoirs, where navigation, flood control, reclamation or stream regulation are of dominant importance, and where they are beyond the capacity or purpose of private or local government capital to construct. In these cases power is often a by-product and should be disposed of by contract or lease. But for the Federal Government deliberately to go out to build up and expand an occasion to the major purpose of a power and manufacturing business is to break down the initiative and enterprise of the American people; it is destruction of equality of opportunity of our people; it is the negation of the ideals upon which our civilization has been based.

This bill raises one of the important issues confronting our people. That is squarely the issue of Federal Government ownership and operation of power and manufacturing business not as a minor by-product but as a major purpose. Involved in this question is the agitation against the conduct of the power industry. The power problem is not to be solved by the project in this bill. The remedy for abuses in the conduct of that industry lies in regulation and not by the Federal Government entering upon the business itself. I have recommended to the Congress on various occasions that action should be taken to establish Federal regulation of interstate power in cooperation with State authorities. This bill would launch the Federal Government upon a policy of ownership and operation of power utilities upon a basis of competition instead of by the proper Government function of regulation for the protection of all the people. I hesitate to contemplate the future of our institutions, of our country if the preoccupation of its officials is to be no longer the promotion of justice and equal opportunity but is to be devoted to barter in the markets. That is not liberalism, it is degeneration.

This proposal can be effectively opposed upon other and perhaps narrower grounds. The establishment of a Federal-operated power business and fertilizer factory in the Tennessee Valley means Federal control from Washington with all the vicissitudes of national politics and the tyrannies of remote bureaucracy imposed upon the people of that valley without voice by them in their own resources, the overriding of State and local government, the undermining of State and local responsibility. The very history of this project over the past 10 years should be a complete demonstration of the ineptness of the Federal Government to administer such enterprise and of the penalties which the local community suffers under it.

This bill distinctly proposes to enter the field of powers reserved to the States. It would deprive the adjacent States of the right to control rates for this power and would deprive them of taxes on property within their borders and would invade and weaken the authority of local government. . . .

The real development of the resources and the industries of the Tennessee Valley can only be accomplished by the people in that valley themselves. Muscle Shoals can only be administered by the people upon the ground, responsible to their own communities, directing them solely for the benefit of their communities and not for purposes of pursuit of social theories or national politics. Any other course deprives them of liberty. . . .

HERBERT HOOVER.

471. THE MOONEY–BILLINGS CASE

Conclusions of the sub-committee of the Section on Lawless Enforcement of Law
of the Wickersham Committee
June, 1931

(The Mooney-Billings Report, Suppressed by the Wickersham Committee, p. 242-3)

On July 22, 1916, a bomb was thrown into a Preparedness parade in San Francisco, killing nine and wounding some forty people. Two days later a Bomb Squad was organized and promptly arrested Thomas Mooney, a labor agitator, his wife, Rena Mooney, Warren K. Billings, a machinist, E. D. Nolan, a labor leader, and Israel Weinberg, a jitney driver, and charged them with the crime. The Grand Jury returned indictments against each of the prisoners for murder. Subsequently the charges against all but Mooney and Billings were dismissed. These two were convicted of murder in the first degree; Billings was sentenced to life imprisonment and Mooney to death. In view of the character of the trial and certain doubts as to the justice of the conviction, President Wilson in September 1917 requested the Mediation Commission to investigate the case. The Commission reported the following January that there was a basis for the feeling that an injustice was done the prisoners and recommended that the President intercede on behalf of the prisoners with the Governor of California. Wilson wrote three letters to the Governor, and eventually the sentence of Mooney was commuted to life imprisonment. The case became a *cause célèbre* and attracted world wide attention. Ceaseless efforts of various groups in the United States to re-open the case or to secure a pardon from the executive of California were without avail. In 1931 a sub-committee of the Wickersham Committee on Law Observance and Enforcement, consisting of Professor Z. Chafee, W. H. Pollack and C. S. Stern, made an extensive report on the Mooney-Billings Case. This Report was not published along with the other reports of the Wickersham Committee, because the Committee felt that it was not proper to inquire into particular cases but only into general principles. Allusions to the Mooney-Billings Report, however, brought a demand for a publication of the document, and when Congress failed to provide for publication it was privately printed. The Wickersham Committee *Report* is in 71 Congress, 2d Session, *House Doc.* No. 252, 14 parts. On the Mooney-Billings Case see also H. T. Hart, *The Case of Thomas J. Mooney and Warren K. Billings: Abstract and Analysis of record before Governor Young of California;* E. J. Hopkins, *What Happened in the Mooney Case.* See also, A. G. Hays, *Trial by Prejudice;* E. M. Borchard, *Convicting the Innocent.*

CONCLUSIONS

Considering the records as a whole, we conclude:

(1) There was never any scientific attempt made, by either the police or the prosecution to discover the perpetrators of the crime. The investigation was in reality turned over to a private detective who used his position to cause the arrest of the defendants. The police investigation was reduced to a hunt for evidence to convict the arrested defendants.

(2) There were flagrant violations of the statutory laws of California by both the police and the prosecution in the manner in which the defendants were arrested and held incommunicado and in the subsequent search of their homes to procure evidence against them.

(3) After the arrest of the defendants, witnesses were brought to the jails to "identify" them, and their "identifications" were accepted by the police and the prosecution, despite the fact that these witnesses were never required to pick the defendants out of a line-up, or to demonstrate their accuracy by any other test.

(4) Immediately after the arrests of the defendants there commenced a deliberate attempt to arouse public prejudice against them, by a series of almost daily interviews given to the press by prosecuting officials.

(5) Witnesses were procured at the trials with information in the hands of the prosecution that seriously challenged the credibility of the witnesses, but this information was deliberately concealed.

(6) Witnesses were permitted to testify at the trials, despite such knowledge in the possession of the prosecution of prior contradictory stories told by these witnesses as to make their mere reproduction a vouching for perjured testimony.

(7) Witnesses were coached in their testimony to a degree that approximated subornation of perjury. There is a strong inference that some of this coaching was done by prosecuting officials, and other evidence points to knowledge by the prosecuting officials that such coaching was being practiced on other witnesses.

(8) The prejudice against the defendants, stimulated by newspaper publicity, was further appealed to at the trials by unfair and intemperate arguments to the jury in the opening and closing statements of the prosecuting attorneys.

(9) After the trials, the disclosures casting doubt on the justice of the convictions were minimized, and every attempt made to defeat the liberation of the defendants, by a campaign of misrepresentation and propaganda carried on by the officials who had prosecuted them.

472. NEW STATE ICE COMPANY v. LIEBMANN
285 U. S. 262
1932

Appeal from the United States Circuit Court of Appeals for the Tenth District. An act of the Oklahoma Legislature, 1925, declared that the manufacture, sale, and distribution of ice is a public business, that no one shall be permitted to manufacture, sell or distribute ice within the State without a license, and that the Corporation Commission in granting a license shall take into consideration the necessity for the manufacture, etc. of ice at the place desired, the extent to which the community was already equipped with such facilities, the responsibility, reliability, and capacity of the persons or corporation applying for the license to furnish facilities, conveniences, and services to the public. One Liebmann set up an ice plant in Oklahoma City, without having first obtained a license, and the New State Ice Company, operating under a license, sought to enjoin him from doing business in Oklahoma City. The Circuit Court dismissed the bill.

SUTHERLAND, J. . . . It must be conceded that all businesses are subject to some measure of public regulation. And that the business of manufacturing, selling, or distributing ice, like that of the grocer, the dairyman, the butcher, or the baker, may be subjected to appropriate regulations in the interest of public health cannot be doubted; but the question here is whether the business is so charged with a public use as to justify the particular restriction above stated. If this legislative restriction be within the constitutional power of the state Legislature, it follows that the license or permit, issued to appellant, constitutes a franchise, to which a court of equity will afford protection against one who seeks to carry on the same business without obtaining from the commission a license or permit to do so. . . . In that view, engagement in the business is a privilege to be exercised only in virtue of a public grant, and not a common right to be exercised independently by any competent person conformably to reasonable regulations equally applicable to all who choose to engage therein. . . .

Here we are dealing with an ordinary business, not with a paramount industry, upon which the prosperity of the state in large measure depends. It is a business as essentially private in its nature as the business of the grocer, the dairyman, the butcher, the baker, the shoemaker, or the tailor, each of whom performs a service which, to a greater or less extent, the community is dependent upon and is interested in having maintained; but which bears no such relation to the public as to warrant its inclusion in the category of businesses charged with a public use. It may be quite true that in Oklahoma ice is, not only an article of prime necessity, but indispensable; but certainly not more so than food or clothing or the shelter of a home. . . .

Plainly, a regulation which has the effect of denying or unreasonably curtailing the common right to engage in a lawful private business, such as that under review, cannot be upheld consistent with the Fourteenth Amendment. Under that amendment nothing is more clearly settled than that it is beyond the power of a state "under the guise of protecting the public, arbitrarily to interfere with private business or prohibit lawful occupations or impose unreasonable and unnecessary restrictions upon them." . . .

The particular requirement before us was evidently not imposed to prevent a practical monopoly of the business, since its tendency is quite to the contrary. Nor is it a case of the protection of natural resources. There is nothing in the product that we can perceive on which to rest a distinction, in respect of this attempted control, from other products in common use which enter into free competition, subject, of course, to reasonable regulations prescribed for the protection of the public and applied with appropriate impartiality.

And it is plain that unreasonable or arbitrary interference or restrictions cannot be saved from the condemnation of that amendment merely by calling them experimental. It is not necessary to challenge the authority of the states to indulge in experimental legislation; but it would be strange and unwarranted doctrine to hold that they may do so by enactments which transcend the limitations imposed on them by the Federal Constitution. The principle is imbedded in our constitutional system that there are certain essentials of liberty with which the state is not entitled to dispense in the interests of experiments. . . .

Judgment affirmed

BRANDEIS, J., dissenting. . . . In my opinion the judgment should be reversed.

First. The Oklahoma statute makes entry into the business of manufacturing ice for sale and distribution dependent, in effect, upon a certificate of public convenience and necessity. Such a certificate was unknown to the common law. It is a creature of the machine age, in which plants have displaced tools and businesses are substituted for trades. The purpose of requiring it is to promote the public interest by preventing waste. Particularly in those businesses in which interest and depreciation charges on plant constitute a large element in the cost of production, experience has taught that the financial burdens incident to unnecessary duplication of facilities are likely to bring high rates and poor service. . . . The introduction in the United States of the certificate of public convenience and necessity marked the growing conviction that under certain circumstances free competition might be harmful to the community, and that, when it was so, absolute freedom to enter the business of one's choice should be denied.

Long before the enactment of the Oklahoma statute here challenged, a like requirement had become common in the United States in some lines of business. . . . As applied to public utilities, the validity under the Fourteenth Amendment of the requirement of the certificate has never been successfully questioned.

Second. Oklahoma declared the business of manufacturing ice for sale and distribution a "public-business"; that is, a public utility. . . . But the conception of a public utility is not static. The welfare of the community may require that the business of supplying ice be made a public utility, as well as the business of supplying water or any other necessary commodity or service. If the business is, or can be made, a public utility, it must be possible to make the issue of a certificate a prerequisite to engaging in it.

Whether the local conditions are such as to justify converting a private business into a public one is a matter primarily for the determination of the state Legislature. . . .

. . . Liebmann rests his defense upon the broad claim that the Federal Constitution gives him the right to enter the business of manufacturing ice for sale even if his doing so be found by the properly constituted authority to be inconsistent with the public welfare. He claims that, whatever the local conditions may demand, to confer upon the commission power to deny that right is an unreasonable, arbitrary, and capricious restraint upon his liberty.

The function of the court is primarily to determine whether the conditions in Oklahoma are such that the Legislature could not reasonably conclude (1) that the public welfare required treating the manufacture of ice for sale and distribution as a "public business"; and (2) that, in order to insure to the inhabitants of some communities an adequate supply of ice at reasonable rates, it was necessary to give the commission power to exclude the establishment of an additional ice plant in places where the community was already well served. Unless the Court can say that the Federal Constitution confers an absolute right to engage anywhere in the business of manufacturing ice for sale, it cannot properly decide that the legislators acted unreasonably without first ascertaining what was the experience of Oklahoma in respect to the ice business. . . .

Can it be said in the light of these facts that it was not an appropriate exercise of legislative discretion to authorize the commission to deny a license to enter the business in localities where necessity for another plant did not exist? The need of some remedy for the evil of destructive competition, where competition existed, had been and was widely felt. Where competition did not exist, the propriety of public regulation had been proven. Many communities were not supplied with ice at all. The particular remedy adopted was not enacted hastily. The statute was based upon a long-established state policy recognizing the public importance of the ice business, and upon 17 years' legislative and administrative experience in the regulation of it. The advisability of treating the ice business as a public utility and of applying to it the certificate of convenience and necessity had been under consideration for many years. Similar legislation had been enacted in Oklahoma under similar circumstances with respect to other public services. The measure bore a substantial relation to the evils found to exist. Under these circumstances, to hold the act void as being unreasonable would, in my opinion, involve the exercise, not of the function of judicial review, but the function of a super-Legislature. . . .

A regulation valid for one kind of business may, of course, be invalid for another, since the reasonableness of every regulation is dependent upon the relevant facts. But so far as concerns the power to regulate, there is no difference, in essence, between a business called private and one called a public utility or said to be "affected with a public interest." . . . The notion of a distinct category of business "affected with a public interest," employing property "devoted to a public use," rests upon historical error. The consequences which it is sought to draw from those phrases are belied by the meaning in which they were first used centuries ago, and by the decision of this Court, in *Munn* v. *Illinois,* 94 U.S. 113, which first introduced them into the law of the Constitution. In my opinion, the true principle is that the state's power extends to every regulation of any business reasonably required and appropriate for the public protection. I find in the due process clause no other limitation upon the character or the scope of regulation permissible. . . .

The people of the United States are now confronted with an emergency more serious than war. Misery is widespread, in a time, not of scarcity, but of overabundance. The long-continued depression has brought unprecedented unemployment, a catastrophic fall in commodity prices, and a volume of economic losses which threatens our financial institutions. . . . But rightly or wrongly, many persons think that one of the major contributing causes has been unbridled competition. Increasingly, doubt is expressed whether it is economically wise, or morally right, that men should be permitted to add to the producing facilities of an industry which is already suffering from overcapacity. . . . Many insist there must be some form of economic control. There are plans for pro-ration. There are many proposals for stabilization. And some thoughtful men of wide business experience insist that all projects for stabilization and pro-ration must prove futile unless, in some way, the equivalent of the certificate of public convenience and necessity is made a prerequisite to embarking new capital in an industry in which the capacity already exceeds the production of schedules.

Whether that view is sound nobody knows. The objections to the proposal are obvious and grave. The remedy might bring evils worse than the present disease. The obstacles to success seem insuperable. The economic and social sciences are largely uncharted seas. We have been none too successful in the modest essays in economic control already entered upon. The new proposal involves a vast extension of the area of control. . . .

Some people assert that our present plight is due, in part, to the limitations set by courts upon experimentation in the fields of social and economic science; and to the discouragement to which proposals for betterment there have been subjected otherwise. There must be power in the states and the nation to remould, through experimentation, our economic practices and institutions to meet changing social and economic needs.

I cannot believe that the framers of the Fourteenth Amendment, or the states which ratified it, intended to deprive us of the power to correct the evils of technological unemployment and excess productive capacity which have attended progress in the useful arts.

To stay experimentation in things social and economic is a grave responsibility. Denial of the right to experiment may be fraught with serious consequences to the nation. It is one of the happy incidents of the federal system that a single courageous state may, if its citizens choose, serve as a laboratory, and try novel social economic experiments without risk to the rest of the country. This Court has the power to prevent an experiment. We may strike down the statute which embodies it on the ground that, in our opinion, the measure is arbitrary, capricious, or unreasonable. We have power to do this, because the due process clause has been held by the Court applicable to matters of substantive law as well as to matters of procedure. But, in the exercise of this high power, we must be ever on our guard, lest we erect our prejudices into legal principles. If we would guide by the light of reason, we must let our minds be bold.

473. CONSTITUTION OF THE AMERICAN FEDERATION OF LABOR
1932

(Report of Proceedings of the 52d Annual Convention of the American Federation of Labor, Cincinnati, Ohio, 1932, p. xviii ff.)

The American Federation of Labor was organized first in 1881, and reorganized as a national Federation in 1886. With the decline of the Knights of Labor, it came to be the dominant labor organization in the country, and by 1934 had attained a membership of over five million. The literature on the A. F. of L. is extensive. See, S. Gompers, *Seventy Years of Life and Labor*, 2 Vols.; S. Perlman, *History of Trade Unionism in the United States;* L. Wolman, *Growth of American Trade Unions;* F. T. Carlton, *History and Problems of Organized Labor;* R. F. Hoxie, *Trade Unionism in the United States;* L. L. Lorwin, *The American Federation of Labor.*

PREAMBLE—Whereas, A struggle is going on in all the nations of the civilized world

between the oppressors and the oppressed of all countries, a struggle between the capitalist and the laborer, which grows in intensity from year to year, and will work disastrous results to the toiling millions if they are not combined for mutual protection and benefit. It, therefore, behooves the representatives of the Trade and Labor Unions of America, in convention assembled, to adopt such measures and disseminate such principles among the mechanics and laborers of our country as will permanently unite them to secure the recognition of rights to which they are justly entitled. We, therefore, declare ourselves in favor of the formation of thorough Federation, embracing every Trade and Labor Organization in America, organized under the Trade Union system.

CONSTITUTION

ART. I—Name: This Association shall be known as the American Federation of Labor, and shall consist of such Trade and Labor Unions as shall conform to its rules and regulations.

ART. II—Objects: Sec. 1. The object of this Federation shall be the encouragement and formation of local Trade and Labor Unions, and the closer federation of such societies through the organization of Central Trade and Labor Unions in every city, and the further combination of such bodies into State, Territorial, or Provincial organizations to secure legislation in the interest of the working masses.

Sec. 2. The establishment of National and International Trade Unions, based upon a strict recognition of the autonomy of each trade, and the promotion and advancement of such bodies.

Sec. 3. The establishment of Departments composed of National or International Unions affiliated with the American Federation of Labor, of the same industry, and which Departments shall be governed in conformity with the laws of the American Federation of Labor.

Sec. 4. An American Federation of all National and International Trade Unions, to aid and assist each other; to aid and encourage the sale of union label goods, and to secure legislation in the interest of the working people, and influence public opinion, by peaceful and legal methods, in favor of organized labor.

Sec. 5. To aid and encourage the labor press of America. . . .

Sec. 8. Party politics, whether they be Democratic, Republican, Socialist, Populistic, Prohibition, or any other, shall have no place in the Conventions of the American Federation of Labor. . . .

ART. IX—Executive Council: Sec. 1. It shall be the duty of the Executive Council to watch legislative measures directly affecting the interests of working people, and to initiate, whenever necessary, such legislative action as the Convention may direct.

Sec. 2. The Executive Council shall use every possible means to organize new Na-

tional or International Trade or Labor Unions, and to organize Local Trade and Labor Unions, and connect them with the Federation until such time as there is a sufficient number to form a National or International Union, when it shall be the duty of the President of the Federation to see that such organization is formed. . . .

Sec. 5. While we recognize the right of each trade to manage its own affairs, it shall be the duty of the Executive Council to secure the unification of all labor organizations, so far as to assist each other in any trade dispute. . . .

Sec. 10. All Local Trade Unions and Federal Labor Unions holding charters direct from the American Federation of Labor, desiring the assistance of the American Federation of Labor in trade disputes, shall submit to the President of the American Federation of Labor for approval by the Executive Council the full statement of the grievance, and shall receive within twenty (20) days from the President an answer as to whether they will be sustained or not, and no benefits shall be paid where a strike takes place before the Local Union has received the approval of the Executive Council. . . .

ART. X—Revenue: Sec. 1. The revenue of the Federation shall be derived from a per capita tax to be paid upon the full paid-up membership of all affiliated bodies, as follows: From International or National Trade Unions, a per capita tax of one cent per member per month; from Local Trade Unions and Federal Labor Unions, thirty-five cents per member per month, twelve and one-half cents of which must be set aside to be used only in case of strike or lockout. . . .

ART. XI—Local Central Bodies: . . .

Sec. 2. It shall be the duty of all National and International Unions affiliated with the American Federation of Labor to instruct their Local Unions to join chartered Central Labor Bodies, Departments, and State Federations in their vicinity where such exist. Similar instructions shall be given by the American Federation of Labor to all Trade and Federal Labor Unions under its jurisdiction.

Sec. 3. Where there are one or more Local Unions in any city belonging to any National or International Union affiliated with this Federation they may organize a

Central Labor Union, or shall join such body if already in existence.

Sec. 4. The Executive Council and Local Central Labor Unions shall use all possible means to organize and connect as Local Unions to National or International Unions the organizations in their vicinity to aid the formation of National or International Unions where none exist, and to organize Federal Labor Unions where the number of craftsmen precludes any other form of organization.

Sec. 5. No Central Labor Union, or other central body of delegates, shall have the authority or power to order any organization, affiliated with such Central Labor Union, or other central labor body, on strike, or to take a strike vote, where such organization has a national organization, until the proper authorities of such National or International organization have been consulted and agreed to such action.

Sec. 6. Separate charters may be issued to Central Labor Unions, Local Unions, or Federal Labor Unions, composed exclusively of colored members, where, in the judgment of the Executive Council, it appears advisable and to the best interest of the Trade Union movement to do so.

Sec. 7. No Central Labor Union, or other central body of delegates, shall have authority or power to originate a boycott, nor shall such bodies indorse and order the placing of the name of any person, firm, or corporation on an unfair list until the Local Union desiring the same has, before declaring the boycott, submitted the matter in dispute to the Central Body for investigation, and the best endeavors on its part to effect an amicable settlement. Violation of this section shall forfeit charter. . . .

ART. XII—Assessment in Defense of National and International Unions: Sec. 1. The Executive Council shall have power to declare a levy of one cent per member per week on all affiliated unions for a period not exceeding ten weeks in any one year, to assist in the support of an affiliated National or International Union engaged in a protracted strike or lockout. . . .

ART. XIII—Defense Fund For Local Trade and Federal Labor Unions: Sec. 1. Unless otherwise ordered by the Executive Council the moneys of the defense fund shall be drawn only to sustain strikes or lockouts of Local Trade and Federal Labor Unions when such strikes or lockouts are authorized, indorsed, and conducted in conformity with the following provisions of this Article:

Sec. 2. In the event of a disagreement between a Local Union and an employer which, in the opinion of the Local Union, may result in a strike, such Union shall notify the President of the American Federation of Labor, who shall investigate or cause an investigation to be made of the disagreement, and endeavor to adjust the difficulty. If his efforts should prove futile, he shall take such steps as he shall deem necessary in notifying the Executive Council, and if the majority of said Council shall decide that a strike is necessary such Union shall be authorized to order a strike, but that under no circumstances shall a strike or lockout be deemed legal, or moneys expended from the defense fund on that account, unless the strike or lockout shall have been first authorized and approved by the President and Executive Council. . . .

Sec. 5. When a strike has been inaugurated under the provisions of Sections 2 and 3, the American Federation of Labor shall pay to the bonded officer of the Union involved, or his order, for a period of six weeks, an amount equal to seven ($7) dollars per week for each member. Each Local Union shall require its treasurer to give proper bond for the safekeeping and disbursement of all funds of the Local. No benefit shall be paid for the first two weeks of the strike. The Executive Council shall have the power to authorize the payment of strike benefits for an additional period. . . .

Sec. 7. Any Union inaugurating a strike without the approval of the Executive Council shall not receive benefit on account of said strike. . . .

Sec. 10. Before a strike shall be declared off a special meeting of the Union shall be called for that purpose, and it shall require a majority vote of all members present to decide the question either way.

Sec. 11. In the event of the defense fund becoming dangerously low through protracted strike or lockout, the Executive Council of the American Federation of Labor shall have the power to levy an assessment of ten cents on each member of Local

Trade and Federal Labor Unions, assessments to be restricted to not more than five per year; and further, that there shall always be a surplus of five thousand ($5,000) dollars in the defense fund. . . .

474. NORRIS–LAGUARDIA ANTI-INJUNCTION BILL
March 20, 1932
(*U. S. Statutes at Large,* Vol. XLVII, p. 70 ff.)

This measure was the climax of a quarter century of agitation for the strict limitation of the use of the injunction in labor disputes. The earlier attempt in the Clayton Act, Doc. No. 403, had proved ineffective. See, F. Frankfurter and N. Greene, *The Labor Injunction;* E. E. Witte, *The Government in Labor Disputes;* Brissenden, "The Labor Injunction" 48 Pol. Sci. Qt. 413; Monkemeyer, "Five Years of the Norris-LaGuardia Act," 2 Mo. L. Rev. 1; Hellerstein, "Picketing Legislation and the Courts," 10 N. C. L. Rev. 158; Riddlesbarger, "Federal Anti-Injunction Act," 14 Ore. L. Rev. 242; and note in 48 Yale L. J. 308.

AN ACT to amend the Judicial Code and to define and limit the jurisdiction of courts sitting in equity, and for other purposes.

Be it enacted, That no court of the United States, as herein defined, shall have jurisdiction to issue any restraining order or temporary or permanent injunction in a case involving or growing out of a labor dispute, except in a strict conformity with the provisions of this Act; nor shall any such restraining order or temporary or permanent injunction be issued contrary to the public policy declared in this Act.

Sec. 2. In the interpretation of this Act and in determining the jurisdiction and authority of the courts of the United States, as such jurisdiction and authority are herein defined and limited, the public policy of the United States is hereby declared as follows:

Whereas, under prevailing economic conditions, . . . the individual unorganized worker is commonly helpless to exercise actual liberty of contract and to protect his freedom of labor, and thereby to obtain acceptable terms and conditions of employment, wherefore, though he should be free to decline to associate with his fellows, it is necessary that he should have full freedom of association, self-organization, and designation of representatives of his own choosing, to negotiate the terms and conditions of his employment, and that he shall be free from the interference,

restraint, or coercion of employers of labor, or their agents, in the activities for the purpose of collective bargaining or other mutual aid or protection; therefore, the following definitions of, and limitations upon, the jurisdiction and authority of the courts of the United States are hereby enacted.

Sec. 3. Any undertaking or promise, such as is described in this section, or any other undertaking or promise in conflict with the public policy declared in section 2 of this Act, is hereby declared to be contrary to the public policy of the United States, shall not be enforceable in any court of the United States and shall not afford any basis for the granting of legal or equitable relief by any such court, including specifically the following:

Every undertaking or promise hereafter made, whether written or oral, express or implied, constituting or contained in any contract or agreement of hiring or employment between any individual firm, company, association, or corporation, and any employee or prospective employee of the same, whereby,

a—Either party to such contract or agreement undertakes or promises not to join, become, or remain a member of any labor organization or of any employer organization; or

b—Either party to such contract or agreement undertakes or promises that he will withdraw from any employment relation in the event that he joins, becomes, or remains a member of any labor organization or of any employer organization.

Sec. 4. No court of the United States shall have the jurisdiction to issue any restraining order or temporary or permanent injunction in any case involving or growing out of any labor dispute to prohibit any person or persons participating or interested in such dispute (as these terms are herein defined) from doing, whether singly or in concert, any of the following acts:

(a) Ceasing or refusing to perform any

work or to remain in any relation of employment;

(b) Becoming or remaining a member of any labor organization or of any employer organization, regardless of any such undertaking or promise as is described in section 3 of this Act:

(c) Paying or giving to, or withholding from any person participating or interested in such labor dispute, any strike or employment benefits or insurance, or other moneys or things of value;

(d) By all lawful means aiding any person participating or interested in any labor dispute who is being proceeded against in, or is prosecuting, any action or suit in any court in the United States or of any state;

(e) Giving publicity to the extent of, or the facts involved in any labor dispute whether by advertising, speaking, patrolling, or by any other method not involving fraud or violence;

(f) Assembling peaceably to act or to organize to act in promotion of their interests in a labor dispute;

(g) Advising or notifying any persons of any intentions to do any of the acts heretofore specified;

(h) Agreeing with other persons to do or not to do any of the acts heretofore specified; and

(i) Advising, urging, or otherwise causing or inducing without fraud or violence the acts heretofore specified, regardless of any such undertaking or promise as is described in section 3 of this Act.

Sec. 5. No court of the United States shall have jurisdiction to issue a restraining order or temporary or permanent injunction upon the ground that any of the persons participating or interested in a labor dispute constitute or are engaged in an unlawful combination or conspiracy because of the doing in concert of the acts enumerated in section 4 of this Act.

Sec. 6. No officer or member of any organization or association, and no association or organization participating or interested in a labor dispute, shall be held responsible or liable in any court of the United States for the unlawful acts of individual officers, members, or agents, except upon clear proof of actual participation in, or actual authorization of, such acts, or of ratification of such acts after actual knowledge thereof.

Sec. 7. No court of the United States shall have jurisdiction to issue a temporary or permanent injunction in any case involving or growing out of a labor dispute as herein defined except after hearing the testimony of witnesses in open court (with opportunity for cross-examination) in support of the allegations of a complaint made under oath, and testimony in opposition thereto, if offered, and except after findings of fact by the court, to the effect—

(a) That unlawful acts have been threatened and will be committed unless restrained or have been committed and will be continued unless restrained, but no injunction or temporary restraining order shall be issued on account of any threat or unlawful act excepting against the person or persons, association, or organization making the threat or committing the unlawful act or actually authorizing or ratifying the same after actual knowledge thereof;

(b) That substantial and irreparable injury to complainant's property will follow;

(c) That as to each item of relief granted greater injury will be inflicted upon complainant by the denial of relief than will be inflicted upon defendants by the granting of relief;

(d) That complainant has no adequate remedy at law; and

(e) That the public officers charged with the duty to protect complainant's property are unable or unwilling to furnish adequate protection. . . .

Sec. 9. No restraining order or temporary or permanent injunctions shall be granted in a case involving or growing out of a labor dispute, except on the basis of findings of fact made and filed by the court in the record of the case prior to the issuance of such restraining order or injunction; and every restraining order or injunction granted in a case involving or growing out of a labor dispute shall include only a prohibition of such specific act or acts as may be expressly complained of in the bill of complaint or petition filed in such case and as shall be expressly included in said findings of fact made and filed by the court as provided herein. . . .

Sec. 11. In all cases arising under this Act in which a person shall be charged with contempt in a court of the United States (as herein defined), the accused shall enjoy the right to speedy and public trial by an impartial jury of the state and district wherein the contempt shall have been committed: *Provided,* That this right shall not apply to contempt committed in the presence of the court or so near thereto as to interfere directly with the administration of justice or to apply to the misbehavior, misconduct, or disobedience of any officer of the court in respect to the writs, orders, or process of the court. . . .

Sec. 13. . . .

(c) The term "labor dispute" includes any controversy concerning terms or conditions of employment, or concerning the association or representation of persons negotiating, fixing, maintaining, changing, or seeking to arrange terms or conditions of employment, regardless of whether or not the disputants stand in approximate relation of employer and employee. . . .

475. THE DEMOCRATIC PLATFORM OF 1932
June 30, 1932

(*Proceedings* of the Democratic National Convention of 1932, p. 146)

The failure of the Republican administration to solve the problems presented by the great depression made Democratic chances of success in 1932 very bright. In an atmosphere of optimism the Democrats met at Chicago, June 27, and nominated to the Presidency Governor Franklin D. Roosevelt of New York. The vice-Presidential nomination went to John E. Garner of Texas. The Republicans, meeting likewise at Chicago, renominated President Hoover and vice-President Curtis. In the November election the Democratic ticket polled 22,821,857 popular and 472 electoral votes, the Republican 15,761,841 popular and 59 electoral votes. See E. E. Robinson, *The Presidential Vote, 1896–1932;* R. V. Peel and T. C. Donnelly, *The 1932 Campaign;* D. Dumond, *Roosevelt to Roosevelt;* C. A. and M. R. Beard, *America in Midpassage;* E. K. Lindley, *The Roosevelt Revolution.* Roosevelt's campaign speeches can be found in his *Public Papers and Addresses,* Vol. II.

In this time of unprecedented economic and social distress the Democratic Party declares its conviction that the chief causes of this condition were the disastrous policies pursued by our government since the World War, of economic isolation, fostering the merger of competitive businesses into monopolies and encouraging the indefensible expansion and contraction of credit for private profit at the expense of the public.

Those who were responsible for these policies have abandoned the ideals on which the war was won and thrown away the fruits of victory, thus rejecting the greatest opportunity in history to bring peace, prosperity, and happiness to our people and to the world.

They have ruined our foreign trade; destroyed the values of our commodities and products, crippled our banking system, robbed millions of our people of their life savings, and thrown millions more out of work, produced wide-spread poverty and brought the government to a state of financial distress unprecedented in time of peace.

The only hope for improving present conditions, restoring employment, affording permanent relief to the people, and bringing the nation back to the proud position of domestic happiness and of financial, industrial, agricultural and commercial leadership in the world lies in a drastic change in economic governmental policies.

We believe that a party platform is a covenant with the people to be faithfully kept by the party when entrusted with power, and that the people are entitled to know in plain words the terms of the contract to which they are asked to subscribe. We hereby declare this to be the platform of the Democratic Party:

The Democratic Party solemnly promises by appropriate action to put into effect the principles, policies, and reforms herein advocated, and to eradicate the policies, methods, and practices herein condemned. We advocate an immediate and drastic reduction of governmental expenditures by abolishing useless commissions and offices, consolidating departments and bureaus, and eliminating extravagance, to accomplish a saving of not less than twenty-five per cent in the cost of federal government, and we call upon the Democratic Party in the States to make a zealous effort to achieve a proportionate result.

We favor maintenance of the national credit by a federal budget annually balanced on the basis of accurate executive estimates within revenues, raised by a system of taxation levied on the principle of ability to pay.

We advocate a sound currency to be preserved at all hazards and an international monetary conference called on the invitation of our government to consider the rehabilitation of silver and related questions.

We advocate a competitive tariff for revenue, with a fact-finding tariff commission free from executive interference, reciprocal tariff agreements with other nations, and an international economic conference designed to restore international trade and facilitate exchange.

We advocate the extension of federal credit to the states to provide unemployment relief wherever the diminishing resources of the states make it impossible for them to provide for the needy; expansion of the federal program of necessary and useful construction affected with a public interest, such as adequate flood control and waterways.

We advocate the spread of employment by a substantial reduction in the hours of labor, the encouragement of the shorter week by applying that principle in government service. We advocate advance planning of public works.

We advocate unemployment and old age insurance under state laws.

We favor the restoration of agriculture, the nation's basic industry; better financing of farm mortgages through recognized farm bank agencies at low rates of interest on an amortization plan, giving preference to credits for the redemption of farms and homes sold under foreclosure.

Extension and development of Farm Co-operative movement and effective control of crop surpluses so that our farmers may have the full benefit of the domestic market.

The enactment of every constitutional measure that will aid the farmers to receive for their basic farm commodities prices in excess of cost.

We advocate a Navy and an Army adequate for national defense, based on a survey of all facts affecting the existing establishments, that the people in time of peace may not be burdened by an expenditure fast approaching a billion dollars annually.

We advocate strengthening and impartial enforcement of the anti-trust laws, to prevent monopoly and unfair trade practices, and revision thereof for the better protection of labor and the small producer and distributor.

The conservation, development, and use of the nation's water power in the public interest.

The removal of government from all fields of private enterprise except where necessary to develop public works and natural resources in the common interest.

We advocate protection of the investing public by requiring to be filed with the government and carried in advertisements of all offerings of foreign and domestic stocks and bonds true information as to bonuses, commissions, principal invested, and interests of the sellers.

Regulation to the full extent of federal power of

    (a) Holding companies which sell securities in interstate commerce;

    (b) Rates of utility companies operating across state lines;

    (c) Exchanges in securities and commodities.

We advocate quicker methods of realizing on assets for the relief of depositors of suspended banks, and a more rigid supervision of national banks for the protection of depositors and the prevention of the use of their moneys in speculation to the detriment of local credits.

The severance of affiliated security companies from, and the divorce of the investment banking business from, commercial banks, and further restriction of federal reserve banks in permitting the use of federal reserve facilities for speculative purposes.

We advocate the full measure of justice and generosity for all war veterans who have suffered disability or disease caused by or resulting from actual service in time of war and for their dependents.

We advocate a firm foreign policy, including peace with all the world and the settlement of international dispute by arbitration; no interference in the internal affairs of other nations; the sanctity of treaties and the maintenance of good faith and of good will in financial obligations; adherence to the World Court with appending reservations; the Pact of Paris abolishing war as an instrument of national policy, to be made effective by provisions for consultation and conference in case of threatened violations of treaties.

International agreements for reduction of armaments and cooperation with nations of the Western Hemisphere to maintain the spirit of the Monroe Doctrine.

We oppose cancellation of the debts owing to the United States by foreign nations.

Independence for the Philippines; ultimate statehood for Porto Rico.

The employment of American citizens in the operation of the Panama Canal.

Simplification of legal procedure and reorganization of the judicial system to make the attainment of justice speedy, certain, and at less cost.

Continuous publicity of political contributions and expenditures; strengthening of the Corrupt Practices Act and severe penalties for misappropriation of campaign funds.

We advocate the repeal of the Eighteenth Amendment. To effect such repeal we demand that the Congress immediately propose a Constitutional Amendment to truly representative conventions in the states called to act solely on that proposal. We urge the enactment of such measures by the several states as will actually promote temperance, effectively prevent the return of the saloon and bring the liquor traffic into the open under complete supervision and control by the states.

We demand that the Federal Government effectively exercise its power to enable the states to protect themselves against importation of intoxicating liquors in violation of their laws.

Pending repeal, we favor immediate modification of the Volstead Act to legalize the manufacture and sale of beer and other beverages of such alcoholic content as is permissible under the Constitution and to provide therefrom a proper and needed revenue.

We advocate continuous responsibility of government for human welfare, especially for the protection of children.

We condemn the improper and excessive use of money in political activities.

We condemn paid lobbies of special interests to influence members of Congress and other public servants by personal contact.

We condemn action and utterances of high public officials designed to influence stock exchange prices.

We condemn the open and covert resistance of administration officials to every effort made by Congressional committees to curtail the extravagant expenditures of the government and to revoke improvident subsidies granted to favorite interests.

We condemn the extravagance of the Farm Board, its disastrous action which made the Government a speculator of farm products and the unsound policy of restricting agricultural products to the demands of domestic markets.

We condemn the usurpation of power by the State Department in assuming to pass upon foreign securities offered by international bankers as a result of which billions of dollars in questionable bonds have been sold to the public upon the implied approval of the Federal Government.

We condemn the Hawley-Smoot Tariff Law, the prohibitive rates of which have resulted in retaliatory action by more than forty countries, created international economic hostilities, destroyed international trade, driven our factories into foreign countries, robbed the American farmer of his foreign markets, and increased the cost of production.

In conclusion, to accomplish these purposes and to recover economic liberty we pledge the nominees of this convention the best efforts of a great party whose founder announced the doctrine which guides us now in the hour of our country's need:

Equal rights to all; special privileges to none.

476. F. D. ROOSEVELT'S FIRST INAUGURAL ADDRESS
March 4, 1933

(Pamphlet, Government Printing Office)

This speech is reproduced, with minor variations, in Vol. II of the *Public Papers and Addresses of F. D. Roosevelt*. On Roosevelt, see this five volume collection of public papers, and E. Looker, *This Man Roosevelt;* E. K. Lindley, *The Roosevelt Revolution, First Phase.* For the New Deal program in general see C. A. and M. R. Beard, *America in Midpassage;* L. Hacker, *Short History of the New Deal;* D. Dumond, *Roosevelt to Roosevelt;* C. A. Beard, *The Future Comes;* S. Chase, *A New Deal;* W. F. Ogburn, ed. *Social Change and the New Deal;* S. Wallace, *The New*

Deal in Action; G. Soule, *The Coming American Revolution;* R. Moley, *After Seven Years;* J. Alsop and R. Kitner, *The Men Around the President.*

President Hoover, Mr. Chief Justice, my friends:

This is a day of national consecration, and I am certain that my fellow-Americans expect that on my induction into the Presidency I will address them with a candor and a decision which the present situation of our nation impels.

This is pre-eminently the time to speak the truth, the whole truth, frankly and boldly. Nor need we shrink from honestly facing conditions in our country today. This great nation will endure as it has endured, will revive and will prosper.

So first of all let me assert my firm belief that the only thing we have to fear is fear itself—nameless, unreasoning, unjustified terror which paralyzes needed efforts to convert retreat into advance.

In every dark hour of our national life a leadership of frankness and vigor has met with that understanding and support of the people themselves which is essential to victory. I am convinced that you will again give that support to leadership in these critical days.

In such a spirit on my part and on yours we face our common difficulties. They concern, thank God, only material things. Values have shrunken to fantastic levels; taxes have risen; our ability to pay has fallen, government of all kinds is faced by serious curtailment of income; the means of exchange are frozen in the currents of trade; the withered leaves of industrial enterprise lie on every side; farmers find no markets for their produce; the savings of many years in thousands of families are gone.

More important, a host of unemployed citizens face the grim problem of existence, and an equally great number toil with little return. Only a foolish optimist can deny the dark realities of the moment.

Yet our distress comes from no failure of substance. We are stricken by no plague of locusts. Compared with the perils which our forefathers conquered because they believed and were not afraid, we have still much to be thankful for. Nature still offers her bounty and human efforts have multiplied it. Plenty is at our doorstep, but a generous use of it languishes in the very sight of the supply.

Primarily, this is because the rulers of the exchange of mankind's goods have failed through their own stubbornness and their own incompetence, have admitted their failure and abdicated. Practices of the unscrupulous money changers stand indicted in the court of public opinion, rejected by the hearts and minds of men.

True, they have tried, but their efforts have been cast in the pattern of an outworn tradition. Faced by failure of credit, they have proposed only the lending of more money.

Stripped of the lure of profit by which to induce our people to follow their false leadership, they have resorted to exhortations, pleading tearfully for restored confidence. They know only the rules of a generation of self-seekers.

They have no vision, and when there is no vision the people perish.

The money changers have fled from their high seats in the temple of our civilization. We may now restore that temple to the ancient truths.

The measure of the restoration lies in the extent to which we apply social values more noble than mere monetary profit.

Happiness lies not in the mere possession of money; it lies in the joy of achievement, in the thrill of creative effort.

The joy and moral stimulation of work no longer must be forgotten in the mad chase of evanescent profits. These dark days will be worth all they cost us if they teach us that our true destiny is not to be ministered unto but to minister to ourselves and to our fellow-men.

Recognition of the falsity of material wealth as the standard of success goes hand in hand with the abandonment of the false belief that public office and high political position are to be valued only by the standards of pride of place and personal profit; and there must be an end to a conduct in banking and in business which too often has given to a sacred trust the likeness of callous and selfish wrongdoing.

Small wonder that confidence languishes, for it thrives only on honesty, on honor, on the sacredness of obligations, on faithful protection, on unselfish performance. Without them it cannot live.

Restoration calls, however, not for changes in ethics alone. This nation asks for action, and action now.

Our greatest primary task is to put people to work. This is no unsolvable problem if we face it wisely and courageously.

It can be accomplished in part by direct recruiting by the government itself, treating the task as we would treat the emergency of a war, but at the same time, through this employment, accomplishing greatly needed projects to stimulate and reorganize the use of our natural resources.

Hand in hand with this, we must frankly recognize the overbalance of population in our industrial centers and, by engaging on a national scale in the redistribution, endeavor to provide a better use of the land for those best fitted for the land.

The task can be helped by definite efforts to raise the values of agricultural products and with this the power to purchase the output of our cities.

It can be helped by preventing realistically the tragedy of the growing loss, through foreclosure, of our small homes and our farms.

It can be helped by insistence that the Federal, State and local governments act forthwith on the demand that their cost be drastically reduced.

It can be helped by the unifying of relief activities which today are often scattered, uneconomical and unequal. It can be helped by national planning for and supervision of all forms of transportation and of communications and other utilities which have a definitely public character.

There are many ways in which it can be helped, but it can never be helped merely by talking about it. We must act, and act quickly.

Finally, in our progress toward a resumption of work we require two safeguards against a return of the evils of the old order; there must be a strict supervision of all banking and credits and investments; there must be an end to speculation with other people's money, and there must be provision for an adequate but sound currency.

These are the lines of attack. I shall presently urge upon a new Congress in special session detailed measures for their fulfillment, and I shall seek the immediate assistance of the several States.

Through this program of action we address ourselves to putting our own national house in order and making income balance outgo.

Our international trade relations, though vastly important, are, in point of time and necessity, secondary to the establishment of a sound national economy.

I favor as a practical policy the putting of first things first. I shall spare no effort to restore world trade by international economic readjustment, but the emergency at home cannot wait on that accomplishment.

The basic thought that guides these specific means of national recovery is not narrowly nationalistic.

It is the insistence, as a first consideration, upon the interdependence of the various elements in, and parts of, the United States—a recognition of the old and permanently important manifestation of the American spirit of the pioneer.

It is the way to recovery. It is the immediate way. It is the strongest assurance that the recovery will endure.

In the field of world policy I would dedicate this nation to the policy of the good neighbor—the neighbor who resolutely respects himself and, because he does so, respects the rights of others—the neighbor who respects his obligations and respects the sanctity of his agreements in and with a world of neighbors.

If I read the temper of our people correctly, we now realize as we have never before, our interdependence on each other; that we cannot merely take, but we must give as well; that if we are to go forward we must move as a trained and loyal army willing to sacrifice for the good of a common discipline, because, without such discipline, no progress is made, no leadership becomes effective.

We are, I know, ready and willing to submit our lives and property to such discipline because it makes possible a leadership which aims at a larger good.

This I propose to offer, pledging that the larger purposes will bind upon us all as a sacred obligation with a unity of duty hitherto evoked only in time of armed strife.

With this pledge taken, I assume unhesitatingly the leadership of this great army of our people, dedicated to a disciplined attack upon our common problems.

Action in this image and to this end is feasible under the form of government which we have inherited from our ancestors.

Our Constitution is so simple and practical that it is possible always to meet extraordinary needs by changes in emphasis and arrangement without loss of essential form.

That is why our constitutional system has proved itself the most superbly enduring political mechanism the modern world has produced. It has met every stress of vast expansion of territory, of foreign wars, of bitter internal strife, of world relations.

It is to be hoped that the normal balance of executive and legislative authority may be wholly adequate to meet the unprecedented task before us. But it may be that an unprecedented demand and need for undelayed action may call for temporary departure from that normal balance of public procedure.

I am prepared under my constitutional duty to recommend the measures that a stricken nation in the midst of a stricken world may require.

These measures, or such other measures as the Congress may build out of its experience and wisdom, I shall seek, within my constitutional authority, to bring to speedy adoption.

But in the event that the Congress shall fail to take one of these two courses, and in the event that the national emergency is still critical, I shall not evade the clear course of duty that will then confront me.

I shall ask the Congress for the one remaining instrument to meet the crisis—broad executive power to wage a war against the emergency as great as the power that would be given me if we were in fact invaded by a foreign foe.

For the trust reposed in me I will return the courage and the devotion that befit the time. I can do no less.

We face the arduous days that lie before us in the warm courage of national unity; with the clear consciousness of seeking old and precious moral values; with the clean satisfaction that comes from the stern performance of duty by old and young alike.

We aim at the assurance of a rounded and permanent national life.

We do not distrust the future of essential democracy. The people of the United States have not failed. In their need they have registered a mandate that they want direct, vigorous action.

They have asked for discipline and direction under leadership. They have made me the present instrument of their wishes. In the spirit of the gift I take it.

In this dedication of a nation we humbly ask the blessing of God. May He protect each and every one of us! May He guide me in the days to come!

477. THE AGRICULTURAL ADJUSTMENT ACT
May 12, 1933

(U. S. Statutes at Large, Vol. XLVIII, p. 31)

The failure of the Hoover farm relief program made it imperative that the new Democratic administration give emergency relief to the farmers. This Agricultural Adjustment Act was the most important of several acts which attempted to afford temporary relief from the most pressing ills of the farmer and at the same time to rehabilitate agriculture. One of the major purposes of the Act was to raise the general level of agricultural commodity prices to that of the pre-War period, chiefly through voluntary crop reduction. This Act also authorized the President to devalue the gold dollar by not more than fifty per cent. Parts of the AAA were subsequently nullified by the Court (Doc. No. 478) but those parts were later substantially reënacted. See, H. Wallace, *America Must Choose*, and *New Frontiers;* M. Ezekiel and L. H. Bean, *Economic Bases of the AAA;* E. G. Nourse, et. al. *Three Years of the AAA;* E. G. Nourse, *Marketing Agreements under the AAA;* J. Davis, *Wheat and the AAA;* H. T. Richards, *Cotton and the AAA;* J. D. Black, *Dairy Industry and the AAA.*

AN ACT To relieve the existing national economic emergency by increasing agricultural purchasing power, . . . to provide for the orderly liquidation of joint-stock land banks, and for other purposes.

TITLE I—AGRICULTURAL ADJUSTMENT

DECLARATION OF EMERGENCY

That the present acute economic emergency being in part the consequence of a severe and increasing disparity between the prices of agricultural and other commodities, which disparity has largely destroyed the purchasing power of farmers for industrial products, has broken down the orderly exchange of commodities, and has seriously impaired the agricultural assets supporting the national credit structure, it is hereby declared that these conditions in the basic industry of agriculture have affected transactions in agricultural commodities with a national public interest, have burdened and obstructed the normal currents of commerce in such commodities, and render imperative the immediate enactment of title I of this Act.

DECLARATION OF POLICY

SEC. 2. It is hereby declared to be the policy of Congress—

(1) To establish and maintain such balance between the production and consumption of agricultural commodities, and such marketing conditions therefor, as will reestablish prices to farmers at a level that will give agricultural commodities a purchasing power with respect to articles that farmers buy, equivalent to the purchasing power of agricultural commodities in the base period. The base period in the case of all agricultural commodities except tobacco shall be the prewar period, August 1909–July 1914. In the case of tobacco, the base period shall be the postwar period, August 1919–July 1929.

(2) To approach such equality of purchasing power by gradual correction of the present inequalities therein at as rapid a rate as is deemed feasible in view of the current consumptive demand in domestic and foreign markets.

(3) To protect the consumers' interest by readjusting farm production at such level as will not increase the percentage of the consumers' retail expenditures for agricultural commodities, or products derived therefrom, which is returned to the farmer, above the percentage which was returned to the farmer in the prewar period, August 1909–July 1914. . . .

SEC. 6. (a) The Secretary of Agriculture is hereby authorized to enter into option contracts with the producers of cotton to sell to any such producer an amount of cotton to be agreed upon not in excess of the amount of reduction in production of cotton by such producer below the amount produced by him in the preceding crop year, in all cases where such producer agrees in writing to reduce the amount of cotton produced by him in 1933, below his production in the previous year, by not less than 30 per centum, without increase in commercial fertilization per acre.

(b) To any such producer so agreeing to reduce production the Secretary of Agriculture shall deliver a nontransferable-option contract agreeing to sell to said producer an amount, equivalent to the amount of his agreed reduction, of the cotton in the possession and control of the Secretary.

(c) The producer is to have the option to buy said cotton at the average price paid by the Secretary for the cotton procured under section 3, and is to have the right at any time up to January 1, 1934, to exercise his option, upon proof that he has complied with his contract and with all the rules and regulations of the Secretary of Agriculture with respect thereto, by taking said cotton upon payment by him of his option price and all actual carrying charges on such cotton; or the Secretary may sell such cotton for the account of such producer, paying him the excess of the market price at the date of sale over the average price above referred to after deducting all actual and necessary carrying charges: *Provided,* That in no event shall the producer be held responsible or liable for financial loss incurred in the holding of such cotton or on account of the carrying charges therein: *Provided further,* That such agreement to curtail cotton production shall contain a further provision that such cotton producer shall not use the land taken out of cotton production for the production for sale, directly or indirectly, of any other nationally produced agricultural commodity or product. . . .

PART 2—COMMODITY BENEFITS

GENERAL POWERS

SEC. 8. In order to effectuate the declared policy, the Secretary of Agriculture shall have power—

(1) To provide for reduction in the acreage or reduction in the production for market, or both, of any basic agricultural commodity, through agreements with producers or by other voluntary methods, and to provide for rental or benefit payments in connection therewith or upon that part of the production of any basic agricultural commodity required for domestic consumption, in such amounts as the Secretary deems fair and reasonable, to be paid out of any moneys available for such payments. . . .

(2) To enter into marketing agreements with processors, associations of producers, and others engaged in the handling, in the current of interstate or foreign commerce of any agricultural commodity or project thereof, after due notice and opportunity for hearing to interested parties. The making of any such agreement shall not be held to be in violation of any of the antitrust laws of the United States, and any such agreement shall be deemed to be lawful. . . .

PROCESSING TAX

SEC. 9. (a) To obtain revenue for extraordinary expenses incurred by reason of the national economic emergency, there shall be levied processing taxes as hereinafter provided. When the Secretary of Agriculture determines that rental or benefit payments are to be made with respect to any basic agricultural commodity, he shall proclaim such determination, and a processing tax shall be in effect with respect to such commodity from the beginning of the marketing year therefor next following the date of such proclamation. The processing tax shall be levied, assessed, and collected upon the first domestic processing of the commodity, whether of domestic production or imported, and shall be paid by the processor. . . .

(b) The processing tax shall be at such rate as equals the difference between the current average farm price for the commodity and the fair exchange value of the commodity; except that if the Secretary has reason to believe that the tax at such rate will cause such reduction in the quantity of the commodity or products thereof domestically consumed as to result in the accumulation of surplus stocks of the commodity or products thereof or in the depression of the farm price of the commodity, then he shall cause

an appropriate investigation to be made and afford due notice and opportunity for hearing to interested parties. If thereupon the Secretary finds that such result will occur, then the processing tax shall be at such rate as will prevent such accumulation of surplus stocks and depression of the farm price of the commodity. . . .

(c) For the purposes of part 2 of this title, the fair exchange value of a commodity shall be the price therefor that will give the commodity the same purchasing power, with respect to articles farmers buy, as such commodity had during the base period specified in section 2. . . .

(d) As used in part 2 of this title—

(1) In case of wheat, rice, and corn, the term "processing" means the milling or other processing (except cleaning and drying) of wheat, rice, or corn for market, including custom milling for toll as well as commercial milling, but shall not include the grinding or cracking thereof not in the form of flour for feed purposes only.

(2) In case of cotton, the term "processing" means the spinning, manufacturing, or other processing (except ginning) of cotton; and the term "cotton" shall not include cotton linters.

(3) In case of tobacco, the term "processing" means the manufacturing or other processing (except drying or converting into insecticides and fertilizers) of tobacco.

(4) In case of hogs, the term "processing" means the slaughter of hogs for market.

(5) In the case of any other commodity, the term "processing" means any manufacturing or other processing involving a change in the form of the commodity or its preparation for market, as defined by regulations of the Secretary of Agriculture; and in prescribing such regulations the Secretary shall give due weight to the customs of the industry.

(e) When any processing tax, or increase or decrease therein, takes effect in respect of a commodity the Secretary of Agriculture, in order to prevent pyramiding of the processing tax and profiteering in the sale of the products derived from the commodity, shall make public such information as he deems necessary regarding (1) the relationship between the processing tax and the price paid to producers of the commodity, (2) the effect of the processing tax upon prices to consumers of products of the commodity, (3) the relationship, in previous periods, between prices paid to the producers of the commodity and prices to consumers of the products thereof, and (4) the situation in foreign countries relating to prices paid to producers of the commodity and prices to consumers of the products thereof. . . .

Part 8

"Emergency Farm Mortgage Act of 1933."

Title III—Financing—and Exercising Power Conferred by Section 8 of Article I of the Constitution: To Coin Money and to Regulate the Value Thereof

Sec. 43. Whenever the President finds, upon investigation, that (1) the foreign commerce of the United States is adversely affected by reason of the depreciation in the value of the currency of any other government or governments in relation to the present standard value of gold, or (2) action under this section is necessary in order to regulate and maintain the parity of currency issues of the United States, or (3) an economic emergency requires an expansion of credit, or (4) an expansion of credit is necessary to secure by international agreement a stabilization at proper levels of the currencies of various governments, the President is authorized, in his discretion— . . .

(1) To direct the Secretary of the Treasury to cause to be issued in such amount or amounts as he may from time to time order, United States notes, . . . in the same size and of similar color to the Federal Reserve notes heretofore issued and in denominations of $1, $5, $10, $20, $50, $100, $500, $1,000, and $10,000; but notes issued under this subsection shall be issued only for the purpose of meeting maturing Federal obligations to repay sums borrowed by the United States and for purchasing United States bonds and other interest-bearing obligations of the United States: *Provided,* That when any such notes are used for such purpose the bond or other obligation so acquired or taken up shall be retired and canceled. Such notes shall be issued at such times and in such amounts as the President may approve but the aggregate amount of such notes outstand-

ing at any time shall not exceed $3,000,000,-000. There is hereby appropriated, out of any money in the Treasury not otherwise appropriated, an amount sufficient to enable the Secretary of the Treasury to retire and cancel 4 per centum annually of such outstanding notes, and the Secretary of the Treasury is hereby directed to retire and cancel annually 4 per centum of such outstanding notes. Such notes and all other coins and currencies heretofore or hereafter coined or issued by or under the authority of the United States shall be legal tender for all debts public and private.

(2) By proclamation to fix the weight of the gold dollar in grains nine tenths fine and also to fix the weight of the silver dollar in grains nine tenths fine at a definite fixed ratio in relation to the gold dollar at such amounts as he finds necessary from his investigation to stabilize domestic prices or to protect the foreign commerce against the adverse effect of depreciated foreign currencies, and to provide for the unlimited coinage of such gold and silver at the ratio so fixed, or in case the Government of the United States enters into an agreement with any government or governments under the terms of which the ratio between the value of gold and other currency issued by the United States and by any such government or governments is established, the President may fix the weight of the gold dollar in accordance with the ratio so agreed upon, and such gold dollar, the weight of which is so fixed, shall be the standard unit of value, and all forms of money issued or coined by the United States shall be maintained at a parity with this standard and it shall be the duty of the Secretary of the Treasury to maintain such parity, but in no event shall the weight of the gold dollar be fixed so as to reduce its present weight by more than 50 per centum. . . .

Sec. 45. (a) The President is authorized for a period of six months from the date of the passage of this Act, to accept silver in payment of the whole or any part of the principal or interest now due, or to become due within six months after such date, from any foreign government or governments on account of any indebtedness to the United States, such silver to be accepted at not to exceed the price of 50 cents an ounce in United States currency. The aggregate value of the silver accepted under this section shall not exceed $200,000,000. . . .

(d) The Secretary of the Treasury shall cause silver certificates to be issued in such denominations as he deems advisable to the total number of dollars for which such silver was accepted in payment of debts. Such silver certificates shall be used by the Treasurer of the United States in payment of any obligations of the United States.

(e) The silver so accepted and received under this section shall be coined into standard silver dollars and subsidiary coins sufficient, in the opinion of the Secretary of the Treasury, to meet any demands for redemption of such silver certificates issued under the provisions of this section, and such coins shall be retained in the Treasury for the payment of such certificates on demand. The silver so accepted and received under this section, except so much thereof as is coined under the provisions of this section, shall be held in the Treasury for the sole purpose of aiding in maintaining the parity of such certificates as provided in existing law. Any such certificates or reissued certificates, when presented at the Treasury, shall be redeemed in standard silver dollars, or in subsidiary silver coin, at the option of the holder of the certificates: . . .

(f) When any silver certificates issued under the provisions of this section are redeemed or received into the Treasury from any source whatsoever, and belong to the United States, they shall not be retired, canceled, or destroyed, but shall be reissued and paid out again and kept in circulation; . . .

SEC. 46. Section 19 of the Federal Reserve Act, as amended, is amended by inserting immediately after paragraph (c) thereof the following new paragraph:

"Notwithstanding the foregoing provisions of this section, the Federal Reserve Board, upon the affirmative vote of not less than five of its members and with the approval of the President, may declare that an emergency exists by reason of credit expansion, and may by regulation during such emergency increase or decrease from time to time, in its discretion, the reserve balances required to be maintained against either demand or time deposits."

478. THE UNITED STATES v. BUTLER et. al.
297 U. S. 1
1936

On Writ of Certiorari to the U. S. Circuit Court of Appeals for the First Circuit. The invalidation of the AAA was perhaps the severest blow which the Supreme Court struck at the New Deal and was in large part responsible for the demand for judicial reform (see Doc. No. 515). While apparently accepting the doctrine of the McCulloch case, the Court here took the position that the end here aimed at—e.g., the rehabilitation of agriculture—was not a legitimate one, but was solely under the jurisdiction of the states. The major provisions of the AAA were reënacted by Congress in the Soil Conservation and Domestic Allotment Act of 1936 and the AAA Act of 1938. The literature on this case is large, but see especially: Holmes, "Federal Spending Power and State Rights," 34 Mich. Law. Rev. 637; Hart, "Processing Taxes and Protective Tariffs," 49 Harv. L. Rev. 610; Brebner-Smith, "The Hoosac Mills Case," 25 Georgetown L. J. 2; Post, "Constitutionality of Government Spending for General Welfare," 22 Va. L. Rev. 1; Collier, "Judicial Bootstraps and the General Welfare Clause," 4 Geo. Wash. L. Rev. 211; D. Alfange, *The Supreme Court and the National Will*; W. Hamilton and O. Adair, *The Power to Govern*.

ROBERTS, J. In this case we must determine whether certain provisions of the Agricultural Adjustment Act, 1933, conflict with the federal Constitution.

Title I of the statute is captioned "Agricultural Adjustment." Section 1 recites that an economic emergency has arisen, due to disparity between the prices of agricultural and other commodities, with consequent destruction of farmers' purchasing power and breakdown in orderly exchange, which, in turn, have affected transactions in agricultural commodities with a national public interest and burdened and obstructed the normal currents of commerce, calling for the enactment of legislation.

Section 2 declares it to be the policy of Congress:

"To establish and maintain such balance between the production and consumption of agricultural commodities, and such marketing, conditions therefor, as will reëstablish prices to farmers at a level that will give agricultural commodities a purchasing power with respect to articles that farmers buy, equivalent to the purchasing power of agricultural commodities in the base period."

The base period, in the case of cotton, and all other commodities except tobacco, is designated as that between August, 1909, and July, 1914.

The further policies announced are an approach to the desired equality by gradual correction of present inequalities "at as rapid a rate as is deemed feasible in view of the current consumptive demand in domestic and foreign markets," and the protection of consumers' interest by readjusting farm production at such level as will not increase the percentage of the consumers' retail expenditures for agricultural commodities or products derived therefrom, which is returned to the farmer, above the percentage returned to him in the base period.

Section 8 provides, amongst other things, that "In order to effectuate the declared policy," the Secretary of Agriculture shall have power

"(1) To provide for reduction in the acreage or reduction in the production for market, or both, of any basic agricultural commodity, through agreements with producers or by other voluntary methods, and to provide for rental or benefit payments in connection therewith or upon that part of the production of any basic agricultural commodity required for domestic consumption, in such amounts as the Secretary deems fair and reasonable, to be paid out of any moneys available for such payments." . . .

"(2) To enter into marketing agreements with processors, associations of producers, and others engaged in the handling, in the current of interstate or foreign commerce of any agricultural commodity or product thereof, after due notice and opportunity for hearing to interested parties." . . .

"(3) To issue licenses permitting processors, associations of producers, and others to engage in the handling, in the current of interstate or foreign commerce, of any agricultural commodity or product thereof, or any competing commodity or product thereof."

It will be observed that the Secretary is not required, but is permitted, if, in his un-controlled judgment, the policy of the act will so be promoted, to make agreements with individual farmers for a reduction of acreage or production upon such terms as he may think fair and reasonable.

Section 9 (a) enacts:

"To obtain revenue for extraordinary expenses incurred by reason of the national economic emergency, there shall be levied processing taxes as hereinafter provided. When the Secretary of Agriculture determines that rental or benefit payments are to be made with respect to any basic agricultural commodity, he shall proclaim such determination, and a processing tax shall be in effect with respect to such commodity from the beginning of the marketing year therefor next following the date of such proclamation. The processing tax shall be levied, assessed, and collected upon the first domestic processing of the commodity, whether of domestic production or imported, and shall be paid by the processor." . . .

Section 9 (b) fixes the tax "at such rate as equals the difference between the current average farm price for the commodity and the fair exchange value," with power in the Secretary, after investigation, notice, and hearing, to readjust the tax so as to prevent the accumulation of surplus stocks and depression of farm prices.

Section 9 (c) directs that the fair exchange value of a commodity shall be such a price as will give that commodity the same purchasing power with respect to articles farmers buy as it had during the base period and that the fair exchange value and the current average farm price of a commodity shall be ascertained by the Secretary from available statistics in his department.

Section 12 (a) appropriates $100,000,000 "to be available to the Secretary of Agriculture for administrative expenses under this title and for rental and benefit payments . . ."; and Section 12 (b) appropriates the proceeds derived from all taxes imposed under the act "to be available to the Secretary of Agriculture for expansion of markets and removal of surplus agricultural products . . . Administrative expenses, rental and benefit payments, and refunds on taxes."

Section 15 (d) permits the Secretary, upon certain conditions to impose compensating taxes on commodities in competition with those subject to the processing tax. . . .

On July 14, 1933, the Secretary of Agriculture, with the approval of the President, proclaimed that he had determined rental and benefit payments should be made with respect to cotton; that the marketing year for that commodity was to begin August 1, 1933; and calculated and fixed the rates of processing and floor taxes on cotton in accordance with the terms of the act.

The United States presented a claim to the respondents as receivers of the Hoosac Mills Corporation for processing and floor taxes on cotton levied under sections 9 and 16 of the act. The receivers recommended that the claim be disallowed. The District Court found the taxes valid and ordered them paid. Upon appeal to Circuit Court of Appeals reversed the order. The judgment under review was entered prior to the adoption of the amending act of August 24, 1935, and we are therefore concerned only with the original act.

First. At the outset the United States contends that the respondents have no standing to question the validity of the tax. The position is that the act is merely a revenue measure levying an excise upon the activity of processing cotton,—a proper subject for the imposition of such a tax,—the proceeds of which go into the federal treasury and thus become available for appropriation for any purpose. It is said that what the respondents are endeavoring to do is to challenge the intended use of the money pursuant to Congressional appropriation when, by confession, that money will have become the property of the Government and the taxpayer will no longer have any interest in it. . . .

The tax can only be sustained by ignoring the avowed purpose and operation of the act, and holding it a measure merely laying on excise upon processors to raise revenue for the support of government. Beyond cavil the sole object of the legislation is to restore the purchasing power of agricultural products to a parity with that prevailing in an earlier day; to take money from the processor and bestow it upon farmers who will reduce their acreage for the accomplishment of the proposed end, and, meanwhile, to aid these farmers during the period required to bring the prices of their crops to the desired level.

The tax plays an indispensable part in the plan of regulation. As stated by the Agricultural Adjustment Administrator, it is "the heart of the law"; a means of "accomplishing one or both of two things intended to help farmers attain parity prices and purchasing power." . . .

The statute not only avows an aim foreign to the procurement of revenue for the support of government, but by its operation shows the exaction laid upon processors to be the necessary means for the intended control of agricultural production. . . .

It is inaccurate and misleading to speak of the exaction from processors prescribed by the challenged act as a tax, or to say that as a tax it is subject to no infirmity. A tax, in the general understanding of the term, and as used in the Constitution, signifies an exaction for the support of the Government. The word has never been thought to connote the expropriation of money from one group for the benefit of another. We may concede that the latter sort of imposition is constitutional when imposed to effectuate regulation of a matter in which both groups are interested and in respect of which there is a power of legislative regulation. But manifestly no justification for it can be found unless as an integral part of such regulation. The exaction cannot be rested out of its setting, denominated an excise for raising revenue and legalized by ignoring its purpose as a mere instrumentality for bringing about a desired end. To do this would be to shut our eyes to what all others than we can see and understand. *Child Labor Tax Case,* 259 U. S. 20, 37.

We conclude that the act is one regulating agricultural production; that the tax is a mere incident of such regulation and that the respondents have standing to challenge the legality of the exaction.

It does not follow that as the act is not an exertion of the taxing power and the exaction not a true tax, the statute is void or the exaction uncollectible. For, to paraphrase what was said in *The Head Money Cases (supra),* p. 596, if this is an expedient regulation by Congress, of a subject within one of its granted powers, "and the end to be attained is one falling within that power, the act is not void, because, within a loose and more extended sense than was used in the Constitution," the exaction is called a tax.

Second. The Government asserts that even if the respondents may question the propriety of the appropriation embodied in the statute their attack must fail because Article I, Section 8 of the Constitution authorizes the contemplated expenditure of the funds raised by the tax. This contention presents the great and the controlling question in the case. We approach its decision with a sense of our grave responsibility to render judgment in accordance with the principles established for the governance of all three branches of the Government.

There should be no misunderstanding as to the function of this court in such a case. It is sometimes said that the court assumes a power to overrule or control the action of the people's representatives. This is a misconception. The Constitution is the supreme law of the land ordained and established by the people. All legislation must conform to the principles it lays down. When an act of Congress is appropriately challenged in the courts as not conforming to the constitutional mandate the judicial branch of the Government has only one duty,—to lay the article of the Constitution which is invoked beside the statute which is challenged and to decide whether the latter squares with the former. All the court does, or can do, is to announce its considered judgment upon the question. The only power it has, if such it may be called, is the power of judgment. This court neither approves nor condemns any legislative policy. Its delicate and difficult office is to ascertain and declare whether the legislation is in accordance with, or in contravention of, the provisions of the Constitution; and, having done that, its duty ends.

The question is not what power the federal Government ought to have but what powers in fact have been given by the people. It hardly seems necessary to reiterate that ours is a dual form of government; that in every state there are two governments,—the state and the United States. Each State has all governmental powers save such as the people, by their Constitution, have conferred upon the United States, denied to the States, or reserved to themselves. The federal union is a government of delegated powers. It has only such as are expressly conferred upon it and such as are reasonably to be implied from those granted. In this respect we differ radically from nations where all legislative power, without restriction or limitation, is vested in a parliament or other legislative body subject to no restrictions except the discretion of its members.

Article I, Section 8, of the Constitution vests sundry powers in the Congress. But two of its clauses have any bearing upon the validity of the statute under review.

The third clause endows the Congress with power "to regulate Commerce . . . among the several States." Despite a reference in its first section to a burden upon, and an obstruction of the normal currents of commerce, the act under review does not purport to regulate transactions in interstate or foreign commerce. Its stated purpose is the control of agricultural production, a purely local activity in an effort to raise the prices paid the farmer. Indeed, the Government does not attempt to uphold the validity of the act on the basis of the commerce clause, which, for the purpose of the present case, may be put aside as irrelevant.

The clause thought to authorize the legislation,—the first,—confers upon the Congress power "to lay and collect Taxes, Duties, Imposts and Excises, to pay the Debts and provide for the common Defence and general Welfare of the United States. . . ." It is not contended that this provision grants power to regulate agricultural production upon the theory that such legislation would promote the general welfare. The Government concedes that the phrase "to provide for the general welfare" qualifies the power "to lay and collect taxes." The view that the clause grants power to provide for the general welfare, independently of the taxing power, has never been authoritatively accepted. . . . The true construction undoubtedly is that the only thing granted is the power to tax for the purpose of providing funds for payment of the nation's debts and making provision for the general welfare.

Nevertheless the Government asserts that warrant is found in this clause for the adoption of the Agricultural Adjustment Act. The argument is that Congress may appropriate and authorize the spending of moneys for the "general welfare"; that the phrase should be liberally construed to cover anything conducive to national welfare; that decision as to what will promote such welfare rests with Congress alone, and the courts may not review its determination; and finally that the appropriation under attack was in fact for the general welfare of the United States. . . .

Since the foundation of the nation sharp differences of opinion have persisted as to the true interpretation of the phrase. Madison asserted it amounted to no more than a reference to the other powers enumerated in the subsequent clauses of the same section; that, as the United States is a government of limited and enumerated powers, the grant of power to tax and spend for the general national welfare must be confined to the enumerated legislative fields committed to the Congress. In this view the phrase is mere tautology, for taxation and appropriation are or may be necessary incidents of the exercise of any of the enumerated legislative powers. Hamilton, on the other hand, maintained the clause confers a power separate and distinct from those later enumerated, is not restricted in meaning by the grant of them, and Congress consequently has a substantive power to tax and to appropriate, limited only by the requirement that it shall be exercised to provide for the general welfare of the United States. Each contention has had the support of those whose views are entitled to weight. This court has noticed the question, but has never found it necessary to decide which is the true construction. Mr. Justice Story, in his Commentaries, espouses the Hamiltonian position. We shall not review the writings of public men and commentators or discuss the legislative practice. Study of all these leads us to conclude that the reading advocated by Mr. Justice Story is the correct one. While, therefore, the power to tax is not unlimited, its confines are set in the clause which confers it, and not in those of section 8 which bestow and define the legislative powers of the Congress. It results that the power of Congress to authorize expenditure of public moneys for public purposes is not limited by the direct grants of legislative power found in the Constitution.

But the adoption of the broader construction leaves the power to spend subject to limitations. . . .

That the qualifying phrase must be given effect all advocates of broad construction admit. Hamilton, in his well known Report on Manufactures, states that the purpose must be "general, and not local.". . .

We are not now required to ascertain the scope of the phrase "general welfare of the United States" or to determine whether an appropriation in aid of agriculture falls within it. Wholly apart from that question, another principle embedded in our Constitution prohibits the enforcement of the Agricultural Adjustment Act. The act invades the reserved rights of the states. It is a statutory plan to regulate and control agricultural production, a matter beyond the powers delegated to the federal government. The tax, the appropriation of the funds raised, and the direction for their disbursement, are but parts of the plan. They are but means to an unconstitutional end.

From the accepted doctrine that the United States is a government of delegated powers, it follows that those not expressly granted, or reasonably to be implied from such as are conferred, are reserved to the states or to the people. To forestall any suggestion to the contrary, the Tenth Amendment was adopted. The same proposition, otherwise stated, is that powers not granted are prohibited. None to regulate agricultural production is given, and therefore legislation by Congress for that purpose is forbidden.

It is an established principle that the attainment of a prohibited end may not be accomplished under the pretext of the exertion of powers which are granted. . . .

These principles are as applicable to the power to lay taxes as to any other federal power. . . .

The power of taxation, which is expressly granted, may, of course, be adopted as a means to carry into operation another power also expressly granted. But resort to the taxing power to effectuate an end which is not legitimate, not within the scope of the Constitution, is obviously inadmissible. . . .

Third. If the taxing power may not be used as the instrument to enforce a regulation of matters of state concern with respect to which the Congress has no authority to interfere, may it, as in the present case, be employed to raise the money necessary to purchase a compliance which the Congress is powerless to command? The Government asserts that whatever might be said against the validity of the plan, if compulsory, it is constitutionally sound because the end is accomplished by voluntary cooperation. There are two sufficient answers to the contention. The regulation is not in fact voluntary. The farmer, of course, may refuse to comply, but the price of such refusal is the loss of benefits. The amount offered is intended to be sufficient to exert pressure on him to agree to the proposed regulation. The power to confer or withhold unlimited benefits is the power to coerce or destroy. If the cotton grower elects not to accept the benefits, he will receive less for his crops; those who receive payments will be able to undersell him. The result may well be financial ruin. The coercive purpose and intent of the statute is not obscured by the fact that it has not been perfectly successful. It is pointed out that, because there still remained a minority whom the rental and benefit payments were insufficient to induce to surrender their independence of action, the Congress has gone further and, in the Bankhead Cotton Act, used the taxing power in a more directly minatory fashion to compel submission. This progression only serves more fully to expose the coercive purpose of the so-called tax imposed by the present act. It is clear that the Department of Agriculture has properly described the plan as one to keep a non-cooperating minority in line. This is coercion by economic pressure. The asserted power of choice is illusory. . . .

But if the plan were one for purely voluntary cooperation it would stand no better so far as federal power is concerned. At best it is a scheme for purchasing with federal funds submission to federal regulation of a subject reserved to the states.

It is said that Congress has the undoubted right to appropriate money to executive officers for expenditure under contracts between the government and individuals; that much of the total expenditures is so made. But appropriations and expenditures under contracts for proper governmental purposes cannot justify contracts which are not within federal power. And contracts for the reduction of acreage and the control of production are outside the range of that power. An appropriation to be expended by the United States under contracts calling for violation of a state law clearly would offend the Constitution. Is a statute less objectionable which authorizes expenditure of federal moneys to induce action in a field in which the United States has no power to intermeddle? The Congress cannot invade state jurisdiction to compel individual action; no more can it purchase such action.

We are referred to numerous types of federal appropriation which have been made in the past, and it is asserted no question has been raised as to their validity. We need not stop to examine or consider them. . . .

Congress has no power to enforce its commands on the farmer to the ends sought by the Agricultural Adjustment Act. It must follow that it may not indirectly accomplish those ends by taxing and spending to purchase compliance. The Constitution and the entire plan of our government negative any such use of the power to tax and to spend as the act undertakes to authorize. It does not help to declare that local conditions throughout the nation have created a situation of national concern; for this is but to say that whenever there is a widespread similarity of local conditions, Congress may ignore constitutional limitations upon its own powers and usurp those reserved to the states. If, in lieu of compulsory regulation of subjects within the states' reserved jurisdiction, which is prohibited, the Congress could invoke the taxing and spending power as a means to accomplish the same end, clause 1 of Section 8 of Article I would become the instrument for total subversion of the governmental powers reserved to the individual states.

If the act before us is a proper exercise of the federal taxing power, evidently the regulation of all industry throughout the United States may be accomplished by similar exercises of the same power. It would be possible to exact money from one branch of an industry and pay it to another branch in every field of activity which lies within the province of the states. The mere threat of such a procedure might well induce the surrender of rights and the compliance with federal regulation as the price of continuance in business. A few instances will illustrate the thought. . . .

A possible result of sustaining the claimed federal power would be that every business group which thought itself under-privileged might demand that a tax be laid on its vendors or vendees the proceeds to be appropriated to the redress of its deficiency of income. . . .

Until recently no suggestion of the existence of any such power in the federal government has been advanced. The expressions
of the framers of the Constitution, the decisions of this court interpreting that instrument and the writings of great commentators
will be searched in vain for any suggestion
that there exists in the clause under discussion or elsewhere in the Constitution, the
authority whereby every provision and every
fair implication from that instrument may be
subverted, the independence of the individual
states obliterated, and the United States converted into a central government exercising
uncontrolled police power in every state of
the Union, superseding all local control or
regulation of the affairs or concerns of the
states.

Hamilton himself, the leading advocate of
broad interpretation of the power to tax and
to appropriate for the general welfare, never
suggested that any power granted by the Constitution could be used for the destruction of
local self-government in the states. Story
countenances no such doctrine. It seems never
to have occurred to them, or to those who
have agreed with them, that the general welfare of the United States, (which has aptly
been termed "an indestructible Union, composed of indestructible States,") might be
served by obliterating the constituent members of the Union. But to this fatal conclusion the doctrine contended for would inevitably lead. And its sole premise is that,
though the makers of the Constitution, in
erecting the federal government, intended
sedulously to limit and define its powers, so
as to reserve to the states and the people
sovereign power, to be wielded by the states
and their citizens and not to be invaded by
the United States, they nevertheless by a
single clause gave power to the Congress to
tear down the barriers, to invade the states'
jurisdiction, and to become a parliament of
the whole people, subject to no restrictions
save such as are self-imposed. The argument
when seen in its true character and in the
light of its inevitable results must be rejected.

The judgment is affirmed.

Mr. Justice STONE, dissenting. I think the
judgment should be reversed.

The present stress of widely held and
strongly expressed differences of opinion of
the wisdom of the Agricultural Adjustment
Act makes it important, in the interest of
clear thinking and sound result, to emphasize
at the outset certain propositions which
should have controlling influence in determining the validity of the Act. They are:

1. The power of courts to declare a statute
unconstitutional is subject to two guiding
principles of decision which ought never to
be absent from judicial consciousness. One is
that courts are concerned only with the power
to enact statutes, not with their wisdom. The
other is that while unconstitutional exercise
of power by the executive and legislative
branches of the government is subject to judicial restraint, the only check upon our own
exercise of power is our own sense of self-
restraint. For the removal of unwise laws
from the statute books appeal lies not to the
courts but to the ballot and to the processes
of democratic government.

2. The constitutional power of Congress to
levy an excise tax upon the processing of
agricultural products is not questioned. The
present levy is held invalid, not for any want
of power in Congress to lay such a tax to
defray public expenditures, including those
for the general welfare, but because the use
to which its proceeds are put is disapproved.

3. As the present depressed state of agriculture is nation wide in its extent and effects,
there is no basis for saying that the expenditure of public money in aid of farmers is not
within the specifically granted power of Congress to levy taxes to "provide for the . . .
general welfare." The opinion of the Court
does not declare otherwise. . . .

It is with these preliminary and hardly controverted matters in mind that we should
direct our attention to the pivot on which the
decision of the Court is made to turn. It is
that a levy unquestionably within the taxing
power of Congress may be traced as invalid
because it is a step in a plan to regulate agricultural production and is thus a forbidden
infringement of state power. The levy is not
any the less an exercise of taxing power because it is intended to defray an expenditure
for the general welfare rather than for some
other support of government. Nor is the levy
and collection of the tax pointed to as effecting the regulation. While all federal taxes inevitably have some influence on the internal
economy of the states, it is not contended

that the levy of a processing tax upon manufacturers using agricultural products as raw material has any perceptible regulatory effect upon either their production or manufacture. . . .

Of the assertion that the payments to farmers are coercive, it is enough to say that no such contention is pressed by the taxpayer, and no such consequences were to be anticipated or appear to have resulted from the administration of the Act. The suggestion of coercion finds no support in the record or in any data showing the actual operation of the Act. Threat of loss, not hope of gain, is the essence of economic coercion. . . . The presumption of constitutionality of a statute is not to be overturned by an assertion of its coercive effect which rests on nothing more substantial than groundless speculation.

It is upon the contention that state power is infringed by purchased regulation of agricultural production that chief reliance is placed. It is insisted that, while the Constitution gives to Congress, in specific and unambiguous terms, the power to tax and spend, the power is subject to limitations which do not find their origin in any express provision of the Constitution and to which other expressly delegated powers are not subject.

The Constitution requires that public funds shall be spent for a defined purpose, the promotion of the general welfare. Their expenditure usually involves payment on terms which will insure use by the selected recipients within the limits of the constitutional purpose. Expenditures would fail of their purpose and thus lose their constitutional sanction if the terms of payment were not such that by their influence on the action of the recipients the permitted end would be attained. The power of Congress to spend is inseparable from persuasion to action over which Congress has no legislative control. Congress may not command that the science of agriculture be taught in state universities. But if it would aid the teaching of that science by grants to state institutions, it is appropriate, if not necessary, that the grant be on the condition, incorporated in the Morrill Act, that it be used for the intended purpose. Similarly it would seem to be compliance with the Constitution, not violation of it, for the government to take and the university to give a contract that the grant would be so used.

It makes no difference that there is a promise to do an act which the condition is calculated to induce. Condition and promise are alike valid since both are in furtherance of the national purpose for which the money is appropriated.

These effects upon individual action, which are but incidents of the authorized expenditure of government money, are pronounced to be themselves a limitation upon the granted power, and so the time-honored principle of constitutional interpretation that the granted power includes all those which are incident to it is reversed. "Let the end be legitimate," said the great Chief Justice, "let it be within the scope of the Constitution, and all means which are appropriate, which are plainly adapted to that end, which are not prohibited, but consist with the letter and spirit of the Constitution, are constitutional." *McCulloch* v. *Maryland*. This cardinal guide to constitutional exposition must now be rephrased so far as the spending power of the federal government is concerned. Let the expenditure be to promote the general welfare, still, if it is needful in order to insure its use for the intended purpose to influence any action which Congress cannot command because within the sphere of state government, the expenditure is unconstitutional. And taxes otherwise lawfully levied are likewise unconstitutional if they are appropriated to the expenditure whose incident is condemned. . . .

Such a limitation is contradictory and destructive of the power to appropriate for the public welfare, and is incapable of practical application. The spending power of Congress is in addition to the legislative power and not subordinate to it. This independent grant of the power of the purse, and its very nature, involving in its exercise the duty to insure expenditure within the granted power, presuppose freedom of selection among divers ends and aims, and the capacity to impose such conditions as will render the choice effective. It is a contradiction in terms to say that there is power to spend for the national welfare, while rejecting any power to impose conditions reasonably adapted to the attainment of the end which alone would justify the expenditure.

The limitation now sanctioned must lead to absurd consequences. The government may give seeds to farmers, but may not condition the gift upon their being planted in places where they are most needed or even planted at all. The government may give money to the unemployed, but may not ask that those who get it shall give labor in return, or even use it to support their families. It may give money to sufferers from earthquake, fire, tornado, pestilence or flood, but may not impose conditions—health precautions designed to prevent the spread of disease, or induce the movement of population to safer or more sanitary areas. All that, because it is purchased regulation infringing state powers, must be left for the states, who are unable or unwilling to supply the necessary relief. The government may spend its money for vocational rehabilitation, but it may not, with the consent of all concerned, supervise the process which it undertakes to aid. It may spend its money for the suppression of the boll weevil, but may not compensate the farmers for suspending the growth of cotton in the infected areas. It may aid state reforestation and forest fire prevention agencies, but may not be permitted to supervise their conduct. It may support rural schools, but may not condition its grant by the requirement that certain standards be maintained. It may appropriate moneys to be expended by the Reconstruction Finance Corporation "to aid in financing agriculture, commerce and industry," and to facilitate "the exportation of agricultural and other products." Do all its activities collapse because, in order to effect the permissible purpose, in myriad ways the money is paid out upon terms and conditions which influence action of the recipients within the states, which Congress cannot command? The answer would seem plain. If the expenditure is for a national public purpose, that purpose will not be thwarted because payment is on condition which will advance that purpose. The action which Congress induces by payments of money to promote the general welfare, but which it does not command or coerce, is but an incident to a specifically granted power, but a permissible means to a legitimate end. If appropriation in aid of a program of curtailment of agricultural production is constitutional, and it is not denied that it is, payment to farmers on condition that they reduce their crop acreage is constitutional. It is not any the less so because the farmer at his own option promises to fulfill the condition.

That the governmental power of the purse is a great one is not now for the first time announced. Every student of the history of government and economics is aware of its magnitude and of its existence in every civilized government. Both were well understood by the framers of the Constitution when they sanctioned the grant of the spending power to the federal government, and both were recognized by Hamilton and Story, whose views of the spending power as standing on a parity with the other powers specifically granted, have hitherto been generally accepted.

The suggestion that it must now be curtailed by judicial fiat because it may be abused by unwise use hardly rises to the dignity of argument. So may judicial power be abused. . . . "It must be remembered that legislators are the ultimate guardians of the liberties and welfare of the people in quite as great a degree as the courts." Justice Holmes, in *Missouri, Kansas & Texas R. R. Co.* v. *May.*

A tortured construction of the Constitution is not to be justified by recourse to extreme examples of reckless congressional spending which might occur if courts could not prevent expenditures which, even if they could be thought to effect any national purpose, would be possible only by action of a legislature lost to all sense of public responsibility. Such suppositions are addressed to the mind accustomed to believe that it is the business of courts to sit in judgment on the wisdom of legislative action. Courts are not the only agency of government that must be assumed to have capacity to govern. Congress and the courts both unhappily may falter or be mistaken in the performance of their constitutional duty. But interpretation of our great charter of government which proceeds on any assumption that the responsibility for the preservation of our institutions is the exclusive concern of any one of the three branches of government, or that it alone can save them from destruction is far more likely, in the long run, "to obliterate the constituent members" of "an indestructible union of indestructible states" than the frank recognition that language, even of a constitution, may mean what it says: that the power to tax and spend includes the power to relieve a nation-wide economic maladjustment by conditional gifts of money.

Mr. Justice BRANDEIS and Mr. Justice CARDOZO join in this opinion.

479. THE TENNESSEE VALLEY ACT
May 18, 1933
(*U. S. Statutes at Large,* Vol. XLVIII, p. 58)

The Tennessee Valley Authority, established by this Act, undertook a broad program of economic and social reconstruction of the Tennessee Valley region. The TVA not only constructed dams and transmission lines, but undertook rural electrification, withdrawal of marginal lands, promotion of public health, and many similar activities. The success of the experiment led to the demand for the construction of other power sites and for regional planning by the federal government. See, S. Chase, *Rich Land, Poor Land;* R. Lord, *Behold Our Land;* H. S. Raushenbush, *The Power Fight;* H. S. Raushenbush and H. W. Laidler, *Power Control;* Martell, "Legal Aspects of the TVA," 7 Geo. Wash. L. Rev. 983. On Sen. Norris, chiefly responsible for the passage of the act, see R. L. Neuberger and S. B. Kahn, *George W. Norris.*

AN ACT to improve the navigability and to provide for the flood control of the Tennessee River; to provide for reforestation and the proper use of marginal lands in the Tennessee Valley; to provide for the agricultural and industrial development of said valley; to provide for the national defense by the creation of a corporation for the operation of Government properties at and near Muscle Shoals in the State of Alabama, and for other purposes. . . .

Be it enacted, That for the purpose of maintaining and operating the properties now owned by the United States in the vicinity of Muscle Shoals, Alabama, . . . there is hereby created a body corporate by the name of the "Tennessee Valley Authority." . . .

SEC. 2. . . .

(f) No director shall have financial interest in any public-utility corporation engaged in the business of distributing and selling power to the public nor in any corporation engaged in the manufacture, selling, or distribution of fixed nitrogen or fertilizer, or any ingredients thereof, nor shall any member have any interest in any business that may be adversely affected by the success of the Corporation as a producer of concen-trated fertilizers or as a producer of electric power. . . .

(h) All members of the board shall be persons who profess a belief in the feasibility and wisdom of this Act. . . .

SEC. 3. . . .

All contracts to which the Corporation is a party and which require the employment of laborers and mechanics in the construction, alteration, maintenance, or repair of buildings, dams, locks, or other projects shall contain a provision that not less than the prevailing rate of wages for work of a similar nature prevailing in the vicinity shall be paid to such laborers or mechanics. . . .

SEC. 4. Except as otherwise specifically provided in this Act, the Corporation—

(f) May purchase or lease and hold such real and personal property as it deems necessary or convenient in the transaction of its business, and may dispose of any such personal property held by it. . . .

(h) Shall have power in the name of the United States of America to exercise the right of eminent domain, and in the purchase of any real estate or the acquisition of real estate by condemnation proceedings, the title to such real estate shall be taken in the name of the United States of America, . . .

(i) Shall have power to acquire real estate for the construction of dams, reservoirs, transmission lines, power houses, and other structures, and navigation projects at any point along the Tennessee River, or any of its tributaries, . . .

(j) Shall have power to construct dams, reservoirs, power houses, power structures, transmission lines, navigation projects, and incidental works in the Tennessee River and its tributaries, and to unite the various power installations into one or more systems by transmission lines.

SEC. 5. The board is hereby authorized— . . .

(b) To arrange with farmers and farm organizations for large-scale practical use of the new forms of fertilizers under conditions permitting an accurate measure of the economic return they produce.

(c) To cooperate with National, State, district, or county experimental stations or demonstration farms, for the use of new forms of fertilizer or fertilizer practices during the initial or experimental period of their introduction.

(d) The board in order to improve and cheapen the production of fertilizer is authorized to manufacture and sell fixed nitrogen, fertilizer, and fertilizer ingredients at Muscle Shoals by the employment of existing facilities, by modernizing existing plants, or by any other process or processes that in its judgment shall appear wise and profitable for the fixation of atmospheric nitrogen or the cheapening of the production of fertilizer.

(e) Under the authority of this Act the board may make donations or sales of the product of the plant or plants operated by it to be fairly and equitably distributed through the agency of county demonstration agents, agricultural colleges, or otherwise as the board may direct, for experimentation, education, and introduction of the use of such products in cooperation with practical farmers so as to obtain information as to the value, effect, and best methods of their use.

(f) The board is authorized to make alterations, modifications, or improvements in existing plants and facilities, and to construct new plants.

(g) In the event it is not used for the fixation of nitrogen for agricultural purposes or leased, then the board shall maintain in standby condition nitrate plant numbered 2, or its equivalent, for the fixation of atmospheric nitrogen, for the production of explosives in the event of war or a national emergency, until the Congress shall by joint resolution release the board from this obligation, and if any part thereof be used by the board for the manufacture of phosphoric acid or potash, the balance of nitrate plant numbered 2 shall be kept in stand-by condition.

(h) To establish, maintain, and operate laboratories and experimental plants, and to undertake experiments for the purpose of enabling the Corporation to furnish nitrogen products for military purposes, and nitrogen and other fertilizer products for agricultural purposes in the most economical manner and at the highest standard of efficiency. . . .

(l) To produce, distribute, and sell electric power, as herein particularly specified.

(m) No products of the Corporation shall be sold for use outside of the United States, its Territories and possessions, except to the United States Government for the use of its Army and Navy, or to its allies in case of war.

SEC. 10. The board is hereby empowered and authorized to sell the surplus power not used in its operations, and for operation of locks and other works generated by it, to States, counties, municipalities, corporations, partnerships, or individuals, according to the policies hereinafter set forth; and to carry out said authority, the board is authorized to enter into contracts for such sale for a term not exceeding twenty years, and in the sale of such current by the board it shall give preference to States, counties, municipalities, and cooperative organizations of citizens or farmers, not organized or doing business for profit, but primarily for the purpose of supplying electricity to its own citizens or members: . . . In order to promote and encourage the fullest possible use of electric light and power on farms within reasonable distance of any of its transmission lines the board in its discretion shall have power to construct transmission lines to farms and small villages that are not otherwise supplied with electricity at reasonable rates, and to make such rules and regulations governing such sale and distribution of such electric power as in its judgment may be just and equitable: *Provided further,* That the board is hereby authorized and directed to make studies, experiments, and determinations to promote the wider and better use of electric power for agricultural and domestic use, or for small or local industries, and it may cooperate with State governments, or their subdivisions or agencies, with educational or research institutions, and with cooperatives or other organizations, in the application of electric power to the fuller and better balanced development of the resources of the region.

SEC. 11. It is hereby declared to be the policy of the Government so far as practical to distribute and sell the surplus power generated at Muscle Shoals equitably among the States, counties, and municipalities within transmission distance. This policy is further declared to be that the projects herein provided for shall be considered primarily as for the benefit of the people of the section as a whole and particularly the domestic and rural consumers to whom the power can economically be made available, and accordingly that sale to and use by industry shall be a secondary purpose, to be utilized principally to secure a sufficiently high load factor and revenue returns which will permit domestic and rural use at the lowest possible rates and in such manner as to encourage increased domestic and rural use of electricity. It is further hereby declared to be the policy of the Government to utilize the Muscle Shoals properties so far as may be necessary to improve, increase, and cheapen the production of fertilizer and fertilizer ingredients by carrying out the provision of this Act. . . .

SEC. 22. To aid further the proper use, conservation, and development of the natural resources of the Tennessee River drainage basin and of such adjoining territory as may be related to or materially affected by the development consequent to this Act, and to provide for the general welfare of the citizens of said areas, the President is hereby authorized, by such means or methods as he may deem proper within the limits of appropriations made therefor by Congress, to make such surveys of and general plans for said Tennessee basin and adjoining territory as may be useful to the Congress and to the several States in guiding and controlling the extent, sequence, and nature of development that may be equitably and economically advanced through the expenditure of public funds, or through the guidance or control of public authority, all for the general purpose of fostering an orderly and proper physical, economic, and social development of said areas; and the President is further authorized in making said surveys and plans to cooperate with the States affected thereby, or subdivisions or agencies of such States, or with cooperative or other organizations, and to make such studies, experiments, or demonstrations as may be necessary and suitable to that end.

SEC. 23. The President shall, from time to time, as the work provided for in the preceding section progresses, recommend to Congress such legislation as he deems proper to carry out the general purposes stated in said section, and for the especial purpose of bringing about in said Tennessee drainage basin and adjoining territory in conformity with said general purposes (1) the maximum amount of flood control; (2) the maximum development of said Tennessee River for navigation purposes; (3) the maximum generation of electric power consistent with flood control and navigation; (4) the proper use of marginal lands; (5) the proper method of reforestation of all lands in said drainage basin suitable for reforestation; and (6) the economic and social well-being of the people living in said river basin. . . .

480. ASHWANDER et. al. v. TENNESSEE VALLEY AUTHORITY
297 U. S. 288
1936

On Writs of Certiorari to the U. S. Circuit Court of Appeals for the Fifth District. This decision was one of the few notable victories of the government in the Courts during the first Roosevelt administration. Justices Brandeis, Stone, Roberts and Cardozo concurred in the result but insisted that the plaintiffs should have had no standing in the Court. See, Albertsworth, "Constitutional Issues of the Federal Power Program," 29 Ills. L. Rev. 883; Grant, "Commerce, Production and the Fiscal Powers of Congress," 45 Yale L. J. 751, 991; Boyd, "The Tennessee Valley Litigation," 11 Indiana L. J. 368; and notes in 84 U. of Pa. L. Rev. 787; 34 Mich. L. Rev. 680; 5 U. of Chicago L. Rev. 639.

HUGHES, C. J. On January 4, 1934, the Tennessee Valley Authority, an agency of the Federal Government, entered into a contract with the Alabama Power Company, providing (1) for the purchase by the Authority from the Power Company of certain transmission lines, sub-stations, and auxiliary properties for $1,000,000, (2) for the purchase by the Authority from the Power Company of certain real property for $150,000, (3) for an interchange of hydroelectric energy, and in addition for the sale by the Authority to the Power Company of its "surplus power," on stated terms, and (4) for mutual restrictions as to the areas to be served in the sale of power. The contract was amended and supplemented in minor particulars on February 13 and May 24, 1934.

The Alabama Power Company is a corporation organized under the laws of Alabama and is engaged in the generation of electric energy and its distribution generally throughout that State, its lines reaching 66 counties. The transmission lines to be purchased by the Authority extend from Wilson Dam, at the Muscle Shoals plant owned by the United States on the Tennessee River in northern Alabama, into seven counties in that State, within a radius of about 50 miles. These lines serve a population of approximately 190,000, including about 10,000 individual customers, or about one-tenth of the total number served directly by the Power Company. The real property to be acquired by the Authority (apart from the transmission lines above mentioned and related properties) is adjacent to the area known as the "Joe Wheeler dam site," upon which the Authority is constructing the Wheeler Dam. . . .

Plaintiffs are holders of preferred stock of the Alabama Power Company. Conceiving the contract with the Tennessee Valley Authority to be injurious to the corporate interests and also invalid, because beyond the constitutional power of the Federal Government, they submitted their protest to the board of directors of the Power Company and demanded that steps should be taken to have the contract annulled. . . . Going beyond that particular challenge, and setting for the pronouncements, policies and programs of the Authority, plaintiffs sought a decree restraining these activities as repugnant to the Constitution, and also asked a general declaratory decree with respect to the rights of the Authority in various relations.

The defendants, including the Authority and its directors, the Power Company and its mortgage trustee, and the municipalities within the described area, filed answers and the case was heard upon evidence. The District Court made elaborate findings and entered a final decree annulling the contract of January 4, 1934, and enjoining the transfer of the transmission lines and auxiliary properties. The court also enjoined the defendant municipalities from making or performing any contracts with the Authority for the purchase of power, and from accepting or expending any funds received from the Authority or the Public Works Administration for the purpose of constructing a public distribution system to distribute power which the Authority supplied. The court gave no consideration to plaintiff's request for a general declaratory decree.

The Authority, its directors, and the city of Florence appealed from the decree and the case was severed as to the other defendants. Plaintiffs took a cross appeal.

The Circuit Court of Appeals limited its discussion to the precise issue with respect to the effect and validity of the contract of January 4, 1934. The District Court had found that the electric energy required for the territory served by the transmission lines to be purchased under that contract is available at Wilson Dam without the necessity for any interconnection with any other dam or power plant. The Circuit Court of Appeals accordingly considered the constitutional authority for the construction of Wilson Dam and for the disposition of the electric energy there created. In the view that the Wilson Dam had been constructed in the exercise of the war and commerce powers of the Congress and that the electric energy there available was the property of the United States and subject to its disposition, the Circuit Court of Appeals decided that the decree of the District Court was erroneous and should be reversed. The court also held that plaintiffs should take nothing by their cross appeal. 78 F. (2d) 578. On plaintiffs' application we granted writs of certiorari, 296 U. S.—.

First. The right of plaintiffs to bring this suit. . . .

We think that plaintiffs have made a sufficient showing to entitle them to bring suit and that a constitutional question is properly presented and should be decided.

Second. The scope of the issue. We agree with the Circuit Court of Appeals that the question to be determined is limited to the validity of the contract of January 4, 1934. The pronouncements, policies and program of the Tennessee Valley Authority and its directors, their motives and desires, did not give rise to a justiciable controversy save as they had fruition in action of a definite and concrete character constituting an actual or threatened interference with the rights of the persons complaining. The judicial power does not extend to the determination of abstract questions. . . .

As it appears that the transmission lines in question run from the Wilson Dam and that the electric energy generated at that dam is more than sufficient to supply all the requirements of the contract, the questions that are properly before us relate to the constitutional authority for the construction of the Wilson Dam and for the disposition, as provided in the contract, of the electric energy there generated.

Third. The constitutional authority for the construction of the Wilson Dam. The Congress may not, "under the pretext of executing its powers, pass laws for the accomplishment of objects not entrusted to the government." Chief Justice Marshall, in *McCulloch* v. *Maryland; Linder* v. *United States,* 268 U. S. 15, 17. The Government's argument recognizes this essential limitation. The Government's contention is that the Wilson Dam was constructed, and the power plant connected with it was installed, in the exercise by the Congress of its war and commerce powers, that is, for the purposes of national defense and the improvement of navigation. . . .

We may take judicial notice of the international situation at the time the Act of 1916 was passed, and it cannot be successfully disputed that the Wilson Dam and its auxiliary plants, including the hydro-electric power plant, are, and were intended to be, adapted to the purposes of national defense. While the District Court found that there is no intention to use the nitrate plants or the hydro-electric units installed at Wilson Dam for the production of war materials in time of peace, "the maintenance of said properties in operating condition and the assurance of an abundant supply of electric energy is the event of war, constitute national defense assets." This finding has ample support.

The Act of 1916 also had in view "improvements to navigation." Commerce includes navigation. "All America understands,

and has uniformly understood," said Chief Justice Marshall in *Gibbons* v. *Ogden,* "the word 'commerce,' to comprehend navigation." The power to regulate interstate commerce embraces the power to keep the navigable rivers of the United States free from obstructions to navigation and to remove such obstructions when they exist. "For these purposes," said the Court in *Gilman* v. *Philadelphia,* 3 Wall. 713, 725, "Congress possesses all the powers which existed in the States before the adoption of the national Constitution, and which have always existed in the Parliament in England." . . .

The Tennessee River is a navigable stream, although there are obstructions at various points because of shoals, reefs and rapids. The improvement of navigation on this river has been a matter of national concern for over a century. . . .

While, in its present condition, the Tennessee River is not adequately improved for commercial navigation, and traffic is small, we are not at liberty to conclude either that the river is not susceptible of development as an important waterway, or that Congress has not undertaken that development, or that the construction of the Wilson Dam was not an appropriate means to accomplish a legitimate end.

The Wilson Dam and its power plant must be taken to have been constructed in the exercise of the constitutional functions of the Federal Government.

Fourth. The constitutional authority to dispose of electric energy generated at the Wilson Dam. The Government acquired full title to the dam site, with all riparian rights. The power of falling water was an inevitable incident of the construction of the dam. That water power came into the exclusive control of the Federal Government. The mechanical energy was convertible into electric energy, and the water power, the right to convert it into electric energy, and the electric energy thus produced, constitute property belonging to the United States.

Authority to dispose of property constitutionally acquired by the United States is expressly granted to the Congress by section 3 of Article IV of the Constitution. This section provides:

"The Congress shall have Power to dispose of and make all needful Rules and Regulations respecting the Territory or other Property belonging to the United States; and nothing in this Constitution shall be so construed as to Prejudice any Claims of the United States, or of any particular State."

To the extent that the power of disposition is thus expressly conferred, it is manifest that the Tenth Amendment is not applicable. And the Ninth Amendment (which petitioners also invoke) in insuring the maintenance of the rights retained by the people does not withdraw the rights which are expressly granted to the Federal Government. The question is as to the scope of the grant and whether there are inherent limitations which render invalid the disposition of property with which we are now concerned.

The occasion for the grant was the obvious necessity of making provision for the government of the vast territory acquired by the United States. The power to govern and to dispose of that territory was deemed to be indispensable to the purposes of the cessions made by the States. . . . The grant was made in broad terms, and the power of regulation and disposition was not confined to territory, but extended to "other property belonging to the United States," so that the power may be applied, as Story says, "to the due regulation of all other personal and real property rightfully belonging to the United States." And so, he adds, "it has been constantly understood and acted upon."

This power of disposal was early construed to embrace leases, thus enabling the Government to derive profit through royalties. . . . The policy, early adopted and steadily pursued, of segregating mineral lands from other public lands and providing for leases, pointed to the recognition both of the full power of disposal and of the necessity of suitably adapting the methods of disposal to different sorts of property. . . .

But when Congress thus reserved mineral lands for special disposal, can it be doubted that Congress could have provided for mining directly by its own agents, instead of giving that right to lessees on the payment of royalties? Upon what ground could it be said that the Government could not mine its own gold, silver, coal, lead, or phosphates in the public domain, and dispose of them as property belonging to the United States? That it could dispose of its land but not of what the

land contained? It would seem to be clear that under the same power of disposition which enabled the Government to lease and obtain profit from sales by its lessees, it could mine and obtain profit from its own sales.

The question is whether a more limited power of disposal should be applied to the water power, convertible into electric energy, and to the electric energy thus produced at the Wilson Dam constructed by the Government in the exercise of its constitutional functions. If so, it must be by reason either of (1) the nature of the particular property, or (2) the character of the "surplus" disposed of, or (3) the manner of disposition.

(1) That the water power and the electric energy generated at the dam are susceptible of disposition as property belonging to the United States is well established. . . .

(2) The argument is stressed that, assuming that electric energy generated at the dam belongs to the United States, the Congress has authority to dispose of this energy only to the extent that it is a surplus necessarily created in the course of making munitions of war or operating the works for navigation purposes; that is, that the remainder of the available energy must be lost or go to waste. We find nothing in the Constitution which imposes such a limitation. It is not to be deduced from the mere fact that the electric energy is only potentially available until the generators are operated. The Government has no less right to the energy thus available by letting the water course over its turbines than it has to use the appropriate processes to reduce to possession other property within its control, as, for example, oil which it may recover from a pool beneath its lands, and which is reduced to possession by boring oil wells and otherwise might escape its grasp. And it would hardly be contended that, when the Government reserves coal on its lands, it can mine the coal and dispose of it only for the purpose of heating public buildings or for other governmental operations. Or, if the Government owns a silver mine, that it can obtain the silver only for the purpose of storage or coinage. Or that when the Government extracts the oil it has reserved, it has no constitutional power to sell it. Our decisions recognize no such restriction. The United States owns the coal, or the silver, or the lead, or the oil, it obtains

from its lands, and it lies in the discretion of the Congress, acting in the public interest, to determine of how much of the property it shall dispose.

We think that the same principle is applicable to electric energy. The argument pressed upon us leads to absurd consequences in the denial, despite the broad terms of the constitutional provision, of a power of disposal which the public interest may imperatively require. Suppose, for example, that in the erection of a dam for the improvement of navigation, it became necessary to destroy a dam and power plant which had previously been erected by a private corporation engaged in the generation and distribution of energy which supplied the needs of neighboring communities and business enterprises. Would anyone say that, because the United States had built its own dam and plant in the exercise of its constitutional functions, and had complete ownership and dominion over both, no power could be supplied to the communities and enterprises dependent on it, not because of any unwillingness of the Congress to supply it, or of any overriding governmental need, but because there was no constitutional authority to furnish the supply? Or that, with abundant power available, which must otherwise be wasted, the supply to the communities and enterprises whose very life may be at stake must be limited to the slender amount of surplus unavoidably involved in the operation of the navigation works, because the Constitution does not permit any more energy to be generated and distributed? In the case of the *Green Bay Canal Company,* where the government works supplanted those of the Canal Company, the Court found no difficulty in sustaining the Government's authority to grant to the Canal Company the water powers which it had previously enjoyed, subject, of course, to the dominant control of the Government. And in the case of *United States* v. *Chandler-Dunbar Company, supra,* the statutory provision, to which the Court referred, was "that any excess of water in the St. Marys River at Sault Sainte Marie over and above the amount now or hereafter required for the uses of navigation shall be leased for power purposes by the Secretary of War upon such terms and conditions as shall be best calculated in his judgment to insure the develop-

ment thereof." It was to the leasing, under this provision, "of any excess of power over the needs of the Government" that the Court saw no valid objection. . . .

(3) We come then to the question as to the validity of the method which had been adopted in disposing of the surplus energy generated at the Wilson Dam. The constitutional provision is silent as to the method of disposing of property belonging to the United States. That method, of course, must be an appropriate means of disposition according to the nature of the property, it must be one adopted in the public interest as distinguished from private or personal ends, and we may assume that it must be consistent with the foundation principles of our dual system of government and must not be contrived to govern the concerns reserved to the States. In this instance, the method of disposal embraces the sale of surplus energy by the Tennessee Valley Authority to the Alabama Power Company, the interchange of energy between the Authority and the Power Company, and the purchase by the Authority from the Power Company of certain transmission lines.

As to the mere sale of surplus energy, nothing need be added to what we have said as to the constitutional authority to dispose. The Government could lease or sell and fix the terms. Sales of surplus energy to the Power Company by the Authority continued a practice begun by the Government several years before. The contemplated interchange of energy is a form of disposition and presents no questions which are essentially different from those that are pertinent to sales.

The transmission lines which the Authority undertakes to purchase from the Power Company lead from the Wilson Dam to a large area within about fifty miles of the dam. These lines provide the means of distributing the electric energy, generated at the dam, to a large population. They furnish a method of reaching a market. The alternative method is to sell the surplus energy at the dam, and the market there appears to be limited to one purchaser, the Alabama Power Company, and its affiliated interests. We know of no constitutional ground upon which the Federal Government can be denied the right to seek a wider market. We suppose that in the early days of mining in the West, if the

Government had undertaken to operate a silver mine on its domain, it could have acquired the mules or horses and equipment to carry its silver to market. And the transmission lines for electric energy are but a facility for conveying to market that particular sort of property, and the acquisition of these lines raises no different constitutional question, unless in some way there is an invasion of the rights reserved to the State or to the people. We find no basis for concluding that the limited undertaking with the Alabama Power Company amounts to such an invasion. Certainly, the Alabama Power Company has no constitutional right to insist that it shall be the sole purchaser of the energy generated at the Wilson Dam; that the energy shall be sold to it or go to waste.

We limit our decision to the case before us, as we have defined it. The argument is earnestly presented that the Government by virtue of its ownership of the dam and power plant could not establish a steel mill and make and sell steel products, or a factory to manufacture clothing or shoes for the public, and thus attempt to make its ownership of energy, generated at its dam, a means of carrying on competitive commercial enterprises and thus drawing to the Federal Government the conduct and management of business having no relation to the purposes for which the Federal Government was established. The picture is eloquently drawn but we deem it to be irrelevant to the issue here. The Government is not using the water power at the Wilson Dam to establish any industry or business. It is not using the energy generated at the dam to manufacture commodities of any sort for the public. The

Government is disposing of the energy itself which simply is the mechanical energy, incidental to falling water at the dam, converted into the electric energy which is susceptible of transmission. The question here is simply as to the acquisition of the transmission lines as a facility for the disposal of that energy. And the Government rightly conceded at the bar, in substance, that it was without constitutional authority to acquire or dispose of such energy except as it comes into being in the operation of works constructed in the exercise of some power delegated to the United States. As we have said, these transmission lines lead directly from the dam, which has been lawfully constructed, and the question of the constitutional right of the Government to acquire or operate local or urban distribution systems is not involved. We express no opinion as to the validity of such an effort, as to the status of any other dam or power development in the Tennessee Valley, whether connected with or apart from the Wilson Dam, or as to the validity of the Tennessee Valley Authority Act or of the claims made in the pronouncements and program of the Authority apart from the questions we have discussed in relation to the particular provisions of the contract of January 4, 1934, affecting the Alabama Power Company.

The decree of the Circuit Court of Appeals is affirmed.

Affirmed.

Brandeis, J. delivered a separate opinion in which Justices Stone, Roberts and Cardozo concurred. McReynolds, J. dissented.

---

481. THE ABANDONMENT OF THE GOLD STANDARD

Joint Resolution of Congress Voiding the Gold Clause in Government Obligations
June 5, 1933

(*U. S. Statutes at Large,* Vol. XLVIII, p. 113)

By executive order of April, 1933, all holders of gold were required to turn their gold into the Federal Reserve Banks by May 1. An executive order of April 20 put an end to the export of gold and formally took the nation off the gold standard. The Joint Resolution of June 5, 1933, repudiated the gold clause not only in all private but in government obligations. See J. Donaldson, *The Dollar;* A. Nussbaum, *Money in the Law;*

J. D. Paris, *Monetary Policies of the United States, 1932–1938;* G. Cassel, *The Downfall of the Gold Standard.* For the constitutional aspects of the Resolution see references to Doc. No. 482.

JOINT RESOLUTION to assure uniform value to the coins and currencies of the United States.

Whereas the holding of or dealing in gold

affect the public interest, and are therefore subject to proper regulation and restriction; and

Whereas the existing emergency has disclosed that provisions of obligations which purport to give the obligee a right to require payment in gold or a particular kind of coin or currency of the United States, or in an amount of money of the United States measured thereby, obstruct the power of the Congress to regulate the value of the money of the United States, and are inconsistent with the declared policy of the Congress to maintain at all times the equal power of every dollar, coined or issued by the United States, in the markets and in the payment of debts. Now, therefore, be it

Resolved by the Senate and House of Representatives of the United States of America in Congress assembled, That (a) every provision contained in or made with respect to any obligation which purports to give the obligee a right to require payment in gold or a particular kind of coin or currency, or in an amount in money of the United States measured thereby, is declared to be against public policy; and no such provision shall be contained in or made with respect to any obligation hereafter incurred. Every obligation, heretofore or hereafter incurred, whether or not any such provision is contained therein or made with respect thereto, shall be discharged upon payment, dollar for dollar, in any coin or currency which at the time of payment is legal tender for public and private debts. Any such provision contained in any law authorizing obligations to be issued by or under authority of the United States, is hereby repealed, but the repeal of any such provision shall not invalidate any other provision or authority contained in such law.

(b) As used in this resolution, the term "obligation" means an obligation (including every obligation of and to the United States, excepting currency) payable in money of the United States; and the term "coin or currency" means coin or currency of the United States, including Federal Reserve notes and circulating notes of Federal Reserve banks and national banking associations.

Sec. 2. The last sentence of paragraph (1) of subsection (b) of section 43 of the act entitled "An act to relieve the existing national economic emergency by increasing agricultural purchasing power, to raise revenue for extraordinary expenses incurred by reason of such emergency, to provide emergency relief with respect to agricultural indebtedness, to provide for the orderly liquidation of joint-stock land banks, and for other purposes," approved May 12, 1933, is amended to read as follows:

"All coins and currencies of the United States (including Federal Reserve notes and circulating notes of Federal Reserve banks and national banking associations) heretofore or hereafter coined or issued shall be legal tender for all debts, public and private, public charges, taxes, duties, and dues, except that gold coins, when below the standard weight and limit of tolerance provided by law for the single piece, shall be legal tender only at valuation in proportion to their actual weight."

482. THE GOLD CLAUSE CASES
1935

These were five cases, appealed from various courts, involving the validity of the Joint Resolution of June 5, 1933 repudiating the gold clause in private and public contracts. (Doc. No. 481). Two decisions are given here, the first involving the validity of the resolution with respect to private, the second with respect to government contracts. In the first case the Court sustained unequivocally the right of Congress to alter private contracts. In the second the Court held that the gold clause violated the legal and binding character of the government contract but that plaintiff had failed to show damages. In this case Justice Stone delivered a separate opinion holding that the Court should have confined itself to answering the first question raised. Justice McReynolds, dissenting sharply from both opinions, warned that "the impending legal and moral chaos is appalling." On these cases see, A. Nussbaum, *Money in the Law;* J. D. Paris, *Monetary Policies of the United States, 1932–1938;* Dawson, "The Gold Clause Decisions," 33 Mich. L. Rev. 647; Dickinson, "The Gold Decisions," 85 U. of Pa. L. Rev. 715; Hart, "The Gold Clause in U. S. Bonds," 48 Harv. L. Rev. 1057; Eder, "The Gold Clauses in the Light of History," 23 Georgetown L. J. 359; Carpenter, "The Gold Clause Cases," 8 So. Calif. L. Rev. 181.

1. *Norman* v. *The Baltimore and Ohio Railroad Company.*

HUGHES, C. J. These cases present the question of the validity of the Joint Resolution of the Congress, of June 5, 1933, with respect to the "gold clauses" of private contracts for the payment of money. . . .

In No. 270, the suit was brought upon a coupon of a bond made by the Baltimore and Ohio Railroad Company under date of February 1, 1930, for the payment of $1,000 on February 1, 1960, and interest from date at the rate of 4½ per cent. per annum, payable semi-annually. The bond provided that the payment of principal and interest "will be made . . . in gold coin of the United States of America of or equal to the standard of weight and fineness existing on February 1, 1930." . . . The coupon in suit, for $22.50 was payable on February 1, 1934. On presentation of the coupon, defendant refused to pay the amount in gold, or the equivalent of gold in legal tender of the United States which was alleged to be, on February 1, 1934, according to the standard of weight and fineness existing on February 1, 1930, the sum of $38.10, and plaintiff demanded judgment for that amount. . . .

The Joint Resolution of June 5, 1933, was one of a series of measures relating to the currency. These measures disclose not only the purposes of the Congress but also the situations which existed at the time the Joint Resolution was adopted and when the payments under the "gold clauses" were sought. . . .

On January 30, 1934, the Congress passed the "Gold Reserve Act of 1934" (48 Stat. 337) which, by section 13, ratified and confirmed all the actions, regulations and orders taken or made by the President and the Secretary of the Treasury under the Act of March 9, 1933, or under Section 43 of the Act of May 12, 1933, and, by section 12, with respect to the authority of the President to fix the weight of the gold dollar, provided that it should not be fixed "in any event at more than 60 per centum of its present weight." On January 31, 1934, the President issued his proclamation declaring that he fixed "the weight of the gold dollar to be 15$\frac{5}{21}$ grains nine tenths fine," from and after that date.

We have not attempted to summarize all the provisions of these measures. We are not concerned with their wisdom. The question before the Court is one of power, not of policy. And that question touches the validity of these measures at but a single point, that is, in relation to the Joint Resolution denying effect to "gold clauses" in existing contracts. The Resolution must, however, be considered in its legislative setting and in the light of other measures *in pari materia.*

First. The Interpretation of the gold clauses in suit. In the case of the *Baltimore and Ohio Railroad Company,* the obligor considers the obligation to be one "for the payment of money and not for the delivery of a specified number of grains or ounces of gold"; that it is an obligation payable in money of the United States and not less so because payment is to be made "in a particular kind of money"; that it is not a "commodity contract" which could be discharged by "tender of bullion." . . .

We are of the opinion that the gold clauses now before us were not contracts for payment in gold coin as a commodity, or in bullion, but were contracts for the payment of money. The bonds were severally for the payment of one thousand dollars. We also think that, fairly construed, these clauses were intended to afford a definite standard or measure of value, and thus to protect against a depreciation of the currency and against the discharge of the obligation by a payment of lesser value than that prescribed. When these contracts were made they were not repugnant to any action of the Congress. In order to determine whether effect may now be given to the intention of the parties in the face of the action taken by the Congress, or the contracts may be satisfied by the payment dollar for dollar, in legal tender, as the Congress has now prescribed, it is necessary to consider (1) the power of the Congress to establish a monetary system and the necessary implications of that power; (2) the power of the Congress to invalidate the provisions of existing contracts which interfere with the exercise of its constitutional authority; and (3) whether the clauses in question do constitute such an interference as to bring them within the range of that power.

Second. The power of the Congress to establish a monetary system. It is unnecessary to review the historic controversy as to the extent of this power, or again to go over the ground traversed by the Court in reaching the conclusion that the Congress may make treasury notes legal tender in payment of debts previously contracted, as well as of those subsequently contracted, whether that authority be exercised in course of war or in time of peace. *Knox* v. *Lee*, 12 Wall. 457; *Juilliard* v. *Greenman*, 110 U. S. 421. . . .

The question of the validity of the Joint Resolution of June 5, 1933, must be determined in the light of these settled principles.

Third. The power of the Congress to invalidate the provisions of existing contracts which interfere with the exercise of its constitutional authority. The instant cases involve contracts between private parties, but the question necessarily relates as well to the contracts or obligations of States and municipalities, or of their political subdivisions, that is, to such engagements as are within the reach of the applicable national power. . . .

The contention is that the power of the Congress, broadly sustained by the decisions we have cited in relation to private contracts for the payment of money generally, does not extend to the striking down of express contracts for gold payments. . . .

Here, the Congress has enacted an express interdiction. The argument against it does not rest upon the mere fact that the legislation may cause hardship or loss. Creditors who have not stipulated for gold payments may suffer equal hardship or loss with creditors who have so stipulated. The former, admittedly, have no constitutional grievance. And, while the latter may not suffer more, the point is pressed that their express stipulations for gold payments constitute property, and that creditors who have not such stipulations are without that property right. And the contestants urge that the Congress is seeking not to regulate the currency, but to regulate contracts, and thus has stepped beyond the power conferred.

This argument is in the teeth of another established principle. Contracts, however express, cannot fetter the constitutional authority of the Congress. Contracts may create rights of property, but when contracts deal with a subject matter which lies within the control of the Congress, they have a congenital infirmity. Parties cannot remove their transactions from the reach of dominant

constitutional power by making contracts about them. . . .

The principle is not limited to the incidental effect of the exercise by the Congress of its constitutional authority. There is no constitutional ground for denying to the Congress the power expressly to prohibit and invalidate contracts although previously made, and valid when made, when they interfere with the carrying out of the policy it is free to adopt. . . . To subordinate the exercise of the Federal authority to the continuing operation of previous contracts would be to place to this extent the regulation of interstate commerce in the hands of private individuals and to withdraw from the control of the Congress so much of the field as they might choose by "prophetic discernment" to bring within the range of their agreements. The Constitution recognizes no such limitation.

The same reasoning applies to the constitutional authority of the Congress to regulate the currency and to establish the monetary system of the country. If the gold clauses now before us interfere with the policy of the Congress in the exercise of that authority, they cannot stand.

Fourth. The effect of the gold clauses in suit in relation to the monetary policy adopted by the Congress. Despite the wide range of the discussion at the bar and the earnestness with which the arguments against the validity of the Joint Resolution have been pressed, these contentions necessarily are brought, under the dominant principles to which we have referred, to a single and narrow point. That point is whether the gold clauses do constitute an actual interference with the monetary policy of the Congress in the light of its broad power to determine that policy. Whether they may be deemed to be such an interference depends upon an appraisement of economic conditions and upon determinations of questions of fact. With respect to those conditions and determinations, the Congress is entitled to its own judgment. We may inquire whether its action is arbitrary or capricious, that is, whether it has reasonable relation to a legitimate end. If it is an appropriate means to such an end, the decisions of the Congress as to the degree of the necessity for the adoption of that means, is final. . . .

Can we say that this determination is so destitute of basis that the interdiction of the gold clauses must be deemed to be without any reasonable relation to the monetary policy adopted by the Congress? . . .

The devaluation of the dollar placed the domestic economy upon a new basis. In the currency as thus provided, States and municipalities must receive their taxes; railroads, their rates and fares; public utilities, their charges for services. The income out of which they must meet their obligations is determined by the new standard. Yet, according to the contentions before us, while that income is thus controlled by law, their indebtedness on their "gold bonds" must be met by an amount of currency determined by the former gold standard. Their receipts, in this view, would be fixed on one basis; their interest charges, and the principal of their obligations, on another. It is common knowledge that the bonds issued by these obligors have generally contained gold clauses, and presumably they account for a large part of the outstanding obligations of that sort. It is also common knowledge that a similar situation exists with respect to numerous industrial corporations that have issued their "gold bonds" and must now receive payments for their products in the existing currency. It requires no acute analysis or profound economic inquiry to disclose the dislocation of the domestic economy which would be caused by such a disparity of conditions in which, it is insisted, those debtors under gold clauses should be required to pay one dollar and sixty-nine cents in currency while respectively receiving their taxes, rates, charges and prices on the basis of one dollar of that currency.

We are not concerned with consequences, in the sense that consequences, however serious, may excuse an invasion of constitutional right. We are concerned with the constitutional power of the Congress over the monetary system of the country and its attempted frustration. Exercising that power, the Congress has undertaken to establish a uniform currency, and parity between kinds of currency, and to make that currency, dollar for dollar, legal tender for the payment of debts. In the light of abundant experience, the Congress was entitled to choose such a uniform monetary system, and to reject a dual system, with respect to all obligations within the

range of the exercise of its constitutional authority. The contention that these gold clauses are valid contracts and cannot be struck down proceeds upon the assumption that private parties, and States and municipalities, may make and enforce contracts which may limit that authority. Dismissing that untenable assumption, the facts must be faced. We think that it is clearly shown that these clauses interfere with the exertion of the power granted to the Congress and certainly it is not established that the Congress arbitrarily or capriciously decided that such an interference existed.

The judgment and decree, severally under review, are affirmed.

2. *John N. Perry* v. *The United States.* 294 U. S. 330.

HUGHES, C. J. The certificate from the Court of Claims shows the following facts:

Plaintiff brought suit as the owner of an obligation of the United States for $10,000 known as "Fourth Liberty Loan 4¼% Gold Bond of 1933–1938." This bond was issued pursuant to the Act of September 24, 1917, as amended, and Treasury Department circular No. 121 dated September 28, 1918. The bond provided: "The principal and interest hereof are payable in United States gold coin of the present standard of value." . . .

The Court of Claims has certified the following questions:

1. Is the claimant, being the holder and owner of a Fourth Liberty Loan 4¼% bond of the United States, of the principal amount of $10,000, issued in 1918, which was payable on and after April 15, 1934, and which bond contained a clause that the principal is "payable in United States gold coin of the present standard of value," entitled to receive from the United States an amount in legal tender currency in excess of the face amount of the bond?

2. Is the United States, as obligor in a Fourth Liberty Loan 4¼% gold bond, Series of 1933–1938, as stated in Question One liable to respond in damages in a suit in the Court of Claims on such bond as an express contract by reason of the change in or impossibility of performance in accordance with the tenor thereof, due to the provisions of Public Resolution No. 10, 73rd Congress, abrogating the gold clause in all obligations?

First. The import of the obligation. The bond in suit differs from an obligation of private parties, or of States or municipalities, whose contracts are necessarily made in subjection to the dominant power of the Congress. *Norman* v. *Baltimore & Ohio R. R. Co.*, decided this day. The bond now before us is an obligation of the United States. The terms of the bond are explicit. They were not only expressed in the bond itself, but they were definitely prescribed by the Congress. The Act of September 24, 1917, both in its original and amended form, authorized the moneys to be borrowed, and the bonds to be issued, "on the credit of the United States" in order to meet expenditures needed "for the national security and defense and other public purposes authorized by law." 40 Stat. 288, 503. The circular of the Treasury Department of September 28, 1918, to which the bond refers "for a statement of the further rights of the holders of bonds of said series" also provided that the principal and interest "are payable in United States gold coin of the present standard of value."

This obligation must be fairly construed. The *"present* standard of value" stood in contradistinction to a *lower* standard of value. The promise obviously was intended to afford protection against loss. That protection was sought to be secured by setting up a standard or measure of the Government's obligation. We think that the reasonable import of the promise is that it was intended to assure one who lent his money to the Government and took its bond that he would not suffer loss through depreciation in the medium of payment. . . .

Second. The binding quality of the obligation. The question is necessarily presented whether the Joint Resolution of June 5, 1933 (48 Stat. 113) is a valid enactment so far as it applies to the obligations of the United States. The Resolution declared that provisions requiring "payment in gold or a particular kind of coin or currency" were "against public policy," and provided that "every obligation, heretofore or hereafter incurred, whether or not any such provision is contained therein," shall be discharged "upon payment, dollar for dollar, in any coin or currency which at the time of payment is legal tender for public and private debts." This enactment was expressly extended to obligations of the United States and provisions for payment in gold, "contained in any law authorizing obligations to be issued by or under

authority of the United States," were repealed.

There is no question as to the power of the Congress to regulate the value of money, that is, to establish a monetary system and thus to determine the currency of the country. The question is whether the Congress can use that power so as to invalidate the terms of the obligations which the Government has theretofore issued in the exercise of the power to borrow money on the credit of the United States. In attempted justification of the Joint Resolution in relation to the outstanding bonds of the United States, the Government argues that "earlier Congresses could not validly restrict the 73rd Congress from exercising its constitutional powers to regulate the value of money, borrow money, or regulate foreign and interstate commerce"; and, from this premise, the Government seems to deduce the proposition that when, with adequate authority, the Government borrows money and pledges the credit of the United States, it is free to ignore that pledge and alter the terms of its obligations in case a later Congress finds their fulfillment inconvenient. The Government's contention thus raises a question of far greater importance than the particular claim of the plaintiff. On that reasoning, if the terms of the Government's bond as to the standard of payment can be repudiated, it inevitably follows that the obligation as to the amount to be paid may also be repudiated. The contention necessarily imports that the Congress can disregard the obligations of the Government at its discretion and that, when the Government borrows money, the credit of the United States is an illusory pledge.

We do not so read the Constitution. There is a clear distinction between the power of the Congress to control or interdict the contracts of private parties when they interfere with the exercise of its constitutional authority, and the power of the Congress to alter or repudiate the substance of its own engagements when it has borrowed money under the authority which the Constitution confers. In authorizing the Congress to borrow money, the Constitution empowers the Congress to fix the amount to be borrowed and the terms of payment. By virtue of the power to borrow money *"on the credit of the United States,"* the Congress is authorized to pledge that credit as an assurance of payment as stipulated,—as the highest assurance the Government can give, its plighted faith. To say that the Congress may withdraw or ignore that pledge is to assume that the Constitution contemplates a vain promise, a pledge having no other sanction than the pleasure and convenience of the pledgor. This Court has given no sanction to such a conception of the obligations of our Government. . . .

When the United States, with constitutional authority, makes contracts, it has rights and incurs responsibilities similar to those of individuals who are parties to such instruments. . . .

The argument in favor of the Joint Resolution, as applied to government bonds, is in substance that the Government cannot by contract restrict the exercise of a sovereign power. But the right to make binding obligations is a competence attaching to sovereignty. In the United States, sovereignty resides in the people who act through the organs established by the Constitution. The Congress as the instrumentality of sovereignty is endowed with certain powers to be exerted on behalf of the people in the manner and with the effect the Constitution ordains. The Congress cannot invoke the sovereign power of the people to override their will as thus declared. The powers conferred upon the Congress are harmonious. The Constitution gives to the Congress the power to borrow money on the credit of the United States, an unqualified power, a power vital to the Government,—upon which in an extremity its very life may depend. The binding quality of the promise of the United States is of the essence of the credit which is so pledged. Having this power to authorize the issue of definite obligations for the payment of money borrowed, the Congress has not been vested with authority to alter or destroy those obligations. The fact that the United States may not be sued without its consent is a matter of procedure which does not affect the legal and binding character of its contracts. While the Congress is under no duty to provide remedies through the courts, the contractual obligation still exists and, despite infirmities of procedure, remains binding upon the conscience of the sovereign.

The Fourteenth Amendment, in its fourth section, explicitly declares: "The validity of the public debt of the United States, authorized by law, . . . shall not be questioned." While this provision was undoubtedly inspired by the desire to put beyond question the obligations of the Government issued during the Civil War, its language indicates a broader connotation. We regard it as confirmatory of a fundamental principle which applies as well to the government bonds in question, and to others duly authorized by the Congress, as to those issued before the Amendment was adopted. Nor can we perceive any reason for not considering the expression "the *validity* of the public debt" as embracing whatever concerns the integrity of the public obligations.

We conclude that the Joint Resolution of June 5, 1933, in so far as it attempted to override the obligation created by the bond in suit, went beyond the congressional power.

Third. The question of damages. In this view of the binding quality of the Government's obligations, we come to the question as to the plaintiff's right to recover damages. That is a distinct question. Because the Government is not at liberty to alter or repudiate its obligations, it does not follow that the claim advanced by the plaintiff should be sustained. The action is for breach of contract. As a remedy for breach, plaintiff can recover no more than the loss he has suffered and of which he may rightfully complain. He is not entitled to be enriched. Plaintiff seeks judgment for $16,931.25, in present legal tender currency, on his bond for $10,000. The question is whether he has shown damage to that extent, or any actual damage, as the Court of Claims has no authority to entertain an action for nominal damages. . . .

The change in the weight of the gold dollar did not necessarily cause loss to the plaintiff of the amount claimed. The question of actual loss cannot fairly be determined without considering the economic situation at the time the Government offered to pay him the $10,000, the face of his bond, in legal tender currency. The case is not the same as if gold coin had remained in circulation. That was the situation at the time of the decisions under the legal tender acts of 1862 and 1863.

Before the change in the weight of the gold dollar in 1934, gold coin had been withdrawn from circulation. The Congress had authorized the prohibition of the exportation of gold coin and the placing of restrictions upon

‡ransactions in foreign exchange. .... And the holder of an obligation, or bond, of the United States, payable in gold coin of the former standard, so far as the restraint upon the right to export gold coin or to engage in transactions in foreign exchange is concerned, was in no better case than the holder of gold coin itself.

In considering what damages, if any, the plaintiff has sustained by the alleged breach of his bond, it is hence inadmissible to assume that he was entitled to obtain gold coin for recourse to foreign markets or for dealings in foreign exchange or for other purposes contrary to the control over gold coin which the Congress had the power to exert, and had exerted, in its monetary regulation. Plaintiff's damages could not be assessed without regard to the internal economy of the country at the time the alleged breach occurred. The discontinuance of gold payments and the establishment of legal tender currency on a standard unit of value with which "all forms of money" of the United States were to be "maintained at a parity," had a controlling influence upon the domestic economy. It was adjusted to the new basis. A free domestic market for gold was non-existent.

Plaintiff demands the "equivalent" in currency of the gold coin promised. But "equivalent" cannot mean more than the amount of money which the promised gold coin would be worth to the bondholder for the purposes for which it could legally be used. That equivalence or worth could not properly be ascertained save in the light of the domestic and restricted market which the Congress had lawfully established. In the domestic transactions to which the plaintiff was limited, in the absence of special license, determination of the value of the gold coin would necessarily have regard to its use as legal tender and as a medium of exchange under a single monetary system with an established parity of all currency and coins. And in view of the control of export and foreign exchange, and the restricted domestic use, the question of value, in relation to transactions legally available to the plaintiff, would require a consideration of the purchasing power of the dollars which the plaintiff has received. Plaintiff has not shown, or attempted to show, that in relation to buying power he has sustained any loss whatever. On the contrary, in view of the adjustment of the internal economy to the single measure of value as established by the legislation of the Congress, and the universal availability and use throughout the country of the legal tender currency in meeting all engagements, the payment to the plaintiff of the amount which he demands would appear to constitute not a recoupment of loss in any proper sense but an unjustified enrichment.

Plaintiff seeks to make his case solely upon the theory that by reason of the change in the weight of the dollar he is entitled to one dollar and sixty-nine cents in the present currency for every dollar promised by the bond, regardless of any actual loss he has suffered with respect to any transaction in which his dollars may be used. We think that position is untenable.

In the view that the facts alleged by the petition fail to show a cause of action for actual damages, the first question submitted by the Court of Claims is answered in the negative. It is not necessary to answer the second question.

Question No. 1 is answered "No."

483. EMERGENCY RAILROAD TRANSPORTATION ACT
June 16, 1933

(*U. S. Statutes at Large,* Vol. XLVIII, p. 211)

The railroads had suffered more seriously than had any other public utility from the depression of 1929—, and throughout the Hoover administration plans for a consolidation of resources and service had been broached. One of the first acts of the Roosevelt administration was to provide for the reorganization of the railroads. The Emergency Act of 1933 provided for mergers and consolidation of terminals, etc. under the direction of a federal coördinator. Mr. Joseph Eastman was appointed first federal coördinator, and in his first report of January 20, 1934, recommended eventual government ownership of railroads. See, E. R. Johnson, *Government Regulation of Transportation.*

AN ACT to relieve the existing national emergency in relation to interstate railroad transportation.

TITLE I—EMERGENCY POWERS

. . . SEC. 2. In order to foster and protect interstate commerce in relation to railroad transportation by preventing and relieving obstructions and burdens thereon resulting from the present acute economic emergency, and in order to safeguard and maintain an adequate national system of transportation, there is hereby created the office of Federal Coordinator of Transportation, who shall be appointed by the President, by and with the advice and consent of the Senate, or be designated by the President from the membership of the Commission. If so designated, the Coordinator shall be relieved from other duties as Commissioner during his term of service to such extent as the President may direct; except that the Coordinator shall not sit as a member of the Commission in any proceedings for the review or suspension of any order issued by him as Coordinator. . . .

SEC. 3. The Coordinator shall divide the lines of the carriers into three groups, to wit, an eastern group, a southern group, and a western group, and may from time to time make such changes or subdivisions in such groups as he may deem to be necessary or desirable. At the earliest practicable date . . . three regional coordinating committees shall be created, one for each group, and each committee shall consist of five regular members and two special members. The carriers in each group, acting each through its board of directors . . . shall select the regular members of the committee representing that group, and shall prescribe the rules under which such committee shall operate; but no railroad system shall have more than one representative on any such committee. In such selection each carrier shall have a vote in proportion to its mileage lying within the group. The two special members of each committee shall be selected in such manner as the Coordinator may approve, one to represent the steam railroads within the group which had in 1932 railway operating revenues of less than $1,000,000 and the other to represent electric railways within the group not owned by a steam railroad or operated as a part of a general steam railroad system of transportation. . . .

SEC. 4. The purposes of this title are (1) to encourage and promote or require action on the part of the carriers and of subsidiaries subject to the Interstate Commerce Act, as amended, which will (a) avoid unnecessary duplication of services and facilities of whatsoever nature and permit the joint use of terminals and trackage incident thereto or requisite to such joint use: *Provided,* That no routes now existing shall be eliminated except with the consent of all participating lines or upon order of the Coordinator, (b) control allowances, accessorial services and the charges therefor, and other practices affecting service or operation, to the end that undue impairment of net earnings may be prevented, and (c) avoid other wastes and preventable expense; (2) to promote financial reorganization of the carriers, with due regard to legal rights, so as to reduce fixed charges to the extent required by the public interest and improve carrier credit; and (3) to provide for the immediate study of other means of improving conditions surrounding transportation in all its forms and the preparation of plans therefor. . . .

SEC. 6. (a) The Coordinator shall confer freely with the committees and give them the benefit of his advice and assistance. At his request, the committees, the carriers, the subsidiaries, and the Commission shall furnish him, or his assistants and agents, such information and reports as he may desire in investigating any matter within the scope of his duties under this title; and the Coordinator, his assistants, and agents, and the Commission, shall at all times have access to all accounts, records, and memoranda of the carriers and subsidiaries. . . .

SEC. 7. (a) A labor committee for each regional group of carriers may be selected by those railroad labor organizations which, as representatives duly designated and authorized to act in accordance with the requirements of the Railway Labor Act, entered into the agreements of January 31, 1932, and December 21, 1932, with duly authorized representatives of the carriers, determining the wage payments of the employees of the carriers. A similar labor committee for each regional group of carriers may be selected by such other railroad labor organizations as may be duly designated and authorized to represent employees in accordance with the requirements of the Railway Labor Act. It shall be the duty of the regional coordinating committees and the Coordinator to give reasonable notice to, and to confer with, the appropriate regional labor committee or committees upon the subject matter prior to taking any action or issuing any order which will affect the interest of the employees, and to afford the said labor committee or committees reasonable opportunity to present views upon said contemplated action or order.

(b) The number of employees in the service of a carrier shall not be reduced by reason of any action taken pursuant to the authority of this title below the number as shown by the pay rolls of employees in service during the month of May, 1933, . . . but not more in any one year than 5 per centum of said number in service during May, 1933; nor shall any employee in such service be deprived of employment such as he had during said month of May or be in a worse position with respect to his compensation for such employment, by reason of any action taken pursuant to the authority conferred by this title.

(c) The Coordinator is authorized and directed to establish regional boards of adjustment whenever and wherever action taken pursuant to the authority conferred by this title creates conditions that make necessary such boards of adjustment to settle controversies between carriers and employees. Carriers and their employees shall have equal representation on such boards of adjustment for settlement of such controversies, and said boards shall exercise the functions of boards of adjustment provided for by the Railway Labor Act.

(d) The Coordinator is authorized and directed to provide means for determining the amount of, and to require the carriers to make just compensation for, property losses and expenses imposed upon employees by reason of transfers of work from one locality to another in carrying out the purposes of this title. . . .

SEC. 10. (a) The carriers or subsidiaries subject to the Interstate Commerce Act, as amended, affected by any order of the Coordinator or Commission made pursuant to this title shall, so long as such order is in effect, be, and they are hereby, relieved from the operation of the antitrust laws. . . . *Provided, however,* That nothing herein shall be construed to repeal, amend, suspend, or modify any of the requirements of the Railway Labor Act or the duties and obligations imposed thereunder or through contracts entered into in accordance with the provisions of said Act. . . .

SEC. 13. It shall further be the duty of the Coordinator, and he is hereby authorized and directed, forthwith to investigate and consider means, not provided for in this title, of improving transportation conditions throughout the country, including cost finding in rail transportation and the ability, financial or otherwise, of the carriers to improve their properties and furnish service and charge rates which will promote the commerce and industry of the country and including, also, the stability of railroad labor employment and other improvement of railroad labor conditions and relations; and from time to time he shall submit to the Commission such recommendations calling for further legislation to these ends as he may deem necessary or desirable in the public interest. The Commission shall promptly transmit such recommendations, together with its comments thereon, to the President and to the Congress. . . .

484. THE NATIONAL RECOVERY ACT
June 16, 1933
(*U. S. Statutes at Large*, Vol. XLVIII, p. 195)

The National Industrial Recovery Act, approved the last day of the notable first session of the 73rd Congress, was in some respects the most extraordinary law ever passed by an American Congress. It provided for the federal control of the entire industrial structure of the country through the mechanism of codes drawn up by government administrators and special industries. For a typical code see Doc. No. 485. Gen. Hugh S. Johnson was appointed chief administrator. Widespread dissatisfaction with the actual workings of the NRA led to a sweeping reorganization in September, 1934. Six months later the Supreme Court invalidated the code system (see

Doc. No. 486), whereupon the President terminated the life of the National Recovery Administration as of Jan. 1, 1936. Some important features of the NRA were later reënacted. See, H. Johnson, *The Blue Eagle, from Egg to Earth;* L. Mayers, ed. *A Handbook of the N.R.A.;* L. S. Lyon, et. al. *The National Recovery Administration;* C. L. Dearing, et. al., *The ABC of the NRA;* D. V. Brown, et. al., *The Economics of the Recovery Program;* C. Dougherty, *Labor under the NRA;* A. A. Berle, et. al., *America's Recovery Program;* F. Perkins, *People at Work;* H. Ickes, *Back to Work;* M. F. Gallagher, *Government Rules Industry,* and references for Doc. No. 486.

AN ACT to encourage national industrial recovery, to foster fair competition, and to provide for the construction of certain useful public works, and for other purposes.

TITLE I—INDUSTRIAL RECOVERY

DECLARATION OF POLICE

SEC. 1. A national emergency productive of widespread unemployment and disorganization of industry, which burdens interstate and foreign commerce, affects the public welfare, and undermines the standards of living of the American people, is hereby declared to exist. It is hereby declared to be the policy of Congress to remove obstructions to the free flow of interstate and foreign commerce which tend to diminish the amount thereof; and to provide for the general welfare by promoting the organization of industry for the purpose of cooperative action among trade groups, to induce and maintain united action of labor and management under adequate governmental sanctions and supervision, to eliminate unfair competitive practices, to promote the fullest possible utilization of the present productive capacity of industries, to avoid undue restriction of production (except as may be temporarily required), to increase the consumption of industrial and agricultural products by increasing purchasing power, to reduce and relieve unemployment, to improve standards of labor, and otherwise to rehabilitate industry and to conserve natural resources.

ADMINISTRATIVE AGENCIES

SEC. 2. . . . (c) This title shall cease to be in effect and any agencies established hereunder shall cease to exist at the expiration of two years after the date of enactment of this Act, or sooner if the President shall by proclamation or the Congress shall by joint resolution declare that the emergency recognized by section 1 has ended.

CODES OF FAIR COMPETITION

SEC. 3. (a) Upon the application to the President by one or more trade or industrial associations or groups, the President may approve a code or codes of fair competition for the trade or industry or subdivision thereof, represented by the applicant or applicants, if the President finds (1) that such associations or groups impose no inequitable restrictions on admission to membership therein and are truly representative of such trades or industries or subdivisions thereof, and (2) that such code or codes are not designed to promote monopolies or to eliminate or oppress small enterprises and will not operate to discriminate against them, and will tend to effectuate the policy of this title: *Provided,* That such code or codes shall not permit monopolies or monopolistic practices: *Provided further,* That where such code or codes affect the services and welfare of persons engaged in other steps of the economic process, nothing in this section shall deprive such persons of the right to be heard prior to approval by the President of such code or codes. The President may, as a condition of his approval of any such code, impose such conditions (including requirements for the making of reports and the keeping of accounts) for the protection of consumers, competitors, employees, and others, and in furtherance of the public interest, and may provide such exceptions to and exemptions from the provisions of such code, as the President in his discretion deems necessary to effectuate the policy herein declared.

(b) After the President shall have approved any such code, the provisions of such code shall be the standards of fair competition for such trade or industry or subdivision thereof. Any violation of such standards in any transaction in or affecting interstate or foreign commerce shall be deemed an unfair method of competition in commerce within the meaning of the Federal Trade Commission Act, as amended; but nothing in this title shall be construed to impair the powers of the Federal Trade Commission under such Act, as amended. . . .

(d) Upon his own motion, or if complaint is made to the President that abuses inimical to the public interest and contrary to the policy herein declared are prevalent in any trade or industry or subdivision thereof, and if no code of fair competition therefor has theretofore been approved by the President, the President, after such public notice and hearing as he shall specify, may prescribe and approve a code of fair competition for such trade or industry or subdivision thereof, which shall have the same effect as a code of fair competition approved by the President under subsection (a) of this section. . . .

AGREEMENTS AND LICENSES

SEC. 4. (a) The President is authorized to enter into agreements with, and to approve voluntary agreements between and among, persons engaged in a trade or industry, labor organizations, and trade or industrial organizations, associations, or groups, relating to any trade or industry, if in his judgment such agreements will aid in effectuating the policy of this title with respect to transactions in or affecting interstate or foreign commerce, and will be consistent with the requirements of clause (2) of subsection (a) of section 3 for a code of fair competition.

(b) Whenever the President shall find that destructive wage or price cutting or other activities contrary to the policy of this title are being practiced in any trade or industry or any subdivision thereof, and, after such public notice and hearing as he shall specify, shall find it essential to license business enterprises in order to make effective a code of fair competition or an agreement under this title or otherwise to effectuate the policy of this title, and shall publicly so announce, no person shall, after a date fixed in such announcement, engage in or carry on any business, in or affecting interstate or foreign commerce, specified in such announcement, unless he shall have first obtained a license issued pursuant to such regulations as the President shall prescribe. The President may suspend or revoke any such license, after due notice and opportunity for hearing, for violations of the terms or conditions thereof. Any order of the President suspending or revok-

ing any such license shall be final if in accordance with law. . . .

SEC. 5. While this title is in effect . . . and for sixty days thereafter, any code, agreement, or license approved, prescribed, or issued and in effect under this title, and any action complying with the provisions thereof taken during such period, shall be exempt from the provisions of the antitrust laws of the United States.

Nothing in this Act, and no regulation thereunder, shall prevent an individual from pursuing the vocation of manual labor and selling or trading the products thereof; nor shall anything in this Act, or regulation thereunder, prevent anyone from marketing or trading the produce of his farm.

LIMITATIONS UPON APPLICATION OF TITLE

SEC. 6. (a) No trade or industrial association or group shall be eligible to receive the benefit of the provisions of this title until it files with the President a statement containing such information relating to the activities of the association or group as the President shall by regulation prescribe. . . .

SEC. 7. (a) Every code of fair competition, agreement, and license approved, prescribed, or issued under this title shall contain the following conditions: (1) That employees shall have the right to organize and bargain collectively through representatives of their own choosing, and shall be free from the interference, restraint, or coercion of employers of labor, or their agents, in the designation of such representatives or in self-organization or in other concerted activities for the purpose of collective bargaining or other mutual aid or protection; (2) that no employee and no one seeking employment shall be required as a condition of employment to join any company union or to refrain from joining, organizing, or assisting a labor organization of his own choosing; and (3) that employers shall comply with the maximum hours of labor, minimum rates of pay, and other conditions of employment, approved or prescribed by the President.

(b) The President shall, so far as practicable, afford every opportunity to employers and employees in any trade or industry or subdivision thereof with respect to which the conditions referred to in clauses (1) and (2) of subsection (a) prevail, to establish by mutual agreement, the standards as to the maximum hours of labor, minimum rates of pay, and such other conditions of employment as may be necessary in such trade or industry or subdivision thereof to effectuate the policy of this title; and the standards established in such agreements, when approved by the President, shall have the same effect as a code of fair competition. . . .

(c) Where no such mutual agreement has been approved by the President he may investigate the labor practices, policies, wages, hours of labor, and conditions of employment in such trade or industry or subdivision thereof; and upon the basis of such investigations, and after such hearings as the President finds advisable, he is authorized to prescribe a limited code of fair competition fixing such maximum hours of labor, minimum rates of pay, and other conditions of employment in the trade or industry or subdivision thereof investigated as he finds to be necessary to effectuate the policy of this title, which shall have the same effect as a code of fair competition approved by the President under subsection (a) of section 3. The President may differentiate according to experience and skill of the employees affected and according to the locality of employment; but no attempt shall be made to introduce any classification according to the nature of the work involved which might tend to set a maximum as well as a minimum wage.

(d) As used in this title, the term "person" includes any individual, partnership, association, trust, or corporation; . . .

OIL REGULATION

SEC. 9. (a) The President is further authorized to initiate before the Interstate Commerce Commission proceedings necessary to prescribe regulations to control the operations of oil pipe lines and to fix reasonable, compensatory rates for the transportation of petroleum and its products by pipe lines, and the Interstate Commerce Commission shall grant preference to the hearings and determination of such cases.

(b) The President is authorized to institute proceedings to divorce from any holding company any pipe-line company controlled by such holding company which pipe-line company by unfair practices or by exorbitant

rates in the transportation of petroleum or its products tends to create a monopoly.

(c) The President is authorized to prohibit the transportation in interstate and foreign commerce of petroleum and the products thereof produced or withdrawn from storage in excess of the amount permitted to be produced or withdrawn from storage by any State law or valid regulation or order prescribed thereunder, by any board, commission, officer, or other duly authorized agency of a State. . . .

TITLE II—PUBLIC WORKS AND CONSTRUCTION PROJECTS

FEDERAL EMERGENCY ADMINISTRATION OF PUBLIC WORKS

SECTION 201. (a) To effectuate the purposes of this title, the President is hereby authorized to create a Federal Emergency Administration of Public Works, all the powers of which shall be exercised by a Federal Emergency Administrator of Public Works, . . . and to establish such agencies, to accept and utilize such voluntary and uncompensated services, to appoint, without regard to the civil service laws, such officers and employees, and to utilize such Federal officers and employees, and, with the consent of the State, such State and local officers and employees as he may find necessary, to prescribe their authorities, duties, responsibilities, and tenure, and, without regard to the Classification Act of 1923, as amended, to fix the compensation of any officers and employees so appointed. The President may delegate any of his functions and powers under this title to such officers, agents, and employees as he may designate or appoint.

(b) The Administrator may, without regard to the civil service laws or the Classification Act of 1923, as amended, appoint and fix the compensation of such experts and such other officers and employees as are necessary to carry out the provisions of this title; and may make such expenditures (including expenditures for personal services and rent at the seat of government and elsewhere, for law books and books of reference, and for paper, printing and binding) as are necessary to carry out the provisions of this title. . . .

(d) After the expiration of two years after the date of the enactment of this Act, or sooner if the President shall by proclamation or the Congress shall by joint resolution declare that the emergency recognized by section 1 has ended, the President shall not make any further loans or grants or enter upon any new construction under this title, and any agencies established hereunder shall cease to exist and any of their remaining functions shall be transferred to such departments of the Government as the President shall designate: . . .

SEC. 202. The Administrator, under the direction of the President, shall prepare a comprehensive program of public works, which shall include among other things the following: (a) Construction, repair, and improvement of public highways and park ways, public buildings, and any publicly owned instrumentalities and facilities; (b) conservation and development of natural resources, including control, utilization, and purification of waters, prevention of soil or coastal erosion, development of water power, transmission of electrical energy, and construction of river and harbor improvements and flood control and also the construction of any river or drainage improvement required to perform or satisfy any obligation incurred by the United States through a treaty with a foreign Government heretofore ratified and to restore or develop for the use of any State or its citizens water taken from or denied to them by performance on the part of the United States of treaty obligations heretofore assumed: *Provided,* That no river or harbor improvements shall be carried out unless they shall have heretofore or hereafter been adopted by the Congress or are recommended by the Chief of Engineers of the United States Army; (c) any projects of the character heretofore constructed or carried on either directly by public authority or with public aid to serve the interests of the general public; (d) construction, reconstruction, alteration, or repair under public regulation or control of low-cost housing and slum-clearance projects; (e) any project (other than those included in the foregoing classes) of any character heretofore eligible for loans under subsection (a) of section 201 of the Emergency Relief and Construction Act of 1932, as amended, and paragraph (3) of such subsection (a) shall for such purposes be held to include loans for the construction or completion of hospitals the operation of which is partly financed from public funds, and of reservoirs and pumping plants and for the construction of dry docks; and if in the opinion of the President it seems desirable, the construction of naval vessels within the terms and/or limits established by the London Naval Treaty of 1930 and of aircraft required therefor and construction of heavier-than-air aircraft and technical construction for the Army Air Corps and such Army housing projects as the President may approve, and provision of original equipment for the mechanization or motorization of such Army tactical units as he may designate: *Provided, however,* That in the event of an international agreement for the further limitation of armament, to which the United States is signatory, the President is hereby authorized and empowered to suspend, in whole or in part, any such naval or military construction or mechanization and motorization of Army units. . . .

SEC. 203. (a) With a view to increasing employment quickly (while reasonably securing any loans made by the United States) the President is authorized and empowered, through the Administrator or through such other agencies as he may designate or create, (1) to construct, finance, or aid in the construction or financing of any public-works project included in the program prepared pursuant to section 202; (2) upon such terms as the President shall prescribe, to make grants to States, municipalities, or other public bodies for the construction, repair, or improvement of any such project, but no such grant shall be in excess of 30 per centum of the cost of the labor and materials employed upon such project; (3) to acquire by purchase, or by exercise of the power of eminent domain, any real or personal property in connection with the construction of any such project, and to sell any security acquired or any property so constructed or acquired or to lease any such property with or without the privilege of purchase: *Provided,* That all moneys received from any such sale or lease or the repayment of any loan shall be used to retire obligations issued pursuant to section 209 of this Act, in addition to any other moneys required to be used for such purpose; (4) to aid in the financing of such railroad maintenance and equipment as may be approved by the Interstate Commerce Commission as desirable for the improvement of transportation facilities; . . . *Provided,* That in deciding to extend any aid or grant hereunder to any State, county, or municipality the President may consider whether action is in process or in good faith assured therein reasonably designed to bring the ordinary current expenditures thereof within the prudently estimated revenues thereof. . . .

(d) The President, in his discretion, and under such terms as he may prescribe, may extend any of the benefits of this title to any State, county, or municipality notwithstanding any constitutional or legal restriction or limitation on the right or power of such State, county, or municipality to borrow money or incur indebtedness.

SEC. 204. (a) For the purpose of providing for emergency construction of public highways and related projects, the President is authorized to make grants to the highway departments of the several States in an amount not less than $400,000,000, to be expended by such departments in accordance with the provisions of the Federal Highway Act, approved November 9, 1921, as amended and supplemented. . . .

SEC. 205. (a) Not less than $50,000,000 of the amount made available by this Act shall be allotted for (A) national forest highways, (B) national forest roads, trails, bridges, and related projects, (C) national park roads and trails in national parks owned or authorized, (D) roads on Indian reservations, and (E) roads through public lands, to be expended in the same manner as provided in paragraph (2) of section 301 of the Emergency Relief and Construction Act of 1932, in the case of appropriations allocated for such purposes, respectively, in such section 301, to remain available until expended. . . .

SEC. 206. All contracts let for construction projects and all loans and grants pursuant to this title shall contain such provisions as are necessary to insure (1) that no convict labor shall be employed on any such project; (2) that (except in executive, administrative, and supervisory positions), so far as practicable and feasible, no individual directly employed on any such project shall be permitted to work more than thirty hours in any one week; (3) that all employees shall be paid just and reasonable wages which shall be compensation sufficient to provide, for the hours of labor as limited, a standard of living in decency and comfort; (4) that in the employment of labor in connection with any such project, preference shall be given, where they are qualified, to ex-service men with dependents, and then in the following order: (A) To citizens of the United States and aliens who have declared their intention of becoming citizens, who are bona fide residents of the political subdivision and/or county in which the work is to be performed, and (B) to citizens of the United States and aliens who have declared their intention of becoming citizens, who are bona fide residents of the State, Territory, or district in which the work is to be performed: *Provided,* That these preferences shall apply only where such labor is available and qualified to perform the work to which the employment relates; and (5) that the maximum of human labor shall be used in lieu of machinery wherever practicable and consistent with sound economy and public advantage. . . .

SUBSISTENCE HOMESTEADS

SEC. 208. To provide for aiding the redistribution of the overbalance of population in industrial centers $25,000,000 is hereby made available to the President, to be used by him through such agencies as he may establish and under such regulations as he may make, for making loans for and otherwise aiding in the purchase of subsistence homesteads. The moneys collected as repayment of said loans shall constitute a revolving fund to be administered as directed by the President for the purposes of this section.

485. COTTON TEXTILE CODE
July 17, 1933

(J. D. Magee, W. E. Atkins, E. Stein, *The National Recovery Program,* p. 11 ff.)

This Code of Fair Competition for the cotton textile industry was drawn up in accordance with the provisions of Sec. 3 of the National Recovery Act of 1933. The most significant section of the code provided for the abolition of child labor in the textile industries.

To effectuate the policy of Title I of the National Industrial Recovery Act, during the period of the emergency, by reducing and relieving unemployment, improving the standards of labor, eliminating competitive practices destructive of the interests of the public, employee and employers, relieving the disastrous effects of over-capacity, and otherwise rehabilitating the cotton textile industry and by increasing the consumption of industrial and agricultural products by increasing purchasing power, and in other respects, the following provisions are established as a Code of fair competition for the cotton textile industry: . . .

Definitions

II. On and after the effective date, the minimum wage that shall be paid by employers in the cotton textile industry to any of their employees—except learners during a six weeks' apprenticeship, cleaners and outside employees—shall be at the rate of $12 per week when employed in the Southern section of the industry and at the rate of $13 per week when employed in the Northern section for 40 hours of labor.

III. On and after the effective date, employers in the cotton textile industry shall not operate on a schedule of hours of labor for their employees—except repair shop crews, engineers, electricians, firemen, office and supervisory staff, shipping, watching and outside crews, and cleaners—in excess of 40 hours per week and they shall not operate productive machinery in the cotton textile industry for more than two shifts of 40 hours each per week.

IV. On and after the effective date, employers in the cotton textile industry shall not employ any minor under the age of 16 years. . . . Each person engaged in the cotton textile industry will furnish duly certified reports in substance as follows and in such form as may hereafter be provided: . . .

V. The Cotton-Textile Institute, Inc., 320 Broadway, New York City, is constituted the agency to collect and receive such reports.

VI. To further effectuate the policies of the Act, the Cotton Textile Industry Committee, . . . is set up to co-operate with the

Administrator as a planning and fair practice agency for the cotton textile industry. Such agency may from time to time present to the Administrator recommendations based on conditions in the industry as they may develop from time to time which will tend to effectuate the operation of the provisions of this Code and the policy of the National Industrial Recovery Act. . . .

Such agency is also set up to co-operate with the Administrator in making investigations as to the functioning and observance of any of the provisions of this Code, at its own instance or on complaint by any person affected, and to report the same to the Administrator.

Such agency is also set up for the purpose of investigating and informing the Administrator on behalf of the cotton textile industry as to the importation of competitive articles into the United States in substantial quantities or increasing ratio to domestic production on such terms or under such conditions as to render ineffective or seriously to endanger the maintenance of this Code and as an agency for making complaint to the President on behalf of the cotton textile industry under the provisions of the National Industrial Recovery Act, with respect thereto.

VII. Where the costs of executing contracts entered into in the cotton textile industry prior to the presentation of Congress of the National Industrial Recovery Act are increased by the application of the provisions of that Act to the industry, it is equitable and promotive of the purposes of the Act that appropriate adjustments of such contracts to reflect such increased costs be arrived at by arbitral proceedings or otherwise, and the Cotton Textile Industry Committee, the applicant for this Code, is constituted an agency to assist in effecting such adjustments.

VIII. Employers in the cotton textile industry shall comply with the requirements of the National Industrial Recovery Act as follows: "(1) That employees shall have the right to organize and bargain collectively through representatives of their own choosing, and shall be free from the interference, restraint, or coercion of employers of labor, or their agents, in the designation of such representatives or in self-organization or in other concerted activities for the purpose of collective bargaining or other mutual aid or protection; (2) that no employee and no one seeking employment shall be required as a condition of employment to join any company union or to refrain from joining, organizing or assisting a labor organization of his own choosing, and (3) that employers shall comply with the maximum hours of labor, minimum rates of pay, and other conditions of employment, approved or prescribed by the President." . . .

486. SCHECHTER POULTRY CORP. v. UNITED STATES
295 U. S. 495
1935

On Writs of Certiorari to the U. S. Circuit Court of Appeals for the Second Circuit. This unanimous opinion invalidating the NRA was the first of a series of judicial onslaughts upon New Deal legislation. The invalidation rested upon two grounds: that the NRA act improperly delegated legislative powers to the executive, and that the provisions of the Poultry Code constituted a regulation of intrastate, not interstate, commerce. It was upon this second count, representing an extreme retreat from the historic position of the Court, that criticism was chiefly focussed. See, Black, "Commerce Clause and the New Deal," 20 Corn. L. Qt. 169; Black, "NRA delegation to the President," 19 Corn L. Qt. 389; Boudin, "Is Economic Planning Constitutional?" 21 Georgetown L. J. 253; Carpenter, "Constitutionality of the NIRA and the AAA," 7 So. Calif. L. Rev. 125; Corwin, "The Schechter Case—Landmark or what?" 13 N. Y. U. L. Qt. Rev. 151; Dickinson, "The Major Issues Presented by the Industrial Recovery Act," 33 Col. L. Rev. 1095; Field, "Constitutional Theory of the NIRA," 18 Minn. L. Rev. 269; Grant, "Commerce, Production, and Fiscal Powers of Congress," 44 Yale L. J. 751; McGowen, "An Economic Interpretation of the Doctrine of Delegation of Governmental Powers," 12 Tulane L. Rev. 179; Powell, "Commerce, Pensions, and Codes, II" 49 Harv. L. Rev. 193.

HUGHES, C. J. Petitioners were convicted in the District Court of the United States for the Eastern District of New York on eighteen counts of an indictment charging violations of what is known as the "Live Poultry Code," and on an additional count for conspiracy to commit such violations. By demurrer to the indictment and appropriate motions on the trial, the defendants contended (1) that the Code had been adopted pursuant to an unconstitutional delegation by Congress of legislative power; (2) that it attempted to regulate intrastate transactions which lay outside the authority of Congress; and (3) that in certain provisions it was repugnant to the due process clause of the Fifth Amendment.

The defendants are slaughterhouse operators. . . . A. L. A. Schechter Poultry Corporation and Schechter Live Poultry Market are corporations conducting wholesale poultry slaughterhouse markets in Brooklyn, New York City. Defendants ordinarily purchase their live poultry from commission men at the West Washington Market in New York City or at the railroad terminals serving the City, but occasionally they purchase from commission men in Philadelphia. They buy the poultry for slaughter and resale. After the poultry is trucked to their slaughterhouse markets in Brooklyn, it is there sold, usually within twenty-four hours, to retail poultry dealers and butchers who sell directly to consumers. The poultry purchased from defendants is immediately slaughtered, prior to delivery, by shochtim in defendants' employ. Defendants do not sell poultry in interstate commerce.

The "Live Poultry Code" was promulgated under section 3 of the National Industrial Recovery Act. That section authorizes the President to approve "codes of fair competition." Such a code may be approved for a trade or industry, upon application by one or more trade or industrial associations or groups, if the President finds (1) that such associations or groups "impose no inequitable restrictions on admission to membership therein and are truly representative," and (2) that such codes are not designed "to promote monopolies or to eliminate or oppress small enterprises and will not operate to discriminate against them, and will tend to effectuate the policy" of Title I of the act. Such codes "shall not permit monopolies or monopolistic practices." As a condition of his approval, the President may "impose such conditions (including requirements for the making of reports and the keeping of accounts) for the protection of consumers, competitors, employees, and others, and in furtherance of the public interest, and may provide such exceptions to and exemptions from the provisions of such code as the President in his discretion deems necessary to effectuate the policy herein declared." Where such a code has not been approved, the President may prescribe one, either on his own motion or on complaint. Violation of any provision of a code (so approved or prescribed) "in any transaction in or affecting interstate or foreign commerce" is made a misdemeanor punishable by a fine of not more than $500 for each offense, and each day the violation continues is to be deemed a separate offense.

The "Live Poultry Code" was approved by the President on April 13, 1934. Its divisions indicate its nature and scope. The Code has eight articles entitled (1) purposes, (2) definitions, (3) hours, (4) wages (5) general labor provisions, (6) administration, (7) trade practice provisions, and (8) general.

The declared purpose is "To effect the policies of title I of the National Industrial Recovery Act." The Code is established as "a code for fair competition for the live poultry industry of the metropolitan area in and about the City of New York." That area is described as embracing the five boroughs of New York City, the counties of Rockland, Westchester, Nassau and Suffolk in the State of New York, the counties of Hudson and Bergen in the State of New Jersey, and the county of Fairfield in the State of Connecticut.

The "industry" is defined as including "every person engaged in the business of selling, purchasing for resale, transporting, or handling and/or slaughtering live poultry, from the time such poultry comes into the New York metropolitan area to the time it is first sold in slaughtered form," and such "related branches" as may from time to time be included by amendment. Employers are styled "members of the industry," and the term employee is defined to embrace "any and all persons engaged in the industry, however compensated," except "members."

The Code fixes the number of hours for work-days. It provides that no employee, with certain exceptions, shall be permitted to work in excess of forty (40) hours in any one week, and that no employee, save as stated, "shall be paid in any pay period less than at the rate of fifty (50) cents per hour." The article containing "general labor provisions" prohibits the employment of any person under sixteen years of age, and declares that employees shall have the right of "collective bargaining," and freedom of choice with respect to labor organizations, in the terms of section 7 (a) of the Act. The minimum number of employees, who shall be employed by slaughterhouse operators, is fixed, the number being graduated according to the average volume of weekly sales.

The seventh article, containing "trade practice provisions," prohibits various practices which are said to constitute "unfair methods of competition."

Of the eighteen counts of the indictment upon which the defendants were convicted, aside from the count for conspiracy, two counts charged violation of the minimum wage and maximum hour provisions of the Code, and ten counts were for violation of the requirement (found in the "trade practice provisions") of "straight killing." The charges in the ten counts, respectively, were that the defendants in selling to retail dealers and butchers had permitted "selections of individual chickens taken from particular coops and half coops."

Of the other six counts, one charged the sale to a butcher of an unfit chicken; two counts charged the making of sales without having the poultry inspected or approved in accordance with regulations or ordinances of the City of New York; two counts charged the making of false reports or the failure to make reports relating to the range of daily prices and volume of sales for certain periods; and the remaining count for sales to slaughterers or dealers who were without licenses required by the ordinances and regulations of the City of New York.

First. Two preliminary points are stressed by the Government with respect to the appropriate approach to the important questions presented. We are told that the provision of the statute authorizing the adoption of codes must be viewed in the light of the grave national crisis with which Congress was confronted. Undoubtedly, the conditions to which power is addressed are always to be considered when the exercise of power is challenged. Extraordinary conditions may call for extraordinary remedies. But the argument necessarily stops short of an attempt to justify action which lies outside the sphere of constitutional authority. Extraordinary conditions do not create or enlarge constitutional power. The Constitution established a national government with powers deemed to be adequate, as they have proved to be both in war and peace, but these powers of the national government are limited by the constitutional grants. Those who act under these grants are not at liberty to transcend the imposed limits because they believe that more or different power is necessary. Such assertions of extra-constitutional authority were anticipated and precluded by the explicit terms of the Tenth Amendment,—"The powers not delegated to the United States by the Constitution, nor prohibited by it to the States, are reserved to the States respectively, or to the people."

The further point is urged that the national crisis demanded a broad and intensive cooperative effort by those engaged in trade and industry, and that this necessary cooperation was sought to be fostered by permitting them to initiate the adoption of codes. But the statutory plan is not simply one for voluntary effort. It does not seek merely to endow voluntary trade or industrial associations or groups with privileges or immunities. It involves the coercive exercise of the law-making power. The codes of fair competition, which the statute attempts to authorize, are codes of laws. If valid, they place all persons within their reach under the obligation of positive law, binding equally those who assent and those who do not assent. Violations of the provisions of the codes are punishable as crimes.

Second. The question of the delegation of legislative power. For a statement of the authorized objectives and content of the "codes of fair competition" we are referred repeatedly to the "Declaration of Policy" in section one of Title I of the Recovery Act. Thus, the approval of a code by the President is conditioned on his finding that it "will tend to effectuate the policy of this title." Sec. 3 (a). The President is authorized to impose such conditions "for the protection of consumers, competitors, employees, and others, and in furtherance of the public interest, and may provide such exceptions to and exemptions from the provisions of such code as the President in his discretion deems necessary to ef-

fectuate the policy herein declared." *Id.* The "policy herein declared" is manifestly that set forth in section one. That declaration embraces a broad range of objectives. Among them we find the elimination of "unfair competitive practices." . . .

We think the conclusion is inescapable that the authority sought to be conferred by section 3 was not merely to deal with "unfair competitive practices" which offend against existing law, and could be the subject of judicial condemnation without further legislation, or to create administrative machinery for the application of established principles of law to particular instances of violation. Rather, the purpose is clearly disclosed to authorize new and controlling prohibitions through codes of laws which would embrace what the formulators would propose, and what the President would approve, or prescribe, as wise and beneficent measures for the government of trades and industries in order to bring about their rehabilitation, correction and development, according to the general declaration of policy in section one. Codes of laws of this sort are styled "codes of fair competition."

We find no real controversy upon this point and we must determine the validity of the Code in question in this aspect.

The question, then, turns upon the authority which section 3 of the Recovery Act vests in the President to approve or prescribe. If the codes have standing as penal statutes, this must be due to the effect of the executive action. But Congress cannot delegate legislative power to the President to exercise an unfettered discretion to make whatever laws he thinks may be needed or advisable for the rehabilitation and expansion of trade or industry.

Accordingly we turn to the Recovery Act to ascertain what limits have been set to the exercise of the President's discretion. *First,* the President, as a condition of approval, is required to find that the trade or industrial associations or groups which propose a code, "impose no inequitable restrictions on admission to membership" and are "truly representative." That condition, however, relates only to the status of the initiators of the new laws and not to the permissible scope of such laws. *Second,* the President is required to find that the code is not "designed to promote monopolies or to eliminate or oppress small enterprises and will not operate to discriminate against them." And, to this is added a proviso that the code "shall not permit monopolies or monopolistic practices." But these restrictions leave virtually untouched the field of policy envisaged by section one, and, in that wide field of legislative possibilities, the proponents of a code, refraining from monopolistic designs, may roam at will and the President may approve or disapprove their proposals as he may see fit.

Nor is the breadth of the President's discretion left to the necessary implications of this limited requirement as to his findings. As already noted, the President in approving a code may impose his own conditions, adding to or taking from what is proposed, as "in his discretion" he thinks necessary "to effectuate the policy" declared by the Act. Of course, he has no less liberty when he prescribes a code of his own motion or on complaint, and he is free to prescribe one if a code has not been approved. The Act provides for the creation by the President of administrative agencies to assist him, but the action or reports of such agencies, or of his other assistants,—their recommendations and findings in relation to the making of codes— have no sanction beyond the will of the President, who may accept, modify or reject them as he pleases. Such recommendations or findings in no way limit the authority which section 3 undertakes to vest in the President with no other conditions than those there specified. And this authority relates to a host of different trades and industries, thus extending the President's discretion to all the varieties of laws which he may deem to be beneficial in dealing with the vast array of commercial and industrial activities throughout the country.

Such a sweeping delegation of legislative power finds no support in the decisions upon which the Government especially relies.

To summarize and conclude upon this point: Section 3 of the Recovery Act is without precedent. It supplies no standards for any trade, industry or activity. It does not undertake to prescribe rules of conduct to be applied to particular states of fact determined by appropriate administrative procedure. Instead of prescribing rules of conduct, it authorizes the making of codes to prescribe them. For that legislative undertaking, section 3 sets up no standards, aside from the statement of the general aims of rehabilitation, correction and expansion described in section one. In view of the scope of that broad declaration, and of the nature of the few restrictions that are imposed, the discretion of the President in approving or prescribing codes, and thus enacting laws for the government of trade and industry throughout the country, is virtually unfettered. We think that the code-making authority thus conferred is an unconstitutional delegation of legislative power.

Second. The question of the application of the provisions of the Live Poultry Code to intrastate transactions. This aspect of the case presents the question whether the particular provisions of the Live Poultry Code, which the defendants were convicted for violating and for having conspired to violate, were within the regulating power of Congress.

These provisions relate to the hours and wages of those employed by defendants in their slaughterhouses in Brooklyn and to the sales there made to retail dealers and butchers.

(1) Were these transactions *"in"* interstate commerce? Much is made of the fact that almost all the poultry coming to New York is sent there from other States. But the code provisions, as here applied, do not concern the transportation of the poultry from other States to New York, or the transactions of the commission men or others to whom it is consigned, or the sales made by such consignees to defendants. When defendants had made their purchases, whether at the West Washington Market in New York City or at the railroad terminals serving the City, or elsewhere, the poultry was trucked to their slaughterhouses in Brooklyn for local disposition. The interstate transactions in relation to that poultry then ended. Defendants held the poultry at their slaughterhouse markets for slaughter and local sale to retail dealers and butchers who in turn sold directly to consumers. Neither the slaughtering nor the sales by defendants were transactions in interstate commerce.

The undisputed facts thus afford no warrant for the argument that the poultry handled by defendants at their slaughterhouse markets was in a *"current"* or *"flow"* of interstate commerce and was thus subject to congressional regulation. The mere fact that there may be a constant flow of commodities into a State does not mean that the flow continues after the property has arrived and has become commingled with the mass of property within the State and is there held solely for local disposition and use. So far as the poultry here in question is concerned, the flow in interstate commerce had ceased. The poultry had come to a permanent rest within the State. It was not held, used, or sold by defendants in relation to any further transactions in interstate commerce and was not destined for transportation to other states. Hence, decisions which deal with a stream of interstate commerce—where goods come to rest within a State temporarily and are later to go forward in interstate commerce—and with the regulations of transactions involved in that practical continuity of movement, are not applicable here.

(2) Did the defendants' transactions directly *"affect"* interstate commerce so as to be subject to federal regulation? The power of Congress extends not only to the regulation of transactions which are part of interstate commerce, but to the protection of that commerce from injury.

In determining how far the federal government may go in controlling intrastate transactions upon the ground that they "affect" interstate commerce, there is a necessary and well-established distinction between direct and indirect effects. The precise line can be drawn only as individual cases arise, but the distinction is clear in principle. Direct effects are illustrated by the railroad cases we have cited, as *e. g.,* the effect of failure to use prescribed safety appliances on railroads which are the highways of both interstate and intrastate commerce, injury to an employee engaged in interstate transportation by the negligence of an employee engaged in an intrastate movement, the fixing of rates for intrastate transportation which unjustly discriminate against interstate commerce. But where the effect of intrastate transactions upon interstate commerce is merely indirect, such transactions remain within the domain of state power. If the commerce clause were construed to reach all enterprises and transactions which could be said to have an indirect effect upon interstate commerce, the

federal authority would embrace practically all the activities of the people and the authority of the State over its domestic concerns would exist only by sufferance of the federal government. Indeed, on such a theory, even the development of the State's commercial facilities would be subject to federal control.

The distinction between direct and indirect effects has been clearly recognized in the application of the Anti-Trust Act. Where a combination or conspiracy is formed, with the intent to restrain interstate commerce or to monopolize any part of it, the violation of the statute is clear. But where that intent is absent, and the objectives are limited to intrastate activities, the fact that there may be an indirect effect upon interstate commerce does not subject the parties to the federal statute, notwithstanding its broad provisions.

While these decisions related to the application of the federal statute, and not to its constitutional validity, the distinction between direct and indirect effects of intrastate transactions upon interstate commerce must be recognized as a fundamental one, essential to the maintenance of our constitutional system. Otherwise as we have said, there would be virtually no limit to the federal power and for all practical purposes we should have a completely centralized government. We must consider the provisions here in question in the light of this distinction.

The question of chief importance relates to the provisions of the Code as to the hours and wages of those employed in defendants' slaughterhouse markets. It is plain that these requirements are imposed in order to govern the details of defendants' management of their local business. The persons employed in slaughtering and selling in local trade are not employed in interstate commerce. Their hours and wages have no direct relation to interstate commerce. The question of how many hours these employees should work and what they should be paid differs in no essential respect from similar questions in other local businesses which handle commodities brought into a State and there dealt in as a part of its internal commerce. This appears from an examination of the considerations urged by the Government with respect to conditions in the poultry trade. Thus, the Government argues that hours and wages affect prices; that slaughterhouse men sell at a small margin above operating costs; that labor represents 50 to 60 per cent of these costs; that a slaughterhouse operator paying lower wages or reducing his cost by exacting long hours of work, translates his saving into lower prices; that this results in demands for a cheaper grade of goods; and that the cutting of prices brings about demoralization of the price structure. Similar conditions may be adduced in relation to other businesses. The argument of the Government proves too much. If the federal government may determine the wages and hours of employees in the internal commerce of a State, because of their relation to cost and prices and their indirect effect upon interstate commerce, it would seem that a similar control might be exerted over other elements of cost, also affecting prices, such as the number of employees, rents, advertising, methods of doing business, etc. All the processes of production and distribution that enter into cost could likewise be controlled. If the cost of doing an intrastate business is in itself the permitted object of federal control, the extent of the regulation of cost would be a question of discretion and not of power.

The Government also makes the point that efforts to enact state legislation establishing high labor standards have been impeded by the belief that unless similar action is taken generally, commerce will be diverted from the States adopting such standards, and that this fear of diversion has led to demands for federal legislation on the subject of wages and hours. The apparent implication is that the federal authority under the commerce clause should be deemed to extend to the establishment of rules to govern wages and hours in intrastate trade and industry generally throughout the country, thus overriding the authority of the States to deal with domestic problems arising from labor conditions in their internal commerce. It is not the province of the Court to

consider the economic advantages or disadvantages of such a centralized system. It is sufficient to say that the Federal Constitution does not provide for it. Our growth and development have called for wide use of the commerce power of the federal government in its control over the expanded activities of interstate commerce, and in protecting that commerce from burdens, interferences, and conspiracies to restrain and monopolize it. But the authority of the federal government may not be pushed to such an extreme as to destroy the distinction, which the commerce clause itself establishes, between commerce "among the several States" and the internal concerns of a State. The same answer must be made to the contention that is based upon the serious economic situation which led to the passage of the Recovery Act,—the fall in prices, the decline in wages and employment, and the curtailment of the market for commodities. Stress is laid upon the great importance of maintaining wage distributions which would provide the necessary stimulus in starting "the cumulative forces making for expanding commercial activity." Without in any way disparaging this motive, it is enough to say that the recuperative efforts of the federal government must be made in a manner consistent with the authority granted by the Constitution.

We are of the opinion that the attempt through the provisions of the Code to fix the hours and wages of employees of defendants in their intrastate business was not a valid exercise of federal power.

On both the grounds we have discussed, the attempted delegation of legislative power, and the attempted regulation of intrastate transactions which affect interstate commerce only indirectly, we hold the code provisions here in question to be invalid and that the judgment of conviction must be reversed.

Justice CARDOZO delivered a concurring opinion with which Justice STONE concurred.

487. UNITED STATES v. ONE BOOK CALLED "ULYSSES"
5 Fed. Supp. 182
1933

This is the most notable opinion interpreting that section of the Tariff Act of 1890 which authorized Customs Bureau officials to confiscate imported books which were of an "obscene" character. Senator Cutting had already riddled this provision in his speech of Oct. 10, 1929. This form of censorship must be distinguished from that exercised by the Post Office authorities and by the States. See M. Ernst and W. Seagle, *To the Pure;* Alpert, "Judicial Censorship of Obscene Literature," 52 Harv. L. Rev. 40; M. Ernst and A. Lindey, *The Censor Marches On.*

WOOLSEY, J. The motion for a decree dismissing the libel herein is granted, and, consequently, of course, the Government's motion for a decree of forfeiture and destruction is denied. . . .

II. I have read "Ulysses" once in its entirety and I have read those passages of which the Government particularly complains several times. In fact, for many weeks, my spare time has been devoted to the consideration of the decision which my duty would require me to make in this matter.

III. The reputation of "Ulysses" in the literary world, however, warranted me taking such time as was necessary to enable me to satisfy myself as to the intent with which the book was written, for, of course, in any case where a book is claimed to be obscene it must first be determined, whether the intent with which it was written was what is called, according to the usual phrase, pornographic, —that is, written for the purpose of exploiting obscenity.

If the conclusion is that the book is pornographic that is the end of the inquiry and forfeiture must follow.

But in "Ulysses," in spite of its unusual frankness, I do not detect anywhere the leer of the sensualist. I hold, therefore, that it is not pornographic.

IV. In writing "Ulysses," Joyce sought to make a serious experiment in a new, if not wholly novel, literary genre. He takes persons of the lower middle class living in Dublin in 1904 and seeks not only to describe what they did on a certain day early in June of that year as they went about the City bent on their usual occupation, but also to tell what many of them thought about the while.

Joyce has attempted—it seems to me, with astonishing success—to show how the screen of consciousness with its ever-shifting kaleidoscopic impressions carries, as it were on a plastic palimpsest, not only what is in the focus of each man's observation of the actual things about him, but also in a penumbral zone residua of past impressions, some recent and some drawn up by association from the domain of the subconscious. He shows how each of these impressions affects the life and behavior of the character which he is describing.

What he seeks to get is not unlike the result of a double or, if that is possible, a multiple exposure on a cinema film which would give a clear foreground with a background visible but somewhat blurred and out of focus in varying degrees.

To convey by words an effect which obviously lends itself more appropriately to a graphic technique, accounts, it seems to me, for much of the obscurity which meets a reader of "Ulysses." And it also explains another aspect of the book, which I have further to consider, namely, Joyce's sincerity and his honest effort to show exactly how the minds of his characters operate.

If Joyce did not attempt to be honest in developing the technique which he has adopted in "Ulysses" the result would be psychologically misleading and thus unfaithful to his chosen technique. Such an attitude would be artistically inexcusable.

It is because Joyce has been loyal to his technique and has not funked its necessary implications, but has honestly attempted to tell fully what his characters think about, that he has been the subject of so many attacks and that his purpose has been so often misunderstood and misrepresented. For his attempt sincerely and honestly to realize his objective has required him incidentally to use certain words which are generally considered dirty words and has led at times to what many think is a too poignant preoccupation with sex in the thoughts of his characters.

The words which are criticized as dirty are old Saxon words known to almost all men and, I venture, to many women, and are such words as would be naturally and habitually used, I believe, by the types of folk whose life, physical and mental, Joyce is seeking to describe. In respect of the recurrent emergence of the theme of sex in the minds of his characters, it must always be remembered that his locale was Celtic and his season Spring.

Whether or not one enjoys such a technique as Joyce uses is a matter of taste on which disagreement or argument is futile, but to subject that technique to the standards of some other technique seems to me to be little short of absurd.

Accordingly, I hold that "Ulysses" is a sincere and honest book and I think that the criticisms of it are entirely disposed of by its rationale.

V. Furthermore, "Ulysses" is an amazing *tour de force* when one considers the success which has been in the main achieved with such a difficult objective as Joyce set for himself. As I have stated, "Ulysses" is not an easy book to read. It is brilliant and dull, intelligible and obscure by turns. In many places it seems to me to be disgusting, but although it contains, as I have mentioned above, many words usually considered dirty, I have not found anything that I consider to be dirt for dirt's sake. Each word of the book contributes like a bit of mosaic to the detail of the picture which Joyce is seeking to construct for his readers.

If one does not wish to associate with such folk as Joyce describes, that is one's own choice. In order to avoid indirect contact with them one may not wish to read "Ulysses"; that is quite understandable. But when such a real artist in words, as Joyce undoubtedly is, seeks to draw a true picture of the lower middle class in a European city, ought it to be impossible for the American public legally to see that picture?

To answer this question it is not sufficient merely to find, as I have found above, that Joyce did not write "Ulysses" with what is a commonly called pornographic intent, I must endeavor to apply a more objective standard to his book in order to determine its effect in the result, irrespective of the intent with which it was written.

VI. The statute under which the libel is filed only denounces, in so far as we are here concerned, the importation into the United States from any foreign country of "any obscene book." Section 305 of the Tariff Act of 1930, Title 19 United States Code, Section 1305. It does not marshal against books the spectrum of condemnatory adjectives found, commonly, in laws dealing with matters of this kind. I am therefore, only required to determine whether "Ulysses"

is obscene within the legal definition of that word.

The meaning of the word "obscene" as legally defined by the Courts is: tending to stir the sex impulses or to lead to sexually impure and lustful thoughts. . . .

Whether a particular book would tend to excite such impulses and thoughts must be tested by the Court's opinion as to its effect on a person with average sex instincts—what the French would call *l'homme moyen sensuel* —who plays, in this branch of legal inquiry, the same role of hypothetical reagent as does the "reasonable man" in the law of torts and "the man learned in the art" on questions of invention in patent law.

The risk involved in the use of such a reagent arises from the inherent tendency of the trier of facts, however fair he may intend to be, to make his reagent too much subservient to his own idiosyncrasies. Here, I have attempted to avoid this, if possible, and to make my reagent herein more objective than he might otherwise be, by adopting the following course.

After I had made my decision in regard to the aspect of "Ulysses," now under consideration, I checked my impressions with two friends of mine who in my opinion answered to the above stated requirements for my reagent.

These literary assessors—as I might properly describe them—were called on separately, and neither knew that I was consulting the other. They are men whose opinion on literature and on life I value most highly. They had both read "Ulysses," and, of course, were wholly unconnected with this cause.

Without letting either of my assessors know what my decision was, I gave to each of them the legal definition of obscene and asked each whether in his opinion "Ulysses" was obscene within that definition.

I was interested to find that they both agreed with my opinion: that reading "Ulysses" in its entirety, as a book must be read on such a test as this, did not tend to excite sexual impulses or lustful thoughts but that its net effect on them was only that of somewhat tragic and very powerful commentary on the inner lives of men and women.

It is only with the normal person that the law is concerned. Such a test as I have described, therefore, is the only proper test of obscenity in the case of a book like "Ulysses" which is a sincere and serious attempt to devise a new literary method for the observation and description of mankind.

I am quite aware that owing to some of its scenes "Ulysses" is a rather strong draught to ask some sensitive, though normal, persons to take. But my considered opinion, after long reflection, is that whilst in many places the effect of "Ulysses" on the reader undoubtedly is somewhat emetic, nowhere does it tend to be an aphrodisiac.

"Ulysses" may, therefore, be admitted into the United States.

488. THE RECOGNITION OF SOVIET RUSSIA
November 16, 1933

(Public Papers and Addresses of Franklin D. Roosevelt, Vol. II, p. 471 ff.)

Since the Revolution of 1917 the United States had steadfastly refused to recognize the government of Soviet Russia. The chief objection to recognition was the Soviet policy of supporting subversive propaganda in other countries; behind this was the widespread hostility to communism. The depression brought a need for improved trade relations with Russia, and the advent of the New Deal a more liberal attitude toward the Russian experiment. In an exchange of notes the Soviet government promised to refrain from supporting subversive activities in the United States; after seven years it is clear that that promise was not kept. Further exchanges pledged Russia to secure religious liberty and fair trials for Americans residing in Russia, promised a consular convention, and waived any claims Russia might have against the United States for intervention in Siberia. See F. L. Schuman, *American Policy toward Russia Since 1917;* Graham, "Russian-American Relations, 1917–1933: an Interpretation," 28 Am. Pol. Sci. Rev. 387.

The White House, Washington
November 16, 1933

My dear Mr. Litvinov:

I am very happy to inform you that as a result of our conversations the Government of the United States has decided to establish normal diplomatic relations with the Government of the Union of Soviet Socialist Republics and to exchange ambassadors.

I trust that the relations now established between our peoples may forever remain normal and friendly, and that our Nations henceforth may cooperate for their mutual benefit and for the preservation of the peace of the world.

I am, my dear Mr. Litvinov,
Very sincerely yours,
FRANKLIN D. ROOSEVELT

The White House, Washington
November 16, 1933

My dear Mr. Litvinov:

I am glad to have received the assurance expressed in your note to me of this date that it will be the fixed policy of the Government of the Union of Soviet Socialist Republics:

1. To respect scrupulously the indisputable right of the United States to order its own life within its own jurisdiction in its own way and to refrain from interfering in any manner in the internal affairs of the United States, its territories or possessions.

2. To refrain, and to restrain all persons in Government service and all organizations of the Government or under its direct or indirect control, including organizations in receipt of any financial assistance from it, from any act overt or covert liable in any way whatsoever to injure the tranquillity, prosperity, order, or security of the whole or any part of the United States, its territories or possessions, and, in particular, from any act tending to incite or encourage armed intervention, or any agitation or propaganda having as an aim, the violation of the territorial integrity of the United States, its territories or possessions, or the bringing about by force of a change in the political or social order of the whole or any part of the United States, its territories or possessions.

3. Not to permit the formation or residence on its territory of any organization or group —and to prevent the activity on its territory of any organization or group, or of representatives or officials of any organization or group—which makes claim to be the Government of, or makes attempt upon the territorial integrity of, the United States, its territories or possessions; not to form, sub-

sidize, support or permit on its territory military organizations or groups having the aim of armed struggle against the United States, its territories or possessions, and to prevent any recruiting on behalf of such organizations and groups.

4. Not to permit the formation or residence on its territory of any organization or group —and to prevent the activity on its territory of any organization or group, or of representatives or officials of any organization or group—which has as an aim the overthrow or the preparation for the overthrow of, or the bringing about by force of a change in, the political or social order of the whole or any part of the United States, its territories or possessions.

It will be the fixed policy of the Executive of the United States within the limits of the powers conferred by the Constitution and the laws of the United States to adhere reciprocally to the engagements above expressed.

I am, my dear Mr. Litvinov,

Very sincerely yours,

FRANKLIN D. ROOSEVELT

489. PHILIPPINE INDEPENDENCE ACT
March 24, 1934

(*U. S. Statutes at Large,* Vol. XLVIII, p. 456)

January 13, 1933, Congress passed, over the veto of President Hoover, the Hawes-Cutting Act providing for Philippine independence on certain conditions. These conditions were unacceptable to the Filipinos, and the Act lapsed. The McDuffie-Tydings Bill of 1934 eliminated some of the unsatisfactory provisions of the earlier act, and was accepted by the Philippine legislature. The impetus behind the acts of 1933 and 1934 was not primarily the idealistic one of the anti-imperialist crusade of 1898–1900. Considerations of economics entered very largely into the decision of 1933–1934. Unrest in the Far East and the growing threat of Japanese imperialism after 1937 made it not improbable that the actual consummation of independence might be delayed until a more propitious time. See H. B. Hawes, *Philippine Uncertainty;* G. L. Kirk, *Philippine Independence.*

An Act to provide for the complete independence to the Philippine Islands, to provide for the adoption of a constitution and a form of government for the Philippine Islands, and for other purposes.

CONVENTION TO FRAME CONSTITUTION FOR PHILIPPINE ISLANDS

SEC. 1. The Philippine Legislature is hereby authorized to provide for the election of delegates to a constitutional convention, which shall meet . . . at such time as the Philippine Legislature may fix, but not later than October 1, 1934, to formulate and draft a constitution for the government of the Commonwealth of the Philippine Islands, subject to the conditions and qualifications prescribed in this Act, which shall exercise jurisdiction over all the territory ceded to the United States by the treaty of peace concluded between the United States and Spain on the 10th day of December 1898, ...

CHARACTER OF CONSTITUTION—MANDATORY PROVISIONS

SEC. 2. (a) The constitution formulated and drafted shall be republican in form, shall contain a bill of rights, and shall, either as a part thereof or in an ordinance appended thereto, contain provisions to the effect that, pending the final and complete withdrawal of the sovereignty of the United States over the Philippine Islands—

(1) All citizens of the Philippine Islands shall owe allegiance to the United States.

(2) Every officer of the government of the Commonwealth of the Philippine Islands shall, before entering upon the discharge of his duties, take and subscribe an oath of office, declaring, among other things, that he recognizes and accepts the supreme authority of and will maintain true faith and allegiance to the United States.

(3) Absolute toleration of religious sentiment shall be secured and no inhabitant or religious organization shall be molested in person or property on account of religious belief or mode of worship.

(4) Property owned by the United States, cemeteries, churches, and parsonages or convents appurtenant thereto, and all lands, buildings, and improvements used exclusively

for religious, charitable, or educational purposes shall be exempt from taxation.

(5) Trade relations between the Philippine Islands and the United States shall be upon the basis prescribed in section 6.

(6) The public debt of the Philippine Islands and its subordinate branches shall not exceed limits now or hereafter fixed by the Congress of the United States; and no loans shall be contracted in foreign countries without the approval of the President of the United States.

(7) The debts, liabilities, and obligations of the present Philippine government, its Provinces, municipalities, and instrumentalities, valid and subsisting at the time of the adoption of the constitution, shall be assumed and paid by the new government.

(8) Provision shall be made for the establishment and maintenance of an adequate system of public schools, primarily conducted in the English language.

(9) Acts affecting currency, coinage, imports, exports. and immigration shall not become law until approved by the President of the United States.

(10) Foreign affairs shall be under the direct supervision and control of the United States.

(11) All acts passed by the Legislature of the Commonwealth of the Philippine Islands shall be reported to the Congress of the United States.

(12) The Philippine Islands recognizes the right of the United States to expropriate property for public uses, to maintain military and other reservations and armed forces in the Philippines, and, upon order of the President, to call into the service of such armed forces all military forces organized by the Philippine government.

(13) The decisions of the courts of the Commonwealth of the Philippine Islands shall be subject to review by the Supreme Court of the United States as provided in paragraph (6) of section 7.

(14) The United States may, by Presidential proclamation, exercise the right to intervene for the preservation of the government of the Commonwealth of the Philippine Islands and for the maintenance of the government as provided in the constitution thereof, and for the protection of life, property, and individual liberty and for the dis-

charge of government obligations under and in accordance with the provisions of the constitution.

(15) The authority of the United States High Commissioner to the government of the Commonwealth of the Philippine Islands, as provided in this Act, shall be recognized.

(16) Citizens and corporations of the United States shall enjoy in the commonwealth of the Philippine Islands all the civil rights of the citizens and corporations, respectively, thereof.

(b) The constitution shall also contain the following provisions, effective as of the date of the proclamation of the President recognizing the independence of the Philippine Islands, as hereinafter provided:

(1) That the property rights of the United States and the Philippine Islands shall be promptly adjusted and settled, and that all existing property rights of citizens or corporations of the United States shall be acknowledged, respected, and safeguarded to the same extent as property rights of citizens of the Philippine Islands.

(2) That the officials elected and serving under the constitution adopted pursuant to the provisions of this Act shall be constitutional officers of the free and independent government of the Philippine Islands and qualified to function in all respects as if elected directly under such government, and shall serve their full terms of office as prescribed in the constitution.

(3) That the debts and liabilities of the Philippine Islands, its Provinces, cities, municipalities, and instrumentalities, which shall be valid and subsisting at the time of the final and complete withdrawal of the sovereignty of the United States, shall be assumed by the free and independent government of the Philippine Islands; and that where bonds have been issued under authority of an Act of Congress of the United States by the Philippine Islands, or any Province, city, or municipality therein, the Philippine government will make adequate provision for the necessary funds for the payment of interest and principal, and such obligations shall be a first lien on the taxes collected in the Philippine Islands.

(4) That the government of the Philippine Islands, on becoming independent of the United States, will assume all continuing

obligations assumed by the United States under the treaty of peace with Spain ceding said Philippine Islands to the United States. . . .

SUBMISSION OF CONSTITUTION TO THE PRESIDENT OF THE UNITED STATES

SEC. 3. Upon the drafting and approval of the constitution by the constitutional convention in the Philippine Islands, the constitution shall be submitted within two years after the enactment of this Act to the President of the United States, who shall determine whether or not it conforms with the provisions of this Act. . . .

SUBMISSION OF CONSTITUTION TO FILIPINO PEOPLE

SEC. 4. After the President of the United States has certified that the constitution conforms with the provisions of this Act, it shall be submitted to the people of the Philippine Islands for their ratification or rejection at an election to be held within four months after the date of such certification, on a date to be fixed by the Philippine Legislature, at which election the qualified voters of the Philippine Islands shall have an opportunity to vote directly for or against the proposed constitution and ordinances appended thereto. . . . If a majority of the votes cast shall be for the constitution, such vote shall be deemed an expression of the will of the people of the Philippine Islands in favor of Philippine independence, . . .

If a majority of the votes cast are against the constitution, the existing government of the Philippine Islands shall continue without regard to the provisions of this Act. . . .

RELATIONS WITH THE UNITED STATES PENDING COMPLETE INDEPENDENCE

SEC. 6 After the date of the inauguration of the government of the Commonwealth of the Philippine Islands trade relations between the United States and the Philippine Islands shall be as now provided by law, subject to the following exceptions:

(a) There shall be levied, collected, and paid on all refined sugars in excess of fifty thousand long tons, and on unrefined sugars in excess of eight hundred thousand long tons, coming into the United States from the Philippine Islands in any calendar year, the same rates of duty which are required by the laws of the United States to be levied, collected, and paid upon like articles imported from foreign countries. . . .

(d) In the event that in any year the limit in the case of any article which may be exported to the United States free of duty shall be reached by the Philippine Islands, the amount or quantity of such articles produced or manufactured in the Philippine Islands thereafter that may be so exported to the United States free of duty shall be allocated, under export permits issued by the government of the Commonwealth of the Philippine Islands, to the producers or manufacturers of such articles proportionately on the basis of their exportation to the United States in the preceding year; except that in the case of unrefined sugar the amount thereof to be exported annually to the United States free of duty shall be allocated to the sugar-producing mills of the islands proportionately on the basis of their average annual production for the calendar years 1931, 1932, and 1933, and the amount of sugar from each mill which may be so exported shall be allocated in each year between the mill and the planters on the basis of the proportion of sugar to which the mill and the planters are respectively entitled. The government of the Philippine Islands is authorized to adopt the necessary laws and regulations for putting into effect the allocation hereinbefore provided.

(e) The government of the Commonwealth of the Philippine Islands shall impose and collect an export tax on all articles that may be exported to the United States from the Philippine Islands free of duty under the provisions of existing law as modified by the foregoing provisions of this section, including the articles enumerated in subdivisions (a), (b), and (c), within the limitations therein specified, as follows:

(1) During the sixth year after the inauguration of the new government the export tax shall be 5 per centum of the rates of duty which are required by the laws of the United States to be levied, collected, and paid on like articles imported from foreign countries;

(2) During the seventh year after the inauguration of the new government the export tax shall be 10 per centum. . . .

(3) During the eighth year after the inauguration of the new government the export tax shall be 15 per centum. . . .

(4) During the ninth year after the inauguration of the new government the export tax shall be 20 per centum. . . .

(5) After the expiration of the ninth year after the inauguration of the new government the export tax shall be 25 per centum. . . .

The government of the Commonwealth of the Philippine Islands shall place all funds received from such export taxes in a sinking fund, and such funds shall, in addition to other moneys available for that purpose, be applied solely to the payment of the principal and interest on the bonded indebtedness of the Philippine Islands, its Provinces, municipalities, and instrumentalities, until such indebtedness has been fully discharged. . . .

SEC. 7. Until the final and complete withdrawal of American sovereignty over the Philippine Islands—. . . .

(4) The President shall appoint, by and with the advice and consent of the Senate, a United States High Commissioner to the government of the Commonwealth of the Philippine Islands who shall hold office at the pleasure of the President and until his successor is appointed and qualified. . . .

If the government of the Commonwealth of the Philippine Islands fails to pay any of its bonded or other indebtedness or the interest thereon when due or to fulfill any of its contracts, the United States High Commissioner shall immediately report the facts to the President, who may thereupon direct the High Commissioner to take over the customs offices and administration of the same, administer the same, and apply such part of the revenue received therefrom as may be necessary for the payment of such overdue indebtedness or for the fulfillment of such contracts. . . .

(6) Review by the Supreme Court of the United States of cases from the Philippine Islands shall be as now provided by law; and such review shall also extend to all cases involving the constitution of the Commonwealth of the Philippine Islands.

SEC. 8. (a) Effective upon the acceptance of this Act by concurrent resolution of the Philippine Legislature or by a convention called for that purpose, as provided in section 17—

(1) For the purposes of the Immigration Act of 1917, the Immigration Act of 1924 (except section 13 (c)), this section, and all other laws of the United States relating to the immigration, exclusion, or expulsion of aliens, citizens of the Philippine Islands who are not citizens of the United States shall be considered as if they were aliens. For such purposes the Philippine Islands shall be considered as a separate country and shall have for each fiscal year a quota of fifty. . . .

RECOGNITION OF PHILIPPINE INDEPENDENCE AND WITHDRAWAL OF AMERICAN SOVEREIGNTY

SEC. 10. (a) On the 4th day of July immediately following the expiration of a period of ten years from the date of the inauguration of the new government under the constitution provided for in this Act the President of the United States shall by proclamation withdraw and surrender all right of possession, supervision, jurisdiction, control, or sovereignty then existing and exercised by the United States in and over the territory and people of the Philippine Islands, including all military and other reservations of the Government of the United States in the Philippines (except such naval reservations and fueling stations as are reserved under section 5), and, on behalf of the United States, shall recognize the independence of the Philippine Islands as a separate and self-governing nation and acknowledge the authority and control over the same of the government instituted by the people thereof, under the constitution then in force. . . .

NEUTRALIZATION OF PHILIPPINE ISLANDS

SEC. 11. The President is requested, at the earliest practicable date, to enter into negotiations with foreign powers with a view to the conclusion of a treaty for the perpetual neutralization of the Philippine Islands, if and when Philippine independence shall have been achieved. . . .

TARIFF DUTIES AFTER INDEPENDENCE

SEC. 13. After the Philippine Islands have become a free and independent nation there shall be levied, collected, and paid upon all articles coming into the United States from the Philippine Islands the rates of duty which are required to be levied, collected, and paid upon like articles imported from other foreign countries: *Provided*, That at least one year prior to the date fixed in this Act for the independence of the Philippine Islands, there shall be held a conference of representatives of the Government of the United States and the government of the Commonwealth of the Philippine Islands, . . . for the purpose of formulating recommendations as to future trade relations between the Government of the United States and the independent government of the Philippine Islands. . . .

IMMIGRATION AFTER INDEPENDENCE

SEC. 14. Upon the final and complete withdrawal of American sovereignty over the Philippine Islands the immigration laws of the United States . . . shall apply to persons who were born in the Philippine Islands to the same extent as in the case of other foreign countries. . . .

EFFECTIVE DATE

SEC. 17. The foregoing provisions of this Act shall not take effect until accepted by concurrent resolution of the Philippine Legislature or by a convention called for the purpose of passing upon that question as may be provided by the Philippine Legislature.

490. THE JOHNSON ACT
April 13, 1934
(*U. S. Statutes at Large*, Vol. XLVIII, p. 574)

This law was an expression of the widespread indignation of the American people at the failure of debtor nations to meet their obligations to the United States. On the war debts see, H. G. Moulton and L. Pasvolsky, *World War Debt Settlements,* and *War Debts and World Prosperity;* National Industrial Conference Board, *Inter-Ally Debts and the United States.*

An Act to prohibit financial transactions with any foreign government in default on its obligations to the United States.

Be it enacted, That hereafter it shall be unlawful within the United States or any place subject to the jurisdiction of the United States for any person to purchase or sell the bonds, securities, or other obligations of, any foreign government or political subdivision thereof or any organization or association acting for or on behalf of a foreign government or political subdivision thereof, issued after

a passage of this Act, or to make any loan to such foreign government, political subdivision, organization, or association, except a renewal or adjustment of existing indebtedness while such government, political subdivision, organization, or association, is in default in the payment of its obligations, or any part thereof, to the Government of the United States. Any person violating the provisions of this Act shall upon conviction thereof be fined not more than $10,000 or imprisoned for not more than five years, or both.

SEC. 2. As used in this Act the term "person" includes individual, partnership, corporation, or association other than a public corporation created by or pursuant to special authorization of Congress, or a corporation in which the Government of the United States has or exercises a controlling interest through stock ownership or otherwise.

491. THE ABROGATION OF THE PLATT AMENDMENT
May 29, 1934
(*U. S. Statutes at Large*, Vol. XLVIII, p. 1682)

The Roosevelt-Hull policy of "the good neighbor" was given dramatic substantiation by the negotiation of a treaty abrogating the Platt Amendment. The protracted and violent strife in Cuba during 1933 and 1934 accounted in part for the willingness of the United States to ab-

dicate responsibility for Cuban affairs. See H. F. Guggenheim, *The United States and Cuba;* C. Beals, *The Crime of Cuba;* R. H. Fitzgibbon, *Cuba and the United States, 1900–1935;* P. G. Wright; *The Cuban Situation and Our Treaty Relations.*

The United States of America and the Republic of Cuba, being animated by the desire to fortify the relations of friendship between the two countries, and to modify, with this purpose, the relations established between them by the Treaty of Relations signed at Havana, May 22, 1903, have appointed, with this intention, as their plenipotentiaries: . . .

Who, after having communicated to each other their full powers, which were found to be in good and due form, have agreed upon the following articles:

ART. I. The Treaty of Relations which was concluded between the two contracting parties on May 22, 1903, shall cease to be in force, and is abrogated, from the date on which the present treaty goes into effect.

ART. II. All the acts effected in Cuba by the United States of America during its military occupation of the island, up to May 20, 1902, the date on which the Republic of Cuba was established, have been ratified and held as valid; and all rights legally acquired by virtue of those acts shall be maintained and protected.

ART. III. Until the two contracting parties agree to the modification or abrogation of the stipulations of the agreement in regard to the lease to the United States of America of lands in Cuba for coaling and naval stations signed by the President of the Republic of Cuba on February 16, 1903, and by the President of the United States of America on the 23rd day of the same month and year, the stipulations of that agreement with regard to the naval station of Guantanamo shall continue in effect. The supplementary agreement in regard to naval or coaling stations signed between the two governments on July 2, 1903, shall continue in effect in the same form and on the same conditions with respect to the naval station at Guantanamo. So long as the United States of America shall not abandon the said naval station of Guantanamo or the two governments shall not agree to a modification of its present limits, the station shall continue to have the territorial area that it now has, with the limits that it has on the date of the signature of the present treaty.

ART. IV. If at any time in the future a situation should arise that appears to point to an outbreak of contagious disease in the territory of either of the contracting parties, either of the two governments shall, for its own protection, and without its act being considered unfriendly, exercise freely and at its discretion the right to suspend communications between those of its ports that it may designate and all or part of the territory of the other party, and for the period that it may consider to be advisable.

ART. V. The present Treaty shall be ratified by the contracting parties in accordance with their respective Constitutional methods; and shall go into effect on the date of the exchange of their ratifications, which shall take place in the city of Washington as soon as possible.

492. ANTI-WAR TREATY OF NON-AGGRESSION AND CONCILIATION
Signed October 10, 1933; Ratified June 15, 1934

(Congressional Record, 73d. Congress, 2d. Sess., Vol. LXXVIII, p. 11910 ff.)

This Treaty, concluded at Rio de Janeiro by Argentina, Brazil, Chile, Mexico, Paraguay, and Uruguay and the United States, extended the Kellogg-Briand Pact to the American States and provided additional machinery for conciliation and arbitration.

The states designated below, in the desire to contribute to the consolidation of peace, and to express their adherence to the efforts made by all civilized nations to promote the spirit of universal harmony;

To the end of condemning wars of aggression and territorial acquisitions that may be obtained by armed conquest, making them impossible and establishing their invalidity through the positive provisions of this treaty, and in order to replace them with pacific solutions based on lofty concepts of justice and equity;

Convinced that one of the most effective means of assuring the moral and material benefits which peace offers to the world, is the organization of a permanent system of conciliation for international disputes, to be applied immediately on the violation of the principles mentioned;

Have decided to put these aims of non-aggression and concord in conventional form, by concluding the present treaty, to which end they have appointed the undersigned plenipotentiaries, who, having exhibited their respective full powers, found to be in good and due form, have agreed upon the following:

Art. I. The High Contracting Parties solemnly declare that they condemn wars of aggression in their mutual relations or those with other states, and that the settlement of disputes or controversies of any kind that may arise among them shall be effected only by the pacific means which have the sanction of international law.

Art. II. They declare that as between the High Contracting Parties, territorial questions must not be settled by violence, and that they will not recognize any territorial arrangement which is not obtained by pacific means, nor the validity of the occupation or acquisition of territories that may be brought about by force of arms.

Art. III. In case of non-compliance by any state engaged in a dispute, with the obligations contained in the foregoing articles, the contracting states undertake to make every effort for the maintenance of peace. To that end they will adopt in their character as neutrals a common and solidary attitude; they will exercise the political, juridical or economic means authorized by international law; they will bring the influence of public opinion to bear but will in no case resort to intervention either diplomatic or armed; subject to the attitude that may be incumbent on them by virtue of other collective treaties to which such states are signatories.

Art. IV. The High Contracting Parties obligate themselves to submit to the conciliation procedure established by this treaty, the disputes specially mentioned and any others that may arise in their reciprocal relations, without further limitations than those enumerated in the following article, in all controversies which it has not been possible to settle by diplomatic means within a reasonable period of time.

Art. V. The High Contracting Parties and the states which may in the future adhere to this treaty, may not formulate at the time of signature, ratification or adherence, other limitations to the conciliation procedure than those which are indicated below:

(a) Differences for the solution of which treaties, conventions, pacts or pacific agreements of any kind whatever may have been concluded, which in no case shall be considered as annulled by this agreement, but supplemented thereby in so far as they tend to assure peace; as well as the questions or matters settled by previous treaties;

(b) Disputes which the parties prefer to solve by direct settlement or submit by common agreement to an arbitral or judicial solution;

(c) Questions which international law leaves to the exclusive competence of each state, under its constitutional system, for which reason the parties may object to their being submitted to the conciliation procedure before the national or local jurisdiction has decided definitely; except in the case of manifest denial or delay of justice, in which case the conciliation procedure shall be initiated within a year at the latest;

(d) Matters which affect constitutional precepts of the parties to the controversy. In case of doubt, each party shall obtain the reasoned opinion of its respective tribunal or supreme court of justice, if the latter should be invested with such powers.

The High Contracting Parties may communicate, at any time and in the manner provided for by Article XV, an instrument stating that they have abandoned wholly or in part the limitations established by them in the conciliation procedure.

The effect of the limitations formulated by one of the contracting parties shall be that the other parties shall not consider themselves obligated in regard to that party save in the measure of the exceptions established.

Art. VI. In the absence of a permanent Conciliation Commission or of some other international organization charged with this mission by virtue of previous treaties in effect, the High Contracting Parties undertake to submit their differences to the examination and investigation of a Conciliation Commission which shall be formed as follows, unless there is an agreement to the contrary of the parties in each case; . . .

Art. X. It is the duty of the Commission to secure the conciliatory settlement of the disputes submitted to its consideration.

After an impartial study of the questions

in dispute, it shall set forth in a report the outcome of its work and shall propose to the Parties bases of settlement by means of a just and equitable solution. . . .

493. THE TAYLOR ACT
June 28, 1934
(*U. S. Statutes at Large,* Vol. XLVIII, p. 1269)

The prolonged droughts of the early 1930's and the accompanying dust storms advertised the fact that over-grazing in the Plains area had contributed to the creation of a "dust bowl" and dramatized the necessity of a new policy with respect to the grazing lands of the West. "The grazing resources of these lands" said the Report of the Committee on Public Lands, "are now being used without supervision or regulation, and there is constant competition among the various users who desire to obtain exclusive benefit from the forage growth. The result of this competitive practice has been lack of proper care, with the attendant evils of soil erosion and removal of protection in drainage areas. . . . Without regulation further destruction is inevitable." This Act proposed the creation of new grazing districts up to 80,000,000 acres in order to conserve the public range. On the problem of soil erosion in the High Plains see S. Chase, *Rich Land, Poor Land;* W. P. Webb, *The Great Plains;* U. S. Dept. of Agriculture, "The Western Range"; U. S. Dept. of Interior, "The Future of The Great Plains."

An act to stop injury to the public grazing lands by preventing overgrazing and soil deterioration, to provide for their orderly use, improvement, and development, to stabilize the livestock industry dependent upon the public range, and for other purposes.

Be it enacted, That in order to promote the highest use of the public lands pending its final disposal, the Secretary of the Interior is authorized, in his discretion, by order to establish grazing districts or additions thereto and/or to modify the boundaries thereof, not exceeding in the aggregate an area of eighty million acres, of vacant, unappropriated, and unreserved lands from any part of the public domain of the United States (exclusive of Alaska), which are not in national forests, national parks and monuments, Indian reservations, [etc.] and which in his opinion are chiefly valuable for grazing and raising forage crops: *Provided,* That no lands withdrawn or reserved for any other purpose shall be included in any such district except with the approval of the head of the department having jurisdiction thereof. . . .

SEC. 2. The Secretary of the Interior shall make provision for the protection, administration, regulation, and improvement of such grazing districts as may be created under the authority of the foregoing section, and he shall make such rules and regulations and establish such service, enter into such cooperative agreements, and do any and all things necessary to accomplish the purposes of this Act and to insure the objects of such grazing districts, namely, to regulate their occupancy and use, to preserve the land and its resources from destruction or unnecessary injury, to provide for the orderly use, improvement, and development of the range; and the Secretary of the Interior is authorized to continue the study of erosion and floor control and to perform such work as may be necessary amply to protect and rehabilitate the areas subject to the provisions of this Act, through such funds as may be made available for that purpose, and any willful violation of the provisions of this Act or of such rules and regulations thereunder after actual notice thereof shall be punishable by a fine of not more than $500.

SEC. 3. That the Secretary of the Interior is hereby authorized to issue or cause to be issued permits to graze livestock on such grazing districts to such bona fide settlers, residents, and other stock owners as under his rules and regulations are entitled to participate in the use of the range, upon the payment annually of reasonable fees in each case to be fixed or determined from time to time. . . . Such permits shall be for a period of not more than ten years, subject to the preference right of the permittees to renewal in the discretion of the Secretary of the Interior, who shall specify from time to time numbers of stock and seasons of use. During periods of range depletion due to severe drought or other natural causes, or in case of a general epidemic of disease, during the life of the permit, the Secretary of the Interior is hereby authorized, in his discretion to remit, reduce, refund in whole or in part, or authorize postponement of payment of grazing fees for such depletion period so long as the emergency exists: *Provided further,* That nothing in this Act shall be construed or administered in any way to diminish or impair any right to the possession and use of water for mining, agriculture, manufacturing, or other purposes which has heretofore vested or accrued under existing law validly affecting the public lands or which may be hereafter initiated or acquired and maintained in accordance with such law. So far as consistent with the purposes and provisions of this Act, grazing privileges recognized and acknowledged shall be adequately safeguarded, but the creation of a grazing district or the issuance of a permit pursuant to the provisions of this Act shall not create any right, title, interest, or estate in or to the lands. . . .

SEC. 5. That the Secretary of the Interior shall permit, under regulations to be prescribed by him, the free grazing within such districts of livestock kept for domestic purposes. . . .

SEC. 7. That the Secretary is hereby authorized, in his discretion, to examine and classify any lands within such grazing districts which are more valuable and suitable for the production of agricultural crops than native grasses and forage plants, and to open such lands to homestead entry in tracts not exceeding three hundred and twenty acres in area. Such lands shall not be subject to settlement or occupation as homesteads until after same have been classified and opened to entry after notice to the permittee by the Secretary of the Interior, and the lands shall remain a part of the grazing district until patents are issued therefor, the homesteader to be, after his entry is allowed, entitled to the possession and use thereof: *Provided,* That upon the application of any person qualified to make homestead entry under the public-land laws, filed in the land office of the proper district, the Secretary of the Interior shall cause any tract not exceeding three hundred and twenty acres in any grazing district to be classified, and such application shall entitle the applicant to a preference right to enter such lands when opened to entry as herein provided.

SEC. 8. That where such action will promote the purposes of the district or facilitate its administration, the Secretary is authorized and directed to accept on behalf of the United States any lands within the exterior boundaries of a district as a gift, or, when public interests will be benefited thereby, he is authorized and directed to accept on behalf of the United States title to any privately owned lands within the exterior boundaries of said grazing district, and in exchange therefor to issue patent for not to exceed an equal value of survey grazing district land or of unreserved surveyed public land in the same State or within a distance of not more than fifty miles within the adjoining State nearest the base lands. . . .

SEC. 11. That when appropriated by Congress, 25 per centum of all moneys received from each grazing district on Indian lands ceded to the United States for disposition under the public-land laws during any fiscal year is hereby made available for expenditure by the Secretary of the Interior for the construction, purchase, or maintenance of range improvements; and an additional 25 per centum of the money received from grazing during each fiscal year shall be paid at the end thereof by the Secretary of the Treasury to the State in which said lands are situated, to be expended as the State legislature may prescribe for the benefit of public schools and public roads of the county or counties in which such grazing lands are situated. And the remaining 50 per centum of all money received from such grazing lands shall be deposited to the credit of the Indians pending final disposition under applicable laws, treaties, or agreements.

SEC. 13. That the President of the United States is authorized to reserve by proclamation and place under national-forest administration in any State where national forests may be created or enlarged by Executive order any unappropriated public lands lying within watersheds forming a part of the national forests which, in his opinion, can best be administered in connection with existing national-forest administration units, and to place under the Interior Department administration any lands within national forests, principally valuable for grazing, which, in his opinion, can best be administered under the provisions of this Act.

SEC. 16. Nothing in this Act shall be construed as restricting the respective States from enforcing any and all statutes enacted for police regulation, nor shall the police power of the respective States be, by this Act, impaired or restricted, and all laws heretofore enacted by the respective States or any thereof, or that may hereafter be enacted as regards public health or public welfare, shall at all times be in full force and effect: *Provided, however,* That nothing in this section shall be construed as limiting or restricting the power and authority of the United States.

494. HOME BUILDING AND LOAN ASSOCIATION v. BLAISDELL
290 U. S. 251
1934

Appeal from the Supreme Court of Minnesota. The facts of the case are set forth in the opinion of the court. This was the first notable case involving the interpretation of emergency legislation incident to the depression of 1929—. For an earlier case of the interpretation of. emergency legislation, see Doc. No. 415. See J. P. Clark, "Emergencies and the Law," 49 Pol. Sci. Qt., 268; Corwin, "Moratorium over Minnesota," 82 U. of Pa. L. Rev. 311.

HUGHES, C. J. Appellant contests the validity of Chapter 339 of the Laws of Minnesota of 1933, p. 514, approved April 18, 1933, called the Minnesota Mortgage Moratorium Law, as being repugnant to the contract clause of the Fourteenth Amendment, of the Federal Constitution. The statute was sustained by the Supreme Court of Minnesota (249 N. W. 334, 893) and the case comes here on appeal.

The Act provides that, during the emergency declared to exist, relief may be had through authorized judicial proceedings with respect to foreclosures of mortgages, and execution sales, of real estates; that sales may be postponed and periods of redemption may be extended. . . .

The state court upheld the statute as an emergency measure. Although conceding that the obligations of the mortgage contract were impaired the court decided that what it thus described as an impairment was, notwithstanding the contract clause of the Federal Constitution, within the police power of the State as that power was called into exercise by the public economy emergency which the legislature had found to exist. Attention is thus directed to the preamble and first section of the statute which described the existing emergency in terms that were deemed to justify the temporary relief which the statute affords. . . .

. . . Aside from the extension of time, the other conditions of redemption are unaltered. While the mortgagor remains in possession he must pay the rental value as that value has been determined, upon notice and hearing, by the court. The rental value so paid is devoted to the carrying of the property by the application of the required payments to taxes, insurance, and interest on the mortgage indebtedness. While the mortgagee-purchaser is debarred from actual possession, he has, so far as rental value is concerned, the equivalent of possession during the extended period.

In determining whether the provision for this temporary and conditional relief exceeds the power of the State by reason of the clause in the Federal Constitution prohibiting impairment of the obligations of contracts, we must consider the relation of emergency to constitutional power, the historical setting of the contract clause, the development of the jurisprudence of this court in the construction of that clause, and the principles of construction which we may consider to be established.

Emergency does not create power. Emergency does not increase granted power or remove or diminish the restrictions imposed upon power granted or reserved. The Constitution was adopted in a period of grave emergency. Its grants of power to the Federal government and its limitations of the power of the States were determined in the light of emergency and they are not altered by emergency. What power was thus granted and what limitations were thus imposed are questions which have always been, and always will be, the subject of close examination under our constitutional system.

While emergency does not create power, emergency may furnish the occasion for the exercise of power. . . .

But full recognition of the occasion and general purpose of the clause does not suffice to fix its precise scope. Nor does an examination of the details of prior legislation in the States yield criteria which can be considered controlling. To ascertain the scope of the constitutional prohibition we examine the course of judicial decisions in its application. These put it beyond question that the prohibition is not an absolute one and is not to be read with literal exactness like a mathematical formula. . . .

Not only is the constitutional provision qualified by the measure of control which the State retains over remedial processes, but the State also continues to possess authority to safeguard the vital interests of its people. It does not matter that legislation appropriate to that end "has the result of modifying or abrogating contracts already in effect." *Stephenson* v. *Binford*, 287 U. S. 251, 276. Not only are existing laws read into contracts in order to fix obligations as between the parties, but the reservation of essential attributes of sovereign power is also read into contracts as a postulate of the legal order. The policy of protecting contracts against impairment presupposes the maintenance of a government in virtue of which contractual relations are worth while,—a government which retains adequate authority to secure the peace and good order of society. This principle of harmonizing the constitutional prohibition with the necessary residuum of state power has had progressive recognition in the decisions of this Court.

Undoubtedly, whatever is reserved of state power must be consistent with the fair intent of the constitutional limitation of that power. The reserved power cannot be construed so as to destroy the limitation, nor is the limitation to be construed to destroy the reserved power in its essential aspects. They must be construed in harmony with each other. This principle precludes a construction which would permit the State to adopt as its policy the repudiation of debts or the destruction of contracts or the denial of means to enforce them. But it does not follow that conditions may not arise in which a temporary restraint of enforcement may not be consistent with the spirit and purpose of the constitutional provision and thus found to be within the range of the reserved power

of the State to protect the vital interests of the community. It cannot be maintained that the constitutional prohibition should be so construed as to prevent limited and temporary interpositions with respect to the enforcement of contracts if made necessary by a great public calamity such as fire, flood, or earthquake. See *American Land Co.* v. *Zeiss*, 219 U. S. 47. The reservation of state power appropriate to such extraordinary conditions may be deemed to be as much a part of all contracts as is the reservation of state power to protect the public interest in the other situations to which we have referred. And if state power exists to give temporary relief from the enforcement of contracts in the presence of disasters due to physical causes such as fire, flood, or earthquake, that power cannot be said to be non-existent when the urgent public need demanding such relief is produced by other and economic causes.

It is manifest from this review of our decisions that there has been a growing appreciation of public needs and of the necessity of finding ground for a rational compromise between individual rights and public welfare. The settlement and consequent contraction of the public domain, the pressure of a constantly increasing density of population, the interrelation of the activities of our people and the complexity of our economic interests, have inevitably led to an increased use of the organization of society in order to protect the very bases of individual opportunity. Where, in earlier days, it was thought that only the concerns of individuals or of classes were involved, and that those of the State itself were touched only remotely, it has later been found that the fundamental interests of the State are directly affected; and that the question is no longer merely that of one party to a contract as against another, but of the use of reasonable means to safeguard the economic structure upon which the good of all depends.

It is no answer to say that this public need was not apprehended a century ago, or to insist that what the provision of the Constitution meant to the vision of that day it must mean to the vision of our time. If by the statement that what the Constitution meant at the time of its adoption it means today, it is intended to say that the great clauses of the Constitution must be confined to the interpretation which the framers, with the conditions and outlook of their time would have placed upon them, the statement carries its own refutation. It was to guard against such a narrow conception that Chief Justice Marshall uttered the memorable warning— "We must never forget it is a constitution we are expounding" (*Mc Culloch* v. *Maryland,* 4 Wheat, 316, 407) "a constitution intended to endure for ages to come, and, consequently, to be adapted to the various crises of human affairs." . . .

Nor is it helpful to attempt to draw a fine distinction between the intended meaning of the words of the Constitution and their intended application. When we consider the contract clause and the decisions which have expounded it in harmony with the essential reserve power of the States to protect the security of their peoples, we find no warrant for the conclusion that the clause has been warped by these decisions from its proper significance or that the founders of our Government would have interpreted the clause differently had they had occasion to assume that responsibility in the conditions of the later day. The vast body of law which has been developed was unknown to the fathers but it is believed to have preserved the essential content and the spirit of the Constitution. With a growing recognition of public needs and the relation of individual right to public security, the court has sought to prevent the perversion of the clause through its use as an instrument to throttle the capacity of the States to protect their fundamental interests. This development is a growth from the seeds which the fathers planted. . . .

We are of the opinion that the Minnesota statute as here applied does not violate the contract clause of the Federal Constitution. Whether the legislation is wise or unwise as a matter of policy is a question with which we are not concerned.

SUTHERLAND, J., with whom concurred VAN DEVANTER, J., McREYNOLDS, J., and BUTLER, J., delivered a dissenting opinion.

495. NEBBIA v. NEW YORK
291 U. S. 502
1934

Appeal from the County Court of Monroe County, New York. The facts of this case are stated in the opinion. The importance of the case derives not only from the judicial validation of price fixing, but also from the new interpretation of the historic concept of "affectation with a public interest" and of the nature of the police power. For the background of this question, see especially R. L. Mott, *Due Process of Law; L. P. McGehee, *Due Process of Law under the Federal Constitution;* E. Freund, *The Police Power, Public Policy, and Constitutional Rights;* and the illuminating article by W. Hamilton, "Affectation with a Public Interest," 39 Yale Law J. 1104. On the Nebbia case see, Hale, "The Constitution and the Price System," 34 Col. Law Rev. 401; Goldsmith and Winks, "Price Fixing: From Nebbia to Guffey," 31 Ills. Law Rev. 179; Fraenkel, "Constitutional Issues in the Supreme Court, 1934 Term," 84 U. of Pa. Law Rev. 345; Cohen and Horack, "After the Nebbia Case," 8 U. of Cin. L. Rev. 219.

ROBERTS, J. The Legislature of New York established, by Chapter 158 of the Laws of 1933, a Milk Control Board with power, among other things, to "fix minimum and maximum . . . retail prices to be charged by . . . stores to consumers for consumption off the premises where sold." The Board fixed nine cents as the price to be charged by a store for a quart of milk. Nebbia, the proprietor of a grocery store in Rochester, sold two quarts and a five cent loaf of bread for eighteen cents; and was convicted for violating the Board's order. At his trial he asserted the statute and order contravene the equal protection clause and the due process clause of the Fourteenth Amendment, and renewed the contention in successive appeals to the county court and the Court of Appeals. Both overruled his claim and affirmed the conviction.

The question for a decision is whether the Federal Constitution prohibits a state from so fixing the selling price of milk. We first inquire as to the occasion for the legislation and its history.

During 1932 the prices received by farmers

for milk were much below the cost of production. The decline in prices during 1931 and 1932 was much greater than that of prices generally. The situation of the families of dairy producers had become desperate and called for state aid similar to that afforded the unemployed, if conditions should not improve. . . .

Various remedies were suggested, amongst them united action by producers, the fixing of minimum prices for milk and cream by state authority, and the imposition of certain graded taxes on milk dealers proportioned so as to equalize the cost of milk and cream to all dealers and so remove the cause of price-cutting.

The legislature adopted Chapter 158 as a method of correcting the evils, which the report of the committee showed could not be expected to right themselves through the ordinary play of the forces of supply and demand, owing to the peculiar and uncontrollable factors affecting the industry. . . .

Section 312 (e) on which the prosecution in the present case is founded, provides: "After the board shall have fixed prices to be charged or paid for milk in any form . . . it shall be unlawful for a milk dealer to sell or buy or offer to sell or buy milk at any price less or more than such price . . . and no method or device shall be lawful whereby milk is bought or sold . . . at a price less or more than such price . . . whether by any discount, or rebate, or free service, or advertising allowance, or a combined price for such milk together with another commodity or commodities, or service or services, which is less or more than the aggregate of the prices for the milk and the price or prices for such other commodity or commodities, or service or services, when sold or offered for sale separately or otherwise. . . ."

First. The appellant urges that the order of the Milk Control Board denies him the equal protection of the laws. . . .

Second. The more serious question is whether, in the light of the conditions disclosed, the enforcement of § 312 (e) denied the appellant the due process secured to him by the Fourteenth Amendment.

Save the conduct of railroads, no business has been so thoroughly regimented and regulated by the State of New York as the milk industry. Legislation controlling it in the in-terest of the public health was adopted in 1862 and subsequent statutes, have been carried into the general codification known as the Agriculture and Markets Law. A perusal of these statutes discloses that the milk industry has been progressively subjected to a larger measure of control. The producer or dairy farmer is in certain circumstances liable to have his herd quarantined against bovine tuberculosis; is limited in the importation of dairy cattle to those free from Bang's disease; is subject to rules governing the care and feeding of his cows and the care of the milk produced, the condition and surroundings of his barns and buildings used for production of milk, the utensils used, and the persons employed in milking. Proprietors of milk gathering stations or processing plants are subject to regulation, and persons in charge must operate under license and give bond to comply with the law and regulations; must keep records, pay promptly for milk purchased, abstain from false or misleading statements and from combinations to fix prices. In addition there is a large volume of legislation intended to promote cleanliness and fair trade practices, affecting all who are engaged in the industry. The challenged amendment of 1933 carried regulation much farther than the prior enactments. Appellant insists that it went beyond the limits fixed by the Constitution.

Under our form of government the use of property and the making of contracts are normally matters of private and not of public concern. The general rule is that both shall be free of governmental interference. But neither property rights nor contract rights are absolute; for government cannot exist if the citizen may at will use his property to the detriment of his fellows, or exercise his freedom of contract to work them harm. Equally fundamental with the private right is that of the public to regulate it in the common interest. . . .

The Fifth Amendment, in the field of federal activity, and the Fourteenth, as respects state action, do not prohibit governmental regulation for the public welfare. They merely condition the exertion of the admitted power, by securing that the end shall be accomplished by methods consistent with due process. And the guaranty of due process, as has often been held, demands only that the law shall not be unreasonable, arbitrary or capricious, and that the means selected shall have a real and substantial relation to the object sought to be attained. It results that a regulation valid for one sort of business, or in given circumstances, may be invalid for another sort, or for the same business under other circumstances, because the reasonableness of each regulation depends upon the relevant facts.

The reports of our decisions abound with cases in which the citizens, individual or corporate, has vainly invoked the Fourteenth Amendment in resistance to necessary and appropriate exertion of the police power. . . .

The Constitution does not guarantee the unrestricted privilege to engage in a business or to conduct it as one pleases. Certain kinds of business may be prohibited; and the right to conduct a business, or to pursue a calling, may be conditioned. Regulation of a business to prevent waste of the state's resources may be justified. And statutes prescribing the terms upon which those conducting certain businesses may contract, or imposing terms if they do enter into agreements, are within the state's competency.

Legislation concerning sales of goods, and incidentally affecting prices, has repeatedly been held valid. . . .

But we are told that because the law essays to control prices it denies due process. Notwithstanding the admitted power to correct existing economic ills by appropriate regulation of business, even though an indirect result may be a restriction of the freedom of contract or a modification of charges for services or the price of commodities, the appellant urges that direct fixation of prices is a type of regulation absolutely forbidden. His position is that the Fourteenth Amendment requires us to hold the challenged statute void for this reason alone. The argument runs that the public control of rates or prices is *per se* unreasonable and unconstitutional, save as applied to businesses affected with a public interest; that a business so affected is one in which property is devoted to an enterprise of a sort which the public itself might appropriately undertake, or one whose owner relies on a public grant or franchise for the right to conduct the business, or in which he is bound to serve all who apply; in short, such as is commonly called a public utility; or a business in its nature a monopoly. The milk industry, it is said, possesses none of these

characteristics, and, therefore, not being affected with a public interest, its charges may not be controlled by the state. Upon the soundness of this contention the appellant's case against the statute depends.

We may as well say at once that the dairy industry is not, in the accepted sense of the phrase, a public utility. We think the appellant is also right in asserting that there is in this case no suggestion of any monopoly or monopolistic practice. It goes without saying that those engaged in the business are in no way dependent upon public grants or franchises for the privilege of conducting their activities. But if, as must be conceded, the industry is subject to regulation in the public interest, what constitutional principle bars the state from correcting existing maladjustments by legislation touching prices? We think there is no such principle. The due process clause makes no mention of sales or of prices any more than it speaks of business or contracts or buildings or other incidents of property. The thought seems nevertheless to have persisted that there is something peculiarly sacrosanct about the price one may charge for what he makes or sells, and that, however able to regulate other elements of manufacture or trade, with incidental effect upon price, the state is incapable of directly controlling the price itself. The view was negatived many years ago. *Munn.* v. *Illinois.* . . .

In the further discussion of the principle it is said that when one devotes his property to a use, "in which the public has an interest," he in effect "grants to the public an interest in that use" and must submit to be controlled for the common good. The conclusion is that if Munn and Scott wished to avoid having their business regulated they should not have embarked their property in an industry which is subject to regulation in the public interest.

The true interpretation of the court's language is claimed to be that only property voluntarily devoted to a known public use is subject to regulation as to rates. But obviously Munn and Scott had not voluntarily dedicated their business to a public use. They intended only to conduct it as private citizens, and they insisted that they had done nothing which gave the public an interest in their transactions or conferred any right of regulation. The statement that one has dedicated his property to a public use is, therefore, merely another way of saying that if one embarks in a business which public interest demands shall be regulated, he must know regulation will ensue. . . .

Many other decisions show that the private character of a business does not necessarily remove it from the realm of regulation of charges or prices. . . .

It is clear that there is no closed class or category of businesses affected with a public interest, and the function of courts in the application of the Fifth and Fourteenth Amendments is to determine in each case whether circumstances vindicate the challenged regulation as a reasonable exertion of governmental authority or condemn it as arbitrary or discriminatory. The phrase "affected with a public interest" can, in the nature of things, mean no more than that an industry, for adequate reason, is subject to control for the public good. In several of the decisions of this court wherein the expressions "affected with a public interest," and "clothed with a public use," have been brought forward as the criteria of the validity of price control, it has been admitted that they are not susceptible of definition and form an unsatisfactory test of the constitutionality of legislation directed at business practices or prices. These decisions must rest, finally, upon the basis that the requirements of due process were not met because the laws were found arbitrary in their operation and effect. But there can be no doubt that upon proper occasion and by appropriate measures the state may regulate a business in any of its aspects, including the prices to be charged for the products or commodities it sells.

So far as the requirement of due process is concerned, and in the absence of other constitutional restriction, a state is free to adopt whatever economic policy may reasonably be deemed to promote public welfare, and to enforce that policy by legislation adapted to its purpose. The courts are without authority either to declare such policy, or, when it is declared by the legislature, to override it. If the laws passed are seen to have a reasonable relation to a proper legislative purpose, and are neither arbitrary nor discriminatory, the requirements of due process are satisfied, and judicial determination to that effect renders a court *functus officio*. . . . And it is equally clear that if the legislative policy be to curb unrestrained and harmful competition by measures which are not arbitrary or discriminatory it does not lie with the courts to determine that the rule is unwise. With the wisdom of the policy adopted, with the adequacy or practicability of the law enacted to forward it, the courts are both incompetent and unauthorized to deal. . . .

The law-making bodies have in the past endeavored to promote free competition by laws aimed at trusts and monopolies. The consequent interference with private property and freedom of contract has not availed with the courts to set these enactments aside as denying due process. Where the public interest was deemed to require the fixing of minimum prices, that expedient has been sustained. If the law-making body within its sphere of government concludes that the conditions or practices in an industry make unrestricted competition an inadequate safeguard of the consumer's interests, produce waste harmful to the public, threaten ultimately to cut off the supply of a commodity needed by the public, or portend the destruction of the industry itself, appropriate statutes passed in an honest effort to correct the threatened consequences may not be set aside because the regulation adopted fixes prices reasonably deemed by the legislature to be fair to those engaged in the industry and to the consuming public. And this is especially so where, as here, the economic maladjustment is one of price, which threatens harm to the producer at one end of the series and the consumer at the other. The Constitution does not secure to anyone liberty to conduct his business in such fashion as to inflict injury upon the public at large, or upon any substantial group of the people. Price control, like any other form of regulation, is unconstitutional only if arbitrary, discriminatory, or demonstrably irrelevant to the policy the legislature is free to adopt, and hence an unnecessary and unwarranted interference with individual liberty.

Tested by these considerations we find no basis in the due process clause of the Fourteenth Amendment for condemning the provisions of the Agriculture and Markets Law here drawn into question.

The judgment is affirmed.

Justices McReynolds, Van Devanter, Sutherland and Butler dissented.

496. ROOSEVELT'S VETO OF THE SOLDIERS' BONUS BILL
May 22, 1935

(Public Papers and Addresses of Franklin D. Roosevelt, Vol. IV, p. 182)

As early as the Minneapolis meeting of 1919 the American Legion had considered favorably the suggestion of "adjusted compensation" for veterans of the World War. In 1922 a bonus bill passed both houses of Congress, but was vetoed by President Harding. A second effort, in 1923, was met by a veto from President Coolidge. In 1924, however, Congress passed over the Presidential veto a bill calling for adjusted compensation certificates to mature in 1945. The depression brought a demand for full and immediate payment of these certificates, Congress responded first by permitting veterans to borrow up to fifty per cent of the fact value of the certificates, and finally by complete capitulation. Congress failed to override this veto, but in January 1936 a similar bill was passed over the Presidential veto. President Roosevelt's second veto message can be found in the *Public Papers and Addresses,* Vol. V, p. 67. On the bonus, see K. Durham, *Billions for Veterans;* R. Burlingame, *Peace Veterans;* M. Duffield, *King Legion;* M. James, *History of the American Legion.*

Mr. Speaker, Members of the House of Representatives:

. . . At the outbreak of the war, the President and the Congress sought and established an entirely new policy in order to guide the granting of financial aid to soldiers and sailors. Remembering the unfortunate results that came from the lack of a veterans' policy after the Civil War, they determined that a prudent and sound principle of insurance should supplant the uncertainties and unfairness of direct bounties. At the same time, their policy encompassed the most complete care for those who had suffered disabilities in service. With respect to the grants made within the lines of this general policy, the President and the Congress have fully recognized that those who served in uniform deserved certain benefits to which other citizens of the Republic were not entitled, and in which they could not participate.

In line with these sound and fair principles, many benefits have been provided for veterans. . . .

We may measure the benefits extended from the fact that there has been expended up to the end of the last fiscal year more than $7,800,000,000 for these items in behalf of the veterans of the World War, not including sums spent for home or work relief. With our current annual expenditures of some $450,000,000 and the liquidation of outstanding obligations under term insurance and the payment of the service certificates, it seems safe to predict that by the year 1945 we will have expended $13,500,000,000. This is a sum equal to more than three-fourths of the entire cost of our participation in the World War, and ten years from now most of the veterans of that war will be barely past the half-century mark.

Payments have been made and are being made only to veterans of the World War and their dependents, and not to civilian workers who helped to win that war.

In the light of our established principles and policies let us consider the case of adjusted compensation. Soon after the close of the war a claim was made by several veterans' organizations that they should be paid some adjusted compensation for their time in uniform. After a complete and fair presentation of the whole subject, followed by full debate in the Congress of the United States, a settlement was reached in 1924.

This settlement provided for adjustment in compensation during service by an additional allowance per day for actual service rendered. Because cash payment was not to be made immediately, this basic allowance was increased by 25 per cent and to this was added compound interest for 20 years, the whole to be paid in 1945. The result of this computation was that an amount two and one-half times the original grant would be paid at maturity.

Taking the average case as an example, the Government acknowledged a claim of $400 to be due. This $400, under the provisions of the settlement, with the addition of the 25 per cent for deferred payment and the compound interest from that time until 1945, would amount to the sum of $1,000 in 1945. The veteran was thereupon given a certificate containing an agreement by the Government to pay him this $1,000 in 1945 or to pay it to his family if he died at any time before 1945.

In effect it was a paid-up endowment policy in the average case for $1,000 payable in 1945, or sooner in the event of his death. Under the provisions of this settlement the total obligation of $1,400,000,000 in 1924 produced a maturity or face value of $3,500,000,000 in 1945.

Since 1924 the only major change in the original settlement was the act of 1931, under which veterans were authorized to borrow up to 50 per cent of the face value of their certificates as of 1945. Three million veterans have already borrowed under this provision an amount which, with interest charges, totals $1,700,000,000.

The bill before me provides for the immediate payment of the 1945 value of the certificates. It means paying $1,600,000,000 more than the present value of the certificates. It requires an expenditure of more than $2,200,000,000 in cash for this purpose. It directs payment to the veterans of a much larger sum than was contemplated in the 1924 settlement. It is nothing less than a complete abandonment of that settlement. It is a new straight gratuity or bounty to the amount of $1,600,000,000. It destroys the insurance protection for the dependents of the veterans provided in the original plan. For the remaining period of 10 years they will have lost this insurance.

This proposal, I submit, violates the entire principle of veterans' benefits so carefully formulated at the time of the war and also the entire principle of the adjusted-certificate settlement of 1924.

What are the reasons presented in this bill for this fundamental change in policy? They are set forth with care in a number of "whereas" clauses at the beginning of the bill.

The first of these states as reasons for the cash payment of these certificates at this time: That it will increase the purchasing power of millions of the consuming public; that it will provide relief for many who are in need because of economic conditions; and that it will lighten the relief burden of cities, counties, and States. The second states that payment will not create any additional debt. The third states that payment now will be an effective method of spending money to hasten recovery.

These are the enacted reasons for the passage of this bill. Let me briefly analyze them.

First, the spending of this sum, it cannot be denied, would result in some expansion of retail trade. But it must be noted that retail trade has already expanded to a condition that compares favorably with conditions before the depression. However, to resort to the kind of financial practice provided in this bill would not improve the conditions necessary to expand those industries in which we have the greatest unemployment. The Treasury notes issued under the terms of this bill we know from past experience would return quickly to the banks. We know, too, that the banks have at this moment more than ample credit with which to expand the activities of business and industry generally. The ultimate effect of this bill will not, in the long run, justify the expectations that have been raised by those who argue for it.

The next reason in the first "whereas" clause is that present payment will provide relief for many who are in need because of economic conditions. The Congress has just passed an act to provide work relief for such citizens. Some veterans are on the relief rolls. . . . Assume, however, that such a veteran served in the United States or overseas during the war; that he came through in fine physical shape as most of them did; that he received an honorable discharge; that he is today 38 years old and in full possession of his faculties and health; that like several million other Americans he is receiving from his Government relief and assistance in one of many forms—I hold that that able-bodied citizen should be accorded no treatment different from that accorded to other citizens who did not wear a uniform during the World War.

The third reason given in the first "whereas" clause is that payment today would lighten the relief burden of municipalities. Why, I ask, should the Congress lift that burden in respect only to those who wore the uniform? Is it not better to treat every able-bodied American alike and to carry out the great relief program adopted by this Congress in a spirit of equality to all? This applies to every other unit of government throughout the Nation.

The second "whereas" clause, which states that the payment of certificates will not create an additional debt, raises a fundamental question of sound finance. To meet a claim of one group by this deceptively easy method of payment will raise similar demands for the payment of claims of other groups. It is easy to see the ultimate result of meeting recurring demands by the issuance of Treasury notes. It invites an ultimate reckoning in uncontrollable prices and in the destruction of the value of savings, that will strike most cruelly those like the veterans who seem to be temporarily benefited. The first person injured by sky-rocketing prices is the man on a fixed income. Every disabled veteran on pension or allowance is on fixed income. This bill favors the able-bodied veteran at the expense of the disabled veteran. . . .

The statement in this same second "whereas" clause that payment will discharge and retire an acknowledged contract obligation of the Government is, I regret to say, not in accordance with the fact. It wholly omits and disregards the fact that this contract obligation is due in 1945 and not today. . . .

The final "whereas" clause, stating that spending the money is the most effective means of hastening recovery, is so ill considered that little comment is necessary. Every authorization of expenditure by the 73d Congress in its session of 1933 and 1934, and every appropriation by the 74th Congress to date, for recovery purposes, has been predicated not on the mere spending of money to hasten recovery, but on the sounder principle of preventing the loss of homes and farms, of saving industry from bankruptcy, of safeguarding bank deposits, and most important of all—of giving relief and jobs through public work to individuals and families faced with starvation. These greater and broader concerns of the American people have a prior claim for our consideration at this time. They have the right of way. . . .

To argue for this bill as a relief measure is to indulge in the fallacy that the welfare of the country can be generally served by extending relief on some basis other than actual deserving need.

The core of the question is that man who is sick or under some other special disability because he was a soldier should certainly be assisted as such. But if a man is suffering from economic need because of the depression, even though he is a veteran, he must be placed on a par with all of the other victims of the depression. The veteran who is disabled owes his condition to the war. The healthy veteran who is unemployed owes his troubles to the depression. Each presents a separate and different problem. Any attempt to mingle the two problems is to confuse our efforts.

Even the veteran who is on relief will benefit only temporarily by this measure, because the payment of this sum to him will remove him from the group entitled to relief if the ordinary rules of relief agencies are followed. For him this measure would give but it would also take away. In the end he would be the loser.

The veteran who suffers from this depression can best be aided by the rehabilitation of the country as a whole. His country with honor and gratitude returned him at the end of the war to the citizenry from which he came. He became once more a member of the great civilian population. His interests became identified with its fortunes and also with its misfortunes. . . .

It is generally conceded that the settlement by adjusted-compensation certificates made in 1924 was fair and it was accepted as fair by the overwhelming majority of World War veterans themselves. . . .

It is important to make one more point. In accordance with the mandate of the Congress, our Budget has been set. The public has accepted it. On that basis this Congress has made and is making its appropriations. That Budget asked for appropriations in excess of receipts to the extent of four billion dollars. The whole of that deficit was to be applied for work relief for the unemployed. That was a single-minded, definite purpose. Every unemployed veteran on the relief rolls was included in that proposed deficit; he will be taken care of out of it.

I cannot in honesty assert to you that to increase that deficit this year by two billion two hundred million dollars will in itself bankrupt the United States. Today the credit of the United States is safe. But it cannot ultimately be safe if we engage in a policy of yielding to each and all of the groups that are able to enforce upon the Congress claims for special consideration. To do so is to abandon the principle of government by and for the American people and to put in its place government by and for political coercion by minorities. We can afford all that we need; but we cannot afford all that we want.

I do not need to be a prophet to assert that if these certificates, due in 1945, are paid in full today, every candidate for election to the Senate or to the House of Representatives will in the near future be called upon in the name of patriotism to support general pension legislation for all veterans, regardless of need or age.

Finally I invite your attention to the fact that, solely from the point of view of the good credit of the United States, the complete failure of the Congress to provide additional taxes for an additional expenditure of this magnitude would in itself any by itself alone warrant disapproval of this measure. . . .

I believe the welfare of the Nation, as well as the future welfare of the veterans, wholly justifies my disapproval of this measure.

Therefore, Mr. Speaker, I return, without my approval, House of Representatives bill No. 3896, providing for the immediate payment to veterans of the 1945 face value of their adjusted-service certificates.

497. RAILROAD RETIREMENT BOARD v. ALTON RAILROAD CO.
295 U. S. 330
1935

Certiorari to the U. S. Court of Appeals for the District of Columbia. Congress, in 1934 passed an act establishing compulsory retirement and pensions for all carriers subject to the Interstate Commerce Act. The authority for this law was, apparently, in the commerce clause of the Constitution. The Court, however, held that there was no reasonable relation between pensions and the promotion of efficiency in interstate commerce, and invalidated the act. For an analysis of the role of the Court in restricting the commerce clause see E. S. Corwin, *Commerce Power versus States Rights,* and *Twilight of the Supreme Court,* and E. R. Johnson, *Government Regulation of Transportation.* For an interpretation of the decision, see Powell, "Commerce, Pensions and Codes," 49 Harv. L. Rev. 1 and 193; Gellhorn, "Validity of Federal Compensation for Transportation Employees," 25 Am. Labor Legislation Rev. 71.

ROBERTS, J. The respondents, comprising 134 Class I railroads, two express companies, and the Pullman Company, brought this suit in the Supreme Court of the District of Columbia, asserting the unconstitutionality of the Railroad Retirement Act and praying an injunction against its enforcement. . . .

The Act establishes a compulsory retirement and pension system for all carriers subject to the Interstate Commerce Act. There is provision for the creation of a fund to be deposited in the United States treasury and administered by a Board denominated an independent agency in the executive branch of the Government. The retirement fund for payment of these pensions and for the expenses of administration of the system will arise from compulsory contributions from present and future employees and the carriers. The sums payable by the employees are to be percentages of their current compensation, and those by each carrier double the total payable by its employees. The Board is to determine from time to time what percentage is required to provide the necessary funds, but until that body otherwise determines the employee contribution is to be 2% of compensation. Out of this fund annuities are to be paid to beneficiaries. . . .

The Supreme Court of the District of Columbia declared the establishment of such a system within the competence of Congress; but thought several inseparable features of the Act transcended the legislative power to regulate interstate commerce, and required a holding that the law is unconstitutional in its entirety. Our duty, like that of the court below, is fairly to construe the powers of Congress, and to ascertain whether or not the enactment falls within them, uninfluenced by predilection for or against the policy disclosed in the legislation. The fact that the compulsory scheme is novel is, of course, no evidence of unconstitutionality. Even should we consider the Act unwise and prejudicial to both public and private interest, if it be fairly within delegated power our obligation is to sustain it. On the other hand though we should think the measure embodies a valuable social plan and be in entire sympathy with its purpose and intended results, if the provisions go beyond the boundaries of constitutional power we must so declare. . . .

The petitioners assert that the questioned Act, fairly considered, is a proper and necessary regulation of interstate commerce; its various provisions have reasonable relation to the main and controlling purposes of the enactment, the promotion of efficiency, economy and safety; consequently it falls within the power conferred by the commerce clause and does not offend the principle of due process. The respondents insist that numerous features of the Act contravene the due process guaranty and further that the requirement of pensions for employees of railroads is not a regulation of interstate commerce within the meaning of the Constitution. . . .

. . . Broadly, the record presents the question whether a statutory requirement that retired employees shall be paid pensions is regulation of commerce between the States within Article I, § 8. . . .

5. It results from what has now been said that the Act is invalid because several of its inseparable provisions contravene the due process of law clause of the Fifth Amendment. We are of opinion that it is also bad for another reason which goes to the heart of the law, even if it could survive the loss of the unconstitutional features which we have discussed. The Act is not in purpose or effect a regulation of interstate commerce within the meaning of the Constitution.

Several purposes are expressed in § 2 (a), amongst them: to provide "adequately for the satisfactory retirement of aged employees"; "to make possible greater employment opportunity and more rapid advancement"; to provide by the administration and construction of the Act "the greatest practicable amount of relief from unemployment and the greatest possible use of resources available for said purpose and for the payment of annuities for the relief of superannuated employees." The respondents assert and the petitioners admit that though these may in and of themselves be laudable objects, they have no reasonable relation to the business of interstate transportation. The clause, however, states a further purpose, the promotion of "efficiency and safety in interstate transportation," and the respondents concede that an act, the provisions of which show that it actually is directed to the attainment of such a purpose, falls within the regulatory power conferred upon the Congress; but they contend that here the provisions of the statute emphasize the necessary conclusion that the plan is conceived solely for the promotion of the stated purposes other than efficient and safe operation of the railroads. The petitioners' view is that this is the true and only purpose of the enactment, and the other objects stated are collateral to it and may be disregarded if the law is found apt for the promotion of this legitimate purpose.

From what has already been said with respect to sundry features of the statutory scheme, it must be evident that petitioners' view is that safety and efficiency are promoted by two claimed results of the plan: the abolition of excessive superannuation, and the improvement of morale. . . .

In final analysis, the petitioners' sole reliance is the thesis that efficiency depends upon morale, and morale in turn upon assurance of security for the worker's old age. Thus pensions are sought to be related to efficiency of transportation, and brought within the commerce power. In supporting the Act the petitioners constantly recur to such phrases as "old age security," "assurance of old age security," "improvement of employee morale and efficiency through providing definite assurance of old age security," "assurance of old age support," "mind at ease," and "fear of old age dependency." These expressions are frequently connected with assertions that the removal of the fear of old age dependency will tend to create a better morale throughout the ranks of employees. The theory is that one who has an assurance against future dependency will do his work more cheerfully, and therefore more efficiently. The question at once presents itself whether the fostering of a contented mind on the part of an employee by legislation of this type, is in any just sense a regulation of interstate transportation. If that question be answered in the affirmative, obviously there is no limit to the field of so-called regulation. The catalogue of means and actions which might be imposed upon an employer in any business, tending to the satisfaction and comfort of his employees, seems endless. Provision for free medical attendance and nursing, for clothing, for food, for housing, for the education of children, and a hundred other matters, might with equal propriety be proposed as tending to relieve the employee of mental strain and worry. Can it fairly be said that the power of Congress to regulate interstate commerce extends to the prescription of any or all of these things? Is it not apparent that they are really and essentially related solely to the social welfare of the worker, and therefore remote from any regulation of commerce as such? We think the answer is plain. These matters obviously lie outside the orbit of Congressional power. The answer of the petitioners is that not all such means of promoting contentment have such a close relation to interstate commerce as pensions. This is in truth no answer, for we must deal with the principle involved and not the means adopted. If contentment of the employee were an object for the attainment of which the regulatory power could be exerted, the courts could not question the wisdom of methods adopted for its advancement. . . .

Certainly the argument is inconsistent with any thought that a plan imposed by statute, requiring the payment of a pension, will promote the same loyalty and continuity of service which were the ends and objects of the voluntary plans. It is going far to say, as petitioners do, that Congress chose the more progressive method "already tried in the laboratory of industrial experience," which they claim has been approved and recommended by those qualified to speak. In support of the assertion, however, they cite general works dealing with voluntary pension plans, and not with any such compulsory system as that with which we are concerned. We think it cannot be denied, and, indeed, is in effect admitted, that the sole reliance of the petitioners is upon the theory that contentment and assurance of security are the major purposes of the Act. We cannot agree that these ends if dictated by statute, and not voluntarily extended by the employer, encourage loyalty and continuity of service. We feel bound to hold that a pension plan thus imposed is in no proper sense a regulation of the activity of interstate transportation. It is an attempt for social ends to impose by sheer fiat non-contractual incidents upon the relation of employer and employee, not as a rule or regulation of commerce and transportation between the States, but as a means of assuring a particular class of employees against old age dependency. This is neither a necessary nor an appropriate rule or regulation affecting the due fulfilment of the railroads' duty to serve the public in interstate transportation.

The judgment of the Supreme Court of the District of Columbia is

Affirmed.

HUGHES, C. J., dissenting. I am unable to concur in the decision of this case. The gravest aspect of the decision is that it does not rest simply upon a condemnation of particular features of the Railroad Retirement Act, but denies to Congress the power to pass any compulsory pension act for railroad employees. If the opinion were limited to the particular provisions of the Act, which the majority find to be objectionable and not severable, the Congress would be free to overcome the objections by a new statute. Classes of persons held to be improperly brought within the range of the Act could be eliminated. Criticisms of the basis of payments, of the conditions prescribed for the receipt of benefits, and of the requirements of contributions could be met. Even in place of a unitary retirement system another sort of plan could be worked out. What was thus found to be inconsistent with the requirements of due process could be exercised and other provisions substituted. But after discussing these matters, the majority finally raise a barrier against all legislative action of this nature by declaring that the subject matter itself lies beyond the reach of the congressional authority to regulate interstate commerce. In that view, no matter how suitably limited a pension act for railroad employees might be with respect to the persons to be benefited, or how appropriate the measure of retirement allowances, or how sound actuarilly the plan, or how well adjusted the burden, still under this decision Congress would not be at liberty to enact such a measure. That is a conclusion of such serious and far-reaching importance that it overshadows all other questions raised by the Act. Indeed, it makes their discussion superfluous. The final objection goes, as the opinion states, "to the heart of the law, even if it could survive the loss of the unconstitutional features" which the opinion perceives. I think that the conclusion thus reached is a departure from sound principles and places an unwarranted limitation upon the commerce clause of the Constitution. . . .

. . . I think that it is clear that the morale

of railroad employees has an important bearing upon the efficiency of the transportation service, and that a reasonable pension plan by its assurance of security is an appropriate means to that end. Nor should such a plan be removed from the reach of constitutional power by classing it with a variety of conceivable benefits which have no such close and substantial relation to the terms and conditions of employment. The appropriate relation of the exercise of constitutional power to the legitimate objects of that power is always a subject of judicial scrutiny. With approximately 82 per cent of railroad employees, 90 per cent of those employed in cable, telephone and telegraph companies, and about one-half of those in the servic of electric railways, light, heat and power companies under formal pension plans, with the extensive recognition by national, state and local governments of the benefit of retirement and pension systems for public employees in the interest of both efficiency and economy, it is evident that there is a widespread conviction that the assurance of security through a pension plan for retired employees is closely and substantially related to the proper conduct of business enterprises.

But with respect to the carriers' plans, we are told that as they were framed in the desire to promote loyalty and continuity of service in the employment of particular carriers, the accruing advantages were due to the fact that the plans were of a voluntary character. In short, that the reaction of the employees would be simply one of gratitude for an act of grace. I find no adequate basis for a conclusion that the advantages of a pension plan can be only such as the carriers contemplated or that the benefit which may accrue to the service from a sense of security on the part of employees should be disregarded. In that aspect, it would be the fact that protection was assured, and not the mo-tive in supplying it, which would produce the desired result. That benefit would not be lost because the sense of security was fostered by a pension plan enforced as an act of justice. Indeed, voluntary plans may have the defect of being voluntary, of being subject to curtailment or withdrawal at will. And the danger of such curtailment or abandonment, with the consequent frustration of the hopes of a vast number of railroad workers and its effect upon labor relation in this enterprise of outstanding national importance, might well be considered as an additional reason for the adoption of a compulsory plan. . . .

The fundamental consideration which supports this type of legislation is that industry should take care of its human wastage, whether that is due to accident or age. That view cannot be dismissed as arbitrary or capricious. It is a reasoned conviction based upon abundant experience. The expression of that conviction in law is regulation. When expressed in the government of interstate carriers, with respect to their employees likewise engaged in interstate commerce, it is a regulation of that commerce. As such, so far as the subject matter is concerned, the commerce clause should be held applicable. . . .

The power committed to Congress to govern interstate commerce does not require that its government should be wise, much less that it should be perfect. The power implies a broad discretion and thus permits a wide range even of mistakes. Expert discussion of pension plans reveals different views of the manner in which they should be set up and a close study of advisable methods is in progress. It is not our province to enter that field, and I am not persuaded that Congress in entering it for the purpose of regulating interstate carriers has transcended the limits of the authority which the Constitution confers.

I think the decree should be reversed.

498. HUMPHREY'S EXECUTOR v. UNITED STATES
295 U. S. 602
1935

Certificate from the Court of Claims. Myers v. U. S. (Doc. No. 459) appeared to give judicial sanction to a very broad power of removal by the President. Did this power extend to removal of members of the independent quasi-legislative and quasi-judicial commissions such as the Federal Trade Commission? The Court here held unanimously that it did not. See, E. S. Corwin, *The President's Power of Removal Under the Constitution;* E. P. Herring, *Public Administra-*

tion and the Public Interest; W. E. Binkley, *The Powers of the President;* H. Laski, *The American Presidency.*

SUTHERLAND, J. . . . William E. Humphrey, the decedent, on December 10, 1931, was nominated by President Hoover to succeed himself as a member of the Federal Trade Commission, and was confirmed by the United States Senate. He was duly commissioned for a term of seven years expiring September 25, 1938; and, after taking the required oath of office, entered upon his duties. On July 25, 1933, President Roosevelt addressed a letter to the commissioner asking for his resignation, on the ground "that the aims and purposes of the Administration with respect to the work of the Commission can be carried out most effectively with personnel of my own selection," but disclaiming any reflection upon the commissioner personally or upon his services. The commissioner replied, asking time to consult his friends. After some further correspondence upon the subject, the President on August 31, 1933, wrote the commissioner expressing the hope that the resignation would be forthcoming and saying:

"You will, I know, realize that I do not feel that your mind and my mind go along together on either the policies or the administering of the Federal Trade Commission, and, frankly, I think it is best for the people of this country that I should have a full confidence."

The commissioner declined to resign; and on October 7, 1933, the President wrote him:

"Effective as of this date you are hereby removed from the office of Commissioner of the Federal Trade Commission."

Humphreys never acquiesced in this action, but continued thereafter to insist that he was still a member of the Commission, entitled to perform its duties and receive the compensation provided by law at the rate of $10,000 per annum. Upon these and other facts set forth in the certificate, which we deem it unnecessary to recite, the following questions are certified:

"1. Do the provisions of section 1 of the Federal Trade Commission Act, stating that 'any commissioner may be removed by the President for inefficiency, neglect of duty, or malfeasance in office,' restrict or limit the power of the President to remove a commis-sioner except upon one or more of the causes named?

"If the foregoing question is answered in the affirmative, then—

"2. If the power of the President to remove a commissioner is restricted or limited as shown by the foregoing interrogatory and the answer made thereto, is such a restriction or limitation valid under the Constitution of the United States?" . . .

The Federal Trade Commission Act creates a commission of five members to be appointed by the President by and with the advice and consent of the Senate, and § 1 provides:

"Not more than three of the commissioners shall be members of the same political party. The first commissioners appointed shall continue in office for terms of three, four, five, six, and seven years, respectively, from the date of the taking effect of this Act, the term of each to be designated by the President, but their successors shall be appointed for terms of seven years, except that any person chosen to fill a vacancy shall be appointed only for the unexpired term of the commissioner whom he shall succeed. The Commission shall engage in any other business, vocation, or employment. Any commissioner may be removed by the President for inefficiency, neglect of duty, or malfeasance in office. . . ."

First. The question first to be considered is whether, by the provisions of § 1 of the Federal Trade Commission Act already quoted, the President's power is limited to removal for the specific causes enumerated therein. . . .

The Commission is to be non-partisan; and it must, from the very nature of its duties, act with entire impartiality. It is charged with the enforcement of no policy except the policy of the law. Its duties are neither political nor executive, but predominantly quasi-judicial and quasi-legislative. Like the Interstate Commerce Commission, its members are called upon to exercise the trained judgment of a body of experts "appointed by law and informed by experience." . . .

The legislative reports in both houses of Congress clearly reflect the view that a fixed term was necessary to the effective and fair administration of the law. . . .

The debates in both houses demonstrate that the prevailing view was that the commission was not to be "subject to anybody in the government but . . . only to the people of the United States"; free from "political domination or control" or the "probability or possibility of such a thing"; to be "separate and apart from any existing department of the government—not subject to the orders of the President." . . .

Thus, the language of the act, the legislative reports, and the general purposes of the legislation as reflected by the debates, all combine to demonstrate the Congressional intent to create a body of experts who shall gain experience by length of service—a body which shall be independent of executive authority, *except in its selection,* and free to exercise its judgment without the leave or hindrance of any other official or any department of the government. To the accomplishment of these purposes, it is clear that Congress was of opinion that length and certainty of tenure would vitally contribute. And to hold that, nevertheless, the members of the commission continue in office at the mere will of the President, might be to thwart, in large measure, the very ends which Congress sought to realize by definitely fixing the term of office.

We conclude that the intent of the act is to limit the executive power of removal to the causes enumerated, the existence of none of which is claimed here; and we pass to the second question.

Second. To support its contention that the removal provision of § 1, as we have just construed it, is an unconstitutional interference with the executive power of the President, the government's chief reliance is *Myers* v. *United States,* 272 U. S. 52. . . . In the course of the opinion of the court, expressions occur which tend to sustain the government's contention, but these are beyond the point involved and, therefore, do not come within the rule of *stare decisis.* In so far as they are out of harmony with the views here set forth, these expressions are disapproved. . . .

The office of a postmaster is so essentially unlike the office now involved that the decision in the *Myers* case cannot be accepted as controlling our decision here. A postmaster is an executive officer restricted to the performance of executive functions. He is charged with no duty at all related to either the legislative or judicial power. The actual decision in the *Meyers* case finds support in

the theory that such an officer is merely one of the units in the executive department and, hence, inherently subject to the exclusive and illimitable power of removal by the Chief Executive, whose subordinate and aid he is. Putting aside *dicta,* which may be followed if sufficiently persuasive but which are not controlling, the necessary reach of the decision goes far enough to include all purely executive officers. It goes no farther;—much less does it include an officer who occupies no place in the executive department and who exercises no part of the executive power vested by the Constitution in the President.

The Federal Trade Commission is an administrative body created by Congress to carry into effect legislative policies embodied in the statute in accordance with the legislative standard therein prescribed, and to perform other specified duties as a legislative or as a judicial aid. Such a body cannot in any proper sense be characterized as an arm or an eye of the executive. Its duties are performed without executive leave and, in the contemplation of the statute, must be free from executive control. . . .

We think it plain under the Constitution that illimitable power of removal is not possessed by the President in respect of officers of the character of those just named. The authority of Congress, in creating quasi-legislative or quasi-judicial agencies, to require them to act in discharge of their duties independently of executive control cannot well be doubted; and that authority includes, as an appropriate incident, power to fix the period during which they shall continue in office, and to forbid their removal except for cause in the meantime. For it is quite evident that one who holds his office only during the pleasure of another, cannot be depended upon to maintain an attitude of independence against the latter's will.

The fundamental necessity of maintaining each of the three general departments of government entirely free from the control or coercive influence, direct or indirect, of either of the others, has often been stressed and is hardly open to serious question. . . .

The power of removal here claimed for the President falls within this principle, since its coercive influence threatens the independence of a commission, which is not only wholly disconnected from the executive department, but which, as already fully appears, was created by Congress as a means of carrying into operation legislative and judicial powers, and as an agency of the legislative and judicial departments. . . .

The result of what we now have said is this: Whether the power of the President to remove an officer shall prevail over the authority of Congress to condition the power by fixing a definite term and precluding a removal except for cause, will depend upon the character of the office; the *Myers* decision, affirming the power of the President alone to make the removal, is confined to purely executive officers; and as to officers of the kind here under consideration, we hold that no removal can be made during the prescribed term for which the officer is appointed, except for one or more of the causes named in the applicable statute. . . .

499. GROSJEAN v. AMERICAN PRESS CO.
297 U. S. 233
1935

Appeal from the District Court of the United States for the Eastern District of Louisiana. Louisiana, in 1934 levied a special tax upon newspapers and periodicals carrying advertising matter and with a weekly circulation of twenty thousand copies or over. It was widely thought at the time that this tax represented an effort of the Huey Long regime to punish certain opposition newspapers. Did such a tax infringe upon that freedom of the press guaranteed in the First and Fourteenth Amendments? The Supreme Court, in an opinion notable for its review of the historical background of the First Amendment, held that it did. See G. L. Patterson, *Free Speech and a Free Press;* Z. Chafee, *Freedom of Speech;* Corwin, "Freedom of Speech and Press under the First Amendment," 30 Yale Law J. 48; Willis, "Freedom of Speech and of the Press," 4 Indiana Law J. 445.

SUTHERLAND, J. This suit was brought by appellees, nine publishers of newspapers in the State of Louisiana, to enjoin the enforcement against them of the Provisions of § 1 of the act of the legislature of Louisiana known as Act No. 23, passed and approved July 12, 1934, as follows:

"That every person, firm, association, or corporation, domestic or foreign, engaged in the business of selling, or making any charge for, advertising or for advertisements, whether printed or published, or to be printed or published, in any newspaper, magazine, periodical or publication whatever having a circulation of more than 20,000 copies per week, or displayed and exhibited, or to be displayed and exhibited by means of moving pictures, in the State of Louisiana, shall, in addition to all other taxes and licenses levied and assessed in this State, pay a license tax for the privilege of engaging in such business in this State of two per cent. of the gross receipts of such business."

The nine publishers who brought the suit publish thirteen newspapers; and these thirteen publications are the only ones within the State of Louisiana having each a circulation of more than 20,000 copies per week, although the lower court finds there are four other daily newspapers each having a circulation of "slightly less than 20,000 copies per week" which are in competition with those published by appellees both as to circulation and as to advertising. In addition, there are 120 weekly newspapers published in the state, also in competition, to a greater or less degree, with the newspapers of appellees. The revenue derived from appellees' newspapers comes almost entirely from regular subscribers or purchasers thereof and from payments received for the insertion of advertisements therein. . . .

Failure to file the report or pay the tax as thus provided constitutes a misdemeanor and subjects the offender to a fine not exceeding $500, or imprisonment not exceeding six months, or both, for each violation. Any corporation violating the act subjects itself to the payment of $500 to be recovered by suit. All of the appellees are corporations. The lower court entered a decree for appellees and granted a permanent injunction. . . .

Third. The validity of the act is assailed as violating the Federal Constitution in two particulars—(1) that it abridges the freedom of the press in contravention of the due process clause contained in § 1 of the Fourteenth Amendment; (2) that it denies appellees the equal protection of the laws in contravention of the same Amendment,

1. The first point presents a question of the utmost gravity and importance; for, if well made, it goes to the heart of the natural right of the members of an organized society, united for their common good, to impart and acquire information about their common interests. The First Amendment to the Federal Constitution provides that "Congress shall make no law . . . abridging the freedom of speech, or of the press . . ." While this provision is not a restraint upon the powers of the states, the states are precluded from abridging the freedom of speech or of the press by force of the due process clause of the Fourteenth Amendment. . . .

In Powell v. Alabama, (287 U. S. 45) . . . we concluded that certain fundamental rights, safeguarded by the first eight amendments against federal action, were also safeguarded against state action by the due process of law clause of the Fourteenth Amendment, and among them the fundamental right of the accused to the aid of counsel in a criminal prosecution.

That freedom of speech and of the press are rights of the same fundamental character, safeguarded by the due process of law clause of the Fourteenth Amendment against abridgement by state legislation, has likewise been settled by a series of decisions of this Court beginning with Gitlow v. New York (268 U. S. 652), and ending with Near v. Minnesota (283 U. S. 697). The word "liberty" contained in that amendment embraces not only the right of a person to be free from physical restraint, but the right to be free in the enjoyment of all his faculties as well.

Appellant contends that the Fourteenth Amendment does not apply to corporations; but this is only partly true. A corporation, we have held, is not a "citizen," within the meaning of the privileges and immunities clause. (Paul v. Virginia, 8 Wall. 168.) But a corporation is a "person" within the meaning of the equal protection and due process of law clauses, which are the clauses involved here. (Covington & Lexington Turnpike Co. v. Sandford, 164 U. S. 578; Smyth v. Ames, 169 U. S. 466).

The tax imposed is designated a "license tax for the privilege of engaging in such business"—that is to say, the business of selling, or making any charge for, advertising.

As applied to appellees, it is a tax of two per cent. on the gross receipts derived from advertisements carried in their newspapers when, and only when, the newspapers of each enjoy a circulation of more than 20,000 copies per week. It thus operates as a restraint in a double sense. First, its effect is to curtail the amount of revenue realized from advertising, and, second, its direct tendency is to restrict circulation. This is plain enough when we consider that, if it were increased to a high degree, as it could be if valid, it well might result in destroying both advertising and circulation.

A determination of the question whether the tax is valid in respect of the point now under review, requires an examination of the history and circumstances which antedated and attended the adoption of the abridgement clause of the First Amendment, since that clause expresses one of those "fundamental principles of liberty and justice which lie at the base of all our civil and political institutions," and, as such, is embodied in the concept "due process of law," and, therefore, protected against hostile state invasion by the due process clause of the Fourteenth Amendment. (Cf. Powell v. Alabama, supra, pp. 67–68.) The history is a long one; but for present purposes it may be greatly abbreviated. . . . [reviews history in England, and background of First Amendment.]

It is impossible to concede that by the words "freedom of the press" the framers of the amendment intended to adopt merely the narrow view then reflected by the law of England that such freedom consisted only in immunity from previous censorship; for this abuse had then permanently disappeared from English practice. It is equally impossible to believe that it was not intended to bring within the reach of these words such modes of restraint as were embodied in the two forms of taxation already described.

In the light of all that has now been said, it is evident that the restricted rules of the English law in respect of the freedom of the press in force when the Constitution was adopted were never accepted by the American colonists, and that by the First Amendment it was meant to preclude the national government, and by the Fourteenth Amendment to preclude the states, from adopting any form of previous restraint upon printed publications, or their circulation, including that which had theretofore been effected by these two well-known and odious methods.

This court had occasion in Near v. Minnesota, supra, at pp. 713 et seq., to discuss at some length the subject in its general aspect. The conclusion there stated is that the object of the constitutional provisions was to prevent previous restraints on publication; and the court was careful not to limit the protection of the right to any particular way of abridging it. Liberty of the press within the meaning of the constitutional provision, it was broadly said, meant "principally although not exclusively, immunity from previous restraints or (from) censorship."

Judge Cooley has laid down the test to be applied—"The evils to be prevented were not the censorship of the press merely, but any action of the government by means of which it might prevent such free and general discussion of public matters as seems absolutely essential to prepare the people for an intelligent exercise of their rights as citizens." 2 Cooley's Constitutional Limitations, 8th ed., p. 886.

It is not intended by anything we have said to suggest that the owners of newspapers are immune from any of the ordinary forms of taxation for support of the government. But this is not an ordinary form of tax, but one single in kind, with a long history of hostile misuse against the freedom of the press.

The predominant purpose of the grant of immunity here invoked was to preserve an untrammeled press as a vital source of public information. The newspapers, magazines and other journals of the country, it is safe to say, have shed and continue to shed, more light on the public and business affairs of the nation than any other instrumentality of publicity; and since informed public opinion is the most potent of all restraints upon misgovernment, the suppression or abridgement of the publicity afforded by a free press cannot be regarded otherwise than with grave concern. The tax here involved is bad not because it takes money from the pockets of the appellees. If that were all, a wholly different question would be presented. It is bad because, in the light of its history and of its present setting, it is seen to be a deliberate and calculated device in the guise of a tax to limit the circulation of information to which the public is entitled in virtue of the constitutional guaranties. A free press stands as one of the great interpreters between the government and the people. To allow it to be fettered is to fetter ourselves.

In view of the persistent search for new subjects of taxation, it is not without significance that, with the single exception of the Louisiana statute, so far as we can discover, no state during the one hundred fifty years of our national existence has undertaken to impose a tax like that now in question.

The form in which the tax is imposed is in itself suspicious. It is not measured or limited by the volume of advertisements. It is measured alone by the extent of the circulation of the publication in which the advertisements are carried, with the plain purpose of penalizing the publishers and curtailing the circulation of a selected group of newspapers.

2. Having reached the conclusion that the act imposing the tax in question is unconstitutional under the due process of law clause because it abridges the freedom of the press, we deem it unnecessary to consider the further ground assigned that it also constitutes a denial of the equal protection of the laws.

Decree affirmed.

500. THE NATIONAL LABOR RELATIONS ACT
July 5, 1935
(U. S. Statutes at Large, Vol. XLIX, p. 449)

The invalidation of the NRA necessitated new legislation for the peaceful settlement of labor disputes, and Congress promptly passed this act, commonly known as the Wagner Act after its chief sponsor, Sen. Robert F. Wagner of New York. The act set up an independent Board authorized to investigate complaints, issue cease and desist orders against unfair practices in labor relations affecting interstate commerce, safeguard the right to bargain collectively, and arbitrate labor disputes. Notwithstanding its phenomenal success in the peaceful settlement of disputes, the National Labor Relations Board was under continuous fire both from employers and from the A. F. of L. which charged discrimination in favor of the rival C. I. O. The Government Printing Office publishes annual volumes of the Decisions and Orders of the Board. See J. Rosenfarb, *The National Labor Policy and How It Works;* H. Harris, *American Labor;* R. R. Brooks, *Unions of Their Own Choosing;* E. Levinson, *Labor on the March;* D. Yoder, *Labor Economics and Labor Problems;* H. G. Taylor, *Labor Problems and Labor Law;* N.L.R.B. Division of Economic Research, "Governmental Protection of Labor's Right to Organize"; Garrison, "The National Labor Relations Act," 24 Survey Graphic, 596.

An Act to diminish the causes of labor disputes burdening or obstructing interstate and foreign commerce, to create a National Labor Relations Board, and for other purposes.

Be it enacted,

FINDINGS AND POLICY

SECTION 1. The denial by employers of the right of employees to organize and the refusal by employers to accept the procedure of collective bargaining lead to strikes and other forms of industrial strife or unrest, which have the intent or the necessary effect of burdening or obstructing commerce by (a) impairing the efficiency, safety, or operation of the instrumentalities of commerce; (b) occurring in the current of commerce; (c) materially affecting, restraining, or controlling the flow of raw materials or manufactured or processed goods from or into the channels of commerce, or the prices of such materials or goods in commerce; or (d) causing diminution of employment and wages in such volume as substantially to impair or disrupt the market for goods flowing from or into the channels of commerce.

The inequality of bargaining power between employees who do not possess full freedom of association or actual liberty of contract, and employers who are organized in the corporate or other forms of ownership association substantially burdens and affects the flow of commerce, and tends to aggravate recurrent business depressions, by depressing wage rates and the purchasing power of wage earners in industry and by preventing the stabilization of competitive wage rates and working conditions within and between industries.

Experience has proved that protection by law of the right of employees to organize and bargain collectively safeguards commerce from injury, impairment, or interruption, and promotes the flow of commerce by removing certain recognized sources of industrial strife and unrest, by encouraging practices fundamental to the friendly adjustment of industrial disputes arising out of differences as to wages, hours, or other working conditions, and by restoring equality of bargaining power between employers and employees.

It is hereby declared to be the policy of the United States to eliminate the causes of certain substantial obstructions to the free flow of commerce and to mitigate and eliminate these obstructions when they have occurred by encouraging the practice and procedure of collective bargaining and by protecting the exercise by workers of full freedom of association, self-organization, and designation of representatives of their own choosing, for the purpose of negotiating the terms and conditions of their employment or other mutual aid or protection.

SEC. 2. When used in this Act—

(1) The term "person" includes one or more individuals, partnerships, associations, corporations, legal representatives, trustees, trustees in bankruptcy, or receivers.

(2) The term "employer" includes any person acting in the interest of an employer, directly or indirectly, but shall not include the United States, or any State or political subdivision thereof, or any person subject to the Railway Labor Act, as amended from time to time, or any labor organization (other than when acting as an employer), or anyone acting in the capacity of officer or agent of such labor organization.

(3) The term "employee" shall include any employee, and shall not be limited to the employees of a particular employer, unless the Act explicitly states otherwise, and shall include any individual whose work has ceased as a consequence of, or in connection with, any current labor dispute or because of any unfair labor practice, and who has not obtained any other regular and substantially equivalent employment, but shall not include any individual employed as an agricultural

laborer, or in the domestic service of any family or person at his home, or any individual employed by his parent or spouse. . . .

(5) The term "labor organization" means any organization of any kind, or any agency or employee representation committee or plan, in which employees participate and which exists for the purpose, in whole or in part, of dealing with employers concerning grievances, labor disputes, wages, rates of pay, hours of employment, or conditions of work.

(6) The term "commerce" means trade, traffic, commerce, transportation, or communication among the several States, . . .

(7) The term "affecting commerce" means in commerce, or burdening or obstructing commerce or the free flow of commerce, or having led or tending to lead to a labor dispute burdening or obstructing commerce or the free flow of commerce. . . .

(9) The term "labor dispute" includes any controversy concerning terms, tenure or conditions of employment, or concerning the association or representation of persons in negotiating, fixing, maintaining, changing, or seeking to arrange terms or conditions of employment, regardless of whether the disputants stand in the proximate relation of employer and employee. . . .

NATIONAL LABOR RELATIONS BOARD

SEC. 3. (a) There is hereby created a board, to be known as the "National Labor Relations Board," which shall be composed of three members, who shall be appointed by the President, by and with the advice and consent of the Senate. One of the original members shall be appointed for a term of one year, one for a term of three years, and one for a term of five years, but their successors shall be appointed for terms of five years each, except that any individual chosen to fill a vacancy shall be appointed only for the unexpired term of the member whom he shall succeed. The President shall designate one member to serve as chairman of the Board. Any member of the Board may be removed by the President, upon notice and hearing, for neglect of duty or malfeasance in office, but for no other cause. . . .

SEC. 4. (a) Each member of the Board shall receive a salary of $10,000 a year, shall be eligible for reappointment, and shall not engage in any other business, vocation, or employment. . . . The Board may establish or utilize such regional, local, or other agencies, and utilize such voluntary and uncompensated services, as may from time to time be needed. . . .

SEC. 6. (a) The Board shall have authority from time to time to make, amend, and rescind such rules and regulations as may be necessary to carry out the provisions of this Act. Such rules and regulations shall be effective upon publication in the manner which the Board shall prescribe.

RIGHTS OF EMPLOYEES

SEC. 7. Employees shall have the right of self-organization, to form, join, or assist labor organizations, to bargain collectively through representatives of their own choosing, and to engage in concerted activities, for the purpose of collective bargaining or other mutual aid or protection.

SEC. 8. It shall be an unfair labor practice for an employer—

(1) To interfere with, restrain, or coerce employees in the exercise of the rights guaranteed in section 7.

(2) To dominate or interfere with the formation or administration of any labor organization or contribute financial or other support to it: *Provided,* That subject to rules and regulations made and published by the Board pursuant to section 6 (a), an employer shall not be prohibited from permitting employees to confer with him during working hours without loss of time or pay.

(3) By discrimination in regard to hire or tenure of employment or any term or condition of employment to encourage or discourage membership in any labor organization: *Provided,* That nothing in this Act, or in the National Industrial Recovery Act (U. S. C., Supp. VII, title 15, secs. 701–712), as amended from time to time, or in any code or agreement approved or prescribed thereunder, or in any other statute of the United States, shall preclude an employer from making an agreement with a labor organization (not established, maintained, or assisted by any action defined in this Act as an unfair labor practice) to require as a condition of employment membership therein, if such labor organization is the representative of the employees as pro-

vided in section 9 (a), in the appropriate collective bargaining unit covered by such agreement when made.

(4) To discharge or otherwise discriminate against an employee because he has filed charges or given testimony under this Act.

(5) To refuse to bargain collectively with the representatives of his employees, subject to the provisions of Section 9 (a).

REPRESENTATIVES AND ELECTIONS

SEC. 9. (a) Representatives designated or selected for the purposes of collective bargaining by the majority of the employees in a unit appropriate for such purposes, shall be the exclusive representatives of all the employees in such unit for the purposes of collective bargaining in respect to rates of pay, wages, hours of employment, or other conditions of employment: *Provided*, That any individual employee or a group of employees shall have the right at any time to present grievances to their employer.

(b) The Board shall decide in each case whether, in order to insure to employees the full benefit of their right to self-organization and to collective bargaining, and otherwise to effectuate the policies of this Act, the unit appropriate for the purposes of collective bargaining shall be the employer unit, craft unit, plant unit, or subdivision thereof.

(c) Whenever a question affecting commerce arises concerning the representation of employees, the Board may investigate such controversy and certify to the parties, in writing, the name or names of the representatives that have been designated or selected. In any such investigation, the Board shall provide for an appropriate hearing upon due notice, either in conjunction with a proceeding under section 10 or otherwise, and may take a secret ballot of employees, or utilize any other suitable method to ascertain such representatives.

(d) Whenever an order of the Board made pursuant to section 10 (c) is based in whole or in part upon facts certified following an investigation pursuant to subsection (c) of this section, and there is a petition for the enforcement or review of such order, such certification and the record of such investigation shall be included in the transcript of the entire record required to be filed under subsections 10 (e) or 10 (f), and thereupon

the decree of the court enforcing, modifying, or setting aside in whole or in part the order of the Board shall be made and entered upon the pleadings, testimony, and proceedings set forth in such transcript.

PREVENTION OF UNFAIR LABOR PRACTICES

SEC. 10. (a) The Board is empowered, as hereinafter provided, to prevent any person from engaging in any unfair labor practice (listed in section 8) affecting commerce. This power shall be exclusive, and shall not be affected by any other means of adjustment or prevention that has been or may be established by agreement, code, law, or otherwise.

(b) Whenever it is charged that any person has engaged in or is engaging in any such unfair labor practice, the Board, or any agent or agency designated by the Board for such purposes, shall have power to issue and cause to be served upon such person a complaint stating the charges in that respect, and containing a notice of hearing before the Board or a member thereof, or before a designated agent or agency, at a place therein fixed, not less than five days after the serving of said complaint. Any such complaint may be amended by the member, agent, or agency conducting the hearing or the Board in its discretion at any time prior to the issuance of an order based thereon. The person so complained of shall have the right to file an answer to the original or amended complaint and to appear in person or otherwise and give testimony at the place and time fixed in the complaint. In the discretion of the member, agent or agency conducting the hearing or the Board, any other person may be allowed to intervene in the said proceeding and to present testimony. In any such proceeding the rules of evidence prevailing in courts of law or equity shall not be controlling.

(c) The testimony taken by such member, agent or agency or the Board shall be reduced to writing and filed with the Board. Thereafter, in its discretion, the Board upon notice may take further testimony or hear argument. If upon all the testimony taken the Board shall be of the opinion that any person named in the complaint has engaged in or is engaging in any such unfair labor practice, then the Board shall state its findings of fact and shall issue and cause to be served on such person an order requiring such person to cease and desist from such unfair labor practice, and to take such affirmative action, including reinstatement of employees with or without back pay, as will effectuate the policies of this Act. Such order may further require such person to make reports from time to time showing the extent to which it has complied with the order. If upon all the testimony taken the Board shall be of the opinion that no person named in the complaint has engaged in or is engaging in any such unfair labor practice, then the Board shall state its findings of fact and shall issue an order dismissing the said complaint. . . .

(e) The Board shall have power to petition any circuit court of appeals of the United States, or if all the circuit courts of appeals to which application may be made are in vacation, any district court of the United States, within any circuit or district, respectively, wherein the unfair labor practice in question occurred or wherein such person resides or transacts business, for the enforcement of such order and for appropriate temporary relief or restraining order, and shall certify and file in the court a transcript of the entire record in the proceeding, including the pleadings and testimony upon which such order was entered and the findings and order of the Board. Upon such filing, the court shall cause notice thereof to be served upon such person, and thereupon shall have jurisdiction of the proceeding and of the question determined therein, and shall have power to grant such temporary relief or restraining order as it deems just and proper, and to make and enter upon the pleadings, testimony, and proceedings set forth in such transcript a decree enforcing, modifying, and enforcing as so modified, or setting aside in whole or in part the order of the Board. No objection that has not been urged before the Board, its member, agent or agency, shall be considered by the court, unless the failure or neglect to urge such objection shall be excused because of extraordinary circumstances. The findings of the Board as to the facts, if supported by evidence, shall be conclusive. . . . The Board may modify its findings as to the facts, or make new findings, by reason of additional evidence so taken and filed, and it shall file

such modified or new findings, which, if supported by evidence, shall be conclusive, and shall file its recommendations, if any, for the modification or setting aside of its original order. The jurisdiction of the court shall be exclusive and its judgment and decree shall be final, except that the same shall be subject to review by the appropriate circuit court of appeals if application was made to the district court as hereinabove provided, and by the Supreme Court of the United States upon writ of certiorari or certification. . . .

(f) Any person aggrieved by a final order of the Board granting or denying in whole or in part the relief sought may obtain a review of such order in any circuit court of appeals of the United States in the circuit wherein the unfair labor practice in question was alleged to have been engaged in or wherein such person resides or transacts business. . . .

(g) The commencement of proceedings under subsection (e) or (f) of this section shall not, unless specifically ordered by the court, operate as a stay of the Board's order. . . .

(i) Petitions filed under this Act shall be heard expeditiously, and if possible within ten days after they have been docketed.

INVESTIGATORY POWERS

SEC. 11. For the purpose of all hearings and investigations, . . .

(1) The Board, or its duly authorized agents or agencies, shall at all reasonable times have access to, for the purpose of examination, and the right to copy any evidence of any person being investigated or proceeded against that relates to any matter under investigation or in question. Any member of the Board shall have power to issue subpenas requiring the attendance and testimony of witnesses and the production of any evidence that relates to any matter under investigation or in question, before the Board, its member, agent, or agency conducting the hearing or investigation. . . .

SEC. 12. Any person who shall willfully resist, prevent, impede, or interfere with any member of the Board or any of its agents or agencies in the performance of duties pursuant to this Act shall be punished by a fine of not more than $5,000 or by imprisonment for not more than one year, or both.

LIMITATIONS

SEC. 13. Nothing in this Act shall be construed so as to interfere with or impede or diminish in any way the right to strike. . . .

SEC. 15. If any provision of this Act, or the application of such provision to any person or circumstance, shall be held invalid, the remainder of this Act, or the application of such provision to persons or circumstances other than those as to which it is held invalid, shall not be affected thereby. . . .

501. N. L. R. B. v. JONES & LAUGHLIN STEEL CORPORATION
301 U. S. 1
1937

On Writ of Certiorari to the U. S. Circuit Court of Appeals for the Fifth District. This is the leading case on the constitutionality of the National Labor Relations Act of 1935 (see Doc. No. 500 and references). In the first five years of its existence the National Labor Relations Board was subjected to an attack far more severe than any in the history of the independent commissions, but its record of successes in the Courts was spectacular. See, Nathanson and Lyons, "Judicial Review of the N. L. R. B.," 33 Ills. Law, Rev. 749; Ward, "Discrimination under the N. L. R. Act," 48 Yale Law J. 1152; Gellhorn and Lynfield, "Politics and Labor Relations," 39 Col. Law Rev. 339; Ziskind, "The Use of Economic Data in Labor Cases," 6 U. of Chicago Law Rev., 607; Geffs and Hepburn, "The Wagner Labor Act Cases," 22 Minn. L. Rev. 1; Koening, "The National Labor Relations Act—an Appraisal," 2 Cornell L. Qt. 392; Donoho, "Jurisdiction of the National Labor Relations Board," 6 Geo. Wash. L. Rev. 436.

HUGHES, C. J. In a proceeding under the National Labor Relations Act of 1935, the National Labor Relations Board found that the petitioner, Jones & Laughlin Steel Corporation, had violated the Act by engaging in unfair labor practices affecting commerce. The proceeding was instituted by the Beaver Valley Lodge No. 200, affiliated with the Amalgamated Association of Iron, Steel and Tin Workers of America, a labor organization. The unfair labor practices charged were that the corporation was discriminating against members of the union with regard to hire and tenure of employment, and was coercing and intimidating its employees in order to interfere with their self-organization. The discriminatory and coercive action alleged was the discharge of certain employees.

The National Labor Relations Board, sustaining the charge, ordered the corporation to cease and desist from such discrimination and coercion, to offer reinstatement to ten of the employees named, to make good their losses in pay, and to post for thirty days notices that the corporation would not discharge or discriminate against members, or those desiring to become members, of the labor union. As the corporation failed to comply, the Board petitioned the Circuit Court of Appeals to enforce the order. The court denied the petition, holding that the order lay beyond the range of federal power. 83 F. (2d) 998. We granted certiorari.

The scheme of the National Labor Relations Act may be briefly stated. [See Doc. No. 500.] Respondent, appearing specially for the purpose of objecting to the jurisdiction of the Board, filed its answer. Respondent admitted the discharges, but alleged that they were made because of inefficiency or violation of rules or for other good reasons and were not ascribable to union membership or activities. As an affirmative defense respondent challenged the constitutional validity of the statute and its applicability in the instant case.

Contesting the ruling of the Board, the respondent argues (1) that the Act is in reality a regulation of labor relations and not of interstate commerce; (2) that the Act can have no application to the respondent's relations with its production employees because they are not subject to regulation by the federal government; and (3) that the provisions of the Act violate Section 2 of Article III and the Fifth and Seventh Amendments of the Constitution of the United States.

The facts as to the nature and scope of the business of the Jones & Laughlin Steel Corporation have been found by the Labor Board and, so far as they are essential to the determination of this controversy, they are not in dispute. The Labor Board has found: The corporation is organized under the laws of Pennsylvania and has its principal office at Pittsburgh. It is engaged in the business of manufacturing iron and steel in plants situated in Pittsburgh and nearby Aliquippa, Pennsylvania. It manufactures and distributes a widely diversified line of steel and pig iron, being the fourth largest producer of steel in the United States. With its subsidiaries—nineteen in number—it is a completely integrated enterprise, owning and operating ore, coal and limestone properties, lake and river transportation facilities and terminal railroads located at its manufacturing plants. It owns or controls mines in Michigan and Minnesota. It operates four ore steamships on the Great Lakes, used in the transportation of ore to its factories. It owns coal mines in Pennsylvania. It operates towboats and steam barges used in carrying coal to its factories. It owns limestone properties in various places in Pennsylvania and West Virginia. It owns the Monongahela connecting railroad which connects the plants of the Pittsburgh works and forms an interconnection with the Pennsylvania, New York Central and Baltimore and Ohio Railroad systems. It owns the Aliquippa and Southern Railroad Company which connects the Aliquippa works with the Pittsburgh and Lake Erie, part of the New York Central system. Much of its product is shipped to its warehouses in Chicago, Detroit, Cincinnati and Memphis,—to the last two places by means of its own barges and transportation equipment. In Long Island City, New York, and in New Orleans it operates structural steel fabricating shops in connection with the warehousing of semi-finished materials sent from its works. Through one of its wholly-owned subsidiaries it owns, leases and operates stores, warehouses and yards for the distribution of equipment and supplies for drilling and operating oil and gas mills and for pipe lines, refineries and pumping stations. It has sales offices in twenty cities in the United States and a wholly-owned subsidiary which is devoted exclusively to distributing its product in Canada. Approximately 75 per cent. of its product is shipped out of Pennsylvania.

Summarizing these operations, the Labor Board concluded that the works in Pittsburgh and Aliquippa "might be likened to the heart of a self-contained, highly integrated body. They draw in the raw materials from Michigan, Minnesota, West Virginia, Pennsylvania in part through arteries and by means controlled by the respondent; they transform the materials and then pump them out to all parts of the nation through the vast mechanism which the respondent has elaborated."

To carry on the activities of the entire steel industry, 33,000 men mine ore, 44,000 men mine coal, 4,000 men quarry limestone, 16,000 men manufacture coke, 343,000 men manufacture steel, and 83,000 men transport its product. Respondent has about 10,000 employees in its Aliquippa plant, which is located in a community of about 30,000 persons.

Practically all the factual evidence in the case, except that which dealt with the nature of respondent's business, concerned its relations with the employees in the Aliquippa plant whose discharge was the subject of the complaint. These employees were active leaders in the labor union.

While respondent criticises the evidence and the attitude of the Board, which is described as being hostile toward employers and particularly toward those who insisted upon their constitutional rights, respondent did not take advantage of its opportunity to present evidence to refute that which was offered to show discrimination and coercion. In this situation, the record presents no ground for setting aside the order of the Board so far as the facts pertaining to the circumstances and purpose of the discharge of the employees are concerned. Upon that point it is sufficient to say that the evidence supports the findings of the Board that respondent discharged these men "because of their union activity and for the purpose of discouraging membership in the union." We turn to the questions of law which respondent urges in contesting the validity and application of the Act.

First. The scope of the Act.—The Act is challenged in its entirety as an attempt to regulate all industry, thus invading the reserved powers of the States over their local concerns. It is asserted that the references in the Act to interstate and foreign commerce are colorable at best; that the Act is not a true regulation of such commerce or of matters which directly affect it but on the contrary has the fundamental object of placing under the compulsory supervision of the federal government all industrial labor relations within the nation. The argument seeks support in the broad words of the preamble and in the sweep of the provisions of the Act, and it is further insisted that its legislative history shows an essential universal purpose in the light of which its scope cannot be limited by either construction or by the application of the separability clause.

If this conception of terms, intent and consequent inseparability were sound, the Act would necessarily fall by reason of the limitation upon the federal power which inheres in the constitutional grant, as well as because of the explicit reservation of the Tenth Amendment. *Schechter Corporation* v. *United States,* 295 U. S. 495, 549, 550, 554. The authority of the federal government may not be pushed to such an extreme as to destroy the distinction, which the commerce clause itself establishes, between commerce "among the several States" and the internal concerns of a State. That distinction between what is national and what is local in the activities of commerce is vital to the maintenance of our federal system.

But we are not at liberty to deny effect to specific provisions, which Congress has constitutional power to enact, by superimposing upon them inferences from general legislative declarations of an ambiguous character, even if found in the same statute. The cardinal principle of statutory construction is to save and not to destroy. We have repeatedly held that as between two possible interpretations of a statute, by one of which it would be unconstitutional and by the other valid, our plain duty is to adopt that which will save the act. Even to avoid a serious doubt the rule is the same.

We think it clear that the National Labor Relations Act may be construed so as to operate within the sphere of constitutional authority. The jurisdiction conferred upon the Board, and invoked in this instance, is found in Section 10 (a), which provides:

SEC. 10 (a). The Board is empowered, as hereinafter provided, to prevent any person from engaging in any unfair labor practice (listed in section 8) affecting commerce.

The critical words of this provision, prescribing the limits of the Board's authority in dealing with the labor practices, are "affecting commerce." The Act specifically defines the "commerce" to which it refers (sec. 2 (6)):

There can be no question that the commerce thus contemplated by the Act (aside from that within a Territory or the District of Columbia) is interstate and foreign commerce in the constitutional sense. The Act also defines the term "affecting commerce" (sec. 2 (7)):

This definition is one of exclusion as well as inclusion. The grant of authority to the Board does not purport to extend to the relationship between all industrial employees and employers. Its terms do not impose collective bargaining upon all industry regardless of effects upon interstate or foreign commerce. It purports to reach only what may be deemed to burden or obstruct that commerce and, thus qualified, it must be construed as contemplating the exercise of control within constitutional bounds. It is a familiar principle that acts which directly burden or obstruct interstate or foreign commerce, or its free flow, are within the reach of the congressional power. Acts having that effect are not rendered immune because they grow out of labor disputes. It is the effect upon commerce, not the source of the injury, which is the criterion. Whether or not particular action does affect commerce in such a close and intimate fashion as to be subject to federal control, and hence to lie within the authority conferred upon the Board, is left by the statute to be determined as individual cases arise. We are thus to inquire whether in the instant case the constitutional boundary has been passed.

Second. The unfair labor practices in question.—The unfair labor practices found by the Board are those defined in Section 8, subdivisions (1) and (3). These provide:

SEC. 8. It shall be an unfair labor practice for an employer—

(1) To interfere with, restrain, or coerce employees in the exercise of the rights guaranteed in section 7.

(3) By discrimination in regard to hire or ten-

ure of employment or any term or condition of employment to encourage or discourage membership in any labor organization. . . .

Section 8, subdivision (1), refers to Section 7, which is as follows:

Sec. 7. Employees shall have the right to self-organization, to form, join, or assist labor organizations, to bargain collectively through representatives of their own choosing, and to engage in concerted activities, for the purpose of collective bargaining or other mutual aid or protection.

Thus, in its present application, the statute goes no further than to safeguard the right of employees to self-organization and to select representatives of their own choosing for collective bargaining or other mutual protection without restraint or coercion by their employer.

That is a fundamental right. Employees have as clear a right to organize and select their representatives for lawful purposes as the respondent has to organize its business and select its own officers and agents. Discrimination and coercion to prevent the free exercise of the right of employees to self-organization and representation is a proper subject for condemnation by competent legislative authority. Long ago we stated the reason for labor organizations. We said that they were organized out of the necessities of the situation; that a single employee was helpless in dealing with an employer; that he was dependent ordinarily on his daily wage for the maintenance of himself and family; that if the employer refused to pay him the wages that he thought fair, he was nevertheless unable to leave the employ and resist arbitrary and unfair treatment; that union was essential to give laborers opportunity to deal on an equality with their employer. *American Steel Foundries* v. *Tri-City Central Trades Council*, 257 U. S. 184, 209. We reiterated these views when we had under consideration the Railway Labor Act of 1926. Fully recognizing the legality of collective action on the part of employees in order to safeguard their proper interests, we said that Congress was not required to ignore this right but could safeguard it. Congress could seek to make appropriate collective action of employees an instrument of peace rather than of strife. We said that such collective action would be a mockery if representation were made futile by interference with freedom of choice. Hence the prohibition by Congress of interference with the selection of representatives for the purpose of negotiation and conference between employers and employees, "instead of being an invasion of the constitutional right of either, was based on the recognition of the rights of both." We have reasserted the same principle in sustaining the application of the Railway Labor Act as amended in 1934.

Third. The application of the Act to employees engaged in production.—The principle involved.—Respondent says that whatever may be said of employees engaged in interstate commerce, the industrial relations and activities in the manufacturing department of respondent's enterprise are not subject to federal regulation. The argument rests upon the proposition that manufacturing in itself is not commerce.

The Government distinguishes these cases. The various parts of respondent's enterprise are described as interdependent and as thus involving "a great movement of iron ore, coal and limestone along well-defined paths to the steel mills, thence through them, and thence in the form of steel products into the consuming centers of the country—a definite and well-understood course of business." It is urged that these activities constitute a "stream" or "flow" of commerce, of which the Aliquippa manufacturing plant is the focal point, and that industrial strife at that point would cripple the entire movement. Reference is made to our decision sustaining the Packers and Stockyards Act. The Court found that the stockyards were but a "throat" through which the current of commerce flowed and the transactions which there occurred could not be separated from that movement.

Respondent contends that the instant case presents material distinctions.

We do not find it necessary to determine whether these features of defendant's business dispose of the asserted analogy to the "stream of commerce" cases. The congressional authority to protect interstate commerce from burdens and obstructions is not limited to transactions which can be deemed to be an essential part of a "flow" of interstate or foreign commerce. Burdens and obstructions may be due to injurious action

springing from other sources. The fundamental principle is that the power to regulate
commerce is the power to enact "all appropriate legislation" for "its protection and
advancement"; to adopt measures "to promote its growth and insure its safety"; "to
foster, protect, control and restrain." That
power is plenary and may be exerted to protect interstate commerce "no matter what the
source of the dangers which threaten it."
Although activities may be intrastate in character when separately considered, if they
have such a close and substantial relation to
interstate commerce that their control is essential or appropriate to protect that commerce from burdens and obstructions, Congress cannot be denied the power to exercise
that control. Undoubtedly the scope of this
power must be considered in the light of our
dual system of government and may not be
extended so as to embrace effects upon interstate commerce so indirect and remote that
to embrace them, in view of our complex
society, would effectually obliterate the distinction between what is national and what
is local and create a completely centralized
government. The question is necessarily one
of degree.

That intrastate activities, by reason of
close and intimate relation to interstate commerce, may fall within federal control is
demonstrated in the case of carriers who are
engaged in both interstate and intrastate
transportation. There federal control has been
found essential to secure the freedom of
interstate traffic from interference or unjust
discrimination and to promote the efficiency
of the interstate service. It is manifest that
intrastate rates deal *primarily* with a local
activity. But in rate-making they bear such a
close relation to interstate rates that effective
control of the one must embrace some control over the other. Under the Transportation
Act, 1920, Congress went so far as to authorize the Interstate Commerce Commission to establish a state-wide level of intrastate rates in order to prevent an unjust
discrimination against interstate commerce.
Other illustrations are found in the broad
requirements of the Safety Appliance Act
and the Hours of Service Act. It is said
that this exercise of federal power has relation to the maintenance of adequate instrumentalities of interstate commerce. But the

agency is not superior to the commerce which
uses it. The protective power extends to the
former because it exists as to the latter.

The close and intimate effect which brings
the subject within the reach of federal power
may be due to activities in relation to productive industry although the industry when
separately viewed is local. This has been
abundantly illustrated in the application of
the federal Anti-Trust Act.

Upon the same principle, the Anti-Trust
Act has been applied to the conduct of employees engaged in production.

It is thus apparent that the fact that the
employees here concerned were engaged in
production is not determinative. The question remains as to the effect upon interstate
commerce of the labor practice involved.

*Fourth. Effects of the unfair labor prac-
tice in respondent's enterprise.*—Giving full
weight to respondent's contention with respect to a break in the complete continuity
of the "stream of commerce" by reason of
respondent's manufacturing operations, the
fact remains that the stoppage of those operations by industrial strife would have a
most serious effect upon interstate commerce.
In view of respondent's far-flung activities,
it is idle to say that the effect would be
indirect or remote. It is obvious that it would
be immediate and might be catastrophic. We
are asked to shut our eyes to the plainest
facts of our national life and to deal with
the question of direct and indirect effects in
an intellectual vacuum. Because there may be
but indirect and remote effects upon interstate commerce in connection with a host of
local enterprises throughout the country, it
does not follow that other industrial activities
do not have such a close and intimate relation
to interstate commerce as to make the presence of industrial strife a matter of the most
urgent national concern. When industries organize themselves on a national scale, making
their relation to interstate commerce the
dominant factor in their activities, how can
it be maintained that their industrial labor
relations constitute a forbidden field into
which Congress may not enter when it is
necessary to protect interstate commerce
from the paralyzing consequences of industrial war? We have often said that interstate
commerce itself is a practical conception. It
is equally true that interferences with that

commerce must be appraised by a judgment that does not ignore actual experience.

Experience has abundantly demonstrated that the recognition of the right of employees to self-organization and to have representatives of their own choosing for the purpose of collective bargaining is often an essential condition of industrial peace. Refusal to confer and negotiate has been one of the most prolific causes of strife. This is such an outstanding fact in the history of labor disturbances that it is a proper subject of judicial notice and requires no citation of instances. But with respect to the appropriateness of the recognition of self-organization and representation in the promotion of peace, the question is not essentially different in the case of employees in industries of such a character that interstate commerce is put in jeopardy from the case of employees of transportation companies. And of what avail is it to protect the facility of transportation, if interstate commerce is throttled with respect to the commodities to be transported!

These questions have frequently engaged the attention of Congress and have been the subject of many inquiries. The steel industry is one of the great basic industries of the United States, with ramifying activities affecting interstate commerce at every point. The Government aptly refers to the steel strike of 1919–1920 with its far-reaching consequences. The fact that there appears to have been no major disturbance in that industry in the more recent period did not dispose of the possibilities of future and like dangers to interstate commerce which Congress was entitled to foresee and to exercise its protective power to forestall. It is not necessary again to detail the facts as to respondent's enterprise. Instead of being beyond the pale, we think that it presents in a most striking way the close and intimate relation which a manufacturing industry may have to interstate commerce and we have no doubt that Congress had constitutional authority to safeguard the right of respondent's employees to self-organization and freedom in the choice of representatives for collective bargaining.

Fifth. The means which the Act employs. —Questions under the due process clause and other constitutional restrictions.—Respondent asserts its right to conduct its business in an orderly manner without being subjected to arbitrary restraints. What we have said points to the fallacy in the argument. Employees have their correlative right to organize for the purpose of securing the redress of grievances and to promote agreements with employers relating to rates of pay and conditions of work. Restraint for the purpose of preventing an unjust interference with that right cannot be considered arbitrary or capricious.

The Act does not compel agreements between employers and employees. It does not compel any agreement whatever. It does not prevent the employer "from refusing to make a collective contract and hiring individuals on whatever terms" the employer may by unilateral action determine." The Act expressly provides in Section 9 (a) that any individual employee or a group of employees shall have the right at any time to present grievances to their employer. The theory of the Act is that free opportunity for negotiation with accredited representatives of employees is likely to promote industrial peace and may bring about the adjustments and agreements which the Act in itself does not attempt to compel. As we said in *Texas & N. O. R. Co.* v. *Railway Clerks, supra,* and repeated in *Virginian Railway Co.* v. *System Federation, No. 40,* the cases of *Adair* v. *United States,* 208 U. S. 161, and *Coppage* v. *Kansas,* 236 U. S. 1, are inapplicable to legislation of this character. The Act does not interfere with the normal exercise of the right of the employer to select its employees or to discharge them. The employer may not, under cover of that right, intimidate or coerce its employees with respect to their self-organization and representation, and, on the other hand, the Board is not entitled to make its authority a pretext for interference with the right of discharge when that right is exercised for other reasons than such intimidation and coercion. The true purpose is the subject of investigation with full opportunity to show the facts. It would seem that when employers freely recognize the right of their employees to their own organizations and their unrestricted right of representation there will be much less occasion for controversy in respect to the free and appropriate exercise of the right of selection and discharge.

The Act has been criticised as one-sided in its application; that it fails to provide a more comprehensive plan. But we are dealing with the power of Congress, not with a particular policy or with the extent to which policy should go. We have frequently said that the legislative authority, exerted within its proper field, need not embrace all the evils within its reach. The Constitution does not forbid "cautious advance, step by step," in dealing with the evils which are exhibited in activities within the range of legislative power. The question in such cases is whether the legisla-

ture, in what it does prescribe, has gone beyond constitutional limits.

Our conclusion is that the order of the Board was within its competency and that the Act is valid as here applied. The judgment of the Circuit Court of Appeals is reversed and the cause is remanded for further proceedings in conformity with this opinion.

McREYNOLDS, J., VAN DEVANTER, J., SUTHERLAND, J., and BUTLER, J. dissented.

502. ASSOCIATED PRESS v. NATIONAL LABOR RELATIONS BOARD
301 U. S. 103
1937

On Writ of Certiorari to the U. S. Circuit Court of Appeals for the Second Circuit. The Jones and Laughlin decision (see Doc. No. 501) had already sustained the constitutionality of the Wagner Act on broad grounds. This case involved more particularly the question whether the act, in so far as it affected newspapers, abridged the freedom of the press guaranteed by the First Amendment. For references see Doc. No. 501, and notes in 25 Col. L. Rev. 710, and 32 Ills. L. Rev. 196.

ROBERTS, J. In this case we are to decide whether the National Labor Relations Act, as applied to the petitioner by an order of the National Labor Relations Board, exceeds the power of Congress to regulate commerce pursuant to Article I, Section 8, abridges the freedom of the press guaranteed by the First Amendment, and denies trial by jury in violation of the Seventh Amendment of the Constitution.

In October 1935 the petitioner discharged Morris Watson, an employee in its New York office. The American Newspaper Guild, a labor organization, filed a charge with the Board alleging that Watson's discharge was in violation of Section 7 of the National Labor Relations Act which confers on employes the right to organize, to form, join, or assist labor organizations to bargain collectively through representatives of their own choosing and to engage in concerted activities for the purpose of collective bargaining or other mutual aid or protection; that the petitioner had engaged in unfair labor practices contrary to subsections (1) and (3) of Section 8 by interfering with, restraining or coercing Watson in the exercise of the rights guaranteed him by Section 7 and by discriminating against him in

respect of his tenure of employment and discouraging his membership in a labor organization. The Board served a complaint upon the petitioner charging unfair labor practices affecting commerce within the meaning of the statute. The petitioner answered admitting Watson's discharge but denying that it was due to his joining or assisting the Guild or engaging in union activities, and denying, on constitutional grounds, the validity of the act and the jurisdiction of the Board.

Second. Does the statute, as applied to the petitioner, abridge the freedom of speech or of the press safeguarded by the First Amendment? We hold that it does not. It is insisted that the Associated Press is in substance the press itself, that the membership consists solely of persons who own and operate newspapers, that the news is gathered solely for publication in the newspapers of members. Stress is laid upon the facts that this membership consists of persons of every conceivable political, economic, and religious view, that the one thing upon which the members are united is that the Associated Press shall be wholly free from partisan activity or the expression of opinions, that it shall limit its function to reporting events without bias in order that the citizens of our country, if given the facts, may be able to form their own opinions respecting them. The conclusion which the petitioner draws is that whatever may be the case with respect to employes in its mechanical departments it must have absolute and unrestricted freedom to employ and to discharge those who, like Watson, edit the news, that there must not be the slightest opportunity for any bias or prejudice personally entertained by an editorial employe to color or to distort what he writes, and that the Associated Press cannot be free to furnish unbiased and impartial news reports unless it is equally free to determine for itself the partiality or bias of editorial employes. So it is said that any regulation protective of union activities, or the right collectively to bargain on the part of such employes, is necessarily an invalid invasion of the freedom of the press.

We think the contention not only has no relevance to the circumstances of the instant case but is an unsound generalization. The ostensible reason for Watson's discharge, as embodied in the records of the petitioner, is "solely on the grounds of his work not being on a basis for which he has shown capability." The petitioner did not assert and does not now claim that he had shown bias in the past. It does not claim that by reason of his connection with the union he will be likely, as the petitioner honestly believes, to show bias in the future. The actual reason for his discharge, as shown by the unattacked finding of the Board, was his Guild activity and his agitation for collective bargaining. The statute does not preclude a discharge on the ostensible grounds for the petitioner's action; it forbids discharge for what has been found to be the real motive of the petitioner. These considerations answer the suggestion that if the petitioner believed its policy of impartiality was likely to be subverted by Watson's continued service, Congress was without power to interdict his discharge. No such question is here for decision. Neither before the Board, nor in the court below nor here has the petitioner professed such belief. It seeks to bar all regulation by contending that regulation in a situation not presented would be invalid. Courts deal with cases upon the basis of the facts disclosed, never with nonexistent and assumed circumstances.

The act does not compel the petitioner to employ anyone; it does not require that the petitioner retain in its employ an incompetent editor or one who fails faithfully to edit the news to reflect the facts without bias or prejudice. The act permits a discharge for any reason other than union activity or agitation for collective bargaining with employes. The restoration of Watson to his former position in no sense guarantees his continuance in petitioner's employ. The petitioner is at liberty, whenever occasion may arise, to exercise its undoubted right to sever his relationship for any cause that seems to it proper save only as a punishment for, or discouragement of, such activities as the act declares permissible.

The business of the Associated Press is not immune from regulation because it is an agency of the press. The publisher of a newspaper has no special immunity from the application of general laws. He has no special privilege to invade the rights and liberties of others. He must answer for libel. He may be punished for contempt of court. He is subject to the anti-trust laws. Like others he must pay equitable and nondiscriminatory taxes on his business. The regulation here in question has no relation whatever to the impartial distribution of news. The order of the Board in nowise circumscribes the full freedom and liberty of the petitioner to publish the news as it desires it published or to enforce policies of its own choosing with respect to the editing and rewriting of news for publication, and the petitioner is free at any time to discharge Watson or any editorial employe who fails to comply with the policies it may adopt.

The judgment of the Circuit Court of Appeals is affirmed.

SUTHERLAND, J., VAN DEVANTER, J., MC-REYNOLDS, J., and BUTLER, J. dissented.

503. THE SOCIAL SECURITY ACT
August 14, 1935

(U. S. Statutes at Large, Vol. XLIX, p. 620)

Social security legislation began in the States as early as 1929, but it was not until the depression had run its course for six years that the Federal government took action in the matter.

The assumption of national responsibility for general social security constitutes a notable chapter in the history of federal centralization in the United States. For social security, see A. Epstein,

Insecurity; I. M. Rubinow, *The Quest for Security;* P. Douglas and A. Director, *The Problem of Unemployment;* P. Douglas, *Social Security in the United States;* M. Stevenson and R. Spear, *The Social Security Program;* J. R. Commons, *Unemployment Insurance;* J. B. Ewing, *Job Insurance;* The Social Security Board, *Social Security in America; Economic Security Act: Hearings before the Committee on Finance,* U. S. Sen., 74th Cong. 1st sess. on S 1130; H. Malisoff, "Emergence of Unemployment Compensation" 54 Pol. Sci. Qt.

An Act to provide for the general welfare by establishing a system of Federal old-age benefits, and by enabling the several States to make more adequate provision for aged persons, blind persons, dependent and crippled children, maternal and child welfare, public health, and the administration of their unemployment compensation laws; to establish a Social Security Board; to raise revenue; and for other purposes.

Be it enacted by the Senate and House of Representatives of the United States of America in Congress assembled,

TITLE I—GRANTS TO STATES FOR OLD AGE ASSISTANCE

APPROPRIATION

SECTION 1. For the purpose of enabling each State to furnish financial assistance, as far as practicable under the conditions in such State, to aged needy individuals, there is hereby authorized to be appropriated for the fiscal year ending June 30, 1936, the sum of $49,750,000, and there is hereby authorized to be appropriated for each fiscal year thereafter a sum sufficient to carry out the purposes of this title. The sums made available under this section shall be used for making payments to States which have submitted, and had approved by the Social Security Board established by Title VII, State plans for old-age assistance.

STATE OLD-AGE ASSISTANCE PLANS

SEC. 2. (a) A State plan for old-age assistance must (1) provide that it shall be in effect in all political subdivisions of the State, and, if administered by them, be mandatory upon them; (2) provide for financial participation by the State; (3) either provide for

the establishment or designation of a single State agency to administer the plan, or provide for the establishment or designation of a single State agency to supervise the administration of the plan; (4) provide for granting to any individual, whose claim for old-age assistance is denied, an opportunity for a fair hearing before such State agency; (5) provide such methods of administration (other than those relating to selection, tenure of office, and compensation of personnel) as are found by the Board to be necessary for the efficient operation of the plan; (6) provide that the State agency will make such reports, in such form and containing such information, as the Board may from time to time require, and comply with such provisions as the Board may from time to time find necessary to assure the correctness and verification of such reports; and (7) provide that, if the State or any of its political subdivisions collects from the estate of any recipient of old-age assistance any amount with respect to old-age assistance furnished him under the plan, one-half of the net amount so collected shall be promptly paid to the United States. Any payment so made shall be deposited in the Treasury to the credit of the appropriation for the purposes of this title.

(b) The Board shall approve any plan which fulfills the conditions specified in subsection (a), except that it shall not approve any plan which imposes, as a condition of eligibility for old-age assistance under the plan—

(1) An age requirement of more than sixty-five years, except that the plan may impose, effective until January 1, 1940, an age requirement of as much as seventy years; or

(2) Any residence requirement which excludes any resident of the State who has resided therein five years during the nine years immediately preceding the application for old-age assistance and has resided therein continuously for one year immediately preceding the application; or

(3) Any citizenship requirement which excludes any citizen of the United States.

PAYMENT TO STATES

SEC. 3. (a) From the sums appropriated therefor, the Secretary of the Treasury shall pay to each State which has an approved plan for old-age assistance, for each quarter, beginning with the quarter commencing July 1, 1935, (1) an amount, which shall be used exclusively as old-age assistance, equal to one-half of the total of the sums expended during such quarter as old-age assistance under the State plan with respect to each individual who at the time of such expenditure is sixty-five years of age or older and is not an inmate of a public institution, not counting so much of such expenditure with respect to any individual for any month as exceeds $30, and (2) 5 per centum of such amount, which shall be used for paying the costs of administering the State plan or for old-age assistance, or both, and for no other purpose: *Provided,* That the State plan, in order to be approved by the Board, need not provide for financial participation before July 1, 1937 by the State, in the case of any State which the Board, upon application by the State and after reasonable notice and opportunity for hearing to the State, finds is prevented by its constitution from providing such financial participation.

(b) The method of computing and paying such amounts shall be as follows:

(1) The Board shall, prior to the beginning of each quarter, estimate the amount to be paid to the State for such quarter under the provisions of clause (1) of subsection (a), such estimate to be based on (A) a report filed by the State containing its estimate of the total sum to be expended in such quarter in accordance with the provisions of such clause, and stating the amount appropriated or made available by the State and its political subdivisions for such expenditures in such quarter, and if such amount is less than one-half of the total sum of such estimated expenditures, the source or sources from which the difference is expected to be derived, (B) records showing the number of aged individuals in the State, and (C) such other investigation as the Board may find necessary. . . .

TITLE II—FEDERAL OLD-AGE BENEFITS

OLD-AGE RESERVE ACCOUNT

SECTION 201. (a) There is hereby created an account in the Treasury of the United States to be known as the "Old-Age Reserve Account." . . .

OLD-AGE BENEFIT PAYMENTS

SEC. 202. (a) Every qualified individual shall be entitled to receive, with respect to the period beginning on the date he attains the age of sixty-five, or on January 1, 1942, whichever is the later, and ending on the date of his death, an old-age benefit (payable as nearly as practicable in equal monthly installments) as follows:

(1) If the total wages determined by the Board to have been paid to him, with respect to employment after December 31, 1936, and before he attained the age of sixty-five, were not more than $3,000, the old-age benefit shall be at a monthly rate of one-half of 1 per centum of such total wages;

(2) If such total wages were more than $3,000, the old-age benefit shall be at a monthly rate equal to the sum of the following:

(A) One-half of 1 per centum of $3,000; plus

(B) One-twelfth of 1 per centum of the amount by which such total wages exceeded $3,000 and did not exceed $45,-000; plus

(C) One-twenty-fourth of 1 per cent-um of the amount by which such total wages exceeded $45,000.

(b) In no case shall the monthly rate computed under subsection (a) exceed $85. . . .

PAYMENTS UPON DEATH

SEC. 203. (a) If any individual dies before attaining the age of sixty-five, there shall be paid to his estate an amount equal to 3½ per centum of the total wages determined by the Board to have been paid to him, with respect to employment after December 31, 1936. . . .

PAYMENTS TO AGED INDIVIDUALS NOT QUALIFIED FOR BENEFITS

SEC. 204. (a) There shall be paid in a lump sum to any individual who, upon attaining the age of sixty-five, is not a qualified individual, an amount equal to 3½ per centum of the total wages determined by the Board to have been paid to him, with respect to employment after December 31, 1936, and before he attained the age of sixty-five.

(b) After any individual becomes entitled to any payment under subsection (a), no other payment shall be made under this title in any manner measured by wages paid to him, except that any part of any payment under subsection (a) which is not paid to him before his death shall be paid to his estate. . . .

SEC. 210. . . .

(b) The term "employment" means any service, of whatever nature, performed within the United States by an employee for his employer, except—

(1) Agricultural labor;

(2) Domestic service in a private home;

(3) Casual labor not in the course of the employer's trade or business;

(4) Service performed as an officer or member of the crew of a vessel documented under the laws of the United States or of any foreign country;

(5) Service performed in the employ of the United States Government or of an instrumentality of the United States;

(6) Service performed in the employ of a State, a political subdivision thereof, or an instrumentality of one or more States or political subdivisions;

(7) Service performed in the employ of a corporation, community chest, fund, or foundation, organized and operated exclusively for religious, charitable, scientific, literary, or educational purposes, or for the prevention of cruelty to children or animals, no part of the net earnings of which inures to the benefit of any private shareholder or individual. . . .

TITLE III—GRANTS TO STATES FOR UNEMPLOYMENT COMPENSATION ADMINISTRATION

APPROPRIATION

SECTION 301. For the purpose of assisting the States in the administration of their unemployment compensation laws, there is hereby authorized to be appropriated, for the fiscal year ending June 30, 1936, the sum of $4,000,000, and for each fiscal year thereafter the sum of 49,000,000, to be used as hereinafter provided.

PAYMENTS TO STATES

SEC. 302. (a) The Board shall from time to time certify to the Secretary of the Treasury for payment to each State which has an unemployment compensation law approved by the Board under Title IX, such amounts as the Board determines to be necessary for the proper administration of such law during the fiscal year in which such payment is to be made. The Board's determination shall be based on (1) the population of the State; (2) an estimate of the number of persons covered by the State law and of the cost of proper administration of such law; and (3) such other factors as the Board finds relevant. The Board shall not certify for payment under this section in any fiscal year a total amount in excess of the amount appropriated therefor for such fiscal year. . . .

PROVISIONS OF STATE LAWS

SEC. 303. (a) The Board shall make no certification for payment to any State unless it finds that the law of such State, approved by the Board under Title IX, includes provisions for—

(1) Such methods of administration (other than those relating to selection, tenure of office, and compensation of personnel) as are found by the Board to be reasonably calculated to insure full payment of unemployment compensation when due; and

(2) Payment of unemployment compensation solely through public employment offices in the State or such other agencies as the Board may approve; and

(3) Opportunity for a fair hearing, before an impartial tribunal, for all individuals whose claims for unemployment compensation are denied; and

(4) The payment of all money received in the unemployment fund of such State, immediately upon such receipt, to the Secretary of the Treasury to the credit of the Unemployment Trust Fund established by section 904; and

(5) Expenditure of all money requisitioned by the State agency from the Unemployment Trust Fund, in the payment of unemployment compensation, exclusive of expenses of administration; and

(6) The making of such reports, in such

form and containing such information, as the Board may from time to time require, and compliance with such provisions as the Board may from time to time find necessary to assure the correctness and verification of such reports; and

(7) Making available upon request to any agency of the United States charged with the administration of public works or assistance through public employment, the name, address, ordinary occupation and employment status of each recipient of unemployment compensation, and a statement of such recipient's rights to further compensation under such law.

(b) Whenever the Board, after reasonable notice and opportunity for hearing to the State agency charged with the administration of the State law, finds that in the administration of the law there is—

(1) a denial, in a substantial number of cases, of unemployment compensation to individuals entitled thereto under such law; or

(2) a failure to comply substantially with any provision specified in subsection (a);

the Board shall notify such State agency that further payments will not be made to the State until the Board is satisfied that there is no longer any such denial or failure to comply. Until it is so satisfied it shall make no further certification to the Secretary of the Treasury with respect to such State. . . .

TITLE IV—GRANTS TO STATES FOR AID TO DEPENDENT CHILDREN

APPROPRIATION

SECTION 401. For the purpose of enabling each State to furnish financial assistance, as far as practicable under the conditions in such State, to needy dependent children, there is hereby authorized to be appropriated for the fiscal year ending June 30, 1936, the sum of $24,750,000, and there is hereby authorized to be appropriated for each fiscal year thereafter a sum sufficient to carry out the purposes of this title. The sums made available under this section shall be used for making payments to States which have submitted, and had approved by the Board, State plans for aid to dependent children. . . .

PAYMENT TO STATES

SEC. 403. (a) From the sums appropriated therefor, the Secretary of the Treasury shall pay to each State which has an approved plan for aid to dependent children, for each quarter, beginning with the quarter commencing July 1, 1935, an amount, which shall be used exclusively for carrying out the State plan, equal to one-third of the total of the sums expended during such quarter under such plan, not counting so much of such expenditure with respect to any dependent child for any month as exceeds $18, or if there is more than one dependent child in the same home, as exceeds $18 for any month with respect to one such dependent child and $12 for such month with respect to each of the other dependent children. . . .

DEFINITIONS

SEC. 406. When used in this title—

(a) The term "dependent child" means a child under the age of sixteen who has been deprived of parental support or care by reason of the death, continued absence from the home, or physical or mental incapacity of a parent, and who is living with his father, mother, grandfather, grandmother, brother, sister, stepfather, stepmother, step brother, stepsister, uncle, or aunt, in a place of residence maintained by one or more of such relatives as his or their own home. . . .

TITLE V—GRANTS TO STATES FOR MATERNAL AND CHILD WELFARE

PART 1—MATERNAL AND CHILD HEALTH SERVICES

APPROPRIATION

SECTION 501. For the purpose of enabling each State to extend and improve, as far as practicable under the conditions in such State, services for promoting the health of mothers and children, especially in rural areas and in areas suffering from severe economic distress, there is hereby authorized to be appropriated for each fiscal year, beginning with the fiscal year ending June 30, 1936, the sum of $3,800,000. The sums made available under this section shall be used for making payments to States which have submitted, and had approved by the Chief of the Children's Bureau, State plans for such services.

SEC. 502. (a) Out of the sums appropriated pursuant to section 501 for each fiscal year the Secretary of Labor shall allot to each State $20,000, and such part of $1,800,000 as he finds that the number of live births in such State bore to the total number of live births in the United States, in the latest calendar year for which the Bureau of the Census has available statistics.

(b) Out of the sums appropriated pursuant to section 501 for each fiscal year the Secretary of Labor shall allot to the States $980,000 (in addition to the allotments made under subsection (a)), according to the financial need for each State for assistance in carrying out its State plan, as determined by him after taking into consideration the number of live births in such State. . . .

APPROVAL OF STATE PLANS

SEC. 503. (a) A State plan for maternal and child-health services must (1) provide for financial participation by the State; (2) provide for the administration of the plan by the State health agency or the supervision of the administration of the plan by the State health agency; (3) provide such methods of administration (other than those relating to selection, tenure of office, and compensation of personnel) as are necessary for the efficient operation of the plan; (4) provide that the State health agency will make such reports, in such form and containing such information, as the Secretary of Labor may from time to time require, and comply with such provisions as he may from time to time find necessary to assure the correctness and verification of such reports; (5) provide for the extension and improvement of local maternal and child-health services administered by local child-health units; (6) provide for cooperation with medical, nursing, and welfare groups and organizations; and (7) provide for the development of demonstration services in needy areas and among groups in special need. . . .

PART 2—SERVICES FOR CRIPPLED CHILDREN
APPROPRIATION

SEC. 511. For the purpose of enabling each State to extend and improve (especially in rural areas and in areas suffering from severe economic distress), as far as practicable under the conditions in such State, services for lo-

cating crippled children, and for providing medical, surgical, corrective, and other services and care, and facilities for diagnosis, hospitalization, and aftercare, for children who are crippled or who are suffering from conditions which lead to crippling, there is hereby authorized to be appropriated for each fiscal year, beginning with the fiscal year ending June 30, 1936, the sum of $2,850,000. The sums made available under this section shall be used for making payments to States which have submitted, and had approved by the Chief of the Children's Bureau, State plans for such services.

ALLOTMENTS TO STATES

SEC. 512. (a) Out of the sums appropriated pursuant to section 511 for each fiscal year the Secretary of Labor shall allot to each State $20,000, and the remainder to the States according to the need of each State as determined by him after taking into consideration the number of crippled children in such State in need of the services referred to in section 511 and the cost of furnishing such services to them.

PART 3—CHILD-WELFARE SERVICES

SEC. 521. (a) For the purpose of enabling the United States, through the Children's Bureau, to cooperate with State public-welfare agencies in establishing, extending, and strengthening, especially in predominantly rural areas, public-welfare services (hereinafter in this section referred to as "child-welfare services") for the protection and care of homeless, dependent, and neglected children, and children in danger of becoming delinquent, there is hereby authorized to be appropriated for each fiscal year, beginning with the fiscal year ending June 30, 1936, the sum of $1,500,000. Such amount shall be allotted by the Secretary of Labor for use by cooperating State public-welfare agencies on the basis of plans developed jointly by the State agency and the Children's Bureau, to each State, $10,000, and the remainder to each State on the basis of such plans, not to exceed such part of the remainder as the rural population of such State bears to the total rural population of the United States. The amount so allotted shall be expended for payment of part of the cost of district, county or other local child-welfare services in areas predominantly rural, and for developing State services for the encouragement and assistance of adequate methods of community child-welfare organization in areas predominantly rural and other areas of special need. . . .

PART 4—VOCATIONAL REHABILITATION

SEC. 531. (a) In order to enable the United States to cooperate with the States and Hawaii in extending and strengthening their programs of vocational rehabilitation of the physically disabled, and to continue to carry out the provisions and purposes of the Act entitled "An Act to provide for the promotion of vocational rehabilitation of persons disabled in industry or otherwise and their return to civil employment," approved June 2, 1920, . . . there is hereby authorized to be appropriated for the fiscal years ending June 30, 1936, and June 30, 1937, the sum of $841,000 for each such fiscal year in addition to the amount of the existing authorization, and for each fiscal year thereafter the sum of $1,938,000.

TITLE VI—PUBLIC HEALTH WORK
APPROPRIATION

SECTION 601. For the purpose of assisting States, counties, health districts, and other political subdivisions of the States in establishing and maintaining adequate public-health services, including the training of personnel for State and local health work, there is hereby authorized to be appropriated for each fiscal year, beginning with the fiscal year ending June 30, 1936, the sum of $8,000,000 to be used as hereinafter provided.

STATE AND LOCAL PUBLIC HEALTH SERVICES

SEC. 602. (a) The Surgeon General of the Public Health Service, with the approval of the Secretary of the Treasury, shall, at the beginning of each fiscal year, allot to the States the total of (1) the amount appropriated for such year pursuant to section 601; and (2) the amounts of the allotments under this section for the preceding fiscal year remaining unpaid to the States at the end of such fiscal year. The amounts of such allotments shall be determined on the basis of (1) the population; (2) the special health problems; and (3) the financial needs; of the

respective States. Upon making such allotments the Surgeon General of the Public Health Service shall certify the amounts thereof to the Secretary of the Treasury.

(b) The amount of an allotment to any State under subsection (a) for any fiscal year, remaining unpaid at the end of such fiscal year, shall be available for allotment to States under subsection (a) for the succeeding fiscal year, in addition to the amount appropriated for such year.

(c) Prior to the beginning of each quarter of the fiscal year, the Surgeon General of the Public Health Service shall, with the approval of the Secretary of the Treasury, determine in accordance with rules and regulations previously prescribed by such Surgeon General after consultation with a conference of the State and Territorial health authorities, the amount to be paid to each State for such quarter from the allotment to such State, and shall certify the amount so determined to the Secretary of the Treasury. Upon receipt of such certification, the Secretary of the Treasury shall, through the Division of Disbursement of the Treasury Department and prior to audit or settlement by the General Accounting Office, pay in accordance with such certification.

(d) The moneys so paid to any State shall be expended solely in carrying out the purposes specified in section 601, and in accordance with plans presented by the health authority of such State and approved by the Surgeon General of the Public Health Service.

INVESTIGATIONS

SEC. 603. (a) There is hereby authorized to be appropriated for each fiscal year, beginning with the fiscal year ending June 30, 1936, the sum of $2,000,000 for expenditure by the Public Health Service for investigation of disease and problems of sanitation. . . .

TITLE VII—SOCIAL SECURITY BOARD
ESTABLISHMENT

SECTION 701. There is hereby established a Social Security Board to be composed of three members to be appointed by the President, by and with the advice and consent of the Senate. During his term of membership on the Board, no member shall engage in any other business, vocation, or employment. Not more than two of the members of the Board shall be members of the same political party. Each member shall receive a salary at the rate of $10,000 a year and shall hold office for a term of six years, . . .

DUTIES OF SOCIAL SECURITY BOARD

SEC. 702. The Board shall perform the duties imposed upon it by this Act and shall also have the duty of studying and making recommendations as to the most effective methods of providing economic security through social insurance, and as to legislation and matters of administrative policy concerning old-age pensions, unemployment compensation, accident compensation, and related subjects. . . .

TITLE VIII—TAXES WITH RESPECT TO EMPLOYMENT

INCOME TAX ON EMPLOYEES

SECTION 801. In addition to other taxes, there shall be levied, collected, and paid upon the income of every individual a tax equal to the following percentages of the wages (as defined in section 811) received by him after December 31, 1936, with respect to employment (as defined in section 811) after such date:

(1) With respect to employment during the calendar years 1937, 1938, and 1939, the rate shall be 1 per centum.

(2) With respect to employment during the calendar years 1940, 1941, and 1942, the rate shall be 1½ per centum.

(3) With respect to employment during the calendar years 1943, 1944, and 1945, the rate shall be 2 per centum.

(4) With respect to employment during the calendar years 1946, 1947, and 1948, the rate shall be 2½ per centum.

(5) With respect to employment after December 31, 1948, the rate shall be 3 per centum.

DEDUCTION OF TAX FROM WAGES

SEC. 802. (a) The tax imposed by section 801 shall be collected by the employer of the taxpayer, by deducting the amount of the tax from the wages as and when paid. . . .

EXCISE TAX ON EMPLOYERS

SEC. 804. In addition to other taxes, every employer shall pay an excise tax, with respect to having individuals in his employ, equal to the following percentages of the wages (as defined in section 811) paid by him after December 31, 1936, with respect to employment (as defined in section 811) after such date:

(1) With respect to employment during the calendar years 1937, 1938, and 1939, the rate shall be 1 per centum.

(2) With respect to employment during the calendar years 1940, 1941, and 1942, the rate shall be 1½ per centum.

(3) With respect to employment during the calendar years 1943, 1944, and 1945, the rate shall be 2 per centum.

(4) With respect to employment during the calendar years 1946, 1947, and 1948, the rate shall be 2½ per centum.

(5) With respect to employment after December 31, 1948, the rate shall be 3 per centum. . . .

DEFINITIONS

SEC. 811. When used in this title— . . .

(b) The term "employment" means any service, of whatever nature, performed within the United States by an employee for his employer, except—

(1) Agricultural labor;

(2) Domestic service in a private home;

(3) Casual labor not in the course of the employer's trade or business;

(4) Service performed by an individual who has attained the age of sixty-five;

(5) Service performed as an officer or member of the crew of a vessel documented under the laws of the United States or of any foreign country;

(6) Service performed in the employ of the United States Government or of an instrumentality of the United States;

(7) Service performed in the employ of a State, a political subdivision thereof, or an instrumentality of one or more States or political subdivisions;

(8) Service performed in the employ of a corporation, community chest, fund, or foundation, organized and operated exclusively for religious, charitable, scientific, literary, or educational purposes, or for the

prevention of cruelty to children or animals, no part of the net earnings of which inures to the benefit of any private shareholder or individual.

TITLE IX—TAX ON EMPLOYERS OF EIGHT OR MORE

IMPOSITION OF TAX

SECTION 901. On and after January 1, 1936, every employer shall pay for each calendar year an excise tax, with respect to having individuals in his employ, equal to the following percentages of the total wages payable by him with respect to employment during such calendar year:

(1) With respect to employment during the calendar year 1936 the rate shall be 1 per centum;

(2) With respect to employment during the calendar year 1937 the rate shall be 2 per centum;

(3) With respect to employment after December 31, 1937, the rate shall be 3 per centum. . . .

CERTIFICATION OF STATE LAWS

SEC. 903. (a) The Social Security Board shall approve any State law submitted to it, within thirty days of such submission, which it finds provides that—

(1) All compensation is to be paid through public employment offices in the State or such other agencies as the Board may approve;

(2) No compensation shall be payable with respect to any day of unemployment occurring within two years after the first day of the first period with respect to which contributions are required;

(3) All money received in the unemployment fund shall immediately upon such receipt be paid over to the Secretary of the Treasury to the credit of the Unemployment Trust Fund. . . .

(5) Compensation shall not be denied in such State to any otherwise eligible individual for refusing to accept new work under any of the following conditions: (A) If the position offered is vacant due directly to a strike, lockout, or other labor dispute; (B) if the wages, hours, or other conditions of the work offered are substantially less favorable to the individual than those prevailing for similar work in the locality; (C) if as a condition of being employed the individual would be required to join a company union or to resign from or refrain from joining any bona fide labor organization.

UNEMPLOYMENT TRUST FUND

SEC. 904. (a) There is hereby established in the Treasury of the United States a trust fund to be known as the "Unemployment Trust Fund, . . ."

(b) It shall be the duty of the Secretary of the Treasury to invest such portion of the Fund as is not, in his judgment, required to meet current withdrawals. Such investment may be made only in interest bearing obligations of the United States or in obligations guaranteed as to both principal and interest by the United States. . . .

INTERSTATE COMMERCE

SEC. 906. No person required under a State law to make payments to an unemployment fund shall be relieved from compliance therewith on the ground that he is engaged in interstate commerce, or that the State law does not distinguish between employees engaged in interstate commerce and those engaged in intrastate commerce.

DEFINITIONS

SEC. 907. When used in this title—

(a) The term "employer" does not include any person unless on each of some twenty days during the taxable year, each day being in a different calendar week, the total number of individuals who were in his employ for some portion of the day (whether or not at the same moment of time) was eight or more. . . .

TITLE X—GRANTS TO STATES FOR AID TO THE BLIND

APPROPRIATION

SECTION 1001. For the purpose of enabling each State to furnish financial assistance, as far as practicable under the conditions in such State, to needy individuals who are blind, there is hereby authorized to be appropriated for the fiscal year ending June 30, 1936, the sum of $3,000,000, and there is hereby authorized to be appropriated for each fiscal year thereafter a sum sufficient to carry out the purposes of this title. The sums made available under this section shall be used for making payments to States which have submitted, and had approved by the Social Security Board, State plans for aid to the blind. . . .

504. STEWARD MACHINE CO. v. DAVIS
301 U. S. 548
1937

Writ of Certiorari of U. S. Circuit Court of Appeals. This case involved the constitutionality of the tax imposed by the Social Security Act of 1935. For refs. see Doc. No. 503 and Nicholson, "Recent Decisions on the Power to Spend for the General Welfare," 12 Temple L. Qt. 435; Herbert, "General Welfare Clauses in the Constitution of the U. S.," 7 Fordham L. Rev. 390; Brebner-Smith, "Judicial limitations on Federal appropriations," 25 Virginia L. Rev. 613; Lowndes," "The Supreme Court on Taxation, 1936 Term," 86 U. of Pa. L. Rev. 1; Denby, "The Case against the Constitutionality of the Social Security Act," 3 Law and Contemporary Problems, 315.

CARDOZO, J. The validity of the tax imposed by the Social Security Act on employers of eight or more is here to be determined.

Petitioner, an Alabama corporation, paid a tax in accordance with the statute, filed a claim for refund with the Commissioner of Internal Revenue, and sued to recover the payment (46.14), asserting a conflict between the statute and the Constitution of the United States. Upon demurrer the District Court gave judgment for the defendant dismissing the complaint, and the Circuit Court of Appeals for the Fifth Circuit affirmed. . . . An important question of constitutional law being involved, we granted certiorari.

The Social Security Act is divided into eleven separate titles, of which only Titles IX and III are so related to this case as to stand in need of summary. [See Doc. No. 503]. . . .

The assault on the statute proceeds on an extended front. Its assailants take the ground that the tax is not an excise; that it is not uniform throughout the United States as excises are required to be; that its exceptions are so many and arbitrary as to violate the Fifth Amendment; that its purpose was not revenue, but an unlawful invasion of the reserved powers of the states; and that the states in submitting to it have yielded to coercion and have abandoned governmental functions which they are not permitted to surrender.

The objections will be considered seriatim with such further explanation as may be necessary to make their meaning clear.

First: The tax, which is described in the statute as an excise, is laid with uniformity throughout the United States as a duty, an impost or an excise upon the relation of employment.

1. We are told that the relation of employment is one so essential to the pursuit of happiness that it may not be burdened with a tax. Appeal is made to history. From the precedents of colonial days we are supplied with illustrations of excises common in the colonies. They are said to have been bound up with the enjoyment of particular commodities. Appeal is also made to principle or the analysis of concepts. An excise, we are told, imports a tax upon a privilege; employment, it is said, is a right, not a privilege, from which it follows that employment is not subject to an excise. Neither the one appeal nor the other leads to the desired goal. . . .

The historical prop failing, the prop or fancied prop of principle remains. We learn that employment for lawful gain is a "natural" or "inherent" or "inalienable" right, and not a "privilege" at all. But natural rights, so called, are as much subject to taxation as rights of less importance. An excise is not limited to vocations or activities that may be prohibited altogether. It is not limited to those that are the outcome of a franchise. It extends to vocations or activities pursued as of common right. What the individual does in the operation of a business is amenable to taxation just as much as what he owns, at all events if the classification is not tyrannical or arbitrary. "Business is as legitimate an object of the taxing powers as property." *City of Newton* v. *Atchison,* 31 Kan. 151, 154 (per Brewer, J.). Indeed, ownership itself, as we had occasion to point out the other day, is only a bundle of rights and privileges invested with a single name. *Henneford* v. *Silas Mason Co., Inc.,* March 29, 1937, 300 U. S. 577. . . . Employment is a business relation, if not itself a business. It is a relation without which business could seldom be carried on effectively. The power to tax the activities and relations that constitute a calling considered as a unit is the power to tax any of them. The whole includes the parts.

The subject matter of taxation open to the power of the Congress is as comprehensive as that open to the power of the states, though the method of apportionment may at times be different. "The Congress shall have power to lay and collect taxes, duties, imposts and excises." Art. 1, § 8. If the tax is a direct one, it shall be apportioned according to the census or enumeration. If it is a duty, impost, or excise, it shall be uniform throughout the United States. Together, these classes include every form of tax appropriate to sovereignty. Whether the tax is to be classified as an "excise" is in truth not of critical importance. If not that, it is an "impost" or a "duty." A capitation or other "direct" tax it certainly is not. "Although there have been from time to time intimations that there might be some tax which was not a direct tax nor included under the words 'duties, imposts and excises,' such a tax for more than one hundred years of national existence has as yet remained undiscovered, notwithstanding the stress of particular circumstances has invited thorough investigation into sources of powers." *Pollock* v. *Farmers' Loan and Trust Co.,* 157 U. S. 429, 557. There is no departure from that thought in later cases, but rather a new emphasis of it. Thus, in *Thomas* v. *United States,* 192 U. S. 363, 370, it was said of the words "duties, imposts and excises" that "they were used comprehensively to cover customs and excise duties imposed on importation, consumption, manufacture and sale of certain commodities, privileges, particular business transactions, vocations, occupations and the like." At times taxpayers have contended that the Congress is without power to lay an excise on the enjoyment of a privilege created by state law. The contention has been

put aside as baseless. Congress may tax the transmission of property by inheritance or will, though the states and not Congress have created the privilege of succession. Congress may tax the enjoyment of a corporate franchise, though a state and not Congress has brought the franchise into being. The statute books of the states are strewn with illustrations of taxes laid on occupations pursued of common right. We find no basis for a holding that the power in that regard which belongs by accepted practice to the legislatures of the states, has been denied by the Constitution to the Congress of the nation.

2. The tax being an excise, its imposition must conform to the canon of uniformity. There has been no departure from this requirement. According to the settled doctrine the uniformity exacted is geographical, not intrinsic. . . .

Second: The excise is not invalid under the provisions of the Fifth Amendment by force of its exemptions.

The statute does not apply, as we have seen, to employers of less than eight. It does not apply to agricultural labor, or domestic service in a private home or to some other classes of less importance. Petitioner contends that the effect of these restrictions is an arbitrary discrimination vitiating the tax.

The Fifth Amendment unlike the Fourteenth has no equal protection clause. But even the states, though subject to such a clause, are not confined to a formula of rigid uniformity in framing measures of taxation. They may tax some kinds of property at one rate, and others at another, and exempt others altogether. They may lay an excise on the operations of a particular kind of business, and exempt some other kind of business closely akin thereto. If this latitude of judgment is lawful for the states, it is lawful, a fortiori, in legislation by the Congress, which is subject to restraints less narrow and confining.

The classifications and exemptions directed by the statute now in controversy have support in considerations of policy and practical convenience that cannot be condemned as arbitrary. The classifications and exemptions would therefore be upheld if they had been adopted by a state and the provisions of the Fourteenth Amendment were invoked to annul them. This is held in two cases passed upon today in which precisely the same provisions were the subject of attack, the provisions being contained in the Unemployment Compensation Law of the State of Alabama. *Carmichael* v. *Southern Coal & Coke Co.,* No. 724, 301 U. S. 495, and *Carmichael* v. *Gulf States Paper Corp.,* No. 797, 301 U. S. ——. The opinion rendered in those cases covers the ground fully. It would be useless to repeat the argument. The act of Congress is therefore valid, so far at least as its system of exemptions is concerned, and this though we assume that discrimination, if gross enough, is equivalent to confiscation and subject under the Fifth Amendment to challenge and annulment.

Third: The excise is not void as involving the coercion of the States in contravention of the Tenth Amendment or of restrictions implicit in our federal form of government.

The proceeds of the excise when collected are paid into the Treasury at Washington, and therefore are subject to appropriation like public moneys generally. No presumption can be indulged that they will be misapplied or wasted. Even if they were collected in the hope or expectation that some other and collateral good would be furthered as an incident, that without more would not make the act invalid. This indeed is hardly questioned. The case for the petitioner is built on the contention that here an ulterior aim is wrought into the very structure of the act, and what is even more important that the aim is not only ulterior, but essentially unlawful. In particular, the 90 per cent credit is relied upon as supporting that conclusion. But before the statute succumbs to an assault upon these lines, two propositions must be made out by the assailant. There must be a showing in the first place that separated from the credit the revenue provisions are incapable of standing by themselves. There must be a showing in the second place that the tax and the credit in combination are weapons of coercion, destroying or impairing the autonomy of the states. The truth of each proposition being essential to the success of the assault, we pass for convenience to a consideration of the second, without pausing to inquire whether there has been a demonstration of the first.

To draw the line intelligently between duress and inducement there is need to remind ourselves of facts as to the problem of unemployment that are now matters of common knowledge. . . . The fact developed quickly that the states were unable to give the requisite relief. The problem had become national in area and dimensions. There was need of help from the nation if the people were not to starve. It is too late today for the argument to be heard with tolerance that in a crisis so extreme the use of the moneys of the nation to relieve the unemployed and their dependents is a use for any purpose narrower than the promotion of the general welfare. The nation responded to the call of the distressed. Between January 1, 1933 and July 1, 1936, the states (according to statistics submitted by the Government) incurred obligations of $689,291,802 for emergency relief; local subdivisions an additional $775,675,366. In the same period the obligations for emergency relief incurred by the national government were $2,929,307,125, or twice the obligations of states and local agencies combined. According to the President's budget message for the fiscal year 1938, the national government expended for public works and unemployment relief for the three fiscal years 1934, 1935, and 1936, the stupendous total of $8,681,000,000. The *parens patriae* has many reasons—fiscal and economic as well as social and moral—for planning to mitigate disasters that bring these burdens in their train.

In the presence of this urgent need for some remedial expedient, the question is to be answered whether the expedient adopted has overlept the bounds of power. The assailants of the statute say that its dominant end and aim is to drive the state legislatures under the whip of economic pressure into the enactment of unemployment compensation laws at the bidding of the central government. Supporters of the statute say that its operation is not constraint, but the creation of a larger freedom, the states and the nation joining in a coöperative endeavor to avert a common evil. Before Congress acted, unemployment compensation insurance was still, for the most part, a project and no more. Wisconsin was the pioneer. Her statute was adopted in 1931. At times bills for such insurance were introduced elsewhere, but they did not reach the stage of law. In 1935 four states (California, Massachusetts, New Hampshire and New York) passed unemployment laws on the eve of the adoption of the Social Security Act, and two others did likewise after the federal act and later in the year. The statutes differed to some extent in type, but were directed to a common end. In 1936, twenty-eight other states fell in line, and eight more the present year. But if states had been holding back before the passage of the federal law, inaction was not owing, for the most part to the lack of sympathetic interest. Many held back through alarm lest in laying such a toll upon their industries, they would place themselves in a position of economic disadvantage as compared with neighbors or competitors. See House Report, No. 615, 74th Congress, 1st session, p. 8; Senate Report, No. 628, 74th Congress, 1st session, p. 11. Two consequences ensued. One was that the freedom of a state to contribute its fair share to the solution of a national problem was paralyzed by fear. The other was that in so far as there was failure by the states to contribute relief according to the measure of their capacity, a disproportionate burden, and a mountainous one, was laid upon the resources of the Government of the nation.

The Social Security Act is an attempt to find a method by which all these public agencies may work together to a common end. Every dollar of the new taxes will continue in all likelihood to be used and needed by the nation as long as states are unwilling, whether through timidity or for other motives, to do what can be done at home. At least the inference is permissible that Congress so believed, though retaining undiminished freedom to spend the money as it pleased. On the other hand fulfillment of the home duty will be lightened and encouraged by crediting the taxpayer upon his account with the Treasury of the nation to the extent that his contributions under the laws of the locality have simplified or diminished the problem of relief and the probable demand upon the resources of the fisc. Duplicated taxes, or burdens that approach them, are recognized hardships that government, state or national, may properly avoid. If Congress believed that the general welfare would better be promoted by relief through local units than by the system then in vogue, the coöperating localities ought not in all fairness to pay a second time.

Who then is coerced through the operation of this statute? Not the taxpayer. He pays in fulfilment of the mandate of the local legisla-ture. Not the state. Even now she does not offer a suggestion that in passing the unemployment law she was affected by duress. For all that appears she is satisfied with her choice, and would be sorely disappointed if it were now to be annulled. The difficulty with the petitioner's contention is that it confuses motive with coercion. "Every tax is in some measure regulatory. To some extent it interposes an economic impediment to the activity taxed as compared with others not taxed." *Sonzinsky* v. *United States, supra,* March 29, 1937. In like manner every rebate from a tax when conditioned upon conduct is in some measure a temptation. But to hold that motive or temptation is equivalent to coercion is to plunge the law in endless difficulties. The outcome of such a doctrine is the acceptance of a philosophical determinism by which choice becomes impossible. Till now the law has been guided by a robust common sense which assumes the freedom of the will as a working hypothesis in the solution of its problems. The wisdom of the hypothesis has illustration in this case. Nothing in the case suggests the exertion of a power akin to undue influence, if we assume that such a concept can ever be applied with fitness to the relations between state and nation. Even on that assumption the location of the point at which pressure turns into compulsion, and ceases to be inducement, would be a question of degree, —at times, perhaps, of fact. The point had not been reached when Alabama made her choice. We cannot say that she was acting, not of her unfettered will, but under the strain of a persuasion equivalent to undue influence, when she chose to have relief administered under laws of her own making, by agents of her own selection, instead of under federal laws, administered by federal officers, with all the ensuing evils, at least to many minds, of federal patronage and power. There would be a strange irony, indeed, if her choice were now to be annulled on the basis of an assumed duress in the enactment of a statute which her courts have accepted as a true expression of her will. We think the choice must stand. . . .

Fourth: The statute does not call for a surrender by the states of powers essential to their quasi-sovereign existence.

Argument to the contrary has its source in two sections of the act. One section (903) defines the minimum criteria to which a state compensation system is required to conform if it is to be accepted by the Board as the basis for a credit. The other section (904) rounds out the requirement with complementary rights and duties. Not all the criteria or their incidents are challenged as unlawful. We will speak of them first generally, and then more specifically in so far as they are questioned. . . .

Even if opinion may differ as to the fundamental quality of one or more of the conditions, the difference will not avail to vitiate the statute. In determining essentials Congress must have the benefit of a fair margin of discretion. One cannot say with reason that this margin has been exceeded, or that the basic standards have been determined in any arbitrary fashion. In the event that some particular condition shall be found to be too uncertain to be capable of enforcement, it may be severed from the others, and what is left will still be valid.

We are to keep in mind steadily that the conditions to be approved by the Board as the basis for a credit are not provisions of a contract, but terms of a statute, which may be altered or repealed. Section 903 (a) (6). The state does not bind itself to keep the law in force. It does not even bind itself that the moneys paid into the federal fund will be kept there indefinitely or for any stated time. On the contrary, the Secretary of the Treasury will honor a requisition for the whole or any part of the deposit in the fund whenever one is made by the appropriate officials. The only consequence of the repeal or excessive amendment of the statute, or the expenditure of the money, when requisitioned, for other than compensation uses or administrative expenses, is that approval of the law will end, and with it the allowance of a credit, upon notice to the state agency and an opportunity for hearing. Section 903 (b) (c).

These basic considerations are in truth a solvent of the problem. Subjected to their test, the several objections on the score of abdication are found to be unreal. . . .

Finally and chiefly, abdication is supposed to follow from section 904 of the statute and the parts of section 903 that are complementary thereto. Section 903 (a) (3). By these the Secretary of the Treasury is authorized and directed to receive and hold in the Unemployment Trust Fund all moneys deposited therein by a state agency for a state unemployment fund and to invest in obligations of the United States such portion of the Fund as is not in his judgment required to meet current withdrawals. We are told that Alabama in consenting to that deposit has renounced the plenitude of power inherent in her statehood.

The same pervasive misconception is in evidence again. All that the state has done is to say in effect through the enactment of a statute that her agents shall be authorized to deposit the unemployment tax receipts in the Treasury at Washington. Alabama Unemployment Act of September 14, 1935, section 10 (i). The statute may be repealed. Section 903 (a) (6). The consent may be revoked. The deposits may be withdrawn. The moment the state commission gives notice to the depositary that it would like the moneys back, the Treasurer will return them. To find state destruction there is to find it almost anywhere. With nearly as much reason one might say that a state abdicates its functions when it places the state moneys on deposit in a national bank.

There are very good reasons of fiscal and governmental policy why a State should be willing to make the Secretary of the Treasury the custodian of the fund. His possession of the moneys and his control of investments will be an assurance of stability and safety in times of stress and strain. A report of the Ways and Means Committee of the House of Representatives, quoted in the margin, develops the situation clearly. Nor is there risk of loss or waste. The credit of the Treasury is at all times back of the deposit, with the result that the right of withdrawal will be unaffected by the fate of any intermediate investments, just as if a checking account in the usual form had been opened in a bank.

The inference of abdication thus dissolves in thinnest air when the deposit is conceived of as dependent upon a statutory consent, and not upon a contract effective to create a duty. By this we do not intimate that the conclusion would be different if a contract were discovered. Even sovereigns may contract without derogating from their sovereignty. The states are at liberty, upon obtaining the consent of Congress, to make agreements with one another. Constitution,

Art. I, section 10, par. 3. We find no room for doubt that they may do the like with Congress if the essence of their statehood is maintained without impairment. Alabama is seeking and obtaining a credit of many millions in favor of her citizens out of the Treasury of the nation. Nowhere in our scheme of government—in the limitations express or implied of our federal constitution—do we find that she is prohibited from assenting to conditions that will assure a fair and just requital for benefits received. But we will not labor the point further. An unreal prohibition directed to an unreal agreement will not vitiate an act of Congress, and cause it to collapse in ruin. . . .

The judgment is affirmed.

Justices McReynolds, Sutherland, Butler and Van Devanter dissented.

505. HELVERING et. al. v. DAVIS
301 U. S. 619
1937

On Writ of Certiorari to the U. S. Circuit Court of Appeals for the First Circuit. In the Stewart Machine Co. case the Supreme Court sustained that part of the Social Security Act which imposed an excise upon employers. The present case involved the constitutionality of the tax upon employees and presented the broad question of the nature and limits of taxation for the general welfare. The opinion is notable for its recognition of the economic background and motivation of the legislation under consideration. Compare this opinion with the opinion of the majority in the AAA case, Doc. No. 478. For references see Docs. No. 503 and 504.

Cardozo, J. The Social Security Act is challenged once again. . . .

In this case Titles VIII and II are the subject of attack. Title VIII . . . lays a special income tax upon employees to be deducted from their wages and paid by the employers. Title II provides for the payment of Old Age Benefits, and supplies the motive and occasion, in the view of the assailants of the statute, for the levy of the taxes imposed by Title VIII. . . .

Second: The scheme of benefits created by the provisions of Title II is not in contravention of the limitations of the Tenth Amendment.

Congress may spend money in aid of the "general welfare." Constitution, Art. I, section 8; *United States* v. *Butler*, 297 U. S. 1, 65; *Steward Machine Co.* v. *Davis*. There have been great statesmen in our history who have stood for other views. We will not resurrect the contest. It is now settled by decision. *United States* v. *Butler*. The conception of the spending power advocated by Hamilton and strongly reinforced by Story has prevailed over that of Madison, which has not been lacking in adherents. Yet difficulties are left when the power is conceded. The line must still be drawn between one welfare and another, between particular and general. Where this shall be placed cannot be known through a formula in advance of the event. There is a middle ground or certainly a penumbra in which discretion is at large. The discretion, however, is not confided to the courts. The discretion belongs to Congress, unless the choice is clearly wrong, a display of arbitrary power, not an exercise of judgment. This is now familiar law. "When such a contention comes here we naturally require a showing that by no reasonable possibility can the challenged legislation fall within the wide range of discretion permitted to the Congress." *United States* v. *Butler, supra,* p. 67. Nor is the concept of the general welfare static. Needs that were narrow or parochial a century ago may be interwoven in our day with the well-being of the nation. What is critical or urgent changes with the times.

The purge of nation-wide calamity that began in 1929 has taught us many lessons. Not the least is the solidarity of interests that may once have seemed to be divided. Unemployment spreads from state to state, the hinterland now settled that in pioneer days gave an avenue of escape. Spreading from state to state, unemployment is an ill not particular but general, which may be checked, if Congress so determines, by the resources of the nation. If this can have been doubtful until now, our ruling today in the case of the *Steward Machine Co.* has set the doubt at rest. But the ill is all one or at least not greatly different whether men are thrown out of work because there is no longer work to do or because the disabilities of age make them incapable of doing it. Rescue becomes necessary irrespective of the cause. The hope behind this statute is to save men and women from the rigors of the poor house as well as from the haunting fear that such a lot awaits them when journey's end is near.

Congress did not improvise a judgment when it found that the award of old age benefits would be conducive to the general welfare. The President's Committee on Economic Security made an investigation and report, aided by a research staff of Government officers and employees, and by an Advisory Council and seven other advisory groups. Extensive hearings followed before the House Committee on Ways and Means, and the Senate Committee on Finance. A great mass of evidence was brought together supporting the policy which finds expression in the act. Among the relevant facts are these: The number of persons in the United States 65 years of age or over is increasing proportionately as well as absolutely. What is even more important the number of such persons unable to take care of themselves is growing at a threatening pace. More and more our population is becoming urban and industrial instead of rural and agricultural. The evidence is impressive that among industrial workers the younger men and women are preferred over the older. In time of retrenchment the older are commonly the first to go, and even if retained, their wages are likely to be lowered. The plight of men and women at so low an age as 40 is hard, almost hopeless, when they are driven to seek for reemployment. Statistics are in the brief. A few illustrations will be chosen from many there collected. In 1930, out of 224 American factories investigated, 71, or almost one third, had fixed maximum hiring age limits; in 4 plants the limit was under 40; in 41 it was under 46. In the other 153 plants there were no fixed limits, but in practice few were hired if they were over 50 years of age. With the loss of savings inevitable in periods of idleness, the fate of workers over 65, when thrown out of work, is little less than desperate. A recent study of the Social Security Board informs us that "one-fifth of the aged in the United States were receiving old-age assistance, emergency relief,

institutional care, employment under the works program, or some other form of aid from public or private funds; two-fifths to one-half were dependent on friends and relatives, one-eighth had some income from earnings; and possibly one-sixth had some savings or property. Approximately three out of four persons 65 or over were probably dependent wholly or partially on others for support." We summarize in the margin the results of other studies by state and national commissions. They point the same way.

The problem is plainly national in area and dimensions. Moreover, laws of the separate states cannot deal with it effectively. Congress, at least, had a basis for that belief. States and local governments are often lacking in the resources that are necessary to finance an adequate program of security for the aged. This is brought out with a wealth of illustration in recent studies of the problem. Apart from the failure of resources, states and local governments are at times reluctant to increase so heavily the burden of taxation to be borne by their residents for fear of placing themselves in a position of economic disadvantage as compared with neighbors or competitors. We have seen this in our study of the problem of unemployment compensation. *Steward Machine Co.* v. *Davis*. A system of old age pensions has special dangers of its own, if put in force in one state and rejected in another. The existence of such a system is a bait to the needy and dependent elsewhere, encouraging them to migrate and seek a haven of repose. Only a power that is national can serve the interests of all.

Whether wisdom or unwisdom resides in the scheme of benefits set forth in Title II, it is not for us to say. The answer to such inquiries must come from Congress, not the courts. Our concern here as often is with power, not with wisdom. Counsel for respondent has recalled to us the virtues of self-reliance and frugality. There is a possibility, he says, that aid from a paternal government may sap those sturdy virtues and breed a race of weaklings. If Massachusetts so believes and shapes her laws in that conviction, must her breed of sons be changed, he asks, because some other philosophy of government finds favor in the halls of Congress? But the answer is not doubtful. One might ask with equal reason whether the system of protective tariffs is to be set aside at will in one state or another whenever local policy prefers the rule of *laissez faire*. The issue is a closed one. It was fought out long ago. When money is spent to promote the general welfare, the concept of welfare or the opposite is shaped by Congress, not the states. So the concept

be not arbitrary, the locality must yield. Constitution, Art. VI, Par. 2.

Ordered accordingly.

Mr. Justice McREYNOLDS and Mr. Justice BUTLER are of opinion that the provisions of the Act here challenged are repugnant to the Tenth Amendment, and that the decree of the Circuit Court of Appeals should be affirmed.

506. CANADIAN RECIPROCAL TRADE AGREEMENT

Signed November 15, 1935; Ratified May 14, 1936

(U. S. Dept. of State. Executive Agreements Series, No. 91)

When the Democrats came into office in March 1933 they found in effect the highest tariff in our history. Instead of a general reduction through new tariff legislation, Pres. Roosevelt and his Secretary of State Cordell Hull determined to use the power to lower tariffs for bargaining purposes. The purpose of this policy was not only economic but political as well. The Trade Agreements Act of 1934 authorized the President to make reciprocal agreements with foreign nations lowering tariffs on particular articles up to fifty per cent. Under this authority Sec. Hull, in the following six years, negotiated twenty-two reciprocal pacts. The new policy resulted in a gratifying expansion of American exports and was not without effect in improving American relations with Latin-American nations. The Canadian reciprocity agreement here given aroused widespread opposition especially from Mid-western farming interests. See, R. L. Buell, *The Hull Trade Program and the American System* (World Affairs Pamphlets, no. 2); H. S. Patton, *The Mid-West and the Trade Agreements Program* (Dept. of State Commercial Policy Ser. no. 27); F. B. Sayre, *The Way Forward;* H. J. Tasca, *The Reciprocal Trade Policy of the United States.* For an earlier effort at reciprocity with Canada see L. E. Ellis, *Reciprocity, 1911.*

BY THE PRESIDENT OF THE UNITED STATES
OF AMERICA

A PROCLAMATION

WHEREAS it it provided in the Tariff Àct of 1930 of the Congress of the United States of America, as amended by the Act of June 12, 1934, entitled "AN ACT To Amend the Tariff Act of 1930" (48 Stat. 943), as follows:

"Sec. 350. (a) For the purpose of expanding foreign markets for the products of the United States (as a means of assisting in the present emergency in restoring the American standard of living, in overcoming domestic unemployment and the present economic depression, in increasing the purchasing power of the American public, and in establishing and maintaining a better relationship among various branches of American agriculture, industry, mining, and commerce) by regulating the admission of foreign goods into the United States in accordance with the characteristics and needs of various branches of American production so that foreign markets will be made available to those branches of American production which require and are capable of developing such outlets by affording corresponding market opportunities for foreign products in the United States, the President, whenever he finds as a fact that any existing duties or other import restrictions of the United States or any foreign country are unduly burdening and restricting the foreign trade of the United States and that the purpose above declared will be promoted by the means hereinafter specified, is authorized from time to time—

"(1) To enter into foreign trade agreements with foreign governments or instrumentalities thereof; and

"(2) To proclaim such modifications of existing duties and other import restrictions, or such additional import restrictions, or such continuance, and for such minimum periods, of existing customs or excise treatment of any article covered by foreign trade agreements, as are required or appropriate to carry out any foreign trade agreement that the President has entered into hereunder. No proclamation shall be made increasing or decreasing by more than 50 per centum any existing rate of duty or transferring any article between the dutiable and free lists. The proclaimed duties and other import restrictions shall apply to articles the growth, produce, or manufacture of all foreign countries, whether imported directly, or indirectly: *Provided,* That the President may suspend the application to articles the growth, produce, or manufacture of any country because of its discriminatory treatment of American commerce or because of other acts or policies which in his opinion tend to defeat the purposes set forth in this section; . . .

WHEREAS I, Franklin D. Roosevelt, President of the United States of America, have found as a fact that certain existing duties and other import restrictions of the United States of America and the Dominion of Canada are unduly burdening and restricting the foreign trade of the United States of America and that the purpose declared in the said Tariff Act of 1930, as amended by the said Act of June 12, 1934, will be promoted by a foreign trade agreement between the United States of America and the Dominion of Canada;

WHEREAS reasonable public notice of the intention to negotiate such foreign trade agreement was given and the views presented by persons interested in the negotiation of such agreement were received and considered;

WHEREAS, after seeking and obtaining information and advice with respect thereto from the United States Tariff Commission, the Departments of State, Agriculture, and Commerce, and from other sources, I entered into a foreign Trade Agreement on November 15, 1935, through my duly empowered plenipotentiary, with His Majesty the King of Great Britain, Ireland and the British dominions beyond the Seas, Emperor of India, in respect of the Dominion of Canada, through his duly empowered Plenipotentiary, which Agreement, is as follows:

The President of the United States of America and His Majesty the King of Great Britain, Ireland and the British dominions beyond the Seas, Emperor of India, in respect of the Dominion of Canada, being desirous of facilitating and extending the commercial relations existing between the United States of America and Canada by granting mutual and reciprocal concessions and advantages for the promotion of trade, have resolved to conclude a Trade Agreement as a step toward the lowering of the barriers impeding trade between their two countries, and for this purpose have through their respective Plenipotentiaries agreed upon the following Articles:

ARTICLE I

The United States of America and Canada will grant each other unconditional and unrestricted most-favored-nation treatment in all matters concerning customs duties and subsidiary charges of every kind and in the method of levying duties, and, further, in all matters concerning the rules, formalities and charges imposed in connection with the clearing of goods through the customs, and with respect to all laws or regulations affecting the sale or use of imported goods within the country.

Accordingly, natural or manufactured products having their origin in either of the countries shall in no case be subject, in regard to the matters referred to above, to any duties, taxes or charges other or higher, or to any rules or formalities other or more burdensome, than those to which the like products having their origin in any third country are or may hereafter be subject.

Similarly, natural or manufactured products exported from the territory of the United States of America or Canada and consigned to the territory of the other country shall in no case be subject with respect to exportation and in regard to the above-mentioned matters, to any duties, taxes or charges other or higher, or to any rules or formalities other or more burdensome, than those to which the like products when consigned to the territory of any third country are or may hereafter be subject.

Any advantage, favor, privilege or immunity which has been or may hereafter be granted by the United States of America or Canada in regard to the above-mentioned matters, to a natural or manufactured product originating in any third country or consigned to the territory of any third country shall be accorded immediately and without compensation to the like product originating in or consigned to the territory of Canada or the United States of America, respectively, and irrespective of the nationality of the carrier.

Article II

Neither the United States of America nor Canada shall establish any prohibition or maintain any restriction on imports from the territory of the other country which is not applied to the importation of any like article originating in any third country. Any abolition of an import prohibition or restriction which may be granted even temporarily by either country in favor of an article of a third country shall be applied immediately and unconditionally to the like article originating in the territory of the other country. These provisions equally apply to exports. . . .

Article III

Articles the growth, produce or manufacture of the United States of America, enumerated and described in Schedule I annexed to this Agreement, shall, on their importation into Canada, be exempt from ordinary customs duties in excess of those set forth in the said Schedule. The said articles shall also be exempt from all other duties, taxes, fees, charges, or exactions, imposed on or in connection with importation, in excess of those imposed on the day of the signature of this Agreement or required to be imposed thereafter under laws of Canada in force on the day of the signature of this Agreement. . . .

Article IV

Articles the growth, produce or manufacture of Canada, enumerated and described in Schedule II annexed to this Agreement, shall, on their importation into the United States of America, be exempt from ordinary customs duties in excess of those set forth and provided for in the said Schedule. . . .

Article V

The provisions of Articles III and IV of this Agreement shall not prevent the Government of either country from imposing on the importation of any product a charge equivalent to an internal tax imposed on a like domestic product or on a commodity from which the imported product has been manufactured or produced in whole or in part.

Article VI

Articles the growth, produce or manufacture of the United States of America or Canada shall, after importation into the other country, be exempt from all internal taxes, fees, charges or exactions other or higher than those payable on like articles of national origin or any other foreign origin. . . .

Article VII

No prohibitions, import or customs quotas, import licenses, or any other form of quantitative regulation, whether or not operated in connection with any agency of centralized control, shall be imposed by the United States of America on the importation or sale of any article the growth, produce or manufacture of Canada enumerated and described in Schedule II, nor by Canada on the importation or sale of any article the growth, produce or manufacture of the United States of America enumerated and described in Schedule I, except as specifically provided for in the said Schedules.

The foregoing provision shall not apply to quantitative restrictions in whatever form imposed by either country on the importation or sale of any article the growth, produce or manufacture of the other country in conjunction with governmental measures operating to regulate or control the production, market supply, or prices of like domestic articles, or tending to increase the labor costs of production of such articles. Whenever the Government of either country proposes to establish or change any restriction authorized by this paragraph, it shall give notice thereof in writing to the other Government and shall afford such other Government an opportunity within thirty days after receipt of such notice to consult with it in respect of the proposed action; and if an agreement with respect thereto is not reached within thirty days following receipt of the aforesaid notice, the Government which proposes to take such action shall be free to do so at any time thereafter, and the other Government shall be free within fifteen days after such action is taken to terminate this Agreement in its entirety on thirty days' written notice. . . .

Article IX

The tariff advantages and other benefits provided for in this Agreement are granted by the United States of America and Canada to each other subject to the condition that if the Government of either country shall establish or maintain, directly or indirectly, any form of control of foreign exchange, it shall administer such control so as to insure that the nationals and commerce of the other country will be granted a fair and equitable share in the allotment of exchange. . . .

ARTICLE X

In the event that a wide variation occurs in the rate of exchange between the currencies of the United States of America and Canada, the Government of either country, if it considers the variation so substantial as to prejudice the industries or commerce of the country, shall be free to propose negotiations for the modification of this Agreement; and if an agreement with respect thereto is not reached within thirty days following receipt of such proposal, the Government making such proposal shall be free to terminate this Agreement in its entirety on thirty days' written notice.

ARTICLE XI

In the event that the Government of either country adopts any measure which, even though it does not conflict with the terms of this Agreement, is considered by the Government of the other country to have the effect of nullifying or impairing any object of the Agreement, the Government which has adopted any such measure shall consider such representations and proposals as the other Government may make with a view to effecting a mutually satisfactory adjustment of the matter. . . .

ARTICLE XII

Nothing in this Agreement shall be construed to prevent the adoption of measures prohibiting or restricting the exportation or importation of gold or silver, or to prevent the adoption of such measures as either Government may see fit with respect to the control of the export or sale for export of arms, ammunition, or implements of war, and, in exceptional circumstances, all other military supplies.

Subject to the requirement that there shall be no arbitrary discrimination by either country against the other country in favor of any third country where similar conditions prevail, the provisions of this Agreement shall not extend to prohibitions or restrictions (1) imposed on moral or humanitarian grounds; (2) designed to protect human, animal or plant life; (3) relating to prison-made goods; (4) relating to the enforcement of police or revenue laws; (5) directed against misbranding, adulteration, and other fraudulent practices, such as are provided for in the pure food and drug laws of either country; and (6) directed against unfair practices in import trade. . . .

ARTICLE XIV

The Government of each country reserves the right to withdraw or to modify the concession granted on any article under this Agreement, or to impose quantitative restrictions on any such article if, as a result of the extension of such concession to third countries, such countries obtain the major benefit of such concession and in consequence thereof an unduly large increase in importations of such article takes place. . . .

Done in duplicate, at the City of Washington, this fifteenth day of November, 1935.

For the President of the United States of America:

CORDELL HULL
*Secretary of State
of the United States of America.*

For His Majesty the King of Great Britain, Ireland and the British dominions beyond the Seas, Emperor of India, for the Dominion of Canada:

W. L. MACKENZIE KING
Prime Minister

507. CARTER v. CARTER COAL CO. et. al.
298 U. S. 238
1936

On Writs of Certiorari to the U. S. Court of Appeals for the District of Columbia. The coal industry had long been recognized as "sick" and an appropriate object of federal regulation. The

Guffey Coal Act of 30 Aug., 1935, whose provisions are here set forth in some detail, represented an effort to regulate both production and labor. The Court, in this opinion, not only reaffirmed the doctrine of the Schechter case (see Doc. No. 486) but appeared to return to the position of the E. C. Knight case (see Doc. No. 339). Mr. C. J. Hughes in a separate opinion insisted that the invalidity of the labor provisions of the Guffey Act did not necessarily invalidate the price-fixing provisions. A second Guffey Coal Act was passed, 26 April, 1937. For conditions in the coal industry, see E. E. Hunt, ed. *What the Coal Commission Found:* W. Hamilton and H. R. Wright, *The Case of Bituminous Coal.* For the Carter case see E. S. Corwin, *Twilight of the Supreme Court* and *Commerce Power versus States Rights;* W. Hamilton and O. Adair, *The Power to Govern;* Black, "The Commerce Clause and the New Deal," 20 Cornell L. Qt. 169; Eisenstein, "The Final Phase of the Schechter Episode," 5 Brooklyn L. Rev. 454; Hetsko, "Congressional Power under the Commerce Clause, etc." 34 Mich. L. Rev. 1167.

SUTHERLAND, J. The purpose of the "Bituminous Coal Conservation Act of 1935," involved in these suits, as declared by the title, are to stabilize the bituminous coal-mining industry and promote its interstate commerce; to provide for cooperative marketing of bituminous coal; to levy a tax on such coal and provide for a drawback under certain conditions; to declare the production, distribution, and use of such coal to be affected with a national public interest; to conserve the national resources of such coal; to provide for the general welfare, and for other purposes. C. 824, 49 Stat. 991. The constitutional validity of the act is challenged in each of the suits.

By the terms of the act, every producer of bituminous coal within the United States is brought within its provisions.

Section 1 is a detailed assertion of circumstances thought to justify the act. It declares that the mining and distribution of bituminous coal throughout the United States by the producer are affected with a national public interest; and that the service of such coal in relation to industrial activities, transportation facilities, health and comfort of the people, conservation by controlled production and economical mining and marketing, maintenance of just and rational relations between the public, owners, producers and employees, the right of the public to constant and adequate supplies of coal at reasonable prices, and the general welfare of the nation, require that the bituminous coal industry should be regulated as the act provides.

Section 1, among other things, further declares that the production and distribution by producers of such coal bear upon and directly affect interstate commerce, and render regulation of production and distribution imperative for the protection of such commerce; that certain features connected with the production, distribution, and marketing have led to waste of the national coal resources, disorganization of interstate commerce in such coal, and burdening and obstructing interstate commerce therein; that practices prevailing in the production of such coal directly affect interstate commerce and require regulation for the protection of that commerce; and that the right of mine workers to organize and collectively bargain for wages, hours of labor, and conditions of employment should be guaranteed in order to prevent constant wage cutting and disparate labor costs detrimental to fair interstate competition, and in order to avoid obstructions to interstate commerce that recur in industrial disputes over labor relations at the mines. These declarations constitute not enactments of law, but legislative averments by way of inducement to the enactment which follows.

The substantive legislation begins with § 2, which establishes in the Department of the Interior a National Bituminous Coal Commission, to be appointed and constituted as the section then specifically provides. Upon this commission is conferred the power to hear evidence and find facts upon which its orders and actions may be predicated.

Section 3 provides:

"There is hereby imposed upon the sale or other disposal of all bituminous coal produced within the United States an excise tax of 15 per centum on the sale price at the mine, or in the case of captive coal the fair market value of such coal at the mine, such tax, subject to the later provisions of this section, to be payable to the United States by the producers of such coal, and to be payable monthly for each calendar month, on or before the first business day of the second succeeding month, and under such regulations, and in such manner, as shall be prescribed by the Commissioner of Internal Revenue: *Provided,* That in the case of captive coal produced as aforesaid, the Commissioner of Internal Revenue shall fix a price therefor at the current market price for the comparable kind, quality, and size of coals in the locality where the same is produced: *Provided further,* That any such coal producer who has filed with the National Bituminous Coal Commission his acceptance of the code provided for in section 4 of this Act, and who acts in compliance with the provisions of such code, shall be entitled to a drawback in the form of a credit upon the amount of such tax payable hereunder, equivalent to 90 per centum of the amount of such tax, to be allowed and deducted therefrom at the time settlement therefor is required, in such manner as shall be prescribed by the Commissioner of Internal Revenue. . . .

Section 4 provides that the commission shall formulate the elaborate provisions contained therein into a working agreement to be known as the Bituminous Coal Code. These provisions require the organization of twenty-three coal districts, each with a district board the membership of which is to be determined in a manner pointed out by the act. . . .

Without repeating the long and involved provisions with regard to the fixing of minimum prices, it is enough to say that the act confers the power to fix the minimum price of coal at each and every coal mine in the United States, with such price variations as the board may deem necessary and proper. There is also a provision authorizing the commission, when deemed necessary in the public interest, to establish maximum prices in order to protect the consumer against unreasonably high prices.

All sales and contracts for the sale of coal are subject to the code prices provided for and in effect when such sales and contracts are made. Various unfair methods of competition are defined and forbidden.

The labor provisions of the code, found in Part III of the same section, require that in order to effectuate the purposes of the act the district boards and code members shall accept specified conditions contained in the code, among which are the following:

Employees to be given the right to organize and bargain collectively, through representatives of their own choosing, free from interference, restraint, or coercion of employers or their agents in respect of their concerted activities.

Such employees to have the right of peaceable assemblage for the discussion of the principles of collective bargaining and to se-lect their own check-weighman to inspect the weighing or measuring of coal.

A labor board is created, consisting of three members, to be appointed by the President and assigned to the Department of Labor. Upon this board is conferred authority to adjudicate disputes arising under the provisions just stated, and to determine whether or not an organization of employees had been promoted, or is controlled or dominated by an employer in its organization, management, policy, or election of representatives. The board "may order a code member to meet the representatives of its employees for the purpose of collective bargaining."

Subdivision (g) of Part III provides:

"Whenever the maximum daily and weekly hours of labor are agreed upon in any contract or contracts negotiated between the producers of more than two-thirds the annual national tonnage production for the preceding calendar year and the representatives of more than one-half of the mine workers employed, such maximum hours of labor shall be accepted by all the code members. The wage agreement or agreements negotiated by collective bargaining in any district or group of two or more districts, between representatives of producers of more than two-thirds of the annual tonnage production of such district or each of such districts in a contracting group during the preceding calendar year, and representatives of the majority of the mine workers therein, shall be filed with the Labor Board and shall be accepted as the minimum wages for the various classifications of labor by the code members operating in such district or group of districts." . . .

The questions involved will be considered under the following heads:

1. The right of stockholders to maintain suits of this character.

2. Whether the suits were prematurely brought.

3. Whether the exaction of 15 *per centum* on the sale price of coal at the mine is a tax or a penalty.

4. The purposes of the act as set forth in § 1, and the authority vested in Congress by the Constitution to effectuate them.

5. Whether the labor provisions of the act can be upheld as an exercise of the power to regulate interstate commerce.

6. Whether subdivision (g) of Part III of the Code, is an unlawful delegation of power.

7. The constitutionality of the price-fixing provisions, and the question of severability— that is to say, whether, if either the group of labor provisions or the group of price-fixing provisions be found constitutionally invalid, the other can stand as separable. . . .

Third. The co-called excise tax of 15 *per centum* on the sale price of coal at the mine, or, in the case of captive coal the fair market value, with its drawback allowance of 13½% is clearly not a tax but a penalty. . . .

It is very clear that the "excise tax" is not imposed for revenue but exacted as a penalty to compel compliance with the regulatory provisons of the act. The whole purpose of the exaction is to coerce what is called an agreement—which, of course, it is not, for it lacks the essential element of consent. One who does a thing in order to avoid a monetary penalty does not agree; he yields to compulsion precisely the same as though he did so to avoid a term in jail. . . .

But it is not necessary to pursue the matter further. That the "tax" is in fact a penalty is not seriously in dispute. The position of the government, as we understand it, is that the validity of the exaction does not rest upon the taxing power but upon the power of Congress to regulate interstate commerce; and that if the act in respect of the labor and price-fixing provisions be not upheld, the "tax" must fall with them. With that position we agree and confine our consideration accordingly.

Fourth. Certain recitals contained in the act plainly suggest that its makers were of opinion that its constitutionality could be sustained under some general federal power, thought to exist, apart from the specific grants of the Constitution. The fallacy of that view will be apparent when we recall fundamental principles which, although hitherto often expressed in varying forms of words, will bear repetition whenever their accuracy seems to be challenged. The recitals to which we refer are contained in § 1 (which is simply a preamble to the act), and, among others, are to the effect that the distribution of bituminous coal is of national interest, affecting the health and comfort of the people and the general welfare of the nation; that this circumstance, together with the necessity of maintaining just and rational relations between the public, owners, producers, and employees, and the right of the public to constant and adequate supplies at reasonable prices, require regulation of the industry as the act provides. These affirmations—and the further ones that the production and distribution of such coal "directly affect interstate commerce," because of which and of the waste of the national coal resources and other circumstances, the regulation is necessary for the protection of such commerce—do not constitute an exertion of the *will* of Congress which is legislation, but a recital of considerations which in the *opinion* of that body existed and justified the expression of its will in the present act. Nevertheless, this preamble may not be disregarded. On the contrary it is important, because it makes clear, except for the pure assumption that the conditions described "directly" affect interstate commerce, that the powers which Congress undertook to exercise are not specific but of the most general character—namely, to protect the general public interest and health and comfort of the people, to conserve privately-owned coal, maintain just relations between producers and employees and others, and promote the general welfare, by controling nation-wide production and distribution of coal. These, it may be conceded, are objects of great worth; but are they ends, the attainment of which has been committed by the Constitution to the federal government? This is a vital question; for nothing is more certain than that beneficent aims, however great or well directed, can never serve in lieu of constitutional power.

The ruling and firmly established principle is that the powers which the general government may exercise are only those specifically enumerated in the Constitution, and such implied powers as are necessary and proper to carry into effect the enumerated powers. Whether the end sought to be attained by an act of Congress is legitimate is wholly a matter of constitutional power and not at all of legislative discretion. Legislative congressional discretion begins with the choice of means and ends with the adoption of methods and details to carry the delegated powers into effect. The distinction between these two things—power and discretion—is not only very plain but very important. For while the

powers are rigidly limited to the enumera-
tions of the Constitution, the means which
may be employed to carry the powers into
effect are not restricted, save that they must
be appropriate, plainly adapted to the end,
and not prohibited by, but consistent with, the
letter and spirit of the Constitution. Thus,
it may be said that to a constitutional end
many ways are open; but to an end not within
the terms of the Constitution, all ways are
closed.

The proposition, often advanced and as
often discredited, that the power of the federal government inherently extends to purposes affecting the nation as a whole with
which the states severally cannot deal or
cannot adequately deal, and the related notion that Congress, entirely apart from those
powers delegated by the Constitution, may
enact laws to promote the general welfare,
have never been accepted but always definitely rejected by this court. . . .

The general rule with regard to the respective powers of the national and the state
governments under the Constitution, is not
in doubt. The states were before the Constitution; and, consequently, their legislative
powers antedated the Constitution. Those who
framed and those who adopted that instrument meant to carve from the general mass
of legislative powers, then possessed by the
states, only such portions as it was thought
wise to confer upon the federal government;
and in order that there should be no uncertainty in respect of what was taken and what
was left, the national powers of legislation
were not aggregated but enumerated—with
the result that what was not embraced by the
enumeration remained vested in the states
without change or impairment. . . . While
the states are not sovereign in the true sense
of that term, but only *quasi*-sovereign, yet
in respect of all powers reserved to them
they are supreme—"as independent of the
general government as that government within
its sphere is independent of the States." *The
Collector* v. *Day,* 11 Wall. 113, 124. And
since every addition to the national legislative
power to some extent detracts from or invades the power of the states, it is of vital
moment that, in order to preserve the fixed
balance intended by the Constitution, the
powers of the general government be not so
extended as to embrace any not within the
express terms of the several grants or the implications necessarily to be drawn therefrom.
It is no longer open to question that the
general government, unlike the states, *Hammer* v. *Dagenhart,* 247 U. S. 251, 275, possesses no *inherent* power in respect of the
internal affairs of the states; and emphatically
not with regard to legislation. The question
in respect of the inherent power of that government as to the external affairs of the
nation and in the field of international law is a
wholly different matter which it is not necessary now to consider.

The determination of the Framers Convention and the ratifying conventions to preserve
complete and unimpaired state self-government in all matters not committed to the
general government is one of the plainest facts
which emerges from the history of their deliberations. . . . Every journey to a forbidden end begins with the first step; and the
danger of such a step by the federal government in the direction of taking over the powers
of the states is that the end of the journey
may find the states so despoiled of their
powers, or—what may amount to the same
thing—so relieved of the responsibilities
which possession of the powers necessarily en-
joins, as to reduce them to little more than
geographical subdivisions of the national
domain. It is safe to say that if, when the
Constitution was under consideration, it had
been thought that any such danger lurked
behind its plain words, it would never have
been ratified. . . .

We have set forth, perhaps at unnecessary
length, the foregoing principles, because it
seemed necessary to do so in order to demonstrate that the general purposes which the
act recites, and which, therefore, unless the
recitals be disregarded, Congress undertook
to achieve, are beyond the power of Congress
except so far, and only so far, as they may
be realized by an exercise of some specific
power granted by the Constitution. Proceeding by a process of elimination, which it is
not necessary to follow in detail, we shall
find no grant of power which authorizes Congress to legislate in respect of these general
purposes unless it be found in the commerce
clause—and this we now consider.

Fifth. Since the validity of the act depends
upon whether it as a regulation of interstate
commerce, the nature and extent of the

power conferred upon Congress by the commerce clause becomes the determinative question in this branch of the case. . . . We first inquire, then— What is commerce? The term, as this court many times has said, is one of extensive import. No all-embracing definition has ever been formulated. The question is to be approached both affirmatively and negatively—that is to say, from the points of view as to what it includes and what it excludes.

In *Veazie et al.* v. *Moor,* 14 How. 568, this court, after saying that the phrase could never be applied to transactions wholly internal, significantly added: "Nor can it be properly concluded, that, because the products of domestic enterprise in agriculture or manufactures, or in the arts, may ultimately become the subjects of foreign commerce, that the control of the means or the encouragements by which enterprise is fostered and protected, is legitimately within the import of the phase *foreign commerce,* or fairly implied in any investiture of the power to regulate such commerce. A pretension as far reaching as this, would extend to contracts between citizen and citizen of the same State, would control the pursuits of the planter, the grazier, the manufacturer, the mechanic, the immense operations of the collieries and mines and furnaces of the country; for there is not one of these avocations, the results of which may not become the subjects of foreign commerce, and be borne either by turnpikes, canals, or railroads, from point to point within the several States, towards an ultimate destination, like the one above mentioned. . . ." . . .

That commodities produced or manufactured within a state are intended to be sold or transported outside the state does not render their production or manufacture subject to federal regulation under the commerce clause. . . .

We have seen that the word "commerce" is the equivalent of the phrase "intercourse for the purposes of trade." Plainly, the incidents leading up to and culminating in the mining of coal do not constitute such intercourse. The employment of men, the fixing of their wages, hours of labor and working conditions, the bargaining in respect to these things—whether carried on separately or collectively—each and all constitute intercourse for the purposes of production, not of trade. The latter is a thing apart from the relation of employer and employee, which in all producing occupations is purely local in character. Extraction of coal from the mine is the aim and the completed result of local activities. Commerce in the coal mined is not brought into being by force of these activities, but by negotiations, agreements, and circumstances entirely apart from production. Mining brings the subject matter of commerce into existence. Commerce disposes of it.

A consideration of the foregoing, and of many cases which might be added to those already cited, renders inescapable the conclusion that the effect of the labor provisions of the act, including those in respect of minimum wages wage agreements, collective bargaining, and the Labor Board and its powers, primarily falls upon production and not upon commerce; and confirms the further resulting conclusion that production is a purely local activity. It follows that none of these essential antecedents of production constitutes a transaction in or forms any part of interstate commerce. Everything which moves in interstate commerce has had a local origin. Without local production somewhere, interstate commerce, as now carried on, would practically disappear. Nevertheless, the local character of mining, of manufacturing and of crop growing is a fact, and remains a fact, whatever may be done with the products. . . .

But § 1 (the preamble) of the act now under review declares that all production and distribution of bituminous coal "bear upon and directly affect its interstate commerce"; and that regulation thereof is imperative for the protection of such commerce. The contention of the government is that the labor provisions of the act may be sustained in that view.

That the production of every commodity intended for interstate sale and transportation has some effect upon interstate commerce may be, if it has not already been, freely granted; and we are brought to the final and decisive inquiry, whether here that effect is direct, as the "preamble" recites, or indirect. The distinction is not formal, but substantial in the highest degree, as we pointed out in the *Schechter* case, *supra,* p. 546, *et seq.* . . .

Whether the effect of a given activity or condition is direct or indirect is not always easy to determine. The word "direct" implies

.hat the activity or condition invoked or blamed shall operate proximately—not mediately, remotely, or collaterally—to produce the effect. It connotes the absence of an efficient intervening agency or condition. And the extent of the effect bears no logical relation to its character. The distinction between a direct and an indirect effect turns, not upon the magnitude of either the cause or the effect, but entirely upon the manner in which the effect has been brought about. If the production by one man of a single ton of coal intended for interstate sale and shipment, and actually so sold and shipped, affects interstate commerce indirectly, the effect does not become direct by multiplying the tonnage, or increasing the number of men employed, or adding to the expense or complexities of the business, or by all combined. It is quite true that rules of law are sometimes qualified by considerations of degree, as the government argues. But the matter of degree has no bearing upon the question here, since that question is not— What is the *extent* of the local activity or condition, or the *extent* of the effect produced upon interstate commerce? but— What is the *relation* between the activity or condition and the effect?

Much stress is put upon the evils which come from the struggle between employers and employees over the matter of wages, working conditions, the right of collective bargaining, etc., and the resulting strikes, curtailment and irregularity of production and effect on prices; and it is insisted that interstate commerce is *greatly* affected thereby. But, in addition to what has just been said, the conclusive answer is that the evils are all local evils over which the federal government has no legislative control. The relation of employer and employee is a local relation. At common law, it is one of the domestic relations. The wages are paid for the doing of local work. Working conditions are obviously local conditions. The employees are not engaged in or about commerce, but exclusively in producing a commodity. And the controversies and evils, which it is the object of the act to regulate and minimize, are local controversies and evils affecting local work undertaken to accomplish that local result. Such effect as they may have upon commerce, however extensive it may be, is secondary and indirect.

An increase in the greatness of the effect adds to its importance. It does not alter its character.

The government's contentions in defense of the labor provisions are really disposed of adversely by our decision in the *Schechter* case, *supra*. The only perceptible difference between that case and this is that in the *Schechter* case, the federal power was asserted with respect to commodities which had come to rest after their interstate transportation; while here, the case deals with commodities at rest before interstate commerce has begun. That difference is without significance. . . . A reading of the entire opinion makes clear, what we now declare, that the want of power on the part of the federal government is the same whether the wages, hours of service, and working conditions, and the bargaining about them, are related to production before interstate commerce has begun, or to sale and distribution after it has ended.

Sixth. That the act, whatever it may be in form, in fact is compulsory clearly appears. . . .

Seventh. Finally, we are brought to the price-fixing provisions of the code. The necessity of considering the question of their constitutionality will depend upon whether they are separable from the labor provisions so that they can stand independently. Section 15 of the act provides:

"If any provision of this Act, or the application thereof to any person or circumstances, is held invalid, the remainder of the Act and the application of such provisions to other persons or circumstances shall not be affected thereby."

In the absence of such a provision, the presumption is that the legislature intends an act to be effective as an entirety—that is to say, the rule is against the multilation of a statute; and if any provision be unconstitutional, the presumption is that the remaining provisions fall with it. The effect of the statute is to reverse this presumption in favor of inseparability, and create the opposite one of separability. Under the non-statutory rule, the burden is upon the supporter of the legislation to show the separability of the provisions involved. Under the statutory rule, the burden is shifted to the assailant to show their inseparability. But under either rule, the determination, in the end, is reached by applying the same test—namely, What was the intent of the lawmakers? . . .

The primary contemplation of the act is stabilization of the industry through the regulation of labor *and* the regulation of prices; for, since both were adopted, we must conclude that both were thought essential. The regulations of labor on the one hand and prices on the other furnish mutual aid and support; and their associated force—not one or the other but both combined—was deemed by Congress to be necessary to achieve the end sought. The statutory mandate for a code upheld by two legs at once suggests the improbability that Congress would have assented to a code supported by only one.

This seems plain enough; for Congress must have been conscious of the fact that elimination of the labor provisions from the act would seriously impair, if not destroy, the force and usefulness of the price provisions. The interdependence of wages and prices is manifest. Approximately two-thirds of the cost of producing a ton of coal is represented by wages. Fair prices necessarily depend upon the cost of production; and since wages constitute so large a proportion of the cost, prices cannot be fixed with any proper relation to cost without taking into consideration this major element. If one of them becomes uncertain, uncertainty with respect to the other necessarily ensues. . . .

Thus wages, hours of labor, and working conditions are to be so adjusted as to effectuate the purposes of the act; and prices are to be so regulated as to *stabilize* wages, working conditions, and hours of labor which have been or are to be fixed under the labor provisions. The two are so woven together as to render the probability plain enough that uniform prices, in the opinion of Congress, could not be fairly fixed or effectively regulated, without also regulating these elements of labor which enter so largely into the cost of production.

The conclusion is unavoidable that the price-fixing provisions of the code are so related to and dependent upon the labor provisions as conditions, considerations or compensations, as to make it clearly probable that the latter being held bad, the former would not have been passed. The fall of the latter, therefore, carries down with it the former.

The price-fixing provisions of the code are thus disposed of without coming to the question of their constitutionality; but neither this disposition of the matter, nor anything we have said, is to be taken as indicating that the court is of opinion that these provisions, if separately enacted, could be sustained. . . .

The decrees must be reversed and the causes remanded for further consideration in conformity with this opinion.

It is so ordered.

Mr. Justice CARDOZO, dissenting.

My conclusions compendiously stated are these:

(a) Part II of the statute sets up a valid system of price-fixing as applied to transactions in interstate commerce and to those in intrastate commerce where interstate commerce is directly or intimately affected. The prevailing opinion holds nothing to the contrary.

(b) Part II, with is system of price-fixing, is separable from Part III, which contains the provisions as to labor considered and condemned in the opinion of the court.

(c) Part II being valid, the complainants are under a duty to come in under the code, and are subject to a penalty if they persist in a refusal. . . .

First: I am satisfied that the Act is within the power of the central government in so far as it provides for minimum and maximum prices upon sales of bituminous coal in the transactions of interstate commerce and in those of intrastate commerce where interstate commerce is directly or intimately affected. Whether it is valid also in other provisions that have been considered and condemned in the opinion of the court, I do not find it necessary to determine at this time. Silence must not be taken as importing acquiescence. Much would have to be written if the subject, even as thus restricted were to be explored through all its implications, historical and economic as well as strictly legal. The fact that the prevailing opinion leaves the price provisions open for consideration in the future makes it appropriate to forego a fullness of elaboration that might otherwise be necessary. As a system of price fixing the Act is challenged upon three grounds: (1) because the governance of prices is not within the commerce clause; (2) because it is a denial of due process forbidden by the Fifth Amendment; and (3) because the standards for administrative action are indefinite, with the result that there has been an unlawful delegation of legislative power.

(1) With reference to the first objection, the obvious and sufficient answer is, so far as the Act is directed to interstate transactions, that sales made in such conditions constitute interstate commerce, and do not merely "affect" it. To regulate the price for such transactions is to regulate commerce itself, and not alone its antecedent conditions or its ultimate consequences. The very act of sale is limited and governed. Prices in interstate transactions may not be regulated by the states. They must therefore be subject to the power of the nation unless they are to be withdrawn altogether from the governmental supervision. If such a vacuum were permitted, many a public evil incidental to interstate transactions would be left without a remedy. This does not mean, of course, that prices may be fixed for arbritrary reasons or in an arbitrary way. The commerce power of the nation is subject to the requirement of due process like the police power of the states. Heed must be given to similar considerations of social benefit or detriment in marking the division between reason and oppression. The evidence is overwhelmingly that Congress did not ignore those considerations in the adoption of this Act. What is to be said in that regard may conveniently be postponed to the part of the opinion dealing with the Fifth Amendment.

Regulation of prices being an exercise of the commerce power in respect of interstate transactions, the question remains whether it comes within that power as applied to intrastate sales where interstate prices are directly or intimately affected. Mining and agriculture and manufacture are not interstate commerce considered by themselves, yet their relation to that commerce may be such that for the protection of the one there is need to regulate the other. Sometimes it is said that the relation must be "direct" to bring that power into play. In many circumstances such a description will be sufficiently precise to meet the needs of the occasion. But a great principle of constitutional law is not susceptible of comprehensive statement in an adjective. The underlying thought is merely this, that "the law is not indifferent to considerations of degree." It cannot be indifferent to them without an expansion of the commerce clause that would absorb or imperil the reserved powers of the states. At times, as in the case cited, the waves of causation will have radiated so far that their undulatory motion, if discernible at all, will be too faint or obscure, too broken by cross-currents, to be heeded by the law. In such circumstances the holding is not directed at prices or wages considered in the abstract, but at prices or wages in particular conditions. The relation may be tenuous or the opposite according to the facts. Always the setting of the facts is to be viewed if one would know the closeness of the tie. Perhaps, if one group of adjectives is to be chosen in preference to another, "intimate" and "remote" will be found to be as good as any. At all events, "direct" and "indirect," even if accepted as sufficient, must not be read too narrowly. The power is as broad as the need that evokes it. . . .

Within rulings the most orthodox, the prices for intrastate sales of coal have so inescapable a relation to those for interstate sales that a system of regulation for transactions of the one class is necessary to give adequate protection to the system of regulation adopted for the other. . . .

What has been said in this regard is said with added certitude when complainants' business is considered in the light of the statistics exhibited in the several records. In No. 636, the Carter case, the complainant has admitted that "sustantially all" (over 97½%) of the sales of the Carter Company are made in interstate commerce. In No. 649 the percentages of intrastate sales are, for one of the complaining companies, twenty-five per cent, for another one per cent, and for most of the others two per cent or four. The Carter Company has its mines in West Virginia; the mines of the other companies are located in Kentucky. In each of those states, moreover, coal from other regions is purchased in large quantities, and is thus brought into competition with the coal locally produced. Plainly, it is impossible to say either from the statute itself or from any figures laid before us that interstate sales will not be prejudicially affected in West Virginia and Kentucky if intrastate prices are maintained on a lower level. . . .

(2) The commerce clause being accepted as a sufficient source of power, the next inquiry must be whether the power has been exercised consistently with the Fifth Amendment. In the pursuit of that inquiry, *Nebbia* v. *New York,* lays down the applicable principle. There a statute of New York prescribing a minimum price for milk was upheld against the objection that price fixing was forbidden by the Fourteenth Amendment. We found it a sufficient reason to uphold the challenged system that "the conditions or practices in an industry make unrestricted competition an inadequate safeguard of the consumer's interests, produce waste harmful to the public, threaten ultimately to cut off the supply of a commodity needed by the public, or portend the destruction of the industry itself."

All this may be said, and with equal, if not greater force, of the conditions and practices in the bituminous coal industry, not only at the enactment of this statute in August, 1935, but for many years before. Overproduction was at a point where free competition had been degraded into anarchy. Prices had been cut so low that profit had become impossible for all except a lucky handful. Wages came down along with prices and with profits. There were strikes, at times nation-wide in extent, at other times spreading over broad areas and many mines, with the accompaniment of violence and bloodshed and misery and bitter feeling. The sordid tale is unfolded in many a document and treatise. During the twenty-three years between 1913 and 1935, there were nineteen investigations or hearings by Congress or by specially created commissions with reference to conditions in the coal mines. The hope of betterment was faint unless the industry could be subjected to the compulsion of a code. In the weeks immediately preceding the passage of this Act the country was threatened once more with a strike of ominous proportions. The plight of the industry was not merely a menace to owners and to mine workers: it was and had long been a menace to the public, deeply concerned in a steady and uniform supply of a fuel so vital to the national economy.

Congress was not condemned to inaction in the face of price wars and wage wars so pregnant with disaster. Commerce had been choked and burdened; its normal flow had been diverted from one state to another; there had been bankruptcy and waste and ruin alike for capital and for labor. The liberty protected by the Fifth Amendment does not include the right to persist in this anarchic riot. . . . The free competition so often figured as a social goods imports order and moderation and a decent regard for the welfare of the group. There is testimony in these records, testimony even by the assailants of the statute, that only through a system of regulated prices can the industry be stabilized and set upon the road of orderly and peaceful progress. If further facts are looked for, they are narrated in the findings as well as in congressional reports and a mass of public records. After making every allowance for difference of opinion as to the most efficient cure, the student of the subject is confronted with the indisputable truth that there were ills to be corrected, and ills that had a direct relation to the maintenance of commerce among the states without friction or diversion. An evil existing, and also the power to correct it, the law-makers were at liberty to use their own discretion in the selection of the means.

(3) Finally, and in answer to the third objection to the statute in its price-fixing provisions, there has been no excessive delegation of legislative power. . . .

I am authorized to state that Mr. Justice BRANDEIS and Mr. Justice STONE join in this opinion.

508. THE REPUBLICAN PLATFORM OF 1936
June 11, 1936

(Proceedings of the 21st Republican National Convention, p. 136)

The Republican National Convention met in Cleveland, Ohio, June 9, 1936, nominated Gov. A. F. Landon of Kansas to the Presidency and Col. Frank Knox of Illinois to the Vice-Presidency, and adopted a platform whose theme was expressed in its opening words. The campaign that followed was bitter but scarcely exciting. In the November election the Republican candidates carried two states—Maine and Vermont, and polled a total of 16,681,913 votes. See, Alfred M. Landon, *America at the Crossroads;* D. Dumond, *Roosevelt to Roosevelt;* C. A. and M. R. Beard, *America in Midpassage.*

America is in peril. The welfare of American men and women and the future of our youth are at stake. We dedicate ourselves to the preservation of their political liberty, their individual opportunity and their character as free citizens, which today for the first time are threatened by Government itself.

For three long years the New Deal Administration has dishonored American traditions and flagrantly betrayed the pledges upon which the Democratic Party sought and received public support.

The powers of Congress have been usurped by the President.

The integrity and authority of the Supreme Court have been flouted.

The rights and liberties of American citizens have been violated.

Regulated monopoly has displaced free enterprise.

The New Deal Administration constantly seeks to usurp the rights reserved to the States and to the people.

It has insisted on the passage of laws contrary to the Constitution.

It has intimidated witnesses and interfered with the right of petition.

It has dishonored our country by repudiating its most sacred obligations.

It has been guilty of frightful waste and extravagance, using public funds for partisan political purposes.

It has promoted investigations to harass and intimidate American citizens, at the same time denying investigations into its own improper expenditures.

It has created a vast multitude of new offices, filled them with its favorites, set up a centralized bureaucracy, and sent out swarms of inspectors to harass our people.

It had bred fear and hesitation in commerce and industry, thus discouraging new enterprises, preventing employment and prolonging the depression.

It secretly has made tariff agreements with our foreign competitors, flooding our markets with foreign commodities.

It has coerced and intimidated voters by withholding relief from those opposing its tyrannical policies.

It has destroyed the morale of many of our people and made them dependent upon Government.

Appeals to passion and class prejudice have replaced reason and tolerance.

To a free people these actions are insufferable. This campaign cannot be waged on the traditional differences between the Republican and Democratic parties. The responsibility of this election transcends all previous political divisions. We invite all Americans, irrespective of party, to join us in defense of American institutions.

CONSTITUTIONAL GOVERNMENT AND FREE ENTERPRISE

WE PLEDGE OURSELVES:

1. To maintain the American system of constitutional and local self government, and to resist all attempts to impair the authority of the Supreme Court of the United States, the final protector of the rights of our citizens against the arbitrary encroachments of the legislative and executive branches of Government. There can be no individual liberty without an independent judiciary.

2. To preserve the American system of free enterprise, private competition, and equality of opportunity, and to seek its constant betterment in the interests of all.

REEMPLOYMENT

The only permanent solution of the unemployment problem is the absorption of the unemployed by industry and agriculture. To that end, we advocate:

Removal of restricitons on production.

Abandonment of all New Deal policies that raise production costs, increase the cost of living, and thereby restrict buying, reduce volume and prevent reemployment.

Encouragement instead of hindrance to legitimate business.

Withdrawal of Government from competition with private payrolls.

Elimination of unnecessary and hampering regulations.

Adoption of such policies as will furnish a chance for individual enterprise, industrial expansion, and the restoration of jobs.

RELIEF

The necessities of life must be provided for the needy, and hope must be restored pending recovery. The administration of relief is a major failure of the New Deal. It has been faithless to those who most deserve our sympathy. To end confusion, partisanship, waste and incompetence,

WE PLEDGE:

1. The return of responsibility for relief administration to non-political local agencies familiar with community problems.
2. Federal grants-in-aid to the States and Territories while the need exists, upon compliance with these conditions: (a) a fair proportion of the total relief burden to be provided from the revenues of States and local governments; (b) all engaged in relief administration to be selected on the basis of merit and fitness; (c) adequate provision to be made for the encouragement of those persons who are trying to become self-supporting.
3. Undertaking of Federal public works only on their merits and separate from the administration of relief.
4. A prompt determination of the facts concerning relief and unemployment.

SECURITY

Real security will be possible only when our productive capacity is sufficient to furnish a decent standard of living for all American families and to provide a surplus for future needs and contingencies. For the attainment of that ultimate objective, we look to the energy, self-reliance and character of our people, and to our system of free enterprise.

Society has an obligation to promote the security of the people, by affording some measure of protection against involuntary unemployment and dependency in old age. The New Deal policies, while purporting to provide social security, have, in fact, endangered it.

We propose a system of old age security, . . .

We propose to encourage adoption by the States and Territories of honest and practical measures for meeting the problems of unemployment insurance.

The unemployment insurance and old age annuity sections of the present Social Security Act are unworkable and deny benefits to about two-thirds of our adult population, including professional men and women and all those engaged in agriculture and domestic service, and the self employed, while imposing heavy tax burdens upon all. The so-called reserve fund estimated at forty-seven billion dollars for old age insurance is no reserve at all, because the fund will contain nothing but the Government's promise to pay, while the taxes collected in the guise of premiums will be wasted by the Government in reckless and extravagant political schemes.

LABOR

The welfare of labor rests upon increased production and the prevention of exploitation. We pledge ourselves to:

Protect the right of labor to organize and to bargain collectively through representatives of its own choosing without interference from any source.

Prevent governmental job holders from exercising autocratic powers over labor.

Support the adoption of State laws and interstate compacts to abolish sweatshops and child labor, and to protect women and children with respect to maximum hours, minimum wages and working conditions. We believe that this can be done within the Constitution as it now stands.

AGRICULTURE

The farm problem is an economic and social, not a partisan problem, and we propose to treat it accordingly. . . .

Our paramount object is to protect and foster the family type of farm, traditional in American life, and to promote policies which will bring about an adjustment of agriculture to meet the needs of domestic and foreign markets. As an emergency measure, during the agricultural depression, Federal benefit payments or grants-in-aid when administered within the means of the Federal Government are consistent with a balanced budget.

WE PROPOSE:

1. To facilitate economical production and

increased consumption on a basis of abundance instead of scarcity.

2. A national land-use program, including the acquisition of abandoned and nonproductive farm lands by voluntary sale or lease, subject to approval of the legislative and executive branches of the States concerned, and the devotion of such land to appropriate public use, such as watershed protection and flood prevention, reforestation, recreation, and conservation of wild life.

3. That an agricultural policy be pursued for the protection and restoration of the land resources, designed to bring about such a balance between soil-building and soil-depleting crops as will permanently insure productivity, with reasonable benefits to cooperating farmers on family-type farms, but so regulated as to eliminate the New Deal's destructive policy towards the dairy and live-stock industries.

4. To extend experimental aid to farmers developing new crops suited to our soil and climate.

5. To promote the industrial use of farm products by applied science.

6. To protect the American farmer against the importation of all livestock, dairy, and agricultural products, substitutes therefor, and derivatives therefrom, which will depress American farm prices.

7. To provide effective quarantine against imported livestock, dairy and other farm products from countries which do not impose health and sanitary regulations fully equal to those required of our own producers.

8. To provide for ample farm credit at rates as low as those enjoyed by other industries, including commodity and livestock loans, and preference in land loans to the farmer acquiring or refinancing a farm as a home.

9. To provide for decentralized, non-partisan control of the Farm Credit Administration and the election by National Farm Loan Associations of at least one-half of each Board of Directors of the Federal Land Banks, and thereby remove these institutions from politics.

10. To provide, in the case of agricultural products of which there are exportable surpluses, the payment of reasonable benefits upon the domestically consumed portion of such crops in order to make the tariff effective. These payments are to be limited to the production level of the family-type farm.

11. To encourage and further develop cooperative marketing.

12. To furnish Government assistance in disposing of surpluses in foreign trade by bargaining for foreign markets selectively by countries both as to exports and imports. We strenuously oppose so-called reciprocal treaties which trade off the American farmer.

13. To give every reasonable assistance to producers in areas suffering from temporary disaster, so that they may regain and maintain a self-supporting status.

TARIFF

Nearly sixty per cent of all imports into the United States are now free of duty. The other forty per cent of imports compete directly with the product of our industry. We would keep on the free list all products not grown or produced in the United States in commercial quantites. As to all commodities that commercially compete with our farms, our forests, our mines, our fisheries, our oil wells, our labor and our industries, sufficient protection should be maintained at all times to defend the American farmer and the American wage earner from the destructive competition emanating from the subsidies of foreign Governments and the imports from low-wage and depreciated-currency countries.

We will repeal the present Reciprocal Trade Agreement law. . . .

We will restore the principle of the flexible tariff in order to meet changing economic conditions here and abroad and broaden by careful definition the powers of the Tariff Commission in order to extend this policy along non-partisan lines.

We will adjust tariffs with a view to promoting international trade, the stabilization of currencies, and the attainment of a proper balance between agriculture and industry.

We condemn the secret negotiation of reciprocal trade treaties without public hearing or legislative approval.

MONOPOLIES

A private monopoly is indefensible and intolerable. It menaces and, if continued, will utterly destroy constitutional government and the liberty of the citizen.

We favor the vigorous enforcement of the criminal laws, as well as the civil laws, against monopolies and trusts and their officials, and we demand the enactment of such additional legislation as is necessary to make it impossible for private monopoly to exist in the United States.

We will employ the full powers of the Government to the end that monopoly shall be eliminated and that free enterprise shall be fully restored and maintained.

REGULATION OF BUSINESS

We recognize the existence of a field within which governmental regulation is desirable and salutary. The authority to regulate should be vested in an independent tribunal acting under clear and specific laws establishing definite standards. Their determinations on law and facts should be subject to review by the Courts. We favor Federal regulation, within the Constitution, of the marketing of securities to protect investors. We favor also Federal regulation of the interstate activities of public utilities.

CIVIL SERVICE

Under the New Deal, official authority has been given to inexperienced and incompetent persons. The Civil Service has been sacrificed to create a national political machine. As a result the Federal Government has never presented such a picture of confusion and inefficiency.

We pledge ourselves to the merit system, virtually destroyed by New Deal spoilsmen. It should be restored, improved and extended. . . .

GOVERNMENT FINANCE

The New Deal Administration has been characterized by shameful waste and general financial irresponsibility. It has piled deficit upon deficit. It threatens national bankruptcy and the destruction through inflation of insurance policies and savings bank deposits.

WE PLEDGE OURSELVES TO:

Stop the folly of uncontrolled spending.

Balance the budget—not by increasing taxes but by cutting expenditures, drastically and immediately.

Revise the Federal tax system and coordinate it with State and local tax systems.

Use the taxing power for raising revenue and not for punitive or political purposes.

MONEY AND BANKING

We advocate a sound currency to be preserved at all hazards.

The first requisite to a sound and stable currency is a balanced budget.

We oppose further devaluation of the dollar.

We will restore to the Congress the authority lodged with it by the Constitution to coin money and regulate the value thereof by repealing all the laws delegating this authority to the Executive.

We will cooperate with other countries toward stabilization of currencies as soon as we can do so with due regard for our national interests and as soon as other nations have sufficient stability to justify such action.

FOREIGN AFFAIRS

We pledge ourselves to promote and maintain peace by all honorable means not leading to foreign alliances or political commitments.

Obedient to the traditional foreign policy of America and to the repeatedly expressed will of the American people, we pledge that America shall not become a member of the League of Nations nor of the World Court nor shall America take on any entangling alliances in foreign affairs.

We shall promote, as the best means of securing and maintaining peace by the pacific settlement of disputes, the great cause of international arbitration through the establishment of free, independent tribunals, which shall determine such disputes in accordance with law, equity and justice.

NATIONAL DEFENSE

We favor an army and navy, including air forces, adequate for our National Defense.

We will cooperate with other nations in the limitation of armaments and control of traffic in arms.

BILL OF RIGHTS

We pledge ourselves to preserve, protect and defend, against all intimidation and threat, freedom of religion, speech, press and radio; and the right of assembly and petition and immunity from unreasonable searches and seizures.

We offer the abiding security of a government of laws as against the autocratic perils of a government of men.

FURTHERMORE

1. We favor the construction by the Federal Government of head-water storage basins to prevent floods, subject to the approval of the legislative and executive branches of the government of the States whose lands are concerned. . . .

5. We shall use every effort to collect the war debt due us from foreign countries amounting to $12,000,000,000—one-third of our national debt. No effort has been made by the present administration even to reopen negotiations.

6. We are opposed to legislation which discriminates against women in Federal and State employment.

CONCLUSION

We assume the obligations and duties imposed upon Government by modern conditions. We affirm our unalterable conviction that, in the future as in the past, the fate of the nation will depend, not so much on the wisdom and power of Government, as on the character and virtue, self-reliance, industry and thrift of the people and on their willingness to meet the responsibilities essential to the preservation of a free society.

Finally, as our party affirmed in its first Platform in 1856: "Believing that the spirit of our institutions as well as the Constitution of our country guarantees liberty of conscience and equality of rights among our citizens, we oppose all legislation tending to impair them," and "we invite the affiliation and cooperation of the men of all parties, however differing from us in other respects, in support of the principles herein declared."

The acceptance of the nomination tendered by this Convention carries with it, as a matter of private honor and public faith, an undertaking by each candidate to be true to the principles and program herein set forth.

509. THE DEMOCRATIC PLATFORM OF 1936
June 25, 1936

(*Proceedings* of the Democratic National Convention, 1936, p. 192)

The Democratic National Convention met in Philadelphia June 23, 1936, renominated President Roosevelt and Vice-President Garner, and adopted a platform reaffirming the New Deal. In the ensuing election Mr. Roosevelt carried 46 states, polled 523 electoral and 27,751,612 popular votes. Roosevelt's campaign speeches can be found in his *Public Papers and Addresses*, Vol. V. See also, D. Dumond, *Roosevelt to Roosevelt; C. A. and M. R. Beard, America in Midpassage.*

THE DEMOCRATIC PLATFORM

Adopted by the Democratic Party, in Convention, at Philadelphia, June, 1936

We hold this truth to be self-evident—that the test of a representative government is its ability to promote the safety and happiness of the people.

We hold this truth to be self-evident—that twelve years of Republican leadership left our nation sorely stricken in body, mind and

spirit; and that three years of Democratic leadership have put it back on the road to restored health and prosperity.

We hold this truth to be self-evident—that twelve years of Republican surrender of the dictatorship of a privileged few have been supplanted by a Democratic leadership which has returned the people themselves to the place of authority, and has revived in them new faith and restored the hope which they had almost lost.

We hold this truth to be self-evident—that this three-year recovery in all the basic values of life and the reestablishment of the American way of living has been brought about by humanizing the policies of the Federal Government as they affect the personal, financial, industrial and agricultural well-being of the American people.

We hold this truth to be self-evident—that government in a modern civilization has certain inescapable obligations to its citizens, among which are:

(1) Protection of the family and the home.

(2) Establishment of a democracy of opportunity for all the people.

(3) Aid to those overtaken by disaster.

These obligations, neglected through twelve years of the old leadership, have once more been recognized by American Government. Under the new leadership they will never be neglected.

FOR THE PROTECTION OF THE FAMILY AND THE HOME

. . . .

SAVINGS AND INVESTMENT

(2) We have safeguarded the thrift of our citizens by restraining those who would gamble with other people's savings, by requiring truth in the sale of securities; by putting the brakes upon the use of credit for speculation; by outlawing the manipulation of prices in stock and commodity markets; by curbing the overweening power and unholy practices of utility holding companies; by insuring fifty million banks accounts.

OLD AGE AND SOCIAL SECURITY

(3) We have built foundations for the security of those who are faced with the hazards of unemployment and old age; for the orphaned, the crippled and the blind. On the foundation of the Social Security Act we are determined to erect a structure of economic security for all our people, making sure that this benefit shall keep step with the ever-increasing capacity of America to provide a high standard of living for all its citizens.

CONSUMER

(4) We will act to secure to the consumer fair value, honest sales and a decreased spread between the price he pays and the price the producer receives.

RURAL ELECTRIFICATION

(5) This administration has fostered power rate yardsticks in the Tennessee Valley and in several other parts of the nation. As a result electricity has been made available to the people at a lower rate. We will continue to promote plans for rural electrification and for cheap power by means of the yardstick method.

HOUSING

(6) We maintain that our people are entitled to decent, adequate housing at a price which they can afford. In the last three years the Federal Government, having saved more than two million homes from foreclosure, has taken the first steps in our history to provide decent housing for people of meagre incomes. We believe every encouragement should be given to the building of new homes by private enterprise; and that the Government should steadily extend its housing program toward the goal of adequate housing for those forced through economic necessities to live in unhealthy and slum conditions.

VETERANS

(7) We shall continue just treatment of our war veterans and their dependents.

FOR THE ESTABLISHMENT OF A DEMOCRACY OF OPPORTUNITY

AGRICULTURE

We have taken the farmers off the road to ruin.

We have kept our pledge to agriculture to use all available means to raise farm income towards its pre-war purchasing power. . . .

By Federal legislation we have reduced the farmer's indebtedness and doubled his net income. In cooperation with the States and through the farmers' own committees, we are restoring the fertility of his land and checking the erosion of his soil. We are bringing electricity and good roads to his home.

We shall continue to improve the soil conservation and domestic allotment program with payments to farmers. . . .

We recognize the gravity of the evils of farm tenancy, and we pledge the full cooperation of the Government in the refinancing of farm indebtedness at the lowest possible rates of interest and over a long term of years.

We favor the production of all the market will absorb, both at home and abroad, plus a reserve supply sufficient to insure fair prices to consumers; we favor judicious commodity loans on seasonal surpluses; and we favor assistance within Federal authority to enable farmers to adjust and balance production with demand, at a fair profit to the farmers.

We favor encouragement of sound, practical farm cooperatives.

By the purchase and retirement of ten million acres of sub-marginal land, and assistance to those attempting to eke out an existence upon it, we have made a good beginning toward proper land use and rural rehabilitation.

The farmer has been returned to the road to freedom and prosperity. We will keep him on that road.

LABOR

We have given the army of America's industrial workers something more substantial than the Republicans' dinner pail full of promises. We have increased the worker's pay and shortened his hours; we have undertaken to put an end to the sweated labor of his wife and children; we have written into the law of the land his right to collective bargaining and self-organization free from the interference of employers; we have provided Federal machinery for the peaceful settlement of labor disputes.

We will continue to protect the worker and we will guard his rights, both as wage-earner and consumer, in the production and consumption of all commodities, including coal and water power and other natural-resource products. . . .

BUSINESS

We have taken the American business man out of the red. We have saved his bank and given it a sounder foundation; we have extended credit; we have lowered interest rates; we have undertaken to free him from the ravages of cut-throat competition. . . .

YOUTH

We have aided youth to stay in school; given them constructive occupation; opened the door to opportunity which twelve years of Republican neglect had closed. . . .

MONOPOLY AND CONCENTRATION OF ECONOMIC POWER

Monopolies and the concentration of economic power, the creation of Republican rule and privilege, continue to be the master of the producer, the exploiter of the consumer, and the enemy of the independent operator. This is a problem challenging the unceasing effort of untrammeled public officials in every branch of the Government. We pledge vigorously and fearlessly to enforce the criminal and civil provisions of the existing anti-trust laws, and to the extent that their effectiveness has been weakened by new corporate devices or judicial construction, we propose by law to restore their efficacy in stamping out monopolistic practices and the concentration of economic power. . . .

UNEMPLOYMENT

We believe that unemployment is a national problem, and that it is an inescapable obligational way. . . . Where business fails to supply such employment, we believe that work at prevailing wages should be provided in co-operation with State and local governments on useful public projects, to the end that the national wealth may be increased, the skill and energy of the worker may be utilized, his morale maintained, and the unemployed assured the opportunity to earn the necessities of life.

THE CONSTITUTION

The Republican platform proposes to meet many pressing national problems solely by action of the separate States. We know that drought, dust storms, floods, minimum wages, maximum hours, child labor and working conditions in industry, monopolistic and unfair business practices cannot be adequately handled exclusively by 48 separate State legislatures, 48 separate State administrations and 48 separate State courts. Transactions and activities which inevitably overflow State boundaries call for both State and Federal treatment.

We have sought and will continue to seek to meet these problems through legislation within the Constitution.

If these problems cannot be effectively solved by legislation within the Constitution, we shall seek such clarifying amendment as will assure to the legislatures of the several States and to the Congress of the United States, each within its proper jurisdiction, the power to enact those laws which the State and Federal legislatures, within their respective spheres, shall find necessary in order adequately to regulate commerce, protect public health and safety and safeguard economic security. Thus we propose to maintain the letter and spirit of the Constitution.

THE MERIT SYSTEM IN GOVERNMENT

For the protection of government itself and promotion of its efficiency, we pledge the immediate extension of the merit system through the classified civil service—which was first established and fostered under Democratic auspices—to all non-policy-making positions in the Federal service.

We shall subject to the civil service law all continuing positions which, because of the emergency, have been exempt from its operation.

CIVIL LIBERTIES

We shall continue to guard the freedom of speech, press, radio, religion and assembly which our Constitution guarantees; with equal rights to all and special privileges to none.

GOVERNMENT FINANCE

The Administration has stopped deflation, restored values and enabled business to go ahead with confidence.

When national income shrinks, government income is imperilled. In reviving national income, we have fortified government finance. We have raised the public credit to a position of unsurpassed security. The interest rate on Government bonds has been reduced to the lowest point in twenty-eight years. The same Government bonds which in 1932 sold under eighty-three are now selling over 104.

We approve the objective of a permanently sound currency so stabilized as to prevent the former wide fluctuations in value which injured in turn producers, debtors, and property owners on the one hand, and wage-earners and creditors on the other, a currency which will permit full utilization of the country's resources. We assert that today we have the soundest currency in the world.

We are determined to reduce the expenses of government. . . . Our retrenchment, tax and recovery programs thus reflect our firm determination to achieve a balanced budget and the reduction of the national debt at the earliest possible moment.

FOREIGN POLICY

In our relationship with other nations, this Government will continue to extend the policy of the Good Neighbor. We reaffirm our opposition to war as an instrument of national policy, and declare that disputes between nations should be settled by peaceful means. We shall continue to observe a true neutrality in the disputes of others; to be prepared, resolutely to resist aggression against ourselves; to work for peace and to take the profits out of war; to guard against being drawn, by political commitments, international banking or private trading, into any war which may develop anywhere.

We shall continue to foster the increase in our foreign trade which has been achieved by this administration; to seek by mutual agreement the lowering of those tariff barriers, quotas and embargoes which have been raised against our exports of agricultural and industrial products; but continue as in the past to give adequate protection to our farmers and manufacturers against unfair competition or the dumping on our shores of commodities and goods produced abroad by cheap labor or subsidized by foreign governments.

THE ISSUE

The issue in this election is plain. The American people are called upon to choose between a Republican administration that has and would again regiment them in the service of privileged groups and a Democratic administration dedicated to the establishment of equal economic opportunity for all our people.

We have faith in the destiny of our nation. We are sufficiently endowed with natural resources and with productive capacity to provide for all a quality of life that meets the standards of real Americanism.

Dedicated to a government of liberal American principles, we are determined to oppose equally, the despotism of Communism and the menace of concealed Facism.

We hold this final truth to be self-evident— that the interests, the security and the happiness of the people of the United States of America can be perpetuated only under the democratic government as conceived by the founders of our nation.

510. UNITED STATES v. CURTISS-WRIGHT EXPORT CORP.
299 U. S. 304
1936

Appeal from the District Court of the U. S. for the Southern District of New York. This case involved the question of the delegation of powers in the realm of foreign affairs, and furnished the occasion for an illuminating dissertation on the nature of the American Union. The facts of the case are set forth in the decision. See W. E. Binkley, *The Powers of the President;* Q. Wright, *The Control of American Foreign Relations;* E. S. Corwin, *The President's Control of Foreign Relations.*

SUTHERLAND, J. On January 27, 1936, an indictment was returned in the court below, the first count of which charges that appellees, beginning with the 29th day of May, 1934, conspired to sell in the United States certain arms of war, namely fifteen machine guns, to Bolivia, a country then engaged in armed conflict in the Chaco, in violation of the Joint Resolution of Congress approved May 28, 1934, and the provisions of a proclamation issued on the same day by the President of the United States pursuant to authority conferred by Sec. 1 of the resolution. In pursuance of the conspiracy, the commission of certain overt acts was alleged, details of which need not be stated. The Joint Resolution follows:

"Resolved by the Senate and House of Representatives of the United States of America in Congress assembled, That if the President finds that the prohibition of the sale of arms and munitions of war in the United States to those countries now engaged in armed conflict in the Chaco may contribute to the reestablishment of peace between those countries, and if after consultation with the governments of other American Republics and with their cooperation, as well as that of such other governments as he may deem necessary, he makes proclamation to that effect, it shall be unlawful to sell, except under such limitations and exceptions as the President prescribes, any arms or munitions or war in any place in the United States to the countries now engaged in that armed conflict, or to any person, company, or association acting in the interest of either country, until otherwise ordered by the President or by Congress.

"Sec. 2. Whoever sells any arms or munitions of war in violation of section 1 shall, on conviction, be punished by a fine not exceeding $10,000 or by imprisonment not exceeding two years, or both."

The President's proclamation, after reciting the terms of the Joint Resolution, declares:

"Now, therefore, I Franklin D. Roosevelt, President of the United States of America, acting under and by virtue of the authority conferred in me by the said joint resolution of Congress, do hereby declare and proclaim that I have found that the prohibition of the sale of arms and munitions of war in the United States to those countries now engaged in armed conflict in the Chaco may contribute to the reestablishment of peace between those countries, and that I have consulted with the governments of other American Republics and have been assured of the cooperation of such governments as I have deemed necessary as contemplated by the said joint resolution; and I do hereby admonish all citizens of the United States and every person to abstain from every violation of the provisions of the joint resolution above set forth, hereby made applicable to Bolivia and Paraguay, and I do hereby warn them that all violations of such provisions will be rigorously prosecuted. . . .

On November 14, 1935, this proclamation was revoked in the following termns: . . .

Appellees severally demurred to the first count of the indictment on the grounds (1) that it did not charge facts sufficient to show the commission by appellees of any offense against any law of the United States; . . .

The court below sustained the demurrers upon the first point, . . . The government appealed to this court under the provisions of the Criminal Appeals Act of March 2, 1907. . . .

First. It is contended that by the Joint Resolution, the going into effect and continued operation of the resolution was conditioned (a) upon the President's judgment as to its beneficial effect 'ipon the reestablishment of peace between the countries engaged in armed conflict in the Chaco; (b) upon the making of a proclamation, which was left to his unfettered discretion, thus constituting an attempted substitution of the President's will for that of Congress; (c) upon the making of a proclamation putting an end to the operation of the resolution, which again was left to the President's unfettered discretion; and (d) further, that the extent of its operation in particular cases was subject to limitation and exception by the President, controlled by no standard. In each of these particulars, appellees urge that Congress abdicated its essential functions and delegated them to the Executive.

Whether, if the Joint Resolution had related solely to internal affairs it would be open to the challenge that it constituted an unlawful delegation of legislative power to the Executive, we find it unnecessary to determine. The whole aim of the resolution is to affect a situation entirely external to the United States, and falling within the category of foreign affairs. The determination which we are called to make, therefore, is whether the Joint Resolution, as applied to that situation, is vulnerable to attack under the rule that forbids a delegation of the law-making power. In other words, assuming (but not deciding) that the challenged delegation, if it were confined to internal affairs, would be invalid, may it nevertheless be sustained on the ground that its exclusive aim is to afford a remedy for a hurtful condition within foreign territory?

It will contribute to the elucidation of the question if we first consider the differences between the powers of the federal government in respect of foreign or external affairs and those in respect of domestic or internal affairs. That there are differences between them, and that these differences are fundamental, may not be doubted.

The two classes of powers are different, both in respect of their origin and their nature. The broad statement that the federal government can exercise no powers except those specifically enumerated in the Constitution, and such implied powers as are necessary and proper to carry into effect the enumerated powers, is categorically true only in respect of our internal affairs. In that field, the primary purpose of the Constitution was to carve from the general mass of legislative powers *then possessed by the states* such portions as it was thought desirable to vest in the federal government, leaving those not included in the enumeration still in the States. *Carter* v. *Carter Coal Co.*, 298 U. S. 238, 294. That this doctrine applies only to powers which the states had, is self evident. And since the states severally never possessed international powers, such powers could not have been carved from the mass of state powers but obviously were transmitted to the United States from some other source. During the colonial period, those powers were possessed exclusively by and were entirely under the control of the Crown. By the Declaration of Independence, "the Representatives of the United States of America" declared the United (not the several) Colonies to be free and independent states, and as such to have "full Power to levy War, conclude Peace, contract Alliances, establish Commerce and to do all other Acts and Things which Independent States may of right do."

As a result of the separation from Great Britain by the colonies acting as a unit, the powers of external sovereignty passed from the Crown not to the colonies severally, but to the colonies in their collective and corporate capacity as the United States of America. Even before the Declaration, the colonies were a unit in foreign affairs, acting through a common agency—namely the Continental Congress, composed of delegates from the thirteen colonies. That agency exercised the powers of war and peace, raised an army, created a navy, and finally adopted the Declaration of Independence. Rulers come and go; governments end and forms of government change; but sovereignty survives. A political society cannot endure without a supreme will somewhere. Sovereignty is never held in suspense. When, therefore, the external sovereignty of Great Britain in respect of the colonies ceased, it immediately passed to the Union. *See Penhallow* v. *Doane*, 3 Dall. 54, 80–81. That fact was given practical application almost at once. The treaty of peace, made on September 23, 1783, was concluded between his Britanic Majesty and the "United States of America." 8 Stat.—European Treaties—80.

The Union existed before the Constitution, which was ordained and established among other things to form "a more perfect Union."

Prior to that event, it is clear that the Union, declared by the Articles of Confederation to be "perpetual," was the sole possessor of external sovereignty and in the Union it remained without change save in so far as the Constitution in express terms qualified its exercise. The Framers' Convention was called and exerted its powers upon the irrefutable postulate that though the states were several their people in respect of foreign affairs were one. . . .

It results that the investment of the federal government with the powers of external sovereignty did not depend upon the affirmative grants of the Constitution. The powers to declare and wage war, to conclude peace, to make treaties, to maintain diplomatic relations with other sovereignties, if they had never been mentioned in the Constitution, would have vested in the federal government as necessary concomitants of nationality. Neither the Constitution nor the laws passed in pursuance of it have any force in foreign territory unless in respect of our own citizens; and operations of the nation in such territory must be governed by treaties, international understandings and compacts, and the principles of international law. As a member of the family of nations, the right and power of the United States in that field are equal to the right and power of the other members of the international family. Otherwise, the United States is not completely sovereign. The power to acquire territory by discovery and occupation, the power to expel undesirable aliens, the power to make such international agreements as do not constitute treaties in the constitutional sense; none of which is expressly affirmed by the Constitution, nevertheless exist as inherently inseparable from the conception of nationality. This the court recognized, and in each of the cases cited found the warrant for its conclusions not in the provisions of the Constitution, but in the law of nations. . . .

Not only, as we have shown, is the federal power over external affairs in origin and essential character different from that over internal affairs, but participation in the exercise of the power is significantly limited. In this vast external realm, with its important, complicated, delicate and manifold problems, the President alone has the power to speak or listen as a representative of the nation. He *makes* treaties with the advice and consent of the Senate; but he alone negotiates. Into the field of negotiation the Senate cannot intrude; and Congress itself is powerless to invade it. . . .

It is important to bear in mind that we are here dealing not along with an authority vested in the President by an exertion of legislative power, but with such an authority plus the very delicate, plenary and exclusive power of the President as the sole organ of the federal government in the field of international relations—a power which does not require as a basis for its exercise an act of Congress, but which, of course, like every other governmental power, must be exercised in subordination to the applicable provisions of the Constitution. It is quite apparent that if, in the maintenance of our international relations, embarrassment—perhaps serious embarrassment—is to be avoided and success for our aims achieved, congressional legislation which is to be made effective through negotiation and inquiry within the international field must often accord to the President a degree of discretion and freedom from statutory restriction which would not be admissible were domestic affairs alone involved. Moreover he, not Congress, has the better opportunity of knowing the conditions which prevail in foreign countries, and especially is this true in time of war. He has his confidential sources of information. He has his agents in the form of diplomatic, consular and other officials. Secrecy in respect of information gathered by them may be highly necessary, and the premature disclosure of it productive of harmful results. Indeed, so clearly is this true that the first President refused to accede to a request to lay before the House of Representatives the instructions, correspondence and documents relating to the negotiation of the Jay Treaty. . . .

In the light of the foregoing observations, it is evident that this court should not be in haste to apply a general rule which will have the effect of condemning legislation like that under review as constituting an unlawful delegation of legislative power. The principles which justify such legislation find overwhelming support in the unbroken legislative practice which has prevailed almost from the inception of the national government to the present day.

Let us examine, in chronological order, the acts of legislation which warrant this conclusion: . . . [cites numerous Congressional acts.]

It well may be assumed that these legislative precedents were in mind when Congress passed the joint resolutions of April 22, 1898, March 14, 1912, and January 31, 1922, to prohibit the export of coal or other war material. . . .

We had occasion to review these embargo and kindred acts in connection with an exhaustive discussion of the general subject of delegation of legislative power in a recent case, *Panama Refining Co.* v. *Ryan,* 293 U. S. 388, 421–422, and in justifying such acts, pointed out that they confided to the President "an authority which was cognate to the conduct by him of the foreign relations of the government."

The result of holding that the joint resolution here under attack is void and unenforceable as constituting an unlawful delegation of legislative power would be to stamp this multitude of comparable acts and resolutions as likewise invalid. And while this court may not, and should not, hesitate to declare acts of Congress, however many times repeated, to be unconstitutional if beyond all rational doubt it finds them to be so, an impressive array of legislation such as we have just set forth, enacted by nearly every Congress from the beginning of our national existence to the present day, must be given unusual weight in the process of reaching a correct determination of the problem. A legislative practice such as we have here, evidenced not by only occasional instances, but marked by the movement of a steady stream for a century and a half of time, goes a long way in the direction of proving the presence of unassailable ground for the constitutionality of the practice, to be found in the origin and history of the power involved, or in its nature or in both combined. . . .

The uniform, long-continued and undisputed legislative practice just disclosed rests upon an admissible view of the Constitution which, even if the practice found far less support in principle than we think it does, we should not feel at liberty at this late day to disturb. . . .

The judgment of the court below must be reversed and the cause remanded for further proceedings in accordance with the foregoing opinion.

Reversed.

McREYNOLDS, J. dissented.

511. DE JONGE v. OREGON
299 U. S. 353
1937

Appeal from the Supreme Court of Oregon. The extent to which the due process clause of the Fourteenth Amendment has come to embrace the guarantees of the first eight amendments is here illustrated. The facts of the case are set forth in the opinion of the Court. See, Z. Chafee, *Freedom of Speech;* C. Warren, "The new 'Liberty' under the Fourteenth Amendment," 39 Harv. L. Rev. 431; Spencer, "Criminal Syndicalism—De Jonge v. Oregon," 16 Ore. L. Rev. 278; "The Supreme Court as Protector of Political Minorities," 46 Yale L. J. 862; Jarrett and Mund, "The Right of Assembly," 9 N. Y. U. L. Qt. Rev. 1; and the note on the comparable Hague Injunction case in 48 Yale L. J., 257.

HUGHES, C. J. Appellant, Dirk De Jorge, was indicted in Multnomah County, Oregon, for violation of the Criminal Syndicalism Law of that State. The act defines "criminal syndicalism" as "the doctrine which advocates crime, physical violence, sabotage or any unlawful acts or methods as a means of accomplishing or effecting industrial or political change or revolution."

With this preliminary definition the act proceeds to describe a number of offenses, embracing the teaching of criminal syndicalism, the printing or distribution of books, pamphlets, &c., advocating that doctrine, the organization of a society or assemblage which advocates it, and presiding at or assisting in conducting a meeting of such an organization, society or group. The prohibited acts are made felonies, punishable by imprisonment for not less than one year nor more than ten years, or by a fine of not more than $1,000, or by both.

We are concerned with but one of the described offenses and with the validity of the statute in this particular application. The charge is that appellant assisted in the conduct of a meeting which was called under the auspices of the Communist party, an organization advocating criminal syndicalism. The defense was that the meeting was public and orderly and was held for a lawful purpose; that while it was held under the auspices of the Communist party, neither criminal syndicalism nor any unlawful conduct was taught or advocated at the meeting either by appellant or by others.

Appellant moved for a direction of acquittal, contending that the statute as applied to him, for merely assisting at a meeting called by the Communist party at which nothing unlawful was done or advocated, violated the due process clause of the Fourteenth Amendment of the Constitution of the United States. This contention was overruled. Appellant was found guilty as charged and was sentenced to imprisonment for seven years. The judgment was affirmed by the Supreme Court of the State, which considered the constitutional question and sustained the statute as thus applied. 152 Ore. 315. The case comes here on appeal. . . .

The stipulation, after setting forth the charging part of the indictment, recites in substance the following:

That on July 27, 1934, there was held in Portland a meeting which had been advertised by hand-bills issued by the Portland section of the Communist party; that the number of persons in attendance was variously estimated at from 150 to 300; that some of those present, who were members of the Communist party, estimated that not to exceed 10 to 15 per cent of those in attendance were such members; that the meeting was open to the public without charge and no questions were asked of those entering with respect to their relation to the Communist party; that the notice of the meeting advertised it as a protest against illegal raids on workers' halls and homes and against the shooting of striking longshoremen by Portland police; that the chairman stated that it was a meeting held by the Communist party; that the first speaker dwelt on the activities of the Young Communist League.

That the defendant De Jonge, the second speaker, was a member of the Communist party and went to the meeting to speak in its name; that in his talk he protested against conditions in the county jail, the action of city police in relation to the maritime strike then in progress in Portland and numerous other matters; that he discussed the reason for the raids on the Communist headquarters and workers' halls and offices; that he told the workers that these attacks were due to efforts on the part of the steamship companies and stevedoring companies to break the maritime longshoremen's and seamen's strike; that they hoped to break the strike by pitting the longshoremen and seamen against the Communist movement; that there was also testimony to the effect that defendant asked those present to do more work in obtaining members for the Communist party and requested all to be at the meeting of the party to be held in Portland on the following evening and to bring their friends to show their defiance to local police authority and o assist them in their revolutionary tactics.

That there was also testimony that defendant urged the purchase of certain Communist literature which was sold at the meeting; that while the meeting was still in progress it was raided by the police; that the meeting was conducted in an orderly manner; that defendant and several others who were actively conducting the meeting were arrested by the police and that on searching the hall the police found a quantity of Communist literature.

The stipulation then set forth various extracts from the literature of the Communist party to show its advocacy of criminal syndicalism. The stipulation does not disclose any activity by the defendant as a basis for his prosecution other than his participation in the meeting in question. Nor does the stipulation show that the Communist literature distributed at the meeting contained any advocacy of criminal syndiaclism or of any unlawful conduct.

It was admitted by the Attorney General of the State in his argument at the bar of this court that the literature distributed in the meeting was not of that sort and that the extracts contained in the stipulation were taken from Communist literature found elsewhere. Its introduction in evidence was for the purpose of showing that the Communist party as such did advocate the doctrine of criminal syndicalism, a fact which is not disputed on this appeal.

On the theory that this was a charge that criminal syndicalism and sabotage were advocated at the meeting in question, defendant moved for acquittal insisting that the evidence was insufficient to warrant his conviction. The trial court denied his motion and error in this respect was assigned on appeal.

The Supreme Court of the State put aside that contention by ruling that the indictment did not charge that criminal syndicalism or sabotage was advocated at the meeting described in the evidence, either by defendant or by any one else. . . .

"What the indictment does charge, in plain and concise language, is that the defendant presided at, conducted and assisted in conducting an assemblage of persons, organization, society and group, to wit, the Communist party, which said assemblage of persons, organization, society and group was unlawfully teaching and advocating in Multnomah County the doctrine of criminal syndicalism and sabotage."

In this view, lack of sufficient evidence as to illegal advocacy or action at the meeting became immaterial. Having limited the charge to defendant's participation in a meeting called by the Communist party, the State Court sustained the conviction upon that basis regardless of what was said or done at the meeting.

We must take the indictment as thus construed. Conviction upon a charge not made would be sheer denial of due process. It thus appears that, while defendant was a member of the Communist party, he was not indicted for participating in its organization, or for joining it, or for soliciting members or for distributing its literature. He was not charged with teaching or advocating criminal syndicalism or sabotage or any unlawful acts, either at the meeting or elsewhere.

He was accordingly deprived of the benefit of evidence as to the orderly and lawful conduct of the meeting and that it was not called or used for the advocacy of criminal syndicalism or sabotage or any unlawful action. His sole offense as charged, and for which he was convicted and sentenced to imprisonment for seven years, was that he had assisted in the conduct of a public meeting, albeit otherwise lawful, which was held under the auspices of the Communist party.

The broad reach of the statute as thus applied is plain. While defendant was a member of the Communist party, that membership was not necessary to conviction on such a charge. A like fate might have attended any speaker, although not a member who "assisted in the conduct" of the meeting. However innocuous the object of the meeting, however lawful the subjects and tenor of the addresses, however reasonable and timely the discussion, all those assisting in the conduct of the meeting would be subject to imprisonment as felons if the meeting were held by the Communist party.

This manifest result was brought out sharply at this bar by the concessions which the Attorney General made, and could not avoid, in the light of the decision of the State court. Thus if the Communist party had called a public meeting in Portland to discuss the tariff, or the foreign policy of the government, or taxation, or relief, or candidacies for the offices of President, members of Congress, Governor or State legislators, every speaker who assisted in the conduct of the meeting would be equally guilty with the defendant in this case, upon the charge as here defined and sustained. . . .

While the States are entitled to protect themselves from the abuse of the privileges of our institutions through an attempted substitution of force and violence in the place of peaceful political action in order to effect revolutionary changes in government, none of our decisions go to the length of sustaining such a curtailment of the right of free speech and assembly as the Oregon statute demands in its present application.

Freedom of speech and of the press are fundamental rights which are safeguarded by the due process clause of the Fourteenth Amendment of the Federal Constitution. The right of peaceable assembly is a right cognate to those of free speech and free press and is equally fundamental.

As this court said in *United States* v. *Cruikshank,* "The very idea of a government, republican in form, implies a right on the part of its citizens to met peaceably for consultation in respect to public affairs and to petition for a redress of grievances."

The First Amendment of the Federal Constitution expressly guarantees that right against abridgment by Congress. But explicit mention there does not argue exclusion elsewhere. For the right is one that cannot be denied without violating those fundamental principles of liberty and justice which lie at the base of all civil and political institutions, principles which the Fourteenth Amendment embodies in the general terms of its due process clause.

These rights may be abused by using speech or press or assembly in order to incite to violence and crime. The people, through their Legislatures, may protect themselves against that abuse. But the legislative intervention can find constitutional justification only by dealing with the abuse. The rights themselves must not be curtailed.

The greater the importance of safeguarding the community from incitements to the overthrow of our institutions by force and violence, the more imperative is the need to preserve inviolate the constitutional rights of free speech, free press and free assembly in order to maintain the opportunity for free political discussion, to the end that government may be responsive to the will of the people and that changes, if desired, may be obtained by peaceful means. Therein lies the security of the republic, the very foundation of constitutional government.

It follows from these considerations that, consistently with the Federal Constitution, peaceable assembly for lawful discussion cannot be made a crime. The holding of meetings for peaceable political action cannot be proscribed. Those who assist in the conduct of such meetings cannot be branded as criminals on that score. The question, if the rights of free speech and peaceable assembly are to be preserved, is not as to the auspices under which the meeting is held, but as to its purpose; not as to the relations of the speakers, but whether their utterances transcend the bounds of the freedom of speech which the Constitution protects.

If the persons assemblying have committed crimes elsewhere, if they have formed or are engaged in a conspiracy against the public peace and order, they may be prosecuted for their conspiracy or other violation of valid laws.

But it is a different matter when the State, instead of prosecuting them for such offenses, seizes upon mere participation in a peaceable assembly and a lawful public discussion as the basis for a criminal charge.

We are not called upon to review the findings of the State court as to the objectives of the Communist party. Notwithstanding those objectives, the defendant still enjoyed his personal right of free speech and to take part in a peaceable assembly having a lawful purpose, although called by that party. The defendant was none the less entitled to discuss the public issues of the day and thus in a lawful manner, without incitement to violence or crime, to seek redress of alleged grievances. That was of the essence of his guaranteed personal liberty.

We hold that the Oregon statute as applied to the particular charge as defined by the State court is repugnant to the due process clause of the Fourteenth Amendment. The judgment of conviction is reversed and the cause is remanded for further proceedings not inconsistent with this opinion. It is so ordered.

512. WEST COAST HOTEL CO. v. PARRISH
300 U. S. 379
1937

Appeal from the Supreme Court of the State of Washington. The decision in Adkins v. Children's Hospital (Doc. No. 451) holding the due process clause of the Fifth Amendment a barrier against federal minimum wage legislation, had effectively blocked such legislation for years. In 1933 New York State attempted to legislate minimum wages for women, but this legislation was invalidated in a five to four decision which asserted that legislatures are "without power . . . to prohibit, change, or nullify contracts between employers and adult women workers as to amount of wages to be paid." The present case reversed this as well as the Adkins decision. The history of the Washington statute in dispute is given in the decision. See, Powell, "The Judiciality of Minimum Wage Legislation," 37 Harv. Law Rev. 545; Black, "Wages and Hours Laws in the Courts," 5 U. of Pitt. Law Rev. 223; Brown, "Minimum Wage Cases in the Supreme Court," 11 So. Cal. Law Rev. 256.

HUGHES, C. J., this case presents the question of the constitutional validity of the minimum wage law of the State of Washington.

The Act, entitled "Minimum Wages for Women," authorizes the fixing of minimum wages for women and minors. . . . It provides:

Sec. 1. The welfare of the State of Washington demands that women and minors be protected from conditions of labor which have a pernicious effect on their health and morals. The State of Washington, therefore, exercising herein its police and sovereign power declares that inadequate wages and unsanitary conditions of labor exert such pernicious effect.

Sec. 2. It shall be unlawful to employ women or minors in any industry or occupation within the State of Washington under conditions of labor detrimental to their health or morals; and it shall be unlawful to employ women workers in any industry within the State of Washington at wages which are not adequate for their maintenance.

Sec. 3. There is hereby created a commission to be known as the "Industrial Welfare Commission" for the State of Washington, to establish such standards of wages and conditions of labor for women and minors employed within the State of Washington, as shall be held hereunder to be reasonable and not detrimental to health and morals, and which shall be sufficient for the decent maintenance of women.

Further provisions required the Commission to ascertain the wages and conditions of labor of women and minors within the State. Public hearings were to be held. If after investigation the Commission found that in any occupation, trade or industry the wages paid to women were "inadequate to supply them necessary cost of living and to maintain the workers in health," the Commission was empowered to call a conference of representatives of employers and employees together with disinterested persons representing the public. The conference was to recommend to the Commission, on its request, an estimate of a minimum wage adequate for the purpose above stated, and on the approval of such a recommendation it became the duty

of the Commission to issue an obligatory order fixing minimum wages. Any such order might be reopened and the question reconsidered with the aid of the former conference or a new one. Special licenses were authorized for the employment of women who were "physically defective or crippled by age or otherwise," and also for apprentices, at less than the prescribed minimum wage.

By a later Act the Industrial Welfare Commission was abolished and its duties were assigned to the Industrial Welfare Committee consisting of the Director of Labor and Industries, the Supervisor of Industrial Insurance, the Supervisor of Industrial Relations, the Industrial Statistician and the Supervisor of Women in Industry. Laws of 1921 (Washington) chap. 7.

The appellant conducts a hotel. The appellee Elsie Parrish was employed as a chambermaid and (with her husband) brought this suit to recover the difference between the wages paid her and the minimum wage fixed pursuant to the state law. The minimum wage was $14.50 per week of 48 hours. The appellant challenged the act as repugnant to the due process clause of the Fourteenth Amendment of the Constitution of the United States. The Supreme Court of the State, reversing the trial court, sustained the statute and directed judgment for the plaintiffs. *Parrish* v. *West Coast Hotel Co.*, 185 Wash. 581. The case is here on appeal.

The appellant relies upon the decision of this Court in *Adkins* v. *Children's Hospital,* which held invalid the District of Columbia Minimum Wage Act which was attacked under the due process clause of the Fifth Amendment. . . .

The recent case of *Morehead* v. *New York ex rel. Tipaldo,* 298 U. S. 587, came here on certiorari to the New York court which had held the New York minimum wage act for women to be invalid. A minority of this Court thought that the New York statute was distinguishable in a material feature from that involved in the *Adkins* case and that for that and other reasons the New York statute should be sustained. But the Court of Appeals of New York had said that it found no material difference between the two statutes and this Court held that the "meaning of the statute" as fixed by the decision of the state court "must be accepted here as if the meaning had

been specifically expressed in the enactment."
Id., p. 609. That view led to the affirmance
by this Court of the judgment in the *Morehead* case, as the Court considered that the
only question before it was whether the *Adkins*
case was distinguishable and that reconsideration of that decision had not been sought. . . .

We think that the question which was not
deemed to be open in the *Morehead* case is
open and is necessarily presented here. The
Supreme Court of Washington has upheld the
minimum wage statute of that State. It has
decided that the statute is a reasonable exercise of the police power of the State. In
reaching that conclusion the state court has
invoked principles long established by this
Court in the application of the Fourteenth
Amendment. The state court has refused to
regard the decision in the *Adkins* case as
determinative and has pointed to our decisions
both before and since that case as justifying
its position. We are of the opinion that this
ruling of the state court demands on our part
a reexamination of the *Adkins* case. The importance of the question, in which many States
having similar laws are concerned, the close
division by which the decision in the *Adkins*
case was reached, and the economic conditions which have supervened, and in the light
of which the reasonableness of the exercise
of the protective power of the State must be
considered, make it not only appropriate, but
we think imperative, that in deciding the
present case the subject should receive fresh
consideration.

The history of the litigation of this question
may be briefly stated. The minimum wage
statute of Washington was enacted over
twenty-three years ago. Prior to the decision
in the instant case it had twice been held
valid by the Supreme Court of the State.
Larsen v. *Rice*, 100 Wash. 642; *Spokane
Hotel Co.* v. *Younger*, 113 Wash. 359. The
Washington statute is essentially the same as
that enacted in Oregon in the same year.
Laws of 1913 (Oregon) chap. 62. The validity
of the latter act was sustained by the Supreme
Court of Oregon in *Stettler* v. *O'Hara*, 69
Ore. 519, and *Simpson* v. *O'Hara*, 70 Ore. 261.
These cases, after reargument, were affirmed
here by an equally divided court, in 1917.
243 U. S. 629. The law of Oregon thus con-
tinued in effect. The District of Columbia
Minimum Wage Law (40 Stat. 960) was en-

acted in 1918. The statute was sustained by the
Supreme Court of the District in the *Adkins*
case. Upon appeal the Court of Appeals of
the District first affirmed that ruling but on
rehearing reversed it and the case came before
this Court in 1923. The judgment of the
Court of Appeals holding the Act invalid was
affirmed, but with Chief Justice Taft, Mr.
Justice Holmes and Mr. Justice Sanford dissenting, and Mr. Justice Brandeis taking no
part. The dissenting opinions took the ground
that the decision was at variance with the
principles which this Court had frequently
announced and applied. In 1925 and 1927,
the similar minimum wage statutes of Arizona and Arkansas were held invalid upon the
authority of the *Adkins* case. The Justices
who had dissented in that case bowed to the
ruling and Mr. Justice Brandeis dissented.
Murphy v. *Sardell*, 269 U. S. 530; *Donham*
v. *West-Nelson Co.*, 273 U. S. 657. The question did not come before us again until the last
term in the *Morehead* case, as already noted.
In that case, briefs supporting the New York
statute were submitted by the States of Ohio,
Connecticut, Illinois, Massachusetts, New
Hampshire, New Jersey and Rhode Island.
298 U. S., p. 604, *note*. Throughout this entire
period the Washington statute now under consideration has been in force.

The principle which must control our decision is not in doubt. The constitutional
provision invoked is the due process clause
of the Fourteenth Amendment governing the
States, as the due process clause invoked in
the *Adkins* case governed Congress. In each
case the violation alleged by those attacking
minimum wage regulation for women is deprivation of freedom of contract. What is
this freedom? The Constitution does not speak
of freedom of contract. It speaks of liberty
and prohibits the deprivation of liberty without due process of law. In prohibiting that
deprivation the Constitution does not recognize an absolute and uncontrollable liberty.
Liberty in each of its phases has its history
and connotation. But the liberty safeguarded
is liberty in a social organization which requires the protection of law against the evils
which menace the health, safety, morals and
welfare of the people. Liberty under the Constitution is thus necessarily subject to the
restraints of due process, and regulation
which is reasonable in relation to its subject

and is adopted in the interests of the community is due process.

This essential limitation of liberty in general governs freedom of contract in particular. More than twenty-five years ago we set forth the applicable principle in these words, after referring to the cases where the liberty guaranteed by the Fourteenth Amendment had been broadly described:

> But it was recognized in the cases cited, as in many others, that freedom of contract is a qualified and not an absolute right. There is no absolute freedom to do as one wills or to contract as one chooses. The guaranty of liberty does not withdraw from legislative supervision that wide department of activity which consists of the making of contracts, or deny to government the power to provide restrictive safeguards. Liberty implies the absence of arbitrary restraint, not immunity from reasonable regulations and prohibitions imposed in the interests of the community. *Chicago, Burlington & Quincy R. R. Co. v. McGuire*, 219 U. S. 549, 565.

This power under the Constitution to restrict freedom of contract has had many illustrations. That it may be exercised in the public interest with respect to contracts between employer and employee is undeniable. Thus statutes have been sustained limiting employment in underground mines and smelters to eight hours a day (*Holden* v. *Hardy*); in requiring redemption in cash of store orders or other evidences of indebtedness issued in the payment of wages (*Knoxville Iron Co.* v. *Harbison*, 183 U. S. 13); in forbidding the payment of seamen's wages in advance (*Patterson* v. *Bark Eudora*, 190 U. S. 169); in making it unlawful to contract to pay miners employed at quantity rates upon the basis of screened coal instead of the weight of the coal as originally produced in the mine (*McLean* v. *Arkansas*, 211 U. S. 539); in prohibiting contracts limiting liability for injuries to employees (*Chicago, Burlington & Quincy R. R. Co.* v. *McGuire*); in limiting hours of work of employees in manufacturing establishments (*Bunting* v. *Oregon*); and in maintaining workmen's compensation laws (*New York Central R. Co.* v. *White*, 243 U. S. 188; *Mountain Timber Co.* v. *Washington*, 243 U. S. 219). In dealing with the relation of employer and employed, the legislature has necessarily a wide field of discretion in order that there may be suitable protection of health

and safety, and that peace and good order may be promoted through regulations designed to insure wholesome conditions of work and freedom from oppression. *Chicago, Burlington & Quincy R. R. Co.* v. *McGuire, supra*, p. 570.

The point that has been strongly stressed that adult employees should be deemed competent to make their own contracts was decisively met nearly forty years ago in *Holden* v. *Hardy, supra*, where we pointed out the inequality in the footing of the parties. . . .

It is manifest that this established principle is peculiarly applicable in relation to the employment of women in whose protection the State has a special interest. That phase of the subject received elaborate consideration in *Muller* v. *Oregon*, where the constitutional authority of the State to limit the working hours of women was sustained. . . . Again, in *Quong Wing* v. *Kirkendall*, 223 U. S. 59, 63, in referring to a differentiation with respect to the employment of women, we said that the Fourteenth Amendment did not interfere with state power by creating a "fictitious equality." We referred to recognized classifications on the basis of sex with regard to hours of work and in other matters, and we observed that the particular points at which that difference shall be enforced by legislation were largely in the power of the State. In later rulings this Court sustained the regulation of hours of work of women employees in *Riley* v. *Massachusetts*, 232 U. S. 671 (factories), *Miller* v. *Wilson*, 236 U. S. 373 (hotels), and *Bosley* v. *McLaughlin*, 236 U. S. 385 (hospitals).

This array of precedents and the principles they applied were thought by the dissenting Justices in the *Adkins* case to demand that the minimum wage statute be sustained. The validity of the distinction made by the Court between a minimum wage and a maximum of hours in limiting liberty of contract was especially challenged. That challenge persists and is without any satisfactory answer. . . .

One of the points which was pressed by the Court in supporting its ruling in the *Adkins* case was that the standard set up by the District of Columbia Act did not take appropriate account of the value of the services rendered. . . .

The minimum wage to be paid under the Washington statute is fixed after full consideration by representatives of employers, employees and the public. It may be assumed that the minimum wage is fixed in consideration of the services that are performed in the particular occupations under normal conditions. Provision is made for special licenses at less wages in the case of women who are incapable of full service. The statement of Mr. Justice Holmes in the *Adkins* case is pertinent:

This statute does not compel anybody to pay anything. It simply forbids employment at rates below those fixed as the minimum requirement of health and right living. It is safe to assume that women will not be employed at even the lowest wages allowed unless they earn them, or unless the employer's business can sustain the burden. In short the law in its character and operation is like hundreds of so-called police laws that have been upheld. 261 U. S., p. 570.

And Chief Justice Taft forcibly pointed out the consideration which is basic in a statute of this character:

Legislatures which adopt a requirement of maximum hours or minimum wages may be presumed to believe that when sweating employers are prevented from paying unduly low wages by positive law they will continue their business, abating that part of their profits, which were wrung from the necessities of their employees, and will concede the better terms required by the law; and that while in individual cases hardship may result, the restriction will enure to the benefit of the general class of employees in whose interest the law is passed and so to that of the community at large. *Id.*, p. 563.

We think that the views thus expressed are sound and that the decision in the *Adkins* case was a departure from the true application of the principles governing the regulation by the State of the relation of employer and employed. Those principles have been reenforced by our subsequent decisions. Thus in *Radice* v. *New York*, 264 U. S. 292, we sustained the New York statute which restricted the employment of women in restaurants at night. In *O'Gorman* v. *Hartford Fire Insurance Company*, 282 U. S. 251, which upheld an act regulating the commissions of insurance agents, we pointed to the presumption of the constitutionality of a statute dealing with a subject within the scope of the police power and to the absence of any factual foundation of record for deciding that the limits of power had been transcended. In *Nebbia* v. *New York*, dealing with the New York statute providing for minimum prices for milk, the general subject of the regulation of the use of private property and of the making of private contracts received an exhaustive examination and we again declared that if such laws "have a reasonable relation to a proper legislative purpose, and are neither arbitrary nor discriminatory, the requirements of due process are satisfied"; that "with the wisdom of the policy adopted, with the adequacy or practicability of the law enacted to forward it, the courts are both incompetent and unauthorized to deal"; that "times without number we have said that the legislature is primarily the judge of the necessity of such an enactment, that every possible presumption is in favor of its validity, and that though the court may hold views inconsistent with the wisdom of the law, it may not be annulled unless palpably in excess of legislative power."

With full recognition of the earnestness and vigor which characterize the prevailing opinion in the *Adkins* case, we find it impossible to reconcile that ruling with these well-considered declarations. What can be closer to the public interest than the health of women and their protection from unscrupulous and overreaching employers? And if the protection of women is a legitimate end of the exercise of state power, how can it be said that the requirement of the payment of a minimum wage fairly fixed in order to meet the very necessities of existence is not an admissible means to that end? The legislature of the State was clearly entitled to consider the situation of women in employment, the fact that they are in the class receiving the least pay, that their bargaining power is relatively weak, and that they are the ready victims of those who would take advantage of their necessitous circumstances. The legislature was entitled to adopt measures to reduce the evils of the "sweating system," the exploiting of workers at wages so low as to be insufficient to meet the bare cost of living thus making their very helplessness the occasion of a most injurious competition. The legislature had the right to consider that its minimum wage requirements would be an important aid in carrying out its policy of protection. The adoption of similar requirements by many States evidences a deep-seated conviction both as to the presence of the evil and as to the means adapted to check it. Legislative response to that conviction cannot be regarded as arbitrary or capricious and that is all we have to decide. Even if the wisdom of the policy be regarded as debatable and its effects uncertain, still the legislature is entitled to its judgment.

There is an additional and compelling consideration which recent economic experience has brought into a strong light. The exploitation of a class of workers who are in an unequal position with respect to bargaining power and are thus relatively defenceless against the denial of a living wage is not only detrimental to their health and well being but casts a direct burden for their support upon the community. What these workers lose in wages the taxpayers are called upon to pay. The bare cost of living must be met. We may take judicial notice of the unparalleled demands for relief which arose during the recent period of depression and still continue to an alarming extent despite the degree of economic recovery which has been achieved. It is unnecessary to cite official statistics to establish what is of common knowledge through the length and breadth of the land. While in the instant case no factual brief has been presented, there is no reason to doubt that the State of Washington has encountered the same social problem that is present elsewhere. The community is not bound to provide what is in effect a subsidy for unconscionable employers. The community may direct its law-making power to correct the abuse which springs from their selfish disregard of the public interest. The argument that the legislation in question constitutes an arbitrary discrimination, because it does not extend to men, is unavailing. This Court has frequently held that the legislative authority, acting within its proper field, is not bound to extend its regulation to all cases which it might possibly reach. The legislature "is free to recognize degrees of harm and it may confine its restrictions to those classes of cases where the need is deemed to be clearest." If "the law presumably hits the evil where it is most felt, it is not to be overthrown because there are other instances to which it might have been applied." There is no, "doctrinaire requirement" that the legislation should be couched in all embracing terms. This familiar principle has repeatedly been applied to legislation which singles out women, and particular classes of women, in the exercise of the State's protective power. Their relative need in the presence of the evil, no less than the existence of the evil itself, is a matter for the legislative judgment.

Our conclusion is that the case of *Adkins* v. *Children's Hospital, supra*, should be, and it is, overruled. The judgment of the Supreme Court of the State of Washington is affirmed.

SUTHERLAND, J., VAN DEVANTER, J., MC-REYNOLDS, J., and BUTLER, J. dissented.

513. HERNDON v. LOWRY
301 U. S. 242
1937

Appeal from the Supreme Court of Georgia. One of the most difficult problems which faces the Court is that of drawing the dividing line between the power of the State to protect itself against riot or insurrection and the freedom of speech guaranteed to the individual by the Federal Constitution. This opinion, holding that the mere possession of radical literature does not constitute violation of a law prohibiting the incitement to insurrection, riot or conspiracy, is notable for a more liberal attitude than that revealed in the Gitlow case (Doc. No. 456). See the *Monthly Bulletin* of the International Juridical Association, vol. VI, no. 2, and notes in 50 Harv. L. Rev. 1313, and 35 Mich. L. Rev. 1373.

ROBERTS, J. The appellant claims his conviction in a state court deprived him of his liberty contrary to the guarantees of the Fourteenth Amendment. He assigns as error the action of the Supreme Court of Georgia in overruling his claim and refusing him a discharge upon habeas corpus. The petition for the writ, presented to the Superior Court of Fulton County, asserted the appellant was unlawfully detained by the appellee as sheriff under the supposed authority of a judgment pronouncing him guilty of attempting to incite insurrection, as defined in 56 of the Penal Code and sentencing him to imprisonment for not less than eighteen nor more than twenty years. . . .

At the July Term 1932 of the Superior Court of Fulton County an indictment was returned charging against the appellant an attempt to induce others to join in combined resistance to the lawful authority of the state with intent to deny, to defeat, and to overthrow such authority by open force, violent means, and unlawful acts; alleging that insurrection was intended to be manifested and accomplished by unlawful and violent acts. The indictment specified that the attempt was made by calling and attending public assemblies and by making speeches for the purpose of organizing and establishing groups and combinations of white and colored persons under the name of the Communist Party of Atlanta for the purpose of uniting, combining, and conspiring to incite riots and to embarrass and impede the orderly processes of the courts and offering combined resistance to, and, by force and violence, overthrowing and defeating the authority of the state; that by speech and persuasion, the appellant solicited and attempted to solicit persons to join, confederate with, and become members of the Communist Party and the Young Communist League and introduced into the state and circulated, aided and assisted in introducing and circulating, booklets, papers, and other writings with the same intent and purpose. The charge was founded on § 56 of the Penal Code, one of four related sections. Section 55 defines insurrection, § 56 defines an attempt to incite insurrection, § 57 prescribes the death penalty for conviction of the offenses described in the two preceding sections unless the jury shall recommend mercy, and § 58 penalizes, by imprisonment, the introduction and circulation of printed matter for the purpose of inciting insurrection, riot, conspiracy, etc. . . .

In the present proceeding the Superior Court and Supreme Court of Georgia have considered and disposed of the contentions based upon the Federal Constitution. The scope of a habeas corpus proceeding in the circumstances disclosed is a state and not a federal question and since the state courts treated the proceeding as properly raising issues of federal constitutional right, we have jurisdiction and all such issues are open here. We must, then, inquire whether the statute as applied in the trial denied appellant rights safeguarded by the Fourteenth Amendment.

The evidence on which the judgment rests consists of appellant's admissions and certain documents found in his possession. The appellant told the state's officers that some time prior to his arrest he joined the Communist Party in Kentucky and later came to Atlanta as a paid organizer for the party, his duties being to call meetings, to educate and disseminate information respecting the party, to distribute literature, to secure members, and to work up an organization of the party in Atlanta; and that he had held or attended three meetings called by him. He made no further admission as to what he did as an organizer, or what he said or did at the meetings. When arrested he carried a box containing documents. After he was arrested he conducted the officers to his room where additional documents and bundles of newspapers and periodicals were found, which he stated were sent him from the headquarters of the Communist Party in New York. He gave the names of persons who were members of the organization in Atlanta, and stated he had only five or six actual members at the time of his apprehension. The stubs of membership books found in the box indicated he had enrolled more members than he stated. There was no evidence that he had distributed any of the material carried on his person and found in his room, or had taken any of it to meetings, save two circulars or appeals respecting county relief which are confessedly innocuous.

The newspapers, pamphlets, periodicals, and other documents found in his room were, so he stated, intended for distribution at his meetings. These the appellee concedes were not introduced in evidence. Certain documents in his possession when he was arrested were placed in evidence. . . .

All of these may be dismissed as irrelevant except those falling within the first and second groups. No inference can be drawn from the possession of the books mentioned, either that they embodied the doctrines of the Communist Party or that they represented views advocated by the appellant. The minutes of meetings contain nothing indicating the purposes of the organization or any intent to overthrow organized government; on the contrary, they indicate merely discussion of relief for the unemployed. The two circulars, admittedly distributed by the appellant, had nothing to do with the Communist Party, its aims or purposes, and were not appeals to join the party but were concerned with unemployment relief in the county and included appeals to the white and negro unemployed to organize and represent the need for further county aid. They were characterized by the Supreme Court of Georgia as "more or less harmless."

The documents of the first class disclose the activity of the appellant as an organizer but, in this respect, add nothing to his admissions.

The matter appearing upon the membership blanks is innocent upon its face however foolish and pernicious the aims it suggests. . . .

This vague declaration falls short of an attempt to bring about insurrection either immediately or within a reasonable time but amounts merely to a statement of ultimate ideals. The blanks, however, indicate more specific aims for which members of the Communist Party are to vote. They are to vote Communist for

"1. Unemployment and Social Insurance at the expense of the State and employers.

"2. Against Hoover's wage-cutting policy.

"3. Emergency relief for the poor farmers without restrictions by the government and banks; exemption of poor farmers from taxes and from forced collection of rents or debts.

"4. Equal rights for the Negroes and self-determination for the Black Belt.

"5. Against capitalistic terror: against all forms of suppression of the political rights of the workers.

"6. Against imperialist war; for the defense of the Chinese people and of the Soviet Union."

None of these aims is criminal upon its face. As to one, the 4th, the claim is that criminality may be found because of extrinsic facts. Those facts consist of possession by appellant of booklets and other literature of the second class illustrating the party doctrines. The State contends these show that the purposes of the Communist Party were forcible subversion of the lawful authority of Georgia. They contain, inter alia, statements to the effect that the party bases itself upon the revolutionary theory of Marxism, opposes "bosses' wars,"

approves of the Soviet Union, and desires the "smashing" of the National Guard, the C. M. T. C., and the R. O. T. C. But the State especially relies upon a booklet entitled "The Communist Position on the Negro Question," on the cover of which appears a map of the United States having a dark belt across certain Southern states and the phrase "Self-Determination for the Black Belt." The booklet affirms that the source of the Communist slogan "Right of Self-Determination of the Negroes in the Black Belt" is a resolution of the Communist International on the Negro question in the United States adopted in 1930, which states that the Communist Party in the United States has been actively attempting to win increasing sympathy among the negro population, that certain things have been advocated for the benefit of the Negroes in the Northern states, but that in the Southern portion of the United States the Communist slogan must be "The Right of Self-Determination of the Negroes in the Black Belt." . . .

There is no evidence the appellant distributed any writings or printed matter found in the box he carried when arrested, or any other advocating forcible subversion of governmental authority. There is no evidence the appellant advocated, by speech or written word, at meetings or elsewhere, any doctrine or action implying such forcible subversion. There is evidence tending to prove that the appellant held meetings for the purpose of recruiting members of the Communist Party and solicited contributions for the support of that party and there is proof of the doctrines which that party espouses. Appellant's intent to incite insurrection, if it is to be found, must rest upon his procuring members for the Communist Party and his possession of that party's literature when he was arrested.

Section 55 of the Georgia Penal Code defines insurrection as "combined resistance to the lawful authority of the State, with intent to the denial thereof, when the same is manifested or intended to be manifested by acts of violence." The appellant was not indicted under this section. Section 58 denounces the introduction, printing, or circulation, or assisting to print or circulate any document "for the purpose of inciting insurrection." The appellant was not indicted under this section. Section 56, under which the indictment is laid, makes no reference to force or violence except by the phrase "combined resistance to the lawful authority of the State." The Supreme Court evidently importing from the similar phraseology in § 55 the additional element contained in that section, namely, "manifested or intended to be manifested by acts of violence," has decided that intended resort to force is an essential element of the offense defined by § 56.

To ascertain how the Act is held to apply to the appellant's conduct we turn to the rulings of the state courts in his case. The trial court instructed the jury: "In order to convict the defendant, . . . it must appear clearly by the evidence that immediate serious violence against the State of Georgia was to be expected or advocated." The jury rendered a verdict of guilty. In the Supreme Court the appellant urged that the evidence was wholly insufficient to sustain the verdict under the law as thus construed. . . .

The affirmance of conviction upon the trial record necessarily gives § 56 the construction that one who seeks members for or attempts to organize a local unit of a party which has the purposes and objects disclosed by the documents in evidence may be found guilty of an attempt to incite insurrection.

The questions are whether this construction and application of the statute deprives the accused of the right of freedom of speech and of assembly guaranteed by the Fourteenth Amendment, and whether the statute so construed and applied furnishes a reasonably definite and ascertainable standard of guilt.

The appellant, while admitting that the people may protect themselves against abuses of the freedom of speech safeguarded by the Fourteenth Amendment by prohibiting incitement to violence and crime insists that legislative regulation may not go beyond measures forefending against "clear and present danger" of the use of force against the state. For this position he relies upon our decisions under the Federal Espionage Acts and cognate state legislation. . . .

The State, on the other hand, insists that our decisions uphold state statutes making criminal utterances which have a "dangerous tendency" towards the subversion of government. It relies particularly upon *Gitlow* v. *New York* (268 U. S. 652). There, however, we dealt with a statute which, quite unlike § 56 of the Georgia Criminal Code, denounced as criminal certain acts carefully and adequately described. . . .

It is evident that the decision sustaining the New York statute furnishes no warrant for the appellee's contention that under a law general in its description of the mischief to be remedied and equally general in respect of the intent of the actor, the standard of guilt may be made the "dangerous tendency" of his words.

The power of a state to abridge freedom of speech and of assembly is the exception rather than the rule and the penalizing even of utterances of a defined character must find its justification in a reasonable apprehension of danger to organized government. The judgment of the legislature is not unfettered. The limitation upon individual liberty must have appropriate relation to the safety of the state. Legislation which goes beyond this need violates the principle of the Constitution. If, therefore, a state statute penalize innocent participation in a meeting held with an innocent purpose merely because the meeting was held under the auspices of an organization membership in which, or the advocacy of whose principles, is also denounced as criminal, the law, so construed and applied, goes beyond the power to restrict abuses of freedom of speech and arbitrarily denies that freedom. And where a statute is so vague and uncertain as to make criminal an utterance or an act which may be innocently said or done with no intent to induce resort to violence or on the other hand may be said or done with a purpose violently to subvert government, a conviction under such a law cannot be sustained. . . .

1. The appellant had a constitutional right to address meetings and organize parties unless in so doing he violated some prohibition of a valid statute. The only prohibition he is said to have violated is that of § 56 forbidding incitement or attempted incitement to insurrection by violence. If the evidence fails to show that he did so incite, then, as applied to him, the statute unreasonably limits freedom of speech and freedom of assembly and violates the Fourteenth Amendment. We are of opinion that the requisite proof is lacking. From what has been said above with respect to the evidence offered at the trial it is apparent that the documents found upon the

appellant's person were certainly, as to some of the aims stated therein, innocent and consistent with peaceful action for a change in the laws or the constitution. The proof wholly fails to show that the appellant had read these documents; that he had distributed any of them; that he believed and advocated any or all of the principles and aims set forth in them, or that those he had procured to become members of the party knew or approved of any of these documents.

Thus, the crucial question is not the formal interpretation of the statute by the Supreme Court of Georgia but the application given it. In its application the offense made criminal is that of soliciting members for a political party and conducting meetings of a local unit of that party when one of the doctrines of the party, established by reference to a document not shown to have been exhibited to anyone by the accused, may be said to be ultimate resort to violence at some indefinite future time against organized government. It is to be borne in mind that the legislature of Georgia has not made membership in the Communist Party unlawful by reason of its supposed dangerous tendency even in the remote future. . . .

His membership in the Communist Party and his solicitation of a few members wholly fail to establish an attempt to incite others to insurrection. Indeed, so far as appears, he had but a single copy of the booklet the State claims to be objectionable; that copy he retained. The same may be said with respect to the other books and pamphlets, some of them of more innocent purport. In these circumstances, to make membership in the party and solicitation of members for that party a criminal offense, punishable by death, in the discretion of a jury, is an unwarranted invasion of the right of freedom of speech.

2. The statute, as construed and applied in the appellant's trial, does not furnish a sufficiently ascertainable standard of guilt. The Act does not prohibit incitement to violent interference with any given activity or operation of the state. By force of it, as construed, the judge and jury trying an alleged offender cannot appraise the circumstances and character of the defendant's utterances or activities as begetting a clear and present danger of forcible obstruction of a particular state function. Nor is any specified conduct or utterance of the accused made an offense.

The test of guilt is thus formulated by the Supreme Court of the state. Forcible action must have been contemplated but it would be sufficient to sustain a conviction if the accused intended that an insurrection "should happen at any time within which he might reasonably expect his influence to continue to be directly operative in causing such action by those whom he sought to induce." If the jury conclude that the defendant should have contemplated that any act or utterance of his in opposition to the established order or advocating a change in that order, might, in the distant future, eventuate in a combination to offer forcible resistance to the State, or as the State says, if the jury believe he should have known that his words would have "a dangerous tendency" then he may be convicted. To be guilty under the law, as construed, a defendant need not advocate resort to force. He need not teach any particular doctrine to come within its purview. In deed, he need not be active in the formation of a combination or group if he agitate for a change in the frame of government, however peaceful his own intent. If, by the exercise of prophesy, he can forecast that, as a result of a chain of causation, following his proposed action a group may arise at some future date which will resort to force, he is bound to make the prophecy and abstain, under pain of punishment, possibly of execution. Every person who attacks existing conditions, who agitates for a change in the form of government, must take the risk that if a jury should be of opinion he ought to have foreseen that his utterances might contribute in any measure to some future forcible resistance to the existing government he may be convicted of the offense of inciting insurrection. Proof that the accused in fact believed that his effort would cause a violent assault upon the state would not be necessary to conviction. It would be sufficient if the jury thought he reasonably might foretell that those he persuaded to join the party might, at some time in the indefinite future, resort to forcible resistance of government. The question thus proposed to a jury involves pure speculation as to future trends of thought and action. Within what time might one reasonably expect that an attempted organization of the Communist Party in the

United States would result in violent action by that party? If a jury returned a special verdict saying twenty years or even fifty years the verdict could not be shown to be wrong. The law, as thus construed, licenses the jury to create its own standard in each case. . . .

The statute, as construed and applied, amounts merely to a dragnet which may enmesh anyone who agitates for a change of government if a jury can be persuaded that he ought to have foreseen his words would have some effect in the future conduct of others. No reasonably ascertainable standard of guilt is prescribed. So vague and indeterminate are the boundaries thus set to the freedom of speech and assembly that the law necessarily violates the guarantees of liberty embodied in the Fourteenth Amendment.

The judgment is reversed. . . .

Mr. Justice VAN DEVANTER, with whom joined Mr. Justice MCREYNOLDS, SUTHER-LAND, and BUTLER, dissented.

514. THE NEUTRALITY ACT OF 1937
May 1, 1937

(U. S. Statutes at Large, Vol. L, p. 121)

Disillusionment with the results of American participation in the first World War, growing throughout the twenties, was aggravated by the depression as well as by the continuation of the "old diplomacy" in Europe, and deepened by the findings of the Nye Committee on Munitions Manufactures and by a host of books and articles arguing the desirability of isolation. The outbreak of the Italo-Ethiopian conflict in May, 1935 led to the hasty passage of the Joint Resolution of Aug. 31, 1935 designed to prevent American involvement in any international conflict. The following year Congress strengthened this act by prohibiting loans to belligerents, and in January, 1937 it took cognizance of the problem presented by civil wars by forbidding the export of munitions for the use of either of the opposing forces in the Spanish Civil War. Finally on May 1, 1937 a Joint Resolution recapitulated these earlier resolutions, strengthening them in some particulars and giving larger discretionary powers to the President. A notable characteristic of this neutrality act was its failure to distinguish between aggressor and victim nations. In a curious fashion the neutrality legislation of 1935–37 vindicated the position taken by Sec. of State Bryan in 1914–15. The outbreak of the second World War in September, 1939 forced a reconsideration of this act and the Neutrality Law of 1939 relaxed in important particulars the provisions of the present act. On the problem of neutrality see C. A. and M. R. Beard, *America in Midpassage;* E. Borchard and W. Lage, *Neutrality for the United States;* P. C. Jessup, *Neutrality, Today and Tomorrow;* H. W. Dulles and H. F. Armstrong, *Can America Stay Neutral;* F. P. Davidson and G. Viereck, *Before America Decides;* J. Raushenbush, *The Final Choice;* Dulles, "Cash and Carry Neutrality," 18 Foreign Affairs, 179;

"The Neutrality Act of 1937," For. Pol. Rep. Vol. XIII no. 14.

JOINT RESOLUTION

To amend the joint resolution, approved August 31, 1935, as amended.

Resolved . . .

EXPORT OF ARMS, AMMUNITION, AND IMPLEMENTS OF WAR

SECTION 1. (a) Whenever the President shall find that there exists a state of war between, or among, two or more foreign states, the President shall proclaim such fact, and it shall thereafter be unlawful to export, or attempt to export, or cause to be exported, arms, ammunition, or implements of war from any place in the United States to any belligerent state named in such proclamation, or to any neutral state for transshipment to, or for the use of, any such belligerent state.

(b) The President shall, from time to time, by proclamation, extend such embargo upon the export of arms, ammunition, or implements of war to other states as and when they may become involved in such war.

(c) Whenever the President shall find that a state of civil strife exists in a foreign state and that such civil strife is of a magnitude or is being conducted under such conditions that the export of arms, ammunition, or implements of war from the United States to such foreign state would threaten or endanger the peace of the United States, the President shall proclaim such fact, and it shall thereafter be unlawful to export, or attempt to export, or cause to be exported, arms, ammunition, or implements of war from any place in the United States to such foreign state, or to any neutral state for transshipment to, or for the use of, such foreign state.

(d) The President shall, from time to time by proclamation, definitely enumerate the arms, ammunition, and implements of war, the export of which is prohibited by this section. The arms, ammunition, and implements of war so enumerated shall include those enumerated in the President's proclamation Numbered 2163, of April 10, 1936, but shall not include raw materials or any other articles or materials not of the same general character as those enumerated in the said proclamation, and in the Convention for the Supervision of the International Trade in Arms and Ammunition and in Implements of War, signed at Geneva June 17, 1925.

(e) Whoever, in violation of any of the provisions of this Act, shall export, or attempt to export, or cause to be exported, arms, ammunition, or implements of war from the United States shall be fined not more than $10,000, or imprisoned not more than five years, or both. . . .

(f) In the case of the forfeiture of any arms, ammunition, or implements of war by reason of a violation of this Act, . . . such arms, ammunition, or implements of war shall be delivered to the Secretary of War for such use or disposal thereof as shall be approved by the President of the Unted States.

(g) Whenever, in the judgment of the President, the conditions which have caused him to issue any proclamation under the authority of this section have ceased to exist, he shall revoke the same, and the provisions of this section shall thereupon cease to apply with respect to the state or states named in such proclamation, except with respect to offenses committed, or forfeitures incurred, prior to such revocation.

EXPORT OF OTHER ARTICLES AND MATERIALS

Sec. 2. (a) Whenever the President shall have issued a proclamation under the authority of section 1 of this Act and he shall thereafter find that the placing of restrictions on the shipment of certain articles or materials in addition to arms, ammunition, and implements of war from the United States to belligerent states, or to a state wherein civil strife exists, is necessary to promote the security or preserve the peace of the United States or to protect the lives of citizens of the United States, he shall so proclaim, and it shall thereafter be unlawful, for any American vessel to carry such articles or materials to any belligerent state, or to any state wherein civil strife exists, named in such proclamation issued under the authority of section 1 of this Act, or to any neutral state for transshipment to, or for the use of, any such belligerent state or any such state wherein civil strife exists. The President shall by proclamation from time to time definitely enumerate the articles and materials which it shall be unlawful for American vessels to so transport. . . .

(c) The President shall from time to time by proclamation extend such restrictions as are imposed under the authority of this section to other states as and when they may be declared to become belligerent states under proclamations issued under the authority of section 1 of this Act.

(d) The President may from time to time change, modify, or revoke in whole or in part any proclamations issued by him under the authority of this section.

(e) Except with respect to offenses committed, or forfeitures incurred, prior to May 1, 1939, this section and all proclamations issued thereunder shall not be effective after May 1, 1939.

FINANCIAL TRANSACTIONS

Sec. 3. (a) Whenever the President shall have issued a proclamation under the authority of section 1 of this Act, it shall thereafter be unlawful for any person within the United States to purchase, sell, or exchange bonds, securities, or other obligations of the government of any belligerent state or of any state wherein civil strife exists, named in such proclamation, or of any political subdivision of any such state, or of any person acting for or on behalf of the government of any such state, or of any faction or asserted government within any such state wherein civil strife exists, or of any person acting for or on behalf of any faction or asserted government within any such state wherein civil strife exists, issued after the date of such proclamation, or to make any loan or extend any credit to any such government, political subdivision, faction, asserted government, or person, or to solicit or receive any contribution for any such government, political subdivision, faction, asserted government, or person: *Provided,* That if the President shall find that such action will serve to protect the commercial or cther interests of the United States or its citizens, he may, in his discretion, and to such extent and under such regulations as he may prescribe, except from the operation of this section ordinary commercial credits and short-time obligations in aid of legal transactions and of a character customarily used in normal peacetime commercial transactions. Nothing in this subsection shall be construed to prohibit the solicitation or collection of funds to be used for medical aid and assistance, or for food and clothing to relieve human suffering, when such solicitation or collection of funds is made on behalf of and for use by any person or organization which is not acting for or on behalf of any such government, political subdivision, faction, or asserted government, but all such solicitations and collections of funds shall be subject to the approval of the President and shall be made under such rules and regulations as he shall prescribe. . . .

(c) Whoever shall violate the provisions of this section or of any regulations issued hereunder shall, upon conviction thereof, be fined not more than $50,000 or imprisoned for not more than five years, or both. Should the violation be by a corporation, organization, or association, each officer or agent thereof participating in the violation may be liable to the penalty herein prescribed. . . .

EXCEPTIONS—AMERICAN REPUBLICS

SEC. 4. This Act shall not apply to an American republic or republics engaged in war against a non-American state or states, provided the American republic is not cooperating with a non-American state or states in such war.

NATIONAL MUNITIONS CONTROL BOARD

SEC. 5. (a) There is hereby established a National Munitions Control Board (hereinafter referred to as the 'Board') to carry out the provisions of this Act. The Board shall consist of the Secretary of State, who shall be chairman and executive officer of the Board, the Secretary of the Treasury, the Secretary of War, the Secretary of the Navy, and the Secretary of Commerce. Except as otherwise provided in this Act, or by other law, the administration of this Act is vested in the Department of State. The Secretary of State shall promulgate such rules and regulations with regard to the enforcement of this section as he may deem necessary to carry out its provisions. The Board shall be convened by the chairman and shall hold at least one meeting a year.

(b) Every person who engages in the business of manufacturing, exporting, or importing any of the arms, ammunition, or implements of war referred to in this Act, whether as an exporter, importer, manufacturer, or dealer, shall register with the Secretary of State his name, or business name, principal place of business, and places of business in the United States, and a list of the arms, ammunition, and implements of war which he manufactures, imports, or exports.

(c) Every person required to register under this section shall notify the Secretary of State of any change in the arms, ammunition, or implements of war which he exports, imports, or manufactures; . . .

(d) It shall be unlawful for any person to export, or attempt to export, from the United States to any other state, any of the arms, ammunition, or implements of war referred to in this Act, or to import, or attempt to import, to the United States from any other state, any of the arms, ammunition, or implements of war referred to in this Act, without first having obtained a license therefor. . . .

(k) The President is hereby authorized to proclaim upon recommendation of the Board from time to time a list of articles which shall be considered arms, ammunition, and implements of war for the purposes of this section.

AMERICAN VESSELS PROHIBITED FROM CARRYING ARMS TO BELLIGERENT STATES

SEC. 6. (a) Whenever the President shall have issued a proclamation under the authority of section 1 of this Act, it shall thereafter be unlawful, until such proclamation is revoked, for any American vessel to carry any arms, ammunition, or implements of war to any belligerent state, or to any state wherein civil strife exists, named in such proclamation, or to any neutral state for transshipment to, or for the use of, any such belligerent state or any such state wherein civil strife exists.

(b) Whoever, in violation of the provisions of this section, shall take, or attempt to take, or shall authorize, hire, or solicit another to take, any American vessel carrying such cargo out of port or from the jurisdiction of the United States shall be fined not more than $10,000, or imprisoned not more than five years, or both; and, in addition, such vessel, and her tackle, apparel, furniture, and equipment, and the arms, ammunition, and implements of war on board, shall be forfeited to the United States.

USE OF AMERICAN PORTS AS BASE OF SUPPLY

SEC. 7. (a) Whenever, during any war in which the United States is neutral, the President, or any person thereunto authorized by him, shall have cause to believe that any vessel, domestic or foreign, whether requiring clearance or not, is about to carry out of a port of the United States, fuel, men, arms, ammunition, implements of war, or other supplies to any warship, tender, or supply ship of a belligerent state, but the evidence is not deemed sufficient to justify forbidding the departure of the vessel as provided for by section 1, title V, chapter 30, of the Act approved June 15, 1917, and if, in the President's judgment, such action will serve to maintain peace between the United States and foreign states, or to protect the commercial interests of the United States and its citizens, or to promote the security or neutrality of the United States, he shall have the power and it shall be his duty to require the owner, master, or person in command thereof, before departing from a port of the United States, to give a bond to the United States, with sufficient sureties, in such amount as he shall deem proper, conditioned that the vessel will not deliver the men, or any part of the cargo, to any warship, tender, or supply ship of a belligerent state.

(b) If the President, or any person thereunto authorized by him, shall find that a vessel, domestic or foreign, in a port of the United States, has previously cleared from a port of the United States during such war and delivered its cargo or any part thereof to a warship, tender, or supply ship of a belligerent state, he may prohibit the departure of such vessel during the duration of the war.

SUBMARINES AND ARMED MERCHANT VESSELS

SEC. 8. Whenever, during any war in which the United States is neutral, the President shall find that special restrictions placed on the use of the ports and territorial waters of the United States by the submarines or armed merchant vessels of a foreign state, will serve to maintain peace between the United States and foreign states, or to protect the commercial interests of the United States and its citizens, or to promote the security of the United States, and shall make proclamation therefore, it shall thereafter be unlawful for any such submarine or armed merchant vessel to enter a port or the territorial waters of the United States or to depart therefrom, except under such conditions and subject to such limitations as the President may prescribe. Whenever, in his judgment, the conditions which have caused him to issue his proclamation have ceased to exist, he shall revoke his proclamation and the provisions of this section shall thereupon cease to apply.

TRAVEL ON VESSELS OF BELLIGERENT STATES

SEC. 9. Whenever the President shall have issued a proclamation under the authority of section 1 of this Act it shall thereafter be unlawful for any citizen of the United States to travel on any vessel of the state or states named in such proclamation, except in accordance with such rules and regulations as the President shall prescribe: . . .

ARMING OF AMERICAN MERCHANT VESSELS PROHIBITED

SEC. 10. Whenever the President shall have issued a proclamation under the authority of section 1, it shall thereafter be unlawful, until such proclamation is revoked, for any American vessel engaged in commerce with any belligerent state, or any state wherein civil strife exists, named in such proclamation, to be armed or to carry any armament, arms, ammunition, or implements of war, except small arms and ammunition therefor which the President may deem necessary and shall publicly designate for the preservation of discipline aboard such vessels.

REGULATIONS

SEC. 11. The President may, from time to time, promulgate such rules and regulations.

not inconsistent with law, as may be necessary and proper to carry out any of the provisions of this Act; and he may exercise any power or authority conferred on him by this Act through such officer or officers, or agency or agencies, as he shall direct. . . .

515. REFORM OF THE FEDERAL JUDICIARY
1937
(U. S. 75th Cong. 1st Sess. *Sen. Report* 711)

The judicial invalidation of a large part of the New Deal program revived the oft-expressed demand for judicial reform. President F. D. Roosevelt argued, as had Theodore Roosevelt, that the courts were out of harmony with democracy and that some way should be found to force them in line with the will of the people as expressed through the other branches of the government. President Roosevelt's specific program called for a reorganization of the inferior federal courts to attain greater efficiency, and the appointment of one new justice, up to six in number, for every justice of the Supreme Court who, having passed the age of seventy and served for ten years, failed to retire. The proposal shocked many who felt that it violated the spirit of the American constitutional system of checks and balances and threatened the independence of the judiciary. The ultimate rejection of the proposal by the Senate Judiciary Committee and by Congress was probably the most serious setback which the President suffered during his eight years of office, yet it is clear now that although he lost the battle he won the campaign. We have included here the proposed bill for the reorganization of the judiciary, the President's address on the bill, the adverse report of the Senate Judiciary Committee, and the emasculated reform act which finally emerged. See M. Ernst, *The Ultimate Power;* I. Brant, *Storm over the Constitution;* R. K. Carr, *Democracy and the Supreme Court;* D. Alfange, *The Supreme Court and the National Will;* W. Lippman, *The Supreme Court, Independent or Controlled;* J. Alsop and T. Catledge, *The 168 Days;* C. A. and M. R. Beard, *America in Midpassage;* C. A. Ewing, *Judges of the Supreme Court, 1789–1937;* C. Fairman, "Retirement of Federal Judges," 51 Harv. L. Rev. 397. The Hearings are published, in six parts, in U. S. 75th Cong. 1st Sess. Sen. Comm. on Judiciary, *Hearings* on 1392.

1. PROPOSED BILL.

Be it enacted, That—

(a) When any judge of a court of the United States, appointed to hold his office

during good behavior, has heretofore or hereafter attained the age of seventy years and has held a commission or commissions as judge of any such court or courts at least ten years, continuously or otherwise, and within six months thereafter has neither resigned nor retired, the President, for each such judge who has not so resigned or retired, shall nominate, and by and with the advice and consent of the Senate, shall appoint one additional judge to the court to which the former is commissioned: *Provided,* That no additional judge shall be appointed hereunder if the judge who is of retirement age dies, resigns, or retires prior to the nomination of such additional judge.

(b) The number of judges of any court shall be permanently increased by the number appointed thereto under the provisions of subsection (a) of this section. No more than fifty judges shall be appointed thereunder, nor shall any judge be so appointed if such appointment would result in (1) more than fifteen members of the Supreme Court of the United States, (2) more than two additional members so appointed to a circuit court of appeals, the Court of Claims, the United States Court of Customs and Patent Appeals, or the Customs Court, or (3) more than twice the number of judges now authorized to be appointed for any district or, in the case of judges appointed for more than one district, for any such group of districts. . . .

(d) An additional judge shall not be appointed under the provisions of this section when the judge who is of retirement age is commissioned to an office as to which Congress has provided that a vacancy shall not be filled.

SEC. 2. (a) Any circuit judge hereafter appointed may be designated and assigned from time to time by the Chief Justice of the

United States for service in the circuit court of appeals for any circuit. Any district judge hereafter appointed may be designated and assigned from time to time by the Chief Justice of the United States for service in any district court, or, subject to the authority of the Chief Justice, by the senior circuit judge of his circuit for service in any district court within the circuit. A district judge designated and assigned to another district hereunder may hold court separately and at the same time as the district judge in such district. . . .

The designation and assignment of any judge may be terminated at any time by order of the Chief Justice or the senior circuit judge, as the case may be. . . .

SEC. 3 (a) The Supreme Court shall have power to appoint a proctor. It shall be his duty (1) to obtain and, if deemed by the Court to be desirable, to publish information as to the volume, character, and status of litigation in the district courts and circuit courts of appeals, and such other information as the Supreme Court may from time to time require by order, and it shall be the duty of any judge, clerk, or marshal of any court of the United States promptly to furnish such information as may be required by the proctor; (2) to investigate the need of assigning district and circuit judges to other courts and to make recommendations thereon to the Chief Justice; (3) to recommend, with the approval of the Chief Justice, to any court of the United States methods for expediting cases pending on its dockets; and (4) to perform such other duties consistent with his office as the Court shall direct. . . .

SEC. 5. When used in this Act—

(a) The term "judge of retirement age" means a judge of a court of the United States, appointed to hold his office during good behavior, who has attained the age of seventy years and has held a commission or commissions as judge of any such court or courts at least ten years, continuously or otherwise, and within six months thereafter, whether or not he is eligible for retirement, has neither resigned nor retired. . . .

2. ADDRESS BY THE PRESIDENT OF THE UNITED STATES, MARCH 9, 1937

. . . Tonight, sitting at my desk in the White House, I make my first radio report to the people in my second term of office. . . .

The American people have learned from the depression. For in the last three national elections an overwhelming majority of them voted a mandate that the Congress and the President begin the task of providing that protection—not after long years of debate, but now.

The courts, however, have cast doubts on the ability of the elected Congress to protect us against catastrophe by meeting squarely our modern social and economic conditions.

We are at a crisis in our ability to proceed with that protection. It is a quiet crisis. There are no lines of depositors outside closed banks. But to the far-sighted it is far-reaching in its possibilities of injury to America.

I want to talk with you very simply about the need for present action in this crisis—the need to meet the unanswered challenge of one-third of a nation ill-nourished, ill-clad, ill-housed.

Last Thursday I described the American form of government as a three-horse team provided by the Constitution to the American people so that their field might be plowed. The three horses are, of course, the three branches of government—the Congress, the executive, and the courts. Two of the horses are pulling in unison today; the third is not. Those who have intimated that the President of the United States is trying to drive that team overlook the simple fact that the President, as Chief Executive, is himself one of the three horses.

It is the American people themselves who are in the driver's seat.

It is the American people themselves who want the furrow plowed.

It is the American people themselves who expect the third horse to pull in unison with the other two.

I hope that you have reread the Constitution of the United States. Like the Bible, it ought to be read again and again.

It is an easy document to understand when you remember that it was called into being because the Articles of Confederation under which the Original Thirteen States tried to operate after the Revolution showed the need of a National Government with power enough to handle national problems. In its preamble the Constitution states that it was intended to form a more perfect Union and promote the general welfare; and the powers given to the Congress to carry out those purposes can be best described by saying that they were all the powers needed to meet each and every problem which then had a national character and which could not be met by merely local action.

But the framers went further. Having in mind that in succeeding generations many other problems then undreamed of would become national problems, they gave to the Congress the ample broad powers "to levy taxes * * * and provide for the common defense and general welfare of the United States."

That, my friends, is what I honestly believe to have been the clear and underlying purpose of the patriots who wrote a Federal Constitution to create a National Government with national power, intended as they said, "to form a more perfect union * * * for ourselves and our posterity."

For nearly 20 years there was no conflict between the Congress and the Court. Then, in 1803, . . . The Court claimed the power to declare it [a statute] unconstitutional and did so declare it. But a little later the Court itself admitted that it was an extraordinary power to exercise and through Mr. Justice Washington laid down this limitation upon it: "It is but a decent respect due to the wisdom. the integrity, and the patriotism of the legislative body, by which any law is passed, to presume in favor of its validity until its violation of the Constitution is proved beyond all reasonable doubt."

But since the rise of the modern movement for social and economic progress through legislation, the Court has more and more often and more and more boldly asserted a power to veto laws passed by the Congress and State legislatures in complete disregard of this original limitation.

In the last 4 years the sound rule of giving statutes the benefit of all reasonable doubt has been cast aside. The Court has been acting not as a judicial body, but as a policy-making body.

When the Congress has sought to stabilize national agriculture, to improve the conditions of labor, to safeguard business against unfair competition, to protect our national resources, and in many other ways to serve our clearly national needs, the majority of the Court has

been assuming the power to pass on the wisdom of these acts of the Congress—and to approve or disapprove the public policy written into these laws.

That is not only my accusation. It is the accusation of most distinguished Justices of the present Supreme Court. I have not the time to quote to you all the language used by dissenting Justices in many of these cases. But in the case holding the Railroad Retirement Act unconstitutional, for instance, Chief Justice Hughes said in a dissenting opinion that the majority opinion was "a departure from sound principles," and placed "an unwarranted limitation upon the commerce clause." And three other Justices agreed with him.

In the case holding the A. A. A. unconstitutional, Justice Stone said of the majority opinion that it was a "tortured construction of the Constitution." And two other Justices agreed with him.

In the case holding the New York Minimum Wage Law unconstitutional, Justice Stone said that the majority were actually reading into the Constitution their own "personal economic predilections," and that if the legislative power is not left free to choose the methods of solving the problems of poverty, subsistence, and health of large numbers in the community, then "government is to be rendered impotent." And two other Justices agreed with him.

In the face of these dissenting opinions, there is no basis for the claim made by some members of the Court that something in the Constitution has compelled them regretfully to thwart the will of the people.

In the face of such dissenting opinions, it is perfectly clear that as Chief Justice Hughes has said, "We are under a Constitution, but the Constitution is what the judges say it is."

The Court in addition to the proper use of its judicial functions has improperly set itself up as a third House of the Congress—a superlegislature, as one of the Justices has called it —reading into the Constitution words and implications which are not there, and which were never intended to be there.

We have, therefore, reached the point as a Nation where we must take action to save the Constitution from the Court and the Court from itself. We must find a way to take an appeal from the Supreme Court to the Constitution itself. We want a Supreme Court which will do justice under the Constitution—not over it. In our courts we want a government of laws and not of men.

I want—as all Americans want—an independent judiciary as proposed by the framers of the Constitution. That means a Supreme Court that will enforce the Constitution as written—that will refuse to amend the Constitution by the arbitrary exercise of judicial power—amendment by judicial say-so. It does not mean a judiciary so independent that it can deny the existence of facts universally recognized.

How, then, could we proceed to perform the mandate given us? It was said in last year's Democratic platform, "If these problems cannot be effectively solved within the Constitution, we shall seek such clarifying amendment as will assure the power to enact those laws, adequately to regulate commerce, protect public health and safety, and safeguard economic security." In other words, we said we would seek an amendment only if every other possible means by legislation were to fail.

When I commenced to review the situation with the problem squarely before me, I came by a process of elimination to the conclusion that short of amendments the only method which was clearly constitutional, and would at the same time carry out other much-needed reforms, was to infuse new blood into all our courts. We must have men worthy and equipped to carry out impartial justice. But at the same time we must have judges who will bring to the courts a present-day sense of the Constitution—judges who will retain in the courts the judicial functions of a court and reject the legislative powers which the courts have today assumed.

In 45 out of 48 States of the Union, judges are chosen not for life but for a period of years. In many States judges must retire at the age of 70. Congress has provided financial security by offering life pensions at full pay for Federal judges on all courts who are willing to retire at 70. In the case of Supreme Court Justices, that pension is $20,-000 a year. But all Federal judges, once appointed, can, if they choose, hold office for life no matter how old they may get to be.

What is my proposal? It is simply this:

Whenever a judge or justice of any Federal court has reached the age of 70 and does not avail himself of the opportunity to retire on a pension, a new member shall be appointed by the President then in office, with the approval, as required by the Constitution, of the Senate of the United States.

That plan has two chief purposes: By bringing into the judicial system a steady and continuing stream of new and younger blood, I hope, first, to make the administration of all Federal justice speedier and therefore less costly; secondly, to bring to the decision of social and economic problems younger men who have had personal experience and contact with modern facts and circumstances under which average men have to live and work. This plan will save our National Constitution from hardening of the judicial arteries.

The number of judges to be appointed would depend wholly on the decision of present judges now over 70 or those who would subsequently reach the age of 70.

If, for instance, any one of the six Justices of the Supreme Court now over the age of 70 should retire as provided under the plan, no additional place would be created. Consequently, although there never can be more than 15, there may be only 14, or 13, or 12, and there may be only 9.

There is nothing novel or radical about this idea. It seeks to maintain the Federal bench in full vigor. It has been discussed and approved by many persons of high authority even since a similar proposal passed the House of Representatives in 1869.

Why was the age fixed at 70? Because the laws of many States, the practice of the civil service, the regulations of the Army and Navy, and the rules of many of our universities and of almost every great private business enterprise commonly fix the retirement age at 70 years or less.

The statute would apply to all the courts in the Federal system. There is general approval so far as the lower Federal courts are concerned. The plan has met opposition only so far as the Supreme Court of the United States itself is concerned. If such a plan is good for the lower courts, it certainly ought to be equally good for the highest court, from which there is no appeal.

Those opposing this plan have sought to

arouse prejudice and fear by crying that I am seeking to "pack" the Supreme Court and that a baneful precedent will be established.

What do they mean by the words "packing the Court"?

Let me answer this question with a bluntness that will end all honest misunderstanding of my purposes.

If by that phrase "packing the Court" it is charged that I wish to place on the bench spineless puppets who would disregard the law and would decide specific cases as I wished them to be decided, I make this answer: That no President fit for his office would appoint, and no Senate of honorable men fit for their office would confirm, that kind of appointees to the Supreme Court.

But if by that phrase the charge is made that I would appoint and the Senate would confirm Justices worthy to sit beside present members of the Court who understand those modern conditions; that I will appoint Justices who will not undertake to override the judgment of the Congress on legislative policy; that I will appoint Justices who will act as Justices and not as legislators—if the appointment of such Justices can be called "packing the Courts"—then I say that I, and with me the vast majority of the American people, favor doing just that thing—now.

Is it a dangerous precedent for the Congress to change the number of the Justices? The Congress has always had, and will have, that power. The number of Justices has been changed several times before—in the administrations of John Adams and Thomas Jefferson, both signers of the Declaration of Independence, Andrew Jackson, Abraham Lincoln, and Ulysses S. Grant.

I suggest only the addition of Justices to the bench in accordance with a clearly defined principle relating to a clearly defined age limit. Fundamentally, if in the future America cannot trust the Congress it elects to refrain from abuse of our constitutional usages, democracy will have failed far beyond the importance to it of any kind of precedent concerning the judiciary.

We think it so much in the public interest to maintain a vigorous judiciary that we encourage the retirement of elderly judges by offering them a life pension at full salary. Why then should we leave the fulfillment of this public policy to chance or make it dependent upon the desire or prejudice of any individual Justice?

It is the clear intention of our public policy to provide for a constant flow of new and younger blood into the judiciary. Normally, every President appoints a large number of district and circuit judges and a few members of the Supreme Court. Until my first term practically every President of the United States had appointed at least one member of the Supreme Court. President Taft appointed five members and named a Chief Justice; President Wilson three; President Harding four, including a Chief Justice; President Coolidge one; President Hoover three, including a Chief Justice.

Such a succession of appointments should have provided a court well balanced as to age. But chance and the disinclination of individuals to leave the Supreme Bench have now given us a Court in which five Justices will be over 75 years of age before next June and one over 70. Thus a sound public policy has been defeated.

I now propose that we establish by law an assurance against any such ill-balanced Court in the future. I propose that hereafter, when a judge reaches the age of 70, a new and younger judge shall be added to the Court automatically. In this way I propose to enforce a sound public policy by law instead of leaving the composition of our Federal courts, including the highest, to be determined by chance or the personal decision of individuals.

If such a law as I propose is regarded as establishing a new precedent, is it not a most desirable precedent?

Like all lawyers, like all Americans, I regret the necessity of this controversy. But the welfare of the United States, and indeed of the Constitution itself, is what we all must think about first. Our difficulty with the Court today rises not from the Court as an institution but from human beings within it. But we cannot yield our constitutional destiny to the personal judgment of a few men who, being fearful of the future, would deny us the necessary means of dealing with the present.

This plan of mine is no attack on the Court; it seeks to restore the Court to its rightful and historic place in our system of constitutional government and to have it resume its high task of building anew on the Constitution "a system of living law."

I have thus explained to you the reasons that lie behind our efforts to secure results by legislation within the Constitution. I hope that thereby the difficult process of constitutional amendment may be rendered unnecessary. . . .

I am in favor of action through legislation—

First, because I believe that it can be passed at this session of the Congress.

Second, because it will provide a reinvigorated, liberal-minded judiciary necessary to furnish quicker and cheaper justice from bottom to top.

Third, because it will provide a series of Federal courts willing to enforce the Constitution as written, and unwilling to assert legislative powers by writing into it their own political and economic policies.

During the past half century the balance of power between the three great branches of the Federal Government has been tipped out of balance by the courts in direct contradiction of the high purposes of the framers of the Constitution. It is my purpose to restore that balance. You who know me will accept my solemn assurance that in a world in which democracy is under attack I seek to make American democracy succeed.

3. Adverse Report from the Committee on the Judiciary.

The Committee on the Judiciary, to whom was referred the bill to reorganize the judicial branch of the Government, after full consideration, having unanimously amended the measure, hereby report the bill adversely with the recommendation that it do not pass. . . .

THE ARGUMENT

The committee recommends that the measure be rejected for the following primary reasons:

I. The bill does not accomplish any one of the objectives for which it was originally offered.

II. It applies force to the judiciary and in its initial and ultimate effect would undermine the independence of the courts.

III. It violates all precedents in the history of our Government and would in itself be a dangerous precedent for the future.

IV. The theory of the bill is in direct violation of the spirit of the American Constitution and its employment would permit alteration of the Constitution without the people's consent or approval; it undermines the protection our constitutional system gives to minorities and is subversive of the rights of individuals.

V. It tends to centralize the Federal district judiciary by the power of assigning judges from one district to another at will.

VI. It tends to expand political control over the judicial department by adding to the powers of the legislative and executive departments respecting the judiciary. . . .

OBJECTIVES AS ORIGINALLY STATED

As offered to the Congress, this bill was designed to effectuate only three objectives, described as follows in the President's message:

1. To increase the personnel of the Federal courts "so that cases may be promptly decided in the first instance, and may be given adequate and prompt hearing on all appeals";

2. To "invigorate all the courts by the permanent infusion of new blood";

3. To "grant to the Supreme Court further power and responsibility in maintaining the efficiency of the entire Federal judiciary."

The third of these purposes was to be accomplished by the provisions creating the office of the Proctor and dealing with the assignment of judges to courts other than those to which commissioned.

The first two objectives were to be attained by the provisions authorizing the appointment of not to exceed 50 additional judges when sitting judges of retirement age, as defined in the bill, failed to retire or resign. How totally inadequate the measure is to achieve either of the named objectives, the most cursory examination of the facts reveals. . . .

QUESTION OF AGE NOT SOLVED

The next question is to determine to what extent "the persistent infusion of new blood" may be expected from this bill.

It will be observed that the bill before us does not and cannot compel the retirement of any judge, whether on the Supreme Court or any other court, when he becomes 70 years of age. It will be remembered that the mere attainment of three score and ten by a particular judge does not, under this bill, require the appointment of another. The man on the bench may be 80 years of age, but this bill will not authorize the President to appoint a new judge to sit beside him unless he has served as a judge for 10 years. In other words, age itself is not penalized; the penalty falls only when age is attended with experience.

No one should overlook the fact that under this bill the President, whoever he may be and whether or not he believes in the constant infusion of young blood in the courts, may nominate a man 69 years and 11 months of age to the Supreme Court, or to any court, and if confirmed, such nominee, if he never had served as a judge, would continue to sit upon the bench unmolested by this law until he had attained the ripe age of 79 years and 11 months.

We are told that "modern complexities call also for a constant infusion of new blood in the courts, just as it is needed in executive functions of the Government and in private business." Does this bill provide for such? The answer is obviously no. As has been just demonstrated, the introduction of old and inexperienced blood into the courts is not prevented by this bill.

More than that, the measure, by its own terms, makes impossible the "constant" or "persistent" infusion of new blood. It is to be observed that the word is "new," not "young."

The Supreme Court may not be expanded to more than 15 members. No more than two additional members may be appointed to any circuit court of appeals, to the Court of Claims, to the Court of Customs and Patent Appeals, or to the Customs Court, and the number of judges now serving in any district or group of districts may not be more than doubled. There is, therefore, a specific limitation of appointment regardless of age. That is to say, this bill, ostensibly designed to provide for the infusion of new blood, sets up insuperable obstacles to the "constant" or "persistent" operation of that principle. . . .

It thus appears that the bill before us does not with certainty provide for increasing the personnel of the Federal judiciary, does not remedy the law's delay, does not serve the interest of the "poorer litigant" and does not provide for the "constant" or "persistent

infusion of new blood" into the judiciary. What, then, does it do?

THE BILL APPLIES FORCE TO THE JUDICIARY

The answer is clear. It applies force to the judiciary. It is an attempt to impose upon the courts a course of action, a line of decision which, without that force, without that imposition, the judiciary might not adopt. . . .

Those of us who hold office in this Government, however humble or exalted it may be, are creatures of the Constitution. To it we owe all the power and authority we possess. Outside of it we have none. We are bound by it in every official act.

We know that this instrument, without which we would not be able to call ourselves presidents, judges, or legislators, was carefully planned and deliberately framed to establish three coordinate branches of government, every one of them to be independent of the others. For the protection of the people, for the preservation of the rights of the individual, for the maintenance of the liberties of minorities, for maintaining the checks and balances of our dual system, the three branches of the Government were so constituted that the independent expression of honest difference of opinion could never be restrained in the people's servants and no one branch could overawe or subjugate the others. That is the American system. It is immeasurably more important, immeasurably more sacred to the people of America, indeed, to the people of all the world than the immediate adoption of any legislation however beneficial.

That judges should hold office during good behavior is the prescription. It is founded upon historic experience of the utmost significance. Compensation at stated times, which compensation was not to be diminished during their tenure, was also ordained. Those comprehensible terms were the outgrowths of experience which was deep-seated. . . . This judicial system is the priceless heritage of every American.

By this bill another and wholly different cause is proposed for the intervention of executive influence, namely, age. Age and behavior have no connection; they are unrelated subjects. By this bill, judges who have reached 70 years of age may remain on the bench and have their judgment augmented if they agree with the new appointee, or vetoed if they disagree. This is far from the independence intended for the courts by the framers of the Constitution. This is an unwarranted influence accorded the appointing agency, contrary to the spirit of the Constitution. The bill sets up a plan which has as its stability the changing will or inclination of an agency not a part of the judicial system. Constitutionally, the bill can have no sanction. The effect of the bill, as stated by the Attorney General to the committee, and indeed by the President in both his message and speech, is in violation of the organic law.

OBJECT OF PLAN ACKNOWLEDGED

No amount of sophistry can cover up this fact. The effect of this bill is not to provide for an increase in the number of Justices composing the Supreme Court. The effect is to provide a forced retirement or, failing in this, to take from the Justices affected a free exercise of their independent judgment. . . .

Let us, for the purpose of the argument, grant that the Court has been wrong, wrong not only in that it has rendered mistaken opinions but wrong in the far more serious sense that it has substituted its will for the congressional will in the matter of legislation. May we nevertheless safely punish the Court?

Today it may be the Court which is charged with forgetting its constitutional duties. Tomorrow it may be the Congress. The next day it may be the Executive. If we yield to temptation now to lay the lash upon the Court, we are only teaching others how to apply it to ourselves and to the people when the occasion seems to warrant. Manifestly, if we may force the hand of the Court to secure our interpretation of the Constitution, then some succeeding Congress may repeat the process to secure another and a different interpretation and one which may not sound so pleasant in our ears as that for which we now contend.

There is a remedy for usurpation or other judicial wrongdoing. If this bill be supported by the toilers of this country upon the ground that they want a Court which will sustain legislation limiting hours and providing minimum wages, they must remember

that the procedure employed in the bill could be used in another administration to lengthen hours and to decrease wages. If farmers want agricultural relief and favor this bill upon the ground that it gives them a Court which will sustain legislation in their favor, they must remember that the procedure employed might some day be used to deprive them of every vestige of a farm relief.

When members of the Court usurp legislative powers or attempt to exercise political power, they lay themselves open to the charge of having lapsed from that "good behavior" which determines the period of their official life. But, if you say, the process of impeachment is difficult and uncertain, the answer is, the people made it so when they framed the Constitution. It is not for us, the servants of the people, the instruments of the Constitution, to find a more easy way to do that which our masters made difficult.

But, if the fault of the judges is not so grievous as to warrant impeachment, if their offense is merely that they have grown old, and we feel, therefore, that there should be a "constant infusion of new blood," then obviously the way to achieve that result is by constitutional amendment fixing definite terms for the members of the judiciary or making mandatory their retirement at a given age. Such a provision would indeed provide for the constant infusion of new blood, not only now but at all times in the future. The plan before us is but a temporary expedient which operates once and then never again, leaving the Court as permanently expanded to become once more a court of old men, gradually year by year falling behind the times. . . .

A MEASURE WITHOUT PRECEDENT

This bill is an invasion of judicial power such as has never before been attempted in this country. It is true that in the closing days of the administration of John Adams, a bill was passed creating 16 new circuit judges while reducing by one the number of places on the Supreme Court. It was charged that this was a bill to use the judiciary for a political purpose by providing official positions for members of a defeated party. The repeal of that law was the first task of the Jefferson administration.

Neither the original act nor the repealer

was an attempt to change the course of judicial decision. And never in the history of the country has there been such an act. The present bill comes to us, therefore, wholly without precedent.

It is true that the size of the Supreme Court has been changed from time to time, but in every instance after the Adams administration, save one, the changes were made for purely administrative purposes in aid of the Court, not to control it. . . .

A PRECEDENT OF LOYALTY TO THE CONSTITUTION

Shall we now, after 150 years of loyalty to the constitutional ideal of an untrammeled judiciary, duty bound to protect the constitutional rights of the humblest citizen even against the Government itself, create the vicious precedent which must necessarily undermine our system? The only argument for the increase which survives analysis is that Congress should enlarge the Court so as to make the policies of this administration effective.

We are told that a reactionary oligarchy defies the will of the majority, that this is a bill to "unpack" the Court and give effect to the desires of the majority; that is to say, a bill to increase the number of Justices for the express purpose of neutralizing the views of some of the present members. In justification we are told, but without authority, by those who would rationalize this program, that Congress was given the power to determine the size of the Court so that the legislative branch would be able to impose its will upon the judiciary. This amounts to nothing more than the declaration that when the Court stands in the way of a legislative enactment, the Congress may reverse the ruling by enlarging the Court. When such a principle is adopted, our constitutional system is overthrown!

This, then, is the dangerous precedent we are asked to establish. When proponents of the bill assert, as they have done, that Congress in the past has altered the number of Justices upon the Supreme Court and that this is reason enough for our doing it now, they show how important precedents are and prove that we should now refrain from any action that would seem to establish one which could be followed hereafter whenever a Congress and an executive should become dissatisfied with the decisions of the Supreme Court.

This is the first time in the history of our country that a proposal to alter the decisions of the court by enlarging its personnel has been so boldly made. Let us meet it. Let us now set a salutary precedent that will never be violated. Let us, of the Seventy-fifth Congress, in words that will never be disregarded by any succeeding Congress, declare that we would rather have an independent Court, a fearless Court, a Court that will dare to announce its honest opinions in what it believes to be the defense of the liberties of the people, than a Court that, out of fear or sense of obligation to the appointing power, or factional passion, approves any measure we may enact. We are not the judges of the judges. We are not above the Constitution.

Even if every charge brought against the so-called "reactionary" members of this Court be true, it is far better that we await orderly but inevitable change of personnel than that we impatiently overwhelm them with new members. Exhibiting this restraint, thus demonstrating our faith in the American system, we shall set an example that will protect the independent American judiciary from attack as long as this Government stands. . . .

True it is, that courts like Congresses, should take account of the advancing strides of civilization. True it is that the law, being a progressive science, must be pronounced progressively and liberally; but the milestones of liberal progress are made to be noted and counted with caution rather than merely to be encountered and passed. Progress is not a mad mob march; rather, it is a steady, invincible stride. . . .

If, under the "hydraulic pressure" of our present need for economic justice, we destroy the system under which our people have progressed to a higher degree of justice and prosperity than that ever enjoyed by any other people in all the history of the human race, then we shall destroy not only all opportunity for further advance but everything we have thus far achieved. . . .

Even if the case were far worse than it is alleged to be, it would still be no argument in favor of this bill to say that the courts and some judges have abused their power. The courts are not perfect, nor are the judges. The Congress is not perfect, nor are Senators and Representatives. The Executive is not perfect. These branches of government and the office under them are filled by human beings who for the most part strive to live up to the dignity and idealism of a system that was designed to achieve the greatest possible measure of justice and freedom for all the people. We shall destroy the system when we reduce it to the imperfect standards of the men who operate it. We shall strengthen it and ourselves, we shall make justice and liberty for all men more certain when, by patience and self-restraint, we maintain it on the high plane on which it was conceived.

Inconvenience and even delay in the enactment of legislation is not a heavy price to pay for our system. Constitutional democracy moves forward with certainty rather than with speed. The safety and the permanence of the progressive march of our civilization are far more important to us and to those who are to come after us than the enactment now of any particular law. The Constitution of the United States provides ample opportunity for the expression of popular will to bring about such reforms and changes as the people may deem essential to their present and future welfare. It is the people's charter of the powers granted those who govern them. . . .

SUMMARY

We recommend the rejection of this bill as a needless, futile, and utterly dangerous abandonment of constitutional principle.

It was presented to the Congress in a most intricate form and for reasons that obscured its real purpose.

It would not banish age from the bench nor abolish divided decisions.

It would not affect the power of any court to hold laws unconstitutional nor withdraw from any judge the authority to issue injunctions.

It would not reduce the expense of litigation nor speed the decision of cases.

It is a proposal without precedent and without justification.

It would subjugate the courts to the will of Congress and the President and thereby destroy the independence of the judiciary, the only certain shield of individual rights.

It contains the germ of a system of centralized administration of law that would enable an executive so minded to send his judges into every judicial district in the land to sit

in judgment on controversies between the Government and the citizen.

It points the way to the evasion of the Constitution and establishes the method whereby the people may be deprived of their right to pass upon all amendments of the fundamental law.

It stands now before the country, acknowledged by its proponents as a plan to force judicial interpretation of the Constitution, a proposal that violates every sacred tradition of American democracy.

Under the form of the Constitution it seeks to do that which is unconstitutional.

Its ultimate operation would be to make this Government one of men rather than one of law, and its practical operation would be to make the Constitution what the executive or legislative branches of the Government choose to say it is—an interpretation to be changed with each change of administration.

It is a measure which should be so emphatically rejected that its parallel will never again be presented to the free representatives of the free people of America.

WILLIAM H. KING.
FREDERICK VAN NUYS.
PATRICK MCCARRAN.
CARL A. HATCH.
EDWARD R. BURKE.
TOM CONNALLY.
JOSEPH C. O'MAHONEY.
WILLIAM E. BORAH.
WARREN R. AUSTIN.
FREDERICK STEIWER.

4. Judiciary Reform Act of 1937, August 24, 1937.

An Act to provide for intervention by the United States, direct appeals to the Supreme Court of the United States, and regulation of the issuance of injunctions, in certain cases involving the constitutionality of Acts of Congress, and for other purposes.

Be it enacted, That whenever the constitutionality of any Act of Congress affecting the public interest is drawn in question in any court of the United States in any suit or proceeding to which the United States, or any agency thereof, or any officer or employee thereof, as such officer or employee, is not a party, the court having jurisdiction of the suit or proceeding shall certify such fact to the Attorney General. In any such case the court shall permit the United States to intervene and become a party for presentation of evidence (if evidence is otherwise receivable in such suit or proceeding) and argument upon the question of the constitutionality of such Act. In any such suit or proceeding the United States shall, subject to the applicable provisions of law, have all the rights of a party and the liabilities of a party as to court costs to the extent necessary for a proper presentation of the facts and law relating to the constitutionality of such Act.

SEC. 2. In any suit or proceeding in any court of the United States to which the United States, or any agency thereof, or any officer or employee thereof, as such officer or employee, is a party, or in which the United States has intervened and become a party, and in which the decision is against the constitutionality of any Act of Congress, an appeal may be taken directly to the Supreme Court of the United States by the United States or any other party to such suit or proceeding upon application therefor or notice thereof within thirty days after the entry of a final or interlocutory judgment, decree, or order; and in the event that any such appeal is taken, any appeal or cross-appeal by any party to the suit or proceeding taken previously, or taken within sixty days after notice of an appeal under this section, shall also be or be treated as taken directly to the Supreme Court of the United States. In the event that an appeal is taken under this section, the record shall be made up and the case docketed in the Supreme Court of the United States within sixty days from the time such appeal is allowed, under such rules as may be prescribed by the proper courts. Appeals under this section shall be heard by the Supreme Court of the United States at the earliest possible time and shall take precedence over all other matters not of a like character. This section shall not be construed to be in derogation of any right of direct appeal to the Supreme Court of the United States under existing provisions of law.

SEC. 3. No interlocutory or permanent injunction suspending or restraining the enforcement, operation, or execution of, or setting aside, in whole or in part, any Act of Congress upon the ground that such Act or any part thereof is repugnant to the Con-

stitution of the United States shall be issued or granted by any district court of the United States, or by any judge thereof, or by any circuit judge acting as district judge, unless the application for the same shall be presented to a circuit or district judge, and shall be heard and determined by three judges, of whom at least one shall be a circuit judge. When any such application is presented to a judge, he shall immediately request the senior circuit judge (or in his absence, the presiding circuit judge) of the circuit in which such district court is located to designate two other judges to participate in hearing and determining such application. It shall be the duty of the senior circuit judge or the presiding circuit judge, as the case may be, to designate immediately two other judges from such circuit for such purpose, and it shall be the duty of the judges so designated to participate in such hearing and determination. Such application shall not be heard or determined before at least five days' notice of the hearing has been given to the Attorney General and to such other persons as may be defendants in the suit: *Provided,* That if of opinion that irreparable loss or damage would result to the petitioner unless a temporary restraining order is granted, the judge to whom the application is made may grant such temporary restraining order at any time before the hearing and determination of the application, but such temporary restraining order shall remain in force only until such hearing and determination upon notice as aforesaid, and such temporary restraining order shall contain a specific finding, based upon evidence submitted to the court making the order and identified by reference thereto, that such irreparable loss or damage would result to the petitioner and specifying the nature of the loss or damage. The said court may, at the time of hearing such application, upon a like finding, continue the temporary stay or suspension, in whole or in part, until decision upon the application. The hearing upon any such application for an interlocutory or permanent injunction shall be given precedence and shall be in every way expedited and be assigned for a hearing at the earliest practicable day. An appeal may be taken directly to the Supreme Court of the United States upon application therefor or notice thereof within thirty days after the entry of the order, decree, or judgment granting or denying, after notice and hearing, and interlocutory or permanent injunction in such case. In the event that an appeal is taken under this section, the record shall be made up and the case docketed in the Supreme Court of the United States within sixty days from the time such appeal is allowed, under such rules as may be prescribed by the proper courts. Appeals under this section shall be heard by the Supreme Court of the United States at the earliest possible time and shall take precedence over all other matters not of a like character. This section shall not be construed to be in derogation of any right of direct appeal to the Supreme Court of the United States under existing provisions of law.

SEC. 4. Section 13 of the Judicial Code, as amended, is hereby amended to read as follows:

"SEC. 13. Whenever any district judge by reason of any disability or absence from his district or the accumulation or urgency of business is unable to perform speedily the work of his district, the senior circuit judge of that circuit, or, in his absence, the circuit justice thereof, shall designate and assign any district judge of any district court within the same judicial circuit to act as district judge in such district and to discharge all the judicial duties of a judge thereof for such time as the business of the said district court may require. Whenever it is found impracticable to designate and assign another district judge within the same judicial circuit as above provided and a certificate of the needs of any such district is presented by said senior circuit judge or said circuit justice to the Chief Justice of the United States, he, or in his absence the senior associate justice, shall designate and assign a district judge of an adjoining judicial circuit if practicable, or if not practicable, then of any judicial circuit, to perform the duties of district judge and hold a district court in any such district as above provided.

516. THE WAGNER HOUSING ACT
September 1, 1937
(U. S. Statutes at Large, Vol. L, p.. 888)

Agitation for slum clearance and the construction of good low-cost housing dates back to the nineteenth century, but notwithstanding the efforts of philanthropists and reformers, little was accomplished, and it was notorious that in this field the United States lagged badly behind such countries as Austria, Germany, England, and Sweden. The NRA provided funds for slum clearance and the construction of low cost housing, but these were insufficient to make any real improvement in the situation. The Wagner Housing Act attempted to solve the problem by placing the enormous resources of the federal government behind the slum clearance program. For the background of the slum problem, see R. W. DeForest and L. Veiller, *The Tenement House Problem;* J. Riis, *How the Other Half Lives;* E. E. Wood, *Recent Trends in American Housing;* L. H. Pink, *The New Day in Housing;* L. Post, *The Challenge of Housing;* M. W. Straus and T. Wegg, *Housing Comes of Age.*

An Act to provide financial assistance to the States and political subdivisions thereof for the elimination of unsafe and insanitary housing conditions, for the eradication of slums, for the provision of decent, safe, and sanitary dwellings for families of low income, and for the reduction of unemployment and the stimulation of business activity, to create a United States Housing Authority, and for other purposes.

DECLARATION OF POLICY

SECTION 1. It is hereby declared to be the policy of the United States to promote the general welfare of the Nation by employing its funds and credit, as provided in this Act, to assist the several States and their political subdivisions to alleviate present and recurring unemployment and to remedy the unsafe and insanitary housing conditions and the acute shortage of decent, safe, and sanitary dwellings for families of low income, in rural or urban communities, that are injurious to the health, safety, and morals of the citizens of the Nation.

DEFINITIONS

SEC. 2. When used in this Act—
(1) The term "low-rent housing" means decent, safe, and sanitary dwellings within

the financial reach of families of low income, and developed and administered to promote serviceability, efficiency, economy, and stability, and embraces all necessary appurtenances thereto. The dwellings in low-rent housing as defined in this Act shall be available solely for families whose net income at the time of admission does not exceed five times the rental (including the value or cost to them of heat, light, water, and cooking fuel) of the dwellings to be furnished such families, except that in the case of families with three or more minor dependents, such ratio shall not exceed six to one.

(2) The term "families of low income" means families who are in the lowest income group and who cannot afford to pay enough to cause private enterprise in their locality or metropolitan area to build an adequate supply of decent, safe, and sanitary dwellings for their use.

(3) The term "slum" means any area where dwellings predominate which, by reason of dilapidation, overcrowding, faulty arrangement or design, lack of ventilation, light or sanitation facilities, or any combination of these factors, are detrimental to safety, health, or morals. . . .

UNITED STATES HOUSING AUTHORITY

SEC. 3. (a) There is hereby created in the Department of the Interior and under the general supervision of the Secretary thereof a body corporate of perpetual duration to be known as the United States Housing Authority, which shall be an agency and instrumentality of the United States.

(b) The powers of the Authority shall be vested in and exercised by an Administrator, who shall be appointed by the President, by and with the advice and consent of the Senate. The Administrator shall serve for a term of five years and shall be removable by the President upon notice and hearing for neglect of duty or malfeasance but for no other cause. . . .

SEC. 4. . . .

(e) The Authority, including but not limited to its franchise, capital, reserves, surplus, loans, income, assets, and property of any kind, shall be exempt from all taxation now or hereafter imposed by the United States or by any State, county, municipality, or local taxing authority. Obligations, including interest thereon, issued by public housing agencies in connection with low-rent-housing or slum-clearance projects, and the income derived by such agencies from such projects, shall be exempt from all taxation now or hereafter imposed by the United States. . . .

LOANS FOR LOW-RENT-HOUSING AND SLUM-CLEARANCE PROJECTS

SEC. 9. The Authority may make loans to public-housing agencies to assist the development, acquisition, or administration of low-rent-housing or slum-clearance projects by such agencies. Where capital grants are made pursuant to section 11 the total amount of such loans outstanding on any one project and in which the Authority participates shall not exceed the development or acquisition cost of such project less all such capital grants, but in no event shall said loans exceed 90 per centum of such cost. In the case of annual contributions in assistance of low rentals as provided in section 10 the total of such loans outstanding on any one project and in which the Authority participates shall not exceed 90 per centum of the development or acquisition cost of such project. Such loans shall bear interest at such rate not less than the going Federal rate at the time the loan is made, plus one-half of one per centum, shall be secured in such manner, and shall be repaid within such period not exceeding sixty years, as may be deemed advisable by the Authority.

ANNUAL CONTRIBUTIONS IN ASSISTANCE OF LOW RENTALS

SEC. 10. (a) The Authority may make annual contributions to public housing agencies to assist in achieving and maintaining the low-rent character of their housing projects. The annual contributions for any such project shall be fixed in uniform amounts, and shall be paid in such amounts over a fixed period of years. No part of such annual contributions by the Authority shall be made available for any project unless and until the State, city, county, or other political subdivision in which such project is situated shall contribute, in the form of cash or tax remissions, general or special, or tax exemptions, at least 20 per centum of the annual contributions herein provided. The Authority shall embody the provisions for such annual contributions in a contract guaranteeing their payment over such fixed period: *Provided,* That no annual contributions shall be made, and the Authority shall enter into no contract guaranteeing any annual contribution in connection with the development of any low-rent-housing or slum-clearance project involving the construction of new dwellings, unless the project includes the elimination by demolition, condemnation, and effective closing, or the compulsory repair or improvement of unsafe or insanitary dwellings situated in the locality or metropolitan area, substantially equal in number to the number of newly constructed dwellings provided by the project; except that such elimination may, in the discretion of the Authority, be deferred in any locality or metropolitan area where the shortage of decent, safe, or sanitary housing available to families of low income is so acute as to force dangerous overcrowding of such families.

(b) Annual contributions shall be strictly limited to the amounts and periods necessary, in the determination of the Authority, to assure the low-rent character of the housing projects involved. Toward this end the Authority may prescribe regulations fixing the maximum contributions available under different circumstances, giving consideration to cost, location, size, rent-paying ability of prospective tenants, or other factors bearing upon the amounts and periods of assistance needed to achieve and maintain low rentals. Such regulations may provide for rates of contribution based upon development, acquisition or administration cost, number of dwelling units, number of persons housed, or other appropriate factors. . . .

(e) The Authority is authorized, on and after the date of the enactment of this Act, to enter into contracts which provide for annual contributions aggregating not more than $5,000,000 per annum, on or after July 1, 1938, to enter into additional such contracts which provide for annual contributions aggregating not more than $7,500,000 per annum, and on or after July 1, 1939, to enter into additional such contracts which provide for annual contributions aggregating not more than $7,500,000 per annum. Without further authorization from Congress, no new contracts for annual contributions beyond those herein authorized shall be entered into by the Authority. The faith of the United States is solemnly pledged to the payment of all annual contributions contracted for pursuant to this section, and there is hereby authorized to be appropriated in each fiscal year, out of any money in the Treasury not otherwise appropriated, the amounts necessary to provide for such payments.

CAPITAL GRANTS IN ASSISTANCE OF LOW RENTALS

SEC. 11. (a) As an alternative method of assistance to that provided in section 10, when any public housing agency so requests and demonstrates to the satisfaction of the Authority that such alternative method is better suited to the purpose of achieving and maintaining low rentals and to the other purposes of this Act, capital grants may be made to such agency for such purposes. . . .

(b) Pursuant to subsection (a) of this section, the Authority may make a capital grant for any low-rent-housing or slum-clearance project, which shall in no case exceed 25 per centum of its development or acquisition cost. . . .

(d) The Authority is authorized, on or after the date of the enactment of this Act to make capital grants (pursuant to subsection (b) of this section) aggregating not more than $10,000,000, on or after July 1, 1938, to make additional capital grants aggregating not more than $10,000,000, and on or after July 1, 1939, to make additional capital grants aggregating not more than $10,000,000. Without further authorization from Congress, no capital grants beyond those herein authorized shall be made by the Authority.

(e) To supplement any capital grant made by the Authority in connection with the development of any low-rent-housing or slum-clearance project, the President may allocate to the Authority, from any funds available for the relief of unemployment, an additional capital grant to be expended for payment of labor used in such development: *Provided,* That such additional capital grant shall not exceed 15 per centum of the development cost of the low-rent-housing or slum-clearance project involved.

(f) No capital grant pursuant to this section shall be made for any low-rent-housing or slum-clearance project unless the public housing agency receiving such capital grant shall also receive, from the State, political subdivision thereof, or otherwise, a contribution for such project (in the form of cash, land, or the value, capitalized at the going Federal rate of interest, of community facilities or services for which a charge is usually made, or tax remissions or tax exemptions) in an amount not less than 20 per centum of its development or acquisition cost.

DISPOSAL OF FEDERAL PROJECTS

SEC. 12. . . .

(b) As soon as practicable the Authority shall sell its Federal projects or divest itself of their management through leases.

GENERAL POWERS OF THE AUTHORITY

SEC. 13. . . .

(5) No contract for any loan, annual contribution, or capital grant made pursuant to this Act shall be entered into by the Authority with respect to any project hereafter initiated costing more than $4,000 per family-dwelling-unit or more than $1,000 per room (excluding land, demolition, and non-dwelling facilities); except that in any city the population of which exceeds 500,000 any such contract may be entered into with respect to a project hereafter initiated costing not to exceed $5,000 per family-dwelling-unit or not to exceed $1,250 per room (excluding land, demolition, and non-dwelling facilities), if in the opinion of the Authority such higher family-dwelling-unit cost or cost per room is justified by reason of higher costs of labor and materials and other construction costs. With respect to housing projects on which construction is hereafter initiated, the Authority shall make loans, grants, and annual contributions only for such low-rent-housing projects as it finds are to be undertaken in such a manner (a) that such projects will not be of elaborate or expensive design or materials, and economy will be promoted both in construction and administration, and (b) that the average construction cost of the dwelling units (excluding land, demolition, and non-dwelling facilities) in any such project is not greater than the average construction cost of dwelling units

currently produced by private enterprise, in the locality or metropolitan area concerned, under the legal building requirements applicable to the proposed site, and under labor standards not lower than those prescribed in this Act.

FINANCIAL PROVISIONS

SEC. 17. The Authority shall have a capital stock of $1,000,000, which shall be subscribed by the United States and paid by the Secretary of the Treasury out of any available funds. . . .

SEC. 20. (a) The Authority is authorized to issue obligations, in the form of notes, bonds, or otherwise, which it may sell to obtain funds for the purposes of this Act. The Authority may issue such obligations in an amount not to exceed $100,000,000 on or after the date of enactment of this Act, an additional amount not to exceed $200,000,000 on or after July 1, 1938, and an additional amount not to exceed $200,000,000 on or after July 1, 1939. Such obligations shall . . . bear such rates of interest not exceeding 4 per centum per annum.

(b) Such obligations shall be exempt, both as to principal and interest, from all taxation (except surtaxes, estate, inheritance, and gift taxes) now or hereafter imposed by the United States or by any State, county, municipality, or local taxing authority.

(c) Such obligations shall be fully and unconditionally guaranteed upon their face by the United States as to the payment of both interest and principal, and, in the event that the Authority shall be unable to make any such payment upon demand when due, payments shall be made to the holder by the Secretary of the Treasury with money hereby authorized to be appropriated for such purpose out of any money in the Treasury not otherwise appropriated.

SEC. 21. . . .

(d) Not more than 10 per centum of the funds provided for in this Act, either in the form of a loan, grant, or annual contribution, shall be expended within any one State.

517. THE ECONOMIC CONDITIONS OF THE SOUTH
July 25, 1938

(Report to the President on the Economic Conditions of the South by the National Emergency Council)

"It is my conviction," wrote President Roosevelt, "that the South represents right now the Nation's No. 1 economic problem." This statement and the Report of the National Emergency Council which appeared to substantiate it, aroused widespread criticism. It has been thought best to incorporate in complete form two of the fifteen sections of the Report rather than attempt to give brief excerpts from each section. See, R. Vance, *Human Geography of the South;* H. Odum, *Southern Regions of the United States; Report* of the Land Planning Commission of the National Resources Board, Pt. II; E. A. Woods and C. B. Metzger, *America's Human Wealth.*

SECTION 2
SOIL

Nature gave the South good soil. With less than a third of the Nation's area, the South contains more than a third of the Nation's good farming acreage. It has two-thirds of all the land in America receiving a 40-inch annual rainfall or better. It has nearly half of the land on which crops can grow for 6 months without danger of frost.

This heritage has been sadly exploited. Sixty-one per cent of all the Nation's land badly damaged by erosion is in the Southern States. An expanse of southern farm land as large as South Carolina has been gullied and washed away; at least 22 million acres of once fertile soil has been ruined beyond repair. Another area the size of Oklahoma and Alabama combined has been seriously damaged by erosion. In addition, the sterile sand and gravel washed off this land has covered over a fertile valley acreage equal in size to Maryland.

There are a number of reasons for this wastage:

Much of the South's land originally was so fertile that it produced crops for many years no matter how carelessly it was farmed. For generations thousands of southern farmers plowed their furrows up and down the slopes, so that each furrow served as a ditch to hasten the run-off of silt-laden water after every rain. While many farmers have now learned the importance of terracing their land or plowing it on the contours, thousands still follow the destructive practices of the past.

Half of the South's farmers are tenants, many of whom have little interest in preserving soil they do not own.

The South's chief crops are cotton, tobacco, and corn; all of these are inter-tilled crops— the soil is plowed between the rows, so that it is left loose and bare of vegetation.

The top-soil washes away much more swiftly than from land planted to cover crops, such as clover, soybeans, and small grains. Moreover, cotton, tobacco, and corn leave few stalks and leaves to be plowed under in the fall; and as a result the soil constantly loses its humus and its capacity to absorb rainfall.

Even after harvest, southern land is seldom planted to cover crops which would protect it from the winter rains. This increases erosion tenfold.

Southeastern farms are the smallest in the Nation. The operating units average only 71 acres, and nearly one-fourth of them are smaller than 20 acres. A farmer with so little land is forced to plant every foot of it in cash crops; he cannot spare an acre for soil restoring crops or pasture. Under the customary tenancy system, moreover, he has every incentive to plant all his land to crops which will bring in the largest possible immediate cash return. The landlord often encourages him in this destructive practice of cash-cropping.

Training in better agricultural methods, such as planting soil-restoring crops, terracing, contour-plowing, and rotation, has been spreading, but such training is still unavailable to most southern farmers. Annually the South spends considerably more money for fertilizer than for agricultural training through its land-grant colleges, experiment stations, and extension workers.

Forests are one of the best protections against erosion. Their foliage breaks the force of the rain; their roots bind the soil so that it cannot wash away; their fallen leaves form a blanket of vegetable cover which soaks up the water and checks run-off. Yet the South has cut away a large part of its forest, leaving acres of gullied, useless soil. There has been comparatively little effort at systematic reforestation. Overgrazing, too, has resulted in serious erosion throughout the Southwest.

There is a close relationship between this erosion and floods, which recently have been causing a loss to the Nation estimated at about $35,000,000 annually. Rainfall runs off uncovered land much more rapidly than it does from land planted to cover crops or forest. Recent studies indicate that a single acre of typical corn land lost approximately 127,000 more gallons of rainfall in a single year than a similar field planted to grass. Another experiment showed that land sodded in grass lost less than 1 per cent of a heavy rain through immediate run-off, while nearby land planted to cotton lost 31 per cent. In short, unprotected land not only is in danger of destruction; it also adds materially to the destructive power of the swollen streams into which it drains.

These factors—each one reenforcing all the others—are causing an unparalleled wastage of the South's most valuable asset, its soil. They are steadily cutting down its agricultural income, and steadily adding to its cost of production as compared with other areas of the world which raise the same crops.

For example, it takes quantities of fertilizer to make worn-out, eroded land produce. The South, with only one-fifth of the Nation's income, pays three-fifths of the Nation's fertilizer bill. In 1929 it bought 5½ million tons of commercial fertilizer at a cost of $161,-000,000. And although fertilizer performs a valuable and necessary service, it does not restore the soil. For a year or two it may nourish a crop, but the land still produces meagerly and at high cost.

Moreover, southern farmers cannot pile on fertilizer fast enough to put back the essential minerals which are washing out of their land. Each year, about 27,500,000 tons of nitrogen and phosphorous compounds are leached out of southern soil and sent down the rivers to the sea.

The South is losing more than $300,000,000 worth of fertile topsoil through erosion every year. This is not merely a loss of income—it is a loss of irreplaceable capital.

SECTION 7
HEALTH

For years evidence has been piling up that food, clothing, and housing influence not only the sickness rate and death rate but even the height and weight of school children. In the South, where family incomes are exceptionally low, the sickness and death rates are unusually high. Wage differentials become in fact differentials in health and life; poor health, in turn, affects wages.

The low-income belt of the South is a belt of sickness, misery, and unnecessary death. Its large proportion of low-income citizens are more subject to disease than the people of any similar area. The climate cannot be blamed—the South is as healthful as any section for those who have the necessary care, diet, and freedom from occupational disease.

Several years ago the United States Public Health Service conducted syphilis-control demonstrations in selected rural areas in the South. These studies revealed a much higher ratio of syphilis among Negroes than among whites, but showed further than this higher ratio was not due to physical differences between races. It was found to be due to the greater poverty and lower living conditions of the Negroes. Similar studies of such diseases have shown that individual health cannot be separated from the health of the community as a whole.

The presence of malaria, which infects annually more than 2,000,000 people, is estimated to have reduced the industrial output of the South one-third. One of the most striking examples of the effect of malaria on industry was revealed by the Public Health Service in studies among employees of a cotton mill in eastern North Carolina. Previous to the attempts to control malaria, the records of the mill one month showed 66 looms were idle as a result of ill-health. After completion of control work, no looms were idle for that reason. Before control work, 238,046 pounds of cloth were manufactured in one month. After completion of the work production rose to 316,804 pounds in one month—an increase of 33⅓ per cent.

In reports obtained in 1935 from 9 lumber companies, owning 14 sawmill villages in 5 southern States, there was agreement that malaria was an important and increasing problem among the employees. During the year 7.6 per cent of hospital admissions, 16.4 per cent of physician calls, and 19.7 per cent of dispensary drugs were for malaria. The average number of days off duty per case of malaria was 9, while days in the hospital for the same cause were 5. Ten railroads in the South listed malaria as an economic problem and a costly liability. Four utility companies had full-time mosquito-fighting crews at work during the year. The average case admitted to a company hospital lasted 3 days and the average number of days off duty because of malaria was 11. Each case of malaria was said to cost the companies $40.

If we attempt to place a monetary value on malaria by accepting the figure of $10,000 as the value of an average life and using the death rate of 3.943 for malaria reported by the census for 1936, the annual cost of deaths from this disease is $39,500,000. To this figure could be added the cost of illness, including days of work lost.

The health-protection facilities of the South are limited. For example, there are only one-third as many doctors per capita in South Carolina as there are in California. The South is deficient in hospitals and clinics, as well as in health workers. Many counties have no facilities at all.

The South has only begun to look into its pressing industrial hygiene problems, although it has 26 per cent of the male mine workers in the United States and 14 per cent of the male factory workers. These are the workers with which modern industrial health protection is most concerned.

The experience as to pneumonia and tuberculosis among employees of the Tennessee Coal, Iron & Railroad Co. and their dependents during the 11-year period from 1925 to 1935 gives an indication of health conditions among miners in the South. The situation generally is probably worse than shown by the figures for this company, whose workers have relatively better protection against disease. For this period the number under observation averaged slightly more than 77,000 persons. There were 3,780 cases of pneumonia, of which 739 terminated fatally. This resulted in an average frequency per 1,000 of approximately 4.9 pneumonia cases per year among surface workers, 4.7 among coal miners, and 10.6 among ore miners. The rate of 4.2 for dependents included also the pneumonia of childhood and infancy. A fatality rate of 30.7 deaths per 1,000 cases of pneumonia was found among surface workers, a rate of 26.8 among coal miners, and 24.8 among ore miners. Deaths from tuberculosis occurred at an annual rate of 1.467 per thousand workers among coal miners, 1.232 among ore miners, and 0.566 among surface workers.

Prior to 1936 only one State in the South gave consideration to industrial hygiene. Today, with the aid of Social Security funds, seven additional States have industrial-hygiene units, and approximately 7,000,000 of the 10,000,000 gainful workers are receiving some type of industrial-hygiene service. However, these industrial-hygiene units have started their programs only recently, and it will be some time before adequate health services will be available. The funds now being spent for this activity in the eight States which have industrial-hygiene services do not meet the problem of protecting and improving the health of these workers. Approximately $100,-000 is now being budgeted for this work, although it is known that the economic loss due to industrial injuries and illnesses among these workers is hundreds of millions of dollars.

Reports of one of the largest life-insurance companies show that more people in the southern area than elsewhere die without medical aid. The same company reported in a recent year a rise of 7.3 per cent in the death rate in the nine South Atlantic States, though in no other region had the death rate risen above 4.8 per cent, and in some sections it had declined.

The scourge of pellagra, that affects the South almost exclusively, is a disease chiefly due to inadequate diet; it responds to rather simple preventive measures, including suitable nourishing food. Even in southern cities from 60 to 88 per cent of the families of low incomes are spending for food less than enough to purchase an adequate diet.

518. CONNECTICUT GENERAL LIFE INS. CO. v. JOHNSON
303 U. S. 77
1938

Appeal from the Supreme Court of California. This case involved the constitutionality of a California law taxing the gross premiums of insurance companies doing business in the state. The Connecticut company challenged the constitutionality of the act in so far as it applied to reinsurance premiums on contracts made in and payable in other states. The Court held that the act in question violated the due process clause of the Fourteenth Amendment. Only the dissenting opinion is here given; its importance flows from the fact that it is the first clear-cut protest against the traditional interpretation of the Fourteenth Amendment which has come officially from any member of the Supreme Court for half a century. For the recent interpretation of the meaning of that amendment, see Graham, "The Conspiracy Theory of the Fourteenth Amendment," 47 Yale L. J., 371; Boudin, "Truth and Fiction about the Fourteenth Amendment," 16 N. Y. U. Law Qt. Rev. 19.

BLACK, J., dissenting. I do not believe that this California corporate franchise tax has been proved beyond all reasonable doubt to be in violation of the Federal Constitution and I believe that the judgment of the Supreme Court of California should be affirmed. Traditionally, states have been empowered to grant or deny foreign corporations the right to do business within their borders, and "may exclude them arbitrarily or impose such conditions as [they] will upon their engaging in business within [their] jurisdiction."

California laid an annual tax upon gross insurance premiums which the Supreme Court of California has construed to be "a franchise tax exacted for the privilege of doing business." In measuring this franchise tax imposed upon corporations the state includes reinsurance premiums paid to the corporation on contracts made without the state, *where such reinsurance protects citizens of the State of California.* There is no attempt by this tax to regulate the business of the insurance company in any state except California.

The record does not indicate that California made any contract with this Connecticut corporation guaranteeing it a permanent franchise to do business in California on the same terms and conditions upon which it entered the state. . . .

But it is contended that the due process clause of the Fourteenth Amendment prohibits California from determining what terms and conditions should be imposed upon this Connecticut corporation to promote the welfare of the people of California.

I do not believe the word "person" in the Fourteenth Amendment includes corporations. "The doctrine of stare decisis, however appropriate and even necessary at times, has only a limited application in the field of constitutional law." This Court has many times changed its interpretations of the Constitution when the conclusion was reached that an improper construction had been adopted. . . . A constitutional interpretation that is wrong should not stand. I believe this Court should now overrule previous decisions which interpreted the Fourteenth Amendment to include corporations.

Neither the history nor the language of the Fourteenth Amendment justifies the belief that corporations are included within its protection. The historical purpose of the Fourteenth Amendment was clearly set forth when first considered by this Court in the Slaughter House Cases, . . .

Certainly, when the Fourteenth Amendment was submitted for approval, the people were not told that the states of the South were to be denied their normal relationship with the Federal Government unless they ratified an amendment granting new and revolutionary rights to corporations. This Court, when the Slaughter House Cases were decided in 1873, had apparently discovered no such purpose. The records of the time can be searched in vain for evidence that this amendment was adopted for the benefit of corporations. It is true that in 1882, twelve years after its adoption, and ten years after the Slaughter House Cases, an argument was made in this Court that a journal of the joint Congressional Committee which framed the amendment, secret and undisclosed up to that date, indicated the committee's desire to protect corporations by the use of the word "person." (*San Mateo County* v. *Southern Pacific Railroad,* 116 U. S. 138.) Four years later, in 1886, this Court in the case of *Santa Clara County*

v. *Southern Pacific Railroad*, 118 U. S. 394, decided for the first time that the word "person" in the amendment did in some instances include corporations. A secret purpose on the part of the members of the committee, even if such be the fact, however, would not be sufficient to justify any such construction. The history of the amendment proves that the people were told that its purpose was to protect weak and helpless human beings and were not told that it was intended to remove corporations in any fashion from the control of state governments. The Fourteenth Amendment followed the freedom of a race from slavery. Justice Swayne said in the Slaughter House Cases, that: "By 'any person' was meant *all* persons within the jurisdiction of the State. No distinction is intimated on account of race or color." Corporations have neither race nor color. He knew the amendment was intended to protect the life, liberty, and property of *human* beings.

The langauge of the amendment itself does not support the theory that it was passed for the benefit of corporations.

The first clause of section 1 of the amendment reads: "All *persons* born or naturalized in the United States, and subject to the jurisdiction thereof, are citizens of the United States and of the State wherein they reside." Certainly a corporation cannot be naturalized and "persons" here is not broad enough to include "corporations."

The first clause of the second sentence of section 1 reads: "No State shall make or enforce any law which shall abridge the privileges or immunities of citizens of the United States." While efforts have been made to persuade this Court to allow corporations to claim the protection of *this* clause, these efforts have not been successful.

The next clause of the second sentence reads: "Nor shall any State deprive any *person* of life, liberty, or property, without due process of law." It has not been decided that this clause prohibits a state from depriving a corporation of "life." This Court has expressly held that "the liberty guaranteed by the 14th Amendment against deprivation without due process of law is the liberty of *natural, not artificial persons.*" Thus. the words "life" and "liberty" do not apply to corporations, and of course they could not have been so intended to apply. However, the

decisions of this Court which the majority follow hold that corporations are included in this clause in so far as the word "property" is concerned. In other words, this clause is construed to mean as follows:

"Nor shall any State deprive any *human being* of life, liberty or property without due process of law; nor shall any State deprive any corporation of property without due process of law."

The last clause of this second sentence of section 1 reads: "Nor deny to any person within its jurisdiction the equal protection of the laws." As used here, "person" has been construed to include corporations.

Both Congress and the people were familiar with the meaning of the word "corporation" at the time the Fourteent:. Amendment was submitted and adopted. The judicial inclusion of the word "corporation" in the Fourteenth Amendment has had a revolutionary effect on our form of government. The states did not adopt the amendment with knowledge of its sweeping meaning under its present construction. No section of the amendment gave notice to the people that, if adopted, it would subject every state law and municipal ordinance, affecting corporations (and all administrative actions under them), to censorship of the United States courts. No word in all this amendment gave any hint that its adoption would deprive the states of their long-recognized power to regulate corporations.

The second section of the amendment informed the people that representatives would be apportioned among the several states "according to their respective numbers, counting the whole number of *persons* in each State, excluding Indians not taxed." No citizen could gather the impression *here* that while the word "persons" in the second section applied to human beings, the word "persons" in the first section *in some instances* applied to corporations. Section 3 of the amendment said that "no *person* shall be a Senator or Representative in Congress," (who "engaged in insurrection"). There was no intimation *here* that the word "person" in the first section *in some instances* included corporations.

This amendment sought to prevent discrimination by the states against classes or races. We are aware of this from words spoken in this Court within five years after its adoption, when the people and the courts were personally familiar with the historical background of the amendment. "We doubt very much whether any action of a State not directed by way of discrimination against the negroes as a class, or on account of their race, will ever be held to come within the purview of this provision." Yet, of the cases in this Court in which the Fourteenth Amendment was applied during the first fifty years after its adoption, less than one-half of 1 per cent invoked it in protection of the negro race, and more than 50 per cent asked that its benefits be extended to corporations.

If the people of this nation wish to deprive the states of their sovereign rights to determine what is a fair and just tax upon corporations doing a purely local business within their own state boundaries, there is a way provided by the Constitution to accomplish this purpose. That way does not lie along the course of judicial amendment to that fundamental charter. An amendment having that purpose could be submitted by Congress as provided by the Constitution. I do not believe that the Fourteenth Amendment had that purpose, nor that the people believed it had that purpose, nor that it should be construed as having that purpose.

I believe the judgment of the Supreme Court of California should be sustained.

519. HELVERING v. GERHARDT
304 U. S. 405
1938

On Writs of Certiorari to the U. S. Circuit Court of Appeals for the Second Circuit. The question of reciprocal immunity of state and federal governments from taxation is an old and troublesome one. Marshall, in McCulloch v. Maryland, laid down the principle that the instrumentalities of the national government must be immune from taxation by the states, because the power to tax involved the power to destroy. The same principle was applied to the instrumentalities of the states, notably in Collector v. Day (Doc. No. 282). The immense enlargement of governmental personnel, the growth of government activities—many of them of a quasi-private character, and the acute financial problems presented by the depression all combined to force a reconsideration of these principles. What are governmental instrumentalities, and how far does immunity extend to those employed by state or federal governments? The Court in this and the Graves case attempted to distinguish between instrumentalities essential to the preservation of government and those non-essential—obviously a very difficult and somewhat arbitrary distinction. Justice Black, in his concurring opinion, called sensibly for a reconsideration of the whole question of intergovernmental tax immunity. See on this and the Graves case, U. S. Dept. of Justice, "Taxation of Government Bondholders and Employees— the Immunity Rule and the Sixteenth Amendment"; Graham, "Two Centuries of Tax Immunity," 18 N. Car. L. Rev. 16; Magill, "Problem of Intergovernmental Tax Exemption," 15 Tax Mag. 699; Shaw, "Recent Cases on the Doctrine of Intergovernmental Tax Immunity," 8 Brooklyn L. Rev. 38; Watkins, "The Power of State and Federal Governments to Tax one another," 24 Va. L. Rev. 475; Lewinson, "Tax-Exempt Salaries and Securities," 23 A. B. A. J. 685; Freedman "Government owned Corporations and Intergovernmental Tax Immunity," 24 Wash. U. L. Qt. 46; Lowndes, "Taxation in the Supreme Court 1937 Term," 87 U. of Pa. L. Rev. 1.

STONE, J. The question for decision is whether the imposition of a federal income tax for the calendar years 1932 and 1933 on salaries received by respondents, as employees of the Port of New York Authority, places an unconstitutional burden on the States of New York and New Jersey.

The Port Authority is a bi-state corporation, created by compact between New York and New Jersey. . . .

In conformity to the plan, and pursuant to further legislation of the two states, the Authority has constructed the Outerbridge Crossing Bridge, the Goethals Bridge, the Bayonne Bridge, and the George Washington Bridge [etc.]. . . .

The respondents during the taxable years in question, were respectively a construction engineer and two assistant general managers, employed by the Authority at annual salaries ranging between $8,000 and $15,000. All took oaths of office, although neither the compact nor the related statutes appears to have created any office to which any of the respondents were appointed, or defined their duties or prescribed that they should take an oath. The several respondents having failed to return their respective salaries as income for the taxable years in question, the commissioner determined deficiencies against them. The Board of Tax Appeals found that the Port Authority was engaged in the performance of a public function for the States of New York and New Jersey, and ruled that the compensation received by the Authority's employees was exempt from federal income tax. The Circuit Court of Appeals for the Second Circuit, affirmed without opinion on the authority of *Brush* v. *Commissioner*. We granted certiorari because of the public importance of the question presented.

The Constitution contains no express limitation on the power of either a state or the national government to tax the other, or its instrumentalities. The doctrine that there is an implied limitation stems from *McCulloch* v. *Maryland*, in which it was held that a state tax laid specifically upon the privilege of issuing bank notes, and in fact applicable alone to the notes of national banks, was invalid since it impeded the national government in the exercise of its power to establish and maintain a bank, implied as an incident to the borrowing, taxing, war and other powers specifically granted to the national government by article 1, § 8 of the Constitution. . . .

That the taxing power of the federal goverment is nevertheless subject to an implied restriction when applied to state instrumentalities was first decided in *Collector* v. *Day*, 11 Wall. 113, where the salary of a state officer, a probate judge, was held to be immune from federal income tax. The question there presented to the Court was not one of interference with a granted power in a field in which the federal government is supreme, but a limitation by implication upon the granted federal power to tax. In recognizing that implication for the first time, the Court was concerned with the continued existence of the states as governmental entities, and their preservation from destruction by the national taxing power. The immunity which it implied was sustained only because it was one deemed necessary to protect the states from destruction by the federal taxation of those governmental functions which they were exercising when the Constitution was adopted and which were essential to their continued existence. . . .

It is enough for present purposes that the state immunity from the national taxing power, when recognized in *Collector* v. *Day*, was narrowly limited to a state judicial officer engaged in the performance of a function which pertained to state governments at the time the Constitution was adopted, without which no state "could long preserve its existence."

There are cogent reasons why any constitutional restriction upon the taxing power granted to Congress, so far as it can be properly raised by implication, should be narrowly limited. One, as was pointed out by Chief Justice Marshall in *McCulloch* v. *Maryland*, and *Weston* v. *Charleston*, is that the people of all the states have created the national government and are represented in Congress. Through that representation they exercise the national taxing power. The very fact that when they are exercising it they are taxing themselves serves to guard against its abuse through the possibility of resort to the usual processes of political action which provides a readier and more adaptable means than any which courts can afford, for securing accommodation of the competing demands for national revenue, on the one hand, and for reasonable scope for the independence of state action, on the other.

Another reason rests upon the fact that any allowance of a tax immunity for the protection of state sovereignty is at the expense of the sovereign power of the nation to tax. Enlargement of the one involves diminution of the other. When enlargement proceeds beyond the necessity of protecting the state, the burden of the immunity is thrown upon the national government with benefit only to a privileged class of taxpayers. With the steady expansion of the activity of state governments into new fields they have undertaken the performance of functions not known to the states when the Constitution was adopted, and have taken over the management of business enterprises once conducted exclusively by private individuals subject to the national taxing power. In a complex economic society tax burdens laid upon those who directly or indirectly have dealings with the states, tend, to some extent not capable of precise measurement, to be passed on economically and thus to burden the state government itself. But if every federal tax which is laid on some new form of state activity, or whose economic burden reaches in some measure the state or those who serve it, were to be set aside as an infringement of state sovereignty, it is evident that a restriction upon national power, devised only as a shield to protect the states from curtailment of the essential operations of government which they have exercised from the beginning, would become a ready means for striking down the taxing power of the nation. Once impaired by the recognition of a state immunity found to be excessive, restoration of that power is not likely to be secured through the action of state legislatures; for they are without the inducements to act which have often persuaded Congress to waive immunities thought to be excessive.

In tacit recognition of the limitation which the very nature of our federal system imposes on state immunity from taxation in order to avoid an everexpanding encroachment upon the federal taxing power, this Court has refused to enlarge the immunity substantially beyond those limits marked out in *Collector* v. *Day.* It has been sustained where, as in *Collector* v. *Day,* the function involved was one thought to be essential to the maintenance of a state government. . . .

But the Court has refused to extend the immunity to a state conducted liquor business, or to a street railway business taken over and operated by state officers as a means of effecting a local public policy. It has sustained the imposition of a federal excise tax laid on the privilege of exercising corporate franchises granted by a state to public service companies. In each of these cases it was pointed out that the state function affected was one which could be carried on by private enterprise, and that therefore it was not one without which a state could not continue to exist as a governmental entity. The immunity has been still more narrowly restricted in those cases where some part of the burden of a tax, collected not from a state treasury but from individual taxpayers, is said to be passed on to the state. In these cases the function has been either held or assumed to be of such a character that its performance by the state is immune from direct federal interference; yet the individuals who personally derived profit or compensation from their employment in carrying out the function were

deemed to be subject to federal income tax.

In a period marked by a constant expansion of government activities and the steady multiplication of the complexities of taxing systems, it is perhaps too much to expect that the judicial pronouncements marking the boundaries of state immunity should present a completely logical pattern. But they disclose no purposeful departure from, and indeed definitely establish, two guiding principles of limitation for holding the tax immunity of state instrumentalities to its proper function. The one, dependent upon the nature of the function being performed by the state or in its behalf, excludes from the immunity activities thought not to be essential to the preservation of state governments even though the tax be collected from the state treasury. . . . The other principle, exemplified by those cases where the tax laid upon individuals affects the state only as the burden is passed on to it by the taxpayer, forbids recognition of the immunity when the burden on the state is so speculative and uncertain that if allowed it would restrict the federal taxing power without affording any corresponding tangible protection to the state government; even though the function be thought important enough to demand immunity from a tax upon the state itself, it is not necessarily protected from a tax which well may be substantially or entirely absorbed by private persons.

With these controlling principles in mind we turn to their application in the circumstances of the present case. The challenged taxes are upon the net income of respondents, derived from their employment in common occupations not shown to be different in their methods or duties from those of similar employees in private industry. The taxpayers enjoy the benefits and protection of the laws of the United States. They are under a duty to support its government and are not beyond the reach of its taxing power. A nondiscriminatory tax laid on their net income, in common with that of all other members of the community, could by no reasonable probability be considered to preclude the performance of the function which New York and New Jersey have undertaken, or to obstruct it more than like private enterprises are obstructed by our taxing system. Even though, to some unascertainable extent, the tax deprives the states of the advantage of paying less than the standard rate for the services which they engage, it does not curtail any of those functions which have been thought hitherto to be essential to their continued existence as states. At most it may be said to increase somewhat the cost of the state governments because, in an interdependent economic society, the taxation of income tends to raise (to some extent which economists are not able to measure), the price of labor and materials. The effect of the immunity if allowed would be to relieve respondents of their duty of financial support to the national government, in order to secure to the state a theoretical advantage so speculative in its character and measurement as to be unsubstantial. A tax immunity devised for protection of the states as governmental entities cannot be pressed so far. . . .

The basis upon which constitutional tax immunity of a state has been supported is the protection which it affords to the continued existence of the state. To attain that end it is not ordinarily necessary to confer on the state a competitive advantage over private persons in carrying on the operations of its government. There is no such necessity here, and the resulting impairment of the federal power to tax argues against the advantage. The state and national governments must coexist. Each must be supported by taxation of those who are citizens of both. The mere fact that the economic burden of such taxes may be passed on to a state government and thus increase to some extent, here wholly conjectural, the expense of its operation, infringes no constitutional immunity. Such burdens are but normal incidents of the organization within the same territory of two governments, each possessed of the taxing power. . . .

As was pointed out in *Metcalf & Eddy* v. *Mitchell,* there may be state agencies of such a character and so intimately associated with the performance of an indispensable function of state government that any taxation of it would threaten such interference with the functions of government itself as to be considered beyond the reach of the federal taxing power. If the tax considered in *Collector* v. *Day,* upon the salary of an officer engaged in the performance of an indispensable function of the state which cannot be delegated to private individuals, may be regarded as such an instance, that is not the case presented here.

Expressing no opinion whether a federal tax may be imposed upon the Port Authority itself with respect to its receipt of income or its other activities, we decide only that the present tax neither precludes nor threatens unreasonably to obstruct any function essential to the continued existence of the state government. So much of the burden of the tax laid upon respondents' income as may reach the state is but a necessary incident to the coexistence within the same organized government of the two taxing sovereigns, and hence is a burden the existence of which the Constitution presupposes. The immunity, if allowed, would impose to an inadmissible extent a restriction upon the taxing power which the Constitution has granted to the federal government.

Reversed.

BLACK, J. delivered a concurring opinion.
BUTLER, J. delivered a dissenting opinion in which MCREYNOLDS, J. concurred.

520. GRAVES et. al. v. NEW YORK ex. rel. O'KEEFE
306 U. S. 466
1939

Writ of Certiorari to the Supreme Court of the State of New York. This case involved the validity of a New York State income tax on the salary of an employee of the federal Home Owners' Loan Corporation. For the problem of intergovernmental tax immunity and references, see Doc. No. 519.

STONE, J. We are asked to decide whether the imposition by the State of New York

of an income tax on the salary of an employee of the Home Owners' Loan Corporation places an unconstitutional burden upon the federal government.

Respondent, a resident of New York, was employed during 1934 as an examining attorney for the Home Owners' Loan Corporation at an annual salary of $2,400. In his income tax return for that year he included his salary as subject to the New York state income tax imposed by Art. 16 of the Tax Law of New York. Subdivision 2f of § 359, since repealed, exempted from the tax "Salaries, wages and other compensation received from the United States of officials or employees thereof, including persons in the military or naval forces of the United States. * * * " Petitioners, New York State Tax Commissioners, rejected respondent's claim for a refund of the tax based on the ground that his salary was constitutionally exempt from state taxation because the Home Owners' Loan Corporation is an instrumentality of the United States Government and that he, during the taxable year, was an employee of the federal government engaged in the performance of a governmental function. . . .

The Home Owners' Loan Corporation was created pursuant to § 4(a) of the Home Owners' Loan Act of 1933, which was enacted to provide emergency relief to home owners, particularly to assist them with respect to home mortgage indebtedness. The corporation, which is authorized to lend money to home owners on mortgages and to refinance home mortgage loans within the purview of the Act, is declared to be an instrumentality of the United States. Its shares of stock are wholly government-owned. Its funds are deposited in the Treasury of the United States, and the compensation of its employees is paid by drafts upon the Treasury.

For the purposes of this case we may assume that the creation of the Home Owners' Loan Corporation was a constitutional exercise of the powers of the federal government. As that government derives its authority wholly from powers delegated to it by the Constitution, its every action within its constitutional power is governmental action, and since Congress is made the sole judge of what powers within the constitutional grant are to be exercised, all activities of government constitutionally authorized by Congress must stand on a parity with respect to their constitutional immunity from taxation. And when the national government lawfully acts through a corporation which it owns and controls, those activities are governmental functions entitled to whatever tax immunity attaches to those

functions when carried on by the government itself through its departments.

The single question with which we are now concerned is whether the tax laid by the state upon the salary of respondent, employed by a corporate instrumentality of the federal government, imposes an unconstitutional burden upon that government. The theory of the tax immunity of either government, state or national, and its instrumentalities, from taxation by the other, has been rested upon an implied limitation on the taxing power of each, such as to forestall undue interference, through the exercise of that power, with the governmental activities of the other. That the two types of immunity may not, in all respects, stand on a parity has been recognized from the beginning, and possible differences in application, deriving from differences in the source, nature and extent of the immunity of the governments and their agencies, were pointed out and discussed by this Court in detail during the last term. *Helvering* v. *Gerhardt.*

So far as now relevant, those differences have been thought to be traceable to the fact that the federal government is one of delegated powers in the exercise of which Congress is supreme; so that every agency which Congress can constitutionally create is a governmental agency. And since the power to create the agency includes the implied power to do whatever is needful or appropriate, if not expressly prohibited, to protect the agency, there has been attributed to Congress some scope, the limits of which it is not now necessary to define, for granting or withholding immunity of federal agencies from state taxation. Whether its power to grant tax exemptions as an incident to the exercise of powers specifically granted by the Constitution can ever, in any circumstances, extend beyond the constitutional immunity of federal agencies which courts have implied, is a question which need not now be determined.

Congress has declared in § 4 of the Act that the Home Owners' Loan Corporation is an instrumentality of the United States and that its bonds are exempt, as to principal and interest, from federal and state taxation, except surtaxes, estate, inheritance and gift taxes. The corporation itself, "including its franchise, its capital, reserves and surplus, and its loans and income," is likewise exempted from taxation; its real property is subject to tax to the same extent as other real property. But Congress has given no intimation of any purpose either to grant or withhold immunity from state taxation of the salary of the corporation's employees, and the Congressional intention is not to be gathered from the statute by implication.

It is true that the silence of Congress, when it has authority to speak, may sometimes give rise to an implication as to the Congressional purpose. The nature and extent of that implication depend upon the nature of the Congressional power and the effect of its exercise. But there is little scope for the application of that doctrine to the tax immunity of governmental instrumentalities. The constitutional immunity of either government from taxation by the other, where Congress is silent, has its source in an implied restriction upon the powers of the taxing government. So far as the implication rests upon the purpose to avoid interference with the functions of the taxed government or the imposition upon it of the economic burden of the tax, it is plain that there is no basis for implying a purpose of Congress to exempt the federal government or its agencies from tax burdens which are unsubstantial or which courts are unable to discern. Silence of Congress implies immunity no more than does the silence of the Constitution. It follows that when exemption from state taxation is claimed on the ground that the federal government is burdened by the tax, and Congress has disclosed no intention with respect to the claimed immunity, it is in order to consider the nature and effect of the alleged burden, and if it appears that there is no ground for implying a constitutional immunity, there is equally a want of any ground for assuming any purpose on the part of Congress to create an immunity.

The present tax is a non-discriminatory tax on income applied to salaries at a specified rate. It is not in form or substance a tax upon the Home Owners' Loan Corporation or its property or income, nor is it paid by the corporation or the government from their funds. It is laid upon income which becomes the property of the taxpayer when received as compensation for his services; and the tax laid upon the privilege of receiving it is paid from his private funds and not from the funds of the government, either directly or indirectly. The theory, which once won a qualified approval, that a tax on income is legally or economically a tax on its source, is no longer tenable, and the only possible basis for implying a constitutional immunity from state income tax of the salary of an employee of the national government or of a governmental agency is that the economic burden of the tax is in some way passed on so as to impose a burden on the national government tantamount to an interference by one government with the other in the performance of its functions.

In the four cases in which this Court has held that the salary of an officer or employee of one government or its instrumentality was immune from taxation by the other, it was assumed, without discussion, that the immunity of a government or its instrumentality extends to the salaries of its officers and employees. This assumption, made with respect to the salary of a governmental officer in *Dobbins* v. *Commissioners of Erie County,* 16 Pet. 435, and in Collector v. Day, 11 Wall. 113, was later extended to confer immunity on income derived by a lessee from lands leased to him by a government in the performance of a government function, *Gillespie* v. *Oklahoma,* 257 U. S. 501; *Burnet* v. *Coronado Oil & aGs Co.,* 285 U. S. 393, and cases cited, although the claim of a like exemption from tax on the income of a contractor engaged in carrying out a government project was rejected both in the case of a contractor with a state, *Metcalf & Eddy* v. *Mitchell,* and of a contractor with the national government, *James* v. *Dravo Contracting Co.*

The ultimate repudiation in *Helvering* v. *Mountain Producers Corp.,* supra, of the doctrine that a tax on the income of a lessee derived from a lease of government owned or controlled lands is a forbidden interference with the activities of the government concerned led to the reexamination by this Court, in the Gerhardt case, of the theory underlying the asserted immunity from taxation by one government of salaries of employees of the other. It was there pointed out that the implied immunity of one government and its agencies from taxation by the other should, as a principle of constitutional construction, be narrowly restricted. For the expansion of the immunity of the one government correspondingly curtails the sovereign power of the other to tax, and where that immunity is invoked by the private citizen it tends to operate for his benefit at the expense of the taxing government and without corresponding benefit to the government in whose name the immunity is claimed. It was further pointed out that, as applied to the taxation of salaries of the employees of one government, the purpose of the immunity was not to confer benefits on the employees by relieving them from contributing their share of the financial support of the other government, whose benefits they enjoy, or to give an advantage to that government by enabling it to engage employees at salaries lower than those paid for like services by other employers, public or private, but to prevent undue interference with the one government by imposing on it the tax burdens of the other.

In applying these controlling principles in the Gerhardt case the Court held that the salaries of employees of the New York Port Authority, a state instrumentality created by New York and New Jersey, were not immune from federal income tax, even though the Authority be regarded as not subject to federal taxation. It was said that the taxpayers enjoyed the benefit and protection of the laws of the United States and were under a duty, common to all citizens, to contribute financial support to the government; that the tax laid on their salaries and paid by them could be said to affect or burden their employer, the Port Authority, or the states creating it, only so far as the burden of the tax was economically passed on to the employer; that a non-discriminatory tax laid on the income of all members of the community could not be assumed to obstruct the function which New York and New Jersey had undertaken to perform, or to cast an economic burden upon them, more than does the general taxation of property and income which, to some extent, incapable of measurement by economists, may tend to raise the price level of labor and materials. The Court concluded that the claimed immunity would do no

more than relieve the taxpayers from the duty of financial support to the national government in order to secure to the state a theoretical advantage, speculative in character and measurement and too unsubstantial to form the basis of an implied constitutional immunity from taxation.

The conclusion reached in the Gerhardt case that in terms of constitutional tax immunity a federal income tax on the salary of an employee is not a prohibited burden on the employer makes it imperative that we should consider anew the immunity here claimed for the salary of an employee of a federal instrumentality. As already indicated, such differences as there may be between the implied tax immunity of a state and the corresponding immunity of the national government and its instrumentalities may be traced to the fact that the national government is one of delegated powers, in the exercise of which it is supreme. Whatever scope this may give to the national government to claim immunity from state taxation of all instrumentalities which it may constitutionally create, and whatever authority Congress may possess as incidental to the exercise of its delegated powers to grant or withhold immunity from state taxation, Congress has not sought in this case to exercise such power. Hence these distinctions between the two types of immunity cannot affect the question with which we are now concerned. The burden on government of a non-discriminatory income tax applied to the salary of the employee of a government or its instrumentality is the same, whether a state or national government is concerned. The determination in the Gerhardt case that the federal income tax imposed on the employees of the Port Authority was not a burden on the Port Authority made it unnecessary to consider whether the Authority itself was immune from federal taxation; the claimed immunity failed because even if the Port Authority were itself immune from federal income tax, the tax upon the income of its employees cast upon it no unconstitutional burden.

Assuming, as we do, that the Home Owners' Loan Corporation is clothed with the same immunity from state taxation as the government itself, we cannot say that the present tax on the income of its employees lays any unconstitutional burden upon it. All the reasons for refusing to imply a constitutional prohibition of federal income taxation of salaries of state employees, stated at length in the Gerhardt case, are of equal force when immunity is claimed from state income tax on salaries paid by the national government or its agencies. In this respect we perceive no basis for a difference in result whether the taxed income be salary or some other form of compensation, or whether the taxpayer be an employee or an officer of either a state or the national government, or of its instrumentalities. In no case is there basis for the assumption that any such tangible or certain economic burden is imposed on the government concerned as would justify a court's declaring that the taxpayer is clothed with the implied constitutional tax immunity of the government by which he is employed. That assumption, made in Collector v. Day, and in New York ex. rel. Rogers v. Graves, is contrary to the reasoning and to the conclusions reached in the Gerhardt case and in Metcalf & Eddy v. Mitchell, [etc.]. In their light the assumption can no longer be made. Collector v. Day, and New York ex rel. Rogers v. Graves, are overruled so far as they recognize an implied constitutional immunity from income taxation of the salaries of officers or employees of the national or a state government or their instrumentalities.

So much of the burden of a non-discriminatory general tax upon the incomes of employees of a government, state or national, as may be passed on economically to that government, through the effect of the tax on the price level of labor or materials, is but the normal incident of the organization within the same territory of two governments, each possessing the taxing power. The burden, so far as it can be said to exist or to affect the government in any indirect or incidental way, is one which the Constitution presupposes, and hence it cannot rightly be deemed to be within an implied restriction upon the taxing power of the national and state governments which the Constitution has expressly granted to one and has confirmed to the other. The immunity is not one to be implied from the Constitution, because if allowed it would impose to an inadmissible extent a restriction on the taxing power which the Constitution has reserved to the state governments.

Reversed.

Mr. Chief Justice HUGHES concurs in the result.

Mr. Justice FRANKFURTER, concurring. I join in the Court's opinion but deem it appropriate to add a few remarks. . . .

The arguments upon which McCulloch v. Maryland, rested had their roots in actuality. But they had been distorted by sterile refinements unrelated to affairs. These refinements derived authority from an unfortunate remark in the opinion in McCulloch v. Maryland. Partly as a flourish of rhetoric and partly because the intellectual fashion of the times indulged a free use of absolutes, Chief Justice Marshall gave currency to the phrase that "the power to tax involves the power to destroy." This dictum was treated as though it were a constitutional mandate. But not without protest. One of the most trenchant minds on the Marshall court, Justice William Johnson, early analyzed the dangerous inroads upon the political freedom of the States and the Union within their respective orbits resulting from a doctrinaire application of the generalities uttered in the course of the opinion in McCulloch v. Maryland. The seductive cliché that the power to tax involves the power to destroy was fused with another assumption, likewise not to be found in the Constitution itself, namely the doctrine that the immunities are correlative—because the existence of the national government implies immunities from state taxation, the existence of state governments implies equivalent immunities from federal taxation. When this doctrine was first applied Mr. Justice Bradley registered a powerful dissent, the force of which gathered rather than lost strength with time. Collector v. Day.

All these doctrines of intergovernmental immunity have until recently been moving in the realm of what Lincoln called "pernicious abstractions." The web of unreality spun from Marshall's famous dictum was brushed away by one stroke of Mr. Justice Holmes's pen: "The power to tax is not the power to destroy while this Court sits." Panhandle Oil Co. v. Mississippi, 277 U. S. 218, 223 (dissent). Failure to exempt public functionaries from the universal duties of citizenship to pay for the cost of government was hypothetically transmuted into hostile action of one government against the other. A succession of decisions thereby withdrew from the taxing power of the States and Nation a very considerable range of wealth without regard to the actual workings of our federalism, and this, too, when the financial needs of all governments began steadily to mount. These decisions have encountered increasing dissent. . . . In this Court dissents have gradually become majority opinions, and even before the present decision the rationale of the doctrine had been undermined.

The judicial history of this doctrine of immunity is a striking illustration of an occasional tendency to encrust unwarranted interpretations upon the Constitution and thereafter to consider merely what has been judicially said about the Constitution, rather than to be primarily controlled by a fair conception of the Constitution. Judicial exegesis is unavoidable with reference to an organic art like our Constitution, drawn in many particulars with purposed vagueness so as to leave room for the unfolding future. But the ultimate touchstone of constitutionality is the Constitution itself and not what we have said about it. Neither *Dobbins* v. *Commissioners of Erie County,* and its offspring, nor *Collector* v. *Day,* and its, can stand appeal to the Constitution and its historic purposes. Since both are the starting points of an interdependent doctrine, both should be, as I assume them to be, overruled this day. Whether Congress may, by express legislation, relieve its functionaries from their civic obligations to pay for the benefits of the State governments under which they live is matter for another day.

521. THE CAROLENE PRODUCTS DOCTRINE
1938

(304 *U. S. Supreme Court Reports,* 144, footnote 4)

This famous footnote to an otherwise inconspicuous case announced what has come to be known as the "preferred freedoms" doctrine of the First Amendment; much of the judicial debate of the fifties centered on the validity and relevance of this doctrine as against the "balance of interest" doctrine espoused by Judge Frankfurter. On Carolene Products see A. T. Mason, *Harlan Fiske Stone;* S. J. Konefsky, *Chief Justice Stone and the Supreme Court;* Commager, *Majority Rule and Minority Rights;* Mason, "The Core of Free Government: Mr. Justice Stone and Preferred Freedoms," 65 *Yale Law J.* 597; Luksy, "Minority Rights and Public Interest," 52 *Yale Law. J.* 1; L. Hand, "Chief Justice Stone's Conception of the Judicial Function," 46 *Columbia Law Rev.* 696; H. Wechsler, "Stone and the Constitution," 46 *Columbia L. Rev.* 764; Bernard, "Liberties of the First Amendment," 50 *Mich. Law Rev.* 261.

STONE, C. J. . . . Regulatory legislation affecting ordinary commercial transactions is not to be pronounced unconstitutional unless in the light of the facts made known or generally assumed it is of such a character as to preclude the assumption that it rests upon some rational basis within the knowledge and experience of legislators.[4]

4. There may be narrower scope for operation of the presumption of constitutionality when legislation appears on its face to be within a specific prohibition of the Constitution, such as those of the first ten Amendments which are deemed equally specific when held to be embraced within the Fourteenth.

It is unnecessary to consider now whether legislation which restricts those political processes which can ordinarily be expected to bring about repeal of undesirable legislation, is to be subjected to a more exacting judicial scrutiny under the general prohibitions of the Fourteenth Amendment, than are most other types of legislation. . . .

Nor need we enquire whether similar considerations enter into the review of statutes directed at particular religions . . . or national . . . or racial minorities . . . whether prejudice against discrete and insular minorities may be a special condition, which tends seriously to curtail the operation of those political processes ordinarily to be relied upon to protect minorities, and which may call for a correspondingly more searching judicial inquiry.

522. THE NEW ORDER IN THE FAR EAST

United States Note to Japan Regarding Violations of American Rights in China
December 31, 1938

(U. S. Dept. of State, *Press Release*, Vol. XIX, No. 483)

The invasion of China by Japan in July, 1937, threatened American interests in the Far East and challenged the Open Door doctrine. On October 6, 1938 the United States sent a strong protest to Japan against the violation of American treaty rights and of the Open Door. To this note Japan replied, November 18, to the effect that a "new situation" had developed in the Far East and the Open Door policy was no longer applicable. The note of Dec. 31 is the American reply to this note. In June, 1939 the United States reaffirmed its position and the following month gave evidence of its seriousness by taking the initial step in abrogating the Commercial Treaty of 1911 with Japan. On Recent Far Eastern policy see H. L. Stimson, *The Far Eastern Crisis;* A. W. Griswold, *The Far Eastern Policy of the United States;* S. C. Y. Pan, *American Diplomacy concerning Manchuria;* N. Peffer, *Must We Fight in Asia;* and Foreign Policy Reports, Vol. 13, no. 23, "America's Role in the Far Eastern Conflict."

Text of a note which the American Ambassador to Japan, Mr. Joseph C. Grew, communicated, under instruction, to the Japanese Minister for Foreign Affairs, His Excellency Mr. Hachiro Arita, on December 31, 1938:

The Government of the United States has received and has given full consideration to the reply of the Japanese Government of November 18 to this Government's note of October 6 on the subject of American rights and interests in China.

In the light of facts and experience the Government of the United States is impelled to reaffirm its previously expressed opinion that imposition of restrictions upon the movements and activities of American nationals who are engaged in philanthropic, educational and commercial endeavors in China has placed and will, if continued, increasingly place Japanese interests in a preferred position and is, therefore, unquestionably discriminatory, in its effect, against legitimate American interests. Further, with reference to such matters as exchange control, compulsory currency circulation, tariff revision, and monopolistic promotion in certain areas of China,

the plans and practices of the Japanese authorities imply an assumption on the part of those authorities that the Japanese Government or the regimes established and maintained in China by Japanese armed forces are entitled to act in China in a capacity such as flows from rights of sovereignty and, further, in so acting to disregard and even to declare nonexistent or abrogated the established rights and interests of other countries, including the United States.

The Government of the United States expresses its conviction that the restrictions and measures under reference not only are unjust and unwarranted but are counter to the provisions of several binding international agreements, voluntarily entered into, to which both Japan and the United States, and in some cases other countries, are parties.

In the concluding portion of its note under reference, the Japanese Government states that it is firmly convinced that "in the face of the new situation, fast developing in East Asia, any attempt to apply to the conditions of today and tomorrow inapplicable ideas and principles of the past neither would contribute toward the establishment of a real peace in East Asia nor solve the immediate issues," and that "as long as these points are understood, Japan has not the slightest inclination to oppose the participation of the United States and other powers in the great work of reconstructing East Asia along all lines of industry and trade."

The Government of the United States in its note of October 6 requested, in view of the oft-reiterated assurances proffered by the Government of Japan of its intention to observe the principle of equality of opportunity in its relations with China, and in view of Japan's treaty obligations so to do, that the Government of Japan abide by these obligations and carry out these assurances in practice. The Japanese Government in its reply appears to affirm that it is its intention to make its observance of that principle conditional upon an understanding by the American Government and by other governments of a "new situation" and a "new order" in the Far East as envisaged and fostered by Japanese authorities.

Treaties which bear upon the situation in the Far East have within them provisions relating to a number of subjects. . . . The various provisions agreed upon may be said to have constituted collectively an arrangement for safeguarding, for the benefit of all, the correlated principles on the one hand of national integrity and on the other hand of equality of economic opportunity. Experience has shown that impairment of the former of these principles is followed almost invariably by disregard of the latter. Whenever any government begins to exercise political authority in areas beyond the limits of its lawful jurisdiction there develops inevitably a situation in which the nationals of that government demand and are accorded, at the hands of their government, preferred treatment, whereupon equality of opportunity ceases to exist and discriminatory practices, productive of friction, prevail.

The admonition that enjoyment by the nationals of the United States of nondiscriminatory treatment in China—a general and well-established right—is henceforth to be contingent upon an admission by the Government of the United States of the validity of the conception of Japanese authorities of a "new situation" and a "new order" in East Asia, is, in the opinion of this Government, highly paradoxical.

This country's adherence to and its advocacy of the principle of equality of opportunity do not flow solely from a desire to obtain the commercial benefits which naturally result from the carrying out of that principle. They flow from a firm conviction that observance of that principle leads to economic and political stability, which are conducive both to the internal well-being of nations and to mutually beneficial and peaceful relationships between and among nations; from a firm conviction that failure to observe that principle breeds international friction and ill-will, with consequences injurious to all countries, including in particular those countries which fail to observe it; and from an equally firm conviction that observance of that principle promotes the opening of trade channels thereby making available the markets, the raw materials and the manufactured products of the community of nations on a mutually and reciprocally beneficial basis.

The principle of equality of economic opportunity is, moreover, one to which over a long period and on many occasions the Japanese Government has given definite approval. It is one to the observance of which the Japanese Government has committed itself in various international agreements and understandings. It is one upon observance of which by other nations the Japanese Government has of its own accord and upon its own initiative frequently insisted. It is one to which the Japanese Government has repeatedly during recent months declared itself committed.

The people and the Government of the United States could not assent to the establishment, at the instance of and for the special purposes of any third country, of a regime which would arbitrarily deprive them of the long-established rights of equal opportunity and fair treatment which are legally and justly theirs along with those of other nations.

Fundamental principles, such as the principle of equality of opportunity, which have long been regarded as inherently wise and just, which have been widely adopted and adhered to, and which are general in their application, are not subject to nullification by a unilateral affirmation.

With regard to the implication in the Japanese Government's note that the "conditions of today and tomorrow" in the Far East call for a revision of the ideas and principles of the past, this Government desires to recall to the Japanese Government its position on the subject of revision of agreements.

This Government had occasion in the course of a communication delivered to the Japanese Government on April 29, 1934, to express its opinion that "treaties can lawfully be modified or be terminated, but only by processes prescribed or recognized or agreed upon by the parties to them."

In the same communication this Government also said, "In the opinion of the American people and the American Government no nation can, without the assent of the other nations concerned, rightfully endeavor to make conclusive its will in situations where there are involved the rights, the obligations and the legitimate interests of other sovereign states." . . .

At various times during recent decades various powers, among which have been Japan and the United States, have had occasion to communicate and to confer with regard to situations and problems in the Far East. In the conducting of correspondence and of conferences relating to these matters, the parties involved have invariably taken into consideration past and present facts and they have not failed to perceive the possibility and the desirability of changes in the situation. In the making of treaties they have drawn up and have agreed upon provisions intended to facilitate advantageous developments and at the same time to obviate and avert the arising of friction between and among the various powers which, having interests in the region or regions under reference, were and would be concerned.

In the light of these facts, and with reference especially to the purpose and the character of the treaty provisions from time to time solemnly agreed upon for the very definite purposes indicated, the Government of the United States deprecates the fact that one of the parties to these agreements has chosen to embark—as indicated both by action of its agents and by official statements of its authorities—upon a course directed toward the arbitrary creation by that power by methods of its own selection, regardless of treaty pledges and the established rights of other powers concerned, of a "new order" in the Far East. Whatever may be the changes which have taken place in the situation in the Far East and whatever may be the situation now, these matters are of no less interest and concern to the American Government than have been the situations which have prevailed there in the past, and such changes as may henceforth take place there, changes which may enter into the producing of a "new situation" and a "new order," are and will be of like concern to this Government. This Government is well aware that the situation has changed. This Government is also well aware that many of the changes have been brought about by action

of Japan. This Government does not admit, however, that there is need or warrant for any one power to take upon itself to prescribe what shall be the terms and conditions of a "new order" in areas not under its sovereignty and to constitute itself the repository of authority and the agent of destiny in regard thereto. . . .

The United States has in its international relations rights and obligations which derive from international law and rights and obligations which rest upon treaty provisions. Of those which rest on treaty provisions, its rights and obligations in and with regard to China rest in part upon provisions in treaties between the United States and China, and in part upon provisions in treaties between the United States and several other powers, including both China and Japan. These treaties were concluded in good faith for the purpose of safeguarding and promoting the interests not of one only but of all their signatories. The people and the Government of the United States cannot assent to the abrogation of any of this country's rights or obligations by the arbitrary action of agents or authorities of any other country.

The Government of the United States has, however, always been prepared, and is now, to give due and ample consideration to any proposals based on justice and reason which envisage the resolving of problems in a manner duly considerate of the rights and obligations of all parties directly concerned by processes of free negotiation and new commitment by and among all of the parties so concerned. There has been and there continues to be opportunity for the Japanese Government to put forward such proposals. This Government has been and it continues to be willing to discuss such proposals, if and when put forward, with representatives of the other powers, including Japan and China, whose rights and interests are involved, at whatever time and in whatever place may be commonly agreed upon.

Meanwhile, this Government reserves all rights of the United States as they exist and does not give assent to any impairment of any of those rights.

523. "HANDS OFF THE WESTERN HEMISPHERE"
F. D. Roosevelt's Pan-American Day Address, April 14, 1939

(New York Times, April 15, 1939)

The American family of nations pays honor today to the oldest and most successful association of sovereign governments which exists in the world. . . .

For upwards of half a century the republics of the Western world have been working together to promote their common civilization under a system of peace. That venture, launched so hopefully fifty years ago, has succeeded; the American family is today a great co-operation group facing a troubled world in serenity and calm. . . .

What was it that has protected us from the tragic involvements which are today making the Old World a new cockpit of old struggles? The answer is easily found. A new and powerful ideal—that of the community of nations—sprang up at the same time that the Americans became free and independent. It was nurtured by statesmen, thinkers and plain people for decades. Gradually it brought together the Pan-American group of governments; today it has fused the thinking of the peoples, and the desires of their responsible representatives toward a common objective.

The result of this thinking has been to shape a typically American institution. This is the Pan-American group, which works in open conference, by open agreement. We hold our conferences not as a result of wars, but as the result of our will to peace.

Elsewhere in the world, to hold conferences such as ours, which meet every five years, it is necessary to fight a major war, until exhaustion or defeat at length brings governments together to reconstruct their shattered fabrics.

Greeting a conference at Buenos Aires in 1936, I took occasion to say:

"The madness of a great war in another part of the world would affect us and threaten our good in a hundred ways, and the economic collapse of any nation or nations must of necessity harm our own prosperity. Can we, the republics of the world, help the Old World to avert the catastrophe which impends? Yes, I am confident that we can."

I still have that confidence. There is no fatality which forces the Old World toward new catastrophe. Men are not prisoners of fate, but only prisoners of their own minds. They have within themselves the power to become free at any moment. . . .

No nation on this hemisphere has any will to aggression, or any desire to establish dominance or mastery. Equally, because we are interdependent, and because we know it, no American nation seeks to deny any neighbor access to the economic and other resources which it must have to live in prosperity.

In these circumstances dreams of conquest appear to us as ridiculous as they are criminal. Pledges designed to prevent aggression, accompanied by the open doors of trade and intercourse, and bound together by common will to co-operate peacefully, make warfare between us as outworn and useless as the weapons of the Stone Age. We may proudly boast that we have begun to realize in Pan-American relations what civilization in intercourse between countries really means.

If that process can be successful here, is it too much to hope that a similar intellectual and spiritual process may succeed elsewhere? Do we really have to assume that nations can find no better methods of realizing their destinies than those which were used by the Huns and Vandals fifteen hundred years ago?

The American peace which we celebrate today has no quality of weakness in it. We are prepared to maintain it, and to defend it to the fullest extent of our strength, matching force to force if any attempt is made to subvert our institutions, or to impair the independence of any one of our group.

Should the method of attack be that of economic pressure, I pledge that my own country will also give economic support, so that no American nation need surrender any fraction of its sovereign freedom to maintain its economic welfare. This is the spirit and intent of the declaration of Lima: The solidarity of the continent.

The American family of nations may also rightfully claim, now, to speak to the rest of the world. We have an interest, wider than that of the mere defense of our sea-ringed continent. We know now that the development of the next generation will so narrow the oceans separating us from the Old World, that our customs and our actions are necessarily involved with hers.

Beyond question, within a scant few years air fleets will cross the ocean as easily as to-day they cross the closed European seas. Economic functioning of the world becomes increasingly a unit; no interruption of it anywhere can fail, in the future, to disrupt economic life everywhere.

The past generation in Pan-American matters was concerned with constructing the principles and the mechanisms through which this hemisphere would work together. But the next generation will be concerned with the methods by which the New World can live together with the Old.

The issue is really whether our civilization is to be dragged into the tragic vortex of unending militarism punctuated by periodic wars, or whether we shall be able to maintain the ideal of peace, individuality and civilization as the fabric of our lives. We have the right to say that there shall not be an organization of world affairs which permits us no choice but to turn our countries into barracks unless we are to be vassals of some conquering empire.

The truest defense of the peace of our hemisphere must always lie in the hope that our sister nations beyond the seas will break the bonds of the ideas which constrain them toward perpetual warfare. By example we can at least show them the possibility. We, too, have a stake in world affairs.

Our will to peace can be as powerful as our will to mutual defense; it can command greater loyalty, devotion and discipline than that enlisted elsewhere for temporary conquest or equally futile glory. It will have its voice in determining the order of world affairs.

This is the living message which the New World can send to the Old. It can be light opening on dark waters. It shows the path of peace.

524. F. D. ROOSEVELT'S APPEALS FOR PEACE IN EUROPE
April 14, 1939 and August 23, 1939

(U. S. Dept. of State, *Press Releases*)

During the period from the Munich Conference of September, 1938 to the outbreak of war, September, 1939, Roosevelt's efforts to persuade the European powers, and especially Germany and Italy, to peace were unceasing.

"THE WHITE HOUSE
April 14, 1939

HIS EXCELLENCY ADOLF HITLER, CHANCELLOR OF THE GERMAN REICH,

You realize I am sure that throughout the world hundreds of millions of human beings are living today in constant fear of a new war or even a series of wars.

The existence of this fear—and the possibility of such a conflict—is of definite concern to the people of the United States for whom I speak, as it must also be to the peoples of the other nations of the entire Western Hemisphere. All of them know that any major war, even if it were to be confined to other continents, must bear heavily on them during its continuance and also for generations to come.

Because of the fact that after the acute tension in which the world has been living during the past few weeks there would seem to be at least a momentary relaxation—because no troops are at this moment on the march—this may be an opportune moment for me to send you this message.

On a previous occasion I have addressed you in behalf of the settlement of political, economic, and social problems by peaceful methods and without resort to arms.

But the tide of events seems to have reverted to the threat of arms. If such threats continue, it seems inevitable that much of the world must become involved in common ruin. All the world, victor nations, vanquished nations, and neutral nations will suffer. I refuse to believe that the world is, of necessity, such a prisoner of destiny. On the contrary, it is clear that the leaders of great nations have it in their power to liberate their peoples from the disaster that impends. It is equally clear that in their own minds and in their hearts the peoples themselves desire that their fears be ended.

It is, however, unfortunately necessary to take cognizance of recent facts.

Three nations in Europe and one in Africa have seen their independent existence terminated. A vast territory in another independent nation of the Far East has been occupied by a neighboring state. Reports, which we trust are not true, insist that further acts of aggression are contemplated against still other independent nations. Plainly the world is moving toward the moment when this situation must end in catastrophe unless a more rational way of guiding events is found.

You have repeatedly asserted that you and the German people have no desire for war. If this is true there need be no war.

Nothing can persuade the peoples of the earth that any governing power has any right or need to inflict the consequences of war on its own or any other people save in the cause of self-evident home defense.

In making this statement we as Americans speak not through selfishness or fear or weakness. If we speak now it is with the voice of strength and with friendship for mankind. It is still clear to me that international problems can be solved at the council table.

It is therefore no answer to the plea for peaceful discussion for one side to plead that unless they receive assurances beforehand that the verdict will be theirs, they will not lay aside their arms. In conference rooms, as in courts, it is necessary that both sides enter upon the discussion in good faith, assuming that substantial justice will accrue to both; and it is customary that they leave their arms outside the room where they confer.

I am convinced that the cause of world peace would be greatly advanced if the nations of the world were to obtain a frank statement relating to the present and future policy of governments.

Because the United States, as one of the nations of the Western Hemisphere, is not involved in the immediate controversies which have arisen in Europe, I trust that you may be willing to make such a statement of policy to me as the head of a nation far removed from Europe in order that I, acting only with the responsibility and obligation of a friendly intermediary, may communicate such declaration to other nations now apprehensive as to the course which the policy of your Government may take.

Are you willing to give assurance that your armed forces will not attack or invade the territory or possessions of the following independent nations: Finland, Estonia, Latvia, Lithuania, Sweden, Norway, Denmark, The Netherlands, Belgium, Great Britain and Ireland, France, Portugal, Spain, Switzerland, Liechtenstein, Luxemburg, Poland, Hungary, Rumania, Yugoslavia, Russia, Bulgaria, Greece, Turkey, Iraq, the Arabias, Syria, Palestine, Egypt and Iran.

Such an assurance clearly must apply not only to the present day but also to a future sufficiently long to give every opportunity to work by peaceful methods for a more permanent peace. I therefore suggest that you construe the word "future" to apply to a minimum period of assured non-aggression—ten years at the least—a quarter of a century, if we dare look that far ahead.

If such assurance is given by your Government, I will immediately transmit it to the governments of the nations I have named and I will simultaneously inquire whether, as I am reasonably sure, each of the nations enumerated above will in turn give like assurance for transmission to you.

Reciprocal assurances such as I have outlined will bring to the world an immediate measure of relief.

I propose that if it is given, two essential problems shall promptly be discussed in the resulting peaceful surroundings, and in those discussions the Government of the United States will gladly take part.

The discussions which I have in mind relate to the most effective and immediate manner through which the peoples of the world can obtain progressive relief from the crushing burden of armament which is each day bringing them more closely to the brink of economic disaster. Simultaneously the Government of the United States would be prepared to take part in discussions looking towards the most practical manner of opening up avenues of international trade to the end that every nation of the earth may be enabled to buy and sell on equal terms in the world market as well as to possess assurance of obtaining the materials and products of peaceful economic life.

At the same time, those governments other than the United States which are directly interested could undertake such political discussions as they may consider necessary or desirable.

We recognize complex world problems which affect all humanity but we know that study and discussion of them must be held in an atmosphere of peace. Such an atmosphere of peace cannot exist if negotiations are overshadowed by the threat of force or by the fear of war.

I think you will not misunderstand the spirit of frankness in which I send you this message. Heads of great governments in this hour are literally responsible for the fate of humanity in the coming years. They cannot fail to hear the prayers of their peoples to be protected from the foreseeable chaos of war. History will hold them accountable for the lives and the happiness of all—even unto the least.

I hope that your answer will make it possible for humanity to lose fear and regain security for many years to come.

A similar message is being addressed to the Chief of the Italian Government.

Franklin D. Roosevelt

August 24, 1939

The following is the text of a communication, dispatched yesterday by the President and delivered today to the King of Italy by Ambassador Phillips:

Again a crisis in world affairs makes clear the responsibility of heads of nations for the fate of their own people and indeed of humanity itself. It is because of traditional accord between Italy and the United States and the ties of consanguinity between millions of our citizens that I feel that I can address Your Majesty in behalf of the maintenance of world peace.

It is my belief and that of the American people that Your Majesty and Your Majesty's Government can greatly influence the averting of an outbreak of war. Any general war would cause to suffer all nations whether belligerent or neutral, whether victors or vanquished, and would clearly bring devastation to the peoples and perhaps to the governments of some nations most directly concerned.

The friends of the Italian people and among them the American people could only regard with grief the destruction of great achievements which European nations and the Italian nation in particular have attained during the past generation.

We in America having welded a homogeneous nation out of many nationalities, often find it difficult to visualize the animosities which so often have created crises among nations of Europe which are smaller than ours in population and in territory, but we accept the fact that these nations have an absolute right to maintain their national independence if they so desire. If that be sound doctrine then it must apply to the weaker nations as well as to the stronger.

Acceptance of this means peace, because fear of aggression ends. The alternative, which means of necessity efforts by the strong to dominate the weak, will lead not only to war, but to long future years of oppression on the part of victors and to rebellion on the part of the vanquished. So history teaches us.

On April fourteenth last I suggested in essence an understanding that no armed forces should attack or invade the territory of any other independent nation, and that this being assured, discussions be undertaken to seek progressive relief from the burden of armaments and to open avenues of international trade including sources of raw materials necessary to the peaceful economic life of each nation.

I said that in these discussions the United States would gladly take part. And such peaceful conversations would make it wholly possible for governments other than the United States to enter into peaceful discussions of political or territorial problems in which they were directly concerned.

Were it possible for Your Majesty's Government to formulate proposals for a pacific solution of the present crisis along these lines you are assured of the earnest sympathy of the United States.

The Government of Italy and the United States can today advance those ideals of

Christianity which of late seem so often to have been obscured.

The unheard voices of countless millions of human beings ask that they shall not be vainly sacrificed again.

525. THE HATCH ACT
August 2, 1939
(*U. S. Statutes at Large,* Vol. LIII, p. 1147)

This act, forbidding "pernicious" political activities by federal officeholders, was part of the long-drawn-out struggle for civil service reform, but its immediate background was the widespread resentment against alleged exploitation of relief workers by political organizations. Perhaps its more lasting significance will derive from the extent to which it defederalizes party politics and transfers to local and state leaders power heretofore exercised by national party leaders.

An Act to prevent pernicious political activities.

Be it enacted, That it shall be unlawful for any person to intimidate, threaten, or coerce, or to attempt to intimidate, threaten, or coerce, any other person for the purpose of interfering with the right of such other person to vote or to vote as he may choose, or of causing such other person to vote for, or not to vote for, any candidate for the office of President, Vice President, Presidential elector, Member of the Senate, or Member of the House of Representatives at any election. . . .

SEC. 2. It shall be unlawful for any person employed in any administrative position by the United States, or by any department, independent agency, or other agency of the United States (including any corporation controlled by the United States or any agency thereof, and any corporation all of the capital stock of which is owned by the United States or any agency thereof), to use his official authority for the purpose of interfering with, or affecting the election or the nomination of any candidate for the office of President, Vice President, Presidential elector, Member of the Senate, or Member of the House of Representatives, Delegates or Commissioners from the Territories and insular possessions.

SEC. 3. It shall be unlawful for any person, directly or indirectly, to promise any employment, position, work, compensation, or other benefit, provided for or made possible in whole or in part by any Act of Congress, to any person as consideration, favor, or reward for any political activity or for the support of or opposition to any candidate or any political party in any election.

SEC. 4. Except as may be required by the provisions of subsection (b), section 9 of this Act, it shall be unlawful for any person to deprive, attempt to deprive, or threaten to deprive, by any means, any person of any employment, position, work, compensation, or other benefit provided for or made possible by any Act of Congress appropriating funds for work relief or relief purposes, on account of race, creed, color, or any political activity, support of, or opposition to any candidate or any political party in any election.

SEC. 5. It shall be unlawful for any person to solicit or receive or be in any manner concerned in soliciting or receiving any assessment, subscription, or contribution for any political purpose whatever from any person known by him to be entitled to or receiving compensation, employment, or other benefit provided for or made possible by any Act of Congress appropriating funds for work relief or relief purposes.

SEC. 6. It shall be unlawful for any person for political purposes to furnish or to disclose, or to aid or assist in furnishing or disclosing, any list or names of persons receiving compensation, employment, or benefits provided for or made possible by any Act of Congress appropriating, or authorizing the appropriation of, funds for work relief or relief puposes, to a political candidate, committee, campaign manager, or to any person for delivery to a political candidate, committee, or campaign manager, and it shall be unlawful for any person to receive any such list or names for political purposes.

SEC. 7. No part of any appropriation made by any Act, heretofore or hereafter enacted, making appropriations for work relief, relief, or otherwise to increase employment by providing loans and grants for public-works projects, shall be used for the purpose of, and no authority conferred by any such Act upon any person shall be exercised or administered for the purpose of, interfering with, restraining, or coercing any individual in the exercise of his right to vote at any election.

SEC. 8. Any person who violates any of the foregoing provisions of this Act upon conviction thereof shall be fined not more than $1,000 or imprisoned for not more than one year, or both.

SEC. 9. (a) It shall be unlawful for any person employed in the executive branch of the Federal Government, or any agency or department thereof, to use his official authority or influence for the purpose of interfering with an election or affecting the result thereof. No officer or employee in the executive branch of the Federal Government, or any agency or department thereof, shall take any active part in political management or in political campaigns. All such persons shall retain the right to vote as they may choose and to express their opinions on all political subjects. For the purposes of this section the term "officer" or "employee" shall not be construed to include (1) the President and Vice President of the United States; (2) persons whose compensation is paid from the appropriation for the office of the President; (3) heads and assistant heads of executive departments; (4) officers who are appointed by the President, by and with the advice and consent of the Senate, and who determine

policies to be pursued by the United States in its relations with foreign powers or in the Nation-wide administration of Federal laws.

(b) Any person violating the provisions of this section shall be immediately removed from the position or office held by him, and thereafter no part of the funds appropriated by any Act of Congress for such position or office shall be used to pay the compensation of such person.

SEC. 9A. (1) It shall be unlawful for any person employed in any capacity by any agency of the Federal Government, whose compensation, or any part thereof, is paid from funds authorized or appropriated by any Act of Congress, to have membership in any political party or organization which advocates the overthrow of our constitutional form of government in the United States.

(2) Any person violating the provisions of this section shall be immediately removed from the position or office held by him, and thereafter no part of the funds appropriated by any Act of Congress for such position or office shall be used to pay the compensation of such person.

SEC. 10. All provisions of this Act shall be in addition to, not in substitution for, of existing law.

SEC. 11. If any provision of this Act, or the application of such provision to any person or circumstance, is held invalid, the remainder of the Act, and the application of such provision to other persons or circumstances, shall not be affected thereby.

526. THE DECLARATION OF PANAMA
October 2, 1939

(U. S. Dept. of State *Bull.* I, Oct. 7, 1939)

This attempt of the American nations to establish a new principle of international law by creating a "safety belt" of three hundred miles around the American Continents was shortly flouted by both belligerents in the naval battle off Montevideo, Dec. 13, 1939.

The republics of America, meeting in Panama, have solemnly ratified their position as neutrals in the conflict which disturbs the peace of Europe. But as the present war may reach unexpected derivations, which by their gravitation may affect the fundamental interests of America. it is hereby declared

that nothing can justify that the interests of belligerents prevail over the rights of neutrals, causing upsets and sufferings of peoples who, by their neutrality in the conflict and their distance from the scene of the happenings, should not suffer its fatal dolorous consequences.

During the World War of 1914–1918, the Governments of Argentina, Brazil, Chile, Colombia and Ecuador presented or supported individual proposals seeking in principle a declaration of American republics which entreated the belligerent nations to abstain from engaging in bellicose activities within a prudent distance from the American coasts.

Therefore, it is imperative as a formula of immediate necessity to adopt urgent dispositions based on such precedents, and in guarantee of these interests to avoid a repetition of the damages and sufferings experienced by the American nations and their citizens in the 1914–1918 war.

There is no doubt that the governments of the American republics ought to foresee these dangers as a means of self-protection and to insist upon the determination that in their waters and up to a reasonable distance from their coasts no hostile acts may be engaged in or bellicose activities carried out by participants in a war in which the said [American] governments do not participate.

For these considerations the governments of the American republics resolve and herewith declare:

1. As a measure of continental protection, the American republics, as long as they maintain their neutrality, have the undisputed right to conserve free from all hostile acts by any belligerent non-American nation those waters adjacent to the American continents which they consider of primordial interest and direct utility for their relations, whether such hostile act is attempted or carried out by land, sea or air.

These waters described will be determined in the following manner:

All waters within the limits herewith specified, except the territorial waters of Canada, and of colonies and undisputed possessions of European countries within these limits.

Beginning at a point on the frontier between the United States and Canada at Passamaquoddy Bay, where the 44th degree 46 minutes and 36 seconds of North Latitude crosses the 66th degree 44 minutes and 11 seconds of West Longitude; from there, directly along parallel 44 degrees 46 minutes and 36 seconds to a point crossing 60 degrees West Longitude; from there directly south-

ward to a point at 20 degrees North Latitude; from there by loxodromical line to a point at 5 degrees North Latitude and 24 degrees West Longitude; from there directly south to a point at 20 degrees South Latitude; from there by loxodromical line to a point at 58 degrees South Latitude and 57 degrees West Longitude; thence westward to a point at 80 degrees West Longitude; thence by loxodromical line to a point where the Equator crosses 97 degrees West Longitude; thence by loxodromical line to a point 15 degrees North Latitude and 120 degrees West Longitude thence by loxodromical line to a point at 48 degrees 29 minutes and 38 seconds North Latitude and 136 degrees West Longitude; thence directly east to the termination in the Pacific Ocean, at Jean de Fuqua Strait, on the frontier between the United States and Canada.

2. The governments of the American republics agree to make an effort to seek observance by the belligerents of the dispositions contained in this declaration through joint representations to the governments actually participating in hostilities or those that may participate in the future.

This procedure will in no wise affect the exercise of the individual rights of each State inherent in its sovereignty.

3. The governments of the American republics further declare that, whenever they consider it necessary, they will consult among themselves to determine what measures they can take individually or collectively for the purpose of obtaining fulfillment of the dispositions of this declaration.

4. The American republic, as long as there exists a state of war in which they themselves are not participating and whenever they consider it necessary, may carry out individual or collective patrols, whichever they may decide through mutual agreement or as far as the elements and resources of each one permit, in waters adjacent to their coasts within the zone already defined.

527. THE NEUTRALITY ACT OF 1939
November 4, 1939

(76th Congress, 2nd Session, *Public Resolution* No. 54)

The outbreak of the second World War, September 1939, and the widespread sympathy for England and France forced a reconsideration of the Neutrality Act of 1937. On Sept. 23, 1939 President Roosevelt appealed to Congress so to amend the existing neutrality laws as to permit belligerents to purchase and remove, at their own risk, war munitions and materials. After a long and bitter debate in which the forces of the isolationists were led by Senator Borah, Congress agreed to the "cash and carry" system, retaining, meanwhile, most of the safeguards of the earlier legislation. Of the sections here omitted, those dealing with Restrictions on Use of American Ports, Submarines and Armed Merchant Vessels, National Munitions Control Board, and Regulations, are substantially similar to the comparable provisions in the Act of 1937, Doc. No. 514.

JOINT RESOLUTION

To preserve the neutrality and the peace of the United States and to secure the safety of its citizens and their interests.

Whereas the United States, desiring to preserve its neutrality in wars between foreign states and desiring also to avoid involvement therein, voluntarily imposes upon its nationals by domestic legislation the restrictions set out in this joint resolution; and

Whereas by so doing the United States waives none of its own rights or privileges, or those of any of its nationals, under international law, and expressly reserves all the rights and privileges to which it and its nationals are entitled under the law of nations; and

Whereas the United States hereby expressly reserves the right to repeal, change or modify this joint resolution or any other domestic legislation in the interests of the peace, security or welfare of the United States and its people: Therefore be it *Resolved,*

PROCLAMATION OF A STATE OF WAR BETWEEN FOREIGN STATES

SECTION 1. (a) That whenever the President, or the Congress by concurrent resolution, shall find that there exists a state of war between foreign states, and that it is necessary to promote the security or preserve the peace of the United States or to protect the lives of citizens of the United States, the President shall issue a proclamation naming the states involved; and he shall, from time to time, by proclamation, name other states

as and when they may become involved in the war.

(b) Whenever the state of war which shall have caused the President to issue any proclamation under the authority of this section shall have ceased to exist with respect to any state named in such proclamation, he shall revoke such proclamation with respect to such state.

COMMERCE WITH STATES ENGAGED IN ARMED CONFLICT

SEC. 2. (a) Whenever the President shall have issued a proclamation under the authority of section 1 (a) it shall thereafter be unlawful for any American vessel to carry any passengers or any articles or materials to any state named in such proclamation.

(b) Whoever shall violate any of the provisions of subsection (a) of this section or of any regulations issued thereunder shall, upon conviction thereof, be fined not more than $50,000 or imprisoned for not more than five years, or both. Should the violation be by a corporation, organization, or association, each officer or director thereof participating in the violation shall be liable to the penalty herein prescribed.

(c) Whenever the President shall have issued a proclamation under the authority of section 1 (a) it shall thereafter be unlawful to export or transport, or attempt to export or transport, or cause to be exported or transported, from the United States to any state named in such proclamation, any articles or materials (except copyrighted articles or materials) until all right, title, and interest therein shall have been transferred to some foreign government, agency, institution, association, partnership, corporation, or national. . . .

(g) The provisions of subsections (a) and (c) of this section shall not apply to transportation by American vessels (other than aircraft) of mail, passengers, or any articles or materials (except articles or materials listed in a proclamation referred to in or issued under the authority of section 12 (i)) (1) to any port in the Western Hemisphere south of thirty-five degrees north latitude, (2) to any port in the Western Hemisphere north of thirty-five degrees north latitude and west of sixty-six degrees west longitude,

(3) to any port on the Pacific or Indian Oceans, including the China Sea, the Tasman Sea, the Bay of Bengal, and the Arabian Sea, and any other dependent waters of either of such oceans, seas, or bays, or (4) to any port on the Atlantic Ocean or its dependent waters south of thirty degrees north latitude. The exceptions contained in this subsection shall not apply to any such port which is included within a combat area as defined in section 3 which applies to such vessels. . . .

(i) Every American vessel to which the provisions of subsections (g) and (h) apply, and every neutral vessel to which the provisions of subsection (l) apply, shall, before departing from a port or from the jurisdiction of the United States, file with the collector of customs of the port of departure, or if there is no such collector at such port then with the nearest collector of customs, a sworn statement (1) containing a complete list of all the articles and materials carried as cargo by such vessel, and the names and addresses of the consignees of all such articles and materials, and (2) stating the ports at which such articles and materials are to be unloaded and the ports of call of such vessel. All transportation referred to in subsections (f), (g), (h), and (l) of this section shall be subject to such restrictions, rules, and regulations as the President shall prescribe; but no loss incurred in connection with any transportation excepted under the provisions of subsections (g), (h), and (l) of this section shall be made the basis of any claim put forward by the Government of the United States. . . .

(l) The provisions of subsection (c) of this section shall not apply to the transportation by a neutral vessel to any port referred to in subsection (g) of this section of any articles or materials (except articles or materials listed in a proclamation referred to in or issued under the authority of section 12 (i)) so long as such port is not included within a combat area as defined in section 3 which applies to American vessels.

COMBAT AREAS

SEC. 3. (a) Whenever the President shall have issued a proclamation under the authority of section 1 (a), and he shall thereafter find that the protection of citizens of the United States so requires, he shall, by proclamation, define combat areas, and thereafter it shall be unlawful, except under such rules and regulations as may be prescribed, for any citizen of the United States or any American vessel to proceed into or through any such combat area. The combat areas so defined may be made to apply to surface vessels or aircraft, or both.

(b) In case of the violation of any of the provisions of this section by any American vessel, or any owner or officer thereof, such vessel, owner, or officer shall be fined not more than $50,000 or imprisoned for not more than five years, or both. Should the owner of such vessel be a corporation, organization, or association, each officer or director participating in the violation shall be liable to the penalty hereinabove prescribed. In case of the violation of this section by any citizen traveling as a passenger, such passenger may be fined not more than $10,000 or imprisoned for not more than two years, or both.

(c) The President may from time to time modify or extend any proclamation issued under the authority of this section, and when the conditions which shall have caused him to issue any such proclamation shall have ceased to exist he shall revoke such proclamation and the provisions of this section shall thereupon cease to apply, except as to offenses committed prior to such revocation. . . .

TRAVEL ON VESSELS OF BELLIGERENT STATES

SEC. 5. (a) Whenever the President shall have issued a proclamation under the authority of section 1 (a) it shall thereafter be unlawful for any citizen of the United States to travel on any vessel of any state named in such proclamation, except in accordance with such rules and regulations as may be prescribed.

(b) Whenever any proclamation issued under the authority of section 1 (a) shall have been revoked with respect to any state the provisions of this section shall thereupon cease to apply with respect to such state, except as to offenses committed prior to such revocation.

ARMING OF AMERICAN MERCHANT VESSELS PROHIBITED

SEC. 6. Whenever the President shall have issued a proclamation under the authority of section 1 (a), it shall thereafter be unlawful, until such proclamation is revoked, for any American vessel, engaged in commerce with any foreign state to be armed, except with small arms and ammunition therefor, which the President may deem necessary and shall publicly designate for the preservation of discipline aboard any such vessel.

FINANCIAL TRANSACTIONS

SEC. 7. (a) Whenever the President shall have issued a proclamation under the authority of section 1 (a), it shall thereafter be unlawful for any person within the United States to purchase, sell, or exchange bonds, securities, or other obligations of the government of any state named in such proclamation, or of any political subdivision of any such state, or of any person acting for or on behalf of the government of any such state, or political subdivision thereof, issued after the date of such proclamation, or to make any loan or extend any credit (other than necessary credits accruing in connection with the transmission of telegraph, cable, wireless and telephone services) to any such government, political subdivision, or person. The provisions of this subsection shall also apply to the sale by any person within the United States to any person in a state named in any such proclamation of any articles or materials listed in a proclamation referred to in or issued under the authority of section 12 (i). . . .

SOLICITATION AND COLLECTION OF FUNDS AND CONTRIBUTIONS

SEC. 8. (a) Whenever the President shall have issued a proclamation under the authority of section 1 (a), it shall thereafter be unlawful for any person within the United States to solicit or receive any contribution for or on behalf of the government of any state named in such proclamation or for or on behalf of any agent or instrumentality of any such state. . . .

AMERICAN REPUBLICS

SEC. 9. This joint resolution (except section 12) shall not apply to any American republic engaged in war against a non-American state or states, provided the American republic is not cooperating with a non-American state or states in such war. . . .

NATIONAL MUNITIONS CONTROL BOARD

SEC. 12. (c) Every person required to register under this section shall notify the Secretary of State of any change in the arms, ammunition, or implements of war which he exports, imports, or manufactures; and upon such notification the Secretary of State shall issue to such person an amended certificate of registration, free of charge, which shall remain valid until the date of expiration of the original certificate. Every person required to register under the provisions of this section shall pay a registration fee of $100. Upon receipt of the required registration fee, the Secretary of State shall issue a registration certificate valid for five years, which shall be renewable for further periods of five years upon the payment for each renewal of a fee of $100; but valid certificates of registration (including amended certificates) issued under the authority of section 2 of the joint resolution of August 31, 1935, or section 5 of the joint resolution of August 31, 1935, as amended, shall, without payment of any additional registration fee, be considered to be valid certificates of registration issued under this subsection, and shall remain valid for the same period as if this joint resolution had not been enacted.

(d) It shall be unlawful for any person to export, or attempt to export, from the United States to any other state, any arms, ammunition, or implements of war listed in a proclamation referred to in or issued under the authority of subsection (i) of this section, or to import, or attempt to import, to the United States from any other state, any of the arms, ammunition, or implements of war listed in any such proclamation, without first having submitted to the Secretary of State the name of the purchaser and the terms of sale and having obtained a license therefor. . . .

(g) No purchase of arms, ammunition, or implements of war shall be made on behalf of the United States by any officer, executive department, or independent establishment of the Government from any person who shall have failed to register under the provisions of this joint resolution.

(h) The Board shall make a report to Congress on January 3 and July 3 of each year, copies of which shall be distributed as are other reports transmitted to Congress. Such reports shall contain such information and data collected by the Board as may be considered of value in the determination of questions connected with the control of trade in arms, ammunition, and implements of war, including the name of the purchaser and the terms of sale made under any such license. The Board shall include in such reports a list of all persons required to register under the provisions of this joint resolution, and full information concerning the licenses issued hereunder, including the name of the purchaser and the terms of sale made under any such license.

(i) The President is hereby authorized to proclaim upon recommendation of the Board from time to time a list of articles which shall be considered arms, ammunition, and implements of war for the purposes of this section; but the proclamation Numbered 2237, of May 1, 1937 (50 Stat. 1834) defin-

ing the term "arms, ammunition, and implements of war" shall, until it is revoked, have full force and effect as if issued under the authority of this subsection. . . .

GENERAL PENALTY PROVISION

SEC. 15. In every case of the violation of any of the provisions of this joint resolution or of any rule or regulation issued pursuant thereto where a specific penalty is not herein provided, such violator or violators, upon conviction, shall be fined not more than $10,-000, or imprisoned not more than two years, or both. . . .

REPEALS

SEC. 19. The joint resolution of August 31, 1935, as amended, and the joint resolution of January 8, 1937, are hereby repealed; but offenses committed and penalties, forfeitures, or liabilities incurred under either of such joint resolutions prior to the date of enactment of this joint resolution may be prosecuted and punished, and suits and proceedings for violations of either of such joint resolutions or of any rule or regulation issued pursuant thereto may be commenced and prosecuted, in the same manner and with the same effect as if such joint resolutions had not been repealed.

528. CHAMBERS v. FLORIDA
309 U. S. 227
1940

On Writ of Certiorari to the Supreme Court of the State of Florida. The essential facts of the case are fully set forth in the opinion. On the use of the "third degree" see E. M. Borchard, *Convicting the Innocent; Report* of the Committee on Lawless Enforcement of the Law, 1 American Journal of Political Science, 575; *Report* of the National Commission on Law Observance and Enforcement, vol. IV. For the interpretation of due process as embracing the protections of the Federal bill of rights, see *Twining* v. *New Jersey,* 211 U. S. 78; *Palko* v. *Connecticut,* 302 U. S. 319; *Hague* v. *C. I. O.* 307 U. S. 496.

BLACK, J. The grave question presented by the petition for certiorari, granted in forma

pauperis, is whether proceedings in which confessions were utilized, and which culminated in sentences of death upon four young negro men in the State of Florida, failed to afford the safeguard of that due process of law guaranteed by the Fourteenth Amendment.

Second. The record shows—

About nine o'clock on the night of Saturday, May 13, 1933, Robert Darcy, an elderly white man, was robbed and murdered in Pompano, Florida, a small town in Broward County about twelve miles from Fort Lauderdale, the County seat. The opinion of the Supreme Court of Florida affirming petitioners' conviction for this crime stated that "It was one of those crimes that induced an enraged community . . . ." And, as the dissenting judge pointed out, "The murder and robbery of the elderly Mr. Darcy . . . was a dastardly and atrocious crime. It naturally aroused great and well deserved indignation."

Between 9:30 and 10 o'clock after the murder, petitioner Charlie Davis was arrested, and within the next twenty-four hours from twenty-five to forty negroes living in the community, including petitioners Williamson, Chambers and Woodward, were arrested without warrants and confined in the Broward County jail, at Fort Lauderdale. Evidence of petitioners was that on the way to Miami a motorcycle patrolman drew up to the car in which the men were riding and the sheriff "told the cop that he had some negroes that he . . . taking down to Miami to escape a mob." This statement was not denied by the sheriff in his testimony and Williams did not testify at all.

It is clear from the evidence of both the State and petitioners that from Sunday, May 14, to Saturday, May 20, the thirty to forty negro suspects were subjected to questioning and cross questioning. From the afternoon of Saturday, May 20, until sunrise of the 21st, petitioners and possibly one or two others underwent persistent and repeated questioning.

So far as appears, the prisoners at no time during the week were permitted to see or confer with counsel or a single friend or relative. When carried singly from his cell and subjected to questioning, each found himself, a single prisoner, surrounded in a fourth floor jail room by four to ten men, the county sheriff, his deputies, a convict guard, and other white officers and citizens of the community.

The testimony is in conflict as to whether all four petitioners were continually threatened and physically mistreated until they finally, in hopeless desperation and fear of their lives, agreed to confess on Sunday morning just after daylight. Be that as it may, it is certain that by Saturday, May 20th, five days of continued questioning had elicited no confession. Admittedly, a concentration of effort—directed against a small number of prisoners including petitioners—on the part of the questioners, principally the sheriff and Williams, the convict guard, began about 3:30 that Saturday afternoon. From that hour on, with only short intervals for food and rest for the questioners—"They all stayed up all night." "They bring one of them at a time backwards and forwards . . . until they confessed."

After one week's constant denial of all guilt, petitioners "broke."

Just before sunrise, the State officials got something "worthwhile" from petitioners which the State's attorney would "want"; again he was called; he came; in the presence of those who had carried on and witnessed the all night questioning, he caused his questions and petitioners' answers to be stenographically reported. These are the confessions utilized by the State to obtain the judgments upon which petitioners were sentenced to death. No formal charges had been brought before the confession. Two days thereafter, petitioners were indicted, were arraigned and Williamson and Woodward pleaded guilty; Chambers and Davis pleaded not guilty. Later the sheriff, accompanied by Williams, informed an attorney who presumably had been appointed to defend Davis that Davis wanted his plea of not guilty withdrawn. This was done, and Davis then pleaded guilty. When Chambers was tried, his conviction rested upon his confession and testimony of the other three confessors. The convict guard and the sheriff "were in the Court room sitting down in a seat." And from arrest until sentenced to death, petitioners were never—either in jail or in court—wholly removed from the constant observation, influence, custody and control of those whose persistent pressure brought about the sunrise confessions.

Third. The scope and operation of the Fourteenth Amendment have been fruitful sources of controversy in our constitutional history. However, in view of its historical setting and the wrongs which called it into being, the due process provision of the Fourteenth Amendment—just as that in the Fifth—had led few to doubt that it was intended to guarantee procedural standards adequate and appropriate, then and thereafter, to protect, at all times, people charged with or suspected of crime by those holding positions of power and authority. Tyrannical governments had immemorially utilized dictatorial criminal procedure and punishment to make scape goats of the weak, or of helpless political, religious, or racial minorities and those who differed, who would not conform and who resisted tyranny. The instruments of such governments were in the main, two. Conduct, innocent when engaged in, was subsequently made by fiat criminally punishable without legislation. And a liberty loving people won the principle that criminal punishments could not be inflicted save for that which proper legislative action had already by "the law of the land" forbidden when done. But even more was needed. From the popular hatred and abhorrence of illegal confinement, torture and extortion of confessions of violations of the "law of the land" evolved the fundamental idea that no man's life, liberty or property be forfeited as criminal punishment for violation of that law until there had been a charge fairly made and fairly tried in a public tribunal free of prejudice, passion, excitement and tyrannical power. Thus, as assurance against ancient evils, our country, in order to preserve "the blessings of liberty," wrote into its basic law the requirement, among others, that the forfeiture of the lives, liberties or property of people accused of crime can only follow if procedural safeguards of due process have been obeyed.

The determination to preserve an accused's right to procedural due process sprang in large part from knowledge of the historical truth that the rights and liberties of people accused of crime could not be safely entrusted to secret inquisitorial processes. The testimony of centuries, in governments of varying kinds over populations of different races and beliefs, stood as proof that physical and mental torture and coercion had brought about the tragically unjust sacrifices of some who were the noblest and most useful of their generations. The rack, the thumbscrew, the wheel, solitary confinement, protracted questioning and cross questioning, and other ingenious forms of entrapment of the helpless or unpopular had left their wake of mutilated bodies and shattered minds along the way to the cross, the guillotine, the stake and the hangman's noose. And they who have suffered most from secret and dictatorial proceedings have almost always been the poor,

the ignorant, the numerically weak, the friendless, and the powerless.

This requirement—of conforming to fundamental standards of procedure in criminal trials—was made operative against the States by the Fourteenth Amendment. When one of several accused had limped into the trial court as a result of admitted physical mistreatment inflicted to obtain confessions upon which a jury had returned a verdict of guilty of murder, this Court recently declared, *Brown* v. *Mississippi,* that "It would be difficult to conceive of methods more revolting to the sense of justice than those taken to procure the confessions of these petitioners, and the use of the confessions thus obtained as the basis for conviction and sentence was a clear denial of due process."

Here, the record develops a sharp conflict upon the issue of physical violence and mistreatment, but shows, without conflict, the drag net methods of arrest on suspicion without warrant, and the protracted questioning and cross questioning of these ignorant young colored tenant farmers by State officers and other white citizens, in a fourth floor jail room, where as prisoners they were without friends, advisers or counselors, and under circumstances calculated to break the strongest nerves and the stoutest resistance. Just as our decision in *Brown* v. *Mississippi* was based upon the fact that the confessions were the result of compulsion, so in the present case, the admitted practices were such as to justify the statement that "The undisputed facts showed that compulsion was applied."

For five days petitioners were subjected to interrogations culminating in Saturday's (May 20th) all night examinations. Over a period of five days they steadily refused to confess and disclaimed any guilt. The very circumstances surrounding their confinement and their questioning without any formal charges having been brought, were such as to fill petitioners with terror and frightful misgivings. Some were practical strangers in the community; three were arrested in a one-room farm tenant house which was their home; the haunting fear of mob violence was around them in an atmosphere charged with excitement and public indignation. From virtually the moment of their arrest until their eventual confessions, they never knew just when any one would be called back to the fourth floor room, and there, surrounded by his accusers and others, interrogated by men who held their very lives—so far as these ignorant petitioners could know—in the balance. The rejection of petitioner Woodward's first "confession," given in the early hours of Sunday morning, because it was found wanting, demonstrates the relentless tenacity which "broke" petitioners' will and rendered them helpless to resist their accusers further. To permit human lives to be forfeited upon confessions thus obtained would make of the constitutional requirement of due process of law a meaningless symbol.

We are not impressed by the argument that law enforcement methods such as those under review are necessary to uphold our laws. The Constitution proscribes such lawless means irrespective of the end. And this argument flouts the basic principle that all people must stand on an equality before the bar of justice in every American court.

Today, as in ages past, we are not without tragic proof that the exalted power of some governments to punish manufactured crime dictatorially is the handmaid of tyranny. Under our constitutional system, courts stand against any winds that blow as havens of refuge for those who might otherwise suffer because they are helpless, weak, outnumbered, or because they are non-conforming victims of prejudice and public excitement. Due process of law, preserved for all by our Constitution, commands that no such practice as that disclosed by this record shall send any accused to his death. No higher duty, no more solemn responsibility, rests upon this Court, than that of translating into living law and maintaining this constitutional shield deliberately planned and inscribed for the benefit of every human being subject to our Constitution—of whatever race, creed or persuasion.

The Supreme Court of Florida was in error and its judgment is

Reversed.

---

529. UNITED STATES v. SOCONY-VACUUM OIL CO.
310 U. S. 150
1940

On Writs of Certiorari to the U. S. Circuit Court of Appeals for the Seventh Circuit. Only that portion of the case is presented which concerns the application to the Sherman Anti-Trust Act of the Rule of Reason. For the earlier vicissitudes of the Rule of Reason see Doc. No. 375. Justice Douglas' statement that price fixing agreements had always been unlawful under the Sherman Act appeared to indicate that this decision did not constitute a departure from the Rule of Reason, but many students held that the repudiation of the Rule of Reason was implicit in the opinion.

Douglas, J. . . .

V. *Application of the Sherman Act*
A. Charge to the Jury

The court charged the jury that it was a violation of the Sherman Act for a group of individuals or corporations to act together to raise the prices to be charged for the commodity which they manufactured where they controlled a substantial part of the interstate trade and commerce in that commodity. The court stated that where the members of a combination had the power to raise prices and acted together for that purpose, the combination was illegal; and that it was immaterial how reasonable or unreasonable those prices were or to what extent they had been affected by the combination. It further charged that if such illegal combination existed, it did not matter that there may also have been other factors which contributed to the raising of the prices. In that connection, it referred specifically to the economic factors which we have previously discussed and which respondents contended were primarily responsible for the price rise and the spot markets' stability in 1935 and 1936, viz. control of production, the Connally Act, the price of crude oil, an increase in consumptive demand, control of inventories and manufacturing quotas, and improved business conditions. The court then charged that, unless the jury found beyond a reasonable doubt that the price rise and its continuance were "caused" by the combination and not caused by those other factors, verdicts of "not guilty" should be returned. It also charged that there was no evidence of governmental approval which would exempt the buying programs from the prohibitions of the Sherman Act; and that knowledge or acquiescence of officers of the government or the good intentions of the members of the combination would not give immunity from prosecution under that Act.

The Circuit Court of Appeals held this charge to be reversible error, since it was based upon the theory that such a combination was illegal per se. In its view respondents' activities were not unlawful unless they constituted an unreasonable restraint of trade. Hence, since that issue had not been submitted to the jury and since evidence bearing on it had been excluded, that court reversed and remanded for a new trial so that the character of those activities and their effect on competition could be determined. In answer to the government's petition respondents here contend that the judgment of the Circuit Court of Appeals was correct, since there was evidence that they had affected prices only in the sense that the removal of the competitive evil of distress gasoline by the buying programs had permitted prices to rise to a normal competitive level; that their activities promoted rather than impaired fair competitive opportunities; and therefore that their activities had not unduly or unreasonably restrained trade. And they also contend that certain evidence which was offered should have been admitted as bearing on the purpose and end sought to be attained, the evil believed to exist, and the nature of the restraint and its effect. By their cross-petition respondents contend that the record contains no substantial competent evidence that the combination, either in purpose or effect, unreasonably restrained trade within the meaning of the Sherman Act, and therefore that the Circuit Court of Appeals erred in holding that they were not entitled to directed verdicts of acquittal.

In *United States* v. *Trenton Potteries Co.*, 273 U. S. 392, this Court sustained a conviction under the Sherman Act where the jury was charged that an agreement on the part of the members of a combination, controlling a substantial part of an industry, upon the prices which the members are to charge for their commodity is in itself an unreasonable restraint of trade without regard to the reasonableness of the prices or the good intentions of the combining units. There the combination was composed of those who controlled some 82 per cent of the business of manufacturing and distributing in the United States vitreous pottery. Their object was to fix the prices for the sale of that commodity. In that case the trial court refused various requests to charge that the agreement to fix prices did not itself constitute a violation of law unless the jury also found that it unreasonably restrained interstate commerce. This Court reviewed the various price-fixing cases under the Sherman Act beginning with *United States* v. *Trans-Missouri Freight Association*, 166 U. S. 290, and *United States* v. *Joint Traffic Association*, 171 U. S. 505, and said ". . . it has since often been decided and always assumed that uniform price-fixing by those controlling in any substantial manner a trade or business in interstate commerce is prohibited by the Sherman Law, despite the reasonableness of the particular prices agreed upon." 273 U. S. page 398. This Court pointed out that the so-called "rule of reason" announced in *Standard Oil Co.* v. *United States*, 221 U. S. 1, and in *United States* v. *American Tobacco Co.*, 221 U. S. 106, had not affected this view of the illegality of price-fixing agreements. And in holding that agreements "to fix or maintain prices" are not reasonable restraints of trade under the statute merely because the prices themselves are reasonable, it said:

"The aim and result of every price-fixing agreement, if effective, is the elimination of one form of competition. The power to fix prices, whether reasonably exercised or not involves power to control the market and to fix arbitrary and unreasonable prices. The reasonable price fixed today may through economic and business changes become the unreasonable price of tomorrow. Once established, it may be maintained unchanged because of the absence of competition secured by the agreement for a price reasonable when fixed. Agreements which create such potential power may well be held to be in themselves unreasonable or unlawful restraints without the necessity of minute inquiry whether a particular price is reasonable or unreasonable as fixed and without placing on the government in enforcing the Sherman Law the burden of ascertaining from day to day whether it has become unreasonable through the mere variation of economic conditions. Moreover, in the absence of express legislation requiring it, we should hesitate to adopt a construction making the difference between legal and illegal conduct in the field of business relations depend upon so uncertain a test as whether prices are reasonable ——a determination which can be satisfactorily made only after a complete survey of our economic organization and a choice between rival philosophies."

In conclusion this Court emphasized that the Sherman Act is not only a prohibition against the infliction of a particular type of public injury, but also, as stated in *Standard Sanitary Mfg. Co.* v. *United States,* 226 U. S. 20, a "limitation of rights" which may be "pushed to evil consequences, and therefore restrained."

But respondents claim that other decisions of this Court afford them adequate defenses to the indictment. (Considers alleged precedents and dismisses them as irrelevant.) . . .

Thus for over forty years this Court has consistently and without deviation adhered to the principle that price-fixing agreements are unlawful per se under the Sherman Act and that no showing of so-called competitive abuses or evils which those agreements were designed to eliminate or alleviate may be interposed as a defense. . . .

The reasonableness of prices has no constancy due to the dynamic quality of the business facts underlying price structures. Those who fixed reasonable prices today would perpetuate unreasonable prices tomorrow, since those prices would not be subject to continuous administrative supervision and readjustment in light of changed conditions. Those who controlled the prices would control or effectively dominate the market. And those who were in that strategic position would have it in their power to destroy or drastically impair the competitive system. But the thrust of the rule is deeper and reaches more than monopoly power. Any combination which tampers with price structures is engaged in an unlawful activity. Even though the members of the price-fixing group were in no position to control the market, to the extent that they raised, lowered, or stabilized prices they would be directly interfering with the free play of market forces. The Act places all such schemes beyond the pale and protects that vital part of our economy against any degree of interference. Congress has not left with us the determination of whether or not particular price-fixing schemes are wise or unwise, healthy or destructive. It has not permitted the age-old cry of ruinous competition and competitive evils to be a defense to price-fixing conspiracies. It has no more allowed genuine or fancied competitive abuses as a legal justification for such schemes than it has the good intentions of the members of the combination. If such a shift is to be made, it must be done by the Congress. Certainly Congress has not left us with any such choice. Nor has the Act created or authorized the creation of any special exception in favor of the oil industry. Whatever may be its peculiar problems and characteristics, the Sherman Act, so far as price-fixing agreements are concerned, establishes one uniform rule applicable to all industries alike. There was accordingly no error in the refusal to charge that in order to convict the jury must find that the resultant prices were raised and maintained at "high, arbitrary and non-competitive levels." The charge in the indictment to that effect was surplusage. . . .

Under the Sherman Act a combination formed for the purpose and with the effect of raising, depressing, fixing, pegging, or stabilizing the price of a commodity in interstate or foreign commerce is illegal per se. Where the machinery for price-fixing is an agreement on the prices to be charged or paid for the commodity in the interstate or foreign channels of trade, the power to fix prices exists if the combination has control of a substantial part of the commerce in that commodity. Where the means for price-fixing are purchases or sales of the commodity in a market operation or, as here, purchases of a part of the supply of the commodity for the purpose of keeping it from having a depressive effect on the markets, such power may be found to exist though the combination does not control a substantial part of the commodity. In such a case that power may be established if as a result of market conditions, the resources available to the combinations, the timing and the strategic placement of orders and the like, effective means are at hand to accomplish the desired objective. But there may be effective influence over the market though the group in question does not control it. Price-fixing agreements may have utility to members of the group though the power possessed or exerted falls far short of domination and control. Monopoly power is not the only power which the Act strikes down, as we have said. Proof that a combination was formed for the purpose of fixing prices and that it caused them to be fixed or contributed to that result is proof of the completion of a price-fixing conspiracy under § 1 of the Act. The indictment in this case charged that this combination had that purpose and effect. And there was abundant evidence to support it. . . .

ROBERTS, J., and MCREYNOLDS, J. dissented.

530. F. D. ROOSEVELT'S ADDRESS AT CHARLOTTESVILLE, VIRGINIA
June 10, 1940

(The Public Papers of F. D. Roosevelt, Vol. 9. p. 259)

This address, delivered the day after Italy entered the World War on the side of Germany, indicated that in so far as the President could control American foreign policy the United States had abandoned neutrality for "non-belligerency." The speech met with almost universal approval.

President Newcomb, my friends of the University of Virginia. . . .

Every generation of young men and women in America has questions to ask the world. Most of the time they are the simple but nevertheless difficult questions—questions of work to do, opportunities to find, ambitions to satisfy.

But every now and again in the history of the republic a different kind of question presents itself—a question that asks, not about the future of an individual or even of a generation, but about the future of the country, the future of the American people. . . .

There is such a time again today. Again today the young men and the young women of America ask themselves with earnestness and with deep concern this same question: "What is to become of the country we know?"

Now they ask it with even greater anxiety than before. They ask, not only what the future holds for this republic, but what the future holds for all peoples and all nations that have been living under democratic forms of government—under the free institutions of a free people.

It is understandable to all of us, I think, that they should ask this question. They read the words of those who are telling them that the ideal of individual liberty, the ideal of free franchise, the ideal of peace through justice is a decadent idea!

They read the word and hear the boast of those who say that a belief in force—force directed by self-chosen leaders—is the new and vigorous system which will overrun the earth. They have seen the ascendancy of this philosophy of force in nation after nation where free institutions and individual liberties were once maintained.

It is natural and understandable that the younger generation should first ask itself what the extension of the philosophy of force to all the world would lead to ultimately. We see today, for example, in stark reality some of the consequences of what we call the machine age.

Where control of machines has been retained in the hands of mankind as a whole, untotaled benefits have accrued to mankind. For mankind was then the master: The machine was the servant.

But in this new system of force the mastery of the machine is not in the hands of mankind. It is in the control of infinitely small groups of individuals who rule without a single one of the democratic sanctions that we have known.

The machine in the hands of irresponsible conquerors becomes the master; mankind is not only the servant, it is the victim too. Such mastery abandons with deliberate contempt all of the moral values to which even this young country for more than 300 years has been accustomed and dedicated.

Surely the new philosophy proves from month to month that it could have no possible conception of the way of life or the way of thought of a nation whose origins go back to Jamestown and Plymouth Rock.

And conversely, neither those who sprang from that ancient stock nor those who have come hither in later years can be indifferent to the destruction of freedom in their ancestral lands across the sea.

Perception to danger to our institutions may come slowly or it may come with a rush and shock as it has to the people of the United States in the past few months. This perception of danger—danger in a worldwide arena—has come to us clearly and overwhelmingly. We perceive the peril in this world-wide arena—an arena that may become so narrow that only the Americans will retain the ancient faiths.

Some indeed still hold to the now somewhat obvious delusion that we of the United States can safely permit the United States to become a lone island, a lone island in a world dominated by the philosophy of force.

Such an island may be the dream of those who still talk and vote as isolationists. Such an island represents to me and to the overwhelming majority of Americans today a helpless nightmare, the helpless nightmare of a people without freedom. Yes, the night-

mare of a people lodged in prison, handcuffed, hungry and fed through the bars from day to day by the contemptuous, unpitying masters of other continents.

It is natural also that we should ask ourselves how now we can prevent the building of that prison and the placing of ourselves in the midst of it.

Let us not hesitate—all of us—to proclaim certain truths. Overwhelmingly we, as a nation, and this applies to all the other American nations, we are convinced that military and naval victory for the gods of force and hate would endanger the institutions of democracy in the Western World—and that equally, therefore, the whole of our sympathies lie with those nations that are giving their life blood in combat against those forces.

The people and Government of the United States have seen with the utmost regret and with grave disquiet the decision of the Italian Government to engage in the hostilities now raging in Europe.

More than three months ago the chief of the Italian Government sent me word that because of the determination of Italy to limit, so far as might be possible, the spread of the European conflict, more than two hundred millions of people in the region of the Mediterranean had been enabled to escape the suffering and the devastation of war.

I informed the chief of the Italian Government that this desire on the part of Italy to prevent the war from spreading met with full sympathy and response on the part of the government and the people of the United States, and I expressed the earnest hope of this government and of this people that this policy on the part of Italy might be continued. I made it clear that in the opinion of the Government of the United States any extension of hostilities in the region of the Mediterranean might result in the still greater enlargement of the scene of the conflict, the conflict in the Near East and in Africa, and that if this came to pass no one could foretell how much greater the theatre of the war eventually might become.

Again, upon a subsequent occasion, not so far ago, recognizing that certain aspirations of Italy might form the basis of discussions between the powers most specifically concerned, I offered, in a message addressed to the chief of the Italian Government, to send to the Governments of France and Great Britain such specific indications of the desires of Italy to obtain readjustments with regard to her position as the chief of the Italian Government might desire to transmit through me.

While making it clear that the government of the United States in such an event could not and would not assume responsibility for the nature of the proposals submitted nor for agreements which might thereafter be reached, I proposed that if Italy would refrain from entering the war I would be willing to ask assurances from the other powers concerned that they would faithfully execute any agreement so reached, and that Italy's voice in any future peace conference would have the same authority as if Italy had actually taken part in the war as a belligerent.

Unfortunately, unfortunately to the regret of all of us, and to the regret of humanity, the chief of the Italian Government was unwilling to accept the procedure suggested, and he has made no counter-proposal. This government directed its efforts to doing what it could to work for the preservation of peace in the Mediterranean area, and it likewise expressed its willingness to endeavor to cooperate with the government of Italy when the appropriate occasion arose for the creation of a more stable world order, through the reduction of armaments and through the construction of a more liberal international economic system which would assure to all powers equality of opportunity in the world markets and in the securing of raw materials on equal terms.

I have likewise, of course, felt it necessary in my communications to Signor Mussolini to express the concern of the government of the United States because of the fact that any extension of the war in the region of the Mediterranean would inevitably result in great prejudice to the ways of life and government and to the trade and commerce of all the American republics.

The government of Italy has now chosen to preserve what it terms its "freedom of action" and to fulfill what it states are its promises to Germany. In so doing it has manifested disregard for the rights and se-

curity of other nations, disregard for the lives of the peoples of those nations which are directly threatened by the spread of this war; and has evidenced its unwillingness to find the means through pacific negotiations for the satisfaction of what it believes are its legitimate aspirations.

On this 10th day of June, 1940, the hand that held the dagger has struck it into the back of its neighbor.

On this 10th day of June, 1940, in this university founded by the first great American teacher of democracy we send forth our prayers and our hopes to those beyond the seas who are maintaining with magnificent valor their battle for freedom.

In our unity, in our American unity, we will pursue two obvious and simultaneous courses; we will extend to the opponents of force the material resources of this nation and, at the same time, we will harness and speed up the use of those resources in order that we ourselves in the Americas may have equipment and training equal to the task of any emergency and every defense.

All roads leading to the accomplishment of these objectives must be kept clear of obstructions. We will not slow down or detour. Signs and signals call for speed—full speed ahead.

Yes, it is right that each new generation should ask questions. But in recent months the principal question has been somewhat simplified. Once more the future of the nation and the future of the American people is at stake.

We need not and we will not, in any way, abandon our continuing efforts to make democracy work within our borders. Yes, we still insist on the need for vast improvements in our own social and economic life.

But that, that is a component part of national defense itself.

The program unfolds swiftly and into that program will fit the responsibility and the opportunity of every man and woman in the land to preserve our heritage in days of peril.

I call for effort, courage, sacrifice, devotion. Granting the love of freedom, all of these are possible.

And the love of freedom is still fierce, still steady in the nation today.

531. ALIEN REGISTRATION ACT, 1940
June 28, 1940
(Public Law No. 670, 76th Congress)

This law is notable as the first in which Congress followed the doctrine of guilt by association. It was directed not primarily to the problem of aliens but to subversive activities which were causing grave concern on the eve of war. See Z. Chafee, Jr., *Free Speech in the United States;* M. R. Konvitz, *Aliens and Asiatics in American Law;* W. M. Gilson, *Aliens and the Law.* See Docs. No. 101, 425.

An Act to prohibit certain subversive activities; to amend certain provisions of law with respect to the admission and deportation of aliens; to require the fingerprinting and registration of aliens; and for other purposes.

TITLE I

SECTION 1. (a) It shall be unlawful for any person, with intent to interfere with, impair, or influence the loyalty, morale, or discipline of the military or naval forces of the United States—

(1) to advise, counsel, urge, or in any manner cause insubordination, disloyalty, mutiny, or refusal of duty by any member of the military or naval forces of the United States; or

(2) to distribute any written or printed matter which advises, counsels, or urges insubordination, disloyalty, mutiny, or refusal of duty by any member of the military or naval forces of the United States.

SEC. 2. (a) It shall be unlawful for any person—

(1) to knowingly or willfully advocate, abet, advise, or teach the duty, necessity, desirability, or propriety of overthrowing or destroying any government in the United States by force or violence, or by the assassination of any officer of any such government;

(2) with the intent to cause the overthrow or destruction of any government in the United States, to print, publish, edit, issue, circulate, sell, distribute, or publicly display any written or printed matter advocating, advising, or teaching the duty, necessity, desirability, or propriety of overthrowing or destroying any government in the United States by force or violence;

(3) to organize or help to organize any society, group, or assembly of persons who teach, advocate, or encourage the overthrow or destruction of any government in the United States by force or violence; or to be or become a member of, or affiliate with, any such society, group, or assembly of persons, knowing the purposes thereof.

532. THE GOBITIS CASE
310 U. S. 586
1940

The Gobitis children were expelled from the public schools of Minersville, Pennsylvania, for refusing to salute the American flag as required by the local Board of Education. Their refusal was based on the belief that such an action would be contrary to scripture, an interpretation held by the Watch Tower Bible and Tract Society, the "Jehovah's Witnesses," of which they were members. Their father, Walter Gobitis, brought suit to enjoin the Board from requiring participation in the flag-salute ceremony as a requisite for attending school. The District Court and the Circuit Court both decided in his favor,

and the school board appealed to the Supreme Court. See H. W. Barber, "Religious Liberty vs. the Police Power," *Am. Pol. Sci. Rev.,* Vol. XLI; V. Rotnem and F. G. Folsom, Jr., "Recent Restrictions upon Religious Liberty," *ibid.,* Vol. XXXVI, pp. 1053-1068; H. H. Stroup, *The Jehovah's Witnesses;* H. S. Commager, *Majority Rule and Minority Rights* is an analysis of issues presented by this case; W. G. Fennell, "The 'Reconstructed Court' and Religious Freedom: the Gobitis Case in Retrospect," *19 N.Y.U. Law Quart. Rev.,* 31 ff.; H. S. Commager, "Who is Loyal to America?" *Harpers,* Sept., 1947; T. R.

Powell, "Conscience and Constitution" in *Democracy and National Unity*. A. Mason, *Harlan F. Stone*, ch. 31.

On Writ of Certiorari to the United States Circuit Court of Appeals for the Third Circuit.

FRANKFURTER, J. A grave responsibility confronts this Court whenever in course of litigation it must reconcile the conflicting claims of liberty and authority. But when the liberty invoked is liberty of conscience, and the authority is authority to safeguard the nation's fellowship, judicial conscience is put to its severest test. Of such a nature is the present controversy.

Lillian Gobitis, aged twelve, and her brother William, aged ten, were expelled from the public schools of Minersville, Pennsylvania, for refusing to salute the national flag as part of a daily school exercise. The local Board of Education required both teachers and pupils to participate in this ceremony. The ceremony is a familiar one. The right hand is placed on the breast and the following pledge recited in unison: "I pledge allegiance to my flag, and to the Republic for which it stands; one nation indivisible, with liberty and justice for all." While the words are spoken, teachers and pupils extend their right hands in salute to the flag. The Gobitis family are affiliated with "Jehovah's Witnesses," for whom the Bible as the Word of God is the supreme authority. The children had been brought up conscientiously to believe that such a gesture of respect for the flag was forbidden by command of scripture.

The Gobitis children were of an age for which Pennsylvania makes school attendance compulsory. Thus they were denied a free education and their parents had to put them into private schools. To be relieved of the financial burden thereby entailed, their father, on behalf of the children and in his own behalf, brought this suit. He sought to enjoin the authorities from continuing to exact participation in the flag-salute ceremony as a condition of his children's attendance at the Minersville school. After trial of the issues, Judge Maris gave relief in the District Court on the basis of a thoughtful opinion; his decree was affirmed by the Circuit Court of Appeals. Since this decision ran counter to several per curiam dispositions of this Court, we granted certiorari to give the matter full reconsideration. By their able submissions, the Committee on the Bill of Rights of the American Bar Association and the American Civil Liberties Union, as friends of the Court, have helped us to our conclusion.

We must decide whether the requirement of participation in such a ceremony, exacted from a child who refuses upon sincere religious grounds, infringes without due process of law the liberty guaranteed by the Fourteenth Amendment.

Centuries of strife over the erection of particular dogmas as exclusive or all-comprehending faiths led to the inclusion of a guarantee for religious freedom in the Bill of Rights. The First Amendment, and the Fourteenth through its absorption of the First, sought to guard against repetition of those bitter religious struggles by prohibiting the establishment of a state religion and by securing to every sect the free exercise of its faith. So pervasive is the acceptance of this precious right that its scope is brought into question, as here, only when the conscience of individuals collides with the felt necessities of society.

Certainly the affirmative pursuit of one's convictions about the ultimate mystery of the universe and man's relation to it is placed beyond the reach of law. Government may not interfere with organized or individual expression of belief or disbelief. Propagation of belief—or even of disbelief in the supernatural— is protected, whether in church or chapel, mosque or synagogue, tabernacle or meetinghouse. Likewise the Constitution assures generous immunity to the individual from imposition of penalties for offending, in the course of his own religious activities, the religious views of others, be they a minority or those who are dominant in government.

But the manifold character of man's relations may bring his conception of religious duty into conflict with the secular interests of his fellow-men. When does the constitutional guarantee compel exemption from doing what society thinks necessary for the promotion of some great common end, or from a penalty for conduct which appears dangerous to the general good? To state the problem is to recall the truth that no single principle can answer all of life's complexities. The right to freedom of religious belief, however dissident and however obnoxious to the cherished beliefs of others—even of a majority—is itself the denial of an absolute. But to affirm that the freedom to follow conscience has itself no limits in the life of a society would deny that very plurality of principles which, as a matter of history, underlies protection of religious toleration. Compare Mr. Justice Holmes in Hudson County Water Co. v. McCarter, 209 U.S. 349, 355. Our present task then, as so often the case with courts, is to reconcile two rights in order to prevent either from destroying the other. But, because in safeguarding conscience we are dealing with interests so subtle and so dear, every possible leeway should be given to the claims of religious faith.

In the judicial enforcement of religious freedom we are concerned with a historic concept. See Mr. Justice Cardozo in Hamilton v. Regents, 293 U.S. 245, at page 265. The religious liberty which the Constitution protects has never excluded legislation of general scope not directed against doctrinal loyalties of particular sects. Judicial nullification of legislation cannot be justified by attributing to the framers of the Bill of Rights views for which there is no historic warrant. Conscientious scruples have not, in the course of the long struggle for religious toleration, relieved the individual from obedience to a general law not aimed at the promotion or restriction of religious beliefs. The mere possession of religious convictions which contradict the relevant concerns of a political society does not relieve the citizen from the discharge of political responsibilities. The necessity for this adjustment has again and again been recognized. In a number of situations the exertion of political authority has been sustained, while basic considerations of religious freedom have been left inviolate. Reynolds v. United States, 98 U.S. 145; Davis v. Beason, 133 U.S. 333; Selective Draft Law Cases, 245 U.S. 366; Hamilton v. Regents, 293 U.S. 245. In all these cases the general laws in question, up-

held in their application to those who refused obedience from religious conviction, were manifestations of specific powers of government deemed by the legislature essential to secure and maintain that orderly, tranquil, and free society without which religious toleration itself is unattainable. Nor does the freedom of speech assured by Due Process move in a more absolute circle of immunity than that enjoyed by religious freedom. Even if it were assumed that freedom of speech goes beyond the historic concept of full opportunity to utter and to disseminate views, however heretical or offensive to dominant opinion, and includes freedom from conveying what may be deemed an implied but rejected affirmation, the question remains whether school children, like the Gobitis children, must be excused from conduct required of all the other children in the promotion of national cohesion. We are dealing with an interest inferior to none in the hierarchy of legal values. National unity is the basis of national security. To deny the legislature the right to select appropriate means for its attainment presents a totally different order of problem from that of the propriety of subordinating the possible ugliness of littered streets to the free expression of opinion through distribution of handbills. Compare Schneider v. State of New Jersey, 308 U.S. 147.

Situations like the present are phases of the profoundest problem confronting a democracy—the problem which Lincoln cast in memorable dilemma: "Must a government of necessity be too strong for the liberties of its people, or too weak to maintain its own existence?" No mere textual reading or logical talisman can solve the dilemma. And when the issue demands judicial determination, it is not the personal notion of judges of what wise adjustment requires which must prevail.

Unlike the instances we have cited, the case before us is not concerned with an exertion of legislative power for the promotion of some specific need or interest of secular society—the protection of the family, the promotion of health, the common defense, the raising of public revenues to defray the cost of government. But all these specific activities of government presuppose the existence of an organized political society. The ultimate foundation of a free society is the binding tie of cohesive sentiment. Such a sentiment is fostered by all those agencies of the mind and spirit which may serve to gather up the traditions of a people, transmit them from generation to generation, and thereby create that continuity of a treasured common life which constitutes a civilization. "We live by symbols." The flag is the symbol of our national unity, transcending all internal differences, however large, within the framework of the Constitution. This Court has had occasion to say that ". . . the flag is the symbol of the nation's power,—the emblem of freedom in its truest, best sense. . . . it signifies government resting on the consent of the governed; liberty regulated by law; the protection of the weak against the strong; security against the exercise of arbitrary power; and absolute safety for free institutions against foreign aggression." Halter v. Nebraska, 205 U.S. 34.

The case before us must be viewed as though the legislature of Pennsylvania had itself formally directed the flag-salute for the children of Minersville; had made no exemption for children whose parents were possessed of conscientious scruples like those of the Gobitis family; and had indicated its belief in the desirable ends to be secured by having its public school children share a common experience at those periods of development when their minds are supposedly receptive to its assimilation, by an exercise appropriate in time and place and setting, and one designed to evoke in them appreciation of the nation's hopes and dreams, its sufferings and sacrifices. The precise issue, then, for us to decide is whether the legislatures of the various states and the authorities in a thousand counties and school districts of this country are barred from determining the appropriateness of various means to evoke that unifying sentiment without which there can ultimately be no liberties, civil or religious. To stigmatize legislative judgment in providing for this universal gesture of respect for the symbol of our national life in the setting of the common school as a lawless inroad on that freedom of conscience which the Constitution protects, would amount to no less than the pronouncement of pedagogical and psycho-

logical dogma in a field where courts possess no marked and certainly no controlling competence. The influences which help toward a common feeling for the common country are manifold. Some may seem harsh and others no doubt are foolish. Surely, however, the end is legitimate. And the effective means for its attainment are still so uncertain and so unauthenticated by science as to preclude us from putting the widely prevalent belief in flag-saluting beyond the pale of legislative power. It mocks reason and denies our whole history to find in the allowance of a requirement to salute our flag on fitting occasions the seeds of sanction for obeisance to a leader.

The wisdom of training children in patriotic impulses by those compulsions which necessarily pervade so much of the educational process is not for our independent judgment. Even were we convinced of the folly of such a measure, such belief would be no proof of its unconstitutionality. For ourselves, we might be tempted to say that the deepest patriotism is best engendered by giving unfettered scope to the most crotchety beliefs. Perhaps it is best, even from the standpoint of those interests which ordinances like the one under review seek to promote, to give to the least popular sect leave from conformities like those here in issue. But the court-room is not the arena for debating issues of educational policy. It is not our province to choose among competing considerations in the subtle process of securing effective loyalty to the traditional ideals of democracy, while respecting at the same time individual idiosyncracies among a people so diversified in racial origins and religious allegiances. So to hold would in effect make us the school board for the country. That authority has not been given to this Court, nor should we assume it.

We are dealing here with the formative period in the development of citizenship. Great diversity of psychological and ethical opinion exists among us concerning the best way to train children for their place in society. Because of these differences and because of reluctance to permit a single, iron-cast system of education to be imposed upon a nation compounded of so many strains, we have held that, even though public education is one of our most cherished democratic institutions, the Bill of Rights bars a state from compelling all children to attend the public schools. Pierce v. Society of the Sisters of the Holy Names of Jesus and Mary, 268 U.S. 510. But it is a very different thing for this Court to exercise censorship over the conviction of legislatures that a particular program or exercise will best promote in the minds of children who attend the common schools an attachment to the institutions of their country.

What the school authorities are really asserting is the right to awaken in the child's mind considerations as to the significance of the flag contrary to those implanted by the parent. In such an attempt the state is normally at a disadvantage in competing with the parent's authority, so long—and this is the vital aspect of religious toleration—as parents are unmolested in their right to counteract by their own persuasiveness the wisdom and rightness of those loyalties which the state's educational system is seeking to promote. Except where the transgression of constitutional liberty is too plain for argument, personal freedom is best maintained—so long as the remedial channels of the democratic process remain open and unobstructed —when it is ingrained in a people's habits and not enforced against popular policy by the coercion of adjudicated law. That the flag-salute is an allowable portion of a school program for those who do not invoke conscientious scruples is surely not debatable. But for us to insist that, though the ceremony may be required, exceptional immunity must be given to dissidents, is to maintain that there is no basis for a legislative judgment that such an exemption might introduce elements of difficulty into the school discipline, might cast doubts in the minds of the other children which would themselves weaken the effect of the exercise.

The preciousness of the family relation, the authority and independence which give dignity to parenthood, indeed the enjoyment of all freedom, presuppose the kind of ordered society which is summarized by our flag. A society which is dedicated to the preservation of these ultimate values of civilization may in self-protection utilize the educational process for inculcating those almost unconscious feelings which bind men together in a comprehending loyalty, whatever may be their lesser differences and difficulties. That is to say, the process may be utilized so long as men's right to believe as they please, to win others to their way of belief, and their right to assemble in their chosen places of worship for the devotional ceremonies of their faith, are all fully respected.

Judicial review, itself a limitation on popular government, is a fundamental part of our constitutional scheme. But to the legislature no less than to courts is committed the guardianship of deeply-cherished liberties. Where all the effective means of inducing political changes are left free from interference, education in the abandonment of foolish legislation is itself a training in liberty. To fight out the wise use of legislative authority in the forum of public opinion and before legislative assemblies rather than to transfer such a contest to the judicial arena, serves to vindicate the self-confidence of a free people.

Reversed.

533. WEST VA. STATE BD. v. BARNETTE
319 U. S. 624
1943

Inspired by the decision in the Gobitis case, the West Virginia State Board of Education ordered the flag salute ceremony to be made compulsory in all public schools. Children who disobeyed were to be dismissed from school, and action could be taken against their parents on the grounds that the children were "unlawfully absent." Members of the Jehovah's Witnesses brought suit in the United States District Court to restrain enforcement against their sect; the lower court decided in their favor, and the West Virginia State Board of Education appealed the case directly to the U. S. Supreme Court. Justices Black, Douglas, and Murphy filed concurring decisions, Justices Roberts and Reed dissenting decisions. See previous Document.

JACKSON, J. This case calls upon us to reconsider a precedent decision, as the Court throughout its history often has been required to do. Before turning to the Gobitis case, however, it is desirable to notice certain characteristics by which this controversy is distinguished.

The freedom asserted by these respondents does not bring them into collision with rights asserted by any other individual. It is such conflicts which most frequently require intervention of the State to determine where the rights of one end and those of another begin. But the refusal of these persons to participate in the ceremony does not interfere with or deny rights of others to do so. Nor is there any question in this case that their behavior is peaceable and orderly. The sole conflict is between authority and rights of the individual. The State asserts power to condition access to public education on making a prescribed sign and profession and at the same time to coerce attendance by punishing both parent and child. The latter stand on a right of self-determination in matters that touch individual opinion and personal attitude.

As the present Chief Justice said in dissent in the Gobitis case, the State may "require teaching by instruction and study of all in our history and in the structure and organization of our government, including the guaranties of civil liberty which tend to inspire patriotism and love of country." 310 U.S. at page 604. Here, however, we are dealing with a compulsion of students to declare a belief. They are not merely made acquainted with the flag salute so that they may be informed as to what it is or even what it means. The issue here is whether this slow and easily neglected route to aroused loyalties constitutionally may be short-cut by substituting a compulsory salute and slogan. This issue is not prejudiced by the Court's previous holding that where a State, without compelling attendance, extends college facilities to pupils who voluntarily enroll, it may prescribe military training as part of the course without offense to the Constitution. It was held that those who take advantage of its opportunities may not on ground of conscience refuse compliance with such conditions. In the present case attendance is not optional. That case is also to be distinguished from the present one because, independently of college privileges or requirements, the State has power to raise militia and impose the duties of service therein upon its citizens.

There is no doubt that, in connection with the pledges, the flag salute is a form of utterance. Symbolism is a primitive but effective way of communicating ideas. The use of an emblem or flag to symbolize some system, idea, institution, or personality, is a short cut from mind to mind. Causes and nations, political parties, lodges and ecclesiastical groups seek to knit the loyalty of their followings to a flag or banner, a color or design. The State announces rank, function, and authority through crowns and maces, uniforms and black robes; the church speaks through the Cross, the Crucifix, the altar and shrine, and clerical raiment. Symbols of State often convey political ideas just as religious symbols come to convey theological ones. Associated with many of these symbols are appropriate gestures of acceptance or respect: a salute, a bowed or bared head, a bended knee. A person gets from a symbol the meaning he puts into it, and what is one man's comfort and inspiration is another's jest and scorn. . . .

It is also to be noted that the compulsory flag salute and pledge requires affirmation of a belief and an attitude of mind. It is not clear whether the regulation contemplates that pupils forego any contrary convictions of their own and become unwilling converts to the prescribed ceremony or whether it will be acceptable if they simulate assent by words without belief and by a gesture barren of meaning. It is now a commonplace that censorship or suppression of expression of opinion is tolerated by our Constitution only when the expression presents a clear and present danger of action of a kind the State is empowered to prevent and punish. It would seem that involuntary affirmation could be commanded only on even more immediate and urgent grounds than silence. But here the power of compulsion is invoked without any allegation that remaining passive during a flag salute ritual creates a clear and present danger that would justify an effort even to muffle expression. To sustain the compulsory flag salute we are required to say that a Bill of Rights which guards the individual's right to speak his own mind, left it open to public authorities to compel him to utter what is not in his mind.

Whether the First Amendment to the Constitution will permit officials to order observance of ritual of this nature does not depend upon whether as a voluntary exercise we would think it to be good, bad or merely innocuous. Any credo of nationalism is likely to include what some disapprove or to omit what others think essential, and to give off different overtones as it takes on different accents or interpretations. If official power exists to coerce acceptance of any patriotic creed, what it shall contain cannot be decided by courts, but must be largely discretionary with the ordaining authority, whose power to prescribe would no doubt include power to amend. Hence validity of the asserted power to force an American citizen publicly to profess any statement of belief or to engage in any ceremony of assent to one presents questions of power that must be considered independently of any idea we may have as to the utility of the ceremony in question.

Nor does the issue as we see it turn on one's possession of particular religious views or the sincerity with which they are held. While religion supplies respondents' motive for enduring the discomforts of making the issue in this case, many citizens who do not share these religious views hold such a compulsory rite to infringe constitutional liberty of the individual. It is not necessary to inquire whether non-conformist beliefs will exempt from the duty to salute unless we first find power to make the salute a legal duty.

The Gobitis decision, however, *assumed,* as did the argument in that case and in this, that power exists in the State to impose the flag salute discipline upon school children in general. The Court only examined and rejected a claim based on religious beliefs of immunity from an unquestioned general rule. The question which underlies the flag salute controversy is whether such a ceremony so touching matters of opinion and political attitude may be imposed upon the individual by official authority under powers committed to any political organization under our Constitution. We examine rather than assume existence of this power and, against this broader definition of issues in this case, re-examine specific grounds assigned for the Gobitis decision.

1. It was said that the flag-salute controversy confronted the Court with "the problem which Lincoln cast in memorable dilemma: 'Must a government of necessity be too *strong* for the liberties of its people, or too *weak* to maintain its own existence?' " and that the answer must be in favor of strength. . . . Such oversimplification, so handy in political debate, often lacks the precision necessary to postulates of judicial reasoning. If validly applied to this problem, the utterance cited would resolve every issue of power in favor of those in authority and would require us to override every liberty thought to weaken or delay execution of their policies.

Government of limited power need not be anemic government. Assurance that rights are secure tends to diminish fear and jealousy of strong government, and by making us feel safe to live under it makes for its better support. Without promise of a limiting Bill of Rights it is doubtful if our Constitution could have mustered enough strength to enable its ratification. To enforce those rights today is not to choose weak government over strong government. It is only to adhere as a means of strength to individual freedom of mind in preference to officially disciplined uniformity for which history indicates a disappointing and disastrous end.

The subject now before us exemplifies this principle. Free public education, if faithful to the ideal of secular instruction and political neutrality, will not be partisan or enemy of any class, creed, party, or faction. If it is to impose any ideological discipline, however, each party or denomination must seek to control, or failing that, to weaken the influence of the educational system. Observance of the limitations of the Constitution will not weaken government in the field appropriate for its exercise.

2. It was also considered in the Gobitis case that functions of educational officers in states, counties and school districts were such that to interfere with their authority "would

in effect make us the school board for the country."

The Fourteenth Amendment, as now applied to the States, protects the citizen against the State itself and all of its creatures—Boards of Education not excepted. These have, of course, important, delicate, and highly discretionary functions, but none that they may not perform within the limits of the Bill of Rights. That they are educating the young for citizenship is reason for scrupulous protection of Constitutional freedoms of the individual, if we are not to strangle the free mind at its source and teach youth to discount important principles of our government as mere platitudes.

Such Boards are numerous and their territorial jurisdiction often small. But small and local authority may feel less sense of responsibility to the Constitution, and agencies of publicity may be less vigilant in calling it to account. The action of Congress in making flag observance voluntary and respecting the conscience of the objector in a matter so vital as raising the Army contrasts sharply with these local regulations in matters relatively trivial to the welfare of the nation. There are village tyrants as well as village Hampdens, but none who acts under color of law is beyond reach of the Constitution.

3. The Gobitis opinion reasoned that this is a field "where courts possess no marked and certainly no controlling competence," that it is committed to the legislatures as well as the courts to guard cherished liberties and that it is constitutionally appropriate to "fight out the wise use of legislative authority in the forum of public opinion and before legislative assemblies rather than to transfer such a contest to the judicial arena," since all the "effective means of inducing political changes are left free."

The very purpose of a Bill of Rights was to withdraw certain subjects from the vicissitudes of political controversy, to place them beyond the reach of majorities and officials and to establish them as legal principles to be applied by the courts. One's right to life, liberty, and property, to free speech, a free press, freedom of worship and assembly, and other fundamental rights may not be submitted to vote; they depend on the outcome of no elections.

In weighing arguments of the parties it is important to distinguish between the due process clause of the Fourteenth Amendment as an instrument for transmitting the principles of the First Amendment and those cases in which it is applied for its own sake. The test of legislation which collides with the Fourteenth Amendment, because it also collides with the principles of the First, is much more definite than the test when only the Fourteenth is involved. Much of the vagueness of the due process clause disappears when the specific prohibitions of the First become its standard. The right of a State to regulate, for example, a public utility may well include, so far as the due process test is concerned, power to impose all of the restrictions which a legislature may have a "rational basis" for adopting. But freedoms of speech and of press, of assembly, and of worship may not be infringed on such slender grounds. They are susceptible of restriction only to prevent grave and immediate danger to interests which the state may lawfully protect. It is important to note that while it is the Fourteenth Amendment which bears directly upon the State it is the more specific limiting principles of the First Amendment that finally govern this case.

Nor does our duty to apply the Bill of Rights to assertions of official authority depend upon our possession of marked competence in the field where the invasion of rights occurs. True, the task of translating the majestic generalities of the Bill of Rights, conceived as part of the pattern of liberal government in the eighteenth century, into concrete restraints on officials dealing with the problems of the twentieth century, is one to disturb self-confidence. These principles grew in soil which also produced a philosophy that the individual was the center of society, that his liberty was attainable through mere absence of governmental restraints, and that government should be entrusted with few controls and only the mildest supervision over men's affairs. We must transplant these rights to a soil in which the *laissez-faire* concept or principle of non-interference has withered at least as to economic affairs, and social advancements are increasingly sought through closer integration of society and through expanded and strengthened governmental controls. These changed conditions often deprive precedents of reliability and cast us more than we would choose upon our own judgment. But we act in these matters not by authority of our competence but by force of our commissions. We cannot, because of modest estimates of our competence in such specialties as public education, withhold the judgment that history authenticates as the function of this Court when liberty is infringed.

4. Lastly, and this is the very heart of the Gobitis opinion, it reasons that "National unity is the basis of national security," that the authorities have "the right to select appropriate means for its attainment," and hence reaches the conclusion that such compulsory measures toward "national unity" are constitutional. Upon the verity of this assumption depends our answer in this case.

National unity as an end which officials may foster by persuasion and example is not in question. The problem is whether under our Constitution compulsion as here employed is a permissible means for its achievement.

Struggles to coerce uniformity of sentiment in support of some end thought essential to their time and country have been waged by many good as well as by evil men. Nationalism is a relatively recent phenomenon but at other times and places the ends have been racial or territorial security, support of a dynasty or regime, and particular plans for saving souls. As first and moderate methods to attain unity have failed, those bent on its accomplishment must resort to an ever-increasing severity. As governmental pressure toward unity becomes greater, so strife becomes more bitter as to whose unity it shall be. Probably no deeper division of our people could proceed from any provocation than from finding it necessary to choose what doctrine and whose program public educational officials shall compel youth to unite in embracing. Ultimate futility of such attempts to compel coherence is the lesson of every such effort from the Roman drive to stamp out Christianity as a disturber of its pagan unity, the Inquisition, as a means to religious and dynastic unity, the Siberian exiles as a means to Russian unity, down to the fast failing efforts of our present totalitarian enemies. Those who begin coercive elimination of dissent soon find themselves exterminating dissenters. Compulsory unification of opinion achieves only the unanimity of the graveyard.

It seems trite but necessary to say that the First Amendment to our Constitution was designed to avoid these ends by avoiding these beginnings. There is no mysticism in the American concept of the State or of the nature or origin of its authority. We set up government by consent of the governed, and the Bill of Rights denies those in power any legal opportunity to coerce that consent. Authority here is to be controlled by public opinion, not public opinion by authority.

The case is made difficult not because the principles of its decision are obscure but because the flag involved is our own. Nevertheless, we apply the limitations of the Constitution with no fear that freedom to be intellectually and spiritually diverse or even contrary will disintegrate the social organization. To believe that patriotism will not flourish if patriotic ceremonies are voluntary and spontaneous instead of a compulsory routine is to make an unflattering estimate of the appeal of our institutions to free minds. We can have intellectual individualism and the rich cultural diversities that we owe to exceptional minds only at the price of occasional eccentricity and abnormal attitudes. When they are so harmless to others or to the State as those we deal with here, the price is not too great. But freedom to differ is not limited to things that do not matter much. That would be a mere shadow of freedom. The test of its substance is the right to differ as to things that touch the heart of the existing order.

If here is any fixed star in our constitutional constellation, it is that no official, high or petty, can prescribe what shall be orthodox in politics, nationalism, religion, or other matters of opinion or force citizens to confess by word or act their faith therein. If there are any circumstances which permit an exception, they do not now occur to us.

We think the action of the local authorities in compelling the flag salute and pledge transcends constitutional limitations on their power and invades the sphere of intellect and spirit which it is the purpose of the First Amendment to our Constitution to reserve from all official control.

The decision of this Court in Minersville School District v. Gobitis and the holdings of those few per curiam decisions which preceded and foreshadowed it are overruled, and the judgment enjoining enforcement of the West Virginia Regulation is affirmed.

JJ. Frankfurter, Roberts, Reed, dissenting.

534. THE ACT OF HAVANA
Agreements Reached at the Havana Pan-American Conference
July 29, 1940

(New York Times, July 30, 1940)

The imminent threat of German or Italian occupation or control of French, English or Dutch possessions in the New World and the even more menacing threat of Nazi control of Latin American trade through barter agreements and political and military pressure, led to a notable conference of the American states in July, 1940. Secretary Hull quickly assumed leadership of this conference, and despite the opposition of the delegation from the Argentine succeeded in achieving substantially his objectives.

The text of the convention covering the legal phase of the plan to be acted upon regarding foreign possessions in the New World follows:

The governments represented in the second consultative meeting of American Foreign Ministers considering:

That, as a consequence of the acts which are developing on the European Continent, there might be produced in territories of possessions which some belligerent nations hold in America situations wherein that sovereignty may be extinguished or essentially affected, or the government suffers acephalism (becomes headless), generating peril for the peace of the Continent and creating a situation wherein the dominion of law and order and respect of life, liberty and property of the inhabitants disappears;

That the American republics would consider any transfer or attempt to transfer sovereignty, jurisdiction, possession or any interest or control in any of these regions to another non-American State as contrary to American sentiments, principles and rights of American States to maintain their security and political independence;

That the American republics would not recognize nor accept such transfer or intent to transfer or acquire interests or rights, direct or indirect, in any of these regions, whatever might be the form employed to realize it;

That the American republics reserve the right to judge through their respective organs of government if some transfer or intent to transfer sovereignty, jurisdiction, cession or incorporation of geographical regions in America owned by European countries until Sept. 1, 1939, may impair their political independence even though there has been no formal transfer or change in the status of the regions;

That for this reason it is necessary to establish for unforeseen cases as for any other which may produce acephalism of the government in the said regions a regime of provisional administration, while arriving at the objective for free determination of the peoples;

That the American republics, as an international community which acts integrally and forcefully, supporting itself on political and juridical principles which have been applied for more than a century, have the incontestable right, in order to preserve their unity and security, to take under their administration said regions and to deliberate over their destinies in accordance with their respective degrees of political and economic development;

That the provisional and transitory character of the measures agreed upon does not mean forgetfulness or abrogation of the principle of non-intervention, the regulator of inter-American life, a principle proclaimed by the American Institute, recognized by the celebrated committee of experts on international law which met at Rio de Janeiro and consecrated in all its amplitude in the seventh Pan-American conference held at Montevideo;

That this community, therefore, has the international juridical capacity to act in such matters;

That in such a case the most adequate regime is that of provisional administration.

Desiring to protect their peace and security and to promote the interests of any of the regions to which this (document) refers and which are understood to be within the foregoing consideration;

Have resolved to conclude the following convention:

First—If a non-American State attempts directly or indirectly to substitute for another non-American State in the sovereignty or control which that (other State) exerted over any territory situated in America, thereby threatening the peace of the continent, said territory automatically will be considered to be within the stipulations of this convention, and will be submitted to a regime of provisional administration.

Second—That administration shall be executed—as it is considered advisable in each case—by one or more American States by virtue of previous consent.

Third—When administration is established over a region it shall be executed in the interest of the security of America and to the benefit of the administered region looking toward its well-being and development, until the region is found to be in condition to administer itself or to return to its former status, so long as this is compatible with the security of the American republics.

Fourth—Administration of the territory shall operate under conditions which guarantee freedom of conscience and faith with the restrictions demanded by the maintenance of public order and good habits.

Fifth—The administration shall apply local laws, coordinating them with the objectives of this convention, but it may adopt in addition those decisions necessary to solve situations concerning which no such local laws exist.

Sixth—In all that concerns commerce and industry the American nations shall enjoy equal conditions and the same benefits, and the administrator never shall create a situation of privilege for himself or his compatriots or for any particular nations. Liberty of economic relations with all countries on a basis of reciprocity shall be maintained.

Seventh—The natives of the region shall participate as citizens in the public administration and tribunals of justice, with no other consideration than that of competence.

Eighth—In so far as possible rights of any kind shall be governed by local laws and customs, acquired to be protected in conformity with such laws.

Ninth—Forced labor shall be abolished in regions where it exists.

Tenth—The administration will provide means to diffuse public education in all grades, with the double aim of promoting the wealth of the region and better living conditions of the people, especially in regard to public and individual hygiene, and preparation of the exercise of political autonomy in the shortest time.

Eleventh—The natives of the region under administration shall have their own organic charter, which the administration shall establish, consulting the people in whatever way possible.

Twelfth—The administration shall submit an annual report to the inter-American organization charged with control of the administered regions, on the manner in which it carried out its mission, attaching accounts and measures adopted during the year in said region.

Thirteenth—The organization to which the preceding article refers shall be authorized to take cognizance of petitions which inhabitants of the region transmit through the intermediary of the administration with reference to the operation of the provisional administration. The administration shall remit, along with these petitions, such observations as it considers convenient.

Fourteenth—First the administration shall be authorized for a period of three years, at the termination of which, and in case of necessity, it shall be renewed for successive periods of not longer than a decade.

Fifteenth—Expenses incurred in the exercise of the administration shall be covered by revenues from the administered region, but in case these are insufficient the deficit shall be covered by the administering nation or nations.

Sixteenth—There shall be established a commission which shall be called the "Inter-American Commission of Territorial Administration" and shall be composed of one representative for each of the States which ratify this convention, and it shall be the international organization to which the convention refers.

Any country which ratifies it (the convention) may call the first meeting, indicating the most convenient city. The commission shall elect a president, complete its organization and fix a definite headquarters. Two-thirds of its members shall constitute a quorum and two-thirds of the members present may adopt agreements.

Seventeenth—The commission is authorized to establish a provisional administration over regions to which the present convention

applies; it also is authorized to install the said administration so that it will be operated by the number of States which will be determined according to the case, and to legalize its execution in terms of the preceding articles.

Eighteenth—The present convention will be opened for signatures of the American republics in Havana and shall be ratified by the high contracting parties in accordance with their constitutional procedures. The Secretary of State of the Republic of Cuba shall transmit, as soon as possible, authentic copies certified to the various governments to obtain ratifications. Instruments of ratification shall be deposited in the archives of the Pan-American Union in Washington, which shall notify the signatory governments of said deposit; such notification shall be considered as exchange of ratifications.

Nineteenth—The present convention shall be effective when two-thirds of the American States shall have deposited their respective instruments of ratification.

535. HEMISPHERIC DEFENSE
August 18, 1940
(*Department of State Bulletin,* Aug. 24, 1940)

August 17 President Roosevelt and Prime Minister Mackenzie King of Canada met at Ogdensburg, New York, to discuss mutual Canadian-American problems of defense. The next day they issued the following joint statement:

The Prime Minister and the President have discussed the mutual problems of defense in relation to the safety of Canada and the United States.

It has been agreed that a Permanent Joint Board on Defense shall be set up at once by

the two countries.

This Permanent Joint Board on Defense shall commence immediate studies relating to sea, land and air problems including personnel and matériel.

It will consider in the broad sense the defense of the north half of the Western Hemisphere.

The Permanent Joint Board on Defense will consist of four or five members from each country, most of them from the services. It will meet shortly.

536. EXCHANGE OF DESTROYERS FOR AIR AND NAVAL BASES
September 2, 1940
(*Department of State Bulletin,* Sept. 7, 1940, pp. 199–200)

In his Charlottesville speech the President had promised to "extend to the opponents of force the material resources of this nation." The urgent need of Britain for additional destroyers to protect her far-flung sea-lanes, and the equally urgent

need of the United States for additional air and naval bases, suggested the desirability of an exchange. That exchange, consummated by the interchange of notes between the Marquess of Lothian and Secretary of State Hull, was characterized by the President as "the most important action in the reinforcement of our national defense that has been taken since the Louisiana Purchase."

Washington, September 2, 1940

Sir:

I have the honor under instructions from His Majesty's Principal Secretary of State for Foreign Affairs to inform you that in view of the friendly and sympathetic interests of His Majesty's Government in the United Kingdom in the national security of the United States and their desire to strengthen the ability of the United States to cooperate effectively with the other nations of the Americas in the defense of the Western Hemisphere, His Majesty's Government will secure the grant to the Government of the United States, freely and without consideration, of the lease for immediate establishment and use of naval and air bases and facilities for entrance thereto and the operation and protection thereof, on the Avalon Peninsula and on the southern coast of Newfoundland, and on the east coast and on the Great Bay of Bermuda.

Furthermore, in view of the above and in view of the desire of the United States to acquire additional air and naval bases in the Caribbean and in British Guiana, and with endeavoring to place a monetary or commercial value upon the many tangible and intangible rights and properties involved, His Majesty's Government will make available to the United States for immediate establishment and use naval and air bases and facilities for entrance thereto and the operation and protection thereof, on the eastern side of the Bahamas, the southern coast of Jamaica, the western coast of St. Lucia, the west coast of Trinidad in the Gulf of Paria, in the island of Antigua and in British Guiana within fifty miles of Georgetown, in exchange for naval and military equipment and material which the United States Government will transfer to His Majesty's Government.

All the bases and facilities referred to in the preceding paragraphs will be leased to the United States for a period of ninety-nine years, free from all rent and charges other than such compensation to be mutually agreed on to be paid by the United States in order to compensate the owners of private property for loss by expropriation or damage arising out of the establishment of the bases and facilities in question.

His Majesty's Government, in the leases to be agreed upon, will grant to the United States for the period of the leases all the rights, power and authority within the bases leased, and within the limits of the territorial waters and air spaces adjacent to or in the vicinity of such bases, necessary to provide access to and defense of such bases, and appropriate provisions for their control.

Without prejudice to the above-mentioned rights of the United States authorities and their jurisdiction within the leased areas, the adjustment and reconciliation between the jurisdiction of the authorities of the United States within these areas and the jurisdiction of the authorities of the territories in which these areas are situated, shall be determined by common agreement.

The exact location and bounds of the aforesaid bases, the necessary seaward, coast and anti-aircraft defenses, the location of sufficient military garrisons, stores and other necessary auxiliary facilities shall be determined by common agreement.

His Majesty's Government are prepared to designate immediately experts to meet with experts of the United States for these purposes. Should these experts be unable to agree in any particular situation, except in the case of Newfoundland and Bermuda, the matter shall be settled by the Secretary of State of the United States and His Majesty's Secretary of State for Foreign Affairs.

I have the honor to be, with the highest consideration, sir,

Your most obedient, humble servant.

Lothian.

Department of State
Washington, September 2, 1940

Excellency:

I have received your note of September 2, 1940 . . .

I am directed by the President to reply to your note as follows:

The Government of the United States appreciates the declarations and the generous action of His Majesty's Government as contained in your communication which are destined to enhance the national security of the United States and greatly to strengthen its ability to cooperate effectively with the other nations of the Americas in the defense of the Western Hemisphere. It therefore gladly accepts the proposals.

The Government of the United States will immediately designate experts to meet with experts designated by His Majesty's Government to determine upon the exact location of the naval and air bases mentioned in your communication under acknowledgment.

In consideration of the declarations above quoted, the Government of the United States will immediately transfer to His Majesty's Government fifty United States Navy destroyers generally referred to as the twelve hundred-ton type. . . .

CORDELL HULL.

537. F. D. ROOSEVELT'S "FOUR FREEDOMS" SPEECH
January 6, 1941

(The Public Papers of F. D. Roosevelt, Vol. 9, p. 663)

The "Four Freedoms," formulated in the President's annual message to the Congress, came to be accepted as the most succinct statement of the things for which the American people were prepared to fight.

TO THE CONGRESS OF THE UNITED STATES:

I address you, the Members of the Seventy-Seventh Congress, at a moment unprecedented in the history of the Union. I use the word "unprecedented," because at no previous time has American security been as seriously threatened from without as it is today. . . .

It is true that prior to 1914 the United States often had been disturbed by events in other Continents. We had even engaged in two wars with European nations and in a number of undeclared wars in the West Indies, in the Mediterranean and in the Pacific for the maintenance of American rights and for the principles of peaceful commerce. In no case, however, had a serious threat been raised against our national safety or our independence.

What I seek to convey is the historic truth that the United States as a nation has at all times maintained opposition to any attempt to lock us in behind an ancient Chinese wall while the procession of civilization went past. Today, thinking of our children and their children, we oppose enforced isolation for ourselves or for any part of the Americas.

Even when the World War broke out in 1914, it seemed to contain only small threat of danger to our own American future. But, as time went on, the American people began to visualize what the downfall of democratic nations might mean to our own democracy.

We need not over-emphasize imperfections in the Peace of Versailles. We need not harp on failure of the democracies to deal with problems of world deconstruction. We should remember that the Peace of 1919 was far less unjust than the kind of "pacification" which began even before Munich, and which is being carried on under the new order of tyranny that seeks to spread over every continent today. The American people have unalterably set their faces against that tyranny.

Every realist knows that the democratic way of life is at this moment being directly assailed in every part of the world—assailed either by arms, or by secret spreading of poisonous propaganda by those who seek to destroy unity and promote discord in nations still at peace. During sixteen months this assault has blotted out the whole pattern of democratic life in an appalling number of independent nations, great and small. The assailants are still on the march, threatening other nations, great and small.

Therefore, as your President, performing my constitutional duty to "give to the Congress information of the state of the Union,"

I find it necessary to report that the future and the safety of our country and of our democracy are overwhelmingly involved in events far beyond our borders.

Armed defense of democratic existence is now being gallantly waged in four continents. If that defense fails, all the population and all the resources of Europe, Asia, Africa and Australasia will be dominated by the conquerors. The total of those populations and their resources greatly exceeds the sum total of the population and resources of the whole of the Western Hemisphere—many times over.

In times like these it is immature—and incidentally untrue—for anybody to brag that an unprepared America, single-handed, and with one hand tied behind its back, can hold off the whole world.

No realistic American can expect from a dictator's peace international generosity, or return of true independence, or world disarmament, or freedom of expression, or freedom of religion—or even good business. Such a peace would bring no security for us or for our neighbors. "Those, who would give up essential liberty to purchase a little temporary safety, deserve neither liberty nor safety." As a nation we may take pride in the fact that we are soft-hearted; but we cannot afford to be soft-hearted. We must always be wary of those who with sounding brass and a tinkling cymbal preach the "ism" of appeasement. We must especially beware of that small group of selfish men who would clip the wings of the American eagle in order to feather their own nests.

I have recently pointed out how quickly the tempo of modern warfare could bring into our very midst the physical attack which we must expect if the dictator nations win this war.

There is much loose talk of our immunity from immediate and direct invasion from across the seas. Obviously, as long as the British Navy retains its power, no such danger exists. Even if there were no British Navy, it is not probable that any enemy would be stupid enough to attack us by landing troops in the United States from across thousands of miles of ocean, until it had acquired strategic bases from which to operate. But we learn much from the lessons of the past years in Europe—particularly the lesson of Norway, whose essential seaports were captured by treachery and surprise built up over a series of years. The first phase of the invasion of this Hemisphere would not be the landing of regular troops. The necessary strategic points would be occupied by secret agents and their dupes—and great numbers of them are already here, and in Latin America.

As long as the aggressor nations maintain the offensive, they—not we—will choose the time and the place and the method of their attack. That is why the future of all American Republics is today in serious danger. That is why this Annual Message to the Congress is unique in our history. That is why every member of the Executive branch of the government and every member of the Congress face great responsibility—and great accountability.

The need of the moment is that our actions and our policy should be devoted primarily—almost exclusively—to meeting this foreign peril. For all our domestic problems are now a part of the great emergency. Just as our national policy in internal affairs has been based upon a decent respect for the rights and dignity of all our fellowmen within our gates, so our national policy in foreign affairs has been based on a decent respect for the rights and dignity of all nations, large and small. And the justice of morality must and will win in the end.

Our national policy is this.

First, by an impressive expression of the public will and without regard to partisanship, we are committed to all-inclusive national defense.

Second, by an impressive expression of the public will and without regard to partisanship, we are committed to full support of all those resolute peoples, everywhere, who are resisting aggression and are thereby keeping war away from our Hemisphere. By this support, we express our determination that the democratic cause shall prevail; and we strengthen the defense and security of our own nation.

Third, by an impressive expression of the public will and without regard to partisanship we are committed to the proposition that principles of morality and considerations for our own security will never permit us to acquiesce in a peace dictated by aggressors and sponsored by appeasers. We know that enduring peace cannot be bought at the cost of other people's freedom.

In the recent national election there was no substantial difference between the two great parties in respect to that national policy. No issue was fought out on this line before the American electorate. Today, it is abundantly evident that American citizens everywhere are demanding and supporting speedy and complete action in recognition of obvious danger. Therefore, the immediate need is a swift and driving increase in our armament production. . . .

Our most useful and immediate role is to act as an arsenal for them as well as for ourselves. They do not need man power. They do need billions of dollars worth of the weapons of defense. . . .

Let us say to the democracies: "We Americans are vitally concerned in your defense of freedom. We are putting forth our energies, our resources and our organizing powers to give you the strength to regain and maintain a free world. We shall send you, in ever-increasing numbers, ships, planes, tanks, guns. This is our purpose and our pledge." In fulfillment of this purpose we will not be intimidated by the threats of dictators that they will regard as a breach of international law and as an act of war our aid to the democracies which dare to resist their aggression. Such aid is not an act of war, even if a dictator should unilaterally proclaim it so to be. When the dictators are ready to make war upon us, they will not wait for an act of war on our part. They did not wait for Norway or Belgium or the Netherlands to commit an act of war. Their only interest is in a new one-way international law, which lacks mutuality in its observance, and, therefore, becomes an instrument of oppression.

The happiness of future generations of Americans may well depend upon how effective and how immediate we can make our aid felt. No one can tell the exact character of the emergency situations that we may be called upon to meet. The Nation's hands must not be tied when the Nation's life is in danger. We must all prepare to make the sacrifices that the emergency—as serious as war itself—demands. Whatever stands in the way of speed and efficiency in defense preparations must give way to the national need.

A free nation has the right to expect full cooperation from all groups. A free nation has the right to look to the leaders of business, of labor, and of agriculture to take the lead in stimulating effort, not among other groups but within their own groups. The best way of dealing with the few slackers or trouble makers in our midst is, first, to shame them by patriotic example, and, if that fails, to use the sovereignty of government to save government.

As men do not live by bread alone, they do not fight by armaments alone. Those who man our defenses, and those behind them who build our defenses, must have the stamina and courage which come from an unshakable belief in the manner of life which they are defending. The mighty action which we are calling for cannot be based on a disregard of all things worth fighting for.

The Nation takes great satisfaction and much strength from the things which have been done to make its people conscious of their individual stake in the preservation of democratic life in America. Those things have toughened the fibre of our people, have renewed their faith and strengthened their devotion to the institutions we make ready to protect. Certainly this is no time to stop thinking about the social and economic problems which are the root cause of the social revolution which is today a supreme factor in the world.

There is nothing mysterious about the foundations of a healthy and strong democracy. The basic things expected by our people of their political and economic systems are simple. They are: equality of opportunity for youth and for others; jobs for those who can work; security for those who need it; the ending of special privilege for the few; the preservation of civil liberties for all; the enjoyment of the fruits of scientific progress in a wider and constantly rising standard of living.

These are the simple and basic things that must never be lost sight of in the turmoil and unbelievable complexity of our modern world. The inner and abiding strength of our economic and political systems is dependent upon the degree to which they fulfill these expectations.

Many subjects connected with our social economy call for immediate improvement. As examples: We should bring more citizens under the coverage of old age pensions and unemployment insurance. We should widen the opportunities for adequate medical care. We should plan a better system by which persons deserving or needing gainful employment may obtain it.

I have called for personal sacrifice. I am assured of the willingness of almost all Americans to respond to that call. . . .

In the future days, which we seek to make secure, we look forward to a world founded upon four essential human freedoms.

The first is freedom of speech and expression—everywhere in the world.

The second is freedom of every person to worship God in his own way—everywhere in the world.

The third is freedom from want—which, translated into world terms, means economic understandings which will secure to every nation a healthy peace time life for its inhabitants—everywhere in the world.

The fourth is freedom from fear—which, translated into world terms, means a worldwide reduction of armaments to such a point and in such a thorough fashion that no nation will be in a position to commit an act of physical aggression against any neighbor—anywhere in the world.

That is no vision of a distant millenium. It is a definite basis for a kind of world attainable in our own time and generation. That kind of world is the very antithesis of the so-called new order of tyranny which the dictators seek to create with the crash of a bomb.

To that new order we oppose the greater conception—the moral order. A good society is able to face schemes of world domination and foreign revolutions alike without fear.

Since the beginning of our American history we have been engaged in change—in a perpetual peaceful revolution—a revolution which goes on steadily, quietly adjusting itself to changing conditions—without the concentration camp or the quick-lime in the ditch. The world order which we seek is the cooperation of free countries, working together in a friendly, civilized society.

This nation has placed its destiny in the hands and heads and hearts of its millions of free men and women; and its faith in freedom under the guidance of God. Freedom means the supremacy of human rights everywhere. Our support goes to those who struggle to gain those rights or keep them. Our strength is in our unity of purpose.

To that high concept there can be no end save victory.

538. THE LEND LEASE ACT
March 11, 1941
(*U. S. Statutes at Large,* Vol. LV, p. 31)

Early in January the President submitted to Congress a program designed to enable the United States to aid the Allies notwithstanding the limitations of the Neutrality legislation. The proposal precipitated long and bitter debate but was eventually accepted by both Houses by substantial majorities.

Be it enacted That this Act may be cited as "An Act to Promote the Defense of the United States."

Section 3.

(a) Notwithstanding the provisions of any other law, the President may, from time to time, when he deems it in the interest of national defense, authorize the Secretary of War, the Secretary of the Navy, or the head of any other department or agency of the Government—

(1) To manufacture in arsenals, factories, and shipyards under their jurisdiction, or otherwise procure, to the extent to which funds are made available therefor, or contracts are authorized from time to time by

the Congress, or both, any defense article for the government of any country whose defense the President deems vital to the defense of the United States.

(2) To sell, transfer title to, exchange, lease, lend, or otherwise dispose of, to any such government any defense article, but no defense article not manufactured or procured under paragraph (1) shall in any way be disposed of under this paragraph, except after consultation with the Chief of Staff of the Army or the Chief of Naval Operations of the Navy, or both. The value of defense articles disposed of in any way under authority of this paragraph, and procured from funds heretofore appropriated, shall not exceed $1,300,000,000. The value of such defense articles shall be determined by the head of the department or agency concerned or such other department, agency or officer as shall be designated in the manner provided in the rules and regulations issued hereunder. Defense articles procured from funds hereafter appropriated to any department or agency of the Government, other than from funds authorized to be appropriated under this Act, shall not be disposed of in any way under authority of this paragraph except to the extent hereafter authorized by the Congress in the Acts appropriating such funds or otherwise.

(3) To test, inspect, prove, repair, outfit, recondition, or otherwise to place in good working order, to the extent to which funds are made available therefor, or contracts are authorized from time to time by the Congress, or both, any defense article for any such government, or to procure any or all such services by private contract.

(4) To communicate to any such government any defense information, pertaining to any defense article furnished to such government under paragraph (2) of this subsection.

(5) To release for export any defense article disposed of in any way under this subsection to any such government,

(b) The terms and conditions upon which any such foreign government receives any aid authorized under subsection (a) shall be those which the President deems satisfactory, and the benefit to the United States may be payment or repayment in kind or property, or any other direct or indirect benefit which the President deems satisfactory.

(c) After June 30, 1943, or after the passage of a concurrent resolution by the two Houses before June 30, 1943, which declares that the powers conferred by or pursuant to subsection (a) are no longer necessary to promote the defense of the United States, neither the President nor the head of any department or agency shall exercise any of the powers conferred by or pursuant to subsection (a); except that until July 1, 1946, any of such powers may be exercised to the extent necessary to carry out a contract or agreement with such a foreign government made before July 1, 1943, or before the passage of such concurrent resolution, whichever is the earlier.

(d) Nothing in this Act shall be construed to authorize or to permit the authorization of convoying vessels by naval vessels of the United States.

(e) Nothing in this Act shall be construed to authorize or to permit the authorization of the entry of any American vessel into a combat area in violation of section 3 of the Neutrality Act of 1939.

Section 8

The Secretaries of War and of the Navy are hereby authorized to purchase or otherwise acquire arms, ammunition, and implements of war produced within the jurisdiction of any country to which section 3 is applicable, whenever the President deems such purchase or acquisition to be necessary in the interests of the defense of the United States.

Section 9

The President may, from time to time, promulgate such rules and regulations as may be necessary and proper to carry out any of the provisions of this Act; and he may exercise any power or authority conferred on him by this Act through such department, agency, or officer as he shall direct,

539. THE ATLANTIC CHARTER
August 14, 1941
(The Public Papers of F. D. Roosevelt, Vol. 10, p. 314)

In a dramatic meeting off Newfoundland, President Roosevelt and Winston Churchill formulated this statement of common war aims.

The President of the United States of America and the Prime Minister, Mr. Churchill, representing His Majesty's Government in the United Kingdom, being met together, deem it right to make known certain common principles in the national policies of their respective countries on which they base their hopes for a better future for the world.

First, their countries seek no aggrandizement, territorial or other;

Second, they desire to see no territorial changes that do not accord with the freely expressed wishes of the peoples concerned;

Third, they respect the right of all peoples to choose the form of government under which they will live; and they wish to see sovereign rights and self government restored to those who have been forcibly deprived of them;

Fourth, they will endeavor, with due respect for their existing obligations, to further the enjoyment by all States, great or small, victor or vanquished, of access, on equal terms, to the trade and to the raw materials of the world which are needed for their economic prosperity;

Fifth, they desire to bring about the fullest collaboration between all nations in the economic field with the object of securing, for all, improved labor standards, economic advancement and social security;

Sixth, after the final destruction of the Nazi tyranny, they hope to see established a peace which will afford to all nations the means of dwelling in safety within their own boundaries, and which will afford assurance that all the men in all the lands may live out their lives in freedom from fear and want;

Seventh, such a peace should enable all men to traverse the high seas and oceans without hindrance;

Eighth, they believe that all of the nations of the world, for realistic as well as spiritual reasons must come to the abandonment of the use of force. Since no future peace can be maintained if land, sea or air armaments continue to be employed by nations which threaten, or may threaten, aggression outside of their frontiers, they believe, pending the establishment of a wider and permanent system of general security, that the disarmament of such nations is essential. They will likewise aid and encourage all other practicable measures which will lighten for peace-loving peoples the crushing burden of armaments.

FRANKLIN D. ROOSEVELT
WINSTON S. CHURCHILL

540. PRESIDENT ROOSEVELT'S MESSAGE ASKING FOR WAR AGAINST JAPAN
December 8, 1941
(The Public Papers of F. D. Roosevelt, Vol. 10, p. 514)

The day after the attack on Pearl Harbor, President Roosevelt appeared before Congress and asked for a declaration of war against Japan. Congress responded that same afternoon, without a dissenting vote. H. Feis, *The Road to Pearl Harbor.*

Yesterday, December 7, 1941—a date which will live in infamy—the United States

of America was suddenly and deliberately attacked by naval and air forces of the Empire of Japan.

The United States was at peace with that nation and, at the solicitation of Japan, was still in conversation with its Government and its Emperor looking toward the maintenance of peace in the Pacific. Indeed, one hour after Japanese air squadrons had commenced bombing in Oahu, the Japanese Ambassador to the United States and his colleague delivered to the Secretary of State a formal reply to a recent American message. While this reply stated that it seemed useless to continue the existing diplomatic negotiations, it contained no threat or hint of war or armed attack.

It will be recorded that the distance of Hawaii from Japan makes it obvious that the attack was deliberately planned many days or even weeks ago. During the intervening time the Japanese Government has deliberately sought to deceive the United States by false statements and expressions of hope for continued peace.

The attack yesterday on the Hawaiian Islands has caused severe damage to American naval and military forces. Very many American lives have been lost. In addition American ships have been reported torpedoed on the high seas between San Francisco and Honolulu.

Yesterday the Japanese Government also launched an attack against Malaya. Last night Japanese forces attacked Hong Kong. Last night Japanese forces attacked Guam. Last night Japanese forces attacked the Philippine Islands. Last night the Japanese attacked Wake Island. This morning the Japanese attacked Midway Island.

Japan has, therefore, undertaken a surprise offensive extending throughout the Pacific area. The facts of yesterday speak for themselves. The people of the United States have already formed their opinions and well understand the implications to the very life and safety of our nation.

As Commander-in-Chief of the Army and Navy, I have directed that all measures be taken for our defense.

Always will we remember the character of the onslaught against us.

No matter how long it may take us to overcome this premeditated invasion, the American people in their righteous might will win through to absolute victory.

I believe I interpret the will of the Congress and of the people when I assert that we will not only defend ourselves to the uttermost but will make very certain that this form of treachery shall never endanger us again.

Hostilities exist. There is no blinking at the fact that our people, our territory and our interests are in grave danger.

With confidence in our armed forces—with the unbonded determination of our people—we will gain the inevitable triumph —so help us God.

I ask that the Congress declare that since the unprovoked and dastardly attack by Japan on Sunday, December seventh, a state of war has existed between the United States and the Japanese Empire.

541. DECLARATION OF WAR ON GERMANY
December 11, 1941

(*The Public Papers of F. D. Roosevelt*, Vol. 10, p. 532)

See H. S. Quigley, *Far Eastern War;* Davis and Lindley, *How War Came;* T. A. Bisson et al, "The United States at War," *For. Policy Repts.,* Vol. XVII, 246 ff.; W. P. Maddox, ed., "America and Japan," *An. Am. Ac. Pol. Soc. Sci.* Vol. 238; W. Langer and S. Gleason, *The Undeclared War;* W. Lord, *Day of Infamy.*

To the Congress of the United States:

On the morning of Dec. 11 the Government of Germany, pursuing its course of world conquest. declared war against the United States.

The long-known and the long-expected has thus taken place. The forces endeavoring to enslave the entire world now are moving toward this hemisphere.

Never before has there been a greater challenge to life, liberty and civilization.

Delay invites great danger. Rapid and united effort by all of the peoples of the world who are determined to remain free will insure a world victory of the forces of justice and of righteousness over the forces of savagery and of barbarism.

Italy also has declared war against the United States.

I therefore request the Congress to recognize a state of war between the United States and Germany, and between the United States and Italy.

FRANKLIN D. ROOSEVELT.

THE WAR RESOLUTION

Declaring that a state of war exists between the Government of Germany and the government and the people of the United States and making provision to prosecute the same.

Whereas the Government of Germany has formally declared war against the government and the people of the United States of America:

Therefore, be it

Resolved by the Senate and House of Representatives of the United States of America in Congress assembled, that the state of war between the United States and the Government of Germany which has thus been thrust upon the United States is hereby formally declared; and the President is hereby authorized and directed to employ the entire naval and military forces of the United States and the resources of the government to carry on war against the Government of Germany; and, to bring the conflict to a successful termination, all of the resources of the country are hereby pledged by the Congress of the United States.

542. UNITED STATES v. DARBY LUMBER CO.
312 U. S. 100
1941

The F. W. Darby Lumber Company and Fred W. Darby were indicted for violating Section 15 of the Fair Labor Standards Act. The principal questions in the case were whether Congress has the power to prohibit shipment in interstate Commerce of products made by employees whose wages were lower or whose hours were longer than Congress prescribed, and, secondly, whether Congress may prohibit employment of workers producing goods for interstate commerce, if their working conditions do not meet a standard determined by Congress. The case is particularly important in that the Court in a unanimous decision specifically overruled *Hammer v. Dagenhart,* which had declared government regulation of transportation of products of child labor unconstitutional. See Doc. No. 413.

Appeal from the District Court of the United States for the Southern District of Georgia.

STONE, J. The two principal questions raised by the record in this case are, first, whether Congress has constitutional power to prohibit the shipment in interstate commerce of lumber manufactured by employees whose wages are less than a prescribed minimum or whose weekly hours of labor at that wage are

greater than a prescribed maximum, and, second, whether it has power to prohibit the employment of workmen in the production of goods "for interstate commerce" at other than prescribed wages and hours. . . .

The Fair Labor Standards Act set up a comprehensive legislative scheme for preventing the shipment in interstate commerce of certain products and commodities produced in the United States under labor conditions as respects wages and hours which fail to conform to standards set up by the Act. Its purpose is to exclude from interstate commerce goods produced for the commerce and to prevent their production for interstate commerce, under conditions detrimental to the maintenance of the minimum standards of living necessary for health and general well-being; and to prevent the use of interstate commerce as the means of competition in the distribution of goods so produced, and as the means of spreading and perpetuating such substandard labor conditions among the workers of the several states. . . .

The prohibition of shipment of the proscribed goods in interstate commerce. Section 15 (a) (1) prohibits, and the indictment charges, the shipment in interstate commerce, of goods produced for interstate commerce by employees whose wages and hours of employment do not conform to the requirements of the Act. Since this section is not violated unless the commodity shipped has been produced under labor conditions prohibited by § 6 and § 7, the only question arising under the commerce clause with respect to such shipments is whether Congress has the constitutional power to prohibit them.

While manufacture is not of itself interstate commerce the shipment of manufactured goods interstate is such commerce and the prohibition of such shipment by Congress is undubitably a regulation of the commerce. The power to regulate commerce is the power "to prescribe the rule by which commerce is to be governed." Gibbons v. Ogden, 9 Wheat. 1, 196. It extends not only to those regulations which aid, foster and protect the commerce, but embraces those which prohibit it. It is conceded that the power of Congress to prohibit transportation in interstate commerce includes noxious articles, and articles such as intoxicating liquor or convict made goods, traffic in which is forbidden or restricted by the laws of the state of destination.

But it is said that the present prohibition falls within the scope of none of these categories; that while the prohibition is nominally a regulation of the commerce its motive or purpose is regulation of wages and hours of persons engaged in manufacture, the control of which has been reserved to the states and upon which Georgia and some of the states of destination have placed no restrictions; that the effect of the present statute is not to exclude the prescribed articles from interstate commerce in aid of state regulation as in Kentucky Whip & Collar Co. v. Illinois Central R. Co., but instead, under the guise of a regulation of interstate commerce, it undertakes to regulate wages and hours within the state contrary to the policy of the state which has elected to leave them unregulated.

The power of Congress over interstate commerce "is complete in itself, may be exercised to its utmost extent, and acknowledges no limitations, other than are prescribed by the constitution." That power can neither be enlarged nor diminished by the exercise or non-exercise of state power. Congress, following its own conception of public policy concerning the restrictions which may appropriately be imposed on interstate commerce, is free to exclude from the commerce articles whose use in the states for which they are destined it may conceive to be injurious to the public health, morals or welfare, even though the state has not sought to regulate their use.

Such regulation is not a forbidden invasion of state power merely because either its motive or its consequence is to restrict the use of articles of commerce within the states of destination and is not prohibited unless by other Constitutional provisions. It is no objection to the assertion of the power to regulate interstate commerce that its exercise is attended by the same incidents which attend the exercise of the police power of the states.

The motive and purpose of the present regulation is plainly to make effective the Congressional conception of public policy that interstate commerce should not be made the instrument of competition in the distribution of goods produced under substandard labor conditions, which competition is injurious to the commerce and to the states from and to which the commerce flows. The motive and purpose of a regulation of interstate commerce are matters for the legislative judgment upon the exercise of which the Constitution places no restriction and over which the courts are given no control. "The judicial cannot prescribe to the legislative departments of the government limitations upon the exercise of its acknowledged power." Veazie Bank v. Fenno, 8 Wall, 533, 548. Whatever their motive and purpose, regulations of commerce which do not infringe some constitutional prohibition are within the plenary power conferred on Congress by the Commerce Clause. Subject only to that limitation, presently to be considered, we conclude that the prohibition of the shipment interstate of goods produced under the forbidden substandard labor conditions is within the constitutional authority of Congress.

In the more than a century which has elapsed since the decision of Gibbons v. Ogden, these principles of constitutional interpretation have been so long and repeatedly recognized by this Court as applicable to the Commerce Clause, that there would be little occasion for repeating them now were it not for the decision of this Court twenty-two years ago in Hammer v. Dagenhart, 247 U. S. 251. In that case it was held by a bare majority of the Court over the powerful and now classic dissent of Mr. Justice Holmes setting forth the fundamental issues involved, that Congress was without power to exclude the products of child labor from interstate commerce. The reasoning and conclusion of the Court's opinion there cannot be reconciled with the conclusion which we have reached, that the power of Congress under the Commerce Clause is plenary to exclude any article from interstate commerce subject only to the specific prohibitions of the Constitution.

Hammer v. Dagenhart has not been followed. The distinction on which the decision was rested that Congressional power to prohibit interstate commerce is limited to articles which in themselves have some harmful or deleterious property—a distinction which was novel when made and unsupported by any provision of the Constitution—has long since been abandoned. The thesis of the opinion that the motive of the prohibition or its effect to control in some measure the use or production within the states of the article thus excluded from the commerce can operate to deprive the regulation of its constitutional authority has long since ceased to have force. And finally we have declared "The authority of the Federal Government over interstate commerce does not differ in extent or character from that retained by the states over interstate commerce." United States v. Rock Royal Co-Operative, Inc., 307 U.S. 533, 569.

The conclusion is inescapable that Hammer v. Dagenhart, was a departure from the principles which have prevailed in the interpretation of the commerce clause both before and since the decision and that such vitality, as a precedent, as it then had has long since been exhausted. It should be and now is overruled.

Validity of the wage and hour requirements. Section 15(a)(2) and §§ 6 and 7 require employers to conform to the wage and hour provisions with respect to all employees engaged in the production of goods for interstate commerce. . . . The validity of the prohibition turns on the question whether the employment, under other than the prescribed labor standards, of employees engaged in the production of goods for interstate commerce is so related to the commerce and so affects it as to be within the reach of the power of Congress to regulate it. . . .

Without attempting to define the precise limits of the phrase, we think the acts alleged in the indictment are within the sweep of the statute. The obvious purpose of the Act was not only to prevent the interstate transportation of the proscribed product, but to stop the initial step toward transportation, production with the purpose of so transporting it. Congress was not unaware that most manufacturing businesses shipping their product in interstate commerce make it in their shops without reference to its ultimate destination and then after manufacture select some of it for shipment interstate and some intrastate according to the daily demands of their business, and that it would be practically impossible, without disrupting manufacturing businesses, to restrict the prohibited kind of production to the particular pieces of lumber, cloth, furniture or the like which later move in interstate rather than intrastate commerce. . . .

There remains the question whether such restriction on the production of goods for commerce is a permissible exercise of the commerce power. The power of Congress over interstate commerce is not confined to the regulation of commerce among the states. It extends to those activities intrastate which so affect interstate commerce or the exercise of the power of Congress over it as to make regulation of them appropriate means to the attainment of a legitimate end, the exercise of the granted power of Congress to regulate interstate commerce.

While this Court has many times found state regulation of interstate commerce, when uniformity of its regulation is of national concern, to be incompatible with the Commerce clause even though Congress has not legislated on the subject, the Court has never implied such restraint on state control over matters intrastate not deemed to be regulations of interstate commerce or its instrumentalities even though they affect the commerce. In the absence of Congressional legislation on the subject state laws which are not regulations of the commerce itself or its instrumentalities are not forbidden even though they affect interstate commerce.

But it does not follow that Congress may not by appropriate legislation regulate intrastate activities where they have a substantial effect on interstate commerce. A recent example is the National Labor Relations Act, for the regulation of employer and employee relations in industries in which strikes, induced by unfair labor practices named in the Act, tend to disturb or obstruct interstate commerce. But long before the adoption of the National Labor Relations Act, this Court had many times held that the power of Congress to regulate interstate commerce extends to the regulation through legislative action of activities intrastate which have a substantial effect on the commerce or the exercise of the Congressional power over it. . . .

Sometimes Congress itself has said that a particular activity affects the commerce as it did in the present act, the Safety Appliance Act, and the Railway Labor Act. In passing on the validity of legislation of the class last mentioned the only function of courts is to determine whether the particular activity regulated or prohibited is within the reach of the federal power.

Congress, having by the present Act adopted the policy of excluding from interstate commerce all goods produced for the commerce which do not conform to the specified labor standards, it may choose the means reasonably adapted to the attainment of the permitted end, even though they involve control of intrastate activities. Such legislation has often been sustained with respect to powers, other than the commerce power granted to the national government, when the means chosen, although not themselves within the granted power, were nevertheless deemed appropriate aids to the accomplishment of some purpose within an admitted power of the national government. . . .

We think also that § 15(a) (2), now under consideration, is sustainable independently of § 15(a) (1), which prohibits shipment or transportation of the proscribed goods. As we have said the evils aimed at by the Act are the spread of substandard labor conditions through the use of the facilities of interstate commerce for competition by the goods so produced with those produced under the prescribed or better labor conditions; and the consequent dislocation of the commerce itself caused by the impairment or destruction of local businesses by competition made effective through interstate commerce. The Act is thus directed at the suppression of a method or kind of competition in interstate commerce which it has in effect condemned as "unfair," as the Clayton Act, 38 Stat. 730, has condemned other "unfair methods of competition" made effective through interstate commerce.

The means adopted by § 15(a) (2) for the protection of interstate commerce by the suppression of the production of the condemned goods for interstate commerce is so related to the commerce and so affects it as to be within the reach of the commerce power. Congress, to attain its objective in the suppression of nationwide competition in interstate commerce by goods produced under substandard labor conditions, has made no distinction as to the volume or amount of shipments in the commerce or of production for commerce by any particular shipper or producer. It recognized that in present day industry, competition by a small part may affect the whole and that the total effect of the competition of many small producers may be great. The legislation aimed at a whole embraces all its parts.

543. MITCHELL v. UNITED STATES et. al.
313 U. S. 80
1941

Appeal from the District Court of the U. S. for the Northern District of Illinois. Essential facts of the case are given in the opinion. See M. R. Konvitz, *Constitution and Civil Rights;* C. S. Johnson, *Patterns of Negro Segregation.*

HUGHES, J. Appellant, a Negro resident of Chicago, and a member of the House of Representatives of the United States, left Chicago for Hot Springs on the evening of April 20, 1937, over the lines of the Illinois Central Railroad Company to Memphis, Tennessee, and the Rock Island beyond, traveling on a round-trip ticket he had purchased at three cents per mile. He had requested a bedroom on the Chicago-Hot Springs Pullman sleeping car but none being available he was provided with a compartment as far as Memphis in the sleeper destined to New Orleans. Just before the train reached Memphis, on the morning after leaving Chicago, he had a Pullman porter transfer him to the Chicago-Hot Springs sleeper on the same train. Space was there available and the porter assigned him a particular seat in that car for which he was to pay the established fare of ninety cents. Shortly after leaving Memphis and crossing the Mississippi River into Arkansas, the train conductor took up the Memphis-Hot Springs portion of his ticket but refused to accept payment for the Pullman seat from Memphis and, in accordance with custom, compelled him over his protest and finally under threat of arrest to move into the car provided for colored passengers. This was in purported compliance with an Arkansas statute, requiring segregation of colored from white persons by the use of cars or partitioned sections providing "equal but separate and sufficient accommodations" for both races. Later the conductor returned the portion of the ticket he had taken up and advised appellant that he could get a refund on the basis of the coach fare of two cents

per mile from Memphis. That refund was not claimed from defendants and was not sought before the Commission, but it was found that the carriers stood ready to make it upon application. . . .

The Commission further found that the Pullman car contained ten sections of berths and two compartment drawing rooms; that the use of one of the drawing rooms would have amounted to segregation under the state law and ordinarily such combinations are available to colored passengers upon demand, the ninety cent fare being applicable. Occasionally they are used by colored passengers but in this instance both drawing rooms were already occupied by white passengers. The Pullman car was of modern design and had all the usual facilities and conveniences found in standard sleeping cars. It was air-conditioned, had hot and cold running water and separate flushable toilets for men and women. It was in excellent condition throughout. First-class white passengers had, in addition to the Pullman sleeper, the exclusive use of the train's only dining-car and only observation-parlor car, the latter having somewhat the same accommodations for day use as the Pullman car.

The coach for colored passengers, though of standard size and steel construction, was "an old combination affair," not air-conditioned, divided by partitions into three main parts, one for colored smokers, one for white smokers and one in the center for colored men and women, known as the women's section, in which appellant sat. There was a toilet in each section but only the one in the women's section was equipped for flushing and it was for the exclusive use of colored women. The car was without wash basins, soap, towels or running water, except in the women's section. The Commission stated that, according to appellant, the car was "filthy and foul smelling," but that the testimony of defendants' witnesses was to the contrary. . . .

The Commission, though treating the enforcement of the state law as a matter for state authorities, thought that in deciding the case on the facts presented it must recognize that the state law required the defendants to segregate colored passengers; that in these circumstances the present colored-passenger coach and the Pullman drawing rooms met the requirements of the Act; and that as there was comparatively little colored traffic and no indication that there was likely to be such demand for dining-car and observation-parlor car accommodations by colored passengers as to warrant the running of any extra cars or the construction of partitions, the discrimination and prejudice was "plainly not unjust or undue." The Commission observed that it was only differences in treatment of the latter character that were "unlawful and within the power of this Commission to condemn, remove, and prevent."

From the dismissal of the complaint, five Commissioners dissented.

The United States is a party to this suit to set aside the Commissioner's order. . . . The Government concludes that the Commission erroneously supposed that the Arkansas Separate Coach Law applied to an interstate passenger and erroneously determined that the small number of colored passengers asking for first-class accommodations justified an occasional discrimination against them because of their race. . . .

The undisputed facts showed conclusively that, having paid a first-class fare for the entire journey from Chicago to Hot Springs, and having offered to pay the proper charge for a seat which was available in the Pullman car for the trip from Memphis to Hot Springs, he was compelled, in accordance with custom, to leave that car and to ride in a second-class car and was thus denied the standard conveniences and privileges afforded to first-class passengers. This was manifestly a discrimination against him in the course of his interstate journey and admittedly that discrimination was based solely upon the fact that he was a Negro. The question whether this was a discrimination forbidden by the Interstate Commerce Act is not a question of segregation but one of equality of treatment. The denial to appellant of equality of accommodations because

of his race would be an invasion of a fundamental individual right which is guaranteed against state action by the Fourteenth Amendment and in view of the nature of the right and of our constitutional policy it cannot be maintained that the discrimination as it was alleged was not essentially unjust. In that aspect it could not be deemed to lie outside the purview of the sweeping prohibitions of the Interstate Commerce Act.

We have repeatedly said that it is apparent from the legislative history of the Act that not only was the evil of discrimination the principal thing aimed at, but that there is no basis for the contention that Congress intended to exempt any discriminatory action or practice of interstate carriers affecting interstate commerce which it had authority to reach. . . .

We find no sound reason for the failure to apply this principle by holding the discrimination from which the appellant suffered to be unlawful and by forbidding it in the future. . . .

We take it that the chief reason for the Commission's action was the "comparatively little colored traffic." But the comparative volume of traffic cannot justify the denial of a fundamental right of equality of treatment, a right specifically safeguarded by the provisions of the Interstate Commerce Act. We thought a similar argument with respect to volume of traffic to be untenable in the application of the Fourteenth Amendment. We said that it made the constitutional right depend upon the number of persons who may be discriminated against, whereas the essence of that right is that it is a personal one. While the supply of particular facilities may be conditioned upon there being a reasonable demand therefor, if facilities are provided, substantial equality of treatment of persons traveling under like conditions cannot be refused. It is the individual we said, who is entitled to the equal protection of the laws, —not merely a group of individuals, or a body of persons according to their numbers. And the Interstate Commerce Act expressly extends its prohibitions to the subjecting of "any particular person" to unreasonable discriminations. . . .

The decree of the District Court is reversed and the cause is remanded with directions to set aside the order of the Commission and to remand the case to the Commission for further proceedings in conformity with this opinion.

544. UNITED STATES v. CLASSIC
313 U. S. 299
1941

One of the features of the American political system is that primary elections, while actually an important part of the constitutional structure, are formally under the control of private organizations. In this case the previous position of the Court that party primaries were private affairs was reversed. See Merriam and Overacker, *Primary Elections;* Stoney, "Suffrage in the South," *Survey Graphic,* Vol. 29, p. 163; see also Doc. No. 464.

Appeal from the District Court of the United States for the Eastern District of Louisiana.

STONE, J. Two counts of an indictment found in a federal district court charged that appellees, Commissioners of Elections, conducting a primary election under Louisiana law, to nominate a candidate of the Democratic Party for representative in Congress, willfully altered and falsely counted and certified the ballots of voters cast in the primary election. The questions for decision are whether the right of qualified voters to vote in the Louisiana primary and to have their ballots counted is a right "secured . . . by the Constitution" within the meaning of §§ 19 and 20 of the Criminal Code, and whether the acts of appellees charged in the indictment violate those sections.

The charge based on these allegations, was that the appellees conspired with each other and with others unknown, to injure and oppress citizens in the free exercise and enjoyment of rights and privileges secured to them by the Constitution and Laws of the United States, namely, (1) the right of qualified voters who cast their ballots in the primary election to have their ballots counted as cast for the candidate of their choice, and (2) the right of the candidates to run for the office of Congressman and to

have the votes in favor of their nomination counted as cast. The overt acts alleged were that the appellees altered eighty-three ballots cast for one candidate and fourteen cast for another, marking and counting them as votes for a third candidate, and that they falsely certified the number of votes cast for the respective candidates to the chairman of the Second Congressional District Committee. . . .

Section 19 of the Criminal Code condemns as a criminal offense any conspiracy to injure a citizen in the exercise "of any right or privilege secured to him by the Constitution or laws of the United States." Section 20 makes it a penal offense for anyone who, "acting under color of any law" "willfully subjects, or causes to be subjected, any inhabitant of any State . . . to the deprivation of any rights, privileges, or immunities secured or protected by the Constitution and laws of the United States." The Government argues that the right of a qualified voter in a Louisiana congressional primary election to have his vote counted as cast is a right secured by Article I, §§ 2 and 4 of the Constitution, and that a conspiracy to deprive the citizen of that right is a violation of § 19, and also that the willful action of appellees as state officials, in falsely counting the ballots at the primary election and in falsely certifying the count, deprived qualified voters of that right and of the equal protection of the laws guaranteed by the Fourteenth Amendment, all in violation of § 20 of the Criminal Code.

Article I, § 2 of the Constitution, commands that "The House of Representatives shall be composed of Members chosen every second Year by the People of the several States, and the Electors in each State shall have the qualifications requisite for Electors of the most numerous Branch of the State Legislature." By § 4 of the same article "The

Times, Places and Manner of holding Elections for Senators and Representatives, shall be prescribed in each State by the Legislature thereof; but the Congress may at any time by Law make or alter such Regulations, except as to the Places of chusing Senators." Such right as is secured by the Constitution to qualified voters to choose members of the House of Representatives is thus to be exercised in conformity to the requirements of state law subject to the restrictions prescribed by § 2 and to the authority conferred on Congress by § 4, to regulate the times, places and manner of holding elections for representatives.

We look then to the statutes of Louisiana here involved to ascertain the nature of the right which under the constitutional mandate they define and confer on the voter and the effect upon its exercise of the acts with which appellees are charged, all with the view to determining, first, whether the right or privilege is one secured by the Constitution of the United States, second, whether the effect under the state statute of appellee's alleged acts is such that they operate to injure or oppress citizens in the exercise of that right within the meaning of § 19 and to deprive inhabitants of the state of that right within the meaning of § 20, and finally, whether §§ 19 and 20 respectively are in other respects applicable to the alleged acts of appellees.

. . . The states are given, and in fact exercise a wide discretion in the formulation of a system for the choice by the people of representatives in Congress. In common with many other states Louisiana has exercised that discretion by setting up machinery for the effective choice of party candidates for representative in Congress by primary elections and by its laws it eliminates or seriously restricts the candidacy at the general election of all those who are defeated at the primary. All political parties, which are defined as those that have cast at least 5 per cent of the total vote at specified preceding elections, are required to nominate their candidates for representative by direct primary elections. . . . .

The right to vote for a representative in Congress at the general election is, as a matter of law, thus restricted to the successful party candidate at the primary, to those not candidates at the primary who file nomination papers, and those whose names may be lawfully written into the ballot by the electors. Even if, as appellees argue, contrary to the decision in Serpas v. Trebucq, supra, voters may lawfully write into their ballots, cast at the general election, the name of a candidate rejected at the primary and have their ballots counted, the practical operation of the primary law in otherwise excluding from the ballot on the general election the names of candidates rejected at the primary is such as to impose serious restrictions upon the choice of candidates by the voters save by voting at the primary election. In fact, as alleged in the indictment, the practical operation of the primary in Louisiana, is and has been since the primary election was established in 1900 to secure the election of the Democratic primary nominee for the Second Congressional District of Louisiana.

Interference with the right to vote in the Congressional primary in the Second Congressional District for the choice of Democratic candidate for Congress is thus as a matter of law and in fact an interference with the effective choice of the voters at the only stage of the election procedure when their choice is of significance, since it is at the only stage when such interference could have any practical effect on the ultimate result, the choice of the Congressman to represent the district. The primary in Louisiana is an integral part of the procedure for the popular choice of Congressman. The right of qualified voters to vote at the Congressional primary in Louisiana and to have their ballots counted is thus the right to participate in that choice.

We come then to the question whether that right is one secured by the Constitution. Section 2 of Article I commands that Congressmen shall be chosen by the people of the several states by electors, the qualifications of which it prescribes. . . .

Obviously included within the right to choose, secured by the Constitution, is the right of qualified voters within a state to cast their ballots and have them counted at Congressional elections. This Court has consistently held that this is a right secured by the Constitution. And since the constitutional command is without restriction or limitation, the right unlike those guaranteed by the Fourteenth and Fifteenth Amendments, is secured against the action of individuals as well as of states. Ex parte, Yarbrough, supra; Logan v. United States, supra.

But we are now concerned with the question whether the right to choose at a primary election, a candidate for election as representative, is embraced in the right to choose representatives secured by Article I, § 2. We may assume that the framers of the Constitution in adopting that section, did not have specifically in mind the selection and elimination of candidates for Congress by the direct primary any more than they contemplated the application of the commerce clause to interstate telephone, telegraph and wireless communication which are concededly within it. But in determining whether a provision of the Constitution applies to a new subject matter, it is of little significance that it is one with which the framers were not familiar. For in setting up an enduring framework of government they undertook to carry out for the indefinite future and in all the vicissitudes of the changing affairs of men, those fundamental purposes which the instrument itself discloses. Hence we read its words, not as we read legislative codes which are subject to continuous revision with the changing course of events, but as the revelation of the great purposes which were intended to be achieved by the Constitution as a continuing instrument of government. If we remember that "it is a Constitution we are expounding," we cannot rightly prefer, of the possible meanings of its words, that which will defeat rather than effectuate the Constitutional purpose.

That the free choice of the people of representatives in Congress, subject only to the restrictions to be found in §§ 2 and 4 of Article I and elsewhere in the Constitution, was one of the great purposes of our Constitutional scheme of government cannot be doubted. We cannot regard it as any the less the constitutional purpose or its words as any the less guarantying the integrity of that choice when a state, exercising its privilege in the absence of Congressional action, changes the mode of choice from a single step, a general election, to two, of which the first is the choice at a primary of those candidates from whom, as a second step, the representative in Congress is to be chosen at the election.

Nor can we say that that choice which the Constitution protects is restricted to the second step because § 4 of Article I, as a means of securing a free choice of representatives by the people, has authorized Congress to regulate the manner of elections, without making any mention of primary elections. For we think that the authority of Congress, given by § 4, includes the authority to regulate primary elections when, as in this case, they are a step in the exercise by the people of their choice of representatives in Congress. . . . In Newberry v. United States, supra, four Justices of this Court were of opinion that the term "elections" in § 4 of Article I did not embrace a primary election since that procedure was unknown to the framers. A fifth Justice who with them pronounced the judgment of the Court, was of opinion that a primary, held under a law enacted before the adoption of the Seventeenth Amendment, for the nomination of candidates for Senator, was not an election within the meaning of § 4 of Article I of the Constitution, presumably because the choice of the primary imposed no legal restrictions on the election of Senators by the state legislatures to which their election had been committed by Article I, § 3. The remaining four Justices were of the opinion that a primary election for the choice of candidates for Senator or Representative were elections subject to regulation by Congress within the meaning of § 4 of Article I. The question then has not been prejudged by and decision of this Court.

. . . From time immemorial an election to public office has been in point of substance no more and no less than the expression by qualified electors of their choice of candidates.

Long before the adoption of the Constitution the form and mode of that expression had changed from time to time. There is no historical warrant for supposing that the framers were under the illusion that the method of effecting the choice of the electors would never change or that if it did, the change was for that reason to be permitted to defeat the right of the people to choose representatives for Congress which the Constitution had guaranteed. The right to participate in the choice of representatives for Congress includes, as we have said, the right to cast a ballot and to have it counted at the general election whether for the successful candidate or not. Where the state law has made the primary an integral part of the procedure of choice, or where in fact the primary effectively controls the choice, the right of the elector to have his ballot counted at the primary, is likewise included in the right protected by Article I, § 2. And this right of participation is protected just as is the right to vote at the election, where the primary is by law made an integral part of the election machinery, whether the voter exercises his right in a party primary which invariably, sometimes or never determines the ultimate choice of the representatives. Here, even apart from the circumstance that the Louisiana primary is made by law an integral part of the procedure of choice, the right to choose a representative is in fact controlled by the primary because, as is alleged in the indictment, the choice of candidates at the Democratic primary determines the choice of the elected representative. Moreover, we cannot close our eyes to the fact already mentioned that the practical influence of the choice of candidates at the primary may be so great as to affect profoundly the choice at the general election even though there is no effective legal prohibition upon the rejection at the election of the choice made at the primary and may thus operate to deprive the voter of his constitutional right of choice. This was noted and extensively commented upon by the concurring Justices in Newberry v. United States.

Unless the constitutional protection of the integrity of "elections" extends to primary elections, Congress is left powerless to effect the constitutional purpose, and the popular choice of representatives is stripped of its constitutional protection save only as Congress, by taking over the control of state elections, may exclude from them the influence of the state primaries. Such an expedient would end that state autonomy with respect to elections which the Constitution contemplated that Congress should be free to leave undisturbed, subject only to such minimum regulation as it should find necessary to insure the freedom and integrity of the choice. Words, especially those of a constitution, are not to be read with such stultifying narrowness. The words of §§ 2 and 4 of Article I, read in the sense which is plainly permissible and in the light of the constitutional purpose, require us to hold that a primary election which involves a necessary step in the choice of candidates for election as representatives in Congress, and which in the circumstances of this case controls that choice, is an election within the meaning of the constitutional provision and is subject to congressional regulation as to the manner of holding it. . . .

There remains the question whether §§ 19 and 20 are an exercise of the congressional authority applicable to the acts with which appellees are charged in the indictment. Section 19 makes it a crime to conspire to "injure" or "oppress" any citizen "in the free exercise . . . of any right or privilege secured to him by the Constitution." In Ex parte Yarbrough, supra, and in United States v. Mosley, supra, as we have seen, it was held that the right to vote in a congressional election is a right secured by the Constitution, and that a conspiracy to prevent the citizen from voting or to prevent the official count of this ballot when cast, is a conspiracy to injure and oppress the citizen in the free exercise of a right secured by the Constitution within the meaning of § 19. Conspiracy to prevent the official count of a citizen's ballot, held in United States v. Mosley, supra, to be a violation of § 19 in the case of a congressional election, is equally a conspiracy to injure and oppress the citizen when the ballots are cast in a primary election pre-requisite to the choice of party candidates for a congressional election. In both cases the right infringed is one secured by the Constitution. The injury suffered by the citizen in the exercise of the right is an injury which the statute describes and to which it applies in the one case as in the other.

The right of the voters at the primary to have their votes counted is, as we have stated, a right or privilege secured by the Constitution, and to this § 20 also gives protection. The alleged acts of appellees were committed in the course of their performance of duties under the Louisiana statute requiring them to count the ballots, to record the result of the count, and to certify the result of the election. Misuse of power, possessed by virtue of state law and made possible only because the wrongdoer is clothed with the authority of state law, is action taken "under color of" state law. Here the acts of appellees infringed the constitutional right and deprived the voters of the benefit of it within the meaning of § 20.

Justices DOUGLAS, BLACK, and MURPHY dissenting.

545. EDWARDS v. CALIFORNIA
314 U. S. 160
1941

During the depression of the 1930's thousands of farmers and casual farm laborers were driven from their marginal farm lands in the Southwest prairie states by the economic crisis and the terrible dust storms. Many migrated to California, lured by the climate, the relatively greater prosperity, and the hope for seasonal work picking fruits and vegetables, a trek graphically described in John Steinbeck's *Grapes of Wrath*. As the influx of poverty-stricken "Okies" began to exceed the demand, resentment arose in California against the entrance of more public charges, and a law was passed making it a misdemeanor to bring or aid in bringing into the state any nonresident person known to be indigent. In January, 1940, Fred F. Edwards, a resident of the state of California, went to Texas, picked up his wife's brother, a Texan resident, whom Edwards knew to be indigent, and drove him to his home in Marysville, California. The Justice Court sentenced him to six months' imprisonment for violating the statute, and the Superior Court of Yuba County sustained the verdict. No appeal to a higher court in California was open, so Edwards appealed to the U.S. Supreme Court, contending that the California statute was unconstitutional. It is interesting that the Court nullified the California Act as interference in interstate commerce rather than a violation of the privileges and rights of American citizens. See E. W. Adams, "State Control of Interstate Migration of Indigents," 40 *Mich. L. Rev.* 711 ff.; S. P. Meyers, "Federal Privileges and Immunities: Application to Ingress and Egress," 29 *Cornell L. Q.*, 489 ff.; J. Steinbeck, *Grapes of Wrath;* C. McWilliams, *Factories in the Field*.

Appeal from the Superior Court of the State of California in and for the County of Yuba.

BYRNES, J. The facts of this case are simple and are not disputed. Appellant is a citizen of the United States and a resident of California. In December, 1939, he left his home in Marysville, California, for Spur, Texas, with the intention of bringing back to Marysville, his wife's brother, Frank Duncan, a citizen of the United States and a resident of Texas. When he arrived in Texas, appellant learned that Duncan had last been employed by the Works Progress Administration. Appellant thus became aware of the fact that Duncan was an indigent person and he continued to be aware of it throughout the period involved in this case. The two men agreed that appellant should transport Duncan from Texas to Marysville in appellant's automobile. Accordingly, they left Spur on January 1, 1940, entered California by way of Arizona on January 3, and reached Marysville on January 5. When he left Texas, Duncan had about $20. It had all been spent by the time he reached Marysville. He lived with appellant for about ten days until he obtained financial assistance from the Farm Security Administration. During the ten day interval, he had no employment.

In Justice Court a complaint was filed against appellant under Section 2615 of the Welfare and Institutions Code of California, which provides: "Every person, firm, or corporation, or officer or agent thereof that brings or assists in bringing into the State any indigent person who is not a resident of the State, knowing him to be an indigent person, is guilty of a misdemeanor." . . . Appellant was convicted and sentenced to six months' imprisonment in the county jail, and sentence was suspended. . . .

Article I, Section 8 of the Constitution delegates to the Congress the authority to regulate interstate commerce. And it is settled beyond question that the transportation of persons is "commerce," within the meaning of that provision. It is nevertheless true that the States are not wholly precluded from exercising their police power in matters of local concern even though they may thereby affect interstate commerce. The issue presented in this case, therefore, is whether the prohibition embodied in Section 2615 against the "bringing" or transportation of indigent persons into California is within the police power of that State. We think that it is not, and hold that it is an unconstitutional barrier to interstate commerce.

The gravity and perplexity of the social and economic dislocation which this statute reflects is a matter of common knowledge and concern. We are not unmindful of it. We appreciate that the spectacle of large segments of our population constantly on the move has given rise to urgent demands upon the ingenuity of government. Both the brief of the Attorney General of California and that of the Chairman of the Select Committee of the House of Representatives of the United States as *amicus curiae* have sharpened this appreciation. . . .

In the words of Mr. Justice Cardozo: "The Constitution was framed under the dominion of a political philosophy less parochial in range. It was framed upon the theory that the peoples of the several states must sink or swim together, and that in the long run prosperity and salvation are in union and not division." Baldwin v. Seelig, 294 U.S. 511.

It is difficult to conceive of a statute more squarely in conflict with this theory than the Section challenged here. Its express purpose and inevitable effect is to prohibit the transportation of indigent persons across the California border. The burden upon interstate commerce is intended and immediate; it is the plain and sole function of the statute. Moreover, the indigent non-residents who are the real victims of the statute are deprived of the opportunity to exert political pressure upon the California legislature in order to obtain a change in policy. We think this statute must fail under any known test of the validity of State interference with interstate commerce. . . .

546. JAPANESE RELOCATION ORDER
February 19, 1942
(*Federal Register,* Vol. VII, No. 38)

Alarmed by the supposed danger of Japanese invasion of the Pacific coast after Pearl Harbor and under the apprehension that all persons of Japanese ancestry were a potential threat to the United States, the War Department persuaded the President to authorize the evacuation of some 112,000 West Coast Japanese, two-thirds of them American citizens to "relocation" centers. A Congressional Resolution of March 21, 1942, made it a misdemeanor "to knowingly enter, remain in, or leave prescribed military areas" contrary to the orders of the commanding officer of the area. This Act which, in perspective seems to have been wholly unnecessary, has been called by E. S. Corwin "the most drastic invasion of the rights of citizens of the U.S. by their own government that has thus far occurred in the history of our nation." See Doc. No. 547 and M. Grodzins, *Americans Betrayed.*

EXECUTIVE ORDER
AUTHORIZING THE SECRETARY OF WAR TO PRESCRIBE MILITARY AREAS

Whereas the successful prosecution of the war requires every possible protection against espionage and against sabotage to national-defense materials, national-defense premises, and national-defense utilities. . . .

Now, therefore, by virtue of the authority

vested in me as President of the United States, and Commander in Chief of the Army and Navy, I hereby authorize and direct the Secretary of War, and the Military Commanders whom he may from time to time designate, whenever he or any designated Commander deems such action necessary or desirable, to prescribe military areas in such places and of such extent as he or the appropriate Military Commander may determine, from which any or all persons may be excluded, and with respect to which, the right of any person to enter, remain in, or leave shall be subject to whatever restrictions the Secretary of War or the appropriate Military Commander may impose in his discretion. The Secretary of War is hereby authorized to provide for residents of any such area who are excluded therefrom, such transportation, food, shelter, and other accommodations as may be necessary, in the judgment of the Secretary of War or the said Military Commander, and until other arrangements are made, to accomplish the purpose of this order. The designation of military areas in any region or locality shall supersede designations of prohibited and restricted areas by the Attorney General under the Proclamations of December 7 and 8, 1941,[1] and shall supersede the responsibility and authority of the Attorney General under the said Proclamations in respect of such prohibited and restricted areas.

I hereby further authorize and direct the Secretary of War and the said Military Commanders to take such other steps as he or the appropriate Military Commander may deem advisable to enforce compliance with the restrictions applicable to each Military area hereinabove authorized to be designated, including the use of Federal troops and other Federal Agencies, with authority to accept assistance of state and local agencies.

I hereby further authorize and direct all Executive Departments, independent establishments and other Federal Agencies, to assist the Secretary of War or the said Military Commanders in carrying out this Executive Order, including the furnishing of medical aid, hospitalization, food, clothing, transportation, use of land, shelter, and other supplies, equipment, utilities, facilities, and services. . . .

FRANKLIN D. ROOSEVELT

547. HIRABAYASHI v. UNITED STATES
320 U. S. 81
1943

This was the first of the cases testing the constitutionality of the Presidential evacuation order and the Act of Congress designed to effectuate that order. The facts of the case are set forth in the opinion. The second case, Koremarsu v. U.S., 323 U.S. 214, in general followed this precedent; there were two dissenting opinions, from Justices Murphy and Jackson. A third case, Ex parte Endo, 323 U.A. 283, granted a writ of habeas corpus to a loyal Japanese American, discharging her from custody. See M. Grodzins, *Americans Betrayed;* E. S. Corwin, *Total War and the Constitution;* N. Dembitz, "Racial Discrimination and the Military Judgment," *Col. L. Rev.,* March, 1945; C. Fairman, "Law of Martial Rule and the National Emergency," *Harv. L. Rev.,* June, 1942; E. V. Rostow, "The Japanese-American Cases—a Disaster," *Yale L. J.,* June, 1945.

On Certificate from the United States Circuit Court of Appeals for the Ninth Circuit.

STONE, J. Appellant, an American citizen of Japanese ancestry, was convicted in the district court of violating the Act of Congress of March 21, 1942, . . . which makes it a misdemeanor knowingly to disregard restrictions made applicable by a military commander to persons in a military area prescribed by him as such, all as authorized by an Executive Order of the President.

The questions for our decision are whether

[1] 6 F.R. 6420.

the particular restriction violated, namely that all persons of Japanese ancestry residing in such an area be within their place of residence daily between the hours of 8:00 P.M. and 6:00 A.M., was adopted by the military commander in the exercise of an unconstitutional delegation by Congress of its legislative power, and whether the restriction unconstitutionally discriminated between citizens of Japanese ancestry and those of other ancestries in violation of the Fifth Amendment. . . .

. . . Appellant asserted that the indictment should be dismissed because he was an American citizen who had never been a subject of and had never borne allegiance to the Empire of Japan, and also because the Act of March 21, 1942, was an unconstitutional delegation of Congressional power. . . .

The evidence showed that appellant had failed to report to the Civil Control Station on May 11 or May 12, 1942, as directed, to register for evacuation from the military area. He admitted failure to do so, and stated it had at all times been his belief that he would be waiving his rights as an American citizen by so doing. The evidence also showed that for like reason he was away from his place of residence after 8:00 P.M. on May 9, 1942. The jury returned a verdict of guilty on both counts and appellant was sentenced to imprisonment for a term of three months on each, the sentences to run concurrently. . . .

The curfew order which appellant violated, and to which the sanction prescribed by the Act of Congress has been deemed to attach, purported to be issued pursuant to an Executive Order of the President. In passing upon the authority of the military commander to make and execute the order, it becomes necessary to consider in some detail the official action which preceded or accompanied the order and from which it derives its purported authority. . . .

. . . On February 19, 1942, the President promulgated Executive Order No. 9066. The Order recited that "the successful prosecution of the war requires every possible protection against espionage and against sabotage to national-defense material, national-defense premises, and national-defense utilities. . . ."

. . . On March 2, 1942, General DeWitt promulgated Public Proclamation No. 1. The proclamation recited that the entire Pacific Coast "by its geographical location is particularly subject to attack, to attempted invasion by the armed forces of nations with which the United States is now at war, and in connection therewith, is subject to espionage and acts of sabotage, thereby requiring the adoption of military measures necessary to establish safeguards against such enemy operations" . . . .

On March 24, 1942, General DeWitt issued Public Proclamation No. 3. After referring to the previous designation of military areas by Public Proclamations No. 1 and 2, it recited that ". . . the present situation within these Military Areas and Zones requires as a matter of military necessity the establishment of certain regulations pertaining to all enemy aliens and all persons of Japanese ancestry within said Military Areas and Zones . . ." It accordingly declared and established that from and after March 27, 1942, "all alien Japanese, all alien Germans, all alien Italians, and all persons of Japanese ancestry residing or being within the geographical limits of Military Area No. 1 . . . shall be within their place of residence between the hours of 8:00 P.M. and 6:00 A.M., which period is hereinafter referred to as the hours of curfew." It also imposed certain other restrictions on persons of Japanese ancestry, and provided that any person violating the regulations would be subject to the criminal penalties provided by the Act of Congress of March 21, 1942. . . .

Appellant does not deny that he knowingly failed to obey the curfew order as charged in the second count of the indictment, or that the order was authorized by the terms of Executive Order No. 9066, or that the challenged Act of Congress purports to punish with criminal penalties disobedience of such an order. His contentions are only that Congress unconstitutionally delegated its legislative power to the military commander by authorizing him to impose the challenged regulation, and that, even if the regulation were in other respects lawfully authorized, the Fifth Amendment prohibits the discrimination made between citizens of Japanese descent and those of other ancestry.

It will be evident from the legislative history that the Act of March 21, 1942, contemplated and authorized the curfew order which we have before us. . . .

The conclusion is inescapable that Congress, by the Act of March 21, 1942, ratified and confirmed Executive Order No. 9066. . . .

. . . And so far as it lawfully could, Congress authorized and implemented such curfew orders as the commanding officer should promulgate pursuant to the Executive Order of the President. The question then is not one of Congressional power to delegate to the President the promulgation of the Executive Order, but whether, acting in cooperation, Congress and the Executive have constitutional authority to impose the curfew restriction here complained of. . . .

The war power of the national government is "the power to wage war successfully." See Charles Evans Hughes, War Powers Under the Constitution, 42 A. B.A.Rep. 232, 238. It extends to every matter and activity so related to war as substantially to affect its conduct and progress. The power is not restricted to the winning of victories in the field and the repulse of enemy forces. It embraces every phase of the national defense, including the protection of war materials and the members of the armed forces from injury and from the dangers which attend the rise, prosecution and progress of war. . . . Since the Constitution commits to the Executive and to Congress the exercise of the war power in all the vicissitudes and conditions of warfare, it has necessarily given them wide scope for the exercise of judgment and discretion in determining the nature and extent of the threatened injury or danger and in the selection of the means for resisting it. . . . Where, as they did here, the conditions call for the exercise of judgment and discretion and for the choice of means by those branches of the Government on which the Constitution has placed the responsibility of war-making, it is not for any court to sit in review of the wisdom of their action or substitute its judgment for theirs.

The actions taken must be appraised in the light of the conditions with which the President and Congress were confronted in the early months of 1942, many of which, since disclosed, were then peculiarly within the knowledge of the military authorities. . . .

. . . That reasonably prudent men charged with the responsibility of our national defense had ample ground for concluding that they must face the danger of invasion, take measures against it, and in making the choice of measures consider our internal situation, cannot be doubted.

The challenged orders were defense measures for the avowed purpose of safe-guarding the military area in question, at a time of threatened air raids and invasion by the Japanese forces, from the danger of sabotage and espionage. As the curfew was made applicable to citizens residing in the area only if they were of Japanese ancestry, our inquiry must be whether in the light of all the facts and circumstances there was any substantial basis for the conclusion, in which Congress and the military commander united, that the curfew as applied was a protective measure necessary to meet the threat of sabotage and espionage which would substantially affect the war effort and which might reasonably be expected to aid a threatened enemy invasion. The alternative which appellant insists must be accepted is for the military authorities to impose the curfew on all citizens within the military area, or on none. In a case of threatened danger requiring prompt action, it is a choice between inflicting obviously needless hardship on the many, or sitting passive and unresisting in the presence of the threat. We think that constitutional government, in time of war, is not so powerless and does not compel so hard a choice if those charged with the responsibility of our national defense have reasonable ground for believing that the threat is real. . . .

In the critical days of March, 1942, the danger to our war production by sabotage and espionage in this area seems obvious. . . . At a time of threatened Japanese attack upon this country, the nature of our inhabitants' attachments to the Japanese enemy was consequently a matter of grave concern. Of the 126,000 persons of Japanese descent in the United States, citizens and non-citizens, approximately 112,000 resided in California, Oregon and Washington at the time of the adoption of the military regulations. Of these approximately two-thirds are citizens because born in the United States. Not only did the great majority ·of such persons reside within the Pacific Coast states but they were concentrated in or near three of the large cities, Seattle, Portland and Los Angeles, all in Military Area No. 1.

There is support for the view that social, economic and political conditions which have prevailed since the close of the last century, when the Japanese began to come to this country in substantial numbers, have intensified their solidarity and have in large measure prevented their assimilation as an integral part of the white population. In addition, large numbers of children of Japanese parentage are sent to Japanese language schools outside the regular hours of public schools in the locality. Some of these schools are generally believed to be sources of Japanese nationalistic propaganda, cultivating allegiance to Japan. Considerable numbers, estimated to be approximately 10,000, of American-born children of Japanese parentage have been sent to Japan for all or a part of their education.

Congress and the Executive, including the military commander, could have attributed special significance, in its bearing on the loyalties of persons of Japanese descent, to the maintenance by Japan of its system of dual citizenship. Children born in the United States of Japanese alien parents, and especially those children born before December 1, 1924, are under many circumstances deemed, by Japanese law, to be citizens of Japan. No official census' of those whom Japan regards as having thus retained Japanese citizenship is available, but there is ground for the belief that the number is large. . . .

As a result of all these conditions affecting the life of the Japanese, both aliens and citizens, in the Pacific Coast area, there has been relatively little social intercourse between them and the white population. The restrictions, both practical and legal, affecting the privileges and opportunities afforded to persons of Japanese extraction residing in the United States, have been sources of irritation and may well have tended to increase their isolation, and in many instances their attachments to Japan and its institutions.

Viewing these data in all their aspects, Congress and the Executive could reasonably have concluded that these conditions have encouraged the continued attachment of members of this group to Japan and Japanese institutions. These are only some of the many considerations which those charged with the responsibility for the national defense could take into account in determining the nature and extent of the danger of espionage and sabotage, in the event of invasion or air raid attack. The extent of that danger could be definitely known only after the event and after it was too late to meet it. Whatever views we may entertain regarding the loyalty to this country of the citizens of Japanese ancestry, we cannot reject as unfounded the judgment of the military authorities and of Congress that there were disloyal members of that population, whose number and strength could not be precisely and quickly ascertained. We cannot say that the war-making branches of the. Government did not have ground for believing that in a critical hour such persons could not readily be isolated and separately dealt with, and constituted a menace to the national defense and safety, which demanded that prompt and adequate measures be taken to guard against it.

Appellant does not deny that, given the danger, a curfew was an appropriate measure against sabotage. It is an obvious protection against the perpetration of sabotage most readily committed during the hours of darkness. If it was an appropriate exercise of the war power its validity is not impaired because it has restricted the citizen's liberty. Like every military control of the population of a dangerous zone in war time, it necessarily involves some infringment of individual liberty, just as does the police establishment of fire lines during a fire, or the confinement of people to their houses during an air raid alarm—neither of which could be thought to be an infringement of constitutional right. Like them, the validity of the restraints of the curfew order depends on all the conditions which obtain at the time the curfew is imposed and which support the order imposing it.

But appellant insists that the exercise of the power is inappropriate and unconstitutional because it discriminates against citizens of Japanese ancestry, in violation of the Fifth Amendment. The Fifth Amendment contains no equal protection clause and it restrains only such discriminatory legislation by Congress as amounts to a denial of due process. Congress may hit at a particular danger where it is seen, without providing for others which are not so evident or so urgent.

Distinctions between citizens solely because of their ancestry are by their very nature odious to a free people whose institutions are founded upon the doctrine of equality. For that reason, legislative classification or discrimination based on race alone has often been held to be a denial of equal protection. We may assume that these considerations would be controlling here were it not for the fact that the danger of espionage and sabotage, in time of war and of threatened invasion, calls upon the military authorities to scrutinize every relevant fact bearing on the loyalty of populations in the danger areas. Because racial discriminations are in most circumstances irrelevant and therefore prohibited, it by no means follows that, in dealing with the perils of war, Congress and the Executive are wholly precluded from taking into account those facts and circumstances which are relevant to measures for our national defense and for the successful prosecution of the war, and which may in fact place citizens of one ancestry in a different category from others. "We must never forget, that it is a constitution we are expounding," "a constitution intended to endure for ages to come, and, consequently, to be adapted to the various crises of human affairs." The adoption by Government, in the crisis of war and of threatened invasion, of measures for the public safety, based upon the recognition of facts and circumstances which indicate that a group of one national extraction may menace that safety more than others, is not wholly beyond the limits of the Constitution and is not to be condemned merely because in other and in most circumstances racial distinctions are irrelevant.

Here the aim of Congress and the Executive was the protection against sabotage of war materials and utilities in areas thought to be in danger of Japanese invasion and air attack. We have stated in detail facts and circumstances with respect to the American citizens of Japanese ancestry residing on the Pacific Coast which support the judgment of the war-waging branches of the Government that some restrictive measure was urgent. We cannot say that these facts and circumstances, considered in the particular war setting, could afford no ground for differentiating citizens of Japanese ancestry from other groups in the United States. The fact alone that attack on our shores was threatened by Japan rather than another enemy power set these citizens apart from others who have no particular associations with Japan. . . .

The Constitution as a continuously operating charter of government does not demand the impossible or the impractical. The essentials of the legislative function are preserved when Congress authorizes a statutory command to become operative, upon ascertainment of a basic conclusion of fact by a designated representative of the Government. The present statute, which authorized curfew orders to be made pursuant to Executive Order No. 9066 for the protection of war resources from espionage and sabotage, satisfies those requirements. Under the Executive Order the basic facts, determined by the military commander in the light of knowledge then available, were whether that danger existed and whether a curfew order was an appropriate means of minimizing the danger. Since his findings to that effect were, as we have said, not without adequate support, the legislative function was performed and the sanction of the statute attached to violations of the curfew order. It is unnecessary to consider whether or to what extent such findings would support orders differing from the curfew order.

The conviction under the second count is without constitutional infirmity. Hence we have no occasion to review the conviction on the first count since, as already stated, the sentences on the two counts are to run concurrently and conviction on the second is sufficient to sustain the sentence. For this reason also it is unnecessary to consider the Government's argument that compliance with the order to report at the Civilian Control Station did not necessarily entail confinement in a relocation center.

Affirmed.

548. F. D. ROOSEVELT'S STATEMENT ON NORTH AFRICAN POLICY
November 17, 1942
(*Department of State Bulletin,* Vol. VII, p. 935)

When the armistice between France and Germany was concluded in June, 1940, France was divided into two parts: occupied France under German control, and unoccupied France, ruled by a government in Vichy headed by Marshal Petain, in which outright Nazi sympathizers like Pierre Laval played major roles. In order to maintain a listening post on the continent and to lessen German influence over the Vichy government, the United States continued diplomatic relations with France, a policy widely condemned by liberal groups in this country. When the Allies invaded North Africa in November, 1942, a conservative French army officer, General Henri Giraud, was chosen to attempt to halt French resistance to the landings, and, when his orders were not obeyed, General Eisenhower accepted the assistance of Admiral Darlan, vice-premier of Vichy France and a notorious collaborationist. Although Darlan was assassinated the next month, the Giraud government continued many of the practices and personnel of the Vichy regime. The State Department maintained that support of De Gaulle would be tantamount to choosing the leader of the new French government, a prerogative which belonged to the French people, while the deal with Darlan was defended on the grounds of military expediency. See W. Langer, *Our Vichy Gamble;* K. Pendar, *Adventure in Diplomacy;* Renee Bierre-Gosset, *Conspiracy in Algiers;* S. E. Morison, *Operations in North African Waters;* Ellen Hammer, "Hindsight on Vichy," *Pol. Sci. Q.,* Vol. LXI, pp. 175 ff.; J. MacVane, *Journey Into War.*

President Franklin D. Roosevelt's Statement on Political Arrangements in North Africa made by Lieut. General Dwight D. Eisenhower, Allied Commander in Chief in North Africa. Washington, November 17, 1942:

I have accepted General Eisenhower's political arrangements made for the time being in Northern and Western Africa.

I thoroughly understand and approve the feeling in the United States and Great Britain and among all the other United Nations that in view of the history of the past two years no permanent arrangement should be made with Admiral Darlan. People in the United Nations likewise would never understand the recognition of a reconstituting of the Vichy Government in France or in any French territory.

We are opposed to Frenchmen who support Hitler and the Axis. No one in our Army has any authority to discuss the future Government of France and the French Empire.

The future French Government will be established—not by any individual in metropolitan France or overseas—but by the French people themselves after they have been set free by the victory of the United Nations.

The present temporary arrangement in North and West Africa is only a temporary expedient, justified solely by the stress of battle.

The present temporary arrangement has accomplished two military objectives. The first was to save American and British lives on the one hand, and French lives on the other hand.

The second was the vital factor of time. The temporary arrangement has made it possible to avoid a "mopping up" period in Algiers and Morocco which might have taken a month or two to consummate. Such a period would have delayed the concentration for the attack from the West on Tunis, and we hope on Tripoli.

Every day of delay in the current operation would have enabled the Germans and Italians to build up a strong resistance, to dig in and make a huge operation on our part essential before we could win. Here again, many more lives will be saved under the present speedy offensive, than if we had had to delay it for a month or more.

It will also be noted that French troops, under the command of General Giraud, have already been in action against the enemy in Tunisia, fighting by the side of American and British soldiers for the liberation of their country.

Admiral Darlan's proclamation assisted in making a "mopping up" period unnecessary. Temporary arrangements made with Admiral Darlan apply, without exception, to the current local situation only.

I have requested the liberation of all persons in Northern Africa who had been imprisoned because they opposed the efforts of the Nazis to dominate the world, and I have asked for the abrogation of all laws and decrees inspired by Nazi Governments or Nazi idealogies. Reports indicate that the French of North Africa are subordinating all political questions to the formation of a common front against the common enemy.

549. FEDERAL POWER COMMISSION v. NATURAL GAS PIPELINE CO.
315 U. S. 575
1942

When the Natural Gas Pipeline Co. challenged a regulation of the Federal Power Commission, this crucial decision sustained the findings of administrative boards and established the Court's refusal to go behind the facts. Chief Justice Stone read an opinion sustaining the ruling of the Federal Power Commission. His reasoning, however, seemed timid to three members of the Court and they wrote a concurring opinion carrying the logic of the decision to its conclusion. Because this concurring opinion has commanded increasing support and because it affords a historical review of the whole rate evaluation question, it is given here instead of the opinion of Chief Justice Stone. Justice Frankfurter filed a separate opinion concurring with the findings of Stone. Compare with the Minnesota Rate Cases of 1890, Doc. No. 319. See also the opinion of Justice Brandeis in the Southwestern Bell Telephone Co. case, 262 U.S. 276; the O'Fallon case, 279 U.S. 461; the St. Joseph Stock Yard case, 298 U.S. 38; McCart v. Indianapolis Water Co., 302 U.S. 419. On the problem of valuation and judicial review see Bonbright, Valuation of Property; Hale, "The Fair Value Theory," 33 Ill. L. Rev., 517; Hale, "Conflicting Judicial Criteria of Utility Rates," 38 Col. L. Rev. 959; Henderson, "Railway Valuation and the Courts," 33 Harv. L. Rev. 1031.

BLACK, DOUGLAS, and MURPHY, JJ., concurring.

I.

We concur with the Court's judgment that the rate order of the Federal Power Commission, issued after a fair hearing upon findings of fact supported by substantial evidence, should have been sustained by the court below. But insofar as the Court assumes that, regardless of the terms of the statute, the due process clause of the Fifth Amendment grants it power to invalidate an order as unconstitutional because it finds the charges to be unreasonable, we are unable to join in the opinion just announced.

Rate making is a species of price fixing. In a recent series of cases, this Court has held that legislative price fixing is not prohibited by the due process clause. We believe that in so holding, it has returned in part at least to the constitutional principles which prevailed for the first hundred years of our history. The Munn and Peik cases, decided in 1877, Justices Field and Strong dissenting, emphatically declared price fixing to be a constitutional prerogative of the legislative branch, not subject to judicial review or revision.

In 1886, four of the Justices who had voted with him in the Munn and Peik cases no longer being on the Court, Chief Justice Waite expressed views in an opinion of the Court which indicated a yielding in part to the doctrines previously set forth in Mr. Justice Field's dissenting opinions, although the decision, upholding a state regulatory statute, did not require him to reach this issue. See Railroad Commission Cases, 116 U.S. 307. . . . By 1890, six Justices of the 1877 Court, including Chief Justice Waite, had been replaced by others. The new Court then clearly repudiated the opinion expressed for the Court by Chief Justice Waite in the Munn and Peik cases, in a holding which accorded with the views of Mr. Justice Field. Chicago, etc., Railway Co. v. Minnesota. Under those views, first embodied in a holding of this Court in 1890, "due process" means no less than "reasonableness judicially determined." In accordance with this elastic meaning which, in the words of Mr. Justice Holmes, makes the sky the limit of judicial power to declare legislative acts unconstitutional, the conclusions of judges, substituted for those of legislatures, become a broad and varying standard of constitutionality. We shall not attempt now to set out at length the reasons for our belief that acceptance of such a meaning is historically unjustified and that it transfers to courts powers which, under the Constitution, belong to the legislative branch of government. But we feel that we must record our disagreement from an opinion which, although upholding the action of the Commission on these particular facts, nevertheless gives renewed vitality to a "constitutional" doctrine which we are convinced has no support in the Constitution.

The doctrine which makes of "due process" an unlimited grant to courts to approve or reject policies selected by legislatures in accordance with the judges' notion of reasonableness had its origin in connection with legislative attempts to fix the prices charged by public utilities. And in no field has it had more paralyzing effects.

II.

We have here, to be sure, a statute which expressly provides for judicial review. Congress has provided in § 5 of the Natural Gas Act that the rates fixed by the Commission shall be "just and reasonable." The provision for judicial review states that the "finding of the Commission as to the facts, if supported by substantial evidence, shall be conclusive." But we are not satisfied that the opinion of the Court properly delimits the scope of that review under this Act. Furthermore, since this case starts a new chapter in the regulation of utility rates, we think it important to indicate more explicitly than

has been done the freedom which the Commission has both under the Constitution and under this new statute. While the opinion of the Court erases much which has been written into rate cases during the last half century, we think this is an appropriate occasion to lay the ghost of Smyth v. Ames, which has haunted utility regulation since 1898. That is especially desirable lest the reference by the majority to "constitutional requirements" and to "the limits of due process" be deemed to perpetuate the fallacious "fair-value" theory of rate making in the limited judicial review provided by the Act.

Smyth v. Ames held [See Doc. No. 319], (1) This theory derives from principles of eminent domain. In condemnation cases the "value of property, generally speaking, is determined by its productiveness,—the profits which its use brings to the owner." But those principles have no place in rate regulation. In the first place, the value of a going concern in fact depends on earnings under whatever rates may be anticipated. The present fair value rule creates but offers no solution to the dilemma that value depends upon the rates fixed and the rates upon value. See Mr. Justice Brandeis, State of Missouri ex rel. Southwestern Bell Telephone Co. v. Public Service Commission, 262 U.S. 276. In the second place, when property is taken under the power of eminent domain the owner is "entitled to the full money equivalent of the property taken, and thereby to be put in as good position pecuniarily as it would have occupied, if its property had not been taken." United States v. New River Collieries Co., 262 U.S. 341. But in rate-making the owner does not have any such protection. We know without attempting any valuation that if earnings are reduced the value will be less. But that does not stay the hand of the legislature or its administrative agency in making rate reductions. As we have said, rate-making is one species of price-fixing. Price-fixing, like other forms of social legislation, may well diminish the value of the property which is regulated. But that is no obstacle to its validity. As stated by Mr. Justice Holmes "The fact that tangible property is also visible tends to give rigidity to our conception of our rights in it that we do not attach to others less concretely clothed. But the notion that the former are exempt from the legislative modification required from time to time in civilized life is contradicted not only by the doctrine of eminent domain, under which what is taken is paid for, but by that of the police power in its proper sense, under which property rights may be cut down, and to that extent taken, without pay." Somewhat the same view was expressed in Nebbia v. People of New York, where this Court said: "The due process clause makes no mention of sales or of prices any more than it speaks of business or contracts or buildings or other incidents of property. The thought seems nevertheless to have persisted that there is something peculiarly sacrosanct about the price one may charge for what he makes or sells, and that, however able to regulate other elements of manufacture or trade, with incidental effect upon price, the state is incapable of ·directly controlling the price itself. This view was negatived many years ago. Munn v. Illinois. Explicit recognition of these principles will place the problems of rate-making in their proper setting under this statute."

(2) The rule of Smyth v. Ames, as construed and applied, directs the rate-making body in forming its judgment as to "fairvalue" to take into consideration various elements—capitalization, book cost, actual cost, prudent investment, reproduction cost. But as stated by Mr. Justice Brandeis: "Obviously 'value' cannot be a composite of all these elements. Nor can it be arrived at on all these bases. They are very different, and must, when applied in a particular case, lead to widely different results. The rule of Smyth v. Ames, as interpreted and applied, means merely that all must be considered. What, if any, weight shall be given to any one, must practically rest in the judicial discretion of the tribunal which makes the determination. Whether a desired result is reached may depend upon how any one of many elements is treated." The risks of not giving weight to reproduction cost have been great. The havoc raised by insistence on reproduction cost is now a matter of historical record. Mr. Justice Brandeis in the Southwestern Bell Telephone case demonstrated how the rule of Smyth v. Ames has seriously impaired the power of rate-regulation and how the "fair value" rule has proved to be unworkable by reason of the time required to make the valuations, the heavy expense involved, and the unreliability of the results obtained. The result of this Court's rulings in rate cases since Smyth v. Ames has recently been summarized as follows: "Under the influence of these precedents, commission regulation has become so cumbersome and so ineffective that it may be said, with only slight exaggeration, to have broken down. Even the investor, on whose behalf the constitutional safeguards have been developed, has received no protection against the rebounds from the inflated stock-market prices that are stimulated by the 'fair-value' doctrine." Bonbright, Valuation of Property, p. 1154.

As we read the opinion of the Court, the Commission is now freed from the compulsion of admitting evidence on reproduction cost or of giving any weight to that element of "fair value." The Commission may now adopt, if it chooses, prudent investment as a rate base—the base long advocated by Mr. Justice Brandeis. And for the reasons stated by Mr. Justice Brandeis in the Southwestern Bell Telephone case there could be no constitutional objection if the Commission adhered to that formula and rejected all others.

Yet it is important to note, as we have indicated, that Congress has merely provided in § 5 of the Natural Gas Act that the rates fixed by the Commission shall be "just and reasonable." It has provided no standard beyond that. Congress, to be sure, has provided for judicial review. But § 19(b) states that the "finding of the Commission as to the facts, if supported by substantial evidence, shall be conclusive." In view of these provisions we do not think it is permissible for the courts to concern themselves with any issues as to the economic merits of a rate base. The Commission has a broad area of discretion for selection of an appropriate rate base. The requirements of "just and reasonable" embrace among other factors two phases of the public interest: (1) the investor interest; (2) the consumer interest. The investor interest is adequately served if the utility is allowed the opportunity to earn the cost of the service. That cost has been defined by Mr. Justice Brandeis as follows: "Cost includes, not only operating expenses, but also capital charges. Capital charges cover the allowance, by way of interest, for the use of the capital, whatever the nature of the security issued therefor, the allowance for risk incurred, and enough more to attract capital." State of Missouri ex rel. Southwestern Bell Telephone Co. v. Public Service Commission, 262 U.S. 291. Irrespective of what the return may be on "fair value," if the rate permits the company to operate successfully and to attract capital all questions as to "just and reasonable" are at an end so far as the investor interest is concerned. Various routes to that end may be worked out by the expert administrators charged with the duty of regulation. It is not the function of the courts to prescribe what formula should be used. The fact that one may be fair to investors does not mean that another would be unfair. The decision in each case must turn on considerations of justness and fairness which cannot be cast into a legalistic formula. The rate of return to be allowed in any given case calls for a highly expert judgment. That judgment has been entrusted to the Commission. There it should rest.

One *caveat* however should be entered. The consumer interest cannot be disregarded in determining what is a "just and reasonable" rate. Conceivably a return to the company of the cost of the service might not be "just and reasonable" to the public. The correct principle was announced by this Court in Covington & Lexington Turnpike Co. v. Sandford, 164 U.S. 578.

"It cannot be said that a corporation . . . is entitled as of right, and without reference to the interests of the public, to realize a given per cent, upon its capital stock. When the question arises whether the legislature has exceeded its constitutional power in prescribing rates to be charged by a corporation controlling a public highway, stockholders are not the only persons whose rights or interests are to be considered. The rights of the public are not to be ignored. It is alleged here that the rates prescribed are unreasonable and unjust to the company and its stockholders. But that involves an inquiry as to what is reasonable and just for the public. If the establishing of new lines of transportation should cause a diminution in the number of those who need to use a turnpike road, and, consequently, a diminution in the tolls collected, that is not, in itself, a sufficient reason why the corporation operating the road should be allowed to maintain rates that would be unjust to those who must or do use its property. The public cannot properly be subjected to unreasonable rates in order simply that stockholders may earn dividends."

This problem carries into a field not necessary to develop here. It reemphasizes however, that the investor interest is not the sole interest for protection. The investor and consumer interests may so collide as to warrant the rate-making body in concluding that a return on historical cost or prudent investment though fair to investors would be grossly unfair to the consumers. The possibility of that collision reinforces the view that the problem of rate-making is for the administrative experts not the courts and that the *ex post facto* function previously performed by the courts should be reduced to the barest minimum which is consistent with the statutory mandate for judicial review. That review should be as confined and restricted as the review, under similar statutes, of orders of other administrative agencies.

550. CASABLANCA CONFERENCE
Feb. 12, 1943
(The Public Papers of F. D. Roosevelt, Vol. 12, p. 71)

By the beginning of 1943 the military initiative had passed to the United Nations. The Casablanca Conference was necessary to step up the Tunisian campaign and plan a new offensive in Southern Europe. President Roosevelt outlined the purposes of the Casablanca Conference as

(1) to maintain the initiative, (2) to dispatch all aid to the Russians, and (3) to send assistance to the Chinese. Finally, the conference was called to help resolve the conflict between Giraud and de Gaulle. Roosevelt was the first President to leave the United States in wartime. Only Roosevelt and Churchill met at Casablanca; Stalin was invited but pleaded the necessity of remaining in Russia to give personal direction to the Russian campaign. The conference met from January 14 to 24, 1943. At Roosevelt's request, it was called the "Unconditional Surrender Conference," a phrase taken from Grant's letter to the Confederate commander of Forts Henry and Donelson. The official report of Jan. 24, 1943 did not contain the term "Unconditional Surrender." Because, in perspective, that was the real significance of the conference, we give here President Roosevelt's radio report of Feb. 12, 1943. See Elliott Roosevelt, *As He Saw It;* F. C. Balling, "Unconditional Surrender and a Unilated Declaration of Peace," *Am. Pol. Sci. Rev.* Vol. XXXIX, pp. 474 ff. Carol Thompson, "Casablanca and After," *Current History,* March, 1943.

The decisions reached and the actual plans made at Casablanca were not confined to any one theater of war or to any one continent or ocean or sea. Before this year is out, it will be made known to the world—in actions rather than in words—that the Casablanca Conference produced plenty of news; and it will be bad news for the Germans and Italians—and the Japanese.

We have lately concluded a long, hard battle in the Southwest Pacific and we have made notable gains. That battle started in the Solomons and New Guinea last summer. It has demonstrated our superior power in planes and, most importantly, in the fighting qualities of our individual soldiers and sailors.

American armed forces in the Southwest Pacific are receiving powerful aid from Australia and New Zealand and also directly from the British themselves.

We do not expect to spend the time it would take to bring Japan to final defeat merely by inching our way forward from island to island across the vast expanse of the Pacific.

Great and decisive actions against the Japanese will be taken to drive the invader from the soil of China. Important actions will be taken in the skies over China—and over Japan itself.

The discussions at Casablanca have been continued in Chungking with the Generalissimo by General Arnold and have resulted in definite plans for offensive operations.

There are many roads which lead right to Tokyo. We shall neglect none of them.

In an attempt to ward off the inevitable disaster, the Axis propagandists are trying all of their old tricks in order to divide the United Nations. They seek to create the idea that if we win this war, Russia, England, China, and the United States are going to get into a cat-and-dog fight.

This is their final effort to turn one nation against another, in the vain hope that they may settle with one or two at a time—that any of us may be so gullible and so forgetful as to be duped into making "deals" at the expense of our Allies.

To these panicky attempts to escape the consequences of their crimes we say—all the United Nations say—that the only terms on which we shall deal with an Axis government or any Axis factions are the terms proclaimed at Casablanca: "Unconditional Surrender." In our. uncompromising policy we mean no harm to the common people of the Axis nations. But we do mean to impose punishment and retribution in full upon their guilty, barbaric leaders. . . .

In the years of the American and French revolutions the fundamental principle guiding our democracies was established. The cornerstone of our whole democratic edifice was the principle that from the people and the people alone flows the authority of government.

It is one of our war aims, as expressed in the Atlantic Charter, that the conquered populations of today be again the masters of their destiny. There must be no doubt anywhere that it is the unalterable purpose of the United Nations to restore to conquered peoples their sacred rights.

551. MOSCOW CONFERENCE
October, 1943

(*Dept. of State Bulletin*, Vol. IX, pp. 307 ff.)

By the fall of 1943, almost two years after the entrance of America into the war, no "second front" had been opened on the European continent, and the Soviet Union complained bitterly, while many people, here and abroad, alleged that the failure to establish a "second front" was a political move directed against future Soviet power. The 15,000-mile air trip of Secretary of State Cordell Hull to Moscow and the success of the Moscow Conference in dispelling that atmosphere of distrust was one of the great diplomatic triumphs of the war. The Moscow Conference planned the new military phase of the war which would begin with the establishment of a "second front" in the West. Secretary Hull, Anthony Eden, British Foreign Secretary, and Soviet Foreign Commissar Molotov, together with the Chinese ambassador to the Soviet Union, signed a four power pact pledging their determination to establish a new world organization. The Tripartite Conference of Foreign Ministers met in Spiridonovka House in Moscow from October 19 to November 1 in twelve historic sessions. The conference dealt with political as well as military problems, notably in the appeal to the Austrians to break with Germany, and the decision to create an independent Austria; the plan to establish in London a European commission of foreign ministers; and the decision to revise the Mediterranean Commission to include representatives of Greece and Yugoslavia. See Jan Ciechanowski, *Defeat in Victory*; P. B. Potter, "Moscow; Cairo; Teheran," *Am. J. Int. Law* Vol. 38; S. B. Fay, "The meaning of the Moscow Conference," *Current History*, n.s. Vol. 5, pp. 289-94; Walter Lippmann, "The Four Policemen," *Vital Speeches* Vol. 10, pp. 138 ff.

The Moscow Conference
October, 1943

The conference of foreign secretaries of the United States of America, Mr. Cordell Hull; of the United Kingdom, Mr. Anthony Eden; and of the Soviet Union, Mr. V. M. Molotov; took place at Moscow from 19 to 30 October, 1943. There were twelve meetings. In addition to the foreign secretaries, the following took part in the conference:

For the United States of America: Mr. W. Averell Harriman, Ambassador of the United States; Major General John R. Deane, United States Army; Mr. H. Hackworth, Mr. James C. Dunn and experts.

For the United Kingdom: Sir Archibald Clark Kerr, Ambassador; Mr. William Strang, Lieutenant General Sir Hastings Ismay and experts.

For the Soviet Union: Marshal K. E. Voroshilov, Marshal of the Soviet Union; Mr. A. Y. Vishinsky, Mr. M. M. Litvinov, Deputy People's Commissars for Foreign Affairs; Mr. V. Sergeyev, Deputy People's Commissar for Foreign Trade; Major General A. A. Gryzlov, of the general staff; Mr. G. F. Saksin, senior official for People's Commissariat for Foreign Affairs, and experts.

The agenda included all questions submitted for discussion by the three governments. Some of the questions called for final decisions, and these were taken. On other questions, after discussion, decisions of principle were taken: These questions were referred for detailed consideration to commissions specially set up for the purpose, or reserved for treatment through diplomatic channels. Other questions again were disposed of by an exchange of views. The governments of the United States, the United Kingdom, and the Soviet Union have been in close cooperation in all matters concerning the common war effort, but this is the first time that the foreign secretaries of the three governments have been able to meet together in conference.

In the first place there were frank and exhaustive discussions of the measures to be taken to shorten the war aaginst Germany and her satellites in Europe. Advantage was taken of the presence of military advisers representing the respective chiefs of staff in order to discuss definite military operations with regard to which decisions had been taken and which are already being prepared in order to create a basis for the closest military cooperation in the future between the three countries.

Second only to the importance of hastening the end of the war was the recognition by the three governments that it was essential in their own national interests and in the interest of all peace-loving nations to continue to present close collaboration and cooperation in the conduct of the war into the period following the end of hostilities, and that only in this way could peace be maintained and the political, economic, and social welfare of their people fully promoted.

This conviction is expressed in a declaration in which the Chinese Government joined during the conference and which was signed by the three Foreign Secretaries and the Chinese Ambassador at Moscow on behalf of their governments. This declaration provided for even closer collaboration in the prosecution of the war and in all matters pertaining to the surrender and disarmament of the enemies with which the four countries were respectively at war. It set forth the principles upon which the four governments agreed that a broad system of international cooperation and security should be based. Provision is made for the inclusion of all other peace-loving nations, great and small, in this system.

The conference agreed to set up machinery for insuring the closest cooperation between the three governments in the examination of European questions arising as the war developed. For this purpose the conference decided to establish in London a European advisory commission to study these questions and to make joint recommendations to the three .governments.

Provision was made for continuing when necessary the tri-partite consultations of representatives of the three governments in the respective capitals through the existing diplomatic channels.

The conference also agreed to establish an advisory council for matters relating to Italy, to be composed, in the first instance, of representatives of their three governments and of the French Committee of National Liberation. Provision is made for addition to this council of representatives of Greece and Yugoslavia in view of their special interests arising out of aggressions of Facist Italy upon their territory during the present war.

This council will deal with day to day questions other than military preparations and will make recommendations designed to co-ordinate allied policy with regard to Italy.

The three foreign secretaries considered it appropriate to reaffirm, by a declaration published today, the attitude of the allied governments in favor of the restoration of democracy in Italy.

The three foreign secretaries declared it to be the purpose of their governments to restore the independence of Austria. At the same time they reminded Austria that in the final settlement account will be taken of efforts that Austria may make toward its own liberation.

The foreign secretaries issued at the conference a declaration by President Roosevelt, Prime Minister Churchill and Premier Stalin containing a solemn warning that at the time of granting any armistice to any German government, those German officers and men and members of the Nazi party who have had any connection with atrocities and executions in countries overrun by German forces, will be taken back to the countries in which their abominable crimes were committed to be charged and punished according to the laws of those countries.

In an atmosphere of mutual confidence and understanding which characterized all the work of the conference, consideration was also given to other important questions. These included not only questions of a current nature, but also questions concerning treatment of Hitlerite Germany and its satellites, economic cooperation and assurance of general peace.

JOINT FOUR-NATION DECLARATION

The governments of the United States of America, United Kingdom, the Soviet Union and China;

United in their determination, in accordance with the declaration by the United Nations of January 1942, and subsequent declarations, to continue hostilities against those Axis powers with which they respectively are at war until such powers have laid down their arms on the basis of unconditional surrender;

Conscious of their responsibility to secure the liberation of themselves and the peoples allied with them from the menace of aggression;

Recognizing the necessity of insuring a rapid and orderly transition from war to peace and of establishing and maintaining international peace and security with the least diversion of the world's human and economic resources for armaments;

Jointly declare:

1. That their united action, pledged for the prosecution of the war against their respective enemies, will be continued for the organization and maintenance of peace and security.

2. That those of them at war with a common enemy will act together in all matters relating to the surrender and disarmament of that enemy.

3. That they will take all measures deemed by them to be necessary to provide against any violation of the terms imposed upon the enemy.

4. That they recognize the necessity of establishing at the earliest practicable date a general international organization, based on the principle of the sovereign equality of all peace-loving states, and open to membership by all such states, large and small, for the maintenance of international peace and security.

5. That fot the purpose of maintaining international peace and security pending the re-establishment of law and order and the inauguration of a system of general security they will consult with one another and as occasion requires with other members of the United Nations, with a view to joint action on behalf of the community of nations.

6. That after the termination of hostilities they will not employ their military forces within the territories of other states except for the purposes envisaged in this declaration and after joint consultation.

7. That they will confer and cooperate with one another and with other members of the United Nations to bring about a practicable general agreement with respect to the regulation of armaments in the post-war period.

DECLARATION REGARDING ITALY

The Foreign Secretaries of the United States, the United Kingdom and the Soviet Union have established that their three governments are in complete agreement that

Allied policy toward Italy must be based upon the fundamental principle that Fascism and all its evil influence and configuration shall be completely destroyed and that the Italian people shall be given every opportunity to establish governmental and other institutions based upon democratic principles.

The Foreign Secretaries of the United States and United Kingdom declare that the action of their governments from the inception of the invasion of Italian territory, in so far as paramount military requirements have permitted, has been based upon this policy.

In furtherance of this policy in the future the Foreign Secretaries of the three governments are agreed that the following measures are important and should be put into effect:

1. It is essential that the Italian Government should be made more democratic by inclusion of representatives of those sections of the Italian people who have always opposed Fascism.

2. Freedom of speech, of religious worship, of political belief, of press and of public meeting shall be restored in full measure to the Italian people, who shall be entitled to form anti-Fascist political groups.

3. All institutions and organizations created by the Fascist regime shall be suppressed.

4. All Fascist or pro-Fascist elements shall be removed from the administration and from institutions and organizations of a public character.

5. All political prisoners of the Fascist regime shall be released and accorded full amnesty.

6. Democratic organs of local government shall be created.

7. Fascist chiefs and army generals known or suspected to be war criminals shall be arrested and handed over to justice.

In making this declaration the three Foreign Secretaries recognize that so long as active military operations continue in Italy the time at which it is possible to give full effect to the principles stated above will be determined by the Commander-in-Chief on the basis of instructions received through the combined chiefs of staff.

The three governments, parties to this

declaration, will, at the request of any one of them, consult on this matter. It is further understood that nothing in this resolution is to operate against the right of the Italian people ultimately to choose their own form of government.

DECLARATION ON AUSTRIA

The governments of the United Kingdom, the Soviet Union and the United States of America are agreed that Austria, the first free country to fall a victim to Hitlerite aggression, shall be liberated from German domination.

They regard the annexation imposed on Austria by Germany on March 15, 1938, as null and void. They consider themselves as in no way bound by any changes effected in Austria since that date. They declare that they wish to see re-established a free and independent Austria and thereby to open the way for the Austrian people themselves, as well as those neighboring States which will be faced with similar problems, to find that political and economic security which is the only basis for lasting peace.

Austria is reminded, however, that she has a responsibility, which she cannot evade, for participation in the war at the side of Hitlerite Germany, and that in the final settlement account will inevitably be taken of her own contribution to her liberation.

STATEMENT ON ATROCITIES

Signed by President Roosevelt, Prime Minister Churchill and Premier Stalin

The United Kingdom, the United States and the Soviet Union have received from many quarters evidence of atrocities, massacres and cold-blooded mass executions which are being perpetrated by Hitlerite forces in many of the countries they have overrun and from which they are now being steadily expelled. The brutalities of Nazi domination are no new thing, and all peoples or territories in their grip have suffered from the worst form of government by terror. What is new is that many of the territories are now being redeemed by the advancing armies of the liberating powers, and that in their desperation the recoiling Hitlerites and Huns are redoubling their ruthless cruelties.

This is now evidenced with particular clearness by monstrous crimes on the territory of the Soviet Union which is being liberated from Hitlerites, and on French and Italian territory.

Accordingly, the aforesaid three Allied powers, speaking in the interest of the thirty-two United Nations, hereby solemnly declare and give full warning of their declaration as follows:

At the time of granting of any armistice to any government which may be set up in Germany, those German officers and men and members of the Nazi party who have been responsible for or have taken a consenting part in the above atrocities, massacres and executions will be sent back to the countries in which their abominable deeds were done in order that they may be judged and punished according to the laws of these liberated countries and of free governments which will be erected therein. Lists will be compiled in all possible detail from all these countries having regard especially to invaded parts of the Soviet Union, to Poland and Czechoslovakia, to Yugoslavia and Greece including Crete and other islands, to Norway, Denmark, Netherlands, Belgium, Luxemburg, France and Italy.

Thus, Germans who take part in wholesale shooting of Polish officers or in the execution of French, Dutch, Belgian or Norwegian hostages or Cretan peasants, or who have shared in slaughters inflicted on the people of Poland or in territories of the Soviet Union which are now being swept clear of the enemy, will know they will be brought back to the scene of their crimes and judged on the spot by the peoples whom they have outraged.

Let those who have hitherto not imbued their hands with innocent blood beware lest they join the ranks of the guilty, for most assuredly the three Allied powers will pursue them to the uttermost ends of the earth and will deliver them to their accusors in order that justice may be done.

The above declaration is without prejudice to the case of German criminals, whose offenses have no particular geographical localization and who will be punished by joint decision of the governments of the Allies.

552. CAIRO CONFERENCE
November, 1943

(Dept. of State Bulletin, Vol. IX, p. 393)

By late November, 1943, the European war was going so well that the Allies could afford to fight in the Pacific on almost as great a scale as in Europe. From November 22 to 26, 1943, Roosevelt and Churchill met for the first time with Chiang Kai-Shek at Cairo. The conference was entirely concerned with Asia; hence, Russia was not represented. Military discussions were concerned with fleet allocations and the opening of supply lines to China from India and Burma. The conference gave China UN status as one of the Big Four. See H. G. Butcher, *My Three Years With Eisenhower;* S. B. Fay, "Moscow, Cairo, and Teheran," *Current History,* n.s., Vol. 6, pp. 97 ff.; Chiang Kai-Shek, *Resistance and Reconstruction.*

Released December 1, 1943

The several military missions have agreed upon future military operations against Japan. The Three Great Allies expressed their resolve to bring unrelenting pressure against their brutal enemies by sea, land, and air.

This pressure is already rising.

The Three Great Allies are fighting this war to restrain and punish the aggression of Japan. They covet no gain for themselves and have no thought of territorial expansion. It is their purpose that Japan shall be stripped of all the islands in the Pacific which she has seized or occupied since the beginning of the first World War in 1914, and that all the territories Japan has stolen from the Chinese, such as Manchuria, Formosa, and the Pescadores, shall be restored to the Republic of China. Japan will also be expelled from all other territories which she has taken by violence and greed. The aforesaid three great powers, mindful of the enslavement of the people of Korea, are determined that in due course Korea shall become free and independent.

With these objects in view the three Allies, in harmony with those of the United Nations at war with Japan, will continue to persevere in the serious and prolonged operations necessary to procure the unconditional surrender of Japan.

553. CONNALLY-FULBRIGHT RESOLUTIONS
November 5, 1943

(Congressional Record, Vol. 89, p. 7729, 9222)

One of the great fears of advocates of a world organization was that the United States Senate, which must ratify all treaties by a two-thirds vote, would fail to approve American entrance into such an organization, just as the plans of Woodrow Wilson for American participation in an effective League of Nations had been thwarted after the First World War. On March 16, 1943, Senators Joseph Ball (R., Minn.), Harold Burton (R., Ohio), Carl Hatch (D., N. Mex.), and Lister Hill (D., Ala.) began a bipartisan movement to commit the U.S. Senate to participation in an international organization. After much discussion on October 14, Senate Foreign Relations Committee reported out the Connally resolution. The debate took place while the Moscow Conference was going

on; when the Conference announced its declaration in favor of "a general international organization," the Senate incorporated a new paragraph into the Connally Resolution almost identical with Article 4 of the Moscow Declaration. In order to insure a greater vote for the Resolution, another paragraph was added specifically stating that all treaties enacted to carry out the purposes of the Resolution must be passed on by a vote of two-thirds of the Senate. On November 5, the Senate adopted the Resolution, as amended, by a vote of 85-5, well above the necessary two-thirds vote which would later be required to approve the new international organization. See bibliography for United Nations Participation Act. Also see bibliography for Docs. 435, 436.

The Fulbright Resolution

Passed by the House of Representatives
21 September 1943

RESOLVED by the House of Representatives
(the Senate concurring), that the Congress
hereby expresses itself as favoring the creation of appropriate international machinery
with power adequate to establish and to
maintain a just and lasting peace, among the
nations of the world, and as favoring participation by the United States therein through
its constitutional process.

The Connally Resolution

Passed by the Senate 6 November 1943

RESOLVED, That the war against all our enemies be waged until complete victory is
achieved.

That the United States cooperate with its
comrades-in-arms in securing a just and honorable peace.

That the United States, acting through its
constitutional processes, join free and sovereign nations in the establishment and
maintenance of international authority with
power to prevent aggression and to preserve
the peace of the world.

That the Senate recognize the necessity of
there being established at the earliest practicable date a general international organization, based on the principle of the sovereign
equality of all peace-loving states, and open
to membership by all such states, large and
small, for the maintenance of international
peace and security.

That, pursuant to the Constitution of the
United States, any treaty made to effect
the purpose of this resolution, on behalf of
the Government of the United States with
any other nation or any association of nations, shall be made only by and with the advice and consent of the Senate of the United
States, provided two-thirds of the Senators
present concur.

554. TEHERAN CONFERENCE
December 1, 1943

(Dept. of State Bulletin, Vol. IX, p. 409)

From their conference at Cairo, President
Roosevelt and Prime Minister Churchill flew to
the Iranian capital of Teheran for their first
meeting with Premier Stalin. For four days,
from November 28 to December 1, 1943, the
three men met and dined together constantly,
discussing the military aspects of coordinating
the Russian offensive with the forthcoming
second front. It was at the Teheran conference
that the details of the Allied invasions of France
were worked out; the meetings had been long
awaited, and the end of the second front issue
resulted in increased good feeling among the
Big Three. Only a vague, general communique
was issued at the time of the conference, and
the secrecy of the conference was widely criticized by the press. One of the political problems
decided at the conference was the Iranian question. Iran had been jointly occupied by the Big
Three; they issued a statement at the conference, pledging recall of their troops when the
war ended. Not until March 24, 1947 did the
State Department make public other decisions of
the conference in respect to arming Yugoslav
guerrillas and attempting to get Turkey to declare war against the Axis. See F. R. Dulles,

The Road to Teheran; D. Dallin, The Big
Three; H. C. Nixon, "Big Four," Va. Quart.
Rev., Vol. 19 pp. 513 ff; Elliott Roosevelt, As
He Saw It.

We—The President of the United States,
the Prime Minister of Great Britain, and the
Premier of the Soviet Union, have met these
four days past in this, the Capital of our
Ally, Iran, and have shaped and confirmed
our common policy.

We express our determination that our
nations shall work together in war and in the
peace that will follow.

As to war—our military staffs have joined
in our round table discussions, and we have
concerted our plans for the destruction of
the German forces. We have reached complete agreement as to the scope and timing
of the operations to be undertaken from the
east, west and south.

The common understanding which we have here reached guarantees that victory will be ours.

And as to peace—we are sure that our concord will win an enduring Peace. We recognize fully the supreme responsibility resting upon us and all the United Nations to make a peace which will command the goodwill of the overwhelming mass of the peoples of the world and banish the scourge and terror of war for many generations.

With our Diplomatic advisers we have surveyed the problems of the future. We shall seek the cooperation and active participation of all nations, large and small, whose peoples in heart and mind are dedicated, as are our own peoples, to the elimination of tyranny and slavery, oppression and intolerance. We will welcome them, as they may choose to come, into a world family of Democratic Nations.

No power on earth can prevent our destroying the German armies by land, their U Boats by sea, and their war plants from the air.

Our attack will be relentless and increasing.

Emerging from these cordial conferences we look with confidence to the day when all peoples of the world may live free lives, untouched by tyranny, and according to their varying desires and their own consciences.

We came here with hope and determination. We leave here, friends in fact, in spirit and in purpose.

ROOSEVELT, CHURCHILL and STALIN

Declaration of the Three Powers Regarding Iran

(This declaration was published Dec. 7, 1943.)

The President of the United States, the Premier of the U.S.S.R. and the Prime Minister of the United Kingdom, having consulted with each other and with the Prime Minister of Iran, desire to declare the mutual agreement of their three Governments regarding their relations with Iran.

The Governments of the United States, the U.S.S.R. and the United Kingdom recognize the assistance which Iran has given in the prosecution of the war against the common enemy, particularly by facilitating the transportation of supplies from overseas to the Soviet Union.

The three Governments realize that the war has caused special economic difficulties for Iran, and they are agreed that they will continue to make available to the Government of Iran such economic assistance as may be possible, having regard to the heavy demands made upon them by their worldwide military operations and to the worldwide shortage of transport, raw materials and supplies for civilian consumption.

With respect to the post-war period, the Governments of the United States, the U.S.S.R. and the United Kingdom are in accord with the Government of Iran that any economic problems confronting Iran at the close of hostilities should receive full consideration, along with those of other members of the United Nations, by conferences or international agencies held or created to deal with international economic matters.

The Governments of the United States, the U.S.S.R and the United Kingdom are at one with the Government of Iran in their desire for the maintenance of the independence, sovereignty and territorial integrity of Iran. They count upon the participation of Iran, together with all other peace-loving nations, in the establishment of international peace, security and prosperity after the war, in accordance with the principles of the Atlantic Charter, to which all four Governments have subscribed.

WINSTON S. CHURCHILL
JOSEPH V. STALIN
FRANKLIN D. ROOSEVELT

Washington, March 24, 1947—The text of the military and other conclusions reached at the Teheran conference, as announced today by the State Department:

The conference:

(1) Agreed that the partisans in Yugoslavia should be supported by supplies and equipment to the greatest possible extent, and also by Commando operations;

(2) Agreed that, from the military point of view, it was most desirable that Turkey should come into the war on the side of the Allies before the end of the year;

(3) Took note of Marshal Stalin's statement that if Turkey found herself at war with Germany, and as a result Bulgaria declared war on Turkey or attacked her, the Soviet would immediately be at war with Bulgaria. The conference further took note that this fact could be explicitly stated in the forthcoming negotiations to bring Turkey into the war;

(4) Took note that Operation Overlord [the landings in Normandy] would be launched during May, 1944, in conjunction with an operation against southern France. The latter operation would be undertaken in as great a strength as availability of landing craft permitted. The conference further took note of Marshal Stalin's statement that

the Soviet forces would launch an offensive at about the same time with the object of preventing the German forces from transferring from the eastern to the western front;

(5) Agreed that the military staffs of the three powers should henceforward keep in close touch with each other in regard to the impending operations in Europe. In particular it was agreed that a cover plan to mystify and mislead the enemy as regards these operations should be concerted between the staffs concerned.

FRANKLIN D. ROOSEVELT
JOSEPH V. STALIN
WINSTON S. CHURCHILL

Teheran, December 1, 1943.

555. AN ECONOMIC BILL OF RIGHTS
January 11, 1944

(The Public Papers of F. D. Roosevelt, Vol. 13, p. 32)

President Roosevelt's annual message to Congress in 1944 was especially notable for his espousal of the new bill of rights.

If ever there was a time to subordinate individual or group selfishness to the national good, that time is now. Disunity at home—bickerings, self-seeking partisanship, stoppages of work, inflation, business as usual, politics as usual, luxury as usual—these are the influences which can undermine the morale of the brave men ready to die at the front for us here.

Those who are doing most of the complaining are not deliberately striving to sabotage the national war effort. They are laboring under the delusion that the time is past when we must make prodigious sacrifices—that the war is already won and we can begin to slacken off. But the dangerous folly of that point of view can be measured by the distance that separates our troops from their ultimate objectives in Berlin and Tokyo—and by the sum of all the perils that lie

along the way.

Let us remember the lessons of 1918. In the summer of that year the tide turned in favor of the Allies. But this Government did not relax. In fact, our national effort was stepped up. In August, 1918, the draft age limits were broadened from 21-31 to 18-45. The President called for "force to the utmost," and his call was heeded. And in November, only three months later, Germany surrendered.

That is the way to fight and win a war—all out—and not with half-an-eye on the battlefronts abroad and the other eye-and-a-half on personal, selfish, or political interests here at home.

Therefore, in order to concentrate all our energies and resources on winning the war, and to maintain a fair and stable economy at home, I recommend that the Congress adopt:

1. A realistic tax law—which will tax all unreasonable profits, both individual and corporate, and reduce the ultimate cost of the war to our sons and daughters. The tax bill now under consideration by the Congress does not begin to meet this test.

2. A continuation of the law for the renegotiation of war contracts—which will pre-

vent exorbitant profits and assure fair prices to the Government. For two long years I have pleaded with the Congress to take undue profits out of the war.

3. A cost of food law—which will enable the Government (a) to place a reasonable floor under the prices the farmer may expect for his production, and (b) to place a ceiling on the prices a consumer will have to pay for the food he buys. This should apply to necessities only; and will require public funds to carry out. It will cost in appropriations about 1 per cent of the present annual cost of the war.

4. Early enactment of the stabilization statute of October, 1942. This expires June 30, 1944, and if it is not extended well in advance the country might just as well expect price chaos by summer. We cannot have stabilization by wishful thinking. We must take positive action to maintain the integrity of the American dollar.

5. A national service law—which, for the duration of the war, will prevent strikes, and with certain appropriate exceptions, will make available for war production or for any other essential services every able-bodied adult in the nation.

These five measures together form a just and equitable whole. I would not recommend a national service law unless the other laws were passed to keep down the cost of living, to share equitably the burdens of taxation, to hold the stabilization line, and to prevent undue profits.

The Federal Government already has the basic power to draft capital and property of all kinds for war purposes on a basis of just compensation.

As you know, I have for three years hesitated to recommend a national service act. Today, however, I am convinced of its necessity. Although I believe that we and our Allies can win the war without such a measure, I am certain that nothing less than total mobilization of all our resources of manpower and capital will guarantee an earlier victory, and reduce the toll of suffering and sorrow and blood.

I have received a joint recommendation for this law from the heads of the War Department, the Navy Department, and the Maritime Commission. These are the men who bear responsibility for the procurement of the necessary arms and equipment, and for the successful prosecution of the war in the field. They say:

When the very life of the nation is in peril the responsibility for service is common to all men and women. In such a time there can be no discrimination between the men and women who are assigned by the Government to its defense at the battle front and the men and women assigned to produce the vital materials essential to successful military operations. A prompt enactment of a national service law would be merely an expression of the universality of this responsibility.

It is our duty now to begin to lay plans and determine the strategy for the winning of a lasting peace and the establishment of an American standard of living higher than ever before known. We cannot be content, no matter how high the general standard of living may be, if some fraction of our people—whether it be one-third or one-fifth or one-tenth—is ill-fed, ill-clothed, ill-housed, and insecure.

This Republic had its beginning, and grew to its present strength, under the protection of certain inalienable political rights—among them the right of free speech, free press, free worship, trial by jury, freedom from unreasonable searches and seizures. They were our rights to life and liberty.

As our nation has grown in size and stature, however—as our industrial economy expanded—these political rights proved inadequate to assure us equality in the pursuit of happiness.

We have come to a clear realization of the fact that true individual freedom cannot exist without economic security and independence. "Necessitous men are not free men." People who are hungry and out of a job are the stuff of which dictatorships are made.

In our day these economic truths have become accepted as self-evident. We have accepted, so to speak, a second Bill of Rights under which a new basis of security and prosperity can be established for all, regaurdless of station, race or creed.

Among these are:

The right to a useful and remunerative

job in the industries or shops or farms or mines of the nation;

The right to earn enough to provide adequate food and clothing and recreation;

The right of every farmer to raise and sell his products at a return which will give him and his family a decent living;

The right of every business man, large and small, to trade in an atmosphere of freedom from unfair competition and domination by monopolies at home or abroad;

The right of every family to a decent home;

The right to adequate medical care and the opportunity to achieve and enjoy good health;

The right to adequate protection from the economic fears of old age, sickness, accident and unemployment;

The right to a good education.

All of these rights spell security. And after this war is won we must be prepared to move forward, in the implementation of these rights, to new goals of human happiness and well-being.

America's own rightful place in the world depends in large part upon how fully these and similar rights have been carried into practice for our citizens. For unless there is security here at home there cannot be lasting peace in the world.

FRANKLIN D. ROOSEVELT

THE WHITE HOUSE,
January 11, 1944.

556. SMITH v. ALLWRIGHT
321 U. S. 649
1944

Lonnie E. Smith, a Negro citizen, brought action against S. E. Allwright, Election Judge of the Forty-eighth Precinct of Harris County, Texas, and his assistant, in the United States District Court for the Southern District of Texas, contending that he was denied a ballot in the Democratic primaries in Texas solely on the grounds of his race. His petition was denied and the Circuit Court, basing its action on Grovey v. Townsend, upheld the District Court. This decision overruled Grovey v. Townsend (295 U.S. 45), and the Court in this case took occasion to rehearse the history of judicial reversals and to reject the doctrine of *stare decisis* in the realm of Constitutional law. See Doc. and bibliography in U.S. v. Classic; R. E. Cushman, "The Texas 'White Primary' Case—Smith v. Allwright," 30 *Cornell L. Quart.*, pp. 66 ff.; F. E. Folsom, "Federal Elections and the 'White Primary,'" 33 *Col. L. Rev.*, pp. 1086 ff.; Stevenson, *Race Distinctions in American Law.*

On writ of Certiorari to the United States Circuit Court of Appeals for the Fifth Circuit.

REED, J. . . . The State of Texas by its Constitution and statutes provides that every person, if certain other requirements are met which are not here in issue, qualified by residence in the district or county "shall be deemed a qualified elector." Primary elections for United States Senators, Congressmen and state officers are provided for by Chapters Twelve and Thirteen of the statutes. Under these chapters, the Democratic Party was required to hold the primary which was the occasion of the alleged wrong to petitioned. . . . These nominations are to be made by the qualified voters of the party.

The Democratic Party of Texas is held by the Supreme Court of that state to be a "voluntary association," protected by Section 27 of the Bill of Rights, Art. 1, Constitution of Texas, from interference by the state except that:

"In the interest of fair methods and a fair expression by their members of their preferences in the selection of their nominees, the State may regulate such elections by proper laws."

The Democratic party on May 24, 1932 in a State Convention adopted the following resolution, which has not since been "amended, abrogated, annulled or avoided":

"Be it resolved that all white citizens of the State of Texas who are qualified to vote under the Constitution and laws of the State shall be eligible to membership in the Democratic party and, as such, entitled to participate in its deliberations."

It was by virtue of this resolution that the respondents refused to permit the petitioner to vote.

Texas is free to conduct her elections and limit her electorate as she may deem wise, save only as her action may be affected by the prohibitions of the United States Constitution or in conflict with powers delegated to and exercised by the National Government. The Fourteenth Amendment forbids a state from making or enforcing any law which abridges the privileges or immunities of citizens of the United States and the Fifteenth Amendment specifically interdicts any denial or abridgement by a state of the right of citizens to vote on account of color. Respondents appeared in the District Court and the Circuit Court of Appeals and defended on the ground that the Democratic party of Texas is a voluntary organization with members banded together for the purpose of selecting individuals of the group representing the common political beliefs as candidates in the general election. As such a voluntary organization, it was claimed, the Democratic party is free to select its own membership and limit to whites participation in the party primary. Such action, the answer asserted, does not violate the Fourteenth, Fifteenth or Seventeenth Amendments as officers of government cannot be chosen at primaries and the Amendments are applicable only to general elections where governmental officers are actually elected. Primaries, it is said, are political party affairs, handled by party not governmental officers.

The right of a Negro to vote in the Texas primary has been considered heretofore by this Court. Since Grovey v. Townsend and prior to the present suit, no case from Texas involving primary elections has been before this Court. We did decide, however, United States v. Classic. We there held that Section 4 of Article I of the Constitution authorized Congress to regulate primary as well as general elections, "where the primary is by law made an integral part of the election machinery." Consequently, in the Classic case, we upheld the applicability to frauds in a Louisiana primary of §§ 19 and 20 of the Criminal Code. Thereby corrupt acts of election officers were subjected to Congressional sanctions because that body had power to protect rights of Federal suffrage secured by the Constitution in primary as in general elections. This decision depended, too, on the determination that under the Louisiana statutes the primary was a part of the procedure for choice of Federal officials. By this decision the doubt as to whether or not such primaries were a part of "elections" subject to Federal control, which had remained unanswered since Newberry v. United States, was erased. The Nixon cases were decided under the equal protection clause of the Fourteenth Amendment without a determination of the status of the primary as a part of the electoral process. The exclusion of Negroes from the primaries by action of the State was held invalid under that Amendment. The fusing by the Classic case of the primary and general elections into a single instrumentality for choice of officers has a definite bearing on the permissibility under the Constitution of excluding Negroes from primaries. This is not to say that the Classic case cuts directly into the rationale of Grovey v. Townsend. This latter case was not mentioned in the opinion. Classic bears upon Grovey v. Townsend not because exclusion of Negroes from primaries is any more or less state action by reason of the unitary character of the electoral process but because the recognition of the place of the primary in the electoral scheme makes clear that state delegation to a party of the power to fix the qualifications of primary elections is delegation of a state function that may make the party's action the action of the state. When Grovey v. Townsend was written, the Court looked upon the denial of a vote in a primary as a mere refusal by a party of party membership. As the Louisiana statutes for holding primaries are similar to those of Texas, our ruling in Classic as to the unitary character of the electoral process calls for a reëxamination as to whether or not the exclusion of Negroes from a Texas party primary was state action.

It may now be taken as a postulate that the right to vote in such a primary for the nomination of candidates without discrimination by the State, like the right to vote in a general election, is a right secured by the Constitution.

We are thus brought to an examination

of the qualifications for Democratic primary electors in Texas, to determine whether state action or private action has excluded Negroes from participation.

We think that this statutory system for the selection of party nominees for inclusion on the general election ballot makes the party which is required to follow these legislative directions an agency of the state in so far as it determines the participants in a primary election. The party takes its character as a state agency from the duties imposed upon it by state statutes; the duties do not become matters of private law because they are performed by a political party. The plan of the Texas primary follows substantially that of Louisiana, with the exception that in Louisiana the state pays the cost of the primary while Texas assesses the cost against candidates. In numerous instances, the Texas statutes fix or limit the fees to be charged. Whether paid directly by the state or through state requirements, it is state action which compels. When primaries become a part of the machinery for choosing officials, state and national, as they have here, the same tests to determine the character of discrimination or abridgement should be applied to the primary as are applied to the general election. If the state requires a certain electoral procedure, prescribes a general election ballot made up of party nominees so chosen and limits the choice of the electorate in general elections for state offices, practically speaking, to those whose names appear on such a ballot, it endorses, adopts and enforces the discrimination against Negroes, practiced by a party entrusted by Texas law with the determination of the qualifications of participants in the primary. This is state action within the meaning of the Fifteenth Amendment.

The United States is a constitutional democracy. Its organic law grants to all citizens a right to participate in the choice of elected officials without restriction by any state because of race. This grant to the people of the opportunity for choice is not to be nullified by a state through casting its electoral process in a form which permits a private organization to practice racial discrimination in the election. Constitutional rights would be of little value if they could be thus indirectly denied.

The privilege of membership in a party may be, as this Court said in Grovey v. Townsend, no concern of a state. But when, as here, that privilege is also the essential qualification for voting in a primary to select nominees for a general election, the state makes the action of the party the action of the state. In reaching this conclusion we are not unmindful of the desirability of continuity of decision in constitutional questions. However, when convinced of former error, this Court has never felt constrained to follow precedent. In constitutional questions, where correction depends upon amendment and not upon legislative action this Court throughout its history has freely exercised its power to reëxamine the basis of its constitutional decisions. This has long been accepted practice, and this practice has continued to this day. This is particularly true when the decision believed erroneous is the application of a constitutional principle rather than an interpretation of the Constitution to extract the principle itself. Here we are applying, contrary to the recent decision in Grovey v. Townsend, the well established principle of the Fifteenth Amendment, forbidding the abridgement by a state of a citizen's right to vote. Grovey v. Townsend is overruled.

Judgment reversed.

557. YALTA (CRIMEA) CONFERENCE
February, 1945

(New York Times, March 15, 1945)

By February, 1945, the Allies had assumed the offensive once more in Europe. It was important for the Big Three to meet again to determine a program for the occupation of Germany, to discuss further plans for the new world organization, and to resolve political conflicts. The division of Europe into military spheres had resulted in political friction among the great powers, particularly in respect to unilateral action by Russia in Poland and by Britain in Greece. From February 4 to 11, 1945, the Big Three leaders, Roosevelt, Churchill, and Stalin, met for the second and last time in the summer palace of Czar Nicholas II near Yalta on the southern shore of the Crimean peninsula. Among important matters discussed were the Polish question, voting procedure in the Security Council of the new international organization, and the formation of democratic governments in Axis satellite nations. Probably the most important single result of the Yalta discussions was the calling of the San Francisco Conference to set up the new international organization. Important sections of the agreements were not made public until March 1947. See J. F. Byrnes, *Speaking Frankly;* W. S. Churchill, *Triumph and Tragedy;* J. R. Deane, *The Strange Alliance;* E. R. Stettinius, *Roosevelt and the Russians: The Yalta Conference;* F. O. Wilcox, "The Yalta Voting Formula," *Am. Pol. Sci. Rev.,* Vol. 39, pp. 943 ff.; L. H. Woolsey, "Poland at Yalta and Dumbarton Oaks," 39 *Am. J. Int. L.,* pp. 295 ff.

Washington, March 24—The text of the agreements reached at the Crimea (Yalta) Conference between President Roosevelt, Prime Minister Churchill and Generalissimo Stalin, as released by the State Department today, follows:

PROTOCOL OF PROCEEDINGS OF CRIMEA CONFERENCE

The Crimea Conference of the heads of the Governments of the United States of America, the United Kingdom, and the Union of Soviet Socialist Republics, which took place from Feb. 4 to 11, came to the following conclusions:

I. WORLD ORGANIZATION

It was decided:

1. That a United Nations conference on the proposed world organization should be summoned for Wednesday, 25 April, 1945, and should be held in the United States of America.

2. The nations to be invited to this conference should be:

(a) the United Nations as they existed on 8 Feb., 1945; and

(b) Such of the Associated Nations as have declared war on the common enemy by 1 March, 1945. (For this purpose, by the term "Associated Nations" was meant the eight Associated Nations and Turkey.) When the conference on world organization is held, the delegates of the United Kingdom and United States of America will support a proposal to admit to original membership two Soviet Socialist Republics, i.e., the Ukraine and White Russia.

3. That the United States Government, on behalf of the three powers, should consult the Government of China and the French Provisional Government in regard to decisions taken at the present conference concerning the proposed world organization.

4. That the text of the invitation to be issued to all the nations which would take part in the United Nations conference should be as follows:

"The Government of the United States of America, on behalf of itself and of the Governments of the United Kingdom, the Union of Soviet Socialistic Republics and the Republic of China and of the Provisional Government of the French Republic, invite the Government of ———— to send representatives to a conference to be held on 25 April, 1945, or soon thereafter, at San Francisco, in the United States of America, to prepare a charter for a general international organization for the maintenance of international peace and security.

"The above-named Governments suggest that the conference consider as affording a basis for such a Charter the proposals for the establishment of a general international organization which were made public last October as a result of the Dumbarton Oaks conference and which have now been supplemented by the following provisions for Section C of Chapter VI:

C. *Voting*

"1. Each member of the Security Council should have one vote.

" '2. Decisions of the Security Council on procedural matters should be made by an affirmative vote of seven members.

" '3. Decisions of the Security Council on all matters should be made by an affirmative vote of seven members, including the concurring votes of the permanent members; provided that, in decisions under Chapter VIII, Section A and under the second sentence of Paragraph 1 of Chapter VIII, Section C, a party to a dispute should abstain from voting.'

"Further information as to arrangements will be transmitted subsequently.

"In the event that the Government of ———— desires in advance of the conference to present views or comments concerning the proposals, the Government of the United States of America will be pleased to transmit such views and comments to the other participating Governments."

Territorial trusteeship:

It was agreed that the five nations which will have permanent seats on the Security Council should consult each other prior to the United Nations conference on the question of territorial trusteeship.

The acceptance of this recommendation is subject to its being made clear that territorial trusteeship will only apply to (a) existing mandates of the League of Nations; (b) territories detached from the enemy as a result of the present war; (c) any other territory which might voluntarily be placed under trusteeship; and (d) no discussion of actual territories is contemplated at the forthcoming United Nations conference or in the preliminary consulations, and it will be a matter for subsequent agreement which territories within the above categories will be placed under trusteeship.

[*The section from this point to the next italicized note was published Feb. 13, 1945.*]

II. DECLARATION ON LIBERATED EUROPE

The following declaration has been approved:

The Premier of the Union of Soviet Socialist Republics, the Prime Minister of the United Kingdom and the President of the United States of America have consulted with each other in the common interests of the peoples of their countries and those of liberated Europe. They jointly declare their mutual agreement to concert during the temporary period of instability in liberated Europe the policies of their three Governments in assisting the peoples liberated from the domination of Nazi Germany and the peoples of the former Axis satellite states of Europe to solve by democratic means their pressing political and economic problems.

The establishment of order in Europe and the rebuilding of national economic life must be achieved by processes which will enable the liberated peoples to destroy the last vestiges of nazism and fascism and to create democratic institutions of their own choice. This is a principle of the Atlantic Charter—the right of all peoples to choose the form of government under which they will live—the restoration of sovereign rights and self-government to those peoples who have been forcibly deprived of them by the aggressor nations.

To foster the conditions in which the liberated peoples may exercise these rights, the three Governments will jointly assist the people in any European liberated state or former Axis satellite state in Europe where, in their judgment conditions require, (a) to establish conditions of internal peace; (b) to carry out emergency measures for the relief of distressed peoples; (c) to form interim governmental authorities broadly representative of all democratic elements in the population and pledged to the earliest possible establishment through free elections of Governments responsive to the will of the people; and (d) to facilitate where necessary the holding of such elections.

The three Governments will consult the other United Nations and provisional authorities or other Governments in Europe when matters of direct interest to them are under consideration.

When, in the opinion of the three Governments, conditions in any European liberated state or any former Axis satellite state in Europe make such action necessary, they will immediately consult together on the measures necessary to discharge the joint responsibilities set forth in this declaration.

By this declaration we reaffirm our faith in the principles of the Atlantic Charter, our pledge in the Declaration by the United Nations and our determination to build in cooperation with other peace-loving nations world order, under law, dedicated to peace, security, freedom and general well-being of all mankind.

In issuing this declaration, the three powers express the hope that the Provisional Government of the French Republic may be associated with them in the procedure suggested.

[*Here ends the previously published part of this section of the agreements.*]

III. DISMEMBERMENT OF GERMANY

It was agreed that Article 12 (a) of the Surrender Terms for Germany should be amended to read as follows:

"The United Kingdom, the United States of America and the Union of Soviet Socialist Republics shall possess supreme authority with respect to Germany. In the exercise of such authority they will take such steps, including the complete disarmament, demilitarization and dismemberment of Germany as they deem requisite for future peace and security."

The study of the procedure of the dismemberment of Germany was referred to a committee consisting of Mr. [Anthony] Eden [their Foreign Secretary] (chairman), Mr. [John] Winant [of the United States] and Mr. [Fedor T.] Gusev. This body would consider the desirability of associating with it a French representative.

IV. ZONE OF OCCUPATION FOR THE FRENCH AND CONTROL COUNCIL FOR GERMANY

It was agreed that a zone in Germany, to be occupied by the French forces, should be allocated to France. This zone would be formed out of the British and American zones and its extent would be settled by the British and Americans in consultation with the French Provisional Government.

It was also agreed that the French Provisional Government should be invited to become a member of the Allied Control Council for Germany.

V. REPARATION

The following protocol has been approved:

Protocol

On the Talks Between the Heads of Three Governments at the Crimean Conference on the Question of the German Reparations in Kind

1. Germany must pay in kind for the losses caused by her to the Allied nations in the course of the war. Reparations are to be received in the first instance by those countries which have borne the main burden of the war, have suffered the heaviest losses and have organized victory over the enemy.

2. Reparations in kind is to be exacted from Germany in three following forms:

(a) Removals within two years from the surrender of Germany or the cessation of organized resistance from the national wealth of Germany located on the territory of Germany herself as well as outside her territory (equipment, machine tools, ships, rolling stock, German investments abroad, shares of industrial, transport and other enterprises in Germany, etc.), these removals to be carried out chiefly for the purpose of destroying the war potential of Germany.

(b) Annual deliveries of goods from current production for a period to be fixed.

(c) Use of German labor.

3. For the working out on the above principles of a detailed plan for exaction of reparation from Germany an Allied reparations commission will be set up in Moscow. It will consist of three representatives—one from the Union of Soviet Socialist Republics, one from the United Kingdom and one from the United States of America.

4. With regard to the fixing of the total sum of the reparation as well as the distribution of it among the countries which suffered from the German aggression, the Soviet and American delegations agreed as follows:

"The Moscow reparation commission should take in its initial studies as a basis for discussion the suggestion of the Soviet Government that the total sum of the reparation in accordance with the points (a) and (b) of the Paragraph 2 should be 20 billion dollars and that 50 per cent of it should go to the Union of Soviet Socialist Republics."

The British delegation was of the opinion that, pending consideration of the reparation question by the Moscow reparation commission, no figures of reparation should be mentioned.

The above Soviet-American proposal has been passed to the Moscow reparation commission as one of the proposals to be considered by the commission.

VI. MAJOR WAR CRIMINALS

The conference agreed that the question of the major war criminals should be the subject of inquiry by the three Foreign Secretaries for report in due course after the close of the conference.

[*The section from this point to the next italicized note was published Feb. 13, 1945.*]

VII. POLAND

The following declaration on Poland was agreed by the conference:

"A new situation has been created in Poland as a result of her complete liberation by the Red Army. This calls for the establishment of a Polish Provisional Government which can be more broadly based than was possible before the recent liberation of the western part of Poland. The Provisional Government which is now functioning in Poland should therefore be reorganized on a broader democratic basis with the inclusion of democratic leaders from Poland itself and from Poles abroad. This new Government should then be ·called the Polish Provisional Government of National Unity.

"M. Molotov, Mr. Harriman and Sir A. Clark Kerr are authorized as a commission to consult in the first instance in Moscow with members of the present Provisional Government and with other Polish democratic leaders from within Poland and from abroad, with a view to the reorganization of the present Government along the above lines. This Polish Provisional Government of National Unity shall be pledged to the holding of free and unfettered elections as soon as possible on the basis of universal suffrage and secret ballot. In these elections all democratic and anti-Nazi parties shall have the right to take part and to put forward candidates.

"When a Polish Provisional Government of National Unity has been properly formed in conformity with the above, the Government of the U.S.S.R., which now maintains diplomatic relations with the present Provisional Government of Poland, and the Government of the United Kingdom and the Government of the United States of America will establish diplomatic relations with the new Polish Provisional Government of National Unity, and will exchange Ambassadors by whose reports the respective Governments will be kept informed about the situation in Poland.

"The three heads of Government consider that the eastern frontier of Poland should follow the Curzon Line with digressions from it in some regions of five to eight kilometers in favor of Poland. They recognize that Poland must receive substantial accessions of territory in the north and west. They feel that the opinion of the new Polish Provisional Government of National Unity should be sought in due course of the extent of these accessions and that the final delimitation of the western frontier of Poland should thereafter await the peace conference."

VIII. YUGOSLAVIA

It was agreed to recommend to Marshal Tito and to Dr. [Ivan] Subasitch:

(a) That the Tito-Subasitch agreement should immediately be put into effect and a new Government formed on the basis of the agreement.

(b) That as soon as the new Government has been formed it should declare:

(I) That the Anti-Fascist Assembly of the National Liberation (AVNOJ) will be extended to include members of the last Yugoslav Skupstina who have not compromised themselves by collaboration with the enemy, thus forming a body to be known as a temporary Parliament and

(II) That legislative acts passed by the Anti-Fascist Assembly of National Liberation (AVNOJ) will be subject to subsequent ratification by a Constituent Assembly; and that this statement should be published in the communiqué of the conference.

[*Here ends the previously published section of the agreements.*]

IX. ITALO-YUGOSLAV FRONTIER— ITALO-AUSTRIAN FRONTIER

Notes on these subjects were put in by

the British delegation, and the American and Soviet delegations agreed to consider them and give their views later.

X. YUGOSLAV-BULGARIAN RELATIONS

There was an exchange of views between the Foreign Secretaries on the question of the desirability of a Yugoslav-Bulgarian pact of alliance. The question at issue was whether a state still under an armistice regime could be allowed to enter into a treaty with another state. Mr. Eden suggested that the Bulgarian and Yugoslav Governments should be informed that this could not be approved. Mr. Stettinius suggested that the British and American Ambassadors should discuss the matter further with Mr. Molotov in Moscow. Mr. Molotov agreed with the proposal of Mr. Stettinius.

XI. SOUTHEASTERN EUROPE

The British delegation put in notes for the consideration of their colleagues on the following subjects:

(a) The Control Commission in Bulgaria.

(b) Greek claims upon Bulgaria, more particularly with reference to reparations.

(c) Oil equipment in Rumania.

XII. IRAN

Mr. Eden, Mr. Stettinius and Mr. Molotov exchanged views on the situation in Iran. It was agreed that this matter should be pursued through the diplomatic channel.

[*The section from this point to the next italicized note was published Feb. 13, 1945.*]

XIII. MEETINGS OF THE THREE FOREIGN SECRETARIES

The conference agreed that permanent machinery should be set up for consultation between the three Foreign Secretaries; they should meet as often as necessary, probably about every three or four months.

These meetings will be held in rotation in the three capitals, the first meeting being held in London.

[*Here ends the previously published section of the agreements.*]

XIV. THE MONTREUX CONVENTION AND THE STRAITS

It was agreed that at the next meeting of the three Foreign Secretaries to be held in London, they should consider proposals which it was understood the Soviet Government would put forward in relation to the Montreaux Convention, and report to their Governments. The Turkish Government should be informed at the appropriate moment.

The foregoing protocol was approved and signed by the three Foreign Secretaries at the Crimean Conference Feb. 11, 1945.

E. R. STETTINIUS JR.
M. MOLOTOV
ANTHONY EDEN

AGREEMENT REGARDING JAPAN

The leaders of the three great powers—the Soviet Union, the United States of America and Great Britain—have agreed that in two or three months after Germany has surrendered and the war in Europe has terminated, the Soviet Union shall enter into the war against Japan on the side of the Allies on condition that;

1. The status quo in Outer Mongolia (the Mongolian People's Republic) shall be preserved;

2. The former rights of Russia violated by the treacherous attack of Japan in 1904 shall be restored, viz.:

(a) The southern part of Sakhalin as well as the islands adjacent to it shall be returned to the Soviet Union;

(b) The commercial port of Dairen shall be internationalized, the pre-eminent interests of the Soviet Union in this port being safeguarded, and the lease of Port Arthur as a naval base of the U.S.S.R. restored;

(c) The Chinese-Eastern Railroad and the South Manchurian Railroad, which provide an outlet to Dairen, shall be jointly operated by the establishment of a joint Soviet-Chinese company, it being understood that the pre-eminent interests of the Soviet Union shall be safeguarded and that China shall retain full sovereignty in Manchuria;

3. The Kurile Islands shall be handed over to the Soviet Union.

It is understood that the agreement concerning Outer Mongolia and the ports and railroads referred to above will require concurrence of Generalissimo Chiang Kai-shek. The President will take measures in order to obtain this concurrence on advice from Marshal Stalin.

The heads of the three great powers have agreed that these claims of the Soviet Union shall be unquestionably fulfilled after Japan has been defeated.

For its part, the Soviet Union expresses its readiness to conclude with the National Government of China a pact of friendship and alliance between the U.S.S.R. and China in order to render assistance to China with its armed forces for the purpose of liberating China from the Japanese yoke.

JOSEPH V. STALIN
FRANKLIN D. ROOSEVELT
WINSTON S. CHURCHILL

February 11, 1945.

558. THE ACT OF CHAPULTEPEC
March 6, 1945

(Congressional Record, March 12, 1945, p. 2058)

Senator Connally, as American delegate to the Inter-American Conference on the Problems of the War, observed that the Act of Chapultepec was an adoption by the Latin American States of a multilateral policy of the Monroe Doctrine. The essence of it was the agreement that any attack against the territorial integrity or sovereignty of an American state should be considered an act of aggression against the other states signing the Pact. For background, see Docs. 521, 526, 534, and A. Whitaker, *The Western Hemisphere Idea.*

Part I. The Governments Represented at the Inter-American Conference on Problems of War and Peace Declare:

1. That all sovereign States are juridically equal among themselves.

2. That every State has the right to the respect of its individuality and independence, on the part of the other members of the international community.

3. That every attack of a State against the integrity or the inviolability of the territory, or against the sovereignty or political independence of an American State, shall, conformably to Part III hereof, be considered as an act of aggression against the other States which sign this Act. In any case invasion by armed forces of one State into the territory of another trespassing boundaries established by treaty and demarcated in accordance therewith shall constitute an act of aggression.

4. That in case acts of aggression occur or there are reasons to believe that an aggression is being prepared by any other State against the integrity or inviolability of the territory, or against the sovereignty or political independence of an American State, the States signatory to this Act will consult among themselves in order to agree upon the measures it may be advisable to take.

5. That during the war, and until the treaty recommended in Part II hereof is concluded, the signatories of this Act recognize that such threats and acts of aggression, as indicated in paragraphs 3 and 4 above, constitute an interference with the war effort of the United Nations, calling for such procedures, within the scope of their constitutional powers of a general nature and for war, as may be found necessary, including: recall of chiefs of diplomatic missions; breaking of diplomatic relations; breaking of consular relations; breaking of postal, telegraphic, telephonic, radio-telephonic relations; interruption of economic, commercial and financial relations; use of armed force to prevent or repel aggression.

6. That the principles and procedure contained in this Declaration shall become effective immediately, inasmuch as any act of aggression or threat of aggression during the present state of war interferes with the war effort of the United Nations to obtain victory. Henceforth, and to the end that principles and procedures herein stipulated shall conform with the constitutional processes of each Republic, the respective Governments shall take the necessary steps to perfect this instrument in order that it shall be in force at all times.

Part II. The Inter-American Conference on Problems of War and Peace *Recom-*

mends:

That for the purpose of meeting threats or acts of aggression against any American Republic following the establishment of peace, the Governments of the American Republics consider the conclusion, in accordance with their constitutional processes, of a treaty establishing procedures whereby such threats or acts may be met by the use, by all or some of the signatories of said treaty, of any one or more of the following measures: recall of chiefs of diplomatic missions; breaking of diplomatic relations; breaking of consular relations; breaking of postal, telegraphic, telephonic, radio-tele-phonic relations; interruption of economic, commercial and financial relations; use of armed force to prevent or repel aggression.

Part III. The above Declaration and Recommendation constitute a regional arrangement for dealing with such matters relating to the maintenance of international peace and security as are appropriate for regional action in this Hemisphere. The said arrangement, and the pertinent activities and procedures, shall be consistent with the purposes and principles of the general international organization, when established.

This agreement shall be known as the *"Act of Chapultepec."*

559. NEW YORK STATE ANTI-DISCRIMINATION ACT
March 12, 1945
(Laws of New York, Chapter 118)

Although a long struggle was waged in Congress for a federal anti-discrimination act, the principle was succesful only in the states. See A. Wilson "The Proposed Legislative Knell of Private Discriminatory Practices," 31 *Va. L. Rev.*, pp. 798 ff.; R. C. Weaver, *Negro Labor;* H. R. Bernhardt, "The Right to a Job," 29 *Corn. L. Quart.*, pp. 489 ff.; H. R. Cayton and G. S. Mitchell, *Black Workers and the New Unions.*

An act to amend the executive law, in relation to prevention and elimination of practices of discrimination in employment and otherwise against persons because of race, creed, color or national origin, . . .

§ 125. *Purposes of article.* This article shall be known as the "Law Against Discrimination." It shall be deemed an exercise of the police power of the state for the protection of the public welfare, health and peace of the people of this state, and in fulfillment of the provisions of the constitution of this state concerning civil rights; and the legislature ·hereby finds and declares that practices of discrimination against any of its inhabitants because of race, creed, color or national origin are a matter of state concern, that such discrimination threatens not only the rights and proper privileges of its inhabitants but menaces the institutions and foundation of a free democratic state. A state agency is hereby created with power to eliminate and prevent discrimination in employment because of race, creed, color or national origin, either by employers, labor organizations, employment agencies or other persons, and to take other actions against discrimination because of race, creed, color or national origin, as herein provided; and the commission established hereunder is hereby given general jurisdicition and power for such purposes.

§ 126. *Opportunity for employment without discrimination a civil right.* The opportunity to obtain employment without discrimination because of race, creed, color or national origin is hereby recognized as and declared to be a civil right.

§ 128. *State commission against discrimination.* There is hereby created in the executive department a state commission against discrimination. Such commission shall consist of five members, to be known as commissioners, who shall be appointed by the governor, by and with the advice and consent of the senate, and one of whom shall be designated as chairman by the governor. The term of office of each member of the commission shall be for five years, provided, however, that of the commissioners first appointed, one shall be appointed for a term of one year, one for a term of two years, one for a term of three years, one for a term of four years, and one for a term of five years.

Each member of the commission shall receive a salary of ten thousand dollars a year. . . .

§ 129. *General policies of commission.* The commission shall formulate policies to effectuate the purposes of this article and may make recommendations to agencies and officers of the state or local subdivisions of government in aid of such policies and purposes.

§ 130. *General powers and duties of commission.* The commission shall have the following functions, powers and duties: 1. To establish and maintain its principal office in the city of Albany, and such other offices within the state as it may deem necessary.

5. To adopt, promulgate, amend, and rescind suitable rules and regulations to carry out the provisions of this article, and the policies and practice of the commission in connection therewith.

6. To receive, investigate and pass upon complaints alleging discrimination in employment because of race, creed, color or national origin.

7. To hold hearings, subpoena witnesses, compel their attendance, administer oaths, take the testimony of any person under oath, and in connection therewith, to require the production for examination of any books or papers relating to any matter under investigation or in question before the commission. The commission may make rules as to the issuance of subpoenas by individual commissioners.

8. To create such advisory agencies and conciliation councils, local, regional or statewide, as in its judgment will aid in effectuating the purposes of this article and of section eleven of article one of the constitution of this state, and the commission may empower them to study the problems of discrimination in all or specific fields of human relationships or in specific instances of discrimination because of race, creed, color or national origin, and to foster through community effort or otherwise good-will, cooperation and conciliation among the groups and elements of the population of the state, and make recommendations to the commission for the development of policies and procedures in general and in specific instances, and for programs of formal and informal education which the commission may recommend to the appropriate state agency. Such advisory agencies and conciliation councils shall be composed of representative citizens, serving without pay, but with reimbursement for actual and necessary traveling expenses; and the commission may make provision for technical and clerical assistance to such agencies and councils and for the expenses of such assistance.

9. To issue such publications and such results of investigations and research as in its judgment will tend to promote good-will and minimize or eliminate discrimination because of race, creed, color or national origin.

10. To render each year to the governor and to the legislature a full written report of all its activities and of its recommendations.

§ 131. *Unlawful employment practices.* It shall be an unlawful employment practice: 1. For an employer, because of the race, creed, color or national origin of any individual, to refuse to hire or employ or to bar or to discharge from employment such individual or to discriminate against such individual in compensation or in terms, conditions or privileges of employment.

2. For a labor organization, because of the race, creed, color or national origin of any individual, to exclude or to expel from its membership such individual or to discriminate in any way against any of its members or against any employer or any individual employed by an employer.

3. For any employer or employment agency to print or circulate or cause to be printed or circulated any statement, advertisement or publication, or to use any form of application for employment or to make any inquiry in connection with prospective employment, which expresses, directly or indirectly, any limitation, specification or discrimination as to race, creed, color or national origin, or any intent to make any such limitation, specification or discrimination, unless based upon a bona fide occupational

qualification.

4. For any employer, labor organization or employment agency to discharge, expel or otherwise discriminate against any person because he has opposed any practices forbidden under this article or because he has filed a complaint, testified or assisted in any proceeding under this article.

5. For any person, whether an employer or an employee or not, to aid, abet, incite, compel or coerce the doing of any of the acts forbidden under this article, or to attempt to do so.

§ 132. *Procedure.* Any person claiming to be aggrieved by an alleged unlawful employment practice may, by himself or his attorney-at-law, make, sign and file with the commission a verified complaint in writing which shall state the name and address of the person, employer, labor organization or employment agency alleged to have committed the unlawful employment practice complained of and which shall set forth the particulars thereof and contain such other information as may be required by the commission. The industrial commissioner or attorney-general may, in like manner, make, sign and file such complaint. Any employer whose employees, or some of them, refuse or threaten to refuse to cooperate with the provisions of this article, may file with the commission a verified complaint asking for assistance by conciliation or other remedial action. . . .

§ 135. *Construction.* The provisions of this article shall be construed liberally for the accomplishment of the purposes thereof.

560. BRIDGES v. WIXON
326 U. S. 135
1945

The historical background of the Bridges case is fully set forth in the concurring opinion by Justice Murphy. The opinions in this case, important in themselves, are particularly significant for the light they throw on the whole question of guilt by association. We have given here only those portions of the opinion of the Court that deal with the meaning of the baffling term "affiliation." In the summer of 1949 the government once more instituted deportation proceedings against Bridges, but was again frustrated.

Habeas corpus proceeding by Harry Bridges against I. F. Wixon, as District Director, Immigration and Naturalization Service, Department of Justice.

DOUGLAS, J. . . . The two grounds on which the deportation order rests—that Harry Bridges at one time had been both "affiliated" with the Communist party and a member of it—present different questions with which we deal separately.

. *Affiliation.* The statute defines affiliation as follows:

"For the purpose of this section: (1) the giving, loaning, or promising of money or any thing of value to be used for the advising, advocacy, or teaching of any doctrine above enumerated shall constitute the advising, advocacy, or teaching of such doctrine; and (2) the giving, loaning or promising of money or any thing of value to any organization, association, society, or group of the character above described shall constitute affiliation therewith; but nothing in this paragraph shall be taken as an exclusive definition of advising, advocacy, teaching, or affiliation." 41 Stat. 1009. The doctrine referred to is the overthrow of the government by force or violence. The organizations or groups referred to are those which advise and teach that doctrine or which write, circulate, display and the like or have in their possession for such purpose any written or printed matter of that character.

In ruling on the question whether an alien had been "affiliated" with the Communist party and therefore could be deported, the court in United States ex rel. Kettunen v. Reimer, 2 Cir., 79 F.2d 315, 317, said that such an affiliation was not proved "unless the alien is shown to have so conducted himself that he has brought about a status of mutual recognition that he may be relied on to cooperate with the Communist Party on a fairly permanent basis. He must be more than merely in sympathy with its aims or even willing to aid it in a casual intermittent way. Affiliation includes an element of dependability upon which the organization can rely which, though not equivalent to membership duty, does rest upon a course of conduct that could not be abruptly ended without giving at least reasonable cause for the charge of a breach of good faith." The same idea was expressed by Dean Landis in the first Bridges' report. After stating that "affiliation" implies a "stronger bond" than "association," he went on to say: "In the corporate field its use embraces not the casual affinity of an occasional similarity of objective, but ties and connections that, though less than that complete control which parent possesses over subsidiary, are nevertheless sufficient to create a continuing relationship that embraces both units within the concept of a system. In the field of eleemosynary and political organization the same basic idea prevails." And he concluded: "Persons engaged in bitter industrial struggles tend to seek help and assistance from every available source. But the intermittent solicitation and acceptance of such help must be shown to have ripened into those bonds of mutual cooperation and alliance that entail continuing reciprocal duties and responsibilities before they can be deemed to come within the statutory requirement of affiliation. . . . To expand that statutory definition to embrace within its terms ad hoc cooperation on objectives whose pursuit is clearly allowable under our constitutional system, or friendly associations that have not been shown to have resulted in the employment of illegal means, is warranted neither by reason nor by law."

The legislative history throws little light on the meaning of "affiliation" as used in the statute. It imports, however, less than membership but more than sympathy. By the terms of the statute it includes those who contribute money or anything of value to an organization which believes in, advises, advocates, or teaches the overthrow of our

government by force or violence. That example throws light on the meaning of the term "affiliation." He who renders financial assistance to any organization may generally be said to approve of its objectives or aims. So Congress declared in the case of an alien who contributed to the treasury of an organization whose aim was to overthrow the government by force and violence. But he who cooperates with such an organization only in its *wholly lawful activities* cannot by that fact be said as a matter of law to be "affiliated" with it. Nor is it conclusive that the cooperation was more than intermittent and showed a rather consistent course of conduct. Common sense indicates that the term "affiliation" in this setting should be construed more narrowly. Individuals, like nations, may cooperate in a common cause over a period of months or years though their ultimate aims do not coincide. Alliances for limited objectives are well known. Certainly those who joined forces with Russia to defeat the Nazis may not be said to have made an alliance to spread the cause of Communism. An individual who makes contributions to feed hungry men does not become "affiliated" with the Communist cause because those men are Communists. A different result is not necessarily indicated if aid is given to or received from a proscribed organization in order to win a legitimate objective in a domestic controversy. Whether intermittent or repeated the act or acts tending to prove "affiliation" must be of that quality which indicates an adherence to or a furtherance of the purposes or objectives of the proscribed organization as distinguished from mere cooperation with it in lawful activities. The act or acts must evidence a working alliance to bring the program to fruition.

We are satisfied that the term "affiliation" was not so construed either by Judge Sears or by the Attorney General. The reports made in this case contain no precise formulation of the standard which was employed. But the way in which the term "affiliation" was used and applied convinces us that it was given a looser and more expansive meaning than the statute permits. . . .

. . . When we turn to the facts of this case we have little more than a course of conduct which reveals cooperation with Communist groups for the attainment of wholly lawful objectives.

The associations which Harry Bridges had with various Communist groups seem to indicate no more than cooperative measures to attain objectives which were wholly legitimate. The link by which it is sought to tie him to subversive activities is an exceedingly tenuous one, if it may be said to exist at all. . . . Nor is there any finding that Bridges took over this project with the view of doing more than advancing the lawful cause of unionism. The advice to support for office certain candidates said to be Communists was based entirely on the platform on which they ran—cash relief; abolition of vagrancy laws; no evictions; gas, water and electricity for the unemployed; and unemployment relief. The advice to read Communist literature was not general; it was specifically addressed to the comparative merits of those publications and other papers on the truthfulness of labor news. The use of addresses of Communist organizations, especially stressed by the Attorney General, was said by Judge Sears to demonstrate "a close cooperation with the Communists and Communist Organizations." But close cooperation is not sufficient to establish an "affiliation" within the meaning of the statute. It must evidence a working alliance to bring the proscribed program to fruition.

It must be remembered that the Marine Workers Industrial Union was not a sham or pretense. It was a genuine union. It was found to have, and we assume it did have, the illegitimate objective of overthrowing the government by force. But it also had the objective of improving the lot of its members in the normal trade union sense. One who cooperated with it in promoting its legitimate objectives certainly could not by that fact alone be said to sponsor or approve of its general or unlawful objectives. But unless he also joined in that overall program,

he would not be "affiliated" with the Communist cause in the sense in which the statute uses the term.

Whether one could be a member of that union without becoming "affiliated" with the Communist party within the meaning of the statute, we need not decide. For Harry Bridges was never a member of it. To say that his cooperation with it made him in turn "affiliated" with the Communist party is to impute to him belief in and adherence to its general or unlawful objectives. In that connection, it must be remembered that although deportation technically is not criminal punishment . . . it may nevertheless visit as great a hardship as the deprivation of the right to pursue a vocation or a calling.

We cannot assume that Congress meant to employ the term "affiliation" in a broad, fluid sense which would visit such hardship on an alien for slight or insubstantial reasons. . . .

Inference must be piled on inference to impute belief in Harry Bridges of the revolutionary aims of the groups whose aid and assistance he employed in his endeavor to improve the lot of the workingmen on the water-front. That he enlisted such aid is not denied. He justified that course on the grounds of expediency—to get such help as he could to aid the cause of his union. But there is evidence that he opposed the Communist tactics of formenting strikes; that he believed in the policy of arbitration and direct negotiation to settle labor disputes, with the strike reserved only as a last resort. . . .

. . . We cannot construe "affiliation" as used in the statute to bring such conduct and attitudes within its reach. . . .

Chief Justice STONE, Justice ROBERTS, Justice FRANKFURTER dissenting.

561. ROOSEVELT'S DRAFT OF JEFFERSON DAY ADDRESS
April 13, 1945
(Congressional Record, April 16, 1945)

This address, never delivered, was the last written by Franklin D. Roosevelt. See D. P. Geddes, *Franklin D. Roosevelt: A Memorial;* Frances Perkins, *The Roosevelt I knew;* G. W. Johnson, *Dictator or Democrat;* Alden Hatch, *Franklin D. Roosevelt;* John Gunther, *Roosevelt in Retrospect;* R. Sherwood, *Roosevelt and Hopkins.*

Americans are gathered together this evening in communities all over the country to pay tribute to the living memory of Thomas Jefferson—one of the greatest of all democrats; and I want to make it clear that I am spelling that word "democrats" with a small "d."

I wish I had the power, just for this evening, to be present at all these gatherings.

In this historic year, more than ever before, we do well to consider the character of Thomas Jefferson as an American citizen of the world.

As minister to France, then as our first Secretary of State and as our third President, Jefferson was instrumental in the establishment of the United States as a vital factor in international affairs.

It was he who first sent our Navy into far distant waters to defend our rights. And the promulgation of the Monroe Doctrine was the logical development of Jefferson's far-seeing foreign policy.

Today this Nation which Jefferson helped so greatly to build is playing a tremendous part in the battle for the rights of man all over the world.

Today we are part of the vast Allied force —a force composed of flesh and blood and steel and spirit—which is today destroying the makers of war, the breeders of hate, in Europe and in Asia.

In Jefferson's time our Navy consisted of only a handful of frigates—but that tiny Navy taught nations across the Atlantic that piracy in the Mediterranean—acts of aggression against peaceful commerce and the enslavement of their crews was one of those things which, among neighbors, simply was not done.

Today we have learned in the agony of war that great power involves great responsibility. Today we can no more escape the consequence of German and Japanese aggression than could we avoid the consequences of attacks by the Barbary corsairs a century and a half before.

We, as Americans, do not choose to deny our responsibility.

Nor do we intend to abandon our determination that, within the lives of our children and our children's children, there will not be a third World War.

We seek peace—enduring peace. More than an end to war, we want an end to the beginnings of all wars—yes, an end to this brutal, inhuman and thoroughly impractical method of settling the differences between governments.

The once powerful, malignant Nazi state is crumbling, the Japanese war lords are receiving, in their home land, the retribution for which they asked when they attacked Pearl Harbor.

But the mere conquest of our enemies is not enough.

We must go on to do all in our power to conquer the doubts and the fears, the ignorance and the greed, which made this horror possible.

Thomas Jefferson, himself a distinguished scientist, once spoke of the 'brotherly spirit of science, which unites into one family all its votaries of whatever grade, and however widely dispersed throughout the different quarters of the globe.'

Today, science has brought all the different quarters of the globe so close together that it is impossible to isolate them one from another.

Today we are faced with the pre-eminent fact that, if civilization is to survive, we must cultivate the science of human relationships—the ability of all peoples, of all kinds, to live together and work together in the same world, at peace.

Let me assure you that my hand is the steadier for the work that is to be done, that

I move more firmly into the task, knowing that you—millions and millions of you—are joined with me in the resolve to make this work endure.

The work, my friends, is peace more than an end of this war—an end to the beginning of all wars, yes, an end, forever, to this impractical, unrealistic settlement of the differences between governments by the mass killing of peoples.

Today as we move against the terrible scourge of war—as we go forward toward the greatest contribution that any generation of human beings can make in this world— the contribution of lasting peace, I ask you to keep up your faith. I measure the sound, solid achievement that can be made at this time by the straight edge of your confidence and your resolve. And to you, and to all Americans who dedicate themselves with us to the making of an abiding peace, I say:

The only limit to our realization of tomorrow will be our doubts of today. Let us move forward with strong and active faith.

562. THE SURRENDER OF GERMANY
May 7, 1945
(*Department of State Bulletin,* July 22, 1945)

On March 7, for the first time since the Napoleonic invasion, the Rhine was crossed by foreign armies. As Russian and American armies poured into Germany, east and west, a new phase of the war began: the isolation and conquest of German pockets in central Europe. On May 6 the German commanders, Jodl and Friedeburg, appeared at Allied headquarters to capitulate. At 2:41 a.m., May 7, 1945, at General Eisenhower's headquarters in Rheims, Col. Gen. Gustav Jodl, Chief of Staff of the German Army, completed the signature of four surrender documents, one each for Great Britain, the United States, Russia, and France. After over five and a half years the war in Europe was at an end. See H. C. Butcher, *My Three Years with Eisenhower;* Walter Millis, *The Last Phase;* J. D. Dawson, *European Victory;* H. R. Trevor-Roper, *The Last Days of Hitler;* L. Clay, *Decision in Germany;* W. Churchill, *Triumph and Tragedy.*

Instrument of surrender of all German forces to General Dwight D. Eisenhower, Supreme Commander of the Allied Expeditionary Forces, and to the Soviet High Command

Rheims. *May 7, 1945.*

1. We the undersigned, acting by authority of the German High Command, hereby surrender unconditionally to the Supreme Commander, Allied Expeditionary Force and simultaneously to the Soviet High Command all forces on land, sea, and in the air who are at this date under German control.

2. The German High Command will at once issue orders to all German military, naval and air authorities and to all forces under German control to cease active operations at 2301 hours Central European time on 8 May and to remain in the positions occupied at that time. No ship, vessel, or aircraft is to be scuttled, or any damage done to their hull, machinery or equipment.

3. The German High Command will at once issue to the appropriate commanders, and ensure the carrying out of any further orders issued by the Supreme Commander, Allied Expeditionary Force and by the Soviet High Command.

4. This act of military surrender is without prejudice to, and will be superseded by any general instrument of surrender imposed by, or on behalf of the United Nations and applicable to Germany and the German armed forces as a whole.

5. In the event of the German High Command or any of the forces under their control failing to act in accordance with this Act of Surrender, the Supreme Commander, Allied Expeditionary Force and the Soviet High Command will take such punitive or other action as they deem appropriate.

Signed at Rheims at 0241 on the 7th day of May, 1945.

Statement by the Governments of the United States of America, Union of Soviet Socialist

Republics, the United Kingdom and the provisional Government of the French Republic on zones of occupation in Germany.

1. Germany, within her frontiers as they were on Dec. 31, 1937, will, for the purposes of occupation, be divided into four zones, one to be allotted to each power as follows:

An eastern zone to the Union of Soviet Socialist Republics;

A northwestern zone to the United Kingdom;

A southwestern zone to the United States of America;

A western zone to France.

The occupying forces in each zone will be under a commander in chief designated by the responsible power. Each of the four powers may, at its discretion, include among the forces assigned to occupation duties under the command of its commander in chief, auxiliary contingents from the forces of any other Allied power which has actively participated in military operations against Germany.

2. The area of "Greater Berlin" will be occupied by forces of each of the four powers. An inter-Allied governing authority (in Russian, Komendatura) consisting of four commandants, appointed by their respective commanders-in-chief, will be established to direct jointly its administration.

Statement by the Governments of the United States of America, Union of Soviet Socialist

Republics, United Kingdom, and the Provisional Government of the French Republic on control of machinery in Germany.

1. In the period when Germany is carrying out the basic requirements of unconditional surrender, supreme authority in Germany will be exercised, on instructions from their Governments, by the Soviet, British, United States and French commanders-in-chief, each in his own zone of occupation, and also jointly, in matters affecting Germany as a whole. The four commanders-in-chief will together constitute the Control Council. Each commander-in-chief will be assisted by a political adviser.

2. The Control Council, whose decisions shall be unanimous, will ensure appropriate uniformity of action by the commanders-in-chief in their respective zones of occupation and will reach agreed decisions on the chief questions affecting Germany as a whole.

3. Under the Control Council, there will be a permanent coordinating committee composed of one representative of each of the four commanders-in-chief and a control staff organized in the following divisions (which are subject to adjustment in the light of experience): Military; naval; air; transport; political; economic; finance; reparation, deliveries and restitution; internal affairs and communications; legal; prisoners of war and displaced persons; manpower. There will be four heads of each division, one designated by each power. . . .

563. MILITARY OCCUPATION OF JAPAN
October 4, 1945
(U. S. State Department, *The Axis in Defeat*)

General MacArthur, as supreme commander in the Pacific, was designated to direct the military occupation of Japan. Our occupation policy for Japan was prepared by the State, War and Navy departments and approved by President Truman on September 6, providing for the demilitarization of Japan, the trial of war criminals, the encouragement of democratic institutions, freedom of religious worship, the dissolution of great industrial and banking combines, and the subordination of the Emperor to General MacArthur. On September 10, the Imperial General Staff was ordered dissolved, and within the next week MacArthur ordered the dissolution of the Black Dragon Society and the arrest of its leaders; the establishment of American censorship over the Domei news agency; publication of the names of 40 Japanese leaders wanted as war criminals; and the creation of a program of re-education along democratic lines. On September 27, the Emperor, breaking all precedent, made a personal call on General MacArthur at his headquarters. MacArthur's most important order was announced on October 4, restoring civil liberties, freeing political prisoners, and abolishing the secret police. W. C. Johnstone, *Future of Japan; Occupation of Japan: Policy and Progress*, Dept. of State Publication 2671, Far Eastern Series 17; W. Fleisher, *What to Do With Japan; Report of the U. S. Education Mission to Japan,* Dept. of State Publication 2579, Far Eastern Series 11; Ruth Benedict, *The Chrysanthemum and the Sword.*

1. In order to remove restrictions on political, civil and religious liberties and discrimination on grounds of race, nationality, creed or political opinion, the Imperial Japanese Government will:

a. Abrogate and immediately suspend the operation of all provisions of all laws, decrees, orders, ordinances and regulations which:

(1) Establish or maintain restrictions on freedom of thought, of religion, of assembly and of speech, including the unrestricted discussion of the Emperor, the Imperial Institution and the Imperial Japanese Government.

(2) Establish or maintain restrictions on the collection and dissemination of information.

(3) By their terms or their applications, operate unequally in favor of or against any person by reason of race, nationality, creed or political opinion. . . .

c. Release immediately all persons now detained, imprisoned, under "protection or surveillance," or whose freedom is restricted in any other manner who have been placed in that state of detention, imprisonment, "protection and surveillance," or restriction of freedom:

(1) Under the enactments referred to in Para 1 a and b above.

(2) Without charge.

(3) By charging them technically with a minor offense, when, in reality, the reason for detention, imprisonment, "Protection and Surveillance," or restriction of freedom, was because of their thought, speech, religion, political beliefs, or assembly. The release of all such persons will be accomplished by 10 October 1945.

d. Abolish all organizations or agencies created to carry out the provisions of the enactments referred to in Para 1 a and b above and that part of, or functions of, other offices or sub divisions of other civil departments or organs which supplement or assist them in the execution of such provisions. These include, but are not limited to:

(1) All secret police organs.

(2) Those departments in the Ministry of Home Affairs, such as the Bureau of Police, charged with supervision of publications, supervision of public meetings and organizations, censorship of motion pictures, and such other departments concerned with the control of thought, speech, religion or assembly.

(3) Those departments, such as the special higher police (Tokubetsu, Koto, Keisatsu Bu), in the Tokyo Metropolitan Police, the Osaka Metropolitan Police, and other Metropolitan Police, the Police of the Territorial Administration of Hokkaido and the various prefectural police charged with supervision of publications, supervision of public meetings and organizations, censorship of motion pictures, and such other departments concerned with the control of thought, speech, religion or assembly.

(4) Those departments, such as the Protection and Surveillance Commission, and all Protection and Surveillance Stations responsible thereto, under the Ministry of Justice charged with protection and surveillance and control of thought, speech, religion, or assembly.

e. Remove from office and employment the Minister of Home Affairs, the Chief of the Bureau of Police of the Ministry of Home Affairs, the Chief of the Tokyo Metropolitan Police Board, the Chief of Osaka Metropolitan Police Board, the Chief of any other Metropolitan Police, the Chief of Police of the Territorial Administration of Hokkaido, the Chiefs of each prefectural police department, the entire personnel of the special higher police of all metropolitan, territorial and prefectural police departments, the guiding and protecting officials and all other personnel of the Protection and Surveillance Commission and of the Protection and Surveillance Stations. None of the above persons will be reappointed to any position under the Ministry of Home Affairs, the Ministry of Justice or any police organ in Japan. Any of the above persons whose assistance is required to accomplish the provisions of this directive will be retained until the directive is accomplished and then dismissed.

f. Prohibit any further activity of police officials, members of police forces, and other government, national or local, officials or employees which is related to the enactments referred to in Para 1 a and b above and to the organs and functions abolished by Para 1 d above.

g. Prohibit the physical punishment and mistreatment of all persons detained, imprisoned, or under protection and surveilliance under any and all Japanese enactments, laws, decrees, orders, ordinances and regulations. All such persons will receive at all times ample sustenance.

h. Ensure the security and preservation of all records and any and all other materials of the organs abolished in Para 1 d. These records may be used to accomplish the provisions of this directive, but will not be destroyed, removed, or tampered with in any way.

i. Submit a comprehensive report to this Headquarters not later than 15 October 1945 describing in detail all action taken to comply with all provisions of this directive. This report will contain the following specific information prepared in the form of separate supplementary reports: . . .

2. All officials and subordinates of the Japanese Government affected by the terms of this directive will be held personally responsible and strictly accountable for compliance with and adherence to the spirit and letter of this directive.

564. TRUMAN'S STATEMENT ON FUNDAMENTALS OF AMERICAN FOREIGN POLICY
October 27, 1945

(Department of State Bulletin, XIII, pp. 653 ff.)

This was the first important statement of foreign policy after President Truman's return from the Potsdam Conference. Point 10 anticipated the subsequent fourth point of the Fair Deal program of 1949. H. S. Truman, *Memoirs*, Vol. I.

. . . 1. We seek no territorial expansion or selfish advantage. We have no plans for aggression against any other state, large or small. We have no objective which need clash with the peaceful aims of any other nation.

2. We believe in the eventual return of sovereign rights and self-government to all peoples who have been deprived of them by force.

3. We shall approve no territorial changes in any friendly part of the world unless they accord with the freely expressed wishes of the people concerned.

4. We believe that all peoples who are prepared for self-government should be permitted to choose their own form of government by their own freely expressed choice, without interference from any foreign source. That is true in Europe, in Asia, in Africa, as well as in the Western Hemisphere.

5. By the combined and cooperative action of our war Allies, we shall help the defeated enemy states establish peaceful, democratic governments of their own free choice. And we shall try to attain a world in which Nazism, Fascism, and military aggression cannot exist.

6. We shall refuse to recognize any government imposed upon any nation by the force of any foreign power. In some cases it may be impossible to prevent forceful imposition of such a government. But the United States will not recognize any such government.

7. We believe that all nations should have the freedom of the seas and equal rights to the navigation of boundary rivers and waterways and of rivers and waterways which pass through more than one country.

8. We believe that all states which are accepted in the society of nations should have access on equal terms to the trade and the raw materials of the world.

9. We believe that the sovereign states of

the Western Hemisphere, without interference from outside the Western Hemisphere, must work together as good neighbors in the solution of their common problems.

10. We believe that full economic collaboration between all nations, great and small, is essential to the improvement of living conditions all over the world, and to the establishment of freedom from fear and freedom from want.

11. We shall continue to strive to promote freedom of expression and freedom of religion throughout the peace-loving areas of the world.

12. We are convinced that the preservation of peace between nations requires a United Nations Organization composed of all the peace-loving nations of the world who are willing jointly to use force if necessary to insure peace.

That is the foreign policy which guides the United States now. That is the foreign policy with which it confidently faces the future.

It may not be put into effect tomorrow or the next day. But none the less, it is our policy; and we shall seek to achieve it. It may take a long time, but it is worth waiting for, and it is worth striving to attain. . . .

565. UNITED NATIONS PARTICIPATION ACT
December 20, 1945
(Public Law 264, 79th Congress)

This measure, which passed the Senate by a vote of 65 to 7, the House by 344 to 15, made the United States a member of the United Nations. Readers should consult the text of the United Nations charter, which has been published in many places and is available upon application to the United Nations Secretariat. See P. Bidwell, *The United States and the United Nations;* K. Colegrove, *The American Senate and World Peace;* E. S. Corwin, The *Constitution and World Organization;* L. M. Goodrich and E. Hambro, *Charter of the United Nations;* Emery Reves, *Anatomy of Peace;* J. Robinson, *Human Rights and Fundamental Freedoms in the Charter of the United Nations;* C. Eagleton and F. O. Wilcox, "The United Nations: Peace and Security," *Am. Pol. Sci. Rev.,* Vol. 39, pp. 934 ff; Robert Summers, ed., *Dumbarton Oaks;* Wendell Willkie, *One World;* J. B. Whitton, ed., *The Second Chance: America and the Peace.*

An act—To provide for the appointment of representatives of the United States in the organs and agencies of the United Nations, and to make other provision with respect to the participation of the United States in such organiaztion.

SEC. 2. (a) The President, by and with the advice and consent of the Senate, shall appoint a representative of the United States at the seat of the United Nations who shall have the rank and status of envoy extraordinary and ambassador plenipotentiary, shall receive annual compensation of $20,000, and shall hold office at the pleasure of the President. Such representative shall represent the United States in the Security Council of the United Nations and shall perform such other functions in connection with the participation of the United States in the United Nations as the President may from time to time direct.

(b) The President, by and with the advice and consent of the Senate, shall appoint a deputy representative of the United States to the Security Council who shall have the rank and status of envoy extraordinary and minister plenipotentiary, shall receive annual compensation of $12,000, and shall hold office at the pleasure of the President. Such deputy representative shall represent the United States in the Security Council of the United Nations in the event of the absence or disability of the representative.

(c) The President, by and with the advice and consent of the Senate, shall designate from time to time to attend a specified session or specified sessions of the General Assembly of the United Nations not to exceed five representatives of the United States and such number of alternates as he may determine consistent with the rules of procedure of the General Assembly. One of the representatives shall be designated as the senior representative. Such representatives and alternates shall each be entitled to receive compensation at the rate of $12,000 per annum for such period as the President may specify, except that no member of the Senate or House of Representatives or officer of the United States who is designated under this subsection as a representative of the United States or as an alternate to attend any specified session or specified sessions of the General Assembly shall be entitled to receive such compensation.

(d) The President may also appoint from time to time such other persons as he may deem necessary to represent the United States in the organs and agencies of the United Nations, but the representative of the United States in the Economic and Social Council and in the Trusteeship Council of the United Nations shall be appointed only by and with the advice and consent of the Senate.

(e) Nothing contained in this section shall preclude the President or the Secretary of State, at the direction of the President, from representing the United States at any meeting or session of any organ or agency of the United Nations.

SEC. 3. The representatives provided for in section 2 hereof, when representing the United States in the respective organs and agencies of the United Nations, shall, at all times, act in accordance with the instructions of the President transmitted by the Secretary of State.

SEC. 4. The President shall, from time to time as occasion may require, but not less than once a year, make reports to the Congress of the activities of the United Nations and of the participation of the United States therein.

SEC. 5. (a) Notwithstanding the provisions of any other law, whenever the United States is called upon by the Security Council to apply measures which said Council has decided, pursuant to article 41 of said Charter, are to be employed to give effect to its decisions under said Charter, the President may, to the extent necessary to apply such measures, through any agency which he may designate, and under such orders, rules, and regulations as may be prescribed by him, investigate, regulate, or prohibit, in whole or in part, economic relations or rail, sea, air, postal, telegraphic, radio, and other means of comunication between any foreign country or any national thereof or any person therein and the United States or any person subject to the jurisdiction thereof, or involving any property subject to the jurisdiction of the United States.

SEC. 6. The President is authorized to negotiate a special agreement or agreements with the Security Council which shall be subject to the approval of the Congress by appropriate Act or joint resolution, providing for the numbers and types of armed forces, their degree of readiness and general location, and the nature of facilities and assistance, including rights of passage, to be made available to the Security Council on its call for the purpose of maintaining international peace and security in accordance with article 43 of said Charter. The President shall not be deemed to require the authorization of the Congress to make available to the Security Council on its call in order to take action under article 42 of said Charter and pursuant to such special agreement or agreements the armed forces, facilities, or assistance provided for therein: *Provided,* That nothing herein contained shall be construed as an authorization to the President by the Congress to make available to the Security Council for such purpose armed forces, facilities or assistance in addition to the forces, facilities, and assistance provided for in such special agreement or agreements.

Approved December 20, 1945.

566. CONSTITUTION OF UNESCO
1945

(Department of State Publication 3082, pp. 1-3)

In 1945 UNESCO was set up as one of the specialized agencies of the U. N. Economic and Social Council, and in 1946 the United States joined it, committing herself to its objectives of promoting collaboration through education, science, and culture. The Librarian of Congress, Luther Evans, became Director of UNESCO in 1953. See B. M. Tripp, *UNESCO in Perspective;* H. E. Wilson, *The Development of UNESCO;* J. Huxley, *UNESCO, Its Purpose and Its Philosophy;* T. Besterman, *UNESCO.*

The governments of the States parties to this Constitution on behalf of their peoples declare:

that since wars begin in the minds of men, it is in the minds of men that the defences of peace must be constructed;

that ignorance of each other's ways and lives has been a common cause, throughout the history of mankind, of that suspicion and mistrust between the peoples of the world through which their differences have all too often broken into war;

that the great and terrible war which has now ended was a war made possible by the denial of the democratic principles of the dignity, equality and mutual respect of men, and by the propagation, in their place, through ignorance and prejudice, of the doctrine of the inequality of men and races;

that the wide diffusion of culture, and the education of humanity for justice and liberty and peace are indispensable to the dignity of man and constitute a sacred duty which all the nations must fulfill in a spirit of mutual assistance and concern:

that a peace based exclusively upon the political and economic arrangements of governments would not be a peace which could secure the unanimous, lasting and sincere support of the peoples of the world, and that the peace must therefore be founded, if it is not to fail, upon the intellectual and moral solidarity of mankind.

For These Reasons, the States parties to this Constitution, believing in full and equal opportunities for education for all, in the unrestricted pursuit of objective truth, and in the free exchange of ideas and knowledge, are agreed and determined to develop and to increase the means of communication between their peoples and to employ these means for the purposes of mutual understanding and a truer and more perfect knowledge of each other's lives;

In Consequence Whereof they do hereby create the United Nations Educational, Scientific and Cultural Organization for the purpose of advancing, through the educational and scientific and cultural relations of the peoples of the world, the objectives of international peace and of the common welfare of mankind for which the United Nations Organisation was established and which its Charter proclaims.

ARTICLE I. PURPOSES AND FUNCTIONS

1. The purpose of the Organisation is to contribute to peace and security by promoting collaboration among the nations through education, science and culture in order to further universal respect for justice, for the rule of law and for the human rights and fundamental freedoms which are affirmed for the peoples of the world, without distinction of race, sex, language or religion, by the Charter of the United Nations.

2. To realise this purpose the Organisation will:

(a) collaborate in the work of advancing the mutual knowledge and understanding of peoples, through all means of mass communication and to that end recommend such international agreements as may be necessary to promote the free flow of ideas by word and image;

(b) give fresh impulse to popular education and to the spread of culture;

by collaborating with Members, at their request, in the development of educational activities;

by instituting collaboration among the nations to advance the ideal of equality of educational opportunity without regard to race, sex or any distinctions economic or social;

by suggesting educational methods best

suited to prepare the children of the world for the responsibilities of freedom;

(c) maintain, increase and diffuse knowledge;

by assuring the conservation and protection of the world's inheritance of books, works of art and monuments of history and science, and recommending to the nations concerned the necessary international conventions;

by encouraging cooperation among the nations in all branches of intellectual activity, including the international exchange of persons active in the fields of education, science and culture and the exchange of publications, objects of artistic and scientific interest and other materials of information;

by initiating methods of international cooperation calculated to give the people of all countries access to the printed and published materials produced by any of them.

3. With a view to preserving the independence, integrity and fruitful diversity of the cultures and educational systems of the States Members of this Organisation, the Organisation is prohibited from intervening in matters which are essentially within their domestic jurisdiction. . . .

567. ASSOCIATED PRESS v. UNITED STATES
1946
326 U. S. 1

The Attorney-General filed a bill in a Federal District Court for an injunction against AP, charging that it had violated the Sherman Act as a combination and conspiracy in restraint of trade in news. The Government charged that the bylaws of the AP, which prohibited members from selling news to non-members, and which granted to each member the power to bar non-member competitors from membership, were violations of the Sherman Act, as was a contract between the AP and the Canadian Press, under which both groups agreed to furnish news exclusively to the other. The three-judge District Court enjoined the bylaws restricting admission of a competitor and the distribution of news to non-members and enjoined observance of the Canadian contract until the by-laws were amended. The Associated Press appealed the case to the Supreme Court, and the United States Government also appealed, for it wanted the decree broadened. See Oliver Gramling, *A.P., the Story of News*, Morris Ernst, *The First Freedom;* J. R. Wiggins, *Freedom or Security*.

BLACK, J. The publishers of more than 1200 newspapers are members of the Associated Press (AP), a cooperative association incorporated under the Membership Corporations Law of the State of New York, Consol. Laws c. 35. Its business is the collection, assembly and distribution of news. The news it distributes is originally obtained by direct employees of the Association, employees of the member newspapers, and the employees of foreign independent news agencies with which AP has contractual relations, such as the Canadian Press. Distribution of the news is made through interstate channels of communication to the various newspaper members of the Association, who pay for it under an assessment plan which contemplates no profit to AP.

The United States filed a bill in a Federal District Court for an injunction against AP and other defendants charging that they had violated the Sherman Anti-Trust Act, in that their acts and conduct constituted (1) a combination and conspiracy in restraint of trade and commerce in news among the states, and (2) an attempt to monopolize a part of that trade.

The heart of the government's charge was that appellants had by concerted action set up a system of By-Laws which prohibited all AP members from selling news to non-members, and which granted each member powers to block its non-member competitors from membership. These By-Laws, to which all AP members had assented, were, in the context of the admitted facts, charged to be in violation of the Sherman Act. . . .

To put the issue into proper focus, it becomes necessary at this juncture to examine the By-Laws.

All members must consent to be bound by them. They impose upon members certain duties and restrictions in the conduct of their separate businesses. For a violation of the By-Laws severe disciplinary action may be taken by the Association. The Board of Directors may impose a fine of $1000.00 or suspend a member and such "action . . . shall be final and conclusive. No member shall have any right to question the same." The offending member may also be expelled by the members of the corporation for any reason "which in its absolute discretion it shall deem of such a character as to be prejudicial to the welfare of the corporation and its members, or to justify such expulsion. The action of the regular members of the corporation in such regard shall be final and there shall be no right of appeal against or review of such action."

These By-Laws, for a violation of which members may be thus fined, suspended, or expelled, require that each newspaper member publish the AP news regularly in whole or in part, and that each shall "promptly furnish to the corporation, through its agents or employees, all the news of such member's district, the area of which shall be determined by the Board of Directors." All members are prohibited from selling or furnishing their spontaneous news to any agency or publisher except to AP. Other By-Laws require each newspaper member to "conduct his or its business in such manner that the news furnished by the corporations" shall not be made available to any non-member in advance of publication. The joint effect of these By-Laws is to block all newspaper non-members from any opportunity to buy news from AP or any of its publisher members. Admission to membership in AP thereby becomes a prerequisite to obtaining AP news or buying news from any one of its more than twelve hundred publishers. The erection of obstacles to the acquisition of membership consequently can make it difficult, if not impossible for non-members to get any of the news furnished by AP or any of the individual members of this combination of American newspaper publishers.

The By-Laws provide a very simple and non-burdensome road for admission of a non-competing applicant. The Board of Directors in such case can elect the applicant without payment of money or the imposition of any other onerous terms. In striking contrast are the By-Laws which govern admission of new members who do compete. Historically, as well as presently, applicants who would offer competition to old members have a hard road to travel. . . .

The District Court found that the By-Laws in and of themselves were contracts in restraint of commerce in that the contained provisions designed to stifle competition in the newspaper publishing field. The court also found that AP's restrictive By-Laws had hindered and impeded the growth of competing newspapers. This latter finding, as to the *past* effect of the restrictions, is challenged. We are inclined to think that it is supported by undisputed evidence, but we do not stop to labor the point. For the court below found, and we think correctly, that the By-Laws on their face, and without regard to their past effect, constitute restraints of trade. Combinations are no less unlawful because they have not as yet resulted in restraint. An agreement or combination to follow a course of conduct which will necessarily restrain or monopolize a part of trade or commerce may violate the Sherman Act, whether it be "wholly nascent or abortive on the one hand, or successful on the other." For these reasons the argument, repeated here in various forms, that AP had not yet achieved a complete monopoly is wholly irrelevant. Undisputed evidence did show, however, that its By-Laws had tied the hands of all of its numerous publishers, to the extent that they could not and did not reach any of their non-member competitors. In this respect the Court did find, and that finding cannot possibly be challenged, that AP's By-Laws had hindered and restrained the sale of interstate news to non-members who competed with members.

Inability to buy news from the largest news agency, or any one of its multitude of members, can have most serious effects on the publication of competitive newspapers, both those presently published and those which but for these restrictions, might be published in the future. This is illustrated by the District Court's finding that in 26 cities of the United States, existing newspapers already have contracts for AP news and the same newspapers have contracts with United Press and International News Service under which new newspapers would be required to pay the contract holders large sums to enter the field. The net effect is seriously to limit the opportunity of any new paper to enter these cities. Trade restraints of this character, aimed at the destruction of competition, tend to block the initiative which brings newcomers into a field of business and to frustrate the free enterprise system which it was the purpose of the Sherman Act to protect.

We need not again pass upon the contention that trade in news carried on among the states is not interstate commerce, Associated Press v. National Labor Relations Board, 301 U.S. 103, or that because AP's activities are cooperative, they fall outside the sphere of business, American Medical Ass'n v. United States, 317 U.S. 519. It is significant that when Congress has desired to permit cooperatives to interfere with the competitive system of business, it has done so expressly by legislation.

Nor can we treat this case as though it merely involved a reporter's contract to deliver his news reports exclusively to a single newspaper, or an exclusive agreement as to news between two newspapers in different cities. For such trade restraints might well be "reasonable," and therefore not in violation of the Sherman Act. But however innocent such agreements might be, standing alone, they would assume quite a different aspect if utilized as essential features of a program to hamper or destroy competition. It is in this light that we must view this case.

It has been argued that the restrictive By-Laws should be treated as beyond the prohibitions of the Sherman Act, since the owner of the property can choose his associates and can, as to that which he has produced by his own enterprise and sagacity, efforts or ingenuity, decide for himself whether and to whom to sell or not to sell. While it is true in a very general sense that one can dispose of his property as he pleases, he cannot "go beyond the exercise of this right, and by contracts or combinations, express or implied, unduly hinder or obstruct the free and natural flow of commerce

in the channels of interstate trade." The Sherman Act was specifically intended to prohibit independent businesses from becoming "associates" in a common plan which is bound to reduce their competitor's opportunity to buy or sell the things in which the groups compete. Victory of a member of such a combination over its business rivals achieved by such collective means cannot consistently with the Sherman Act or with practical, everyday knowledge be attributed to *individual* "enterprise and sagacity"; such hampering of business rivals can only be attributed to that which really makes it possible—the collective power of an unlawful combination. That the object of sale is the creation or product of a man's ingenuity does not alter this principle. It is obviously fallacious to view the By-Laws here in issue as instituting a program to encourage and permit full freedom of sale and disposal of property by its owners. Rather, these publishers have, by concerted arrangements, pooled their power to acquire, to purchase, and to dispose of news reports through the channels of commerce. They have also pooled their economic and news control power and, in exerting that power, have entered into agreements which the District Court found to be "plainly designed in the interest of preventing competition." . . .

Finally, the argument is made that to apply the Sherman Act to this association of publishers constitutes an abridgment of the freedom of the press guaranteed by the First Amendment. Perhaps it would be a sufficient answer to this contention to refer to the decisions of this Court in Associated Press v. N. L. R. B., and Indiana Farmer's Guide Publishing Co. v. Prairie Farmer Publishing Co., 293 U.S. 268. It would be strange indeed however if the grave concern for freedom of the press which prompted adoption of the First Amendment should be read as a command that the government was without power to protect that freedom. The First Amendment, far from providing an argument against application of the Sherman Act, here provides powerful reasons to the contrary. That Amendment rests on the assumption that the widest possible dissemination of information from diverse and antagonistic sources is essential to the welfare of the public, that a free press is a condition of a free society. Surely a command that the government itself shall not impede the free flow of ideas does not afford non-governmental combinations a refuge if they impose restraints upon that constitutionally guaranteed freedom. Freedom to publish means freedom for all and not for some. Freedom to publish is guaranteed by the Constitution, but freedom to combine to keep others from publishing is not Freedom of the press from governmental interference under the First Amendment does not sanction repression of that freedom by private interests. The First Amendment affords not the slightest support for the contention that a combination to restrain trade in news and views has any constitutional immunity. . . .

Affirmed.

568. UNITED STATES v. LOVETT, WATSON, AND DODD
328 U. S. 303
1946

Section 304 of the Emergency Deficiency Appropriation Act of 1943 provided that, after November 15, 1943, no salary was to be paid to Robert Morss Lovett, Secretary of the Virgin Islands, Goodwin B. Watson, and William E. Dodd, Jr., both on the staff of the Federal Communications Commission, for any government work. This action arose from a speech on February 1, 1943, by Rep. Martin Dies, chairman of the House Committee on Un-American Activities, stating that thirty-nine government employees were members of subversive, communist organizations, and that Congress should refuse to appropriate funds for their salaries. A special sub-committee of the House Committee on Appropriation investigated the charges and decided that three of the thirty-nine, Watson, Dodd, and Lovett were guilty, after which the House passed the act in question. The Senate voted down this section, 69-0, but the House was adamant, and the Senate was forced to concur in order to get the appropriations act passed. Lovett, Watson, and Dodd continued to work for the government after November 15, 1943, without salary, and filed suit in the Court of Claims for back salary, contending that the section was unconstitutional, violating the Fifth Amendment, being a bill of attainder, and a Congressional usurpation of executive power of removal. The Court of Claims found in favor of the plaintiffs, and the Government appealed the case to the Supreme Court. See Doc. No. 528; F. L. Schuman, " 'Bill of Attainder' in the Seventy-Eighth Congress," *Am. Pol. Sci. Rev.,* Vol. 37; A. R. Ogden, *The Dies Committee;* W. Gellerman, *Martin Dies;* M. Dies, *The Trojan Horse in America;* H. S. Commager, "Who is Loyal to America?" *Harper's,* September, 1947.

On Writs of Certiorari to the Court of Claims.

BLACK, J. In 1943 the respondents, Lovett, Watson, and Dodd, were and had been for several years working for the Government. The Government agencies which had lawfully employed them were fully satisfied with the quality of their work and wished to keep them employed on their jobs. Over the protest of those employing agencies, Congress provided in Section 304 of the Urgent Deficiency Appropriation Act of 1943, by way of an amendment attached to the House bill, that after November 15, 1943, no salary or compensation should be paid respondents out of any monies then or thereafter appropriated except for services as jurors or members of the armed forces, unless they were prior to November 15, 1943 again appointed to jobs by the President with the advice and consent of the Senate. Notwithstanding the Congressional enactment, and the failure of the President to reappoint respondents, the agencies kept all the respondents at work on their jobs for varying periods after November 15, 1943; but their compensation was discontinued after that date. To secure compensation for this post-November 15th work, respondents brought these actions in the Court of Claims. They urged that Section 304 is unconstitutional and void on the grounds that: (1) The Section, properly interpreted, shows a Congressional purpose to exercise the power to remove executive employees, a power not entrusted to Congress but to the Executive Branch of Government under Article II, Sections 1, 2, 3, and 4 of the Constitution; (2) the Section violates Article I, Section 9, Clause 3, of the Constitution which provides that "no bill of attainder or ex post facto law shall be passed";

(3) the Section violates the Fifth Amendment, in that it singles out these three respondents and deprives them of their liberty and property without due process of law. . . .

Our inquiry is thus confined to whether the actions in the light of a proper construction of the Act present justiciable controversies and if so whether Section 304 is a bill of attainder against these respondents involving a use of power which the Constitution unequivocally declares Congress can never exercise. . . .

We hold that the purpose of Section 304 was not merely to cut off respondents' compensation through regular disbursing channels but permanently to bar them from government service, and that the issue of whether it is constitutional is justiciable. The Section's language as well as the circumstances of its passage which we have just described show that no mere question of compensation procedure or of appropriations was involved, but that it was designed to force the employing agencies to discharge respondents and to bar their being hired by any other governmental agency. Any other interpretation of the Section would completely frustrate the purpose of all who sponsored Section 304, which clearly was to "purge" the then existing and all future lists of Government employees of those whom Congress deemed guilty of "subversive activities" and therefore "unfit" to hold a federal job. What was challenged therefore is a statute which, because of what Congress thought to be their political beliefs, prohibited respondents from ever engaging in any government work, except as jurors or soldiers. Respondents claimed that their discharge was unconstitutional; that they consequently rightfully continued to work for the Government and that the Government owes them compensation for services performed under contracts of employment. Congress has established the Court of Claims to try just such controversies. What is involved here is a Congressional proscription of Lovett, Watson, and Dodd, prohibiting their ever holding a Government job. Were this case to be not justiciable, Congressional action, aimed at three named individuals, which stigmatized their reputation and seriously impaired their chance to earn a living,

could never be challenged in any court. Our Constitution did not contemplate such a result. To quote Alexander Hamilton, ". . . a limited constitution . . . [is] one which contains certain specified exceptions to the legislative authority; such, for instance, as that it shall pass no bills of attainder, no ex post facto laws, and the like. Limitations of this kind can be preserved in practice no other way than through the medium of the courts of justice; whose duty it must be to declare all acts contrary to the manifest tenor of the Constitution void. Without this, all the reservations of particular rights or privileges would amount to nothing."

We hold that Section 304 falls precisely within the category of Congressional actions which the Constitution barred by providing that "No Bill of Attainder or ex post facto Law shall be passed." In Cummings v. State of Missouri, this Court said, "A bill of attainder is a legislative act which inflicts punishment without a judicial trial. If the punishment be less than death, the act is termed a bill of pains and penalties. Within the meaning of the Constitution, bills of attainder include bills of pains and penalties."

Section 304 was designed to apply to particular individuals. Just as the statute in the two cases mentioned it "operates as a legislative decree of perpetual exclusion" from a chosen vocation. This permanent proscription from any opportunity to serve the Government is punishment, and of a most severe type. It is a type of punishment which Congress has only invoked for special types of odious and dangerous crimes, such as treason; acceptance of bribes by members of Congress; or by other government officials; and interference with elections by Army and Navy officers.

Section 304, thus, clearly accomplishes the punishment of named individuals without a judicial trial. The fact that the punishment is inflicted through the instrumentality of an Act specifically cutting off the pay of certain named individuals found guilty of disloyalty, makes it no less galling or effective than if it had been done by an Act which designated the conduct as criminal. No one would think that Congress could have passed a valid law, stating that after investigation it had found Lovett, Dodd, and Watson "guilty" of the crime of engaging in "subversive activities," defined that term for the first time, and sentenced them to perpetual exclusion from any government employment. Section 304, while it does not use that language, accomplishes that result. The effect was to inflict punishment without the safeguards of a judicial trial and "determined by no previous law or fixed rule." The Constitution declares that that cannot be done either by a state or by the United States.

Those who wrote our Constitution well knew the danger inherent in special legislative acts which take away the life, liberty, or property of particular named persons, because the legislature thinks them guilty of conduct which deserves punishment. They intended to safeguard the people of this country from punishment without trial by duly constituted courts. . . . When our Constitution and Bill of Rights were written, our ancestors had ample reason to know that legislative trials and punishments were too dangerous to liberty to exist in the nation of free men they envisioned. And so they proscribed bills of attainder. Section 304 is one. Much as we regret to declare that an Act of Congress violates the Constitution, we have no alternative here.

569. CONSTITUTION OF THE CONGRESS OF INDUSTRIAL ORGANIZATIONS
1946

The failure of the American Federation of Labor to organize the unorganized and its adherence to the craft form of organization led to a breach within the ranks of organized labor. The Committee for Industrial Organization, formed in 1935, acquired members with great rapidity, and in 1937 took on the name, Congress of Industrial Organizations. This independent Constitution, adopted in 1946, was a consequence of the general conviction in the C.I.O. that unity between the two great labor organizations was unlikely in the calculable future. By 1947 the C.I.O. unions claimed a total paid membership of 6,000,000. Compare the Constitution of the A. F. of L., Doc. No. 473; see R. R. Brooks, *When Labor Organizes;* B. Stolberg, *The Story of the C.I.O.;* H. Harris, *American Labor;* E. Levinson, *Labor on the March.* See Doc. No. 626.

action into labor unions for their mutual aid and protection.

Second. To extend the benefits of collective bargaining and to secure for the workers means to establish peaceful relations with their employers, by forming labor unions capable of dealing with modern aggregates of industry and finance.

Third. To maintain determined adherence to obligations and responsibilities under collective bargaining and wage agreements.

Fourth. To secure legislation safeguarding the economic security and social welfare of the workers of America, to protect and extend our democratic institutions and civil rights and liberties, and thus to perpetuate the cherished traditions of our democracy.

ARTICLE I

NAME

This organization shall be known as the "Congress of Industrial Organizations" (CIO).

ARTICLE II

OBJECTS

The objects of the organization are:

First. To bring about the effective organization of the working men and women of America regardless of race, creed, color, or nationality, and to unite them for common

ARTICLE III

AFFILIATES

SECTION 1. The Organization shall be composed of affiliated national and international unions, organizing committees, local industrial unions and industrial union councils.

SEC. 2. Certificates of affiliation shall be issued to national and international unions and organizing committees by the Executive Board.

SEC. 3. Certificates of affiliation shall be issued to local industrial unions by the Executive Board. The Executive Board shall issue rules governing the conduct, activities, affairs, and the suspension and expulsion of local industrial unions. It shall be the duty of the Executive Board to combine local industrial unions into national or international unions or organizing committees. Any local industrial union or group of local industrial unions may request the Executive Board to authorize such combination. The decision of the Executive Board may be appealed to the convention, provided, however, that pending the appeal the decision shall remain in full force and effect.

SEC. 4. Certificates of affiliation shall be issued to industrial union councils by the Executive Board. Industrial Union Councils shall be organized upon a city, state or other regional basis as may be deemed advisable by the Executive Board and shall be composed of the locals of national unions, international unions and organizing committees, and local industrial unions and local industrial union councils within the territorial limits of such council. It shall be the duty of national and international unions and organizing committees to direct their locals to affiliate with the proper industrial union councils. It shall be the duty of all local industrial unions and local industrial union councils to affiliate with the proper industrial union councils. The Executive Board shall issue rules governing the conduct, activities, affairs, and the suspension and expulsion of industrial union councils. The decision of the Executive Board may be appealed to the convention, provided, however, that pending the appeal the decision shall remain in full force and effect.

SEC. 6. National or international unions and organizing committees may not be suspended or expelled except upon a two-thirds vote at the convention. This provision may not be amended except by a two-thirds vote at the convention.

ARTICLE IV

OFFICERS AND EXECUTIVE BOARD

SECTION 1. The officers shall consist of a president, secretary-treasurer, and nine vice presidents. Each officer shall be a member of an affiliate, shall be elected by a majority of the votes cast at each regular convention, shall serve for the term of one year and shall assume office immediately upon election. In the event that more than two candidates are nominated for any one of the foregoing offices, and no one candidate receives a majority of the votes cast, all except the two candidates receiving the highest votes shall be eliminated from the list of candidates, and a second vote taken. . . .

SEC. 3. The convention shall elect the Executive Board which shall be composed of one member from each affiliated national and international union and organizing committee. Each such affiliate shall nominate one of its duly qualified officers for such membership to the Executive Board. The President, Secretary-Treasurer and Vice Presidents shall be members of the Executive Board by virtue of their office. . . .

SEC. 5. National headquarters shall be maintained at Washington, D. C.

ARTICLE V

THE DUTIES OF THE OFFICERS

PRESIDENT

SECTION 1. The President shall preside over the convention and meetings of the Executive Board, exercise supervision of the affairs of the Organization, and function as the chief executive officer.

SEC. 2. The President shall interpret the meaning of the Constitution and his interpretation shall be subject to review by the Executive Board. Between sessions of the Executive Board he shall have full power to direct the affairs of the Organization, and his acts shall be reported to the Executive Board for its approval.

SEC. 3. The President shall have authority, subject to the approval of the Executive Board, to appoint, direct, suspend or remove, such organizers, representatives, agents and employees as he may deem necessary.

SEC. 4. The President shall make full reports of the administration of his office and of the affairs of the Organization to the convention. . . .

ARTICLE VI

DUTIES OF THE EXECUTIVE BOARD

SECTION 1. The Executive Board shall enforce the constitution and carry out the instructions of the conventions, and between conventions shall have power to direct the affairs of the Organization.

SEC. 7. The Executive Board shall have the power to file charges and conduct hearings on such charges against any officer of the Organization or other member of the Executive Board, on the ground that such person is guilty of malfeasance or maladministration, and to make a report to the convention recommending appropriate action. The Executive Board must serve such officer with a copy of the written charges a reasonable time before the hearing.

ARTICLE VII

CONVENTION

SECTION 1. The convention shall be the supreme authority of the Organization and except as otherwise provided in the Constitution, its decisions shall be by a majority vote.

SEC. 2. A convention shall be held each year during the months of October or November at a time and place designated by the Executive Board. The Executive Board shall give at least 30 days' notice of the time and place which it so designatés. Special conventions may be called upon 30 days' notice by the Executive Board.

SEC. 3. The Call for a special convention must include a statement of the particular subject or subjects to be considered at the convention and no other business shall be transacted at such convention. A special convention shall be governed by the provisions for regular conventions.

SEC. 4. A majority of the delegates seated shall constitute a quorum.

SEC. 5. Each national and international union and organizing committee and each local industrial union shall be entitled to one vote for each member. Each industrial union council shall be entitled to one vote.

SEC. 6. Each national or international union and organizing committee shall be entitled to the number of· delegates indicated in the following scale:

Up to   5,000 membership, 2 delegates
Over   5,000 membership, 3 delegates
Over   10,000 membership, 4 delegates
Over   25,000 membership, 5 delegates
Over   50,000 membership, 6 delegates
Over   75,000 membership, 7 delegates
100,000 membership, 8 delegates for the first 100,000 members and one additional delegate for each additional 50,000 or majority fraction thereof.

Each local industrial union and industrial union council shall be entitled to one delegate. Local industrial unions may combine with other local industrial unions in a reasonable distance of one another and elect delegates to represent them.

570. EMPLOYMENT ACT OF 1946
February 20, 1946

(*Public Law 304, 79th Congress*)

The Employment Act of 1946 marked a new approach to the formulation of national economic policy by making explicit the government's responsibility for full employment. The act set up a Council of Economic Advisers authorized to study economic trends and to recommend to the President policies to alleviate the negative effects of the business cycle. Under the leadership of economists like Leon Keyserling and Arthur Burns, the Council came to exercise profound influence on the formulation of economic policies. See E. G. Nourse, *The 1950's Come First;* E. G. Nourse, *Economics in the Public Service;* S. E. Harris, *Economic Planning;* S. K. Bailey, *Congress Makes A Law.*

AN ACT

To declare a national policy on employment, production, and purchasing power, and for other purposes. . . .

SEC. 2. The Congress hereby declares that it is the continuing policy and responsibility of the Federal Government to use all practicable means consistent with its needs and obligations and other essential considerations of national policy, with the assistance and cooperation of industry, agriculture, labor, and State and local governments, to coordinate and utilize all its plans, functions, and resources for the purpose of creating and maintaining, in a manner calculated to foster and promote free competitive enterprise and the general welfare, conditions under which there will be afforded useful employment opportunities, including self-employment, for those able, willing, and seeking to work, and to promote maximum employment, production, and purchasing power.

SEC. 3. (a) The President shall transmit to the Congress within sixty days after the beginning of each regular session (commencing with the year 1947) an economic report setting forth (1) the levels of employment, production, and purchasing power obtaining in the United States and such levels needed to carry out the policy declared in section 2; (2) current and foreseeable trends in the levels of employment, production, and purchasing power; (3) a review of the economic program of the Federal Government and a review of economic conditions affecting employment in the United States or any considerable portion thereof during the preceding year and of their effect upon employment, production, and purchasing power; and (4) a program for carrying out the policy declared in section 2, together with such recommendations for legislation as he may deem necessary or desirable. . . .

SEC. 4. (a) There is hereby created in the Executive Office of the President a Council of Economic Advisers. The Council shall be composed of three members who shall be appointed by the President, by and with the advice and consent of the Senate, and each of whom shall be a person who, as a result of his training, experience, and attainments, is exceptionally qualified to analyze and interpret economic developments, to appraise programs and activities of the Government in the light of the policy declared in section 2, and to formulate and recommend national economic policy to promote employment, production, and purchasing power under free competitive enterprise. Each member of the Council shall receive compensation at the rate of $15,000 per annum. The President shall designate one of the members of the Council as chairman and one as vice chair-

man, who shall act as chairman in the absence of the chairman. . . .

(c) It shall be the duty and function of the Council—

(1) to assist and advise the President in the preparation of the Economic Report;

(2) to gather timely and authoritative information concerning economic developments and economic trends, both current and prospective, to analyze and interpret such information in the light of the policy declared in section 2 for the purpose of determining whether such developments and trends are interfering, or are likely to interfere, with the achievement of such policy, and to compile and submit to the President studies relating to such developments and trends;

(3) to appraise the various programs and activities of the Federal Government in the light of the policy declared in section 2 for the purpose of determining the extent to which such programs and activities are contributing, and the extent to which they are not contributing, to the achievement of such policy, and to make recommendations to the President with respect thereto;

(4) to develop and recommend to the President national economic policies to foster and promote free competitive enterprise, to avoid economic fluctuations or to diminish the effects thereof, and to maintain employment, production, and purchasing power;

(5) to make and furnish such studies, reports thereon, and recommendations with respect to matters of Federal economic policy and legislation as the President may request.

(d) The Council shall make an annual report to the President in December of each year. . . .

SEC. 5. (a) There is hereby established a Joint Committee on the Economic Report, to be composed of seven Members of the Senate, to be appointed by the President of the Senate, and seven Members of the House of Representatives, to be appointed by the

Speaker of the House of Representatives. The party representation on the joint committee shall as nearly as may be feasible reflect the relative membership of the majority and minority parties in the Senate and House of Representatives.

(b) It shall be the function of the joint committee—

(1) to make a continuing study of matters relating to the Economic Report;

(2) to study means of coordinating programs in order to further the policy of this Act; and

(3) as a guide to the several com-

mittees of the Congress dealing with legislation relating to the Economic Report, not later than May 1 of each year (beginning with the year 1947) to file a report with the Senate and the House of Representatives containing its findings and recommendations with respect to each of the main recommendations made by the President in the Economic Report, and from time to time to make such other reports and recommendations to the Senate and House of Representatives as it deems advisable. . . .

571. THE CONTROL OF ATOMIC ENERGY
November 15, 1946
(79th Congress, 2nd Session. Senate Comm. Monograph No. 1)

The atomic bomb had been created by the scientists of the United States, Great Britain, and Canada. The end of the war and the creation of the United Nations at once raised, in critical form, the question of the control of the new weapon. The American public, alarmed by the potentialities of Russian control of the atom bomb, insisted upon keeping the "secret" of the bomb, though physicists were generally agreed that this was a secret that could not be kept. American policy on the atomic bomb was formulated in a declaration made jointly by President Truman, the Prime Minister of the United Kingdom, and the Prime Minister of Canada. On January 24, 1946, the United Nations established an Atomic Energy Commission. The American position, as presented by Bernard Baruch, was that the atomic weapon should not be made available to other nations until adequate provisions for security and inspection had been agreed upon; the Russian position, as presented by Andrei Gromyko, was that manufacture of the bomb should be outlawed and stock piles destroyed at once, and that the American plan for control and inspection would involve an unwarranted interference with the domestic affairs of sovereign states. The American plan was, in effect, adopted. On the problem of atomic control, see Bernard Brodie, *Absolute Weapon;* P. S. M. Blackett, *Fear, War, and the Bomb;* Dexter Masters, ed. *One World or None;* E. L. Woodward, *Some Political Consequences of the Atomic Bomb;* U.S. Govt. Printing Office, *Essential Information on*

Atomic Energy; J. P. Baxter, *Scientists Against Time.*

Text of the agreed declaration on atomic energy by the President of the United States, the Prime Minister of the United Kingdom, and the Prime Minister of Canada

The President of the United States, the Prime Minister of the United Kingdom, and the Prime Minister of Canada have issued the following statement:

1. We recognize that the application of recent scientific discoveries to the methods and practice of war has placed at the disposal of mankind means of destruction hitherto unknown, against which there can be no adequate military defense, and in the employment of which no single nation can in fact have a monopoly.

2. We desire to emphasize that the responsibility for devising means to insure that the new discoveries shall be used for the benefit of mankind, instead of as a means of destruction, rests not on our nations alone, but upon the whole civilized world. Nevertheless, the progress that we have

made in the development and use of atomic energy demands that we take an initiative in the matter, and we have accordingly met together to consider the possibility of international action—

(*a*) to prevent the use of atomic energy for destructive purposes;

(*b*) to promote the use of recent and future advances in scientific knowledge, particularly in the utilization of atomic energy, for peaceful and humanitarian ends.

3. We are aware that the only complete protection for the civilized world from the destructive use of scientific knowledge lies in the prevention of war. No system of safeguards that can be devised will of itself provide an effective guaranty against production of atomic weapons by a nation bent on aggression. Nor can we ignore the possibility of the development of other weapons or of new methods of warfare which may constitute as great a threat to civilization as the military use of atomic energy.

4. Representing, as we do, the three countries which possess the knowledge essential to the use of atomic energy, we declare at the outset our willingness, as a first contribution, to proceed with the exchange of fundamental scientific information and the interchange of scientists and scientific literature for peaceful ends with any nation that will fully reciprocate.

5. We believe that the fruits of scientific research should be made available to all nations, and that freedom of investigation and free interchange of ideas are essential to the progress of knowledge. In pursuance of this policy, the basic scientific information essential to the development of atomic energy for peaceful purposes has already been made available to the world. It is our intention that all further information of this character that may become available from time to time should be similarly treated. We trust that other nations will adopt the same policy, thereby creating an atmosphere of reciprocal confidence in which political agreement and cooperation will flourish.

6. We have considered the question of the disclosure of detailed information concerning the practical industrial application of atomic energy. The military exploitation of atomic energy depends, in large part, upon the same methods and processes as would be required for industrial uses.

We are not convinced that the spreading of the specialized information regarding the practical application of atomic energy, before it is possible to devise effective, reciprocal, and enforceable safeguards acceptable to all nations, would contribute to a constructive solution of the problem of the atomic bomb. On the contrary, we think it might have the opposite effect. We are, however, prepared to share, on a reciprocal basis with others of the United Nations, detailed information concerning the practical industrial application of atomic energy just as soon as effective enforceable safeguards against its use for destructive purposes can be devised.

7. In order to attain the most effective means of entirely eliminating the use of atomic energy for destructive purposes and promoting its widest use for industrial and humanitarian purposes, we are of the opinion that at the earliest practicable date a commission should be set up under the United Nations Organization to prepare recommendations for submission to the Organization.

The Commission should be instructed to proceed with the utmost dispatch and should be authorized to submit recommendations from time to time dealing with separate phases of its work.

In particular the Commission should make specific proposals—

(*a*) for extending between all nations the exchange of basic scientific information for peaceful ends;

(*b*) for control of atomic energy to the extent necessary to insure its use only for peaceful purposes;

(*c*) for the elimination from national armaments of atomic weapons and of all other major weapons adaptable to mass destruction;

(*d*) for effective safeguards by way of inspection and other means to protect complying States against the hazards of violations and evasions.

8. The work of the Commission should proceed by separate stages, the successful completion of each one of which will develop the necessary confidence of the world before the next stage is undertaken. Specifically it

is considered that Commission might well devote its attention first to the wide exchange of scientists and scientific information, and as a second stage to the development of full knowledge concerning natural resources of raw materials.

9. Faced with the terrible realities of the application of science to destruction, every nation will realize more urgently than before the overwhelming need to maintain the rule of law among nations and to banish the scourge of war from the earth. This can only be brought about by giving whole-hearted support to the United Nations Organization, and by consolidating and extending its authority, thus creating conditions of mutual trust in which all peoples will be free to devote themselves to the arts of peace. It is our firm resolve to work without reservation to achieve these ends.

HARRY S. TRUMAN,
President of the United States.
C. R. ATTLEE,
Prime Minister of the United Kingdom.
W. L. MACKENZIE KING,
Prime Minister of Canada.

572. THE ATOMIC ENERGY COMMISSION
August 1, 1946

(Public Law 585, 79th Congress, 2nd Session)

The general background of this measure is stated in Section 1. The act was amended in 1954 to provide for greater cooperation among the free nations and increased use of atomic power by private industry. See, H. D. Smyth, *Atomic Energy for Military Purposes,* B. Brodie, ed., *The Absolute Weapon: Atomic Power and the World Order;* Julia E. Johnsen, *The Atomic Bomb.*

AN ACT

For the development and control of atomic energy.

DECLARATION OF POLICY

SECTION 1. (a) FINDINGS AND DECLARATION.—Research and experimentation in the field of nuclear chain reaction have attained the stage at which the release of atomic energy on a large scale is practical. The significance of the atomic bomb for military purposes is evident. The effect of the use of atomic energy for civilian purposes upon the social, economic, and political structures of today cannot now be determined. It is a field in which unknown factors are involved. Therefore, any legislation will necessarily be subject to revision from time to time. It is reasonable to anticipate, however, that tapping this new source of energy will cause profound changes in our present way of life. Accordingly, it is hereby declared to be the policy of the people of the United States that, subject at all times to the paramount objective of assuring the common defense and security, the development and utilization of atomic energy shall, so far as practicable, be directed toward improving the public welfare, increasing the standard of living, strengthening free competition in private enterprise, and promoting world peace.

(b) PURPOSE OF ACT.—It is the purpose of this Act to effectuate the policies set out in section 1 (a) by providing, among others, for the following major programs relating to atomic energy:

(1) A program of assisting and fostering private research and development to encourage maximum scientific progress;

(2) A program for the control of scientific and technical information which will permit the dissemination of such information to encourage scientific progress, and for the sharing on a reciprocal basis of information concerning the practical industrial application of atomic energy as soon as effective and enforceable safeguards against its use for destructive purposes can be devised;

(3) A program of federally conducted research and development to assure the Government of adequate scientific and technical accomplishment;

(4) A program for Government control of the production, ownership, and use of fissionable material to assure the common defense and security and to insure the broadest possible exploitation of the fields; and

(5) A program of administration which

will be consistent with the foregoing policies and with international arrangements made by the United States, and which will enable the Congress to be currently informed so as to take further legislative action as may hereafter be appropriate.

ORGANIZATION

SEC. 2. (a) ATOMIC ENERGY COMMISSION.—

(1) There is hereby established an Atomic Energy Commission (herein called the Commission), which shall be composed of five members. Three members shall constitute a quorum of the Commission. The President shall designate one member as Chairman of the Commission.

(2) Members of the Commission shall be appointed by the President, by and with the advice and consent of the Senate. . . .

RESEARCH

SEC. 3. (a) RESEARCH ASSISTANCE.—The Commission is directed to exercise its powers in such manner as to insure the continued conduct of research and development activities in the fields specified below by private or public institutions or persons and to assist in the acquisition of an ever-expanding fund of theoretical and practical knowledge in such fields. To this end the Commission is authorized and directed to make arrangements (including contracts, agreements, and loans) for the conduct of research and development activities relating to—

(1) nuclear processes;

(2) the theory and production of atomic energy, including processes, materials, and devices related to such production;

(3) utilization of fissionable and radioactive materials for medical, biological, health, or military purposes;

(4) utilization of fissionable and radioactive materials and processes entailed in the production of such materials for all other purposes, including industrial uses; and

(5) the protection of health during research and production activities.

PRODUCTION OF FISSIONABLE MATERIAL

SEC. 4.

. . . (b) PROHIBITION.—It shall be unlawful for any person to own any facilities for the production of fissionable material or for any person to produce fissionable material, except to the extent authorized by subsection (c).

(c) OWNERSHIP AND OPERATION OF PRODUCTION FACILITIES.—

(1) OWNERSHIP OF PRODUCTION FACILITIES.—The Commission, as agent of and on behalf of the United States, shall be the exclusive owner of all facilities for the production of fissionable material other than facilities which (A) are useful in the conduct of research and development activities in the fields specified in section 3, and (B) do not, in the opinion of the Commission, have a potential production rate adequate to enable the operator of such facilities to produce within a reasonable period of time a sufficient quantity of fissionable material to produce an atomic bomb or any other atomic weapon.

(2) OPERATION OF THE COMMISSION'S PRODUCTION FACILITIES.—The Commission is authorized and directed to produce or to provide for the production of fissionable material in its own facilities.

(e) MANUFACTURE OF PRODUCTION FACILITIES.—Unless authorized by a license issued by the Commission, no person may manufacture, produce, transfer, or acquire any facilities for the production of fissionable material.

CONTROL OF MATERIALS

SEC. 5. (a) FISSIONABLE MATERIALS.—

(2) GOVERNMENT OWNERSHIP OF ALL FISSIONABLE MATERIAL.—All right, title, and interest within or under the jurisdiction of the United States, in or to any fissionable material, now or hereafter produced, shall be the property of the Commission, and shall be deemed to be vested in the Commission by virtue of this Act.

(4) DISTRIBUTION OF FISSIONABLE MATERIAL.—Without prejudice to its continued ownership thereof, the Commission is authorized to distribute fissionable material

owned by it, with or without charge, to applicants requesting such material (A) for the conduct of research or development activities either independently or under contract or other arrangement with the Commission, (B) for use in medical therapy, or (C) for use pursuant to a license issued under the authority of section 7.

(7) PUBLIC LANDS.—All uranium, thorium, and all other materials determined pursuant to paragraph (1) of this subsection to be peculiarly essential to the production of fissionable material, contained, in whatever concentration, in deposits in the public lands are hereby reserved for the use of the United States subject to valid claims, rights, or privileges existing on the date of the enactment of this Act: The Secretary of the Interior shall cause to be inserted in every patent, conveyance, lease, permit, or other authorization hereafter granted to use the public lands or their mineral resources, under any of which there might result the extraction of any materials so reserved, a reservation to the United States of all such materials, whether or not of commercial value, together with the right of the United States through its authorized agents or representatives at any time to enter upon the land and prospect for, mine, and remove the same, making just compensation for any damage or injury occasioned thereby.

MILITARY APPLICATIONS OF ATOMIC ENERGY

SEC. 6. (a) AUTHORITY.—The Commission is authorized to—

(1) conduct experiments and do research and development work in the military application of atomic energy; and

(2) engage in the production of atomic bombs, atomic bomb parts, or other military weapons utilizing fissionable materials; except that such activities shall be carried on only to the extent that the express consent and direction of the President of the United States has been obtained, which consent and direction shall be obtained at least once each year.

The President from time to time may direct the Commission (1) to deliver such quantities of fissionable materials or weapons to the armed forces for such use as he deems necessary in the interest of national defense or (2) to authorize the armed forces to manufacture, produce, or acquire any equipment or device utilizing fissionable material or atomic energy as a military weapon.

INTERNATIONAL ARRANGEMENTS

SEC. 8.

. . . (b) EFFECT OF INTERNATIONAL ARRANGEMENTS.—Any provision of this Act or any action of the Commission to the extent that it conflicts with the provisions of any international arrangement made after the date of enactment of this Act shall be deemed to be of no further force or effect.

PROPERTY OF THE COMMISSION

SEC. 9. (a) The President shall direct the transfer to the Commission of all interests owned by the United States or any Government agency in the following property:

(1) All fissionable material; all atomic weapons and parts thereof; all facilities, equipment and materials for the processing, production, or utilization of fissionable material or atomic energy; all processes and technical information of any kind, and the source thereof (including data, drawings, specifications, patents, patent applications, and other sources) relating to the processing, production, or utilization of fissionable material or atomic energy; and all contracts, agreements, leases, patents, applications for patents, inventions and discoveries (whether patented or unpatented), and other rights of any kind concerning any such items;

(2) All facilities, equipment, and materials, devoted primarily to atomic energy research and development; and

(3) Such other property owned by or in the custody or control of the Manhattan Engineer District or other Government agencies as the President may determine.

CONTROL OF INFORMATION

SEC. 10. (a) POLICY.—It shall be the policy of the Commission to control the dissemination of restricted data in such a manner as to assure the common defense and security. Consistent with such policy, the Commission shall be guided by the following principles:

(1) That until Congress declares by joint resolution that effective and enforceable international safeguards against the use of atomic energy for destructive purposes have been established, there shall be no exchange of information with other nations with respect to the use of atomic energy for industrial purposes; and

(2) That the dissemination of scientific and technical information relating to atomic energy should be permitted and encouraged so as to provide that free interchange of ideas and criticisms which is essential to scientific progress.

(3) Whoever, with intent to injure the United States or with intent to secure an advantage to any foreign nation, acquires or attempts or conspires to acquire any document, writing, sketch, photograph, plan, model, instrument, appliance, note or information involving or incorporating restricted data shall, upon conviction thereof, be punished by death or imprisonment for life (but the penalty of death or imprisonment for life may be imposed only upon recommendation of the jury and only in cases where the offense was committed with intent to injure the United States); or by a fine of not more than $20,000 or imprisonment for not more than twenty years, or both. . . .

GENERAL AUTHORITY

Sec. 12. (a) In the performance of its functions the Commission is authorized to—

(1) establish advisory boards to advise with and make recommendations to the Commission on legislation, policies, administration, research, and other matters;

(2) establish by regulation or order such standards and instructions to govern the possession and use of fissionable and byproduct materials as the Commission may deem necessary or desirable to protect health or to minimize danger from explosions and other hazards to life or property. . . .

JOINT COMMITTEE ON ATOMIC ENERGY

Sec. 15. (a) There is hereby established a Joint Committee on Atomic Energy to be composed of nine Members of the Senate to be appointed by the President of the Senate, and nine Members of the House of Representatives to be appointed by the Speaker of the House of Representatives. In each instance not more than five members shall be members of the same political party.

(b) The joint committee shall make continuing studies of the activities of the Atomic Energy Commission and of problems relating to the development, use, and control of atomic energy. The Commission shall keep the joint committee fully and currently informed with respect to the Commission's activities. All bills, resolutions, and other matters in the Senate or the House of Representatives relating primarily to the Commission or to the development, use, or control of atomic energy shall be referred to the joint committee. The members of the joint committee who are Members of the Senate shall from time to time report to the Senate, and the members of the joint committee who are Members of the House of Representatives shall from time to time report to the House, by bill or otherwise, their recommendations with respect to matters within the jurisdiction of their respective Houses which are (1) referred to the joint committee or (2) otherwise within the jurisdiction of the joint committee.

573.   THE FULBRIGHT ACT
August 1, 1946
(Public Law 584, 79th Congress, 2nd Session)

At the close of the war millions of dollars worth of surplus war materials were left in Allied countries. Senator Fulbright of Arkansas proposed that the money received from the sale of such war surplus to Allied governments should be used to finance cultural and educational interchange. A precedent for this plan could be found in the arrangements whereby the United

States appropriated half of the indemnity received from China after the Boxer uprising to bring Chinese students to the United States.

An Act to Amend the Surplus Property Act of 1944.

SEC. 2. Section 32 (b) (2) In carrying out the provisions of this section, the Secretary of State is hereby authorized to enter into an executive agreement or agreements with any foreign government for the use of currencies, or credits for currencies, of such government acquired as a result of such surplus property disposals, for the purpose of providing, by the formation of foundations or otherwise, for (A) financing studies, research, instruction, and other educational activities of or for American citizens in schools and institutions of higher learning located in such foreign country, or of the citizens of such foreign country in American schools and institutions of higher learning located outside the continental United States, Hawaii, Alaska (including the Aleutian Islands), Puerto Rico, and the Virgin Islands, including payment for transportation, tuition, maintenance, and other expenses incident to scholastic activities; or (B) furnishing transportation for citizens of such foreign country who desire to attend American schools and institutions of higher learning in the continental United States, Hawaii, Alaska (including the Aleutian Islands), Puerto Rico, and the Virgin Islands, and whose attendance will not deprive citizens of the United States of an opportunity to attend such schools and institutions: *Provided, however,* That no such agreement or agreements shall provide for the use of an aggregate amount of the currencies, or credits for currencies, of any one country in excess of $20,000,000 or for the expenditure of the currencies, or credits for currencies, of any one foreign country in excess of $1,000,000 annually at the official rate of exchange for such currencies, unless otherwise authorized by Congress, nor shall any such agreement relate to any subject other than the use and expenditure of such currencies or credits for currencies for the purposes herein set forth: *Provided further,* That for the purpose of selecting students and educational institutions qualified to participate in this program, and to supervise the exchange program authorized herein, the President of the United States is hereby authorized to appoint a Board of Foreign Scholarships, consisting of ten members, who shall serve without compensation, composed of representatives of cultural, educational, student and war veterans groups, and including representatives of the United States Office of Education, the United States Veterans' Administration, State educational institutions, and privately endowed educational institutions: *And Provided further,* That in the selection of American citizens for study in foreign countries under this paragraph preference shall be given to applicants who shall have served in the military or naval forces of the United States during World War I or World War II, and due consideration shall be given to applicants from all geographical areas of the United States.

574. YAMASHITA v. STYER
327 U.S. 1
1946

Original proceeding: as an application by General Tomoyuki Yamashita for leave to file petition for writ of habeas corpus and for writ of petition. General Yamashita had been the commanding general of the Fourteenth Army Group of the Imperial Japanese Army in the Philippines at the end of World War II. When the war ended, he surrendered to American forces and was indicted for violating the laws of war by failing to control the operation of his troops, by "permitting them to commit" atrocities against civilians and prisoners of war. He was not accused of having authorized the acts for which he was indicted, or even having specific knowledge of their occurrence. Nonetheless, he was convicted and sentenced to death by an American military commission. His counsel argued that Yamashita was denied all the trial protections contained in the 1929 Prisoner-of-War Convention, and appealed to the United States Supreme Court. Justice Jackson did not participate in the case; and Justices Rutledge and Murphy dissented. See A. F. Reel, *The Case of General Yamashita;* T. Taylor, *Nuremberg and Vietnam;* W. Bosch, *Judgment at Nuremberg;* R. Minear, *Victors' Justice.*

STONE, C. J. . . . The petitions for habeas corpus set up that the detention of petitioner for the purpose of the trial was unlawful for reasons which are now urged as showing that the military commission was without lawful authority or jurisdiction to place petitioner on trial, as follows:

(a) That the military commission which tried and convicted petitioner was not lawfully created, and that no military commission to try petitioner for violations of the law of war could lawfully be convened after the cessation of hostilities between the armed forces of the United States and Japan;

(b) that the charge preferred against petitioner fails to charge him with a violation of the law of war;

(c) that the commission was without authority and jurisdiction to try and convict petitioner because the order governing the procedure of the commission permitted the admission in evidence of depositions, affidavits and hearsay and opinion evidence, and because the commission's rulings admitting such evidence were in violation of the 25th and 38th Articles of War (10 U.S.C. §§ 1496, 1509, 10 U.S.C.A. §§ 1496, 1509) and the Geneva Convention (47 Stat. 2021), and deprived petitioner of a fair trial in violation of the due process clause of the Fifth Amendment;

(d) that the commission was without authority and jurisdiction in the premises because of the failure to give advance notice of petitioner's trial to the neutral power representing the interests of Japan as a belligerent as required by Article 60 of the Geneva Convention, 47 Stat. 2021, 2051. . . .

The authority to create the Commission. General Styer's order for the appointment of the commission was made by him as Commander of the United States Armed Forces, Western Pacific. . . .

Here the commission was not only created by a commander competent to appoint it, but his order conformed to the established policy of the Government and to higher military commands authorizing his action. . . .

By direction of the President, the Joint Chiefs of Staff of the American Military Forces, on September 12, 1945, instructed General MacArthur, Commander in Chief, United States Army Forces, Pacific, to proceed with the trial, before appropriate military tribunals, of such Japanese war criminals "as have been or may be apprehended." By order of General MacArthur of September 24, 1945, General Styer was specifically directed to proceed with the trial of petitioner upon the charge here involved. This order was accompanied by detailed rules and regulations which General MacArthur prescribed for the trial of war criminals. These regulations directed, among other things, that review of the sentence imposed by the commission should be by the officer convening it, with "authority to approve, mitigate, remit, commute, suspend, reduce or otherwise alter the sentence imposed," and directed that no sentence of death should be carried into effect until confirmed by the Commander in Chief, United States Army Forces, Pacific.

It thus appears that the order creating the commission for the trial of petitioner was authorized by military command, and was in complete conformity to the Act of Congress sanctioning the creation of such tribunals for the trial of offenses against the law of war committed by enemy combatants. And we turn to the question whether the authority to create the commission and direct the trial by military order continued after the cessation of hostilities.

An important incident to the conduct of war is the adoption of measures by the military commander, not only to repel and defeat the enemy, but to seize and subject to disciplinary measures those enemies who, in their attempt to thwart or impede our military effort, have violated the law of war. . . . The trial and punishment of enemy combatants who have committed violations of the law of war is thus not only a part of the conduct of war operating as a preventive measure against such violations, but is an exercise of the authority sanctioned by Congress to administer the system of military justice recognized by the law of war. That sanction is without qualification as to the exercise of this authority so long as a state of war exists—from its declaration until peace is proclaimed. . . .

The Charge. Neither Congressional action nor the military orders constituting the commission authorized it to place petitioner on trial unless the charge preferred against him is of a violation of the law of war. The charge, so far as now relevant, is that petitioner, between October 9, 1944 and September 2, 1945, in the Philippine Islands, "while commander of armed forces of Japan at war with the United States of America and its allies, unlawfully disregarded and failed to discharge his duty as commander to control the operations of the members of his command, permitting them to commit brutal atrocities and other high crimes against people of the United States and of its allies and dependencies, particularly the Philippines; and he . . . thereby violated the laws of war."

Bills of particulars, filed by the prosecution by order of the commission, allege a series of acts, one hundred and twenty-three in number, committed by members of the forces under petitioner's command, during the period mentioned. The first item specifies the execution of "a deliberate plan and purpose to massacre and exterminate a large part of the civilian population of Batangas Province, and to devastate and destroy public, private and religious property therein, as a result of which more than 25,000 men, women and children, all unarmed noncombatant civilians, were brutally mistreated and killed, without cause or trial, and entire settlements were devastated and destroyed wantonly and without military necessity." Other items specify acts of violence, cruelty and homicide inflicted upon the civilian population and prisoners of war, acts of wholesale pillage and the wanton destruction of religious monuments.

It is not denied that such acts directed against the civilian population of an occupied country and against prisoners of war

are recognized in international law as violations of the law of war. . . . But it is urged that the charge does not allege that petitioner has either committed or directed the commission of such acts, and consequently that no violation is charged as against him. But this overlooks the fact that the gist of the charge is an unlawful breach of duty by petitioner as an army commander to control the operations of the members of his command by "permitting them to commit" the extensive and widespread atrocities specified. The question then is whether the law of war imposes on an army commander a duty to take such appropriate measures as are within his power to control the troops under his command for the prevention of the specified acts which are violations of the law of war and which are likely to attend the occupation of hostile territory by an uncontrolled soldiery, and whether he may be charged with personal responsibility for his failure to take such measures when violations result. That this was the precise issue to be tried was made clear by the statement of the prosecution at the opening of the trial.

It is evident that the conduct of military operations by troops whose excesses are unrestrained by the orders or efforts of their commander would almost certainly result in violations which it is the purpose of the law of war to prevent. Its purpose to protect civilian populations and prisoners of war from brutality would largely be defeated if the commander of an invading army could with impunity neglect to take reasonable measures for their protection. Hence the law of war presupposes that its violation is to be avoided through the control of the operations of war by commanders who are to some extent responsible for their subordinates.

This is recognized by the Annex to Fourth Hague Convention of 1907, respecting the laws and customs of war on land. Article I lays down as a condition which an armed force must fulfill in order to be accorded the rights of lawful belligerents, that it must be "commanded by a person responsible for his subordinates." 36 Stat. 2295. Similarly Article 19 of the Tenth Hague Convention, relating to bombardment by naval vessels, provides that commanders in chief of the belligerent vessels "must see that the above Articles are properly carried out." 36 Stat. 2389. And Article 26 of the Geneva Red Cross Convention of 1929, 47 Stat. 2074, 2092, for the amelioration of the condition of the wounded and sick in armies in the field, makes it "the duty of the commanders-in-chief of the belligerent armies to provide for the details of execution of the foregoing articles [of the convention], as well as for unforeseen cases." And, finally, Article 43 of the Annex of the Fourth Hague Convention, 36 Stat. 2306, requires that the commander of a force occupying enemy territory, as was petitioner, "shall take all the measures in his power to restore, and ensure, as far as possible, public order and safety, while respecting, unless absolutely prevented, the laws in force in the country."

These provisions plainly imposed on petitioner, who at the time specified was military governor of the Philippines, as well as commander of the Japanese forces, an affirmative duty to take such measures as were within his power and appropriate in the circumstances to protect prisoners of war and the civilian population. This duty of a commanding officer has heretofore been recognized, and its breach penalized by our own military tribunals. . . .

We do not here appraise the evidence on which petitioner was convicted. . . . It is plain that the charge on which petitioner was tried charged him with a breach of his duty to control the operations of the members of his command, by permitting them to commit the specified atrocities. This was enough to require the commission to hear evidence tending to establish the culpable failure of petitioner to perform the duty imposed on him by the law of war and to pass upon its sufficiency to establish guilt.

Obviously charges of violations of the law of war triable before a military tribunal need not be stated with the precision of a common law indictment. . . . But we conclude that the allegations of the charge, tested by any reasonable standard, adequately allege a violation of the law of war and that the commission had authority to try and decide the issue which it raised. . . .

It thus appears that the order convening the commission was a lawful order, that the commission was lawfully constituted, that petitioner was charged with violation of the law of war, and that the commission had authority to proceed with the trial, and in doing so did not violate any military, statutory or constitutional command. We have considered, but find it unnecessary to discuss other contentions which we find to be without merit. We therefore conclude that the detention of petitioner for trial and his detention upon his conviction, subject to the prescribed review by the military authorities were lawful, and that the petition for certiorari, and leave to file in this Court petitions for writs of habeas corpus and prohibition should be, and they are

Denied.

Writs denied.

575. THE TRUMAN DOCTRINE
March 12, 1947
(*Congressional Record,* March 12, 1947)

The immediate background of this message to Congress is stated in the text. The idea that the United States was to underwrite the defense of free states against "totalitarian regimes" was widely hailed as a sharp new turn in American foreign policy, a world-wide equivalent of the Monroe Doctrine. In the Soviet Union it was held to be an open threat on the part of the United States against Russian-dominated areas and Russian expansion. See F. L. Schuman, *Soviet Politics;* E. H. Carr, *The Soviet Impact on the Western World;* E. A. Speiser, *The United States and the Near East;* D. E. Webster, *The Turkey of Ataturk;* H. Truman, *Memoirs,* Vol. II.

The gravity of the situation which confronts the world today necessitates my appearance before a joint session of the Congress. The foreign policy and the national security of this country are involved.

One aspect of the present situation, which I wish to present to you at this time for your consideration and decision, concerns Greece and Turkey.

The United States has received from the Greek Government an urgent appeal for financial and economic assistance. Preliminary reports from the American Economic Mission now in Greece and reports from the American Ambassador in Greece corroborate the statement of the Greek Government that assistance is imperative if Greece is to survive as a free nation.

I do not believe that the American people and the Congress wish to turn a deaf ear to the appeal of the Greek Government.

The very existence of the Greek state is today threatened by the terrorist activities of several thousand armed men, led by Communists, who defy the Government's authority at a number of points, particularly along the northern boundaries. A commission appointed by the United Nations Security Council is at present investigating disturbed conditions in Northern Greece and alleged border violations along the frontiers between Greece on the one hand and Albania, Bulgaria and Yugoslavia on the other.

Meanwhile, the Greek Government is unable to cope with the situation. The Greek Army is small and poorly equipped. It needs supplies and equipment if it is to restore the authority to the Government throughout Greek territory.

Greece must have assistance if it is to become a self-supporting and self-respecting democracy. The United States must supply this assistance. We have already extended to Greece certain types of relief and economic aid but these are inadequate. There is no other country to which democratic Greece can turn. No other nation is willing and able to provide the necessary support for a democratic Greek Government.

The British Government, which has been helping Greece, can give no further financial or economic aid after March 31. Great Britain finds itself under the necessity of reducing or liquidating its commitments in several parts of the world, including Greece.

We have considered how the United Nations might assist in this crisis. But the situation is an urgent one requiring immediate action, and the United Nations and its related organizations are not in a position to extend help of the kind that is required. . . .

Greece's neighbor, Turkey, also deserves our attention. The future of Turkey as an independent and economically sound state is clearly no less important to the freedom-loving peoples of the world than the future of Greece. The circumstances in which Turkey finds itself today are considerably different from those of Greece. Turkey has been spared the disasters that have beset Greece. And during the war, the United States and Great Britain furnished Turkey with material aid. Nevertheless, Turkey now needs our support.

Since the war Turkey has sought additional financial assistance from Great Britain and the United States for the purpose of effecting the modernization necessary for the maintenance of its national integrity. That integrity is essential to the preservation of order in the Middle East.

The British Government has informed us that, owing to its own difficulties, it can no longer extend financial or economic aid to Turkey. As in the case of Greece, if Turkey is to have the assistance it needs, the United States must supply it. We are the only country able to provide that help.

I am fully aware of the broad implications involved if the United States extends assistance to Greece and Turkey, and I shall discuss these implications with you at this time.

One of the primary objectives of the foreign policy of the United States is the creation of conditions in which we and other nations will be able to work out a way of life free from coercion. This was a fundamental issue in the war with Germany and Japan. Our victory was won over countries which sought to impose their will, and their way of life, upon other nations.

To ensure the peaceful development of nations, free from coercion, the United States has taken a leading part in establishing the United Nations. The United Nations is designed to make possible lasting freedom and independence for all its members. We shall not realize our objectives, however, unless we are willing to help free peoples to maintain their free institutions and their national integrity against aggressive movements that seek to impose on them totalitarian regimes. This is no more than a frank recognition that totalitarian regimes imposed on free peoples, by direct or indirect aggression, undermine the foundations of international peace and hence the security of the United States.

The peoples of a number of countries of the world have recently had totalitarian regimes forced upon them against their will. The Government of the United States has made frequent protests against coercion and intimidation, in violation of the Yalta Agreement, in Poland, Rumania and Bulgaria. I must also state that in a number of other countries there have been similar developments.

At the present moment in world history nearly every nation must choose between alternative ways of life. The choice is too often not a free one.

One way of life is based upon the will of the majority, and is distinguished by free institutions, representative government, free elections, guarantees of individual liberty, freedom of speech and religion, and freedom from political oppression.

The second way of life is based upon the will of the minority forcibly imposed upon the majority. It relies upon terror and oppression, a controlled press and radio, fixed elections, and the suppression of personal freedoms.

I believe that it must be the policy of the United States to support free peoples who are resisting attempted subjugation by armed minorities or by outside pressures.

I believe that we must assist free peoples to work out their own destinies in their own way.

I believe that our help should be primarily through economic and financial aid which is essential to economic stability and orderly political processes.

The world is not static, and the status quo is not sacred. But we cannot allow changes in the status quo in violation of the charter of the United Nations by such methods as coercion, or by such subterfuges as political infiltration. In helping free and independent nations to maintain their freedom, the United States will be giving effect to the principles of the charter of the United Nations.

It is necessary only to glance at a map to realize that the survival and integrity of the Greek nation are of grave importance in a much wider situation. If Greece should fall under the control of an armed minority, the effect upon its neighbor, Turkey, would be immediate and serious. Confusion and disorder might well spread throughout the entire Middle East.

Moreover, the disappearance of Greece as an independent state would have a profound effect upon those countries in Europe whose peoples are struggling against great difficulties to maintain their freedoms and their independence while they repair the damages of war.

It would be an unspeakable tragedy if these countries, which have struggled so long against overwhelming odds, should lose that victory for which they sacrificed so much. Collapse of free institutions and loss of independence would be disastrous not only for them but for the world. Discouragement and possibly failure would quickly be the lot of neighboring peoples striving to maintain their freedom and independence.

Should we fail to aid Greece and Turkey in this fateful hour, the effect will be far reaching to the west as well as to the east. We must take immediate and resolute action.

I therefore ask the Congress to provide authority for assistance to Greece and Turkey in the amount of $400,000,000 for the period ending June 30, 1948.

In addition to funds, I ask the Congress to authorize the detail of American civilian and military personnel to Greece and Turkey, at the request of those countries, to assist in the tasks of reconstruction, and for the purpose of supervising the use of such financial and material assistance as may be furnished. I recommend that authority also be provided for the instruction and training of selected Greek and Turkish personnel.

Finally, I ask that the Congress provide authority which will permit the speediest and most effective use, in terms of needed commodities, supplies, and equipment, of such funds as may be authorized. . . .

The seeds of totalitarian regimes are nurtured by misery and want. They spread and grow in the evil soil of poverty and strife. They reach their full growth when the hope of a people for a better life has died. We must keep that hope alive. The free peoples of the world look to us for support in maintaining their freedoms.

If we falter in our leadership, we may endanger the peace of the world—and we shall surely endanger the welfare of this nation.

Great responsibilities have been placed upon us by the swift movement of events. I am confident that the Congress will face these responsibilities squarely.

576. AMERICAN AID TO GREECE AND TURKEY
MAY 22, 1947
(80th Congress, 1st Session, *Senate Doc.* No. 111)

Truman called, originally, for $400 million to implement the Truman Doctrine (see Doc. No. 575). As of Jan. 1, 1949, Congress had appropriated $625 million for Greece and Turkey, and as the Greek Civil War continued unabated it was clear that further appropriations would be required.

An Act to provide for assistance to Greece and Turkey.

Whereas the Governments of Greece and Turkey have sought from the Government of the United States immediate financial and other assistance which is necessary for the maintenance of their national integrity and their survival as free nations; and

Whereas the national integrity and survival of these nations are of importance to the security of the United States and of all freedom-loving peoples and depend upon the receipt at this time of assistance; and . . .

Whereas the furnishing of such assistance to Greece and Turkey by the United States will contribute to the freedom and independence of all members of the United Nations in conformity with the principles and purposes of the Charter: Now, therefore,

Be it enacted that, notwithstanding the provisions of any other law, the President may from time to time when he deems it in the interest of the United States furnish assistance to Greece and Turkey, upon request of their governments, and upon terms and conditions determined by him—

(1) by rendering financial aid in the form of loans, credits, grants, or otherwise, to those countries;

(2) by detailing to assist those countries any persons in the employ of the Govern-

ment of the United States; . . .

(3) by detailing a limited number of members of the military services of the United States to assist those countries, in an advisory capacity only; . . .

(4) by providing for (A) the transfer to, and the procurement for by manufacture or otherwise and the transfer to, those countries of any articles, services, and information, and (B) the instruction and training of personnel of those countries; . . .

SEC. 3. As a condition precedent to the receipt of any assistance pursuant to this Act, the government requesting such assistance shall agree (a) to permit free access of United States Government officials for the purpose of observing whether such assistance is utilized effectively and in accordance with the undertakings of the recipient government; (b) to permit representatives of the press and radio of the United States to observe freely and to report fully regarding the utilization of such assistance; . . . and (f) to give full and continuous publicity within such country as to the purpose, source, character, scope, amounts, and progress of United States economic assistance carried on therein pursuant to this Act.

SEC. 4. . . . (b) There is hereby authorized to be appropriated to the President not to exceed $400,000,000 to carry out the provisions of this act. . . .

SEC. 5. . . . The President is directed to withdraw any or all aid authorized herein under any of the following circumstances:

(1) If requested by the Government of Greece or Turkey, respectively, representing a majority of the people of either such nation;

(2) If the Security Council finds (with respect to which finding the United States waives the exercise of any veto) or the Gen-

eral Assembly finds that action taken or assistance furnished by the United Nations makes the continuance of such assistance unnecessary or undesirable;

(3) If the President finds that any purposes of the Act have been substantially accomplished by the action of any other intergovernmental organizations or finds that the purposes of the Act are incapable of satisfactory accomplishment; and

(4) If the President finds that any of the assurances given pursuant to section 3 are not being carried out.

SEC. 6. Assistance to any country under this Act may, unless sooner terminated by the President, be terminated by concurrent resolution by the two Houses of the Congress. . . .

SEC. 8. The chief of any mission to any country receiving assistance under this Act shall be appointed by the President, by and with the advice and consent of the Senate, and shall perform such functions relating to the administration of this Act as the President shall prescribe.

Approved May 22, 1947.

577. TRUMAN LOYALTY ORDER
March 22, 1947
(*Federal Register,* Vol. 12, p. 1935)

See H. S. Commager, "Washington Witch-Hunt," 164 *Nation* 385; G. Seldes, *Witch Hunt;* A. Barth, *Loyalty of Free Men;* H. D. Lasswell, *National Security and Individual Freedom;* J. L. O'Brian, *National Security and Individual Freedom.*

PART I
INVESTIGATION OF APPLICANTS

1. There shall be a loyalty investigation of every person entering the civilian employment of any department or agency of the Executive Branch of the Federal Government.

A. Investigations of persons entering the competitive service shall be conducted by the Civil Service Commission, except in such cases as are covered by a special agreement between the commission and any given department or agency.

B. Investigations of persons other than those entering the competitive service shall be conducted by the employing department or agency. Departments and agencies without investigative organizations shall utilize the investigative facilities of the Civil Service Commission.

2. The investigations of persons entering the employ of the Executive Branch may be conducted after any such person enters upon actual employment therein, but in any such case the appointment of such person shall be conditioned upon a favorable determination with respect to his loyalty. . . .

3. An investigation shall be made of all applicants at all available pertinent sources of information and shall include reference to:

A. Federal Bureau of Investigation files.

B. Civil Service Commission files.

C. Military and Naval Intelligence files.

D. The files of any other appropriate government investigative or intelligence agency.

E. House Committee on un-American Activities files.

F. Local law-enforcement files at the place of residence and employment of the applicant, including municipal, county and state law-enforcement files.

G. Schools and colleges attended by applicant.

H. Former employers of applicant.

I. References given by applicant.

J. Any other appropriate source.

4. Whenever derogatory information with respect to loyalty of an applicant is revealed, a full field investigation shall be conducted. A full field investigation shall also be conducted of those applicants, or of applicants for particular positions, as may be designated by the head of the employing department or agency, such designations to be based on the determination by any such head of the best interests of national security.

PART II

INVESTIGATION OF EMPLOYES

1. The head of each department and agency in the Executive Branch of the Government shall be personally responsible for an effective program to assure that disloyal civilian officers or employes are not retained in employment in his department or agency.

A. He shall be responsible for prescribing and supervising the loyalty determination procedures of his department or agency, in accordance with the provisions of this order, which shall be considered as providing minimum requirements.

B. The head of a department or agency which does not have an investigative organization shall utilize the investigative facilities of the Civil Service Commission.

2. The head of each department and agency shall appoint one or more loyalty boards, each composed of not less than three representatives of the department or agency concerned, for the purpose of hearing loyalty cases arising within such department or agency and making recommendations with respect to the removal of any officer or employe of such department or agency on grounds relating to loyalty, and he shall prescribe regulations for the conduct of the proceedings before such boards.

A. An officer or employe who is charged with being disloyal shall have a right to an administrative hearing before a loyalty board in the employing department or agency. He may appear before such board personally, accompanied by counsel or representative of his own choosing, and present evidence on his own behalf, through witnesses or by affidavit.

B. The officer or employe shall be served with a written notice of such hearing in sufficient time, and shall be informed therein of the nature of the charges against him in sufficient detail, so that he will be enabled to prepare his defense. The charges shall be stated as specifically and completely as, in the discretion of the employing department or agency, security considerations permit, and the officer or employe shall be informed in the notice (1) of his right to reply to such charges in writing within a specified reason-

able period of time, (2) of his right to an administrative hearing on such charges before a loyalty board, and (3) of his right to appear before such board personally, to be accompanied by counsel or representative of his own choosing, and to present evidence on his behalf, through witness or by affidavit.

3. A recommendation of removal by a loyalty board shall be subject to appeal by the officer or employe affected, prior to his removal, to the head of the employing department or agency or to such person or persons as may be designated by such head, under such regulations as may be prescribed by him, and the decision of the department or agency concerned shall be subject to appeal to the Civil Service Commission's Loyalty Review Board, hereinafter provided for, for an advisory recommendation.

4. The rights of hearing, notice thereof, and appeal therefrom shall be accorded to every officer or employe prior to his removal on grounds of disloyalty, irrespective of tenure, or of manner, method, or nature of appointment, but the head of the employing department or agency may suspend any officer or employe at any time pending a determination with respect to loyalty.

5. The loyalty boards of the various departments and agencies shall furnish to the Loyalty Review Board, hereinafter provided for, such reports as may be requested concerning the operation of the loyalty program in any such department or agency.

PART III

RESPONSIBILITIES OF CIVIL SERVICE COMMISSION

1. There shall be established in the Civil Service Commission a Loyalty Review Board of not less than three impartial persons, the members of which shall be officers or employes of the commission.

A. The board shall have authority to review cases involving persons recommended for dismissal on grounds relating to loyalty by the loyalty board of any department or agency and to make advisory recommendations thereon to the head of the employing department or agency. Such cases may be referred to the board either by the employing department or agency, or by the officer or employe concerned.

B. The board shall make rules and regulations, not inconsistent with the provisions of this order, deemed necessary to implement statutes and executive orders relating to employe loyalty.

C. The Loyalty Review Board shall also:

(1) Advise all departments and agencies on all problems relating to employe loyalty.

(2) Disseminate information pertinent to employe loyalty programs.

(3) Coordinate the employe loyalty policies and procedures of the several departments and agencies.

(4) Make reports and submit recommendations to the Civil Service Commission for transmission to the President from time to time as may be necessary to the maintenance of the employe loyalty program.

2. There shall also be established and maintained in the Civil Service Commission a central master index covering all persons on whom loyalty investigations have been made by any department or agency since Sept. 1, 1939. Such master index shall contain the name of each person investigated, adequate identifying information concerning each such person, and a reference to each department and agency which has conducted a loyalty investigation concerning the person involved. . . .

B. The reports and other investigative material and information developed by the investigating department or agency shall be retained by such department or agency in each case.

3. The Loyalty Review Board shall currently be furnished by the Department of Justice the name of each foreign or domestic organization, association, movement, group or combination of persons which the Attorney General, after appropriate investigation and determination, designates as totalitarian, Fascist, Communist or subversive, or as having adopted a policy of advocating or approving the commission of acts of force or violence to deny others their rights under the Constitution of the United States, or as seeking to alter the form of government of the United States by unconstitutional means.

A. The Loyalty Review Board shall disseminate such information to all departments and agencies.

PART IV

SECURITY MEASURES IN INVESTIGATIONS

1. At the request of the head of any department or agency of the Executive Branch an investigative agency shall make available to such head, personally, all investigative material and information collected by the investigative agency concerning any employe or prospective employe of the requesting department or agency, or shall make such material and information available to any officer or officers designated by such head and approved by the investigative agency.

2. Notwithstanding the foregoing requirement, however, the investigative agency may refuse to disclose the names of confidential informants, provided it furnishes sufficient information about such informants on the basis of which the requesting department or agency can make an adequate evaluation of the information furnished by them, and provided it advises the requesting department or agency in writing that it is essential to the protection of the informants or to the investigation of other cases that the identity of the informants not be revealed. Investigative agencies shall not use this discretion to decline to reveal sources of information where such action is not essential.

3. Each department and agency of the Executive Branch should develop and maintain, for the collection and analysis of information relating to the loyalty of its employes and prospective employes, a staff specially trained in security techniques, and an effective security control system for protecting such information generally and for protecting confidential sources of such information particularly.

PART V

STANDARDS

1. The standard for the refusal of employment or the removal from employment

in an executive department or agency on grounds relating to loyalty shall be that, on all the evidence, reasonable grounds exist for belief that the person involved is disloyal to the Government of the United States.

2. Activities and associations of an applicant or employe which may be considered in connection with the determination of disloyalty may include one or more of the following:

A. Sabotage, espionage, or attempts or preparations therefor, knowingly associating with spies or saboteurs;

B. Treason or sedition or advocacy thereof;

C. Advocacy of revolution of force or violence to alter the constitutional form of Government of the United States;

D. Intentional, unauthorized disclosure to any person, under circumstances which may indicate disloyalty to the United States, of documents or information of a confidential or non-public character obtained by the person making the disclosure as a result of his employment by the Government of the United States;

E. Performing or attempting to perform his duties, or *otherwise acting, so as to serve the interests of another government in preference to the interests of the United States.*

F. Membership in, affiliation with or *sympathetic association* with any foreign or *domestic* organization, association, movement, *group or combination* of persons, designated by the Attorney General as totalitarian, Fascist, Communist, or *subversive,* or as having adopted a policy of advocating or approving the commission of acts of force or violence to deny other persons their rights under the Constitution of the United States, or as seeking to alter the form of Government of the United States by unconstitutional means.

578. THE MARSHALL PLAN
June 5, 1947
(*Congressional Record,* June 30, 1947)

On June 5, 1947, at a Harvard commencement, Secretary of State George C. Marshall delivered a notable address setting forth the basic principles of American policy toward the postwar rehabilitation of Europe. Secretary Marshall viewed the European economy as a unit, and suggested that European countries in need of American aid should join together in drawing up a program stating their needs. Great Britain and France, after consulting with Prime Minister Molotov of the Soviet Union, issued an invitation on July 3, 1947 to twenty-two European countries to participate in a conference, the purpose of which was to draw up a blueprint of European reconstruction to present to the United States. The Soviet Union took an increasingly hostile view of the undertaking, saw the Marshall Plan as the beginning of an anti-Russian bloc, and refused to participate. The conference of European countries opened at Paris on July 12, and submitted a general report on European needs, September 23, 1947. See S. B. Fay, "The Marshall Plan," *Current History,* September 1947; *New York Times,* September 24, 1947, for the conference report.

Remarks by the Honorable George C. Marshall, Secretary of State, at Harvard University on June 5, 1947.

I need not tell you gentlemen that the world situation is very serious. That must be apparent to all intelligent people. I think one difficulty is that the problem is one of such enormous complexity that the very mass of facts presented to the public by press and radio make it exceedingly difficult for the man in the street to reach a clear appraisement of the situation. Furthermore, the people of this country are distant from the troubled areas of the earth and it is hard for them to comprehend the plight and consequent reactions of the long-suffering peoples, and the effect of those reactions on their governments in connection with our efforts to promote peace in the world.

In considering the requirements for the rehabilitation of Europe the physical loss of life, the visible destruction of cities, factories, mines, and railroads was correctly estimated, but it has become obvious during recent months that this visible destruction was probably less serious than the dislocation of the entire fabric of European economy. For the past 10 years conditions have been highly abnormal. The feverish preparation for war and the more feverish maintenance of the war effort engulfed all aspects of national economies. Machinery has fallen into disrepair or is entirely obsolete. Under the arbitrary and destructive Nazi rule, virtually every possible enterprise was geared into the German war machine. Long-standing commercial ties, private institutions, banks, insurance companies and shipping companies disappeared, through loss of capital, absorption through nationalization or by simple destruction. In many countries, confidence in the local currency has been severely shaken. The breakdown of the business structure of Europe during the war was complete. Recovery has been seriously retarded by the fact that 2 years after the close of hostilities a peace settlement with Germany and Austria has not been agreed upon. But even given a more prompt solution of these difficult problems, the rehabilitation of the economic structure of Europe quite evidently will require a much longer time and greater effort than had been foreseen.

There is a phase of this matter which is both interesting and serious. The farmer has always produced the foodstuffs to exchange with the city dweller for the other necessities of life. This division of labor is the basis of modern civilization. At the present time it is threatened with breakdown. The town and city industries are not producing adequate goods to exchange with the food-producing farmer. Raw materials and fuel are in short supply. Machinery is lacking or worn out. The farmer or the peasant cannot find the goods for sale which he desires to purchase. So the sale of his farm produce for money which he cannot use seems to him an unprofitable transaction. He, therefore, has withdrawn many fields from crop cultivation and is using them for grazing. He feeds more grain to stock and finds for himself and his family an ample supply of food, however short he may be on clothing and the other ordinary gadgets of civilization.

Meanwhile people in the cities are short of food and fuel. So the governments are forced to use their foreign money and credits to procure these necessities abroad. This process exhausts funds which are urgently needed for reconstruction. Thus a very serious situation is rapidly developing which bodes no good for the world. The modern system of the division of labor upon which the exchange of products is based is in danger of breaking down.

The truth of the matter is that Europe's requirements for the next 3 or 4 years of foreign food and other essential products—principally from America—are so much greater than her present ability to pay that she must have substantial additional help, or face economic, social, and political deterioration of a very grave character.

The remedy lies in breaking the vicious circle and restoring the confidence of the European people in the economic future of their own countries and of Europe as a whole. The manufacturer and the farmer throughout wide areas must be able and willing to exchange their products for currencies the continuing value of which is not open to question.

Aside from the demoralizing effect on the world at large and the possibilities of disturbances arising as a result of the desperation of the people concerned, the consequences to the economy of the United States should be apparent to all. It is logical that the United States should do whatever it is able to do to assist in the return of normal economic health in the world, without which there can be no political stability and no assured peace. Our policy is directed not against any county or doctrine but against hunger, poverty, desperation, and chaos. Its purpose should be the revival of a working economy in the world so as to permit the emergence of political and social conditions in which free institutions can exist. Such assistance, I am convinced, must not be on a piecemeal basis as various crises develop. Any assistance that this Government may render in the future should provide a cure rather than a mere palliative. Any government that is willing to assist in the task of recovery will find full cooperation, I am sure, on the part of the United States Government. Any government which maneuvers to block the recovery of other countries cannot expect help from us. Furthermore, governments, political parties, or groups which seek to perpetuate human misery in order to profit therefrom politically or otherwise will encounter the opposition of the United States.

It is already evident that, before the United States Government can proceed much further in its efforts to alleviate the situation and help start the European world on its way to recovery, there must be some agreement among the countries of Europe as to the requirements of the situation and the part those countries themselves will take in order to give proper effect to whatever action might be undertaken by this Government. It would be neither fitting nor efficacious for this Government to undertake to draw up unilaterally a program designed

to place Europe on its feet economically. This is the business of the Europeans. The initiative, I think, must come from Europe. The role of this country should consist of friendly aid in the drafting of a European program and of later support of such a program so far as it may be practical for us to do so. The program should be a joint one, agreed to by a number, if not all European nations.

An essential part of any successful action on the part of the United States is an understanding on the part of the people of America of the character of the problem and the remedies to be applied. Political passion and prejudice should have no part. With foresight, and a willingness on the part of our people to face up to the vast responsibility which history has clearly placed upon our country, the difficulties I have outlined can and will be overcome.

579. EVERSON v. BOARD OF EDUCATION
330 U.S. 1
1947

The rising costs of education during the war and postwar years led to demands from parochial and independent schools for some form of governmental aid. The Board of Education of Ewing, New Jersey, provided for free transportation for all pupils to public and parochial schools alike. The challenge to this act reintroduced the old controversy over the separation of church and state. The concurring and dissenting opinions in this case give abundant historical analysis and bibliographical references; see, also, J. M. O'Neill, *Religion and Education Under the Constitution;* A. W. Johnson, *Legal Status of Church-State Relationships in the United States;* Leo Pfeffer, *Church, State, and Freedom;* Leo Pfeffer, "Church and State, Something Less than Separation," 19 *U. of Chicago Law Rev.* 1; E. S. Corwin, "Supreme Court as National School Board," 14 *Law and Cont. Problems* 3.

Appeal from the Court of Errors and Appeals of the State of New Jersey.
Affirmed.

BLACK, J. . . . A New Jersey statute authorizes its local school districts to make

rules and contracts for the transportation of children to and from schools. The appellee, a township board of education, acting pursuant to this statute authorized reimbursement to parents of money expended by them for the bus transportation of their children on regular busses operated by the public transportation system. Part of this money was for the payment of transportation of some children in the community to Catholic parochial schools. . . .

The appellant, in his capacity as a district taxpayer, filed suit in a State court challenging the right of the Board to reimburse parents of parochial school students. He contended that the statute and the resolution passed pursuant to it violated both the State and the Federal Constitutions. . . .

The only contention here is that the State statute and the resolution, in so far as they authorized reimbursement to parents of children attending parochial schools, violate the Federal Constitution in these two respects, which to some extent, overlap. First. They authorize the State to take by taxation the private property of some and bestow it upon others, to be used for their own private purposes. This, it is alleged violates the due process clause of the Fourteenth Amendment. Second. The statute and the resolution forced inhabitants to pay taxes to help support and maintain schools which are dedicated to, and which regularly teach, the Catholic Faith. This is alleged to be a use of State power to support church schools contrary to the prohibition of the First Amendment which the Fourteenth Amendment made applicable to the states. . . .

Insofar as the second phase of the due process argument may differ from the first, it is by suggesting that taxation for transportation of children to church schools constitutes support of a religion by the State. But if the law is invalid for this reason, it is because it violates the First Amendment's prohibition against the establishment of religion by law. This is the exact question raised by appellant's second contention, to consideration of which we now turn.

Second. The New Jersey statute is challenged as a "law respecting an establishment of religion." The First Amendment, as made applicable to the states by the Fourteenth, commands that a state "shall make no law respecting an establishment of religion, or prohibiting the free exercise thereof." These words of the First Amendment reflected in the minds of early Americans a vivid mental picture of conditions and practices which they fervently wished to stamp out in order to preserve liberty for themselves and for their posterity. Doubtless their goal has not been entirely reached; but so far has the Nation moved toward it that the expression "law respecting an establishment of religion," probably does not so vividly remind present-day Americans of the evils, fears, and political problems that caused that expression to be written into our Bill of Rights. Whether this New Jersey law is one respecting the "establishment of religion" requires an understanding of the meaning of that language, particularly with respect to the imposition of taxes. Once again, therefore, it is not inappropriate briefly to review the background and environment of the period in which that constitutional language was fashioned and adopted. . . .

This Court has previously recognized that the provisions of the First Amendment, in the drafting and adoption of which Madison and Jefferson played such leading roles, had the same objective and were intended to provide the same protection against governmental intrusion on religious liberty as the Virginia statute. Reynolds v. United States, supra, 98 U.S. at page 164, [etc.]. Prior to the adoption of the Fourteenth Amendment, the First Amendment did not apply as a restraint against the states. Most of them did soon provide similar constitutional protections for religious liberty. But some states persisted for about half a century in imposing restraints upon the free exercise of religion and in discriminating against particular religious groups. In recent years, so far as the provision against the establishment of a religion is concerned, the question has most frequently arisen in connection with proposed state aid to church schools and efforts to carry on religious teachings in the public schools in accordance with the tenets of a particular sect. Some churches have either sought or accepted state financial support for their schools. Here again the efforts to obtain state aid or acceptance of it have not been limited to any one particular faith. The state courts, in the main, have remained faithful to the language of their own constitutional provisions designed to protect religious freedom and to separate religions and governments. Their decisions, however, show the difficulty in drawing the line between tax legislation which provides funds for the welfare of the general public and that which is designed to support institutions which teach religion.

The meaning and scope of the First Amendment, preventing establishment of religion or prohibiting the free exercise thereof, in the light of its history and the evils it was designed forever to suppress, have been several times elaborated by the decisions of this Court prior to the application of the First Amendment to the states by the Fourteenth. The broad meaning given the Amendment by these earlier cases has been accepted by this Court in its decisions concerning an individual's religious freedom rendered since the Fourteenth Amendment was interpreted to make the prohibitions of the First applicable to state action abridging religious freedom. There is every reason to give the same application and broad interpretation to the "establishment of religion" clause. The interrelation of these complementary clauses was well summarized in a statement of the Court of Appeals of South Carolina, quoted with approval by this Court, in Watson v. Jones, 13 Wall. 679: "The structure of our government has, for the preservation of civil liberty, rescued the temporal institutions from religious interference. On the other hand, it has secured religious liberty from the invasions of the civil authority."

The "establishment of religion" clause of the First Amendment means at least this: Neither a state nor the Federal Government can set up a church. Neither can pass laws which aid one religion, aid all religions, or prefer one religion over another. Neither can force nor influence a person to go to or to remain away from church against his will or force him to profess a belief or disbelief in any religion. No person can be punished for entertaining or professing religious beliefs or disbeliefs, for church attendance or non-attendance. No tax in any amount, large or small, can be levied to support any religious activities or institutions, whatever they may be called, or whatever form they may adopt to teach or practice religion. Neither a state nor the Federal Government can, openly or secretly, participate in the affairs of any religious organizations or groups and vice versa. In the words of Jefferson, the clause against establishment of religion by law was intended to erect "a wall of separation between Church and State." Reynolds v. United States, supra, 98 U.S. at page 164.

We must consider the New Jersey statute in accordance with the foregoing limitations imposed by the First Amendment. But we must not strike that state statute down if it is within the state's constitutional power even though it approaches the verge of that power. New Jersey cannot consistently with the "establishment of religion" clause of the First Amendment contribute tax-raised funds to the support of an institution which teaches the tenets and faith of any church. On the other hand, other language of the amendment commands that New Jersey can-

not hamper its citizens in the free exercise of their own religion. Consequently, it cannot exclude individual Catholics, Lutherans, Mohammedans, Baptists, Jews, Methodists, Non-believers, Presbyterians, or the members of any other faith, *because of their faith, or lack of it,* from receiving the benefits of public welfare legislation. While we do not mean to intimate that a state could not provide transportation only to children attending public schools, we must be careful, in protecting the citizens of New Jersey against state-established churches, to be sure that we do not inadvertently prohibit New Jersey from extending its general State law benefits to all its citizens without regard to their religious belief.

Measured by these standards, we cannot say that the First Amendment prohibits New Jersey from spending tax-raised funds to pay the bus fares of parochial school pupils as a part of a general program under which it pays the fares of pupils attending public and other schools. It is undoubtedly true that children are helped to get to church schools. There is even a possibility that some of the children might not be sent to the church schools if the parents were compelled to pay their children's bus fares out of their own pockets when transportation to a public school would have been paid for by the State. The same possibility exists where the state requires a local transit company to provide reduced fares to school children including those attending parochial schools, or where a municipally owned transportation system undertakes to carry all school children free of charge. Moreover, state-paid policemen, detailed to protect children going to and from church schools from the very real hazards of traffic, would serve much the same purpose and accomplish much the same result as state provisions intended to guarantee free transportation of a kind which the state deems to be best for the school children's welfare. And parents might refuse to risk their children to the serious danger of traffic accidents going to and from parochial schools, the approaches to which were not protected by policemen. Similarly, parents might be reluctant to permit their children to attend schools which the state had cut off from such general government services as ordinary police and fire protection, connections for sewage disposal, public highways and sidewalks. Of course, cutting off church schools from these services, so separate and so indisputably marked off from the religious function, would make it far more difficult for the schools to operate. But such is obviously not the purpose of the First Amendment. That Amendment requires the state to be a neutral in its relations with groups of religious believers and non-believers; it does not require the state to be their adversary. State power is no more to be used so as to handicap religions, than it is to favor them.

This Court has said that parents may, in the discharge of their duty under state compulsory education laws, send their children to a religious rather than a public school if the school meets the secular educational requirements which the state has power to impose. See Pierce v. Society of Sisters, 268 U.S. 510. It appears that these parochial schools meet New Jersey's requirements. The state contributes no money to the schools. It does not support them. Its legislation, as applied, does no more than provide a general program to help parents get their children, regardless of their religion, safely and expeditiously to and from accredited schools.

The First Amendment has erected a wall between church and state. That wall must be kept high and impregnable. We could not approve the slightest breach. New Jersey has not breached it here.

Affirmed.

580. TAFT-HARTLEY ACT
June 23, 1947
(Public Law 101, 80th Congress)

The National Labor Relations Act of 1935 placed limitations on the conduct of employers in labor-management disputes. See Doc. No. 500. The Taft-Hartley Act placed limitations on the conduct of trade unions in labor-management disputes. Some of the important provisions of the act banned the closed shop, permitted employers to sue unions for breaking contracts, forbade union contributions to political campaigns, and required unions to give 60 days' notice before inaugurating strikes. President Truman vetoed the act, but it was passed over his veto by a vote of 331 to 83 in the House and 68 to 25 in the Senate. After 1947, the trade union movement conducted a continuous campaign to repeal or amend this law. See H. A. Millis and E. C. Brown, *From the Wagner Act to Taft-Hartley;* J. Seidman, *American Labor from Defense to Reconversion;* F. A. Hartley, *Our New National Labor Policy.*

An Act to amend the National Labor Relations Act, to provide additional facilities for the mediation of labor disputes affecting commerce, to equalize legal responsibilities of labor organizations and employers, and for other purposes. . . .

SEC. 101. The National Labor Relations Act is hereby amended to read as follows: . . . .

"SEC. 3. (a) The National Labor Relations Board (hereinafter called the 'Board') created by this Act prior to its amendment by the Labor Management Relations Act, 1947, is hereby continued as an agency of the United States, except that the Board shall consist of five instead of three members, appointed by the President by and with the advice and consent of the Senate. . . .

"SEC. 7. Employees shall have the right to self-organization, to form, join, or assist labor organizations, to bargain collectively through representatives of their own choosing, and to engage in other concerted activities for the purpose of collective bargaining or other mutual aid or protection, and shall also have the right to refrain from any or all of such activities except to the extent that such right may be affected by an agreement requiring membership in a labor organization as a condition of employment as authorized in section 8 (a) (3).

"SEC. 8. (a) It shall be an unfair labor practice for an employer—

"(1) to interfere with, restrain, or coerce employees in the exercise of the rights guaranteed in section 7;

"(2) to dominate or interfere with the formation or administration of any labor organization or contribute financial or other support to it: *Provided,* That subject to rules and regulations made and published by the Board pursuant to section 6, an employer, shall not be prohibited from permitting employees to confer with him during working hours without loss of time or pay;

"(3) by discrimination in regard to hire or tenure of employment or any term or condition of employment to encourage or discourage membership in any labor organization: *Provided,* That nothing in this Act, or in any other statute of the United States, shall preclude an employer from making an agreement with a labor organization . . . to require as a condition of employment membership therein, (i) if such labor organization is the representative of the employees as provided in section 9 (a), in the appropriate collective-bargaining unit covered by such agreement when made; and (ii) if, following the most recent election held as provided in section 9 (e) the Board shall have certified that at least a majority of the employees eligible to vote in such election have voted to authorize such labor organization to make such an agreement: *Provided further,* That no employer shall justify any discrimination against an employee for nonmembership in a labor organization (A) if he has reasonable grounds for believing that such membership was not available to the employee on the same terms and conditions generally applicable to other members, or (B) if he has reasonable grounds for believing that membership was denied or terminated for reasons other than the failure of the employee to tender the periodic dues and the initiation fees uniformly required as a condition of acquiring or retaining membership;

"(4) to discharge or otherwise discriminate against an employee because he has filed charges or given testimony under this Act;

"(5) to refuse to bargain collectively with the representatives of his employees, subject to the provisions of section 9 (a).

"(b) It shall be an unfair labor practice for a labor organization or its agents—

"(1) to restrain or coerce (A) employees in the exercise of the rights guaranteed in section 7: *Provided,* That this paragraph shall not impair the right of a labor organization to prescribe its own rules with respect to the acquisition or retention of membership therein; or (B) an employer in the selection of his representatives for the purposes of collective bargaining or the adjustment of grievances;

"(2) to cause or attempt to cause an employer to discriminate against an employee in violation of subsection (a) (3) or to discriminate against an employee with respect to whom membership in such organization has been denied or terminated on some ground other than his failure to tender the periodic dues and the initiation fees uniformly required as a condition of acquiring or retaining membership;

"(3) to refuse to bargain collectively with an employer, provided it is the representative of his employees subject to the provision of section 9 (a);

"(4) to engage in, or to induce or encourage the employees of any employer to engage in, a strike or a concerted refusal in the course of their employment to use, manufacture, process, transport, or otherwise handle or work on any goods, articles, materials, or commodities or to perform any services, where an object thereof is: (A) forcing or requiring any employer or self-employed person to join any labor or employer organization or any employer or other person to cease using, selling, handling, transporting, or otherwise dealing in the products of any other producer, processor, or manufacturer, or to cease doing business with any other person; (B) forcing or requiring any other employer to recognize or bargain with a labor organization as the representative of his employees unless such labor organization has been certified as the representative of such employees under the provisions of section 9; (C) forcing or requiring any employer to recognize or bargain with a particular labor organization as the representative of his employees if another labor organization has been certified as the representative of such employees under the provisions of section 9; (D) forcing or requiring any employer to assign particular work to employees in a particular labor organization or in a particular trade, craft, or class rather than to employees in another labor organization or in another trade, craft, or class, unless such employer is failing to conform to an order or certification of the Board determining the bargaining representative for employees performing such work: *Provided,* That nothing contained in this subsection (b) shall be construed to make unlawful a refusal by any person to enter upon the premises of any employer (other than his own employer), if the employees of such employer are engaged in a strike ratified or approved by a representative of such employees whom such employer is required to recognize under this Act;

"(5) to require of employees covered by an agreement authorized under subsection (a) (3) the payment, as a condition precedent to becoming a member of such organization, of a fee in an amount which the Board finds excessive or discriminatory under all the circumstances. In making such a finding, the Board shall consider, among other relevant factors, the practices and customs of labor organizations in the particular industry, and the wages currently paid to the employees affected; and

"(6) to cause or attempt to cause an employer to pay or deliver or agree to pay or deliver any money or other thing of value, in the nature of an exaction, for services which are not performed or not to be performed.

"(c) The expressing of any views, argument, or opinion, or the dissemination thereof, whether in written, printed, graphic, or visual form, shall not constitute or be evidence of an unfair labor practice under any of the provisions of this Act, if such expression contains no threat of reprisal or force or promise of benefit.

"(d) . . . That where there is in effect a collective-bargaining contract covering employees in an industry affecting commerce, the duty to bargain collectively shall also mean that no party to such contract shall terminate or modify such contract, unless the party desiring such termination or modification—

"(1) serves a written notice upon the other party to the contract of the proposed termination or modification sixty days prior to the expiration date thereof, or in the event such contract contains no expiration date, sixty days prior to the time it is proposed to make such termination or modification;

"(2) offers to meet and confer with the other party for the purpose of negotiating a new contract or a contract containing the proposed modifications;

"(3) notifies the Federal Mediation and Conciliation Service within thirty days after such notice of the existence of a dispute, and simultaneously therewith notifies any State or Territorial agency established to mediate and conciliate disputes within the State or Territory where the dispute occurred, provided no agreement has been reached by that time; and

"(4) continues in full force and effect without resorting to strike or lock-out, all the terms and conditions of the existing contract for a period of sixty days after such notice is given or until the expiration date of such contract, whichever occurs later: . . .

"(h) No investigation shall be made by the Board of any question affecting commerce concerning the representation of employees, raised by a labor organization under subsection (c) of this section, no petition under section 9 (e) (1) shall be entertained, and no complaint shall be issued pursuant to a charge made by a labor organization under subsection (b) of section 10, unless there is on file with the Board an affidavit executed contemporaneously or within the preceding twelve-month period by each officer of such labor organization and the officers of any national or international labor organization of which it is an affiliate or constituent unit that he is not a member of the Communist Party or affiliated with such party, and that he does not believe in, and is not a member of or supports any organization that believes in or teaches, the overthrow of the United States Government by force or by any illegal or unconstitutional methods. The provisions of section 35 A of the Criminal Code shall be applicable in respect to such affidavits. . . .

SEC. 301. . . . (b) Any labor organization which represents employees in an industry affecting commerce as defined in this Act and any employer whose activities affect commerce as defined in this Act shall be bound by the acts of its agents. Any such labor organization may sue or be sued as an entity and in behalf of the employees whom it represents in the courts of the United States. Any money judgment against a labor organization in a district court of the United States shall be enforceable only against the organization as an entity and against its assets, and shall not be enforceable against any individual member or his assets. . . .

SEC. 303. (a) It shall be unlawful, for the purposes of this section only, in an industry or activity affecting commerce, for any labor organization to engage in, or to induce or encourage the employees of any employer to engage in, a strike or a concerted refusal in the course of their employment to use, manufacture, process, transport, or otherwise handle or work on any goods, articles, materials, or commodities or to perform any services, where an object thereof is—

(1) forcing or requiring any employer or self-employed person to join any labor or employer organization or any employer or other person to cease using, selling, handling, transporting, or otherwise dealing in the products of any other producer, processor or manufacturer, or to cease doing business with any other person;

(2) forcing or requiring any other employer to recognize or bargain with a labor organization as the representative of his employees unless such labor organization has been certified as the representative of such employees under the provisions of section 9 of the National Labor Relations Act;

(3) forcing or requiring any employer to recognize or bargain with a particular labor organization as the representative of his employees if another labor organization has been certified as the representative of such employees under the provi-

sions of section 9 of the National Labor Relations Act;

(4) forcing or requiring any employer to assign particular work to employees in a particular labor organization or in a particular trade, craft, or class rather than to employees in another labor organization or in another trade, craft, or class unless such employer is failing to conform to an order of certification of the National Labor Relations Board determining the bargaining representative for employees performing such work. Nothing contained in this subsection shall be construed to make unlawful a refusal by any person to enter upon the premises of any employer (other than his own employer), if the employees of such employer are engaged in a strike ratified or approved by a representative of such employees whom such employer is required to recognize under the National Labor Relations Act.

(b) Whoever shall be injured in his business or property by reason of any violation of subsection (a) may sue therefor in any district court of the United States subject to the limitations and provisions of section 301 hereof without respect to the amount in controversy, or in any other court having jurisdiction of the parties, and shall recover the damages by him sustained and the cost of the suit. . . .

SEC. 304. Section 313 of the Federal Corrupt Practices Act, 1925 (U.S.C., 1940 edition, title 2, sec. 251; Supp. V, title 50, App., sec. 1509), as amended, is amended to read as follows:

"SEC. 313. It is unlawful for any national bank, or any corporation organized by authority of any law of Congress, to make a contribution or expenditure in connection with any election to any political office, or in connection with any primary election or political convention or caucus held to select candidates for any political office, or for any corporation whatever, or any labor organization to make a contribution or expenditure in connection with any election at which Presidential and Vice Presidential electors or a Senator or Representative in or a Delegate or Resident Commissioner to Congress are to be voted for, or in connection with any primary election or political convention or caucus held to select candidates for any of the foregoing offices, or for any candidate, political committee, or other person to accept or receive any contribution prohibited by this section. . . .

SEC. 305. It shall be unlawful for any individual employed by the United States or any agency thereof including wholly owned Government corporations to participate in any strike. Any individual employed by the United States or by any such agency who strikes shall be discharged immediately from his employment, and shall forfeit his civil service status, if any, and shall not be eligible for reemployment for three years by the United States or any such agency. . . .

581. NATIONAL SECURITY ACT OF 1947
July 26, 1947
(Public Law 253, 80th Congress)

This act provided for the unification of the armed forces under the supervision of a new cabinet officer, the Secretary of Defense. It also provided for the creation of a National Security Council to coordinate the domestic, foreign, and military policies of the government relating to national security. The Security Council speedily became a kind of super-cabinet operating in the broad field of national security. See R. Cutler, "The Development of the National Security Council," 34 *Foreign Affairs* 441; D. Anderson, "The President and National Security," *Atlantic Monthly,* January 1956.

An Act to promote the national security by providing for a Secretary of Defense; for a National Military Establishment; for a Department of the Army, a Department of the Navy, and a Department of the Air Force; and for the coordination of the activities of the National Military Establishment with other departments and agencies of the Government concerned with the national security.

SEC. 101. (a) There is hereby established a council to be known as the National Security Council (hereinafter in this section referred to as the "Council").

The President of the United States shall preside over meetings of the Council: *Provided,* That in his absence he may designate a member of the Council to preside in his place.

The function of the Council shall be to advise the President with respect to the integration of domestic, foreign, and military policies relating to the national security so as to enable the military services and the other departments and agencies of the Government to cooperate more effectively in matters involving the national security.

The Council shall be composed of the President; the Secretary of State; the Secretary of Defense; the Secretary of the Army; the Secretary of the Navy; the Secretary of the Air Force; the Chairman of the National Security Resources Board; and such of the following named officers as the President may designate from time to time: The Secretaries of the executive departments, the Chairman of the Munitions Board, and the Chairman of the Research and Development Board; but no such additional member shall be designated until the advice and consent of the Senate has been given to his appointment to the office the holding of which authorizes his designation as a member of the Council.

(b) In addition to performing such other functions as the President may direct, for the purpose of more effectively coordinating the policies and functions of the departments and agencies of the Government relating to the national security, it shall, subject to the direction of the President, be the duty of the Council—

(1) to assess and appraise the objectives, commitments, and risks of the United States in relation to our actual and potential military power in the interest of national security, for the purpose of making recommendations to the President in connection therewith; and

(2) to consider policies on matters of common interest to the departments and agencies of the Government concerned

with the national security, and to make recommendations to the President in connection therewith. . . .

(d) The Council shall, from time to time, make such recommendations, and such other reports to the President as it deems appropriate or as the President may require.

SEC. 102. (a) There is hereby established under the National Security Council a Central Intelligence Agency with a Director of Central Intelligence, who shall be the head thereof. . . .

(d) For the purpose of coordinating the intelligence activities of the several Government departments and agencies in the interest of national security, it shall be the duty of the Agency, under the direction of the National Security Council—. . . .

(3) to correlate and evaluate intelligence relating to the national security, and provide for the appropriate dissemination of such intelligence within the Government using where appropriate existing agencies and facilities: . . . .

SEC. 103. (a) There is hereby established a National Security Resources Board (hereinafter in this section referred to as the "Board") to be composed of the Chairman of the Board and such heads or representatives of the various executive departments and independent agencies as may from time to time be designated by the President to be members of the Board. . . .

(c) It shall be the function of the Board to advise the President concerning the coordination of military, industrial, and civilian mobilization, including—

(1) policies concerning industrial and civilian mobilization in order to assure the most effective mobilization and maximum utilization of the Nation's manpower in the event of war;

(2) programs for the effective use in time of war of the Nation's natural and industrial resources for military and civilian needs, for the maintenance and stabilization of the civilian economy in time of war, and for the adjustment of such economy to war needs and conditions; . . . .

SEC. 201. (a) There is hereby established the National Military Establishment, and the Secretary of Defense shall be the head thereof.

(b) The National Military Establishment shall consist of the Department of the Army, the Department of the Navy, and the Department of the Air Force, together with all other agencies created under title II of this Act.

SEC. 202. (a) There shall be a Secretary of Defense, who shall be appointed from civilian life by the President, by and with the advice and consent of the Senate: *Provided,* That a person who has within ten years been on active duty as a commissioned officer in a Regular component of the armed services shall not be eligible for appointment as Secretary of Defense. The Secretary of Defense shall be the principal assistant to the President in all matters relating to the national security. Under the direction of the President and subject to the provisions of this Act he shall perform the following duties:

(1) Establish general policies and programs for the National Military Establishment and for all of the departments and agencies therein;

(2) Exercise general direction, authority, and control over such departments and agencies;

(3) Take appropriate steps to eliminate unnecessary duplication or overlapping in the fields of procurement, supply, transportation, storage, health, and research;

(4) Supervise and coordinate the preparation of the budget estimates of the departments and agencies comprising the National Military Establishment; formulate and determine the budget estimates for submittal to the Bureau of the Budget; and supervise the budget programs of such departments and agencies under the applicable appropriation Act: . . . .

SEC. 210. There shall be within the National Military Establishment a War Council composed of the Secretary of Defense, as Chairman, who shall have power of decision; the Secretary of the Army; the Secretary of the Navy; the Secretary of the Air Force; the Chief of Staff, United States Army; the Chief of Naval Operations; and the Chief of Staff, United States Air Force. The War Council shall advise the Secretary of Defense on matters of broad policy relating to the armed forces, and shall consider and report on such other matters as the Secretary of Defense may direct.

SEC. 211. (a) There is hereby established within the National Military Establishment the Joint Chiefs of Staff, which shall consist of the Chief of Staff, United States Army; the Chief of Naval Operations; the Chief of Staff, United States Air Force; and the Chief of Staff to the Commander in Chief, if there be one.

(b) Subject to the authority and direction of the President and the Secretary of Defense, it shall be the duty of the Joint Chiefs of Staff—

(1) to prepare strategic plans and to provide for the strategic direction of the military forces;

(2) to prepare joint logistic plans and to assign to the military services logistic responsibilities in accordance with such plans;

(3) to establish unified commands in strategic areas when such unified commands are in the interest of national security;

(4) to formulate policies for joint training of the military forces; . . . .

(c) The Joint Chiefs of Staff shall act as the principal military advisers to the President and the Secretary of Defense and shall perform such other duties as the President and the Secretary of Defense may direct or as may be prescribed by law. . . .

582. THE VANDENBERG RESOLUTION
May 19, 1948
(80th Congress, 2nd Session, *Senate Resolution* 239)

During and after World War II Senator Vandenberg of Michigan emerged as one of the leaders of internationalism and one of the architects of the bipartisan foreign policy. This Resolution was commonly regarded as the forerunner of the Atlantic Pact.

WHEREAS peace with justice and the defense of human rights and fundamental freedoms require international cooperation through more effective use of the United Nations: Therefore be it

Resolved, That the Senate reaffirm the policy of the United States to achieve international peace and security through the United Nations so that armed force shall not be used except in the common interest, and that the President be advised of the sense of the Senate that this Government, by constitutional process, should particularly pursue the following objectives within the United Nations Charter:

(1) Voluntary agreement to remove the veto from all questions involving pacific settlements of international disputes and situations, and from the admission of new members.

(2) Progressive development of regional and other collective arrangements for individual and collective self-defense in accordance with the purposes, principles, and provisions of the Charter.

(3) Association of the United States, by Constitutional process, with such regional and other collective arrangements as are based on continuous and effective self-help and mutual aid, and as affect its national security.

(4) Contributing to the maintenance of peace by making clear its determination to exercise the right of individual or collective self-defense under article 51 should any armed attack occur affecting its national security.

(5) Maximum efforts to obtain agreements to provide the United Nations with armed forces as provided by the Charter, and to obtain agreement among member nations upon universal regulation and reduction of armaments under adequate and dependable guaranty against violation.

(6) If necessary, after adequate effort toward strengthening the United Nations, review of the Charter at an appropriate time by a General Conference called under article 109 or by the General Assembly.

583.   McCOLLUM v. BOARD OF EDUCATION
333 U.S. 203
1948

Another aspect of the rising church-state controversy of the forties emerged from the widespread practice of devoting "released time" to religious instruction in the public schools. As of 1947 over two million pupils in some 2,200 communities participated in released time programs. The Program of the Board of Education of Champaign County, Illinois, was challenged by Vashti McCollum on the ground that it violated the prohibitions of the First Amendment as embraced in the Fourteenth. The concurring opinion, by Justice Frankfurter, presents a full analysis of the historical background and many bibliographical references. See also J. M. O'Neill, *Religion and Education under the Constitution;* and, for a sharply critical review of the decision, E. S. Corwin, "The Supreme Court as National School Board," 23 *Thought* 665; A. W. Johnson and F. H. Yost, *Separation of Church and State;* R. F. Cushman, "Holy Bible and Public Schools," 40 *Cornell L. Q.* 475.

Appeal from the Supreme Court of the State of Illinois.

Action for mandamus by the People of the State of Illinois, on the relation of Vashti McCollum, against the Board of Education of School District No. 71, Champaign County, Ill., and others to require the Board of Education to adopt and enforce rules and regulations prohibiting all instruction in and teaching of all religious education in all public schools in the district and in all public school houses and buildings in the district when occupied by public schools.

BLACK, J. This case relates to the power of a state to utilize its tax-supported public school system in aid of religious instruction insofar as that power may be restricted by the First and Fourteenth Amendments to the Federal Constitution.

The appellant, Vashti McCollum, began this action for mandamus against the Champaign Board of Education in the Circuit Court of Champaign County, Illinois. Her asserted interest was that of a resident and taxpayer of Champaign and of a parent whose child was then enrolled in the Champaign public schools. Illinois has a compulsory education law which, with exceptions, requires parents to send their children, aged seven to sixteen, to its tax-supported public schools where the children are to remain in attendance during the hours when the schools are regularly in session. Parents who violate this law commit a misdemeanor punishable by fine unless the children attend private or parochial schools which meet educational standards fixed by the State. District boards of education are given general supervisory powers over the use of the public school buildings within the school districts.

Appellant's petition for mandamus alleged that religious teachers, employed by private religious groups, were permitted to come weekly into the school buildings during the regular hours set apart for secular teaching, and then and there for a period of thirty minutes substitute their religious teaching for the secular education provided under the compulsory education law. The petitioner charged that this joint public-school, religious-group program violated the First and Fourteenth Amendments to the United States Constitution. . . .

Although there are disputes between the parties as to various inferences that may or may not properly be drawn from the evidence concerning the religious program, the following facts are shown by the record without dispute. In 1940 interested members of the Jewish, Roman Catholic, and a few of the Protestant faiths formed a voluntary association called the Champaign Council on Religious Education. They obtained permission from the Board of Education to offer classes in religious instruction to public school pupils in grades four to nine inclusive. Classes were made up of pupils whose parents signed printed cards requesting that their children be permitted to attend; they were held weekly, thirty minutes for the lower grades, forty-five minutes for the higher. The council employed the religious teachers at no expense to the school authorities, but the instructors were subject to the approval and supervision of the superintendent of schools. The classes were taught in three separate religious groups by Protestant teachers, Catholic priests, and a Jewish rabbi, although for the past several years there have apparently been no classes instructed in the Jewish religion. Classes were conducted in the regular classrooms of the school building. Students who did not choose to take the religious instruction were not released from public school duties; they were required to leave their classrooms and go to some other place in the school building for pursuit of their secular studies. On the other hand, students who were released from secular study for the religious instructions were required to be present at the religious classes. Reports of their presence or absence were to be made to their secular teachers.

The foregoing facts, without reference to others that appear in the record, show the use of tax-supported property for religious instruction and the close cooperation between the school authorities and the religious council in promoting religious education. The operation of the state's compulsory education system thus assists and is integrated with the program of religious instruction carried on by separate religious sects. Pupils compelled by law to go to school for secular education are released in part from their legal duty upon the condition that they attend the religious classes. This is beyond all question a utilization of the tax-established and tax-supported public school system to aid religious groups to spread their faith. And it falls squarely under the ban of the First Amendment (made applicable to the States by the Fourteenth) as we interpreted it in Everson v. Board of Education, 330 U.S. 1, 67 S.Ct. 504. There we said: "Neither a state nor the Federal Government can set up a church. Neither can pass laws which aid one religion, aid all religions, or prefer one religion over another. Neither can force nor influence a person to go to or to remain away from church against his will or force him to profess a belief or disbelief in any religion. No person can be punished for entertaining or professing religious beliefs or disbeliefs, for church attendance or nonattendance. No tax in any amount, large or small, can be levied to support any religious activities or institutions, whatever they may be called, or whatever form they may adopt to teach or practice religion. Neither a state nor the Federal Government can, openly or secretly, participate in the affairs of any religious organizations or groups, and vice versa. In the words of Jefferson, the clause against establishment of religion by law was intended to erect 'a wall of separation between Church and State.' " The majority in the Everson case, and the minority as shown by quotations from the dissenting views agreed that the First Amendment's language, properly interpreted, had erected a wall of separation between Church and State. They disagreed as to the facts shown by the record and as to the proper application of the First Amendment's language to those facts.

Recognizing that the Illinois program is barred by the First and Fourteenth Amendments if we adhere to the views expressed both by the majority and the minority in the Everson case, counsel for the respondents challenge those views as dicta and urge that we reconsider and repudiate them. They argue that historically the First Amendment was intended to forbid only government preference of one religion over another, not an impartial governmental assistance of all religions. In addition they ask that we distinguish or overrule our holding in the Everson case that the Fourteenth Amendment made the "establishment of religion" clause of the First Amendment applicable as a prohibition against the States. After giving full consideration to the arguments presented we are unable to accept either of these contentions.

To hold that a state cannot consistently with the First and Fourteenth Amendments utilize its public school system to aid any or all religious faiths or sects in the dissemination of their doctrines and ideals does not, as counsel urge, manifest a governmental hostility to religions or religious teachings. A manifestation of such hostility would be at war with our national tradition as embodied in the First Amendment's guaranty of the free exercise of religion. For the First Amendment rests upon the premise that both religion and government can best work to achieve their lofty aims if each is left free from the other within its respective sphere. Or, as we said in the Everson case, the First Amendment has erected a wall between Church and State which must be kept high and impregnable.

Here not only are the state's tax-supported public school buildings used for the dissemination of religious doctrines. The State also affords sectarian groups an invaluable aid in that it helps to provide pupils for their religious classes through use of the state's compulsory public school machinery. This is not separation of Church and State.

The cause is reversed and remanded to the State Supreme Court for proceedings not inconsistent with this opinion.

584. SELECTIVE SERVICE ACT OF 1948
June 24, 1948
(Public Law 759, 80th Congress)

In 1916 and again in 1940, Congress made provision for drafting men during peacetime. Both of these acts were directed to a crisis in which war seemed imminent. In 1948, Congress acted to deal with a long-run situation of tension in the world. In this sense, the act of 1948 set a precedent. See President's Advisory Commission on Universal Training, *A Program for National Security;* W. Millis, *Arms and Men;* S. P. Huntington, *The Soldier and the State;* A. A. Ekirch, Jr., *The Civilian and the Military;* G. B. Turner, ed., *History of Military Affairs in Western Society,* chs. 14, 15.

An Act to provide for the common defense by increasing the strength of the armed forces of the United States, including the reserve components thereof, and for other purposes.

SEC. 1. (a) This Act may be cited as the "Selective Service Act of 1948."

(b) The Congress hereby declares that an adequate armed strength must be achieved and maintained to insure the security of this Nation.

(c) The Congress further declares that in a free society the obligations and privileges of serving in the armed forces and the reserve components thereof should be shared generally, in accordance with a system of selection which is fair and just, and which is consistent with the maintenance of an effective national economy. . . .

SEC. 2. Notwithstanding any other provision of law, the authorized active duty personnel strength of the armed forces . . . is hereby established as follows: (1) Of the Army of the United States, 837,000 plus 110,000 one-year enlistees; (2) of the Navy, including the Marine Corps, the present authorized statutory strength of 666,882, plus 36,000 one-year enlistees; and (3) of the Air Force of the United States, 502,000 plus 15,000 one-year enlistees. The strength herein established for each of the armed forces shall mean the daily average number of persons on active duty therein during the fiscal year.

SEC. 3. Except as otherwise provided in this title, it shall be the duty of every male citizen of the United States, and every other male person residing in the United States, who, on the day or days fixed for the first or any subsequent registration, is between the ages of eighteen and twenty-six, to present himself for and submit to registration at such time or times and place or places, and in such manner, as shall be determined by proclamation of the President and by rules and regulations prescribed hereunder.

SEC. 4. (a) Except as otherwise provided in this title, every male citizen of the United States, and every other male person residing in the United States, who is between the ages of nineteen and twenty-six, at the time fixed for his registration, or who attains the age of nineteen after having been required to register pursuant to section 3 of this title, shall be liable for training and service in the armed forces of the United States. . . . The President is authorized from time to time, whether or not a state of war exists, to select and induct into the armed forces of the United States for training and service in the manner provided in this title such number of persons as may be required to provide and maintain the personnel strengths (other than one-year enlistee personnel strengths) of the respective armed forces authorized by section 2 of this title. . . .

SEC. 5. (a) The selection of persons for training and service under section 4 shall be made in an impartial manner, under such rules and regulations as the President may prescribe, from the persons who are liable for such training and service and who at the time of selection are registered and classified, but not deferred or exempted. . . .

585. UNITED STATES NOTE ON BERLIN BLOCKADE AND AIRLIFT
July 6, 1948
(Department of State Bulletin, Vol. XIX, p. 86)

At the Potsdam Conference a four-power command was set up to govern Berlin. Although Berlin was surrounded by Soviet-occupied territory, the city itself was divided into four zones occupied by American, British, French, and Russian troops. On June 20 and June 22, 1948, the Soviet occupation officials declared that they considered Berlin an integral part of the Soviet zone of Germany and would henceforth govern the city on a unilateral basis. On June 24, they halted all land and water traffic between the Western zones of Germany and Berlin. The United States and Britain responded with an air-lift of food, coal, etc., to the beleaguered citizens of the Western zones. At its height, a plane was landing on the Berlin airstrips every minute, and the Allies were delivering some 4,500 tons of supplies daily. On May 12, 1949, the Soviets abandoned their blockade and normal traffic was restored between the Western zones of Germany and Berlin. See H. Truman, *Memoirs*, Vol. II; L. Clay, *Decision in Germany*.

The United States Government wishes to call to the attention of the Soviet Government the extremely serious international situation which has been brought about by the actions of the Soviet Government in imposing restrictive measures on transport which amount now to a blockade against the sectors in Berlin occupied by the United States, United Kingdom and France. The United States Government regards these measures of blockade as a clear violation of existing agreements concerning the administration of Berlin by the four occupying powers.

The rights of the United States as a joint occupying power in Berlin derive from the total defeat and unconditional surrender of Germany. The international agreements undertaken in connection therewith by the Governments of the United States, United Kingdom, France and the Soviet Union defined the zones in Germany and the sectors in Berlin which are occupied by these powers. They established the quadripartite control of Berlin on a basis of friendly cooperation which the Government of the United States earnestly desires to continue to pursue.

These agreements implied the right of free access to Berlin. This right has long been confirmed by usage. It was directly specified in a message sent by President Truman to Premier Stalin on June 14, 1945, which agreed to the withdrawal of United States forces to the zonal boundaries provided satisfactory arrangements could be entered into between the military commanders, which would give access by rail, road and air to United States forces in Berlin. Premier Stalin replied on June 16 suggesting a change in date but no other alteration in the plan proposed by the President. Premier Stalin then gave assurances that all necessary measures would be taken in accordance with the plan. Correspondence in a similar sense took place between Premier Stalin and Mr. Churchill. In accordance with this understanding, the United States, whose armies had penetrated deep into Saxony and Thuringia, parts of the Soviet zone, withdrew its forces to its own area of occupation in Germany and took up its position in its own sector in Berlin. Thereupon the agreements in regard to the occupation of Germany and Berlin went into effect. The United States would not have so withdrawn its troops from a large area now occupied by the Soviet Union had there been any doubt whatsoever about the observance of its agreed right of free access to its sector of Berlin. The right of the United States to its position in Berlin thus stems from precisely the same source as the right of the Soviet Union. It is impossible to assert the latter and deny the former.

It clearly results from these undertakings that Berlin is not a part of the Soviet zone, but is an international zone of occupation. Commitments entered into in good faith by the zone commanders and subsequently confirmed by the Allied Control Authority, as well as practices sanctioned by usage, guarantee the United States together with other powers, free access to Berlin for the purpose of fulfilling its responsibilities as an occupying power. The facts are plain. Their meaning is clear. Any other interpretation would offend all the rules of comity and reason.

In order that there should be no misunderstanding whatsoever on this point, the United States Government categorically asserts that it is in occupation of its sector in Berlin with free access thereto as a matter of established right deriving from the defeat and surrender of Germany and confirmed by formal agreements among the principal Allies. It further declares that it will not be induced by threats, pressures or other actions to abandon these rights. It is hoped

that the Soviet Government entertains no doubts whatsoever on this point. . . .

The responsibility which this Government bears for the physical well-being and the safety of the German population in its sector of Berlin is outstandingly humanitarian in character. This population includes hundreds of thousands of women and children, whose health and safety are dependent on the continued use of adequate facilities for moving food, medical supplies and other items indispensable to the maintenance of human life in the western sectors of Berlin. The most elemental of these human rights which both our Governments are solemnly pledged to protect are thus placed in jeopardy by these restrictions. It is intolerable that any one of the occupying authorities should attempt to impose a blockade upon the people of Berlin.

The United States Government is therefore obliged to insist that in accordance with existing agreements the arrangements for the movement of freight and passenger traffic between the western zones and Berlin be fully restored. There can be no question of delay in the restoration of these essential services, since the needs of the civilian population in the Berlin area are imperative. . . .

586. THE NORTH ATLANTIC TREATY
Signed April 4, 1949
(81st Congress, 1st Session, *Executive Document* L)

The North Atlantic Pact, as it was popularly known, was designed to provide collective security to the democratic nations of the Atlantic Community against possible overt action by Russia or her satellite states. It was patterned closely on the Treaty of Rio de Janeiro of 1947. Although it marked a sharp departure from traditional American foreign policy, it was clearly consistent with the Truman Doctrine, the Marshall Plan, and the Vandenberg Resolution of May 19, 1948. Other signatory countries were Belgium, Canada, Denmark, France, Iceland, Italy, Luxembourg, Netherlands, Norway, Portugal, and the United Kingdom.

The Parties to this Treaty reaffirm their faith in the purposes and principles of the

Charter of the United Nations and their desire to live in peace with all peoples and all governments.

They are determined to safeguard the freedom, common heritage and civilization of their peoples, founded on the principles of democracy, individual liberty and the rule of law.

They seek to promote stability and well-being in the North Atlantic area.

They are resolved to unite their efforts for collective defense and for the preservation of peace and security.

They therefore agree to this North Atlantic Treaty:

ART. 1. The Parties undertake, as set forth in the Charter of the United Nations, to settle any international disputes in which they may be involved by peaceful means in such a manner that international peace and security, and justice, are not endangered, and to refrain in their international relations from the threat or use of force in any manner inconsistent with the purposes of the United Nations.

ART. 2. The Parties will contribute toward the further development of peaceful and friendly international relations by strengthening their free institutions, by bringing about a better understanding of the principles upon which these institutions are founded, and by promoting conditions of stability and well-being. They will seek to eliminate conflict in their international economic policies and will encourage economic collaboration between any or all of them.

ART. 3. In order more effectively to achieve the objectives of this Treaty, the Parties, separately and jointly, by means of continuous and effective self-help and mutual aid, will maintain and develop their individual and collective capacity to resist armed attack.

ART. 4. The Parties will consult together whenever, in the opinion of any of them, the territorial integrity, political independence or security of any of the Parties is threatened.

ART. 5. The Parties agree that an armed attack against one or more of them in Europe or North America shall be considered an attack against them all; and consequently they agree that, if such an armed attack occurs, each of them, in exercise of the right of individual or collective self-defense recognized by Article 51 of the Charter of the United Nations, will assist the Party or Parties so attacked by taking forthwith, individually and in concert with the other Parties, such action as it deems necessary, including the use of armed force, to restore and maintain the security of the North Atlantic area.

Any such armed attack and all measures taken as a result thereof shall immediately be reported to the Security Council. Such measures shall be terminated when the Security Council has taken the measures necessary to restore and maintain international peace and security.

ART. 6. For the purpose of Article 5 an armed attack on one or more of the Parties is deemed to include an armed attack on the territory of any of the Parties in Europe or North America, on the Algerian departments of France, on the occupation forces of any Party in Europe, on the islands under the jurisdiction of any Party in the North Atlantic area north of the Tropic of Cancer or on the vessels or aircraft in this area of any of the Parties.

ART. 7. This Treaty does not affect, and shall not be interpreted as affecting, in any way the rights and obligations under the Charter of the Parties which are members of the United Nations, or the primary responsibility of the Security Council for the maintenance of international peace and security.

ART. 8. Each Party declares that none of the international engagements now in force between it and any other of the Parties or any third state is in conflict with the provisions of this Treaty, and undertakes not to enter into any international engagement in conflict with this Treaty.

ART. 9. The Parties hereby establish a council, on which each of them shall be represented, to consider matters concerning the implementation of this Treaty. The council shall be so organized as to be able to meet promptly at any time. The council shall set up such subsidiary bodies as may be necessary; in particular it shall establish immediately a defense committee which shall recommend measures for the implementation of Articles 3 and 5.

ART. 10. The Parties may, by unanimous agreement, invite any other European state in a position to further the principles of this Treaty and to contribute to the security of the North Atlantic area to accede to this Treaty. Any state so invited may become a party to the Treaty by depositing its instrument of accession with the Government of the United States of America. The Government of the United States of America will inform each of the Parties of the deposit of each such instrument of accession.

ART. 11. . . . The Treaty shall enter into force between the states which have ratified it as soon as the ratifications of the majority of the signatories, including the ratifications of Belgium, Canada, France, Luxembourg, the Netherlands, the United Kingdom and the United States, have been deposited and shall come into effect with respect to other states on the date of the deposit of their ratifications.

ART. 12. After the Treaty has been in force for ten years, or at any time thereafter, the Parties shall, if any of them so requests, consult together for the purpose of reviewing the Treaty, having regard for the factors then affecting peace and security in the North Atlantic area, including the development of universal as well as regional arrangements under the Charter of the United Nations for the maintenance of international peace and security.

ART. 13. After the Treaty has been in force for twenty years, any Party may cease to be a party one year after its notice of denunciation has been given to the Government of the United States of America, which will inform the Governments of the other Parties of the deposit of each notice of denunciation.

587. RECOGNITION OF ISRAEL
1948–49
(White House Press Releases, May 14, 1948, and January 31, 1949)

In 1947, the General Assembly of the United Nations adopted a plan for the partition of Palestine into independent Jewish and Arab states. On May 14, 1948, the Jewish community of Palestine proclaimed the creation of the independent state of Israel. On the same day, President Truman announced that the United States accorded *de facto* recognition to the government of Israel. *De jure* recognition was granted on January 31, 1949. The quick response of the United States to the Israeli plea for recognition established close relations between the two governments. These relations were further cemented when the United States supported Israel's successful application for admission to the United Nations in 1949. See J. C. Hurewitz, *The Struggle for Palestine;* J. C. Hurewitz, *Diplomacy in the Near and Middle East;* Abba Eban, *The Voice of Israel;* E. Rackman, *Israel's Emerging Constitution, 1948–1951.*

1. STATEMENT BY PRESIDENT TRUMAN

May 14, 1949

This Government has been informed that a Jewish state has been proclaimed in Palestine, and recognition has been requested by the provisional government thereof.

The United States recognizes the provisional government as the *de facto* authority of the new State of Israel.

2. STATEMENT BY PRESIDENT TRUMAN

January 31, 1949

On October 24, 1948, the President stated that when a permanent government was elected in Israel, it would promptly be given *de jure* recognition. Elections for such a government were held on January 25th. The votes have now been counted, and this Government has been officially informed of the results. The United States Government is therefore pleased to extend *de jure* recognition to the Government of Israel as of this date.

588. TRUMAN'S POINT FOUR PROGRAM
June 24, 1949
(81st Congress, 1st Session, *House Doc.* No. 240)

Following a proposal made in his inaugural address, President Truman sent a special message to Congress urging a program of technical assistance to underdeveloped areas. The President recommended a modest initial appropriation of $45 million to be expanded as future needs required. Congress enacted the President's proposal on June 5, 1950, and thus took another important step in the assumption of international responsibilities. See W. A. Brown, *American Foreign Assistance;* R. T. Mack, *Raising the World's Standard of Living;* M. Curti and K. Beir, *Prelude to Point Four;* J. B. Bingham, *Shirt-Sleeve Diplomacy.*

To the Congress of the United States:

In order to enable the United States, in cooperation with other countries, to assist the peoples of economically underdeveloped areas to raise their standards of living, I recommend the enactment of legislation to authorize an expanded program of technical assistance for such areas, and an experimental program for encouraging the outflow of private investment beneficial to their economic development. These measures are the essential first steps in an undertaking which will call upon private enterprise and voluntary organizations in the United States, as well as the government, to take part in a constantly growing effort to improve economic conditions in the less developed regions of the world.

The grinding poverty and the lack of economic opportunity for many millions of people in the economically underdeveloped parts of Africa, the Near and Far East, and certain regions of Central and South America, constitute one of the greatest challenges of the world today. In spite of their age-old economic and social handicaps, the peoples in these areas have, in recent decades, been stirred and awakened. The spread of industrial civilization, the growing understanding of modern concepts of government, and the impact of two World Wars have changed their lives and their outlook. They are eager to play a greater part in the community of nations.

All these areas have a common problem. They must create a firm economic base for the democratic aspirations of their citizens. Without such an economic base, they will be unable to meet the expectations which the modern world has aroused in their peoples. If they are frustrated and disappointed, they may turn to false doctrines which hold that the way of progress lies through tyranny. . . .

For these various reasons, assistance in the development of the economically underdeveloped areas has become one of the major elements of our foreign policy. In my inaugural address, I outlined a program to help the peoples of these areas to attain greater production as a way to prosperity and peace.

The major effort in such a program must be local in character; it must be made by the people of the underdeveloped areas themselves. It is essential, however, to the success of their effort that there be help from abroad. In such cases, the peoples of these areas will be unable to begin their part of this great enterprise without initial aid from other countries.

The aid that is needed falls roughly into two categories. The first is the technical, scientific, and managerial knowledge necessary to economic development. This category includes not only medical and educational knowledge, and assistance and advice in such basic fields as sanitation, communications, road building, and governmental services, but also, and perhaps most important, assistance in the survey of resources and in planning for long-range economic development.

The second category is production goods —machinery and equipment—and financial assistance in the creation of productive enterprises. The underdeveloped areas need capital for port and harbor development, roads and communications, irrigation and drainage projects, as well as for public utilities and the whole range of extractive, processing, and manufacturing industries. Much of the capital required can be provided by these areas themselves, in spite of their low standards of living. But much must come from abroad.

The two categories of aid are closely related. Technical assistance is necessary to lay the ground-work for productive investment. Investment, in turn, brings with it technical assistance. In general, however, technical surveys of resources and of the possibilities of economic development must precede substantial capital investment. Furthermore, in many of the areas concerned, technical assistance in improving sanitation, communications, or education is required to create conditions in which capital investment can be fruitful. . . .

It has already been shown that experts in these fields can bring about tremendous improvements. For example, the health of the people of many foreign communities has been greatly improved by the work of United States sanitary engineers in setting up modern water supply systems. The food supply of many areas has been increased as the result of the advice of United States agricultural experts in the control of animal diseases and the improvement of crops. These are only examples of the wide range of benefits resulting from the careful application of modern techniques to local problems. The benefits which a comprehensive program of expert assistance will make possible can only be revealed by studies and surveys undertaken as a part of the program itself.

To inaugurate the program, I recommend a first year appropriation of not to exceed 45 million dollars. This includes 10 million dollars already requested in the 1950 Budget for activities of this character. The sum recommended will cover both our participation in the programs of the international agencies and the assistance to be provided directly by the United States.

In every case, whether the operation is conducted through the United Nations, the other international agencies, or directly by the United States, the country receiving the benefit of the aid will be required to bear a substantial portion of the expense.

589. TRUMAN ANNOUNCES HYDROGEN BOMB PROGRAM
January 31, 1950
(*Department of State Bulletin,* Vol. XXII, p. 229)

The first Russian atomic explosion of 1949 intensified the race to develop new and more efficient weapons of destruction. On January 31, 1950, President Truman announced the inauguration of an all-out effort to develop a hydrogen bomb substantially more powerful than existing atomic weapons. This program achieved its initial objective in November, 1952, when the first hydrogen bomb was detonated. See W. L. Laurence, *The Hell Bomb;* H. D. Smyth, *Atomic Energy for Military Purposes;* A. H. Compton, *Atomic Quest;* J. W. Campbell, *The Atomic Story;* G. Dean, *Report on the Atom.*

It is part of my responsibility as Commander-in-Chief of the armed forces to see to it that our country is able to defend itself against any possible aggressor. Accordingly, I have directed the Atomic Energy Commission to continue its work on all forms of atomic weapons, including the so-called hydrogen or super-bomb. Like all other work in the field of atomic weapons, it is being and will be carried forward on a basis consistent with the over-all objectives of our program for peace and security.

This we shall continue to do until a satisfactory plan for international control of atomic energy is achieved. We shall also continue to examine all those factors that affect our program for peace and this country's security.

The activities necessary to carry out our program of technical aid will be diverse in character and will have to be performed by a number of different government agencies and private instrumentalities. It will be necessary to utilize not only the resources of international agencies and the United States Government, but also the facilities and the experience of the private business and nonprofit organizations that have long been active in this work. . . .

In the economically underdeveloped areas of the world today there are new creative energies. We look forward to the time when these countries will be stronger and more independent than they are now, and yet more closely bound to us and to other nations by ties of friendship and commerce, and by kindred ideals. On the other hand, unless we aid the newly awakened spirit in these peoples to find the course of fruitful development, they may fall under the control of those whose philosophy is hostile to human freedom, thereby prolonging the unsettled state of the world and postponing the achievement of permanent peace.

Before the peoples of these areas we hold out the promise of a better future through the democratic way of life. It is vital that we move quickly to bring the meaning of that promise home to them in their daily lives.

HARRY S TRUMAN.

590. TRUMAN'S STATEMENT ON THE KOREAN WAR
June 27, 1950
(Department of State Press Release)

At the Cairo and Potsdam conferences, the Allied Powers promised the Korean people independence and self-government. After the defeat of Japan, the United States established a military government in Korea south of the 38th parallel and the USSR established a similar government north of the parallel. A joint American-Soviet commission to work out the details of Korean unification failed to agree. Intervention by the United Nations was of no avail. Finally in 1948, the U.S. and the UN sponsored elections in South Korea, and shortly thereafter a government of the Republic of Korea was established to rule South Korea. In 1949, the United States granted de jure recognition and withdrew its troops. The Soviets responded by creating a North Korean government. On June 25, 1950, the North Koreans launched a full-scale attack on the South. Two days later the UN Security Council called on all members of the UN to assist South Korea to repel the attack and restore peace. President Truman then issued the following statement. See H. Truman, *Memoirs*, Vol. II; M. Clark, *From the Danube to the Yalu*; L. M. Goodrich, *Korea: A Study of U.S. Policy in the United Nations*; R. T. Oliver, *Why War Came in Korea*; Council on Foreign Relations, *The U. S. in World Affairs, 1950*.

In Korea the Government forces, which were armed to prevent border raids and to preserve internal security, were attacked by invading forces from North Korea. The Security Council of the United Nations called upon the invading troops to cease hostilities and to withdraw to the 38th parallel. This they have not done, but on the contrary have pressed the attack. The Security Council called upon all members of the United Nations to render every assistance to the United Nations in the execution of this resolution. In these circumstances I have ordered United States air and sea forces to give the Korean Government troops cover and support.

The attack upon Korea makes it plain beyond all doubt that Communism has passed beyond the use of subversion to conquer independent nations and will now use armed invasion and war. It has defied the orders of the Security Council of the United Nations issued to preserve international peace and security. In these circumstances the occupation of Formosa by Communist forces would be a direct threat to the security of the Pacific area and to the United States forces performing their lawful and necessary functions in that area. Accordingly I have ordered the Seventh Fleet to prevent any attack on Formosa. As a corollary of this action I am calling upon the Chinese Government on Formosa to cease all air and sea operations against the mainland. The Seventh Fleet will see that this is done. The determination of the future status of Formosa must await the restoration of security in the Pacific, a peace settlement with Japan, or consideration by the United Nations.

I have also directed that United States Forces in the Philippines be strengthened and that military assistance to the Philippine Government be accelerated.

I have similarly directed acceleration in the furnishing of military assistance to the forces of France and the Associated States in Indo-China and the dispatch of a military mission to provide close working relations with those forces.

I know that all members of the United Nations will consider carefully the consequences of this latest aggression in Korea in defiance of the Charter of the United Nations. A return to the rule of force in international affairs would have far reaching effects. The United States will continue to uphold the rule of law.

I have instructed Ambassador Austin, as the representative of the United States to the Security Council, to report these steps to the Council.

591. McCARRAN INTERNAL SECURITY ACT
September 23, 1950
(Public Law 831, 81st Congress)

The growth of Communist power in the postwar world aroused deep fears among many Americans who believed that Communism menaced America not only from without but from within. In 1947, President Truman inaugurated a loyalty program designed to keep the federal government free from subversive influence. See Doc. No. 577. In 1950, Congress went beyond the Truman program and acted to limit the operation of "subversive" groups in all areas of American life. Ignoring President Truman's warning that the act was unconstitutional, Congress overrode his veto by a voice-vote. Section 103, which would establish detention centers for suspected subversives, was repealed in September, 1971. See W. Gellhorn, *Individual Freedom and Governmental Restraints;* M. Ernst and D. L. Loth, *Report on the American Communist;* F. Biddle, *The Fear of Freedom;* C. Wilcox, ed., *Civil Liberties Under Attack;* H. D. Lasswell, *National Security and Individual Freedom;* C. McWilliams, *Witch Hunt;* S. A. Stouffer, *Communism, Conformity, and Civil Liberties;* H. Truman, *Memoirs,* Vol. II.

An act to protect the United States against certain un-American and subversive activities by requiring registration of Communist organizations, and for other purposes.

SEC. 2. As a result of evidence adduced before various committees of the Senate and House of Representatives, the Congress hereby finds that—

(1) There exists a world Communist movement which, in its origins, its development, and its present practice, is a world-wide revolutionary movement whose purpose it is, by treachery, deceit, infiltration into other groups (governmental and

otherwise), espionage, sabotage, terrorism, and any other means deemed necessary, to establish a Communist totalitarian dictatorship in the countries throughout the world through the medium of a world-wide Communist organization. . . .

(4) The direction and control of the world Communist movement is vested in and exercised by the Communist dictatorship of a foreign country.

(5) The Communist movement in the United States is an organization numbering thousands of adherents, rigidly and ruthlessly disciplined. Awaiting and seeking to advance a moment when the United States may be so far extended by foreign engagements, so far divided in counsel, or so far in industrial or financial straits, that overthrow of the Government of the United States by force and violence may seem possible of achievement, it seeks converts far and wide by an extensive system of schooling and indoctrination. Such preparations by Communist organizations in other countries have aided in supplanting existing governments. The Communist organization in the United States, pursuing its stated objectives, the recent successes of Communist methods in other countries, and the nature and control of the world Communist movement itself, present a clear and present danger to the security of the United States and to the existence of free American institutions, and make it necessary that Congress, in order to provide for the common defense, to preserve the sovereignty of the United States as an independent nation, and to guarantee to each State a republican form of government, enact appropriate legislation recognizing the existence of such world-wide

conspiracy and designed to prevent it from accomplishing its purpose in the United States. . . .

SEC. 4. (a) It shall be unlawful for any person knowingly to combine, conspire, or agree with any other person to perform any act which would substantially contribute to the establishment within the United States of a totalitarian dictatorship, as defined in paragraph (15) of section 3 of this title, the direction and control of which is to be vested in, or exercised by or under the domination or control of, any foreign government, foreign organization, or foreign individual: *Provided, however,* That this subsection shall not apply to the proposal of a constitutional amendment. . . .

(f) Neither the holding of office nor membership in any Communist organization by any person shall constitute per se a violation of subsection (a) or subsection (c) of this section or of any other criminal statute. The fact of the registration of any person under section 7 or section 8 of this title as an officer or member of any Communist organization shall not be received in evidence against such person in any prosecution for any alleged violation of subsection (a) or subsection (c) of this section or for any alleged violation of any other criminal statute. . . .

SEC. 7. (a) Each Communist-action organization (including any organization required, by a final order of the Board, to register as a Communist-action organization) shall, within the time specified in subsection (c) of this section, register with the Attorney General, or on a form prescribed by him by regulations, as a Communist-action organization.

(b) Each Communist-front organization . . . shall . . . register with the Attorney General, on a form prescribed by him by regulations, as a Communist-front organization. . . .

(d) Upon the registration of each Communist organization under the provisions of this title, the Attorney General shall publish in the Federal Register the fact that such organization has registered as a Communist-action organization, or as a Communist-front organization, as the case may be, and the publication thereof shall constitute notice to all members of such organization that such organization has so registered. . . .

SEC. 12. (a) There is hereby established a board, to be known as the Subversive Activities Control Board, which shall be composed of five members, who shall be appointed by the President, by and with the advice and consent of the Senate. Not more than three members of the Board shall be members of the same political party. Two of the original members shall be appointed for a term of one year, two for a term of two years, and one for a term of three years, but their successors shall be appointed for terms of three years each, except that any individual chosen to fill a vacancy shall be appointed only for the unexpired term of the member whom he shall succeed. The President shall designate one member to serve as Chairman of the Board. Any member of the Board may be removed by the President, upon notice and hearing, for neglect of duty or malfeasance in office, but for no other cause. . . .

(e) It shall be the duty of the Board—

(1) upon application made by the Attorney General under section 13 (a) of this title, or by any organization under section 13 (b) of this title, to determine whether any organization is a "Communist-action organization" within the meaning of paragraph (3) of section 3 of this title, or a "Communist-front organization" within the meaning of paragraph (4) of section 3 of this title; and

(2) upon application made by the Attorney General under section 13 (a) of this title, or by any individual under section 13 (b) of this title, to determine whether any individual is a member of any Communist-action organization registered, or by final order of the Board required to be registered, under section 7 (a) of this title. . . .

SEC. 22. The Act of October 16, 1918 . . . is hereby amended to read as follows: "That any alien who is a member of any one of the following classes shall be excluded from admission into the United States:

"(1) Aliens who seek to enter the United States whether solely, principally, or incidentally, to engage in activities which would be prejudicial to the public interest, or would endanger the welfare or safety of the United States;

"(2) Aliens who, at any time, shall be or shall have been members of any of the following classes:

"(A) Aliens who are anarchists;

"(B) Aliens who advocate or teach, or who are members of or affiliated with any organization that advocates or teaches, opposition to all organized government;

"(C) Aliens who are members of or affiliated with (i) the Communist Party of the United States; (ii) any other totalitarian party of the United States; (iii) the Communist Political Association; (iv) the Communist or other totalitarian party of any State of the United States, of any foreign state, or of any political or geographical subdivision of any foreign state; (v) any section, subsidiary, branch, affiliate, or subdivision of any such association or party; or (vi) the direct predecessors or successors of any such association or party, regardless of what name such group or organization may have used, may now bear, or may hereafter adopt;

"(D) Aliens not within any of the other provisions of this paragraph (2) who advocate the economic, international, and governmental doctrines of world communism or the economic and governmental doctrines of any other form of totalitarianism, or who are members of or affiliated with any organization that advocates the economic, international, and governmental doctrines of world communism, or the economic and governmental doctrines of any other form of totalitarianism, either through its own utterances or through any written or printed publications issued or published by or with the permission or consent of or under the authority of such organization or paid for by the funds of such organization. . . .

"(F) Aliens who advocate or teach or who are members of or affiliated with any organization that advocates or teaches (i) the overthrow by force or violence or other unconstitutional means of the Government of the United States or of all forms of law; or (ii) the duty, necessity, or propriety of the unlawful assaulting or killing of any officer or officers (either of specific individuals or of officers generally) of the Government of the United States or of any other organized government, because of his or their official character; or (iii) the unlawful damage, injury, or destruction of property; or (iv) sabotage;

"(G) Aliens who write or publish, or cause to be written or published, or who knowingly circulate, distribute, print, or display, or knowingly cause to be circulated, distributed, printed, published, or displayed, or who knowingly have in their possession for the purpose of circulation, publication, or display, any written or printed matter, advocating or teaching opposition to all organized government, or advocating (i) the overthrow by force or violence or other unconstitutional means of the Government of the United States or of all forms of law; or (ii) the duty, necessity, or propriety of the unlawful assaulting or killing of any officer or officers (either of specific individuals or of officers generally) of the Government of the United States or of any other organized government; or (iii) the unlawful damage, injury, or destruction of property; or (iv) sabotage; or (v) the economic, international, and governmental doctrines of world communism or the economic and governmental doctrines of any other form of totalitarianism. . . .

SEC. 102. (a) In the event of any one of the following:

(1) Invasion of the territory of the United States or its possessions,

(2) Declaration of war by Congress, or

(3) Insurrection within the United States in aid of a foreign enemy,

and if, upon the occurrence of one or more of the above, the President shall find that the proclamation of an emergency pursuant to this section is essential to the preservation, protection and defense of the Constitution, and to the common defense and safety of the territory and people of the United States, the President is authorized to make public proclamation of the existence of an "Internal Security Emergency."

(b) A state of "Internal Security Emergency" (hereinafter referred to as the "emergency") so declared shall continue in existence until terminated by proclamation of the

President or by concurrent resolution of the Congress. . . .

SEC. 103. (a) Whenever there shall be in existence such an emergency, the President, acting through the Attorney General, is hereby authorized to apprehend and by order detain, pursuant to the provisions of this title, each person as to whom there is reasonable ground to believe that such person probably will engage in, or probably will conspire with others to engage in, acts of espionage or of sabotage. . . .

592. TRUMAN'S VETO OF THE McCARRAN ACT
September 22, 1950
(81st Congress, 2nd Session, *House Doc.* No. 708)

To the House of Representatives:

I return herewith, without my approval, H. R. 9490, the proposed Internal Security Act of 1950.

I am taking this action only after the most serious study and reflection and after consultation with the security and intelligence agencies of the Government. The Department of Justice, the Department of Defense, the Central Intelligence Agency, and the Department of State have all advised me that the bill would seriously damage the security and the intelligence operations for which they are responsible. They have strongly expressed the hope that the bill would not become law.

This is an omnibus bill containing many different legislative proposals with only one thing in common: they are all represented to be "anti-Communist." But when the many complicated pieces of the bill are analyzed in detail, a startling result appears.

H. R. 9490 would not hurt the Communists. Instead, it would help them.

It has been claimed over and over again that this is an "anti-Communist" bill—a "Communist control" bill. But in actual operation the bill would have results exactly the opposite of those intended.

It would actually weaken our existing internal security measures and would seriously hamper the Federal Bureau of Investigation and our other security agencies. . . .

I therefore most earnestly request the Congress to reconsider its action. I am confident that on more careful analysis most Members of Congress will recognize that this bill is contrary to the best interests of our country at this critical time.

H. R. 9490 is made up of a number of different parts. In summary, their purposes and probable effects may be described as follows: . . . (Analysis of secs. 1-21, and 23)

Sections 22 and 25 of this bill would make sweeping changes in our laws governing the admission of aliens to the United States and their naturalization as citizens.

The ostensible purpose of these provisions is to prevent persons who would be dangerous to our national security from entering the country or becoming citizens. In fact, present law already achieves that objective.

What these provisions would actually do is to prevent us from admitting to our country, or to citizenship, many people who could make real contributions to our national strength. The bill would deprive our Government and our intelligence agencies of the valuable services of aliens in security operations. It would require us to exclude and to deport the citizens of some friendly non-Communist countries. Furthermore, it would actually make it easier for subversive aliens to become United States citizens. Only the Communist movement would gain from such actions.

Section 24 and sections 26 through 30 of this bill make a number of minor changes in the naturalization laws. None of them is of great significance—nor are they particularly relevant to the problem of internal security. These provisions, for the most part, have received little or no attention in the legislative process. I believe that several of them would not be approved by the Congress if they were considered on their merits, rather than as parts of an omnibus bill.

Section 31 of this bill makes it a crime to attempt to influence a judge or jury by public demonstration, such as picketing. While the courts already have considerable power to punish such actions under existing law, I have no objection to this section.

Sections 100 through 117 of this bill (title II) are intended to give the Government power, in the event of invasion, war, or insurrection in the United States in aid of a foreign enemy, to seize and hold persons who could be expected to attempt acts of espionage or sabotage, even though they had as yet committed no crime. It may be that legislation of this type should be on the statute books. But the provisions in H. R. 9490 would very probably prove ineffective to achieve the objective sought, since they would not suspend the writ of habeas corpus, and under our legal system to detain a man not charged with a crime would raise serious constitutional questions unless the writ of habeas corpus were suspended. Furthermore, it may well be that other persons than those covered by these provisions would be more important to detain in the event of emergency. This whole problem, therefore, should clearly be studied more thoroughly before further legislative action along these lines is considered.

In brief, when all the provisions of H. R. 9490 are considered together, it is evident that the great bulk of them are not directed toward the real and present dangers that exist from communism. Instead of striking blows at communism, they would strike blows at our own liberties and at our position in the forefront of those working for freedom in the world. At a time when our young men are fighting for freedom in Korea, it would be tragic to advance the objectives of communism in this country, as this bill would do.

Because I feel so strongly that this legislation would be a terrible mistake, I want to discuss more fully its worst features: sections 1 through 17 and sections 22 and 25. . . .

Unfortunately, these provisions are not merely ineffective and unworkable. They represent a clear and present danger to our institutions.

Insofar as the bill would require registration by the Communist Party itself, it does not endanger our traditional liberties. However, the application of the registration requirements to so-called Communist-front or-

ganizations can be the greatest danger to freedom of speech, press and assembly, since the alien and sedition laws of 1798. This danger arises out of the criteria or standards to be applied in determining whether an organization is a Communist-front organization.

There would be no serious problem if the bill required proof that an organization was controlled and financed by the Communist Party before it could be classified as a Communist-front organization. However, recognizing the difficulty of proving those matters, the bill would permit such a determination to be based solely upon "the extent to which the positions taken or advanced by it from time to time on matters of policy do not deviate from those" of the Communist movement.

This provision could easily be used to classify as a Communist-front organization any organization which is advocating a single policy or objective which is also being urged by the Communist Party or by a Communist foreign government. In fact, this may be the intended result, since the bill defines "organization" to include "a group of persons . . . permanently or temporarily associated together for joint action on any subject or subjects." Thus, an organization which advocates low-cost housing for sincere humanitarian reasons might be classified as a Communist-front organization because the Communists regularly exploit slum conditions as one of their fifth-column techniques.

It is not enough to say that this probably would not be done. The mere fact that it could be done shows clearly how the bill would open a Pandora's box of opportunities for official condemnation of organizations and individuals for perfectly honest opinions which happen to be stated also by Communists.

The basic error of these sections is that they move in the direction of suppressing opinion and belief. This would be a very dangerous course to take, not because we have any sympathy for Communist opinions, but because any governmental stifling of the free expression of opinion is a long step toward totalitarianism.

There is no more fundamental axiom of American freedom than the familiar statement: In a free country we punish men for the crimes they commit but never for the opinions they have. And the reason this is so fundamental to freedom is not, as many suppose, that it protects the few unorthodox from suppression by the majority. To permit freedom of expression is primarily for the benefit of the majority, because it protects criticism, and criticism leads to progress.

We can and we will prevent espionage, sabotage, or other actions endangering our national security. But we would betray our finest traditions if we attempted, as this bill would attempt, to curb the simple expression of opinion. This we should never do, no matter how distasteful the opinion may be to the vast majority of our people. The course proposed by this bill would delight the Communists, for it would make a mockery of the Bill of Rights and of our claims to stand for freedom in the world.

And what kind of effect would these provisions have on the normal expression of political views? Obviously, if this law were on the statute books, the part of prudence would be to avoid saying anything that might be construed by someone as not deviating sufficiently from the current Communist-propaganda line. And since no one could be sure in advance what views were safe to express, the inevitable tendency would be to express no views on controversial subjects.

The result could only be to reduce the vigor and strength of our political life—an outcome that the Communists would happily welcome, but that freemen should abhor.

We need not fear the expression of ideas —we do need to fear their suppression.

Our position in the vanguard of freedom rests largely on our demonstration that the free expression of opinion, coupled with government by popular consent, leads to national strength and human advancement. Let us not, in cowering and foolish fear, throw away the ideals which are the fundamental basis of our free society.

Not only are the registration provisions of this bill unworkable and dangerous, they are also grossly misleading in that all but one of the objectives which are claimed for them are already being accomplished by other and superior methods—and the one objective which is not now being accomplished would

not in fact be accomplished under this bill either.

It is claimed that the bill would provide information about the Communist Party and its members. The fact is, the FBI already possesses very complete sources of information concerning the Communist movement in this country. If the FBI must disclose its sources of information in public hearings to require registration under this bill, its present sources of information, and its ability to acquire new information, will be largely destroyed.

It is claimed that this bill would deny income-tax exemptions to Communist organizations. The fact is that the Bureau of Internal Revenue already denies income-tax exemptions to such organizations.

It is claimed that this bill would deny passports to Communists. The fact is that the Government can and does deny passports to Communists under existing law.

It is claimed that this bill would prohibit the employment of Communists by the Federal Government. The fact is that the employment of Communists by the Federal Government is already prohibited and, at least in the executive branch, there is an effective program to see that they are not employed.

It is claimed that this bill would prohibit the employment of Communists in defense plants. The fact is that it would be years before this bill would have any effect of this nature—if it ever would. Fortunately, this objective is already being substantially achieved under the present procedures of the Department of Defense, and if the Congress would enact one of the provisions I have recommended—which it did not include in this bill—the situation would be entirely taken care of, promptly and effectively. . . .

Sections 22 and 25 of this bill are directed toward the specific questions of who should be admitted to our country, and who should be permitted to become a United States citizen. I believe there is general agreement that the answers to those questions should be: We should admit to our country, within the available quotas, anyone with a legitimate purpose who would not endanger our security, and we should admit to citizenship any immigrant who will be a loyal and constructive member of the community. Those are essentially the standards set by existing law. Under present law we do not admit to our country known Communists because we believe they work to overthrow our Government, and we do not admit Communists to citizenship because we believe they are not loyal to the United States.

The changes which would be made in the present law by sections 22 and 25 would not reinforce those sensible standards. Instead, they would add a number of new standards, which, for no good and sufficient reason, would interfere with our relations with other countries and seriously damage our national security.

Section 22 would, for example, exclude from our country anyone who advocates any form of totalitarian or one-party government. We, of course, believe in the democratic system of competing political parties, offering a choice of candidates and policies. But a number of countries with which we maintain friendly relations have a different form of government.

Until now no one has suggested that we should abandon cultural and commercial relations with a country merely because it has a form of government different from ours. Yet section 22 would require that. As one instance, it is clear that under the definitions of the bill the present Government of Spain, among others, would be classified as "totalitarian." As a result, the Attorney General would be required to exclude from the United States all Spanish businessmen, students, and other nonofficial travelers who support the present Government of their country. I cannot understand how the sponsors of this bill can think that such an action would contribute to our national security. . . .

Section 22 is so contrary to our national interests that it would actually put the Government into the business of thought control by requiring the deportation of any alien who distributes or publishes, or who is affiliated with an organization which distributes or publishes, any written or printed matter advocating (or merely expressing belief in) the economic and governmental doctrines of any form of totalitarianism. This provision does not require an evil intent or purpose

on the part of the alien, as does a similar provision in the Smith Act. Thus, the Attorney General would be required to deport any alien operating or connected with a well-stocked bookshop containing books on economics or politics written by supporters of the present Governments of Spain, of Yugoslavia, or any one of a number of other countries. Section 25 would make the same aliens ineligible for citizenship. There should be no room in our laws for such hysterical provisions. The next logical step would be to "burn the books."

This illustrates the fundamental error of these immigration and naturalization provisions. It is easy to see that they are hasty and ill-considered. But far more significant—and far more dangerous—is their apparent underlying purpose. Instead of trying to encourage the free movement of people, subject only to the real requirements of national security, these provisions attempt to bar movement to anyone who is, or once was, associated with ideas we dislike and, in the process, they would succeed in barring many people whom it would be to our advantage to admit.

Such an action would be a serious blow to our work for world peace. We uphold—or have upheld till now, at any rate—the concept of freedom on an international scale. That is the root concept of our efforts to bring unity among the free nations and peace in the world.

The Communists, on the other hand, attempt to break down in every possible way the free interchange of persons and ideas. It will be to their advantage, and not ours, if we establish for ourselves an "iron curtain" against those who can help us in the fight for freedom. . . .

I do not undertake lightly the responsibility of differing with the majority in both Houses of Congress who have voted for this bill. We are all Americans; we all wish to safeguard and preserve our constitutional liberties against internal and external enemies. But I cannot approve this legislation, which instead of accomplishing its avowed purpose would actually interfere with our liberties and help the Communists against whom the bill was aimed.

This is a time when we must marshal all

our resources and all the moral strength of our free system in self-defense against the threat of Communist aggression. We will fail in this, and we will destroy all that we seek to preserve, if we sacrifice the liberties of our citizens in a misguided attempt to achieve national security.

There is no reason why we should fail. Our country has been through dangerous times before, without losing our liberties to external attack or internal hysteria. Each of us, in Government and out, has a share in guarding our liberties. Each of us must search his own conscience to find whether he is doing all that can be done to preserve and strengthen them.

No considerations of expediency can justify the enactment of such a bill as this, a bill which would so greatly weaken our liberties and give aid and comfort to those who would destroy us. I have, therefore, no alternative but to return this bill without my approval, and I earnestly request the Congress to reconsider its action.

HARRY S TRUMAN.

593. DENNIS v. U.S.
341 U. S. 494
1951

The Truman administration opened its drive against internal Communism in 1948 by obtaining the indictment of eleven high-ranking Communist leaders for conspiring to teach and advocate the violent overthrow of the government in violation of the Smith Act of 1940 (see Doc. No. 531). Convicted in the lower courts, the Communists carried their case to the Supreme Court, which voted 6 to 2 to sustain the Smith Act and the conviction of the Communist leaders. This decision modified the "clear and present danger" doctrine of Justice Holmes by holding that offenders could be punished for conspiring to teach and advocate revolution. See M. L. Ernst and D. L. Loth, *Report on the American Communist;* C. H. Pritchett, *Civil Liberties and the Vinson Court;* W. Mendelson, "Clear and Present Danger—From Schenck to Dennis," 52 *Columbia Law Rev.* 313; N. L. Nathanson, "Communist Trial and the Clear and Present Danger Test" 63 *Harvard Law Rev.* 1167; H. S. Commager, *Freedom, Loyalty and Dissent;* T. Draper, *Roots of American Communism.*

Appeal from the United States Court of Appeals for the second Circuit.

VINSON, C. J. Petitioners were indicted in July, 1948, for violation of the conspiracy provisions of the Smith Act, § 11, during the period of April, 1945, to July, 1948. . . . A verdict of guilty as to all the petitioners was returned by the jury on October 14, 1949. The Court of Appeals affirmed the convictions. 183 F. 2d 201. We granted certiorari limited to the following two questions: (1) Whether either § 2 or § 3 of the Smith Act, inherently or as construed and applied in the instant case, violates the First Amendment and other provisions of the Bill of Rights; (2) whether either § 2 or § 3 of the Act, inherently or as construed and applied in the instant case, violates the First and Fifth Amendments because of indefiniteness. . . .

The indictment charged the petitioners with willfully and knowingly conspiring (1) to organize as the Communist Party of the United States of America a society, group and assembly of persons who teach and advocate the overthrow and destruction of the Government of the United States by force and violence, and (2) knowingly and willfully to advocate and teach the duty and necessity of overthrowing and destroying the Government of the United States by force and violence. The indictment further alleged that § 2 of the Smith Act proscribes these acts and that any conspiracy to take such action is a violation of § 3 of the Act. . . .

The obvious purpose of the statute is to protect existing Government, not from change by peaceable, lawful and constitutional means, but from change by violence, revolution and terrorism. That it is within the *power* of the Congress to protect the Government of the United States from armed rebellion is a proposition which requires little discussion. Whatever theoretical merit there may be to the argument that there is a "right" to rebellion against dictatorial governments is without force where the existing structure of the government provides for peaceful and orderly change. We reject any principle of governmental helplessness in the face of preparation for revolution, which principle, carried to its logical conclusion, must lead to anarchy. No one could conceive that it is not within the power of Congress to prohibit acts intended to overthrow the Government by force and violence. The question with which we are concerned here is not whether Congress has such *power,* but whether the *means* which it has employed conflict with the First and Fifth Amendments to the Constitution.

One of the bases for the contention that the means which Congress has employed are invalid takes the form of an attack on the face of the statute on the grounds that by its terms it prohibits academic discussion of the merits of Marxism-Leninism, that it stifles ideas and is contrary to all concepts of a free speech and a free press. . . .

The very language of the Smith Act negates the interpretation which petitioners would have us impose on that Act. It is directed at advocacy, not discussion. Thus, the trial judge properly charged the jury that they could not convict if they found that petitioners did "no more than pursue peaceful studies and discussions or teaching and advocacy in the realm of ideas." He further charged that it was not unlawful "to conduct in an American college and university a course explaining the philosophical theories set forth in the books which have been placed in evidence." Such a charge is in strict accord with the statutory language, and illustrates the meaning to be placed on those words. Congress did not intend to eradicate the free discussion of political theories, to destroy the traditional rights of Americans to discuss and evaluate ideas without fear of governmental sanction. Rather Congress was concerned with the very kind of activity in which the evidence showed these petitioners engaged.

But although the statute is not directed at the hypothetical cases which petitioners have conjured, its application in this case has resulted in convictions for the teaching and advocacy of the overthrow of the Government by force and violence, which, even though coupled with the intent to accomplish that overthrow, contains an element of speech. For this reason, we must pay special heed to the demands of the First Amendment marking out the boundaries of speech.

We pointed out in *Douds, supra,* that the basis of the First Amendment is the hypothesis that speech can rebut speech, propaganda will answer propaganda, free debate of ideas will result in the wisest governmental policies. It is for this reason that this Court has recognized the inherent value of free discourse. An analysis of the leading cases in this Court which have involved direct limitations on speech, however, will demonstrate that both the majority of the Court and the dissenters in particular cases have recognized that this is not an unlimited, unqualified right, but that the societal value of speech must, on occasion, be subordinated to other values and considerations. . . .

The rule we deduce from these cases is that where an offense is specified by a statute in nonspeech or nonpress terms, a conviction relying upon speech or press as evidence of violation may be sustained only when the speech or publication created a "clear and present danger" of attempting or accomplishing the prohibited crime. . . .

In this case we are squarely presented with the application of the "clear and present danger" test, and must decide what that phrase imports. . . .

Obviously, the words cannot mean that before the Government may act, it must wait until the *putsch* is about to be executed, the plans have been laid and the signal is awaited. If Government is aware that a group aiming at its overthrow is attempting to indoctrinate its members and to commit them to a course whereby they will strike when the leaders feel the circumstances permit, action by the Government is required. The argument that there is no need for Government to concern itself, for Government is strong, it possesses ample powers to put down a rebellion, it may defeat the revolution with ease needs no answer. For that is not the question. Certainly an attempt to overthrow the Government by force, even though doomed from the outset because of inadequate numbers or power of the revolutionists, is a sufficient evil for Congress to prevent. The damage which such attempts create both physically and politically to a nation makes it impossible to measure the validity in terms of the probability of success, or the immediacy of a successful attempt. In the instant case the trial judge charged the jury that they could not convict unless they found that petitioners intended to overthrow the Government "as speedily as circumstances would permit." This does not mean, and could not properly mean, that they would not strike until there was certainty of success. What was meant was that the revolutionists would strike when they thought the time was ripe. We must therefore reject the contention that success or probability of success is the criterion. . . .

The mere fact that from the period 1945 to 1948 petitioners' activities did not result in an attempt to overthrow the Government by force and violence is of course no answer to the fact that there was a group that was ready to make the attempt. The formation by petitioners of such a highly organized conspiracy, with rigidly disciplined members subject to call when the leaders, these petitioners, felt that the time had come for action, coupled with the inflammable nature of world conditions, similar uprisings in other countries, and the touch-and-go nature of our relations with countries with whom petitioners were in the very least ideologically attuned, convince us that their convictions were justified on this score. And this analysis disposes of the contention that a conspiracy to advocate, as distinguished from the advocacy itself, cannot be constitutionally restrained, because it comprises only the preparation. It is the existence of the conspiracy which creates the danger. Cf. *Pinkerton* v. *United States,* 328 U.S. 640 (1946); *Goldman* v. *United States,* 245 U.S. 474 (1918); *United States* v. *Rabinowich,* 238 U.S. 78 (1915). If the ingredients of the reaction are present, we cannot bind the Government to wait until the catalyst is added. . . .

We hold that § § 2 (a) (1), 2 (a) (3) and 3 of the Smith Act, do not inherently, or as construed or applied in the instant case, violate the First Amendment and other provisions of the Bill of Rights, or the First and Fifth Amendments because of indefiniteness. Petitioners intended to overthrow the Government of the United States as speedily as the circumstances would permit. Their conspiracy to organize the Communist Party and to teach and advocate the overthrow of the Government of the United States by force and violence created a "clear and present danger" of an attempt to overthrow the Government by force and violence. They were properly and constitutionally convicted for violation of the Smith Act. The judgments of conviction are

Affirmed.

JACKSON, V., concurring. This prosecution is the latest of never-ending, because never successful, quests for some legal formula that will secure an existing order against revolutionary radicalism. It requires us to reappraise, in the light of our own times and conditions, constitutional doctrines devised under other circumstances to strike a balance between authority and liberty.

Activity here charged to be criminal is conspiracy—that defendants conspired to teach and advocate, and to organize the Communist Party to teach and advocate, overthrow and destruction of the Government by force and violence. There is no charge of actual violence or attempt at overthrow.

The principal reliance of the defense in this Court is that the conviction cannot stand under the Constitution because the conspiracy of these defendants presents no "clear and present danger" of imminent or foreseeable overthrow. . . .

If we must decide that this Act and its application are constitutional only if we are convinced that petitioner's conduct creates a "clear and present danger" of violent overthrow, we must appraise imponderables, including international and national phenomena which baffle the best informed foreign offices and our most experienced politicians. We would have to foresee and predict the effectiveness of Communist propaganda, opportunities for infiltration; whether, and when, a time will come that they consider propitious for action, and whether and how fast our existing government will deteriorate. And we would have to speculate as to whether an approaching Communist *coup* would not be anticipated by a nationalistic fascist movement. No doctrine can be sound whose application requires us to make a prophecy of that sort in the guise of a legal decision. The judicial process simply is not adequate to a trial of such far-flung issues. The answers given would reflect our own political predilections and nothing more.

The authors of the clear and present danger test never applied it to a case like this, nor would I. If applied as it is proposed here, it means that the Communist plotting is protected during its period of incubation; its preliminary stages of organization and preparation are immune from the law; the Government can move only after imminent action is manifest, when it would, of course, be too late.

The highest degree of constitutional protection is due to the individual acting without conspiracy. But even an individual cannot claim that the Constitution protects him in advocating or teaching overthrow of government by force or violence. I should suppose no one would doubt that Congress has power to make such attempted overthrow a crime. But the contention is that one has the constitutional right to work up a public desire and will to do what is a crime to attempt. I think direct incitement by speech or writing can be made a crime, and I think there can be a conviction without also proving that the odds favored its success by 99 to 1, or some other extremely high ratio.

The names of Mr. Justice Holmes and Mr. Justice Brandeis cannot be associated with such a doctrine of governmental disability. After the *Schenck* case, in which they set forth the clear and present danger test, they joined in these words of Mr. Justice Holmes, spoken for a unanimous Court:

". . . [T]he First Amendment while prohibiting legislation against free speech as such cannot have been, and obviously was not, intended to give immunity for every possible use of language. *Robertson* v. *Baldwin*, 165 U.S. 275, 281. We venture

to believe that neither Hamilton nor Madison, nor any other competent person then or later, ever supposed that to make criminal the counselling of a murder within the jurisdiction of Congress would be an unconstitutional interference with free speech." *Frohwerk* v. *United States*, 249 U.S. 204.

The same doctrine was earlier stated in *Fox* v. *Washington*, 236 U.S. 273, 277, and that case was recently and with approval cited in *Giboney* v. *Empire Storage & Ice Co.*, 336 U.S. 490, 502.

As aptly stated by Judge Learned Hand in *Masses Publishing Co.* v. *Patten*, 244 F. 535, 540: "One may not counsel or advise others to violate the law as it stands. Words are not only the keys of persuasion, but the triggers of action, and those which have no purport but to counsel the violation of law cannot by any latitude of interpretation be a part of that public opinion which is the final source of government in a democratic state." . . .

BLACK, J., dissenting. . . .

At the outset I want to emphasize what the crime involved in this case is, and what it is not. These petitioners were not charged with an attempt to overthrow the Government. They were not charged with nonverbal acts of any kind designed to overthrow the Government. They were not even charged with saying anything or writing anything designed to overthrow the Government. The charge was that they agreed to assemble and to talk and publish certain ideas at a later date: The indictment is that they conspired to organize the Communist Party and to use speech or newspapers and other publications in the future to teach and advocate the forcible overthrow of the Government. No matter how it is worded, this is a virulent form of prior censorship of speech and press, which I believe the First Amendment forbids. I would hold § 3 of the Smith Act authorizing this prior restraint unconstitutional on its face and as applied.

But let us assume, contrary to all constitutional ideas of fair criminal procedure, that petitioners although not indicted for the crime of actual advocacy, may be punished for it. Even on this radical assumption, the only way to affirm these convictions, as the dissent of MR. JUSTICE DOUGLAS shows, is to qualify drastically or wholly repudiate the established "clear and present danger" rule. This the Court does in a way which greatly restricts the protections afforded by the First Amendment. The opinions for affirmance show that the chief reason for jettisoning the rule is the expressed fear that advocacy of Communist doctrine endangers the safety of the Republic. Undoubtedly, a governmental policy of unfettered communication of ideas does entail dangers. To the Founders of this Nation, however, the benefits derived from free expression were worth the risk. They embodied this philosophy in the First Amendment's command that Congress "shall make no law abridging . . . the freedom of speech, or of the press . . . ." I have always believed that the First Amendment is the keystone of our Government, that the freedoms it guarantees provide the best insurance against destruction of all freedom. At least as to speech in the realm of public matters, I believe that the "clear and present danger" test does not "mark the furthermost constitutional boundaries of protected expression" but does "no more than recognize a minimum compulsion of the Bill of Rights." *Bridges* v. *California,* 314 U.S. 252, 263.

So long as this Court exercises the power of judicial review of legislation, I cannot agree that the First Amendment permits us to sustain laws suppressing freedom of speech and press on the basis of Congress' or our own notions of mere "reasonableness." Such a doctrine waters down the First Amendment so that it amounts to little more than an admonition to Congress. The Amendment as so construed is not likely to protect any but those "safe" or orthodox views which rarely need its protection. . . .

Public opinion being what it now is, few will protest the conviction of these Communist petitioners. There is hope, however, that in calmer times, when present pressures, passions and fears subside, this or some later Court will restore the First Amendment liberties to the high preferred place where they belong in a free society.

DOUGLAS, J., dissenting. If this were a case where those who claimed protection under the First Amendment were teaching the techniques of sabotage, the assassination of the President, the filching of documents from public files, the planting of bombs, the art of street warfare, and the like, I would have no doubts. The freedom to speak is not absolute; the teaching of methods of terror and other seditious conduct should be beyond the pale along with obscenity and immorality. . . .

So far as the present record is concerned, what petitioners did was to organize people to teach and themselves teach the Marxist-Leninist doctrine contained chiefly in four books: *Foundations of Leninism* by Stalin (1924), *The Communist Manifesto* by Marx and Engels (1848), *State and Revolution* by Lenin (1917), *History of the Communist Party of the Soviet Union* (B) (1939). . . .

I repeat that we deal here with speech alone, not with speech *plus* acts of sabotage or unlawful conduct. Not a single seditious act is charged in the indictment.

Free speech has occupied an exalted position because of the high service it has given our society. Its protection is essential to the very existence of a democracy. The airing of ideas releases pressures which otherwise might become destructive. When ideas compete in the market for acceptance, full and free discussion exposes the false and they gain few adherents. Full and free discussion even of ideas we hate encourages the testing of our own prejudices and preconceptions. Full and free discussion keeps a society from becoming stagnant and unprepared for the stresses and strains that work to tear all civilizations apart.

Full and free discussion has indeed been the first article of our faith. We have founded our political system on it. It has been the safeguard of every religious, political, philosophical, economic, and racial group amongst us. We have counted on it to keep us from embracing what is cheap and false; we have trusted the common sense of our people to choose the doctrine true to our genius and to reject the rest. This has been the one single outstanding tenet that has made our institutions the symbol of freedom and equality. We have deemed it more costly to liberty to suppress a despised minority than to let them vent their spleen. We have above all else feared the political censor. We have wanted a land where our people can be exposed to all the diverse creeds and cultures of the world.

There comes a time when even speech loses its constitutional immunity. Speech innocuous one year may at another time fan such destructive flames that it must be halted in the interests of the safety of the Republic. That is the meaning of the clear and present danger test. When conditions are so critical that there will be no time to avoid the evil that the speech threatens, it is time to call a halt. Otherwise, free speech which is the strength of the Nation will be the cause of its destruction.

Yet free speech is the rule, not the exception. The restraint to be constitutional must be based on more than fear, on more than passionate opposition against the speech, on more than a revolted dislike for its contents. There must be some immediate injury to society that is likely if speech is allowed. . . .

The nature of Communism as a force on the world scene would, of course be relevant to the issue of clear and present danger of petitioners' advocacy within the United States. But the primary consideration is the strength and tactical position of petitioners and their converts in this country. On that there is no evidence in the record. If we are to take judicial notice of the threat of Communists within the nation, it should not be difficult to conclude that *as a political party* they are of little consequence. Communists in this country have never made a respectable or serious showing in any election. I would doubt that there is a village, let alone a city or county or state which the Communists could carry. Communism in the world scene is no bogey-man; but Communism as a political faction or party in this country plainly is. Communism has been so thoroughly exposed in this country that it has been crippled as a political force. Free speech has destroyed it as an effective political party. It is inconceivable that those who went up and down this country preaching the doctrine of revolution which petitioners espouse would have any success. In days of trouble and confusion when bread lines were long, when the unemployed walked the streets, when people were starving, the advocates of a short-cut by revolution might have a chance to gain adherents. But today there are no such conditions. The country is not in despair; the people know Soviet Communism; the doctrine of Soviet revolution is exposed in all of its ugliness and the American people want none of it.

How it can be said that there is a clear and present danger that this advocacy will succeed is, therefore, a mystery. Some nations less resilient than the United States, where illiteracy is high and where democratic traditions are only budding, might have to take drastic steps and jail these men for merely speaking their creed. But in America they are miserable merchants of unwanted ideas; their wares remain unsold. The fact that their ideas are abhorrent does not make them powerful. . . .

The First Amendment provides that "Congress shall make no law . . . abridging the freedom of speech." The Constitution provides no exception. This does not mean, however, that the Nation need hold its hand until it is in such weakened condition that there is no time to protect itself from incitement to revolution. Seditious conduct can always be punished. But the command of the First Amendment is so clear that we should not allow Congress to call a halt to free speech except in the extreme case of peril from the speech itself. The First Amendment makes confidence in the common sense of our people and in their maturity of judgment the great postulate of our democracy. Its philosophy is that violence is rarely, if ever, stopped by denying civil liberties to those advocating resort to force. The First Amendment reflects the philosophy of Jefferson "that it is time enough for the rightful purposes of civil government for its officers to interfere when principles break out into overt acts against peace and good order." The political censor has no place in our public debates. Unless and until extreme and necessitous circumstances are shown our aim should be to keep speech unfettered and to allow the processes of law to be invoked only when the provocateurs among us move from speech to action.

Vishinsky wrote in 1948 in *The Law of the Soviet State,* "In our state, naturally there can be no place for freedom of speech, press, and so on for the foes of socialism."

Our concern should be that we accept no such standard for the United States. Our faith should be that our people will never give support to these advocates of revolution, so long as we remain loyal to the purposes for which our Nation was founded. . . .

594. THE RECALL OF GENERAL DOUGLAS MacARTHUR
April 11, 1951
(Department of State Bulletin, April 16, 1951)

The question of military strategy in the Korean War involved the over-all foreign policy of the United States. In October, 1950, the Chinese Communist government sent troops to aid the faltering North Koreans. To meet this situation, the commander of United States and United Nations troops in Korea, General Douglas MacArthur, proposed the use of air and naval forces to extend the war to Chinese territory. President Truman rejected this proposal and ordered MacArthur to conduct a limited war on the Korean peninsula. When MacArthur continued to press for more extensive military operations against the Chinese, President Truman relieved him of his command. Truman explained the reasons for his action in this address to the nation. See H. Truman, *Memoirs*, Vol. II; Council on Foreign Relations, *The United States in World Affairs, 1950–1953*; R. H. Rovere and A. M. Schlesinger, Jr., *The General and the President*; C. Whitney, *MacArthur: His Rendezvous with History*; C. A. Willoughby and J. Chamberlain, *MacArthur, 1944–1951*. For his speech (April 19, 1951) to joint session of Congress, see U.S. Senate Committee on Armed Services and Committee on Foreign Relations, 82nd Congress, *Joint Statement . . . on Relief of General MacArthur and on American Policy in Far East*, and *House Doc.* No. 36.

I want to talk plainly to you tonight about what we are doing in Korea and about our policy in the Far East.

In the simplest terms, what we are doing in Korea is this: We are trying to prevent a third world war.

I think most people in this country recognized that fact last June. And they warmly supported the decision of the Government to help the Republic of Korea against the Communist aggressors. Now, many persons, even some who applauded our decision to defend Korea, have forgotten the basic reason for our action.

It is right for us to be in Korea. It was right last June. It is right today.

I want to remind you why this is true.

The Communists in the Kremlin are engaged in a monstrous conspiracy to stamp out freedom all over the world. If they were to succeed, the United States would be numbered among their principal victims. It must be clear to everyone that the United States cannot—and will not—sit idly by and await foreign conquest. The only question is: When is the best time to meet the threat and how?

The best time to meet the threat is in the beginning. It is easier to put out a fire in the beginning when it is small than after it has become a roaring blaze.

And the best way to meet the threat of aggression is for the peace-loving nations to act together. If they don't act together, they are likely to be picked off, one by one. . . .

This is the basic reason why we joined in creating the United Nations. And since the end of World War II we have been putting that lesson into practice—we have been working with other free nations to check the aggressive designs of the Soviet Union before they can result in a third world war.

That is what we did in Greece, when that nation was threatened by the aggression of international communism.

The attack against Greece could have led to general war. But this country came to the aid of Greece. The United Nations supported Greek resistance. With our help, the determination and efforts of the Greek people defeated the attack on the spot.

Another big Communist threat to peace was the Berlin blockade. That too could have led to war. But again it was settled because free men would not back down in an emergency. . . .

The question we have had to face is whether the Communist plan of conquest can be stopped without general war. Our Government and other countries associated with us in the United Nations believe that the best chance of stopping it without general war is to meet the attack in Korea and defeat it there.

That is what we have been doing. It is a difficult and bitter task.

But so far it has been successful.

So far, we have prevented World War III.

So far, by fighting a limited war in Korea, we have prevented aggression from succeeding and bringing on a general war. And the ability of the whole free world to resist Communist aggression has been greatly improved.

We have taught the enemy a lesson. He has found out that aggression is not cheap or easy. Moreover, men all over the world who want to remain free have been given new courage and new hope. They know now that the champions of freedom can stand up and fight and that they will stand up and fight.

Our resolute stand in Korea is helping the forces of freedom now fighting in Indochina and other countries in that part of the world. It has already slowed down the timetable of conquest. . . .

We do not want to see the conflict in Korea extended. We are trying to prevent a world war—not to start one. The best way to do this is to make plain that we and the other free countries will continue to resist the attack.

But you may ask: Why can't we take other steps to punish the aggressor? Why don't we bomb Manchuria and China itself? Why don't we assist Chinese Nationalist troops to land on the mainland of China?

If we were to do these things we would be running a very grave risk of starting a general war. If that were to happen, we would have brought about the exact situation we are trying to prevent.

If we were to do these things, we would become entangled in a vast conflict on the continent of Asia and our task would become immeasurably more difficult all over the world.

What would suit the ambitions of the Kremlin better than for our military forces to be committed to a full-scale war with Red China? . . .

The course we have been following is the one best calculated to avoid an all-out war. It is the course consistent with our obligation to do all we can to maintain international peace and security. Our experience in Greece and Berlin shows that it is the most effective course of action we can follow. . . .

If the Communist authorities realize that they cannot defeat us in Korea, if they realize it would be foolhardy to widen the hostilities beyond Korea, then they may recognize the folly of continuing their aggression. A peaceful settlement may then be possible. The door is always open.

Then we may achieve a settlement in Korea which will not compromise the principles and purposes of the United Nations.

I have thought long and hard about this question of extending the war in Asia. I have discussed it many times with the ablest military advisers in the country. I believe with all my heart that the course we are following is the best course.

I believe that we must try to limit war to Korea for these vital reasons: to make sure that the precious lives of our fighting men are not wasted; to see that the security of our country and the free world is not needlessly jeopardized; and to prevent a third world war.

A number of events have made it evident that General MacArthur did not agree with that policy. I have therefore considered it essential to relieve General MacArthur so that there would be no doubt or confusion as to the real purpose and aim of our policy.

It was with the deepest personal regret that I found myself compelled to take this action. General MacArthur is one of our greatest military commanders. But the cause of world peace is more important than any individual.

The change in commands in the Far East means no change whatever in the policy of the United States. We will carry on the fight in Korea with vigor and determination in an effort to bring the war to a speedy and successful conclusion.

The new commander, Lt. Gen. Matthew Ridgway, has already demonstrated that he has the great qualities of military leadership needed for this task.

We are ready, at any time, to negotiate for a restoration of peace in the area. But we will not engage in appeasement. We are only interested in real peace.

Real peace can be achieved through a settlement based on the following factors:

One: the fighting must stop.

Two: concrete steps must be taken to insure that the fighting will not break out again.

Three: there must be an end to the aggression.

A settlement founded upon these elements would open the way for the unification of Korea and the withdrawal of all foreign forces.

In the meantime, I want to be clear about our military objective. We are fighting to resist an outrageous aggression in Korea. We are trying to keep the Korean conflict from spreading to other areas. But at the same time we must conduct our military activities so as to insure the security of our forces.

This is essential if they are to continue the fight until the enemy abandons its ruthless attempt to destroy the Republic of Korea.

That is our military objective—to repel attack and to restore peace.

In the hard fighting in Korea, we are proving that collective action among nations is not only a high principle but a workable means of resisting aggression. Defeat of aggression in Korea may be the turning point in the world's search for a practical way of achieving peace and security.

The struggle of the United Nations in Korea is a struggle for peace.

The free nations have united their strength in an effort to prevent a third world war.

That war can come if the Communist rulers want it to come. But this Nation and its allies will not be responsible for its coming.

We do not want to widen the conflict. We will use every effort to prevent that disaster. And in so doing we know that we are following the great principles of peace, freedom, and justice.

595. EUROPEAN RECOVERY PROGRAM
December 30, 1951
(*Department of State Bulletin,* Vol. XXVI, p. 43)

The Marshall Plan for aid to Europe was given practical effect by the Economic Cooperation Act of 1948. This act appropriated money for the rehabilitation of Europe and created an Economic Cooperation Administration to spend it. Additional legislation provided for aid to other parts of the world. Under the authority thus granted, the ECA gave assistance to countries throughout the world including Communist Yugoslavia after the Tito-Stalin break of 1948. The heart of the American program of economic aid remained the effort to secure the recovery of Western Europe. The terminal report of December 30, 1951, summarized the achievements of the ECA in Western Europe. See S. E. Harris, *The European Recovery Program;* J. A. Krout, ed., "American Foreign Aid Program," 23 *Proc. of Am. Academy of Pol. Sci.* 345; J. K. Galbraith, "European Recovery: The Longer View," 12 *Rev. of Politics* 165; J. H. Williams, "End of the Marshall Plan," 30 *Foreign Affairs* 593.

The recovery of Europe from the chaos of 1947, when it was hungry, cold, disorderly, and frightened, can be measured in cold statistics: Industrial production, 64 percent above 1947 and 41 percent above prewar; steel production, nearly doubled in less than 4 years; coal production, slightly below prewar but still 27 percent higher than in 1947; aluminum, copper, and cement production, up respectively 69, 31, and 90 percent from 1947; food production, 24 percent above 1947 and 9 percent above prewar levels.

The Economic Cooperation Administration has expended nearly 12 billion dollars in grants and loans in carrying out the European Recovery Program—equal to nearly 80 dollars for every man, woman, and child in the United States. To this, the countries of Europe have added the equivalent of another 9 billion dollars in its own currencies to match the American grant-aid dollars. Of the U.S. funds, about 5.5 billion dollars have been used to purchase industrial commodities, mostly from the United States, and another 5.2 billion dollars for the purchase of food and other agricultural commodities such as cotton. Over 800 million dollars has alone gone into the cost of ocean freight for goods sent to Europe. The U.S. contribution to the setting up of the EPU was 350 million dollars and another 100 million dollars has been used since then to help the payments union over rough spots.

In their turn, the Marshall Plan countries in the past 3 years completed or are pushing to completion a total of 27 major projects for the increase of power and 32 major projects for modernizing and expanding the production of iron and steel. Major petroleum refining works number 11 and the volume of refining has quadrupled over prewar. Other industrial projects costing the equivalent of a million dollars or more bring the total of such projects to 132, costing the equivalent of over two billion dollars. About half a billion dollars of the U.S. commodity and technical aid has gone into these projects.

Into other major recovery projects have gone also the equivalent of billions of dollars of the counterpart currencies generated in the Marshall Plan countries to match American dollar aid. Such counterpart funds are used by the respective countries for recovery projects approved by the ECA. Biggest single use—equivalent to more than a billion dollars—has been for the improvement of electric, gas, and power facilities, an improvement that is helping to make possible Europe's rearmament program today.

Similarly vital to Europe's defense has been the rehabilitation of the continent's run-down and war-smashed railway network, with approved projects for use of counterpart funds totaling more than the equivalent of half a billion dollars. Similarly, counterpart projects for the reconstruction of merchant fleets, port and shipping facilities, and inland waterways have been completed or are in the process of completion in the Marshall Plan countries. Airports, too, have been built or improved with ECA-generated local currencies.

Through such double-barreled use of dollar aid and local funds, Marshall Plan nations, in less than 4 years, have rebuilt their economies to a point that could well persuade the Kremlin that the Europe which looked like such easy pickings in 1946 and 1947 is indeed a formidable bastion today.

Steel production, for example, so necessary to a strong peace or war economy, has risen from less than 31 million tons in 1947 to nearly 60 million tons in 1951. Soviet Russia and her satellites combined have a steel production rate of about 35 million tons.

The average volume of crude oil refined in Europe in prewar years was 12 million tons annually. In 1950–51 the volume of refined products reached 46.8 million tons, or nearly four times prewar.

In 1947, Europe's average monthly electrical production was 13½ million kilowatt hours. In mid-1951 the wheels of Europe's industry were being turned with 20½ million kilowatt hours per month. From a monthly cement production average of less than 2 million metric tons in 1947, Europe's production rose to 4 million tons monthly during the first half of 1951.

Cotton-yarn production in free Europe has risen from a monthly average of 82,000 metric tons in 1947 to 125,000 tons in 1951; wool yarn production is up from 33,000 tons monthly in 1947 to 44,000 tons in 1951.

One of the most dramatic improvements, and one closely tied to Europe's defense capabilities, is in the production of motor vehicles. Monthly production, running at the rate of 54,000 vehicles in 1947, is up to 145,000 vehicles in 1951.

Agricultural production is up 9 percent over prewar and 24 percent over 1947–48, but at the same time there are many more mouths to feed (population is up from 250 million in 1938 to over 275 million in 1951) and Europe is not yet self-sufficient in food production.

Overall, Europe's gross national product—the total sum of its production of goods and services—rose by nearly 25 percent in the less than 4 years of Marshall Plan aid to over 125 billion dollars in 1950. This is a 15 percent increase over prewar levels.

But Europe by no means considers its job finished. Member countries of the OEEC recently issued a manifesto declaring their intention to work for an expansion of total production in Western Europe by 25 percent over the next 5 years.

With her industrial plant rebuilt to better than prewar years, Europe's hope for meeting or surpassing this goal must rest on improved production methods and greater productivity—increased output of goods with the same amount of manpower, machines, and management.

596. MUTUAL SECURITY ACT OF 1951
October 10, 1951
(Public Law 165, 82nd Congress)

The Truman Doctrine and the Marshall Plan committed the United States to large-scale programs of military and economic aid to friendly nations. The Military Defense Assistance Act of 1949 authorized military aid and the Economic Cooperation Acts of 1948 and 1949 and the Point Four Program of 1950 authorized economic and technical assistance to free nations throughout the world. See Docs. No. 575, 578, 588. At the end of 1951, Congress assigned the function of administering both the economic and the military aid programs to a new agency, the Mutual Security Administration. The significance of the Mutual Security Act of 1951 was twofold: first, it provided for the coordination of the military and economic aid programs; second, it marked a new emphasis of American policy on military, rather than economic aid. See D. Middleton, *Defense of Western Europe;* H. L. Marx, ed., *Defense and National Security;* U.S. President, *Report to Congress on the Mutual Security Program,* 1951–.

An Act to maintain the security and promote the foreign policy and provide for the general welfare of the United States by furnishing assistance to friendly nations in the interest of international peace and security.

SEC. 2. The Congress declares it to be the purpose of this Act to maintain the security and to promote the foreign policy of the United States by authorizing military, economic, and technical assistance to friendly countries to strengthen the mutual security and individual and collective defenses of the free world, to develop their resources in the interest of their security and independence and the national interest of the United States and to facilitate the effective participation of those countries in the United Nations system

for collective security. The purposes of the Mutual Defense Assistance Act of 1949, as amended (22 U.S.C. 1571–1604), the Economic Cooperation Act of 1948, as amended, and the Act for International Development (22 U.S.C. 1557) shall hereafter be deemed to include this purpose.

TITLE I
EUROPE

SEC. 101. (a) In order to support the freedom of Europe through assistance which will further the carrying out of the plans for defense of the North Atlantic area, while at the same time maintaining the economic stability of the countries of the area so that they may meet their responsibilities for defense, and to further encourage the economic unification and the political federation of Europe, there are hereby authorized to be appropriated to the President for the fiscal year 1952 for carrying out the provisions and accomplishing the policies and purpose of this Act—

(1) not to exceed $5,028,000,000 for assistance pursuant to the provisions of the Mutual Defense Assistance Act of 1949, as amended, for countries which are parties to the North Atlantic Treaty and for any country of Europe (other than a country covered by another title of this Act), which the President determines to be of direct importance to the defense of the North Atlantic area and whose increased ability to defend itself the President determines is important to the preservation of the peace and security of the North Atlantic area and to the security of the United States. . . .

(2) not to exceed $1,022,000,000 for assistance pursuant to the provisions of the Economic Cooperation Act of 1948, as amended (including assistance to further European military production), for any country of Europe covered by paragraph (1) of this subsection and for any other country covered by section 103 (a) of the said Economic Cooperation Act of 1948, as amended. . . .

TITLE II
NEAR EAST AND AFRICA

SEC. 201. In order to further the purpose of this Act by continuing to provide military assistance to Greece, Turkey, and Iran, there are hereby authorized to be appropriated to the President for the fiscal year 1952, not to exceed $396,250,000 for furnishing assistance to Greece and Turkey pursuant to the provisions of the Act of May 22, 1947, as amended, and for furnishing assistance to Iran pursuant to the provisions of the Mutual Defense Assistance Act of 1949, as amended (22 U.S.C. 1571–1604). In addition, unexpected balances of appropriations heretofore made for assistance to Greece and Turkey, available for the fiscal year 1951, pursuant to the Act of May 22, 1947, as amended, and for assistance to Iran pursuant to the Mutual Defense Assistance Act of 1949, as amended, are hereby authorized to be continued available through June 30, 1952, and to be consolidated with the appropriation authorized by this section.

SEC. 202. Whenever the President determines that such action is essential for the purpose of this Act, he may provide assistance, pursuant to the provisions of the Mutual Defense Assistance Act of 1949, as amended, to any country of the Near East area (other than those covered by section 201) and may utilize not to exceed 10 per centum of the amount made available (excluding balances of prior appropriations continued available) pursuant to section 201 of this Act: *Provided,* That any such assistance may be furnished only upon determination by the President that (1) the strategic location of the recipient country makes it of direct importance to the defense of the Near

East area, (2) such assistance is of critical importance to the defense of the free nations, and (3) the immediately increased ability of the recipient country to defend itself is important to the preservation of the peace and security of the area and to the security of the United States.

SEC. 203. In order to further the purpose of this Act in Africa and the Near East, there are hereby authorized to be appropriated to the President, for the fiscal year 1952, not to exceed $160,000,000 for economic and technical assistance in Africa and the Near East in areas other than those covered by section 103 (a) of the Economic Cooperation Act of 1948, as amended. . . .

TITLE III
ASIA AND PACIFIC

SEC. 301. In order to carry out in the general area of China (including the Republic of the Philippines and the Republic of Korea) the provisions of subsection (a) of section 303 of the Mutual Defense Assistance Act of 1949, as amended, there are hereby authorized to be appropriated to the President for the fiscal year 1952, not to exceed $535,250,000. . . .

SEC. 302. (a) In order to further the purpose of this Act through the strengthening of the area covered in section 301 of this Act (but not including the Republic of Korea), there are hereby authorized to be appropriated to the President, for the fiscal year 1952, not to exceed $237,500,000 for economic and technical assistance in those portions of such area which the President deems to be not under Communist control. Funds appropriated pursuant to authority of this section shall be available under the applicable provisions of the Economic Cooperation Act of 1948, as amended, and of the Act for International Development. . . .

TITLE IV
AMERICAN REPUBLICS

SEC. 401. In order to further the purpose of this Act through the furnishing of military assistance to the other American Republics, there are hereby authorized to be appropriated to the President, for the fiscal year 1952, not to exceed $38,150,000 for carrying out the purposes of this section under the provisions of the Mutual Defense Assistance Act of 1949, as amended. . . .

TITLE V
ORGANIZATION AND GENERAL PROVISIONS

SEC. 501. (a) In order that the programs of military, economic, and technical assistance authorized by this Act may be administered as parts of a unified program in accordance with the intent of Congress and to fix responsibility for the coordination and supervision of these programs in a single person, the President is authorized to appoint in the Executive Office of the President a Director for Mutual Security. The Director on behalf of the President and subject to his direction, shall have primary responsibility for—

(1) continuous supervision and general direction of the assistance programs under this Act to the end that such programs shall be (A) effectively integrated both at home and abroad, and (B) administered so as to assure that the defensive strength of the free nations of the world shall be built as quickly as possible on the basis of continuous and effective self-help and mutual aid;

(2) preparation and presentation to the Congress of such programs of foreign military, economic, and technical assistance as may be required in the interest of the security of the United States;

(3) preparation for the President of the report to the Congress required by section 518 of this Act. . . .

SEC. 502. (a) The Economic Cooperation Administration and the offices of Administrator for Economic Cooperation, Deputy Administrator, United States Special Representative in Europe, and Deputy Special Representative are hereby abolished.

(b) To assist in carrying out the purpose of this Act—

(1) there is hereby established, its principle office at the seat of the government, a Mutual Security Agency, hereinafter referred to as the Agency, which shall be headed by the Director for Mutual Security; and

(2) there shall be transferred to the Director the powers, functions, and responsibilities conferred upon the Administration for Economic Cooperation by the Economic Cooperation Act of 1948, as amended, and by any other law, but no such powers, functions, and responsibilities, shall be exercised after June 30, 1952, except as provided in subsection (c) of this section.

(c) Not later than April 1, 1952, the President shall inform the Committee on Foreign Relations of the Senate and the Committee on Foreign Affairs of the House of Representatives which of the powers, functions, and responsibilities transferred to the Director by subsection (b) (2) are found by the President to be necessary to enable the Director after June 30, 1952, to carry out the duties conferred upon him by section 503. The termination provisions of section 122 of the Economic Cooperation Act of 1948, as amended, shall come into effect on June 30, 1952, and none of the powers, functions, and responsibilities conferred by that Act shall be exercised after that date, except those powers, functions, and responsibilities found necessary to enable the Director to carry out the duties conferred on him by section 503 of this Act, which powers, functions, and responsibilities unless otherwise provided by law shall continue in effect until June 30, 1954. . . .

SEC. 503. After June 30, 1952, the Director, on behalf of the President and subject to his direction, shall, in consultation with the Secretaries of State and Defense, continue to have primary responsibility for—

(a) The development and administration of programs of assistance designed to sustain and increase military effort, including production, construction, equipment and matériel in each country or in groups of countries which receive United States military assistance;

(b) the provision of such equipment, materials, commodities, services, financial, or other assistance as he finds to be necessary for carrying out mutual defense programs; and

(c) the provision of limited economic assistance to foreign nations for which the United States has responsibility as a result of participation in joint control arrangements when the President finds that the provision of such economic assistance is in the interest of the security of the United States. . . .

SEC. 513. Whenever the President determines it to be necessary for the purpose of this Act, not to exceed 10 per centum of the funds made available under any title of this Act may be transferred to and consolidated with funds made available under any other title of this Act in order to furnish, to a different area, assistance of the kind for which such funds were available before transfer. Whenever the President makes any such determination, he shall forthwith notify the Committee on Foreign Relations of the Senate and the Committee on Foreign Affairs of the House of Representatives. In the case of the transfer of funds available for military purposes, he shall also forthwith notify the Committees on Armed Services of the Senate and House of Representatives.

SEC. 516. It is hereby declared to be the policy of the Congress that this Act shall be administered in such a way as (1) to eliminate the barriers to, and provide the incentives for, a steadily increased participation of free private enterprise in developing the resources of foreign countries consistent with the policies of this Act, (2) to the extent that it is feasible and does not interfere with the achievement of the purposes set forth in this Act, to discourage the cartel and monopolistic business practices prevailing in certain countries receiving aid under this Act which result in restricting production and increasing prices, and to encourage where suitable competition and productivity, and (3) to encourage where suitable the development and strengthening of the free labor union movements as the collective bargaining agencies of labor within such countries. . . .

SEC. 529. If the President determines that the furnishing of assistance to any nation—

(a) is no longer consistent with the national interest or security of the United States or the policies and purpose of this Act; or

(b) would contravene a decision of the Security Council of the United Nations; or

(c) would be inconsistent with the principle that members of the United Nations should refrain from giving assistance to any nation against which the Security Council or the General Assembly has recommended measures in case of a threat to, or breach of, the peace, or act of aggression, he shall terminate all or part of any assistance furnished pursuant to this Act. The function conferred herein shall be in addition to all other functions heretofore conferred with respect to the termination of military, economic, or technical assistance. . . .

597. YOUNGSTOWN SHEET & TUBE CO. v. SAWYER
343 U.S. 579
1952

This decision is one of the few instances in our history where the court has restrained the executive power. In December, 1951, in the midst of the Korean War, steelworkers gave notice of intent to strike. Intervention by the Federal Mediation Service and the Wage Stabilization Board failed, and the steelworkers' union called a strike for April 4, 1952. On the ground that a strike would jeopardize national security, President Truman directed Secretary of Commerce Sawyer to take over and operate the affected steel mills. One of the mills challenged the constitutionality of this order and asked for an injunction against the Secretary of Commerce; the district court granted the injunction; the court of appeals stayed the injunction, and the case came on appeal to the Supreme Court. See H. Truman, *Memoirs,* Vol. II; C. Rossiter, *Supreme Court and the Commander in Chief;* C. Rossiter, *Constitutional Dictatorship;* E. S. Corwin, *The President, Office and Powers;* B. M. Rich, *The Presidents and Civil Disorder;* Grover Cleveland, *The Government in the Chicago Strike of 1894;*

E. Berman, *Labor Disputes and the President;*
E. S. Corwin, "Steel Seizure Case," 53 *Columbia
Law Rev.* 53. Appendix I to this case provides
a "synoptic analysis of Legislation authorizing
seizure of Industrial Property."

BLACK, J. We are asked to decide whether
the President was acting within his constitutional power when he issued an order
directing the Secretary of Commerce to take
possession of and operate most of the Nation's steel mills. The mill owners argue that
the President's order amounts to lawmaking,
a legislative function which the Constitution
has expressly confided to the Congress and
not to the President. The Government's position is that the order was made on findings
of the President that his action was necessary to avert a national catastrophe which
would inevitably result from a stoppage of
steel production, and that in meeting this
grave emergency the President was acting
within the aggregate of his constitutional
powers as the Nation's Chief Executive and
the Commander in Chief of the Armed
Forces of the United States. . . .

Two crucial issues have developed: *First.*
Should final determination of the constitutional validity of the President's order be
made in this case which has proceeded no
further than the preliminary injunction
stage? *Second.* If so, is the seizure order
within the constitutional power of the President? . . .

The President's power, if any, to issue the
order must stem either from an act of Congress or from the Constitution itself. There
is no statute that expressly authorizes the
President to take possession of property as
he did here. Nor is there any act of Congress
to which our attention has been directed
from which such a power can fairly be implied. Indeed, we do not understand the Government to rely on statutory authorization
for this seizure. There are two statutes which
do authorize the President to take both personal and real property under certain conditions. However, the Government admits that
these conditions were not met and that the
President's order was not rooted in either of
the statutes. The Government refers to the
seizure provisions of one of these statutes
(Sec. 201 (b) of the Defense Production
Act) as "much too cumbersome, involved,
and time-consuming for the crisis which was
at hand."

Moreover, the use of the seizure technique
to solve labor disputes in order to prevent
work stoppages was not only unauthorized
by any congressional enactment; prior to this
controversy, Congress had refused to adopt
that method of settling labor disputes. When
the Taft-Hartley Act was under consideration in 1947, Congress rejected an amendment which would have authorized such
governmental seizures in cases of emergency.
Apparently it was thought that the technique
of seizure, like that of compulsory arbitration, would interfere with the process of collective bargaining. Consequently, the plan
adopted in that Act did not provide for seizure under any circumstances. Instead, the
plan sought to bring about settlements by
use of the customary devices of mediation,
conciliation, investigation by boards of inquiry, and public reports. In some instances
temporary injunctions were authorized to
provide cooling-off periods. All this failing,
unions were left free to strike after a secret
vote by employees as to whether they wished
to accept their employer's final settlement
offer.

It is clear that if the President had authority to issue the order he did, it must be
found in some provisions of the Constitution. And it is not claimed that express constitutional language grants this power to the
President. The contention is that presidential
power should be implied from the aggregate
of his powers under the Constitution. Particular reliance is placed on provisions in Article II which say that "the executive Power
shall be vested in a President . . ."; that
"he shall take Care that the Laws be faithfully executed"; and that he "shall be Commander in Chief of the Army and Navy of
the United States."

The order cannot properly be sustained as
an exercise of the President's military power
as Commander in Chief of the Armed Forces.
The Government attempts to do so by citing
a number of cases upholding broad powers in
military commanders engaged in day-to-day
fighting in a theater of war. Such cases need

not concern us here. Even though "theater of war" be an expanding concept, we cannot with faithfulness to our constitutional system hold that the Commander in Chief of the Armed Forces has the ultimate power as such to take possession of private property in order to keep labor disputes from stopping production. This is a job for the Nation's lawmakers, not for its military authorities.

Nor can the seizure order be sustained because of the several constitutional provisions that grant executive power to the President. In the framework of our Constitution, the President's power to see that the laws are faithfully executed refutes the idea that he is to be a lawmaker. The Constitution limits his functions in the lawmaking process to the recommending of laws he thinks wise and the vetoing of laws he thinks bad. And the Constitution is neither silent nor equivocal about who shall make laws which the President is to execute. The first section of the first article says that "All legislative Powers herein granted shall be vested in a Congress of the United States. . . ." After granting many powers to the Congress, Article I goes on to provide that Congress may "make all Laws which shall be necessary and proper for carrying into Execution the foregoing Powers and all other Powers vested by this Constitution in the Government of the United States, or in any Department or Officer thereof."

The President's order does not direct that a congressional policy be executed in a manner prescribed by Congress—it directs that a presidential policy be executed in a manner prescribed by the President. The preamble of the order itself, like that of many statutes, sets out reasons why the President believes certain policies should be adopted, proclaims that these policies as rules of conduct to be followed, and again, like a statute, authorizes a government official to promulgate additional rules and regulations consistent with the policy proclaimed and needed to carry that policy into execution. The power of Congress to adopt such public policies as those proclaimed by the order is beyond question. It can authorize the taking of private property for public use. It can make laws regulating the relationships between employers and employees, prescribing rules de-

signed to settle labor disputes, and fixing wages and working conditions in certain fields of our economy. The Constitution did not subject this law-making power of Congress to presidential or military supervision or control.

It is said that other Presidents without congressional authority have taken possession of private business enterprises in order to settle labor disputes. But even if this be true, Congress has not thereby lost its exclusive constitutional authority to make laws necessary and proper to carry out the powers vested by the Constitution "in the Government of the United States, or in any Department or Officer thereof."

The Founders of this Nation entrusted the law-making power to the Congress alone in both good and bad times. It would do no good to recall the historical events, the fears of power and the hopes for freedom that lay behind their choice. Such a review would but confirm our holding that this seizure order cannot stand.

The Judgment of the District Court is affirmed.

VINSON, C. J., dissenting: . . . In passing upon the question of Presidential powers in this case, we must first consider the context in which those powers were exercised.

Those who suggest that this is a case involving extraordinary powers should be mindful that these are extraordinary times. A world not yet recovered from the devastation of World War II has been forced to face the threat of another and more terrifying global conflict. . . . For almost two full years, our armed forces have been fighting in Korea, suffering casualties of over 108,000 men. Hostilities have not abated. The "determination of the United Nations to continue its action in Korea to meet the aggression" has been reaffirmed. Congressional support of the action in Korea has been manifested by provisions for increased military manpower and equipment and for economic stabilization, as hereinafter described. . . .

Even this brief review of our responsibilities in the world community discloses the enormity of our undertaking. Success of these measures may, as has often been observed, dramatically influence the lives of many generations of the world's peoples yet unborn.

Alert to our responsibilities, which coincide with our own self preservation through mutual security, Congress has enacted a large body of implementing legislation. . . .

Congress recognized the impact of these defense programs upon the economy. Following the attack in Korea, the President asked for authority to requisition property and to allocate and fix priorities for scarce goods. In the Defense Production Act of 1950, Congress granted the powers requested and, *in addition,* granted power to stabilize prices and wages and to provide for settlement of labor disputes arising in the defense program. . . .

The President has the duty to execute the foregoing legislative programs. Their successful execution depends upon continued production of steel and stabilized prices for steel. Accordingly, when the collective bargaining agreements between the Nation's steel producers and their employees, represented by the United Steel Workers, were due to expire on December 31, 1951, and a strike shutting down the entire basic steel industry was threatened, the President acted to avert a complete shutdown of steel production. . . . We . . . assume without deciding that the courts may go behind a President's finding of fact that an emergency exists. But there is not the slightest basis for suggesting that the President's finding in this case can be undermined. Plaintiffs moved for a preliminary injunction before answer or hearing. Defendant opposed the motion, filing uncontroverted affidavits of Government officials describing the facts underlying the President's order.

Secretary of Defense Lovett swore that "a work stoppage in the steel industry will result immediately in serious curtailment of production of essential weapons and munitions of all kinds." He illustrated by showing that 84% of the national production of certain alloy steel is currently used for production of military-end items and that 35% of total production of another form of steel goes into ammunition, 80% of such ammunition now going to Korea. The Secretary of Defense stated that: "We are holding the line (in Korea) with ammunition and not with the lives of our troops."

Affidavits of the Chairman of the Atomic Energy Commission, the Secretary of the Interior, defendant as Secretary of Commerce, and the Administrators of the Defense Production Administration, the National Production Authority, the General Services Administration and the Defense Transport Administration were also filed in the District Court. These affidavits disclose an enormous demand for steel in such vital defense programs as the expansion of facilities in atomic energy, petroleum, power, transportation and industrial production, including steel production. Those charged with administering allocations and priorities swore to the vital part steel production plays in our economy. The affidavits emphasize the critical need for steel in our defense program, the absence of appreciable inventories of steel, and the drastic results of any interruption in steel production. . . .

Accordingly, if the President has any power under the Constitution to meet a critical situation in the absense of express statutory authorization, there is no basis whatever for criticizing the exercise of such power in this case.

The steel mills were seized for a public use. The power of eminent domain, invoked in this case, is an essential attribute of sovereignty and has long been recognized as a power of the Federal Government. . . .

Admitting that the Government could seize the mills, plaintiffs claim that the implied power of eminent domain can be exercised only under an Act of Congress; under no circumstances, they say, can that power be exercised by the President unless he can point to an express provision in enabling legislation. This was the view adopted by the District Judge when he granted the preliminary injunction. . . .

Under this view, the President is left powerless at the very moment when the need for action may be most pressing and when no one, other than he, is immediately capable of action. Under this view, he is left powerless because a power not expressly given to Congress is nevertheless found to rest exclusively with Congress.

Consideration of this view of executive impotence calls for further examination of the nature of the separation of powers under our tripartite system of Government. . . .

The whole of the "executive Power" is vested in the President. Before entering office, the President swears that he "will faithfully execute the Office of President of the United States, and will to the best of (his) ability, preserve, protect and defend the Constitution of the United States." Art. II, sec. 1.

This comprehensive grant of the executive power to a single person was bestowed soon after the country had thrown the yoke of monarchy. Only by instilling initiative and vigor in all of the three departments of Government, declared Madison, could tyranny in any form be avoided. . . . It is thus apparent that the Presidency was deliberately fashioned as an office of power and independence. Of course, the Framers created no autocrat capable of arrogating any power unto himself at any time. But neither did they create an automaton impotent to exercise the powers of Government at a time when the survival of the Republic itself may be at stake.

In passing upon the grave constitutional question presented in this case, we must never forget, as Chief Justice Marshall admonished, that the Constitution is "intended to endure for ages to come, and consequently, to be adapted to the various *crises* of human affairs," and that "(i)ts means are adequate to its ends." Cases do arise presenting questions which could not have been foreseen by the Framers. In such cases, the Constitution has been treated as a living document adaptable to new situations. But we are not called upon today to expand the Constitution to meet a new situation. For, in this case, we need only look to history and time-honored principles of constitutional law— principles that have been applied consistently by all branches of the Government throughout our history. It is those who assert the in-

validity of the Executive Order who seek to amend the Constitution in this case. . . .

The broad executive power granted by Article II to an officer on duty 365 days a year cannot, it is said, be invoked to avert disaster. Instead, the President must confine himself to sending a message to Congress recommending action. Under this messenger-boy concept of the Office, the President cannot even act to preserve legislative programs from destruction so that Congress will have something left to act upon. There is no judicial finding that the executive action was unwarranted because there was in fact no basis for the President's finding of the existence of an emergency for, under this view, the gravity of the emergency and the immediacy of the threatened disaster are considered irrelevant as a matter of law.

Seizure of the plaintiffs' property is not a pleasant undertaking. Similarly unpleasant to a free country are the draft which disrupts the home and military procurement which causes economic dislocation and compels adoption of price controls, wage stabilization and allocation of materials. The President informed Congress that even a temporary Government operation of plaintiffs' properties was "thoroughly distasteful" to him, but was necessary to prevent immediate paralysis of the mobilization program. Presidents have been in the past, and any man worthy of the Office should be in the future, free to take at least interim action necessary to execute legislative programs essential to survival of the Nation. A sturdy judiciary should not be swayed by the unpleasantness or unpopularity of necessary executive action, but must independently determine for itself whether the President was acting, as required by the Constitution, to "take Care that the laws be faithfully executed."

598.   TRUMAN'S VETO OF THE McCARRAN-WALTER IMMIGRATION ACT
(82nd Congress, 2nd Session, *House Doc.* No. 520)

June 25, 1952

The McCarran-Walter Immigration Act continued the basic quota system of immigration adopted in 1924. It included new provisions to

prevent the admission of possible subversives and to permit the expulsion of dangerous aliens. President Truman vetoed the bill on constitutional and other grounds, but Congress passed it over his veto by a vote of 278 to 133 in the House and 57 to 26 in the Senate. See P. Tyler, ed., *Immigration and the United States;* U.S. President's Commission on Immigration and Naturalization, *Whom We Shall Welcome;* B. M. Ziegler, ed., *Immigration.*

To the House of Representatives:

I return herewith, without my approval, H. R. 5678, the proposed Immigration and Nationality Act.

In outlining my objections to this bill, I want to make it clear that it contains certain provisions that meet with my approval. This is a long and complex piece of legislation. It has 164 separate sections, some with more than 40 subdivisions. It presents a difficult problem of weighing the good against the bad, and arriving at a judgment on the whole.

H. R. 5678 is an omnibus bill which would revise and codify all of our laws relating to immigration, naturalization, and nationality.

A general revision and modernization of these laws unquestionably is needed and long overdue, particularly with respect to immigration. But this bill would not provide us with an immigration policy adequate for the present world situation. Indeed, the bill, taking all its provisions together, would be a step backward and not a step forward. In view of the crying need for reform in the field of immigration, I deeply regret that I am unable to approve H. R. 5678.

In recent years our immigration policy has become a matter of major national concern Long dormant questions about the effect of our immigration laws now assume first-rate importance. What we do in the field of immigration and naturalization is vital to the continued growth and internal development of the United States—to the economic and social strength of our country—which is the core of the defense of the free world. Our immigration policy is equally, if not more, important to the conduct of our foreign relations and to our responsibilities of moral leadership in the struggle for world peace.

In one respect, this bill recognizes the great international significance of our immigration and naturalization policy, and takes a step to improve existing laws. All racial bars to naturalization would be removed, and at least some minimum immigration quota would be afforded to each of the free nations of Asia.

I have long urged that racial or national barriers to naturalization be abolished. This was one of the recommendations in my civil-rights message to the Congress on February 2, 1948. On February 19, 1951, the House of Representatives unanimously passed a bill to carry it out.

But now this most desirable provision comes before me embedded in a mass of legislation which would perpetuate injustices of long standing against many other nations of the world, hamper the efforts we are making to rally the men of the east and west alike to the cause of freedom, and intensify the repressive and inhumane aspects of our immigration procedures. The price is too high and, in good conscience, I cannot agree to pay it. . . .

In addition to removing racial bars to naturalization, the bill would permit American women citizens to bring their alien husbands to this country as nonquota immigrants, and enable alien husbands of resident women aliens to come in under the quota in a preferred status. These provisions would be a step toward preserving the integrity of the family under our immigration laws, and are clearly desirable. . . .

But these few improvements are heavily outweighed by other provisions of the bill which retain existing defects in our laws, and add many undesirable new features.

The bill would continue, practically without change, the national origins quota system, which was enacted into law in 1924, and put into effect in 1929. This quota system—always based upon assumptions at variance with our American ideals—is long since out of date and more than ever unrealistic in the face of present world conditions.

This system hinders us in dealing with current immigration problems, and is a constant handicap in the conduct of our foreign relations. As I stated in my message to Congress on March 24, 1952, on the need for an emergency program of immigration from Europe:

"Our present quota system is not only

inadequate to meet present emergency needs, it is also an obstacle to the development of an enlightened and satisfactory immigration policy for the long-run future."

The inadequacy of the present quota system has been demonstrated since the end of the war, when we were compelled to resort to emergency legislation to admit displaced persons. If the quota system remains unchanged, we shall be compelled to resort to similar emergency legislation again, in order to admit any substantial portion of the refugees from communism or the victims of overcrowding in Europe.

With the idea of quotas in general there is no quarrel. Some numerical limitation must be set, so that immigration will be within our capacity to absorb. But the over-all limitation of numbers imposed by the national origins quota system is too small for our needs today, and the country by country limitations create a pattern that is insulting to large numbers of our finest citizens, irritating to our allies abroad, and foreign to our purposes and ideals.

The over-all quota limitation, under the law of 1924, restricted annual immigration to approximately 150,000. This was about one-seventh of 1 percent of our total population in 1920. Taking into account the growth in population since 1920, the law now allows us but one-tenth of 1 percent of our total population. And since the largest national quotas are only partly used, the number actually coming in has been in the neighborhood of one-fifteenth of 1 percent. This is far less than we must have in the years ahead to keep up with the growing needs of our Nation for manpower to maintain the strength and vigor of our economy.

The greatest vice of the present quota system, however, is that it discriminates, deliberately and intentionally, against many of the peoples of the world. The purpose behind it was to cut down and virtually eliminate immigration to this country from southern and eastern Europe. A theory was invented to rationalize this objective. The theory was that in order to be readily assimilable, European immigrants should be admitted in proportion to the numbers of persons of their respective national stocks already here

as shown by the census of 1920. Since Americans of English, Irish, and German descent were most numerous, immigrants of those three nationalities got the lion's share—more than two-thirds—of the total quota. The remaining third was divided up among all the other nations given quotas.

The desired effect was obtained. Immigration from the newer sources of Southern and Eastern Europe was reduced to a trickle. The quotas allotted to England and Ireland remained largely unused, as was intended. Total quota immigration fell to a half or a third—and sometimes even less—of the annual limit of 154,000. People from such countries as Greece, or Spain, or Latvia were virtually deprived of any opportunity to come here at all, simply because Greeks or Spaniards or Latvians had not come here before 1920 in any substantial numbers.

The idea behind this discriminatory policy was, to put it baldly, that Americans with English or Irish names were better people and better citizens than Americans with Italian or Greek or Polish names. It was thought that people of West European origin made better citizens than Rumanians or Yugoslavs or Ukrainians or Hungarians or Balts or Austrians. Such a concept is utterly unworthy of our traditions and our ideals. It violates the great political doctrine of the Declaration of Independence that "all men are created equal." It denies the humanitarian creed inscribed beneath the Statue of Liberty proclaiming to all nations, "Give me your tired, your poor, your huddled masses yearning to breathe free."

It repudiates our basic religious concepts, our belief in the brotherhood of man, and in the words of St. Paul that "there is neither Jew nor Greek, there is neither bond nor free, . . . for ye are all one in Christ Jesus."

The basis of this quota system was false and unworthy in 1924. It is even worse now. At the present time this quota system keeps out the very people we want to bring in. It is incredible to me that, in this year of 1952, we should again be enacting into law such a slur on the patriotism, the capacity, and the decency of a large part of our citizenry. . . .

The time to shake off this dead weight of past mistakes is now. The time to develop a decent policy of immigration—a fitting instrument for our foreign policy and a true reflection of the ideals we stand for, at home and abroad—is now. In my earlier message on immigration, I tried to explain to the Congress that the situation we face in immigration is an emergency—that it must be met promptly. I have pointed out that in the last few years, we have blazed a new trail in immigration, through our displaced persons program. Through the combined efforts of the Government and private agencies, working together not to keep people out, but to bring qualified people in, we summoned our resources of good will and human feeling to meet the task. In this program we have found better techniques to meet the immigration problems of the 1950's.

None of this fruitful experience of the last 3 years is reflected in this bill before me. None of the crying human needs of this time of trouble is recognized in this bill. But it is not too late. The Congress can remedy these defects, and it can adopt legislation to meet the most critical problems before adjournment. . . .

I now wish to turn to the other provisions of the bill, those dealing with the qualifications of aliens and immigrants for admission, with the administration of the laws, and with problems of naturalization and nationality. In these provisions, too, I find objections that preclude my signing this bill.

The bill would make it even more difficult to enter our country. Our resident aliens would be more easily separated from homes and families under grounds of deportation, both new and old, which would specifically be made retroactive. Admission to our citizenship would be made more difficult; expulsion from our citizenship would be made easier. Certain rights of native-born, first-generation Americans would be limited. All our citizens returning from abroad would be subjected to serious risk of unreasonable invasions of privacy. Seldom has a bill exhibited the distrust evidenced here for citizens and aliens alike—at a time when we need unity at home and the confidence of our friends abroad. . . .

I am asked to approve the reenactment of highly objectionable provisions now contained in the Internal Security Act of 1950 —a measure passed over my veto shortly after the invasion of South Korea. Some of these provisions would empower the Attorney General to deport any alien who has engaged or has had a purpose to engage in activities "prejudicial to the public interest" or "subversive to the national security." No standards or definitions are provided to guide discretion in the exercise of powers so sweeping. To punish undefined "activities" departs from traditional American insistence on established standards of guilt. To punish an undefined "purpose" is thought control.

These provisions are worse than the infamous Alien Act of 1798, passed in a time of national fear and distrust of foreigners, which gave the President power to deport any alien deemed "dangerous to the peace and safety of the United States." Alien residents were thoroughly frightened and citizens much disturbed by that threat to liberty.

Such powers are inconsistent with our democratic ideals. Conferring powers like that upon the Attorney General is unfair to him as well as to our alien residents. Once fully informed of such vast discretionary powers vested in the Attorney General, Americans now would and should be just as alarmed as Americans were in 1798 over less drastic powers vested in the President.

Heretofore, for the most part, deportation and exclusion have rested upon findings of fact made upon evidence. Under this bill, they would rest in many instances upon the "opinion" or "satisfaction" of immigration or consular employees. The change from objective findings to subjective feelings is not compatible with our system of justice. The result would be to restrict or eliminate judicial review of unlawful administrative action. . . .

Many of the aspects of the bill which have been most widely criticized in the public debate are reaffirmations or elaborations of existing statutes or administrative procedures. Time and again, examination discloses that the revisions of existing law that would be made by the bill are intended to solidify some restrictive practice of our immigration authorities, or to overrule or modify some ameliorative decision of the Supreme Court or other Federal courts. By and large, the changes that would be made by the bill do not depart from the basically restrictive spirit of our existing laws—but intensify and reinforce it.

These conclusions point to an underlying condition which deserves the most careful study. Should we not undertake a reassessment of our immigration policies and practices in the light of the conditions that face us in the second half of the twentieth century? The great popular interest which this bill has created, and the criticism which it has stirred up, demand an affirmative answer. I hope the Congress will agree to a careful reexamination of this entire matter. . . .

HARRY S TRUMAN.

599. EISENHOWER'S SECURITY PROGRAM— EXECUTIVE ORDER 10450
April 27, 1953
(*Federal Register,* Vol. 18, p. 2489)

President Eisenhower reorganized the government's security program in 1953. Executive Order 10450 extended the security system to all agencies of the government and replaced the Truman criterion of disloyalty as the basis for dismissing government employees with the new criterion of "security risk." See Doc. No. 577. This new criterion permitted the discharge of any person whose employment was for any reason not "clearly consistent with the interests of national security." In 1956 the Supreme Court held that this order applied only to workers in "sensitive" positions. See Doc. No. 615. See A. Yarmolinsky, *Case Studies in Personal Security;* W. Gellhorn, *Individual Freedom and Governmental Restraints;* J. R. Wiggins, "Freedom or Security," *Current History,* October 1955.

WHEREAS the interests of the national security require that all persons privileged to be employed in the departments and agencies of the Government shall be reliable, trustworthy, of good conduct and character, and of complete and unswerving loyalty to the United States; and

WHEREAS the American tradition that all persons should receive fair, impartial, and equitable treatment at the hands of the Government requires that all persons seeking the privilege of employment or privileged to be employed in the departments and agencies of the Government be adjudged by mutually consistent and no less than minimum standards and procedures among the departments and agencies governing the employment and retention in employment of persons in the Federal service . . . it is hereby ordered as follows:

SEC. 1. In addition to the departments and agencies specified in the said act of August 26, 1950, and Executive Order No. 10237 of April 26, 1951, the provisions of that act shall apply to all other departments and agencies of the Government.

SEC. 2. The head of each department and agency of the Government shall be responsible for establishing and maintaining within his department or agency an effective program to insure that the employment and retention in employment of any civilian officer or employee within the department or agency is clearly consistent with the interests of the national security.

SEC. 3. (a) The appointment of each civilian officer or employee in any department or agency of the Government shall be made subject to investigation. The scope of the investigation shall be determined in the first instance according to the degree of adverse effect the occupant of the position sought to be filled could bring about, by virtue of the nature of the position, on the national security, but in no event shall the investigation include less than a national agency check (including a check of the fingerprint files of the Federal Bureau of Investigation), and written inquiries to appropriate local law-enforcement agencies, former employers and supervisors, references, and schools attended by the person under investigation: *Provided,* that upon request of the head of the department or agency concerned, the Civil Service Commission may, in its discretion, authorize such less investigation as may meet the requirements of the national security with respect to per-diem, intermittent, temporary, or seasonal employees, or aliens employed outside the United States. Should there develop at any stage of investigation information indicating that the employment of any such person may not be clearly consistent with the interests of the national security, there shall be conducted with respect to such person a full field investigation, or such less investigation as shall be sufficient to enable the head of the department or agency concerned to determine whether retention of such person is clearly consistent with the interests of the national security. . . .

SEC. 6. Should there develop at any stage of investigation information indicating that the employment of any officer or employee of the Government may not be clearly consistent with the interests of the national security, the head of the department or agency concerned or his representative shall immediately suspend the employment of the person involved if he deems such suspension necessary in the interests of the national security and, following such investigation and review as he deems necessary, the head of the department or agency concerned shall terminate the employment of such suspended officer or employee whenever he shall determine such termination necessary or advisable in the interests of the national security, in accordance with the said act of August 26, 1950.

SEC. 7. Any person whose employment is suspended or terminated under the authority granted to heads of departments and agencies by or in accordance with the said act of August 26, 1950, or pursuant to the said Executive Order No. 9835 or any other security or loyalty program relating to officers or employees of the Government, shall not be reinstated or restored to duty or re-employed in the same department or agency, and shall not be reemployed in any other department or agency, unless the head of the department or agency concerned finds that such reinstatement, restoration, or reemployment is clearly consistent with the interests of the national security, which finding shall

be made a part of the records of such department or agency: *Provided,* that no person whose employment has been terminated under such authority thereafter may be employed by any other department or agency except after a determination by the Civil Service Commission that such person is eligible for such employment.

SEC. 8. (a) The investigations conducted pursuant to this order shall be designed to develop information as to whether the employment or retention in employment in the Federal service of the person being investigated is clearly consistent with the interests of the national security. Such information shall relate, but shall not be limited, to the following:

(1) Depending on the relation of the Government employment to the national security:

(i) Any behavior, activities, or associations which tend to show that the individual is not reliable or trustworthy.

(ii) Any deliberate misrepresentations, falsifications, or omission of material facts.

(iii) Any criminal, infamous, dishonest, immoral, or notoriously disgraceful conduct, habitual use of intoxicants to excess, drug addiction, or sexual perversion.

(iv) An adjudication of insanity, or treatment for serious mental or neurological disorder without satisfactory evidence of cure.

(v) Any facts which furnish reason to believe that the individual may be subjected to coercion, influence, or pressure which may cause him to act contrary to the best interests of the national security.

(2) Commission of any act of sabotage, espionage, treason, or sedition, or attempts thereat or preparation therefor, or conspiring with, or aiding or abetting, another to commit or attempt to commit any act of sabotage, espionage, treason, or sedition.

(3) Establishing or continuing a sympathetic association with a saboteur, spy, traitor, seditionist, anarchist, or revolutionist, or with an espionage or other secret agent or representative of a foreign nation, or any representative of a foreign nation whose interests may be inimical to the interests of the United States, or with any person who advocates the use of force or violence to

overthrow the government of the United States or the alteration of the form of government of the United States by unconstitutional means.

(4) Advocacy of use of force or violence to overthrow the government of the United States, or of the alteration of the form of government of the United States by unconstitutional means.

(5) Membership in, or affiliation or sympathetic association with, any foreign or domestic organization, association, movement, group, or combination of persons which is totalitarian, Fascist, Communist, or subversive, or which has adopted, or shows, a policy of advocating or approving the commission of acts of force or violence to deny other persons their rights under the Constitution of the United States, or which seeks to alter the form of government of the United States by unconstitutional means.

(6) Intentional, unauthorized disclosure to any person of security information, or of other information disclosure of which is prohibited by law, or willful violation or disregard of security regulations.

(7) Performing or attempting to perform his duties, or otherwise acting, so as to serve the interests of another government in preference to the interests of the United States. . . .

DWIGHT D. EISENHOWER.

600. SUBMERGED LANDS ACT OF 1953
May 22, 1953
(Public Law 31, 83rd Congress)

This act settled a long-standing controversy over the development of natural resources, particularly oil, off the shores of the United States. The issue of state versus federal control over these resources involved two further questions: first, should these resources be exploited for the benefit of individual states or for the benefit of the nation as a whole; second, should these resources be developed by private corporations or by public agencies. In 1947 and again in 1950, the Supreme Court declared that the federal government had exclusive rights to these submerged lands; see *U.S.* v. *California* 332 U.S. 19, *U.S.* v. *Louisiana* 339 U.S. 699, and *U.S.* v. *Texas* 339 U.S. 707. In 1952, President Truman assigned the offshore oil resources to the Navy as a reserve for use in time of war. These actions were nullified by the Submerged Lands Act of 1953, which assigned federal rights to the offshore lands to the seaboard states. The question of the extent of state title to tidelands, however, remained to vex future administrations. See E. R. Bartley, *The Tidelands Oil Controversy;* Fulton, *Sovereignty of the Sea;* Masterson, *Jurisdiction in Marginal Seas;* Jessup, *Law of Territorial Waters and Maritime Jurisdiction.*

An Act to confirm and establish the titles of the States to lands beneath navigable waters within State boundaries and to the natural resources within such lands and waters, to provide for the use and control of said lands and resources, and to confirm the jurisdiction and control of the United States over the natural resources of the seabed of the Continental Shelf seaward of State boundaries.

SEC. 3. *Rights of the States.*—

(a) It is hereby determined and declared to be in the public interest that (1) title to and ownership of the lands beneath navigable waters within the boundaries of the respective States, and the natural resources within such lands and waters and (2) the right and power to manage, administer, lease, develop, and use the said lands and natural resources all in accordance with applicable State law be, and they are hereby, subject to the provisions hereof, recognized, confirmed, established, and vested in and assigned to the respective States or the persons who were on June 5, 1950, entitled thereto under the law of the respective States in which the land is located, and the respective grantees, lessees, or successors in interest thereof;

(b) (1) The United States hereby releases and relinquishes unto said States and persons aforesaid, except as otherwise reserved herein, all right, title, and interest of the United States, if any it has, in and to all said lands, improvements, and natural resources; (2) the United States hereby releases and relinquishes all claims of the United States, if any it has, for money or damages arising out of any operations of said States or persons pursuant to State authority upon or within said lands and navigable waters; . . . .

(d) Nothing in this Act shall affect the use, development, improvement, or control by or under the constitutional authority of the United States of said lands and waters for the purposes of navigation or flood control or the production of power, or be construed as the release or relinquishment of any rights of the United States arising under the constitutional authority of Congress to regulate or improve navigation, or to provide for flood control, or the production of power; . . . .

SEC. 4. *Seaward Boundaries.*—The seaward boundary of each original coastal State is hereby approved and confirmed as a line three geographical miles distant from its coast line or, in the case of the Great Lakes, to the international boundary. Any State admitted subsequent to the formation of the Union which has not already done so may extend its seaward boundaries to a line three geographical miles distant from its coast line, or to the international boundaries of the United States in the Great Lakes or any other body of water traversed by such boundaries. Any claim heretofore or hereafter asserted either by constitutional provision, statute, or otherwise, indicating the intent of a State so to extend its boundaries is hereby approved and confirmed, without prejudice to its claim, if any it has, that its boundaries extend beyond that line. Nothing in this section is to be construed as questioning or in any manner prejudicing the existence of any State's seaward boundary beyond three geographical miles if it was so provided by its constitution or laws prior to or at the time such State became a member of the Union, or if it has been heretofore approved by Congress. . . .

SEC. 6. *Powers Retained by the United States.*—(a) The United States retains all its navigational servitude and rights in and powers of regulation and control of said lands and navigable waters for the constitutional purposes of commerce, navigation, national defense, and international affairs, all of which shall be paramount to, but shall not be deemed to include, proprietary rights of ownership, or the rights of management, administration, leasing, use, and development of the lands and natural resources which are specifically recognized, confirmed, established, and vested in and assigned to the respective States and others by section 3 of this Act.

(b) In time of war or when necessary for national defense, and the Congress or the President shall so prescribe, the United States shall have the right of first refusal to purchase at the prevailing market price, all or any portion of the said natural resources, or to acquire and use any portion of said lands by proceeding in accordance with due process of law and paying just compensation therefor. . . .

601. EISENHOWER'S ATOMS FOR PEACE PROGRAM
December 8, 1953
(*Department of State Publication* 5314)

Atomic power misused theatened to end human life; wisely used it held out the promise of a better life for all mankind. At the end of 1953, President Eisenhower directed the attention of the world community to the enormous potential for good inherent in the development of atomic energy. In a speech to the United Nations he proposed that the major scientific nations of the world jointly contribute to a pool of atomic power resources to be used for socially desirable purposes. The President thus aroused the hopes of the world that in the long run atomic energy would redound to the benefit of the world community. See International Conference on the Peaceful Uses of Atomic Energy, *Proceedings 1955;* A. H. Compton, *Atomic Quest;* G. Dean, *Report on the Atom;* R. E. Lapp, *Atoms and People;* U.S. Congress Joint Committee on Atomic Energy, *Peaceful Uses of Atomic Energy.*

Madame President, Members of the General Assembly:

I feel impelled to speak today in a language that in a sense is new—one which I, who have spent so much of my life in the military profession, would have preferred never to use.

That new language is the language of atomic warfare.

The atomic age has moved forward at such a pace that every citizen of the world should have some comprehension, at least in comparative terms, of the extent of this development, of the utmost significance to every one of us. Clearly, if the peoples of the world are to conduct an intelligent search for peace, they must be armed with the significant facts of today's existence.

My recital of atomic danger and power is necessarily stated in United States terms, for these are the only incontrovertible facts that I know. I need hardly point out to this Assembly, however, that this subject is global, not merely national in character.

On July 16, 1945, the United States set off the world's first atomic explosion.

Since that date in 1945, the United States of America has conducted 42 test explosions.

Atomic bombs today are more than 25 times as powerful as the weapons with which the atomic age dawned, while hydrogen weapons are in the ranges of millions of tons of TNT equivalent.

Today, the United States' stockpile of atomic weapons, which, of course, increases daily, exceeds by many times the explosive equivalent of the total of all bombs and all shells that came from every plane and every gun in every theatre of war in all of the years of World War II.

A single air group, whether afloat or land-based, can now deliver to any reachable target a destructive cargo exceeding in power all the bombs that fell on Britain in all of World War II.

In size and variety, the development of atomic weapons has been no less remarkable. The development has been such that atomic weapons have virtually achieved conventional status within our armed services. In the United States, the Army, the Navy, the Air Force, and the Marine Corps are all capable of putting this weapon to military use.

But the dread secret, and the fearful engines of atomic might, are not ours alone.

In the first place, the secret is possessed by our friends and allies, Great Britain and Canada, whose scientific genius made a tremendous contribution to our original discoveries, and the designs of atomic bombs.

The secret is also known by the Soviet Union.

The Soviet Union has informed us that, over recent years, it has devoted extensive resources to atomic weapons. During this period, the Soviet Union has exploded a series of atomic devices, including at least one involving thermo-nuclear reactions.

If at one time the United States possessed what might have been called a monopoly of atomic power, that monopoly ceased to exist several years ago. Therefore, although our earlier start has permitted us to accumulate what is today a great quantitative advantage, the atomic realities of today comprehend two facts of even greater significance.

First, the knowledge now possessed by several nations will eventually be shared by others—possibly all others.

Second, even a vast superiority in numbers of weapons, and a constant capability of devastating retaliation, is no preventive, of itself, against the fearful material damage and toll of human lives that would be inflicted by surprise aggression.

The free world, at least dimly aware of these facts, has naturally embarked on a large program of warning and defense systems. That program will be accelerated and expanded.

But let no one think that the expenditure of vast sums for weapons and systems of defense can guarantee absolute safety for the cities and citizens of any nation. The awful arithmetic of the atomic bomb does not permit of any such easy solution. Even against the most powerful defense, an aggressor in possession of the effective minimum number of atomic bombs for a surprise attack could probably place a sufficient number of his bombs on the chosen targets to cause hideous damage.

Should such an atomic attack be launched against the United States, our reactions would be swift and resolute. But for me to say that the defense capabilities of the United States are such that they could inflict terrible losses upon an aggressor—for me to say that the retaliation capabilities of the United States are so great that such an aggressor's land would be laid waste—all this, while fact, is not the true expression of the purpose and the hope of the United States.

To pause there would be to confirm the hopeless finality of a belief that two atomic colossi are doomed malevolently to eye each other indefinitely across a trembling world. To stop there would be to accept helplessly the probability of civilization destroyed—the annihilation of the irreplaceable heritage of mankind handed down to us generation from generation—and the condemnation of mankind to begin all over again the age-old struggle upward from savagery toward decency, and right, and justice.

Surely no sane member of the human race could discover victory in such desolation. Could anyone wish his name to be coupled by history with such human degradation and destruction?

Occasional pages of history do record the faces of the "Great Destroyers" but the whole book of history reveals mankind's never-ending quest for peace, and mankind's God-given capacity to build.

It is with the book of history, and not with isolated pages, that the United States will ever wish to be identified. My country wants to be constructive, not destructive. It wants agreements, not wars, among nations. It wants itself to live in freedom, and in the confidence that the people of every other nation enjoy equally the right of choosing their own way of life.

So my country's purpose is to help us move out of the dark chamber of horrors into the light, to find a way by which the minds of men, the hopes of men, the souls of men everywhere, can move forward toward peace and happiness and well being.

In this quest, I know that we must not lack patience.

I know that in a world divided, such as ours today, salvation cannot be attained by one dramatic act.

I know that many steps will have to be taken over many months before the world can look at itself one day and truly realize that a new climate of mutually peaceful confidence is abroad in the world.

But I know, above all else, that we must start to take these steps—NOW. . . .

There is at least one new avenue of peace which has not yet been well explored—an avenue now laid out by the General Assembly of the United Nations.

In its resolution of November 18th, 1953, this General Assembly suggested—and I quote—"that the Disarmament Commission study the desirability of establishing a subcommittee consisting of representatives of the Powers principally involved, which should seek in private an acceptable solution . . . and report on such a solution to the General Assembly and to the Security Council not later than 1 September 1954."

The United States, heeding the suggestion of the General Assembly of the United Nations, is instantly prepared to meet privately with such other countries as may be "principally involved," to seek "an acceptable solution" to the atomic armaments race which overshadows not only the peace, but the very life, of the world.

We shall carry into these private or diplomatic talks a new conception.

The United States would seek more than the mere reduction or elimination of atomic materials for military purposes.

It is not enough to take this weapon out of the hands of the soldiers. It must be put into the hands of those who will know how to strip its military casing and adapt it to the arts of peace.

The United States knows that if the fearful trend of atomic military buildup can be reversed, this greatest of destructive forces can be developed into a great boon, for the benefit of all mankind.

The United States knows that peaceful power from atomic energy is no dream of the future. That capability, already proved, is here—now—today. Who can doubt, if the entire body of the world's scientists and engineers had adequate amounts of fissionable material with which to test and develop their ideas, that this capability would rapidly be transformed into universal, efficient, and economic usage.

To hasten the day when fear of the atom will begin to disappear from the minds of people, and the governments of the East and West, there are certain steps that can be taken now.

I therefore make the following proposals:

The Governments principally involved, to the extent permitted by elementary prudence, to begin now and continue to make joint contributions from their stockpiles of normal uranium and fissionable materials to an International Atomic Energy Agency. We would expect that such an agency would be set up under the aegis of the United Nations.

The ratios of contributions, the procedures and other details would properly be within the scope of the "private conversations" I have referred to earlier.

The United States is prepared to undertake these explorations in good faith. Any partner of the United States acting in the same good faith will find the United States a not unreasonable or ungenerous associate.

Undoubtedly initial and early contributions to this plan would be small in quantity. However, the proposal has the great virtue that it can be undertaken without the irritations and mutual suspicions incident to any attempt to set up a completely acceptable system of world-wide inspection and control.

The Atomic Energy Agency could be made responsible for the impounding, storage, and protection of the contributed fissionable and other materials. The ingenuity of our scientists will provide special safe conditions under which such a bank of fissionable material can be made essentially immune to surprise seizure.

The more important responsibility of this Atomic Energy Agency would be to devise methods whereby this fissionable material would be allocated to serve the peaceful pursuits of mankind. Experts would be mobilized to apply atomic energy to the needs of agriculture, medicine, and other peaceful activities. A special purpose would be to provide abundant electrical energy in the power-starved areas of the world. Thus the contributing powers would be dedicating some of their strength to serve the needs rather than the fears of mankind.

The United States would be more than willing—it would be proud to take up with others "principally involved" the development of plans whereby such peaceful use of atomic energy would be expedited.

Of those "principally involved" the Soviet Union must, of course, be one.

I would be prepared to submit to the Congress of the United States, and with every expectation of approval, any such plan that would:

First—encourage world-wide investigation into the most effective peacetime uses of fissionable material, and with the certainty that they had all the material needed for the conduct of all experiments that were appropriate;

Second—to begin to diminish the potential destructive power of the world's atomic stockpiles;

Third—allow all peoples of all nations to see that, in this enlightened age, the great powers of the earth, both of the East and of the West, are interested in human aspirations first, rather than in building up the armaments of war;

Fourth—open up a new channel for peaceful discussion, and initiate at least a new approach to the many difficult problems that must be solved in both private and public conversations, if the world is to shake off the inertia imposed by fear, and is to make positive progress toward peace.

Against the dark background of the atomic bomb, the United States does not wish merely to present strength, but also the desire and the hope for peace.

The coming months will be fraught with fateful decisions. In this Assembly; in the capitals and military headquarters of the world; in the hearts of men everywhere, be they governors or governed, may they be the decisions which will lead this world out of fear and into peace.

To the making of these fateful decisions, the United States pledges before you—and therefore before the world—its determination to help solve the fearful atomic dilemma —to devote its entire heart and mind to find the way by which the miraculous inventiveness of man shall not be dedicated to his death, but consecrated to his life. . . .

602. THE BRICKER AMENDMENT
January–February, 1954
(*Congressional Record,* January 28, February 4, 26, 1954)

The internationalist tendency of American foreign policy did not receive unanimous support from the American people. A powerful minority of neo-isolationists sought to check our increasing involvement in world affairs through the so-called Bricker amendment, the purpose of which was to restrict the power of the executive branch to make treaties and agreements that might limit American sovereignty. President Eisenhower expressed opposition to the Bricker amendment in a letter sent to the majority leader of the Senate on January 25, 1954. The Senate rejected the Bricker proposal on February 25 by a vote of 42 to 50. On February 26, Senator Walter F. George proposed a watered-down version of the Bricker amendment. This version received an affirmative two-thirds majority of 61 to 30 in its first test in the Senate. On the crucial motion to send the proposed amendment to the states the vote was 60 to 31, one less than the necessary two-thirds majority. This marked the high tide of support for the proposal to limit the treaty-making powers of the President. The whole incident is important not only as a manifestation of the struggle over interventionism in foreign policy but also as an example of the recurring struggle for power between the President and Congress. See G. A. Schubert, Jr., "Politics and the Constitution: the Bricker Amendment during 1953," 16 *Journal of Politics* 257; Q. Wright, "Congress and the Treaty-Making Power," *Amer. Soc. of Int'l. Law Proceedings* (1952), 43; H. S. Commager, "The Perilous Folly of Senator Bricker," *Reporter,* October 13, 1953.

1. PROPOSED AMENDMENT
"Article—

SEC. 1. Clause 2 of Article VI of the Constitution of the United States is hereby amended by adding at the end thereof; Notwithstanding the foregoing provisions of this clause, no treaty made after the establishment of this Constitution shall be the supreme law of the land unless made in pursuance of this Constitution.

SEC. 2. A provision of a treaty or other international agreement which conflicts with this Constitution shall not be of any force or effect.

SEC. 3. A treaty or other international agreement shall become effective as internal law in the United States only through legislation by the Congress unless in advising and consenting to a treaty the Senate, by a vote of two-thirds of the Senators present and voting, shall provide that such treaty may become effective as internal law without legislation by the Congress.

SEC. 4. On the question of consenting to the ratification of a treaty the vote shall be determined by yeas and nays, and the names of the persons voting for and against shall be entered on the Journal of the Senate.

2. EISENHOWER LETTER ON THE BRICKER AMENDMENT

The White House
Washington, January 25, 1954.

Dear Senator Knowland:

In response to your inquiry, I give the following as my attitude toward the proposal for amending the treaty-making functions of the Federal Government.

I am unalterably opposed to the Bricker Amendment as reported by the Senate Judiciary Committee. It would so restrict the conduct of foreign affairs that our country could not negotiate the agreements necessary for the handling of our business with the rest of the world. Such an amendment would make it impossible for us to deal effectively with friendly nations for our mutual defense and common interests.

These matters are fundamental. We cannot hope to achieve and maintain peace if we shackle the Federal Government so that it is no longer sovereign in foreign affairs. The President must not be deprived of his historic position as the spokesman for the nation in its relations with other countries.

Adoption of the Bricker Amendment in its present form by the Senate would be notice to our friends as well as our enemies abroad that our country intends to withdraw from its leadership in world affairs. The inevitable reaction would be of major proportion. It would impair our hopes and plans for peace and for the successful achievement of the important international matters now under discussion. This would include the diversion of atomic energy from warlike to peaceful purposes.

I fully subscribe to the proposition that no treaty or international agreement can contravene the Constitution. I am aware of the feeling of many of our citizens that a treaty may override the Constitution. So that there can be no question on this point, I will gladly support an appropriate amendment that will make this clear for all time.

Sincerely,

DWIGHT D. EISENHOWER.

3. THE GEORGE RESOLUTION
"Article—

SEC. 1.   A provision of a treaty or other international agreement which conflicts with this Constitution shall not be of any force or effect.

SEC. 2.   An international agreement other than a treaty shall become effective as internal law in the United States only by an act of the Congress.

SEC. 3.   On the question of advising and consenting to the ratification of a treaty the vote shall be determined by yeas and nays, and the names of the persons voting for and against shall be entered on the Journal of the Senate.

SEC. 4.   This article shall be inoperative unless it shall have been ratified as an amendment to the Constitution by the legislatures of three-fourths of the several States within 7 years from the date of its submission.

603. SECRETARY DULLES' STRATEGY OF MASSIVE RETALIATION
January 12, 1954
(*Department of State Bulletin,* Vol. XXX, pp. 107–10)

The Eisenhower administration made two changes in the nation's military policy. First, the size of the military establishment was cut. Second, a new emphasis was placed upon atomic weapons in the nation's military planning. Secretary of State Dulles explained these changes as a new approach to military strategy, declaring that the United States planned in the future to rely on the threat of "massive retaliation" to "deter" Communist aggression. See J. R. Beal, *John Foster Dulles;* W. Reitzel, M. Kaplan and C. Coblenz, *United States Foreign Policy 1945–1955;* C. B. Marshall, *The Limits of Foreign Policy;* G. F. Kennan, *Realities of American Foreign Policy;* P. H. Nitze, "Atoms, Strategy and Policy," 34 *Foreign Affairs* 187; T. K. Finletter, *Power and Policy;* H. A. Kissinger, "Military Policy and Defense of the 'Grey' Areas," 33 *Foreign Affairs* 416.

We live in a world where emergencies are always possible, and our survival may de-

pend upon our capacity to meet emergencies. Let us pray that we shall always have that capacity. But, having said that, it is necessary also to say that emergency measures—however good for the emergency—do not necessarily make good permanent policies. Emergency measures are costly; they are superficial; and they imply that the enemy has the initiative. They cannot be depended on to serve our long-time interests.

This "long time" factor is of critical importance. The Soviet Communists are planning for what they call "an entire historical era," and we should do the same. They seek, through many types of maneuvers, gradually to divide and weaken the free nations by overextending them in efforts which, as Lenin put it, are "beyond their strength, so that they come to practical bankruptcy." Then, said Lenin, "our victory is assured." Then, said Stalin, will be "the moment for the decisive blow."

In the face of this strategy, measures

cannot be judged adequate merely because they ward off an immediate danger. It is essential to do this, but it is also essential to do so without exhausting ourselves.

When the Eisenhower administration applied this test, we felt that some transformations were needed. It is not sound military strategy permanently to commit U.S. land forces to Asia to a degree that leaves us no strategic reserves. It is not sound economics, or good foreign policy, to support permanently other countries; for in the long run, that creates as much ill will as good will. Also, it is not sound to become permanently committed to military expenditures so vast they lead to "practical bankruptcy."

Change was imperative to assure the stamina needed for permanent security. But it was equally imperative that change should be accompanied by understanding of our true purposes. Sudden and spectacular change had to be avoided. Otherwise, there might have been a panic among our friends and miscalculated aggression by our enemies. We can, I believe, make a good report in these respects.

We need allies and collective security. Our purpose is to make these relations more effective, less costly. This can be done by placing more reliance on deterrent power and less dependence on local defensive power.

This is accepted practice so far as local communities are concerned. We keep locks on our doors, but we do not have an armed guard in every home. We rely principally on a community security system so well equipped to punish any who break in and steal that, in fact, would-be aggressors are generally deterred. That is the modern way of getting maximum protection at a bearable cost. What the Eisenhower administration seeks is a similar international security system. We want, for ourselves and the other free nations, a maximum deterrent at a bearable cost.

Local defense will always be important. But there is no local defense which alone will contain the mighty land power of the Communist world. Local defenses must be reinforced by the further deterrent of massive retaliatory power. A potential aggressor must know that he cannot always prescribe battle conditions that suit him. Otherwise, for example, a potential aggressor, who is glutted with manpower, might be tempted to attack in confidence that resistance would be confined to manpower. He might be tempted to attack in places where his superiority was decisive.

The way to deter aggression is for the free community to be willing and able to respond vigorously at places and with means of its own choosing.

So long as our basic policy concepts were unclear, our military leaders could not be selective in building our military power. If an enemy could pick his time and place and method of warfare—and if our policy was to remain the traditional one of meeting aggression by direct and local opposition—then we needed to be ready to fight in the Arctic and in the Tropics; in Asia, the Near East, and in Europe; by sea, by land, and by air; with old weapons and with new weapons. . . .

Before military planning could be changed, the President and his advisers, as represented by the National Security Council, had to make some basic policy decisions. This has been done. The basic decision was to depend primarily upon a great capacity to retaliate, instantly, by means and at places of our choosing. Now the Department of Defense and the Joint Chiefs of Staff can shape our military establishment to fit what is *our* policy, instead of having to try to be ready to meet the enemy's many choices. That permits of a selection of military means instead of a multiplication of means. As a result, it is now possible to get, and share, more basic security at less cost.

Let us now see how this concept has been applied to foreign policy, taking first the Far East.

In Korea this administration effected a major transformation. The fighting has been stopped on honorable terms. That was possible because the aggressor, already thrown back to and behind his place of beginning, was faced with the possibility that the fighting might, to his own great peril, soon spread beyond the limits and methods which he had selected.

The cruel toll of American youth and the nonproductive expenditure of many billions have been stopped. Also our armed forces are no longer largely committed to the Asian mainland. We can begin to create a strategic reserve which greatly improves our defensive posture.

This change gives added authority to the warning of the members of the United Nations which fought in Korea that, if the Communists renewed the aggression, the United Nations response would not necessarily be confined to Korea.

I have said in relation to Indochina that, if there were open Red Chinese army aggression there, that would have "grave consequences which might not be confined to Indochina." . . .

In the ways I outlined we gather strength for the long-term defense of freedom. We do not, of course, claim to have found some magic formula that insures against all forms of Communist successes. It is normal that at some times and at some places there may be setbacks to the cause of freedom. What we do expect to insure is that any setbacks will have only temporary and local significance, because they will leave unimpaired those free world assets which in the long run will prevail.

If we can deter such aggression as would mean general war, and that is our confident resolve, then we can let time and fundamentals work for us. . . .

---

604. ATOMIC ENERGY COMMISSION DECISION IN OPPENHEIMER CASE
June 29, 1954
(U.S. Atomic Energy Commission Press Release)

Dr. J. Robert Oppenheimer played a major role in the development of the atomic bomb by American scientists during World War II. After the war, Dr. Oppenheimer served as consultant to the Atomic Energy Commission. In the spring of 1954, a special Personnel Security Board headed by Gordon Gray voted 2 to 1 to class Dr. Oppenheimer as a security risk, deny him access to restricted government data, and suspend him from his position as consultant to the Atomic Energy Program. The decision was accompanied by an unusual opinion which pronounced Oppenheimer devotedly loyal, unusually discreet, and a public servant whose contribution could never be repaid. On June 29, 1954, the Atomic Energy Commission upheld the decision of the Gray Board by a vote of 4 to 1. The majority and minority opinions of the AEC not only reflected basic differences in judgment of Dr. Oppenheimer but also basic differences in judgment concerning the proper approach to the problem of security in a democratic state. Informed opinion throughout the country was sharply critical of the conclusions of the majority of the Commission. See J. and S. Alsop, *We Accuse;* W. Gellhorn, *Security, Loyalty, and Science;* U.S. Atomic Energy Commission, *In the Matter of J. Robert Oppenheimer;* E. Rabinowitch, "What Is a Security Risk?" *Bulletin of Atomic Scientists,* June 1954; C. P. Curtis, *The Oppenheimer Case;* E. Bontecou, *The Federal Loyalty-Security Program;* M. Grodzins, *The Loyal and the Disloyal;* A. Westin, *The Constitution and Loyalty Programs;* A. Barth, *Government by Investigation.*

UNITED STATES ATOMIC ENERGY COMMISSION

Washington 25, D.C., June 29, 1954

The issue before the Commission is whether the security of the United States warrants Dr. J. Robert Oppenheimer's continued access to restricted data of the Atomic Energy Commission. The data to which Dr. Oppenheimer has had until recently full access include some of the most vital secrets in the possession of the United States.

Having carefully studied the pertinent documents—the transcript of the hearings before the Personnel Security Board (Gray Board), the findings and recommendation of the Board, the briefs of Dr. Oppenheimer's counsel, and the findings and recommendation of the General Manager—we have concluded that Dr. Oppenheimer's clearance for access to restricted data should not be reinstated.

The Atomic Energy Act of 1946 lays upon

the Commissioners the duty to reach a determination as to "the character, associations, and loyalty" of the individuals engaged in the work of the Commission. Thus, disloyalty would be one basis for disqualification, but it is only one. Substantial defects of character and imprudent and dangerous associations, particularly with known subversives who place the interests of foreign powers above those of the United States, are also reasons for disqualification.

On the basis of the record before the Commission, comprising the transcript of the hearing before the Gray Board as well as reports of Military Intelligence and the Federal Bureau of Investigation, we find Dr. Oppenheimer is not entitled to the continued confidence of the Government and of this Commission because of the proof of fundamental defects in his "character."

In respect to the criterion of "associations," we find that his associations with persons known to him to be Communists have extended far beyond the tolerable limits of prudence and self-restraint which are to be expected of one holding the high positions that the Government has continuously entrusted to him since 1942. These associations have lasted too long to be justified as merely the intermittent and accidental revival of earlier friendships. . . .

In weighing the matter at issue, we have taken into account Dr. Oppenheimer's past contributions to the atomic energy program. At the same time, we have been mindful of the fact that the positions of high trust and responsibility which Dr. Oppenheimer has occupied carried with them a commensurately high obligation of unequivocal character and conduct on his part. A Government official having access to the most sensitive areas of restricted data and to the innermost details of national war plans and weapons must measure up to exemplary standards of reliability, self-discipline, and trustworthiness. Dr. Oppenheimer has fallen far short of acceptable standards.

The record shows that Dr. Oppenheimer has consistently placed himself outside the rules which govern others. He has falsified in matters wherein he was charged with grave responsibilities in the national interest. In his associations he has repeatedly exhibited a willful disregard of the normal and proper obligations of security. . . .

Dr. Oppenheimer's persistent and willful disregard for the obligations of security is evidence by his obstruction of inquiries by security officials. The record shows . . . instances where Dr. Oppenheimer has refused to answer inquiries of Federal officials on security matters or has been deliberately misleading.

"Associations" is a factor which, under the law, must be considered by the Commission. Dr. Oppenheimer's close association with Communists is another part of the pattern of his disregard of the obligations of security.

Dr. Oppenheimer, under oath, admitted to the Gray Board that from 1937 to at least 1942 he made regular and substantial contributions in cash to the Communist Party. He has admitted that he was a "fellow traveler" at least until 1942. He admits that he attended small evening meetings at private homes at which most, if not all, of the others present were Communist Party members. He was in contact with officials of the Communist Party, some of whom had been engaged in espionage. His activities were of such a nature that these Communists looked upon him as one of their number.

However, Dr. Oppenheimer's early Communist associations are not in themselves a controlling reason for our decision.

They take on importance in the context of his persistent and continuing association with Communists, including his admitted meetings with Haakon Chevalier in Paris as recently as last December—the same individual who had been intermediary for the Soviet Consulate in 1943.

On February 25, 1950, Dr. Oppenheimer wrote a letter to Chevalier attempting "to clear the record with regard to your alleged involvement in the atom business." Chevalier used this letter in connection with his application to the State Department for a United States passport. Later that year Chevalier came and stayed with Dr. Oppenheimer for several days at the latter's home. In December 1953, Dr. Oppenheimer visited with Chevalier privately on two occasions in Paris, and lent his name to Chevalier's dealings with the United States Embassy in Paris on a problem which, according to Dr.

Oppenheimer, involved Chevalier's clearance. Dr. Oppenheimer admitted that today he has only a "strong guess" that Chevalier is not active in Communist Party affairs.

These episodes separately and together present a serious picture. It is clear that for one who has had access for so long to the most vital defense secrets of the Government and who would retain such access if his clearance were continued, Dr. Oppenheimer has defaulted not once but many times upon the obligations that should and must be willingly borne by citizens in the national service.

Concern for the defense and security of the United States requires that Dr. Oppenheimer's clearance should not be reinstated.

Dr. J. Robert Oppenheimer is hereby denied access to restricted data.

LEWIS L. STRAUSS, *Chairman.*
EUGENE M. ZUCKERT, *Commissioner.*
JOSEPH CAMPBELL, *Commissioner.*

DISSENTING OPINION
OF HENRY DE WOLF SMYTH

I dissent from the action of the Atomic Energy Commission in the matter of Dr. J. Robert Oppenheimer. I agree with the "clear conclusion" of the Gray Board that he is completely loyal and I do not believe he is a security risk. It is my opinion that his clearance for access to restricted data should be restored.

In a case such as this, the Commission is required to look into the future. It must determine whether Dr. Oppenheimer's continued employment by the Government of the United States is in the interests of the people of the United States. This prediction must balance his potential contribution to the positive strength of the country against the possible danger that he may weaken the country by allowing important secrets to reach our enemies.

Since Dr. Oppenheimer is one of the most knowledgeable and lucid physicists we have, his services could be of great value to the country in the future. Therefore, the only question being determined by the Atomic Energy Commission is whether there is a possibility that Dr. Oppenheimer will intentionally or unintentionally reveal secret information to persons who should not have it. To me, this is what is meant within our security system by the term security risk. Character and associations are important only insofar as they bear on the possibility that secret information will be improperly revealed.

In my opinion the most important evidence in this regard is the fact that there is no indication in the entire record that Dr. Oppenheimer has ever divulged any secret information. The past 15 years of his life have been investigated and reinvestigated. For much of the last 11 years he has been under actual surveillance, his movements watched, his conversations noted, his mail and telephone calls checked. This professional review of his actions has been supplemented by enthusiastic amateur help from powerful personal enemies.

After reviewing the massive dossier and after hearing some forty witnesses, the Gray Board reported on May 27, 1954, that Dr. Oppenheimer "seems to have had a high degree of discretion reflecting an unusual ability to keep to himself vital secrets." My own careful reading of the complete dossier and of the testimony leads me to agree with the Gray Board on this point. I am confident that Dr. Oppenheimer will continue to keep to himself all the secrets with which he is entrusted. . . .

The history of Dr. Oppenheimer's contributions to the development of nuclear weapons stands untarnished.

It is clear that Dr. Oppenheimer's past associations and activities are not newly discovered in any substantial sense. They have been known for years to responsible authorities who have never been persuaded that they rendered Dr. Oppenheimer unfit for public service. Many of the country's outstanding men have expressed their faith in his integrity.

In spite of all this, the majority of the Commission now concludes that Dr. Oppenheimer is a security risk. I cannot accept this conclusion or the fear behind it. In my opinion the conclusion cannot be supported by a fair evaluation of the evidence.

To be effective a security system must be

realistic. In the words of the Atomic Energy Commission security criteria:

"The facts of each case must be carefully weighed and determination made in the light of all the information presented, whether favorable or unfavorable. The judgment of responsible persons as to the integrity of the individuals should be considered. The decision as to security clearance is an overall, commonsense judgment, made after consideration of all the relevant information as to whether or not there is risk that the granting of security clearance would endanger the common defense or security."

Application of this standard of overall commonsense judgment to the whole record destroys any pattern of suspicious conduct or catalog of falsehoods and evasions, and leaves a picture of Dr. Oppenheimer as an able, imaginative human being with normal human weaknesses and failings. In my opinion the conclusion drawn by the majority from the evidence is so extreme as to endanger the security system. . . .

With respect to the alleged disregard of the security system, I would suggest that the system itself is nothing to worship. It is a necessary means to an end. Its sole purpose, apart from the prevention of sabotage, is to protect secrets. If a man protects the secrets he has in his hands and his head, he has shown essential regard for the security system.

In addition, cooperation with security officials in their legitimate activities is to be ex-pected of private citizens and Government employees. The security system has, however, neither the responsibility nor the right to dictate every detail of a man's life. I frankly do not understand the charge made by the majority that Dr. Oppenheimer has shown a persistent and willful disregard for the obligations of security, and that therefore he should be declared a security risk. No gymnastics of rationalization allow me to accept this argument. If in any recent instances, Dr. Oppenheimer has misunderstood his obligation to security, the error is occasion for reproof but not for a finding that he should be debarred from serving his country. Such a finding extends the concept of "security risk" beyond its legitimate justification and constitutes a dangerous precedent.

In these times, failure to employ a man of great talents may impair the strength and power of this country. Yet I would accept this loss if I doubted the loyalty of Dr. Oppenheimer or his ability to hold his tongue. I have no such doubts.

I conclude that Dr. Oppenheimer's employment "will not endanger the common defense and security" and will be "clearly consistent with the interests of the national security." I prefer the positive statement that Dr. Oppenheimer's further employment will continue to strengthen the United States.

I therefore have voted to reinstate Dr. Oppenheimer's clearance.

HENRY D. SMYTH, *Commissioner.*

605. AMERICAN INTERVENTION IN GUATEMALA
June 30, 1954
(State Department Press Release, June 30, 1954)

American diplomats devoted little time to the problems of Latin America in the years following World War II. Their activities centered upon Europe and Asia. During this period, Communism gained its first foothold in Latin America. The tiny state of Guatemala came under the control of a government willing and able to do business with the Communist bloc. When Guatemala received a shipment of arms from Communist Czechoslovakia, Secretary of State Dulles reacted vigorously. He secured the support of all North and South American states except Guatemala for a declaration condemning the spread of Communist influence to the Western Hemisphere, then encouraged anti-Communist groups in Guatemala to stage a successful revolt against the pro-Communist government. To allay widespread criticism of American policy, Secretary Dulles analyzed the whole Guatemalan situation in a radio address of June 30, 1954. See C. Urrutia-Aparitio, "Guatemala's Withdrawal from the Organization of Central American States," 48 *Amer. J. of Int'l. Law* 145; A. P. Whitaker, *The Hemispheric Idea;* J. Gillin and K. H. Silvert, "Ambiguities in Guatemala," 34 *Foreign Affairs* 469.

. . . In Guatemala, international Communism had an initial success. It began ten years ago when a revolution occurred in Guatemala. The revolution was not without justification. But the Communists seized on it, not as an opportunity for real reforms, but as a chance to gain political power.

Communist agitators devoted themselves to infiltrating the public and private organizations of Guatemala. They sent recruits to Russia and other Communist countries for revolutionary training and indoctrination in such institutions as the Lenin School in Moscow. Operating in the guise of "reformers" they organized the workers and peasants under Communist leadership. Having gained control of what they call "mass organizations" they moved on to take over the official press and radio of the Guatemalan Government. They dominated the Social Security organization and ran the agrarian reform program. Through the technique of the "popular front" they dictated to the Congress and the President.

The judiciary made one valiant attempt to protect its integrity and independence. But the Communists, using their control of the legislative body, caused the Supreme Court to be dissolved when it refused to give approval to a Communist-contrived law. Arbenz, who until this week was President of Guatemala, was openly manipulated by the leaders of Communism.

Guatemala is a small country. But its power, standing alone, is not a measure of the threat. The master plan of international Communism is to gain a solid political base in this hemisphere, a base that can be used to extend Communist penetration to the other peoples of the other American Governments. It was not the power of the Arbenz Government that concerned us but the power behind it.

If world Communism captures any American State, however small, a new and perilous front is established which will increase the danger to the entire free world and require even greater sacrifices from the American people.

This situation in Guatemala had become so dangerous that the American States could not ignore it. At Caracas last March the American States held their Tenth Inter-American Conference. They then adopted a momentous statement. They declared that "the domination or control of the political institutions of any American State by the international communist movement . . . would constitute a threat to the sovereignty and political independence of the American States, endangering the peace of America."

There was only one American State that voted against this Declaration. That State was Guatemala.

This Caracas Declaration precipitated a dramatic chain of events. From their European base the Communist leaders moved rapidly to build up the military power of their agents in Guatemala. In May a large shipment of arms moved from behind the Iron Curtain into Guatemala. The shipment was sought to be secreted by false manifests and false clearances. Its ostensible destination was changed three times while en route.

At the same time, the agents of international Communism in Guatemala, intensified efforts to penetrate and subvert the neighboring Central American States. They attempted political assassinations and political strikes. They used consular agents for political warfare.

Many Guatemalan people protested against their being used by Communist dictatorship to serve the Communist's lust for power. The response was mass arrests, the suppression of constitutional guarantees, the killing of opposition leaders and other brutal tactics normally employed by Communism to secure the consolidation of its power.

In the face of these events and in accordance with the spirit of the Caracas Declaration, the nations of this hemisphere laid further plans to grapple with the danger. The Arbenz Government responded with an effort to disrupt the inter-American system. Because it enjoyed the full support of Soviet Russia, which is on the Security Council, it tried to bring the matter before the Security Council. It did so without first referring the matter to the American regional organization as is called for both by the United Nations Charter itself and by the treaty creating the American Organization.

The Foreign Minister of Guatemala openly connived in this matter with the Foreign Minister of the Soviet Union. The two were in open correspondence and ill-concealed privity. The Security Council at first voted overwhelmingly to refer the Guatemala matter to the Organization of American States. The vote was ten to one. But that one negative vote was a Soviet veto.

Then the Guatemalan Government, with a Soviet backing, redoubled its efforts to supplant the American States system by Security Council jurisdiction.

However, last Friday, the United Nations Security Council decided not to take up the Guatemalan matter, but to leave it in the first instance to the American States themselves. That was a triumph for the system of balance between regional organization and world organization, which the American States had fought for when the Charter was drawn up at San Francisco.

The American States then moved promptly to deal with the situation. Their "peace commission" left yesterday for Guatemala. Earlier the Organization of American States had voted overwhelmingly to call a meeting of their Foreign Ministers to consider the penetration of international Communism in Guatemala and the measures required to eliminate it. Never before has there been so clear a call uttered with such a sense of urgency and strong resolve.

Throughout the period I have outlined, the Guatemalan Government and Communist agents throughout the world have persistently attempted to obscure the real issue —that of Communist imperialism—by claiming that the United States is only interested in protecting American business. We regret that there have been disputes between the Guatemalan Government and the United Fruit Company. We have urged repeatedly that these disputes be submitted for settlement to an international tribunal or to international arbitration. That is the way to dispose of problems of this sort. But this issue is relatively unimportant. All who know the temper of the U.S. people and Government must realize that our overriding concern is that which, with others, we recorded at Caracas, namely the endangering by international Communism of the peace and security of this hemisphere.

The people of Guatemala have now been heard from. Despite the armaments piled up by the Arbenz Government, it was unable to enlist the spiritual cooperation of the people.

Led by Colonel Castillo Armas, patriots arose in Guatemala to challenge the Communist leadership—and to change it. Thus, the situation is being cured by the Guatemalans themselves.

Last Sunday, President Arbenz of Guatemala resigned and seeks asylum. Others are following his example.

Tonight, just as I speak, Colonel Castillo Armas is in conference in El Salvador with Colonel Monzon, the head of the Council which has taken over the power in Guatemala City. It was this power that the just wrath of the Guatemalan people wrested from President Arbenz who then took flight.

Now the future of Guatemala lies at the disposal of the Gautemalan people themselves. It lies also at the disposal of leaders loyal to Guatemala who have not treasonably become the agents of an alien despotism which sought to use Guatemala for its own evil ends.

606. COMMUNIST CONTROL ACT OF 1954
August 24, 1954
(Public Law 637, 83rd Congress)

The government's program to prevent subversion from within culminated in the Communist Control Act of 1954 outlawing the Communist Party. See Docs. No. 531, 577, 591, 599; S. H. Hofstadter, *The Fifth Amendment and the Immunity Act of 1954;* C. A. Auerbach, "Communist Control Act of 1954," 23 *U. of Chicago Law Rev.* 173; M. L. Ernst and D. L. Loth, *Report on the American Communist;* R. K.

Carr, *The House Committee on Un-American Activities, 1945–1950.*

An Act to outlaw the Communist Party, to prohibit members of Communist organizations from serving in certain representative capacities, and for other purposes.

SEC. 2. The Congress hereby finds and declares that the Communist Party of the United States, although purportedly a political party, is in fact an instrumentality of a conspiracy to overthrow the Government of the United States. It constitutes an authoritarian dictatorship within a republic, demanding for itself the rights and privileges accorded to political parties, but denying to all others the liberties guaranteed by the Constitution. Unlike political parties, which evolve their policies and programs through public means, by the reconciliation of a wide variety of individual views, and submit those policies and programs to the electorate at large for approval or disapproval, the policies and programs of the Communist Party are secretly prescribed for it by the foreign leaders of the world Communist movement. Its members have no part in determining its goals, and are not permitted to voice dissent to party objectives. Unlike members of political parties, members of the Communist Party are recruited for indoctrination with respect to its objectives and methods, and are organized, instructed, and disciplined to carry into action slavishly the assignments given them by their hierarchical chieftains. Unlike political parties, the Communist Party acknowledges no constitutional or statutory limitations upon its conduct or upon that of its members. The Communist Party is relatively small numerically, and gives scant indication of capacity ever to attain its ends by lawful political means. The peril inherent in its operation arises not from its numbers, but from its failure to acknowledge any limitation as to the nature of its activities, and its dedication to the proposition that the present constitutional Government of the United States ultimately must be brought to ruin by any available means, including resort to force and violence. Holding that doctrine, its role as the agency of a hostile foreign power renders its existence a clear present and continuing danger to the security of the United States. It is the means whereby individuals are seduced into the service of the world Communist movement, trained to do its bidding, and directed and controlled in the conspiratorial performance of their revolutionary services. Therefore, the Communist Party should be outlawed.

SEC. 3. The Communist Party of the United States, or any successors of such party regardless of the assumed name, whose object or purpose is to overthrow the Government of the United States, or the government of any State, Territory, District, or possession thereof, or the government of any political subdivision therein by force and violence, are not entitled to any of the rights, privileges, and immunities attendant upon legal bodies created under the jurisdiction of the laws of the United States or any political subdivision thereof; and whatever rights, privileges, and immunities which have heretofore been granted to said party or any subsidiary organization by reason of the laws of the United States or any political subdivision thereof, are hereby terminated: *Provided, however,* That nothing in this section shall be construed as amending the Internal Security Act of 1950, as amended.

SEC. 4. Whoever knowingly and willfully becomes or remains a member of (1) the Communist Party, or (2) any other organization having for one of its purposes or objectives the establishment, control, conduct, seizure, or overthrow of the Government of the United States, or the government of any State or political subdivision thereof, by the use of force or violence, with knowledge of the purpose or objective of such organization, shall be subject to all the provisions and penalties of the Internal Security Act of 1950, as amended, as a member of a "Communist-action" organization. . . .

607. SOUTHEAST ASIA TREATY ORGANIZATION
September 8, 1954
(Department of State Bulletin, September 20, 1954)

The French withdrawal from Vietnam, together with the growing alarm at the spread of Communism in the undeveloped world (or the fear of such expansion), prompted Secretary of State John Foster Dulles to negotiate a defensive alliance, patterned after the NATO treaty, with certain governments of Southeast Asia and other interested parties—excluding, however, China, Vietnam, and Formosa. The treaty was signed in Manila by representatives of the United States, Australia, France, New Zealand, Pakistan, the Republic of the Philippines, Thailand, and the United Kingdom.

The Parties to this Treaty,

Recognizing the sovereign equality of all the Parties,

Reiterating their faith in the purposes and principles set forth in the Charter of the United Nations and their desire to live in peace with all peoples and all governments,

Reaffirming that, in accordance with the Charter of the United Nations, they uphold the principle of equal rights and self-determination of peoples, and declaring that they will earnestly strive by every peaceful means to promote self-government and to secure the independence of all countries whose peoples desire it and are able to undertake its responsibilities,

Desiring to strengthen the fabric of peace and freedom and to uphold the principles of democracy, individual liberty and the rule of law, and to promote the economic well-being and development of all peoples in the treaty area,

Intending to declare publicly and formally their sense of unity, so that any potential aggressor will appreciate that the Parties stand together in the area, and

Desiring further to coordinate their efforts for collective defense for the preservation of peace and security,

Therefore agree as follows:

ARTICLE I

The Parties undertake, as set forth in the Charter of the United Nations, to settle any international disputes in which they may be involved by peaceful means in such a manner that international peace and security and justice are not endangered, and to refrain in their international relations from the threat or use of force in any manner inconsistent with the purposes of the United Nations.

ARTICLE II

In order more effectively to achieve the objectives of this Treaty, the Parties, separately and jointly, by means of continuous and effective self-help and mutual aid will maintain and develop their individual and collective capacity to resist armed attack and to prevent and counter subversive activities directed from without against their territorial integrity and political stability.

ARTICLE III

The Parties undertake to strengthen their free institutions and to cooperate with one another in the further development of economic measures, including technical assistance, designed both to promote economic progress and social well-being and to further the individual and collective efforts of governments toward these ends.

ARTICLE IV

1. Each Party recognizes that aggression by means of armed attack in the treaty area against any of the Parties or against any State or territory which the Parties by unanimous agreement may hereafter designate, would endanger its own peace and safety, and agrees that it will in the event act to meet the common danger in accordance with its constitutional processes. Measures taken under this paragraph shall be immediately reported to the Security Council of the United Nations.

2. If, in the opinion of any of the Parties, the inviolability or the integrity of the territory or the sovereignty or political independence of any Party in the treaty area or of any other State or territory to which the provisions of paragraph 1 of this Article from time to time apply is threatened in any way other than by armed attack or is affected or threatened by any fact or situation which might endanger the peace of the area, the Parties shall consult immediately in order to agree on the measures which should be taken for the common defense.

3. It is understood that no action on the territory of any State designated by unani-

mous agreement under paragraph 1 of this Article or on any territory so designated shall be taken except on the invitation or with the consent of the government concerned. . . .

608. EISENHOWER'S LETTER TO NGO DINH DIEM
October 23, 1954
(Department of State Bulletin, November 15, 1954)

In the spring of 1954, after years of civil war, Vietnamese nationalists under the Communist leader Ho Chi Minh defeated the French army at Dienbienphu. The Geneva Agreements of July 1954 formalized the end of French control in Vietnam, prohibited military intervention in the area by any other foreign power, and provided for democratic elections and the eventual re-unification of both halves of the country. Ngo Dinh Diem, a Vietnamese Catholic and aristocrat, who had opposed both the Communists and the French, became premier of South Vietnam with the strong moral backing of groups of influential Americans, whom he had impressed both with his anti-Communism and with his apparent enthusiasm for social reform. Eisenhower, however, was skeptical of any large-scale American commitment to Diem, and assured him only of economic assistance, and that in the most general terms. See B. Fall, *The Two Vietnams;* J. Lacouture, *Vietnam: Between Two Truces;* R. Scheer, *How the United States Got Involved in Vietnam.*

Dear Mr. President:

I have been following with great interest the course of developments in Vietnam, particularly since the conclusion of the conference at Geneva. The implications of the agreement concerning Vietnam have caused grave concern regarding the future of a country temporarily divided by an artificial military grouping, weakened by a long and exhausting war, and faced with enemies without and by their subversive collaborators within.

Your recent requests for aid to assist in the formidable project of the movement of several hundred thousand loyal Vietnamese citizens away from areas which are passing under a *de facto* rule and political ideology which they abhor, are being fulfilled. I am glad that the United States is able to assist in this humanitarian effort.

We have been exploring ways and means to permit our aid to Vietnam to be more effective and to make a greater contribution to the welfare and stability of the Government of Vietnam. I am, accordingly, instructing the American Ambassador to Vietnam [Donald R. Heath] to examine with you in your capacity as Chief of Government, how an intelligent program of American aid given directly to your Government can serve to assist Vietnam in its present hour of trial, provided that your Government is prepared to give assurances as to the standards of performance it would be able to maintain in the event such aid were supplied.

The purpose of this offer is to assist the Government of Vietnam in developing and maintaining a strong, viable state, capable of resisting attempted subversion or aggression through military means. The Government of the United States expects that this aid will be met by performance on the part of the Government of Vietnam in undertaking needed reforms. It hopes that such aid, combined with your own continuing efforts, will contribute effectively toward an independent Vietnam endowed with a strong Government. Such a Government would, I hope, be so responsive to the nationalist aspirations of its people, so enlightened in purpose and effective in performance, that it will be respected both at home and abroad and discourage any who might wish to impose a foreign ideology on your free people.

609. SENATE CENSURE OF SENATOR McCARTHY
December 2, 1954
(83rd Congress, 2nd Session, *Senate Resolution* 301)

Early in 1950, Senator Joseph R. McCarthy of Wisconsin inaugurated a campaign to prove that the government was infested with Communists and Communist sympathizers. At various times thereafter, he charged that Communist sympathizers had dictated American policy decisions and that such noted Americans as General George C. Marshall were Communist dupes. McCarthy's activities reached a climax in a full-scale investigation of "Communist infiltration in the army." These hearings resulted in charges on the part of Army Secretary Stevens that McCarthy attempted to secure special privileges for his former aide Private G. David Schine and counatercharges by Senator McCarthy that Stevens attempted to hide evidence of Communist infiltration from his committee and the public. On July 30, 1954, Senator Ralph Flanders of Vermont introduced a resolution in the Senate censuring McCarthy for improper conduct, especially during the army investigation. A Senate committee headed by Senator Watkins of Utah recommended censure; and the Senate accepted this recommendation by a vote of 67 to 22. Following this action by the Senate, McCarthy's influence waned. See J. Anderson and R. W. May, *McCarthy;* J. R. McCarthy, *McCarthyism, the Fight for America;* W. F. Buckley and L. B. Bozell, *McCarthy and His Enemies;* "McCarthy; A Documented Record," *The Progressive,* April 1954; U.S. Senate Government Operations Committee, 83rd Congress, *Special Senate Investigation on charges and countercharges Involving Secretary of Army Robert T. Stevens . . . and Senator Joe McCarthy . . . pursuant to S. Res. 189;* U.S. Senate Select Committee to Study Censure Charges, 83rd Congress, *Hearings . . . pursuant to S. Res. 301.*

Resolved, That the Senator from Wisconsin, Mr. McCarthy, failed to cooperate with the Subcommittee on Privileges and Elections of the Senate Committee on Rules and Administration in clearing up matters referred to that subcommittee which concerned his conduct as a Senator and affected the honor of the Senate and, instead, repeatedly abused the subcommittee and its members who were trying to carry out assigned duties, thereby obstructing the constitutional processes of the Senate, and that this conduct of the Senator from Wisconsin, Mr. McCarthy, is contrary to senatorial traditions and is hereby condemned.

SEC. 2. The Senator from Wisconsin, Mr. McCarthy, in writing to the chairman of the Select Committee to Study Censure Charges (Mr. Watkins) after the Select Committee had issued its report and before the report was presented to the Senate charging three members of the Select Committee with "deliberate deception" and "fraud" for failure to disqualify themselves; in stating to the press on November 4, 1954, that the special Senate session that was to begin November 8, 1954, was a "lynch party"; in repeatedly describing this special Senate session as a "lynch bee" in a nationwide television and radio show on November 7, 1954; in stating to the public press on November 13, 1954, that the chairman of the Select Committee (Mr. Watkins) was guilty of "the most unusual, most cowardly things I've heard of" and stating further: "I expected he would be afraid to answer the questions, but didn't think he'd be stupid enough to make a public statement"; and in characterizing the said committee as the "unwitting handmaiden," "involuntary agent" and "attorneys-in-fact" of the Communist Party and in charging that the said committee in writing its report "imitated Communist methods—that it distorted, misrepresented, and omitted in its effort to manufacture a plausible rationalization" in support of its recommendations to the Senate, which characterizations and charges were contained in a statement released to the press and inserted in the *Congressional Record* of November 10, 1954, acted contrary to senatorial ethics and tended to bring the Senate into dishonor and disrepute, to obstruct the constitutional processes of the Senate, and to impair its dignity; and such conduct is hereby condemned.

610. BROWN v. BOARD OF EDUCATION OF TOPEKA
347 U.S. 483
1954

This case tested the validity of state laws providing for racial segregation in the public schools. The Court reversed the doctrine of *Plessy* v. *Ferguson,* 163 U.S. 537, that the Fourteenth Amendment does not outlaw segregation so long as equal facilities are provided for each race. The Court here ruled that "Separate educational facilities are inherently unequal." The Court followed this ruling with another on May 31, 1955, which established the principle that desegregation must proceed with "all deliberate speed" and assigned to the lower courts the responsibility for applying this principle: 349 U.S. 294. These rulings inaugurated a substantial revolution in the legal status of Negroes not only in the field of education but in other areas as well. On November 7, 1955, the Interstate Commerce Commission followed the Court's reasoning in a ruling that segregation was illegal on interstate trains and buses, *NAACP* v. *St. Louis–San Francisco Railway Company.* Following these decisions, the struggle over segregation shifted from the realm of law to the realm of politics. See B. H. Nelson, *The Fourteenth Amendment and the Negro Since 1920;* H. S. Ashmore, *The Negro and the Schools;* P. A. Freund, "Understanding the School Decision," *Congressional Record,* March 28, 1956; J. D. Hyman, "Segregation and the Fourteenth Amendment," 4 *Vanderbilt Law Rev.* 555; T. Marshall et. al., *Brief for Appellants in the case of Brown v. Board of Education,* filed in the U.S. Supreme Court, November 16, 1953; T. Marshall, "Supreme Court as Protector of Civil Rights," *Annals of the Am. Aca. of Pol. and Soc. Sci.,* May 1951.

Appeal from the U.S. Dist. Court, District of Kansas.

WARREN, C. J. These cases come to us from the States of Kansas, South Carolina, Virginia, and Delaware. They are premised on different facts and different local conditions, but a common legal question justifies their consideration together in this consolidated opinion.

In each of the cases, minors of the Negro race, through their legal representatives, seek the aid of the courts in obtaining admission to the public schools of their community on a nonsegregated basis. In each instance, they have been denied admission to schools attended by white children under laws requiring or permitting segregation according to race. This segregation was alleged to deprive the plaintiffs of the equal protection of the laws under the Fourteenth Amendment. In each of the cases other than the Delaware case, a three-judge federal district court denied relief to the plaintiffs on the so-called "separate but equal" doctrine announced by this Court in Plessy v. Ferguson, 163 U.S. 537. Under that doctrine, equality of treatment is accorded when the races are provided substantially equal facilities, even though these facilities be separate. In the Delaware case, the Supreme Court of Delaware adhered to that doctrine, but ordered that the plaintiffs be admitted to the white schools because of their superiority to the Negro schools.

The plaintiffs contend that segregated public schools are not "equal" and cannot be made "equal," and that hence they are deprived of the equal protection of the laws. Because of the obvious importance of the question presented, the Court took jurisdiction. Argument was heard in the 1952 Term, and reargument was heard this Term on certain questions propounded by the Court.

Reargument was largely devoted to the circumstances surrounding the adoption of the Fourteenth Amendment in 1868. It covered exhaustively consideration of the Amendment in Congress, ratification by the states, then existing practices in racial segregation, and the views of proponents and opponents of the Amendment. This discussion and our own investigation convince us that, although these sources cast some light, it is not enough to resolve the problem with which we are faced. At best, they are inconclusive. The most avid proponents of the post-War Amendments undoubtedly intended them to remove all legal distinctions among "all persons born or naturalized in the United

States." Their opponents, just as certainly, were antagonistic to both the letter and the spirit of the Amendments and wished them to have the most limited effect. What others in Congress and the state legislatures had in mind cannot be determined with any degree of certainty.

An additional reason for the inconclusive nature of the Amendment's history, with respect to segregated schools, is the status of public education at that time. In the South, the movement toward free common schools, supported by general taxation, had not yet taken hold. Education of white children was largely in the hands of private groups. Education of Negroes was almost nonexistent, and practically all of the race were illiterate. In fact, any education of Negroes was forbidden by law in some states. Today, in contrast, many Negroes have achieved outstanding success in the arts and sciences as well as in the business and professional world. It is true that public education had already advanced further in the North, but the effect of the Amendment on Northern States was generally ignored in the congressional debates. Even in the North, the conditions of public education did not approximate those existing today. The curriculum was usually rudimentary; ungraded schools were common in rural areas; the school term was but three months a year in many states; and compulsory school attendance was virtually unknown. As a consequence, it is not surprising that there should be so little in the history of the Fourteenth Amendment relating to its intended effect on public education.

In the first cases in this Court construing the Fourteenth Amendment, decided shortly after its adoption, the Court interpreted it as proscribing all state-imposed discriminations against the Negro race. The doctrine of "separate but equal" did not make its appearance in this Court until 1896 in the case of Plessy v. Ferguson, supra, involving not education but transportation. American courts have since labored with the doctrine for over half a century. In this Court, there have been six cases involving the "separate but equal" doctrine in the field of public education. In Cumming v. Board of Education of Richmond County, 175 U.S. 528, and Gong Lum v. Rice, 275 U.S. 78, the validity of the doctrine itself was not challenged. In more recent cases, all on the graduate school level, inequality was found in that specific benefits enjoyed by white students were denied to Negro students of the same educational qualifications. State of Missouri ex rel. Gaines v. Canada, 305 U.S. 337; Sipuel v. Board of Regents of University of Oklahoma, 332 U.S. 631; Sweatt v. Painter, 339 U.S. 629; McLaurin v. Oklahoma State Regents, 339 U.S. 637. In none of these cases was it necessary to reexamine the doctrine to grant relief to the Negro plaintiff. And in Sweatt v. Painter, supra, the Court expressly reserved decision on the question whether Plessy v. Ferguson should be held inapplicable to public education.

In the instant cases, that question is directly presented. Here, unlike Sweatt v. Painter, there are findings below that the Negro and white schools involved have been equalized, or are being equalized, with respect to buildings, curricula, qualifications and salaries of teachers, and other "tangible" factors. Our decision, therefore, cannot turn on merely a comparison of these tangible factors in the Negro and white schools involved in each of the cases. We must look instead to the effect of segregation itself on public education.

In approaching this problem, we cannot turn the clock back to 1868 when the Amendment was adopted, or even to 1896 when Plessy v. Ferguson was written. We must consider public education in the light of its full development and its present place in American life throughout the Nation. Only in this way can it be determined if segregation in public schools deprives these plaintiffs of the equal protection of the laws.

Today, education is perhaps the most important function of state and local governments. Compulsory school attendance laws and the great expenditures for education both demonstrate our recognition of the importance of education to our democratic society. It is required in the performance of our most basic public responsibilities, even service in the armed forces. It is the very foundation of good citizenship. Today it is a principal instrument in awakening the child to cultural values, in preparing him for later professional training, and in helping him to adjust normally to his environment. In these days, it is doubtful that any child may reasonably be expected to succeed in life if he is denied the opportunity of an education. Such an opportunity, where the state has undertaken to provide it, is a right which must be made available to all on equal terms.

We come then to the question presented: Does segregation of children in public schools solely on the basis of race, even though the physical facilities and other "tangible" factors may be equal, deprive the children of the minority group of equal educational opportunities? We believe that it does.

In Sweatt v. Painter, supra [339 U.S. 629, 70 S.Ct. 850], in finding that a segregated law school for Negroes could not provide them equal educational opportunities, this Court relied in large part on "those qualities which are incapable of objective measurement but which make for greatness in a law school." In McLaurin v. Oklahoma State Regents, supra [339 U.S. 637, 70 S.Ct. 853], the Court, in requiring that a Negro admitted to a white graduate school be treated like all other students, again resorted to intangible considerations: ". . . his ability to study, to engage in discussions and exchange views with other students, and, in general, to learn his profession." Such considerations apply with added force to children in grade and high schools. To separate them from others of similar age and qualifications solely because of their race generates a feeling of inferiority as to their status in the community that may affect their hearts and minds in a way unlikely ever to be undone. The effect of this separation on their educational opportunities was well stated by a finding in the Kansas case by a court which nevertheless felt compelled to rule against the Negro plaintiffs:

"Segregation of white and colored children in public schools has a detrimental effect upon the colored children. The impact is greater when it has the sanction of the law; for the policy of separating the races is usually interpreted as denoting the inferiority of the Negro group. A sense of inferiority affects the motivation of a child to learn. Segregation with the sanction of law, therefore, has a tendency to retard the educational and mental development of Negro children and to deprive them of some of the benefits they would receive in a racially integrated school system."

Whatever may have been the extent of psychological knowledge at the time of Plessy v. Ferguson, this finding is amply supported by modern authority. Any language in Plessy v. Ferguson contrary to this finding is rejected.

We conclude that in the field of public education the doctrine of "separate but equal" has no place. Separate educational facilities are inherently unequal. Therefore, we hold that the plaintiffs and others similarly situated for whom the actions have been brought are, by reason of the segregation complained of, deprived of the equal protection of the laws guaranteed by the Fourteenth Amendment. This deposition makes unnecessary any discussion whether such segregation also violates the Due Process Clause of the Fourteenth Amendment.

Because these are class actions, because of the wide applicability of this decision, and because of the great variety of local conditions, the formulation of decrees in these cases presents problems of considerable complexity. On reargument, the consideration of appropriate relief was necessarily subordinated to the primary question—the constitutionality of segregation in public education. We have now announced that such segregation is a denial of the equal protection of the laws. In order that we may have the full assistance of the parties in formulating decrees, the cases will be restored to the docket, and the parties are requested to present further argument. . . . The Attorney General of the United States is again invited to participate. The Attorneys General of the states requiring or permitting segregation in public education will also be permitted to appear as *amici curiae* upon request to do so by September 15, 1954, and submission of briefs by October 1, 1954.

It is so ordered.

611. CONGRESSIONAL RESOLUTION ON THE DEFENSE
OF FORMOSA
January 29, 1955
(Public Law, 84th Congress)

Communist China threatened in 1955 to attack and overcome the last strongholds of the Chinese nationalist government on Formosa and the neighboring Pescadores islands. At the urging of President Eisenhower, Congress passed a resolution declaring that Formosa and the neighboring islands were essential to American military security and authorizing the President to use American troops to defend the islands from Communist attack. This is a rare instance of Congressional action giving the President authority to involve the nation in war at his own discretion. See Doc. No. 650; A. Dean, "United States Foreign Policy and Formosa," 33 *Foreign Affairs* 360; J. W. Ballantine, *Formosa, A Problem for United States Foreign Policy;* R. A. Smith, *The Rebirth of Formosa;* H. Feis, *The China Tangle.*

Whereas the primary purpose of the United States, in its relations with all other nations, is to develop and sustain a just and enduring peace for all; and

Whereas certain territories in the West Pacific under the jurisdiction of the Republic of China are now under armed attack, and threats and declarations have been and are being made by the Chinese Communists that such armed attack is in aid of and in preparation for armed attack on Formosa and the Pescadores;

Whereas such armed attack if continued would gravely endanger the peace and security of the West Pacific Area and particularly of Formosa and the Pescadores; and

Whereas the secure possession by friendly governments of the Western Pacific Island chain, of which Formosa is a part, is essential to the vital interests of the United States and all friendly nations in or bordering upon the Pacific Ocean; and

Whereas the President of the United States on January 6, 1955, submitted to the Senate for its advice and consent to ratification a Mutual Defense Treaty between the United States of America and the Republic of China, which recognizes that an armed attack in the West Pacific area directed against territories, therein described, in the region of Formosa and the Pescadores, would be dangerous to the peace and safety of the parties to the treaty: Therefore be it

Resolved by the Senate and House of Representatives of the United States of America in Congress assembled, That the President of the United States be and he hereby is authorized to employ the Armed Forces of the United States as he deems necessary for the specific purpose of securing and protecting Formosa and the Pescadores against armed attack, this authority to include the security and protection of such related positions and territories of that area now in friendly hands and the taking of such other measures as he judges to be required or appropriate in assuring the defense of Formosa and the Pescadores.

This resolution shall expire when the President shall determine that the peace and security of the area is reasonably assured by international conditions created by action of the United Nations or otherwise, and shall so report to the Congress.

612. EISENHOWER'S OPEN SKIES PROPOSAL
Statement on Disarmament Presented at the Geneva Conference
July 21, 1955
(The Public Papers of the Presidents: Dwight D. Eisenhower, 1955, no. 166)

All through the fifties the competition for nuclear weapons and the search for a formula for disarmament commanded the most anxious attention of statesmen. During the "thaw" in Soviet–United States relations brought on by the truce in Korea, the cease-fire in the Formosa

Strait, and the compromise peace in Vietnam, Eisenhower attended a summit conference in Geneva, announced that "the American people want to be friends with the Soviet peoples" and proposed disarmament and "open skies" inspection. The Russians would not hear of this proposal, however, and countered with a proposal for the prohibition of the manufacture of atomic weapons and a drastic limitation on ground forces of the great powers. For the problem of disarmament in a nuclear age see P. Gallois, *The Balance of Terror;* B. Brodie, *The Absolute Weapon;* H. Kahn, *On Thermonuclear War;* G. Kennan, *Russia, the Atom and the West;* H. Kissinger, *Nuclear Weapons and Foreign Policy;* R. Lapp, *Atoms and Peace;* J. Warburg, *Disarmament, The Challenge of the 1960s;* F. O. Miksche, *The Failure of Atomic Strategy;* L. Pearson, *Diplomacy in the Nuclear Age;* A. Nutting, *Disarmament;* P. Quigg, "Open Skies and Open Space," *Foreign Affairs,* October 1958.

Disarmament is one of the most important subjects on our agenda. It is also extremely difficult. In recent years the scientists have discovered methods of making weapons many, many times more destructive of opposing armed forces—but also of homes, and industries and lives—than ever known or even imagined before. These same scientific discoveries have made much more complex the problems of limitation and control and reduction of armament. . . .

The United States government is prepared to enter into a sound and reliable agreement making possible the reduction of armament. I have directed that an intensive and thorough study of this subject be made within our own government. From these studies, which are continuing, a very important principle is emerging to which I referred in my opening statement on Monday.

No sound and reliable agreement can be made unless it is completely covered by an inspection and reporting system adequate to support every portion of the agreement.

The lessons of history teach us that disarmament agreements without adequate reciprocal inspection increase the dangers of war and do not brighten the prospects of peace.

Thus it is my view that the priority attention of our combined study of disarmament should be upon the subject of inspection and reporting. . . .

Gentlemen, since I have been working on this memorandum to present to this Conference, I have been searching my heart and mind for something that I could say here that could convince everyone of the great sincerity of the United States in approaching this problem of disarmament.

I should address myself for a moment principally to the delegates from the Soviet Union, because our two great countries admittedly possess new and terrible weapons in quantities which do give rise in other parts of the world, or reciprocally, to the fears and dangers of surprise attack.

I propose, therefore, that we take a practical step, that we begin an arrangement, very quickly, as between ourselves—immediately. These steps would include:

To give to each other a complete blueprint of our military establishments, from beginning to end, from one end of our countries to the other; lay out the establishments and provide the blueprints to each other.

Next, to provide within our countries facilities for aerial photography to the other country—we to provide you the facilities within our country, ample facilities for aerial reconnaissance, where you can make all the pictures you choose and take them to your own country to study, you to provide exactly the same facilities for us and we to make these examinations, and by this step to convince the world that we are providing as between ourselves against the possibility of great surprise attack, thus lessening danger and relaxing tension. Likewise we will make more easily attainable a comprehensive and effective system of inspection and disarmament, because what I propose, I assure you, would be but a beginning. . . .

The quest for peace is the statesman's most exacting duty. Security of the nation entrusted to his care is his greatest responsibility. Practical progress to lasting peace is his fondest hope. Yet in pursuit of his hope he must not betray the trust placed in him as guardian of the people's security. A sound peace—with security, justice, wellbeing, and freedom for the people of the world—*can be achieved, but only by patiently and* thoughtfully following a hard and sure and tested road.

613. UNITED STATES v. LATTIMORE
127 Fed. Supp. 405
1955

Senator McCarthy's drive against alleged "Communist sympathizers" focused in 1952 upon one man, Professor Owen J. Lattimore, distinguished Far Eastern expert at the Johns Hopkins University. Testifying before a Senate subcommittee in 1952, Lattimore denied under oath that he was a "follower of the Communist line" or a "promoter of Communist causes." These statements were used as grounds for a perjury indictment against him. Federal Judge Luther Youngdahl dismissed the charges as too vague to be adjudicated in a court of law. See O. Lattimore, *Ordeal by Slander;* U.S. Senate Internal Security Subcommittee of Judiciary Committee, *Hearings on Subversive Influence in Educational Process . . . Feb. 10–March 10, 1953.*

YOUNGDAHL, District Judge.

Owen Lattimore was indicted October 7, 1954, on two counts of perjury allegedly committed before the Senate Internal Security Subcommittee on or about February 27, 1952.

The first count charges that Lattimore perjured himself when he denied that he was a "follower of the Communist line." It avers that in his positions and policies as to political, diplomatic, military, economic and social matters, there can be found expressed in his statements and writings from 1935 to 1950, several hundred instances in which he followed the Communist line, meaning that he:

". . . followed in time, conformed to, complied with and paralleled the positions taken, the policies expressed and propaganda issued on the same matters by the Government of the Soviet Union, the Communist Party of the Soviet Union, the Comintern and its successors, the various Communist governments, parties and persons adhering to Communism and accepting the leadership of the Soviet Com-

munist Party." (Count I, paragraph 5).

The second count charges that Lattimore perjured himself when he testified he had never been a "promoter of Communist interests." Such a person is defined as one who:

". . . knowingly and intentionally contributed to the growth, enlargement and prosperity of Communism by acting to further, encourage and advance those objectives of political, diplomatic, military, economic and social interest to the Government of the Soviet Union, the Communist party of the Soviet Union, the Comintern and its successors, the various Communist governments, parties and persons adhering to Communism and accepting the leadership of the Soviet Communist party." (Count II, paragraph 5).

Defendant moved to dismiss the indictment, alleging that each of the two counts violate both the First and Sixth Amendments to the United States Constitution. The Court's holding that both counts should be dismissed on the ground of vagueness renders unnecessary a determination of their constitutionality under the First Amendment. . . .

When passing upon the Motion to Dismiss, ". . . the allegations of the indictment must be accepted as they are written." This we do, and are of the opinion that it does not, as a matter of law, inform the accused of the nature and cause of the accusation against him. Neither does it charge an offense with reasonable clarity so that the accused can make his defense, nor furnish the accused with such a description of the charge that he would be able to avail himself of his conviction or acquittal for protection against a further prosecution for the same cause.

In upholding the dismissal of the first count in the prior indictment Judge Prettyman, speaking for the Court of Appeals, aptly stated,

"Not only is it a basic rule that 'Criminal statutes must have an ascertainable standard of guilt or they fall for vagueness', but it is equally well established that an indictment must charge an offense with such reasonable certainty that the accused can make his defense. The cases on the point are myriad, as reference to any authority quickly reveals."

Testing the two counts against this principle, the Court is satisfied that they fail to meet the prescribed standard of definiteness and so must fall for vagueness.

Under Count I, perjury is charged to the statement by Lattimore that he was not a follower of the Communist line. The Government supplies a definition of this phrase in the indictment. The Government is prompt to concede that no such definition was presented to the defendant at the Committee hearing in 1952; that it was formulated after Lattimore testified; that it was prepared after independent research conducted by the United States Attorney's Office. The sources of such research, however, do not appear. The Government contends that it is a matter of common knowledge as to what is meant by "follower of the Communist line" and that people differ but little in their understanding of the term; that it is not a minimal requirement of following the Communist line to zig and zag with it, since it does not always zigzag; and that the Communist line means the Soviet Communist line and all other organizations that followed the Soviet line. The Government claims a right to prove, by men who are familiar with the common usage of the phrase and by documents of defendant's, that the definition found in the indictment was the same definition which Lattimore had in mind when he testified; that the jury should be left to determine what is the Communist line, what it means to follow such a line, what Lattimore understood as the Communist line, what Lattimore meant by the word "follow," and lastly, having decided the above, that Lattimore, when he said he was not a follower of the Communist line, did not at that time believe in the truth of such testimony according to the meaning he ascribed to these words.

While the proper test of perjury is subjective, insofar as it is based upon the understanding of the witness himself regarding the words that he used, a criminal prosecution must have certain objective standards. Most often in perjury cases the objective standard is not hard to come by; what the accused considered his statements to mean is not in issue since the words or phrases involved have one clear, accepted and recognized meaning. Here, the phrase "follower of the Communist line" is subject to varying interpretations. It has no universally accepted definition. The Government has defined it in one way and seeks to impute its definition to the defendant. Defendant has declined to adopt it, offering a definition of his own. It would not necessitate great ingenuity to think up definitions differing from those offered either by the Government or defendant. By groundless surmise only could the jury determine which definition defendant had in mind.

The Court cannot escape the conclusion that "follower of the Communist line" is not a phrase with a meaning about which men of ordinary intellect could agree, nor one which could be used with mutual understanding by a questioner and answerer unless it were defined at the time it were sought and offered as testimony. This count, even with its apparent definition, is an open invitation to the jury to substitute, by conjecture, their understanding of the phrase for that of the defendant. The meaning of such a phrase varies according to a particular individual's political philosophy. To ask twelve jurors to agree and then decide that the definition of the Communist line found in the indictment is the definition that defendant had in mind and denied believing in, is to ask the jury to aspire to levels of insight to which the ordinary person is incapable, and upon which speculation no criminal indictment should hinge. We cannot debase the principle that:

"The accused is entitled under the Constitution to be advised as to every element in respect to which it is necessary for him to prepare a defense."

When elements in an indictment are so easily subject to divergent interpretation, the accused is not adequately apprised of the charges as to enable him to prepare a defense. It therefore fails to conform to the requirements of the Sixth Amendment and Federal Rules. It cannot be cured by a bill of particulars.

The second count charges that Lattimore perjured himself when he testified he had never been a "promoter of Communist interest."

This entire perjury indictment arises out of, and is essentially founded upon, the statements, correspondence, and editorial comments of defendant. It does not rest upon alleged acts of espionage or such an act as membership in the Communist party. The Government pointed to the activities of an espionage agent as an example of how one might knowingly promote Communist interests without also being a knowing follower of the Communist line—whatever that may be. But the Government was quick to state that it was not charging defendant with being an espionage agent. It should be kept in mind that under this count only written comments and opinions are involved and are said to have produced a certain effect, namely, to have promoted Communist interests. Such writings and comments are not alleged to have produced the designated result over a short period of time, and in isolated instances, but over a fifteen-year period. By no stretch of the imagination can we comprehend how this consistent result (promoting Communist interests) could have been so attained had not the commentator been both aware of what the Communists were asserting during this extended period, and then knowingly adhered to these assertions (followed the Communist line). If defendant had contradicted the Communists' assertions, he could hardly be said to have promoted their interests.

Count II, thus dependent upon Count I, cannot stand, being anchored to, partaking of, and plagued by, all its vagueness and indefiniteness. While some paragraphs of Count II specifically refer to Count I, either for the definition of the Communist line or for topical references wherein defendant promoted Communist interests, all of the paragraphs, realistically appraised, are rooted in, and presume a prior finding of, the meaning of the phrase "follower of the Communist line."

The charges here serve only to inform the defendant that his sworn statements are to be tested against all his writings for chance parallelism with, or indirect support of, Communism regardless of any deliberate intent on his part. They demonstrate that the Government seeks to establish that at some time, in some way, in some places, in all his vast writings, over a fifteen-year period, Lattimore agreed with something it calls and personally defines as following the Communist line and promoting Communist interests.

Jury inquiries would be limitless. No charge by the Court could embody objective standards to circumscribe and guide the jury in its determination of what the witness might have meant regarding words he used. With so sweeping an indictment with its many vague charges, and with the existing atmosphere of assumed and expected loathing for Communism, it would be neither surprising nor unreasonable were the jury subconsciously impelled to substitute its own understanding for that of defendant.

To require defendant to go to trial for perjury under charges so formless and obscure as those before the Court would be unprecedented and would make a sham of the Sixth Amendment and the Federal Rule requiring specificity of charges.

The indictment will therefore be dismissed.

614. CONSTITUTION OF THE AFL-CIO
1955
(Report of the First Constitutional Convention of the AFL-CIO, 1955)

Labor's civil war ended in 1955 when the American Federation of Labor and the Congress of Industrial Organizations merged into a single federation of unions, the AFL-CIO. See Doc. No. 569. This brought into a single labor organization some 15 million workers. The constitution of the new organization granted to the new Federation more power over national union affairs than the constitution of the old American Federation of Labor. See Doc. No. 473. This reflected an increase in the importance of the functions performed by the central agencies of the labor movement. See A. J. Goldberg, *AFL-CIO Labor United;* E. Levinson, *Labor on the March;* J. Seidman, *American Labor from Defense to Reconversion.*

Preamble

The establishment of this Federation through the merger of the American Federation of Labor and the Congress of Industrial Organizations is an expression of the hopes and aspirations of the working people of America.

We seek the fulfillment of these hopes and aspirations through democratic processes within the framework of our constitutional government and consistent with our institutions and traditions.

At the collective bargaining table, in the community, in the exercise of the rights and responsibilities of citizenship, we shall responsibly serve the interests of the American people.

We pledge ourselves to the more effective organization of working men and women; to the securing to them of full recognition and enjoyment of the rights to which they are justly entitled; to the achievement of ever higher standards of living and working conditions; to the attainment of security for all the people; to the enjoyment of the leisure which their skills make possible; and to the strengthening and extension of our way of life and the fundamental freedoms which are the basis of our democratic society.

We shall combat resolutely the forces which seek to undermine the democratic institutions of our nation and to enslave the human soul. We shall strive always to win full respect for the dignity of the human individual whom our unions serve.

With Divine guidance, grateful for the fine traditions of our past, confident of meeting the challenge of the future, we proclaim this constitution. . . .

ARTICLE II
Objects and Principles

The objects and principles of this Federation are:

1. To aid workers in securing improved wages, hours and working conditions with due regard for the autonomy, integrity and jurisdiction of affiliated unions.

2. To aid and assist affiliated unions in extending the benefits of mutual assistance and collective bargaining to workers and to promote the organization of the unorganized into unions of their own choosing for their mutual aid, protection and advancement, giving recognition to the principle that both craft and industrial unions are appropriate, equal and necessary as methods of union organization.

3. To affiliate national and international unions with this Federation and to establish such unions; to form organizing committees and directly affiliated local unions and to secure their affiliation to appropriate national and international unions affiliated with or chartered by the Federation; to establish, assist and promote state and local central bodies composed of local unions of all affiliated organizations and directly affiliated local unions; to establish and assist trade departments composed of affiliated national and international unions and organizing committees.

4. To encourage all workers without regard to race, creed, color, national origin or ancestry to share equally in the full benefits of union organization.

5. To secure legislation which will safeguard and promote the principle of free collective bargaining, the rights of workers, farmers and consumers, and the security and welfare of all the people and to oppose legislation inimical to these objectives.

6. To protect and strengthen our democratic institutions, to secure full recognition and enjoyment of the rights and liberties to which we are justly entitled, and to preserve and perpetuate the cherished traditions of our democracy.

7. To give constructive aid in promoting the cause of peace and freedom in the world and to aid, assist and cooperate with free

and democratic labor movements throughout the world.

8. To preserve and maintain the integrity of each affiliated union in the organization to the end that each affiliate shall respect the established bargaining relationships of every other affiliate and that each affiliate shall refrain from raiding the established bargaining relationship of any other affiliate and, at the same time, to encourage the elimination of conflicting and duplicating organizations and jurisdictions through the process of voluntary agreement or voluntary merger in consultation with the appropriate officials of the Federation, to preserve, subject to the foregoing, the organizing jurisdiction of each affiliate.

9. To aid and encourage the sale and use of union made goods and union services through the use of the union label and other symbols; to promote the labor press and other means of furthering the education of the labor movement.

10. To protect the labor movement from any and all corrupt influences and from the undermining efforts of communist agencies and all others who are opposed to the basic principles of our democracy and free and democratic unionism.

11. To safeguard the democratic character of the labor movement and to protect the autonomy of each affiliated national and international union.

12. While preserving the independence of the labor movement from political control, to encourage workers to register and vote, to exercise their full rights and responsibilities of citizenship, and to perform their rightful part in the political life of the local, state and national communities. . . .

ARTICLE VIII

Executive Council

Sec. 1.   The Executive Council shall consist of the President, the Vice Presidents and the Secretary-Treasurer.

Sec. 2.   The Executive Council shall be the governing body of this Federation between conventions. It is authorized and empowered to take such action and render such decisions as may be necessary to carry out fully and adequately the decisions and instructions of the conventions and to enforce the provisions contained in this constitution. Between conventions it shall have the power to direct the affairs of the Federation and to take such actions and render such decisions as are necessary and appropriate to safeguard and promote the best interests of the Federation and its affiliated unions, including the organization of unorganized industries by means most appropriate for that purpose.

Sec. 3.   The Executive Council shall meet upon the call of the President at least three times within each year at a time and place designated by the President.

Sec. 4.   It shall be the duty of the Executive Council to watch legislative measures directly affecting the interests of working people, and to initiate, wherever necessary, such legislative action as the convention may direct.

Sec. 5.   The Executive Council shall prepare and present to the convention in printed form a statement of all matters of interest to the convention and of the activities of the Federation between conventions.

Sec. 6.   The Executive Council shall have power to make rules to govern matters consistent with this constitution and shall report accordingly to the Federation.

Sec. 7.   It is a basic principle of this Federation that it must be and remain free from any and all corrupt influences and from the undermining efforts of communist, fascist or other totalitarian agencies who are opposed to the basic principles of our democracy and of free and democratic trade unionism. The Executive Council, when requested to do so by the President or by any other member of the Executive Council, shall have the power to conduct an investigation, directly or through an appropriate standing or special committee appointed by the President, of any situation in which there is reason to believe that any affiliate is dominated, controlled or substantially influenced in the conduct of its affairs by any corrupt influence, or that the policies or activities of any affiliate are consistently directed toward the advocacy, support, advancement or achievement of the program or of the purposes of the Communist Party, any fascist organization or other totalitarian movement. Upon the completion of such an investigation, including a hearing if requested, the Executive Council shall have the authority to make recommendations or give directions to the affiliate involved and shall have the further authority, upon a two-thirds vote, to suspend any affiliate found guilty of a violation of this section. Any action of the Executive Council under this section may be appealed to the convention, provided, however, that such action shall be effective when taken and shall remain in full force and effect pending any appeal.

SEC. 8. Subject to the provisions of Article III, Section 7, the Executive Council shall use every possible means to assist affiliated unions in the organization of the unorganized and to organize new national and international unions, organizing committees, and directly affiliated local unions. . . .

SEC. 9. In carrying out the provisions of this Article the Executive Council shall recognize that both craft and industrial unions are appropriate, equal and necessary as methods of trade union organization and that all workers whatever their race, color, creed or national origin are entitled to share in the full benefits of trade union organization.

SEC. 10. A majority of the members of the Executive Council shall constitute a quorum for the transaction of the business of the Council.

SEC. 11. The Executive Council shall have the power to file charges and conduct hearings on such charges against any Executive Officer of the Federation or other member of the Executive Council on the ground that such person is guilty of malfeasance, or maladministration, and to make a report to the convention recommending appropriate action. The Executive Council must serve such officer with a copy of the written charges a reasonable time before the hearing. . . .

ARTICLE XI

DEPARTMENT OF ORGANIZATION

SEC. 1. The organizing work of this Federation as set forth in Article VIII, Section 8, shall be conducted by the Department of Organization under the general supervision of the President. The Department of Organization shall be provided the staff and resources necessary to conduct such activities.

SEC. 2. The Department of Organization shall be headed by a Director of Organization who shall be appointed by the President after consultation with the Executive Committee, subject to the approval of the Executive Council. . . .

ARTICLE XIII

COMMITTEES AND STAFF DEPARTMENTS

SEC. 1. The President of the Federation shall appoint the following standing committees and such other committees as may from time to time be necessary. The President with the approval of the Executive Council may combine standing committees. The committees, under the direction of the President, and subject to the authority of the Executive Council and the convention, shall carry out their functions as described herein:

(a) The Committee on Legislation shall undertake to carry out the policies and programs of the Federation in the Congress and in the legislatures of state and local governments;

(b) The Committee on Civil Rights shall be vested with the duty and responsibility to assist the Executive Council to bring about at the earliest possible date the effective implementation of the principle stated in this constitution of non-discrimination in accordance with the provisions of this constitution;

(c) The Committee on Political Education shall be vested with the duty and responsibility to assist the Executive Council in meeting the need for sound political education and in bringing about the effective implementation of the objectives stated in this constitution of encouraging workers to register and vote, to exercise their full rights and responsibilities of citizenship and to perform their rightful part in the political life of the city, state, and national communities;

(d) The Committee on Ethical Practices shall be vested with the duty and responsibility to assist the Executive Council in carrying out the constitutional determination of the Federation to keep the Federation free from any taint of corruption or communism, in accordance with the provisions of this constitution;

(e) The Committee on International Affairs shall be concerned with international developments facing our nation and the Federation's relationships with the international trade union movement;

(f) The Committee on Education shall promote the widest possible understanding among union members of the aims of the Federation, shall assist affiliated unions in developing their own educational programs and shall implement the Federation's interest in providing the nation with the highest standard of education at all levels;

(g) The Committee on Social Security

shall have the responsibility of providing guidance and information in the fields of social insurance and welfare;

(h) The Committee on Economic Policy shall undertake to recommend programs and policies toward the end of promoting prosperity, full employment and full utilization of our resources. . . .

ARTICLE XVII

AMENDMENTS

This constitution can be amended or altered only by the convention, by a two-thirds vote of those present and voting, either by a show of hands, or, if a roll-call is properly demanded as provided in this constitution, by such roll-call. . . .

615. COLE v. YOUNG
351 U.S. 536
1956

This case dealt with the application of the Internal Security Act of 1950, Doc. No. 592, to government employees who have no contact with restricted information. The Court voided that part of Executive Order 10450 which extended the security program to all government employees. Following this decision, President Eisenhower ordered the Attorney General to modify the government's security program to apply only to sensitive positions in which employees have direct contact with restricted government documents. See 70 *Harvard Law Rev.* 165; 42 *Am. Bar Assoc. J.* 764.

Appeal from the United States Court of Appeals for the District of Columbia.

HARLAN, J. This case presents the question of the meaning of the term "national security" as used in the Act of August 26, 1950, giving to the heads of certain departments and agencies of the Government summary suspension and unreviewable dismissal powers over their civilian employees, when deemed necessary "in the interest of the national security of the United States."

Petitioner, a preference-eligible veteran under § 2 of the Veterans' Preference Act of 1944, 58 Stat. 387, held a position in the classified civil service as a food and drug inspector for the New York District of the Food and Drug Administration, Department of Health, Education, and Welfare. In November 1953 he was suspended without pay from his position pending investigation to determine whether his employment should be terminated. . . .

Thereafter the Secretary of the Department of Health, Education, and Welfare, after "a study of all the documents in [petitioner's] case," determined that petitioner's continued employment was not "clearly consistent with the interests of national security" and ordered the termination of his employment. . . .

The Act authorizes dismissals only upon a determination by the Secretary that the dismissal is "necessary or advisable in the interest of the national security." That determination requires an evaluation of the risk of injury to the "national security" that the employee's retention would create, which in turn would seem necessarily to be a function not only of the character of the employee and the likelihood of his misconducting himself, but also of the nature of the position he occupies and its relationship to the "national security." That is, it must be determined whether the position is one in which the employee's misconduct would affect the "national security." That of course would not be necessary if "national security" were used in the Act in a sense so broad as to be involved in *all* activities of the Government, for then the relationship to the "national security" would follow from the very fact of employment. For the reasons set forth below, however, we conclude (1) that the term "national security" is used in the Act in a definite and limited sense and relates only to those activities which are directly concerned with the Nation's safety, as distinguished from the general welfare; and (2) that no determination has been made that petitioner's position was affected with the "national security" as that term is used in the Act. It follows that his dismissal was not authorized by the 1950 Act.

As noted above, the issue turns on the meaning of "national security" as used in the Act. While that term is not defined in the Act, we think it clear from the statute as a whole that that term was intended to comprehend only those activities of the Government that are directly concerned with the protection of the Nation from internal subversion or foreign aggression, and not those which contribute to the strength of the Nation only through their impact on the general welfare.

Virtually conclusive of this narrow meaning of "national security" is the fact that had Congress intended the term in a sense broad enough to include all activities of the Government, it would have granted the power to terminate employment "in the interest of the national security" to all agencies of the Government. Instead, Congress specified 11 named agencies to which the Act should apply, the character of which reveals, without doubt, a purpose to single out those agencies which are directly concerned with the national defense and which have custody over information the compromise of which might endanger the country's security, the so-called "sensitive" agencies. Thus, of the 11 named agencies, 8 are concerned with military operations or weapons development, and the other 3, with international relations, internal security, and the stock-piling of strategic materials. . . .

It is clear, therefore, both from the face of the Act and the legislative history, that "national security" was not used in the Act in an all-inclusive sense but was intended to refer only to the protection of "sensitive" activities. It follows that an employee can be dismissed "in the interest of the national security" under the Act only if he occupies a "sensitive" position, and thus that a condition precedent to the exercise of the dismissal authority is a determination by the agency head that the position occupied is one affected with the "national security." . . .

From our holdings (1) that not all positions in the Government are affected with the "national security" as that term is used in the 1950 Act and (2) that no determination has been made that petitioner's position was one in which he could adversely affect the "national security," it necessarily follows that petitioner's discharge was not authorized by the 1950 Act. . . . Since petitioner's discharge was not authorized by the 1950 Act and hence violated the Veterans' Preference Act, the judgment of the Court of Appeals is reversed and the case is remanded to the District Court for further proceedings not inconsistent with this opinion.

Reversed and remanded.

616. PENNSYLVANIA v. NELSON
350 U.S. 497
1956

This case tested the validity of the sedition acts of Pennsylvania and several other states. The Court declared that the defense of the federal government from sedition was properly a function of the federal government rather than the states, and concluded that since Congress had preempted the field with a whole series of laws, the sedition acts of the various states were void. For an earlier example of this reasoning, see *Prigg* v. *Pennsylvania,* Doc. No. 158. See Hunt, "Federal Supremacy and State Legislation," 53 *Michigan Law Rev.* 407.

Appeal from the decision of the Pennsylvania State Supreme Court.

WARREN, C. J. The respondent Steve Nelson, an acknowledged member of the Communist Party, was convicted in the Court of Quarter Sessions of Allegheny County, Pennsylvania, of a violation of the Pennsylvania Sedition Act and sentenced to imprisonment for twenty years and to a fine of $10,000 and to costs of prosecution in the sum of $13,000. The Superior Court affirmed the conviction. 172 Pa.Super. 125. The Supreme Court of Pennsylvania, recognizing but not reaching many alleged serious trial errors and conduct of the trial court infringing upon respondent's right to due process of law, decided the case on the narrow issue of supersession of the state law by the Federal Smith Act. In its opinion, the court stated:

"And, while the Pennsylvania statute proscribes sedition against either the Government of the United States or the Government of Pennsylvania, it is only alleged sedition against the United States with which the instant case is concerned. Out of all the voluminous testimony, we have not found, nor has anyone pointed to, a single word indicating a seditious act or even utterance directed against the Government of Pennsylvania."

The precise holding of the court, and all that is before us for review, is that the Smith Act of 1940, as amended in 1948, which prohibits the knowing advocacy of the overthrow of the Government of the United States by force and violence, supersedes the enforceability of the Pennsylvania Sedition Act which proscribes the same conduct. . . .

Where, as in the instant case, Congress has not stated specifically whether a federal statute has occupied a field in which the States are otherwise free to legislate, differ-

ent criteria have furnished touchstones for decision. Thus,

"[t]his Court, in considering the validity of state laws in the light of . . . federal laws touching the same subject, has made use of the following expressions: conflicting; contrary to; occupying the field; repugnance; difference; irreconcilability; inconsistency; violation; curtailment; and interference. But none of these expressions provides an infallible constitutional test or an exclusive constitutional yardstick. In the final analysis, there can be no one crystal clear distinctly marked formula." Hines v. Davidowitz. 312 U.S. 52, 67, 61.

And see Rice v. Santa Fe Elevator Corp., 331 U.S. 218, 230–321. In this case, we think that each of several tests of supersession is met.

First, "[t]he scheme of federal regulation [is] so pervasive as to make reasonable the inference that Congress left no room for the States to supplement it." Rice v. Santa Fe Elevator Corp., 331 U.S. at page 230. The Congress determined in 1940 that it was necessary for it to reenter the field of antisubversive legislation, which had been abandoned by it in 1921. In that year, it enacted the Smith Act which proscribes advocacy of the overthrow of any government—federal, state or local—by force and violence and organization of and knowing membership in a group which so advocates. Conspiracy to commit any of these acts is punishable under the general criminal conspiracy provisions in 18 U.S.C. § 371, 18 U.S.C.A. § 371. The Internal Security Act of 1950 is aimed more directly at Communist organizations. It distinguishes between "Communist-action organizations" and "Communist-front organizations," requiring such organizations to register and to file annual reports with the Attorney General giving complete details as to their officers and funds. Members of Communist-action organizations who have not been registered by their organization must register as individuals. Failure to register in accordance with the requirements of Sections 786–787 is punishable by a fine of not more than $10,000 for an offending organization and by a fine of not more than $10,000 or imprisonment for not more than five years or both for an individual offender—each day of failure to register constituting a separate offense. And the Act imposes certain sanctions upon both "action" and "front" organizations and their members. The Communist Control Act of 1954 declares "that the Communist Party of the United States, although purportedly a political party, is in fact an instrumentality of a conspiracy to overthrow the Government of the United States" and that "its role as the agency of a hostile foreign power renders its existence a clear present and continuing danger to the security of the United States." It also contains a legislative finding that the Communist Party is a " 'Communist-action' organization" within the meaning of the Internal Security Act of 1950 and provides that "knowing" members of the Communist Party are "subject to all the provisions and penalties" of that Act. It furthermore sets up a new classification of "Communist-infiltrated organizations" and provides for the imposition of sanctions against them.

We examine these Acts only to determine the congressional plan. Looking to all of them in the aggregate, the conclusion is inescapable that Congress has intended to occupy the field of sedition. Taken as a whole, they evince a congressional plan which makes it reasonable to determine that no room has been left for the States to supplement it. Therefore, a state sedition statute is superseded regardless of whether it purports to supplement the federal law. As was said by Mr. Justice Holmes in Charlestown & Western Carolina R. Co. v. Varnville Furniture Co., 237 U.S. 597, 604.

"When Congress has taken the particular subject-matter in hand, coincidence is as ineffective as opposition, and a state law is not to be declared a help because it attempts to go farther than Congress has seen fit to go."

Second, the federal statutes "touch a field in which the federal interest is so dominant that the federal system [must] be assumed to preclude enforcement of state laws on the same subject." Rice v. Santa Fe Elevator Corp., 331 U.S. at page 230, citing Hines v. Davidowitz, supra. Congress has devised an all embracing program for resistance to the various forms of totalitarian aggression. Our external defenses have been strengthened, and a plan to protect against internal subversion has been made by it. It has appropriated vast sums, not only for our own protection, but also to strengthen freedom throughout the world. It has charged the Federal Bureau of Investigation and the Central Intelligence Agency with responsibility for intelligence concerning Communist seditious activities against our Government, and has denominated such activities as part of a world conspiracy. It accordingly proscribed sedition against all government in the nation—national, state and local. Congress declared that these steps were taken "to provide for the common defense, to preserve the sovereignty of the United States as an independent nation, and to guarantee to each State a republican form of government. . . . Congress having thus treated seditious conduct as a matter of vital national concern, it is in no sense a local enforcement problem. As was said in the court below:

"Sedition against the United States is not a *local* offense. It is a crime against the *Nation*. As such, it should be prosecuted and punished in the Federal courts where this defendant has in fact been prosecuted and convicted and is now under sentence. It is not only important but vital that such prosecutions should be exclusively within the control of the Federal Government. . . ."

Third, enforcement of state sedition acts presents a serious danger of conflict with the administration of the federal program. . . .

In his brief, the Solicitor General states that forty-two States plus Alaska and Hawaii have statutes which in some form prohibit advocacy of the violent overthrow of established government. These statutes are entitled anti-sedition statutes, criminal anarchy laws, criminal syndicalist laws, etc. Although all of them are primarily directed against the overthrow of the United States Government, they are in no sense uniform. And our attention has not been called to any case where the prosecution has been successfully directed against an attempt to destroy state or local government. Some of these Acts are studiously drawn and purport to protect fundamental rights by appropriate definitions, standards of proof and orderly procedures in keeping with the avowed congressional purpose "to protect freedom from those who would destroy it, without infringing upon the freedom of all our people." Others are vague and are almost wholly without such safeguards. Some even purport to punish mere membership in subversive organizations which the federal statutes do not punish where federal registration requirements have been fulfilled.

When we were confronted with a like situation in the field of labor-management relations, Mr. Justice Jackson wrote:

"A multiplicity of tribunals and a diversity of procedures are quite as apt to produce incompatible or conflicting adjudications as are different rules of substantive law."

Should the States be permitted to exercise a concurrent jurisdiction in this area, federal enforcement would encounter not only the difficulties mentioned by Mr. Justice Jackson, but the added conflict engendered by different criteria of substantive offenses.

Since we find that Congress has occupied the field to the exclusion of parallel state legislation, that the dominant interest of the Federal Government precludes state intervention, and that administration of state Acts would conflict with the operation of the federal plan, we are convinced that the decision of the Supreme Court of Pennsylvania is unassailable.

We are not unmindful of the risk of compounding punishments which would be created by finding concurrent state power. In our view of the case, we do not reach the question whether double or multiple punishment for the same overt acts directed against the United States has constitutional sanction. Without compelling indication to the contrary, we will not assume that Congress intended to permit the possibility of double punishment. Cf. Houston v. Moore, 5 Wheat. 1, 31, 75; Jerome v. United States, 318 U.S. 101, 105.

The judgment of the Supreme Court of Pennsylvania is affirmed.

Affirmed.

Justices Reed, Burton, and Minton dissenting.

617. SOUTHERN DECLARATION ON INTEGRATION
March 12, 1956
(*New York Times,* March 12, 1956)

In the second *Brown* v. *Board of Education* decision (349 U.S. 294) the Court directed that integration proceed "with all deliberate speed." In the event, the deliberateness was far more conspicuous than the speed. Though there was at first some disposition to acquiesce in the judicial mandate, opposition grew and hardened. Hastily organized White Citizens Councils conspired to frustrate the operation of the *Brown* decision. On March 12 ninety-six Southern Congressmen—it was practically unanimous—issued a Declaration denouncing the Supreme Court decision as a violation of the Constitution and calling on their states to refuse obedience to it, and pledging themselves to resist it "by all lawful means." See A. P. Blaustein and C. C. Ferguson, *Desegregation and the Law;* Sutherland, "The American Judiciary and Racial Segregation" 20 *Modern Law Rev.* 201; B. M. Ziegler, ed., *Segregation and the Supreme Court;* H. H. Hyman and P. B. Sheatsley, "Attitudes toward Desegration," 195 *Scientific American* 35; J. F. Byrnes, "The Supreme Court Must Be Curbed," *U.S. News and World Report,* May 18, 1956; R. B. McKay, "With All Deliberate Speed," 31 *N.Y.U. Law Rev.* 991; and R. McKay, "With All Deliberate Speed: Legislative Reaction and Judicial Development, 1956–57," 43 *Virginia Law Rev.* 1205; A. Bickel "The Original Understanding and the Segregation Decision," 69 *Harvard Law Rev.* 1; C. V. Woodward, *Strange Career of Jim Crow.*

We regard the decision of the Supreme Court in the school cases as clear abuse of judicial power. It climaxes a trend in the Federal judiciary undertaking to legislate, in derogation of the authority of Congress, and to encroach upon the reserved rights of the states and the people.

The original Constitution does not mention education. Neither does the Fourteenth Amendment nor any other amendment. The debates preceding the submission of the Fourteenth Amendment clearly show that there was no intent that it should affect the systems of education maintained by the states.

The very Congress which proposed the amendment subsequently provided for segregated schools in the District of Columbia.

When the amendment was adopted in 1868, there were thirty-seven states of the Union. Every one of the twenty-six states that had any substantial racial differences among its people either approved the operation of segregated schools already in existence or subsequently established such schools by action of the same law-making body which considered the Fourteenth Amendment.

As admitted by the Supreme Court in the public school case (Brown v. Board of Education), the doctrine of separate but equal schools "apparently originated in Roberts v. City of Boston (1849), upholding school segregation against attack as being violative of a state constitutional guarantee of equality." This constitutional doctrine began in the North—not in the South—and it was followed not only in Massachusetts, but in Connecticut, New York, Illinois, Indiana, Michigan, Minnesota, New Jersey, Ohio, Pennsylvania and other northern states until they, exercising their rights as states through the constitutional processes of local self-government, changed their school systems.

In the case of Plessy v. Ferguson in 1896 the Supreme Court expressly declared that under the Fourteenth Amendment no person was denied any of his rights if the states provided separate but equal public facilities. This decision has been followed in many other cases. It is notable that the Supreme Court, speaking through Chief Justice Taft, a former President of the United States, unanimously declared in 1927 in Lum v. Rice that the "separate but equal" principle is ". . . within the discretion of the state in regulating its public schools and does not conflict with the Fourteenth Amendment."

This interpretation, restated time and again, became a part of the life of the people of many of the states and confirmed their habits, customs, traditions and way of life. It is founded on elemental humanity and common sense, for parents should not be deprived by Government of the right to direct the lives and education of their own children.

Though there has been no constitutional amendment or act of Congress changing this established legal principle almost a century old, the Supreme Court of the United States, with no legal basis for such action, undertook to exercise their naked judicial power and substituted their personal political and social ideas for the established law of the land.

This unwarranted exercise of power by the court, contrary to the Constitution, is creating chaos and confusion in the states principally affected. It is destroying the amicable relations between the white and Negro races that have been created through ninety years of patient effort by the good people of both races. It has planted hatred and suspicion where there has been heretofore friendship and understanding.

Without regard to the consent of the governed, outside agitators are threatening immediate and revolutionary changes in our public school systems. If done, this is certain to destroy the system of public education in some of the states.

With the gravest concern for the explosive and dangerous condition created by this decision and inflamed by outside meddlers:

We reaffirm our reliance on the Constitution as the fundamental law of the land.

We decry the Supreme Court's encroachments on rights reserved to the states and to the people, contrary to established law and to the Constitution.

We commend the motives of those states which have declared the intention to resist forced integration by any lawful means.

We appeal to the states and people who are not directly affected by these decisions to consider the constitutional principles involved against the time when they too, on issues vital to them, may be the victims of judicial encroachment.

Even though we constitute a minority in the present Congress, we have full faith that a majority of the American people believe in the dual system of government which has enabled us to achieve our greatness and will in time demand that the reserved rights of the states and of the people be made secure against judicial usurpation.

We pledge ourselves to use all lawful means to bring about a reversal of this decision which is contrary to the Constitution and to prevent the use of force in its implementation.

In this trying period, as we all seek to right this wrong, we appeal to our people not to be provoked by the agitators and troublemakers invading our states and to scrupulously refrain from disorder and lawless acts.

618. BUTLER v. MICHIGAN
352 U.S. 380
1957

This is the first major censorship case to reach the Supreme Court; while technically it addressed itself only to the issue of applying standards of what was fit for children to the whole realm of literature, its implications are wide. See Z. Chafee, *The Blessings of Liberty;* A. Meiklejohn, *Free Speech: and its Relation to Self Government;* W. Gellhorn, *Individual Freedom and Governmental Restraints,* ch. 2; M. L. Ernst and W. Seagle, *To the Pure;* M. Jahoda, *The Impact of Literature;* P. Blanshard, *The Right to Read;* F. Thayer, *Legal Control of the Press;* Lockhart and McClure, "Literature, the Law of Obscenity, and the Constitution," 38 *Minnesota Law Rev.* 295; Alpert, "Judicial Censorship of Obscene Literature" 52 *Harvard Law Rev.* 40; Z. Chafee, "Censorship of Books and Plays," 1 *Bill of Rights Rev.* 16.

FRANKFURTER, J. This appeal from a judgment of conviction entered by the Recorder's Court of the City of Detroit, Michigan, challenges the constitutionality of the following provision, § 343, of the Michigan Penal Code, Comp. Laws Supp. 1954, § 750.343:

"Any person who shall import, print, publish, sell, possess with the intent to sell, design, prepare, loan, give away, distribute or offer for sale, any book, magazine, newspaper, writing, pamphlet, ballad, printed paper, print, picture, drawing, photograph, publication or other thing, including any recordings, containing obscene, immoral, lewd or lascivious language, or obscene, immoral, lewd or lascivious prints, pictures, figures or descriptions, tending to incite minors to violent or depraved or immoral acts, manifestly tending to the corruption of the morals of youth, or shall introduce into any family, school or place of education or shall buy, procure, receive or have in his possession, any such book, pamphlet, magazine, newspaper, writing, ballad, printed paper, print, picture, drawing, photograph, publication or other thing, either for the purpose of sale, exhibition, loan or circulation, or with intent to introduce the same into any family, school or place of education, shall be guilty of a misdemeanor."

Appellant was charged with its violation for selling to a police officer what the trial judge characterized as "a book containing obscene, immoral, lewd, lascivious language, or descriptions, tending to incite minors to violent or depraved or immoral acts, manifestly tending to the corruption of the morals of youth." Appellant moved to dismiss the proceeding on the claim that application of § 343 unduly restricted freedom of speech as protected by the Due Process Clause of the Fourteenth Amendment in that the statute (1) prohibited distribution of a book to the general public on the basis of the undesirable influence it may have upon youth; (2) damned a book and proscribed its sale merely because of some isolated passages that appeared objectionable when divorced from the book as a whole; and (3) failed to provide a sufficiently definite standard of guilt. After hearing the evidence, the trial judge denied the motion, and, in an oral opinion, held that "the defendant is guilty because he sold a book in the City of Detroit containing this language [the passages deemed offensive], and also because the

Court feels that even viewing the book as a whole, it [the objectionable language] was not necessary to the proper development of the theme of the book nor of the conflict expressed therein." Appellant was fined $100. . . .

It is clear on the record that appellant was convicted because Michigan, by § 343, made it an offense for him to make available for the general reading public (and he in fact sold to a police officer) a book that the trial judge found to have a potentially deleterious influence upon youth. The State insists that, by thus quarantining the general reading public against books not too rugged for grown men and women in order to shield juvenile innocence, it is exercising its power to promote the general welfare. Surely, this is to burn the house to roast the pig. Indeed, the Solicitor General of Michigan has, with characteristic candor, advised the Court that Michigan has a statute specifically designed to protect its children against obscene matter "tending to the corruption of the morals of youth." But the appellant was not convicted for violating this statute.

We have before us legislation not reasonably restricted to the evil with which it is said to deal. The incidence of this enactment is to reduce the adult population of Michigan to reading only what is fit for children. It thereby arbitrarily curtails one of those liberties of the individual, now enshrined in the Due Process Clause of the Fourteenth Amendment, that history has attested as the indispensable conditions for the maintenance and progress of a free society. We are constrained to reverse this conviction.

Reversed.

619.   EISENHOWER ADDRESS ON AMERICAN POLICY IN THE MIDDLE EAST
February 20, 1957
(*New York Times,* February 21, 1957)

Bowing to American pressure and world opinion, Great Britain and France evacuated their troops from Egyptian territory at the end of 1956. See Doc. No. 620. Israeli troops were withdrawn from all occupied territory except the Gulf of Aqaba and the Gaza strip, which had been used by Egypt for hostile acts against Israel. President Eisenhower assured the Israelis that the United States would support efforts to prevent the resumption of hostile acts by Egypt if Israel would withdraw her troops from these two areas. This commitment became binding when Israel complied with the President's request. The exact character of the commitment however, was clouded in semantic ambiguity. See "United States Policy in the Middle East Sept. 1956–June 1957: Documents," Dept. of State Publication 6505.

I come to you again to talk about the situation in the Middle East. The future of the United Nations and peace in the Middle East may be at stake.

In the four months since I talked to you about the crisis in that area, the United Nations has made considerable progress in resolving some of the difficult problems. We are now, however, faced with a fateful moment as the result of the failure of Israel to withdraw its forces behind the Armistice lines, as contemplated by the United Nations Resolutions on this subject. . . .

When I talked to you last October, I pointed out that the United States fully realized that military action against Egypt resulted from grave and repeated provocations. But also I said that the use of military force to solve international disputes could not be reconciled with the principles and purposes of the United Nations, to which we had all subscribed. I added that our country could not believe that resort to force and war would for long serve the permanent interests of the attacking nations, which were Britain, France and Israel.

So I pledged that the United States would seek through the United Nations to end the conflict and to bring about a recall of the forces of invasion, and then make a renewed and earnest effort through that organization to secure justice, under international law, for all of the parties concerned.

Since that time much has been achieved and many of the dangers implicit in the situation have been avoided. The governments of Britain and France have withdrawn their forces from Egypt. Thereby they showed respect for the opinions of mankind as expressed almost unanimously by the eighty-nation members of the United Nations General Assembly. . . .

The Prime Minister of Israel, in answer to a personal communication, assured me early in November that Israel would willingly withdraw its forces if and when there should be created a United Nations force to move into the Suez Canal area. This force was, in fact, created and has moved into the canal area.

Subsequently, Israel forces were withdrawn from much of the territory of Egypt which they had occupied. However, Israeli forces still remain outside the armistice lines, notably at the mouth of the Gulf of Aqaba which is about 100 miles from the nearest Israeli territory and in the Gaza Strip which, by the armistice agreement, was to be occupied by Egypt. This fact creates the present crisis. . . .

In view of the valued friendly relations which the United States has always had with the state of Israel, I wrote to Prime Minister Ben-Gurion on Feb. 3. I recalled his statement to me of Nov. 8 to the effect that the Israeli forces would be withdrawn under certain conditions, and I urged that, in view of the General Assembly resolutions of Feb. 2, Israel should complete that withdrawal.

However, the Prime Minister, in his reply, took the position that Israel would not evacuate its military forces from the Gaza Strip unless Israel retained the civil administration and police. This would be in contradiction to the armistice agreement. Also, the reply said that Israel would not withdraw from the Straits of Aqaba unless freedom of passage through the straits was assured.

It was a matter of keen disappointment to us that the Government of Israel, despite the United Nations action, still felt unwilling to withdraw.

However, in a further effort to meet the views of Israel in these respects, Secretary of State Dulles, at my direction, gave to the Government of Israel on Feb. 11 a statement of United States policy. This has now been made public. It pointed out that neither the United States nor the United Nations had authority to impose upon the parties a substantial modification of the Armistice agreement which was freely signed by Israel and Egypt. Nevertheless, the statement said, the United States as a member of the United Nations would seek such disposition of the United Nations Emergency Force as would assure that the Gaza Strip could no longer be a source of armed infiltration and reprisals.

The Secretary of State orally informed the Israeli Ambassador that the United States would be glad to urge and support, also, some participation by the United Nations, with the approval of Egypt, in the administration of the Gaza Strip. The principal population of the strip consists of about 300,000 Arab refugees, who exist largely as a charge upon the benevolence of the United Nations and its members.

With reference to the passage into and through the Gulf of Aqaba, we expressed the conviction that the gulf constitutes international waters and that no nation has the right to prevent free and innocent passage in the gulf. We announced that the United States was prepared to exercise this right itself and to join with others to secure general recognition of this right. . . .

We should not assume that if Israel withdraws, Egypt will prevent Israeli shipping from using the Suez Canal or the Gulf of Aqaba. If, unhappily, Egypt does hereafter violate the Armistice agreement or other international obligation, then this should be dealt with firmly by the society of nations.

The present moment is a grave one, but we are hopeful that reason and right will prevail. Since the events of last October and November, solid progress has been made, in conformity with the Charter of the United Nations. There is the cease-fire, the forces of Britain and France have been withdrawn, the forces of Israel have been partially withdrawn, and the clearing of the Canal nears completion. When Israel completes its withdrawal, it will have removed a definite block to further progress.

Once this block is removed, there will be serious and creative tasks for the United Nations to perform. There needs to be respect for the right of Israel to national existence and to internal development. Complicated provisions insuring the effective international use of the Suez Canal will need to be worked out in detail. The Arab refugee problem must be solved. As I said in my special message to Congress on Jan. 5, it must be made certain that all the Middle East is kept free from aggression and infiltration.

Finally, all who cherish freedom, including

ourselves, should help the nations of the Middle East achieve their just aspirations for improving the well-being of their peoples.

What I have spoken about tonight is only one step in a long process calling for patience and diligence, but at this moment it is the critical issue on which future progress depends.

It is an issue which can be solved if only we will apply the principles of the United Nations.

That is why, my fellow Americans, I know you want the United States to continue to use its maximum influence to sustain those principles as the world's best hope for peace.

620. THE EISENHOWER DOCTRINE
March 9, 1957
(Public Law 7, 85th Congress)

The Suez crisis of 1956–57 created a situation which appeared to be highly favorable to Communist infiltration or overt attack. After persuading Britain, France, and Israel to withdraw their forces from Egyptian territory, President Eisenhower turned his attention to the larger problem of protecting the Middle East from Communist attack. The President asked for authority to send financial and military aid, at his discretion, to any Middle Eastern country threatened by Communist aggression. Congress endorsed the proposal for economic aid and modified the proposal dealing with military aid. Compare this doctrine with the Truman Doctrine, Doc. No. 575. See J. C. Hurewitz, *Middle East Dilemmas;* J. C. Campbell, "From 'Doctrine' to Policy in the Middle East," 35 *Foreign Affairs* 441.

Resolved, That the President be and hereby is authorized to cooperate with and assist any nation or group of nations in the general area of the Middle East desiring such assistance in the development of economic strength dedicated to the maintenance of national independence.

SEC. 2. The President is authorized to undertake, in the general area of the Middle East, military assistance programs with any

nation or group of nations of that area desiring such assistance. Furthermore, the United States regards as vital to the national interest and world peace the preservation of the independence and integrity of the nations of the Middle East. To this end, if the President determines the necessity thereof, the United States is prepared to use armed force to assist any such nation or group of nations requesting assistance against armed aggression from any country controlled by international communism: *Provided,* That such employment shall be consonant with the treaty obligations of the United States and with the Constitution of the United States.

SEC. 3. The President is hereby authorized to use during the balance of the fiscal year 1957 for economic and military assistance under this joint resolution not to exceed $200,000,000 from any appropriation now available for carrying out the provisions of the Mutual Security Act of 1954. . . .

SEC. 4. The President should continue to furnish facilities and military assistance, within the provisions of applicable law and established policies, to the United Nations Emergency Force in the Middle East, with a view to maintaining the truce in that region.

SEC. 5. The President shall within the

months of January and July of each year report to the Congress his action hereunder.

SEC. 6. This joint resolution shall expire when the President shall determine that the peace and security of the nations in the general area of the Middle East are reason-ably assured by international conditions created by action of the United Nations or otherwise except that it may be terminated earlier by a concurrent resolution of the two Houses of Congress.

621. EISENHOWER'S ADDRESS ON THE SITUATION IN LITTLE ROCK
September 24, 1957
(Public Papers of the Presidents: Dwight D. Eisenhower, 1957, no. 198)

With the passing of time, Southern resistance to desegregation grew and became "massive." Within a few months, in 1956, five Southern states adopted forty-two segregation measures. Georgia made it a felony for any school official to spend tax money for public schools in which the races were mixed; Mississippi made it a crime for any organization to institute desegregation proceedings in the state courts; Virginia went to the extreme of closing some of her public schools altogether. State resistance came to a head in Arkansas. In the late summer of 1957 Governor Orville Faubus called out the state National Guard under orders not to protect Negro children in their right to attend school, but to prevent them from exercising that right. These troops were withdrawn on order of the federal district judge. Mobs, aided and abetted by the local authorities, then prevented Negroes from entering the local high school. On September 24, President Eisenhower dispatched federal troops to Little Rock to preserve order and at the same time he addressed the nation on this subject. The people of Arkansas responded by reelecting Faubus to the governorship, and Faubus persisted in his tactics of obstruction until the following year. Eventually order was restored, the troops withdrawn, and token desegregation took place. See A. T. Mason and W. M. Beaney, *The Supreme Court in a Free Society;* C. V. Woodward, *The Strange Career of Jim Crow;* C. S. Mangum, *The Legal Status of the Negro;* H. Ashmore, *The Negro and the Schools;* W. Peters, *The Southern Temper;* D. Shoemaker, ed., *With All Deliberate Speed;* A. Blaustein and C. Ferguson, *Desegregation and the Law;* B. Ziegler, *Desegregation and the Supreme Court.*

My Fellow Citizens. . . . I must speak to you about the serious situation that has arisen in Little Rock. . . . In that city, under the leadership of demagogic extremists, disorderly mobs have deliberately prevented the carrying out of proper orders from a federal court. Local authorities have not eliminated that violent opposition and, under the law, I yesterday issued a proclamation calling upon the mob to disperse.

This morning the mob again gathered in front of the Central High School of Little Rock, obviously for the purpose of again preventing the carrying out of the court's order relating to the admission of Negro children to that school.

Whenever normal agencies prove inadequate to the task and it becomes necessary for the executive branch of the federal government to use its powers and authority to uphold federal courts, the President's responsibility is inescapable.

In accordance with that responsibility, I have today issued an Executive Order directing the use of troops under federal authority to aid in the execution of federal law at Little Rock, Arkansas. This became necessary when my Proclamation of yesterday was not observed, and the obstruction of justice still continues.

It is important that the reasons for my action be understood by all our citizens.

As you know, the Supreme Court of the United States has decided that separate public educational facilities for the races are inherently unequal and therefore compulsory school segregation laws are unconstitutional. . . .

During the past several years, many communities in our southern states have instituted public school plans for gradual progress in the enrollment and attendance of school children of all races in order to bring themselves into compliance with the law of the land.

They thus demonstrated to the world that we are a nation in which laws, not men, are supreme.

I regret to say that this truth—the cornerstone of our liberties—was not observed in this instance. . . .

Here is the sequence of events in the development of the Little Rock school case.

In May of 1955, the Little Rock School Board approved a moderate plan for the gradual desegregation of the public schools in that city. It provided that a start toward integration would be made at the present term in the high school, and that the plan would be in full operation by 1963. . . . Now this Little Rock plan was challenged in the courts by some who believed that the period of time as proposed in the plan was too long.

The United States Court at Little Rock, which has supervisory responsibility under the law for the plan of desegregation in the public schools, dismissed the challenge, thus approving a gradual rather than an abrupt change from the existing system. The court found that the school board had acted in good faith in planning for a public school system free from racial discrimination.

Since that time, the court has on three separate occasions issued orders directing that the plan be carried out. All persons were instructed to refrain from interfering with the efforts of the school board to comply with the law.

Proper and sensible observance of the law then demanded the respectful obedience which the nation has a right to expect from all its people. This, unfortunately, has not been the case at Little Rock. Certain misguided persons, many of them imported into Little Rock by agitators, have insisted upon defying the law and have sought to bring it into disrepute. The orders of the court have thus been frustrated.

The very basis of our individual rights and freedoms rests upon the certainty that the President and the Executive Branch of Government will support and insure the carrying out of the decisions of the federal courts,

even, when necessary, with all the means at the President's command. . . .

Mob rule cannot be allowed to override the decisions of our courts.

Now, let me make it very clear that federal troops are not being used to relieve local and state authorities of their primary duty to preserve the peace and order of the community. . . .

The proper use of the powers of the Executive Branch to enforce the orders of a federal court is limited to extraordinary and compelling circumstances. Manifestly, such an extreme situation has been created in Little Rock. This challenge must be met and with such measures as will preserve to the people as a whole their lawfully protected rights in a climate permitting their free and fair exercise.

The overwhelming majority of our people in every section of the country are united in their respect for observance of the law— even in those cases where they may disagree with that law. . . .

A foundation of our American way of life is our national respect for law.

In the South, as elsewhere, citizens are keenly aware of the tremendous disservice that has been done to the people of Arkansas in the eyes of the nation, and that has been done to the nation in the eyes of the world.

At a time when we face grave situations abroad because of the hatred that communism bears toward a system of government based on human rights, it would be difficult to exaggerate the harm that is being done to the prestige and influence, and indeed to the safety, of our nation and the world.

Our enemies are gloating over this incident and using it everywhere to misrepresent our whole nation. We are portrayed as a violator of those standards of conduct which the peoples of the world united to proclaim in the Charter of the United Nations. There they affirmed "faith in fundamental human rights" and "in the dignity and worth of the human person" and they did so "without distinction as to race, sex, language or religion."

And so, with deep confidence, I call upon the citizens of the State of Arkansas to assist in bringing to an immediate end all interference with the law and its processes. If resistance to the federal court orders ceases at once, the further presence of federal troops will be unnecessary and the City of Little Rock will return to its normal habits of peace and order and a blot upon the fair name and high honor of our nation in the world will be removed.

Thus will be restored the image of America and of all its parts as one nation, indivisible, with liberty and justice for all.

622. YATES v. UNITED STATES
354 U.S. 298 at 339
1957

Appeal from U.S. District Court for Southern District of California. This case, involving the alleged violation of the terms of the Smith Act by fourteen members of the Communist Party, qualified the *Dennis* decision in important particulars. We give here not the opinion of the Court, through Justice Harlan, but the concurring opinion by Justices Black and Douglas, which covers somewhat broader ground more briefly. See references for Doc. No. 593, and A. Meiklejohn, *Free Speech and Its Relation to Self-Government;* Richardson, "Freedom of Expression and the Functions of the Courts," 65 *Harvard Law Rev.* 1.

Mr. Justice BLACK, with whom Mr. Justice DOUGLAS joins, concurring in part and dissenting in part:

I would reverse every one of these convictions and direct that all the defendants be acquitted. In my judgment the statutory provisions on which these prosecutions are based abridge freedom of speech, press, and assembly in violation of the First Amendment to the United States Constitution. See my dissent and that of Mr. Justice Douglas in Dennis v. United States, 341 U.S. 494, 579. Also see my opinion in American Communications Ass'n, C. I. O. v. Douds, 339 U.S. 382, 445.

The kind of trials conducted here are wholly dissimilar to normal criminal trials. Ordinarily these "Smith Act" trials are prolonged affairs lasting for months. In part this is attributable to the routine introduction in evidence of massive collections of books, tracts, pamphlets, newspapers, and manifestoes discussing communism, socialism, capitalism, feudalism and governmental institutions in general, which, it is not too much to say, are turgid, diffuse, abstruse, and just plain dull. Of course, no juror can or is expected to plow his way through this jungle of verbiage. The testimony of witnesses is comparatively insignificant. Guilt or innocence may turn on what Marx or Engels or someone else wrote or advocated as much as a hundred or more years ago. Elaborate, refined distinctions are drawn between "communism," "Marxism," "Leninism," "Trotskyism," and "Stalinism." When the propriety of obnoxious or unorthodox views about government is in reality made the crucial issue, as it must be in cases of this kind, prejudice makes conviction inevitable except in the rarest circumstances.

Since the Court proceeds on the assumption that the statutory provisions involved are valid, however, I feel free to express my views about the issues it considers. . . .

I agree with the Court insofar as it holds that the trial judge erred in instructing that persons could be punished under the Smith Act for teaching and advocating forceful overthrow as an abstract principle. But on the other hand, I cannot agree that the instruction which the Court indicates it might approve is constitutionally permissible. The Court says that persons can be punished for advocating action to overthrow the Government by force and violence, where those to whom the advocacy is addressed are urged "to *do* something, now or in the future, rather than merely to *believe* in something." Under the Court's approach, defendants could still be convicted simply for agreeing to talk as distinguished from agreeing to act. I believe that the First Amendment forbids Congress to punish people for talking about public affairs, whether or not such discussion incites to action, legal or illegal. As the Virginia Assembly said in 1785, in its "Statute for Religious Liberty," written by Thomas Jefferson, "it is time enough for the rightful purposes of civil government, for its officers to interfere when principles break out into overt acts against peace and good order." . . .

The section under which this conspiracy indictment was brought, requires proof of an overt act done "to effect the object of the conspiracy." Originally, 11 such overt acts were charged here. These 11 have now dwindled to 2, and as the Court says:

"Each was a public meeting held under Party auspices at which speeches were made by one or more of the petitioners extolling leaders of the Soviet Union and criticizing various aspects of the foreign policy of the United States. At one of the meetings an appeal for funds was made. Petitioners contend that these meetings do not satisfy the requirement of the statute that there be shown an act done by one of the conspirators 'to effect the object of the conspiracy.' The Government concedes that nothing unlawful was shown to have been said or done at these meetings, but contends that these occurrences nonetheless sufficed as overt acts under the jury's findings."

The Court holds that attendance at these lawful and orderly meetings constitutes an "overt act" sufficient to meet the statutory requirements. I disagree.

The requirement of proof of an overt act in conspiracy cases is no mere formality, particularly in prosecutions like these which in many respects are akin to trials for treason. Article III, Sect. 3, of the Constitution provides that "No Person shall be convicted of Treason unless on the Testimony of two Witnesses to the same overt Act, or on Confession in open Court." One of the objects of this provision was to keep people from being convicted of disloyalty to government during periods of excitement when passions and prejudices ran high, merely because they expressed "unacceptable" views. See Cramer v. United States, 325 U.S. 1, 48. The same reasons that make proof of overt acts so important in treason cases apply here. The only overt act which is now charged against these defendants is that they went to a constitutionally protected public assembly where they took part in lawful discussion of public questions, and where neither they nor anyone else advocated or suggested overthrow of the United States Government. Many years ago this Court said that "The very idea of a government, republican in form, implies a right on the part of its citizens to meet peaceably for consultation in respect to public affairs and to petition for a redress of grievances." United States v. Cruikshank, 92 U.S. 542. In my judgment defendants' attendance at these public meetings cannot be viewed as an overt act to effectuate the object of the conspiracy charged.

In essence, petitioners were tried upon the charge that they believe in and want to foist upon this country a different and to us a despicable form of authoritarian government in which voices criticizing the existing order are summarily silenced. I fear that the present type of prosecutions are more in line with the philosophy of authoritarian government than with that expressed by our First Amendment.

Doubtlessly, dictators have to stamp out causes and beliefs which they deem subversive to their evil regimes.

But governmental suppression of causes and beliefs seems to me to be the very antithesis of what our Constitution stands for. The choice expressed in the First Amendment in favor of free expression was made against a turbulent background by men such as Jefferson, Madison, and Mason—men who believed that loyalty to the provisions of this Amendment was the best way to assure a long life for this new nation and its Government. Unless there is complete freedom for expression of all ideas, whether we like them or not, concerning the way government should be run and who shall run it, I doubt if any views in the long run can be secured against the censor. The First Amendment provides the only kind of security system that can preserve a free government— one that leaves the way wide open for people to favor, discuss, advocate, or incite causes and doctrines however obnoxious and antagonistic such views may be to the rest of us.

Mr. Justice CLARK dissented.

623. EISENHOWER ANNOUNCES DISPATCH OF U.S. TROOPS TO LEBANON
July 15, 1958
(Public Papers of the Presidents: Dwight D. Eisenhower, 1958, no. 171)

When in the spring of 1958 Syria and Egypt undertook to subvert the pro-Western government of Lebanon, President Chamoun appealed to the United Nations for help. The UN machinery worked slowly—or not at all—and when Iraq broke out in revolt, Chamoun turned directly to the United States for help. Eisenhower responded by ordering the Sixth Fleet to steam into the eastern Mediterranean and by dispatching eventually 14,000 Marines to Lebanon. An American proposal to turn the whole thing over to the United Nations was vetoed by the Soviet. When nearby Arab states agreed to refrain from intervention in Lebanon, and Chamoun agreed to retire, peace returned to the little country. In October, Eisenhower withdrew the Marines. See Doc. No. 620; C. Coon, *The Story of the Middle East;* Caractacus, *Revolution in Iraq;* J. C. Campbell, *Defense of the Middle East;* N. Ziadeh, *Syria and Lebanon;* W. Z. Laqueur, *The Soviet Union and the Middle East.*

Yesterday morning, I received from President Chamoun of Lebanon an urgent plea that some United States forces be stationed in Lebanon to help maintain security and to evidence the concern of the United States for the integrity and independence of Lebanon. President Chamoun's appeal was made with the concurrence of all the members of the Lebanese Cabinet.

President Chamoun made clear that he considered an immediate United States response imperative if Lebanon's independence, already menaced from without, were to be preserved in the face of the grave developments which occurred yesterday in Baghdad whereby the lawful government was violently overthrown and many of its members martyred.

In response to this appeal from the government of Lebanon, the United States has dispatched a contingent of United States forces to Lebanon to protect American lives and by their presence there to encourage the Lebanese government in defense of Lebanese sovereignty and integrity. These forces have not been sent as any act of war. They will demonstrate the concern of the United States for the independence and integrity of Lebanon, which we deem vital to the national interest and world peace. Our concern will also be shown by economic assistance. We shall act in accordance with these legitimate concerns.

The United States, this morning, will report its action to an emergency meeting of the United Nations Security Council. As the United Nations charter recognizes, there is an inherent right of collective self-defense. In conformity with the spirit of the charter, the United States is reporting the measures taken by it to the Security Council of the United Nations, making clear that these measures will be terminated as soon as the Security Council has itself taken the measures necessary to maintain international peace and security.

The United States believes that the United Nations can and should take measures which are adequate to preserve the independence and integrity of Lebanon. It is apparent, however, that in the face of the tragic and shocking events that are occurring nearby, more will be required than the team of United Nations observers now in Lebanon. Therefore, the United States will support in the United Nations measures which seem to be adequate to meet the new situation and which will enable the United States forces promptly to be withdrawn.

Lebanon is a small peace-loving state with which the United States has traditionally had the most friendly relations. There are in Lebanon about 2500 Americans and we cannot, consistently with our historic relations and with the principles of the United Nations, stand idly by when Lebanon appeals itself for evidence of our concern and when Lebanon may not be able to preserve internal order and to defend itself against indirect aggression.

624. NATIONAL DEFENSE EDUCATION ACT
September 2, 1958
(72 *U.S. Statutes at Large* 1580 ff. Public Law 85–864)

The "baby-bulge" of the forties, which brought additional millions of children to schools and colleges, the rising costs of education, and the rapid obsolescence of existing facilities, created an acute crisis in the decade of the fifties. As local school authorities found it difficult to raise enough money to do the job adequately, demand for federal aid became insistent. In 1947–48 the President's Commission on Higher Education proposed increased federal spending for higher education and in 1956 the President's Committee for the White House Conference on Education advocated an expanded program of federal support for primary and secondary education. President Eisenhower proposed a $2 billion school aid program in 1956, and President Kennedy asked for $3 billion in 1961, but such proposals invariably encountered strong opposition both from religious interests demanding aid for parochial schools and from states-rights conservatives who feared increasing federal control over education. At the college level, agreement was somewhat easier to achieve, and Congress in 1958 passed the National Defense Education Act, which was extended and broadened by subsequent acts of 1961, 1963, and 1964. The emphasis on science, readily apparent from the portions given below, reflected current alarm over Soviet successes in missile development—the "missile gap"—while the Communist disclaimer was a reminder that cold-war considerations gave an important impetus to the passage of this legislation. Later the scope of the program was broadened to include non-scientific subjects, and the Communist disclaimer was dropped.

TITLE I
GENERAL PROVISIONS

SEC. 101. The Congress hereby finds and declares that the security of the Nation requires the fullest development of the mental resources and technical skills of its young men and women. The present emergency demands that additional and more adequate educational opportunities be made available. The defense of this Nation depends upon the mastery of modern techniques developed from complex scientific principles. It depends as well upon the discovery and development of new principles, new techniques, and new knowledge.

We must increase our efforts to identify and educate more of the talent of our Nation. This requires programs that will give assurance that no student of ability will be denied an opportunity for higher education because of financial need; will correct as rapidly as possible the existing imbalances in our educational programs which have led to an insufficient proportion of our population educated in science, mathematics, and modern foreign languages and trained in technology.

The Congress reaffirms the principle and declares that the States and local communities have and must retain control over and primary responsibility for public education. The national interest requires, however, that the Federal Government give assistance to education for programs which are important to our defense.

To meet the present educational emergency requires additional effort at all levels of government. It is therefore the purpose of this Act to provide substantial assistance in various forms to individuals, and to States and their subdivisions, in order to insure trained manpower of sufficient quality and quantity to meet the national defense needs of the United States.

SEC. 102. Nothing contained in this Act shall be construed to authorize any department, agency, officer, or employee of the United States to exercise any direction, supervision, or control over the curriculum, program of instruction, administration, or personnel of any educational institution or school system.

TITLE II

Loans to Students in Institutions of Higher Education

Sec. 201. For the purpose of enabling the Commissioner to stimulate and assist in the establishment at institutions of higher education of funds for the making of low-interest loans to students in need thereof to pursue their courses of study in such institutions, there are hereby authorized to be appropriated $47,500,000 for the fiscal year ending June 30, 1959, $75,000,000 for the fiscal year ending June 30, 1960, $82,500,000 for the fiscal year ending June 30, 1961, $90,000,000 for the fiscal year ending June 30, 1962, and such sums for the fiscal year ending June 30, 1963, and each of the three succeeding fiscal years as may be necessary to enable students who have received a loan for any school year ending prior to July 1, 1962, to continue or complete their education. . . .

(b) In no case may the total of such Federal capital contributions to any institution of higher education for any fiscal year exceed $250,000.

Sec. 204. An agreement with any institution of higher education for Federal capital contributions by the Commissioner under this title shall—

(1) provide for establishment of a student loan fund by such institution; . . .

(4) provide that in the selection of students to receive loans from such student loan fund special consideration shall be given to (A) students with a superior academic background who express a desire to teach in elementary or secondary schools, and (B) students whose academic background indicates a superior capacity or preparation in science, mathematics, engineering, or a modern foreign language. . . .

Sec. 207. (a) Upon application by any institution of higher education with which he has made an agreement under this title, the Commissioner may make a loan to such institution for the purpose of helping to finance the institution's capital contributions to a student loan fund established pursuant to such agreement. . . .

TITLE III

Financial Assistance for Strengthening Science, Mathematics, and Modern Foreign Language Instruction

Sec. 301. There are hereby authorized to be appropriated $70,000,000 for the fiscal year ending June 30, 1959, and for each of the three succeeding fiscal years, for (1) making payments to State educational agencies under this title for the acquisition of equipment (suitable for use in providing education in science, mathematics, or modern foreign language) and . . . (2) making loans authorized in section 305. . . .

TITLE IV

National Defense Fellowships

Sec. 401. There are hereby authorized to be appropriated such sums as may be necessary to carry out the provisions of this title.

Sec. 402. During the fiscal year ending June 30, 1959, the Commissioner is authorized to award one thousand fellowships under the provisions of this title, and during each of the three succeeding fiscal years he is authorized to award one thousand five hundred such fellowships. Such fellowships shall be for periods of study not in excess of three academic years.

Sec. 403. (a) The Commissioner shall award fellowships under this title to individuals accepted for study in graduate programs approved by him under this section. The Commissioner shall approve a graduate program of an institution of higher education only upon application by the institution and only upon his finding:

(1) that such program is a new program or an existing program which has been expanded,

(2) that such new program or expansion of an existing program will substantially further the objective of increasing the facilities available in the Nation for the graduate training of college or univer-

sity level teachers and of promoting a wider geographical distribution of such facilities throughout the Nation, and

(3) that in the acceptance of persons for study in such programs preference will be given to persons interested in teaching in institutions of higher education.

SEC. 404 (a) Each person awarded a fellowship under the provisions of this title shall receive a stipend of $2,000 for the first academic year of study after the baccalaureate degree, $2,200 for the second such year, and $2,400 for the third such year, plus an additional amount of $400 for each such year on account of each of his dependents.

(b) In addition to the amounts paid to persons pursuant to subsection (a) there shall be paid to the institution of higher education at which each such person is pursuing his course of study such amount, not more than $2,500 per academic year, as is determined by the Commissioner to constitute that portion of the cost of the new graduate program or of the expansion in an existing graduate program in which such person is pursuing his course of study, which is reasonably attributable to him.

TITLE V

GUIDANCE, COUNSELING, AND TESTING; IDENTIFICATION AND ENCOURAGEMENT OF ABLE STUDENTS

SEC. 501. There are hereby authorized to be appropriated $15,000,000 for the fiscal

year ending June 30, 1959, and for each of the three succeeding fiscal years, for making grants to State educational agencies under this part to assist them to establish and maintain programs of testing and guidance and counseling. . . .

TITLE X

MISCELLANEOUS PROVISIONS

. . . (f) No part of any funds appropriated or otherwise made available for expenditure under authority of this Act shall be used to make payments or loans to any individual unless such individual (1) has executed and filed with the Commissioner an affidavit that he does not believe in, and is not a member of and does not support any organization that believes in or teaches, the overthrow of the United States Government by force or violence or by any illegal or unconstitutional methods, and (2) has taken and subscribed to an oath or affirmation in the following form: "I do solemnly swear (or affirm) that I will bear true faith and allegiance to the United States of America and will support and defend the Constitution and laws of the United States against all its enemies, foreign and domestic." The provisions of section 1001 of title 18, United States Code, shall be applicable with respect to such affidavits. . . .

625. NAACP v. ALABAMA
357 U.S. 449
1958

Appeal from the Supreme Court of Alabama. The NAACP had spearheaded the struggle for Negro rights in the South. One method whereby Southern whites fought back against the *Brown* decision and the new program for civil rights was a rash of laws harassing the NAACP. On the surface these laws merely required of the NAACP—and of other organizations—full disclosure: membership lists, records, finances, and

so forth. Clearly membership lists gave state and local authorities an opportunity to bring social or economic pressure on members of unpopular organizations. The task of weighing the right of the state to information about organizations against the right of privacy, the interest of society in full disclosure and the interest of society in voluntary association, was a difficult one. See Robison, "Protection of Associations from Compulsory Disclosure," 58 *Columbia Law Rev.* 614; Rankwich, "The Right of Privacy," 27 *Notre Dame Law Rev.* 499; Fly, "Full Disclosure: Public Safeguard," 168 *The Nation* 299; and the elaborate discussion of some of these questions in *American Communications Association* v. *Douds,* 339 U.S. 382.

MR. JUSTICE HARLAN. We review from the standpoint of its validity under the Federal Constitution a judgment of civil contempt entered against the National Association for the Advancement of Colored People, in the courts of Alabama. The question presented is whether Alabama, consistently with the Due Process Clause of the Fourteenth Amendment, can compel petitioner to reveal to the State's Attorney General the names and addresses of all its Alabama members and agents, without regard to their positions or functions in the Association. The judgment of contempt was based upon petitioner's refusal to comply fully with a court order requiring in part the production of membership lists. Petitioner's claim is that the order, in the circumstances shown by this record, violated rights assured to petitioner and its members under the Constitution. . . .

Petitioner produced substantially all the data called for . . . except its membership lists, as to which it contended that Alabama could not constitutionally compel disclosure. . . .

The Association both urges that it is constitutionally entitled to resist official inquiry into its membership lists, and that it may assert, on behalf of its members, a right personal to them to be protected from compelled disclosure by the State of their affiliation with the Association as revealed by the membership lists. We think that petitioner argues more appropriately the rights of its members, and that its nexus with them is sufficient to permit that it act as their representative before this Court. In so concluding, we reject respondent's argument that the Association lacks standing to assert here constitutional rights pertaining to the members, who are not of course parties to the litigation. . . .

If petitioner's rank-and-file members are constitutionally entitled to withhold their connection with the Association despite the production order, it is manifest that this right is properly assertable by the Association. To require that it be claimed by the members themselves would result in nullification of the right at the very moment of its assertion. . . .

We thus reach petitioner's claim that the production order in the state litigation trespasses upon fundamental freedoms protected by the Due Process Clause of the Fourteenth Amendment. Petitioner argues that in view of the facts and circumstances shown in the record, the effect of compelled disclosure of the membership lists will be to abridge the rights of its rank-and-file members to engage in lawful association in support of their common beliefs. It contends that governmental action which, although not directly suppressing association, nevertheless carries this consequence, can be justified only upon some overriding valid interest of the State.

Effective advocacy of both public and private points of view, particularly controversial ones, is undeniably enhanced by group association, as this Court has more than once recognized by remarking upon the close nexus between the freedoms of speech and assembly.

It is beyond debate that freedom to engage in association for the advancement of beliefs and ideas is an inseparable aspect of the "liberty" assured by the Due Process Clause of the Fourteenth Amendment, which embraces freedom of speech. [Cites cases] Of course, it is immaterial whether the beliefs sought to be advanced by association pertain to political, economic, religious or cultural matters, and state action which may have the effect of curtailing the freedom to associate is subject to the closest scrutiny.

The fact that Alabama, so far as is relevant to the validity of the contempt judgment presently under review, has taken no direct action to restrict the right of petitioner's members to associate freely, does not end inquiry into the effect of the production order. In the domain of these indispensable liberties, whether of speech, press, or association, the decisions of this Court recognize that abridgement of such rights, even though unintended, may inevitably follow from varied forms of governmental action. . . .

It is hardly a novel perception that compelled disclosure of affiliation with groups engaged in advocacy may constitute as effective a restraint on freedom of association as the forms of governmental action in the cases above were thought likely to produce upon the particular constitutional rights there involved. This Court has recognized the vital relationship between freedom to associate and privacy in one's associations. When referring to the varied forms of governmental action which might interfere with freedom of assembly, it said in American Communications Ass'n v. Douds, 339 U.S. 402, "A requirement that adherents of particular religious faiths or political parties wear identifying arm-bands, for example, is obviously of this nature." Compelled disclosure of membership in an organization engaged in advocacy of particular beliefs is of the same order. Inviolability of privacy in group association may in many circumstances be indispensable to preservation of freedom of association, particularly where a group espouses dissident beliefs.

We think that the production order, in the respects here drawn in question, must be regarded as entailing the likelihood of a substantial restraint upon the exercise by petitioner's members of their right to freedom of association. Petitioner has made an uncontroverted showing that on past occasions revelation of the identity of its rank-and-file members has exposed these members to economic reprisal, loss of employment, threat of physical coercion, and other manifestations of public hostility. . . .

It is not sufficient to answer, as the State does here, that whatever repressive effect compulsory disclosure of names of petitioner's members may have upon participation by Alabama citizens in petitioner's activities follows not from *state* action but from *private* community pressures. The crucial factor is the interplay of governmental and private action, for it is only after the initial exertion of state power represented by the production order that private action takes hold. . . .

626. FIRST UNITARIAN CHURCH v. LOS ANGELES COUNTY
357 U.S. 513 at 529
1958

Appeal from Supreme Court of California. A California statute denied tax exemption to any "person or organization which advocates the overthrow of the government of the United States or of the State by force or violence . . ." and required that all who claimed tax exemption sign an elaborate loyalty oath. The law affected veterans who were entitled to tax exemption under the provisions of the California Constitution; in *Speiser* v. *Randall,* 357 U.S. 513, the Court struck down this application of the act as a violation of freedom of speech. We give here the concurring opinion in a case involving the right of a church to tax exemption; because it covers both the free speech and the freedom of religion issues, we give the concurring opinion of Justice Black. See L. Pfeffer, *Church, State and Freedom;* H. Hyman, *To Try Men's Souls;* and notes in 44 *Am. Bar Assoc. J.* 1196; 72 *Harvard Law Rev.* 185; 12 *Vanderbilt Law Rev.* 275.

Mr. Justice BLACK, whom Mr. Justice DOUGLAS joins, concurring. . . . California, in effect, has imposed a tax on belief and expression. In my view, a levy of this nature is wholly out of place in this country; so far as I know such a thing has never even been attempted before. I believe that it constitutes a palpable violation of the First Amendment, which of course is applicable in all its particulars to the states. . . . The mere fact that California attempts to exact this ill-concealed penalty from individuals and churches and that its validity has to be considered in this Court only emphasizes how dangerously far we have departed from the fundamental principles of freedom declared in the First Amendment. We should never forget that the freedoms secured by that Amendment—Speech, Press, Religion, Petition and Assembly—are absolutely indispensable for the preservation of a free society in which government is based upon the consent of an informed citizenry and is dedicated to the protection of the rights of all, even the most despised minorities . . .

This case offers just another example of wide-scale effort by government in this country to impose penalties and disabilities on everyone who is or is suspected of being a "Communist" or who is not ready at all times and all places to swear his loyalty to state and nation. Government employees, lawyers, doctors, teachers, pharmacists, veterinarians, subway conductors, industrial workers and a multitude of others have been denied an opportunity to work at their trade or profession for these reasons. Here a tax is levied unless the taxpayer makes an oath that he does not and will not in the future advocate certain things; in Ohio those without jobs have been denied unemployment insurance unless they are willing to swear that they do not hold specific views; and Congress has even attempted to deny public housing to needy families unless they first demonstrate their loyalty. These are merely random samples; I will not take time here to refer to innumerable others, such as oaths for hunters and fishermen, wrestlers and boxers and junk dealers.

I am convinced that this whole business of penalizing people because of their views and expressions concerning government is hopelessly repugnant to the principles of freedom upon which this nation was founded and which have helped to make it the greatest in the world. As stated in prior cases, I believe "that the First Amendment grants an absolute right to believe in any governmental system, [to] discuss all governmental affairs and [to] argue for desired changes in the existing order. This freedom is too dangerous for bad, tyrannical governments to permit. But those who wrote and adopted our First Amendment weighed those dangers against the dangers of censorship and deliberately chose the First Amendment's unequivocal command that freedom of assembly, petition, speech and press shall not be abridged. I happen to believe this was a wise choice and that our free way of life enlists such respect and love that our nation cannot be imperiled by mere talk."

Loyalty oaths, as well as other contemporary "security measures," tend to stifle all forms of unorthodox or unpopular thinking or expression—the kind of thought and expression which has played such a vital and beneficial role in the history of this nation. The result is a stultifying conformity which in the end may well turn out to be more destructive to our free society than foreign agents could ever hope to be. The course which we have been following the last decade is not the course of a strong, free, secure people, but that of the frightened, the insecure, the intolerant. I am certain that loyalty to the United States can never be secured by the endless proliferation of "loyalty" oaths; loyalty must arise spontaneously from the hearts of people who love their country and respect their government. I also adhere to the proposition that the "First Amendment provides the only kind of security system that can preserve a free government—one that leaves the way wide open for people to favor, discuss, advocate, or incite causes and doctrines however obnoxious and antagonistic such views may be to the rest of us." Yates v. United States, 345 U.S. 298, 344.

627. COOPER v. AARON
358 U.S. 1
1958

Certiorari to the Court of Appeals for the Eighth District. The background of this case is set forth in Doc. No. 621, and the legal situation fully analyzed in the body of the opinion. The case is notable because it was not only a unanimous judgment, but one in which each judge concurred by name and of which each judge was presumably joint author. See, in addition to references in Doc. No. 621, Leflar and Davis, "Segregation in Public Schools," 67 *Harvard*

Law Rev. 377; McKay, "With All Deliberate Speed," 31 *N.Y.U. Law Rev.* 991; Charles Black, "The Lawfulness of the Segregation Decision," 69 *Yale Law J.* 421; Pollak, "Racial Discrimination and Judicial Integrity," 108 *U. of Pa. Law Rev.* 1; Charles Fairman, "Attack on Segregation Cases," 70 *Harvard Law Rev.* 83.

Opinion of the Court by CHIEF JUSTICE WARREN, Mr. Justice BLACK, Mr. Justice FRANKFURTER, Mr. Justice DOUGLAS, Mr. Justice BURTON, Mr. Justice CLARK, Mr. Justice HARLAN, Mr. Justice BRENNAN, and Mr. Justice WHITTAKER:

As this case reaches us it raises questions of the highest importance to the maintenance of our federal system of government. It necessarily involves a claim by the governor and legislature of a state that there is no duty on state officials to obey federal court orders resting on this Court's considered interpretation of the United States Constitution. Specifically it involves actions by the governor and legislature of Arkansas upon the premise that they are not bound by our holding in Brown v. Board of Education, 347 U.S. 483. . . .

On May 17, 1954, this Court decided that enforced racial segregation in the public schools of a state is a denial of the equal protection of the laws enjoined by the Fourteenth Amendment. Brown v. Board of Education.

The Court postponed, pending further argument, formulations of a decree to effectuate this decision. That decree was rendered May 31, 1955. Brown v. Board of Education, 349 U.S. 294. In the formulation of that decree the Court recognized that good faith compliance with the principles declared in Brown might in some situations "call for elimination of a variety of obstacles in making the transition to school systems operated in accordance with the constitutional principles set forth in our May 17, 1954, decision." . . .

Under such circumstances, the district courts were directed to require "a prompt and reasonable start toward full compliance," and to take such action as was necessary to bring about the end of racial segregation in the schools "with all deliberate speed." . . .

On May 20, 1954, three days after the first Brown opinion, the Little Rock District School Board adopted, and on May 23, 1954, made public, a statement of policy entitled "Supreme Court Decision—Segregation in the Public Schools." In this statement the Board recognized that "It is our responsibility to comply with Federal Constitutional Requirements and we intend to do so when the Supreme Court of the United States outlines the method to be followed."

Thereafter the Board undertook studies of the administrative problems confronting the transition to a desegregated public school system in Little Rock. It instructed the Superintendent of Schools to prepare a plan. . . . The plan provided for desegregation at the senior high school level (grades 10 through 12) as the first stage. Desegregation at the junior high and elementary levels was to follow. It was contemplated that desegregation at the high school level would commence in the fall of 1957, and the expectation was that complete desegregation of the school system would be accomplished by 1963. . . .

While the School Board was thus going forward with its preparation for desegregating the Little Rock school system, other state authorities, in contrast, were actively pursuing a program designed to perpetuate in Arkansas the system of racial segregation which this Court had held violated the Fourteenth Amendment. First came, in November 1956, an amendment to the State Constitution flatly commanding the Arkansas General Assembly to oppose "in every Constitutional manner the Unconstitutional desegregation decisions of May 17, 1954 and May 31, 1955 of the United States Supreme Court," Ark. Const. Amend. 44, and, through the initiative, a pupil assignment law. Pursuant to this state constitutional command, a law relieving school children from compulsory attendance at racially mixed schools, was enacted by the General Assembly in February, 1957. . . .

On September 2, 1957, the day before these Negro students were to enter Central High, the school authorities were met with drastic opposing action on the part of the

Governor of Arkansas who dispatched units of the Arkansas National Guard to the Central High School grounds, and placed the school "off limits" to colored students. As found by the District Court in subsequent proceedings, the Governor's action had not been requested by the school authorities, and was entirely unheralded . . .

The next school day was Monday, September 23, 1957. The Negro children entered the high school . . . under the protection of the Little Rock Police Department and members of the Arkansas State Police. But the officers caused the children to be removed from the school during the morning because they had difficulty controlling a large and demonstrating crowd which had gathered at the high school. On September 25, however, the President of the United States dispatched federal troops to Central High School and admission of the Negro students to the school was thereby effected. Regular army troops continued at the high school until November 27, 1957. They were then replaced by federalized National Guardsmen who remained throughout the balance of the school year. Eight of the Negro students remained in attendance at the school throughout the school year.

We come now to the aspect of the proceedings presently before us. On February 20, 1958, the School Board and the Superintendent of Schools filed a petition in the District Court seeking a postponement of their program of desegregation. Their position in essence was that because of extreme hostility, which they stated had been engendered largely by the official attitudes and actions of the Governor and the Legislature, the maintenance of a sound education program at Central High School, with the Negro students in attendance, would be impossible. The Board therefore proposed that the Negro students already admitted to the school be withdrawn and sent to segregated schools, and that all further steps to carry out the Board's desegregation program be postponed for a period later suggested by the Board to be two and one-half years. . . .

One may well sympathize with the position of the Board in the face of the frustrating conditions which have confronted it, but, regardless of the Board's good faith, the actions of the other state agencies responsible for those conditions compel us to reject the Board's legal position. . . .

The constitutional rights of respondents are not to be sacrificed or yielded to the violence and disorder which have followed upon the actions of the Governor and Legislature. . . .

. . . the constitutional rights of children not to be discriminated against in school admission on grounds of race or color declared by this Court in the Brown case can neither be nullified openly and directly by state legislators or state executive or judicial officers, nor nullified indirectly by them through evasive schemes for segregation whether attempted "ingeniously or ingenuously." Smith v. Texas, 311 U.S. 128.

What has been said, in the light of the facts developed, is enough to dispose of the case. However, we should answer the premise of the actions of the Governor and Legislature that they are not bound by our holding in the Brown case. It is necessary only to recall some basic constitutional propositions which are settled doctrine.

Article VI of the Constitution makes the Constitution the "supreme Law of the Land." In 1803, Chief Justice Marshall, speaking for a unanimous Court, referring to the Constitution as "the fundamental and paramount law of the nation," declared in the notable case of Marbury v. Madison that "It is emphatically the province and duty of the judicial department to say what the law is." This decision declared the basic principle that the federal judiciary is supreme in the exposition of the law of the Constitution, and that principle has ever since been respected by this Court and the country as a permanent and indispensable feature of our constitutional system. It follows that the interpretation of the Fourteenth Amendment enunciated by this Court in the Brown case is the supreme law of the land . . .

No state legislator or executive or judicial officer can war against the Constitution without violating his undertaking to support it . . .

It is, of course, quite true that the responsibility for public education is primarily the concern of the states, but it is equally true that such responsibilities, like all other state activity, must be exercised consistently with federal constitutional requirements as they apply to state action. The Constitution created a government dedicated to equal justice under law. The Fourteenth Amendment embodied and emphasized that idea. State support of segregated schools through any arrangement, management, funds, or property cannot be squared with the Amendment's command that no state shall deny to any person within its jurisdiction the equal protection of the laws. The right of a student not to be segregated on racial grounds in schools so maintained is indeed so fundamental and pervasive that it is embraced in the concept of due process of law. Bolling v. Sharpe, 347 U.S. 497. The basic decision in Brown was unanimously reached by this Court only after the case had been briefed and twice argued and the issue had been given the most serious consideration. Since the first Brown opinion three new Justices have come to the Court. They are at one with the Justices still on the Court who participated in that basic decision as to its correctness, and that decision is now unanimously reaffirmed. The principles announced in that decision and the obedience of the states to them, according to the command of the Constitution, are indispensable for the protection of the freedoms guaranteed by our fundamental charter for all of us. Our constitutional ideal of equal justice under law is thus made a living truth.

628. EISENHOWER'S VETO OF WATER POLLUTION CONTROL ACT
February 23, 1959
(Public Papers of the Presidents: Dwight D. Eisenhower, 1960, no. 43)

With the industrialization of almost the entire country, and the rapid growth of big cities, the problem of the pollution of streams and lakes, and even of seashores, became of urgent importance. Gradually the conviction grew that only the national government could deal adequately with the problem. Congress responded with an act voting substantial federal funds to fight water pollution. See "Water Pollution Control," Hearings of the sub-committee of the Committee on Public Works, 87 Cong. 1st sess. on Sen. Re. 805; R. J. Hammond, *Benefit Cost Analysis and Water Pollution Control;* O. Eckstein, *Water Resource Development;* C. B. Haver, *History and Status of Federal Resource Development Activities;* L. Klein, *Aspects of River Pollution;* B. Morrell, *Our Nation's Water Resources.*

federal grants to municipalities for assistance in the construction of sewage treatment works from $50 million to $90 million annually, and from $500 million to $900 million in the aggregate.

Because water pollution is a uniquely local blight, primary responsibility for solving the problem lies not with the federal government but rather must be assumed and exercised, as it has been, by state and local governments. This being so, the defects of H. R. 3610 are apparent. By holding forth the promise of a large-scale program of long-term federal support, it would tempt municipalities to delay essential water pollution abatement efforts while they waited for federal funds. . . .

Polluted water is a threat to the health and well-being of all our citizens. Yet, pollution and its correction are so closely involved with local industry processes and with public water supply and sewage treatment, that the problem can be successfully met only by state and local action rather than providing excuses for inaction—which an expanded program under H. R. 3610 would do . . .

I am requesting the Secretary of Health, Education and Welfare to arrange for a national conference on water pollution to be held next December.

To the House of Representatives:

I am returning herewith, without my approval, H. R. 3610, an enrolled bill "To amend the Federal Water Pollution Control Act to increase grants for construction of sewage treatment works, and for other purposes."

The bill would authorize an increase in

629. UPHAUS v. WYMAN
360 U.S. 72
1959

No case since *Dennis* attracted such widespread attention as did the case of the Rev. Willard Uphaus and his World Fellowship v. the State of New Hampshire. Constitutionally the case is interesting because it involved complex problems of freedom of association, freedom of religion, the right of privacy, as well as the more familiar problem of the authority of the state to investigate and its right to know. The facts of the case are set forth fully in the dissenting opinion. See notes in 45 *Am. Bar Assoc. J.* 1069; 47 *California Law Rev.* 930; 61 *Columbia Law Rev.* 725; 73 *Harvard Law Rev.* 161; 38 *Texas Law Rev.* 330.

Mr. Justice CLARK: This case is here again on appeal from a judgment of civil contempt entered against appellant by the Merrimack County Court and affirmed by the Supreme Court of New Hampshire. It arises out of appellant's refusal to produce certain documents before a New Hampshire legislative investigating committee which was authorized and directed to determine, *inter alia*, whether there were subversive persons or organizations present in the State of New Hampshire. Upon the first appeal from the New Hampshire court, we vacated the judgment, and remanded the case to it for consideration in the light of Sweezy v. State of New Hampshire, 1957, 354 U.S. 234. That court reaffirmed its former decision, 101 N.H. 139, deeming Sweezy not to control the issues in the instant case. For reasons which will appear, we agree with the Supreme Court of New Hampshire.

As in Sweezy, the Attorney General of New Hampshire, who had been constituted a one-man legislative investigating committee by Joint Resolution of the Legislature, was conducting a probe of subversive activities in the state. In the course of his investigation the Attorney General called appellant, Executive Director of World Fellowship, Inc., a voluntary corporation organized under the laws of New Hampshire and maintaining

a summer camp in the state. Appellant testified concerning his own activities, but refused to comply with two subpoenas *duces tecum* which called for the production of certain corporate records for the years 1954 and 1955. The information sought consisted of: (1) a list of the names of all the camp's nonprofessional employees for those two summer seasons; (2) the correspondence which appellant had carried on with and concerning those persons who came to the camp as speakers; and (3) the names of all persons who attended the camp during the same periods of time. Met with appellant's refusal, the Attorney General, in accordance with state procedure, petitioned the Merrimack County Court to call appellant before it and require compliance with the subpoenas.

In court, appellant again refused to produce the information. He claimed that by the Smith Act, as construed by this Court in Commonwealth of Pennsylvania v. Nelson, 1956, 350 U.S. 497, Congress had so completely occupied the field of subversive activities that the states were without power to investigate in that area. Additionally, he contended that the Due Process Clause precluded enforcement of the subpoenas, first, because the resolution under which the Attorney General was authorized to operate was vague and, second, because the documents sought were not relevant to the inquiry. Finally, appellant argued the enforcement would violate his rights of free speech and association.

The Merrimack County Court sustained appellant's objection to the production of the names of the nonprofessional employees. The Attorney General took no appeal from that ruling, and it is not before us. Appellant's objections to the production of the names of the camp's guests were overruled, and he was ordered to produce them. Upon his refusal, he was adjudged in contempt of court and ordered committed to jail until he should have complied with the court order. On the demand for the correspondence and the objection thereto, the trial court made no ruling but transferred the question to the Supreme Court of New Hampshire. That court affirmed the trial court's action in regard to the guest list. Concerning the requested production of the correspondence, the Supreme Court entered no order, but directed that on remand the trial court "may exercise its discretion with respect to the entry of an order to enforce the command of the subpoena for the production of correspondence." 100 N. H. at page 448. No remand having yet been effected, the trial court has not acted upon this phase of the case, and there is no final judgment requiring the appellant to produce the letters. We therefore do not treat with that question. We now pass to a consideration of the sole question before us, namely, the validity of the order of contempt for refusal to produce the list of guests at World Fellowship, Inc., during the summer seasons of 1954 and 1955. In addition to the arguments appellant made to the trial court, he urges here that the "indefinite sentence" imposed upon him constitutes such cruel and unusual punishment as to be a denial of due process.

Appellant vigorously contends that the New Hampshire Subversive Activities Act of 1951 and the resolution creating the committee have been superseded by the Smith Act, as amended. In support of this position appellant cites Com. of Pennsylvania v. Nelson, *supra*. The argument is that Nelson, which involved a prosecution under a state sedition law, held that "Congress has intended to occupy the field of sedition." [350 U.S. 505, 76 S. Ct. 481.] This rule of decision, it is contended, should embrace legislative investigations made pursuant to an effort by the Legislature to inform itself of the presence of subversives within the state and possibly to enact laws in the subversive field. The appellant's argument sweeps too broad. In Nelson itself we said that the "precise holding of the court . . . is that the Smith Act . . . which prohibits the knowing advocacy of the overthrow of the Government of the United States by force and violence, supersedes the enforceability of the Pennsylvania Sedition Act which proscribes the *same conduct*." 350 U.S. at page 499. The basis of Nelson thus rejects the notion that it stripped the states of the right to protect themselves. All the

opinion proscribed was a race between federal and state prosecutors to the courthouse door. The opinion made clear that a state could proceed with prosecutions for sedition against the state itself; that it can legitimately investigate in this area follows *a fortiori*. In Sweezy v. State of New Hampshire, *supra*, where the same contention was made as to the identical state Act, it was denied *sub silentio*. Nor did our opinion in Nelson hold that the Smith Act had proscribed state activity in protection of itself either from actual or threatened "sabotage or attempted violence of all kinds." In footnote 8 of the opinion it is pointed out that the state had full power to deal with internal civil disturbances. Thus registration statutes, *quo warranto* proceedings as to subversive corporations, the subversive instigation of riots and a host of other subjects directly affecting state security furnish grist for the state's legislative mill. Moreover, the right of the state to require the production of corporate papers of a state-chartered corporation in an inquiry to determine whether corporate activity is violative of state policy is, of course, not touched upon in Nelson and today stands unimpaired, either by the Smith Act or the Nelson opinion.

Appellant's other objections can be capsuled into the single question of whether New Hampshire, under the facts here, is precluded from compelling the production of the documents by the Due Process Clause of the Fourteenth Amendment. Let us first clear away some of the underbrush necessarily surrounding the case because of its setting.

First, the academic and political freedoms discussed in Sweezy v. State of New Hampshire, *supra*, are not present here in the same degree, since World Fellowship is neither a university nor a political party. Next, since questions concerning the authority of the committee to act as it did are questions of state law, Dreyer v. People of State of Illinois, 1902, 187 U.S. 71, 84, we accept as controlling the New Hampshire Supreme Court's conclusion that "[t]he legislative history makes it clear beyond a reasonable doubt that it [the Legislature] did and does desire an answer to these questions." Finally, we assume, without deciding, that Uphaus had sufficient standing to assert any rights of the guests whose identity the committee seeks to determine. See National Association for Advancement of Colored People v. State of Alabama, 1958, 357 U.S. 449. The interest of the guests at World Fellowship in their associational privacy having been asserted, we have for decision the federal question of whether the public interests overbalance these conflicting private ones. Whether there was "justification" for the production order turns on the "substantiality" of New Hampshire's interests in obtaining the identity of the guests when weighed against the individual interests which the appellant asserts. National Association for Advancement of Colored People v. State of Alabama, *supra.* What was the interest of the state? The Attorney General was commissioned to determine if there were any subversive persons within New Hampshire. The obvious starting point of such an inquiry was to learn what persons were within the state. It is, therefore, clear that the requests relate directly to the Legislature's area of interest, i.e., the presence of subversives in the state, as announced in its resolution. Nor was the demand of the subpoena burdensome; as to time, only a few months of each of the two years were involved; as to place, only the camp conducted by the corporation; nor as to the lists of names, which included about 300 each year.

Moreover, the Attorney General had valid reason to believe that the speakers and guests at World Fellowship might be subversive persons within the meaning of the New Hampshire Act. The Supreme Court of New Hampshire found Uphaus' contrary position "unrelated to reality." Although the evidence as to the nexus between World Fellowship and subversive activities may not be conclusive, we believe it sufficiently relevant to support the Attorney General's action. The New Hampshire definition of subversive persons was born of the legislative determination that the Communist movement posed a serious threat to the security of the state. The record reveals that appellant had participated in "Communist front" activities and that "[n]ot less than nineteen speakers invited by Uphaus to talk at World Fellowship had either been members of the Communist Party or had connections or af-

filiations with it or with one or more of the organizations cited as subversive or Communist controlled in the United States Attorney General's list." While the Attorney General's list is designed for the limited purpose of determining fitness for federal employment, Wieman v. Updegraff, 1952, 344 U.S. 183, and guilt by association remains a thoroughly discredited doctrine, it is with a legislative investigation—not a criminal prosecution—that we deal here. Certainly the investigatory power of the state need not be constricted until sufficient evidence of subversion is gathered to justify the institution of criminal proceedings.

The nexus between World Fellowship and subversive activities disclosed by the record furnished adequate justification for the investigation we here review. The Attorney General sought to learn if subversive persons were in the state because of the legislative determination that such persons, statutorily defined with a view toward the Communist Party, posed a serious threat to the security of the state. The investigation was, therefore, undertaken in the interest of self-preservation, "the ultimate value of any society," Dennis v. United States, 1951, 341 U.S. 494, 509. This governmental interest outweighs individual rights in an associational privacy which, however real in other circumstances, cf. National Association for Advancement of Colored People v. State of Alabama, *supra,* were here tenuous at best. The camp was operating as a public one, furnishing both board and lodging to persons applying therefor. As to them, New Hampshire law requires that World Fellowship, Inc., maintain a register, open to inspection of sheriffs and police officers. It is contended that the list might be "circulated throughout the states and the Attorney Generals throughout the states have cross-indexed files, so that any guest whose name is mentioned in that kind of proceeding immediately becomes suspect, even in his own place of residence." Record, p. 7. The record before us, however, only reveals a report to the Legislature of New Hampshire made by the Attorney General in accordance with the requirements of the resolution. We recognize, of course, that compliance with the subpoena will result in exposing the fact that the persons therein named were guests at World Fellowship. But so long as a committee must report to its legislative parent, exposure—in the sense of disclosure—is an inescapable incident of an investigation into the presence of subversive persons within a state. And the governmental interest in self-preservation is sufficiently compelling to subordinate the interest in associational privacy of persons who, at least to the extent of the guest registration statute, made public at the inception the association they now wish to keep private. In the light of such a record we conclude that the state's interest has not been "pressed, in this instance, to a point where it has come into fatal collision with the overriding" constitutionally protected rights of appellant and those he may represent. Cantwell v. State of Connecticut, 1940, 310 U.S. 296, 307.

We now reach the question of the validity of the sentence. The judgment of contempt orders the appellant confined until he produces the documents called for in the subpoenas. He himself admitted to the court that although they were at hand, not only had he failed to bring them with him to court, but that, further, he had no intention of producing them. In view of appellant's unjustified refusal we think the order a proper one. As was said in Green v. United States, 1958, 356 U.S. 165, 197 (dissenting opinion): "Before going any further, perhaps it should be emphasized that we are not at all concerned with the power of courts to impose conditional imprisonment for the purpose of compelling a person to obey a valid order. Such coercion, where the defendant carries the keys to freedom in his willingness to comply with the court's directive, is essentially a civil remedy designed for the benefit of other parties and has quite properly been exercised for centuries to secure compliance with judicial decrees."

We have concluded that the committee's demand for the documents was a legitimate one; it follows that the judgment of contempt for refusal to produce them is valid. We do not impugn appellant's good faith in the assertion of what he believed to be his rights. But three courts have disagreed with him in interpreting those rights. If appellant chooses to abide by the result of the adjudication and obey the order of New Hampshire's courts, he need not face jail. If, however, he continues to disobey, we find on this record no constitutional objection to the exercise of the traditional remedy of contempt to secure compliance.

Affirmed.

Mr. Justice BRENNAN, with whom the CHIEF JUSTICE, Mr. Justice BLACK, and Mr. Justice DOUGLAS join, dissenting: The Court holds today that the constitutionally protected rights of speech and assembly of appellant and those whom he may represent are to be subordinated to New Hampshire's legislative investigation because, as applied in the demands made on him, the investigation is rationally connected with a discernible legislative purpose. With due respect for my Brothers' views, I do not agree that a showing of any requisite legislative purpose or other state interest that constitutionally can subordinate appellant's rights is to be found in this record. Exposure purely for the sake of exposure is not such a valid subordinating purpose. Watkins v. United States, 354 U.S. 178, 187; Sweezy v. State of New Hampshire, 354 U.S. 234; NAACP v. State of Alabama, 357 U.S. 449. This record, I think, not only fails to reveal any interest of the state sufficient to subordinate appellant's constitutionally protected rights, but affirmatively shows that the investigatory objective was the impermissible one of exposure for exposure's sake. I therefore dissent from the judgment of the Court. . . .

Only recently has the Court been required to begin a full exploration of the impact of the governmental investigatory function on these freedoms. Here is introduced the weighty consideration that the power of investigation, whether exercised in aid of the governmental legislative power, or in aid of the governmental power to adjudicate disputes, is vital to the functioning of free governments and is therefore necessarily broad. But where the exercise of the investigatory power collides with constitutionally guaranteed freedoms, that power too has inevitable limitations, and the delicate and always difficult accommodation of the two with minimum sacrifice of either is the hard task of the judiciary and ultimately of this Court. . . .

Of course . . . Government must have freedom to make an appropriate investigation where there appears a rational connection with the lawmaking process, the processes of adjudication, or other essential governmental functions. . . . But guide lines must be marked out by the courts. . . . On the facts of this case I think that New Hampshire's investigation, as applied to the appellant, was demonstrably and clearly outside the wide limits of the power which must be conceded to the state even though it be attended by some exposure. In demonstration of this I turn to the detailed examination of the facts which this case requires. . . .

The appellant, Uphaus, is executive director of a group called World Fellowship which runs a discussion program at a summer camp in New Hampshire, at which the public is invited to stay. Various speakers come to the camp primarily for discussion of political, economic, and social matters. The appellee reports that Uphaus and some of the speakers have been said by third persons to have a history of association with "Communist front" movements, to have followed the "Communist line," signed amnesty petitions and *amicus curiae* briefs, and carried on similar activities of a sort which have recently been viewed hostilely and suspiciously by many Americans. A strain of pacifism runs through the appellant's thinking, and the appellee apparently would seek to determine whether there should be drawn therefrom an inference of harm for our institutions; he conjectures, officially, whether "the advocacy of this so-called peace crusade is for the purpose of achieving a quicker and a cheaper occupation by the Soviet Union and Communism." There is no evidence that any activity of a sort that violates the law of New Hampshire or could in fact be constitutionally punished went on at the camp. What is clear was that there was some sort of assemblage at the camp that was oriented toward the discussion of political and other public matters. The activities going on were those of private citizens. The views expounded obviously were minority views. But the assemblage was, on its face, for purposes to which the First and Fourteenth Amendments give constitutional protection against incursion by the powers of government. . . .

The Legislature, upon receiving the report, extended the investigation for a further two years. It was during this period that the refusals of the appellant to furnish information with which we are now concerned took place. The Attorney General had already published the names of speakers at the World Fellowship camp. Now he wanted the correspondence between Uphaus and the speakers. The Attorney General admitted that it was unlikely that the correspondence between Uphaus and the speakers was going to contain a damning admission of a purpose to advocate the overthrow of the government (presumably of New Hampshire) by force and violence. He said that it might indicate a sinister purpose behind the advocacy of pacifism— "the purpose of achieving a quicker and a cheaper occupation by the Soviet Union and Communism." The guest list, the nonavailability of which to the Attorney General was commented on in the passage from the 1955 report was also desired. Appellant's counsel, at the hearing in court giving rise to the contempt finding under review, protested that appellant did not want to allow the Attorney General to have the names to expose them. The Attorney General also wished the names of the nonprofessional help at the camp—the cooks and dishwashers and the like. It was objected that the cooks and dishwashers were hired from the local labor pool and that if such employment were attended by a trip to the Attorney General's office and the possibility of public exposure, help might become hard to find at the camp. This last objection was sustained in the trial court, but the other two inquiries were allowed and appellant's failure to respond to the one relating to the guest list was found contemptuous. . . .

In examining the right of the State to obtain this information from the appellant by compulsory process, we must recollect what we so recently said in NAACP v. State of Alabama:

"Effective advocacy of both public and private points of view, particularly controversial ones, is undeniably enhanced by group association, as this Court has more than once recognized by remarking upon the close nexus between the freedoms of speech and assembly. It is beyond debate that freedom to engage in association for the advancement of beliefs and ideals is an inseparable aspect of the "liberty" assured by the Due Process Clause of the Fourteenth Amendment which embraces freedom of speech. Of course, it is immaterial whether the beliefs sought to be advanced by association pertain to political, economic, religious or cultural matters, and state action which may have the effect of curtailing the freedom to associate is subject to the closest scrutiny."

And in examining the state's interest in carrying out a legislative investigation, as was said in a similar context in United States v. Rumley, *supra*, we must strive not to be "that 'blind' Court, against which Mr. Chief Justice Taft admonished in a famous passage . . . that does not see what '[a]ll others can see and understand.' " The problem of protecting the citizen's constitutional rights from legislative investigation and exposure is a practical one, and we must take a practical, realistic approach to it. . . .

One may accept the Court's truism that preservation of the state's existence is undoubtedly a proper purpose for legislation. But, in descending from this peak of abstraction to the facts of this case, one must ask the question: What relation did this investigation of individual conduct have to

legislative ends here? If bills of attainder were still a legitimate legislative end, it is clear that the investigations and reports might naturally have furnished the starting point (though only that) for a legislative adjudication of guilt under the 1951 Act. But what other legislative purpose was actually being fulfilled by the course taken by this investigation, with its overwhelming emphasis on individual associations and conduct?

The investigation, as revealed by the report, was overwhelmingly and predominantly a roving, self-contained investigation of individual and group behavior, and behavior in compulsory disclosure itself tends to have a repressive effect. We deal only with the power of the state to *compel* such a disclosure. We are asked, in this narrow context, only to give meaning to our statement in Watkins v. United States, "that the mere semblance of a legislative purpose would not justify an inquiry in the face of the Bill of Rights." Here we must demand some initial showing by the state sufficient to counterbalance the interest in privacy as it relates to freedom of speech and assembly. On any basis that has practical meaning, New Hampshire has not made such a showing here. I would reverse the judgment of the New Hampshire Supreme Court.

630.   BARENBLATT v. U.S.
360 U.S. 109
1959

This was probably the most exhaustively argued of the many cases involving the reach of the investigatory power of Congresssional committees. In the *Watkins* case, 354 U.S. 178, the Court had reversed a contempt citation of a witness before a Congressional committee because the committee had failed to make clear the pertinence of its questions to a legitimate legislative purpose, and the *Sweezy* case (*Sweezy v. New Hampshire,* 354 U.S. 234) had radiated the same doctrine. *Barenblatt* did not so much reverse as circumscribe the reach of these two decisions. See T. Taylor, *Grand Inquest;* C. Fairman, *Mr. Justice Miller and the Supreme Court;* E. J. Eberling, *Congressional Investigations;* J. E. Johnson, *The Investigating Powers*

of Congress; M. N. McGeary, *The Developments of Congressional Investigative Power;* Wittke, *The History of English Parliamentary Privilege;* Finer, "Congressional Investigations: The British System," 18 *U. of Chicago Law Rev.* 521; Landis, "Constitutional Limitations on the Congressional Power of Investigation," 40 *Harvard Law Rev.* 153; Potts, "Power of Legislative Bodies to Punish for Contempt," 74 *U. of Pa. Law Rev.* 691; C. H. Pritchett, *The Political Offender and the Warren Court;* and notes in 47 *California Law Rev.* 930; 45 *Cornell Law Rev.* 354; 73 *Harvard Law Rev.* 159; 58 *Michigan Law Rev.* 406; and 27 *U. of Chicago Law Rev.* 315.

Mr. Justice HARLAN: Once more the Court is required to resolve the conflicting constitutional claims of Congressional power and of an individual's right to resist its exercise. The Congressional power in question concerns the internal process of Congress in moving within its legislative domain; it involves the utilization of its committees to secure "testimony needed to enable it efficiently to exercise a legislative function belonging to it under the Constitution." . . . The scope of the power of inquiry, in short, is as penetrating and far-reaching as the potential power to enact and appropriate under the Constitution.

Broad as it is, the power is not, however, without limitations. Since Congress may only investigate into those areas in which it may potentially legislate or appropriate, it cannot inquire into matters which are within the exclusive province of one or the other branch of the government. Lacking the judicial power given to the Judiciary, it cannot inquire into matters that are exclusively the concern of the Judiciary. Neither can it supplant the Executive in what exclusively belongs to the Executive. And the Congress, in common with all branches of the government, must exercise its powers subject to the limitations placed by the Constitution on governmental action, more particularly in the context of this case the relevant limitations of the Bill of Rights. . . .

In the present case Congressional efforts to learn the extent of a nationwide, indeed worldwide, problem have brought one of its investigating committees into the field of education. Of course, broadly viewed, inquiries cannot be made into the teaching that is pursued in any of our educational institutions. When academic teaching-freedom and its corollary learning-freedom, so essential to the well-being of the Nation, are claimed, this Court will always be on the alert against intrusion by Congress into this constitutionally protected domain. But this does not mean that the Congress is precluded from interrogating a witness merely because he is a teacher. An educational institution is not a constitutional sanctuary from inquiry into matters that may otherwise be within the constitutional legislative domain merely for

the reason that inquiry is made of someone within its walls. . . .

We here review petitioner's conviction for contempt of Congress, arising from his refusal to answer certain questions put to him by a Subcommittee of the House Committee on Un-American Activities during the course of an inquiry concerning alleged Communist infiltration into the field of education. . . .

Pursuant to a subpoena, petitioner on June 28, 1954, appeared as a witness before this Congressional Subcommittee. After answering a few preliminary questions and testifying that he had been a graduate student and teaching fellow at the University of Michigan from 1947 to 1950 and an instructor in psychology at Vassar College from 1950 to shortly before his appearance before the Subcommittee, petitioner objected generally to the right of the Subcommittee to inquire into his "political" and "religious" beliefs or any "other personal and private affairs" or "associational activities," upon grounds set forth in a previously prepared memorandum which he was allowed to file with the Subcommittee. Thereafter petitioner specifically declined to answer each of the following five questions:

"Are you now a member of the Communist Party?
"Have you ever been a member of the Communist Party?
"Now, you have stated that you knew Francis Crowley. Did you know Francis Crowley as a member of the Communist Party?
"Were you ever a member of the Haldane Club of the Communist Party while at the University of Michigan?
"Were you a member while a student of the University of Michigan Council of Arts, Sciences, and Professions?"

In each instance the grounds of refusal were those set forth in the prepared statement. Petitioner expressly disclaimed reliance upon "the Fifth Amendment." . . .

We conceive the ultimate issue in this case to be whether petitioner could properly be convicted of contempt for refusing to answer questions relating to his participation in or knowledge of alleged Communist Party activities at educational institutions in this country. . . .

Petitioner's various contentions resolve themselves into three propositions: First, the compelling of testimony by the Subcommittee was neither legislatively authorized nor constitutionally permissible because of the vagueness of Rule XI of the House of Representatives, Eighty-third Congress, the charter of authority of the parent Committee. Second, petitioner was not adequately apprised of the pertinency of the Subcommittee's questions to the subject matter of the inquiry. Third, the questions petitioner refused to answer infringed rights protected by the First Amendment. . . .

The precise constitutional issue confronting us is whether the Subcommittee's inquiry into petitioner's past or present membership in the Communist Party transgressed the provisions of the First Amendment which of course reach and limit Congressional investigations.

The Court's past cases establish sure guides to decision. Undeniably, the First Amendment in some circumstances protects an individual from being compelled to disclose his associational relationships. However, the protections of the First Amendment unlike a proper claim of the privilege against self-incrimination under the Fifth Amendment, do not afford a witness the right to resist inquiry in all circumstances. Where First Amendment rights are asserted to bar governmental interrogation, resolution of the issue always involves a balancing by the courts of the competing private and public interests at stake in the particular circumstances shown. These principles were recognized in the Watkins case, where, in speaking of the First Amendment in relation to Congressional inquiries, we said: "It is manifest that despite the adverse effects which follow upon compelled disclosure of private matters, not all such inquiries are barred. . . . The critical element is the existence of, and the weight to be ascribed to, the interest of the Congress in demanding disclosures from an unwilling witness." . . .

The first question is whether this investigation was related to a valid legislative purpose, for Congress may not constitutionally require an individual to disclose his political relationships or other private affairs except in relation to such a purpose.

That Congress has wide power to legislate in the field of Communist activity in this Country, and to conduct appropriate investigations in aid thereof, is hardly debatable. The existence of such power has never been questioned by this Court, and it is sufficient to say, without particularization, that Congress has enacted or considered in this field a wide range of legislative measures, not a few of which have stemmed from recommendations of the very Committee whose actions have been drawn in question here. In the last analysis this power rests on the right of self-preservation, "the ultimate value of any society," Dennis v. United States, 341 U.S. 494, 509. Justification for its exercise in turn rests on the long and widely accepted view that the tenets of the Communist Party include the ultimate overthrow of the Government of the United States by force and violence, a view which has been given formal expression by the Congress. . . .

We think that investigatory power in this domain is not to be denied Congress solely because the field of education is involved. . . . Indeed we do not understand petitioner here to suggest that Congress in no circumstances may inquire into Communist activity in the field of education. Rather his position is in effect that this particular investigation was aimed not at the revolutionary aspects but at the theoretical classroom discussion of communism.

In our opinion this position rests on a too constricted view of the nature of the investigatory process. . . . Nor can it fairly be concluded that this investigation was directed at controlling what is being taught at our universities rather than at overthrow. . . .

Nor can we accept the further contention that this investigation should not be deemed to have been in furtherance of a legislative purpose because the true objective of the Committee and of the Congress was purely "exposure." So long as Congress acts in pursuance of its constitutional power, the judiciary lacks the authority to intervene on the basis of the motives which spurred the exercise of that power. . . .

Finally, the record is barren of other factors which in themselves might sometimes lead to the conclusion that the individual interests at stake were not subordinate to those of the state. There is no indication in this record that the Subcommittee was attempting to pillory witnesses. Nor did petitioner's appearance as a witness follow from indiscriminate dragnet procedures, lacking in probable cause for belief that he possessed information which might be helpful to the Subcommittee. And the relevancy of the questions put to him by the Subcommittee is not open to doubt.

We conclude that the balance between the individual and the governmental interests here at stake must be struck in favor of the latter, and that therefore the provisions of the First Amendment have not been offended.

We hold that the judgment of the Court of Appeals must be affirmed.

Mr. Justice BLACK, with whom the CHIEF JUSTICE, Justice DOUGLAS concur, dissenting. . . . The First Amendment says in no equivocal language that Congress shall pass no law abridging freedom of speech, press, assembly or petition. The activities of this Committee, authorized by Congress, do precisely that, through exposure, obloquy, and public scorn. The Court does not really deny this fact but relies on a combination of three reasons for permitting the infringement: (A) The notion that despite the First Amendment's command Congress can abridge speech and association if this Court decides that the governmental interest in abridging speech is greater than an individual's interest in exercising that freedom, (B) the Government's right to "preserve itself," (C) the fact that the Committee is only after Communists or suspected Communists in this investigation.

(A) I do not agree that laws directly abridging First Amendment freedoms can be justified by a Congressional or judicial balancing process. There are, of course, cases suggesting that a law which primarily regulates conduct but which might also indirectly affect speech can be upheld if the effect on speech is minor in relation to the need for control of the conduct. . . . But even such laws governing conduct, we emphasized, must be tested, though only by a balancing process, if they indirectly affect ideas. On one side of the balance, we pointed out, is the interest of the United States in seeing that

its fundamental law protecting freedom of communication is not abridged; on the other the obvious interest of the state to regulate conduct within its boundaries. . . .

To apply the Court's balancing test under such circumstances is to read the First Amendment to say "Congress shall pass no law abridging freedom of speech, press, assembly and petition, unless Congress and the Supreme Court reach the joint conclusion that on balance the interests of the government in stifling these freedoms is greater than the interest of the people in having them exercised." This is closely akin to the notion that neither the First Amendment nor any other provision of the Bill of Rights should be enforced unless the Court believes it is *reasonable* to do so. Not only does this violate the genius of our *written* Constitution, but it runs expressly counter to the injunction to Court and Congress made by Madison when he introduced the Bill of Rights. "If they [the first ten amendments] are incorporated into the Constitution, independent tribunals of justice will consider themselves in a peculiar manner the guardians of those rights; they will be an impenetrable bulwark against *every* assumption of power in the Legislative or Executive; they will be naturally led to resist *every* encroachment upon rights expressly stipulated for in the Constitution by the declaration of rights." Unless we return to this view of our judicial function, unless we once again accept the notion that the Bill of Rights means what it says and that this Court must enforce that meaning, I am of the opinion that our great charter of liberty will be more honored in the breach than in the observance.

But even assuming what I cannot assume, that some balancing is proper in this case, I feel that the Court after stating the test ignores it completely. At most it balances the right of the government to preserve itself, against Barenblatt's right to refrain from revealing Communist affiliations. Such a balance, however, mistakes the factors to be weighed. In the first place, it completely leaves out the real interest in Barenblatt's silence, the interest of the people as a whole in being able to join organizations, advocate causes, and make political "mistakes" without later being subjected to governmental penalties for having dared to think for themselves. It is this right, the right to err politically, which keeps us strong as a nation. For no number of laws against communism can have as much effect as the personal conviction which comes from having heard its arguments and rejected them, or from having once accepted its tenets and later recognized their worthlessness. Instead, the obloquy which results from investigations such as this not only stifles "mistakes" but prevents all but the most courageous from hazarding any views which might at some later time become disfavored. This result, whose importance cannot be overestimated, is doubly crucial when it affects the universities, on which we must largely rely for the experimentation and development of new ideas essential to our country's welfare. It is these interests of society, rather than Barenblatt's own right to silence, which I think the Court should put on the balance against the demands of the government, if any balancing process is to be tolerated. Instead they are not mentioned, while on the other side the demands of the government are vastly overstated and called "self-preservation." It is admitted that this Committee can only seek information for the purpose of suggesting laws, and that Congress' power to make laws in the realm of speech and association is quite limited, even on the Court's test. Its interest in making such laws in the field of education, primarily a state function, is clearly narrower still. Yet the Court styles this attenuated interest self-preservation and allows it to overcome the need our country has to let us all think, speak, and associate politically as we like and without fear of reprisal. Such a result reduces "balancing" to a mere play on words and is completely inconsistent with the rules this Court has previously given for applying a "balancing test" where it is proper. . . .

(B) Moreover, I cannot agree with the Court's notion that First Amendment freedoms must be abridged in order to "preserve" our country. That notion rests on the unarticulated premise that this nation's security hangs upon its power to punish people because of what they think, speak or write about, or because of those with whom they associate for political purposes. The government, in its brief, virtually admits this position when it speaks of the "communication of unlawful ideas." I challenge this premise, and deny that ideas can be proscribed under our Constitution. I agree that despotic governments cannot exist without stifling the voice of opposition to their oppressive practices. The First Amendment means to me, however, that the only constitutional way our government can preserve itself is to leave its people the fullest possible freedom to praise, criticize or discuss, as they see fit, all governmental policies and to suggest, if they desire, that even its most fundamental postulates are bad and should be changed; "Therein lies the security of the Republic, the very foundation of constitutional government." On that premise this land was created, and on that premise it has grown to greatness. Our Constitution assumes that the common sense of the people and their attachment to our country will enable them, after free discussion, to withstand ideas that are wrong. To say that our patriotism must be protected against false ideas by means other than these is, I think, to make a baseless charge. Unless we can rely on these qualities—if, in short, we begin to punish speech—we cannot honestly proclaim ourselves to be a free nation and we have lost what the Founders of this land risked their lives and their sacred honors to defend.

(C) The Court implies, however, that the ordinary rules and requirements of the Constitution do not apply because the Committee is merely after Communists and they do not constitute a political party but only a criminal gang. . . . By accepting this charge and allowing it to support treatment of the Communist Party and its members which would violate the Constitution if applied to other groups, the Court, in effect, declares that Party outlawed. It has been only a few years since there was a practically unanimous feeling throughout the country and in our courts that this could not be done in our free land. . . . But the Party as a whole and innocent members of it could not be attained merely because it had some illegal aims and because some of its members were lawbreakers. . . .

The fact is that once we allow any group

which has some political aims or ideas to be driven from the ballot and from the battle for men's minds because some of its members are bad and some of its tenets are illegal, no group is safe. Today we deal with Communists or suspected Communists. In 1920, instead, the New York Assembly duly elected legislators on the ground that, being Socialist, they were disloyal to the country's principles. In the 1830's the Masons were hunted as outlaws and subversives, and abolitionists were considered revolutionaries of the most dangerous kind in both North and South. Earlier still, at the time of the universally unlamented alien and sedition laws, Thomas Jefferson's party was attacked and its members derisively called "Jacobins." . . . History should teach us then, that in times of high emotional excitement minority parties and groups which advocate extremely unpopular social or governmental innovations will always be typed as criminal gangs and attempts will always be made to drive them out. It was knowledge of this fact, and of its great dangers, that caused the Founders of our land to enact the First Amendment as a guarantee that neither Congress nor the people would do anything to hinder or destroy the capacity of individuals and groups to seek converts and votes for any cause, however radical or unpalatable their principles might seem under the accepted notions of the time. Whatever the states were left free to do, the First Amendment sought to leave Congress devoid of any kind or quality of power to direct any type of national laws against the freedom of individuals to think what they please, advocate whatever policy they choose, and join with others to bring about the social, religious, political and governmental changes which seem best to them. Today's holding, in my judgment, marks another major step in the progressively increasing retreat from the safeguards of the First Amendment.

Ultimately all the questions in this case, really boil down to one—whether we as a people will try fearfully and futilely to preserve democracy by adopting totalitarian methods, or whether in accordance with our traditions and our Constitution we will have the confidence and courage to be free.

I would reverse this conviction.

Mr. Justice BRENNAN, dissenting: I would reverse this conviction. It is sufficient that I state my complete agreement with my Brother Black that no purpose for the investigation of Barenblatt is revealed by the record except exposure purely for the sake of exposure. This is not a purpose to which Barenblatt's rights under the First Amendment can validly be subordinated. An investigation in which the processes of lawmaking and law-evaluating are submerged entirely in exposure of individual behavior—in adjudication of a sort, through the exposure process—is outside the constitutional pale of Congressional inquiry. Watkins v. United States, 354 U.S. 178; see also Sweezy v. State of New Hampshire, 354 U.S. 234; NAACP v. State of Alabama, 357 U.S. 449; Uphaus v. Wyman, 360 U.S. 72.

631. THE U-2 AFFAIR
1960

Nineteen fifty-nine saw a brief thaw in the relations between the Soviet Union and the United States. In the fall of 1959, Premier Khrushchev toured the United States, visited President Eisenhower at Camp David, and invited the President to make a return visit to Russia. Meantime the two leaders planned for yet another summit conference, to meet in Paris in May. But on May 5 Khrushchev announced that the Russians had brought down an American reconnaissance plane deep in the heart of Russia and captured its pilot, Francis Powers.

We give here the Soviet note on the U-2 affair, the brief official statement of the State Department, and the more elaborate explanation by President Eisenhower. Meantime Powers was tried in Russia for espionage and condemned to ten years imprisonment; in less than two years he was released and returned to the United States. Eisenhower called off further reconnaissance flights over Russia; when Khrushchev demanded apology, disavowal, and punishment, the President refused, and the Soviet Premier broke up the summit conference. See J. Davids,

America and the World of Our Time; R. Osgood, *Limited War;* R. Stebbins, *The United States in World Affairs, 1960;* W. W. Rostow, *The United States in the World Arena;* C. Bowles, *The Coming Political Breakthrough;* J. Lukacs, *A History of the Cold War;* G. Kennan, "Peaceful Coexistence: A Western View," *Foreign Affairs,* January 1960.

1. SOVIET NOTE ON THE U-2 INCIDENT
May 10, 1960
(*Department of State Bulletin,* May 30, 1960)

On May 1 of this year at 5 hours 36 minutes, Moscow time, a military aircraft violated the boundary of the Union of Soviet Socialist Republics and intruded across the borders of the Soviet Union for a distance of more than 2,000 kilometers. The government of the Union of Soviet Socialist Republics naturally could not leave unpunished such a flagrant violation of Soviet state boundaries. When the intentions of the violating aircraft became apparent, it was shot down by Soviet rocket troops in the area of Sverdlovsk.

Upon examination by experts of all data at the disposal of the Soviet side, it was incontrovertibly established that the intruder aircraft belonged to the United States of America, was permanently based in Turkey and was sent through Pakistan into the Soviet Union with hostile purposes. . . .

Exact data from the investigation leave no doubts with respect to the purpose of the flight of the American aircraft which violated the U.S.S.R. border on May 1. This aircraft was specially equipped for reconnaissance and diversionary flight over the territory of the Soviet Union. It had on board apparatus for aerial photography for detecting the Soviet radar network and other special radio-technical equipment which form part of U.S.S.R. anti-aircraft defenses. At the disposal of the Soviet expert commission which carried out the investigation, there is indisputable proof of the espionage-reconnaissance mission of the American aircraft: films of Soviet defense and industrial establishments, a tape record-

ing of signals of Soviet radar stations and other data.

Pilot Powers, . . . has indicated that he did everything in full accordance with the assignment given him. On the flight map taken from him there was clearly and accurately marked the entire route he was assigned after takeoff from the city of Adana (Turkey): Peshawar (Pakistan)–the Ural Sea–Sverdlovsk–Archangel–Murmansk, followed by a landing at the Norwegian airfield at Bude. The pilot has also stated that he served in subunit number 10–10 which under cover of the National Aeronautics and Space Administration is engaged in high altitude military reconnaissance. . . .

After it had been incontrovertibly proven that the American aircraft intruded across the borders of the Soviet Union for aggressive reconnaissance purposes, a new announcement was made by the U.S. State Department on May 7 which contained the forced admission that the aircraft was sent into the Soviet Union for military reconnaissance purposes and, by that very fact, it was admitted that the flight was pursuing aggressive purposes.

2. STATE DEPARTMENT STATEMENT ON THE U-2 INCIDENT
May 7, 1960
(*Department of State Bulletin,* May 23, 1960)

The Department has received the text of Mr. Khrushchev's further remarks about the unarmed plane which is reported to have been shot down in the Soviet Union. As previously announced, it was known that a U-2 plane was missing. As a result of the inquiry ordered by the President it has been established that insofar as the authorities in Washington are concerned there was no authorization for any such flight as described by Mr. Khrushchev.

Nevertheless it appears that in endeavoring to obtain information now concealed behind the Iron Curtain a flight over Soviet territory was probably undertaken by an unarmed civilian U-2 plane.

It is certainly no secret that, given the

state of the world today, intelligence collection activities are practiced by all countries, and postwar history certainly reveals that the Soviet Union has not been lagging behind in this field.

The necessity for such activities as measures for legitimate national defense is enhanced by the excessive secrecy practiced by the Soviet Union in contrast to the free world.

One of the things creating tension in the world today is apprehension over surprise attack with weapons of mass destruction.

To reduce mutual suspicion and to give a measure of protection against surprise attack the United States in 1955 offered its open-skies proposal—a proposal which was rejected out of hand by the Soviet Union. It is in relation to the danger of surprise attack that planes of the type of unarmed civilian U-2 aircraft have made flights along the frontiers of the free world for the past 4 years.

3. EISENHOWER'S STATEMENT ON THE U-2 INCIDENT
May 25, 1960

(Public Papers of the Presidents: Dwight D. Eisenhower, 1960, no. 163)

You recall, of course, why I went to Paris ten days ago.

Last summer and fall I had many conversations with world leaders; some of these were with Chairman Khrushchev, here in America. Over those months a small improvement in relations between the Soviet Union and the West seemed discernible. A possibility developed that the Soviet leaders might at last be ready for serious talks about our most persistent problems—those of disarmament, mutual inspection, atomic control, and Germany, including Berlin.

To explore that possibility, our own and the British and French leaders met together, and later we agreed, with the Soviet leaders, to gather in Paris on May 16. . . .

Our safety, and that of the free world, demand, of course, effective systems for gathering information about the military capabilities of other powerful nations, especially those that make a fetish of secrecy. This involves many techniques and methods. In these times of vast military machines and nuclear-tipped missiles, the ferreting out of this information is indispensable to free-world security.

This has long been one of my most serious preoccupations. It is part of my grave responsibility, within the over-all problem of protecting the American people, to guard ourselves and our allies against surprise attack.

During the period leading up to World War II we learned from bitter experience the imperative necessity of a continuous gathering of intelligence information, the maintenance of military communications and contact, and alertness of command.

An additional word seems appropriate about this matter of communications and command. While the Secretary of Defense and I were in Paris, we were, of course, away from our normal command posts. He recommended that under the circumstances we test the continuing readiness of our military communications. I personally approved. Such tests are valuable and will be frequently repeated in the future.

Moreover, as President, charged by the Constitution with the conduct of America's foreign relations, and as Commander-in-Chief, charged with the direction of the operations and activities of our Armed Forces and their supporting services, I take full responsibility for approving all the various programs undertaken by our government to secure and evaluate military intelligence.

It was in the prosecution of one of these intelligence programs that the widely publicized U-2 incident occurred.

Aerial photography has been one of many methods we have used to keep ourselves and the free world abreast of major Soviet military developments. The usefulness of this work has been well established through four years of effort. The Soviets were well aware of it. Chairman Khrushchev has stated that he became aware of these flights several years ago. Only last week, in his Paris press conference, Chairman Khrushchev confirmed that he knew of these flights when he visited the United States last September.

Incidentally, this raises the natural question—why all the furor concerning one particular flight? He did not, when in America last September charge that these flights were any threat to Soviet safety. He did not then see any reason to refuse to confer with American representatives.

This he did only about the flight that unfortunately failed, on May 1, far inside Russia.

Now, two questions have been raised about this particular flight; first, as to its timing, considering the imminence of the summit meeting; second, our initial statements when we learned the flight had failed.

As to the timing, the question was really whether to halt the program and thus forgo the gathering of important information that was essential and that was likely to be unavailable at a later date. The decision was that the program should not be halted.

The plain truth is this: when a nation needs intelligence activity, there is no time when vigilance can be relaxed. Incidentally, from Pearl Harbor we learned that even negotiation itself can be used to conceal preparations for a surprise attack.

Next, as to our government's initial statement about the flight, this was issued to protect the pilot, his mission, and our intelligence processes, at a time when the true facts were still undetermined.

Our first information about the failure of this mission did not disclose whether the pilot was still alive, was trying to escape, was avoiding interrogation, or whether both plane and pilot had been destroyed. Protection of our intelligence system and the pilot, and concealment of the plane's mission, seemed imperative. It must be remembered that over a long period these flights had given us information of the greatest importance to the nation's security. In fact, their success has been nothing short of remarkable. . . .

I then made two facts clear to the public: first, our program of aerial reconnaissance had been undertaken with my approval; second, this government is compelled to keep abreast, by one means or another, of military activities of the Soviets, just as their government has for years engaged in espionage activities in our country and throughout the world. . . .

In fact, before leaving Washington I had directed that these U-2 flights be stopped. Clearly their usefulness was impaired. Moreover, continuing this particular activity in these new circumstances could not but complicate the relations of certain of our allies with the Soviets.

At the four-power meeting on Monday morning, he demanded of the United States four things: First, condemnation of U-2 flights as a method of espionage; second, assurance that they would not be continued; third, a public apology on behalf of the United States; and, fourth, punishment of all those who had any responsibility respecting this particular mission.

I replied by advising the Soviet leader that I had, during the previous week, stopped these flights and that they would not be resumed. I offered also to discuss the matter with him in personal meetings, while the regular business of the summit might proceed. Obviously, I would not respond to his extreme demands. He knew, of course, by holding to those demands the Soviet Union was scuttling the summit conference. . . .

A major American goal is a world of open societies.

Here in our country anyone can buy maps and aerial photographs showing our cities, our dams, our plants, our highways—indeed, our whole industrial and economic complex. We know that Soviet attachés regularly collect this information. Last fall Chairman Khrushchev's train passed no more than a few hundred feet from an operational ICBM, in plain view from his window. Our thousands of books and scientific journals, our magazines, newspapers and official publications, our radio and television, all openly describe to all the world every aspect of our society.

This is as it should be. We are proud of our freedom.

Soviet distrust, however, does still remain. To allay these misgivings I offered five years ago to open our skies to Soviet reconnaissance aircraft on a reciprocal basis. The Soviets refused. That offer is still open. At an appropriate time America will submit such a program to the United Nations, together with the recommendation that the United Nations itself conduct this reconnaissance.

Should the United Nations accept this proposal, I am prepared to propose that America supply part of the aircraft and equipment required.

632. SHELTON v. TUCKER
364 U.S. 479
1960

Appeal from U.S. District Court for Eastern District of Arkansas. The question presented here was similar to that presented in *NAACP v. Alabama,* 357 U.S. 449 (see Doc. No. 625), and raised some of the questions raised by *Adler* v. *Board of Education,* 342 U.S. 485 and *Belian* v. *Board of Higher Education, 357 U.S. 399:* how far may the state (or the school authorities) go in requiring full disclosure of membership and activities as a prerequisite for teaching in its schools? While on the surface the Arkansas statute proclaimed an interest of the state in all associations and affiliations, there was reason to suppose that it was primarily concerned with membership in the NAACP and similar organizations. See Freund, "Competing Freedoms in American Constitutional Law," 13 *U. of Chicago Conference Series* 26; Richardson, "Freedom of Expression and the Function of the Courts," 65 *Harvard Law Rev.* 1.

Mr. Justice STEWART: An Arkansas statute compels every teacher, as a condition of employment in a state-supported school or college, to file annually an affidavit listing without limitation every organization to which he has belonged or regularly contributed within the preceding five years. At issue in these two cases is the validity of that statute under the Fourteenth Amendment to the Constitution . . .

The statute in question is Act 10 of the Second Extraordinary Session of the Arkansas General Assembly of 1958. The provisions of the Act are summarized in the opinion of the District Court as follows:

"Act 10 provides in substance that no person shall be employed or elected to employment as a superintendent, principal or teacher in any public school in Arkansas, or as an instructor, professor or teacher in any public institution of higher learning in that state until such person shall have submitted to the appropriate hiring authority an affidavit listing all organizations to which he at the time belongs and to which he has belonged during the past five years, and also listing all organizations to which he at the time is paying regular dues or is making regular contributions, or to which within the past five years he has paid such dues or made such contributions. . . ."

The plaintiffs in the Federal District Court (appellants here) were B. T. Shelton, a teacher employed in the Little Rock Public School System, suing for himself and others similarly situated, together with the Arkansas Teachers Association. Shelton . . . declined to file the affidavit, and his contract for the ensuing school year was not renewed. At the trial the evidence showed that he was not a member of the Communist Party or of any organization advocating the overthrow of the government by force, and that he was a member of the National Association for the Advancement of Colored People. The court upheld Act 10, finding the information it required was "relevant," and relying on several decisions of this Court. . . .

It is urged here, as it was unsuccessfully urged throughout the proceedings in both the federal and state courts, that Act 10 deprives teachers in Arkansas of their rights to personal, associational, and academic liberty, protected by the Due Process Clause of the Fourteenth Amendment from invasion by state action. In considering this contention, we deal with two basic postulates.

First. There can be no doubt of the right of a state to investigate the competence and fitness of those whom it hires to teach in its schools, as this Court before now has had occasion to recognize. . . .

Second. It is not disputed that to compel a teacher to disclose his every associational tie is to impair that teacher's right of free association, a right closely allied to freedom of speech and a right which, like free speech, lies at the foundation of a free society. Such interference with personal freedom is conspicuously accented when the teacher serves at the absolute will of those to whom the disclosure must be made—those who any year can terminate the teacher's employment without a hearing, without affording an op- without a hearing, without affording an opportunity to explain.

The statute does not provide that the information it requires be kept confidential. Each school board is left free to deal with the information as it wishes. The record contains evidence to indicate that fear of public disclosure is neither theoretical nor groundless. Even if there were no disclosure to the general public, the pressure upon a teacher to avoid any ties which might displease those who control his professional destiny would be constant and heavy. Public exposure, bringing with it the possibility of public pressures upon school boards to discharge teachers who belong to unpopular or minority organizations, would simply operate to widen and aggravate the impairment of constitutional liberty. . . .

The question to be decided here is not whether the State of Arkansas can ask certain of its teachers about all their organizational relationships. It is not whether the state can ask all of its teachers about certain of their associational ties. It is not whether teachers can be asked how many organizations they belong to, or how much time they spend in organizational activity. The question is whether the state can ask every one of its teachers to disclose every single organization with which he has been associated over a five-year period. The scope of the inquiry required by Act 10 is completely unlimited. The statute requires a teacher to reveal the church to which he belongs, or to which he has given financial support. It requires him to disclose his political party, and every political organization to which he may have contributed over a five-year period. It requires him to list, without number, every conceivable kind of associational tie—social, professional, political, avocational, or religious. Many such relationships could have no possible bearing upon the teacher's occupational competence or fitness.

In a series of decisions this Court has held that, even though the governmental purpose be legitimate and substantial, that purpose cannot be pursued by means that broadly stifle fundamental personal liberties when the end can be more narrowly achieved. The breadth of legislative abridgment must be viewed in the light of less drastic means for achieving the same basic purpose. . . .

The unlimited and undiscriminate sweep of the statute now before us brings it within the ban of our prior cases. The statute's comprehensive interference with associational freedom goes far beyond what might be justified in the exercise of the state's legitimate inquiry into the fitness and competency of its teachers. The judgments in both cases must be reversed.

It is so ordered.

Judgments reversed.

Justices FRANKFURTER, CLARK, HARLAN and WHITTAKER, dissenting.

---

633. EISENHOWER'S FAREWELL ADDRESS
January 17, 1961

(Public Papers of the Presidents: Dwight D. Eisenhower, 1960–61, no. 421)

On Eisenhower see S. Adams, *First-Hand Report: Story of the Eisenhower Administration;* M. Childs, *Eisenhower: Captive Hero;* R. J. Donavan, *Eisenhower, the Inside Story;* L. Koenig, *The Invisible Presidency;* M. J. Pusey, *Eisenhower the President;* R. Rovere, *The Eisenhower Years: Affairs of State.*

My fellow Americans:

Three days from now, after half a century in the service of our country, I shall lay down the responsibilities of office as, in traditional and solemn ceremony, the authority of the Presidency is vested in my successor. . . .

We now stand ten years past the midpoint of a century that has witnessed four major wars among great nations. Three of them involved our own country. Despite these holocausts America is today the strongest, the most influential and most productive nation in the world. Understandably proud of this pre-eminence we yet realize that America's leadership and prestige depend, not merely upon our unmatched material progress, riches and military strength, but on how we use our power in the interests of world peace and human betterment.

Throughout America's adventure in free government, our basic purposes have been to keep the peace; to foster progress in human achievement, and to enhance liberty, dignity and integrity among people and among nations. To strive for less would be unworthy of a free and religious people. Any failure traceable to arrogance, or our lack of comprehension or readiness to sacrifice would inflict upon us grievous hurt both at home and abroad.

Progress toward these noble goals is persistently threatened by the conflict now engulfing the world. It commands our whole attention, absorbs our very beings. We face a hostile ideology—global in scope, atheistic in character, ruthless in purpose, and insidious in method. Unhappily the danger it poses promises to be of indefinite duration. To meet it successfully, there is called for, not so much the emotional and transitory sacrifices of crisis, but rather those which enable us to carry forward steadily, surely, and without complaint the burdens of a prolonged and complex struggle—with liberty the stake. Only thus shall we remain, despite every provocation, on our charted course toward permanent peace and human betterment. . . .

A vital element in keeping the peace is our military establishment. Our arms must be mighty, ready for instant action, so that no potential aggressor may be tempted to risk his own destruction.

Our military organization today bears little relation to that known by any of my predecessors in peacetime, or indeed by the fighting men of World War II or Korea.

Until the latest of our world conflicts, the United States had no armaments industry. American makers of plowshares could, with time and as required, make swords as well. But now we can no longer risk emergency improvisation of national defense; we have been compelled to create a permanent armaments industry of vast proportions. Added to this, three and a half million men and women are directly engaged in the defense establishment. We annually spend on military security more than the net income of all United States corporations.

This conjunction of an immense military establishment and a large arms industry is new in the American experience. The total influence—economic, political, even spiritual—is felt in every city, every statehouse, every office of the federal government. We recognize the imperative need for this development. Yet we must not fail to comprehend its grave implications. Our toil, resources, and livelihood are all involved; so is the very structure of our society.

In the councils of government, we must guard against the acquisition of unwarranted influence, whether sought or unsought, by the military-industrial complex. The potential for the disastrous rise of misplaced power exists and will persist.

We must never let the weight of this combination endanger our liberties or democratic processes. We should take nothing for granted. Only an alert and knowledgeable citizenry can compel the proper meshing of the huge industrial and military machinery of defense with our peaceful methods and goals, so that security and liberty may prosper together.

Akin to, and largely responsible for the sweeping changes in our industrial-military posture, has been the technological revolution during recent decades.

In this revolution, research has become central; it also becomes more formalized, complex, and costly. A steadily increasing share is conducted for, by, or at the direction of, the federal government. . . .

The prospect of domination of the nation's scholars by federal employment, project allocations, and the power of money is ever present—and is gravely to be regarded.

Yet, in holding scientific research and discovery in respect, as we should, we must also be alert to the equal and opposite danger that public policy could itself become the captive of a scientific-technological elite.

It is the task of statesmanship to mold, to balance, and to integrate these and other forces, new and old, within the principles of our democratic system—ever aiming toward the supreme goals of our free society.

Another factor in maintaining balance involves the element of time. As we peer into society's future, we—you and I, and our government—must avoid the impulse to live only for today, plundering, for our own ease and convenience, the precious resources of tomorrow. We cannot mortgage the material assets of our grandchildren without risking the loss also of their political and spiritual heritage. We want democracy to survive for all generations to come, not to become the insolvent phantom of tomorrow.

Down the long lane of the history yet to be written America knows that this world of ours, ever growing smaller, must avoid becoming a community of dreadful fear and hate, and be, instead, a proud confederation of mutual trust and respect.

Such a confederation must be one of equals. The weakest must come to the conference table with the same confidence as do we, protected as we are by our moral, economic, and military strength. That table, though scarred by many past frustrations, cannot be abandoned for the certain agony of the battlefield.

Disarmament, with mutual honor and confidence, is a continuing imperative. Together we must learn how to compose differences, not with arms, but with intellect and decent purpose. Because this need is so sharp and apparent I confess that I lay down my official responsibilities in this field with a definite sense of disappointment. As one who has witnessed the horror and the lingering sadness of war—as one who knows that another war could utterly destroy this civilization which has been so slowly and painfully built over thousands of years—I wish I could say tonight that a lasting peace is in sight.

Happily, I can say that war has been avoided. Steady progress toward our ultimate goal has been made. But, so much remains to be done. As a private citizen, I shall never cease to do what little I can to help the world advance along that road. . . .

634. JOHN F. KENNEDY'S INAUGURAL ADDRESS
January 20, 1961
(*Department of State Bulletin,* February 6, 1961)

Nominated on the first ballot at the Democratic convention in Los Angeles, Senator Kennedy won the 1960 election by a slim popular margin of 118,000 votes and a substantial majority of 303 to 219 votes in the electoral college. On Kennedy see T. White, *The Making of the President, 1960;* D. Acheson, *A Democrat Looks at his Party;* J. McG. Burns, *John F. Kennedy;* and Kennedy's own *The Strategy of Peace, Let Us Begin,* and *To Turn the Tide.*

an end as well as a beginning—signifying renewal as well as change. For I have sworn before you and Almighty God the same solemn oath our forebearers prescribed nearly a century and three-quarters ago.

The world is very different now. For man holds in his mortal hands the power to abolish all forms of human poverty and all forms of human life. And yet the same revolutionary beliefs for which our forebearers fought are still at issue around the globe—the belief that the rights of man come not from the generosity of the state but from the hand of God.

We dare not forget today that we are the heirs of that first revolution. Let the word go forth from this time and place, to friend and foe alike, that the torch has been passed to a new generation of Americans—born in this

Vice-President Johnson, Mr. Speaker, Mr. Chief Justice, President Eisenhower, Vice-President Nixon, President Truman, Reverend Clergy, Fellow Citizens:

We observe today not a victory of party but a celebration of freedom—symbolizing century, tempered by war, disciplined by a hard and bitter peace, proud of our ancient heritage—and unwilling to witness or permit the slow undoing of those human rights to which this nation has always been committed, and to which we are committed today at home and around the world.

Let every nation know, whether it wishes us well or ill, that we shall pay any price, bear any burden, meet any hardship, support any friend, oppose any foe to assure the survival and the success of liberty.

This much we pledge—and more.

To those old allies whose cultural and spiritual origins we share, we pledge the loyalty of faithful friends. United, there is little we cannot do in a host of co-operative ventures. Divided, there is little we can do—for we dare not meet a powerful challenge at odds and split asunder.

To those new states whom we welcome to the ranks of the free, we pledge our word that one form of colonial control shall not have passed away merely to be replaced by a far more iron tyranny. We shall not always expect to find them supporting our view. But we shall always hope to find them strongly supporting their own freedom—and to remember that, in the past, those who foolishly sought power by riding the back of the tiger ended up inside.

To those people in the huts and villages of half the globe struggling to break the bonds of mass misery, we pledge our best efforts to help them help themselves, for whatever period is required—not because the Communists may be doing it, not because we seek their votes, but because it is right. If a free society cannot help the many who are poor, it cannot save the few who are rich.

To our sister republics south of our border, we offer a special pledge—to convert our good words into good deeds—in a new alliance for progress—to assist free men and free governments in casting off the chains of poverty. But this peaceful revolution of hope cannot become the prey of hostile powers. Let all our neighbors know that we shall join with them to oppose aggression or subversion anywhere in the Americas. And let every other power know that this hemisphere intends to remain the master of its own house.

To that world assembly of sovereign states, the United Nations, our last best hope in an age where the instruments of war have far outpaced the instruments of peace, we renew our pledge of support—to prevent it from becoming merely a forum for invective—to strengthen its shield of the new and the weak—and to enlarge the area in which its writ may run.

Finally, to those nations who would make themselves our adversary, we offer not a pledge but a request: that both sides begin anew the quest for peace, before the dark powers of destruction unleashed by science engulf all humanity in planned or accidental self-destruction.

We dare not tempt them with weakness. For only when our arms are sufficient beyond doubt can we be certain beyond doubt that they will never be employed.

But neither can two great and powerful groups of nations take comfort from our present course—both sides overburdened by the cost of modern weapons, both rightly alarmed by the steady spread of the deadly atom, yet both racing to alter that uncertain balance of terror that stays the hand of mankind's final war.

So let us begin anew—remembering on both sides that civility is not a sign of weakness, and sincerity is always subject to proof. Let us never negotiate out of fear. But let us never fear to negotiate.

Let both sides explore what problems unite us instead of belaboring those problems which divide us.

Let both sides, for the first time, formulate serious and precise proposals for the inspection and control of arms—and bring the absolute power to destroy other nations under the absolute control of all nations.

Let both sides seek to invoke the wonders of science instead of its terrors. Together let us explore the stars, conquer the deserts, eradicate disease, tap the ocean depths, and encourage the arts and commerce.

Let both sides unite to heed in all corners of the earth the command of Isaiah—to "undo the heavy burdens . . . [and] let the oppressed go free."

And if a beachhead of co-operation may push back the jungle of suspicion, let both sides join in creating a new endeavor, not a new balance of power, but a new world of law, where the strong are just and the weak secure and the peace preserved.

All this will not be finished in the first one hundred days. Nor will it be finished in the first one thousand days, nor in the life of this administration, nor even perhaps in our lifetime on this planet. But let us begin.

In your hands, my fellow citizens, more than mine, will rest the final success or failure of our course. Since this country was founded, each generation of Americans has been summoned to give testimony to its national loyalty. The graves of young Americans who answered the call to service surround the globe.

Now the trumpet summons us again—not as a call to bear arms, though arms we need —not as a call to battle, though embattled we are—but a call to bear the burden of a long twilight struggle, year in and year out, "rejoicing in hope, patient in tribulation"— a struggle against the common enemies of man: tyranny, poverty, disease, and war itself.

Can we forge against these enemies a grand and global alliance, North and South, East and West, that can assure a more fruit-ful life for all mankind? Will you join in that historic effort?

In the long history of the world, only a few generations have been granted the role of defending freedom in its hour of maximum danger. I do not shrink from this responsibility—I welcome it. I do not believe that any of us would exchange places with any other people or any other generation. The energy, the faith, the devotion which we bring to this endeavor will light our country and all who serve it—and the glow from that fire can truly light the world.

And so, my fellow Americans: ask not what your country can do for you—ask what you can do for your country.

My fellow citizens of the world: ask not what America will do for you, but what together we can do for the freedom of man.

Finally, whether you are citizens of America or citizens of the world, ask of us here the same high standards of strength and sacrifice which we ask of you. With a good conscience our only sure reward, with history the final judge of our deeds, let us go forth to lead the land we love, asking His blessing and His help, but knowing that here on earth God's work must truly be our own.

---

635. KENNEDY'S MESSAGE ON FEDERAL AID TO EDUCATION
February 20, 1961

(Public Papers of the Presidents: John F. Kennedy, 1961, no. 46)

Between 1920 and 1960 the population increased by about 75 per cent and the high school population by 500 per cent, while college and university enrollment increased sixfold. Inability of the poorer states to support public schools and universities adequately led to a widespread demand for federal aid to education at every level. In the late forties Senator Taft introduced a bill appropriating up to $250 million a year to aid public schools in the poorer states and guaranteeing appropriations of $40 a year for every schoolchild in the country. This bill failed of passage as did similar bills during the Eisenhower administration. Meantime, however, federal appropriations for research in colleges and universities, and for scholarships to students of science had mounted to substantial sums. President Kennedy came to office committed to a program of federal aid to education at all levels, but his proposals ran into intransigent opposition from states rightists and from those who feared a crack in the "wall of separation between church and state." See J. Conant, *The American High School Today;* J. Conant, *Slums and Suburbs;* F. Butts, *The American Tradition in Religion and Education;* L. Pfeffer, *Church, State and Freedom;* J. O'Neill, *Religion and Education Under the Constitution;* A. Schlesinger, Jr., *A Thousand Days;* T. Sorenson, *The Kennedy Legacy.*

1. ASSISTANCE TO PUBLIC ELEMENTARY AND SECONDARY SCHOOLS

. . . I recommend to the Congress a three-year program of general federal assistance for public elementary and secondary classroom construction and teachers' salaries.

Based essentially on the bill which passed the Senate last year (S. 8), although beginning at a more modest level of expenditures, this program would assure every state of no less than $15 for every public school student in average daily attendance, with the total amount appropriated ($666 million being authorized in the first year, rising to $866 million over a three-year period) distributed according to the equalization formula contained in the last year's Senate bill, and already familiar to the Congress by virtue of its similarity to the formulas contained in the Hill-Burton Hospital Construction and other acts. Ten per cent of the funds allocated to each state in the first year, and an equal amount thereafter, is to be used to help meet the unique problems of each state's "areas of special educational need"— depressed areas, slum neighborhoods, and others.

This is a modest program with ambitious goals. The sums involved are relatively small when we think in terms of more than 36 million public school children, and the billions of dollars necessary to educate them properly. Nevertheless, a limited beginning now—consistent with our obligations in other areas of responsibility—will encourage all states to expand their facilities to meet the increasing demand and enrich the quality of education offered, and gradually assist our relatively low-income states in the elevation of their educational standards to a national level.

The bill which will follow this message has been carefully drawn to eliminate disproportionately large or small inequities, and to make the maximum use of a limited number of dollars. In accordance with the clear prohibition of the Constitution, no elementary or secondary school funds are allocated for constructing church schools or paying church-school teachers' salaries; and thus nonpublic school children are rightfully not counted in determining the funds each state will receive for its public schools. Each state will be expected to maintain its own effort or contribution; and every state whose effort is below the national average will be expected to increase that proportion of its income which is devoted to public elementary and secondary education.

This investment will pay rich dividends in the years ahead—in increased economic growth, in enlightened citizens, in national excellence. For some 40 years, the Congress has wrestled with this problem and searched for a workable solution. I believe that we now have such a solution; and that this Congress in this year will make a land-mark contribution to American education. . . .

2. Construction of Colleges and University Facilities

The burden of increased enrollments—imposed upon our elementary and secondary schools already in the fifties—will fall heavily upon our colleges and universities during the sixties. By the autumn of 1966, an estimated one million more students will be in attendance at institutions of higher learning than enrolled last fall—for a total more than twice as high as the total college enrollment of 1950. Our colleges, already hard-pressed to meet rising enrollments since 1950 during a period of rising costs, will be in critical straits merely to provide the necessary facilities, much less the cost of quality education.

The country as a whole is already spending nearly $1 billion a year on academic and residential facilities for higher education— some 20 per cent of the total spent for higher education. Even with increased contributions from state, local, and private sources, a gap of $2.9 billion between aggregate needs and expenditures is anticipated by 1965, and a gap of $5.2 billion by 1970.

The national interest requires an educational system on the college level sufficiently financed and equipped to provide every student with adequate physical facilities to meet his instructional, research, and residential needs.

I therefore recommend legislation which will:

(1) Extend the current College Housing Loan Program with a five year $250 million a year program designed to meet the federal government's appropriate share of residential housing for students and faculty. As a start, additional lending authority is necessary to speed action during fiscal 1961 on approvable loan applications already at hand.

(2) Establish a new, though similar, long-term, low-interest rate loan program for academic facilities, authorizing $300 million in loans each year for five years to assist in the construction of classrooms, laboratories, libraries, and related structures—sufficient to enable public and private higher institutions to accommodate the expanding enrollments they anticipate over the next five years; and also to assist in the renovation, rehabilitation, and modernization of such facilities.

. . . I recommend the establishment of a five-year program with an initial authorization of $26,250,000 of state-administered scholarships for talented and needy young people which will supplement but not supplant those programs of financial assistance to students which are now in operation.

Funds would be allocated to the states during the first year for a total of twenty-five thousand scholarships averaging $700 each, 37,500 scholarships the second year, and 50,000 for each succeeding year thereafter. These scholarships, which would range according to need up to a maximum stipend of $1000, would be open to all young persons, without regard to sex, race, creed, or color, solely on the basis of their ability—as determined on a competitive basis—and their financial need. They would be permitted to attend the college of their choice, and free to select their own program of study. Inasmuch as tuition and fees do not normally cover the institution's actual expenses in educating the student, additional allowances to the college or university attended should accompany each scholarship to enable these institutions to accept the additional students without charging an undue increase in fees or suffering an undue financial loss.

636. KENNEDY'S MESSAGE ON THE PEACE CORPS
March 1, 1961
(*Department of State Bulletin,* March 20, 1961)

The Peace Corps was to the 1960s what Lend-Lease had been to the 1940s; like Lend-Lease it caught the popular imagination not only at home but abroad. The idea apparently originated with the President's brother-in-law, Sargent Shriver, who was appointed its first director. In his message to Congress the President noted that the idea of a Peace Corps had received strong support from members of Congress, and from universities, student groups, labor unions, and others. First established on a pilot basis by Executive Order of March 1, the Peace Corps was put on a permanent statutory basis on September 22, when Congress appropriated $40 million for its operation during the fiscal year of 1962. The Peace Corps provided an effective outlet for the idealism of American youth. As the President said in his statement on signing the Executive Order, "Life in the Peace Corps will not be easy. There will be no salary, and allowances will be at a level sufficient only to maintain health and meet basic needs. . . . But every American who participates in the Peace Corps . . . will know that he or she is sharing in the great common task of bringing to man that decent way of life which is the foundation of freedom and a condition of peace." See L. Fuchs, *"Those Peculiar Americans": The Peace Corps and American* *National Character;* S. Shriver, "Two Years of the Peace Corps," 41 *Foreign Affairs* 694; T. Sorenson, *Kennedy;* R. Hoopes, *The Peace Corps Experience;* M. Windmiller, *The Peace Corps and Pax Americana.*

To the Congress of the United States:

I recommend to the Congress the establishment of a permanent Peace Corps—a pool of trained American men and women sent overseas by the U.S. Government or through private organizations and institutions to help foreign countries meet their urgent needs for skilled manpower. . . .

Throughout the world the people of the newly developing nations are struggling for economic and social progress which reflects their deepest desires. Our own freedom, and the future of freedom around the world, depend, in a very real sense, on their ability to build growing and independent nations where men can live in dignity, liberated from the bonds of hunger, ignorance, and poverty.

One of the greatest obstacles to the achievement of this goal is the lack of trained men and women with the skill to teach the young and assist in the operation of development projects—men and women with the capacity to cope with the demands of swiftly evolving economies, and with the dedication to put that capacity to work in the villages, the mountains, the towns, and the factories of dozens of struggling nations.

The vast task of economic development urgently requires skilled people to do the work of the society—to help teach in the schools, construct development projects, demonstrate modern methods of sanitation in the villages, and perform a hundred other tasks calling for training and advanced knowledge.

To meet this urgent need for skilled manpower we are proposing the establishment of a Peace Corps—an organization which will recruit and train American volunteers, sending them abroad to work with the people of other nations.

This organization will differ from existing assistance programs in that its members will supplement technical advisers by offering the specific skills needed by developing nations if they are to put technical advice to work. They will help provide the skilled manpower necessary to carry out the development projects planned by the host governments, acting at a working level and serving at great personal sacrifice. There is little doubt that the number of those who wish to serve will be far greater than our capacity to absorb them. . . .

Last session, the Congress authorized a study of these possibilities. Preliminary reports of this study show that the Peace Corps is feasible, needed, and wanted by many foreign countries.

Most heartening of all, the initial reaction to this proposal has been an enthusiastic response by student groups, professional organizations, and private citizens everywhere —a convincing demonstration that we have in this country an immense reservoir of dedicated men and women willing to devote their energies and time and toil to the cause of world peace and human progress.

Among the specific programs to which Peace Corps members can contribute are teaching in primary and secondary schools, especially as part of national English language teaching programs; participation in the worldwide program of malaria eradication; instruction and operation of public health and sanitation projects; aiding in village development through school construction and other programs; increasing rural agricultural productivity by assisting local farmers to use modern implements and techniques. The initial emphasis of these programs will be on teaching. Thus the Peace Corps members will be an effective means of implementing the development programs of the host countries—programs which our technical assistance operations have helped to formulate.

The Peace Corps will not be limited to the young, or to college graduates. All Americans who are qualified will be welcome to join this effort. But undoubtedly the corps will be made up primarily of young people as they complete their formal education. . . .

. . . Each new recruit will receive a training and orientation period varying from 6 weeks to 6 months. This training will include courses in the culture and language of the country to which they are being sent and specialized training designed to increase the work skills of recruits. In some cases training will be conducted by participant agencies and universities in approved training programs. Other training programs will be conducted by the Peace Corps staff.

Length of service in the Corps will vary depending on the kind of project and the country, generally ranging from 2 to 3 years. Peace Corps members will often serve under conditions of physical hardship, living under primitive conditions among the people of developing nations. For every Peace Corps member service will mean a great financial sacrifice. They will receive no salary. Instead they will be given an allowance which will only be sufficient to meet their basic needs and maintain health. It is essential that Peace Corps men and women live simply and unostentatiously among the people they have come to assist. At the conclusion of their tours, members of the Peace Corps will receive a small sum in the form of severance pay based on length of service abroad to assist them during their first weeks back in the United States. Service with the Peace Corps will not exempt volunteers from selective service.

637. KENNEDY'S PROPOSAL FOR THE ALLIANCE FOR PROGRESS
March 13, 1961
(Department of State Bulletin, April 3, 1961)

Kennedy inherited a difficult and highly sensitive Latin-American situation, and tackled it with immense energy. For the background of the Latin-American problem see the analysis in Kennedy's address of March 13, which we give here. The formal charter of Punta del Este, Uruguay, was designed to implement the proposals set forth by the President. See A. Stevenson, "The Alliance for Progress: A Road Map to New Achievements," *Dept. of State Bull.,* August 21, 1961; W. Benton, *The Voice of Latin America;* C. Bowles, *An American Purpose;* W. Manger, ed., *The Alliance for Progress: A Critical Appraisal;* V. Alba, *Alliance Without Allies: The Mythology of Progress in Latin America;* J. Dreier, *The Alliance for Progress: Problems and Perspectives;* W. Krause, *The United States and Latin America: The Alliance for Progress Program;* H. K. May, *Problems and Perspectives of the Alliance for Progress: A Critical Examination;* P. Nehemkis, *Latin America: Myth and Reality;* H. Perloff, *Alliance for Progress: A Social Innovation in the Making;* R. Steel, *Pax Americana;* J. Levinson and J. De Onis, *The Alliance that Lost Its Way.*

children are deprived of the education or the jobs which are the gateway to a better life. And each day the problems grow more urgent. Population growth is outpacing economic growth, low living standards are even further endangered, and discontent—the discontent of a people who know that abundance and the tools of progress are at last within their reach—that discontent is growing. In the words of José Figueres, "once dormant peoples are struggling upward toward the sun, toward a better life."

If we are to meet a problem so staggering in its dimensions, our approach must itself be equally bold, an approach consistent with the majestic concept of Operation Pan America. Therefore I have called on all people of the hemisphere to join in a new Alliance for Progress—*Alianza para Progreso*—a vast co-operative effort, unparalleled in magnitude and nobility of purpose, to satisfy the basic needs of the American people for homes, work and land, health and schools—*techo, trabajo y tierra, salud y escuela.*

TEN-YEAR PLAN FOR THE AMERICAS

. . . One hundred and thirty-nine years ago the United States, stirred by the heroic struggle of its fellow Americans, urged the independence and recognition of the new Latin-American republics. It was then, at the dawn of freedom throughout this hemisphere, that Bolívar spoke of his desire to see the Americas fashioned into the greatest region in the world, "greatest," he said, "not so much by virtue of her area and her wealth, as by her freedom and her glory."

Never, in the long history of our hemisphere, has this dream been nearer to fulfillment, and never has it been in greater danger. . . .

Throughout Latin America—a continent rich in resources and in the spiritual and cultural achievements of its people—millions of men and women suffer the daily degradations of hunger and poverty. They lack decent shelter or protection from disease. Their

First, I propose that the American republics begin on a vast new ten-year plan for the Americas, a plan to transform the 1960's into an historic decade of democratic progress. These ten years will be the years of maximum progress, maximum effort—the years when the greatest obstacles must be overcome, the years when the need for assistance will be the greatest.

And if we are successful, if our effort is bold enough and determined enough, then the close of this decade will mark the beginning of a new era in the American experience. The living standards of every American family will be on the rise, basic education will be available to all, hunger will be a forgotten experience, the need for massive outside help will have passed, most nations will have entered a period of self-sustaining growth, and, although there will be still much to do, every American republic will be the master of its own revolution and its own hope and progress. . . .

If the countries of Latin America are ready to do their part—and I am sure they are—then I believe the United States, for its part, should help provide resources of a scope and magnitude sufficient to make this bold development plan a success, just as we helped to provide, against nearly equal odds, the resources adequate to help rebuild the economies of Western Europe. For only an effort of towering dimensions can insure fulfillment of our plan for a decade of progress.

Second, I will shortly request a ministerial meeting of the Inter-American Economic and Social Council, a meeting at which we can begin the massive planning effort which will be at the heart of the Alliance for Progress.

For if our alliance is to succeed, each Latin nation must formulate long-range plans for its own development—plans which establish targets and priorities, insure monetary stability, establish the machinery for vital social change, stimulate private activity and initiative, and provide for a maximum national effort. These plans will be the foundation of our development effort and the basis for the allocation of outside resources. . . .

Third, I have this evening signed a request to the Congress for $500 million as a first step in fulfilling the Act of Bogotá. This is the first large-scale inter-American effort —instituted by my predecessor President Eisenhower—to attack the social barriers which block economic progress. The money will be used to combat illiteracy, improve the productivity and use of their land, wipe out disease, attack archaic tax and land-tenure structures, provide educational opportunities, and offer a broad range of projects designed to make the benefits of increasing abundance available to all. We will begin to commit these funds as soon as they are appropriated.

Fourth, we must support all economic integration which is a genuine step toward larger markets and greater competitive opportunity. The fragmentation of Latin-American economies is a serious barrier to industrial growth. Projects such as the Central American common market and free-trade areas in South America can help to remove these obstacles.

Fifth, the United States is ready to co-operate in serious, case-by-case examinations of commodity market problems. Frequent violent changes in commodity prices seriously injure the economies of many Latin-American countries, draining their resources and stultifying their growth. Together we must find practical methods of bringing an end to this pattern.

Sixth, we will immediately step up our food-for-peace emergency program, help to establish food reserves in areas of recurrent drought, and help provide school lunches for children and offer feed grains for use in rural development. For hungry men and women cannot wait for economic discussions or diplomatic meetings; their need is urgent, and their hunger rests heavily on the conscience of their fellow men.

Seventh, all the people of the hemisphere must be allowed to share in the expanding wonders of science—wonders which have captured man's imagination, challenged the powers of his mind, and given him the tools for rapid progress. I invite Latin-American scientists to work with us in new projects in fields such as medicine and agriculture, physics and astronomy, and desalinization, and to help plan for regional research laboratories in these and other fields, and to strengthen co-operation between American universities and laboratories.

We also intend to expand our science-teacher training programs to include Latin-American instructors, to assist in establishing such programs in other American countries, and translate and make available revolutionary new teaching materials in physics, chemistry, biology, and mathematics so that the young of all nations may contribute their skills to the advance of science.

Eighth, we must rapidly expand the training of those needed to man the economies of rapidly developing countries. This means expanded technical training programs, for which the Peace Corps, for example, will be available when needed. It also means assistance to Latin-American universities, graduate schools, and research institutes.

We welcome proposals in Central America for intimate co-operation in higher education, co-operation which can achieve a regional effort of increased effectiveness and excellence. We are ready to help fill the gap in trained manpower, realizing that our ultimate goal must be a basic education for all who wish to learn.

Ninth, we reaffirm our pledge to come to the defense of any American nation whose independence is endangered. As confidence in the collective security system of the Organization of American States spreads, it will be possible to devote to constructive use a major share of those resources now spent on the instruments of war. Even now, as the government of Chile has said, the time has come to take the first steps toward sensible limitations of arms. And the new generation of military leaders has shown an increasing awareness that armies can not only defend their countries—they can, as we have learned through our own Corps of Engineers, help to build them.

Tenth, we invite our friends in Latin America to contribute to the enrichment of life and culture in the United States. We need teachers of your literature and history and tradition, opportunities for our young people to study in your universities, access to your music, your art, and the thought of your great philosophers. For we know we have much to learn.

In this way you can help bring a fuller spiritual and intellectual life to the people of the United States and contribute to understanding and mutual respect among the nations of the hemisphere.

With steps such as these we propose to complete the revolution of the Americas, to build a hemisphere where all men can hope for a suitable standard of living and all can live out their lives in dignity and in freedom.

POLITICAL FREEDOM AND SOCIAL PROGRESS

To achieve this goal political freedom must accompany material progress. Our Alliance for Progress is an alliance of free governments—and it must work to eliminate tyranny from a hemisphere in which it has no rightful place. Therefore let us express our special friendship to the people of Cuba and the Dominican Republic—and the hope

they will soon rejoin the society of free men, uniting with us in our common effort.

This political freedom must be accompanied by social change. For unless necessary social reforms, including land and tax reform, are freely made, unless we broaden the opportunity of all of our people, unless the great mass of Americans share in increasing prosperity, then our alliance, our revolution, our dream, and our freedom will fail. But we call for social change by free men—change in the spirit of Washington and Jefferson, of Bolívar and San Martín and Martí—not change which seeks to impose on men tyrannies which we cast out a century and a half ago. Our motto is what it has always been—progress yes, tyranny no—*progreso sí, tiranía no!*

But our greatest challenge comes from within—the task of creating an American civilization where spiritual and cultural values are strengthened by an ever-broadening base of material advance, where, within the rich diversity of its own traditions, each nation is free to follow its own path toward progress.

The completion of our task will, of course, require the efforts of all the governments of our hemisphere. But the efforts of governments alone will never be enough. In the end the people must choose and the people must help themselves.

And so I say to the men and women of the Americas—to the *campesino* in the fields, to the *obrero* in the cities, to the *estudiante* in the schools—prepare your mind and heart for the task ahead, call forth your strength, and let each devote his energies to the betterment of all so that your children and our children in this hemisphere can find an ever richer and a freer life.

Let us once again transform the American Continent into a vast crucible of revolutionary ideas and efforts, a tribute to the power of the creative energies of free men and women, an example to all the world that liberty and progress walk hand in hand. Let us once again awaken our American revolution until it guides the struggles of people everywhere—not with an imperialism of force or fear but the rule of courage and freedom and hope for the future of man.

638. THE BAY OF PIGS: AMBASSADOR STEVENSON'S STATEMENTS
1961
(Department of State Bulletin, May 8, 1961)

American opinion had, at first, welcomed the overthrow of the Cuban dictator, Batista, and the accession to power of the revolutionary leader Fidel Castro. Castro, however, speedily embarked upon three policies which alienated not only American but Latin-American sympathy as well: reckless confiscation of American and other foreign property without compensation; infiltration and subversion of other Latin-American states; and a close rapprochement to Soviet Russia. On January 3, 1961 Castro, in what amounted to an open declaration of hostility, ordered that the American Embassy be reduced to eleven persons; President Eisenhower countered by severing relations with Cuba. Meantime thousands of refugees from the Castro dictatorship had fled to nearby states in Latin America, and particularly to Florida, where they planned and drilled for a return to their home island and the overthrow of the dictator. There is no doubt that in this they were supported, financed, and armed by the U.S. Central Intelligence Agency. Castro charged that the United States was planning to invade his island, but at a press conference April 12 President Kennedy stated that "there will not under any conditions be . . . an intervention in Cuba by United States armed forces. This Government will do everything it possibly can—and I think it can meet its responsibilities—to make sure that there are no Americans involved in any actions inside Cuba." On the morning of April 15, airplanes stationed in Florida bombed the Cuban mainland, and on the morning of the 17th, the Cuban refugees took off from Florida and Guatemala in an attempted invasion of their home country. The invasion was a failure; almost all of the invaders were killed or captured. Cuba—supported by the Soviet— promptly charged that the United States had invaded her, and called upon the UN to brand her action that of an aggressor. We give here portions of Ambassador Adlai Stevenson's replies to these charges. See, C. W. Mills, *Listen, Yankee;* N. Weyl, *Red Star Over Cuba;* H. Matthews, *The Cuban Story;* R. F. Smith, *The United States and Cuba, 1917–1960;* T. Szulc and K. Meyer, *The Cuban Invasion;* R. Scheer & M. Zeitlin, *Cuba: Tragedy in Our Hemisphere;* T. Sorenson, *The Kennedy Legacy;* P. Salinger, *With Kennedy;* A. Schlesinger, Jr., *A Thousand Days;* H. Johnson, *The Bay of Pigs: The Leader's Story.*

STATEMENT OF APRIL 17

Let me make it clear that we do not regard the Cuban problem as a problem between Cuba and the United States. The challenge is not to the United States but to the hemiphere and its duly constituted body, the Organization of American States. The Castro regime has betrayed the Cuban revolution. It is now collaborating in organized attempts by means of propaganda, agitation, and subversion to bring about the overthrow of existing governments by force and replace them with regimes subservient to an extracontinental power. These events help to explain why the Cuban government continues to bypass the Organization of American States, even if they do not explain why Cuba, which is thus in open violation of its obligations under inter-American treaties and agreements, continues to charge the United States with violations of these same obligations.

Soon after the Castro government assumed power, it launched a program looking to the export of its system to other countries of the hemisphere, particularly in the Caribbean area. The intervention of Cuban diplomatic personnel in the internal affairs of other nations of the hemisphere has become flagrant. Cuban diplomatic and consular establishments are used as distribution points for propaganda material calling on the peoples of Latin America to follow Cuba's example. Even Cuban diplomatic pouches destined for various Latin-American countries have been found to contain inflammatory and subversive propaganda directed against friendly governments.

In public support of these activities Prime Minister Castro, President Dorticós, Dr. Roa himself, and many other high-ranking members of the revolutionary government have openly stated that "the peoples of Latin America should follow Cuba's example." They have frankly declared that the Cuban system is for export. . . .

Statements of Soviet Russian and Chinese Communist leaders indicate that, by Dr. Castro's own actions, the Cuban revolution has become an instrument of the foreign policies of these extracontinental powers. The increasingly intimate relationship between Cuba and the Soviet Union, the People's Republic of China, and other countries associated with them, in conjunction with the huge shipments of arms, munitions, and other equipment from the Sino-Soviet bloc, must therefore be matters of deep concern to independent governments everywhere.

The Castro regime has mercilessly destroyed the hope of freedom the Cuban people had briefly glimpsed at the beginning of 1959. Cuba has never witnessed such political persecution as exists today. The arrests, the prisons bulging with political prisoners, and the firing squads testify to this. Since the Castro regime came to power, more than 600 persons have been executed, with a shocking disregard of the standards of due process of law and fair trial generally accepted and practiced in the civilized community of nations. The government has even threatened to replace its slogan for this year—"the year of education"—with a new slogan—"the year of the execution wall."

There is no democratic participation of the Cuban people in their determination of their destiny. Staged rallies, at which small percentages of the population are harangued and asked to express approval of policies by shouts or show of hands, represent the procedure of a totalitarian demagog and not free and democratic expression of opinion through the secret ballot.

The Cuban farm worker who was promised his own plot of land finds that he is an employee of the state working on collective or state-run farms. The independent labor movement, once one of the strongest in the hemisphere, is today in chains. Freely elected Cuban labor leaders, who as late as the end of 1960 protested the destruction of workers' rights, were imprisoned for their pains, or took asylum in foreign embassies, or fled the country to escape imprisonment.

When in addition the people are confronted, despite aid from the Sino-Soviet bloc, with a drastic reduction in their stan-

dard of living, it is not surprising opposition to their present master grows. . . .

The problem created in the Western Hemisphere by the Cuban revolution is not one of revolution. . . . The problem is that every effort is being made to use Cuba as a base to force totalitarian ideology into other parts of the Americas.

The Cuban government has disparaged the plans of the American states to pool their resources to accelerate social and economic development in the Americas. At the Bogotá meeting of the Committee of 21 in September, 1960, the Cuban delegation missed few opportunities to insult the representatives of other American states and to play an obstructionist role. They refused to sign the Act of Bogotá and thereby to take part in the hemisphere-wide co-operative effort of social reform to accompany programs of economic development. The Cuban official reaction to President Kennedy's Alliance for Progress program for the Americas was in a similar vein. In a speech on March 12, 1961, Dr. Castro denounced the program, portraying it as a program of "alms" using "usurious dollars" to buy the economic independence and national dignity of the countries which participate in the program. . . .

Dr. Castro has carefully and purposefully destroyed the great hope the hemisphere invested in him when he came to power two years ago. No one in his senses could have expected to embark on such a course as this with impunity. No sane man would suppose that he could speak Dr. Castro's words, proclaim his aggressive intentions, carry out his policies of intervention and subversion—and at the same time retain the friendship, the respect, and the confidence of Cuba's sister republics in the Americas. He sowed the wind and reaps the whirlwind.

It is not the United States which is the cause of Dr. Castro's trouble: It is Dr. Castro himself. It is not Washington which has turned so many thousands of his fellow countrymen against his regime—men who fought beside him in the Cuban hills, men who risked their lives for him in the underground movements in Cuban cities, men who lined Cuban streets to hail him as the liberator from tyranny, men who occupied the most prominent places in the first government of the Cuban revolution. It is these men who constitute the threat—if threat there is—to Dr. Castro's hope of consolidating his power and intensifying his tyranny. . . .

The problem which the United States confronts today is our attitude toward such men as these. Three years ago many American citizens looked with sympathy on the cause espoused by Castro and offered hospitality to his followers in their battle against the tyranny of Batista. We cannot expect Americans today to look with less sympathy on those Cubans who, out of love for their country and for liberty, now struggle against the tyranny of Castro.

If the Castro regime has hostility to fear, it is the hostility of Cubans, not of Americans. If today Castro's militia are hunting down guerrillas in the hills where Castro himself once fought, they are hunting down Cubans, not Americans. If the Castro regime is overthrown, it will be overthrown by Cubans, not by Americans.

I do not see that it is the obligation of the United States to protect Dr. Castro from the consequences of his treason to the promises of the Cuban revolution, to the hopes of the Cuban people, and to the Democratic aspirations of the Western Hemisphere. . . .

Our only hope is that the Cuban tragedy may awaken the people and governments of the Americas to a profound resolve—a resolve to concert every resource and energy to advance the cause of economic growth and social progress throughout the hemisphere, but to do so under conditions of human freedom and political democracy. This cause represents the real revolution of the Americas. To this struggle to expand freedom and abundance and education and culture for all the citizens of the New World the free states of the hemisphere summon all the peoples in nations where freedom and independence are in temporary eclipse. We confidently expect that Cuba will be restored to the American community and will take a leading role to win social reform and economic opportunity, human dignity and democratic government, not just for the people of Cuba but for all the people of the hemisphere.

STATEMENT OF APRIL 18

The current uprising in Cuba is the product of the progressively more violent opposition of the Cuban people to the policies and practices of this regime. Let us not forget that there have been hundreds of freedom fighters in the mountains of central Cuba for almost a year; that during the last six months skirmishes with the Castro police, attacks upon individual members of his armed forces, nightly acts of sabotage by the revolutionaries, have been increasing in number and intensity. Protest demonstrations have taken place by workers whose trade-union rights have been betrayed, by Catholics whose freedom of expression and worship has been circumscribed, by professional men whose right to free association has been violated. The response of the Castro regime has been repression, arrests without warrant, trial without constitutional guarantees, imprisonment without term and without mercy, and, finally, the execution wall.

Let me be absolutely clear: that the present events are the uprising of the Cuban people against an oppressive regime which has never given them the opportunity in peace and by democratic process to approve or to reject the domestic and foreign policies which it has followed.

For our part, our attitude is clear. Many Americans looked with sympathy, as I have said, on the cause espoused by Dr. Castro when he came to power. They look with the same sympathy on the men who today seek to bring freedom and justice to Cuba—not for foreign monopolies, not for the economic or political interests of the United States or any foreign power, but for Cuba and for the Cuban people.

It is hostility of Cubans, not Americans, that Dr. Castro has to fear. It is not our obligation to protect him from the consequences of his treason to the revolution, to the hopes of the Cuban people, and to the democratic aspirations of the hemisphere.

The United States sincerely hopes that any difficulties which we or other American countries may have with Cuba will be settled peacefully. We have committed no aggression against Cuba. We have no aggressive purposes against Cuba. We intend no military intervention in Cuba. We seek to see a restoration of the friendly relations which once prevailed between Cuba and the United States. We hope that the Cuban people will settle their own problems in their own interests and in a manner which will assure social justice, true independence, and political liberty to the Cuban people. . . .

STATEMENT OF APRIL 20

I have some final words that I should like to say in this debate. I am grateful to those of my colleagues who have expressed respect for my country and for the honesty of its spokesmen here and in Washington.

First let me say that we don't deny that the exiles from Cuba have received the sympathy of many people inside and outside the United States—even as Dr. Castro had the sympathy of many in the United States, Mexico, and elsewhere. But the extent to which so many speakers have deliberately confused this with intervention and aggression by the United States Government has exceeded all bounds of fact or fancy.

Obviously the incessant repetition of such charges as though they had been proved reveals a greater anxiety to mislead and to corrupt world opinion than to keep the discussion on the tracks. . . .

I have heard a torrent—a deluge—of ugly words from Communist speakers here accusing the United States of aggression and invasion against Cuba. I will resist the temptation to invite attention to the record of aggression of the countries represented by some of those speakers—or to inquire as to which country has *really* intervened in Cuba, which country has perverted the Cuban revolution, and why these same speakers are so emotional about the revolt of the Cuban refugees against the new tyranny in Cuba and the new imperialism in the world.

Let me just ask—if this was a United States military operation, do you think it would succeed or fail? How long do you think Cuba could resist the military power

of the United States? Perhaps the best evidence of the falsity of the shrill charges of American aggression in Cuba is the melancholy fact that this blow for freedom has not yet succeeded. And if the United States had been in charge I submit that fighting would hardly have broken out on the day debate was to start in this committee. . . .

The Cuban people have not spoken.

Their yearning to be free of Castro's executions, of his betrayal of the revolution, of his controlled press, and of his yoke and rule by mailed fist has not been extinguished. The more than 100,000 refugees from his tyranny are undeniable proof of the historic aspirations of the Cuban people for freedom. The Cubans will continue to look forward to the day when they can determine their own future by democratic processes and through free institutions.

And what are the lessons to be learned? For those Cuban patriots who gave their lives, the lesson is one of tragic finality. But what of those who live on and will shape the future? The events of the last few days are indelible reminders to all of us in the Western Hemisphere. The penetration of force from outside our hemisphere, dominating a puppet government and providing it with arms, tanks, and fighter aircraft, is already dangerously strong and deep. It is now demonstrably stronger, deeper, and more dangerous to all of us who value freedom than most Americans—and most of our neighbors in the Western Hemisphere—have been willing to think.

If there is hope in the events of the last few days it is that it will awaken all of us in the Americas to a renewed determination to mobilize every resource and energy to advance the cause of economic growth and social progress throughout the hemisphere—to foster conditions of freedom and political democracy. They summon all of us to expand freedom and abundance with education of all peoples. If we dedicate ourselves with renewed resolve to bringing greater social reform, greater economic opportunity, greater human dignity, the sacrifices of the last few days will not have been in vain. . . .

639. THE BERLIN CRISIS
1961

(Department of State Bulletin, August 14, 1961)

The long-simmering Berlin crisis reached another of its many climaxes in midsummer of 1961. In the alternating seasons of thaw and freeze in Russian policy towards the West, this was a season of deep freeze. On June 4, Premier Khrushchev proposed the effective ending of the three-power control of West Berlin and the creation of a "demilitarized city" for Berlin. "The occupation regime now being maintained," he wrote, "has already outlived itself and has lost all connection with the purposes for which it was established, as well as with the Allied agreements concerning Germany that established the basis for its existence. The occupation rights will naturally be terminated upon the conclusion of a German peace treaty, whether it is signed with both German States or only with the German Democratic Republic [i.e., East Germany] within whose territory West Berlin is located." The West reacted sharply to this proposal; President Kennedy's address of July 25 breathed determination and defiance. The Soviet response was just as decided. On August 13, East German authorities—supported of course by the Soviet—closed the boundaries between the Eastern and the Western sectors of the hapless city. Not withstanding vigorous protests from the Western powers, East Germany then proceeded to erect a vast concrete wall between the two sectors, in part to prevent the continuous flow of refugees and escapees to the Western sector, in part to dramatize the separation of the two Berlins and to isolate the West Berliners. We give here President Kennedy's address of July 25 and the formal protest of the Western Commandants of August 15. The story can be followed in the successive issues of the *Department of State Bulletin* during the summer and fall of 1961.

An important by-product of the Berlin crisis was a lively public controversy over fall-out shelters, touched off by Kennedy's plea for a greatly enlarged program of civil defense. A wide variety of critics opposed large-scale construction of shelters on the grounds that it increased the risk of nuclear war and that in any case there was no adequate defense against all-out nuclear attack. The combination of this criticism and public apathy defeated efforts to commit the country to what was, in effect, a new nuclear strategy (as distinguished from the old strategy of deterrence by threat of retaliation)—the proposition that the country could

survive a nuclear war and might therefore, under certain circumstances, be able to undertake a "preemptive first strike." See T. Sorenson, *The Kennedy Legacy;* A. Schlesinger, Jr., *A Thousand Days.*

1. KENNEDY'S REPORT
July 25, 1961

Seven weeks ago tonight I returned from Europe to report on my meeting with Premier Khrushchev and the others. His grim warnings about the future of the world, his aide memoire on Berlin, his subsequent speeches and threats which he and his agents have launched, and the increase in the Soviet military budget that he has announced have all prompted a series of decisions by the administration and a series of consultations with the members of the NATO organization. In Berlin, as you recall, he intends to bring to an end, through a stroke of the pen, first, our legal rights to be in West Berlin and, secondly, our ability to make good on our commitment to the 2 million free people of that city. That we cannot permit.

We are clear about what must be done—and we intend to do it. I want to talk frankly with you tonight about the first steps that we shall take. These actions will require sacrifice on the part of many of our citizens. More will be required in the future. They will require, from all of us, courage and perseverance in the years to come. But if we and our allies act out of strength and unity of purpose—with calm determination and steady nerves, using restraint in our words as well as our weapons—I am hopeful that both peace and freedom will be sustained.

The immediate threat to free men is in West Berlin. But that isolated outpost is not an isolated problem. The threat is worldwide. Our effort must be equally wide and strong and not be obsessed by any single manufactured crisis. We face a challenge in Berlin, but there is also a challenge in southeast Asia, where the borders are less guarded, the enemy harder to find, and the danger of communism less apparent to those who have so little. We face a challenge in our own hemisphere and indeed wherever else the freedom of human beings is at stake.

Let me remind you that the fortunes of war and diplomacy left the free people of West Berlin in 1945 110 miles behind the Iron Curtain. . . .

We are there as a result of our victory over Nazi Germany, and our basic rights to be there deriving from that victory include both our presence in West Berlin and the enjoyment of access across East Germany. These rights have been repeatedly confirmed and recognized in special agreements with the Soviet Union. Berlin is not a part of East Germany, but a separate territory under the control of the allied powers. Thus our rights there are clear and deep-rooted. But in addition to those rights is our commitment to sustain—and defend, if need be—the opportunity for more than 2 million people to determine their own future and choose their own way of life.

Thus our presence in West Berlin, and our access thereto, cannot be ended by any act of the Soviet Government. The NATO shield was long ago extended to cover West Berlin, and we have given our word that an attack in that city will be regarded as an attack upon us all.

For West Berlin, lying exposed 110 miles inside East Germany, surrounded by Soviet troops and close to Soviet supply lines, has many roles. It is more than a showcase of liberty, a symbol, an island of freedom in a Communist sea. It is even more than a link with the free world, a beacon of hope behind the Iron Curtain, an escape hatch for refugees.

West Berlin is all of that. But above all it has now become, as never before, the great testing place of Western courage and will, a focal point where our solemn commitments, stretching back over the years since 1945, and Soviet ambitions now meet in basic confrontation.

It would be a mistake for others to look upon Berlin, because of its location, as a tempting target. The United States is there, the United Kingdom and France are there, the pledge of NATO is there, and the people of Berlin are there. It is as secure, in that sense, as the rest of us, for we cannot separate its safety from our own.

I hear it said that West Berlin is militarily untenable. And so was Bastogne. And so, in fact, was Stalingrad. Any dangerous spot is tenable if men—brave men—will make it so.

We do not want to fight, but we have fought before. And others in earlier times have made the same dangerous mistake of assuming that the West was too selfish and too soft and too divided to resist invasions of freedom in other lands. Those who threaten to unleash the forces of war on a dispute over West Berlin should recall the words of the ancient philosopher: "A man who causes fear cannot be free from fear."

We cannot and will not permit the Communists to drive us out of Berlin, either gradually or by force. . . .

In the days and months ahead, I shall not hesitate to ask the Congress for additional measures or exercise any of the Executive powers that I possess to meet this threat to peace. Everything essential to the security of freedom must be done; and if that should require more men, or more taxes, or more controls, or other new powers, I shall not hesitate to ask them. The measures proposed today will be constantly studied, and altered as necessary. But while we will not let panic shape our policy, neither will we permit timidity to direct our program.

Accordingly I am now taking the following steps:

(1) I am tomorrow requesting of the Congress for the current fiscal year an additional $3,247,000,000 of appropriations for the Armed Forces.

(2) To fill out our present Army divisions and to make more men available for prompt deployment, I am requesting an increase in the Army's total authorized strength from 875,000 to approximately 1 million men.

(3) I am requesting an increase of 29,000 and 63,000 men, respectively, in the active-duty strength of the Navy and the Air Force.

(4) To fulfill these manpower needs, I

am ordering that our draft calls be doubled and tripled in the coming months. . . .

And let me add that I am well aware of the fact that many American families will bear the burden of these requests. Studies or careers will be interrupted; husbands and sons will be called away; incomes in some cases will be reduced. But these are burdens which must be borne if freedom is to be defended. Americans have willingly borne them before, and they will not flinch from the task now.

We have another sober responsibility. To recognize the possibilities of nuclear war in the missile age without our citizens' knowing what they should do and where they should go if bombs begin to fall would be a failure of responsibility. In May I pledged a new start on civil defense. Last week I assigned, on the recommendation of the Civil Defense Director, basic responsibility for this program to the Secretary of Defense, to make certain it is administered and coordinated with our continental defense efforts at the highest civilian level. Tomorrow I am requesting of the Congress new funds for the following immediate objectives: to identify and mark space in existing structures—public and private—that could be used for fallout shelters in case of attack; to stock those shelters with food, water, first-aid kits, and other minimum essentials for survival; to increase their capacity; to improve our air-raid warning and fallout detection systems, including a new household warning system which is now under development; and to take other measures that will be effective at an early date to save millions of lives if needed.

In the event of an attack, the lives of those families which are not hit in a nuclear blast and fire can still be saved—*if* they can be warned to take shelter and *if* that shelter is available. We owe that kind of insurance to our families—and to our country. In contrast to our friends in Europe, the need for this kind of protection is new to our shores. But the time to start is now. In the coming months I hope to let every citizen know what steps he can take without delay to protect his family in case of attack. I know that you will want to do no less. . . .

2. NOTE OF WESTERN COMMANDANTS TO SOVIET COMMANDANTS
August 15, 1961
(Department of State Bulletin, September 4, 1961)

During the night of August 12–13 the East German authorities put into effect illegal measures designed to turn the boundaries between the West sectors of Berlin and the Soviet sector into an arbitrary barrier to movement of German citizens resident in East Berlin and East Germany.

Not since the imposition of the Berlin blockade had there been such a flagrant violation of the four-power agreements concerning Berlin. The agreement of June 20, 1949, in which the U.S.S.R. pledged itself to facilitate freedom of movement within Berlin and between Berlin and the rest of Germany, had also been violated.

In disregard of these arrangements and of the wishes of the population of this city, for the welfare of which the four powers are jointly responsible, freedom of circulation throughout Berlin has been severely curtailed. Traffic between the East sector and the Western sectors of Berlin has been disrupted by the cutting of S-Bahn and U-Bahn service, the tearing up of streets, the erection of road blocks, and the stringing of barbed wire. In carrying out these illegal actions, military, and paramilitary units, which were formed in violation of four-power agreements and whose very presence in East Berlin is illegal, turned the Soviet sector of Berlin into an armed camp.

Moreover, the East German authorities have now prohibited the many inhabitants of East Berlin and East Germany who were employed in West Berlin from continuing to pursue their occupations in West Berlin. They have thus denied to the working population under their control the elementary right of free choice of place of employment.

It is obvious that the East German authorities have taken these repressive measures because the people under their control, deeply perturbed by the threats on Berlin recently launched by Communist leaders, were fleeing in large numbers to the West.

We must protest against the illegal measures introduced on August 13 and hold you responsible for the carrying out of the relevant agreements.

640. KENNEDY'S LETTER TO NGO DINH DIEM
December 14, 1961

(Department of State Bulletin, January 1, 1962)

For the background of the Vietnamese situation see Doc. No. 608. In spite of the reluctance of the Eisenhower administration to commit itself to full-scale support of Diem, the latter found many influential friends in this country, both in the government and without. The American Friends of Vietnam, organized by liberals in 1955, promoted Diem as a democratic alternative to Communism, and a group of political scientists at Michigan State University, supported by the Central Intelligence Agency (CIA), helped to organize the police force which in the absence of long-awaited land reforms became the mainstay of Diem's regime. Senator John F. Kennedy, introduced to Diem in 1952 by Supreme Court Justice William O. Douglas, became an early supporter of Diem, although it was under Kennedy's administration that the United States in 1963 finally abandoned the Diem regime to its fate—largely, it would appear, because Diem seemed finally to be more interested, in Kennedy's estimation, in quelling local opposition than in fighting the Communists. In the meantime, however—still hoping that Diem would become the nucleus of a workable democratic nationalism—Kennedy, accepting Diem's thesis that North Vietnam was seeking "to take over your country," stepped up American support by sending military "advisers" to South Vietnam, thereby drawing the United States further into a situation from which there seemed to be no turning back, yet the advantages of which became increasingly difficult to perceive. See Docs. No. 650, 653, 654, 662, 665; also G. M. Kahin and J. W. Lewis, *The United States in Vietnam;* B. Fall, *Vietnam Witness: 1953–1966;* R. Hilsman, *To Move a Nation;* T. Sorenson, *Kennedy;* A. Schlesinger, Jr., *A Thousand Days;* T. Draper, *Abuse of Power;* A. Buchan, "Questions about Vietnam," in R. Falk, ed., *The Vietnam War and International Law,* II, 35–44; F. Schurmann, *The Politics of Escalation;* E. Weintal and C. Bartlett, *Facing the Brink.*

Dear Mr. President:

I have received your recent letter in which you described so cogently the dangerous condition caused by North Vietnam's efforts to take over your country. The situation in your embattled country is well known to me and to the American people. We have been deeply disturbed by the assault on your country. Our indignation has mounted as the deliberate savagery of the Communist program of assassination, kidnapping, and wanton violence became clear.

Your letter underlines what our own information has convincingly shown—that the campaign of force and terror now being waged against your people and your Government is supported and directed from the outside by the authorities at Hanoi. They have thus violated the provisions of the Geneva Accords designed to ensure peace in Vietnam and to which they bound themselves in 1954.

At that time, the United States, although not a party to the Accords, declared that it "would view any renewal of the aggression in violation of the Agreements with grave concern and as seriously threatening international peace and security." We continue to maintain that view.

In accordance with that declaration, and in response to your request, we are prepared to help the Republic of Vietnam to protect its people and to preserve its independence. We shall promptly increase our assistance to your defense effort as well as help relieve the destruction of the floods which you describe. I have already given the orders to get these programs underway.

The United States, like the Republic of Vietnam, remains devoted to the cause of peace and our primary purpose is to help your people maintain their independence. If the Communist authorities in North Vietnam will stop their campaign to destroy the Republic of Vietnam, the measures we are taking to assist your defense efforts will no longer be necessary. We shall seek to persuade the Communists to give up their attempts of force and subversion. In any case, we are confident that the Vietnamese people will preserve their independence and gain the

peace and prosperity for which they have sought so hard and so long.

641. BAKER v. CARR
369 U.S. 186
1962

Appeal from District Court for the Middle District of Tennessee. Not since *Brown* v. *Topeka* had any decision been awaited as eagerly as was this decision on the power of the courts to rule on questions of legislative apportionment in the states. The situation was familiar and widespread: rural control of state legislatures through the power over apportionment, and the refusal—often in the face of clear constitutional mandate—to carry through periodic reapportionments. A case involving issues similar to those in this case, *Colegrove* v. *Green,* 328 U.S. 549 (1946), had been dismissed because the issue was held to be of a peculiarly political nature; but that case had been decided by a close vote of 4 to 3. Only one of the four was still on the Court in 1962—Frankfurter—while two of the dissenters—Black and Douglas—participated in the *Baker* v. *Carr* case. See on the whole question of legislative apportionment and judicial review, Griffith, *Rise and Development of the Gerrymander;* Bone, "States Attempting to Comply with Reapportionment Requirements," 17 *Law and Contemporary Problems* 387; Harvey, "Reapportionments of State Legislatures," 17 *Law and Contemporary Problems* 364; Walter, "Reapportionment and Urban Representation," 105 *Annals of Am. Aca. of Pol. and Soc. Sci.* 11; Lewis, "Legislative Apportionment and the Federal Courts," 71 *Harvard Law Rev.* 1057; Durfee "Apportionment or Representation in the Legislature," 43 *Michigan Law Rev.* 1091; Senator Clark in 106 *Congressional Record,* 13827–42 (June 29, 1960); A. E. Banfield, "Baker v Carr: New Light on the Constitutional Guarantees of Republican Government," 50 *California Law Rev.* 243; R. Dixon, "Legislative Apportionment and the Federal Constitution," 27 *Law and Contemporary Problems* 329; S. H. Friedelbaum, "Baker v Carr: The New Doctrine of Judicial Intervention and Its Implications for American Federalism," 29 *U. of Chicago Law Rev.* 673; R. B. McKay, "Political Thickets and Crazy Quilts: Reapportionment and Equal Protection," 61 *Michigan Law Rev.* (February 1963); Robert McCloskey, "Forward: The Reapportionment Case," 76 *Harvard Law Rev.* 54; R. Dixon, *Democratic Representation;* A. Cox, *The Warren Court;*

P. C. Neal, "Baker v Carr: Politics in Search of Law," *Supreme Court Review, 1962;* R. Cortner, *The Apportionment Cases;* C. Auerbach, "The Reapportionment Cases: One Person, One Vote—One Vote, One Value," in P. B. Kurland, ed., *The Supreme Court Review, 1964,* 188.

Mr. Justice BRENNAN:

This civil action was brought to redress the alleged deprivation of federal constitutional rights. The complaint, alleging that by means of a 1901 statute of Tennessee apportioning the members of the General Assembly among the state's 95 counties, "these plaintiffs and others similarly situated, are denied the equal protection of the laws accorded them by the Fourteenth Amendment to the Constitution of the United States by virtue of the debasement of their votes," was dismissed by a three-judge court in the Middle District of Tennessee. The court held that it lacked jurisdiction of the subject matter and also that no claim was stated upon which relief could be granted. We hold that the dismissal was error, and remand the cause to the District Court for trial and further proceedings consistent with this opinion. . . .

The Tennessee Constitution provides in Article II as follows:

"SEC. 4. *Census.*—An enumeration of the qualified voters, and an apportionment of the Representatives in the General Assembly, shall be made in the year one thousand eight hundred and seventy-one, and within every subsequent term of ten years.

"SEC. 5. *Apportionment of representatives.*—The number of Representatives shall, at the several periods of making the enumeration, be apportioned among the several counties or districts, according to the number of qualified voters in each. . . .

"SEC. 6. *Apportionment of senators.*— The number of Senators shall, at the several periods of making the enumeration, be apportioned among the several counties or districts according to the number of qualified electors in each, and shall not exceed one-third in the number of representatives. . . ."

Thus, Tennessee's standard for allocating legislative representation among her counties is the total number of qualified voters resident in the respective counties, subject only to minor qualifications. Decennial reapportionment in compliance with the constitutional scheme was effected by the General Assembly each decade from 1871 to 1901. . . .

In the more than 60 years since that action, all proposals in both Houses of the General Assembly for reapportionment have failed to pass.

Between 1901 and 1961, Tennessee has experienced substantial growth and redistribution of her population. In 1901, the population was 2,020,616, of whom 487,380 were eligible to vote. The 1960 federal census reports the State's population at 3,567,089, of whom 2,092,891 are eligible to vote. The relative standings of the counties in terms of qualified voters have changed significantly. It is primarily the continued application of the 1901 Apportionment Act to this shifted and enlarged voting population which gives rise to the present controversy.

Indeed, the complaint alleges that the 1901 statute, even as of the time of its passage, "made no apportionment of Representatives and Senators in accordance with the constitutional formula . . . , but instead arbitrarily and capriciously apportioned representatives in the Senate and House without reference . . . to any logical or reasonable formula whatever." It is further alleged that "because of the population changes since 1900, and the failure of the legislature to reapportion itself since 1901," the 1901 statute became "unconstitutional and obsolete." Appellants also argue that, because of the composition of the legislature effected by the 1901 apportionment act, redress in the form of a state constitutional amendment to change

the entire mechanism for reapportioning, or any other change short of that, is difficult or impossible. The complaint concludes that "these plaintiffs and others similarly situated, are denied the equal protection of the laws accorded them by the Fourteenth Amendment to the Constitution of the United States by virtue of the debasement of their votes." They seek a declaration that the 1901 statute is unconstitutional and an injunction restraining the appellees from acting to conduct any further elections under it. They also pray that unless and until the General Assembly enacts a valid reapportionment, the District Court should either decree a reapportionment by mathematical application of the Tennessee constitutional formulae to the most recent federal census figures, or direct the appellees to conduct legislative elections, primary and general, at large. They also pray for such other and further relief as may be appropriate. . . .

In light of the District Court's treatment of the case, we hold today only that (a) that the court possessed jurisdiction of the subject matter; (b) that a justiciable cause of action is stated upon which appellants would be entitled to appropriate relief; and (c) because appellees raise the issue before this Court, that the appellants have standing to challenge the Tennessee apportionment statutes. Beyond noting that we have no cause at this stage to doubt the District Court will be able to fashion relief if violations of constitutional rights are found, it is improper now to consider what remedy would be most appropriate if appellants prevail at the trial. . . .

Article III, Sect. 2 of the federal Constitution provides that "the judicial Power shall extend to all Cases, in Law and Equity, arising under this Constitution, the Laws of the United States, and Treaties made, or which shall be made, under their Authority; . . ." It is clear that the cause of action is one which "arises under" the federal Constitution. The complaint alleges that the 1901 statute effects an apportionment that deprives the appellants of the equal protection of the laws in violation of the Fourteenth Amendment. Dismissal of the complaint upon the ground of lack of jurisdiction of the subject matter would, therefore, be justified only if that claim were "so attenuated and unsubstantial as to be absolutely devoid of merit." . . .

Since the complaint plainly sets forth a case arising under the Constitution, the subject matter is within the federal judicial power defined in Art. III, Sect. 2, and so within the power of Congress to assign to the jurisdiction of the District Courts. Congress has exercised that power. . . .

An unbroken line of our precedents sustains the federal courts' jurisdiction of the subject matter of federal constitutional claims of this nature.

A federal court cannot "pronounce any statute, either of a state or of the United States, void, because irreconcilable with the Constitution, except as it is called upon to adjudge the legal rights of litigants in actual controversies."

Have the appellants alleged such a personal stake in the outcome of the controversy as to assure that concrete adverseness which sharpens the presentation of issues upon which the court so largely depends for illumination of difficult constitutional questions? This is the gist of the question of standing. It is, of course, a question of federal law. . . .

We hold that the appellants do have standing to maintain this suit. Our decisions plainly support this conclusion. Many of the cases have assumed rather than articulated the premise in deciding the merits of similar claims. And Colegrove v. Green, squarely held that voters who allege facts showing disadvantage to themselves as individuals have standing to sue. A number of cases decided after Colegrove recognized the standing of the voters there involved to bring those actions.

These appellants seek relief in order to protect or vindicate an interest of their own, and of those similarly situated. Their constitutional claim is, in substance, that the 1901 statute constitutes arbitrary and capricious state action, offensive to the Fourteenth Amendment in its irrational disregard of the standard of apportionment prescribed by the state's constitution or of any standard, effecting a gross disproportion of representation to voting population. . . . A citizen's right to a vote free of arbitrary impairment by state action has been judicially recognized as a right secured by the Constitution, when such impairment resulted from dilution by a false tally, cf. United States v. Classic, 313 U.S. 299, or by a refusal to count votes from arbitrarily selected precincts, cf. United States v. Mosley, 238 U.S. 383, or by a stuffing of the ballot box, cf. Ex parte Siebold, 100 U.S. 371.

It would not be necessary to decide whether appellants' allegations of impairment of their votes by the 1901 apportionment will, ultimately, entitle them to any relief, in order to hold that they have standing to seek it. If such impairment does produce a legally cognizable injury, they are among those who have sustained it. They are asserting "a plain, direct and adequate interest in maintaining the effectiveness of their votes," Coleman v. Miller, 307 U.S. at 438. They are entitled to a hearing and to the District Court's decision on their claims. "The very essence of civil liberty certainly consists in the right of every individual to claim the protection of the laws, whenever he receives an injury." Marbury v. Madison, 5 U.S. 137, 163.

In . . . Colegrove v. Green, the court stated: "From a review of these decisions there can be no doubt that the federal rule . . . is that the federal courts . . . will not intervene in cases of this type to compel legislative reapportionment." 179 F. Supp. at 826. We understand the District Court to have read the cited cases as compelling the conclusion that since the appellants sought to have a legislative apportionment held unconstitutional, their suit presented a "political question" and was therefore nonjusticiable. We hold that this challenge to an apportionment presents no nonjusticiable "political question." The cited cases do not hold the contrary.

Of course the mere fact that the suit seeks protection of a political right does not mean it presents a political question. . . .

But it is argued that this case shares the characteristics of decisions that constitute a category not yet considered, cases concerning the Constitution's guaranty, in Art. IV, Sect. 4, of a republican form of government. A conclusion as to whether the case at bar does present a political question cannot be confidently reached until we have considered those cases with special care. We shall discover that Guaranty Clause claims involve those elements which define a "political question," and for that reason and no other, they are nonjusticiable. In particular, we shall discover that the nonjusticiability of such claims has nothing to do with their touching upon matters of state governmental organization. . . .

We come, finally, to the ultimate inquiry whether our precedents as to what constitutes a nonjusticiable "political question" bring the case before us under the umbrella of that doctrine. A natural beginning is to note whether any of the common characteristics which we have been able to identify and label descriptively are present. We find none: The question here is the consistency of state action with the federal Constitution. We have no question decided, or to be decided, by a political branch of government coequal with this Court. Nor do we risk embarrassment of our government abroad, or grave disturbance at home if we take issue with Tennessee as to the constitutionality of her action here challenged. Nor need the appellants, in order to succeed in this action, ask the Court to enter upon policy determinations for which judicially manageable standards are lacking. Judicial standards under the Equal Protection Clause are well developed and familiar, and it has been open to courts since the enactment of the Fourteenth Amendment to determine, if on the

particular facts they must, that a discrimination reflects *no* policy, but simply arbitrary and capricious action.

This case does, in one sense, involve the allocation of political power within a state, and the appellants might conceivably have added a claim under the Guaranty Clause. Of course, as we have seen, any reliance on that clause would be futile. But, because any reliance on the Guaranty Clause could not have succeeded it does not follow that appellants may not be heard on the Equal Protection claim which in fact they tender. True, it must be clear that the Fourteenth Amendment claim is not so enmeshed with those political question elements which render Guaranty Clause claims nonjusticiable as actually to present a political question itself. But we have found that not to be the case here. . . .

We conclude that the complaint's allegations of a denial of equal protection present a justiciable constitutional cause of action upon which appellants are entitled to a trial and a decision. The right asserted is within the reach of judicial protection under the Fourteenth Amendment.

The judgment of the District Court is reversed. . . .

Justices DOUGLAS, CLARK, and STEWART, filed concurring opinions. FRANKFURTER and HARLAN dissented.

642.　THE CUBAN MISSILE CRISIS
October 27, 1962
(*Department of State Bulletin,* November 12, 1962)

For reasons that are not altogether clear, the Soviet Union, at Fidel Castro's request, decided to place intermediate-range ballistic missiles on Cuba—a reckless act which may have contributed to Khrushchev's downfall in October 1964. Kennedy's decision to force removal of the missiles brought the world to the gravest crisis it had experienced since World War II, perhaps the gravest military crisis in history, since it carried with it the possibility of all-out nuclear war. For a week, the world trembled on the edge of catastrophe. Publicly the Russians proposed a deal: Russian missiles to be withdrawn from Cuba in return for the removal of Ameri-

can missiles from Turkey, combined with pledges of nonaggression on the part of both major powers. Privately, in a letter the substance of which is repeated in Kennedy's reply (given here in its entirety), Khrushchev made no mention of a bargain and asked merely for an American assurance not to invade Cuba—a reminder, incidentally, that the Bay of Pigs incident had played some part in bringing about the present crisis. In effect, Khrushchev backed down, and Kennedy's prompt and gracious acceptance of his capitulation brought the crisis to an end. See Doc. No. 638; L. Lockwood, *Castro's Cuba, Cuba's Fidel;* M. Zeitlin and

R. Scheer, *Cuba: Tragedy in Our Hemisphere;*
T. Draper, *Castro's Revolution: Myths and
Realities;* K. E. Meyer and T. Szulc, *The Cuban
Invasion: The Chronicle of a Disaster;* E. Abel,
The Missile Crisis; T. Sorenson, *Kennedy;*
A. Schlesinger, Jr., *A Thousand Days;* E. Weintal
and C. Bartlett, *Facing the Brink;* D. Horowitz,
"Showdown: The Cuban Crisis," in A. D. Don-
ald, ed., *John F. Kennedy and the New Fron-
tier;* H. Thomas, *Cuba: The Pursuit of Free-
dom;* R. Hagen and B. Bernstein, "Military
Value of Missiles in Cuba," 19 *Bull. of the
Atomic Scientists* 8; R. Kennedy, *Thirteen
Days;* R. Divine, ed., *The Cuban Missile Crisis;*
G. T. Allison, *Essence of Decision: Explaining
the Cuban Missile Crisis.*

Dear Mr. Chairman:

I have read your letter of October 26th
with great care and welcomed the statement
of your desire to seek a prompt solution to
the problem. The first thing that needs to
be done, however, is for work to cease on
offensive missile bases in Cuba and for all
weapons systems in Cuba capable of offensive use to be rendered inoperable, under effective United Nations arrangements.

Assuming this is done promptly, I have
given my representatives in New York instructions that will permit them to work out
this weekend—in cooperation with the Acting Secretary General and your representative—an arrangement for a permanent solution to the Cuban problem along the lines
suggested in your letter of October 26th. As
I read your letter, the key elements of your
proposals—which seem generally acceptable
as I understand them—are as follows:

1) You would agree to remove these
weapons systems from Cuba under appropriate United Nations observation and supervision; and undertake, with suitable safe-

guards, to halt the further introduction of
such weapons systems into Cuba.

2) We, on our part, would agree—upon
the establishment of adequate arrangements
through the United Nations to ensure the
carrying out and continuation of these commitments—(a) to remove promptly the quarantine measures now in effect and (b) to
give assurances against an invasion of Cuba.
I am confident that other nations of the
Western Hemisphere would be prepared to
do likewise.

If you will give your representative similar instructions, there is no reason why we
should not be able to complete these arrangements and announce them to the world
within a couple of days. The effect of such
a settlement on easing world tensions would
enable us to work toward a more general arrangement regarding "other armaments", as
proposed in your second letter which you
made public. I would like to say again that
the United States is very much interested in
reducing tensions and halting the arms race;
and if your letter signifies that you are prepared to discuss a detente affecting NATO
and the Warsaw Pact, we are quite prepared
to consider with our allies any useful proposals.

But the first ingredient, let me emphasize,
is the cessation of work on missile sites in
Cuba and measures to render such weapons
inoperable, under effective international guarantees. The continuation of this threat, or a
prolonging of this discussion concerning Cuba
by linking these problems to the broader
questions of European and world security,
would surely lead to an intensification of
the Cuban crisis and a grave risk to the
peace of the world. For this reason I hope
we can quickly agree along the lines outlined
in this letter and in your letter of October
26th.

643. KENNEDY'S SPEECH AT AMERICAN UNIVERSITY
June 10, 1963

(Public Papers of the Presidents: John F. Kennedy, 1963, no. 232)

Both the USSR and the United States emerged
somewhat sobered and chastened from the near-
disaster of the Cuban missile crisis. In the
spring of 1963, they initiated a series of quiet

diplomatic conversations about disarmament
and the general reduction of tensions; and
whereas in the past disarmament negotiations
had always degenerated into propaganda con-

tests, this time both sides showed a serious interest in reducing the risk of nuclear confrontations like the one through which they had so recently passed. Kennedy's commencement speech at American University gave public notice that he had been reconsidering the whole question of Soviet-American relations and had come to the conclusion that it was time, in effect, to liquidate the cold war in Europe. At the time, this speech seemed to herald a new departure in American foreign policy—an abandonment of the anti-Communist crusade abroad and a renewed attack on mounting problems at home. In retrospect, one can see that the détente with the Soviet Union in Europe merely freed the United States for a more active role in Asia. The rapprochement with the USSR and Kennedy's enlarged commitments to Diem (see Doc. No. 640) were pieces of the same large pattern. Nevertheless, Kennedy's American University speech had an important effect on public discussion. For the first time, it became politically respectable to discuss foreign affairs without resorting automatically to the rhetoric of the cold war. See T. Sorenson, *Kennedy;* A. Schlesinger, Jr., *A Thousand Days;* H. K. Jacobson and E. Stein, *Diplomats, Scientists, and Politicians.*

. . . Some say that it is useless to speak of world peace or world law or world disarmament—and that it will be useless until the leaders of the Soviet Union adopt a more enlightened attitude. I hope they do. I believe we can help them do it. But I also believe that we must reexamine our own attitude—as individuals and as a Nation—for our attitude is as essential as theirs. And every graduate of this school, every thoughtful citizen who despairs of war and wishes to bring peace, should begin by looking inward—by examining his own attitude toward the possibilities of peace, toward the Soviet Union, toward the course of the cold war and toward freedom and peace here at home.

First: Let us examine our attitude toward peace itself. Too many of us think it is impossible. Too many think it unreal. But that is a dangerous, defeatist belief. It leads to the conclusion that war is inevitable—that mankind is doomed—that we are gripped by forces we cannot control. . . .

Second: Let us reexamine our attitude toward the Soviet Union. . . .

No government or social system is so evil that its people must be considered as lacking in virtue. As Americans, we find communism profoundly repugnant as a negation of personal freedom and dignity. But we can still hail the Russian people for their many achievements—in science and space, in economic and industrial growth, in culture and in acts of courage.

Among the many traits the peoples of our two countries have in common, none is stronger than our mutual abhorrence of war. Almost unique, among the major world powers, we have never been at war with each other. And no nation in the history of battle ever suffered more than the Soviet Union suffered in the course of the Second World War. At least 20 million lost their lives. Countless millions of homes and farms were burned or sacked. A third of the nation's territory, including nearly two thirds of its industrial base, was turned into a wasteland—a loss equivalent to the devastation of this country east of Chicago.

Today, should total war ever break out again—no matter how—our two countries would become the primary targets. It is an ironic but accurate fact that the two strongest powers are the two in the most danger of devastation. All we have built, all we have worked for, would be destroyed in the first 24 hours. And even in the cold war, which brings burdens and dangers to so many countries, including this Nation's closest allies—our two countries bear the heaviest burdens. For we are both devoting massive sums of money to weapons that could be better devoted to combating ignorance, poverty, and disease. We are both caught up in a vicious and dangerous cycle in which suspicion on one side breeds suspicion on the other, and new weapons beget counterweapons.

In short, both the United States and its allies, and the Soviet Union and its allies, have a mutually deep interest in a just and genuine peace and in halting the arms race. Agreements to this end are in the interests of the Soviet Union as well as ours—and even the most hostile nations can be relied upon to accept and keep those treaty obligations, and only those treaty obligations, which are in their own interest.

So, let us not be blind to our differences—but let us also direct attention to our common interests and to the means by which those differences can be resolved. And if we cannot end now our differences, at least we can help make the world safe for diversity. For, in the final analysis, our most basic common link is that we all inhabit this small planet. We all breathe the same air. We all cherish our children's future. And we are all mortal.

Third: Let us reexamine our attitude toward the cold war, remembering that we are not engaged in a debate, seeking to pile up debating points. We are not here distributing blame or pointing the finger of judgment. We must deal with the world as it is, and not as it might have been had the history of the last 18 years been different. . . .

. . . The United States will make no deal with the Soviet Union at the expense of other nations and other peoples, not merely because they are our partners, but also because their interests and ours converge.

Our interests converge, however, not only in defending the frontiers of freedom, but in pursuing the paths of peace. It is our hope—and the purpose of allied policies—to convince the Soviet Union that she, too, should let each nation choose its own future, so long as that choice does not interfere with the choices of others. The Communist drive to impose their political and economic system on others is the primary cause of world tension today. For there can be no doubt that, if all nations could refrain from interfering in the self-determination of others, the peace would be much more assured.

This will require a new effort to achieve world law—a new context for world discussions. It will require increased understanding between the Soviets and ourselves. And increased understanding will require increased contact and communication. One step in this direction is the proposed arrangement for a direct line between Moscow and Washington, to avoid on each side the dangerous delays, misunderstandings, and misreadings of the other's actions which might occur at a time of crisis.

We have also been talking in Geneva about other first-step measures of arms control, designed to limit the intensity of the arms race and to reduce the risks of accidental war. Our primary long-range interest in Geneva, however, is general and complete disarmament—designed to take place by stages, permitting parallel political developments to build the new institutions of peace which would take the place of arms. The pursuit of disarmament has been an effort of this Government since the 1920's. It has been urgently sought by the past three administrations. And however dim the prospects may be today, we intend to continue this effort—to continue it in order that all countries, including our own, can better grasp what the problems and possibilities of disarmament are.

The one major area of these negotiations where the end is in sight, yet where a fresh start is badly needed, is in a treaty to outlaw nuclear tests. The conclusion of such a treaty, so near and yet so far, would check the spiraling arms race in one of its most dangerous areas. It would place the nuclear powers in a position to deal more effectively with one of the greatest hazards which man faces in 1963, the further spread of nuclear arms. It would increase our security—it would decrease the prospects of war. Surely this goal is sufficiently important to require our steady pursuit, yielding neither to the temptation to give up the whole effort nor the temptation to give up our insistence on vital and responsible safeguards.

I am taking this opportunity, therefore, to announce two important decisions in this regard.

First: Chairman Khrushchev, Prime Minister Macmillan, and I have agreed that high-level discussions will shortly begin in Moscow looking toward early agreement on a comprehensive test ban treaty. Our hopes must be tempered with the caution of history—but with our hopes go the hopes of all mankind.

Second: To make clear our good faith and solemn convictions on the matter, I now declare that the United States does not propose to conduct nuclear tests in the atmosphere so long as other states do not do so.

We will not be the first to resume. Such a declaration is no substitute for a formal binding treaty, but I hope it will help us achieve one. Nor would such a treaty be a substitute for disarmament, but I hope it will help us achieve it. . . .

. . . The United States, as the world knows, will never start a war. We do not want a war. We do not now expect a war. This generation of Americans has already had enough—more than enough—of war and hate and oppression. We shall be prepared if others wish it. We shall be alert to try to stop it. But we shall also do our part to build a world of peace where the weak are safe and the strong are just. We are not helpless before that task or hopeless of its success. Confident and unafraid, we labor on —not toward a strategy of annihilation but toward a strategy of peace.

644. SCHOOL DISTRICT OF ABINGTON TOWNSHIP, PENNSYLVANIA v. SCHEMPP
374 U.S. 203
1963

This decision involved a Pennsylvania law requiring Bible reading in public schools and a similar rule of the Baltimore school board which had given rise to the case of *Murray* v. *Curlett*, covered in the same opinion. In the first case, referred to in the Court's opinion as No. 142, a lower court had ruled that religious exercises in public schools amounted to an establishment of religion by the State and therefore violated the Constitution; in the Maryland case (No. 119), the lower court sided with the school board. The Supreme Court, in a controversial decision, upheld the former interpretation, Justice Stewart filing a lone dissent. See P. G. Kauper, *Religion and the Constitution;* J. H. Laubach, *School Prayers;* D. Fellman, "Religion in American Public Law," 44 *Boston U. Law Rev.,* 287; "Religion and the Constitution—A Symposium on the Supreme Court Decisions on Prayer and Bible Reading in Public Schools," 13 *J. of Public Law* 247; D. A. Gianella, "Religious Liberty, Nonestablishment, and Doctrinal Development; Pt. I: The Religious Liberty Guarantee," 80 *Harvard Law Rev.* 1381; M. Galenter, "Religious Freedom in the United States: A Turning Point?" *Wisconsin Law Rev.* (1966); M. Rudd, "Toward an Understanding of the Landmark Federal Decisions Affecting Relations Between Church and State," 36 *U. of Cincinnati Law Rev.* (Summer 1967); A. Schwartz, "No Imposition of Religion: The Establishment Clause Value," 78 *Yale Law J.* 692; J. M. Dodge II, "Free Exercise of Religion: A Sociological Approach," 67 *Michigan Law Rev.,* W. Katz, *Religion and American Constitutions;* M. De Wolfe Howe, *The Garden and the Wilderness;* P. Kurland, "The School Prayer Cases," in D. H. Oaks, ed., *The Wall Between Church and State;* Note, "The Free Exercise and Establishment Clauses: Conflict or Coordination," 48 *Minnesota Law Rev.* 929; P. G. Kauper, "The Warren Court: Religious Liberty and Church State Relations," in R. Sayler et al., eds., *The Warren Court;* W. Beaney and E. Beiser, "Prayer and Politics: The Impact of Engle and Schempp on the Political Process," in T. Becker, ed., *The Impact of Supreme Court Decisions.*

Applying the Establishment Clause principles to the cases at bar we find that the States are requiring the selection and reading at the opening of the school day of verses from the Holy Bible and the recitation of the Lord's Prayer by the students in unison. These exercises are prescribed as part of the curricular activities of students who are required by law to attend school. They are held in the school buildings under the supervision and with the participation of teachers employed in those schools. The trial court in No. 142 has found that such an opening exercise is a religious ceremony and was intended by the State to be so. We agree with the trial court's finding as to the religious character of the exercises. Given that finding, the exercises and the law requiring them are in violation of the Establishment Clause.

There is no such specific finding as to the religious character of the exercises in No. 119, and the State contends (as does the

State in No. 142) that the program is an effort to extend its benefits to all public school children without regard to their religious belief. Included within its secular purposes, it says, are the promotion of moral values, the contradiction to the materialistic trends of our times, the perpetuation of our institutions and the teaching of literature. The case came up on demurrer, of course, to a petition which alleged that the uniform practice under the rule had been to read from the King James version of the Bible and that the exercise was sectarian. The short answer, therefore, is that the religious character of the exercise was admitted by the State. But even if its purpose is not strictly religious, it is sought to be accomplished through readings, without comment, from the Bible. Surely the place of the Bible as an instrument of religion cannot be gainsaid, and the State's recognition of the pervading religious character of the ceremony is evident from the rule's specific permission of the alternative use of the Catholic Douay version as well as the recent amendment permitting nonattendance at the exercises. None of these factors is consistent with the contention that the Bible is here used either as an instrument for nonreligious moral inspiration or as a reference for the teaching of secular subjects.

The conclusion follows that in both cases the laws require religious exercises and such exercises are being conducted in direct violation of the rights of the appellees and petitioners. Nor are these required exercises mitigated by the fact that individual students may absent themselves upon parental request, for that fact furnishes no defense to a claim of unconstitutionality under the Establishment Clause. Further, it is no defense to urge that the religious practices here may be relatively minor encroachments on the First Amendment. The breach of neutrality that is today a trickling stream may all too soon become a raging torrent and, in the words of Madison, "it is proper to take alarm at the first experiment on our liberties."

It is insisted that unless these religious exercises are permitted a "religion of secularism" is established in the schools. We agree of course that the State may not establish a "religion of secularism" in the

sense of affirmatively opposing or showing hostility to religion, thus "preferring those who believe in no religion over those who do believe." We do not agree, however, that this decision in any sense has that effect. In addition, it might well be said that one's education is not complete without a study of comparative religion or the history of religion and its relationship to the advancement of civilization. It certainly may be said that the Bible is worthy of study for its literary and historic qualities. Nothing we have said here indicates that such study of the Bible or of religion, when presented objectively as part of a secular program of education, may not be effected consistently with the First Amendment. But the exercises here do not fall into those categories. They are religious exercises, required by the States in violation of the command of the First Amendment that the Government maintain strict neutrality, neither aiding nor opposing religion.

Finally, we cannot accept that the concept of neutrality, which does not permit a State to require a religious exercise even with the consent of the majority of those affected, collides with the majority's right to free exercise of religion. While the Free Exercise Clause clearly prohibits the use of state action to deny the rights of free exercise to *anyone*, it has never meant that a majority could use the machinery of the State to practice its beliefs. Such a contention was effectively answered by Mr. Justice Jackson for the Court in West Virginia Board of Education v. Barnette, 319 U.S. 624:

> "The very purpose of a Bill of Rights was to withdraw certain subjects from the vicissitudes of political controversy, to place them beyond the reach of majorities and officials and to establish them as legal principles to be applied by the courts. One's right to . . . freedom of worship . . . and other fundamental rights may not be submitted to vote; they depend on the outcome of no elections."

The place of religion in our society is an exalted one, achieved through a long tradition of reliance on the home, the church and the inviolable citadel of the individual heart and mind. We have come to recognize through bitter experience that it is not within the power of government to invade that cita-del, whether its purpose or effect be to aid or oppose, to advance or retard. In the rela-tionship between man and religion, the State is firmly committed to a position of neutral-ity. Though the application of that rule re-quires interpretation of a delicate sort, the rule itself is clearly and concisely stated in

the word of the First Amendment. Applying that rule to the facts of these cases, we af-firm the judgment in No. 142. In No. 119, the judgment is reversed and the cause re-manded to the Maryland Court of Appeals for further proceedings consistent with this opinion. . . .

645. THE NUCLEAR TEST BAN TREATY
September 24, 1963

(Department of State Bulletin, August 12, 1963)

This was the first fruit of the new Soviet–American détente—the unexpected outcome of the Cuban missile crisis (Doc. No. 642). The treaty was signed on July 25, 1963 and ratified by the Senate on September 24 by a vote of 80 to 19, by the Soviet Union the next day, and by Great Britain—a third party to the negotia-tions—the following month. Eventually ninety-nine other nations ratified the treaty, with the conspicuous exception of France, at that time the fourth nuclear power. De Gaulle's refusal to sign reflected, among other things, his grow-ing belief that France could no longer rely on the military protection of NATO and, in gen-eral, his wish to pursue a course independent of the United States in all things. See H. Bethe, "The Case for Ending Nuclear Tests," *The At-lantic Monthly*, August 1960; P. M. S. Blackett, "The First Real Chance for Disarmament," *Harper's*, January 1963; D. Horowitz, *Free World Colossus*; M. Willrich, "The Treaty on Non-Proliferation of Nuclear Weapons: Nuclear Technology Confronts World Politics," 77 *Yale Law J.* 1447; J. Weisner and W. York, "Na-tional Security and the Nuclear Test Ban," *Scientific American*, October 1964; T. Sorenson, *Kennedy*; A. Schlesinger, Jr., *A Thousand Days*; H. Jacobson and E. Stein, *Diplomats, Scientists, and Politicians*.

The Governments of the United States of America, the United Kingdom of Great Britain and Northern Ireland, and the Union of Soviet Socialist Republics, hereinafter re-ferred to as the "Original Parties",

Proclaiming as their principal aim the speediest possible achievement of an agree-ment on general and complete disarmament under strict international control in accor-

dance with the objectives of the United Na-tions which would put an end to the arma-ments race and eliminate the incentive to the production and testing of all kinds of weapons, including nuclear weapons,

Seeking to achieve the discontinuance of all test explosions of nuclear weapons for all time, determined to continue negotiations to this end, and desiring to put an end to the contamination of man's environment by ra-dioactive substances,

Have agreed as follows:

ARTICLE I

1. Each of the Parties to this Treaty un-dertakes to prohibit, to prevent, and not to carry out any nuclear weapon test explosion, or any other nuclear explosion, at any place under its jurisdiction or control:

(a) in the atmosphere; beyond its limits, including outer space; or underwater, in-cluding territorial waters or high seas; or

(b) in any other environment if such ex-plosion causes radioactive debris to be pres-ent outside the territorial limits of the State under whose jurisdiction or control such ex-plosion is conducted. It is understood in this connection that the provisions of this sub-paragraph are without prejudice to the con-clusion of a treaty resulting in the perma-nent banning of all nuclear test explosions, including all such explosions underground, the conclusion of which, as the Parties have stated in the Preamble to this Treaty, they seek to achieve.

2. Each of the Parties to this Treaty un-dertakes furthermore to refrain from caus-

ing, encouraging, or in any way participating in, the carrying out of any nuclear weapon test explosion, or any other nuclear explosion, anywhere which would take place in any of the environments described, or have the effect referred to, in paragraph 1 of this Article. . . .

ARTICLE III

1. This Treaty shall be open to all States for signature. Any State which does not sign this Treaty before its entry into force in accordance with paragraph 3 of this Article may accede to it at any time. . . .
3. This Treaty shall enter into force after

its ratification by all the Original Parties and the deposit of their instruments of ratification. . . .

ARTICLE IV

This Treaty shall be of unlimited duration. Each Party shall in exercising its national sovereignty have the right to withdraw from the Treaty if it decides that extraordinary events, related to the subject matter of this Treaty, have jeopardized the supreme interests of its country. It shall give notice of such withdrawal to all other Parties to the Treaty three months in advance. . . .

646. REYNOLDS v. SIMS
377 U.S. 533
1964

Wesberry v. *Sanders,* 376 U.S. 1, dealt with apportionment in the House of Representatives—specifically a 1931 Georgia law under which urban districts (as in most states) were heavily underrepresented in the House. A six-man majority held that the state's malapportioned congressional districts contravened Article I, Section 2 of the Constitution, which in effect, they argued, laid down the "one man, one vote" principle. The present case raised the issue of apportionment in state legislatures. In language even more sweeping than that of the *Baker* or *Wesberry* decisions, the Court now invoked the Equal Protection Clause of the Fourteenth Amendment to support its decision that both houses of a state legislature must be apportioned on the basis of population. The Court argued further that analogies with the system of representation in Congress, in which one house is based on population and the other on geography, were irrelevant to the case of state legislatures. In the subsequent cases of *WMCA, Inc.* v. *Lomenzo* and *Lucas* v. *Forty-fourth General Assembly of Colorado* (1964), the Court applied the same reasoning to apportionment schemes proposed by New York and Colorado, both of which it invalidated. Justice Harlan, dissenting in the present case as in the other apportionment cases, accused the Court of unwarranted judicial interference in political affairs—a charge that was soon taken up by the Court's critics in the country as a whole. See Note, J. A. Friedman, "Beyond *Wesberry*: State Apportionment and Equal Protection," 39 *N.Y.U.*

Law Rev., 264; Note, "Wesberry v. Sanders: Deep in the Thicket," 32 *George Washington Law Rev.,* 1076; J. Weiss, "Analysis of Wesberry v. Sanders," 38 *Southern California Law Rev.,* 67; M. Jewell, "Minority Representation: A Political or Judicial Question," 53 *Kentucky Law Journal,* 267; B. T. L. Calvin, *One Man, One Vote;* L. Ratner, "Reapportionment and the Constitution," 38 *Southern California Law Rev.,* 540; R. McKay, "Reapportionment: Success Story of the Warren Court," in R. Sayler et al., eds., *The Warren Court,* 32; R. Dixon, *Democratic Representation;* R. Cortner, *The Apportionment Cases.*

WARREN, C. J. . . . Undoubtedly, the right of suffrage is a fundamental matter in a free and democratic society. Especially since the right to exercise the franchise in a free and unimpaired manner is preservative of other basic civil and political rights, any alleged infringement of the right of citizens to vote must be carefully and meticulously scrutinized.

Legislators represent people, not trees or acres. Legislators are elected by voters, not farms or cities or economic interests. As long as ours is a representative form of government, and our legislatures are those instruments of government elected directly by and directly representative of the people, the right to elect legislators in a free and unimpaired fashion is a bedrock of our political system. It could hardly be gainsaid that a constitutional claim had been asserted by an allegation that certain otherwise qualified voters had been entirely prohibited from voting for members of their state legislature. And, if a State should provide that the votes of citizens in one part of the State should be given two times, or five times, or 10 times the weight of votes of citizens in another part of the State, it could hardly be contended that the right to vote of those residing in the disfavored areas had not been effectively diluted. It would appear extraordinary to suggest that a state could be constitutionally permitted to enact a law providing that certain of the state's voters could vote two, five, or 10 times for their legislative representatives, while voters living elsewhere could vote only once. And it is inconceivable that a state law to the effect that, in counting votes for legislators, the votes of citizens in one part of the State would be multiplied by two, five, or 10, while the votes of persons in another area would be counted only at face value, could be constitutionally sustainable. Of course, the effect of state legislative districting schemes which give the same number of representatives to unequal numbers of constituents is identical. Overweighting and overvaluation of the votes of those living here has the certain effect of dilution and undervaluation of the votes of those living there. The resulting discrimination against those individual voters living in disfavored areas is easily demonstrable mathematically. Their right to vote is simply not the same right to vote as that of those living in a favored part of the State. Two, five, or 10 of them must vote before the effect of their voting is equivalent to that of their favored neighbor. Weighting the votes of citizens differently, by any method or means, merely because of where they happen to reside, hardly seems justifiable. One must be ever aware that the Constitution forbids sophisticated as well as simpleminded modes of discrimination." . . .

 . . . Since the achieving of fair and effective representation for all citizens is conced-edly the basic aim of legislative apportionment, we conclude that the Equal Protection Clause guarantees the opportunity for equal participation by all voters in the election of state legislators. Diluting the weight of votes because of place of residence impairs basic constitutional rights under the Fourteenth Amendment just as much as invidious discriminations based upon factors such as race, *Brown* v. *Board of Education,* 347 U.S. 483, [or economic status, *Griffin* v. *Illinois,* 351 U.S. 12, *Douglas* v. *California,* 372 U.S. 353]. Our constitutional system amply provides for the protection of minorities by means other than giving them majority control of state legislatures. And the democratic ideals of equality and majority rule, which have served this Nation so well in the past, are hardly of any less significance for the present and the future.

We are told that the matter of apportioning representation in a state legislature is a complex and many-faceted one. We are advised that States can rationally consider factors other than population in apportioning legislative representation. We are admonished not to restrict the power of the States to impose differing views as to political philosophy on their citizens. We are cautioned about the dangers of entering into political thickets and mathematical quagmires. Our answer is this: a denial of constitutionally protected rights demands judicial protection; our oath and our office require no less of us. . . .

We hold that, as a basic constitutional standard, the Equal Protection Clause requires that the seats in both houses of a bicameral state legislature must be apportioned on a population basis. Simply stated, an individual's right to vote for state legislators is unconstitutionally impaired when its weight is in a substantial fashion diluted when compared with votes of citizens living in other parts of the State. Since, under neither the existing apportionment provisions nor under either of the proposed plans was either of the houses of the Alabama Legislature apportioned on a population basis, the District Court correctly held that all three of these schemes were constitutionally invalid. Furthermore, the existing apportionment, and also to a lesser extent the apportionment under the Crawford-Webb Act, presented little more than crazy quilts, completely lacking in rationality, and could be found invalid on that basis alone. . . .

Since neither of the houses of the Alabama Legislature under any of the three plans considered by the District Court was apportioned on a population basis, we would be justified in proceeding no further. However, one of the proposed plans, that contained in the so-called 67-Senator Amendment, at least superficially resembles the scheme of legislative representation followed in the Federal Congress. Under this plan, each of Alabama's 67 counties is allotted one senator, and no counties are given more than one Senate seat. Arguably, this is analogous to the allocation of two Senate seats, in the Federal Congress, to each of the 50 States, regardless of population. Seats in the Alabama House, under the proposed constitutional amendment, are distributed by giving each of the 67 counties at least one, with the remaining 49 seats being allotted among the more populous counties on a population basis. This scheme, at least at first glance, appears to resemble that prescribed for the Federal House of Representatives, where the 435 seats are distributed among the States on a population basis, although each State, regardless of its population, is given at least one Congressman. Thus, although there are substantial differences in underlying rationale and result, the 67-Senator Amendment, as proposed by the Alabama Legislature, at least arguably presents for consideration a scheme analogous to that used for apportioning seats in Congress.

Much has been written since our decision in *Baker* v. *Carr* about the applicability of the so-called federal analogy to state legislative apportionment arrangements. After considering the matter, the court below concluded that no conceivable analogy could be drawn between the federal scheme and the apportionment of seats in the Alabama Legislature under the proposed constitutional amendment. We agree with the District Court, and find the federal analogy inapposite and irrelevant to state legislative districting schemes. Attempted reliance on federal analogy appears often to be little more than an after-the-fact rationalization

offered in defense of maladjusted state apportionment arrangements. The original constitutions of 36 of our States provided that representation in both houses of the state legislatures would be based completely, or predominantly, on population. And the Founding Fathers clearly had no intention of establishing a pattern or model for the apportionment of seats in state legislatures when the system of representation in the Federal Congress was adopted. Demonstrative of this is the fact that the Northwest Ordinance, adopted in the same year, 1787, as the Federal Constitution, provided for the apportionment of seats in territorial legislatures solely on the basis of population.

Thus, we conclude that the plan contained in the 67-Senator Amendment for apportioning seats in the Alabama Legislature cannot be sustained by recourse to the so-called federal analogy. Nor can any other inequitable state legislative apportionment scheme be justified on such an asserted basis. This does not necessarily mean that such a plan is irrational or involves something other than a "republican form of government." We conclude simply that such a plan is impermissible for the States under the Equal Protection Clause, since perforce resulting, in virtually every case, in submergence of the equal-population principle in at least one house of a state legislature.

Since we find the so-called federal analogy inapposite to a consideration of the constitutional validity of state legislative apportionment schemes, we necessarily hold that the Equal Protection Clause requires both houses of a state legislature to be apportioned on a population basis. . . .

HARLAN, J., dissenting. . . . The Court's elaboration of its new "constitutional" doctrine indicates how far—and how unwisely —it has strayed from the appropriate bounds of its authority. The consequence of today's decision is that in all but the handful of States which may already satisfy the new requirements the local District Court or, it may be, the state courts, are given blanket authority and the constitutional duty to supervise apportionment of the state legislatures. It is difficult to imagine a more intolerable and inappropriate interference by the judiciary with the independent legislatures of the States.

. . . These decisions give support to a current mistaken view of the Constitution and the constitutional function of this Court. This view, in a nutshell, is that every major social ill in this country can find its cure in some constitutional "principle," and that this Court should "take the lead" in promoting reform when other branches of government fail to act. The Constitution is not a panacea for every blot upon the public welfare, nor should this Court, ordained as a judicial body, be thought of as a general haven for reform movements. The Constitution is an instrument of government, fundamental to which is the premise that in a diffusion of governmental authority lies the greatest promise that this Nation will realize liberty for all its citizens. This Court, limited in function in accordance with that premise, does not serve its high purpose when it exceeds its authority, even to satisfy justified impatience with the slow workings of the political process. For when, in the name of constitutional interpretation, the Court *adds* something to the Constitution that was deliberately excluded from it, the Court in reality substitutes its view of what should be so for the amending process. . . .

647. ESCOBEDO v. ILLINOIS
378 U.S. 478
1964

The most important decisions of the Warren Court concerned themselves, broadly speaking, with four major areas: civil rights, reapportionment, religious freedom, and procedures of criminal investigation under the Bill of Rights. In the last of these, the general drift of the Court's opinions—opinions that were no less controversial than those concerning civil rights and reapportionment—was to set strict limits to the powers of the state in apprehending, interrogating, and prosecuting suspected criminals. In *Mapp* v. *Ohio* (1961) the Court held that evidence obtained by search and seizure in violation of the Fourth Amendment was inadmissible in state as well as federal courts; in *Gideon* v. *Wainwright* (1963), it affirmed the right to counsel in state criminal cases; in *Jackson* v. *Denno* (1964), it tightened its rule against forced confessions; and in the *Miranda* case (1966), it imposed additional restrictions on self-incrimination. In all of these cases, the chief constitutional issue was whether the guarantees contained in the Bill of Rights applied to the states as well as to agencies of the federal government, but even when that question was settled, additional issues, of enormous practical importance, remained. In the present case, Danny Escobedo, a twenty-two-year old of Mexican extraction, had been convicted of murder on the basis of a confession secured before his formal indictment, during an interrogation in which he was denied access to his lawyer. The Supreme Court of Illinois first reversed the conviction and then, in a rehearing, ruled that the right to counsel applied only to persons formally indicted for a crime. See I. Silver, "The Supreme Court, the State Judiciary, and State Criminal Procedure: An Example of Uncreative Federalism," 41 *St. John's Law Rev.*, 331; A. Blumberg, *Criminal Justice;* W. W. Van Alstyne, "In Gideon's Wake: Harsher Penalties and the Successful Criminal Appellant," 74 *Yale Law J.* 606; D. Dowling, Jr., "Escobedo and Beyond: The Need for a Fourteenth Amendment Code of Criminal Procedure," 56 *J. of Crim. Law, Criminology, and Police Science* 143; D. Robinson, Jr., "Massiah, Escobedo and Rationales for the Exclusion of Confessions," 56 *J. of Crim. Law, Criminology, and Police Science* 412; S. H. Elsen and A. Enrer, "Counsel for the Suspect: *Massiah* v. *United States* and *Escobedo* v. *Illinois*," 49 *Minnesota Law Rev.* 47; L. Herman, "The Supreme Court and Restrictions on Police Interrogation," 25 *Ohio State Law J.* 449.

GOLDBERG, J. . . . The critical question in this case is whether, under the circumstances, the refusal by the police to honor petitioner's request to consult with his lawyer during the course of an interrogation constitutes a denial of "the Assistance of Counsel" in violation of the Sixth Amendment to the Constitution as "made obligatory upon the States by the Fourteenth Amendment," *Gideon v. Wain-*

wright, 372 U.S. 335, 342, and thereby renders inadmissible in a state criminal trial any incriminating statement elicited by the police during the interrogation. . . .

The interrogation here was conducted before petitioner was formally indicted. But in the context of this case, that fact should make no difference. When petitioner requested, and was denied, an opportunity to consult with his lawyer, the investigation had ceased to be a general investigation of "an unsolved crime." Petitioner had become the accused, and the purpose of the interrogation was to "get him" to confess his guilt despite his constitutional right not to do so. At the time of his arrest and throughout the course of the interrogation, the police told petitioner that they had convincing evidence that he had fired the fatal shots. Without informing him of his absolute right to remain silent in the face of this accusation, the police urged him to make a statement. . . . Petitioner, a layman, was undoubtedly unaware that under Illinois law an admission of "mere" complicity in the murder plot was legally as damaging as an admission of firing of the fatal shots. . . . The "guiding hand of counsel" was essential to advise petitioner of his rights in this delicate situation. . . . This was the "stage when legal aid and advice" were most critical to petitioner. . . . It would exalt form over substance to make the right to counsel, under these circumstances, depend on whether at the time of the interrogation, the authorities had secured a formal indictment. Petitioner had, for all practical purposes, already been charged with murder. . . .

In *Gideon v. Wainwright,* 372 U.S. 335, we held that every person accused of a crime, whether state or federal, is entitled to a lawyer at trial. The rule sought by the State here, however, would make the trial no more than an appeal from the interrogation; and the "right to use counsel at the formal trial [would be] a very hollow thing [if], for all practical purposes, the conviction is already assured by pretrial examination." *In re Groban,* 352 U.S. 330, 344 (Black, J., dissenting). "One can imagine a cynical prosecutor saying: 'Let them have the most illustrious counsel, now. They can't escape the noose. There is nothing that coun-

sel can do for them at the trial.' " *Ex parte Sullivan,* 107 F. Supp. 514, 517–18.

We have learned the lesson of history, ancient and modern, that a system of criminal law enforcement which comes to depend on the "confession" will, in the long run, be less reliable and more subject to abuses than a system which depends on extrinsic evidence independently secured through skillful investigation. . . .

We have also learned the companion lesson of history that no system of criminal justice can, or should, survive if it comes to depend for its continued effectiveness on the citizens' abdication through unawareness of their constitutional rights. No system worth preserving should have to *fear* that if an accused is permitted to consult with a lawyer, he will become aware of, and exercise, these rights. If the exercise of constitutional rights will thwart the effectiveness of a system of law enforcement, then there is something very wrong with that system.

We hold, therefore, that where, as here, the investigation is no longer a general inquiry into an unsolved crime but has begun to focus on a particular suspect, the suspect has been taken into police custody, the police carry out a process of interrogations that lends itself to eliciting incriminating statements, the suspect has requested and been denied an opportunity to consult with his lawyer, and the police have not effectively warned him of his absolute constitutional right to remain silent, the accused has been denied "the Assistance of Counsel" in violation of the Sixth Amendment to the Constitution as "made obligatory upon the States by the Fourteenth Amendment," and that no statement elicited by the police during the interrogation may be used against him at a criminal trial. . . .

Nothing we have said today affects the powers of the police to investigate "an unsolved crime," by gathering information from witnesses and by other "proper investigative efforts." We hold only that when the process shifts from investigatory to accusatory—when its focus is on the accused and its purpose is to elicit a confession—our adversary system begins to operate, and, under the circumstances here, the accused must be permitted to consult with his lawyer.

648. BELL v. MARYLAND
378 U.S. 226
1964

The issue here was whether the Fourteenth Amendment outlaws private discrimination as well as discrimination by state governments. The plaintiff in the case had been arrested in a sit-in at a segregated lunch counter. As in earlier cases involving the same question, the Court found grounds to evade the central issue. In a separate opinion, given below, Justices Douglas and Goldberg confronted this issue and argued for outright reversal of the conviction of civil rights demonstrators in the Maryland courts. Justices Black, Harlan, and White dissented on the grounds that an attack on private discrimination was an attack on property. See I. M. Heyman, "Civil Rights 1964 Term: Responses to Direct Action," P. Kurland (ed.), *Supreme Court Review*, 1965, 33; J. Greenberg, "The Supreme Court, Civil Rights, and Civil Dissonance," 77 *Yale Law J.* 1520; L. Miller, *The Petitioners: The Story of the Supreme Court of the United States and the Negro*.

The problem in this case, and in the other sit-in cases before us, is presented as though it involved the situation of "a private operator conducting his own business on his own premises and exercising his own judgment" as to whom he will admit to the premises.

The property involved is not, however, a man's home or his yard or even his fields. Private property is involved, but it is property that is serving the public. As my Brother GOLDBERG says, it is a "civil" right, not a "social" right, with which we deal. Here it is a restaurant refusing service to a Negro. But so far as principle and law are concerned it might just as well be a hospital refusing admission to a sick or injured Negro (cf. Simkins v. Moses H. Cone Memorial Hospital, 4 Cir., 323 F.2d 959), or a drug store refusing antibiotics to a Negro, or a bus denying transportation to a Negro, or a telephone company refusing to install a telephone in a Negro's home.

The problem with which we deal has no relation to opening or closing the door of one's home. The home of course is the essence of privacy, in no way dedicated to public use, in no way extending an invitation to the public. Some businesses, like the classical country store where the owner lives overhead or in the rear, make the store an extension, so to speak, of the home. But such is not this case. The facts of these sit-in cases have little resemblance to any institution of property which we customarily associate with privacy. . . .

The revolutionary change effected by an affirmance in these sit-in cases would be much more damaging to an open and free society than what the Court did when it gave the corporation the sword and the shield of the Due Process and Equal Protection Clauses of the Fourteenth Amendment. Affirmance finds in the Constitution a corporate right to refuse service to anyone "it" chooses and to get the State to put people in jail who defy "its" will. . . .

Affirmance would make corporate management the arbiter of one of the deepest conflicts in our society: corporate management could then enlist the aid of state police, state prosecutors, and state courts to force *apartheid* on the community they served, if *apartheid* best suited the corporate need; or, if its profits would be better served by lowering the barriers of segregation, it could do so. . . .

The point is that corporate motives in the retail field relate to corporate profits, corporate prestige, and corporate public relations. Corporate motives have no tinge of an individual's choice to associate only with one class of customers, to keep members of one race from his "property," to erect a wall of privacy around a business in the manner that one is erected around the home. . . .

BLACK, J., with whom Justice HARLAN and Justice WHITE, join, dissenting.

We are admonished that in deciding this case we should remember that "it is *a constitution* we are expounding." We conclude as we do because we remember that it *is* a Constitution and that it is our duty "to bow with respectful submission to its provisions." And in recalling that it is a Constitution "intended to endure for ages to come," we also remember that the Founders wisely provided the means for that endurance: changes in the Constitution, when thought necessary, are to be proposed by Congress or conventions and ratified by the States. The Founders gave no such amending power to this Court. Our duty is simply to interpret the Constitution, and in doing so the test of constitutionality is not whether a law is offensive to our conscience or to the "good old common law," but whether it is offensive to the Constitution. Confining ourselves to our constitutional duty to construe, not to rewrite or amend, the Constitution, we believe that section 1 of the Fourteenth Amendment does not bar Maryland from enforcing its trespass laws so long as it does so with impartiality.

This Court has done much in carrying out its solemn duty to protect people from unlawful discrimination. And it will, of course, continue to carry out this duty in the future as it has in the past. But the Fourteenth Amendment of itself does not compel either a black man or a white man running his own private business to trade with anyone else against his will. We do not believe that section 1 of the Fourteenth Amendment was written or designed to interfere with a storekeeper's right to choose his customers or with a property owner's right to choose his social or business associates, so long as he does not run counter to valid state or federal regulation. The case before us does not involve the power of the Congress to pass a law compelling privately owned businesses to refrain from discrimination on the basis of race and to trade with all if they trade with any. We express no views as to the power of Congress, acting under one or another provision of the Constitution, to prevent racial discrimination in the operation of privately owned businesses, nor upon any particular form of legislation to that end. Our sole conclusion is that section 1 of the Fourteenth Amendment, standing alone, does not prohibit privately owned restaurants from choosing their own customers. It does not destroy what has until very recently been universally recognized in this country as the unchallenged right of a man who owns a business to run the business in his own way so long as some valid regulatory statute does not tell him to do otherwise. . . .

649. CIVIL RIGHTS ACT OF 1964
July 2, 1964
(78 *U.S. Statutes at Large* 241 ff. Public Law 88-352)

The Civil Rights Act of 1957 was the first since Reconstruction and went part of the way toward meeting President Eisenhower's request for federal enforcement of those guarantees of civil rights written into the Constitution. Dissatisfaction with it had led to the passage of another civil rights law in 1960, addressed primarily to the problem of voting but, like its predecessor, ineffective. Mounting pressure from the civil rights movement forced President Kennedy in 1963 to demand federal legislation against segregation in all businesses involved in interstate commerce and against job discrimination. President Johnson continued Kennedy's efforts. After a long struggle, capped by a three-month filibuster, Congress finally passed a bill, stronger than Kennedy's original proposal but weaker than some of the alternatives proposed by the House. It prohibited discrimination in places of public accommodation, forbade discrimination in employment, forbade discrimination in voting, and set up machinery of enforcement. This was the strongest civil rights measure since Reconstruction, but in practice it was a qualified success at best. See I. M. Heyman, "Civil Rights 1964 Term: Responses to Direct Action," P. Kurland (ed.), *Supreme Court Review*, 1965, 33; H. Abraham, *Freedom and the Court;* J. Greenberg, "The Supreme Court, Civil Rights and Civil Dissonance," 77 *Yale Law J.* 1150; A. Cox, *The Warren Court;* A. Lewis, *Portrait of a Decade;* A. Wolk, *The President and Black Civil Rights.*

TITLE I
VOTING RIGHTS

SEC. 101 (2). No person acting under color of law shall—

(A) in determining whether any individual is qualified under State law or laws to vote in any Federal election, apply any standard, practice, or procedure different from the standards, practices, or procedures applied under such law or laws to other individuals within the same county, parish, or similar political subdivision who have been found by State officials to be qualified to vote; . . .

(C) employ any literacy test as a qualification for voting in any Federal election unless (i) such test is administered to each individual wholly in writing; and (ii) a certified copy of the test and of the answers given by the individual is furnished to him within twenty-five days of the submission of his request made within the period of time during which records and papers are required to be retained and preserved pursuant to title III of the Civil Rights Act of 1960. . . .

TITLE II

INJUNCTIVE RELIEF AGAINST DISCRIMINATION IN PLACES OF PUBLIC ACCOMMODATION

SEC. 201. (a) All persons shall be entitled to the full and equal enjoyment of the goods, services, facilities, privileges, advantages, and accommodations of any place of public accommodation, as defined in this section, without discrimination or segregation on the ground of race, color, religion, or national origin.

(b) Each of the following establishments which serves the public is a place of public accommodation within the meaning of this title if its operations affect commerce, or if discrimination or segregation by it is supported by State action:

(1) any inn, motel, or other establishment which provides lodging to transient guests, other than an establishment located within a building which contains not more than five rooms for rent or hire and which is actually occupied by the proprietor of such establishment as his residence;

(2) any restaurant, cafeteria, lunch room, lunch counter, soda fountain, or other facility principally engaged in selling food for consumption on the premises . . .

(3) any motion picture house, theater, concert hall, sports arena, stadium or other place of exhibition or entertainment. . . .

(d) Discrimination or segregation by an establishment is supported by State action within the meaning of this title if such discrimination or segregation (1) is carried on under color of any law, statute, ordinance, or regulation; or (2) is carried on under color of any custom or usage required or enforced by officials of the State or political subdivision thereof. . . .

SEC. 202. All persons shall be entitled to be free, at any establishment or place, from discrimination or segregation of any kind on the ground of race, color, religion, or national origin, if such discrimination or segregation is or purports to be required by any law, statute, ordinance, regulation, rule, or order of a State or any agency or political subdivision thereof. . . .

SEC. 206. (a) Whenever the Attorney General has reasonable cause to believe that any person or group of persons is engaged in a pattern or practice of resistance to the full enjoyment of any of the rights secured by this title, the Attorney General may bring a civil action in the appropriate district court of the United States by filing with it a complaint . . . requesting such preventive relief, including an application for a permanent or temporary injunction, restraining order or other order against the person or persons responsible for such pattern or practice, as he deems necessary to insure the full enjoyment of the rights herein described.

TITLE VI

NONDISCRIMINATION IN FEDERALLY ASSISTED PROGRAMS

SEC. 601. No person in the United States shall, on the ground of race, color, or national origin, be excluded from participation in, be denied the benefits of, or be subjected to discrimination under any program or activity receiving Federal financial assistance.

650. THE TONKIN GULF INCIDENT
1964

After the fall of Diem (see introduction to Docs. No. 608 and 640), the South Vietnamese civil war entered a new phase. Communist-led guerillas (the National Liberation Front or Vietcong) gained control of larger and larger areas of the country, and a succession of military dictators proved ineffective in dealing with them. The Johnson administration, like the Kennedy administration, interpreted the guerrilla warfare in the south as evidence of North Vietnamese aggression, and increased its military and naval support of the South Vietnamese government. In August 1964, during the Presidential campaign in which Goldwater was accusing Johnson of laxity in combating Communism, the administration claimed that North Vietnamese gunboats had fired on American destroyers in the Tonkin Gulf off the coast of North Vietnam. Johnson ordered aerial retaliation and then asked Congress to give him broad discretionary power to combat Communism in Southeast Asia. The House unanimously and the Senate with only two dissenting votes (Morse of Oregon and Gruening of Alaska) passed a joint resolution to this effect on August 7. This resolution furnished the legal basis for the subsequent escalation of the war (see Doc. No. 653). It was repealed by an 81–10 Senate vote on June 24, 1971. See C. Cooper, *The Lost Crusade;* J. Galloway, *The Gulf of Tonkin Resolution;* L. Velvel, *Undeclared War and Civil Disobedience;* I. F. Stone, *In a Time of Torment;* F. Schurmann et al., *The Politics of Escalation in Vietnam;* R. Falk, "Six Legal Dimensions of the United States Involvement in the Vietnam War," in R. Falk, ed., *The Vietnam War and International Law,* II, 216; E. Weintal and C. Bartlett, *Facing the Brink;* C. Roberts, *L.B.J.'s Inner Circle;* J. Goulden, *Truth Is the First Casualty;* E. G. Windchy, *Tonkin Gulf;* A. Austin, *The President's War.*

1. PRESIDENT JOHNSON'S MESSAGE TO CONGRESS
August 5, 1964

(Department of State Bulletin, August 24, 1964)

Last night I announced to the American people that the North Vietnamese regime had conducted further deliberate attacks against U.S. naval vessels operating in international waters, and that I had therefore directed air action against gunboats and supporting facilities used in these hostile operations. This air action has now been carried out with substantial damage to the boats and facilities. Two U.S. aircraft were lost in the action.

After consultation with the leaders of both parties in the Congress, I further announced a decision to ask the Congress for a resolution expressing the unity and determination of the United States in supporting freedom and in protecting peace in southeast Asia.

These latest actions of the North Vietnamese regime have given a new and grave turn to the already serious situation in southeast Asia. Our commitments in that area are well known to the Congress. They were first made in 1954 by President Eisenhower. They were further defined in the Southeast Asia Collective Defense Treaty approved by the Senate in February 1955.

This treaty with its accompanying protocol obligates the United States and other members to act in accordance with their constitutional processes to meet Communist aggression against any of the parties or protocol states.

Our policy in southeast Asia has been consistent and unchanged since 1954. I summarized it on June 2 in four simple propositions:

1. *America keeps her word.* Here as elsewhere, we must and shall honor our commitments.

2. *The issue is the future of southeast Asia as a whole.* A threat to any nation in that region is a threat to all, and a threat to us.

3. *Our purpose is peace.* We have no military, political, or territorial ambitions in the area.

4. *This is not just a jungle war, but a struggle for freedom on every front of human activity.* Our military and economic assistance to South Vietnam and Laos in particular has the purpose of helping these

countries to repel aggression and strengthen their independence.

The threat to the free nations of southeast Asia has long been clear. The North Vietnamese regime has constantly sought to take over South Vietnam and Laos. This Communist regime has violated the Geneva accords for Vietnam. It has systematically conducted a campaign of subversion, which includes the direction, training, and suppy of personnel and arms for the conduct of guerrilla warfare in South Vietnamese territory. In Laos, the North Vietnamese regime has maintained military forces, used Laotian territory for infiltration into South Vietnam, and most recently carried out combat operations—all in direct violation of the Geneva agreements of 1962.

In recent months, the actions of the North Vietnamese regime have become steadily more threatening. . . .

As President of the United States I have concluded that I should now ask the Congress, on its part, to join in affirming the national determination that all such attacks will be met, and that the United States will continue in its basic policy of assisting the free nations of the area to defend their freedom.

As I have repeatedly made clear, the United States intends no rashness, and seeks no wider war. We must make it clear to all that the United States is united in its determination to bring about the end of Communist subversion and aggression in the area. We seek the full and effective restoration of the international agreements signed in Geneva in 1954, with respect to South Vietnam, and again in Geneva in 1962, with respect to Laos. . . .

2. JOINT RESOLUTION OF CONGRESS
H. J. Res. 1145
August 7, 1964

(*Department of State Bulletin,*
August 24, 1964)

To promote the maintenance of international peace and security in southeast Asia.

WHEREAS naval units of the Communist regime in Vietnam, in violation of the principles of the Charter of the United Nations and of international law, have deliberately and repeatedly attacked United States naval vessels lawfully present in international waters, and have thereby created a serious threat to international peace; and

WHEREAS these attacks are part of a deliberate and systematic campaign of aggression that the Communist regime in North Vietnam has been waging against its neighbors and the nations joined with them in the collective defense of their freedom; and

WHEREAS the United States is assisting the peoples of southeast Asia to protect their freedom and has no territorial, military or political ambitions in that area, but desires only that these peoples should be left in peace to work out their own destinies in their own way; Now, therefore, be it

Resolved by the Senate and House of Representatives of the United States of America in Congress assembled, That the Congress approves and supports the determination of the President, as Commander in Chief, to take all necessary measures to repel any armed attack against the forces of the United States and to prevent further aggression.

SEC. 2. The United States regards as vital to its national interest and to world peace the maintenance of international peace and security in southeast Asia. Consonant with the Constitution of the United States and the Charter of the United Nations and in accordance with its obligations under the Southeast Asia Collective Defense Treaty, the United States is, therefore, prepared, as the President determines, to take all necessary steps, including the use of armed force, to assist any member or protocol state of the Southeast Asia Collective Defense Treaty requesting assistance in defense of its freedom.

SEC. 3. This resolution shall expire when the President shall determine that the peace and security of the area is reasonably assured by international conditions created by action of the United Nations or otherwise, except that it may be terminated earlier by concurrent resolution of the Congress.

651. ECONOMIC OPPORTUNITY ACT OF 1964
August 20, 1964
(78 *U.S. Statutes at Large* 580 ff. Public Law 88–452)

Next to the Civil Rights Act of 1964 (Doc. No. 649), the present legislation, which initiated the "war on poverty," was the most important item in President Johnson's program, one of the principal components of his "Great Society." Whereas the Civil Rights Act had been inherited from the Kennedy administration, the "antipoverty" bill originated with Johnson, having been proposed in his State of the Union message of January 1964. Overcoming the considerable opposition in Congress was an impressive feat of executive leadership; and the measure was passed much as the President had asked. It created an Office of Economic Opportunity (as director of which the President appointed Sargent Shriver) and provided a great variety of measures against poverty, the most important of which are indicated in the excerpts that follow. The whole program, however, was chronically short of funds. See J. A. Kershaw, *Government Against Poverty;* L. C. Thurow, *Poverty and Discrimination;* S. Levitan, *The Great Society's Poor Law;* R. Davidson and S. Levitan, *Anti-Poverty House-Keeping: The Administration of the Economic Opportunity Act.*

. . . SEC. 2. Although the economic well-being and prosperity of the United States have progressed to a level surpassing any achieved in world history, and although these benefits are widely shared throughout the Nation, poverty continues to be the lot of a substantial number of our people. The United States can achieve its full economic and social potential as a nation only if every individual has the opportunity to contribute to the full extent of his capabilities and to participate in the workings of our society. It is, therefore, the policy of the United States to eliminate the paradox of poverty in the midst of plenty in this Nation by opening to everyone the opportunity for education and training, the opportunity to work, and the opportunity to live in decency and dignity. It is the purpose of this Act to strengthen, supplement, and coordinate efforts in furtherance of that policy.

TITLE I
YOUTH PROGRAMS

PART A—JOB CORPS

SEC. 101. The purpose of this part is to prepare for the responsibilities of citizenship and to increase the employability of young men and young women aged sixteen through twenty-one by providing them in rural and urban residential centers with education, vocational training, useful work experience, including work directed toward the conservation of natural resources, and other appropriate activities.

SEC. 102. In order to carry out the purposes of this part, there is hereby established within the Office of Economic Opportunity (hereinafter referred to as the "Office"), established by title VI, a Job Corps (hereinafter referred to as the "Corps").

SEC. 103. The Director of the Office (hereinafter referred to as the "Director") is authorized to—

(a) enter into agreements with any Federal, State, or local agency or private organization for the establishment and operation, in rural and urban areas, of conservation camps and training centers; . . .

(b) arrange for the provision of education and vocational training of enrollees in the Corps . . .

(c) provide or arrange for the provision of programs of useful work experience and other appropriate activities for enrollees . . .

SEC. 105. (a) Enrollees may be provided with such living, travel, and leave allowances, and such quarters, subsistence, transportation, equipment, clothing, recreational services, medical, dental, hospital, and other health services, and other expenses as the Director may deem necessary or appropriate for their needs. Transportation and travel allowances may also be provided, in such circumstances as the Director may determine, for applicants for enrollment to or from places of enrollment, and for former enrollees from places of termination to their homes. . . .

PART B—WORK-TRAINING PROGRAMS

SEC. 111. The purpose of this part is to provide useful work experience opportunities for unemployed young men and young women, through participation in State and community work-training programs, so that their employability may be increased or their education resumed or continued and so that public agencies and private nonprofit organizations (other than political parties) will be enabled to carry out programs which will permit or contribute to an undertaking or service in the public interest that would not otherwise be provided, or will contribute to the conservation and development of natural resources and recreational areas. . . .

PART C—WORK-STUDY PROGRAMS

SEC. 121. The purpose of this part is to stimulate and promote the part-time employment of students in institutions of higher education who are from low-income families and are in need of the earnings from such employment to pursue courses of study at such institutions. . . .

SEC. 123. The Director is authorized to enter into agreements with institutions of higher education (as defined by section 401 (f) of the Higher Education Facilities Act of 1963 (P.L. 88–204)) under which the Director will make grants to such institutions to assist in the operation of work-study programs as hereinafter provided.

SEC. 124. An agreement entered into pursuant to section 123 shall—

(a) provide for the operation by the institution of a program for the part-time employment of its students in work—

(1) for the institution itself, or

(2) for a public or private nonprofit organization when the position is obtained through an arrangement between the institution and such an organization and—

(A) the work is related to the student's educational objective, or

(B) such work (i) will be in the public interest and is work which would not otherwise be provided, (ii) will not result in the displacement of employed workers

or impair eixsting contracts for services, and (iii) will be governed by such conditions of employment as will be appropriate and reasonable in light of such factors as the type of work performed, geographical region, and proficiency of the employee:

Provided, however, That no such work shall involve the construction, operation, or maintenance of so much of any facility used or to be used for sectarian instruction or as a place for religious worship . . .

TITLE II

URBAN AND RURAL COMMUNITY ACTION PROGRAMS

PART A—GENERAL COMMUNITY ACTION PROGRAMS

SEC. 201. The purpose of this part is to provide stimulation and incentive for urban and rural communities to mobilize their resources to combat poverty through community action programs.

SEC. 202. (a) The term "community action program" means a program—

(1) which mobilizes and utilizes resources, public or private, of any urban or rural, or combined urban and rural, geographical area (referred to in this part as a "community"), including but not limited to a State, metropolitan area, county, city, town, multicity unit, or multicounty unit in an attack on poverty;

(2) which provides services, assistance, and other activities of sufficient scope and size to give promise of progress toward elimination of poverty or a cause or causes of poverty through developing employment opportunities, improving human performance, motivation, and productivity, or bettering the conditions under which people live, learn, and work;

(3) which is developed, conducted, and administered with the maximum feasible participation of residents of the areas and members of the groups served; and

(4) which is conducted, administered, or coordinated by a public or private non-

profit agency (other than a political party), or a combination thereof.

(b) The Director is authorized to prescribe such additional criteria for programs carried on under this part as he shall deem appropriate. . . .

PART B—ADULT BASIC EDUCATION PROGRAMS

SEC. 212. It is the purpose of this part to initiate programs of instruction for individuals who have attained age eighteen and whose inability to read and write the English language constitutes a substantial impairment of their ability to get or retain employment commensurate with their real ability, so as to help eliminate such inability and raise the level of education of such individuals with a view of making them less likely to become dependent on others, improving their ability to benefit from occupational training and otherwise increasing their opportunities for more productive and profitable employment, and making them better able to meet their adult responsibilities.

SEC. 213. (a) From the sums appropriated to carry out this title, the Director shall make grants to States which have State plans approved by him under this section. . . .

PART C—VOLUNTARY ASSISTANCE PROGRAM FOR NEEDY CHILDREN

SEC. 219. The purpose of this part is to allow individual Americans to participate in a personal way in the war on poverty, by voluntarily assisting in the support of one or more needy children, in a program coordinated with city or county social welfare agencies.

SEC. 220. (a) In order to carry out the purposes of this part, the Director is authorized to establish a section within the Office of Economic Opportunity to act as an information and coordination center to encourage voluntary assistance for deserving and needy children. Such section shall collect the names of persons who voluntarily desire to assist financially such children and shall secure from city or county social welfare agencies such information concerning deserving and needy children as the Director shall deem appropriate. . . .

TITLE III

SPECIAL PROGRAM TO COMBAT POVERTY IN RURAL AREAS

SEC. 301. It is the purpose of this title to meet some of the special problems of rural poverty and thereby to raise and maintain the income and living standards of low-income rural families and migrant agricultural employees and their families.

PART A—AUTHORITY TO MAKE GRANTS AND LOANS

SEC. 302. (a) The Director is authorized to make—

(1) loans having a maximum maturity of 15 years and in amounts not exceeding $2,500 in the aggregate to any low income rural family where, in the judgment of the Director, such loans have a reasonable possibility of effecting a permanent increase in the income of such families by assisting or permitting them to—

(A) acquire or improve real estate or reduce encumbrances or erect improvements thereon,

(B) operate or improve the operation of farms not larger than family sized, including but not limited to the purchase of feed, seed, fertilizer, livestock, poultry, and equipment, or

(C) participate in cooperative associations; and/or to finance nonagricultural enterprises which will enable such families to supplement their income. . . .

PART B—ASSISTANCE FOR MIGRANT, AND OTHER SEASONALLY EMPLOYED, AGRICULTURAL EMPLOYEES AND THEIR FAMILIES

SEC. 311. The Director shall develop and implement as soon as practicable a program to assist the States, political subdivisions of States, public and nonprofit agencies, institutions, organizations, farm associations, or individuals in establishing and operating programs of assistance for migrant, and other seasonally employed, agricultural employees and their families which programs shall be limited to housing, sanitation, education, and day care of children. Institutions, organizations, farm associations, or individuals shall be limited to direct loans. . . .

652. THE WARREN REPORT
September 24, 1964

On November 22, 1963, President Kennedy was assassinated while riding in a motorcade in Dallas. The Dallas police arrested Lee Harvey Oswald, a former Marine, and charged him with the crime. Before Oswald could be brought to trial, he himself was assassinated (November 24) by Jack Ruby, a nightclub operator, while being transferred, before millions of television viewers, from the police headquarters to the Dallas county jail. One of Lyndon Johnson's first acts as President was to appoint an official commission, headed by Chief Justice Earl Warren, to conduct a full investigation into the assassination of President Kennedy and the murder of Oswald. The commission, which included Senators Russell and Cooper, Representatives Hale Boggs and Gerald Ford, Allen Dulles (former director of CIA), and John J. McCloy (former U.S. High Commissioner for Germany), concluded that Oswald had acted alone, that there was no relationship between Oswald and Ruby, and that there was no conspiracy to assassinate the President. The issues surrounding the case, however, were extremely complicated, and the Warren Report did not silence speculation about a possible conspiracy. See Leo Sauvage, *The Oswald Affair;* E. J. Epstein, *Inquest: The Warren Commission and the Establishment of Truth;* M. Brener, *The Garrison Case;* W. Manchester, *The Death of the President: November 20–November 25, 1963; The Official Warren Commission Report on the Assassination of President John F. Kennedy.*

. . . These conclusions represent the reasoned judgment of all members of the Commission and are presented after an investigation which has satisfied the Commission that it has ascertained the truth concerning the assassination of President Kennedy to the extent that a prolonged and thorough search makes this possible.

1. The shots which killed President Kennedy and wounded Governor Connally were fired from the sixth floor window at the southeast corner of the Texas School Book Depository. This determination is based upon the following:

(*a*) Witnesses at the scene of the assassination saw a rifle being fired from the sixth floor window of the Depository Building, and some witnesses saw a rifle in the window immediately after the shots were fired.

(*b*) The nearly whole bullet found on Governor Connally's stretcher at Parkland Memorial Hospital and the two bullet fragments found in the front seat of the Presidential limousine were fired from the 6.5-millimeter Mannlicher-Carcano rifle found on the sixth floor of Depository Building to the exclusion of all other weapons.

(*c*) The three used cartridge cases found near the window on the sixth floor at the southeast corner of the building were fired from the same rifle which fired the above-described bullet and fragments, to the exclusion of all other weapons.

(*d*) The windshield in the Presidential limousine was struck by a bullet fragment on the inside surface of the glass, but was not penetrated.

(*e*) The nature of the bullet wounds suffered by President Kennedy and Governor Connally and the location of the car at the time of the shots establish that the bullets were fired from above and behind the Presidential limousine, striking the President and the Governor as follows:

(1) President Kennedy was first struck by a bullet which entered at the back of his neck and exited through the lower front portion of his neck, causing a wound which would not necessarily have been lethal. The President was struck a second time by a bullet which entered the right-rear portion of his head, causing a massive and fatal wound.

(2) Governor Connally was struck by

a bullet which entered on the right side of his back and traveled downward through the right side of his chest, exiting below his right nipple. This bullet then passed through his right wrist and entered his left thigh where it caused a superficial wound.

(f) There is no credible evidence that the shots were fired from the Triple Underpass, ahead of the motorcade, or from any other location.

2. The weight of the evidence indicates that there were three shots fired.

3. Although it is not necessary to any essential findings of the Commission to determine just which shot hit Governor Connally, there is very persuasive evidence from the experts to indicate that the same bullet which pierced the President's throat also caused Governor Connally's wounds. However, Governor Connally's testimony and certain other factors have given rise to some difference of opinion as to this probability but there is no question in the mind of any member of the Commission that all the shots which caused the President's and Governor Connally's wounds were fired from the sixth floor window of the Texas School Book Depository.

4. The shots which killed President Kennedy and wounded Governor Connally were fired by Lee Harvey Oswald. This conclusion is based upon the following:

(a) The Mannlicher-Carcano 6.5-millimeter Italian rifle from which the shots were fired was owned by and in the possession of Oswald.

(b) Oswald carried this rifle into the Depository Building on the morning of November 22, 1963.

(c) Oswald, at the time of the assassination, was present at the window from which the shots were fired.

(d) Shortly after the assassination, the Mannlicher-Carcano rifle belonging to Oswald was found partially hidden between some cartons on the sixth floor and the improvised paper bag in which Oswald brought the rifle to the Depository was found close by the window from which the shots were fired.

(e) Based on testimony of the experts and their analysis of films of the assassination, the Commission has concluded that a rifleman of Lee Harvey Oswald's capabilities could have fired the shots from the rifle used in the assassination within the elapsed time of the shooting. The Commission has concluded further that Oswald possessed the capability with a rifle which enabled him to commit the assassination.

(f) Oswald lied to the police after his arrest concerning important substantive matters.

(g) Oswald had attempted to kill Maj. Gen. Edwin A. Walker (Resigned, U.S. Army) on April 10, 1963, thereby demonstrating his disposition to take human life.

5. Oswald killed Dallas Police Patrolman J. D. Tippit approximately 45 minutes after the assassination. . . .

9. The Commission has found no evidence that either Lee Harvey Oswald or Jack Ruby was part of any conspiracy, domestic or foreign, to assassinate President Kennedy. . . .

(f) No direct or indirect relationship between Lee Harvey Oswald and Jack Ruby has been discovered by the Commission, nor has it been able to find any credible evidence that either knew the other, although a thorough investigation was made of the many rumors and speculations of such a relationship.

(g) The Commission has found no evidence that Jack Ruby acted with any other person in the killing of Lee Harvey Oswald.

11. On the basis of the evidence before the Commission it concludes that Oswald acted alone. Therefore, to determine the motives for the assassination of President Kennedy, one must look to the assassin himself. Clues to Oswald's motives can be found in his family history, his education or lack of it, his acts, his writings, and the recollections of those who had close contacts with him throughout his life. The Commission has presented with this report all of the background information bearing on motivation which it could discover. Thus, others may study Lee Oswald's life and arrive at their own conclusions as to his possible motives.

The Commission could not make any definitive determination of Oswald's motives. It has endeavored to isolate factors which contributed to his character and which might have influenced his decision to assassinate President Kennedy. These factors were:

(*a*) His deep-rooted resentment of all authority which was expressed in a hostility toward every society in which he lived;

(*b*) His inability to enter into meaningful relationships with people, and a continuous pattern of rejecting his environment in favor of new surroundings;

(*c*) His urge to try to find a place in history and despair at times over failures in his various undertakings;

(*d*) His capacity for violence as evidenced by his attempt to kill General Walker;

(*e*) His avowed commitment to Marxism and communism, as he understood the terms and developed his own interpretation of them; this was expressed by his antagonism toward the United States, by his defection to the Soviet Union, by his failure to be reconciled with life in the United States even after his disenchantment with the Soviet Union, and by his efforts, though frustrated, to go to Cuba. Each of these contributed to his capacity to risk all in cruel and irresponsible actions. . . .

653. "AGGRESSION FROM THE NORTH": STATE DEPARTMENT WHITE PAPER ON VIETNAM
February 27, 1965
(*Department of State Bulletin,* March 22, 1965)

Following his overwhelming defeat of Goldwater, and armed with the Congressional mandate he had received after the Tonkin Gulf incident (Doc. No. 650), President Johnson embarked on a new military strategy for defeating the Communists in Vietnam—strategic bombing of North Vietnam. Hitherto the fighting had been confined to South Vietnam, and Americans had participated in the role of military "advisers" to the Army of the Republic of Vietnam. The new policy required not only the saturation bombing of North Vietnam but the dispatch of large numbers of American troops to South Vietnam, until the total by 1967 had reached almost 500,000. Both measures presupposed an interpretation of the conflict as "aggression from the North"—not, as critics of the war insisted, a civil war between the National Liberation Front (Vietcong) and the successive military regimes in Saigon. This thesis—that South Vietnam was the victim of "aggression" analogous to the invasion of South Korea in 1950 or of Czechoslovakia in 1938—was spelled out at length in the State Department's "White Paper" of February 1965, which became the justification of subsequent escalations of the American effort in Southeast Asia. See E. Goldman, *The Tragedy of Lyndon Johnson;* G. M. Kahin and J. Lewis, *The United States in Vietnam;* C. Cooper, *The Lost Crusade;* R. Barnet, *Intervention and Revolution;* F. Schurmann et al., *The Politics of Escalation in Vietnam.*

South Vietnam is fighting for its life against a brutal campaign of terror and armed attack inspired, directed, supplied, and controlled by the Communist regime in Hanoi. This flagrant aggression has been going on for years, but recently the pace has quickened and the threat has now become acute.

The war in Vietnam is a new kind of war, a fact as yet poorly understood in most parts of the world. Much of the confusion that prevails in the thinking of many people, and even many governments, stems from this basic misunderstanding. For in Vietnam a totally new brand of aggression has been loosed against an independent people who want to make their own way in peace and freedom.

Vietnam is *not* another Greece, where indigenous guerrilla forces used friendly neighboring territory as a sanctuary.

Vietnam is *not* another Malaya, where Communist guerrillas were, for the most part, physically distinguishable from the peaceful majority they sought to control.

Vietnam is *not* another Philippines, where Communist guerrillas were physically separated from the source of their moral and physical support.

Above all, the war in Vietnam is *not* a spontaneous and local rebellion against the established government.

There are elements in the Communist program of conquest directed against South Vietnam common to each of the previous areas of aggression and subversion. But there is one fundamental difference. In Vietnam a Communist government has set out deliberately to conquer a sovereign people in a neighboring state. And to achieve its end, it has used every resource of its own government to carry out its carefully planned program of concealed aggression. North Vietnam's commitment to seize control of the South is no less total than was the commitment of the regime in North Korea in 1950. But knowing the consequences of the latter's undisguised attack, the planners in Hanoi have tried desperately to conceal their hand. They have failed and their aggression is as real as that of an invading army.

This report is a summary of the massive evidence of North Vietnamese aggression obtained by the Government of South Vietnam. This evidence has been jointly analyzed by South Vietnamese and American experts.

The evidence shows that the hard core of the Communist forces attacking South Vietnam were trained in the North and ordered into the South by Hanoi. It shows that the key leadership of the Vietcong (VC), the officers and much of the cadre, many of the technicians, political organizers, and propagandists have come from the North and operate under Hanoi's direction. It shows that the training of essential military personnel and their infiltration into the South is directed by the Military High Command in Hanoi.

The evidence shows that many of the weapons and much of the ammunition and other supplies used by the Vietcong have been sent into South Vietnam from Hanoi. In recent months new types of weapons have been introduced in the VC army, for which all ammunition must come from outside sources. Communist China and other Communist states have been the prime suppliers of these weapons and ammunition, and they have been channeled primarily through North Vietnam.

The directing force behind the effort to conquer South Vietnam is the Communist Party in the North, the Lao Dong (Workers) Party. As in every Communist state, the party is an integral part of the regime itself. North Vietnamese officials have expressed their firm determination to absorb South Vietnam into the Communist world.

Through its Central Committee, which controls the Government of the North, the Lao Dong Party directs the total political and military effort of the Vietcong. The Military High Command in the North trains the military men and sends them into South Vietnam. The Central Research Agency, North Vietnam's central intelligence organization, directs the elaborate espionage and subversion effort. . . .

Under Hanoi's overall direction the Communists have established an extensive machine for carrying on the war within South Vietnam. The focal point is the Central Office for South Vietnam with its political and military subsections and other specialized agencies. A subordinate part of this Central Office is the Liberation Front for South Vietnam. The front was formed at Hanoi's order in 1960. Its principal function is to influence opinion abroad and to create the false impression that the aggression in South Vietnam is an indigenous rebellion against the established Government.

For more than 10 years the people and the Government of South Vietnam, exercising the inherent right of self-defense, have fought back against these efforts to extend Communist power south across the 17th parallel. The United States has responded to the appeals of the Government of the Republic of Vietnam for help in this defense of the freedom and independence of its land and its people.

In 1961 the Department of State issued a report called *A Threat to the Peace*. It described North Vietnam's program to seize South Vietnam. The evidence in that report had been presented by the Government of the Republic of Vietnam to the International Control Commission (ICC). A special report by the ICC in June 1962 upheld the validity of that evidence. The Commission held that there was "sufficient evidence to show beyond reasonable doubt" that North Vietnam had sent arms and men into South Vietnam to carry out subversion with the aim of overthrowing the legal Government there. The ICC found the authorities in Hanoi in specific violation of four provisions of the Geneva Accords of 1954.

Since then, new and even more impressive evidence of Hanoi's aggression has accumulated. The Government of the United States believes that evidence should be presented to its own citizens and to the world. It is important for free men to know what has been happening in Vietnam, and how, and why. That is the purpose of this report. . . .

The record is conclusive. It establishes beyond question that North Vietnam is carrying out a carefully conceived plan of aggression against the South. It shows that North Vietnam has intensified its efforts in the years since it was condemned by the International Control Commission. It proves that Hanoi continues to press its systematic program of armed aggression into South Vietnam. This aggression violates the United

Nations Charter. It is directly contrary to the Geneva Accords of 1954 and of 1962 to which North Vietnam is a party. It shatters the peace of Southeast Asia. It is a fundamental threat to the freedom and security of South Vietnam.

The people of South Vietnam have chosen to resist this threat. At their request, the United States has taken its place beside them in their defensive struggle.

The United States seeks no territory, no military bases, no favored position. But we have learned the meaning of aggression elsewhere in the post-war world, and we have met it.

If peace can be restored in South Vietnam, the United States will be ready at once to reduce its military involvement. But it will not abandon friends who want to remain free. It will do what must be done to help them. The choice now between peace and continued and increasingly destructive conflict is one for the authorities in Hanoi to make.

654. JOHNSON'S SPEECH ON VIETNAM, JOHNS HOPKINS UNIVERSITY
April 7, 1965
(*Department of State Bulletin,* April 26, 1965)

At the time of its delivery, this speech was widely taken as an indication of the Johnson administration's willingness to negotiate a conclusion to the Vietnamese war—a solution, it seemed, that was prevented only by the intransigence of North Vietnam. Later it became clear that the administration had consistently passed up opportunities for negotiation—a fact which suggested that the United States still hoped for decisive military victory. President Johnson's speech is notable not so much for his commitment to "unconditional negotiations" —a phrase that in practice proved to be open to a great variety of interpretations—as for his reiteration, once again, of the ideological justification for a greatly expanded American intervention. Once again Johnson insisted that the war in South Vietnam was the result of aggression from the North. The speech also resorts to the "domino theory" of Asian politics, according to which a Communist victory in South Vietnam would almost automatically lead to a Communist victory in Thailand, which would in

turn lead to a Communist victory in Burma, and so on until all of Asia had fallen under the Communist yoke. This interpretation presupposed a conspiratorial view of revolution, according to which wars of national liberation were planned and directed, in the last resort, from Peking; and it also implied a military view of history which gave very little weight to the local, nonmilitary sources of social revolution. Such at least was the argument of Johnson's critics. See P. Geyelin, *Lyndon B. Johnson and the World;* E. Goldman, *The Tragedy of Lyndon Johnson;* F. Schurmann, *The Politics of Escalation;* M. Gettleman, ed., *Vietnam;* A. Schlesinger, Jr., *The Bitter Heritage.*

. . . Over this war, and all Asia, is the deepening shadow of Communist China. The rulers in Hanoi are urged on by Peking. This is a regime which has destroyed freedom in

Tibet, attacked India, and been condemned by the United Nations for aggression in Korea. It is a nation which is helping the forces of violence in almost every continent. The contest in Vietnam is part of a wider pattern of aggressive purpose.

Why are these realities our concern? Why are we in South Vietnam? We are there because we have a promise to keep. Since 1954 every American President has offered support to the people of South Vietnam. We have helped to build, and we have helped to defend. Thus, over many years, we have made a national pledge to help South Vietnam defend its independence. And I intend to keep our promise.

To dishonor that pledge, to abandon this small and brave nation to its enemy, and to the terror that must follow, would be an unforgivable wrong.

We are also there to strengthen world order. Around the globe, from Berlin to Thailand, are people whose well-being rests, in part, on the belief that they can count on us if they are attacked. To leave Vietnam to its fate would shake the confidence of all these people in the value of American commitment, the value of America's word. The result would be increased unrest and instability, and even wider war.

We are also there because there are great stakes in the balance. Let no one think for a moment that retreat from Vietnam would bring an end to conflict. The battle would be renewed in one country and then another. The central lesson of our time is that the appetite of aggression is never satisfied. To withdraw from one battlefield means only to prepare for the next. We must say in Southeast Asia, as we did in Europe, in the words of the Bible: "Hitherto shalt thou come, but no further."

There are those who say that all our effort there will be futile, that China's power is such it is bound to dominate all Southeast Asia. But there is no end to that argument until all the nations of Asia are swallowed up.

There are those who wonder why we have a responsibility there. We have it for the same reason we have a responsibility for the defense of freedom in Europe. World War II was fought in both Europe and Asia, and when it ended we found ourselves with continued responsibility for the defense of freedom.

Our objective is the independence of South Vietnam, and its freedom from attack. We want nothing for ourselves, only that the people of South Vietnam be allowed to guide their own country in their own way.

We will do everything necessary to reach that objective. And we will do only what is absolutely necessary.

In recent months, attacks on South Vietnam were stepped up. Thus it became necessary to increase our response and to make attacks by air. This is not a change of purpose. It is a change in what we believe that purpose requires.

We do this in order to slow down aggression.

We do this to increase the confidence of the brave people of South Vietnam who have bravely borne this brutal battle for so many years and with so many casualties.

And we do this to convince the leaders of North Vietnam, and all who seek to share their conquest, of a very simple fact:

We will not be defeated.

We will not grow tired.

We will not withdraw, either openly or under the cloak of a meaningless agreement. . . .

Once this is clear, then it should also be clear that the only path for reasonable men is the path of peaceful settlement.

Such peace demands an independent South Vietnam securely guaranteed and able to shape its own relationships to all others, free from outside interference, tied to no alliance, a military base for no other country.

These are the essentials of any final settlement.

We will never be second in the search for such a peaceful settlement in Vietnam.

There may be many ways to this kind of peace: in discussion or negotiation with the governments concerned; in large groups or in small ones; in the reaffirmation of old agreements or their strengthening with new ones.

We have stated this position over and over again fifty times and more, to friend and foe alike. And we remain ready, with this purpose, for unconditional discussions.

700 DOCUMENTS OF AMERICAN HISTORY

And until that bright and necessary day of peace we will try to keep conflict from spreading. We have no desire to see thousands die in battle, Asians or Americans. We have no desire to devastate that which the people of North Vietnam have built with toil and sacrifice. We will use our power with restraint and with all the wisdom we can command. But we will use it. . . .

We will always oppose the effort of one nation to conquer another nation.

We will do this because our own security is at stake.

But there is more to it than that. For our generation has a dream. It is a very old dream. But we have the power and now we have the opportunity to make it come true.

For centuries, nations have struggled among each other. But we dream of a world where disputes are settled by law and reason. And we will try to make it so.

For most of history men have hated and killed one another in battle. But we dream of an end to war. And we will try to make it so.

For all existence most men have lived in poverty, threatened by hunger. But we dream of a world where all are fed and charged with hope. And we will help to make it so.

The ordinary men and women of North Vietnam and South Vietnam—of China and India—of Russia and America—are brave people. They are filled with the same proportions of hate and fear, of love and hope. Most of them want the same things for themselves and their families. Most of them do not want their sons ever to die in battle, or see the homes of others destroyed. . . .

Every night before I turn out the lights to sleep, I ask myself this question: Have I done everything that I can do to unite this country? Have I done everything I can to help unite the world, to try to bring peace and hope to all the peoples of the world? Have I done enough?

Ask yourselves that question in your homes and in this hall tonight. Have we done all we could? Have we done enough? . . .

---

655. JOHNSON'S STATEMENT ON AMERICAN INTERVENTION IN THE DOMINICAN REPUBLIC
May 2, 1965
(State Department Bulletin, May 17, 1965)

In April 1965, as recounted in the following press release, the administration received alarming reports from the Dominican Republic that a movement to restore former President Juan Bosch, a democrat earlier driven from office by a military coup, had been captured by Communists under the influence of Fidel Castro. With great dispatch, and without inquiring any further into the accuracy of these reports, President Johnson ordered American forces to the Dominican Republic. Despite his professions of neutrality, the effect of this maneuver was to assist the military junta in preventing the restoration of Bosch. As for the alleged threat of a Communist takeover, it seems to have existed only in the imaginations of Ambassador W. Tapley Bennett, Jr. and the CIA. President Johnson was bitterly criticized for this action, one of the most controversial of his Presidency. See A. J. Thomas, Jr. and A. Van Wynen Thomas, The Dominican Republic Crisis: 1965; P. Geyelin, Lyndon B. Johnson and the World;

L. B. Johnson, "The Search for a Durable Peace in the Dominican Republic," Dept. of State Bull., June 21, 1965; T. Szulc, Dominican Diary; R. Barnet, Intervention and Revolution; D. Kurzman, Santo Domingo: Revolt of the Damned; T. Draper, The Dominican Revolt; A Case Study in American Policy; H. J. Morgenthau, "To Intervene or Not to Intervene," 45 Foreign Affairs 425; R. Steel, Pax Americana; J. B. Martin, Overtaken by Events: The Dominican Crisis from the Fall of Trujillo to Civil War; A. Schlesinger, Jr., A Thousand Days; A. F. Lowenthal, The Dominican Intervention.

. . . Last week our observers warned of an approaching political storm in the Dominican Republic. I immediately asked our

Ambassador to return to Washington at once so that we might discuss the situation and might plan a course of conduct. But events soon outran our hopes for peace.

Saturday, April 24—8 days ago—while Ambassador Bennett was conferring with the highest officials of your Government, revolution erupted in the Dominican Republic. Elements of the military forces of that country overthrew their government. However, the rebels themselves were divided. Some wanted to restore former President Juan Bosch. Others opposed his restoration. President Bosch, elected after the fall of Trujillo and his assassination, had been driven from office by an earlier revolution in the Dominican Republic.

Those who opposed Mr. Bosch's return formed a military committee in an effort to control that country. The others took to the street, and they began to lead a revolt on behalf of President Bosch. Control and effective government dissolved in conflict and confusion. . . .

On Wednesday afternoon there was no longer any choice for the man who is your President. I was sitting in my little office reviewing the world situation with Secretary Rusk, Secretary McNamara, and Mr. McGeorge Bundy. Shortly after 3 o'clock I received a cable from our Ambassador, and he said that things were in danger; he had been informed the chief of police and governmental authorities could no longer protect us. We immediately started the necessary conference calls to be prepared.

At 5:14, almost 2 hours later, we received a cable that was labeled "critic," a word that is reserved for only the most urgent and immediate matters of national security.

The cable reported that Dominican law enforcement and military officials had informed our Embassy that the situation was completely out of control and that the police and the government could no longer give any guarantee concerning the safety of Americans or any foreign nationals.

Ambassador Bennett, who is one of our most experienced Foreign Service officers, went on in that cable to say that only an immediate landing of American forces could safeguard and protect the lives of thousands of Americans and thousands of other citizens of some 30 other countries. Ambassador Bennett urged your President to order an immediate landing.

In this situation hesitation and vacillation could mean death for many of our people, as well as many of the citizens of other lands.

I thought that we could not and we did not hesitate. Our forces, American forces, were ordered in immediately to protect American lives. They have done that. They have attacked no one, and although some of our servicemen gave their lives, not a single American civilian or the civilian of any other nation, as a result of this protection, lost their lives. . . .

The revolutionary movement took a tragic turn. Communist leaders, many of them trained in Cuba, seeing a chance to increase disorder, to gain a foothold, joined the revolution. They took increasing control. And what began as a popular democratic revolution, committed to democracy and social justice, very shortly moved and was taken over and really seized and placed into the hands of a band of Communist conspirators. . . .

The American nations cannot, must not, and will not permit the establishment of another Communist government in the Western Hemisphere. This was the unanimous view of all the American nations when, in January 1962, they declared, and I quote: 'The principles of communism are incompatible with the principles of the Inter-American system.' . . .

To those who fight only for liberty and justice and progress I want to join with the Organization of American States in saying—in appealing to you tonight to lay down your arms and to assure you there is nothing to fear. The road is open for you to share in building a Dominican democracy, and we in America are ready and anxious and willing to help you. Your courage and your dedication are qualities which your country and all the hemisphere need for the future. You are needed to help shape that future. And neither we nor any other nation in this hemisphere can or should take it upon itself to ever interfere with the affairs of your country or any other country.

We believe that change comes, and we are glad it does, and it should come through peaceful process. But revolution in any country is a matter for that country to deal with. It becomes a matter calling for hemispheric action only—repeat, only—when the object is the establishment of a Communist dictatorship.

Let me also make clear tonight that we support no single man or any single group of men in the Dominican Republic. Our goal is a simple one. We are there to save the lives of our citizens and to save the lives of all people. Our goal, in keeping with the great principles of the inter-American system, is to help prevent another Communist state in this hemisphere. And we would like to do this without bloodshed or without large-scale fighting.

The form and the nature of the free Dominican government, I assure you, is solely a matter for the Dominican people . . .

656. GRISWOLD v. CONNECTICUT
381 U.S. 479
1965

Appellants in this case gave contraceptive information and advice to married persons, in violation of a Connecticut law forbidding the use of contraceptive devices and punishing anyone assisting in this offense. Their conviction was upheld in lower courts. By a 7 to 2 majority, the Supreme Court held that the Connecticut birth control law unconstitutionally violated the right of privacy. Justice Harlan concurred on narrower grounds. In this case as in *Bell* v. *Maryland* (Doc. No. 648), Justice Black, joined in dissent by Justice Stewart, emerged rather unexpectedly as an advocate of judicial self-restraint, arguing that the Court was now reading its own prejudices into the Constitution, in the area of civil liberties, just as earlier justices had done in the field of economic legislation. See T. I. Emerson, "The Griswold Penumbra: Constitutional Charter for an Expanded Law of Privacy?" 64 *Michigan Law Rev.* 219; P. Kauper, "Penumbras, Peripheries, Emanations, Things Fundamental and Things Forgotten: The Griswold Case," 64 *Michigan Law Rev.* 235; R. B. McKay, "The Right of Privacy: Emanation and Intimation," 64 *Michigan Law Rev.* 259; M. Franklin, "The Ninth Amendment as Civil Law Method and its Implications for the Republican Form of Government: Griswold v. Connecticut," 40 *Tulane Law Rev.* (April 1966); W. M. Beaney, "The Griswold Case and the Expanded Right to Privacy," *Wisconsin Law Rev.*, 1966, 969; E. Katin, "Griswold v. Connecticut: The Justices and Connecticut's 'Uncommonly Silly Law,'" 42 *Notre Dame Lawyer*, 680; N. Dorsen, *Frontiers of Civil Liberties;* A. Sutherland, "Privacy in Connecticut," 64 *Michigan Law Rev.* 283; H. Gross, "The Concept of Privacy," 42 *N. Y. U. Law Rev.* 34.

Appeal from Connecticut Supreme Court of Errors.

DOUGLAS, J. . . . We have had many controversies over these penumbral rights of "privacy and repose." . . . These cases bear witness that the right of privacy which presses for recognition here is a legitimate one.

The present case, then, concerns a relationship lying within the zone of privacy created by several fundamental constitutional guarantees. And it concerns a law which, in forbidding the *use* of contraceptives rather than regulating their manufacture or sale, seeks to achieve its goals by means having a maximum destructive impact upon that relationship. Such a law cannot stand in light of the familiar principle, so often applied by this Court, that a "governmental purpose to control or prevent activities constitutionally subject to state regulation may not be achieved by means which sweep unnecessarily broadly and thereby invade the area of protected freedoms." NAACP v. Alabama, 377 U.S. 288, 307. Would we allow the police to search the sacred precincts of marital bedrooms for telltale signs of the use of contraceptives? The very idea is repulsive to the notions of privacy surrounding the marriage relationship.

We deal with a right of privacy older than the Bill of Rights—older than our political parties, older than our school system. Mar-

riage is a coming together for better or for worse, hopefully enduring, and intimate to the degree of being sacred. It is an association that promotes a way of life, not causes; a harmony in living, not political faiths; a bilateral loyalty, not commercial or social projects. Yet it is an association for as noble a purpose as any involved in our prior decisions.
Reversed.

BLACK, J., with whom Justice STEWART joined, dissenting. . . . The Court talks about a constitutional "right of privacy" as though there is some constitutional provision or provisions forbidding any law ever to be passed which might abridge the "privacy" of individuals. But there is not. There are, of course, guarantees in certain specific constitutional provisions which are designed in part to protect privacy at certain times and places with respect to certain activities. Such, for example, is the Fourth Amendment's guarantee against "unreasonable searches and seizures." But I think it belittles that Amendment to talk about it as though it protects nothing but "privacy." To treat it that way is to give it a niggardly interpretation, not the kind of liberal reading I think any Bill of Rights provision should be given. The average man would very likely not have his feelings soothed any more by having his property seized openly than by having it seized privately and by stealth. He simply wants his property left alone. And a person can be just as much, if not more, irritated,

annoyed and injured by an unceremonious public arrest by a policeman as he is by a seizure in the privacy of his office or home.

One of the most effective ways of diluting or expanding a constitutionally guaranteed right is to substitute for the crucial word or words of a constitutional guarantee another word, more or less flexible and more or less restricted in its meaning. This fact is well illustrated by the use of the term "right of privacy" as a comprehensive substitute for the Fourth Amendment's guarantee against "unreasonable searches and seizures." "Privacy" is a broad, abstract and ambiguous concept which can easily be shrunken in meaning but which can also, on the other hand, easily be interpreted as a constitutional ban against many things other than searches and seizures. I have expressed the view many times that First Amendment freedoms, for example, have suffered from a failure of the courts to stick to the simple language of the First Amendment in construing it, instead of invoking multitudes of words substituted for those the Framers used. . . . For these reasons I get nowhere in this case by talk about a constitutional "right of privacy" as an emanation from one or more constitutional provisions. I like my privacy as well as the next one, but I am nevertheless compelled to admit that government has a right to invade it unless prohibited by some specific constitutional provision. For these reasons I cannot agree with the Court's judgment and the reasons it gives for holding this Connecticut law unconstitutional. . . .

657. SOCIAL SECURITY AMENDMENTS OF 1965 (MEDICARE)
July 30, 1965
(79 U.S. Statutes at Large 286 ff. Public Law 89–97)

When the Social Security Acts (Doc. No. 503) were debated in 1935, some advocates of social security insisted that it ought to provide not only retirement benefits but a system of health insurance for people over 65. The strongest opposition to such a program came from the American Medical Association and its allies in Congress, who attacked it as "socialized medicine." In 1962 President Kennedy revived the issue, but Congress rejected his proposal. In

1964 Congress once again defeated a bill providing medical care for elderly people. Finally, after Johnson's landslide victory in the Presidential election of 1964, a health insurance program was adopted by Congress over the strong opposition of the AMA. An amendment to the Social Security Act, the bill provided a basic plan which automatically covered anyone over 65 (except aliens with less than five years' residence, aliens without status as permanent residents, and federal employees eligible for government health insurance under another law) and paid for hospitalization, nursing home care, home visits, and diagnostic services according to rather complicated rules laid down in Title XVIII, part A and elsewhere in the measure. In addition, a voluntary supplementary plan (part B), to which subscribers paid $3 a month, covered physicians' charges—not covered in the basic plan—together with additional home visits and diagnostic services. The basic plan contained a $40 deductible, the supplementary plan a deductible of $50. The whole program was to be financed in part from increases in the social security tax and in part from other revenues. In addition to the medical features of the bill, it also extended retirement benefits under the Social Security Act to include some categories of persons not previously covered and raised the amount one could earn and still qualify for retirement benefits from $1,200 to $1,500 a year. Only the medical provisions are given below. See R. J. Myers, *Medicare*; H. M. Somers and A. R. Somers, *Medicare and The Hospitals: Issues and Prospects*; U.S. Congress, *1968 Annual Report of Board of Trustees of Federal Hospital Insurance Trust Fund*, House Doc. 91–47; U.S. Department of HEW, *Medicare, A Bibliography of Selected References, 1966–67*; U.S. Department of HEW, *Reimbursement Incentives for Hospital and Medical Care*, Social Security Administration Research Report No. 24; W. J. Cohen, "Social Security Amendments of 1965: Summary and Legislative History," *Soc. Sec. Bull.*, 28 (September 1965); W. J. Cohen, "Social Security Amendments of 1967: Summary and Legislative History," *Soc. Sec. Bull.*, 31 (February 1968).

TITLE XVIII

Health Insurance for the Aged

PART A—HOSPITAL INSURANCE BENEFITS FOR THE AGED

. . . Sec. 1812. (a) The benefits provided to an individual by the insurance program under this part shall consist of entitlement to have payment made on his behalf (subject to the provisions of this part) for—

(1) inpatient hospital services for up to 90 days during any spell of illness;

(2) post-hospital extended care services for up to 100 days during any spell of illness;

(3) post-hospital home health services for up to 100 visits . . . after the beginning of one spell of illness and before the beginning of the next; and

(4) outpatient hospital diagnostic services. . . .

PART B—SUPPLEMENTARY MEDICAL INSURANCE BENEFITS FOR THE AGED

Sec. 1831. There is hereby established a voluntary insurance program to provide medical insurance benefits in accordance with the provisions of this part for individuals 65 years of age or over who elect to enroll under such program, to be financed from premium payments by enrollees together with contributions from funds appropriated by the Federal Government.

Sec. 1832. (a) The benefits provided to an individual by the insurance program established by this part shall consist of—

(1) entitlement to have payment made to him or on his behalf (subject to the provisions of this part) for medical and other health services, except those described in paragraph (2) (B); and

(2) entitlement to have payment made on his behalf (subject to the provisions of this part) for—

(A) home health services for up to 100 visits during a calendar year; and

(B) medical and other health services (other than physicians' services unless furnished by a resident or intern of a hospital) furnished by a provider of services or by others under arrangements with them made by a provider of services.

(b) For definitions of 'spell of illness', 'medical and other health services', and other terms used in this part, see section 1861.

Sec. 1833. (a) Subject to the succeeding provisions of this section, there shall be paid from the Federal Supplementary Medical Insurance Trust Fund, in the case of each individual who is covered under the insurance program established by this part and incurs expenses for services with respect to which benefits are payable under this part, amounts equal to—

(1) in the case of services described in section 1832(a)(1)—80 percent of the reasonable charges for the services . . . and

(2) in the case of services described in section 1832(a)(2)—80 percent of the reasonable cost of the services. . . .

(b) Before applying subsection (a) with respect to expenses incurred by an individual during any calendar year, the total amount of the expenses incurred by such individual during such year (which would, except for this subsection, constitute incurred expenses from which benefits payable under subsection (a) are determinable) shall be reduced by a deductible of $50 . . .

SEC. 1839. (a) The monthly premium of each individual enrolled under this part for each month before 1968 shall be $3. . . .

PART C—MISCELLANEOUS PROVISIONS
DEFINITIONS OF SERVICES,
INSTITUTIONS, ETC.

SEC. 1861. For purposes of this title—

(a) The term 'spell of illness' with respect to any individual means a period of consecutive days—

(1) beginning with the first day (not included in a previous spell of illness) (A) on which such individual is furnished inpatient hospital services or extended care services, and (B) which occurs in a month for which he is entitled to benefits under part A, and

(2) ending with the close of the first period of 60 consecutive days thereafter on each of which he is neither an inpatient of a hospital nor an inpatient of an extended care facility.

(b) The term 'inpatient hospital services' means the following items and services furnished to an inpatient of a hospital and (except as provided in paragraph (3) by the hospital)—

(1) bed and board;

(2) such nursing services and other related services, such use of hospital facilities, and such medical social services as are ordinarily furnished by the hospital for the care and treatment of inpatients, and

such drugs, biologicals, supplies, appliances, and equipment, for use in the hospital, as are ordinarily furnished by such hospital for the care and treatment of inpatients; and

(3) such other diagnostic or therapeutic items or services, furnished by the hospital or by others under arrangements with them made by the hospital, as are ordinarily furnished to inpatients either by such hospital or by others under such arrangements;

excluding, however—

(4) medical or surgical services provided by a physician, resident, or intern; and

(5) the services of a private-duty nurse or other private-duty attendant. . . .

(s) The term 'medical and other health services' means any of the following items or services (unless they would otherwise constitute inpatient hospital services, extended care services, or home health services):

(1) physicians' services;

(2) services and supplies (including drugs and biologicals which cannot, as determined in accordance with regulations, be self-administered) furnished as an incident to a physician's professional service, of kinds which are commonly furnished in physicians' offices and are commonly either rendered without charge or included in the physicians' bills, and hospital services (including drugs and biologicals which cannot, as determined in accordance with regulations, be self-administered) incident to physicians' services rendered to outpatients;

(3) diagnostic X-ray tests, diagnostic laboratory tests, and other diagnostic tests;

(4) X-ray, radium, and radioactive isotope therapy, including materials and services of technicians;

(5) surgical dressings, and splints, casts, and other devices used for reduction of fractures and dislocations;

(6) rental of durable medical equipment, including iron lungs, oxygen tents, hospital beds, and wheelchairs used in the patient's home (including an institution used as his home);

(1) ambulance service where the use of

other methods of transportation is contraindicated by the individual's condition, but only to the extent provided in regulations;

(8) prosthetic devices (other than dental) which replace all or part of an internal body organ, including replacement of such devices; and

(9) leg, arm, back, and neck braces, and artificial legs, arms, and eyes, including replacements if required because of a change in the patient's physical condition. No diagnostic tests performed in any laboratory which is independent of a physician's office or a hospital shall be included within paragraph (3) unless such laboratory—

(10) if situated in any State in which State or applicable local law provides for licensing of establishments of this nature, (A) is licensed pursuant to such law, or (B) is approved, by the agency of such State or locality responsible for licensing establishments of this nature, as meeting the standards established for such licensing; and

(11) meets such other conditions relating to the health and safety of individuals with respect to whom such tests are performed as the Secretary may find necessary. . . .

SEC. 1862. (a) Notwithstanding any other provision of this title, no payment may be made under part A or part B for any expenses incurred for items or services—

(7) where such expenses are for routine physical checkups, eyeglasses or eye examinations for the purpose of prescribing, fitting, or changing eyeglasses, hearing aids or examinations therefor, or immunizations; . . .

(10) where such expenses are for cosmetic surgery or are incurred in connection therewith, except as required for the prompt repair of accidental injury or for improvement of the functioning of a malformed body member; . . .

(12) where such expenses are for services in connection with the care, treatment, filling, removal, or replacement of teeth or structures directly supporting teeth. . . .

SEC. 106. (a) Subsection (a) of section 213 of the Internal Revenue Code of 1954 (relating to allowance of deduction) is amended to read as follows:

(a) *Allowance of Deduction.*—There shall be allowed as a deduction the following amounts, not compensated for by insurance or otherwise—

(1) the amount by which the amount of the expenses paid during the taxable year (reduced by any amount deductible under paragraph (2) for medical care of the taxpayer, his spouse, and dependents (as defined in section 152) exceeds 3 percent of the adjusted gross income, and

(2) an amount (not in excess of $150) equal to one-half of the expenses paid during the taxable year for insurance which constitutes medical care for the taxpayer, his spouse, and dependents. . . .

658. UNITED STATES v. SEEGER
380 U.S. 163, 246
1965

Writ of certiorari to U.S. Circuit Court of Appeals, Second Circuit. This case is one of three critically important recent decisions (see *Welsh* v. *U.S.* and the *Gillette* decision, Doc. No. 682) dealing with the right of a draftee to refuse military service on ethical grounds. Daniel Seeger had been reared a Roman Catholic, attended Quaker meetings, and was a close student of Quaker belief, from which he claimed to derive much of his thought. He argued that

Section 6(j) of the 1948 Universal Military Training and Service Act violated the establishment and free exercise of religion clauses of the First Amendment as well as the due process clause of the Fifth and the religious test clause of Article VI. The district court found for the government; appellate court reversed the holding, stating that exemption from compulsory military service given *only* to those "who rely on a belief in a Supreme Being as the foundation of their objection is an invalid legislative classification that violated the due process clause of the Fifth Amendment." Underlying the legal issue was the twin claim that asserts that loyalty to conscience is superior to country, and that "conscience" has a moral as well as religious connotation. The Supreme Court gave the statutory phrase, "supreme being," a lower-case meaning, thus extending exemption to nontheistic as well as theistic objectors. See N. Dorsen and D. Rudovsky, "On Selective Conscientious Objection," 11 *Forum* 44; D. Cutler, *The Religious Situation, 1969;* J. H. Sherk, "The Position of the Conscientious Objector," 55 *Current History* (1968); N. Redlich and K. Feinberg, "Individual Conscience and the Selective Conscientious Objector: The Right Not to Kill," 44 *N. Y. U. Law Rev.* 875; P. Donnici, "Governmental Encouragement of Religious Ideology: A Study of the Current Conscientious Objector Exemption from Military Service," 12 *J. of Public Law* 16; Comment, "Constitutionality of Requiring Belief in Supreme Being for Draft Exemption as Conscientious Objector," 64 *Columbia Law Rev.* 938; J. Finn, ed., *A Conflict of Loyalties;* J. B. Tietz, "Deity Belief: Necessity for Draft Status," 38 *Southern California Law Rev.* 529; A. Brodie and H. Southerland, "Conscience, the Constitution and the Supreme Court: The Riddle of the United States v. Seeger," *Wisconsin Law Rev.* 1966, 302; N. Dorsen, *Frontiers of Civil Liberties;* M. Konvitz, *Religious Liberty and Conscience.*

CLARK, J. . . . These cases involve claims of conscientious objectors under § 6(j) of the Universal Military Training and Service Act, . . . which exempts from combatant training and service in the armed forces of the United States those persons who by reason of their religious training and belief are conscientiously opposed to participation in war in any form. The cases were consolidated for argument and we consider them together although each involves different facts and circumstances. The parties raise the basic question of the constitutionality of the section which defines the term "religious training and belief," as used in the Act, as "an individual's belief in a relation to a Supreme Being involving duties superior to those arising from any human re-lation, but [not including] essentially political, sociological, or philosophical views or a merely personal moral code." The constitutional attack is launched under the First Amendment's Establishment and Free Exercise Clauses and is twofold: (1) The section does not exempt nonreligious conscientious objectors; and (2) it discriminates between different forms of religious expression in violation of the Due Process Clause of the Fifth Amendment. . . .

. . . Seeger was convicted in the District Court for the Southern District of New York of having refused to submit to induction in the armed forces. He was originally classified 1–A in 1953 by his local board, but this classification was changed in 1955 to 2–S (student) and he remained in this status until 1958 when he was reclassified 1–A. He first claimed exemption as a conscientious objector in 1957 after successive annual renewals of his student classification. Although he did not adopt verbatim the printed Selective Service System form, he declared that he was conscientiously opposed to participation in war in any form by reason of his "religious" belief; that he preferred to leave the question as to his belief in a Supreme Being open, "rather than answer 'yes' or 'no'; that his "skepticism or disbelief in the existence of God" did "not necessarily mean lack of faith in anything whatsoever"; that his was a "belief in and devotion to goodness and virtue for their own sakes, and a religious faith in a purely ethical creed." He cited such personages as Plato, Aristotle and Spinoza for support of his ethical belief in intellectual and moral integrity "without belief in God, except in the remotest sense." His belief was found to be sincere, honest, and made in good faith; and his conscientious objection to be based upon individual training and belief, both of which included research in religious and cultural fields. Seeger's claim, however, was denied solely because it was not based upon a "belief in a relation to a Supreme Being" as required by § 6(j) of the Act. . . .

1. The crux of the problem lies in the phrase "religious training and belief" which Congress has defined as "belief in a relation to a Supreme Being involving duties superior

to those arising from any human relation." In assigning meaning to this statutory language we may narrow the inquiry by noting briefly those scruples expressly excepted from the definition. The section excludes those persons who, disavowing religious belief, decide on the basis of essentially political, sociological or economic considerations that war is wrong and that they will have no part of it. These judgments have historically been reserved for the Government, and in matters which can be said to fall within these areas the conviction of the individual has never been permitted to override that of the state. United States v. Macintosh, supra (dissenting opinion). The statute further excludes those whose opposition to war stems from a "merely personal moral code," a phrase to which we shall have occasion to turn later in discussing the application of § 6(j) to these cases. We also pause to take note of what is not involved in this litigation. No party claims to be an atheist or attacks the statute on this ground. The question is not, therefore, one between theistic and atheistic beliefs. We do not deal with or intimate any decision on that situation in these cases. Nor do the parties claim the monotheistic belief that there is but one God; what they claim (with the possible exception of Seeger who bases his position here not on factual but on purely constitutional grounds) is that they adhere to theism, which is the "Belief in the existence of a god or gods; . . . Belief in superhuman powers or spiritual agencies in one or many gods," as opposed to atheism. Our question, therefore, is the narrow one: Does the term "Supreme Being" as used in § 6(j) mean the orthodox God or the broader concept of a power or being, or a faith, "to which all else is subordinate or upon which all else is ultimately dependent"? . . .

In spite of the elusive nature of the inquiry, we are not without certain guidelines. In amending the 1940 Act, Congress adopted almost intact the language of Chief Justice Hughes in United States v. Macintosh, supra:

"The essence of religion is belief in a relation to *God* involving duties superior to those arising from any human relation." At 633–634 of 283 U.S., 51 S.Ct. at 578. (Emphasis supplied.)

By comparing the statutory definition with those words, however, it becomes readily apparent that the Congress deliberately broaden them by substituting the phrase "Supreme Being" for the appellation "God." And in so doing it is also significant that Congress did not elaborate on the form or nature of this higher authority which it chose to designate as "Supreme Being." . . . It appears, therefore, that we need only look to this clear statement of congressional intent as set out in the report. Under the 1940 Act it was necessary only to have a conviction based upon religious training and belief; we believe that is all that is required here. Within that phrase would come all sincere religious beliefs which are based upon a power or being, or upon a faith, to which all else is subordinate or upon which all else is ultimately dependent. The test might be stated in these words: A sincere and meaningful belief which occupies in the life of its possessor a place parallel to that filled by the God of those admittedly qualifying for the exemption comes within the statutory definition. This construction avoids imputing to Congress an intent to classify different religion beliefs, exempting some and excluding others, and is in accord with the well-established congressional policy of equal treatment for those whose opposition to service is grounded in their religious tenets.

. . . Section 6(j), then, is no more than a clarification of the 1940 provision involving only certain "technical amendments", to use the words of Senator Gurney. As such it continues the congressional policy of providing exemption from military service for those whose opposition is based on grounds that can fairly be said to be "religious." To hold otherwise would not only fly in the face of Congress' entire action in the past; it would ignore the historic position of our country on this issue since its founding.

659. VOTING RIGHTS ACT OF 1965
August 6, 1965
(79 *U.S. Statutes at Large* 437)

This measure was debated at a time of turbulence. Sit-ins, demonstrations, and protest marches—such as that at Selma, Alabama, led by the Rev. Martin Luther King—swept the nation, with the South and Washington, D.C., especially hard-hit. It was against this backdrop that the Johnson administration submitted its voting rights proposal to Congress. The act won strong bipartisan support as well as the endorsement of most civil rights leaders. It had its constitutional basis in the Fifteenth Amendment. See L. Miller, *The Petitioners;* N. Dorsen, *Frontiers of Civil Liberties;* A. Cox, *The Warren Court: Constitutional Decision as an Instrument of Social Reform;* D. S. Strong, *Negroes, Ballots, and Judges: National Voting Rights Legislation in the Federal Courts;* W. Christopher, "The Constitutionality of the Voting Rights Act of 1965," *Stanford Law Rev.,* 1966; A. Bickel, "The Voting Rights Cases," *Supreme Court Rev.,* 1966; E. P. Tuttle, "Equality and the Vote," 41 *N.Y.U. Law Rev.* (April 1966).

Be it enacted by the Senate and House of Representatives of the United States of America in Congress assembled, That this Act shall be known as the "Voting Rights Act of 1965."

SEC. 2. No voting qualification or prerequisite to voting, or standard, practice, or procedure shall be imposed or applied by any State or political subdivision to deny or abridge the right of any citizen of the United States to vote on account of race or color.

SEC. 3. (a) Whenever the Attorney General institutes a proceeding under any statute to enforce the guarantees of the fifteenth amendment in any State or political subdivision the court shall authorize the appointment of Federal examiners by the United States Civil Service Commission in accordance with section 6 to serve for such period of time and for such political subdivisions as court shall determine is appropriate to enforce the guarantees of the fifteenth amendment (1) as part of any interlocutory order if the court determines that the appointment of such examiners is necessary to enforce such guarantees or (2) as part of any final judgment if the court finds that violations of the fifteenth amendment justifying equitable relief have occurred in such State or subdivision: *Provided,* That the court need not authorize the appointment of examiners if any incidents of denial or abridgement of the right to vote on account of race or color (1) have been few in number and have been promptly and effectively corrected by State or local action, (2) the continuing effect of such incidents has been eliminated, and (3) there is no reasonable probability of their recurrence in the future.

(b) If in a proceeding instituted by the Attorney General under any statute to enforce the guarantees of the fifteenth amendment in any State or political subdivision the court finds that a test or device has been used for the purpose or with the effect of denying or abridging the right of any citizen of the United States to vote on account of race or color, it shall suspend the use of tests and devices in such State or political subdivisions as the court shall determine is appropriate and for such period as it deems necessary.

(c) If in any proceeding instituted by the Attorney General under any statute to enforce the guarantees of the fifteenth amendment in any State or political subdivision the court finds that violations of the fifteenth amendment justifying equitable relief have occurred within the territory of such State or political subdivision, the court, in addition to such relief as it may grant, shall retain jurisdiction for such period as it may deem appropriate and during such period no voting qualification or prerequisite to voting, or standard, practice, or procedure with respect to voting different from that in force or effect at the time the proceeding was commenced shall be enforced unless and until the court finds that such qualification, prerequisite, standard, practice, or procedure does not have the purpose and will not have the effect of denying or abridging the right to vote on account of race or color: *Provided,* That such qualification, prerequisite, standard, practice, or procedure may be enforced if the qualification, prerequisite, standard, practice, or procedure has been submitted by the chief legal officer or other appropriate official of such State or subdivision to the Attorney General and the Attorney General has not interposed an objection within sixty days after such submission, except that neither the court's finding nor the Attorney General's failure to object shall bar a subsequent action to enjoin enforcement of such qualification, prerequisite, standard, practice, or procedure.

SEC. 4. (a) To assure that the right of citizens of the United States to vote is not denied or abridged on account of race or color, no citizen shall be denied the right to vote in any Federal, State, or local election because of his failure to comply with any test or device in any State. . . .

(c) The phrase "test or device" shall mean any requirement that a person as a prerequisite for voting or registration for voting (1) demonstrate the ability to read, write, understand, or interpret any matter, (2) demonstrate any educational achievement or his knowledge of any particular subject, (3) possess good moral character, or (4) prove his qualifications by the voucher of registered voters or members of any other class. . . .

(e) (1) Congress hereby declares that to secure the rights under the fourteenth amendment of persons educated in American-flag schools in which the predominant classroom language was other than English, it is necessary to prohibit the States from conditioning the right to vote of such persons on ability to read, write, understand, or interpret any matter in the English language.

(2) No person who demonstrates that he has successfully completed the sixth primary grade in a public school in, or a private school accredited by, any State or territory, the District of Columbia, or the Commonwealth of Puerto Rico in which the predominant classroom language was other than English, shall be denied the right to vote in any Federal, State, or local election because of his inability to read, write, understand, or interpret any matter in the English

language. . . . Attorney General certifies with respect to any political subdivision named in, or included within the scope of, determinations made under section 4(b) that (1) he has received complaints in writing from twenty or more residents of such political subdivision alleging that they have been denied the right to vote under color of law on account of race or color, and that he believes such complaints to be meritorious, or (2) that in his judgment (considering, among other factors, whether the ratio of nonwhite persons to white persons registered to vote within such subdivision appears to him to be reasonably attributable to violations of the fifteenth amendment or whether substantial evidence exists that bona fide efforts are being made within such subdivision to comply with the fifteenth amendment), the appointment of examiners is otherwise necessary to enforce the guarantees of the fifteenth amendment, the Civil Service Commission shall appoint as many examiners for such subdivision as it may deem appropriate to prepare and maintain lists of persons eligible to vote in Federal, State, and local elections.

(b) Any person whom the examiner finds, in accordance with instructions received under section 9(b), to have the qualifications prescribed by State law not inconsistent with the Constitution and laws of the United States shall promptly be placed on a list of eligible voters. . . . The appropriate State or local election official shall place such names on the official voting list. Any person whose name appears on the examiner's list shall be entitled and allowed to vote in the election district of his residence unless and until the appropriate election officials shall have been notified that such person has been removed from such list in accordance with subsection (d): *Provided,* That no person shall be entitled to vote in any election by virtue of this Act unless his name shall have been certified and transmitted on such a list to the offices of the appropriate election officials at least forty-five days prior to such election.

(c) The examiner shall issue to each person whose name appears on such a list a certificate evidencing his eligibility to vote.

(d) A person whose name appears on

such a list shall be removed therefrom by an examiner if (1) such person has been successfully challenged in accordance with the procedure prescribed in section 9, or (2) he has been determined by an examiner to have lost his eligibility to vote under State law not inconsistent with the Constitution and the laws of the United States. . . .

SEC. 10. (a) The Congress finds that the requirement of the payment of a poll tax as a precondition to voting (i) precludes persons of limited means from voting or imposes unreasonable financial hardship upon such persons as a precondition to their exercise of the franchise, (ii) does not bear a reasonable relationship to any legitimate State interest in the conduct of elections, and (iii) in some areas has the purpose or effect of denying persons the right to vote because of race or color. Upon the basis of these findings, Congress declares that the constitutional right of citizens to vote is denied or abridged in some areas by the requirement of the payment of a poll tax as a precondition to voting.

(b) In the exercise of the powers of Congress under section 5 of the fourteenth amendment and section 2 of the fifteenth amendment, the Attorney General is authorized and directed to institute forthwith in the name of the United States such actions, including actions against States or political subdivisions, for declaratory judgment or injunctive relief against the enforcement of any requirement of the payment of a poll tax as a precondition to voting, or substitute therefor enacted after November 1, 1964, as will be necessary to implement the declaration of subsection (a) and the purposes of this section. . . .

660. SOUTH CAROLINA v. KATZENBACH
383 U.S. 301
1966

The Civil Rights Act of 1965, which for the first time provided effective federal protection for Negroes who wished to register and vote, brought startling results in mounting black registration throughout the South. South Carolina, which lagged behind most states in registering blacks, brought suit to enjoin certain provisions of the Act, particularly those suspending literacy and other tests, providing for federal voting examiners, challenges to eligibility listings, and enforcement through criminal contempt suits. The crucial constitutional question was whether this legislation was "appropriate" under the terms of the Fifteenth Amendment. Chief Justice Warren spoke for a unanimous court in sustaining the constitutionality of these provisions. See R. Bardolph, ed., *The Civil Rights Record;* H. Abraham, *Freedom and the Court;* A. M. Bickel, "The Voting Rights Cases," in P. Kurland, ed., *The Supreme Court Review,* 1966.

WARREN, C. J. . . . By leave of the Court, South Carolina has filed a bill of complaint, seeking a declaration that selected provisions of the Voting Rights Act of 1965 violate the Federal Constitution, and asking for an injunction against enforcement of these provisions by the Attorney General. . . .

Recognizing that the questions presented were of urgent concern to the entire country, we invited all of the States to participate in this proceeding as friends of the Court. A majority responded by submitting or joining in briefs on the merits, some supporting South Carolina and others the Attorney General. . . .

. . . The Voting Rights Act was designed by Congress to banish the blight of racial discrimination in voting, which has infected the electoral process in parts of our country for nearly a century. The Act creates stringent new remedies for voting discrimination where it persists on a pervasive scale, and in addition the statute strengthens existing remedies for pockets of voting discrimination elsewhere in the country. Congress assumed the power to prescribe these remedies from § 2 of the Fifteenth Amendment, which authorizes the national legislature to effectuate by "appropriate" measures the constitutional prohibition against racial discrimination in voting. We hold that the sections of the Act which are properly before us are an appropriate means for carrying out Congress' constitutional responsibilities and are consonant with all other provisions of the Constitution. We therefore deny South Carolina's request that enforcement of these sections of the Act be enjoined.

The constitutional propriety of the Voting Rights Act of 1965 must be judged with reference to the historical experience which it reflects. . . .

Two points emerge vividly from the voluminous legislative history of the Act contained in the committee hearings and floor debates. First: Congress felt itself confronted by an insidious and pervasive evil which had been perpetuated in certain parts of our country through unremitting and ingenious defiance of the Constitution. Second: Congress concluded that the unsuccessful remedies which it had prescribed in the past would have to be replaced by sterner and more elaborate measures in order to satisfy the clear commands of the Fifteenth Amendment. . . .

According to the results of recent Justice Department voting suits, . . . discriminatory administration of voting qualifications has been found in all eight Alabama cases, in all nine Louisiana cases, and in all nine Mississippi cases which have gone to final judgment. Moreover, in almost all of these cases, the courts have held that the discrimination was pursuant to a widespread "pattern or practice." White applicants for registration have often been excused altogether from the literacy and understanding tests or have been given easy versions, have received extensive help from voting officials, and have been registered despite serious errors in their answers. Negroes, on the other hand, have typically been required to pass difficult versions of all the tests, without any outside assistance and without the slightest error. The good morals requirement is so vague and subjective that it has constituted an open invitation to abuse at the hands of voting officials. Negroes obliged to obtain vouchers from registered voters have found it virtually impossible to comply in areas where almost no Negroes are on the rolls.

In recent years, Congress has repeatedly tried to cope with the problem by facilitating case-by-case litigation against voting discrimination. . . .

Despite the earnest efforts of the Justice Department and of many federal judges, these new laws have done little to cure the problem of voting discrimination. According to estimates by the Attorney General during hearings on the Act, registration of voting age Negroes in Alabama rose only from 10.2% to 19.4% between 1958 and 1964; in Louisiana it barely inched ahead from 31.7% to 31.8% between 1956 and 1965; and in Mississippi it increased only from 4.4% to 6.4% between 1954 and 1964. In each instance, registration of voting age whites ran roughly 50 percentage points or more ahead of Negro registration.

The previous legislation has proved ineffective for a number of reasons. Voting suits are unusually onerous to prepare, sometimes requiring as many as 6,000 man-hours spent combing through registration records in preparation for trial. Litigation has been exceedingly slow, in part because of the ample opportunities for delay afforded voting officials and others involved in the proceedings. Even when favorable decisions have finally been obtained, some of the States affected have merely switched to discriminatory devices not covered by the federal decrees or have enacted difficult new tests designed to prolong the existing disparity between white and Negro registration. Alternatively, certain local officials have defied and evaded court orders or have simply closed their registration offices to freeze the voting rolls. The provision of the 1960 law authorizing registration by federal officers has had little impact on local maladministration because of its procedural complexities.

During the hearings and debates on the Act, Selma, Alabama, was repeatedly referred to as the pre-eminent example of the ineffectiveness of existing legislation. In Dallas County, of which Selma is the seat, there were four years of litigation by the Justice Department and two findings by the federal courts of widespread voting discrimination. Yet in those four years, Negro registration rose only from 156 to 383, although there are approximately 15,000 Negroes of voting age in the county. . . .

The Voting Rights Act of 1965 reflects Congress' firm intention to rid the country of racial discrimination in voting. The heart of the Act is a complex scheme of stringent remedies aimed at areas where voting discrimination has been most flagrant. . . .

. . . The first of the remedies, contained in § 4(a), is the suspension of literacy tests and similar voting qualifications for a period of five years from the last occurrence of substantial voting discrimination. Section 5 prescribes a second remedy, the suspension of all new voting regulations pending review by federal authorities to determine whether their use would perpetuate voting discrimination. The third remedy . . . is the assignment of federal examiners by the Attorney General to list qualified applicants who are thereafter entitled to vote in all elections. . . . Section 8 authorizes the appointment of federal poll-watchers in places to which federal examiners have already been assigned. Section 10(d) excuses those made eligible to vote . . . from paying accumulated past poll taxes for state and local elections. Section 12(e) provides for balloting by persons denied access to the polls in areas where federal examiners have been appointed.

The remaining remedial portions of the Act are aimed at voting discrimination in any area of the country where it may occur . . .

These provisions of the Voting Rights Act of 1965 are challenged on the fundamental ground that they exceed the powers of Congress and encroach on an area reserved to the States by the Constitution. South Caro-lina and certain of the *amici curiae* also . . . argue that the coverage formula prescribed in § 4(a)-(d) violates the principle of the equality of States, denies due process by employing an invalid presumption and by barring judicial review of administrative findings, constitutes a forbidden bill of attainder, and impairs the separation of powers by adjudicating guilt through legislation. . . .

The ground rules for resolving this question are clear. The language and purpose of the Fifteenth Amendment, the prior decisions construing its several provisions, and the general doctrines of constitutional interpretation, all point to one fundamental principle. As against the reserved powers of the States, Congress may use any rational means to effectuate the constitutional prohibition of racial discrimination in voting. . . .

Section 1 of the Fifteenth Amendment declares that "the right of citizens of the United States to vote shall not be denied or abridged by the United States or by any State on account of race, color, or previous condition of servitude." This declaration has always been treated as self-executing and has repeatedly been construed, without further legislative specification, to invalidate state voting qualifications or procedures which are discriminatory on their face or in practice. . . .

We therefore reject South Carolina's argument that Congress may appropriately do no more than to forbid violations of the Fifteenth Amendment in general terms—that the task of fashioning specific remedies or of applying them to particular localities must necessarily be left entirely to the courts. . . .

661. MIRANDA v. ARIZONA
384 U.S. 436
1966

Certiorari to the Supreme Court of Arizona, which had held that Miranda's constitutional rights were not violated. The case involved interrogation of petitioner, Ernesto Miranda, by two Phoenix, Arizona police officers, and his oral confession to the charge of kidnapping and rape. The Supreme Court in these years was continually faced with the necessity of setting strict procedural limitations upon the power of the police in apprehending, interrogating, and prosecuting criminal suspects. Defendant rights, then, became a vitally important due process issue, one that preoccupied the justices as they sought to bring order out of what some regarded as the chaos of constitutional doctrines affecting confessions. The Court was here concerned with the use of the privilege against self-incrimination as affecting those detained by the police for "custodial" interrogation. In *Malloy* v. *Hogan*, 378 U.S. 1 (1964), the Court had held the privilege fully applicable to the states through the due process clause of the Fourteenth Amendment. *Escobedo* (Doc. No. 647) spawned multiple decisions involving forced confessions and the right to counsel. It accelerated nationwide controversy at a time when "handcuffing the police" had already become an explosive social-political issue. The *Miranda* case unleashed further debate. It also illustrates the workings of Parkinson's law as right-to-counsel litigation proliferated, and major cases followed dealing with postindictment police lineups, probation revocation hearings, juvenile delinquency hearings, etc. The Court majority here reversed the lower court's decision, with Justice Harlan speaking for three of the four dissenters. See F. Graham, *The Self-Inflicted Wound;* I. Silver, "The Supreme Court, the State Judiciary, and State Criminal Procedure," 41 *St. John's Law Rev.* 331; E. Pringle and H. Garfield, "The Expanding Power of Police to Search and Seize: Effect of Recent U.S. Supreme Court Decisions on Criminal Investigation," 40 *U. of Colorado Law Rev.* 491; A. Blumberg, *Criminal Justice;* A. Cox, *The Warren Court;* R. Pitler, " 'The Fruit of the Poisoned Tree' Revisited and Shepardized," 56 *California Law Rev.* 579; B. J. George, Jr., "The Fruits of Miranda: Scope of the Exclusionary Rule," 39 *U. of Colorado Law Rev.* 478; A. K. Pye, "The Warren Court and Criminal Procedure," in Richard Sayler et al., eds., *The Warren Court;* Sutherland, "Crime and Confession," 79 *Harvard Law Rev.* 29; Herman, "Supreme Court and Restrictions in Police Interrogation," 25 *Ohio State Law Rev.* 449.

WARREN, C. J. . . . The cases before us raise questions which go to the roots of our concepts of American criminal jurisprudence: the restraints society must observe consistent with the Federal Constitution in prosecuting individuals for crime. More specifically, we deal with the admissibility of statements obtained from an individual who is subjected to custodial police interrogation and the necessity for procedures which assure that the individual is accorded his privilege under the Fifth Amendment to the Constitution not to be compelled to incriminate himself.

We start here, as we did in *Escobedo,* with the premise that our holding is not an innovation in our jurisprudence, but is an application of principles long recognized and applied in other settings. We have undertaken a thorough re-examination of the *Escobedo* decision and the principles it announced, and we reaffirm it. That case was but an explication of basic rights that are enshrined in our Constitution—that "No person . . . shall be compelled in any criminal case to be a witness against himself," and that "the accused shall . . . have the Assistance of Counsel"—rights which were put in jeopardy in that case through official overbearing. These precious rights were fixed in our Constitution only after centuries of persecution and struggle. And in the words of Chief Justice Marshall, they were secured "for ages to come, and . . . designed to approach immortality as nearly as human institutions can approach it," *Cohens* v. *Virginia.* . . .

The constitutional issue we decide in each of these cases is the admissibility of statements obtained from a defendant questioned while in custody or otherwise deprived of his freedom of action in any significant way. In each, the defendant was questioned by police officers, detectives, or a prosecuting attorney in a room in which he was cut off from the outside world. In none of these cases was the defendant given a full and effective warning of his rights at the outset of the interrogation process. In all the cases, the questioning elicited oral admissions, and in three of them, signed statements as well which were admitted at their trials. They all thus share salient features—incommunicado interrogation of individuals in a police-dominated atmosphere, resulting in self-incriminating statements without full warnings of Constitutional rights. . . .

Even without employing brutality, the "third degree" or the specific stratagems described above, the very fact of custodial interrogation exacts a heavy toll on individual liberty and trades on the weakness of individuals. . . .

In the cases before us today, given this background, we concern ourselves primarily with this interrogation atmosphere and the evils it can bring. In *Miranda* v. *Arizona,* the police arrested the defendant and took him to a special interrogation room where they secured a confession. . . .

In these cases, we might not find the defendants' statements to have been involuntary in traditional terms. Our concern for adequate safeguards to protect precious Fifth Amendment rights is, of course, not lessened in the slightest. In each of the cases, the defendant was thrust into an unfamiliar atmosphere and run through menacing police interrogation procedures. The potentiality for compulsion is forcefully apparent, for example, in *Miranda*, where the indigent Mexican defendant was a seriously disturbed individual with pronounced sexual fantasies. . . .

It is obvious that such an interrogation environment is created for no purpose other than to subjugate the individual to the will of his examiner. This atmosphere carries its own badge of intimidation. To be sure, this is not physical intimidation, but it is equally destructive of human dignity. The current practice of incommunicado interrogation is at odds with one of our Nation's most cherished principles—that the individual may not be compelled to incriminate himself. Unless adequate protective devices are employed to dispel the compulsion inherent in custodial surroundings, no statement obtained from the defendant can truly be the product of his free choice.

From the foregoing, we can readily perceive an intimate connection between the privilege against self-incrimination and police custodial questioning. It is fitting to turn to history and precedent underlying the Self-Incrimination Clause to determine its applicability in this situation. . . .

Today, then, there can be no doubt that the Fifth Amendment privilege is available outside of criminal court proceedings and serves to protect persons in all settings in which their freedom of action is curtailed in any significant way from being compelled to incriminate themselves. We have concluded that without proper safeguards the process of in-custody interrogation of persons suspected or accused of crime contains inherently compelling pressures which work to undermine the individual's will to resist and to compel him to speak where he would not otherwise do so freely. In order to combat these pressures and to permit a full opportunity to exercise the privilege against self-incrimination, the accused must be adequately and effectively apprised of his rights and the exercise of those rights must be fully honored.

It is impossible for us to foresee the potential alternatives for protecting the privilege which might be devised by Congress or the States in the exercise of their creative rule-making capacities. Therefore we cannot say that the Constitution necessarily requires adherence to any particular solution for the inherent compulsions of the interrogation process as it is presently conducted. Our decision in no way creates a constitutional straitjacket which will handicap sound efforts at reform, nor is it intended to have this effect. We encourage Congress and the States to continue their laudable search for increasingly effective ways of protecting the rights of the individual while promoting efficient enforcement of our criminal laws. However, unless we are shown other procedures which are at least as effective in apprising accused persons of their right of silence and in assuring a continuous opportunity to exercise it, the following safeguards must be observed.

At the outset, if a person in custody is to be subjected to interrogation, he must first be informed in clear and unequivocal terms that he has the right to remain silent. For those unaware of the privilege, the warning is needed simply to make them aware of it— the threshold requirement for an intelligent decision as to its exercise. More important, such a warning is an absolute prerequisite in overcoming the inherent pressures of the interrogation atmosphere. It is not just the subnormal or woefully ignorant who succumb to an interrogator's imprecations, whether implied or expressly stated, that the interrogation will continue until a confession is obtained or that silence in the face of accusation is itself damning and will bode ill when presented to a jury. Further, the warning will show the individual that his interrogators are prepared to recognize his privilege should he choose to exercise it.

The Fifth Amendment privilege is so fundamental to our system of constitutional rule and the expedient of giving an adequate warning as to the availability of the privilege so simple, we will not pause to inquire in individual cases whether the defendant was aware of his rights without a warning being given. Assessments of the knowledge the defendant possessed, based on information as to his age, education, intelligence, or prior contact with authorities, can never be more than speculation; a warning is a clear-cut fact. More important, whatever the background of the person interrogated, a warning at the time of the interrogation is indispensable to overcome its pressures and to insure that the individual knows he is free to exercise the privilege at that point in time.

The warning of the right to remain silent must be accompanied by the explanation that anything said can and will be used against the individual in court. This warning is needed in order to make him aware not only of the privilege, but also of the consequences of forgoing it. It is only through an awareness of these consequences that there can be any assurance of real understanding and intelligent exercise of the privilege. Moreover, this warning may serve to make the individual more acutely aware that he is faced with a phase of the adversary system —that he is not in the presence of persons acting solely in his interest.

The circumstances surrounding in-custody interrogation can operate very quickly to overbear the will of one merely made aware of his privilege by his interrogators. Therefore, the right to have counsel present at the interrogation is indispensable to the protection of the Fifth Amendment privilege under the system we delineate today. Our aim is to assure that the individual's right to choose between silence and speech remains unfettered throughout the interrogation process. A once-stated warning, delivered by those who will conduct the interrogation, cannot itself suffice to that end among those who most require knowledge of their rights. A mere warning given by the interrogators is not alone sufficient to accomplish that end. Prosecutors themselves claim that the admonishment of the right to remain silent without more "will benefit only the recidivist and the professional. . . ."

Accordingly we hold that an individual held for interrogation must be clearly informed that he has the right to consult with a lawyer and to have the lawyer with him during interrogation under the system for protecting the privilege we delineate today. As with the warnings of the right to remain silent and that anything stated can be used in evidence against him, this warning is an absolute prerequisite to interrogation. No amount of circumstantial evidence that the person may have been aware of this right will suffice to stand in its stead. Only through such a warning is there ascertainable assurance that the accused was aware of this right.

If an individual indicates that he wishes the assistance of counsel before any interrogation occurs, the authorities cannot rationally ignore or deny his request on the basis that the individual does not have or cannot afford a retained attorney. The financial ability of the individual has no relationship to the scope of the rights involved here. The privilege against self-incrimination secured by the Constitution applies to all individuals. The need for counsel in order to protect the privilege exists for the indigent as well as the affluent. In fact, were we to limit these constitutional rights to those who can retain an attorney, our decisions today would be of little significance. The cases before us as well as the vast majority of confession cases with which we have dealt in the past involve those unable to retain counsel. While authorities are not required to relieve the accused of his poverty, they have the obligation not to take advantage of indigence in the administration of justice. Denial of counsel to the indigent at the time of interrogation while allowing an attorney to those who can afford one would be no more supportable by reason or logic than the similar situation at trial and on appeal struck down in *Gideon* v. *Wainwright,* 372 U.S. 335 (1963), and *Douglas* v. *California,* 372 U.S. 353 (1963).

In order fully to apprise a person interrogated of the extent of his rights under this system then, it is necessary to warn him not only that he has the right to consult with an attorney, but also that if he is indigent a lawyer will be appointed to represent him. Without this additional warning, the admonition of the right to consult with counsel would often be understood as meaning only that he can consult with a lawyer if he has one or has the funds to obtain one. The warning of a right to counsel would be hollow if not couched in terms that would convey to the indigent—the person most often subjected to interrogation—the knowledge that he too has a right to have counsel present. As with the warnings of the right to remain silent and of the general right to counsel, only by effective and express explanation to the indigent of this right can there be assurance that he was truly in a position to exercise it.

Once warnings have been given, the subsequent procedure is clear. If the individual indicates in any manner, at any time prior to or during questioning, that he wishes to remain silent, the interrogation must cease. At this point he has shown that he intends to exercise his Fifth Amendment privilege; any statement taken after the person invokes his privilege cannot be other than the product of compulsion, subtle or otherwise. Without the right to cut off questioning, the setting of in-custody interrogation operates on the individual to overcome free choice in producing a statement after the privilege has been once invoked. If the individual states that he wants an attorney, the interrogation must cease until an attorney is present. At

that time, the individual must have an opportunity to confer with the attorney and to have him present during any subsequent questioning. If the individual cannot obtain an attorney and he indicates that he wants one before speaking to police, they must respect his decision to remain silent. . . . any evidence that the accused was threatened, tricked, or cajoled into a waiver will, of course, show that the defendant did not voluntarily waive his privilege. The requirement of warnings and waiver of rights is a fundamental with respect to the Fifth Amendment privilege and not simply a preliminary ritual to existing methods of interrogation. . . .

The principles announced today deal with the protection which must be given to the privilege against self-incrimination when the individual is first subjected to police interrogation while in custody at the station or otherwise deprived of his freedom of action in any significant way. It is at this point that our adversary system of criminal proceedings commences, distinguishing itself at the outset from the inquisitorial system recognized in some countries. Under the system of warnings we delineate today or under any other system which may be devised and found effective, the safeguards to be erected about the privilege must come into play at this point. . . .

662. LYNDON B. JOHNSON ADDRESS ON AGGRESSION IN VIETNAM
September 29, 1967

(*Department of State Bulletin*, October 23, 1967)

By autumn 1967, 480,000 men were engaged in Vietnam and the dollar cost of the war exceeded $25 billion annually. Rising domestic opposition prompted President Johnson's San Antonio formula, and the tone of a message that balanced moderation against militancy. See T. Hoopes, *The Limits of Intervention;* F. Schurmann et al., *The Politics of Escalation in Vietnam;* P. Geyelin, *Lyndon B. Johnson and the World.*

This evening I came here to speak to you about Vietnam.

I do not have to tell you that our people are profoundly concerned about that struggle.

There are passionate convictions about the wisest course for our nation to follow. There are many sincere and patriotic Americans who harbor doubts about sustaining the commitment that three Presidents and half a million of our young men have made.

Doubt and debate are enlarged because the problems of Vietnam are quite complex. They are a mixture of political turmoil—of poverty—of religious and factional strife— of ancient servitude and modern longing for freedom. Vietnam is all of these things.

Vietnam is also the scene of a powerful aggression that is spurred by an appetite for conquest.

It is the arena where Communist expansionism is most aggressively at work in the world today—where it is crossing international frontiers in violation of international agreements; where it is killing and kidnaping; where it is ruthlessly attempting to bend free people to its will.

Into this mixture of subversion and war, of terror and hope, America has entered—with its material power and with its moral commitment.

Why? . . .

But the key to all we have done is really our own security. At times of crisis, before asking Americans to fight and die to resist aggression in a foreign land, every American President has finally had to answer this question:

Is the aggression a threat not only to the immediate victim but to the United States of America and to the peace and security of the entire world of which we in America are a very vital part?

That is the question which Dwight Eisenhower and John Kennedy and Lyndon Johnson had to answer in facing the issue in Vietnam.

That is the question that the Senate of the United States answered by a vote of 82 to 1 when it ratified and approved the SEATO treaty in 1955, and to which the members of the United States Congress responded in a resolution [Tonkin Bay] that it passed in 1964 by a vote of 504 to 2:

. . . the United States is, therefore, prepared, as the President determines, to take all necessary steps, including the use of armed force, to assist any member or protocol state of the Southeast Asia Collective Defense Treaty requesting assistance in defense of its freedom.

Those who tell us now that we should abandon our commitment, that securing South Vietnam from armed domination is not worth the price we are paying, must also answer this question. And the test they must meet is this: What would be the consequence of letting armed aggression against South Vietnam succeed? What would follow in the time ahead? What kind of world are they prepared to live in five months or five years from tonight?

For those who have borne the responsibility for decision during these past ten years, the stakes to us have seemed clear—and have seemed high. . . .

I cannot tell you tonight as your President —with certainty—that a Communist conquest of South Vietnam would be followed by a Communist conquest of Southeast Asia. But I do know there are North Vietnamese troops in Laos. I do know that there are North Vietnamese-trained guerrillas tonight in northeast Thailand. I do know that there are Communist-supported guerrilla forces operating in Burma. And a Communist coup was barely averted in Indonesia, the fifth largest nation in the world.

So your American President cannot tell you—with certainty—that a Southeast Asia dominated by Communist power would bring a third world war much closer to terrible reality. One could hope that this would not be so.

But all that we have learned in this tragic century strongly suggests to me that it would be so. As President of the United States, I am not prepared to gamble on the chance that it is not so. I am not prepared to risk the security—indeed, the survival—of this American Nation on mere hope and wishful thinking. I am convinced that by seeing this struggle through now we are greatly reducing the chances of a much larger war—perhaps a nuclear war. I would rather stand in Vietnam in our time, and by meeting this danger now and facing up to it, thereby reduce the danger for our children and for our grandchildren.

The price of these efforts, of course, has been heavy. But the price of not having made them at all, not having seen them through, in my judgment would have been vastly greater.

Our goal has been the same: in Europe, in Asia, in our own hemisphere. It has been —and it is now—peace.

And peace cannot be secured by wishes; peace cannot be preserved by noble words and pure intentions. Enduring peace—Franklin D. Roosevelt said—cannot be bought at the cost of other people's freedom. . . .

The true peacekeepers in the world tonight are not those who urge us to retire from the field in Vietnam, who tell us to try to find the quickest, cheapest exit from that tormented land, no matter what the consequences to us may be.

The true peacekeepers are those men who stand out there on the DMZ at this very hour taking the worst that the enemy can give. The true peacekeepers are the soldiers who are breaking the terrorist's grip around the villages of Vietnam, the civilians who are bringing medical care and food and education to people who have already suffered a generation of war.

And so I report to you that we are going to continue to press forward. Two things we must do. Two things we shall do.

First, we must not mislead our enemy. Let him not think that debate and dissent will produce wavering and withdrawal. For I can assure you they won't. Let him not think that protests will produce surrender. Because they won't. Let him not think that he will wait us out. For he won't.

Second, we will provide all that our brave men require to do the job that must be done. And that job is going to be done. . . .

Let the world know that the keepers of peace will endure through every trial—and that with the full backing of their countrymen, they are going to prevail.

663.   AFROYIM v. RUSK
387 U.S. 253
1967

Petitioner, Beys Afroyim, a naturalized citizen, had voted in the Israeli elections. In an effort to renew his American passport, he sought declaratory judgment that the provision of the 1940 Neutrality Act forfeiting citizenship for voluntarily voting in a foreign election was void. District and appeals courts had ruled that Congress possessed constitutional power to expatriate a citizen for so voting. The Supreme Court, in a 5 to 4 decision, reversed *Perez v. Brownell* and followed a pattern in which it "chipped away" at Congressional power over expatriation. See R. Young, "Review of Recent Supreme Court Decisions," 53 *Am. Bar Assoc. J.* 750; R. B. Gonzales, "Expatriation: Congress versus the Courts," 7 *The Southern Quarterly* 433.

BLACK, J. . . . [I]n the other cases decided with and since *Perez,* this Court has consistently invalidated on a case-by-case basis various other statutory sections providing for involuntary expatriation. It has done so on various grounds and has refused to hold that citizens can be expatriated without their voluntary renunciation of citizenship. These cases, as well as many commentators, have cast great doubt upon the soundness of *Perez.* Under these circumstances we granted certiorari to reconsider it. . . .

The fundamental issue before this Court here, as it was in *Perez,* is whether Congress can consistently with the Fourteenth Amendment enact a law stripping an American of his citizenship which he has never voluntarily renounced or given up. The majority in *Perez* held that Congress could do this. . . .

First we reject the idea expressed in *Perez* that, aside from the Fourteenth Amendment, Congress has any general power, express or implied, to take away an American citizen's citizenship without his assent. This power cannot, as *Perez* indicated, be sustained as an implied attribute of sovereignty possessed by all nations. Other nations are governed by their own constitutions, if any, and we can draw no support from theirs. In our country the people are sovereign and the Government cannot sever its relationship to the people by taking away their citizenship. Our Constitution governs us and we must never forget that our Constitution limits the Government to those powers specifically granted or those that are necessary and proper to carry out the specifically granted ones. The Constitution of course, grants Congress no express power to strip people of their citizenship, whether in the exercise of the implied power to regulate foreign affairs or in the exercise of any specifically granted power. And even before the adoption of the Fourteenth Amendment, views were expressed in Congress and by this Court that under the Constitution the Government was granted no power, even under its express power to pass a uniform rule of naturalization, to determine what conduct should and should not result in the loss of citizenship. . . .

This undeniable purpose of the Fourteenth Amendment to make citizenship of Negroes permanent and secure would be frustrated by holding that the Government can rob a citizen of his citizenship without his consent by simply proceeding to act under an implied general power to regulate foreign affairs or some other power generally granted. Though the framers of the Amendment were not particularly concerned with the problem of expatriation, it seems undeniable from the language they used that they wanted to put citizenship beyond the power of any governmental unit to destroy. . . .

Because the legislative history of the Fourteenth Amendment and the expatriation proposals which preceded and followed it, like most other legislative history, contains many statements from which conflicting inferences can be drawn, our holding might be unwarranted if it rested entirely or principally upon that legislative history. But it does not. Our holding we think is the only one that can stand in view of the language and

the purpose of the Fourteenth Amendment, and our construction of that Amendment, we believe, comports more nearly than *Perez* with the principles of liberty and equal justice to all that the entire Fourteenth Amendment was adopted to guarantee. Citizenship is no light trifle to be jeopardized any moment Congress decides to do so under the name of one of its general or implied grants of power. In some instances, loss of citizenship can mean that a man is left without the protection of citizenship in any country in the world—as a man without a country. Citizenship in this Nation is a part of a cooperative affair. Its citizenry is the country and the country is its citizenry. The very nature of our free government makes it completely incongruous to have a rule of law under which a group of citizens temporarily in office can deprive another group of citizens of their citizenship. We hold that the Fourteenth Amendment was designed to, and does, protect every citizen of this Nation against a congressional forcible destruction of his citizenship, whatever his creed, color, or race. Our holding does no more than to give to this citizen that which is his own, a constitutional right to remain a citizen in a free country unless he voluntarily relinquishes that citizenship.

Perez v. Brownell is overruled. The judgment is reversed.

Reversed.

664.   JONES v. ALFRED MAYER CO.
392 U.S. 409
1967

Certiorari to the United States Court of Appeals for the Eighth Circuit. Petitioners alleged that the Alfred Mayer Co. refused to sell them a home for the sole reason that Joseph Lee Jones was a Negro. Filing a complaint that sought injunctive and other relief in the district court, they relied in part on the Civil Rights Act of 1866 passed after the Thirteenth Amendment, and reenacted in 1870, an obscure section (Section 1982) of which barred all racial discrimination, public as well as private, in the sale or rental of property. The district court dismissed the suit and the court of appeals affirmed on the ground that the Reconstruction measures applied only to state action and not to private refusals to sell. The Supreme Court, in

a 7 to 2 ruling, reversed the lower courts. See G. Casper, "Jones v. Mayer: Clio, Bemused and Confused Muse," *Supreme Court Rev.,* 1968; J. M. Galbraith, "The Unconstitutionality of Proposition 14: An Extension of Prohibited State Action," 19 *Stanford Law. Rev.* (November 1966); C. Black, Jr., "Forward: State Action, Equal Protection, and California's Proposition 14," 81 *Harvard Law Rev.* (November 1967).

STEWART, J. . . . At the outset, it is important to make clear precisely what this case does *not* involve. Whatever else it may be, 42 U.S.C. § 1982 is not a comprehensive open housing law. In sharp contrast to the Fair Housing Title (Title VIII) of the Civil Rights Act of 1968, Pub. L. 90–284, 82 Stat. 81, the statute in this case deals only with racial discrimination and does not address itself to discrimination on grounds of religion or national origin. It does not deal specifically with discrimination in the provision of services or facilities in connection with the sale or rental of a dwelling. It does not prohibit advertising or other representations that indicate discriminatory preferences. It does not refer explicitly to discrimination in financing arrangements or in the provision of brokerage services. It does not empower a federal administrative agency to assist aggrieved parties. It makes no provision for intervention by the Attorney General. And, although it can be enforced by injunction, it contains no provision expressly authorizing a federal court to order the payment of damages.

Thus, although § 1982 contains none of the exemptions that Congress included in the Civil Rights Act of 1968, it would be a serious mistake to suppose that § 1982 in any way diminishes the significance of the law recently enacted by Congress. . . .

We begin with the language of the statute itself. In plain and unambiguous terms, § 1982 grants to all citizens, without regard to race or color, "the same right" to purchase and lease property "as is enjoyed by white citizens." . . .

On its face, therefore, § 1982 appears to prohibit *all* discrimination against Negroes in the sale or rental of property—discrimination by private owners as well as discrimination by public authorities. Indeed, even the respondents seem to concede that, if § 1982 "means what it says"—to use the words of the respondents' brief—then it must encompass every racially motivated refusal to sell or rent and cannot be confined to officially sanctioned segregation in housing. Stressing

what they consider to be the revolutionary implications of so literal a reading of § 1982, the respondents argue that Congress cannot possibly have intended any such result. Our examination of the relevant history, however, persuades us that Congress meant exactly what it said. . . .

In light of the concerns that led Congress to adopt it and the contents of the debates that preceded its passage, it is clear that the Act was designed to do just what its terms suggest: to prohibit all racial discrimination, whether or not under color of law, with respect to the rights enumerated therein—including the right to purchase or lease property. . . .

Against this background, it would obviously make no sense to assume, without any historical support whatever, that Congress made a silent decision in 1870 to exempt private discrimination from the operation of the Civil Rights Act of 1866. . . .

The remaining question is whether Congress has power under the Constitution to do what § 1982 purports to do: to prohibit all racial discrimination, private and public, in the sale and rental of property. Our starting point is the Thirteenth Amendment. . . .

Negro citizens, North and South, who saw in the Thirteenth Amendment a promise of freedom—freedom to "go and come at pleasure" and to "buy and sell when they please" —would be left with "a mere paper guarantee" if Congress were powerless to assure that a dollar in the hands of a Negro will purchase the same thing as a dollar in the hands of a white man. At the very least, the freedom that Congress is empowered to secure under the Thirteenth Amendment includes the freedom to buy whatever a white man can buy, the right to live wherever a white man can live. If Congress cannot say that being a free man means at least this much, then the Thirteenth Amendment made a promise the Nation cannot keep. . . .

The judgment is

Reversed.

665. JOHNSON'S ADDRESS ON A NEW STEP TOWARD PEACE
March 31, 1968
(*Department of State Bulletin,* April 15, 1968)

"I can't get out. I can't finish it with what I got. So what the hell can I do?" President Johnson is reported to have said as early as March 1965. The spectacular Tet offensive of the North Vietnamese exposed him to a deeply pessimistic assessment of the Asian conflict and led to a military request for another 200,000 troops. Another and new approach was demanded, the President concluded, and he called a halt to the open-ended escalation of the war that he had initiated; then, almost as a postscript, he announced his own withdrawal from the national political scene at the end of his term of office. See T. Hoopes, *The Limits of Intervention;* D. Kraslow and S. H. Loory, *The Secret Search for Peace in Vietnam;* M. Kalb and E. Abel, *Roots of Involvement.*

Good evening, my fellow Americans. Tonight I want to speak to you of peace in Vietnam and Southeast Asia.

No other question so preoccupies our people. No other dream so absorbs the 250 million human beings who live in that part of the world. No other goal motivates American policy in Southeast Asia.

For years, representatives of our Government and others have traveled the world seeking to find a basis for peace talks.

Since last September, they have carried the offer that I made public at San Antonio.

That offer was this: that the United States would stop its bombardment of North Vietnam when that would lead promptly to productive discussions—and that we would assume that North Vietnam would not take military advantage of our restraint.

Hanoi denounced this offer, both privately and publicly. Even while the search for peace was going on, North Vietnam rushed their preparations for a savage assault on the people, the Government, and the allies of South Vietnam.

Their attack—during the Tet holidays— failed to achieve its principal objectives.

It did not collapse the elected government of South Vietnam or shatter its army, as the Communists had hoped.

It did not produce a "general uprising" among the people of the cities, as they had predicted.

The Communists were unable to maintain control of any of the more than thirty cities that they attacked. And they took very heavy casualties.

But they did compel the South Vietnamese and their allies to move certain forces from the countryside into the cities. They caused widespread disruption and suffering. Their attacks, and the battles that followed, made refugees of half a million human beings.

The Communists may renew their attack any day. They are, it appears, trying to make 1968 the year of decision in South Vietnam —the year that brings, if not final victory or defeat, at least a turning point in the struggle.

This much is clear: If they do mount another round of heavy attacks, they will not succeed in destroying the fighting power of South Vietnam and its allies.

But tragically, this is also clear: Many men—on both sides of the struggle—will be lost. A nation that has already suffered twenty years of warfare will suffer once again. Armies on both sides will take new casualties. And the war will go on.

There is no need for this to be so.

There is no need to delay the talks that could bring an end to this long and this bloody war.

Tonight I renew the offer I made last August—to stop the bombardment of North Vietnam. We ask that talks begin promptly, that they be serious talks on the substance of peace. We assume that during those talks Hanoi will not take advantage of our restraint.

We are prepared to move immediately toward peace through negotiations.

So tonight, in the hope that this action will lead to early talks, I am taking the first step to deescalate the conflict. We are reducing—substantially reducing—the present level of hostilities. And we are doing so unilaterally and at once.

Tonight I have ordered our aircraft and our naval vessels to make no attacks on North Vietnam, except in the area north of the demilitarized zone where the continuing enemy buildup directly threatens Allied forward positions and where the movements of their troops and supplies are clearly related to that threat.

The area in which we are stopping our attacks includes almost 90 percent of North Vietnam's population and most of its territory. Thus there will be no attacks around the principal populated areas or in the food-producing areas of North Vietnam.

Even this very limited bombing of the North could come to an early end if our restraint is matched by restraint in Hanoi. But I cannot in good conscience stop all bombing so long as to do so would immediately and directly endanger the lives of our men and our allies. Whether a complete bombing halt becomes possible in the future will be determined by events.

Our purpose in this action is to bring about a reduction in the level of violence that now exists.

It is to save the lives of brave men and to save the lives of innocent women and children. It is to permit the contending forces to move closer to a political settlement.

And tonight I call upon the United Kingdom and I call upon the Soviet Union, as cochairmen of the Geneva conferences and as permanent members of the United Nations Security Council, to do all they can to move from the unilateral act of deescalation that I have just announced toward genuine peace in Southeast Asia.

Now, as in the past, the United States is ready to send its representatives to any forum, at any time, to discuss the means of bringing this ugly war to an end.

I am designating one of our most distinguished Americans, Ambassador Averell Harriman, as my personal representative for such talks. In addition, I have asked Am-

bassador Llewellyn Thompson, who returned from Moscow for consultation, to be available to join Ambassador Harriman at Geneva or any other suitable place just as soon as Hanoi agrees to a conference.

I call upon President Ho Chi Minh to respond positively and favorably to this new step toward peace.

But if peace does not come now through negotiations, it will come when Hanoi understands that our common resolve is unshakable and our common strength is invincible. . . .

We applaud this evidence of determination on the part of South Vietnam. Our first priority will be to support their effort.

We shall accelerate the reequipment of South Vietnam's armed forces in order to meet the enemy's increased firepower. This will enable them progressively to undertake a larger share of combat operations against the Communist invaders.

On many occasions I have told the American people that we would send to Vietnam those forces that are required to accomplish our mission there. So, with that as our guide, we have previously authorized a force level of approximately 525,000. . . .

. . . let it never be forgotten: Peace will come also because America sent her sons to help secure it.

It has not been easy—far from it. During the past four and a half years, it has been my fate and my responsibility to be Commander in Chief. I lived daily and nightly with the cost of this war. I know the pain that it has inflicted. I know perhaps better than anyone the misgivings that it has aroused.

Throughout this entire long period, I have been sustained by a single principle: that what we are doing now in Vietnam is vital not only to the security of Southeast Asia, but it is vital to the security of every American.

Surely we have treaties which we must respect. Surely we have commitments that we are going to keep. Resolutions of the Congress testify to the need to resist aggression in the world and in Southeast Asia.

But the heart of our involvement in South Vietnam—under three different Presidents, three separate administrations—has always been America's own security.

And the larger purpose of our involvement has always been to help the nations of Southeast Asia become independent and stand alone, self-sustaining as members of a great world community—at peace with themselves and at peace with all others.

With such an Asia, our country—and the world—will be far more secure than it is tonight.

I believe that a peaceful Asia is far nearer to reality because of what America has done in Vietnam. I believe that the men who endure the dangers of battle—fighting there for us tonight—are helping the entire world avoid far greater conflicts, far wider wars, far more destruction, than this one. . . .

Yet I believe that we must always be mindful of this one thing, whatever the trials and the tests ahead: The ultimate strength of our country and our cause will lie not in powerful weapons or infinite resources or boundless wealth but will lie in the unity of our people.

This I believe very deeply.

Throughout my entire public career I have followed the personal philosophy that I am a free man, an American, a public servant, and a member of my party, in that order always and only.

For thirty-seven years in the service of our nation, first as a Congressman, as a Senator and as Vice President and now as your President, I have put the unity of the people first. I have put it ahead of any divisive partisanship.

And in these times as in times before, it is true that a house divided against itself by the spirit of faction, of party, of region, of religion, of race, is a house that cannot stand.

There is division in the American house now. There is divisiveness among us all tonight. And holding the trust that is mine, as President of all the people, I cannot disregard the peril to the progress of the American people and the hope and the prospect of peace for all peoples.

So I would ask all Americans, whatever their personal interests or concern, to guard against divisiveness and all its ugly consequences.

Fifty-two months and ten days ago, in a moment of tragedy and trauma, the duties of this Office fell upon me. I asked then for your help and God's, that we might continue America on its course, binding up our wounds, healing our history, moving forward in new unity, to clear the American agenda and to keep the American commitment for all of our people.

United we have kept that commitment. United we have enlarged that commitment.

Through all time to come, I think America will be a stronger nation, a more just society, and a land of greater opportunity and fulfillment because of what we have all done together in these years of unparalleled achievement.

Our reward will come in the life of freedom, peace, and hope that our children will enjoy through ages ahead.

What we won when all of our people united just must not now be lost in suspicion, distrust, selfishness, and politics among any of our people.

Believing this as I do, I have concluded that I should not permit the Presidency to become involved in the partisan divisions that are developing in this political year.

With America's sons in the fields far away, with America's future under challenge right here at home, with our hopes and the world's hopes for peace in the balance every day, I do not believe that I should devote an hour or a day of my time to any personal partisan causes or to any duties other than the awesome duties of this Office—the Presidency of your country.

Accordingly, I shall not seek, and I will not accept, the nomination of my party for another term as your President.

But let men everywhere know, however, that a strong, a confident, and a vigilant America stands ready tonight to seek an honorable peace—and stands ready tonight to defend an honored cause—whatever the price, whatever the burden, whatever the sacrifices that duty may require.

666. CIVIL RIGHTS ACT OF 1968
April 11, 1968
62 *U.S. Statutes at Large* 696 ff. Public Law 90–284

The fifth major civil rights measure to be passed since 1957, this administration-backed bill was notable for its strong open-housing provision, which prohibited discrimination on the basis of race, religion, or national origin in selling or renting houses, and which represented a major victory for civil rights groups. It also included civil rights protection, Indian rights, and antiriot clauses. The last section, authored mainly by Senator Strom Thurmond of South Carolina, was the legal basis for the indictment of the self-named "Chicago Eight," and for their 1969–70 trial in federal district court in Chicago. The defendants were charged with conspiracy to cross state lines with the intent of organizing, encouraging, promoting, and inciting a riot in violation of the "antiriot" clause, and the case was the first court test of this provision. The "riot" in question involved disturbances that occurred during the August 1968 Democratic Convention in Chicago. The antiriot clause depends upon the constitutional power to regulate interstate commerce; and, as the trial made dramatically clear, it clashes with constitutional norms about freedom of speech and dissent. See J. Kirby, "The Right to Vote," in Dorsen, ed., *The Rights of Americans.*

An Act to prescribe penalties for certain acts of violence or intimidation, and for other purposes.

TITLE I

INTERFERENCE WITH FEDERALLY PROTECTED ACTIVITIES

CHAPTER 102—RIOTS

SEC. 2101. *Riots.*

(a) (1) Whoever travels in interstate or foreign commerce or uses any facility of interstate or foreign commerce, including, but not limited to, the mail, telegraph, telephone, radio, or television, with intent—

(A) to incite a riot; or

(B) to organize, promote, encourage, participate in, or carry on a riot; or

(C) to commit any act of violence in furtherance of a riot; or

(D) to aid or abet any person in inciting or participating in or carrying on a riot or committing any act of violence in furtherance of a riot;

and who either during the course of any such travel or use or thereafter performs or attempts to perform any other overt act for any purpose specified [above]—

Shall be fined not more than $10,000, or imprisoned not more than five years, or both.

(b) In any prosecution under this section, proof that a defendant engaged or attempted to engage in one or more of the overt acts described [above] and (1) has traveled in interstate or foreign commerce, or (2) has use of or used any facility of interstate or foreign commerce, including but not limited to, mail, telegraph, telephone, radio, or television, to communicate with or broadcast to any person or group of persons prior to such overt acts, such travel or use shall be admissible proof to establish that such defendant traveled in or used such facility of interstate or foreign commerce.

SEC. 2102. *Definitions.*

(a) As used in this chapter, the term "riot" means a public disturbance involving (1) an act or acts of violence by one or more persons part of an assemblage of three or more persons, which act or acts shall constitute a clear and present danger of, or shall result in, damage or injury to the property of any other person or to the person of any other individual or (2) a threat or threats of the commission of an act or acts of violence by one or more persons part of an assemblage of three or more persons having, individually or collectively, the ability of immediate execution of such threat or threats, where the performance of the threatened act or acts of violence would constitute a clear and present danger of, or would result in, damage or injury to the property of any other person or to the person of any other individual.

(b) As used in this chapter, the term "to incite a riot," or "to organize, promote, encourage, participate in, or carry on a riot," includes, but is not limited to, urging or instigating other persons to riot, but shall not be deemed to mean the mere oral or written (1) advocacy of ideas or (2) expression of belief, not involving advocacy of any act or acts of violence or assertion of the rightness of, or the right to commit, any such act or acts.

TITLE X

CIVIL OBEDIENCE

CIVIL DISORDERS

(a)(1) Whoever teaches or demonstrates to any other person the use, application, or making of any firearm or explosive or incendiary device, or technique capable of causing injury or death to persons, knowing or having reason to know or intending that the same will be unlawfully employed for use in, or in furtherance of, a civil disorder which may in any way or degree obstruct, delay, or adversely affect commerce or the movement of any article or commodity in commerce or the conduct or performance of any federally protected function; or

(2) Whoever transports or manufactures for transportation in commerce any firearm, or explosive or incendiary device, knowing or having reason to know or intending that the same will be used unlawfully in furtherance of a civil disorder; or

(3) Whoever commits or attempts to commit any act to obstruct, impede, or interfere with any fireman or law enforcement officer lawfully engaged in the lawful performance of his official duties incident to and during the commission of a civil disorder which in any way or degree obstructs, delays, or adversely affects commerce or the movement of any article or commodity in commerce or the conduct or performance of any federally protected function—

Shall be fined not more than $10,000 or imprisoned not more than five years, or both.

667. OMNIBUS CRIME CONTROL AND SAFE STREETS ACT
June 19, 1968
(82 *U.S. Statutes at Large* 198 ff. Public Law 90–351)

A Harris poll of 1968 found that 81 per cent of the American people thought law and order had broken down; and all candidates in this Presidential election year campaigned on the assumption that the crime rate was rising uncontrollably. This Omnibus Crime Control Act, then, accurately reflected the public mood. Sensitive to public pressures, troubled by urban riots, themselves anxious about the highly visible crime rate, congressmen voted overwhelmingly for this measure: only twenty-three representatives and four senators dared to vote against it. The act involved only federal prosecution, to be sure (hence *Miranda, Escobedo,* etc. remained intact), but its sections on immunity and wiretapping, among others, had a powerful impact on state legislators. Title III on electronic eavesdropping—the most controversial aspect of the measure—opened wider the gates to legalized police surveillance and complicated the pervasive problem of privacy that became increasingly evident by the late 1960s. See F. P. Graham, "A Contemporary History of American Crime," in H. D. Graham and T. R. Gurr, *Violence in America;* A. K. Pye, "The Warren Court and Criminal Procedure," in R. H. Sayler et al., eds., *The Warren Court;* "From Private Places to Personal Privacy: A Post-Katz Study of Fourth Amendment Protection," 43 *N.Y.U. Law Rev.* 968; I. Younger, "Wiretapping, Electronic Eavesdropping, and the Police: A Note on the Present State of the Law," 42 *N.Y.U. Law Rev.* 82; D. Marcell, "Privacy and the American Character," 66 *South Atlantic Quarterly* 1.

An Act to assist State and local governments in reducing the incidence of crime, to increase the effectiveness, fairness, and coordination of law enforcement and criminal justice systems at all levels of government, and for other purposes.

TITLE I

Law Enforcement Assistance

Declarations and Purpose

Congress finds that the high incidence of crime in the United States threatens the peace, security, and general welfare of the Nation and its citizens. To prevent crime and to insure the greater safety of the people, law enforcement efforts must be better coordinated, intensified, and made more effective at all levels of government.

Congress finds further that crime is essentially a local problem that must be dealt with by State and local governments if it is to be controlled effectively.

It is therefore the declared policy of the Congress to assist State and local governments in strengthening and improving law enforcement at every level by national assistance. It is the purpose of this title to (1) encourage States and units of general local government to prepare and adopt comprehensive plans based upon their evaluation of State and local problems of law enforcement; (2) authorize grants to States and units of local government in order to improve and strengthen law enforcement; and (3) encourage research and development directed toward the improvement of law enforcement and the development of new methods for the prevention and reduction of crime and the detection and apprehension of criminals.

TITLE III

Wiretapping and Electronic Surveillance

Findings

. . . To safeguard the privacy of innocent persons, the interception of wire or oral communications where none of the parties to the communication has consented to the interception should be allowed only when authorized by a court of competent jurisdiction and should remain under the control and supervision of the authorizing court. Interception of wire and oral communications should further be limited to certain major types of offenses and specific categories of crime with assurances that the interception is justified and that the information obtained thereby will not be misused. . . .

Sec. 2511. *Interception and disclosure of wire or oral communications prohibited.*

(1) Except as otherwise specifically provided in this chapter any person who—

(a) willfully intercepts, endeavors to intercept, or procures any other person to intercept or endeavor to intercept, any wire or oral communication. . . .

(c) willfuly discloses, or endeavors to disclose, to any other person the contents of any wire or oral communication, knowing or having reason to know that the information was obtained through the interception of a wire or oral communication in violation of this subsection; or

(d) willfully uses, or endeavors to use, the contents of any wire or oral communication, knowing or having reason to know that the information was obtained through the interception of a wire or oral communication in violation of this subsection;

shall be fined not more than $10,000 or imprisoned not more than five years, or both. . . .

(3) Nothing contained in this chapter or in section 605 of the Communications Act of 1934 (48 Stat. 1143; 47 U.S.C. 605) shall limit the constitutional power of the President to take such measures as he deems necessary to protect the Nation against actual or potential attack or other hostile acts of a foreign power, to obtain foreign intelligence information deemed essential to the security of the United States, or to protect national security information against foreign intelligence activities. Nor shall anything contained in this chapter be deemed to limit the constitutional power of the President to take such measures as he deems necessary to protect the United States against the overthrow of the Government by force or other unlawful means, or against any other clear and present danger to the structure or existence of the Government. The contents of any wire or oral communication intercepted by authority of the President in the exercise of the foregoing powers may be received in

evidence in any trial hearing, or other proceeding only where such interception was reasonable, and shall not be otherwise used or disclosed except as is necessary to implement that power.

SEC. 2514. *Immunity of witnesses.* Whenever in the judgment of a United States attorney the testimony of any witness, or the production of books, papers, or other evidence by any witness, in any case or proceeding before any grand jury or court of the United States involving any violation of this chapter or any of the offenses enumerated in section 2516, or any conspiracy to violate this chapter or any of the offenses enumerated in section 2516 is necessary to the public interest, such United States attorney, upon the approval of the Attorney General, shall make application to the court that the witness shall be instructed to testify or produce evidence subject to the provisions of this section, and upon order of the court such witness shall not be excused from testifying or from producing books, papers, or other evidence on the ground that the testimony or evidence required of him may tend to incriminate him or subject him to a penalty or forfeiture. No such witness shall be prosecuted or subjected to any penalty or forfeiture for or on account of any transaction, matter or thing concerning which he is compelled, after having claimed his privilege against self-incrimination, to testify or produce evidence, nor shall testimony so compelled be used as evidence in any criminal proceeding (except in a proceeding described in the next sentence) against him in any court. No witness shall be exempt under this section from prosecution for perjury or contempt committed while giving testimony or producing evidence under compulsion as provided in this section.

SEC. 2515. *Prohibition of use as evidence of intercepted wire or oral communications.* Whenever any wire or oral communication has been intercepted, no part of the contents of such communication and no evidence derived therefrom may be received in evidence in any trial, hearing, or other proceeding in or before any court, grand jury, department, officer, agency, regulatory body, legislative committee, or other authority of the United States, a State, or a political subdivision thereof if the disclosure of that information would be in violation of this chapter.

SEC. 2516. *Authorization for interception of wire or oral communications.*

(1) The Attorney General, or any Assistant Attorney General specially designated by the Attorney General, may authorize an application to a Federal judge of competent jurisdiction for, and such judge may grant in conformity with section 2518 of this chapter an order authorizing or approving the interception of wire or oral communications by the Federal Bureau of Investigation, or a Federal agency having responsibility for the investigation of the offense as to which the application is made, when such interception may provide or has provided evidence of—

(a) any offense punishable by death or by imprisonment for more than one year under sections 2274 through 2277 of title 42 of the United States Code (relating to the enforcement of the Atomic Energy Act of 1954), or under the following chapters of this title: chapter 37 (relating to espionage), chapter 105 (relating to sabotage), chapter 115 (relating to treason), or chapter 102 (relating to riots);

(b) a violation of section 186 or section 501(c) of title 29, United States Code (dealing with restrictions on payments and loans to labor organizations), or any offense which involves murder, kidnapping, robbery, or extortion, and which is punishable under this title;

(c) any offense which is punishable under the following sections of this title: section 201 (bribery of public officials and witnesses), section 224 (bribery in sporting contests), section 1084 (transmission of wagering information), section 1503 (influencing or injuring an officer, juror, or witness generally), section 1510 (obstruction of criminal investigations), section 1751 (Presidential assassinations, kidnapping, and assault), section 1951 (interference with commerce by threats or violence), section 1952 (interstate and foreign travel or transportation in aid of racketeering enterprises), section 1954 (offer, acceptance, or solicitation to influence operations of employee benefit plan), section 659 (theft from interstate shipment).

section 664 (embezzlement from pension and welfare funds), or sections 2314 and 2315 (interstate transportation of stolen property);

(d) any offense involving counterfeiting punishable under section 471, 472, or 473 of this title;

(e) any offense involving bankruptcy fraud or the manufacture, importation, receiving, concealment, buying, selling, or otherwise dealing in narcotic drugs, marihuana, or other dangerous drugs, punishable under any law of the United States;

(f) any offense including extortionate credit transactions under sections 892,893, or 894 of this title; or

(g) any conspiracy to commit any of the foregoing offenses.

(2) The principal prosecuting attorney of any State, or the principal prosecuting attorney of any political subdivision thereof, if such attorney is authorized by a statute of that State to make application to a State court judge of competent jurisdiction for an order authorizing or approving the interception of wire or oral communications. . . .

SEC. 2517. *Authorization for disclosure and use of intercepted wire or oral communications.*

. . . (3) Any person who has received, by any means authorized by this chapter, any information concerning a wire or oral communication, or evidence derived therefrom intercepted in accordance with the provisions of this chapter may disclose the contents of that communication or such derivative evidence while giving testimony under oath or affirmation in any criminal proceeding in any court of the United States or of any State or in any Federal or State grand jury proceeding. . . .

(5) When an investigative or law enforcement officer, while engaged in intercepting wire or oral communications in the manner authorized herein, intercepts wire or oral communications relating to offenses other than those specified in the order of authorization or approval, the contents thereof, and evidence derived therefrom, may be disclosed. . . .

SEC. 2518. *Procedure for interception of wire or oral communications.*

(1) Each application for an order authorizing or approving the interception of a wire or oral communication shall be made in writing upon oath or affirmation to a judge of competent jurisdiction and shall state the applicant's authority to make such application. Each application shall include the following information: . . .

(d) a statement of the period of time for which the interception is required to be maintained. . . .

(e) a full and complete statement of the facts concerning all previous applications known to the individual authorizing and making the application, made to any judge for authorization to intercept, or for approval of interceptions of, wire or oral communications involving any of the same persons, facilities or places specified in the application, and the action taken by the judge on each such application. . . .

(5) No order entered under this section may authorize or approve the interception of any wire or oral communication for any period longer than is necessary to achieve the objective of the authorization, nor in any event longer than thirty days. Extensions of an order may be granted, but only upon application for an extension. . . . The period of extension shall be no longer than the authorizing judge deems necessary to achieve the purposes for which it was granted and in no event for longer than thirty days. Every order and extension thereof shall contain a provision that the authorization to intercept shall be executed as soon as practicable, shall be conducted in such a way as to minimize the interception of communications not otherwise subject to interception under this chapter, and must terminate upon attainment of the authorized objective, or in any event in thirty days.

(6) Whenever an order authorizing interception is entered pursuant to this chapter, the order may require reports to be made to the judge who issued the order showing what progress has been made toward achievement of the authorized objective and the need for continued interception. Such reports shall be made at such intervals as the judge may require.

(7) Notwithstanding any other provision of this chapter, any investigative or law enforcement officer, specially designated by the

Attorney General or by the principal prosecuting attorney of any State or subdivision thereof acting pursuant to a statute of that State, who reasonably determines that—

(a) an emergency situation exists with respect to conspiratorial activities threatening the national security interest or to conspiratorial activities characteristic of organized crime that requires a wire or oral communication to be intercepted before an order authorizing such interception can with due diligence be obtained, and

(b) there are grounds upon which an order could be entered under this chapter to authorize such interception,

may intercept such wire or oral communication if an application for an order approving the interception is made in accordance with this section within forty-eight hours after the interception has occurred, or begins to occur. In the absence of an order, such interception shall immediately terminate when the communication sought is obtained or when the application for the order is denied, whichever is earlier. In the event such application for approval is denied, or in any other case where the interception is terminated without an order having been issued, the contents of any wire or oral communication intercepted shall be treated as having been obtained in violation of this chapter, and an inventory shall be served as provided for in subsection (d) of this section on the person named in the application.

(8)(a) The contents of any wire or oral communication intercepted by any means authorized by this chapter shall, if possible, be recorded on tape or wire or other comparable device. The recording of the contents of any wire or oral communication under this subsection shall be done in such way as will protect the recording from editing or other alterations. Immediately upon the expiration of the period of the order, or extensions thereof, such recordings shall be made available to the judge issuing such order and sealed under his directions. Custody of the recordings shall be wherever the judge orders. They shall not be destroyed except upon an order of the issuing or denying judge and in any event shall be kept for ten years. . . . The judge, upon the filing of a motion, may in his discretion make

available to such person or his counsel for inspection such portions of the intercepted communications, applications and orders as the judge determines to be in the interest of justice. On an ex parte showing of good cause to a judge of competent jurisdiction the serving of the inventory required by this subsection may be postponed.

(9) The contents of any intercepted wire or oral communication or evidence derived therefrom shall not be received in evidence or otherwise disclosed in any trial, hearing, or other proceeding in a Federal or State court unless each party, not less than ten days before the trial, hearing, or proceeding, has been furnished with a copy of the court order, and accompanying application, under which the interception was authorized or approved. This ten-day period may be waived by the judge if he finds that it was not possible to furnish the party with the above information ten days before the trial, hearing, or proceeding and that the party will not be prejudiced by the delay in receiving such information.

(10)(a) Any aggrieved person in any trial, hearing, or proceeding in or before any court, department, officer, agency, regulatory body, or other authority of the United States, a State, or a political subdivision thereof, may move to suppress the contents of any intercepted wire or oral communication, or evidence derived therefrom, on the grounds that—

(i) the communication was unlawfully intercepted;

(ii) the order of authorization or approval under which it was intercepted is insufficient on its face; or

(iii) the interception was not made in conformity with the order of authorization or approval.

Such motion shall be made before the trial, hearing, or proceeding unless there was no opportunity to make such motion or the person was not aware of the grounds of the motion. If the motion is granted, the contents of the intercepted wire or oral communication, or evidence derived therefrom, shall be treated as having been obtained in violation of this chapter. The judge, upon the filing of such motion by the aggrieved person, may in his discretion make available to the aggrieved person or his counsel for inspection such portions of the intercepted communication or evidence derived there-

from as the judge determines to be in the interests of justice.

668. NUCLEAR NONPROLIFERATION TREATY
March 13, 1969
(Department of State Bulletin, July 1, 1968)

As early as 1953 President Eisenhower had submitted to the United Nations an "Atoms for Peace" plan; see Doc. No. 601. The Test Ban Treaty of 1963 (see Doc. No. 645) discouraged nonnuclear countries from developing nuclear weapons, and in 1966 the Senate adopted the Pastore Resolution calling for a nonproliferation treaty. Lengthy consultations with the USSR and the NATO countries brought about a nonproliferation treaty that was recommended by a United Nations Resolution on June 12, 1968 and received the formal signature of the nuclear powers on July 1. Senate ratification came on March 13, 1969. See M. Willrich, "The Treaty on Non-Proliferation of Nuclear Weapons: Nuclear Technology Confronts World Politics," 77 *Yale Law J.* 1447; M. Willrich, *Non-Proliferation Treaty: Framework of Nuclear Arms Control;* G. Bunn, "The Nuclear Nonproliferation Treaty," *Wisconsin Law Rev.,* 1968, 766; B. Boskey and M. Willrich, eds., *Nuclear Proliferation: Prospects for Control.*

PRESIDENT JOHNSON'S MESSAGE

I consider this treaty to be the most important international agreement limiting nuclear arms since the nuclear age began. It is a triumph of sanity and of man's will to survive.

The treaty takes a major step toward a goal the United States has been seeking for the past twenty-two years.

Its central purpose is to prevent the spread of nuclear weapons. Its basic undertaking was deliberately patterned after United States atomic energy legislation, which forbids transfers of our nuclear weapons to others. The treaty not only makes such a prohibition binding on all nuclear powers; it reinforces the prohibition by barring non-nuclear countries from receiving them from any source, from manufacturing or otherwise ac-

quiring them, and from seeking or receiving any assistance in their manufacture.

The treaty, however, does more than just prohibit the spread of nuclear weapons. It would also promote the further development of nuclear energy for peaceful purposes under safeguards.

This is the goal of the International Atomic Energy Agency (IAEA), which resulted from President Eisenhower's "Atoms for Peace" plan. The IAEA is charged with the primary responsibility for safeguards under the nonproliferation treaty. It already has considerable experience in applying safeguards under international agreements for cooperation in the civil uses of nuclear energy.

I believe that this treaty will greatly advance the goal of nuclear cooperation for peaceful purposes under international safeguards.

It will require that all parties which export nuclear materials and equipment to nonnuclear-weapon states for peaceful purposes make sure that such materials, and those used or produced in such equipment, are under international safeguards.

It will require all non-nuclear parties to accept international safeguards on *all* peaceful nuclear activities within their territories, under their jurisdiction, or carried out under their control anywhere.

It will help insure cooperation in the field of peaceful uses of nuclear energy, and the exchange of scientific and technological information on such peaceful applications.

It will enable all countries to assist non-nuclear parties to the treaty with their peaceful nuclear activities, confident that their assistance will not be diverted to the making of nuclear weapons.

It obligates the nuclear-weapon parties to make potential benefits from any peaceful applications of nuclear explosions available— on a non-discriminatory basis, and at the lowest possible cost—to parties to the treaty that are required to give up the right to have their own nuclear explosives.

By 1985 the world's peaceful nuclear power stations will probably be turning out enough by-product plutonium for the production of tens of nuclear bombs every day. This capability must not be allowed to result in the further spread of nuclear weapons. The consequences would be nuclear anarchy, and the energy designed to light the world could plunge it into darkness.

But the treaty has a significance that goes beyond its furtherance of these important aspects of United States nuclear policy. In the great tradition of the Nuclear Test Ban Treaty, it represents another step on the journey toward world peace. I believe that its very achievement, as well as its provisions, enhances the prospects of progress toward disarmament.

On Monday, July 1—as this treaty was signed on behalf of the United States—I announced that agreement had been reached with the Soviet Union to enter into discussions in the nearest future on the limitation and reduction of both offensive nuclear weapons systems, and systems of defense against ballistic missiles. Thus there is hope that this treaty will mark the beginning of a new phase in the quest for order and moderation in international affairs.

I urgently recommend that the Senate move swiftly to enhance our security and that of the entire world by giving its consent to the ratification of this treaty.

TREATY ON THE NON-PROLIFERATION OF NUCLEAR WEAPONS

Considering the devastation that would be visited upon all mankind by a nuclear war and the consequent need to make every effort to avert the danger of such a war and to take measures to safeguard the security of peoples,

Believing that the proliferation of nuclear weapons would seriously enhance the danger of nuclear war,

In conformity with resolutions of the United Nations General Assembly calling for the conclusion of an agreement on the prevention of wider dissemination of nuclear weapons, . . .

Declaring their intention to achieve at the earliest possible date the cessation of the nuclear arms race and to undertake effective measures in the direction of nuclear disarmament,

Urging the co-operation of all States in the attainment of this objective,

Recalling the determination expressed by the Parties to the 1963 Treaty banning nuclear weapon tests in the atmosphere, in outer space and under water in its preamble to seek to achieve the discontinuance of all test explosions of nuclear weapons for all time and to continue negotiations to this end,

Desiring to further the easing of international tension and the strengthening of trust between States in order to facilitate the cessation of the manufacture of nuclear weapons, the liquidation of all their existing stockpiles, and the elimination from national arsenals of nuclear weapons and the means of their delivery pursuant to a Treaty on general and complete disarmament under strict and effective international control,

Recalling that, in accordance with the Charter of the United Nations, States must refrain in their international relations from the threat or use of force against the territorial integrity or political independence of any State, or in any other manner inconsistent with the Purposes of the United Nations, and that the establishment and maintenance of international peace and security are to be promoted with the least diversion for armaments of the world's human and economic resources,

Have agreed as follows:

ARTICLE I

Each nuclear-weapon State Party to the Treaty undertakes not to transfer to any recipient whatsoever nuclear weapons or other nuclear explosive devices or control over such weapons or explosive devices directly, or indirectly; and not in any way to assist, encourage, or induce any non-nuclear-weapon State to manufacture or otherwise acquire nuclear weapons or other nuclear explosive devices, or control over such weapons or explosive devices.

ARTICLE II

Each non-nuclear-weapon State Party to the Treaty undertakes not to receive the transfer from any transferor whatsoever of nuclear weapons or other nuclear explosive devices or of control over such weapons or explosive devices directly, or indirectly; not to manufacture or otherwise acquire nuclear weapons or other nuclear explosive devices; and not to seek or receive any assistance in the manufacture of nuclear weapons or other nuclear explosive devices.

ARTICLE III

1. Each non-nuclear-weapon State Party to the Treaty undertakes to accept safeguards, as set forth in an agreement to be negotiated and concluded with the International Atomic Energy Agency in accordance with the Statute of the International Atomic Energy Agency and the Agency's safeguards system, for the exclusive purpose of verification of the fulfilment of its obligations assumed under this Treaty with a view to preventing diversion of nuclear energy from peaceful uses to nuclear weapons or other nuclear explosive devices. Procedures for the safeguards required by this article shall be followed with respect to source or special fissionable material whether it is being produced, processed or used in any principal nuclear facility or is outside any such facility. The safeguards required by this article shall be applied on all source or special fissionable material in all peaceful nuclear activities within the territory of such State, under its jurisdiction, or carried out under its control anywhere.

2. Each State Party to the Treaty undertakes not to provide: (a) source or special fissionable material, or (b) equipment or material especially designed or prepared for the processing, use or production of special fissionable material, to any non-nuclear-weapon State for peaceful purposes, unless the source or special fissionable material shall be subject to the safeguards required by this article.

3. The safeguards required by this article shall be implemented in a manner designed to comply with article IV of this Treaty, and to avoid hampering the economic or technological development of the parties or international co-operation in the field of peaceful nuclear activities, including the international exchange of nuclear material and equipment for the processing, use or production of nuclear material for peaceful purposes in accordance with the provisions of this article and the principle of safeguarding set forth in the preamble.

4. Non-nuclear-weapon States Party to the Treaty shall conclude agreements with the International Atomic Energy Agency to meet the requirements of this article either individually or together with other States in accordance with the Statute of the International Atomic Energy Agency. Negotiation of such agreements shall commence within 180 days from the original entry into force of this Treaty. For States depositing their instruments of ratification or accession after the 180-day period, negotiation of such agreements shall commence not later than the date of such deposit. Such agreements shall enter into force not later than eighteen months after the date of initiation of negotiations.

ARTICLE IV

1. Nothing in this Treaty shall be interpreted as affecting the inalienable right of all the Parties to the Treaty to develop research, production and use of nuclear energy for peaceful purposes without discrimination and in conformity with articles I and II of this Treaty.

2. All the Parties to the Treaty undertake to facilitate, and have the right to participate in, the fullest possible exchange of equipment, materials and scientific and technological information for the peaceful uses of nuclear energy. Parties to the Treaty in a position to do so shall also co-operate in contributing alone or together with other States or international organizations to the further development of the applications of

nuclear energy for peaceful purposes, especially in the territories of non-nuclear-weapon States Party to the Treaty, with due consideration for the needs of the developing areas of the world.

ARTICLE V

Each Party to the Treaty undertakes to take appropriate measures to ensure that, in accordance with this Treaty, under appropriate international observation and through appropriate international procedures, potential benefits from any peaceful applications of nuclear explosions will be made available to non-nuclear-weapon States Party to the Treaty on a non-discriminatory basis and that the charge to such Parties for the explosive devices used will be as low as possible and exclude any charge for research and development. Non-nuclear-weapon States Party to the Treaty shall be able to obtain such benefits, pursuant to a special international agreement or agreements, through an appropriate international body wtih adequate representation of non-nuclear-weapon States. Negotiations on this subject shall commence as soon as possible after the Treaty enters into force. Non-nuclear-weapon States Party to the Treaty so desiring may also obtain such benefits pursuant to bilaterial agreements.

ARTICLE VI

Each of the Parties to the Treaty undertakes to pursue negotiations in good faith on effective measures relating to cessation of the nuclear arms race at an early date and to nuclear disarmament, and on a Treaty on general and complete disarmament under strict and effective international control.

ARTICLE VII

Nothing in this Treaty affects the right of any group of States to conclude regional treaties in order to assure the total absence of nuclear weapons in their respective territories.

. . . This Treaty shall enter into force after its ratification by the States, the Governments of which are designated Depositaries of the Treaty, and forty other States signatory to this Treaty and the deposit of their instruments of ratification. For the purposes of this Treaty, a nuclear-weapon State is one which has manufactured and exploded a nuclear weapon or other nuclear explosive device prior to 1 January 1967. . . .

ARTICLE X

1. Each Party shall in exercising its national sovereignty have the right to withdraw from the Treaty if it decides that extraordinary events, related to the subject matter of this Treaty, have jeopardized the supreme interests of its country. It shall give notice of such withdrawal to all other Parties to the Treaty and to the United Nations Security Council three months in advance. Such notice shall include a statement of the extraordinary events it regards as having jeopardized its supreme interests.

669. NIXON'S STATEMENT ON THE ANTIBÁLLISTIC MISSILE DEFENSE SYSTEM
March 14, 1969

(*Department of State Bulletin,* March 31, 1969)

The search for a defense against intercontinental ballistic missiles began in the early 1950s and took the form, in 1956, of a Nike Zeus system designed to intercept single-missile attacks. So great were the technical deficiencies of this system that the Kennedy administration decided not to deploy it. Under great pressure from military and business communities, Secretary McNamara proposed deployment of the so-called Sentinel system, aimed specifically at the alleged threat of a Chinese nuclear attack. President Nixon decided to modify this system, apparently out of concern with the SS9, a Soviet intercontinental ballistic missile. His announcement, and disclosure of some of the ABM sites—near large urban centers—provoked widespread debate, with a majority of scientists noting serious technical limitations in the entire ABM system. Reflecting public and scientific hostility to the ABM were the long and heated Congressional debates; in the end the ABM measure passed by a 51–49 vote in the Senate, and by substantial majorities in the House. See American Enterprise Institute for Policy Research, *The Safeguard ABM System. With 1970 Supplement;* A. Chayes and J. Weisner, eds., *ABM: An Evaluation of the Decision to Deploy an Antiballistic Missile System; Nuclear Proliferation: Prospects for Control;* R. Stein, "The ABM, Proliferation and International Stability," 46 *Foreign Affairs* 487.

Immediately after assuming office, I requested the Secretary of Defense to review the program initiated by the last administration to deploy the Sentinel ballistic missile defense system. . . .

After carefully considering the alternatives, I have reached the following conclusions: (1) the concept on which the Sentinel program of the previous administration was based should be substantially modified; (2) the safety of our country requires that we should proceed now with the development and construction of the new system in a carefully phased program; (3) this program will be reviewed annually from the point of view of (a) technical developments, (b) the threat, (c) the diplomatic context, including any talks on arms limitation.

The modified system has been designed so that its defensive intent is unmistakable. It will be implemented not according to some fixed, theoretical schedule but in a manner clearly related to our periodic analysis of the threat. The first deployment covers two missile sites; the first of these will not be completed before 1973. Any further delay would set this date back by at least two additional years. The program for fiscal year 1970 is the minimum necessary to maintain the security of our nation.

This measured deployment is designed to fulfill three objectives:

1. Protection of our land-based retaliatory forces against a direct attack by the Soviet Union;

2. Defense of the American people against the kind of nuclear attack which Communist China is likely to be able to mount within the decade;

3. Protection against the possibility of accidental attacks from any source. . . .

The Sentinel system approved by the previous administration provided more capabilities for the defense of cities than the program I am recommending, but it did not provide protection against some threats to our retaliatory forces which have developed subsequently. Also, the Sentinel system had the disadvantage that it could be misinterpreted as the first step toward the construction of a heavy system.

Giving up all construction of missile defense poses too many risks. Research and development does not supply the answer to many technical issues that only operational experience can provide. The Soviet Union has engaged in a buildup of its strategic forces larger than was envisaged in 1967, when the decision to deploy Sentinel was made. The following is illustrative of recent Soviet activity. . . .

In addition to these developments, the Chinese threat against our population, as well as the danger of an accidental attack, cannot be ignored. By approving this system, it is possible to reduce U.S. fatalities to a minimal level in the event of a Chinese nuclear attack in the 1970s, or in an accidental attack from any source. No President with the responsibility for the lives and security of the American people could fail to provide this protection. . . .

The present estimate is that the total cost of installing this system will be $6–$7 billion. However, because of the deliberate pace of the deployment, budgetary requests for the coming year can be substantially less —by about one-half—than those asked for by the previous administration for the Sentinel system.

In making this decision, I have been mindful of my pledge to make every effort to move from an era of confrontation to an era of negotiation. The program I am recommending is based on a careful assessment of the developing Soviet and Chinese threats. I have directed the President's Foreign Intelligence Advisory Board—a non-partisan group of distinguished private citizens—to make a yearly assessment of the threat, which will supplement our regular intelligence assessment. Each phase of the deployment will be reviewed to insure that we are doing as much as necessary but no more than that required by the threat existing at that time. Moreover, we will take maximum advantage of the information gathered from the initial deployment in designing the later phases of the program.

Since our deployment is to be closely re-lated to the threat, it is subject to modification as the threat changes, either through negotiations or through unilateral actions by the Soviet Union or Communist China.

The program is not provocative. The Soviet retaliatory capability is not affected by our decision. The capability for surprise attack against our strategic forces is reduced. In other words, our program provides an incentive for a responsible Soviet weapons policy and for the avoidance of spiraling U.S. and Soviet strategic arms budgets. . . .

670. THE NATIONAL COMMITMENTS RESOLUTION
June 25, 1969

(*Congressional Record*, Vol. 115, Pt. 13, p. 17245)

Growing disillusioned with the Vietnam War and apprehensive over the nonconsultative actions of successive chief executives, many senators concluded that Congressional power to declare war had been seriously undermined. The original version of this resolution had been authored by J. W. Fulbright, chairman of the Senate Foreign Relations Committee in 1967. Reintroduced in February 1969, the compromise version below (S Res 85), drawn up by Senator John S. Cooper with Fulbright's endorsement, reflected anxiety over the issue of Congressional prerogatives and concern with the need to reassert a Congressional voice in decisions committing the United States militarily. While not legally binding on the Chief Executive, it nonetheless suggests the "sense" of the Senate that the executive powers section of the Constitution was not to be construed as a grant of unlimited power enabling the President to wage war without Senatorial consent. Clearly no one questioned the Executive's delegated authority to repel a sudden attack, but an overwhelming majority—the vote was 70 to 16—seemed to believe that a four-year course of escalation, as in Vietnam, was another matter indeed. See L. Velvel, "The War in Vietnam: Unconstitutional, Justiciable and Jurisdictionably Attainable," F. Wormath, "The Vietnam War: The President Versus the Constitution," R. Falk, "Six Legal Dimensions of the U.S. Involvement in the Vietnam War," in R. Falk, ed., *The*

Vietnam War and International Law, II; "Congress, the President, and the Power to Commit Forces to Combat," 81 *Harvard Law Rev.* (1968) ; B. Hollander, "The President and Congress—Operational Control of the Armed Forces," 27 *Military Law Rev.* (1965).

Whereas accurate definition of the term "national commitment" in recent years has become obscured: Now, therefore, be it

Resolved, that a national commitment for the purpose of this resolution means the use of the armed forces on foreign territory, or a promise to assist a foreign country, government or people by the use of the armed forces or financial resources of the United States, either immediately or upon the happening of certain events, and

That it is the sense of the Senate that a national commitment by the United States results only from affirmative action taken by the Legislative and Executive Branches of the United States Government by means of a treaty, statute, or concurrent resolution of both Houses of Congress specifically providing for such commitment.

671. PROHIBITION ON THE EMPLACEMENT OF NUCLEAR WEAPONS ON THE SEABED
October 7, 1969
(*Department of State Bulletin,* November 3, 1969)

On October 7, 1969, the United States and the USSR presented, at the Conference of the Committee on Disarmament of Geneva, a joint draft treaty banning the emplacement of nuclear weapons and other weapons of mass destruction on the seabed and in the subsoil thereof. Russia and the United States, designated below as the "Depository Governments," jointly worked out this treaty, which, it was hoped, would be ratified by twenty-two countries, the precedent established by the 1958 Geneva law of the sea conventions.

DRAFT TREATY ON THE PROHIBITION OF THE EMPLACEMENT OF NUCLEAR WEAPONS AND OTHER WEAPONS OF MASS DESTRUCTION ON THE SEABED AND THE OCEAN FLOOR AND IN THE SUBSOIL THEREOF

The States Parties to this Treaty,

Recognizing the common interest of mankind in the progress of the exploration and use of the seabed and the ocean floor for peaceful purposes,

Considering that the prevention of a nuclear arms race on the seabed and ocean floor serves the interests of maintaining world peace, reduces international tensions, and strengthens friendly relations among States,

Convinced that this Treaty constitutes a step towards the exclusion of the seabed, the ocean floor and the subsoil thereof from the arms race, and determined to continue negotiations concerning further measures leading to this end,

Convinced that this Treaty constitutes a step towards a treaty on general and complete disarmament under strict and effective international control, and determined to continue negotiations to this end,

Convinced that this Treaty will further the purposes and principles of the Charter of the United Nations, in a manner consistent with the principles of international law

and without infringing the freedoms of the high seas;

Have agreed as follows:

ARTICLE I

1. The States Parties to this Treaty undertake not to emplant or emplace on the seabed and the ocean floor and in the subsoil thereof beyond the maximum contiguous zone provided for in the 1958 Geneva Convention on the Territorial Sea and the Contiguous Zone any objects with nuclear weapons or any other types of weapons of mass destruction, as well as structures, launching installations or any other facilities specifically designed for storing, testing or using such weapons.

2. The States Parties to this Treaty undertake not to assist, encourage or induce any State to commit actions prohibited by this Treaty and not to participate in any other way in such actions. . . .

ARTICLE III

1. In order to promote the objectives and ensure the observance of the provisions of this Treaty, the States Parties to the Treaty shall have the right to verify the activities of other States Parties to the Treaty on the seabed and the ocean floor and in the subsoil thereof beyond the maximum contiguous zone, referred to in Article II, if these activities raise doubts concerning the fulfillment of the obligations assumed under this Treaty, without interfering with such activities or otherwise infringing rights recognized under international law, including the freedoms of the high seas.

2. The right of verification recognized by the States Parties in paragraph 1 of this Article may be exercised by any State Party using its own means or with the assistance of any other State Party.

3. The States Parties to the Treaty un-

dertake to consult and to cooperate with a view to removing doubts concerning the ful- fillment of the obligations assumed under this Treaty. . . .

672. NIXON'S ADDRESS ON VIETNAMIZING THE WAR
November 3, 1969
(*Department of State Bulletin* November 24, 1969)

Like his predecessors, Richard Nixon was un- willing to see any part of the "free world" fall to Communist domination, and he ruled out an American defeat in Vietnam as well as any political accommodation that might result in a coalition government for South Vietnam. During the 1968 Presidential campaign, Mr. Nixon had claimed to have a plan "to move off dead cen- ter." His policy, however, like those of previous chief executives, was based on a stable anti- Communist government supported by American money and firepower. Toward this end, the President felt that more time was needed for the withdrawal of American ground combat troops and for his "Vietnamization" program. This aim should be placed against a backdrop of mounting antiwar sentiments, specifically the October 15, 1969 Moratorium Day demonstra- tions in Washington, the most impressive peace march to date. Believing such protests gave aid and comfort to the enemy, the President re- sponded by appealing for the support of the "silent majority."

. . . Tonight I want to talk to you on a subject of deep concern to all Americans and to many people in all parts of the world— the war in Vietnam.

I believe that one of the reasons for the deep division about Vietnam is that many Americans have lost confidence in what their Government has told them about our policy. The American people cannot and should not be asked to support a policy which involves the overriding issues of war and peace unless they know the truth about that policy. . . .

In January I could only conclude that the precipitate withdrawal of American forces from Vietnam would be a disaster not only for South Vietnam but for the United States and for the cause of peace.

For the South Vietnamese, our precipitate withdrawal would inevitably allow the Com-

munists to repeat the massacres which fol- lowed their takeover in the North fifteen years before. . . .

For the United States, this first defeat in our nation's history would result in a col- lapse of confidence in American leadership not only in Asia but throughout the world.

Three American Presidents have recog- nized the great stakes involved in Vietnam and understood what had to be done. . . .

For the future of peace, precipitate with- drawal would thus be a disaster of immense magnitude.

—A nation cannot remain great if it be- trays its allies and lets down its friends.

—Our defeat and humiliation in South Vietnam without question would promote recklessness in the councils of those great powers who have not yet abandoned their goals of world conquest.

—This would spark violence wherever our commitments help maintain the peace—in the Middle East, in Berlin, eventually even in the Western Hemisphere.

Ultimately, this would cost more lives. It would not bring peace; it would bring more war.

For these reasons I rejected the recom- mendation that I should end the war by im- mediately withdrawing all our forces. I chose instead to change American policy on both the negotiating front and the battlefront.

In order to end a war fought on many fronts, I initiated a pursuit for peace on many fronts.

In a television speech on May 14, in a speech before the United Nations, and on a number of other occasions, I set forth our peace proposals in great detail.

—We have offered the complete with- drawal of all outside forces within one year.

—We have proposed a cease-fire under in- ternational supervision.

—We have offered free elections under international supervision, with the Communists participating in the organization and conduct of the elections as an organized political force. The Saigon Government has pledged to accept the result of the elections.

We have not put forth our proposals on a take-it-or-leave-it basis. We have indicated that we are willing to discuss the proposals that have been put forth by the other side. We have declared that anything is negotiable, except the right of the people of South Vietnam to determine their own future. At the Paris peace conference, Ambassador Lodge has demonstrated our flexibility and good faith in forty public meetings.

Hanoi has refused even to discuss our proposals. They demand our unconditional acceptance of their terms, which are that we withdraw all American forces immediately and unconditionally and that we overthrow the Government of South Vietnam as we leave.

We have not limited our peace initiatives to public forums and public statements. I recognized in January that a long and bitter war like this usually cannot be settled in a public forum. That is why, in addition to the public statements and negotiations, I have explored every possible private avenue that might lead to a settlement. . . .

But the effect of all the public, private, and secret negotiations which have been undertaken since the bombing halt a year ago and since this administration came into office on January 20 can be summed up in one sentence: No progress whatever has been made except agreement on the shape of the bargaining table.

Now, who is at fault?

It has become clear that the obstacle in negotiating an end to the war is not the President of the United States. It is not the South Vietnamese Government.

The obstacle is the other side's absolute refusal to show the least willingness to join us in seeking a just peace. It will not do so while it is convinced that all it has to do is to wait for our next concession, and our next concession after that one, until it gets everything it wants.

There can now be no longer any question that progress in negotiation depends only on Hanoi's deciding to negotiate, to negotiate seriously. . . .

Now let me turn, however, to a more encouraging report on another front.

At the time we launched our search for peace, I recognized we might not succeed in bringing an end to the war through negotiation.

I therefore put into effect another plan to bring peace—a plan which will bring the war to an end regardless of what happens on the negotiating front. It is in line with a major shift in U.S. foreign policy which I described in my press conference at Guam on July 25.

Let me briefly explain what has been described as the Nixon doctrine—a policy which not only will help end the war in Vietnam but which is an essential element of our program to prevent future Vietnams. . . .

I laid down in Guam three principles as guidelines for future American policy toward Asia:

—First, the United States will keep all of its treaty commitments.

—Second, we shall provide a shield if a nuclear power threatens the freedom of a nation allied with us or of a nation whose survival we consider vital to our security.

—Third, in cases involving other types of aggression, we shall furnish military and economic assistance when requested in accordance with our treaty commitments. But we shall look to the nation directly threatened to assume the primary responsibility of providing the manpower for its defense.

After I announced this policy, I found that the leaders of the Philippines, Thailand, Vietnam, South Korea, and other nations which might be threatened by Communist aggression welcomed this new direction in American foreign policy.

The defense of freedom is everybody's business—not just America's business. And it is particularly the responsibility of the people whose freedom is threatened. In the previous administration we Americanized the war in Vietnam. In this administration we are Vietnamizing the search for peace.

The policy of the previous administration

not only resulted in our assuming the primary responsibility for fighting the war but, even more significantly, did not adequately stress the goal of strengthening the South Vietnamese so that they could defend themselves when we left. . . .

Let me now turn to our program for the future.

We have adopted a plan which we have worked out in cooperation with the South Vietnamese for the complete withdrawal of all U.S. combat ground forces and their replacement by South Vietnamese forces on an orderly scheduled timetable. This withdrawal will be made from strength and not from weakness. As South Vietnamese forces become stronger, the rate of American withdrawal can become greater.

I have not and do not intend to announce the timetable for our program. There are obvious reasons for this decision, which I am sure you will understand. As I have indicated on several occasions, the rate of withdrawal will depend on developments on three fronts.

One of these is the progress which can be, or might be, made in the Paris talks. An announcement of a fixed timetable for our withdrawal would completely remove any incentive for the enemy to negotiate an agreement. They would simply wait until our forces had withdrawn and then move in.

The other two factors on which we will base our withdrawal decisions are the level of enemy activity and the progress of the training program of the South Vietnamese forces. I am glad to be able to report tonight progress on both of these fronts has been greater than we anticipated when we started the program in June for withdrawal. As a result, our timetable for withdrawal is more optimistic now than when we made our first estimates in June.

This clearly demonstrates why it is not wise to be frozen in on a fixed timetable. We must retain the flexibility to base each withdrawal decision on the situation as it is at that time rather than on estimates that are no longer valid.

Along with this optimistic estimate, I must in all candor leave one note of caution: If the level of enemy activity significantly increases, we might have to adjust our timetable accordingly.

However, I want the record to be completely clear on one point.

At the time of the bombing halt just a year ago, there was some confusion as to whether there was an understanding on the part of the enemy that if we stopped the bombing of North Vietnam, they would stop the shelling of cities in South Vietnam. I want to be sure that there is no misunderstanding on the part of the enemy with regard to our withdrawal program.

We have noted the reduced level of infiltration, the reduction of our casualties, and are basing our withdrawal decisions partially on those factors.

If the level of infiltration or our casualties increase while we are trying to scale down the fighting, it will be the result of a conscious decision by the enemy.

Hanoi could make no greater mistake than to assume that an increase in violence will be to its advantage. If I conclude that increased enemy action jeopardizes our remaining forces in Vietnam, I shall not hesitate to take strong and effective measures to deal with that situation.

This is not a threat. This is a statement of policy which as Commander in Chief of our Armed Forces I am making in meeting my responsibility for the protection of American fighting men wherever they may be.

My fellow Americans, I am sure you can recognize from what I have said that we really only have two choices open to us if we want to end this war:

—I can order an immediate, precipitate withdrawal of all Americans from Vietnam without regard to the effects of that action.

—Or we can persist in our search for a just peace, through a negotiated settlement if possible or through continued implementation of our plan for Vietnamization if necessary—a plan in which we will withdraw all of our forces from Vietnam on a schedule in accordance with our program, as the South Vietnamese become strong enough to defend their own freedom.

I have chosen this second course. It is not the easy way. It is the right way. It is a plan which will end the war and serve the cause of peace, not just in Vietnam, but in the Pacific and in the world.

In speaking of the consequences of a precipitate withdrawal, I mentioned that our allies would lose confidence in America.

Far more dangerous, we would lose confidence in ourselves. Oh, the immediate reaction would be a sense of relief that our men were coming home. But as we saw the consequences of what we had done, inevitable remorse and divisive recrimination would scar our spirit as a people.

We have faced other crises in our history and have become stronger by rejecting the easy way out and taking the right way in meeting our challenges. Our greatness as a nation has been our capacity to do what had to be done when we knew our course was right.

I recognize that some of my fellow citizens disagree with the plan for peace I have chosen. . . . I would be untrue to my oath of office if I allowed the policy of this nation to be dictated by the minority who hold that point and who try to impose it on the Nation by mounting demonstrations in the street.

For almost two hundred years, the policy of this nation has been made under our Constitution by those leaders in the Congress and in the White House elected by all of the people. If a vocal minority, however fervent its cause, prevails over reason and the will of the majority, this nation has no future as a free society.

And now I would like to address a word, if I may, to the young people of this nation who are particularly concerned—and I understand why they are concerned—about this war.

I respect your idealism.

I share your concern for peace.

I want peace as much as you do. . . .

I have chosen a plan for peace. I believe it will succeed.

If it does succeed, what the critics say now won't matter. If it does not succeed, anything I say then won't matter.

I know it may not be fashionable to speak of patriotism or national destiny these days. But I feel it is appropriate to do so on this occasion.

Two hundred years ago this nation was weak and poor. But even then, America was the hope of millions in the world. Today we have become the strongest and richest nation in the world. The wheel of destiny has turned so that any hope the world has for the survival of peace and freedom will be determined by whether the American people have the moral stamina and the courage to meet the challenge of free-world leadership.

Let historians not record that when America was the most powerful nation in the world we passed on the other side of the road and allowed the last hopes for peace and freedom of millions of people to be suffocated by the forces of totalitarianism. . . .

673. CHEMICAL AND BIOLOGICAL DEFENSE POLICIES AND PROGRAMS
1969–70

The widespread use of chemical defoliants in Vietnam, which had questionable effect upon the Vietcong and possibly produced birth defects in children, as well as the highly publicized Pentagon plan to transport unwanted nerve gas across the country and dump it into the ocean, were among the factors which combined to produce a major public challenge to the automatic priority given to CBW research and development programs. Rising concern about the dangers of ill-considered application of such weaponry and their side effects, and even about the necessity of these weapons, generated an administrative review of these programs. The presidential statements below encouraged opponents of chemical and biological weapons research. Tear gas was implicitly excluded from the prohibition. See S. Rose, ed., *CBW: Chemical and Biological Warfare;* R. Clarke, *The Silent Weapons;* R. McCarthy, *The Ultimate Folly: War by Pestilence, Asphyxiation and Defoliation;* F. J. Brown, *Chemical Warfare;* S. Hersh, *Chemical and Biological Warfare: America's Hidden Arsenal; The Problem of Chemical and Biological Warfare: A Study of the Historical, Technical, Military, Legal and Political Aspects of CBW and Possible Disarmament Measures,* vols. III, IV, V.

1. STATEMENT BY PRESIDENT NIXON
November 25, 1969
(Department of State Bulletin, December 15, 1969)

Soon after taking office I directed a comprehensive study of our chemical and biological defense policies and programs. There had been no such review in over fifteen years. As a result, objectives and policies in this field were unclear and programs lacked definition and direction. . . .

As to our chemical warfare program, the United States:

—Reaffirms its oft-repeated renunciation of the first use of lethal chemical weapons.

—Extends this renunciation to the first use of incapacitating chemicals.

Consonant with these decisions, the administration will submit to the Senate, for its advice and consent to ratification, the Geneva protocol of 1925, which prohibits the first use in war of "asphyxiating, poisonous or other gases and of bacteriological methods of warfare." The United States has long supported the principles and objectives of this protocol. We take this step toward formal ratification to reinforce our continuing advocacy of international constraints on the use of these weapons.

Biological weapons have massive, unpredictable, and potentially uncontrollable consequences. They may produce global epidemics and impair the health of future generations. I have therefore decided that:

—The United States shall renounce the use of lethal biological agents and weapons and all other methods of biological warfare.

—The United States will confine its biological research to defensive measures, such as immunization and safety measures.

—The Department of Defense has been asked to make recommendations as to the disposal of existing stocks of bacteriological weapons.

In the spirit of these decisions, the United States associates itself with the principles and objectives of the United Kingdom draft convention, which would ban the use of biological methods of warfare. We will seek, however, to clarify specific provisions of the draft to assure that necessary saefguards are included.

2. NIXON'S MESSAGE TO THE SENATE ON THE GENEVA PROTOCOL
August 10, 1970
(Department of State Bulletin, September 7, 1970)

With a view to receiving the advice and consent of the Senate to ratification, I transmit herewith the Protocol for the Prohibition of the Use in War of Asphyxiating, Poisonous or Other Gases, and of Bacteriological Methods of Warfare, signed at Geneva June 17, 1925. I transmit also the report by the Secretary of State which sets forth the understandings and the proposed reservation of the United States with respect to the Protocol.

In submitting this Protocol for approval, I consider it desirable and appropriate to make the following statements:

—The United States has renounced the first-use of lethal and incapacitating chemical weapons.

—The United States has renounced any use of biological and toxin weapons.

—Our biological and toxin programs will be confined to research for defensive purposes, strictly defined. By the example we set, we hope to contribute to an atmosphere of peace, understanding and confidence between nations and among men. The policy of the United States Government is to support international efforts to limit biological and toxin research programs to defensive purposes.

—The United States will seek further agreement on effective arms-control measures in the field of biological and chemical warfare.

Today, there are 85 parties, including all other major powers, to this basic international agreement which the United States proposed and signed in 1925. The United States always has observed the principles and objectives of this Protocol.

I consider it essential that the United States now become a party to this Protocol, and urge the Senate to give its advice and consent to ratification with the reservation set forth in the Secretary's report.

674. MASSACHUSETTS ACT LIMITING U.S. AUTHORITY OVER DRAFTEES
April 2, 1970
(*Laws of Massachusetts,* 1970, Chapter 174)

The war in Southeast Asia inevitably raised constitutional questions about Presidential authority in warmaking and about the legality of the operation of the Selective Service Act. In 1970, the Massachusetts General Court passed the Wells-Shea Bill, which attempted to protect inhabitants of the state from military service outside the territorial limits of the United States in any war not authorized by Congressional declaration. This potentially dangerous challenge to the operation of the selective service, and to the war itself, was carried to the Supreme Court, which refused to hear argument. See J. Wells, ed., *The People vs. Presidential War;* L. Velvel, *Undeclared War and Civil Disobedience;* R. Fall, "The Six Legal Dimensions of the Vietnam War," and F. Wormuth, "The Vietnam War, the President Versus the Constitution," in R. Falk, ed., *The Vietnam War and International Law,* II.

An Act defining the rights of inhabitants of the Commonwealth inducted or serving in the military forces of the United States.

SEC. 1. No inhabitant of the commonwealth inducted or serving in the military forces of the United States shall be required to serve outside the territorial limits of the United States in the conduct of armed hostilities not an emergency and not otherwise authorized in the powers granted to the President of the United States in Article II, Section 2, of the Constitution of the United States designating the President as the Commander-in-Chief, unless such hostilities were initially authorized or subsequently ratified by a congressional declaration of war according to the constitutionally established procedures in Article I, Section 8, of the Constitution of the United States.

SEC. 2. The attorney general shall, in the name and on behalf of the commonwealth and on behalf of any inhabitants thereof who are required to serve in the armed forces of the United States in violation of section one of this act, bring an appropriate action in the Supreme Court of the United States as the court having original jurisdiction thereof under clause two of section 2 of Article III of the Constitution of the United States to defend and enforce the rights of such inhabitants and of the commonwealth under section one; but if it shall be finally determined that such action is not one of which the Supreme Court of the United States has original jurisdiction, then he shall bring another such action in an appropriate inferior federal court. Any inhabitant of the commonwealth who is required to serve in the armed forces of the United States in violation of section one of this act may notify the attorney general thereof, and all such inhabitants so notifying the attorney general shall be joined as parties in such action. If such action shall be commenced hereunder in an inferior federal court, the attorney general shall take all steps necessary and within his power to obtain favorable action thereon, including a decision by the Supreme Court of the United States.

675. NEW YORK STATE ANTIABORTION LAW
April 11, 1970
(*Laws of New York,* 1970, Chapter 127)

Most state antiabortion laws date from the nineteenth century. The movement to legalize abortion emerged in the mid-sixties, and between 1967 and 1970, twelve states enacted legislation substantially broadening the justification for therapeutic abortion. New York State was one of three (with Alaska and Hawaii) that repealed outright antiabortion statutes. For a major Court decision dealing with the use of contraceptive devices and the "marital right of privacy," see *Griswold* v. *Connecticut*, 1965 (Doc. No. 656). On the abortion issue, see *Congressional Quarterly,* July 24, 1970; C. Lister, "The Right to Control the Use of One's Body," in Dorsen, ed., *The Rights of Americans.*

SEC. 1. Subdivision three of section 125.05 of the penal law is hereby amended to read as follows:

3. "Justifiable abortional act." An abortional act is justifiable when committed upon a female *with her consent* by a duly licensed physician acting (*a*) under a reasonable belief that such is necessary to preserve [the]

her life [of such female], *or,* (*b*) *within twenty-four weeks from the commencement of her pregnancy.* A pregnant female's commission of an abortional act upon herself is justifiable when she acts upon the advice of a duly licensed physician (*1*) that such *act* is necessary to preserve her life, *or,* (*2*) *within twenty-four weeks from the commencement of her pregnancy.* The submission by a female to an abortional act is justifiable when she believes that it is being committed by a duly licensed physician [and when she acts upon the advice of a duly licensed physician] *acting under a reasonable belief* that such *act* is necessary to preserve her life, *or within twenty-four weeks from the commencement of her pregnancy.*

SEC. 2 This act shall take effect July first, nineteen hundred seventy.

676. NIXON'S STATEMENT ON THE INVASION OF CAMBODIA
April 30, 1970
(Department of State Bulletin, May 18, 1970)

On May 18, the pro-American General Lon Nol overthrew the reigning Prince Sihanouk and made himself premier of Cambodia. A month later, President Nixon approved the shipment of captured rifles to the new government and a program for training its troops, and on April 24 he asked the American commanding general Creighton Abrams to submit plans for a military "incursion" into Cambodia to provide protection for the more rapid withdrawal of U.S. troops from Vietnam. On April 30, he announced to the American people this extension of the war into Cambodia; the announcement set off nationwide demonstrations of protest. On June 30, the President declared the sixty-day operation a success and withdrew American "combat" forces from Cambodia. See D. Kirk, *Wider War: The Struggle for Cambodia, Thailand and Laos;* Committee of Concerned Asian Scholars, *The Indochina Story;* J. S. Grant et al., eds., *Cambodia: The Widening War in Indochina;* M. Gettleman et al., eds., *Conflict in Indochina: A Reader on the Widening War in Laos and Cambodia.*

. . . American policy . . . has been to scrupulously respect the neutrality of the Cambodian people. . . .

North Vietnam, however, has not respected that neutrality.

For the past five years, . . . North Vietnam has occupied military sanctuaries all along the Cambodian frontier with South Vietnam.

North Vietnam in the last two weeks has stripped away all pretense of respecting the sovereignty or the neutrality of Cambodia. Thousands of their soldiers are invading the country from the sanctuaries; they are encircling the capital of Phnom Penh. Coming from these sanctuaries, as you see here, they have moved into Cambodia and are encircling the capital.

Cambodia, as a result of this, has sent out a call to the United States, to a number of other nations, for assistance. Because if this enemy effort succeeds, Cambodia would become a vast enemy staging area and a springboard for attacks on South Vietnam along six hundred miles of frontier, a refuge where enemy troops could return from combat without fear of retaliation.

North Vietnamese men and supplies could then be poured into that country, jeopardizing not only the lives of our own men but the people of South Vietnam as well.

. . . [T]his is the decision I have made.

In cooperation with the armed forces of South Vietnam, attacks are being launched this week to clean out major enemy sanctuaries on the Cambodian–Vietnam border.

A major responsibility for the ground operations is being assumed by South Vietnamese forces. . . .

Tonight American and South Vietnamese units will attack the headquarters for the entire Communist military operation in South Vietnam. This key control center has been occupied by the North Vietnamese and Vietcong for five years in blatant violation of Cambodia's neutrality.

This is not an invasion of Cambodia. The areas in which these attacks will be launched are completely occupied and controlled by North Vietnamese forces. Our purpose is not to occupy the areas. Once enemy forces are driven out of these sanctuaries and once their military supplies are destroyed, we will withdraw.

These actions are in no way directed at the security interests of any nation. Any government that chooses to use these actions as a pretext for harming relations with the United States will be doing so on its own responsibility and on its own initiative, and we will draw the appropriate conclusions.

Now, let me give you the reasons for my decision.

A majority of the American people, a majority of you listening to me, are for the withdrawal of our forces from Vietnam. The action I have taken tonight is indispensable for the continuing success of that withdrawal program.

A majority of the American people want to end this war rather than to have it drag on interminably. The action I have taken tonight will serve that purpose.

A majority of the American people want to keep the casualties of our brave men in Vietnam at an absolute minimum. The action I take tonight is essential if we are to accomplish that goal.

We take this action not for the purpose of expanding the war into Cambodia, but for the purpose of ending the war in Vietnam and winning the just peace we all desire. We have made and we will continue to make every possible effort to end this war through

negotiation at the conference table rather than through more fighting on the battlefield.

Let us look again at the record. We have stopped the bombing of North Vietnam. We have cut air operations by over 20 percent. We have announced withdrawal of over 250,000 of our men. We have offered to withdraw all of our men, if they will withdraw theirs. We have offered to negotiate all issues with only one condition—and that is that the future of South Vietnam be determined not by North Vietnam, not by the United States, but by the people of South Vietnam themselves.

The answer of the enemy has been intransigence at the conference table, belligerence in Hanoi, massive military aggression in Laos and Cambodia, and stepped-up attacks in South Vietnam designed to increase American casualties.

This attitude has become intolerable. We will not react to this threat to American lives merely by plaintive diplomatic protests. If we did, the credibility of the United States would be destroyed in every area of the world where only the power of the United States deters aggression.

Tonight I again warn the North Vietnamese that if they continue to escalate the fighting when the United States is withdrawing its forces, I shall meet my responsibility as Commander in Chief of our Armed Forces to take the action I consider necessary to defend the security of our American men.

The action that I have announced tonight puts the leaders of North Vietnam on notice that we will be patient in working for peace, we will be conciliatory at the conference table, but we will not be humiliated. We will not be defeated. We will not allow American men by the thousands to be killed by an enemy from privileged sanctuaries.

The time came long ago to end this war through peaceful negotiations. We stand ready for those negotiations. We have made major efforts, many of which must remain secret. I say tonight that all the offers and approaches made previously remain on the conference table whenever Hanoi is ready to negotiate seriously.

But if the enemy response to our most conciliatory offers for peaceful negotiation continues to be to increase its attacks and humiliate and defeat us, we shall react accordingly.

My fellow Americans, we live in an age of anarchy, both abroad and at home. We see mindless attacks on all the great institutions which have been created by free civilizations in the last five hundred years. Even here in the United States, great universities are being systematically destroyed. Small nations all over the world find themselves under attack from within and from without.

If, when the chips are down, the world's most powerful nation, the United States of America, acts like a pitiful, helpless giant, the forces of totalitarianism and anarchy will threaten free nations and free institutions throughout the world.

It is not our power but our will and character that is being tested tonight. The question all Americans must ask and answer tonight is this: Does the richest and strongest nation in the history of the world have the character to meet a direct challenge by a group which rejects every effort to win a just peace, ignores our warning, tramples on solemn agreements, violates the neutrality of an unarmed people, and uses our prisoners as hostages?

If we fail to meet this challenge, all other nations will be on notice that despite its overwhelming power the United States, when a real crisis comes, will be found wanting.

During my campaign for the Presidency, I pledged to bring Americans home from Vietnam. They are coming home.

I promised to end this war. I shall keep that promise.

I promised to win a just peace. I shall keep that promise.

We shall avoid a wider war. But we are also determined to put an end to this war. . . .

No one is more aware than I am of the political consequences of the action I have taken. It is tempting to take the easy political path: to blame this war on previous administrations and to bring all of our men home immediately, regardless of the consequences, even though that would mean defeat for the United States; to desert 18 million South Vietnamese people who have put their trust in us and to expose them to the same slaughter and savagery which the leaders of North Vietnam inflicted on hundreds of thousands of North Vietnamese who chose freedom when the Communists took over North Vietnam in 1954; to get peace at any price now, even though I know that a peace of humiliation for the United States would lead to a bigger war or surrender later.

I have rejected all political considerations in making this decision.

Whether my party gains in November is nothing compared to the lives of 400,000 brave Americans fighting for our country and for the cause of peace and freedom in Vietnam. Whether I may be a one-term President is insignificant compared to whether by our failure to act in this crisis the United States proves itself to be unworthy to lead the forces of freedom in this critical period in world history. I would rather be a one-term President and do what I believe is right than to be a two-term President at the cost of seeing America become a second-rate power and to see this nation accept the first defeat in its proud 190-year history. . . .

677. ORGANIZED CRIME CONTROL ACT
October 17, 1970
Public Law 91–452, 91st Congress

The rapid increase in violent crime, mounting instances of urban riots and political confrontation, and hostility to judicial decisions thought to "handcuff the police," combined to produce this measure. Labeled an "organized crime" measure, it included provisions that applied indiscriminately to a wide range of offenses— from bad-check passing and burglary to conspiracy. This legislation, reflecting popular anxi- eties, passed the Senate with only one negative vote and with only twenty-six House members recorded against it.

An Act relating to the control of organized crime in the United States.

STATEMENT OF FINDINGS AND PURPOSE

The Congress finds that (1) organized crime in the United States is a highly sophisticated, diversified, and widespread activity that annually drains billions of dollars from America's economy by unlawful conduct and the illegal use of force, fraud, and corruption; (2) organized crime derives a major portion of its power through money obtained from such illegal endeavors as syndicated gambling, loan sharking, the theft and fencing of property, the importation and distribution of narcotics and other dangerous drugs, and other forms of social exploitation; (3) this money and power are increasingly used to infiltrate and corrupt legitimate business and labor unions and to subvert and corrupt our democratic processes; (4) organized crime activities in the United States weaken the stability of the Nation's economic system, harm innocent investors and competing organizations, interfere with free competition, seriously burden interstate and foreign commerce, threaten the domestic security, and undermine the general welfare of the Nation and its citizens; and (5) organized crime continues to grow because of defects in the evidence-gathering process of the law inhibiting the development of the legally admissible evidence necessary to bring criminal and other sanctions or remedies to bear on the unlawful activities of those engaged in organized crime and because the sanctions and remedies available to the Government are unnecessarily limited in scope and impact.

It is the purpose of this Act to seek the eradication of organized crime in the United States by strengthening the legal tools in the evidence-gathering process, by establishing new penal prohibitions, and by providing enhanced sanctions and new remedies to deal with the unlawful activities of those engaged in organized crime.

TITLE I

SPECIAL GRAND JURY

. . . (a) A special grand jury impaneled by any district court, with the concurrence of a majority of its members, may, upon comple-

tion of its original term, or each extension thereof, submit to the court a report—

(1) concerning noncriminal misconduct, malfeasance, or misfeasance in office involving organized criminal activity by an appointed public officer or employee as the basis for a recommendation of removal or disciplinary action; or

(2) regarding organized crime conditions in the district. . . .

TITLE II

GENERAL IMMUNITY

. . . Whenever a witness refuses, on the basis of his privilege against self-incrimination, to testify or provide other information in a proceeding before or ancillary to—

(1) a court or grand jury of the United States,

(2) an agency of the United States, or

(3) either House of Congress, a joint committee of the two Houses, or a committee or a subcommittee of either House, and the person presiding over the proceeding communicates to the witness an order issued under this part, the witness may not refuse to comply with the order on the basis of his privilege against self-incrimination; but no testimony or other information compelled under the order (or any information directly or indirectly derived from such testimony or other information) may be used against the witness in any criminal case, except a prosecution for perjury, giving a false statement, or otherwise failing to comply with the order.

SEC. 6003. *Court and grand jury proceedings.*

(a) In the case of any individual who has been or may be called to testify or provide other information at any proceeding before or ancillary to a court of the United States or a grand jury of the United States, the United States district court for the judicial district in which the proceeding is or may be held shall issue, in accordance with subsection (b) of this section, upon the request of the United States attorney for such district, an order requiring such individual to give testimony or provide other information which he refuses to give or provide on the basis of his privilege against self-incrimina-

tion, such order to become effective as provided in section 6002 of this part.

(b) A United States attorney may, with
the approval of the Attorney General, the
Deputy Attorney General, or any designated
Assistant Attorney General, request an order
under subsection (a) of this section when in
his judgment—

(1) the testimony or other information
from such individual may be necessary to
the public interest; and

(2) such individual has refused or is
likely to refuse to testify or provide other
information on the basis of his privilege
against self-incrimination. . . .

TITLE III

RECALCITRANT WITNESSES

SEC. 301. (a) Chapter 119, title 28,
United States Code, is amended by adding
at the end thereof the following new section:
SEC. 1826. *Recalcitrant witnesses.*

(a) Whenever a witness in any proceeding
before or ancillary to any court or grand
jury of the United States refuses without
just cause shown to comply with an order of
the court to testify or provide other information, including any book, paper, document, record, recording or other material,
the court, upon such refusal, or when such
refusal is duly brought to its attention, may
summarily order his confinement at a suitable
place until such time as the witness is willing to give such testimony or provide such
information. No period of such confinement
shall exceed the life of—

(1) the court proceeding, or

(2) the term of the grand jury, including extensions,

before which such refusal to comply with
the court order occurred, but in no event
shall such confinement exceed eighteen
months.

(b) No person confined pursuant to subsection (a) of this section shall be admitted
to bail pending the determination of an appeal taken by him from the order for his
confinement if it appears that the appeal
is frivolous or taken for delay. Any appeal
from an order of confinement under this sec-

tion shall be disposed of as soon as practicable, but not later than thirty days from the
filing of such appeal. . . .

TITLE X

DANGEROUS SPECIAL OFFENDER
SENTENCING

SEC. 1001. (a) Chapter 227, title 18,
United States Code, is amended by adding
at the end thereof the following new sections:
SEC. 3575. *Increased sentence for dangerous special offenders.*

(a) Whenever an attorney charged with
the prosecution of a defendant in a court of
the United States for an alleged felony committed when the defendant was over the age
of twenty-one years has reason to believe
that the defendant is a dangerous special offender such attorney, a reasonable time before trial or acceptance by the court of a
plea of guilty or nolo contendere, may sign
and file with the court, and may amend, a
notice (1) specifying that the defendant is
a dangerous special offender who upon conviction for such felony is subject to the imposition of a sentence under subsection (b)
of this section, and (2) setting out with particularity the reasons why such attorney believes the defendant to be a dangerous special offender. In no case shall the fact that
the defendant is alleged to be a dangerous
special offender be an issue upon the trial of
such felony, be disclosed to the jury, or be
disclosed before any plea of guilty or nolo
contendere or verdict or finding of guilty to
the presiding judge without the consent of
the parties. If the court finds that the filing
of the notice as a public record may prejudice fair consideration of a pending criminal
matter, it may order the notice sealed and
the notice shall not be subject to subpoena
or public inspection during the pendency of
such criminal matter, except on order of the
court, but shall be subject to inspection by
the defendant alleged to be a dangerous special offender and his counsel.

(b) Upon any plea of guilty or nolo contendere or verdict or finding of guilty of the
defendant of such felony, a hearing shall be

held, before sentence is imposed, by the court sitting without a jury. The court shall fix a time for the hearing, and notice thereof shall be given to the defendant and the United States at least ten days prior thereto. The court shall permit the United States and counsel for the defendant, or the defendant if he is not represented by counsel, to inspect the presentence report sufficiently prior to the hearing as to afford a reasonable opportunity for verification. In extraordinary cases, the court may withhold material not relevant to a proper sentence, diagnostic opinion which might seriously disrupt a program of rehabilitation, any source of information obtained on a promise of confidentiality, and material previously disclosed in open court. A court withholding all or part of a presentence report shall inform the parties of its action and place in the record the reasons therefor. The court may require parties inspecting all or part of a presentence report to give notice of any part thereof intended to be controverted. In connection with the hearing, the defendant and the United States shall be entitled to assistance of counsel, compulsory process, and cross-examination of such witnesses as appear at the hearing. A duly authenticated copy of a former judgment or commitment shall be prima facie evidence of such former judgment or commitment. If it appears by a preponderance of the information, including information submitted during the trial of such felony and the sentencing hearing and so much of the presentence report as the court relies upon, that the defendant is a dangerous special offender, the court shall sentence the defendant to imprisonment for an appropriate term not to exceed twenty-five years and not disproportionate in severity to the maximum term otherwise authorized by law for such felony. Otherwise it shall sentence the defendant in accordance with the law prescribing penalties for such felony. The court shall place in the record its findings, including an identification of the information relied upon in making such findings, and its reasons for the sentence imposed.

(c) This section shall not prevent the imposition and execution of a sentence of death or of imprisonment for life or for a term exceeding twenty-five years upon any person convicted of an offense so punishable.

(d) Notwithstanding any other provision of this section, the court shall not sentence a dangerous special offender to less than any mandatory minimum penalty prescribed by law for such felony. This section shall not be construed as creating any mandatory minimum penalty.

(e) A defendant is a special offender for purposes of this section if—

(1) the defendant has previously been convicted in courts of the United States, a State, the District of Columbia, the Commonwealth of Puerto Rico, a territory or possession of the United States, any political subdivision, or any department, agency, or instrumentality thereof for two or more offenses committed on occasions different from one another and from such felony and punishable in such courts by death or imprisonment in excess of one year, for one or more of such convictions the defendant has been imprisoned prior to the commission of such felony, and less than five years have elapsed between the commission of such felony and either the defendant's release, on parole or otherwise, from imprisonment for one such conviction or his commission of the last such previous offense or another offense punishable by death or imprisonment in excess of one year under applicable laws of the United States, a State, the District of Columbia, the Commonwealth of Puerto Rico, a territory or possession of the United States, any political subdivision, or any department, agency or instrumentality thereof; or

(2) the defendant committed such felony as part of a pattern of conduct which was criminal under applicable laws of any jurisdiction, which constituted a substantial source of his income, and in which he manifested special skill or expertise; or

(3) such felony was, or the defendant committed such felony in furtherance of, a conspiracy with three or more other persons to engage in a pattern of conduct criminal under applicable laws of any jurisdiction, and the defendant did, or agreed that he would, initiate, organize, plan, finance, direct, manage, or supervise all or part of such conspiracy or conduct, or give

or receive a bribe or use force as all or part of such conduct. . . .

SEC. 3577. *Use of information for sentencing.* No limitation shall be placed on the information concerning the background, character, and conduct of a person convicted of an offense which a court of the United States may receive and consider for the purpose of imposing an appropriate sentence. . . .

678. RESTRICTING PRESIDENTIAL AUTHORITY IN CAMBODIA
January 5, 1971
(84 *U.S. Statutes at Large* 1942)

The United States military "incursion" into Cambodia in April 1970 touched off widespread protests against American foreign policy. It deepened popular anxiety over national commitments in Asia and further stirred a Congress restive about unilateral presidential initiatives ever since the Tonkin Bay Resolution. Sponsored by Senators John Sherman Cooper and Frank Church, this amendment to the foreign aid authorization act (HR 19911)—or, as it was formally called, the Special Foreign Assistance Act—reflected senatorial desire to limit the Cambodian operation and prevent its recurrence. Originally attached to the Military Sales Act (HR 15628) and passed on June 30, 1970, it was watered down and finally eliminated from this Act; but revised and attached to the foreign aid authorization measure, it was passed by a bipartisan coalition on January 5, 1971.

SEC. 8. The Foreign Assistance Act of 1961 is amended by adding at the end thereof the following new section:

SEC. 652. *Limitation Upon Additional Assistance to Cambodia.* The President shall not exercise any special authority granted to him under . . . this Act for the purpose of providing additional assistance to Cambodia, unless the President, at least thirty days prior to the date he intends to exercise any such authority on behalf of Cambodia (or ten days prior to such date if the President certifies in writing that an emergency exists requiring immediate assistance to Cambodia), notifies the Speaker of the House of Representatives and the Committee on Foreign Relations of the Senate in writing of each such intended exercise, the section of this Act under which such authority is to be exercised, and the justification for, and the extent of, the exercise of such authority.

679. THE SALT NEGOTIATIONS: ABM LIMITATION AGREEMENT
May 20, 1971
(*Congressional Quarterly,* May 28, 1971)

In 1967 President Johnson urged that United States–USSR talks be held to forestall installation of the antiballistic missile system; at the same time the Soviet Union suggested broadening the scope of the talks to include offensive as well as defensive weapons. The Strategic Arms Limitation Talks (SALT) formally began in November 1969 in Helsinki and entered their fourth round on March 15, 1970 in Vienna. President Nixon proposed a step-by-step procedure to achieve limitations on different weapons, taking one system at a time. On May 20, 1971, he announced that the United States and the Soviet Union had agreed at the nineteen-month-old SALT rounds to concentrate on limiting defensive antiballistic missile (ABM) systems. A joint communiqué, given here, stated that after agreement was reached the two governments would take up limitation of offensive strategic weapons. See Doc. No. 688.

The governments of the United States and the Soviet Union, after reviewing the course of their talks on the limitations of strategic armaments, have agreed to concentrate this year on working out an agreement for the limitation of the deployment of antiballistic missile systems (ABMs). They have also agreed that, together with concluding an agreement to limit ABMs, they will agree on certain measures with respect to the limitation of offensive strategic weapons.

The two sides are taking this course in the conviction that it will create more favorable conditions for further negotiations to limit all strategic arms. These negotiations will be actively pursued.

680. NIXON REVIVES THE SUBVERSIVE ACTIVITIES CONTROL BOARD
July 2, 1971
(*Federal Register,* Vol. 36, No. 131, pp. 12831–32)

The Subversive Activities Control Board was an independent and semijudicial agency created in 1950, at the peak of the cold war. By the late 1960s, its work had fallen off almost completely, and it heard only three witnesses in 1970. Congressional critics complained that the Board was nonfunctioning and a needless expense; in response, the Nixon administration moved to strengthen rather than to dismantle it. Among other things, the President's executive order (11605) gave the Board authority to determine what organizations should be classified as subversive by the Attorney General, a function which up to now had been the sole responsibility of the Attorney General himself.

. . . The Subversive Activities Control Board shall, upon petition of the Attorney General, conduct appropriate hearings to determine whether any organization is totalitarian, fascist, communist, subversive, or whether it has adopted a policy of unlawfully advocating the commission of acts of force or violence to deny others their rights under the Constitution or laws of the United States or of any State, or which seeks to overthrow the government of the United States or any State or subdivision thereof by unlawful means.

(d) The Board may determine that an organization has adopted a policy of unlawfully advocating the commission of acts of force or violence to deny others their constitutional or statutory rights or that an organization seeks to overthrow the government of the United States or any State or subdivision thereof by unlawful means if it is found that such group engages in, unlawfully advocates, or has among its purposes or objectives, or adopts as a means of obtaining any of its purposes or objectives.—

(1) The commission of acts of force or violence or other unlawful acts to deny others their rights or benefits guaranteed by the Constitution or laws of the United States or of the several States or political subdivisions thereof; or

(2) The unlawful damage or destruction of property; or injury to persons; or

(3) The overthrow or destruction of the government of the United States or the government of any State, Territory, district, or possession thereof, or the government of any political subdivision therein, by unlawful means; or

(4) The commission of acts which violate laws pertaining to treason, rebellion or insurrection, riots or civil disorders, seditious conspiracy, sabotage, trading with the enemy, obstruction of the recruiting and enlistment service of the United States, impeding officers of the United States, or related crimes or offenses.

(e) The Board may determine an organization to be "totalitarian" if it is found that such organization engages in activities which seek by unlawful means the establishment of a system of government in the United States which is autocratic and in which control is centered in a single individual, group, or political party, allowing no effective representation to opposing individuals, groups, or parties and providing no practical opportunity for dissent.

(f) The Board may determine an organization to be "fascist" if it is found that such organization engages in activities which seek by unlawful means the establishment of a system of government in the United States which is characterized by rigid one-party dictatorship, forcible suppression of the opposition, ownership of the means of production under centralized governmental control and which fosters racism.

(g) The Board may determine an organization to be "communist" if it is found that such organization engages in activities which seek by unlawful means the establishment of a government in the United States which is based upon the revolutionary principles of Marxism-Leninism, which interprets history as a relentless class war aimed at the destruction of the existing society and the establishment of the dictatorship of the proletariat, the government ownership of the means of production and distribution of property, and the establishment of a single authoritarian party.

(h) The Board may determine an organization to be "subversive" if it is found that such organization engages in activities which seek the abolition or destruction by unlawful means of the government of the United States or any State, or subdivision thereof.

681. PRESIDENT NIXON AND CHINA
1971

President Nixon's speech of July 15, 1971, in which he announced his intention to visit mainland China, startled the country and the world. Scholars had seen in the relaxation of trade and travel restrictions, the resumption of the United States–China talks in Warsaw in 1970, and the selective licensing of goods for export to the People's Republic, early signs of a thaw. Mr. Nixon's announcement came as a surprise nonetheless. It signaled the abandonment of a policy of unyielding hostility toward the People's Republic. It dealt a fateful blow to Nationalist Chinese aspirations, and it meant a shift in the United States position at the United Nations—where the American delegation now outlined a "two-China" policy (i.e., recognition of both the People's Republic and Nationalist China on Taiwan) and rejected consideration of any proposal that might withdraw recognition from Taiwan as China's representative to the world organization.

1. NIXON'S ANNOUNCEMENT
July 15, 1971
(*Department of State Bulletin,*
August 2, 1971)

. . . As I have pointed out on a number of occasions over the past three years, there can be no stable and enduring peace without the participation of the People's Republic of China and its 750 million people. That is why I have undertaken initiatives in several areas to open the door for more normal relations between our two countries.

In pursuance of that goal, I sent Dr. Kissinger, my Assistant for National Security Affairs, to Peking during his recent world tour for the purpose of having talks with Premier Chou En-lai.

The announcement I shall now read is being issued simultaneously in Peking and in the United States:

"Premier Chou En-lai and Dr. Henry Kissinger, President Nixon's Assistant for National Security Affairs, held talks in Peking from July 9 to 11, 1971. Knowing of President Nixon's expressed desire to visit the People's Republic of China, Premier Chou En-lai on behalf of the Government of the People's Republic of China has extended an invitation to President Nixon to visit China at an appropriate date before May, 1972.

"President Nixon has accepted the invitation with pleasure.

"The meeting between the leaders of China and the United States is to seek the normalization of relations between the two countries and also to exchange views on questions of concern to the two sides."

In anticipation of the inevitable speculation which will follow this announcement, I want to put our policy in the clearest possible context. Our action in seeking a new relationship with the People's Republic of China will not be at the expense of our old friends.

It is not directed against any other nation.

We seek friendly relations with all nations. Any nation can be our friend without being any other nation's enemy.

I have taken this action because of my profound conviction that all nations will gain from a reduction of tensions and a better relationship between the United States and the People's Republic of China.

It is in this spirit that I will undertake what I deeply hope will become a journey for peace—peace not just for our generation but for future generations on this earth we share together.

2. U.S. RESOLUTIONS ON CHINA ISSUE
September 22, 1971

(New York Times, September 23, 1971)

FIRST RESOLUTION

The General Assembly, recalling the provisions of the Charter, decides that any proposal in the United Nations General Assembly which would result in depriving the Republic of China of representation in the United Nations is an important question under Article 18 of the Charter.

SECOND RESOLUTION

The General Assembly, having considered the item entitled "the Representation of China in the United Nations,"

Noting that since the founding of the United Nations, fundamental changes have occurred in China,

Having regard for the existing factual situation,

Noting that the Republic of China has been continuously represented as a member of the United Nations since 1945,

Believing that the People's Republic of China should be represented in the United Nations,

Recalling that Article 1, Paragraph 4, of the Charter of the United Nations establishes the United Nations as a center for harmonizing the actions of nations,

Believing that an equitable resolution of this problem should be sought in the light of the above-mentioned considerations and without prejudice to the eventual settlement of the conflicting claims involved,

Hereby affirms the right of representation of the People's Republic of China and recommends that it be seated as one of the five permanent members of the Security Council,

Affirms the continued right of representation of the Republic of China;

Recommends that all United Nations bodies and the specialized agencies take into account the provisions of this resolution in deciding the question of Chinese representation.

682. GILLETTE v. UNITED STATES
401 U.S. 437
1971

Certiorari to the U.S. Court of Appeals, 2nd Circuit. This court had upheld the U.S. District Court for the Northern District of California, which had denied petitioner's postinduction habeas corpus petition. The Supreme Court in the *Seeger* (see Doc. No. 659) and *Welsh* cases recognized the necessity of expanding the constitutional basis of the conscientious objector status beyond the First Amendment's free exercise and establishment clauses. *Welsh* v. *U.S.* found that a claimant opposed to all wars need only demonstrate the sincerity of his belief; no religious basis for the belief need exist. Here the Court decided whether selective conscientious objection—objection to a particular war—was constitutionally acceptable. Petitioner, Guy

Gillette, refused to report for induction and claimed that he was entitled to conscientious objector status on the grounds of opposition only to the war in Vietnam. His appeal was decided upon simultaneously with that of Louis Negre, another petitioner for selective conscientious objector exemption. See Hochstadt, "The Right to Exemption from Military Service of a Constitutional Objector to a Particular War," 3 *Harvard Civil Liberties–Civil Rights Law Rev.* (1967); M. E. Tigar, "The Right of Selective Service Registrants," in N. Dorsen, ed., *The Rights of Americans;* K. Greenawalt, "All or Nothing at All: The Defeat of Selective Conscientious Objection," in P. Kurland, ed., *The Supreme Court Review,* 1971.

MARSHALL, J. . . . These cases present the question whether conscientious objection to a particular war, rather than objection to war as such, relieves the objector from responsibilities of military training and service. Specifically, we are called upon to decide whether conscientious scruples relating to a particular conflict are within the purview of established provisions relieving conscientious objectors to war from military service. Both petitioners also invoke constitutional principles barring government interference with the exercise of religion and requiring governmental neutrality in matters of religion.

In No. 85, petitioner Gillette was convicted of wilful failure to report for induction into the armed forces. Gillette defended on the ground that he should have been ruled exempt from induction as a conscientious objector to war. In support of his unsuccessful request for classification as a conscientious objector, this petitioner had stated his willingness to participate in a war of national defense or a war sponsored by the United Nations as a peace-keeping measure, but declared his opposition to American military operations in Vietnam, which he characterized as "unjust." Petitioner concluded that he could not in conscience enter and serve in the armed forces during the period of the Vietnam conflict. Gillette's view of his duty to abstain from any involvement in a war seen as unjust is, in his words, "based on a humanist approach to religion," and his personal decision concerning military service was guided by fundamental principles of conscience and deeply held views about the purpose and obligation of human existence. . . .

We granted certiorari in these cases, . . . in order to resolve vital issues concerning the exercise of congressional power to raise and support armies, as affected by the religious guaranties of the First Amendment. We affirm the judgments below in both cases.

Each petitioner claims a nonconstitutional right to be relieved of the duty of military service in virtue of his conscientious scruples. Both claims turn on the proper construction of § 6(j) of the Military Selective Service Act of 1967, 50 U.S.C. App. § 456(j), which provides:

"Nothing contained in this title . . . shall be construed to require any person to be subject to combatant training and service in the armed forces of the United States who, by reason of religious training and belief, is conscientiously opposed to participation in war in any form."

This language controls Gillette's claim to exemption, which was asserted administratively prior to the point of induction. Department of Defense Directive No. 1300.6 (May 10, 1968), prescribes that post-induction claims to conscientious objector status shall be honored, if valid, by the various branches of the armed forces. Section 6(j) of the Act, as construed by the courts, is incorporated by the various service regulations issued pursuant to the Directive, and thus the standards for measuring claims of in-service objectors, such as Negre, are the same as the statutory tests applicable in a pre-induction situation.

For purposes of determining the statutory status of conscientious objection to a particular war, the focal language of § 6(j) is the phrase, "conscientiously opposed to participation in war in any form." This language, on a straightforward reading, can bear but one meaning; that conscientious scruples relating to war and military service must amount to conscientious opposition to participating personally in any war and all war. . . .

. . . the legislative materials simply do not support the view that Congress intended to recognize any conscientious claim whatever as a basis for relieving the claimant from the general responsibility or the various incidents of military service. The claim that is recognized by § 6(j) is a claim of conscience running against war as such. This claim, not one involving opposition to a particular war only, was plainly the focus of congressional concern.

Finding little comfort in the wording or the legislative history of § 6(j), petitioners rely heavily on dicta in the decisional law dealing with objectors whose conscientious scruples ran against war as such, but who indicated certain reservations of an abstract nature. It is instructive that none of the cases relied upon embraces an interpretation of § 6(j) at variance with the construction we adopt today.

. . . Rather we hold that Congress intended to exempt persons who oppose participating in all war—"participation in war in any form"—and that persons who object solely to participation in a particular war are not within the purview of the exempting section, even though the latter objection may have such roots in a claimant's conscience and personality that it is "religious" in character. . . .

Both petitioners argue that § 6(j), construed to cover only objectors to all war, violates the religious clauses of the First Amendment. . . .

The critical weakness of petitioners' establishment claim arises from the fact that § 6(j), on its face, simply does not discriminate on the basis of religious affiliation or religious belief, apart of course from beliefs concerning war. The section says that anyone who is conscientiously opposed to all war shall be relieved of military service. The specified objection must have a grounding in "religious training and belief," but no particular sectarian affiliation or theological position is required. . . .

Properly phrased, petitioners' contention is that the special statutory status accorded conscientious objection to all war, but not objection to a particular war, works a de facto discrimination among religions. This happens, say petitioners, because some religious faiths themselves distinguish between personal participation in "just" and in "unjust" wars, commending the former and forbidding the latter, and therefore adherents of some religious faiths—and individuals whose personal beliefs of a religious nature include the distinction—cannot object to all wars consistently with what is regarded as the true imperative of conscience. Of course this contention of de facto religious discrimination, rendering § 6(j) fatally underinclusive, cannot simply be brushed aside. The question of governmental neutrality is not concluded by the observation that § 6(j) on its face makes no discrimination between religions, for the Establishment Clause forbids subtle departures from neutrality, "religious gerrymanders," as well as obvious abuses. . . .

We conclude not only that the affirmative purposes underlying § 6(j) are neutral and secular, but also that valid neutral reasons exist for limiting the exemption to objectors to all war, and that the section therefore cannot be said to reflect a religious preference. . . .

For their part, petitioners make no attempt to provide a careful definition of the claim to exemption which they ask the courts to carve out and protect. They do not explain why objection to a particular conflict—much less an objection that focuses on a particular facet of a conflict—should excuse the objector from all military service whatever, even from military operations that are connected with the conflict at hand in remote or tenuous ways. They suggest no solution to the problems arising from the fact that altered circumstances may quickly render the objection to military service moot.

Petitioners' remaining contention is that Congress interferes with the free exercise of religion by conscripting persons who oppose a particular war on grounds of conscience and religion. Strictly viewed, this complaint does not implicate problems of comparative treatment of different sorts of objectors, but rather may be examined in some isolation from the circumstance that Congress has chosen to exempt those who conscientiously object to all war. And our holding that § 6(j) comports with the Establishment Clause does not automatically settle the present issue. For despite a general harmony of purpose between the two religious clauses of the First Amendment, the Free Exercise Clause no doubt has a reach of its own. . . .

Nonetheless, our analysis of § 6(j) for Establishment Clause purposes has revealed governmental interests of a kind and weight sufficient to justify under the Free Exercise Clause the impact of the conscription laws on those who object to particular wars.

Our cases do not at their farthest reach support the proposition that a stance of conscientious opposition relieves an objector from any colliding duty fixed by a democratic government. . . . However, our analysis of § 6(j) shows that the impact of conscription on objectors to particular wars is far from unjustified. The conscription laws, applied to such persons as to others, are not designed to interfere with any religious ritual or practice, and do not work a penalty against any theological position. The incidental burdens felt by persons in petitioners' position are strictly justified by substantial governmental interests that relate directly to the very impacts questioned. And more broadly, of course, there is the Government's interest in procuring the manpower necessary for military purposes, pursuant to the constitutional grant of power to Congress to raise and support armies. Art. I, § 8.

Since petitioners' statutory and constitutional claims to relief from military service are without merit, it follows that in Gillette's case (No. 85) there was a basis in fact to support administrative denial of exemption, and that in Negre's case (No. 325) there was a basis in fact to support the Army's denial of a discharge. Accordingly, the judgments below are affirmed.

Affirmed.

683. SWANN v. CHARLOTTE-MECKLENBURG BOARD OF EDUCATION
402 U.S. 1
1971

Certiorari from U.S. Court of Appeals for the Fourth District. The most sweeping school desegregation action since the *Brown* decision of 1954, this ruling upheld a busing decree for Charlotte-Mecklenburg County in North Carolina, which had required massive crosstown busing of children in an effort to approximate in each elementary school the ratio of 71 per cent white and 29 per cent black children that obtained in the state school system generally. The court of appeals had sustained this program only in relation to secondary schools, finding it "unreasonably burdensome" for elementary schools. The unanimous decision of the Supreme Court inaugurated a prolonged, acrimonious nationwide controversy over busing that threatened to erupt into a major political issue. See R. Carter, "The Right to Equal Educational Opportunity," in N. Dorsen, ed., *The Rights of Americans.*

Burger, C. J. We granted certiorari in this case to review important issues as to the duties of school authorities and the scope of powers of federal courts under this Court's mandates to eliminate racially separate public schools established and maintained by state action. . . .

This case and those argued with it arose in states having a long history of maintaining two sets of schools in a single school system deliberately operated to carry out a governmental policy to separate pupils in schools solely on the basis of race. That was what *Brown* v. *Board of Education* was all about. These cases present us with the problem of defining in more precise terms than heretofore the scope of the duty of school authorities and district courts in implementing *Brown I* and the mandate to eliminate dual systems and establish unitary systems at once. Meanwhile district courts and courts of appeals have struggled in hundreds of cases with a multitude and variety of problems under this Court's general directive. Understandably, in an area of evolving remedies, those courts had to improvise and experiment without detailed or specific guidelines. This Court, in *Brown I,* appropriately dealt with the large constitutional principles; other federal courts had to grapple with the flinty, intractable realities of day-to-day implementation of those constitutional commands. Their efforts, of necessity, embraced a process of "trial and error," and our effort to formulate guidelines must take into account their experience. . . .

The central issue in this case is that of student assignment, and there are essentially four problem areas:

(1) to what extent racial balance or racial quotas may be used as an implement in a remedial order to correct a previously segregated system;

(2) whether every all-Negro and all-white school must be eliminated as an indispensable part of a remedial process of desegregation;

(3) what are the limits, if any, on the rearrangement of school districts and attendance zones, as a remedial measure; and

(4) what are the limits, if any, on the

use of transportation facilities to correct state-enforced racial school segregation.

(1) RACIAL BALANCES OR RACIAL QUOTAS

The constant theme and thrust of every holding from *Brown I* to date is that state-enforced separation of races in public schools is discrimination that violates the Equal Protection Clause. The remedy commanded was to dismantle dual school systems.

We are concerned in these cases with the elimination of the discrimination inherent in the dual school systems, not with myriad factors of human existence which can cause discrimination in a multitude of ways on racial, religious, or ethnic grounds. The target of the cases from *Brown I* to the present was the dual school system. The elimination of racial discrimination in public schools is a large task and one that should not be retarded by efforts to achieve broader purposes lying beyond the jurisdiction of school authorities. One vehicle can carry only a limited amount of baggage. It would not serve the important objective of *Brown I* to seek to use school desegregation cases for purposes beyond their scope, although desegregation of schools ultimately will have impact on other forms of discrimination. We do not reach in this case the question whether a showing that school segregation is a consequence of other types of state action, without any discriminatory action by the school authorities, is a constitutional violation requiring remedial action by a school desegregation decree. This case does not present that question and we therefore do not decide it.

Our objective in dealing with the issues presented by these cases is to see that school authorities exclude no pupil of a racial minority from any school, directly or indirectly, on account of race; it does not and cannot embrace all the problems of racial prejudice, even when those problems contribute to disproportionate racial concentrations in some schools.

In this case it is urged that the District Court has imposed a racial balance requirement of 71%–29% on individual schools. The fact that no such objective was actually achieved—and would appear to be impossible—tends to blunt that claim, yet in the opinion and order of the District Court of December 1, 1969, we find that court directing:

"that efforts should be made to reach a 71–29 ratio in the various schools so that there will be no basis for contending that one school is racially different from the others . . . , that no school [should] be operated with an all-black or predominantly black student body, [and] that pupils of all grades [should] be assigned in such a way that as nearly as practicable the various schools at various grade levels have about the same proportion of black and white students."

The District Judge went on to acknowledge that variation "from that norm may be unavoidable." This contains intimations that the "norm" is a fixed mathematical racial balance reflecting the pupil constituency of the system. If we were to read the holding of the District Court to require, as a matter of substantive constitutional right, any particular degree of racial balance or mixing, that approach would be disapproved and we would be obliged to reverse. The constitutional command to desegregate schools does not mean that every school in every community must always reflect the racial composition of the school system as a whole. . . .

We see therefore that the use made of mathematical ratios was no more than a starting point in the process of shaping a remedy, rather than an inflexible requirement. From that starting point the District Court proceeded to frame a decree that was within its discretionary powers, an equitable remedy for the particular circumstances. As we said in *Green*, a school authority's remedial plan or a district court's remedial decree is to be judged by its effectiveness. Awareness of the racial composition of the whole school system is likely to be a useful starting point in shaping a remedy to correct past constitutional violations. In sum, the very limited use made of mathematical ratios was within the equitable remedial discretion of the District Court.

(2) ONE-RACE SCHOOLS

The record in this case reveals the familiar phenomenon that in metropolitan areas minority groups are often found concentrated in one part of the city. In some circumstances certain schools may remain all or largely of one race until new schools can be provided or neighborhood patterns change. Schools all or predominantly of one race in a district of mixed population will require close scrutiny to determine that school assignments are not part of state-enforced segregation.

In light of the above, it should be clear that the existence of some small number of one-race, or virtually one-race, schools within a district is not in and of itself the mark of a system which still practices segregation by law. The district judge or school authorities should make every effort to achieve the greatest possible degree of actual desegregation and will thus necessarily be concerned with the elimination of one-race schools. No *per se* rule can adequately embrace all the difficulties of reconciling the competing interests involved; but in a system with a history of segregation the need for remedial criteria of sufficient specificity to assure a school authority's compliance with its constitutional duty warrants a presumption against schools that are substantially disproportionate in their racial composition. Where the school authority's proposed plan for conversion from a dual to a unitary system contemplates the continued existence of some schools that are all or predominantly of one race, they have the burden of showing that such school assignments are genuinely nondiscriminatory. The court should scrutinize such schools, and the burden upon the school authorities will be to satisfy the court that their racial composition is not the result of present or past discriminatory action on their part.

An optional majority-to-minority transfer provision has long been recognized as a useful part of every desegregation plan. Provision for optional transfer of those in the majority racial group of a particular school to other schools where they will be in the minority is an indispensable remedy for those students willing to transfer to other schools in order to lessen the impact on them of the state-imposed stigma of segregation. In order to be effective, such a transfer arrangement must grant the transferring student free transportation and space must be made available in the school to which he desires to move. . . .

(3) REMEDIAL ALTERING OF ATTENDANCE ZONES

The maps submitted in these cases graphically demonstrate that one of the principal tools employed by school planners and by courts to break up the dual school system has been a frank—and sometimes drastic—gerrymandering of school districts and attendance zones. An additional step was pairing, "clustering," or "grouping" of schools with attendance assignments made deliberately to accomplish the transfer of Negro students out of formerly segregated Negro schools and transfer of white students to formerly all-Negro schools. More often than not, these zones are neither compact nor contiguous; indeed they may be on opposite ends of the city. As an interim corrective measure, this cannot be said to be beyond the broad remedial powers of a court.

Absent a constitutional violation there would be no basis for judicially ordering assignment of students on a racial basis. All things being equal, with no history of discrimination, it might well be desirable to assign pupils to schools nearest their homes. But all things are not equal in a system that has been deliberately constructed and maintained to enforce racial segregation. The remedy for such segregation may be administratively awkward, inconvenient and even bizarre in some situations and may impose burdens on some; but all awkwardness and inconvenience cannot be avoided in the interim period when remedial adjustments are being made to eliminate the dual school systems.

No fixed or even substantially fixed guidelines can be established as to how far a court can go, but it must be recognized that there are limits. The objective is to dismantle the dual school system. "Racially neutral" assignment plans proposed by school authorities to a district court may be inadequate; such plans may fail to counteract the continuing effects of past school segregation resulting from discriminatory location of school sites or distortion of school size in order to achieve or maintain an artificial racial separation. When school authorities present a district court with a "loaded game board," affirmative action in the form of remedial altering of attendance zones is proper to achieve truly nondiscriminatory assignments. In short, an assignment plan is not acceptable simply because it appears to be neutral.

In this area, we must of necessity rely to a large extent, as this Court has for more than sixteen years, on the informed judgment of the district courts in the first instance and on courts of appeals.

We hold that the pairing and grouping of non-contiguous school zones is a permissible tool and such action is to be considered in light of the objectives sought. Judicial steps in shaping such zones going beyond combinations of contiguous areas should be examined in light of what is said [above] concerning the objectives to be sought. Maps do not tell the whole story since non-contiguous school zones may be more accessible to each other in terms of the critical travel time, because of traffic patterns and good highways, than schools geographically closer together. Conditions in different localities will vary so widely that no rigid rules can be laid down to govern all situations.

(4) TRANSPORTATION OF STUDENTS

The scope of permissible transportation of students as an implement of a remedial decree has never been defined by this Court and by the very nature of the problem it cannot be defined with precision. No rigid guidelines as to student transportation can be given for application to the infinite variety of problems presented in thousands of situations. Bus transportation has been an integral part of the public education system for years, and was perhaps the single most important factor in the transition from the one-room schoolhouse to the consolidated school. Eighteen million of the nation's public school children, approximately 39%, were transported to their schools by bus in 1969–1970 in all parts of the country.

The importance of bus transportation as a normal and accepted tool of educational policy is readily discernible in this and the companion case. The Charlotte school authorities did not purport to assign students on the basis of geographically drawn zones until 1965 and then they allowed almost unlimited transfer privileges. The District Court's conclusion that assignment of children to the school nearest their home serving their grade would not produce an effective dismantling of the dual system is supported by the record.

Thus the remedial techniques used in the District Court's order were within that court's power to provide equitable relief; implementation of the decree is well within the capacity of the school authority.

The decree provided that the buses used to implement the plan would operate on direct routes. Students would be picked up at schools near their homes and transported to the schools they were to attend. The trips for elementary school pupils average about seven miles and the District Court found that they would take "not over thirty-five minutes at the most." This system compares favorably with the transportation plan previously operated in Charlotte under which each day 23,600 students on all grade levels were transported an average of fifteen miles one way for an average trip requiring over an hour. In these circumstances, we find no basis for holding that the local school authorities may not be required to employ bus transportation as one tool of school desegregation. Desegregation plans cannot be limited to the walk-in school.

An objection to transportation of students may have validity when the time or distance of travel is so great as to risk either the health of the children or significantly impinge on the educational process. District courts must weigh the soundness of any transportation plan in light of what is said . . . above. It hardly needs stating that the limits on time of travel will vary with many factors, but probably with none more than the age of the students. The reconciliation of competing values in a desegregation case is, of course, a difficult task with many sensitive facets but fundamentally no more so than remedial measures courts of equity have traditionally employed.

The Court of Appeals, searching for a term to define the equitable remedial power of the district courts, used the term "reasonableness." In *Green, supra,* this Court used the term "feasible" and by implication, "workable," "effective," and "realistic" in the mandate to develop "a plan that promises realistically to work, and . . . to work *now."* On the facts of this case, we are unable to conclude that the order of the District Court is not reasonable, feasible and workable. However, in seeking to define the scope of remedial power or the limits on remedial power of courts in an area as sensitive as we deal with here, words are poor instruments to convey the sense of basic fairness inherent in equity. Substance, not semantics, must govern, and we have sought to suggest the nature of limitations without frustrating the appropriate scope of equity.

At some point, these school authorities and others like them should have achieved full compliance with this Court's decision in *Brown I.* The systems will then be "uni-

tary" in the sense required by our decisions in *Green* and *Alexander.*

It does not follow that the communities served by such systems will remain demographically stable, for in a growing, mobile society, few will do so. Neither school authorities nor district courts are constitutionally required to make year-by-year adjustments of the racial composition of student bodies once the affirmative duty to desegregate has been accomplished and racial discrimination through official action is eliminated from the system. This does not mean that federal courts are without power to deal with future problems; but in the absence of a showing that either the school authorities or some other agency of the State has deliberately attempted to fix or alter demographic patterns to affect the racial composition of the schools, further intervention by a district court should not be necessary.

For the reasons herein set forth, the judgment of the Court of Appeals is affirmed as to those parts in which it affirmed the judgment of the District Court. The order of the District Court dated August 7, 1970, is also affirmed. It is so ordered.

684. NEW YORK TIMES CO. v. UNITED STATES
403 U.S. 713
1971

Writ of certiorari to the U.S. Court of Appeals for the Second Circuit. This dramatic case involved the right of the *New York Times*—as well as the *Washington Post* and other newspapers throughout the land—to publish substantial extracts from the so-called Pentagon Papers, a secret history of the war prepared for Secretary of Defense McNamara and classified "top secret." These papers had been removed from the temporary custody of the Rand Corporation by Daniel Ellsberg and made available to numerous newspapers. As they contained documents bearing on high-level military, diplomatic, and military decisions, the Justice Department argued that their publication would work "irreparable injury" to the "national security" and asked—for the first time in American history—for prior censorship. Two circuit courts granted temporary injunctions, but on appeal the Supreme Court rejected these on constitutional grounds. The issues of the case were not par-

ticularly complex but the opinions of the Court were: the justices wrote altogether nine opinions for a total of some 11,000 words, with no one opinion commanding the support of more than three judges. We give here the majority opinion by Justice Black—his last major opinion before his death three months later—and excerpts from the most respectable of the dissenting opinions, that of Justice Harlan. See H. Kalven, Jr., "The Right to Publish," in N. Dorsen, ed., *The Rights of Americans;* "Media and the First Amendment in a Free Society," 60 *Georgetown Law J.* (March 1972).

MR. JUSTICE BLACK, with whom MR. JUSTICE DOUGLAS joins, concurring.

I adhere to the view that the Government's case against the Washington Post should have been dismissed and that the injunction against the New York Times should have been vacated without oral argument when the cases were first presented to this Court. I believe that every moment's continuance of the injunctions against these newspapers amounts to a flagrant, indefensible, and continuing violation of the First Amendment. Furthermore, after oral arguments, I agree completely that we must affirm the judgment of the Court of Appeals for the District of Columbia and reverse the judgment of the Court of Appeals for the Second Circuit for the reasons stated by my Brothers Douglas and Brennan. In my view it is unfortunate that some of my Brethren are apparently willing to hold that the publication of news may sometimes be enjoined. Such a holding would make a shambles of the First Amendment.

Our Government was launched in 1789 with the adoption of the Constitution. The Bill of Rights, including the First Amendment, followed in 1791. Now, for the first time in the 182 years since the founding of the Republic, the federal courts are asked to hold that the First Amendment does not mean what it says, but rather means that the Government can halt the publication of current news of vital importance to the people of this country.

In seeking injunctions against these newspapers and in its presentation to the Court, the Executive Branch seems to have forgotten the essential purpose and history of the First Amendment. . . .

. . . The amendments were offered to *curtail* and *restrict* the general powers granted to the Executive, Legislative, and Judicial branches two years before in the original Constitution. The Bill of Rights changed the original Constitution into a new charter under which no branch of government could abridge the people's freedoms of press, speech, religion, and assembly. Yet the Solicitor General argues and some members of the Court appear to agree that the general powers of the Government adopted in the original Constitution should be interpreted to limit and restrict the specific and emphatic guarantees of the Bill of Rights adopted later. I can imagine no greater perversion of history. . . .

In the First Amendment the Founding Fathers gave the free press the protection it must have to fulfill its essential role in our democracy. The press was to serve the governed, not the governors. The Government's power to censor the press was abolished so that the press would remain forever free to censure the Government. The press was protected so that it could bare the secrets of government and inform the people. Only a free and unrestrained press can effectively expose deception in government. And paramount among the responsibilities of a free press is the duty to prevent any part of the government from deceiving the people and sending them off to distant lands to die of foreign fevers and foreign shot and shell. In my view, far from deserving condemnation for their courageous reporting, the New York Times, the Washington Post, and other newspapers should be commended for serving the purpose that the Founding Fathers saw so clearly. In revealing the workings of government that led to the Vietnam war, the newspapers nobly did precisely that which the Founders hoped and trusted they would do. . . .

. . . [W]e are asked to hold that despite the First Amendment's emphatic command, the Executive Branch, the Congress, and the Judiciary can make laws enjoining publication of current news and abridging freedom of the press in the name of "national security." The Government does not even attempt to rely on any act of Congress. Instead it makes the bold and dangerously far-reaching contention that the courts should take it upon themselves to "make" a law abridging freedom of the press in the name of equity, presidential power and national security, even when the representatives of the people in Congress have adhered to the command of the First Amendment and refused to make such a law. . . . To find that the President has "inherent power" to halt the publication of news by resort to the courts would wipe out the First Amendment and destroy the fundamental liberty and security of the very people the Government hopes to make "secure." No one can read the history of the adoption of the First Amendment without being convinced beyond any doubt that it was injunctions like those sought here that

Madison and his collaborators intended to outlaw in this Nation for all time.

The word "security" is a broad, vague generality whose contours should not be invoked to abrogate the fundamental law embodied in the First Amendment. The guarding of military and diplomatic secrets at the expense of informed representative government provides no real security for our Republic. The Framers of the First Amendment, fully aware of both the need to defend a new nation and the abuses of the English and Colonial governments, sought to give this new society strength and security by providing that freedom of speech, press, religion, and assembly should not be abridged. This thought was eloquently expressed in 1937 by Mr. Chief Justice Hughes—great man and great Chief Justice that he was—when the Court held a man could not be punished for attending a meeting run by Communists.

"The greater the importance of safeguarding the community from incitements to the overthrow of our institutions by force and violence, the more imperative is the need to preserve inviolate the constitutional rights of free speech, free press and free assembly in order to maintain the opportunity for free political discussion, to the end that government may be responsive to the will of the people and that changes, if desired, may be obtained by peaceful means. Therein lies the security of the Republic, the very foundation of constitutional government."

MR. JUSTICE HARLAN, with whom THE CHIEF JUSTICE and MR. JUSTICE BLACKMUN join, dissenting.

These cases forcefully call to mind the wise admonition of Mr. Justice Holmes, dissenting in *Northern Securities Co.* v. *United States,* 193 U.S. 197, 400–401 (1904):

"Great cases like hard cases make bad law. For great cases are called great, not by reason of their real importance in shaping the law of the future, but because of some accident of immediate overwhelming interest which appeals to the feelings and distorts the judgment. These immediate interests exercise a kind of hydraulic pressure which makes what previously was clear seem doubtful, and before which

even well settled principles of law will bend."

With all respect, I consider that the Court has been almost irresponsibly feverish in dealing with these cases. . . .

This frenzied train of events took place in the name of the presumption against prior restraints created by the First Amendment. Due regard for the extraordinarily important and difficult questions involved in these litigations should have led the Court to shun such a precipitate timetable. In order to decide the merits of these cases properly, some or all of the following questions should have been faced:

1. Whether the Attorney General is authorized to bring these suits in the name of the United States. Compare *In re Debs,* 158 U.S. 564 (1895), with *Youngstown Sheet & Tube Co.* v. *Sawyer,* 343 U.S. 579 (1952). This question involves as well the construction and validity of a singularly opaque statute—the Espionage Act, 18 U.S.C. § 793(e).

2. Whether the First Amendment permits the federal courts to enjoin publication of stories which would present a serious threat to national security. See *Near* v. *Minnesota,* 283 U.S. 697, 716 (1931) (dictum).

3. Whether the threat to publish highly secret documents is of itself a sufficient implication of national security to justify an injunction on the theory that regardless of the contents of the documents harm enough results simply from the demonstration of such a breach of secrecy.

4. Whether the unauthorized disclosure of any of these particular documents would seriously impair the national security.

5. What weight should be given to the opinion of high officers in the Executive Branch of the Government with respect to questions 3 and 4.

6. Whether the newspapers are entitled to retain and use the documents not withstanding the seemingly uncontested facts that the documents, or the originals of which they are duplicates, were purloined from the Government's possession and that the newspapers received them with knowledge that they had been feloniously acquired. Cf. *Liberty Lobby, Inc.* v. *Pearson,* 390 F.2d 489 (1968).

7. Whether the threatened harm to the

national security or the Governmnet's possessory interest in the documents justifies the issuance of an injunction against publication in light of—

a. The strong First Amendment policy against prior restraints on publication;

b. The doctrine against enjoining conduct in violation of criminal statutes; and

c. The extent to which the materials at issue have apparently already been otherwise disseminated.

These are difficult questions of fact, of law, and of judgment; the potential consequences of erroneous decision are enormous. The time which has been available to us, to the lower courts, and to the parties has been wholly inadequate for giving these cases the kind of consideration they deserve. It is a reflection on the stability of the judicial process that these great issues—as important as any that have arisen during my time on the Court—should have been decided under the pressures engendered by the torrent of publicity that has attended these litigations from their inception.

Forced as I am to reach the merits of these cases, I dissent from the opinion and judgments of the Court. Within the severe limitations imposed by the time constraints under which I have been required to operate, I can only state my reasons in telescoped form, even though in different circumstances I would have felt constrained to deal with the cases in the fuller sweep indicated above.

It is a sufficient basis for affirming the Court of Appeals for the Second Circuit in the *Times* litigation to observe that its order must rest on the conclusion that because of the time elements the Government had not been given an adequate opportunity to present its case to the District Court. At the least this conclusion was not an abuse of discretion.

In the *Post* litigation the Government had more time to prepare; this was apparently the basis for the refusal of the Court of Appeals for the District of Columbia Circuit on rehearing to conform its judgment to that of the Second Circuit. But I think there is another and more fundamental reason why this judgment cannot stand—a reason which also furnishes an additional ground

for not reinstating the judgment of the District Court in the *Times* litigation, set aside by the Court of Appeals. It is plain to me that the scope of the judicial function in passing upon the activities of the Executive Branch of the Government in the field of foreign affairs is very narrowly restricted. This view is, I think, dictated by the concept of separation of powers upon which our constitutional system rests.

In a speech on the floor of the House of Representatives, Chief Justice John Marshall, then a member of that body, stated:

"The President is the sole organ of the nation in its external relations, and its sole representative with foreign nations." 10 Annals of Cong. 613 (1800).

From that time, shortly after the founding of the Nation, to this, there has been no substantial challenge to this description of the scope of executive power. See *United States* v. *Curtiss-Wright Corp.,* 299 U.S. 304, 319–321 (1936), collecting authorities.

From this constitutional primacy in the field of foreign affairs, it seems to me that certain conclusions necessarily follow. Some of these were stated concisely by President Washington, declining the request of the House of Representatives for the papers leading up to the negotiation of the Jay Treaty:

"The nature of foreign negotiations requires caution, and their success must often depend on secrecy; and even when brought to a conclusion a full disclosure of all the measures, demands, or eventual concessions which may have been proposed or contemplated would be extremely impolitic; for this might have a pernicious influence on future negotiations, or produce immediate inconveniences, perhaps danger and mischief, in relation to other powers." 1 J. Richardson, Messages and Papers of the Presidents 194–195 (1896).

The power to evaluate the "pernicious influence" of premature disclosure is not, however, lodged in the Executive alone. I agree that, in performance of its duty to protect the values of the First Amendment against political pressures, the judiciary must review the initial Executive determination to the point of satisfying itself that the subject matter of the dispute does lie within the proper compass of the President's foreign relations power. Constitutional considerations forbid "a complete abandonment of judicial control." Cf. *United States* v. *Reynolds,* 345 U.S. 1, 8 (1953). Moreover, the judiciary may properly insist that the determination that disclosure of the subject matter would irreparably impair the national security be made by the head of the Executive Department concerned—here the Secretary of State or the Secretary of Defense—after actual personal consideration by that officer. This safeguard is required in the analogous area of executive claims of privilege for secrets of state. See *id.,* at 8 and n. 20; *Duncan* v. *Cammell, Laird & Co.,* [1942] A. C. 624, 638 (House of Lords).

But in my judgment the judiciary may not properly go beyond these two inquiries and redetermine for itself the probable impact of disclosure on the national security.

"[T]he very nature of executive decisions as to foreign policy is political, not judicial. Such decisions are wholly confided by our Constitution to the political departments of the government, Executive and Legislative. They are delicate, complex, and involve large elements of prophecy. They are and should be undertaken only by those directly responsible to the people whose welfare they advance or imperil. They are decisions of a kind for which the Judiciary has neither aptitude, facilities nor responsibility and which has long been held to belong in the domain of political power not subject to judicial intrusion or inquiry." *Chicago & Southern Air Lines* v. *Waterman Steamship Corp.,* 333 U.S. 103, 111 (1948) (Jackson, J.).

Even if there is some room for the judiciary to override the executive determination, it is plain that the scope of review must be exceedingly narrow. I can see no indication in the opinions of either the District Court or the Court of Appeals in the *Post* litigation that the conclusions of the Executive were given even the deference owing to an administrative agency, much less that owing to a co-equal branch of the Government operating within the field of its constitutional prerogative.

Accordingly, I would vacate the judgment of the Court of Appeals for the District of Columbia Circuit on this ground and remand the case for further proceedings in the District Court. Before the commencement of such further proceedings, due opportunity should be afforded the Government for procuring from the Secretary of State or the Secretary of Defense or both an expression of their views on the issue of national security. The ensuing review by the District Court should be in accordance with the views expressed in this opinion. And for the reasons stated above I would affirm the judgment of the Court of Appeals for the Second Circuit.

Pending further hearings in each case conducted under the appropriate ground rules, I would continue the restraints on publication. I cannot believe that the doctrine prohibiting prior restraints reaches to the point of preventing courts from maintaining the *status quo* long enough to act responsibly in matters of such national importance as those involved here.

685. JOINT CHINESE–UNITED STATES COMMUNIQUÉ ISSUED AT SHANGHAI
February 27, 1972
(*Department of State Bulletin,* March 20, 1972)

This joint Sino-U.S. communiqué is one of the considerable ironies of recent history. Richard Nixon had been a leading protagonist of the bipartisan cold war with both the Soviet Union and China, and had advocated military containment, political quarantine, and exclusion from the United Nations. In 1972, he decisively

reversed this China policy. Following a mismanaged American defeat at the United Nations, China was admitted to this international organization; shortly after this development, President Nixon visited China itself. On the last day of his unprecedented mission, the President and Premier Chou En-lai released a joint 1,800-word statement indicating that their talks had resulted in agreement upon the need for increased Sino-American contacts and for eventual withdrawal of U.S. troops from Formosa. This communiqué began with a general account of President Nixon's vision of the future for both countries; then each recorded separately its views on Far Eastern policy and issues. The sections given here are what followed. See M. Oksenberg, "The Strategies of Peking," and J. Cohen, "Recognizing China," *Foreign Affairs,* October 1971.

The U.S. side stated: Peace in Asia and peace in the world requires efforts both to reduce immediate tensions and to eliminate the basic causes of conflict. The United States will work for a just and secure peace: just, because it fulfills the aspirations of peoples and nations for freedom and progress; secure, because it removes the danger of foreign aggression. The United States supports individual freedom and social progress for all the peoples of the world, free of outside pressure or intervention. The United States believes that the effort to reduce tensions is served by improving communication between countries that have different ideologies so as to lessen the risks of confrontation through accident, miscalculation or misunderstanding. Countries should treat each other with mutual respect and be willing to compete peacefully, letting performance be the ultimate judge. No country should claim infallibility and each country should be prepared to re-examine its own attitudes for the common good. The United States stressed that the peoples of Indochina should be allowed to determine their destiny without outside intervention; its constant primary objective has been a negotiated solution; the eight-point proposal put forward by the Republic of Vietnam and the United States on January 27, 1972 represents a basis for the attainment of that objective; in the absence of a negotiated settlement the United States envisages the ultimate withdrawal of all U.S. forces from the region consistent with the aim of self-determination for each country of Indochina. The United States will maintain its close ties with and support for the Republic of Korea; the United States will support efforts of the Republic of Korea to seek a relaxation of tension and increased communication in the Korean peninsula. The United States places the highest value on its friendly relations with Japan; it will continue to develop the existing close bonds. Consistent with the United Nations Security Council Resolution of December 21, 1971, the United States favors the continuation of the ceasefire between India and Pakistan and the withdrawal of all military forces to within their own territories and to their own sides of the ceasefire line in Jammu and Kashmir; the United States supports the right of the peoples of South Asia to shape their own future in peace, free of military threat, and without having the area become the subject of great power rivalry.

The Chinese side stated: Wherever there is oppression, there is resistance. Countries want independence, nations want liberation and the people want revolution—this has become the irresistible trend of history. All nations, big or small, should be equal; big nations should not bully the small and strong nations should not bully the weak. China will never be a superpower and it opposes hegemony and power politics of any kind. The Chinese side stated that it firmly supports the struggles of all the oppressed people and nations for freedom and liberation and that the people of all countries have the right to choose their social systems according to their own wishes and the right to safeguard the independence, sovereignty and territorial integrity of their own countries and oppose foreign aggression, interference, control and subversion. All foreign troops should be withdrawn to their own countries.

The Chinese side expressed its firm support to the peoples of Vietnam, Laos and Cambodia in their efforts for the attainment of their goal and its firm support to the seven-point proposal of the Provisional Revolutionary Government of the Republic of South Vietnam and the elaboration of February this year on the two key problems in the proposal, and to the Joint Declaration of the Summit Conference of the Indochinese Peoples. It firmly supports the eight-point program for the peaceful unification of Korea put forward by the Government of the Democratic People's Republic of Korea on April 12, 1971, and the stand for the abolition of the "U.N. Commission for the Unification and Rehabilitation of Korea." It firmly opposes the revival and outward expansion of Japanese militarism and firmly supports the Japanese people's desire to build an independent, democratic, peaceful and neutral Japan. It firmly maintains that India and Pakistan should, in accordance with the United Nations resolutions on the India-Pakistan question, immediately withdraw all their forces to their respective territories and to their own sides of the ceasefire line in Jammu and Kashmir and firmly supports the Pakistan Government and people in their struggle to preserve their independence and sovereignty and the people of Jammu and Kashmir in their struggle for the right of self-determination.

There are essential differences between China and the United States in their social systems and foreign policies. However, the two sides agreed that countries, regardless of their social systems, should conduct their relations on the principles of respect for the sovereignty and territorial integrity of all states, non-aggression against other states, non-interference in the internal affairs of other states, equality and mutual benefit, and peaceful coexistence. International disputes should be settled on this basis, without resorting to the use or threat of force. The United States and the People's Republic of China are prepared to apply these principles to their mutual relations.

With these principles of international relations in mind the two sides stated that:

—progress toward the normalization of relations between China and the United States is in the interests of all countries;
—both wish to reduce the danger of international military conflict;
—neither should seek hegemony in the Asia-Pacific region and each is opposed to efforts by any other country or group of countries to establish such hegemony; and
—neither is prepared to negotiate on behalf of any third party or to enter into agreements or understandings with the other directed at other states.

Both sides are of the view that it would be against the interests of the peoples of the world for any major country to collude with another against other countries, or for major countries to divide up the world into spheres of interest.

The two sides reviewed the long-standing serious disputes between China and the United States. The Chinese side reaffirmed its position: The Taiwan question is the crucial question obstructing the normalization of relations between China and the United States; the Government of the People's Republic of China is the sole legal government of China; Taiwan is a province of China which has long been returned to the motherland; the liberation of Taiwan is China's internal affair in which no other country has the right to interfere; and all U.S. forces and military installations must be withdrawn from Taiwan. The Chinese Government firmly opposes any activities which aim at the creation of "one China, one Taiwan," "one China, two governments," "two Chinas," and "independent Taiwan" or advocate that "the status of Taiwan remains to be determined."

The U.S. side declared: The United States acknowledges that all Chinese on either side of the Taiwan Strait maintain there is but one China and that Taiwan is a part of China. The United States Government does not challenge that position. It reaffirms its interest in a peaceful settlement of the Taiwan question by the Chinese themselves. With this prospect in mind, it affirms the ultimate objective of the withdrawal of all U.S. forces and military installations from Taiwan. In the meantime, it will progressively reduce its forces and military installations on Taiwan as the tension in the area diminishes.

The two sides agreed that it is desirable to broaden the understanding between the two peoples. To this end, they discussed specific areas in such fields as science, technology, culture, sports and journalism, in which people-to-people contacts and exchanges would be mutually beneficial. Each side undertakes to facilitate the further development of such contacts and exchanges.

Both sides view bilateral trade as another area from which mutual benefit can be derived, and agreed that economic relations based on equality and mutual benefit are in the interest of the peoples of the two countries. They agree to facilitate the progressive development of trade between their two countries.

The two sides agreed that they will stay in contact through various channels, including the sending of a senior U.S. representative to Peking from time to time for concrete consultations to further the normalization of relations between the two countries and continue to exchange views on issues of common interest.

The two sides expressed the hope that the gains achieved during this visit would open up new prospects for the relations between the two countries. They believe that the normalization of relations between the two countries is not only in the interest of the Chinese and American peoples but also contributes to the relaxation of tension in Asia and the world. . . .

686. PRESIDENT NIXON'S RESPONSE TO NORTH VIETNAM'S SPRING OFFENSIVE
May 8, 1972
(Department of State Bulletin, May 29, 1972)

On January 25, 1972, President Nixon announced to the nation that he had submitted to the North Vietnamese through secret channels an eight-point program, "an equitable proposal for peace." Largely repetitious of unyielding administration proposals of the past, it was followed by public and private discussions, the latter conducted by Henry Kissinger, Presidential Assistant for National Security Affairs, in Moscow and Paris. These talks maintained the same intractable spirit of earlier "peace plans." The Easter 1972 North Vietnamese offensive, the administration claimed, was further proof that the Hanoi government was the real obstacle to peace in Southeast Asia, that it would agree to a cessation of hostilities only on its own unyielding terms, and that it now violated the 1968 "agreement" between the two countries. According to the terms of this unofficial "understanding," which had resulted in President Johnson's bombing halt, both sides made concessions: North Vietnam would refrain from indiscriminate attacks on South Vietnam's major cities or through the demilitarized zone, and would tolerate American reconnaissance flights over its territory; while the United States, for its part, would halt its bombing raids north of the DMZ and fly only "protective reaction" missions—that is, attack missile and antiaircraft sites when its surveillance aircraft above the DMZ came under attack. But President Nixon early broke the "understanding." In May 1970, directly after American forces invaded Cambodia and four days after Secretary of Defense Melvin Laird stated that the agreement had "been fairly well lived up to by Hanoi" (and that "our aerial reconnaissance had been interfered with only rarely"), the President ordered a 555-plane raid on the North. He again violated the agreement, and again described the violation as a "protective reaction" raid, in November 1970, with a series of heavy American air attacks on North Vietnamese supply dumps. Now, in May 1972, in a nationwide television and radio address, President Nixon charged that North Vietnam had broken this understanding by its "massive invasion of South Vietnam." His response included sending in an armada of 800 fighter-bombers, as many as seven aircraft carriers, thirty-five destroyers and cruisers, more than 150 B-52 strategic air force bombers, upwards of 16,000 naval and air force personnel, and unleashing a bombing campaign of unprecedented ferocity. Shortly after it began, it was learned that General John Lavelle, commander of the Seventh Air Force, was relieved of his command because of unauthorized bombing missions, some twenty in all, prior to the North Vietnamese offensive across the DMZ, and because he falsified the after-action reports of these missions. Such raids on unauthorized targets were termed "protective reaction" missions. In addition to undermining civilian control of the military, these raids destroyed the credibility of President Nixon's claim that North Vietnam first violated the 1968 understanding.

Good evening.

Five weeks ago, on Easter weekend, the Communist armies of North Vietnam launched a massive invasion of South Vietnam, an invasion that was made possible by tanks, artillery, and other advanced offensive weapons supplied to Hanoi by the Soviet Union and other Communist nations.

The South Vietnamese have fought bravely to repel this brutal assault. Casualties on both sides have been very high. Most tragically, there have been over 20,000 civilian casualties, including women and children, in the cities which the North Vietnamese have shelled in wanton disregard of human life.

As I announced in my report to the Nation twelve days ago, the role of the United States in resisting this invasion has been limited to air and naval strikes on military targets in North and South Vietnam. As I also pointed out in that report, we have responded to North Vietnam's massive military offensive by undertaking wide-ranging new peace efforts aimed at ending the war through negotiation. . . . .

We now have a clear, hard choice among three courses of action: immediate withdrawal of all American forces, continued attempts at negotiation, or decisive military action to end the war.

I know that many Americans favor the first course of action, immediate withdrawal. They believe the way to end the war is for the United States to get out and to remove the threat to our remaining forces by simply withdrawing them.

From a political standpoint, this would be a very easy choice for me to accept. After all, I did not send over one-half million Americans to Vietnam. I have brought 500,000 men home from Vietnam since I took office. But abandoning our commitment in Vietnam here and now would mean turning 17 million South Vietnamese over to Communist tyranny and terror. It would mean leaving hundreds of American prisoners in Communist hands with no bargaining leverage to get them released.

An American defeat in Vietnam would encourage this kind of aggression all over the world, aggression in which smaller nations armed by their major allies could be tempted to attack neighboring nations at will in the Mideast, in Europe, and other areas. World peace would be in grave jeopardy.

The second course of action is to keep on trying to negotiate a settlement. Now, this is the course we have preferred from the beginning, and we shall continue to pursue it. We want to negotiate, but we have made every reasonable offer and tried every possible path for ending this war at the conference table.

The problem is, as you all know, it takes two to negotiate and now, as throughout the past four years, the North Vietnamese arrogantly refuse to negotiate anything but an imposition, an ultimatum that the United States impose a Communist regime on 17 million people in South Vietnam who do not want a Communist government.

It is plain then that what appears to be a choice among three courses of action for the United States is really no choice at all. The killing in this tragic war must stop. By simply getting out, we would only worsen the bloodshed. By relying solely on negotiations, we would give an intransigent enemy the time he needs to press his aggression on the battlefield.

There is only one way to stop the killing. That is to keep the weapons of war out of the hands of the international outlaws of North Vietnam.

Throughout the war in Vietnam, the United States has exercised a degree of restraint unprecedented in the annals of war. That was our responsibility as a great nation, a nation which is interested—and we can be proud of this as Americans—as America has always been, in peace not conquest.

However, when the enemy abandons all restraint, throws its whole army into battle in the territory of its neighbor, refuses to negotiate, we simply face a new situation. In these circumstances, with 60,000 Americans threatened, any President who failed to act decisively would have betrayed the trust of his country and betrayed the cause of world peace.

I therefore concluded that Hanoi must be denied the weapons and supplies it needs to continue the aggression. In full coordination with the Republic of Vietnam I have ordered the following measures, which are being implemented as I am speaking to you:

All entrances to North Vietnamese ports will be mined to prevent access to these ports and North Vietnamese naval operations from these ports.

United States forces have been directed to take appropriate measures within the internal and claimed territorial waters of North Vietnam to interdict the delivery of any supplies.

Rail and all other communications will be cut off to the maximum extent possible.

Air and naval strikes against military targets in North Vietnam will continue.

These actions are not directed against any other nation. Countries with ships presently in North Vietnamese ports have already been notified that their ships will have three daylight periods to leave in safety. After that time, the mines will become active and any ships attempting to leave or enter these ports will do so at their own risk.

These actions I have ordered will cease when the following conditions are met:

First, all American prisoners of war must be returned.

Second, there must be an internationally supervised cease-fire throughout Indochina.

Once prisoners of war are released, once the internationally supervised cease-fire has begun, we will stop all acts of force throughout Indochina, and at that time we will proceed with a complete withdrawal of all American forces from Vietnam within four months.

Now, these terms are generous terms. They are terms which would not require surrender and humiliation on the part of anybody. They would permit the United States to withdraw with honor. They would end the killing. They would bring our POW's home. They would allow negotiations on a political settlement between the Vietnamese themselves. They would permit all the nations which have suffered in this long war—Cambodia, Laos, North Vietnam, South Vietnam—to turn at last to the urgent works of healing and of peace. They deserve immediate acceptance by North Vietnam. . . .

687. JOHNSON v. LOUISIANA
92 Supreme Court Reporter 1643
1972

Appellant Frank Johnson was arrested for robbery, identified by the victim of another robbery, and tried for the latter offense before a twelve-man jury, which rendered a 9 to 3 verdict for conviction. The Louisiana Supreme Court affirmed the conviction, rejecting appellant's challenge to the jury trial provision of Louisiana law as a violation of the due process and the equal protection clauses. Justice White, joined by the four Nixon appointees, delivered the majority opinion, which upheld the state law that permitted juries to convict in state criminal cases by a less-than-unanimous vote. Dissenting, Justice Douglas charged that the majority opinion undermined the presumption of innocence, jeopardized the doctrine of guilt beyond a reasonable doubt, and affected the chances of fair trial for political and social minorities. See I. R. Kaufman, "Harbingers of Jury Reform," 58 *Am. Bar Assoc. J.* 675.

WHITE, J. . . . Under both the Louisiana Constitution and Code of Criminal Procedure, criminal cases in which the punishment is necessarily at hard labor are tried to a jury of twelve, and the vote of nine jurors is sufficient to return either a guilty or not guilty verdict. The principal question in this case is whether these provisions allowing less than unanimous verdicts in certain cases are valid under the Due Process and Equal Protection Clauses of the Fourteenth Amendment. . . .

Appellant argues that in order to give substance to the reasonable doubt standard which the State, by virtue of the Due Process Clause of the Fourteenth Amendment, must satisfy in criminal cases . . . that clause must be construed to require a unanimous jury verdict in all criminal cases. In so contending, appellant does not challenge the instructions in this case. Concededly, the jurors were told to convict only if convinced of guilt beyond a reasonable doubt. Nor is there any claim that, if the verdict in this case had been unanimous, the evidence would have been insufficient to support it. Appellant focuses instead on the fact that less than all jurors voted to convict and argues that, because three voted to acquit, the reasonable doubt standard has not been satisfied and his conviction is therefore infirm.

We note at the outset that this Court has never held jury unanimity to be a requisite of due process of law. . . .

Entirely apart from these cases, however, it is our view that the fact of three dissenting votes to acquit raises no question of constitutional substance about either the integrity or the accuracy of the majority verdict of guilt. Appellant's contrary argument breaks down into two parts, each of which we shall consider separately: first, that nine individual jurors will be unable to vote conscientiously in favor of guilt beyond a reasonable doubt when three of their colleagues are arguing for acquittal, and second, that guilt cannot be said to have been proved beyond a reasonable doubt when one or more of a jury's members at the conclusion of deliberation still possess such a doubt. Neither argument is persuasive. . . .

. . . In considering the first branch of appellant's argument, we can find no basis for holding that the nine jurors who voted for his conviction failed to follow their instructions concerning the need for proof beyond such a doubt or that the vote of any one of the nine failed to reflect an honest belief that guilt had been so proved. . . . Appellant offers no evidence that majority jurors simply ignore the reasonable doubts of their colleagues or otherwise act irresponsibly in casting their votes in favor of conviction, and before we alter our own longstanding perceptions about jury behavior and overturn a considered legislative judgment that unanimity is not essential to reasoned jury verdicts, we must have some basis for doing so other than unsupported assumptions.

We conclude, therefore, that, as to the nine jurors who voted to convict, the State satisfied its burden of proving guilt beyond any reasonable doubt. The remaining question under the Due Process Clause is whether the vote of three jurors for acquittal can be said to impeach the verdict of the other nine

and to demonstrate that guilt was not in fact proved beyond such doubt. We hold that it cannot. . . .

. . . [N]ine jurors—a substantial majority of the jury—were convinced by the evidence. In our view disagreement of three jurors does not alone establish reasonable doubt, particularly when such a heavy majority of the jury, after having considered the dissenters' views, remains convinced of guilt. That rational men disagree is not in itself equivalent to a failure of proof by the State, nor does it indicate infidelity to the reasonable doubt standard.

. . . We conclude, therefore, that verdicts rendered by nine out of twelve jurors are not automatically invalidated by the disagreement of the dissenting three. Appellant was not deprived of due process of law.

Appellant also attacks as violative of the Equal Protection Clause the provisions of Louisiana law requiring unanimous verdicts in capital and five-man jury cases, but permitting less-than-unanimous verdicts in cases such as his. We conclude, however, that the Louisiana statutory scheme serves a rational purpose and is not subject to constitutional challenge.

. . . Louisiana has permitted less serious crimes to be tried by five jurors with unanimous verdicts, more serious crimes have required the assent of nine of twelve jurors, and for the most serious crimes a unanimous verdict of twelve jurors is stipulated. In appellant's case, nine jurors rather than five or twelve were required for a verdict. We discern nothing invidious in this classification. . . . We perceive nothing unconstitutional or invidiously discriminatory, however, in a State's insisting that its burden of proof be carried with more jurors where more serious crimes or more severe punishments are at issue. . . . Appellant might well have been ultimately acquitted had he committed a capital offense. But as we have indicated, this does not constitute a denial of equal protection of the law; the State may treat capital offenders differently without violating the constitutional rights of those charged with lesser crimes. . . . We remain unconvinced by anything appellant has presented that this legislative judgment was defective in any constitutional sense. . . .

The judgment of the Supreme Court of Louisiana is therefore

Affirmed.

MR. JUSTICE DOUGLAS, with whom MR. JUSTICE BRENNAN and MR. JUSTICE MARSHALL concur, dissenting.

Appellant in the Louisiana case and petitioners in the Oregon case were convicted by juries that were less than unanimous. This procedure is authorized by both the Louisiana and Oregon Constitutions. Their claim, rejected by the majority, is that this procedure is a violation of their federal constitutional rights. With due respect to the majority, I dissent from this radical departure from American traditions. . . .

These civil rights—whether they concern speech, searches and seizures, self-incrimination, criminal prosecutions, bail, or cruel and unusual punishments extend of course to everyone, but in cold reality touch mostly the lower castes in our society. I refer of course to the Blacks, the Chicanos, the one-mule farmers, the agricultural workers, the off-beat students, the victims of the ghetto. Are we giving the States the power to experiment in diluting their civil rights? It has long been thought that the Thou Shalt Nots in the Constitution and Bill of Rights protect everyone against governmental intrusion or overreaching. The idea has been obnoxious that there are some who can be relegated to second-class citizenship. But if we construe the Bill of Rights and the Fourteenth Amendment to permit States to "experiment" with the basic rights of people, we open a veritable Pandora's box. For hate and prejudice are versatile forces that can degrade the constitutional scheme.

That, however, is only one of my concerns when we make the Bill of Rights, as applied to the States, a "watered down" version of what that charter guarantees. My chief concern is one often expressed by the late Justice Black who was alarmed at the prospect of nine men appointed for life sitting as a super-legislative body to determine whether government has gone too far. The balancing was done when the Constitution and Bill of Rights were written and adopted. For this Court to determine, say, whether one person but not another is entitled to free speech is a power never granted it. But that is the ultimate reach of a decision that lets the States, subject to our veto, to experiment with rights guaranteed by the Bill of Rights.

I would construe the Sixth Amendment, when applicable to the States, precisely as I would when applied to the Federal Government.

The plurality approves a procedure which diminishes the reliability of jury. First, it eliminates the circumstances in which a minority of jurors (a) could have rationally persuaded the entire jury to acquit, or (b) while unable to persuade the majority to acquit, nonetheless could have convinced them to convict only on a lesser-included offense. Second, it permits prosecutors in Oregon and Louisiana to enjoy a conviction-acquittal ratio substantially greater than that ordinarily returned by unanimous juries.

The diminution of verdict reliability flows from the fact that nonunanimous juries need not debate and deliberate as fully as must unanimous juries. As soon as the requisite majority is attained, further consideration is not required either by Oregon or by Louisiana even though the dissident jurors might, if given the chance, be able to convince the majority. . . .

We therefore have always held that in criminal cases we would err on the side of letting the guilty go free rather than sending the innocent to jail. We have required proof beyond a reasonable doubt as "concrete substance for the presumption of innocence."

That procedure has required a degree of patience on the part of the jurors, forcing them to deliberate in order to reach a unanimous verdict. Up until today the price has never seemed too high. Now a "law and order" judicial mood causes these barricades to be lowered.

The requirements of a unanimous jury verdict in criminal cases and proof beyond a reasonable doubt are so embedded in our constitutional law and touch so directly all the citizens and are such important barricades of liberty that if they are to be changed they should be introduced by constitutional amendment.

Today the Court approves a nine to three verdict. Would the Court relax the standard of reasonable doubt still further by resorting to eight to four verdicts or even a majority rule? Moreover, in light of today's holdings and that of *Williams* v. *Florida,* in the future would it invalidate three to two or even two to one convictions? . . .

The vast restructuring of American law which is entailed in today's decisions is for political not for judicial action. Until the Constitution is rewritten, we have the present one to support and construe. It has served us well. We lifetime appointees, who sit here only by happenstance, are the last who should sit as a Committee of Revision on rights as basic as those involved in the present cases.

Proof beyond a reasonable doubt and unanimity of criminal verdicts and the presumption of innocence are basic features of the accusatorial system. What we do today is not in that tradition but more in the tradition of the inquisition. Until amendments are adopted setting new standards, I would let no man be fined or imprisoned in derogation of what up to today was indisputably the law of the land.

688.   STRATEGIC ARMS LIMITATIONS AGREEMENTS
May 26, 1972
(*Department of State Bulletin,* June 26, 1972)

Richard Nixon was the first President to visit Moscow. On May 23, one day after his arrival there, United States and Russian officials agreed to work together on health and environmental problems; and they signed accords on May 24 on space cooperation and joint scientific and technical activities. Two days later, President Nixon and Leonid Brezhnev, General Secretary of the Russian Communist Party, signed an arms treaty that for the first time placed limits on strategic weapons. They also signed, on the same date, an interim accord on offensive systems that froze land-based and submarine-based intercontinental missiles at the level in operation or under construction at the time. See A. Pierre, "Nuclear Diplomacy: Britain, France, and America," *Foreign Affairs,* January 1971; W. Kintner and R. Pfaltzgraff, Jr., eds., *SALT: Implications for Arms Control in the 1970s.*

strategic offensive arms and would lead to a decrease in the risk of outbreak of war involving nuclear weapons,

Proceeding from the premise that the limitation of anti-ballistic missile systems, as well as certain agreed measures with respect to the limitation of strategic offensive arms, would contribute to the creation of more favorable conditions for further negotiations on limiting strategic arms,

Mindful of their obligations under Article VI of the Treaty on the Non-Proliferation of Nuclear Weapons,

Declaring their intention to achieve at the earliest possible date the cessation of the nuclear arms race and to take effective measures toward reductions in strategic arms, nuclear disarmament, and general and complete disarmament,

Desiring to contribute to the relaxation of international tension and the strengthening of trust between States,

Have agreed as follows:

TREATY ON ANTI-BALLISTIC MISSILE SYSTEMS

The United States of America and the Union of Soviet Socialist Republics, hereinafter referred to as the Parties,

Proceeding from the premise that nuclear war would have devastating consequences for all mankind,

Considering that effective measures to limit anti-ballistic missile systems would be a substantial factor in curbing the race in

ARTICLE I

1. Each Party undertakes to limit anti-ballistic missile (ABM) systems and to adopt other measures in accordance with the provisions of this Treaty.

2. Each Party undertakes not to deploy ABM systems for a defense of the territory of its country and not to provide a base for

such a defense, and not to deploy ABM systems for defense of an individual region except as provided for in Article III of this Treaty. . . .

ARTICLE III

Each Party undertakes not to deploy ABM systems or their components except that:

(a) within one ABM system deployment area having a radius of one hundred and fifty kilometers and centered on the Party's national capital, a Party may deploy: (1) no more than one hundred ABM launchers and no more than one hundred ABM interceptor missiles at launch sites, and (2) ABM radars within no more than six ABM radar complexes, the area of each complex being circular and having a diameter of no more than three kilometers; and

(b) within one ABM system deployment area having a radius of one hundred and fifty kilometers and containing ICBM silo launchers, a Party may deploy: (1) no more than one hundred ABM launchers and no more than one hundred ABM interceptor missiles at launch sites, (2) two large phased-array ABM radars comparable in potential to corresponding ABM radars operational or under construction on the date of signature of the Treaty in an ABM system deployment area containing ICBM silo launchers, and (3) no more than eighteen ABM radars each having a potential less than the potential of the smaller of the above-mentioned two large phased-array ABM radars.

ARTICLE IV

The limitations provided for in Article III shall not apply to ABM systems or their components used for development or testing, and located within current or additionally agreed test ranges. Each Party may have no more than a total of fifteen ABM launchers at test ranges.

ARTICLE V

1. Each Party undertakes not to develop, test, or deploy ABM systems or components which are sea-based, air-based, space-based, or mobile land-based.

2. Each Party undertakes not to develop, test, or deploy ABM launchers for launching more than one ABM interceptor missile at a time from each launcher, nor to modify deployed launchers to provide them with such a capability, nor to develop, test, or deploy automatic or semi-automatic or other similar systems for rapid reload of ABM launchers.

ARTICLE VI

To enhance assurance of the effectiveness of the limitations on ABM systems and their components provided by this Treaty, each Party undertakes:

(a) not to give missiles, launchers, or radars, other than ABM interceptor missiles, ABM launchers, or ABM radars, capabilities to counter strategic ballistic missiles or their elements in flight trajectory, and not to test them in an ABM mode; and

(b) not to deploy in the ·future radars for early warning of strategic ballistic missile attack except at locations along the periphery of its national territory and oriented outward.

ARTICLE VII

Subject to the provisions of this Treaty, modernization and replacement of ABM systems or their components may be carried out.

ARTICLE VIII

ABM systems or their components in excess of the numbers or outside the areas specified in this Treaty, as well as ABM systems or their components prohibited by this Treaty, shall be destroyed or dismantled under agreed procedures within the shortest possible agreed period of time.

ARTICLE IX

To assure the viability and effectiveness of this Treaty, each Party undertakes not to transfer to other States, and not to deploy outside its national territory, ABM systems or their components limited by this Treaty.

ARTICLE X

Each Party undertakes not to assume any international obligations which would conflict with this Treaty.

ARTICLE XI

The Parties undertake to continue active negotiations for limitations on strategic offensive arms.

ARTICLE XII

1. For the purpose of providing assurance of compliance with the provisions of this Treaty, each Party shall use national technical means of verification at its disposal in a manner consistent with generally recognized principles of international law.

2. Each Party undertakes not to interfere with the national technical means of verification of the other Party operating in accordance with paragraph 1 of this Article.

3. Each Party undertakes not to use deliberate concealment measures which impede verification by national technical means of compliance with the provisions of this Treaty. This obligation shall not require changes in current construction, assembly, conversion, or overhaul practices.

ARTICLE XIII

1. To promote the objectives and implementation of the provisions of this Treaty, the Parties shall establish promptly a Standing Consultative Commission, within the framework of which they will:

(a) consider questions concerning compliance with the obligations assumed and related situations which may be considered ambiguous;

(b) provide on a voluntary basis such information as either Party considers necessary to assure confidence in compliance with the obligations assumed;

(c) consider questions involving unintended interference with national technical means of verification;

(d) consider possible changes in the strategic situation which have a bearing on the provisions of this Treaty;

(e) agree upon procedures and dates for destruction or dismantling of ABM systems or their components in cases provided for by the provisions of this Treaty;

(f) consider, as appropriate, possible proposals for further increasing the viability of this Treaty, including proposals for amendments in accordance with the provisions of this Treaty;

(g) consider, as appropriate, proposals for further measures aimed at limiting strategic arms.

2. The Parties through consultation shall establish, and may amend as appropriate, Regulations for the Standing Consultative Commission governing procedures, composition and other relevant matters.

ARTICLE XIV

1. Each Party may propose amendments to this Treaty. Agreed amendments shall enter into force in accordance with the procedures governing the entry into force of this Treaty.

2. Five years after entry into force of this Treaty, and at five year intervals thereafter, the Parties shall together conduct a review of this Treaty.

ARTICLE XV

1. This Treaty shall be of unlimited duration.

2. Each Party shall, in exercising its national sovereignty, have the right to withdraw from this Treaty if it decides that extraordinary events related to the subject matter of this Treaty have jeopardized its supreme interests. It shall give notice of its decision to the other Party six months prior to withdrawal from the Treaty. Such notice shall include a statement of the extraordinary events the notifying Party regards as having jeopardized its supreme interests.

ARTICLE XVI

1. This Treaty shall be subject to ratification in accordance with the constitutional procedures of each Party. The Treaty shall enter into force on the day of the exchange of instruments of ratification.

2. This Treaty shall be registered pursuant to Article 102 of the Charter of the United Nations.

DONE at Moscow on May 26, 1972, in two copies, each in the English and Russian languages, both texts being equally authentic.

For the United States of America:

RICHARD NIXON

President of the United States of America

For the Union of Soviet Socialist Republics:

LEONID I. BREZHNEV

General Secretary of the Central Committee of the CPSU

INTERIM AGREEMENT ON LIMITATION OF STRATEGIC OFFENSIVE ARMS

The United States of America and the Union of Soviet Socialist Republics, hereinafter referred to as the Parties,

Convinced that the Treaty on the Limitation of Anti-Ballistic Missile Systems and this Interim Agreement on Certain Measures with Respect to the Limitation of Strategic Offensive Arms will contribute to the creation of more favorable conditions for active negotiations on limiting strategic arms as well as to the relaxation of international tension and the strengthening of trust between States,

Taking into account the relationship between strategic offensive and defensive arms,

Mindful of their obligations under Article VI of the Treaty on the Non-Proliferation of Nuclear Weapons,

Have agreed as follows:

ARTICLE I

The Parties undertake not to start construction of additional fixed land-based intercontinental ballistic missile (ICBM) launchers after July 1, 1972.

ARTICLE II

The Parties undertake not to convert land-based launchers for light ICBMs, or for ICBMs of older types deployed prior to 1964, into land-based launchers for heavy ICBMs of types deployed after that time.

ARTICLE III

The Parties undertake to limit submarine-launched ballistic missile (SLBM) launchers and modern ballistic missile submarines to the numbers operational and under construction on the date of signature of this Interim Agreement, and in addition to launchers and submarines constructed under procedures established by the Parties as replacements for an equal number of ICBM launchers of older types deployed prior to 1964 or for launchers on older submarines. . . .

ARTICLE IV

Subject to the provisions of this Interim Agreement, modernization and replacement of strategic offensive ballistic missiles and launchers covered by this Interim Agreement may be undertaken.

ARTICLE V

1. For the purpose of providing assurance of compliance with the provisions of this Interim Agreement, each Party shall use national technical means of verification at its disposal in a manner consistent with generally recognized principles of international law.

2. Each Party undertakes not to interfere with the national technical means of verification of the other Party operating in accordance with paragraph 1 of this Article.

3. Each Party undertakes not to use deliberate concealment measures which impede verification by national technical means of compliance with the provisions of this Interim Agreement. This obligation shall not require changes in current construction, assembly, conversion, or overhaul practices.

ARTICLE VI

To promote the objectives and implementation of the provisions of this Interim Agreement, the Parties shall use the Standing Consultative Commission established under Article XIII of the Treaty on the Limitation of Anti-Ballistic Missile Systems in accordance with the provisions of that Article.

ARTICLE VII

The Parties undertake to continue active negotiations for limitations on strategic offensive arms. The obligations provided for in this Interim Agreement shall not prejudice the scope or terms of the limitations on strategic offensive arms which may be worked out in the course of further negotiations.

ARTICLE VIII

1. This Interim Agreement shall enter into force upon exchange of written notices of acceptance by each Party, which exchange shall take place simultaneously with the exchange of instruments of ratification of the Treaty on the Limitation of Anti-Ballistic Missile Systems.

2. This Interim Agreement shall remain in force for a period of five years unless replaced earlier by an agreement on more complete measures limiting strategic offensive arms. It is the objective of the Parties to conduct active follow-on negotiations with the aim of concluding such an agreement as soon as possible. . . .

PROTOCOL TO INTERIM AGREEMENT

The United States of America and the Union of Soviet Socialist Republics, hereinafter referred to as the Parties,

Having agreed on certain limitations relating to submarine-launched ballistic missile launchers and modern ballistic missile submarines, and to replacement procedures, in the Interim Agreement,

Have agreed as follows:

The Parties understand that, under Article III of the Interim Agreement, for the period during which that Agreement remains in force:

The US may have no more than 710 ballistic missile launchers on submarines (SLBMs) and no more than 44 modern ballistic missile submarines. The Soviet Union may have no more than 950 ballistic missile launchers on submarines and no more than 62 modern ballistic missile submarines.

Additional ballistic missile launchers on submarines up to the above-mentioned levels, in the U.S.—over 656 ballistic missile launchers on nuclear-powered submarines, and in the U.S.S.R.—over 740 ballistic missile launchers on nuclear-powered submarines, operational and under construction, may become operational as replacements for equal numbers of ballistic missile launchers of older types deployed prior to 1964 or of ballistic missile launchers on older submarines.

The deployment of modern SLBMs on any submarine, regardless of type, will be counted against the total level of SLBMs permitted for the U.S. and the U.S.S.R.

This Protocol shall be considered an integral part of the Interim Agreement. . . .

689. LLOYD CORP., LTD. v. TANNER et al.
92 Supreme Court Reporter   2219
1972

Certiorari from the U.S. Court of Appeals for the Ninth Circuit denied. At stake in this case was the right to distribute leaflets opposed to the draft and to the Vietnam War in the interior mall area of a large, privately owned shopping center. The Lloyd shopping center had a strict no-handbilling rule and its security guards requested those distributing the handbills, under threat of arrest, to resume their activities outside the mall, which they did. They claimed that this action violated their First Amendment rights and brought suit for injunctive relief. The district court upheld their contention, finding that the shopping center is "open to the general public" and is "the functional equivalent of a public business district," and the Court of Appeals for the Ninth Circuit affirmed. The Supreme Court, however, held that the shopping center was indeed private property, and that the First Amendment could not be extended to an invasion of such property. Justice Powell rendered the opinion for a majority of five, which included the other three Nixon appointees as well as Justice White. Justice Marshall spoke for the dissenters, Justices Douglas, Brennan, and Stewart.

POWELL, J. . . . The Center embodies a relatively new concept in shopping center design. The stores are all located within a single large, multi-level building complex sometimes referred to as the "Mall." . . . Some of the stores open directly on the outside public sidewalks, but most open on the interior privately owned malls. Some stores open on both. There are no public streets or public sidewalks within the building complex, which is enclosed and entirely covered except for the landscaped portions of some of the interior malls.

The distribution of the handbills occurred in the malls. . . .

. . . the Center pursues policies comparable to those of major stores and shopping centers across the country, although the Center affords superior facilities for these purposes. Groups and organizations are permitted, by invitation and advance arrangement, to use the auditorium and other facilities. Rent is charged for use of the auditorium except with respect to certain civic and charitable organizations, such as the Cancer Society, Boy and Girl Scouts. The Center also allows limited use of the malls by the American Legion to sell "Buddy Poppies" for disabled veterans, and by the Salvation Army and Volunteers of America to solicit Christmas contributions. It has denied similar use to other civic and charitable organizations. Political use is also forbidden, except that presidential candidates of both parties have been allowed to speak in the auditorium. . . .

The District Court observed that Lloyd Center invites schools to hold football rallies, presidential candidates to give speeches, and service organizations to hold Veteran's Day ceremonies on its premises. The court also observed that the Center permits the Salvation Army, the Volunteers of America, and the American Legion to solicit funds in the Mall. Thus, the court concluded that the Center was already open to First Amendment activities, and that respondents could not constitutionally be excluded from leafletting solely because Lloyd Center was not enamored of the form or substance of their speech. . . .

. . . In other words, the District Court found that Lloyd Center had deliberately chosen to open its private property to a broad range of expression and that having done so it could not constitutionally exclude respondents, and the Court of Appeals affirmed this finding. . . .

On Veteran's Day, Lloyd Center allows organizations to parade through the Center with flags, drummers, and color guard units and to have a speaker deliver an address on the meaning of Veteran's Day and the valor of American soldiers. Presidential candidates have been permitted to speak without restriction on the issues of the day, which presumably include war and peace. The American Legion is annually given permission to sell poppies in the Mall because Lloyd Center believes that "veterans . . . deserves [sic] some comfort and support by the people of the United States." In light of these facts, I perceive no basis for depriving respondents of the opportunity to distribute leaflets inviting patrons of the Center to attend a meeting in which different points of view would be expressed than those held by the organizations and persons privileged to use Lloyd Center as a forum for parading their ideas and symbols. . . .

B. If respondents had distributed handbills complaining about one or more stores in Lloyd Center or about the Center itself, petitioner concedes that our decision in *Logan Valley* would insulate that conduct from proscription by the Center. I cannot see any logical reason to treat differently speech that is related to subjects other than the Center and its member stores.

We must remember that it is a balance that we are striking—a balance between the freedom to speak, a freedom that is given a preferred place in our hierarchy of values, and the freedom of a private property-owner to control his property. When the competing interests are fairly weighted, the balance can only be struck in favor of speech.

Members of the Portland community are able to see doctors, dentists, lawyers, bankers, travel agents, and persons offering countless other services in Lloyd Center. They can buy almost anything that they want or need there. For many Portland citizens, Lloyd Center will so completely satisfy their wants that they will have no reason to go elsewhere for goods or services. If speech is to reach these people, it must reach them in Lloyd Center. The Center itself recognizes this. For example, in 1964 its director of public relations offered candidates for President and Vice-President the use of the center for political speeches, boasting "that our convenient location and setting would provide the largest audience [the candidates] could attract in Oregon."

For many persons who do not have easy access to television, radio, the major newspapers, and the other forms of mass media, the only way they can express themselves to a broad range of citizens on issues of general public concern is to picket, or to handbill, or to utilize other free or relatively inexpensive means of communication. The only hope that these people have to be able to communicate effectively is to be permitted to speak in those areas in which most of their fellow citizens can be found. One such area is the business district of a city or town or its functional equivalent. And this is why respondents have a tremendous need to express themselves within Lloyd Center.

Petitioner's interests, on the other hand, pale in comparison. For example, petitioner urges that respondents' First Amendment activity would disturb the Center's customers. It is undisputed that some patrons will be disturbed by any First Amendment activity that goes on, regardless of its object. But, there is no evidence to indicate that speech directed to topics unrelated to the shopping center would be more likely to impair the motivation of customers to buy than speech directed to the uses to which the Center is put, which petitioner concedes is constitutionally protected under *Logan Valley*. On

the contrary, common sense would indicate that speech that is critical of a shopping center or one or more of its stores is more likely to deter consumers from purchasing goods or services than speech on any other subject. Moreover, petitioner acknowledges that respondents have a constitutional right to leaflet on any subject on public streets and sidewalks within Lloyd Center. It is difficult for me to understand why leafletting in the Mall would be so much more disturbing to the Center's customers. . . .

The basic issue in this case is whether respondents, in the exercise of asserted First Amendment rights, may distribute handbills on Lloyd's private property contrary to its wishes and contrary to a policy enforced against *all* handbilling. In addressing this issue, it must be remembered that the First and Fourteenth Amendments safeguard the rights of free speech and assembly by limitations on *state* action, not on action by the owner of private property used nondiscriminatorily for private purposes only. . . .

The argument reaches too far. The Constitution by no means requires such an attenuated doctrine of dedication of private property to public use. . . .

Nor does property lose its private character merely because the public is generally invited to use it for designated purposes. Few would argue that a free standing store, with abutting parking space for customers, assumes significant public attributes merely because the public is invited to shop. Nor is size alone the controlling factor. The essentially private character of a store and its privately owned abutting property does not change by virtue of being large or clustered with other stores in a modern shopping center. This is not to say that no differences may exist with respect to government regulation or rights of citizens arising by virtue of the size and diversity of activities carried on within a privately owned facility serving the public. There will be, for example, problems with respect to public health and safety which vary in degree and in the appropriate government response, depending upon the size and character of a shopping center, an office building, a sports arena or other large facility serving the public for commercial purposes. We do say that the Fifth and

Fourteenth Amendment rights of private property owners, as well as the First Amendment rights of all citizens, must be respected and protected. The Framers of the Constitution certainly did not think these fundamental rights of a free society are incompatible with each other. There may be situations where accommodations between them, and the drawing of lines to assure due protection of both, are not easy. But on the facts presented in this case, the answer is clear.

We hold that there has been no such dedication of Lloyd's privately owned and operated shopping center to public use as to entitle respondents to exercise therein the asserted First Amendment rights. Accordingly, we reverse the judgment and remand the case to the Court of Appeals with directions to vacate the injunction.

It is so ordered.

690. UNITED STATES v. U.S. DISTRICT COURT
92 Supreme Court Reporter 2125
1972

Certiorari from U.S. Court of Appeals for the Sixth Circuit. *Katz* v. *United States,* 1967, specifically overruled Chief Justice Taft's majority opinion in the *Olmstead* case and found electronic surveillance subject to the warrant provision of the Fourth Amendment. Debate continued to rage over whether evidence obtained by electronic surveillance in internal security cases violates the protections guaranteed by this amendment. The problem is recurrent for two reasons: (1) electronic technology has made wiretapping crude and practically obsolete, and has rendered the invasion of privacy easy and inexpensive; and (2) the Justice Department, in President Nixon's administration, claimed that the executive has *inherent* power to override the Fourth Amendment and to use electronic surveillance without judicial warrant in domestic security cases. Literal compliance with the Fourth Amendment and with the terms of the 1968 Omnibus Crime Control and Safe Streets Act (Doc. No. 668), which it sponsored, argued the administration, "would create serious potential dangers to the national security and to the lives of informants and agents." The Court unanimously rejected this invocation of "national security" to justify diminishing the protection afforded by the Bill of Rights. In this case three defendants were charged with conspiracy to destroy, and one with destroying, government property. Defendants claimed that the government had engaged in electronic surveillance; the government answered that the wiretaps had been approved by the executive for the purpose of gathering "intelligence information deemed necessary to protect the nation," and alleged such wiretaps lawful as a reasonable exercise of presidential power to protect the national security. The U.S. District Court for the Eastern District of Michigan re-jected the government's contention. On appeal, the circuit court held that, in dealing with the threat of domestic subversion, the entire executive branch, including the Attorney General, is subject to the warrant provision of the Fourth Amendment. See K. Greenawalt, "The Right to Privacy," in N. Dorsen, ed., *The Rights of Americans;* A. Westin, *Privacy and Freedom;* "The United States Courts of Appeals: 1970–1971 Term Criminal Law and Procedure," 60 *Georgetown Law J.* (November 1971); A. Breckenridge, *The Right to Privacy;* P. A. Thompson, "Wiretapping—Power of United States Attorney General to Authorize Wiretapping Without Judicial Warrant," 60 *Kentucky Law J.* 245; G. Kenny, "The 'National Security Wiretap': Presidential Prerogative or Judicial Responsibility," 45 *South. California Law Rev.* 888.

POWELL, J. . . .

Title III of the Omnibus Crime Control and Safe Streets Act, 18 U.S.C. §§ 2510–2520, authorizes the use of electronic surveillance for classes of crimes carefully specified in 18 U.S.C. § 2516. Such surveillance is subject to prior court order. Section 2518 sets forth the detailed and particularized application necessary to obtain such an order as well as carefully circumscribed conditions for its use. The Act represents a comprehensive attempt by Congress to promote more effective control of crime while protecting the privacy of individual thought and expression. . . .

The Government . . . argues that "in excepting national security surveillances from the Act's warrant requirement Congress recognized the President's authority to conduct such surveillances without prior judicial approval." The section thus is viewed as a recognition or affirmance of a constitutional authority in the President to conduct warrantless domestic security surveillance such as that involved in this case.

We think the language of § 2511(3), as well as the legislative history of the statute, refutes this interpretation.

The relevant language is that:

"Nothing contained in this chapter . . . shall limit the constitutional power of the President to take such measures as he deems necessary to protect . . ."

against the dangers specified. At most, this is an implicit recognition that the President does have certain powers in the specified areas. Few would doubt this, as the section refers—among other things—to protection "against actual or potential attack or other hostile acts of a foreign power." But so far as the use of the President's electronic surveillance power is concerned, the language is essentially neutral.

Section 2511(3) certainly confers no power, as the language is wholly inappropriate for such a purpose. It merely provides that the Act shall not be interpreted to limit or disturb such power as the President may have under the Constitution. . . .

One could hardly expect a clearer expression of congressional neutrality. The debate above explicitly indicates that nothing in § 2511(3) was intended to *expand* or to *contract* or to *define* whatever presidential surveillance powers existed in matters affecting the national security. If we could accept the Government's characterization of § 2511(3) as a congressionally prescribed exception to the general requirement of a warrant, it would be necessary to consider the question of whether the surveillance in this case came within the exception and, if so, whether the statutory exception was itself constitutionally valid. But viewing § 2511(3) as a congressional disclaimer and expression of neutrality, we hold that the statute is not the measure of the executive authority asserted in this case. Rather, we must look to the constitutional powers of the President. . . .

It is important at the outset to emphasize the limited nature of the question before the Court. This case raises no constitutional challenge to electronic surveillance as specifically authorized by Title III of the Omnibus Crime Control and Safe Streets Act of 1968. . . . Further, the instant case requires no judgment on the scope of the President's surveillance power with respect to the activities of foreign powers, within or without this country. The Attorney General's affidavit in this case states that the surveillances were "deemed necessary to protect the nation from attempts of *domestic organizations* to attack and subvert the existing structure of Government" (emphasis supplied). There is no evidence of any involvement, directly or indirectly, of a foreign power.

Our present inquiry, though important, is therefore a narrow one. . . . The determination of this question requires the essential Fourth Amendment inquiry into the "reasonableness" of the search and seizure in question. . . .

We begin the inquiry by noting that the President of the United States has the fundamental duty, under Art. II, § 1, of the Constitution, "to preserve, protect, and defend the Constitution of the United States." Implicit in that duty is the power to protect our Government against those who would subvert or overthrow it by unlawful means. In the discharge of this duty, the President —through the Attorney General—may find it necessary to employ electronic surveillance to obtain intelligence information on the plans of those who plot unlawful acts against the Government. . . .

. . . History abundantly documents the tendency of Government—however benevolent and benign its motives—to view with suspicion those who most fervently dispute its policies. Fourth Amendment protections become the more necessary when the targets of official surveillance may be those suspected of unorthodoxy in their political beliefs. The danger to political dissent is acute where the Government attempts to act under so vague a concept as the power to protect "domestic security." Given the difficulty of defining the domestic security interest, the danger of abuse in acting to protect that interest becomes apparent. . . .

The price of lawful public dissent must not be a dread of subjection to an unchecked surveillance power. Nor must the fear of unauthorized official eavesdropping deter vigorous citizen dissent and discussion of Government action in private conversation. For private dissent, no less than open public discourse, is essential to our free society. . . .

As the Fourth Amendment is not absolute in its terms, our task is to examine and balance the basic values at stake in this case: the duty of Government to protect the domestic security, and the potential danger posed by unreasonable surveillance to individual privacy and free expression. If the legitimate need of Government to safeguard domestic security requires the use of electronic surveillance, the question is whether the needs of citizens for privacy and free expression may not be better protected by requiring a warrant before such surveillance is undertaken. We must also ask whether a warrant requirement would unduly frustrate the efforts of Government to protect itself from acts of subversion and overthrow directed against it. . . .

Fourth Amendment freedoms cannot properly be guaranteed if domestic security surveillances may be conducted solely within the discretion of the executive branch. The Fourth Amendment does not contemplate the executive officers of Government as neutral and disinterested magistrates. Their duty and responsibility is to enforce the laws, to investigate and to prosecute. . . . But those charged with this investigative and prosecutorial duty should not be the sole judges of when to utilize constitutionally sensitive means in pursuing their tasks. The historical judgment, which the Fourth Amendment accepts, is that unreviewed executive discretion may yield too readily to pressures to obtain incriminating evidence and overlook potential invasions of privacy and protected speech. . . .

. . . We do not think a case has been made for the requested departure from Fourth Amendment standards. The circumstances described do not justify complete exemption of domestic security surveillance from prior judicial scrutiny. Official surveillance, whether its purpose be criminal investigation or on-going intelligence gathering, risks infringement of constitutionally protected privacy of speech. Security surveillances are especially sensitive because of the inherent vagueness of the domestic security concept, the necessarily broad and continuing nature of intelligence gathering, and the temptation to utilize such surveillances to oversee political dissent. We recognize, as we have before, the constitutional basis of the President's domestic security role, but we think it must be exercised in a manner compatible with the Fourth Amendment. In this case we hold that this requires an appropriate prior warrant procedure.

We cannot accept the Government's argument that internal security matters are too subtle and complex for judicial evaluation. Courts regularly deal with the most difficult issues of our society. There is no reason to believe that federal judges will be insensitive to or uncomprehending of the issues involved in domestic security cases. Certainly courts can recognize that domestic security surveillance involves different considerations from the surveillance of ordinary crime. If the threat is too subtle or complex for our senior law enforcement officers to convey its significance to a court, one may question whether there is probable cause for surveillance.

Nor do we believe prior judicial approval will fracture the secrecy essential to official intelligence gathering. The investigation of criminal activity has long involved imparting sensitive information to judicial officers who have respected the confidentialities involved. Judges may be counted upon to be especially conscious of security requirements in national security cases. Title III of the Omnibus Crime Control and Safe Streets Act already has imposed this responsibility on the judiciary in connection with such crimes as espionage, sabotage and treason, § 2516 (1)(a)(c), each of which may involve domestic as well as foreign security threats. Moreover, a warrant application involves no public or adversary proceedings: it is an *ex parte* request before a magistrate or judge. Whatever security dangers clerical and secretarial personnel may pose can be minimized by proper administrative measures, possibly to the point of allowing the Government itself to provide the necessary clerical assistance.

Thus, we conclude that the Government's concerns do not justify departure in this case from the customary Fourth Amendment requirement of judicial approval prior to initiation of a search or surveillance. Although some added burden will be imposed upon the Attorney General, this inconvenience is justified in a free society to protect constitutional values. Nor do we think the Government's domestic surveillance powers will be impaired to any significant degree. A prior warrant establishes presumptive validity of the surveillance and will minimize the burden of justification in post-surveillance judicial review. By no means of least importance will be the reassurance of the public generally that indiscriminate wiretapping and bugging of law-abiding citizens cannot occur.

691. UNITED STATES v. EARL CALDWELL
92 Supreme Court Reporter 2686
1972

On appeal from the U.S. Court of Appeals for the Ninth Circuit. Earl Caldwell, a black reporter for the *New York Times,* was assigned to cover the Black Panther Party as well as other black militant groups. He gained the full confidence of the Panthers and wrote in-depth articles about them. A subpoena was served on Caldwell, directing him to appear before the grand jury and to bring his notes as well as tapes covering interviews with Panther members. He objected to the scope of the subpoena on the grounds that it was unlimited in nature and that his appearance before the grand jury would destroy his working relationship with the Black Panther Party. The district court ruled that he had to appear, but need not reveal confidential communications—unless the court was satisfied that there was a "compelling and overriding national interest" at stake. Caldwell refused to appear and was held in contempt. The court of appeals decision—that to reveal confidential sources jeopardized a First Amendment freedom and that Caldwell need not appear before the grand jury—was appealed to the Supreme Court. Justice White, supported by President Nixon's four appointees, firmly rejected the theory that the First Amendment shields newsmen from having to testify when the result would be to cut off news sources and deprive the public of news. The participation of Judge Rehnquist, the newest appointee, was crucial; precedent required that he disqualify himself because he represented the Justice Department on the issue in 1970 and because he helped prepare the Department's guidelines for subpoenaing newsmen. Justice Stewart, dissenting, spoke for Justices Brennan and Marshall. Justice Douglas filed a separate dissent. See N. Isaacs, "Beyond 'Caldwell'—1: 'There May Be Worse To Come from This Court,'" and B. Schmitt, Jr, "Beyond 'Caldwell'—2: 'The Decision Is Tentative,'" *Columbia Journalism Rev.* (Sept./Oct. 1972); "Media and the First Amendment in a Free Society," 60 *Georgetown Law J.* (March 1972); D. A. Pember, *Privacy and the Press: The Law, the Media, and the First Amendment.*

WHITE, J. . . . The issue in these cases is whether requiring newsmen to appear and testify before State or federal grand juries abridges the freedom of speech and press guaranteed by the First Amendment. We hold that it does not.

. . . The sole issue before us is the obligation of reporters to respond to grand jury subpoenas as other citizens do and to answer questions relevant to an investigation into the commission of crime. Citizens generally are not constitutionally immune from grand jury subpoenas; and neither the First Amendment nor other constitutional provision protects the average citizen from disclosing to a grand jury information that he has received in confidence. The claim is, however, that reporters are exempt from these obligations because if forced to respond to subpoenas and identify their sources or disclose other confidences, their informants will refuse or be reluctant to furnish newsworthy information in the future. This asserted burden on news gathering is said to make compelled testimony from newsmen constitutionally suspect and to require a privileged position for them.

It is clear that the First Amendment does not invalidate every incidental burdening of the press that may result from the enforcement of civil or criminal statutes of general applicability. Under prior cases, otherwise valid laws serving substantial public interests may be enforced against the press as against others, despite the possible burden that may be imposed. . . .

The prevailing view is that the press is not free with impunity to publish everything and anything it desires to publish. Although it may deter or regulate what is said or published, the press may not circulate knowing or reckless falsehoods damaging to private reputation without subjecting itself to liability for damages, including punitive damages, or even criminal prosecution. . . .

A number of States have provided newsmen a statutory privilege of varying breadth, but the majority have not done so, and none has been provided by federal statute. Until now the only testimonial privilege for unofficial witnesses that is rooted in the Federal Constitution is the Fifth Amendment privilege against compelled self-incrimination. We are asked to create another by interpreting the First Amendment to grant newsmen a testimonial privilege that other citizens do not enjoy. This we decline to do. Fair and effective law enforcement aimed at providing security for the person and property of the individual is a fundamental function of government, and the grand jury plays an important, constitutionally mandated role in this process. On the records now before us, we perceive no basis for holding that the public interest in law enforcement and in ensuring effective grand jury proceedings is insufficient to override the consequential, but uncertain, burden on news gathering which is said to result from insisting that reporters, like other citizens, respond to relevant questions put to them in the course of valid grand jury investigation or criminal trial.

This conclusion itself involves no restraint on what newspapers may publish or on the type or quality of information reporters may seek to acquire, nor does it threaten the vast bulk of confidential relationships between reporters and their sources. Grand juries address themselves to the issues of whether crimes have been committed and who committed them. Only where news sources themselves are implicated in crime or possess information relevant to the grand jury's task need they or the reporter be concerned about grand jury subpoenas. Nothing before us indicates that a large number or percentage of *all* confidential news sources fall into either category and would in any way be deterred by our holding that the Constitution does not, as it never has, exempt the newsman from performing the citizen's normal duty of appearing and furnishing information relevant to the grand jury's task.

The preference for anonymity of those confidential informants involved in actual criminal conduct is presumably a product of their desire to escape criminal prosecution, and this preference, while understandable, is hardly deserving of constitutional protection. It would be frivolous to assert—and no one does in these cases—that the First Amendment, in the interest of securing news or otherwise, confers a license on either the reporter or his news sources to violate otherwise valid criminal laws. Although stealing documents or private wiretapping could provide newsworthy information, neither reporter nor source is immune from conviction for such conduct, whatever the impact on the flow of news. Neither is immune, on First Amendment grounds, from testifying against the other, before the grand jury or at a criminal trial. The Amendment does not reach so far as to override the interest of the public in ensuring that neither reporter nor source is invading the rights of other citizens through reprehensible conduct forbidden to all other persons. . . .

Thus, we cannot seriously entertain the notion that the First Amendment protects a newsman's agreement to conceal the criminal conduct of his source, or evidence thereof, on the theory that it is better to write about crime than to do something about it. Insofar as any reporter in these cases undertook not to reveal or testify about the crime he witnessed, his claim of privilege under the First Amendment presents no substantial question. The crimes of news sources are no less reprehensible and threatening to the public interest when witnessed by a reporter than when they are not. . . .

. . . grand juries characteristically conduct secret proceedings, and law enforcement officers are themselves experienced in dealing with informers and have their own methods for protecting them without interference with the effective administration of justice. There is little before us indicating that informants whose interest in avoiding exposure is that it may threaten job security, personal safety, or peace of mind, would in fact, be in a worse position, or would think they would be, if they risked placing their trust in public officials as well as reporters. We doubt if the informer who prefers anonymity but is sincerely interested in furnishing evidence of crime will always or very often be deterred by the prospect of dealing with those public authorities characteristically charged with the duty to protect the public interest as well as his.

Accepting the fact, however, that an undetermined number of informants not themselves implicated in crime will nevertheless, for whatever reason, refuse to talk to newsmen if they fear identification by a reporter in an official investigation, we cannot accept the argument that the public interest in possible future news about crime from undisclosed, unverified sources must take precedence over the public interest in pursuing and prosecuting those crimes reported to the press by informants and in thus deterring the commission of such crimes in the future. . . .

It is said that currently press subpoenas have multiplied, that mutual distrust and tension between press and officialdom have increased, that reporting styles have changed, and that there is now more need for confidential sources, particularly where the press seeks news about minority cultural and political groups or dissident organizations suspicious of the law and public officials. These developments, even if true, are treacherous grounds for a far-reaching interpretation of the First Amendment fastening a nationwide rule on courts, grand juries, and prosecuting officials everywhere. The obligation to testify in response to grand jury subpoenas will not threaten these sources not involved with criminal conduct and without information

relevant to grand jury investigations, and we cannot hold that the Constitution places the sources in these two categories either above the law or beyond its reach. . . .

Finally, as we have earlier indicated, news gathering is not without its First Amendment protections, and grand jury investigations if instituted or conducted other than in good faith, would pose wholly different issues for resolution under the First Amendment. Official harassment of the press undertaken not for purposes of law enforcement but to disrupt a reporter's relationship with his news sources would have no justification. Grand juries are subject to judicial control and subpoenas to motions to quash. We do not expect courts will forget that grand juries must operate within the limits of the First Amendment as well as the Fifth.

MR. JUSTICE DOUGLAS, dissenting.

. . . The Court of Appeals agreed with the findings of the District Court but held that Caldwell need not appear at all before the grand jury absent a "compelling need" shown by the Government. 434 F. 2d 1081.

It is my view that there is no "compelling need" that can be shown which qualifies the reporter's immunity from appearing or testifying before a grand jury, unless the reporter himself is implicated in a crime. His immunity in my view is therefore quite complete, for absent his involvement in a crime, the First Amendment protects him against an appearance before a grand jury and if he is involved in a crime, the Fifth Amendment stands as a barrier. Since in my view there is no area of inquiry not protected by a privilege, the reporter need not appear for the futile purpose of invoking one to each question. And, since in my view a newsman has an absolute right not to appear before a grand jury it follows for me that a journalist who voluntarily appears before that body may invoke his First Amendment privilege to specific questions. . . . The New York Times, whose reporting functions are at issue here, takes the amazing position that First Amendment rights are to be balanced against other needs or conveniences of government. My belief is that all of the "balancing" was done by those who wrote the Bill of Rights. By casting the First Amendment in absolute terms, they repudiated, the timid, watered-down, emasculated versions of the First Amendment which both the Government and the New York Times advances in the case.

My view is close to that of the late Alexander Meiklejohn . . .

He . . . believed that "Self-government can exist only insofar as the voters acquire the intelligence, integrity, sensitivity, and generous devotion to the general welfare that, in theory, casting a ballot is assumed to express," and that "[p]ublic discussions of public issues, together with the spreading of information and opinion bearing on those issues, must have a freedom unabridged by our agents. Though they govern us, we in a deeper sense, govern them. Over our governing, they have no power. Over their governing we have sovereign power."

Two principles which follow from this understanding of the First Amendment are at stake here. One is that the people, the ultimate governors, must have absolute freedom of and therefore privacy of their individual opinions and beliefs regardless of how suspect or strange they may appear to others. Ancillary to that principle is the conclusion that an individual must also have absolute privacy over whatever information he may generate in the course of testing his opinions and beliefs. In this regard, Caldwell's status as a reporter is less relevant than is his status as a student who affirmatively pursued empirical research to enlarge his own intellectual viewpoint. The second principle is that effective self-government cannot succeed unless the people are immersed in a steady, robust, unimpeded, and uncensored flow of opinion and reporting which are continuously subjected to critique, rebuttal, and re-examination. In this respect, Caldwell's status as a newsgatherer and an integral part of that process becomes critical.

Government has many interests that compete with the First Amendment. . . .

The Court has not always been consistent in its protection of these First Amendment rights and has sometimes allowed a government interest to override the absolutes of the First Amendment. For example, under the banner of the "clear and present danger" test, and later under the influence of the "balancing" formula, the Court has permitted men to be penalized not for any harmful conduct but solely for holding unpopular beliefs.

In recent years we have said over and again that where First Amendment rights are concerned any regulation "narrowly drawn," must be "compelling" and not merely "rational" as is the case where other activities are concerned. But the "compelling" interest in regulation neither includes paring down or diluting the right, nor embraces penalizing one solely for his intellectual viewpoint; it concerns the State's interest, for example, in regulating the time and place or perhaps manner of exercising First Amendment rights. Thus one has an undoubted right to read and proclaim the First Amendment in the classroom or in a park. But he would not have the right to blare it forth from a sound truck rolling through the village or city at 2 a.m. The distinction drawn in *Cantwell* v. *Connecticut*, 310 U.S. 296, 303–304, 60 S. Ct. 900, 903, 84 L. Ed. 1213 should still stand: "[T]he Amendment embraces two concepts, —freedom to believe and freedom to act. The first is absolute but, in the nature of things, the second cannot be."

Under these precedents there is no doubt that Caldwell could not be brought before the grand jury for the sole purpose of exposing his political beliefs. Yet today the Court effectively permits that result under the guise of allowing an attempt to elicit from him "factual information." To be sure, the inquiry will be couched only in terms of extracting Caldwell's recollection of what was said to him during the interviews, but the fact remains that his questions to the Panthers and therefore the respective answers were guided by Caldwell's own preconceptions and views about the Black Panthers. His entire experience was shaped by his intellectual viewpoint. Unlike the random bystander, those who affirmatively set out to test an hypothesis, as here, have no tidy means of segregating subjective opinion from objective facts.

Sooner or later any test which provides less than blanket protection to beliefs and associations will be twisted and relaxed so as to provide virtually no protection at all. . . .

Today's decision will impede the wide open and robust dissemination of ideas and counterthought which a free press both fosters and protects and which is essential to the success of intelligent self-government. Forcing a reporter before a grand jury will have two retarding effects upon the ear and the pen of the press. Fear of exposure will cause dissidents to communicate less openly to trusted reporters. And, fear of accountability will cause editors and critics to write with more restrained pens.

I see no way of making mandatory the disclosure of a reporter's confidential source of the information on which he bases his news story.

The press has a preferred position in our constitutional scheme not to enable it to make money, not to set newsmen apart as a favored class, but to bring fulfillment to the public's right to know. The right to know is crucial to the governing powers of the people, to paraphrase Alexander Meiklejohn. Knowledge is essential to informed decisions.

As Mr. Justice Black said in *New York Times Co.* v. *United States,* 403 U.S. 713, 717 (concurring opinion), "The press was to serve the governed, not the governors. . . . The press was protected so that it could bare the secrets of government and inform the people."

Government has an interest in law and order; and history shows that the trend of rulers—the bureaucracy and the police—is to suppress the radical and his ideas and to arrest him rather than the hostile audience. . . .

The people who govern are often far removed from the cabals that threaten the regime; the people are often remote from the sources of truth even though they live in the city where the forces that would undermine society operate. The function of the press is to explore and investigate events, inform the people what is going on, and to expose the harmful as well as the good influences at work. There is no higher function performed under our constitutional regime. Its performance means that the press is often engaged in projects that bring anxiety or even fear to the bureaucracies or departments or officials of government. The whole weight of government is therefore often brought to bear against a paper or a reporter.

A reporter is no better than his source of information. Unless he has a privilege to withhold the identity of his source, he will be the victim of governmental intrigue or aggression. If he can be summoned to testify in secret before a grand jury, his sources will dry up and the attempted exposure, the effort to enlighten the public, will be ended. If what the Court sanctions today becomes settled law, then the reporter's main function in American society will be to pass on to the public the press releases which the various departments of government issue.

It is no answer to reply that the risk that a newsman will divulge one's secrets to the grand jury is no greater than the threat that he will in any event inform to the police. Even the most trustworthy reporter may not be able to withstand relentless badgering before a grand jury.

The record in this case is replete with weighty affidavits from responsible newsmen, telling how important are the sanctity of their sources of information. When we deny newsmen that protection, we deprive the people of the information needed to run the affairs of the Nation in an intelligent way. . . .

Today's decision is more than a clog upon news gathering. It is a signal to publishers and editors that they should exercise caution in how they use whatever information they can obtain. Without immunity they may be summoned to account for their criticism. . . .

The intrusion of government into this domain is symptomatic of the disease of this society. As the years pass the power of government becomes more and more pervasive. It is a power to suffocate both people and causes. Those in power, whatever their politics, want only to perpetuate it. Now that the fences of the law and the tradition that has protected the press are broken down, the people are the victims. The First Amendment, as I read it, was designed precisely to prevent that tragedy.

MR. JUSTICE STEWART, with whom MR. JUSTICE BRENNAN and MR. JUSTICE MARSHALL join, dissenting.

The Court's crabbed view of the First

Amendment reflects a disturbing insensitivity to the critical role of an independent press in our society. . . . The Court in these cases holds that a newsman has no First Amendment right to protect his sources when called before a grand jury. The Court thus invites state and federal authorities to undermine the historic independence of the press by attempting to annex the journalistic profession as an investigative arm of government. Not only will this decision impair performance of the press' constitutionally protected functions, but it will, I am convinced, in the long run, harm rather than help the administration of justice.

I respectfully dissent.

The reporter's constitutional right to a confidential relationship with his source stems from the broad societal interest in a full and free flow of information to the public. It is this basic concern that underlies the Constitution's protection of a free press, *Grosjean* v. *American Press Co.*, 297 U.S. 233, *New York Times* v. *Sullivan*, 376 U.S. 254, because the guarantee is "not for the benefit of the press so much as for the benefit of us all." *Time, Inc.* v. *Hill*, 385 U.S. 374. . . .

In keeping with this tradition, we have held that the right to publish is central to the First Amendment and basic to the existence of constitutional democracy. . . .

A corollary of the right to publish must be the right to gather news. The full flow of information to the public protected by the free press guarantee would be severely curtailed if no protection whatever were afforded to the process by which news is assembled and disseminated. We have, therefore, recognized that there is a right to publish without prior governmental approval. . . .

No less important to the news dissemination process is the gathering of information. News must not be unnecessarily cut off at its source, for without freedom to acquire information the right to publish would be impermissibly compromised. Accordingly, a right to gather news, of some dimensions, must exist. . . .

The right to gather news implies, in turn, a right to a confidential relationship between a reporter and his source. This proposition follows as a matter of simple logic once three factual predicates are recognized: (1) newsmen require informants to gather news; (2) confidentiality—the promise or understanding that names or certain aspects of communications will be kept off-the-record—is essential to the creation and maintenance of a news-gathering relationship with informants; and (3) the existence of an unbridled subpoena power—the absence of a constitutional right protecting, in *any* way, a confidential relationship from compulsory process—will either deter sources from divulging information or deter reporters from gathering and publishing information.

It is obvious that informants are necessary to the news-gathering process as we know it today. If it is to perform its constitutional mission, the press must do far more than merely print public statements or publish prepared handouts. Familiarity with the people and circumstances involved in the myriad background activities that result in the final product called "news" is vital to complete and responsible journalism, unless the press is to be a captive mouthpiece of "newsmakers."

It is equally obvious that the promise of confidentiality may be a necessary prerequisite to a productive relationship between a newsman and his informants. . . .

Finally, and most important, when governmental officials possess an unchecked power to compel newsmen to disclose information received in confidence, sources will clearly be deterred from giving information, and reporters will clearly be deterred from publishing it, because uncertainty about exercise of the power will lead to "self-censorship." . . .

The impairment of the flow of news cannot, of course, be proven with scientific precision, as the Court seems to demand. Obviously, not every news-gathering relationship requires confidentiality. And it is difficult to pinpoint precisely how many relationships do require a promise or understanding of non-disclosure. But we have never before demanded that First Amendment rights rest on elaborate empirical studies demonstrating beyond any conceivable doubt that deterrent effects exist; we have never before required proof of the exact number of people potentially affected by governmental action, who would actually be dissuaded from engaging in First Amendment activity.

Rather, on the basis of common sense and available information, we have asked, often implicitly, (1) whether there was a rational connection between the cause (the governmental action) and the effect (the deterrence or impairment of First Amendment activity) and (2) whether the effect would occur with some regularity. . . .

Thus, when an investigation impinges on First Amendment rights, the government must not only show that the inquiry is of "compelling and overriding importance" but it must also "convincingly" demonstrate that the investigation is "substantially related" to the information sought. . . .

Accordingly, when a reporter is asked to appear before a grand jury and reveal confidences, I would hold that the government must (1) show that there is probable cause to believe that the newsman has information which is clearly relevant to a specific probable violation of law; (2) demonstrate that the information sought cannot be obtained by alternative means less destructive of First Amendment rights; and (3) demonstrate a

compelling and overriding interest in the information. . . .

The error in the Court's absolute rejection of First Amendemnt interests in these cases seems to me to be most profound. For in the name of advancing the administration of justice, the Court's decision, I think, will only impair the achievement of that goal. People entrusted with law enforcement responsibility, no less than private citizens, need general information relating to controversial social problems. Obviously, press reports have great value to government, even when the newsman cannot be compelled to testify before a grand jury. The sad paradox of the Court's position is that when a grand jury may exercise an unbridled subpoena power, and sources involved in sensitive matters become fearful of disclosing information, the newsman will not only cease to be a useful grand jury witness; he will cease to investigate and publish information about issues of public import. I cannot subscribe to such an anomalous result, for, in my view, the interests protected by the First Amendment are not antagonistic to the administration of justice. . . .

692.   FURMAN v. GEORGIA
92 Supreme Court Reporter 2726
1972

Certiorari from the Supreme Court of Georgia. This case, together with *Jackson* v. *Georgia* and *Branch* v. *Texas,* decided on the same day, climaxed a five-year campaign against capital punishment by the NAACP. This campaign was, in turn, a continuation of agitation against such punishment that had flourished for two centuries, triumphing in many nations and in some states of the Union. At the time of this decision, no one had been executed in the United States since 1967, and an unprecedented total of over 650 men and women languished on death rows across the country. The petitioners had been sentenced to death—one for murder under a Georgia statute and two for rape, in Georgia and Texas—and the Court had to decide the limited question of whether the death penalty constituted cruel and unusual punishment in violation of the Eighth and Fourteenth Amendments; it so found in 243 pages. The five-judge majority, failing to find a common

basis for their decision, issued five separate opinions: three justices (Douglas, Brennan, Marshall) concluded that executions in modern America violated the prohibition against cruel and unusual punishment; the other two (Stewart and White) found that the legal system operates in a cruel and unusual way in that it gives judges an arbitrary discretion to decree life or death. The four Nixon-appointed justices, dissenting, filed four opinions. They denied the contention that the death penalty or its erratic application was cruel and unusual punishment. Chief Justice Burger suggested that legislation could meet the objections of Justices Stewart and White, by stating the conditions under which a judge or jury can impose the death penalty (e.g., rape accompanied by vicious assault) or by reverting to a century-old practice which imposed mandatory death sentences for the commission of certain crimes. In effect, all four dissenters implied or charged that the majority had usurped the prerogative of the state legislatures by their decision.

Brennan, J. . . . At bottom, then, the Cruel and Unusual Punishments Clause prohibits the infliction of uncivilized and inhuman punishments. The State, even as it punishes, must treat its members with respect for their intrinsic worth as human beings. A punishment is "cruel and unusual," therefore, if it does not comport with human dignity.

This formulation, of course, does not of itself yield principles for assessing the constitutional validity of particular punishments. Nevertheless, even though "[t]his Court has had little occasion to give precise content to the [Clause]," *ibid.*, there are principles recognized in our cases and inherent in the Clause sufficient to permit a judicial determination whether a challenged punishment comports with human dignity.

The primary principle is that a punishment must not be so severe as to be degrading to the dignity of human beings. Pain, certainly, may be a factor in the judgment. . . .

More than the presence of pain, however, is comprehended in the judgment that the extreme severity of a punishment makes it degrading to the dignity of human beings. The barbaric punishments condemned by history, "punishments which inflict torture, such as the rack, the thumb-screw, the iron boot, the stretching of limbs, and the like," are, of course, "attended with acute pain and suffering." O'Neil v. Vermont, 144 U.S. 323, 339, 12 S.Ct. 693, 699, 36 L.Ed. 450 (1892) (Field, J., dissenting). When we consider why they have been condemned, however, we realize that the pain involved is not the only reason. The true significance of these punishments is that they treat members of the human race as nonhumans, as objects to be toyed with and discarded. They are thus inconsistent with the fundamental premise of the Clause that even the vilest criminal remains a human being possessed of common human dignity.

In determining whether a punishment comports with human dignity, we are aided also by a second principle inherent in the Clause—that the State must not arbitrarily inflict a severe punishment. This principle derives from the notion that the State does not respect human dignity when, without reason, it inflicts upon some people a severe punishment that it does not inflict upon others. Indeed, the very words "cruel and unusual punishments" imply condemnation of the arbitrary infliction of severe punishments. . . .

A third principle inherent in the Clause is that a severe punishment must not be unacceptable to contemporary society. Rejection by society, of course, is a strong indication that a severe punishment does not comport with human dignity. . . .

The question under this principle, then, is whether there are objective indicators from which a court can conclude that contemporary society considers a severe punishment unacceptable. Accordingly, the judicial task is to review the history of a challenged punishment and to examine society's present practices with respect to its use. Legislative authorization, of course, does not establish acceptance. The acceptability of a severe punishment is measured not by its availability, for it might become so offensive to society as never to be inflicted, but by its use.

The final principle inherent in the Clause is that a severe punishment must not be excessive. A punishment is excessive under this principle if it is unnecessary: The infliction of a severe punishment by the State cannot comport with human dignity when it is nothing more than the pointless infliction of suffering. If there is a significantly less severe punishment adequate to achieve the purposes for which the punishment is inflicted . . . , the punishment inflicted is unnecessary and therefore excessive. . . . Although the determination that a severe punishment is excessive may be grounded in a judgment that it is disproportionate to the crime, the more significant basis is that the punishment serves no penal purpose more effectively than a less severe punishment. This view of the principle was explicitly recognized by the Court in Weems v. United States. . . . The test, then, will ordinarily be a cumulative one: If a punishment is unusually severe, if there is a strong probability that it is inflicted arbitrarily, if it is substantially rejected by contemporary society, and if there is no reason to believe that it serves any penal purpose more effectively than some less severe punishment, then the continued infliction of that punishment violates the command of the Clause that the State may not inflict inhuman and uncivilized punishments upon those convicted of crimes.

The punishment challenged in these cases is death. . . .

The question, then, is whether the deliberate infliction of death is today consistent with the command of the Clause that the State may not inflict punishments that do not comport with human dignity. I will analyze the punishment of death in terms of the principles set out above and the cumulative test to which they lead: It is a denial of human dignity for the State arbitrarily to subject a person to an unusually severe punishment that society has indicated it does not regard as acceptable and that cannot be shown to serve any penal purpose more effectively than a significantly less drastic punishment. Under these principles and this test, death is today a "cruel and unusual" punishment.

Death is a unique punishment in the United States. In a society that so strongly affirms the sanctity of life, not surprisingly the common view is that death is the ultimate sanction. This natural human feeling appears all about us. There has been no national debate about punishment, in general or by imprisonment, comparable to the debate about the punishment of death. No other punishment has been so continuously restricted. . . .

. . . This Court, too, almost always treats death cases as a class apart. And the unfortunate effect of this punishment upon the functioning of the judicial process is well known; no other punishment has a similar effect.

The only explanation for the uniqueness of death is its extreme severity. Death is today an unusually severe punishment, unusual in its pain, in its finality, and in its enormity. No other existing punishment is comparable to death in terms of physical and mental suffering. . . .

The unusual severity of death is manifested most clearly in its finality and enormity. Death, in these respects, is in a class by itself. . . .

Death is truly an awesome punishment. The calculated killing of a human being by the State involves, by its very nature, a denial of the executed person's humanity. The contrast with the plight of a person punished by imprisonment is evident. An individual in prison does not lose "the right to have rights." A prisoner retains, for example, the constitutional rights to the free exercise of religion, to be free of cruel and unusual punishments, and to treatment as a "person" for purposes of due process of law and the equal protection of the laws. A prisoner remains a member of the human family. . . .

In comparison to all other punishments today, then, the deliberate extinguishment of human life by the State is uniquely degrading to human dignity. I would not hesitate to hold, on that ground alone, that death is today a "cruel and unusual" punishment, were it not that death is a punishment of longstanding usage and acceptance in this country. I therefore turn to the second principle—that the State may not arbitrarily inflict an unusually severe punishment.

The outstanding characteristic of our present practice of punishing criminals by death is the infrequency with which we resort to it. The evidence is conclusive that death is not the ordinary punishment for any crime.

There has been a steady decline in the infliction of this punishment in every decade since the 1930's, the earliest period for which accurate statistics are available. . . .

Thus, although "the death penalty has been employed throughout our history," . . . in fact the history of this punishment is one of successive restriction. What was once a common punishment has become, in the context of a continuing moral debate, increasingly rare. . . .

The progressive decline in and the current rarity of the infliction of death demonstrate that our society seriously questions the appropriateness of this punishment today. The

States point out that many legislatures authorize death as the punishment for certain crimes and that substantial segments of the public, as reflected in opinion polls and referendum votes, continue to support it. Yet the availability of this punishment through statutory authorization, as well as the polls and referenda, which amount simply to approval of that authorization, simply underscores the extent to which our society has in fact rejected this punishment. . . . And today society will inflict death upon only a small sample of the eligible criminals. Rejection could hardly be more complete without becoming absolute. At the very least, I must conclude that contemporary society views this punishment with substantial doubt. . . . Obviously, concepts of justice change; no immutable moral order requires death for murderers and rapists. The claim that death is a just punishment necessarily refers to the existence of certain public beliefs. The claim must be that for capital crimes death alone comports with society's notion of proper punishment. As administered today, however, the punishment of death cannot be justified as a necessary means of exacting retribution from criminals. When the overwhelming number of criminals who commit capital crimes go to prison, it cannot be concluded that death serves the purpose of retribution more effectively than imprisonment. The asserted public belief that murderers and rapists deserve to die is flatly inconsistent with the execution of a random few. As the history of the punishment of death in this country shows, our society wishes to prevent crime; we have no desire to kill criminals simply to get even with them.

In sum, the punishment of death is inconsistent with all four principles: Death is an unusually severe and degrading punishment; there is a strong probability that it is inflicted arbitrarily; its rejection by contemporary society is virtually total; and there is no reason to believe that it serves any penal purpose more effectively than the less severe punishment of imprisonment. The function of these principles is to enable a court to determine whether a punishment comports with human dignity. Death, quite simply, does not.

When this country was founded, memories of the Stuart horrors were fresh and severe corporal punishments were common. Death was not then a unique punishment. The practice of punishing criminals by death, moreover, was widespread and by and large acceptable to society. Indeed, without developed prison systems, there was frequently no workable alternative. Since that time successive restrictions, imposed against the background of a continuing moral controversy, have drastically curtailed the use of this punishment. Today death is a uniquely and unusually severe punishment. When examined by the principles applicable under the Cruel and Unusual Punishments Clause, death stands condemned as fatally offensive to human dignity. The punishment of death is therefore "cruel and unusual," and the States may no longer inflict it as a punishment for crimes. . . .

MR. JUSTICE BLACKMUN, dissenting.

I join the respective opinions of THE CHIEF JUSTICE, MR. JUSTICE POWELL, and MR. JUSTICE REHNQUIST, and add only the following, somewhat personal, comments.

1. Cases such as these provide for me an excruciating agony of the spirit. I yield to no one in the depth of my distaste, antipathy, and, indeed, abhorrence, for the death penalty, with all its aspects of physical distress and fear and of moral judgment exercised by finite minds. That distaste is buttressed by a belief that capital punishment serves no useful purpose that can be demonstrated. For me, it violates childhood's training and life's experiences, and is not compatible with the philosophical convictions I have been able to develop. It is antagonistic to any sense of "reverence for life." Were I a legislator, I would vote against the death penalty for the policy reasons argued by counsel for the respective petitioners and expressed and adopted in the several opinions filed by the Justices who vote to reverse these convictions.

3. I, perhaps alone among the present members of the Court, am on judicial record as to this. As a member of the United States Court of Appeals I first struggled silently with the issue of capital punishment. . . .

4. The several majority opinions acknowl-

edge, as they must, that until today capital punishment was accepted and assumed as not unconstitutional *per se* under the Eighth Amendment or the Fourteenth Amendment. . . .

Suddenly, however, the course of decision is now the opposite way, with the Court evidently persuaded that somehow the passage of time has taken us to a place of greater maturity and outlook. The argument, plausible and high-sounding as it may be, is not persuasive, for it is only one year since *Mc-Gautha*, only eight and one-half years since *Rudolph*, fourteen years since *Trop*. . . .

My problem, however, as I have indicated, is the suddenness of the Court's perception of progress in the human attitude since decisions of only a short while ago.

5. To reverse the judgments in these cases is, of course, the easy choice. It is easier to strike the balance in favor of life and against death. It is comforting to relax in the thoughts—perhaps the rationalizations—that this is the compassionate decision for a maturing society; that this is the moral and the "right" thing to do; that thereby we convince ourselves that we are moving down the road toward human decency; that we value life even though that life has taken another or others or has grievously scarred another or others and their families; and that we are less barbaric than we were in 1878 or in 1890 or in 1910 or in 1947 or in 1958 or in 1963 or a year ago in 1971 when *Wilkerson, Kimmler, Weems, Francis, Trop, Rudolph,* and *McGautha* were respectively decided.

This, for me, is good argument, and it makes some sense. But it is good argument and it makes sense only in a legislative and executive way and not as a judicial expedient. As I have said above, were I a legislator, I would do all I could to sponsor and to vote for legislation abolishing the death penalty. And were I the chief executive of a sovereign State, I would be sorely tempted to exercise executive clemency as Governor Rockefeller of Arkansas did recently just before he departed from office. There—on the Legislative Branch of the State or Federal Government, and secondarily, on the Executive Branch—is where the authority and responsibility for this kind of action lies.

The authority should not be taken over by the judiciary in the modern guise of an Eighth Amendment issue.

I do not sit on these cases, however, as a legislator, responsive, at least in part, to the will of constituents. Our task here, as must so frequently be emphasized and re-emphasized, is to pass upon the constitutionality of legislation that has been enacted and that is challenged. This is the sole task for judges. We should not allow our personal preferences as to the wisdom of legislative and congressional action, or our distaste for such action, to guide our judicial decision in cases such as these. The temptations to cross that policy line are very great. In fact, as today's decision reveals, they are almost irresistible.

6. The Court, in my view, is somewhat propelled toward its result by the interim decision of the California Supreme Court, with one justice dissenting, that the death penalty is violative of that State's constitution.

7. I trust the Court fully appreciates what it is doing when it decides these cases the way it does today. Not only are the capital punishment laws of 39 States and the District of Columbia stricken down, but also all those provisions of the federal statutory structure that permit the death penalty apparently are voided. No longer is capital punishment possible, I suspect, for, among other crimes, treason, . . . or assassination of the President, the Vice President, or those who stand elected to those positions. . . .

8. It is of passing interest to note a few voting facts with respect to recent federal death penalty legislation:

A. The aircraft piracy statute . . . was enacted September 5, 1961. . . .

B. The presidential assassination statute, . . . was approved August 28, 1965. . . .

C. The Omnibus Crime Control Act of 1970 was approved January 2, 1971. Title IV thereof added the congressional assassination statute. . . .

Although personally I may rejoice at the Court's result, I find it difficult to accept or to justify as a matter of history, of law, or of constitutional pronouncement. I fear the Court has overstepped. It has sought and has achieved an end.

693. AGREEMENT ON ENDING THE WAR AND RESTORING PEACE IN VIETNAM

January 24, 1973

(*Department of State Bulletin,* February 12, 1973)

On January 24, Henry Kissinger, principal American negotiator, announced an agreement between the United States and North Vietnam which was to go into effect on January 27. Consisting of the text and four protocols or annexes, the Vietnam accord contained clauses pertaining to cease-fire in South Vietnam, troop withdrawals, prisoners of war, truce supervision, and the character of future government in South Vietnam. Kissinger claimed that the settlement was "fair and just," and confessed "a firm expectation" that the cease-fire would soon extend to both Laos and Cambodia as well. In this he proved mistaken.

CHAPTER I

THE VIETNAMESE PEOPLE'S FUNDAMENTAL NATIONAL RIGHTS

ARTICLE 1

The United States and all other countries respect the independence, sovereignty, unity, and territorial integrity of Vietnam as recognized by the 1954 Geneva Agreements on Vietnam.

CHAPTER II

CESSATION OF HOSTILITIES— WITHDRAWAL OF TROOPS

ARTICLE 2

A cease-fire shall be observed throughout South Vietnam as of 2400 hours G.M.T., on January 27, 1973.

At the same hour, the United States will stop all its military activities against the territory of the Democratic Republic of Vietnam by ground, air and naval forces, wherever they may be based, and end the mining of the territorial waters, ports, harbors, and waterways of the Democratic Republic of Vietnam. The United States will remove, permanently deactivate or destroy all the

mines in the territorial waters, ports, harbors, and waterways of North Vietnam as soon as this Agreement goes into effect.

The complete cessation of hostilities mentioned in this Article shall be durable and without limit of time.

ARTICLE 3

The parties undertake to maintain the cease-fire and to ensure a lasting and stable peace.

As soon as the cease-fire goes into effect:

(a) The United States forces and those of the other foreign countries allied with the United States and the Republic of Vietnam shall remain in-place pending the implementation of the plan of troop withdrawal. The Four-Party Joint Military Commission described in Article 16 shall determine the modalities.

(b) The armed forces of the two South Vietnamese parties shall remain in-place. The Two-Party Joint Military Commission described by Article 17 shall determine the areas controlled by each party and the modalities of stationing.

(c) The regular forces of all services and arms and the irregular forces of the parties in South Vietnam shall stop all offensive activities against each other and shall strictly abide by the following stipulations:

—All acts of force on the ground, in the air, and on the sea shall be prohibited;

—All hostile acts, terrorism and reprisals by both sides will be banned.

ARTICLE 4

The United States will not continue its military involvement or intervene in the internal affairs of South Vietnam.

ARTICLE 5

Within sixty days of the signing of this Agreement, there will be a total withdrawal from South Vietnam of troops, military advisers, and military personnel, including technical military personnel and military personnel associated with the pacification program, armaments, munitions, and war material of the United States and those of the other foreign countries mentioned in Article 3 (a). Advisers from the above-mentioned countries to all paramilitary organizations and the police force will also be withdrawn within the same period of time.

ARTICLE 6

The dismantlement of all military bases in South Vietnam of the United States and of the other foreign countries mentioned in Article 3 (a) shall be completed within sixty days of the signing of this Agreement.

ARTICLE 7

From the enforcement of the cease-fire to the formation of the government provided for in Articles 9 (b) and 14 of this Agreement, the two South Vietnamese parties shall not accept the introduction of troops, military advisers, and military personnel including technical military personnel, armaments, munitions, and war material into South Vietnam.

The two South Vietnamese parties shall be permitted to make periodic replacement of armaments, munitions and war material which have been destroyed, damaged, worn out or used up after the cease-fire, on the basis of piece-for-piece, of the same characteristics and properties, under the supervision of the Joint Military Commission of the two South Vietnamese parties and of the International Commission of Control and Supervision.

CHAPTER III

THE RETURN OF CAPTURED MILITARY PERSONNEL AND FOREIGN CIVILIANS, AND CAPTURED AND DETAINED VIETNAMESE CIVILIAN PERSONNEL

ARTICLE 8

(a) The return of captured military personnel and foreign civilians of the parties shall be carried out simultaneously with and completed not later than the same day as the troop withdrawal mentioned in Article 5. The parties shall exchange complete lists of the above-mentioned captured military personnel and foreign civilians on the day of the signing of this Agreement.

(b) The parties shall help each other to get information about those military personnel and foreign civilians of the parties missing in action, to determine the location and take care of the graves of the dead so as to facilitate the exhumation and repatriation of the remains, and to take any such other measures as may be required to get information about those still considered missing in action.

(c) The question of the return of Vietnamese civilian personnel captured and detained in South Vietnam will be resolved by the two South Vietnamese parties on the basis of the principles of Article 21 (b) of the Agreement on the Cessation of Hostilities in Vietnam of July 20, 1954. The two South Vietnamese parties will do so in a spirit of national reconciliation and concord, with a view to ending hatred and enmity, in order to ease suffering and to reunite families. The two South Vietnamese parties will do their utmost to resolve this question within ninety days after the cease-fire comes into effect.

CHAPTER IV

THE EXERCISE OF THE SOUTH VIETNAMESE PEOPLE'S RIGHT TO SELF-DETERMINATION

ARTICLE 9

The Government of the United States of America and the Government of the Democratic Republic of Vietnam undertake to respect the following principles for the exercise of the South Vietnamese people's right to self-determination:

(a) The South Vietnamese people's right to self-determination is sacred, inalienable, and shall be respected by all countries.

(b) The South Vietnamese people shall decide themselves the political future of South Vietnam through genuinely free and democratic general elections under international supervision.

(c) Foreign countries shall not impose any political tendency or personality on the South Vietnamese people.

ARTICLE 10

The two South Vietnamese parties undertake to respect the cease-fire and maintain peace in South Viĕtnam, settle all matters of contention through negotiations, and avoid all armed conflict.

ARTICLE 11

Immediately after the cease-fire, the two South Vietnamese parties will:

—achieve national reconciliation and concord, end hatred and enmity, prohibit all acts of reprisal and discrimination against individuals or organizations that have collaborated with one side or the other;

—ensure the democratic liberties of the people: personal freedom, freedom of speech, freedom of the press, freedom of meeting, freedom of organization, freedom of political activities, freedom of belief, freedom of movement, freedom of residence, freedom of work, right to property ownership, and right to free enterprise.

ARTICLE 12

(a) Immediately after the cease-fire, the two South Vietnamese parties shall hold consultations in a spirit of national reconciliation and concord, mutual respect, and mutual non-elimination to set up a National Council of National Reconciliation and Concord of three equal segments. The Council shall operate on the principle of unanimity. After the National Council of National Reconciliation and Concord has assumed its functions, the two South Vietnamese parties will consult about the formation of councils at lower levels. The two South Vietnamese parties shall sign an agreement on the internal matters of South Vietnam as soon as possible and do their utmost to accomplish this within ninety days after the cease-fire comes into effect, in keeping with the South Vietnamese people's aspirations for peace, independence and democracy.

(b) The National Council of National Reconciliation and Concord shall have the task of promoting the two South Vietnamese parties' implementation of this Agreement, achievement of national reconciliation and concord and ensurance of democratic liberties. The National Council of National Reconciliation and Concord will organize the free and democratic general elections provided for in Article 9 (b) and decide the procedures and modalities of these general elections. The institutions for which the general elections are to be held will be agreed upon through consultations between the two South Vietnamese parties. The National Council of National Reconciliation and Concord will also decide the procedures and modalities of such local elections as the two South Vietnamese parties agree upon.

ARTICLE 13

The question of Vietnamese armed forces in South Vietnam shall be settled by the two South Vietnamese parties in a spirit of national reconciliation and concord, equality and mutual respect, without foreign interference, in accordance with the postwar situation. Among the questions to be discussed by the two South Vietnamese parties are steps to reduce their military effectives and to demobilize the troops being reduced. The two South Vietnamese parties will accomplish this as soon as possible.

ARTICLE 14

South Vietnam will pursue a foreign policy of peace and independence. It will be prepared to establish relations with all countries irrespective of their political and social systems on the basis of mutual respect for independence and sovereignty and accept economic and technical aid from any country with no political conditions attached. The acceptance of military aid by South Vietnam in the future shall come under the authority of the government set up after the general elections in South Vietnam provided for in Article 9 (b).

CHAPTER V

THE REUNIFICATION OF VIETNAM AND THE RELATIONSHIP BETWEEN NORTH AND SOUTH VIETNAM

ARTICLE 15

The reunification of Vietnam shall be carried out step by step through peaceful means on the basis of discussions and agreements between North and South Vietnam, without coercion or annexation by either party, and without foreign interference. The time for reunification will be agreed upon by North and South Vietnam.

Pending reunification:

(a) The military demarcation line between the two zones at the 17th parallel is only provisional and not a political or territorial boundary, as provided for in paragraph 6 of the Final Declaration of the 1954 Geneva Conference.

(b) North and South Vietnam shall respect the Demilitarized Zone on either side of the Provisional Military Demarcation Line. . . .

(d) North and South Vietnam shall not join any military alliance or military bloc and shall not allow foreign powers to maintain military bases, troops, military advisers, and military personnel on their respective territories, as stipulated in the 1954 Geneva Agreements on Vietnam.

CHAPTER VI

THE JOINT MILITARY COMMISSIONS, THE INTERNATIONAL COMMISSION OF CONTROL AND SUPERVISION, THE INTERNATIONAL CONFERENCE

ARTICLE 16

(a) The Parties participating in the Paris Conference on Vietnam shall immediately designate representatives to form a Four-Party Joint Military Commission with the task of ensuring joint action by the parties in implementing the . . . provisions of this Agreement. . . .

(c) The Four-Party Joint Military Commission shall begin operating immediately after the signing of this Agreement and end its activities in sixty days, after the completion of the withdrawal of U.S. troops and those of the other foreign countries mentioned in Article 3 (a) and the completion of the return of captured military personnel and foreign civilians of the parties. . . .

ARTICLE 17

(a) The two South Vietnamese parties shall immediately designate representatives to form a Two-Party Joint Military Commission with the task of ensuring joint action by the two South Vietnamese parties in implementing the . . . provisions of this Agreement. . . .

(c) After the signing of this Agreement, the Two-Party Joint Military Commission shall agree immediately on the measures and organization aimed at enforcing the cease-fire and preserving peace in South Vietnam.

ARTICLE 18

(a) After the signing of this Agreement, an International Commission of Control and Supervision shall be established immediately.

(b) Until the International Conference provided for in Article 19 makes definitive arrangements, the International Commission of Control and Supervision will report to the four parties on matters concerning the control and supervision of the implementation . . . of this Agreement. . . .

[c] The International Commission of Control and Supervision shall form control teams for carrying out its tasks. The two South Vietnamese parties shall agree immediately on the location and operation of these teams. The two South Vietnamese parties will facilitate their operation.

(d) The International Commission of Control and Supervision shall be composed of representatives of four countries: Canada, Hungary, Indonesia and Poland. The chairmanship of this Commission will rotate among the members for specific periods to be determined by the Commission. . . .

ARTICLE 19

The parties agree on the convening of an International Conference within thirty days of the signing of this Agreement to acknowledge the signed agreements; to guarantee the ending of the war, the maintenance of peace in Vietnam, the respect of the Vietnamese people's fundamental national rights, and the South Vietnamese people's right to self-determination; and to contribute to and guarantee peace in Indochina.

The United States and the Democratic Republic of Vietnam, on behalf of the parties participating in the Paris Conference on Vietnam, will propose to the following parties that they participate in this International Conference: the People's Republic of China, the Republic of France, the Union of Soviet Socialist Republics, the United Kingdom, the four countries of the International Commission of Control and Supervision, and the Secretary General of the United Nations, together with the parties participating in the Paris Conference on Vietnam. . . .

CHAPTER VIII

THE RELATIONSHIP BETWEEN THE UNITED STATES AND THE DEMOCRATIC REPUBLIC OF VIETNAM

ARTICLE 21

The United States anticipates that this Agreement will usher in an era of reconciliation with the Democratic Republic of Vietnam as with all the peoples of Indochina. In pursuance of its traditional policy, the United States will contribute to healing the wounds of war and to postwar reconstruction of the Democratic Republic of Vietnam and throughout Indochina. . . .

DONE in Paris this 27th day of January, 1973, in Vietnamese and English. The Vietnamese and English texts are official and equally authentic.

PROTOCOL ON PRISONERS AND DETAINEES

PROTOCOL TO THE AGREEMENT ON ENDING THE WAR AND RESTORING PEACE IN VIETNAM CONCERNING THE RETURN OF CAPTURED MILITARY PERSONNEL AND FOREIGN CIVILIANS AND CAPTURED AND DETAINED VIETNAMESE CIVILIAN PERSONNEL.

The Parties participating in the Paris Conference on Vietnam,

In implementation of Article 8 of the Agreement on Ending the War and Restoring Peace in Vietnam signed on this date providing for the return of captured military personnel and foreign civilians, and captured and detained Vietnamese civilian personnel,

Have agreed as follows:

THE RETURN OF CAPTURED MILITARY PERSONNEL AND FOREIGN CIVILIANS

ARTICLE 1

The parties signatory to the Agreement shall return the captured military personnel of the parties mentioned in Article 8 (a) of the Agreement as follows:

—all captured military personnel of the United States and those of the other foreign countries mentioned in Article 3 (a) of the Agreement shall be returned to United States authorities;

—all captured Vietnamese military personnel, whether belonging to regular or irregular armed forces, shall be returned to the two South Vietnamese parties; they shall be returned to that South Vietnamese party under whose command they served.

ARTICLE 2

All captured civilians who are nationals of the United States or of any other foreign countries mentioned in Article 3 (a) of the Agreement shall be returned to United States authorities. All other captured foreign civilians shall be returned to the authorities of their country of nationality by any one of the parties willing and able to do so. . . .

ARTICLE 6

Each party shall return all captured persons mentioned in Articles 1 and 2 of this Protocol without delay and shall facilitate their return and reception. The detaining parties shall not deny or delay their return for any reason, including the fact that captured persons may, on any grounds, have been prosecuted or sentenced.

THE RETURN OF CAPTURED AND DETAINED VIETNAMESE CIVILIAN PERSONNEL

ARTICLE 7

(a) The question of the return of Vietnamese civilian personnel captured and detained in South Vietnam will be resolved by the two South Vietnamese parties on the basis of the principles of Article 21 (b) of the Agreement on the Cessation of Hostilities in Vietnam of July 20, 1954. . . .

TREATMENT OF CAPTURED PERSONS DURING DETENTION

ARTICLE 8

(a) All captured military personnel of the parties and captured foreign civilians of the parties shall be treated humanely at all times, and in accordance with international practice.

They shall be protected against all violence to life and person, in particular against murder in any form, mutilation, torture and cruel treatment, and outrages upon personal dignity. These persons shall not be forced to join the armed forces of the detaining party.

They shall be given adequate food, clothing, shelter, and the medical attention required for their state of health. They shall be allowed to exchange post cards and letters with their families and receive parcels.

(b) All Vietnamese civilian personnel captured and detained in South Vietnam shall be treated humanely at all times, and in accordance with international practice.

They shall be protected against all violence to life and person, in particular against murder in any form, mutilation, torture and cruel treatment, and outrages against personal dignity. The detaining parties shall not deny or delay their return for any reason, including the fact that captured persons may, on any grounds, have been prosecuted or sentenced. These persons shall not be forced to join the armed forces of the detaining party.

They shall be given adequate food, clothing, shelter, and the medical attention required for their state of health. They shall be allowed to exchange post cards and letters with their families and receive parcels. . . .

694. ROE et al. v. WADE, District Attorney of Dallas County
Supreme Court Reporter
1973

On appeal from the U. S. District Court for the Northern District of Texas. Jane Roe, the pseudonym of a young Dallas woman, unmarried and pregnant, who could not afford to leave the state to get an abortion, challenged the constitutionality of an 1854 Texas criminal abortion law which proscribed procuring or attempting an abortion except on medical advice for the purpose of saving the mother's life. James H. Hallford, a Dallas physician who had two criminal abortion suits pending against him, was permitted to intervene. A childless married couple (John and Mary Doe) from Dallas separately attacked the Texas antiabortion laws on the ground of injury through the future possibilities of contraceptive failure, pregnancy, unpreparedness for parenthood, and impairment of the wife's health. Roe and the Does were joined in their suit by Hallford. A three-judge district court held that Roe and Hallford, and members of their classes, had standing to sue and that they presented justiciable controversies, and declared the abortion statutes void as vague and overly broad infringements upon the plaintiffs' Ninth and Fourteenth Amendment rights. At the same time, however, the court ruled the Does's complaint not justiciable, and denied an injunction against prosecution of Hallford and other doctors similarly indicted. As a result, the status quo remained in effect, and Henry Wade, Dallas district attorney, announced his intention to continue prosecuting under the state law. The plaintiffs appealed directly to the Supreme Court for a decision on the constitutionality of the Texas statute. These Texas cases were joined with *Doe* v. *Bolton,* which involved a 1972 Georgia antiabortion law and which eventually decided peripheral matters relating to fetal life. The Court decided that Roe had standing to sue, that the Does did not since their complaint was based upon contingencies too speculative to present an actual case or controversy, that Hallford did not have standing and should have been denied (by the district court) declarative as well as injunctive relief. But in the two remaining cases—that of Roe and *Doe* v. *Bolton*—the Court majority through J. Blackmun improvised a solution of the abortion problem: namely, a three-part formula whose practical effect would require repeal of most antiabortion statutes in the forty-six out of fifty states where they were currently the law. The decision was based on the constitutional right to privacy, a concept evolved out of the due process clause of the Fourteenth Amendment. Erecting its theory of fetal life into constitutional law, the Court struck down a Texas measure typical of the criminal statutes of the last half of the nineteenth century and introduced peculiar wording—"the capability of meaningful life outside the mother's womb"—to define a time when the state's interest in potential life is sufficiently "compelling" to allow for proscription of abortion. In the companion case of *Doe* v. *Bolton,* the health of the mother is so broadly defined that the decision for abortion amounts to a simple medical judgment about its necessity.

BLACKMUN, J. . . . We forthwith acknowledge our awareness of the sensitive and emotional nature of the abortion controversy, of the vigorous opposing views, even among physicians, and of the deep and seemingly absolute convictions that the subject inspires. One's philosophy, one's experiences, one's exposure to the raw edges of human existence, one's religious training, one's attitudes toward life and family and their values, and the moral standards one establishes and seeks to observe, are all likely to influence and to color one's thinking and conclusions about abortion.

In addition, population growth, pollution, poverty, and racial overtones tend to complicate and not to simplify the problem.

Our task, of course, is to resolve the issue by constitutional measurement free of emotion and of predilection. We seek earnestly to do this, and, because we do, we have inquired into, and in this opinion place some emphasis upon, medical and medical-legal history and what that history reveals about man's attitudes toward the abortive procedure over the centuries. . . .

The Texas statutes that concern us here are Arts. 1191–1194 and 1196 of the State Penal Code. These make it a crime to "procure an abortion," as therein defined, or to attempt one, except with respect to "an abortion procured or attempted by medical advice for the purpose of saving the life of the mother." Similar statutes are in existence in a majority of the states. . . .

The principal thrust of appellant's attack on the Texas statutes is that they improperly invade a right, said to be possessed by the pregnant woman, to choose to terminate her pregnancy. Appellant would discover this right in the concept of personal "liberty" embodied in the Fourteenth Amendment's Due Process Clause; or in personal, marital, familial, and sexual privacy said to be protected by the Bill of Rights or its penumbras, see *Griswold* v. *Connecticut,* 381 U. S. 479 (1965); *Eisenstadt* v. *Baird,* 405 U. S. 438 (1972); *id.,* at 460 (WHITE, J., concurring); or among those rights reserved to the people by the Ninth Amendment, *Griswold* v. *Connecticut,* 381 U. S., at 486 (Goldberg, J., concurring). . . .

The Constitution does not explicitly mention any right of privacy. In a line of decisions, however, going back perhaps as far as *Union Pacific R. Co.* v. *Botsford,* 141 U. S. 250, 251 (1891), the Court has recognized that a right of personal privacy, or a guarantee of certain areas or zones of privacy, does exist under the Constitution. . . .

This right of privacy, whether it be founded in the Fourteenth Amendment's concept of personal liberty and restrictions upon state action, as we feel it is, or, as the District Court determined, in the Ninth Amendment's reservation of rights to the people, is broad enough to encompass a woman's decision whether or not to terminate her pregnancy. The detriment that the state would impose upon the pregnant woman by denying this choice altogether is apparent. Specific and direct harm medically diagnosable even in early pregnancy may be involved. Maternity, or additional offspring, may force upon the woman a distressful life and future. Psychological harm may be imminent. Mental and physical health may be taxed by child care. There is also the distress, for all concerned, associated with the unwanted child, and there is the problem of bringing a child into a family already unable, psychologically and otherwise, to care for it. In other cases, as in this one, the additional difficulties and continuing stigma of unwed motherhood may be involved. All these are factors the woman and her responsible physician necessarily will consider in consultation.

On the basis of elements such as these, appellants and some *amici* argue that the woman's right is absolute and that she is entitled to terminate her pregnancy at whatever time, in whatever way, and for whatever reason she alone chooses. With this we do not agree. Appellants' arguments that Texas either has no valid interest at all in regulating the abortion decision, or no interest strong enough to support any limitation upon the woman's sole determination, is unpersuasive. The Court's decisions recognizing a right of privacy also acknowledge that some state regulation in areas protected by that right is appropriate. As noted above, a state may properly assert important interests in safeguarding health, in maintaining medical standards, and in protecting potential life. At some point in pregnancy, these respective interests become sufficiently compelling to sustain regulation of the factors that govern the abortion decision. The privacy right involved, therefore, cannot be said to be absolute. . . .

We therefore conclude that the right of personal privacy includes the abortion decision, but that this right is not unqualified and must be considered against important state interests in regulation.

We note that those federal and state courts that have recently considered abortion law challenges have reached the same conclusion. . . .

The appellee and certain *amici* argue that the fetus is a "person" within the language and meaning of the Fourteenth Amendment. In support of this they outline at length and in detail the well-known facts of fetal development. If this suggestion of personhood is established, the appellant's case, of course, collapses, for the fetus' right to life is then guaranteed specifically by the Amendment. The appellant conceded as much on reargument. On the other hand, the appellee conceded on reargument that no case could be cited that holds that a fetus is a person within the meaning of the Fourteenth Amendment.

The Constitution does not define "person" in so many words. Section 1 of the Fourteenth Amendment contains three references to "person." The first, in defining "citizens," speaks of "persons born or naturalized in the United States." The word also appears both in the Due Process Clause and in the Equal Protection Clause. "Person" is used in other places in the Constitution. . . . in nearly all these instances, the use of the word is such that it has application only postnatally. None indicates, with any assurance, that it has any possible pre-natal application.

Texas urges that, apart from the Fourteenth Amendment, life begins at conception and is present throughout pregnancy, and that, therefore, the state has a compelling interest in protecting that life from and after conception. We need not resolve the difficult question of when life begins. When those trained in the respective disciplines of medicine, philosophy, and theology are unable to arrive at any consensus, the judiciary, at this point in the development of man's knowledge, is not in a position to speculate as to the answer. . . .

In areas other than criminal abortion the law has been reluctant to endorse any theory that life, as we recognize it, begins before live birth or to accord legal rights to the unborn except in narrowly defined situations and except when the rights are contingent upon live birth. . . .

In short, the unborn have never been recognized in the law as persons in the whole sense. . . .

In view of all this, we do not agree that, by adopting one theory of life, Texas may override the rights of the pregnant woman that are at stake. We repeat, however, that the state does have an important and legitimate interest in preserving and protecting the health of the pregnant woman, whether she be a resident of the state or a nonresident who seeks medical consultation and treatment there, and that it has still *another* important and legitimate interest in protecting the potentiality of human life. These interests are separate and distinct. Each grows in substantiality as the woman approaches term and, at a point during pregnancy, each becomes "compelling."

With respect to the state's important and legitimate interest in the health of the mother, the "compelling" point, in the light of present medical knowledge, is at approximately the end of the first trimester. This is so because of the now established medical fact, referred to above . . . , that until the end of the first trimester mortality in abortion is less than mortality in normal childbirth. It follows that, from and after this point, a state may regulate the abortion procedure to the extent that the regulation reasonably relates to the preservation and protection of maternal health. . . .

With respect to the state's important and legitimate interest in potential life, the "compelling" point is at viability. This is so because the fetus then presumably has the capability of meaningful life outside the mother's womb. State regulation protective of fetal life after viability thus has both logical and biological justifications. If the state is interested in protecting fetal life after viability, it may go so far as to proscribe abortion during that period except when it is necessary to preserve the life or health of the mother.

Measured against these standards, Art. 1196 of the Texas Penal Code, in restricting legal abortions to those "procured or attempted by medical advice for the purpose of saving the life of the mother," sweeps too broadly. The statute makes no distinction between abortions performed early in pregnancy and those performed later, and it limits to a single reason, "saving" the mother's life, the legal justification for the procedure. The statute, therefore, cannot survive the constitutional attack made upon it here. . . .

To summarize and to repeat:

1. A state criminal abortion statute of the current Texas type, that excepts from criminality only a *life saving* procedure on behalf of the mother, without regard to pregnancy stage and without recognition of the other interests involved, is violative of the Due Process Clause of the Fourteenth Amendment.

(a) For the stage prior to approximately the end of the first trimester, the abortion decision and its effectuation must be left to the medical judgment of the pregnant woman's attending physician.

(b) For the stage subsequent to approximately the end of the first trimester, the state, in promoting its interest in the health of the mother, may, if it chooses, regulate the abortion procedure in ways that are reasonably related to maternal health.

(c) For the stage subsequent to viability the state, in promoting its interest in the potentiality of human life, may, if it chooses, regulate, and even proscribe, abortion except where it is necessary, in appropriate medical judgment, for the preservation of the life or health of the mother. . . .

695. MILLER v. CALIFORNIA
June 21, 1973

The Court, in five cases decided on the same day, handed down a new set of guidelines on obscenity after ineffectively tinkering on the subject for sixteen years. It sharply tightened up on the rules, rejected the old test of "redeeming social value," made it difficult if not impossible for producers of magazines and films to have any advance assurance that their works would not subject them to criminal penalties, and enabled local and state lawmakers to ban books, plays, and films that might be permitted elsewhere. These decisions were all decided by a five-to-four vote, with the four Nixon appointees, together with Justice White, casting a bloc vote. Chief Justice Burger wrote the majority opinion in the *Miller* v. *California* and *Paris Adult Theater* v. *Slaton* cases. Mr. Justice Douglas delivered the dissent in *Miller;* Mr. Justice Brennan rendered it in *Paris Theater.*

BURGER, C. J. . . . This is one of a group of "obscenity-pornography" cases being reviewed by the Court in a reexamination of standards enunciated in earlier cases involving what Mr. Justice Harlan called "the intractable obscenity problem."

This case involves the application of a state's criminal obscenity statute to a situation in which sexually explicit materials have been thrust by aggressive sales action upon unwilling recipients who had in no way indicated any desire to receive such materials.

This Court has recognized that the states have a legitimate interest in prohibiting dissemination or exhibition of obscene material when the mode of dissemination carries with it a significant danger of offending the sensibilities of unwilling recipients or of exposure to juveniles.

It is in this context that we are called on to define the standards which must be used to identify obscene material that a state may regulate without infringing the First Amendment as applicable to the states through the 14th Amendment.

Since the Court now undertakes to formulate standards more concrete than those in the past, it is useful for us to focus on two of the landmark cases in the somewhat tortured history of the Court's obscenity decisions. . . .

We have seen "a variety of views among the members of the Court unmatched in any other course of constitutional adjudication." This is not remarkable for in the area of freedom of speech and press the courts must always remain sensitive to any infringement on genuinely serious literary, artistic, political or scientific expression. This is an area in which there are few eternal verities.

This much has been categorically settled by the Court: that obscene material is unprotected by the First Amendment.

We acknowledge, however, the inherent dangers of undertaking to regulate any form of expression. State statutes designed to regulate obscene materials must be carefully limited. As a result, we now confine the permissible scope of such regulations to works which depict or describe sexual conduct.

That conduct must be specifically defined by the applicable state law, as written or authoritatively construed. A state offense must also be limited to works which, taken as a whole, appeal to the prurient interest in sex, which portray sexual conduct in a patently offensive way, and which, taken as a whole, do not have serious literary, artistic, political or scientific value.

The basic guidelines for the tryer of fact must be: (a) whether "the average person, applying contemporary community standards" would find that the work, taken as a whole, appeals to the prurient interest; (b) whether the work depicts or describes, in a patently offensive way, sexual conduct specifically defined by the applicable state law, and (c) whether the work, taken as a whole, lacks serious literary, artistic, political, or scientific value.

We do not adopt as a constitutional standard the "utterly without redeeming social value" test [of *Roth* v *U. S.* (1957)]. That concept has never commanded the adherence of more than three justices at one time. . . .

. . . [T]oday, for the first time since Roth was decided in 1957, a majority of this Court has agreed on concrete guidelines to isolate "hard-core" pornography for expression protected by the First Amendment.

This may not be an easy road, freed from difficulty. But no amount of "fatigue" should lead us to adopt a convenient "institutional rationale—an absolutist, anything goes view of the First Amendment—because it will lighten our burdens."

Under a national constitution, fundamental First Amendment limitations on the powers of the states do not vary from community to community, but this does not mean that there are, or should or can be, fixed, uniform national standards of precisely what appeals to the "prurient interest" or "patently offensive."

It is neither realistic nor constitutionally sound to read the First Amendment as requiring that the people of Maine or Mississippi accept public depiction of conduct found tolerable in Las Vegas, or New York City. . . .

. . . [I]n our view, to equate the free and robust exchange of ideas and political debate with commercial exploitation of obscene material demeans the grand conception of the First Amendment and its high purposes in the historic struggle for freedom. . . .

One can concede that the "sexual revolution" of recent years may have had useful by-products in striking layers of prudery from a subject long irrationally kept from needed ventilation. But it does not follow that no regulation of patently offensive "hard-core" material is needed or permissible; civilized people do not allow unregulated access to heroin because it is a derivative of medicinal morphine. . . .

DOUGLAS, J. dissenting . . . Today we leave open the way for California to send a man to prison for distributing brochures that advertise books and a movie under freshly written standards defining obscenity which until today's decision were never the part of any law.

The court has worked hard to define obscenity and concededly has failed.

But even those members of this Court who created the new and changing standards of "obscenity" could not agree on their application.

Today the Court retreats from the earlier formulations of the constitutional test and undertakes to make new definitions. This effort, like the earlier ones, is earnest and well-intentioned.

The difficulty is that we do not deal with constitutional terms, since "obscenity" is not mentioned in the Constitution or Bill of Rights. And the First Amendment makes no such exemption necessarily implied, for there was no recognized exception to the free press at the time the Bill of Rights was adopted which treated "obscene" publications differently from other types of papers, magazines, and books.

So there are no constitutional guidelines for deciding what is and what is not "obscene." We deal here with problems of censorship which, if adopted, should be done by constitutional amendment after full debate by the people.

Obscenity cases usually generate tremendous emotional outbursts. They have no business being in the courts.

While the right to know is the corollary of the right to speak or publish, no one can be forced by Government to listen to disclosure that he finds offensive.

There is no "captive audience" problem in these obscenity cases. No one is being compelled to look or to listen.

The idea that the First Amendment permits Government to ban publications that are "offensive" to some people puts an ominous gloss on freedom of the press. That test would make it possible to ban any paper or any journal or magazine in some benighted place.

BURGER, C. J. [in this Paris Theater Case] . . . It should be clear from the outset that we do not undertake to tell the states what they must do, but rather to define the area in which they may chart their own course in dealing with obscene material.

We categorically disapprove the theory, apparently adopted by the trial judge, that obscene, pornographic films acquire constitutional immunity from state regulation simply because they are exhibited for consenting adults only.

Although we have often pointedly recognized the high importance of the state interest in regulating the exposure of obscene materials to juveniles and unconsenting adults, this Court has never declared these to be the only legitimate state interests permitting regulation of obscene material.

The states have a long-recognized legitimate interest in regulating the use of obscene material in local commerce and in all places of public accommodation, as long as these regulations do not run afoul of specific constitutional prohibitions.

In particular, we hold that there are legitimate state interests at stake in stemming the tide of commercialized obscenity, even assuming it is feasible to enforce effective safeguards against exposure to juveniles and to the passerby. Rights and interests "other than those of the advocates are involved." These include the interest of the public in the quality of life and the total community environment, the tone of commerce in the great city centers, and, possibly, the public safety itself. . . .

From the beginning of civilized societies legislators and judges have acted on various unprovable assumptions. Such assumptions underlie much lawful state regulation of commercial and business affairs.

If we accept the unprovable assumption that a complete education requires certain books, and the well nigh universal belief that good books, plays, and art lift the spirit, improve the mind, enrich the human personality and develop character, can we then say that a state legislature may not act on the corollary assumption that commerce in obscene books, or public exhibitions focused on obscene conduct, have a tendency to exert a corrupting and debasing impact leading to antisocial behavior?

It is argued that individual "free will" must govern, even in activities beyond the protection of the First Amendment and other constitutional guarantees of privacy, and that government cannot legitimately impede an individual's desire to see or acquire obscene plays, movies, and books.

We do indeed base our society on certain assumptions that people have the capacity for free choice. Most exercises of individual free choice—those in politics, religion, and expression of ideas—are explicitly protected by the Constitution. Totally unlimited play for free will, however, is not allowed in ours or any other society. . . .

BRENNAN, J. dissenting . . . If, as the Court today assumes, "a state legislature may act on the assumption that commerce in obscene books, or public exhibitions focused on obscene conduct, have a tendency to exert a corrupting and debasing impact leading to antisocial behavior," then it is hard to see how state-ordered regimentation of our minds can ever be forestalled.

For if a state may, in an effort to maintain or create a particular moral tone, prescribe what its citizens cannot read or cannot see, then it would seem to follow that in pursuit of that same objective a state could decree that its citizens must read certain books or must view certain films.

However laudable its goal—and that is obviously a question on which reasonable minds may differ—the state cannot proceed by means that violate the Constitution.

Even a legitimate, sharply focused state concern for the morality of the community cannot, in other words, justify an assault on the protections of the First Amendment. Where the state interest in regulation of morality is vague and ill-defined, interference with the guarantees of the First Amendment is even more difficult to justify.

In short, while I cannot say that the interests of the state—apart from the question of juveniles and unconsenting adults—are trivial or nonexistent, I am compelled to conclude that these interests cannot justify the substantial damage to constitutional rights and to this nation's judicial machinery that inevitably results from state efforts to bar the distribution even of unprotected material to consenting adults.

I would hold, therefore, that at least in the absence of distribution to juveniles or obtrusive exposure to unconsenting adults, the First and Fourteenth Amendments prohibit the state and Federal governments from attempting wholly to suppress sexually oriented materials on the basis of their allegedly "obscene" contents. . . .

APPENDIX

THE CONSTITUTION OF THE UNITED STATES

(Richardson, ed. *Messages and Papers,* Vol. I, p. 21 ff.)

WE THE PEOPLE of the United States, in Order to form a more perfect Union, establish Justice, insure domestic Tranquility, provide for the common defence, promote the general Welfare, and secure the Blessings of Liberty to ourselves and our Posterity, do ordain and establish this Constitution for the United States of America.

ARTICLE I

SEC. 1. All legislative Powers herein granted shall be vested in a Congress of the United States, which shall consist of a Senate and House of Representatives.

SEC. 2. The House of Representatives shall be composed of Members chosen every second Year by the People of the several States, and the Electors in each State shall have the Qualifications requisite for Electors of the most numerous Branch of the State Legislature.

No Person shall be a Representative who shall not have attained to the Age of twenty five Years, and been seven Years a Citizen of the United States, and who shall not, when elected, be an Inhabitant of that State in which he shall be chosen.

Representatives and direct Taxes shall be apportioned among the several States which may be included within this Union, according to their respective Numbers, which shall be determined by adding to the whole Number of free Persons, including those bound to Service for a Term of Years, and excluding Indians not taxed, three fifths of all other Persons. The actual Enumeration shall be made within three Years after the first Meeting of the Congress of the United States, and within every subsequent Term of ten Years, in such Manner as they shall by Law direct. The Number of Representatives shall not exceed one for every thirty Thousand, but each State shall have at Least one Representative; and until such enumeration shall be made, the State of New Hampshire

shall be entitled to chuse three, Massachusetts eight, Rhode-Island and Providence Plantations one, Connecticut five, New-York six, New Jersey four, Pennsylvania eight, Delaware one, Maryland six, Virginia ten, North Carolina five, South Carolina five, and Georgia three.

When vacancies happen in the Representation from any State, the Executive Authority thereof shall issue Writs of Election to fill such Vacancies.

The House of Representatives shall chuse their Speaker and other Officers; and shall have the sole Power of Impeachment.

SEC. 3. The Senate of the United States shall be composed of two Senators from each State, chosen by the Legislature thereof, for six Years; and each Senator shall have one Vote.

Immediately after they shall be assembled in Consequence of the first Election, they shall be divided as equally as may be into three Classes. The Seats of the Senators of the first Class shall be vacated at the Expiration of the second Year, of the second Class at the Expiration of the fourth Year, and of the third Class at the Expiration of the sixth Year, so that one third may be chosen every second Year; and if Vacancies happen by Resignation, or otherwise, during the Recess of the Legislature of any State, the Executive thereof may make temporary Appointments until the next Meeting of the Legislature, which shall then fill such Vacancies.

No Person shall be a Senator who shall not have attained to the Age of thirty Years, and been nine Years a Citizen of the United States, and who shall not, when elected, be an Inhabitant of that State for which he shall be chosen.

The Vice President of the United States shall be President of the Senate, but shall have no Vote, unless they be equally divided.

The Senate shall chuse their other Officers, and also a President pro tempore, in the

Absence of the Vice President, or when he shall exercise the Office of President of the United States.

The Senate shall have the sole Power to try all Impeachments. When sitting for that Purpose, they shall be on Oath or Affirmation. When the President of the United States is tried, the Chief Justice shall preside: And no Person shall be convicted without the Concurrence of two thirds of the Members present.

Judgment in Cases of Impeachment shall not extend further than to removal from Office, and disqualification to hold and enjoy any Office of honor, Trust or Profit under the United States: but the Party convicted shall nevertheless be liable and subject to Indictment, Trial, Judgment and Punishment, according to Law.

SEC. 4. The Times, Places and Manner of holding Elections for Senators and Representatives, shall be prescribed in each State by the Legislature thereof; but the Congress may at any time by Law make or alter such Regulations, except as to the Places of chusing Senators.

The Congress shall assemble at least once in every Year, and such Meeting shall be on the first Monday in December, unless they shall by Law appoint a different Day.

SEC. 5. Each House shall be the Judge of the Elections, Returns and Qualifications of its own Members, and a Majority of each shall constitute a Quorum to do Business; but a smaller Number may adjourn from day to day, and may be authorized to compel the Attendance of absent Members, in such Manner, and under such Penalties as each House may provide.

Each House may determine the Rules of its Proceedings, punish its Members for disorderly Behaviour, and, with the Concurrence of two thirds, expel a Member.

Each House shall keep a Journal of its Proceedings, and from time to time publish the same, excepting such Parts as may in their Judgment require Secrecy; and the Yeas and Nays of the Members of either House on any question shall, at the Desire of one fifth of those Present, be entered on the Journal.

Neither House, during the Session of Congress, shall, without the Consent of the other, adjourn for more than three days, nor to any other Place than that in which the two Houses shall be sitting.

SEC. 6. The Senators and Representatives shall receive a Compensation for their Services, to be ascertained by Law, and paid out of the Treasury of the United States. They shall in all Cases, except Treason, Felony and Breach of the Peace, be privileged from Arrest during their Attendance at the Session of their respective Houses, and in going to and returning from the same; and for any Speech or Debate in either House, they shall not be questioned in any other Place.

No Senator or Representative shall, during the Time for which he was elected, be appointed to any civil Office under the Authority of the United States which shall have been created, or the Emoluments whereof shall have been encreased during such time; and no Person holding any Office under the United States, shall be a Member of either House during his Continuance in Office.

SEC. 7. All Bills for raising Revenue shall originate in the House of Representatives; but the Senate may propose or concur with Amendments as on other Bills.

Every Bill which shall have passed the House of Representatives and the Senate, shall, before it become a Law, be presented to the President of the United States; If he approve he shall sign it, but if not he shall return it, with his Objections to that House in which it shall have originated, who shall enter the Objections at large on their Journal, and proceed to reconsider it. If after such Reconsideration two thirds of that House shall agree to pass the Bill, it shall be sent, together with the Objections, to the other House, by which it shall likewise be reconsidered, and if approved by two thirds of that House, it shall become a Law. But in all such Cases the Votes of both Houses shall be determined by Yeas and Nays, and the Names of the Persons voting for and against the Bill shall be entered on the Journal of each House respectively. If any Bill shall not be returned by the President within ten Days (Sundays excepted) after it shall have been presented to him, the Same shall be a Law, in like

Manner as if he had signed it, unless the Congress by their Adjournment prevent its Return, in which Case it shall not be a Law.

Every Order, Resolution, or Vote to which the Concurrence of the Senate and House of Representatives may be necessary (except on a question of Adjournment) shall be presented to the President of the United States; and before the Same shall take Effect, shall be approved by him, or being disapproved by him, shall be repassed by two thirds of the Senate and House of Representatives, according to the Rules and Limitations prescribed in the Case of a Bill.

SEC. 8. The Congress shall have Power To lay and collect Taxes, Duties, Imposts and Excises, to pay the Debts and provide for the common Defence and general Welfare of the United States; but all Duties, Imposts and Excises shall be uniform throughout the United States;

To borrow Money on the credit of the United States;

To regulate Commerce with foreign Nations, and among the several States, and with the Indian Tribes;

To establish an uniform Rule of Naturalization, and uniform Laws on the subject of Bankruptcies throughout the United States;

To coin Money, regulate the Value thereof, and of foreign Coin, and fix the Standard of Weights and Measures;

To provide for the Punishment of counterfeiting the Securities and current Coin of the United States;

To establish Post Offices and post Roads;

To promote the Progress of Science and useful Arts, by securing for limited Times to Authors and Inventors the exclusive Right to their respective Writings and Discoveries;

To constitute Tribunals inferior to the supreme Court;

To define and punish Piracies and Felonies committed on the high Seas, and Offences against the Law of Nations;

To declare War, grant Letters of Marque and Reprisal, and make Rules concerning Captures on Land and Water;

To raise and support Armies, but no Appropriation of Money to that Use shall be for a longer Term than two Years;

To provide and maintain a Navy;

To make Rules for the Government and Regulation of the land and naval Forces;

To provide for calling forth the Militia to execute the Laws of the Union, suppress Insurrections and repel Invasions;

To provide for organizing, arming, and disciplining, the Militia, and for governing such Part of them as may be employed in the Service of the United States, reserving to the States respectively, the Appointment of the Officers, and the Authority of training the Militia according to the discipline prescribed by Congress;

To exercise exclusive Legislation in all Cases whatsoever, over such District (not exceeding ten Miles square) as may, by Cession of particular States, and the Acceptance of Congress, become the Seat of the Government of the United States, and to exercise like Authority over all Places purchased by the Consent of the Legislature of the State in which the Same shall be, for the Erection of Forts, Magazines, Arsenals, dock-Yards, and other needful Buildings;—And

To make all Laws which shall be necessary and proper for carrying into Execution the foregoing Powers, and all other Powers vested by this Constitution in the Government of the United States, or in any Department or Officer thereof.

SEC. 9. The Migration or Importation of such Persons as any of the States now existing shall think proper to admit, shall not be prohibited by the Congress prior to the Year one thousand eight hundred and eight, but a Tax or duty may be imposed on such Importation, not exceeding ten dollars for each Person.

The Privilege of the Writ of Habeas Corpus shall not be suspended, unless when in Cases of Rebellion or Invasion the public Safety may require it.

No Bill of Attainder or ex post facto Law shall be passed.

No Capitation, or other direct, Tax shall be laid, unless in Proportion to the Census or Enumeration herein before directed to be taken.

No Tax or Duty shall be laid on Articles exported from any State.

No Preference shall be given by any Regulation of Commerce or Revenue to the Ports of one State over those of another:

nor shall Vessels bound to, or from, one State, be obliged to enter, clear, or pay Duties in another.

No Money shall be drawn from the Treasury, but in Consequence of Appropriations made by Law; and a regular Statement and Account of the Receipts and Expenditures of all public Money shall be published from time to time.

No Title of Nobility shall be granted by the United States: And no Person holding any Office of Profit or Trust under them, shall, without the Consent of the Congress, accept of any present, Emolument, Office, or Title, of any kind whatever, from any King, Prince or foreign State.

SEC. 10. No State shall enter into any Treaty, Alliance, or Confederation; grant Letters of Marque and Reprisal; coin Money; emit Bills of Credit; make any Thing but gold and silver Coin a Tender in Payment of Debts; pass any Bill of Attainder, ex post facto Law, or Law impairing the Obligation of Contracts, or grant any Title of Nobility.

No State shall, without the Consent of Congress, lay any Imposts or Duties on Imports or Exports, except what may be absolutely necessary for executing it's inspection Laws: and the net Produce of all Duties and Imposts, laid by any State on Imports or Exports, shall be for the Use of the Treasury of the United States; and all such Laws shall be subject to the Revision and Controul of the Congress.

No State shall, without the Consent of Congress, lay any Duty of Tonnage, keep Troops, or Ships of War in time of Peace, enter into any Agreement or Compact with another State, or with a foreign Power, or engage in War, unless actually invaded, or in such imminent Danger as will not admit of delay.

ARTICLE II

SEC. 1. The executive Power shall be vested in a President of the United States of America. He shall hold his Office during the Term of four Years, and, together with the Vice President, chosen for the same Term, be elected, as follows

Each State shall appoint, in such Manner as the Legislature thereof may direct, a Number of Electors, equal to the whole Number of Senators and Representatives to which the State may be entitled in the Congress: but no Senator or Representative, or Person holding an Office of Trust or Profit under the United States, shall be appointed an Elector.

The Electors shall meet in their respective States, and vote by Ballot for two Persons, of whom one at least shall not be an Inhabitant of the same State with themselves. And they shall make a List of all the Persons voted for, and of the Number of Votes for each; which List they shall sign and certify, and transmit sealed to the Seat of the Government of the United States, directed to the President of the Senate. The President of the Senate shall, in the Presence of the Senate and House of Representatives, open all the Certificates, and the Votes shall then be counted. The Person having the greatest Number of Votes shall be the President, if such Number be a Majority of the whole Number of Electors appointed; and if there be more than one who have such Majority, and have an equal Number of Votes, then the House of Representatives shall immediately chuse by Ballot one of them for President; and if no person have a Majority, then from the five highest on the List the said House shall in like Manner chuse the President. But in chusing the President, the Votes shall be taken by States, the Representation from each State having one Vote; A quorum for this Purpose shall consist of a Member or Members from two thirds of the States, and a Majority of all the States shall be necessary to a Choice. In every Case, after the Choice of the President, the Person having the greatest Number of Votes of the Electors shall be the Vice President. But if there should remain two or more who have equal Votes, the Senate shall chuse from them by Ballot the Vice President.

The Congress may determine the Time of chusing the Electors, and the Day on which they shall give their Votes; which Day shall be the same throughout the United States.

No Person except a natural born Citizen, or a Citizen of the United States, at the time of the Adoption of this Constitution, shall be eligible to the Office of President; neither shall any Person be eligible to that Office who shall not have attained to the Age of thirty five Years, and been fourteen Years a Resident within the United States.

In Case of the Removal of the President from Office, or of his Death, Resignation, or Inability to discharge the Powers and Duties of the said Office, the Same shall devolve on the Vice President, and the Congress may by Law provide for the Case of Removal, Death, Resignation or Inability, both of the President and Vice President, declaring what Officer shall then act as President, and such Officer shall act accordingly, until the Disability be removed, or a President shall be elected.

The President shall, at stated Times, receive for his Services, a Compensation, which shall neither be encreased nor diminished during the Period for which he shall have been elected, and he shall not receive within that Period any other Emolument from the United States, or any of them.

Before he enter on the Execution of his Office, he shall take the following Oath or Affirmation:—"I do solemnly swear (or affirm) that I will faithfully execute the Office of President of the United States, and will to the best of my Ability, preserve, protect and defend the Constitution of the United States."

SEC. 2. The President shall be Commander in Chief of the Army and Navy of the United States, and of the Militia of the several States, when called into the actual Service of the United States; he may require the Opinion, in writing, of the principal Officer in each of the executive Departments, upon any Subject relating to the Duties of their respective Offices, and he shall have Power to grant Reprieves and Pardons for Offenses against the United States, except in Cases of Impeachment.

He shall have Power, by and with the Advice and Consent of the Senate, to make Treaties, provided two thirds of the Senators present concur; and he shall nominate, and by and with the Advice and Consent of the Senate, shall appoint Ambassadors, other public Ministers and Consuls, Judges of the supreme Court, and all other Officers of the United States, whose Appointments are not herein otherwise provided for, and which shall be established by Law: but the Congress may by Law vest the Appointment of such inferior Officers, as they think proper, in the President alone, in the Courts of Law, or in the Heads of Departments.

The President shall have Power to fill up all Vacancies that may happen during the Recess of the Senate, by granting Commissions which shall expire at the End of their next Session.

SEC. 3. He shall from time to time give to the Congress Information of the State of the Union, and recommend to their Consideration such Measures as he shall judge necessary and expedient; he may, on extraordinary Occasions, convene both Houses, or either of them, and in Case of Disagreement between them, with Respect to the Time of Adjournment, he may adjourn them to such Time as he shall think proper; he shall receive Ambassadors and other public Ministers; he shall take Care that the Laws be faithfully executed, and shall Commission all the Officers of the United States.

SEC. 4. The President, Vice President and all civil Officers of the United States, shall be removed from Office on Impeachment for, and Conviction of, Treason, Bribery, or other high Crimes and Misdemeanors.

ARTICLE III

SEC. 1. The judicial Power of the United States, shall be vested in one supreme Court, and in such inferior Courts as the Congress may from time to time ordain and establish. The Judges, both of the supreme and inferior Courts, shall hold their Offices during good Behaviour, and shall, at stated Times, receive for their Services, a Compensation, which shall not be diminished during their Continuance in Office.

SEC. 2. The judicial Power shall extend to all Cases, in Law and Equity, arising under this Constitution, the Laws of the United States, and Treaties made, or which shall be made, under their Authority;—to all Cases affecting Ambassadors, other public Ministers and Consuls;—to all Cases of admiralty and maritime Jurisdiction;—to Controversies to which the United States shall be a Party;—to Controversies between two or more States;—between a State and Citizens of another State;—between Citizens of different States,—between Citizens of the same State claiming Lands under Grants of different States, and between a State, or the Citizens thereof, and foreign States, Citizens or Subjects.

In all Cases affecting Ambassadors, other public Ministers and Consuls, and those in which a State shall be Party, the supreme Court shall have original Jurisdiction. In all the other Cases before mentioned, the supreme Court shall have appellate Jurisdiction, both as to Law and Fact, with such Exceptions, and under such Regulations as the Congress shall make.

The Trial of all Crimes, except in Cases of Impeachment, shall be by Jury; and such Trial shall be held in the State where the said Crimes shall have been committed; but when not committed within any State, the Trial shall be at such Place or Places as the Congress may by Law have directed.

SEC. 3.   Treason against the United States, shall consist only in levying War against them, or in adhering to their Enemies, giving them Aid and Comfort. No Person shall be convicted of Treason unless on the Testimony of two Witnesses to the same overt Act, or on Confession in open Court.

The Congress shall have Power to declare the Punishment of Treason, but no Attainder of Treason shall work Corruption of Blood, or Forfeiture except during the Life of the Person attained.

ARTICLE IV

SEC. 1.   Full faith and Credit shall be given in each State to the Public Acts, Records, and judicial Proceedings of every other State. And the Congress may by general Laws prescribe the Manner in which such Acts, Records and Proceedings shall be proved, and the Effect thereof.

SEC. 2.   The Citizens of each State shall be entitled to all Privileges and Immunities of Citizens in the several States.

A Person charged in any State with Treason, Felony, or other Crime, who shall flee from Justice, and be found in another State, shall on Demand of the executive Authority of the State from which he fled, be delivered up, to be removed to the State having Jurisdiction of the Crime.

No Person held to Service or Labour in one State, under the Laws thereof, escaping into another, shall, in Consequence of any Law or Regulation therein, be discharged from such Service or Labour, but shall be delivered up on Claim of the Party to whom such Service or Labour may be due.

SEC. 3.   New States may be admitted by the Congress into this Union; but no new States shall be formed or erected within the Jurisdiction of any other State; nor any State be formed by the Junction of two or more States, or Parts of States, without the Consent of the Legislatures of the States concerned as well as of the Congress.

The Congress shall have Power to dispose of and make all needful Rules and Regulations respecting the Territory or other Property belonging to the United States; and nothing in this Constitution shall be so construed as to Prejudice any Claims of the United States, or of any particular State.

SEC. 4.   The United States shall guarantee to every State in this Union a Republican Form of Government, and shall protect each of them against Invasion; and on Application of the Legislature, or of the Executive (when the Legislature cannot be convened) against domestic violence.

ARTICLE V

The Congress, whenever two thirds of both Houses shall deem it necessary, shall propose Amendments to this Constitution, or, on the Application of the Legislatures of two thirds of the several States, shall call a Convention for proposing Amendments, which, in either Case, shall be valid to all Intents and Purposes, as Part of this Constitution, when ratified by the Legislatures of three fourths of the several States, or by Conventions in three fourths thereof, as the one or the other Mode of Ratification may be proposed by the Congress; Provided that no Amendment which may be made prior to the Year One thousand eight hundred and eight shall in any Manner affect the first and fourth Clauses in the Ninth Section of the first Article; and that no State, without its Consent, shall be deprived of it's equal Suffrage in the Senate.

ARTICLE VI

All Debts contracted and Engagements entered into, before the Adoption of this Constitution, shall be as valid against the United States under this Constitution, as under the Confederation.

This Constitution, and the Laws of the United States which shall be made in Pursuance thereof; and all Treaties made, or which shall be made, under the Authority of the United States, shall be the supreme Law of the Land; and the Judges in every State shall be bound thereby, any Thing in the Constitution or Laws of any State to the Contrary notwithstanding.

The Senators and Representatives before mentioned, and the Members of the several State Legislatures, and all executive and judicial Officers, both of the United States and of the several States, shall be bound by Oath or Affirmation, to support this Constitution; but no religious Test shall ever be required as a Qualification to any Office or public Trust under the United States.

ARTICLE VII

The Ratification of the Conventions of nine States, shall be sufficient for the Establishment of this Constitution between the States so ratifying the Same.

Done in Convention by the Unanimous Consent of the States present the Seventeenth Day of September in the Year of our Lord one thousand seven hundred and Eighty seven and of the Independence of the United States of America the Twelfth. In witness thereof We have hereunto subscribed our Names,

G° WASHINGTON—Presid^t
and deputy from Virginia

New Hampshire	JOHN LANGDON NICHOLAS GILMAN
Massachusetts	NATHANIEL GORHAM RUFUS KING
Connecticut	W^M SAM^L JOHNSON ROGER SHERMAN
New York	ALEXANDER HAMILTON
New Jersey	WIL: LIVINGSTON DAVID BREARLEY W^M PATERSON JONA: DAYTON
Pennsylvania	B FRANKLIN THOMAS MIFFLIN ROB^T MORRIS GEO. CLYMER THO^S FITZSIMONS JARED INGERSOLL JAMES WILSON GOUV MORRIS

Delaware	GEO: READ GUNNING BEDFORD jun JOHN DICKINSON RICHARD BASSETT JACO: BROOM
Maryland	JAMES M^{C}HENRY DAN OF S^T THO^S JENIFER DAN^L CARROLL
Virginia	JOHN BLAIR— JAMES MADISON JR.
North Carolina	W^M BLOUNT RICH^D DOBBS SPAIGHT HU WILLIAMSON
South Carolina	J. RUTLEDGE CHARLES COTESWORTH PINCKNEY CHARLES PINCKNEY PIERCE BUTLER
Georgia	WILLIAM FEW ABR BALDWIN

Articles in addition to, and Amendment of the Constitution of the United States of America, proposed by Congress, and ratified by the Legislatures of the several States, pursuant to the fifth Article of the original Constitution.

[The first ten amendments went into effect November 3, 1791.]

ARTICLE I

Congress shall make no law respecting an establishment of religion, or prohibiting the free exercise thereof; or abridging the freedom of speech, or of the press; or the right of the people peaceably to assemble, and to petition the government for a redress of grievances.

ARTICLE II

A well regulated Militia, being necessary to the security of a free State, the right of the people to keep and bear Arms, shall not be infringed.

ARTICLE III

No soldier shall, in time of peace be quartered in any house, without the consent of the Owner, nor in time of war, but in a manner to be prescribed by law.

ARTICLE IV

The right of the people to be secure in their persons, houses, papers, and effects, against unreasonable searches and seizures, shall not be violated, and no Warrants shall issue, but upon probable cause, supported by Oath or affirmation, and particularly describing the place to be searched, and the persons or things to be seized.

ARTICLE V

No person shall be held to answer for a capital, or otherwise infamous crime, unless on a presentment or indictment of a Grand Jury, except in cases arising in the land or naval forces, or in the Militia, when in actual service in time of War or public danger;

nor shall any person be subject for the same offence to be twice put in jeopardy of life or limb; nor shall be compelled in any criminal case to be a witness against himself, nor be deprived of life, liberty, or property, without due process of law; nor shall private property be taken for public use, without just compensation.

ARTICLE VI

In all criminal prosecutions, the accused shall enjoy the right to a speedy and public trial, by an impartial jury of the State and district wherein the crime shall have been committed, which district shall have been previously ascertained by law, and to be informed of the nature and cause of the accusation; to be confronted with the witnesses against him; to have compulsory process for obtaining witnesses in his favor, and to have the Assistance of Counsel for his defence.

ARTICLE VII

In Suits at common law, where the value in controversy shall exceed twenty dollars, the right of trial by jury shall be preserved, and no fact tried by a jury, shall be otherwise re-examined in any Court of the United States, than according to the rules of the common law.

ARTICLE VIII

Excessive bail shall not be required, nor excessive fines imposed, nor cruel and unusual punishments inflicted.

ARTICLE IX

The enumeration in the Constitution, of certain rights, shall not be construed to deny or disparage others retained by the people.

ARTICLE X

The powers not delegated to the United States by the Constitution, nor prohibited by it to the States, are reserved to the States respectively, or to the people.

ARTICLE XI
Jan. 8, 1798

The Judicial power of the United States shall not be construed to extend to any suit in law or equity, commenced or prosecuted against one of the United States by Citizens of another State, or by Citizens or Subjects of any Foreign State.

ARTICLE XII
Sept. 25, 1804

The Electors shall meet in their respective states, and vote by ballot for President and Vice-President, one of whom, at least, shall not be an inhabitant of the same state with themselves; they shall name in their ballots the person voted for as President, and in distinct ballots the person voted for as Vice-President, and they shall make distinct lists of all persons voted for as President, and of all persons voted for as Vice-President, and of the number of votes for each, which lists they shall sign and certify, and transmit sealed to the seat of the government of the United States, directed to the President of the Senate;—The President of the Senate shall, in the presence of the Senate and House of Representatives, open all the certificates and the votes shall then be counted;—The person having the greatest number of votes for President, shall be the President, if such number be a majority of the whole number of Electors appointed; and if no person have such majority, then from the persons having the highest numbers not exceeding three on the list of those voted for as President, the House of Representatives shall choose immediately, by ballot, the President. But in choosing the President, the votes shall be taken by states, the representation from each state having one vote; a quorum for this purpose shall consist of a member or members from two-thirds of the states, and a majority of all the states shall be necessary to a choice. And if the House of Representatives shall not choose a President whenever the right of choice shall devolve upon them, before the fourth day of March next following, then the Vice-President shall act as President, as in the case of the death or other constitutional disability of the President.—The person having the greatest number of votes as Vice-President, shall be the Vice-President, if such number be a majority of the whole number of Electors appointed, and if no person have a majority, then from the two highest numbers on the list, the Senate shall choose the Vice-President; a quorum for the purpose shall consist of two-thirds of the whole number of Senators, and a majority of the whole number shall be necessary to a choice. But no person constitutionally ineligible to the office of President shall be eligible to that of Vice-President of the United States.

ARTICLE XIII
Dec. 18, 1865

SEC. 1. Neither slavery nor involuntary servitude, except as a punishment for crime whereof the party shall have been duly convicted, shall exist within the United States, or any place subject to their jurisdiction.

SEC. 2. Congress shall have power to enforce this article by appropriate legislation.

ARTICLE XIV
July 28, 1868

SEC. 1. All persons born or naturalized in the United States, and subject to the jurisdiction thereof, are citizens of the United States and of the State wherein they reside. No State shall make or enforce any law which shall abridge the privileges or immunities of citizens of the United States; nor shall any State deprive any person of life, liberty, or property, without due process of law; nor deny to any person within its jurisdiction the equal protection of the laws.

SEC. 2. Representatives shall be apportioned among the several States according to their respective numbers, counting the whole number of persons in each State, excluding Indians not taxed. But when the right to vote at any election for the choice of electors for President and Vice President of the United States, Representatives in Congress, the Executive and Judicial officers of a State, or the members of the Legislature thereof, is denied to any of the male inhabitants of such State, being twenty-one years of age, and citizens of the United States, or in any way abridged, except for participation in rebellion, or other crime, the basis of representation therein shall be reduced in the proportion which the number of such male citizens shall bear to the whole number of male citizens twenty-one years of age in such State.

SEC. 3. No person shall be a Senator or Representative in Congress, or elector of President and Vice President, or hold any office, civil or military, under the United States, or under any State, who, having previously taken an oath, as a member of Congress, or as an officer of the United States, or as a member of any State legislature, or as an executive or judicial officer of any State, to support the Constitution of the United States, shall have engaged in insurrection or rebellion against the same, or given aid or comfort to the enemies thereof. But Congress may by a vote of two-thirds of each House, remove such disability.

SEC. 4. The validity of the public debt of the United States, authorized by law, including debts incurred for payment of pensions and bounties for services in suppressing insurrection or rebellion, shall not be questioned. But neither the United States nor any State shall assume or pay any debt or obligation incurred in aid of insurrection or rebellion against the United States, or any claim for the loss or emancipation of any slave; but all such debts, obligations and claims shall be held illegal and void.

SEC. 5. The Congress shall have power to enforce, by appropriate legislation, the provisions of this article.

ARTICLE XV
May 30, 1870

SEC. 1. The right of citizens of the United States to vote shall not be denied or abridged by the United States or by any State on account of race, color, or previous condition of servitude—

SEC. 2. The Congress shall have power to enforce this article by appropriate legislation—

ARTICLE XVI
February 25, 1913

The Congress shall have power to lay and collect taxes on incomes, from whatever source derived, without apportionment among the several States and without regard to any census or enumeration.

ARTICLE XVII
May 31, 1913

The Senate of the United States shall be composed of two senators from each State, elected by the people thereof, for six years; and each Senator shall have one vote. The electors in each State shall have the qualifications requisite for electors of the most numerous branch of the State legislature.

When vacancies happen in the representation of any State in the Senate, the executive authority of such State shall issue writs of election to fill such vacancies: *Provided,* That the legislature of any State may empower the executive thereof to make temporary appointments until the people fill the vacancies by election as the legislature may direct.

This amendment shall not be so construed as to affect the election or term of any senator chosen before it becomes valid as part of the Constitution.

ARTICLE XVIII
January 29, 1919

After one year from the ratification of this article, the manufacture, sale or transportation of intoxicating liquors within, the importation thereof into, or the exportation thereof from the United States and all territory subject to the jurisdiction thereof for beverage purposes is hereby prohibited.

The Congress and the several States shall have concurrent power to enforce this article by appropriate legislation.

This article shall be inoperative unless it shall have been ratified as an amendment to the Constitution by the legislatures of the several States, as provided in the Constitution, within seven years from the date of the submission hereof to the States by Congress.

ARTICLE XIX
August 26, 1920

The right of citizens of the United States to vote shall not be denied or abridged by the United States or by any States on account of sex.

The Congress shall have power by appropriate legislation to enforce the provisions of this article.

Article XX
February 6, 1933

Sec. 1. The terms of the President and Vice-President shall end at noon on the twentieth day of January, and the terms of Senators and Representatives at noon on the third day of January, of the years in which such terms would have ended if this article had not been ratified; and the terms of their successors shall then begin.

Sec. 2. The Congress shall assemble at least once in every year, and such meeting shall begin at noon on the third day of January, unless they shall by law appoint a different day.

Sec. 3. If, at the time fixed for the beginning of the term of the President, the President-elect shall have died, the Vice-President-elect shall become President. If a President shall not have been chosen before the time fixed for the beginning of his term, or if the President-elect shall have failed to qualify, then the Vice-President-elect shall act as President until a President shall have qualified; and the Congress may by law provide for the case wherein neither a President-elect nor a Vice-President-elect shall have qualified, declaring who shall then act as President, or the manner in which one who is to act shall be selected, and such person shall act accordingly until a President or Vice-President shall have qualified.

Sec. 4. The Congress may by law provide for the case of the death of any of the persons from whom the House of Representatives may choose a President whenever the right of choice shall have devolved upon them, and for the case of the death of any of the persons from whom the Senate may choose a Vice-President whenever the right of choice shall have devolved upon them.

Sec. 5. Sections 1 and 2 shall take effect on the 15th day of October following the ratification of this article.

Sec. 6. This article shall be inoperative unless it shall have been ratified as an amendment to the Constitution by the legislatures of three-fourths of the several States within seven years from the date of its submission.

Article XXI
December 5, 1933

Sec. 1. The eighteenth article of amendment to the Constitution of the United States is hereby repealed. . . .

Article XXII
February 26, 1951

Sec. 1. No person shall be elected to the office of the President more than twice, and no person who has held the office of President, or acted as President for more than two years of a term to which some other person was elected President shall be elected to the office of the President more than once. But this Article shall not apply to any person holding the office of President when this Article was proposed by the Congress, and shall not prevent any person who may be holding the office of President, or acting as President, during the term within which this Article becomes operative from holding the office of President or acting as President during the remainder of such term.

Article XXIII
March 29, 1961

Sec. 1. The District constituting the seat of Government of the United States shall appoint in such manner as the Congress may direct:

A number of electors of President and Vice-President equal to the whole number of Senators and Representatives in Congress to which the District would be entitled if it were a State, but in no event more than the least populous state; they shall be in addition to those appointed by the states, but they shall be considered, for the purposes of the election of President and Vice-President, to be electors appointed by a state; and they shall meet in the District and perform such duties as provided by the twelfth article of amendment.

Sec. 2. The Congress shall have power to enforce this article by appropriate legislation.

ARTICLE XXIV
January 24, 1964

SEC. 1. The right of citizens of the United States to vote in any primary or other election for President or Vice-President, for electors for President or Vice-President, or for Senator or Representative in Congress, shall not be denied or abridged by the United States or any state by reason of failure to pay any poll tax or other tax.

SEC. 2. The Congress shall have power to enforce this article by appropriate legislation.

ARTICLE XXV
February 23, 1967

SEC. 1. In case of the removal of the President from office or his death or resignation, the Vice-President shall become President.

SEC. 2. Whenever there is a vacancy in the office of the Vice-President, the President shall nominate a Vice-President who shall take the office upon confirmation by a majority vote of both houses of Congress.

SEC. 3. Whenever the President transmits to the President pro tempore of the Senate and the Speaker of the House of Representatives his written declaration that he is unable to discharge the powers and duties of his office, and until he transmits to them a written declaration to the contrary, such powers and duties shall be discharged by the Vice-President as Acting President.

SEC. 4. Whenever the Vice-President and a majority of either the principal officers of the executive departments, or of such other body as Congress may by law provide, transmit to the President pro tempore of the Senate and the Speaker of the House of Representatives their written declaration that the President is unable to discharge the powers and duties of his office, the Vice-President shall immediately assume the powers and duties of the office as Acting President.

Thereafter, when the President transmits to the President pro tempore of the Senate and the Speaker of the House of Representatives his written declaration that no inability exists, he shall resume the powers and duties of his office unless the Vice-President and a majority of either the principal officers of the executive department, or of such other body as Congress may by law provide, transmit within four days to the President pro tempore of the Senate and the Speaker of the House of Representatives their written declaration that the President is unable to discharge the powers and duties of his office. Thereupon Congress shall decide the issue, assembling within 48 hours for that purpose if not in session. If the Congress, within 21 days after receipt of the latter written declaration, or, if Congress is not in session, within 21 days after Congress is required to assemble, determines by two-thirds vote of both houses that the President is unable to discharge the powers and duties of his office, the Vice-President shall continue to discharge the same as Acting President; otherwise, the President shall resume the powers and duties of his office.

ARTICLE XXVI
July 7, 1971

SEC. 1. The right of citizens of the United States, who are eighteen years of age or older, to vote shall not be denied or abridged by the United States or by any State on account of age.

SEC. 2. The Congress shall have power to enforce this article by appropriate legislation.

ARTICLE XXVII
Passed by Congress March 22, 1972;
Not yet ratified

SEC. 1. Equality of rights under the law shall not be denied or abridged by the United States or by any State on account of sex.

SEC. 2. The Congress shall have the power to enforce, by appropriate legislation, the provisions of this article.

SEC. 3. This amendment shall take effect two years after the date of ratification.

INDEX

(The references in this index are to document numbers, not pages.)

817